doing business with

CHINA

With more than 130 years presence in China, Cable & Wireless is committed to continuing to strengthen its relationships with its Chinese partners, to deliver innovative telecommunications solutions for its many multi-national customers in China.

www.cw.com

Tel: 0086 10 6561 6622

CABLE & WIRELESS

GLOBAL MARKET BRIEFING

doing business with
CHINA

FOURTH EDITION

FOREWORDS BY
SHI GUANGSHENG
PASCAL LAMY
ROBERT A CAPP

CONSULTANT EDITORS
JONATHAN REUVID AND LI YONG

IN ASSOCIATION WITH
THE CHINA ASSOCIATION OF INTERNATIONAL TRADE
MINISTRY OF FOREIGN TRADE AND ECONOMIC COOPERATION
CHINALINK

KOGAN
PAGE

Publisher's note

Every possible effort has been made to ensure that the information contained in this handbook is accurate at the time of going to press and neither the publishers nor any of the authors can accept responsibility for any errors or omissions, however caused. No responsibility for loss or damage occasioned to any person acting, or refraining from action, as a result of material in this publication can be accepted by the editor, the publisher or any of the authors.

This (fourth) edition first published in Great Britain and the United States in 2003 by Kogan Page Limited.

Kogan Page Ltd
120 Pentonville Road
London N1 9JN

Kogan Page US
22883 Quicksilver Drive
Sterling VA 20166-2012

Web site: www.kogan-page.co.uk

© Kogan Page and contributors 2003

ISBN 0 7494 39114

British Library Cataloguing-in-Publication Data

A CIP record for this book is available from the British Library

---

Library of Congress Cataloging-in-Publication Data

Doing business with China / consultant editors Jonathan Reuvid and Li
Yong. -- 4th ed.
    p. cm. -- (Global market briefing)
Includes index.
  ISBN 0-7494-3911-4
  1. China--Economic conditions--2000- 2. China--Commercial policy. 3.
China--Foreign economic relations. 4. Business enterprises,
Foreign--Government policy--China. 5. Investments, Foreign--China. I.
Reuvid, Jonathan. II. Li, Yong. III. Series.
  HC427.95.D65 2003
  330.951--dc21

2002156017

Typeset by JS Typesetting Ltd, Wellingborough, Northants
Printed and bound in Great Britain by Biddles Ltd, Guildford and King's Lynn

Erratum

On page 519, Table 7.46.1, the GDP for 2001 should read 46.099 not 460.99.

On page 520, line 6, US$57.86 billion should read US$5.786 billion.

relationships

关系 – Guanxi

Offices:

UK
+44 (0)20 8679 3888

China
+86 (0)311 785 2536

Email: consult@eastbridgeassociates.co.uk
Website: www.eastbridgeassociates.co.uk

The Integrated Approach
The key to business success in China

China's competitive environment is changing rapidly. The post-WTO influx of foreign businesses and products, a growing Chinese private sector, and the continuing shakeout of state owned enterprises are raising the competitive bar. As competition becomes stiffer, companies will have to look harder for competitive advantages. China Concept Consulting believes that foreign firms can find such competitive advantages in the strategic use of "guanxi" – the Chinese term for relationships – combined with rigorous business analysis.

China Concept Consulting has long believed the key to business success in China is the combination of realistic market analyses, localization of products and services, prudent financial management, operational excellence and the proper use of guanxi. This is the integrated approach – combining Chinese business culture with rigorous Western business analysis – China Concept brings to all of our projects.

Guanxi encompasses the relationships that businesses build with the government and other stakeholders. It includes government lobbying for industry-friendly policies as well as the networking that builds and smoothes business relationships. The rules of the guanxi game are not very different from networking in the West, but guanxi's relative importance is greater due in part to China's imperfect market and legal systems, and

the Chinese culture that emphasize relationships.

One of the most important uses of guanxi will be to facilitate the execution of business strategies. Lured by the great potential of the Chinese market, foreign businesses are eager to enter the market, but few have a clear idea of how business is done in China. While guanxi is no longer an important element in determining whether businesses could get approval to operate in China, it still has a great impact on how things are done. To do so, relations with your customers, suppliers, investors, employees and other key stakeholders must be maintained and nurtured.

From the perspective of government lobbying, the greater transparency of rules and regulations that WTO promises to bring will mean less overt government intervention. While companies will be thankful that more business can be conducted according to market principles, the government regulators will not simply disappear. Firms will have to use government communication to subtly communicate their interests and to influence government policy directions.

Although WTO will change who does business in China and what products and services can be marketed, it will not drastically change how business is conducted. Guanxi is an integral part of the Chinese culture, and it will not disappear overnight.

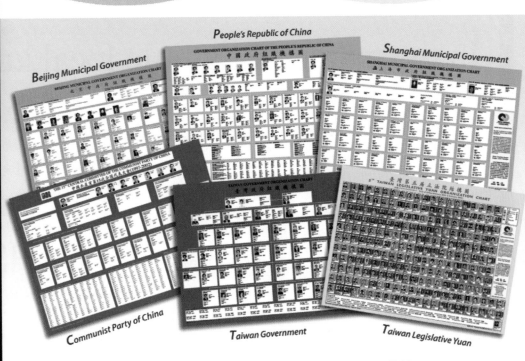

International Market

International Market

International Market

In the market for a little local knowledge?

Buying or selling in some international markets can become a baffling, energy-sapping business. Yet armed with reliable local knowledge you'll be able to take it all in your stride.

With offices in 81 countries, HSBC is providing global exporters, importers and major foreign manufacturers operating in China with banking services, trade payments and market information. Use our local knowledge to help you minimise language and business practise obstacles and maximise operating efficiency.

HSBC

The world's local bank

Issued by The Hongkong and Shanghai Banking Corporation Limited

Contents

PART ONE: CHINA'S ECONOMY AND ADMINISTRATION SYSTEM

Business Gateway to China

Market consultancy and project facilitation
Market entry strategy planning
Event management and marketing promotion in China & UK
International liaison & networking
Bilingual consultant for contract negotiation
Import and export
Regional Investment facilitation
Shanghai Centre

おもてなしのエアライン

/It's tough doing business in China
without the right connections

When you need to be in the right place at the right time, go with the airline that has
more connections across China than any other.

Shenyang
Dalian
Beijing
Qingdao
Shanghai
Xiamen
Hong Kong
Tokyo

50 million guests fly ANA

ANA

A STAR ALLIANCE MEMBER

How to fail to do business in China

Translation *vs* Localisation:
Methods and processes for assuring content integrity

It is a matter of commonsense and courtesy that you do not deliberately insult people with whom you wish to do business. So why do companies trying to do business in China continue to make the same mistakes?

Direct Image Marketing & Communications is the UK's largest provider of Chinese, Japanese and Korean publishing services. We have been serving international airlines, professional firms, publishers, exporters and government departments for over ten years.

We recently conducted research amongst translation houses and their clients to determine how they control quality.

In today's economic climate most translation companies are grateful for the work and are reluctant to specify processes, which will increase their charges. Clients also do not have a systematic way of ensuring that they get the highest quality translations. Very few clients also organise a third party check of translated content. Moreover, many companies use translations after only one proofing stage. Typically this aims only to detect spelling, grammatical and typographical errors, as opposed to carrying out a more rigorous process to assure true meaning has been captured, communication objectives have been met and overall quality preserved. This process requires more detailed cross-checks and specialist editorial/copywriting capabilities, addressing issues such as communicative mission, nature of audience, idiom usage, nuance, tone and register.

Experience shows that companies which understand the need for a systematic approach to localisation are those which produce the highest quality Chinese. The two most important elements of the localisation process are the initial communications brief to the providers and the editorial stage. Use of experienced editors is the crucial element in ensuring the quality of localised material. Many times we have been horrified by the poor results, where there has clearly been little, or no editorial input. In our view it makes the difference between items that are merely a rote translation and those like ours that are indiscernible from well-constructed material actually originated in China. By way of analogy, how many times have we all laughed at the shaky English translations we have read in instructions with imported consumer goods?

This is an important issue for companies, who are consistently very careful with the English language material they produce. Nobody would ignore the importance of corporate image, branding, marketing efficacy, technical accuracy and even legality. Contrast that with what sometimes seems to be an almost inexplicable 'blind faith' in sub-contracted translation, or perhaps a tacit acceptance of a lowered quality cross-bar for foreign language material.

British companies, like their competitors need to balance issues of quality assurance and budget constraint. True localisations that encompass drawing up a communications brief and a proper editorial process are invariably more costly, but to return to our starting point: can you really expect to do business with China if you cannot even communicate in good Chinese?

For more information, contact Lynette Quah, Senior Account Manager for the Chinese Section at Direct Image Marketing & Communications on **020 7336 6579**.

Flap as the butterfly, sting as the bee.

谁与争锋

If you want to be a heavyweight contender in foreign markets, just how far can you trust direct translations? The above caption, actual raw results of English to Chinese to English translation* performed by independent commercial translators, demonstrates the very real hazards of relying on the translation process alone. Our guess is Ali wouldn't be impressed.

For Direct Image, translation is just one step along the path to assuring content integrity. Our native Chinese, Japanese and Korean designers, editors and marketing support staff ensure your message reaches East Asia intact and fully localised to suit the target market.

From print communications including brochures, ads, annual reports, magazines, newsletters, financial journals and technical documents through to websites and digital media, we take the business of communicating in foreign languages seriously.

Because that's exactly how we want *you* to be regarded abroad.

Source text: Float like a butterfly, sting like a bee (your hands can't hit what your eyes can't see) - Muhammad Ali

■ Translation & editorial services ■ Website localisation ■ Design /typesetting/printing ■ Marketing support

Direct Image Marketing & Communications Limited

CHINESE   JAPANESE   KOREAN

Karen House, 1-11 Bache's Street, London N1 6DL, UK
Telephone +44 (0)20 7336 6579   Fax +44 (0)20 7336 7156
Email dimc@direct-image.co.uk   Website www.dimc.co.uk

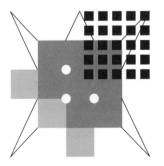

PART SEVEN: LOCAL ECONOMIES – THE 49 PROVINCES, AUTONOMOUS REGIONS, LEADING CITIES AND SPECIAL ADMINISTRATIVE REGIONS

APPENDICES

PART ONE

*Please note: Following the State Council reorganization in March 2003, MOFTEC has been merged with elements of the State Economics and Trade Commission to become the new Ministry of Commerce.

Legal documents available online in Chinese and English

ContractStore has recently published a collection of dual language – Chinese and English – commercial contracts which can be purchased and downloaded from its website at **www.contractstore.com**

Founded in 2000 by an English solicitor, Giles Dixon, the company – The ContractStore Limited – provides a wide range of commercial and construction contracts. Customers include the business community in the UK and China and throughout the world.

All ContractStore documents are prepared by qualified commercial lawyers with substantial international experience. The legal team includes two Chinese lawyers who, working with their English counterparts, have developed Chinese versions of a number of ContractStore contracts suitable for use in China. All the documents come with helpful explanatory notes.

As Xie Rong, Asian marketing director of ContractStore, says "China's recent accession to the World Trade Organisation is going to bring a lot of new foreign companies to China for investment. ContractStore not only offers useful commercial contracts in both languages. We also provide advice to foreign companies on doing business in China and we assist in locating lawyers for them throughout the PRC.

"In addition, we help Chinese lawyers and businesses with their international contracts and with business links to the UK."

The ContractStore's offer presents new opportunities for international business.

在线销售中英文法律文件

合同商店近期在网站上开始销售双语 — 中英文本的商业合同法律文件，这些文件可以直接从 www.contractstore.com 网站上购买并下载。

合同商店有限公司于 2000 年在英国由英国律师 Giles Dixon 投资注册开办，宗旨是在网上提供内容广泛的商业法和建筑法合同。客户包括在英国和中国的商业机构，并广及国际范围。

合同商店的文件由一批相当有经验的从事国际商法的律师起草，其中包括二位中国律师，他们和英国同行一起工作，完成了筛选和翻译适合在中国使用的合同文件。所有的文件都附有有助理解的解释。

如同合同商店的亚洲市场经理谢蓉所说："中国近期的加入 WTO 将会引来很多新的外国公司投资中国。合同商店不仅提供适用的双语商业合同，同时还向外国公司提供到中国进行商务的建议，并协助推荐中国境内的当地律师。

另外，我们也协助中国律师和商界的朋友们建立与英国以及国际间的联系和业务合作。"

合同商店提供面向国际业务的新商机。

www.contractstore.com
enquiries@contractstore.com

ChinaLink LIVERPOOL CHAMBER OF COMMERCE & INDUSTRY
英国利物浦工商会英中贸易联络中心

ChinaLink is a market leader in providing specialist China market consultancy and facilitation service for British companies and organisations. *ChinaLink* has helped hundreds of companies from across the UK in finding partners, locating agents and distributors, setting up representative offices and joint ventures, sourcing products, searching manufacturers, and doing other projects in China.

ChinaLink is a one-stop-shop for Chinese companies interested in the UK market. Several hundreds of Chinese companies have visited the UK market through the arrangement of *ChinaLink*.

Accredited by Trade Partners UK to operate British government schemes in China, *ChinaLink* has provided event management service in China including organisation of tens of inward and outward missions, exhibitions, showcases, trade seminars, trade fairs and other promotion activities each year in China.

ChinaLink's liaison service has facilitated the twinning of Liverpool and Shanghai and has provided advice to support other UK-China cities to work together.

ChinaLink services are open to all. With its head office based in Liverpool Chamber of Commerce, *ChinaLink* operates within the 62 accredited and approved chambers of the British Chamber of Commerce network. In China, *ChinaLink* has teamed up with 19 Chinese chambers including the national Chamber of Commerce to support its operations in China.

"I was very impressed by the valuable work that ChinaLink s doing to enhance business ties between the UK and China. Your undoubted dedication has clearly been a major factor in its success to date and the excellent reputation the organisation holds."
– Dr. Denis MacShane, MP and Minister of Foreign and Commonwealth Office, UK *(22 April 2002)*

"It is obvious from the onset that ChinaLink have vast and personal experience of the country visited. This unique insight makes them a most suitable leadership and can help avoid many of the local pitfalls."
– Denis Sowler, Export Manager, Tithebarn Ltd, UK *(May 2002)*

"It wouldn't have been possible to bring back the £3 million pound contract from China if not for the commercial, diplomatic and linguistic skills of ChinaLink's consultant during the negotiation."
– Alistair Duncan, KPMG consultant and Managing Director, Telescope Technology Ltd, UK *(Jan. 2002)*

Head Office:
Dr. Kegang Wu, Director, *ChinaLink*, One Old Hall Street, Liverpool, L3 9HG UK
Tel: 0151 227 1233/4 Fax: 0151 236 0121 Web: www.chinalink.org.uk Email: chinalink@liverpoolchamber.org.uk

Shanghai Office:
Ms H. Hua, *ChinaLink*, Liverpool Chamber of Commerce & Industry Shanghai Representative Office,
Suite 806, No. 2 Jin Ling Dong Lu, Shanghai 200002
Tel: 021 6232 7703 Fax: 021 6323 7704 Email: chinalink@online.sh.cn

Associated Partner Offices:
Beijing • Shanghai • Guangdong • Guangzhou • Shenzhen • Zhejiang • Jiangsu • Tianjing • Harbin •
Liaoning • Shaanxi • Chengdu • Dalian • Anhui • Yantai • Dongying • Shantou

Foreword

It is my great pleasure to learn that the fourth edition of the book *Doing Business with China* is going to be published soon. I hereby extend my warm congratulations! At the same, I hope that the readers will be able to deepen their understanding about China through the book, and increase their confidence in their trade and investment with China.

The 16th National Congress of the Communist Party concluded not long ago has put forward the grand vision of future objectives, such as 'full engagement in the building of a well-off society' and 'striving to quadruple the 2000 GDP by year 2020'. As a major component of China's national economy, foreign trade will play an important role in achieving the goals of building a well-off society, quadrupling GDP and reaching the level of a mid-developed country. According to the goal of quadrupled GDP, China's total import and export value will hopefully reach US$2 trillion by year 2020, which is equivalent to the total trade of today's world largest trading country. This goal is grand, although gaining it will require arduous efforts. However, I believe that with unremitting effort it is achievable.

In 2002, China saw an increase of 21.8 per cent year on year in its total trade value, registering a new high of US$620.79 billion, which is likely to advance China's ranking in the world from 6th to 5th. Meanwhile, China's absorption of foreign investment in 2002 has reached a total of US$82.77 billion in contract value and US$52.74 billion in actually utilized value, up 19.62 per cent and 12.51 per cent respectively from 2001.

The year 2002 was the first year of China's accession to the WTO and, within the year, China has witnessed a relatively stable and predictable international trade environment, which has facilitated the rapid growth of China's foreign trade and economic cooperation while at the same time offering development opportunities for the international community. In response to China's accession to the WTO, China has rectified, amended and legislated a large number of laws and regulations, which have further driven the perfection process of China's socialist market economy. Joining the WTO has enhanced the recognition by government departments, particularly those government officials who are in the departments of economic management and administration, and Chinese entrepreneurs of the need to participate in international competition and expanded their understanding of international rules. China's accession to the WTO has not only had important implications on China's further opening up and active participation in the economic globalization process in the year 2002, but will also continue to play an important role in that regard for a considerable period of time in the future. Upon China's entry into the WTO, China has lowered tariffs, further opened up the market for goods and gradually opened the service sectors, all of which will have important facilitating effects on the development of the national economy and foreign trade.

On 10 December 2002, the WTO completed its review of China's trade policy. China's serious and responsible attitude and its work in carrying out its commitments have won just and objective appraisal and affirmation from most of the WTO members. At the same time, as a new member of the WTO, China has also been actively involved in the new-round of multilateral trade negotiations, in which China has interacted with other WTO members in a concerted effort to pursue a balanced interest between developing and developed members in the multilateral trade system. Thereby, China has played a constructive role in the multilateral trade system.

China's opening up has entered a new era after its WTO accession. The positive effect on China's economic development is being further demonstrated. In order to adapt to the new circumstances in the development of economic globalization, China will walk in the world with an even more active posture and continue to further an all-round, multi-tiered and wider range of opening up. All those efforts will continue to provide even greater room and more and better opportunities for foreign investments and various other forms of economic and technological cooperation.

Shi Guangsheng
Minister, Ministry of Foreign Trade and Economic Cooperation

Foreword

Pascal Lamy, EU Trade Commissioner

To say that China figured prominently on our trade and economic agenda in the last few years would be an understatement.

The deepening of our bilateral trade and economic relations – both imports and exports have more than doubled in just the last five years – has been reflected in the dramatic increase in the bilateral contacts at all levels between the European Commission and the Chinese authorities. This is not only due to the fact that increased trade flows also mean a more complex relationship (including more trade disputes, inevitably), but also to the recognition that China immediately became a key player within the multilateral trading system, and in particular in the context of the Doha Development Agenda, the new round of multilateral trade negotiations launched in 2001.

So China, quite frankly, now sits at the top table in terms of world trade, a position which comes with responsibilities, as well as rights. The signs are positive that China is ready to take up both aspects of this role, and thereby play a key role in the new global economic order.

In particular, China's accession to the WTO on 11 December 2001 has opened up a new period of dramatic changes, both for China and her trading partners including the EU and the multilateral trading system. The accession came indeed as a crowning point of the policy of opening launched in the 1970s by China based on the conviction of the Chinese leadership that accession to the WTO would benefit the Chinese economy enormously and would underpin the reform process towards a market economy. The EU has always been a staunch supporter of this accession, since the emergence of a stable and prosperous China, moreover a China that is well integrated into the international trading system, is without any doubt in our own interests.

Of course, now it is for China to ensure that the substantial commitments made in the context of the accession negotiations are implemented on the ground, not least because China is now the fourth largest trader in the world (counting the EU as one entity). One year after China's accession, it is fair to say that China has made impressive efforts to meet her WTO obligations, especially in the legislative areas. Hundreds of laws and regulations have been updated. The legal framework is not yet fully WTO compatible in each and every aspect, but given the starting point one year ago, achieving the current level is already a remarkable performance. The EU, as I think all trade partners of China, acknowledges that the Chinese leadership is eager to demonstrate that China will abide by her WTO obligations.

However, there is no time for complacency and much remains to be done. First of all, many of China's commitments are due to enter into force over a transitional period, which means that the benefits will only flow through over the years to come. Second, in some areas, we have witnessed the establishment of non-trade barriers which are in part neutralizing the liberalization brought by WTO accession. Third, if it is not always easy to respect the letter of WTO obligation (eg the reduction of some tariff lines), it is even more difficult to ensure that the core principles of WTO – among which the rule of law, the transparency and the predictability – are fully integrated into the daily task of the administrative and judiciary system.

So the EU has developed, in liaison with the Chinese authorities, a number of technical assistance projects, the main objective of which is to help the Chinese administration in charge of implementing China's WTO obligations. Current projects total 22 million euros, and the design of a new 15 million euro project is being finalized. This is, thus, the largest technical assistance programme supporting China's integration into the international trading system.

The European Commission, in liaison with EU Member States and EU stakeholders, and in particular the European Chamber of Commerce in China, has closely monitored the implementation by China of her WTO commitments during the past twelve months. Implementation issues have been raised, particularly in the framework of the Transitional Review Mechanism, the mechanism foreseen within WTO to review China's accession on an annual basis. The results of this exercise offer a good snapshot of Chinese WTO implementation.

In this context, while 2002 had a special character with China's first steps within the WTO, 2003 will be crucial since the months to come will see the confirmation of China's involvement within the multilateral trading system. The new leaders, who will be at the helm from next March onwards, have in this respect a formidable task ahead.

And while the Chinese new leadership is not expected to implement dramatic changes in terms of economic and trade policy, the EU is eager to maintain and develop the same multi-layered, multi-faceted relationship with the new generation of leaders that we have had with the current generation.

So in this context, the fourth edition of *Doing Business with China*, by presenting the different points of view of the various players and their insight into the dramatic changes going on in China, will serve as a most valuable tool.

Foreword

Robert A Kapp, President, United States-China Business Council

'Doing Business with China' is a hallowed term, rich with the flavour of those early years of China's commercial re-engagement with the global economy following its decision to 'open to the outside world' in 1978.

In the 1970s and early eighties, 'Doing Business with China' was the title of a thousand seminars, most of which informed their participants that Beijing was in the north and Guangzhou in the south; that the Yangtze and other major rivers flowed from west to east; that the Chinese economy was experimenting with various departures from the Maoist-Stalinist planning system of the first decades of communist rule; and other elementary observations that still, in those days of broad foreign unfamiliarity with the PRC, constituted business-useful information.

With the passage of years, 'Doing Business with China' lost much of its electrifying appeal. By the 1990s, major firms in the developed economies – particularly multinationals – were engaging with China in increasingly significant and complex ways. Following the downturn in international confidence caused by the traumatic events of the spring and summer of 1989 and their aftermath, global business interest in China bounded ahead in the mid-1990s, reassured by then-leader Deng Xiaoping's evident commitment to preserve the overall policy direction known as 'Reform and Opening'. Foreign direct investment in China soared throughout that decade and companies gradually added to their store of on-the-ground experience. Meanwhile, China presented itself to the world, through its products and its people. Tens of thousands of able and motivated Chinese went abroad for study, research, and practical training. The exoticism of China declined in international business circles as it became more and more integrated into the global business plans of large companies worldwide. 'Doing Business with China,' in the older sense of the term, became the label for more and more humble exercises aimed at passers-by in the business world and at those whose lack of initiative or resources had kept them on the sidelines of China's growing international commercial engagement.

Now, it can well be argued, 'Doing Business with China' is in for a new life, of which this massive compendium of information and analysis is a perfect illustration. This publication is most welcome, and will be important to wide audiences for years to come.

Let me explain what I mean by 'a new life' for the notion of 'Doing Business with China'.

First of all, with China's entry into the World Trade Organization, we are very likely to see a quantum increase in the number of businesses both Chinese and non-Chinese that set out to find and maximize their opportunities in Sino-foreign trade and investment. Under the WTO, 'trading rights' – the right to import and export directly – are being provided to thousands upon thousands of Chinese firms, many of them private and non-governmental, who could not do international business before. We are seeing a huge increase in the number of Chinese companies and individuals hoping to break into international markets in any of a myriad of ways. One aspect of the new 'Doing Business with China' is that the 'China' with whom people outside of the PRC can 'do business' is changing before our eyes.

Second, as China normalizes its trade and economic relations with the world under the reassuring umbrella of WTO-defined standards of behaviour, legions of foreign firms that until recently had refrained from contemplating direct business relations with China are deciding that there is no time like the present, and taking their own steps to familiarize themselves with the business environment in the PRC. We see, certainly in the United States at any rate, a powerful wave of interest among smaller firms, for example, in finding opportunities to grow their businesses with, or in, China.

Large or small, American companies' heightened interest in China in recent years has been linked to increased corporate investment within China, as it improves its investment climate and proves to be both a growing domestic market and a solid producer of goods for global absorption. While many remain to be fully realized over a period of years, China's extensive WTO commitments define a range of truly historic transformations of its economic and commercial environment, and represent a fundamental commitment at the highest levels of China's political leadership to harmonizing China's trade and economic policies with those of the global trading system.

This process of law and policy change under the WTO is clearly leading to heightened international business interest in setting up operations on the ground in China and in establishing the chains of supply, finance, marketing and service that characterize modern global business. That, in turn, has led many multinationals to encourage their own international vendors and suppliers to come to China in the wake of the megafirms' decisions to operate there. These new entrants into the Chinese business environment at the start of the 21st century also need to know how to 'Do Business with China', and are a factor in the revitalization of this old and familiar phrase.

Even in companies with decades of experience with China, 'Doing Business with China' will resonate anew. For one thing, those companies that have built extensive business operations in China, or who have established solid and vital trading relationships with PRC counterparts, now pump a constant and growing flow of staff members through the China mill. Most company personnel now working on China have strong foundations of technical and business experience within their firms, but China represents a 'normal' assignment, a little different from other international postings or, for that matter, from appointments to any number of corporate positions at home.

It is not necessary now – and in fact, it never really was – to have a PhD in Chinese studies and linguistic fluency to function effectively in business with China. But it is necessary for business people to know what China is, and what its economic and political and social milieux consists of, and how they are distinct from, say,

comparable milieux in France or South Africa or Korea or India. For these corporate professionals, then, a comprehensive and wide-ranging volume like this will provide a convenient companion, as they bring their corporate experience and business skills to bear on the normal business tasks they seek to accomplish in China.

Finally, the new incarnation of the idea of 'Doing Business with China' embodied in this massive and comprehensive book brings home the point that we at the United States-China Business Council have known for three decades: one can never know all there is to know about business with the PRC, because the PRC itself is so massive, so complex, and constantly evolving. The company that concludes it has reached a level of understanding of China so strong that it needs to reach no further is a company in peril. Intelligent companies know better, and adopt a posture with regard to China that is both humble and intellectually curious; they build on what they know from experience, and what they learn from other firms' experiences through the medium of business associations like the organization I serve. They continually ask themselves whether their current approaches both to long-range goals and immediate operational challenges are the best choices in the contemporary environment. They weigh perceived opportunities and perceived risks. They ponder the current policy and regulatory systems of China, the legal uncertainties attendant upon China operations, the chances of success of one business model versus another.

All of this requires information, both at the baseline and in real time. The week's news of policy shifts, new laws and regulations, changes of political personnel, trade negotiations, and so forth is important, and the best entrants into the burgeoning field of China business information (such as the magazine, *The China Business Review*, published by my Council) provide business readers and planners with material they need each day, week, and month.

But real-time information cannot stand alone. Baseline information, brought up to date periodically to reflect the changed Chinese business environment, is equally important. That is where *Doing Business with China* – the book, as opposed to the phrase – will serve well.

Let me close this Foreword with a note of caution. There is no single, universal interpretation of any of the topics covered in this wide-ranging volume. While Chinese and non-Chinese perspectives on the Chinese business environment have often converged over the past two and one-half decades, they frequently differ.

Moreover, if China ever saw these subjects with a single mind, those days are long past and it is possible in today's China to find multiple views and interpretations of all the core topics of interest to international business. Thus, the essays contained in this fine volume must not be seen as the only descriptions and analyses available, but as baseline guides, to be tested and refined by individual readers as they move through their own experiences and consult with a multiplicity of advisers and colleagues.

Second, at the US-China Business Council we are very aware that China's immense business relations with the world take place within the context of both Chinese domestic politics and of international political relations. China's international commercial behaviour is inextricably linked to the state of China's economy, its society, and its politics, on the one hand, and to China's broader political relations with key trading partners such as the United States, the European Union, Japan, and Taiwan. *Doing Business with China* does not plumb these topics, which are the domain of legions of China scholars and analysts worldwide. But China, like other countries, has politics; it makes its laws and regulations, and carries them out in a complex environment of personal relationships, densely ramified institutions, evolving and increasingly complex legal structures, difficult social issues, shifting central-local authority relationships, and multifaceted relations among bureaucracies. The obscurity of Chinese political behaviour at times makes business decision-making more speculative than business people would wish.

Much of this more politically-inflected reality is normally left undiscussed by Chinese writers, perhaps for a couple of principal reasons. First, writing for public consumption about the political manoeuvrings and power relationships undergirding China's changing international business environment might not be good for one's own political health; such observations can involve closely guarded bureaucratic or even personal interests which are better left beyond the reach of prying eyes. Second, the play of political, personal, and interest-group forces on the making of the Chinese business environment is itself subject to widely varying interpretations. There is no one single definitive description suitable for use in a Baedeker Guide to business with China, and readers seeking unitary guidance through the political thickets surrounding the Chinese economic and commercial environment would be on a fool's errand.

So it is no tragedy that *Doing Business with China* has not delved deeply into these realms. But it is worth remembering, as one courses through the dozens of valuable entries in this compendium, that in practice, 'on the ground,' the texture of operational realities will continue to challenge the curiosity of business people in every field, in every province, in every city.

To conclude, I welcome this massive volume, its familiar title endowed with new life in a new era of Sino-global business, and expect that it will serve as a baseline resource for business people worldwide for years to come.

Robert A Kapp has been president of the United States-China Business Council since 1994. Founded in 1973, the Council (www.uschina.org) is the principal organization of American companies engaged in trade and investment with China, serving several hundred corporate members from its headquarters in Washington and field offices in Beijing and Shanghai. The Council also publishes the authoritative China Business Review (www.chinabusinessreview.com).

Dr Kapp was educated at Swarthmore and Yale, receiving his PhD in modern Chinese history from Yale in 1970. He taught on the faculties of Rice University (Houston) and the University of Washington (Seattle) between 1970 and 1980, serving as editor of The Journal of Asian Studies from 1978 to 1980. From 1980 to 1994 he led two trade associations in Washington State. On behalf of the US-China Business Council, Dr Kapp is active in the field of US-China relations, and writes regularly on US-China issues.

THE 48 GROUP CLUB
"The Icebreakers"

The 48 Group Club, whose origins stretch back to 1953, has maintained its high profile and excellent relationship with Chinese commerce at all levels and in all regions. The Club continues to act as an effective bridge for Chinese and British businesses.

Whether you are newcomer to China or an 'old hand', you will find a warm welcome in **The 48 Group Club**.

For membership or Club details please contact:
The 48 Group Club
42 Heath Drive
London SW20 9BG

Tel/Fax: 020 8542 8857
Email: carolinejcook@blueyonder.co.uk

Promoting Positive Trade and Cultural Relations with People's Republic of China

Introduction

Jonathan Reuvid and Li Yong

The publication of this fourth edition of *Doing Business with China* marks China's first two historic events of the twenty-first century. On 11 December 2001, the country finally became a member of the World Trade Organization (WTO), and on 15 November of that year, with the official announcement of Mr Hu Jintao's appointment as Mr Jiang Zemin's successor, the smooth transfer of government to China's fourth generation of leaders was accomplished.

WTO membership

The immediate impact on foreign trade and foreign direct investment (FDI) of China's WTO entry in 2002 is summarised below and in the first chapter of the book by Li Shantong of the Development Research Centre of the State Council. The longer term implications of WTO membership, both for investment and trade in the context of China's further opening up, are explored in depth in Parts One and Two by an array of Chinese and foreign authors ranging from Liu Xiangdong, Vice Ministerial Chair and Hu Jingyan, Director General, Department of Foreign Investment, MOFTEC, and Shi Yonghai, Chairman, China Association of International Trade, to the Brussels office partners of law firm Herbert Smith.

These different perspectives on WTO entry, supported by the prefaces of Lord Brittan, former EU Trade Commissioner and Shen Jueren, Honorary President of China Association of International Trade, contribute to the central theme of this book: China's overwhelming sense of purpose in becoming an active player in the world economy. Readers will be struck by the wholehearted nature of the commitments China has made to the WTO and in particular the determination to infuse international standards of transparency into the regulation of the economy and business management practice.

China's resilient economy

The sustained growth of China's economy continues to impress commentators and critics alike. GDP growth for the full year 2002 is set to reach 8 per cent at the time of writing, while industrial production in the 12 months ending October 2002 increased by 14.2 per cent, ahead of all other developing countries and in marked contrast to the lacklustre economies of the EU and the United States. The first fruits of WTO entry have been the doubling of China's monthly trade surplus to US$4.75 billion in October 2002, raising the 12 month trade surplus to US$30.0 billion, and the resurgent foreign direct investment (FDI) which is likely to exceed US$50 billion for 2002, a record new annual inflow.

However, critics of China's macro-economic management continue to focus on the unresolved weaknesses of the state-owned banking sector and the non-performing debts of state-owned enterprises (SOEs), which equate to a significant proportion of GDP. After this year's experience of major corporate collapses in western financial markets, finger-pointing at irregularities in China carries less conviction and the tough strategy which China has promulgated for the restructure of SOEs (see Chapter 1.8), if carried through, will address public sector indebtedness over time.

Perhaps because they are now too accustomed to economic life in low-growth economies, western observers tend to overlook the momentum and accelerator effects of China's high growth and high FDI business environment on the creation of national wealth. Visitors to any of China's buoyant cities are struck by the pervasive growth-orientated outlook which differentiates business development in China from business back home.

In his valedictory address to congress of 9 November, Mr Jiang Zemin laid emphasis on continuing economic stability and growth, setting the target of a four-fold increase in GDP by 2020. Continued annual growth of at least 7 per cent is probably necessary to offset the problems already mentioned, as well as the threat of rising unemployment as inefficient and uneconomic SOEs are culled. In this context, the positive stimulus to the economy provided by WTO entry is of paramount importance.

Market entry and operations in China

Part Two of the book brings readers up to date on the regulation and mechanics of foreign trade as both tariff and non-tariff barriers are lowered further or withdrawn in stages over the coming years.

Parts Three and Four will be more familiar to readers of previous editions of *Doing Business with China*. In Part Three, essential briefings are given by two British law firms practising in China, Herbert Smith and Denton Wilde Sapte, on the regulatory and reporting requirements for setting up business entities and investing directly in China.

The Beijing office of PricewaterhouseCoopers has updated its previous chapters on accounting and auditing requirements, taxation and the differences between PRC Accounting Regulations and International Accounting Standards. Finally, in Part Three, CCPIT Patents Trademark Law Office has provided trademark and patent administration guidance.

Part Four, although familiar, focuses more thoroughly than before on the marketing and business development aspects of doing business successfully in China. For corporate readers who have taken the primary decision to engage in the Chinese market as importers, exporters or investors, we urge you to treat the whole of Part Four as required background reading.

Part Five is intended specifically for those businesses whose involvement will include the opening and operation of bank accounts in China in local and/or foreign currency. As restrictions on the activities of authorised foreign banks in handling RMB accounts are lifted over the next five years, the increased competition in banking will cause Chinese banks to conform more closely to international best practice. Part Five concludes with an overview of the organisation and supervision of China's securities market.

Market segmentation

The manufacturing and service industries profiled in Part Six are those which we have identified as offering growing opportunities for foreign companies, either to invest, as shareholders restrictions are relaxed, or to trade profitably as tariff barriers or quotas are progressively reduced.

Part Seven profiles the local economies of China's 49 provinces, autonomous regions, leading cities and the two special administrative regions (SARs), Hong Kong and Macao. Statistics and commentaries are more comprehensive than in previous editions.

Appendices

In earlier editions, appendices pertinent to content were positioned at the end of the respective Parts and only the general appendices were grouped at the end of the book. For this edition, for ease of reading, we have gathered all appendices at the end of the book, grouped according to the relevant Parts.

Acknowledgements

As always, we offer our grateful thanks to the many individual authors whose collective contributions have made this wide-ranging compendium possible. Most are listed individually in the Contents list at the front of the book and all their names and contact details are listed in Appendix I – Contributors Contact List, at the end of the book. However, particular words of appreciation are due to our colleague, Professor Liu Baocheng of the University of International Business and Economics, Beijing, who has contributed chapters on a variety of topics throughout the book, and also to Chen Duo, Deputy Director General of Hong Kong & Macao Research Institute who provided the profiles of the two SARs in Part Seven. We also owe special thanks to Ms Long Miao of China Import and Export Bank and Ms Pang Kuixia of China Securities Regulatory Commission for their efforts in contributing two insightful chapters on behalf of their respective organisations. In addition, we would like to express our gratitude to the students of the University of International Business and Economics, Lang Yigang, Tian Jie, Li Guanghua, Chai Hua, Mo Ye, Zhang Wei, Li Jiayin and Li Han, for their research and secretarial support.

We wish to convey our sincere and respectful thanks for their Forewords to Minister Shi Guangsheng of

MOFTEC, EU Trade Commissioner Pascal Lamy and Dr Robert Kapp, President, United States-China Business Council, and again to Mr Shen Jueren and Lord Brittan, now Vice-Chairman, UBS Warburg, for their Prefaces.

Finally, we express our appreciation and that of Kogan Page to HSBC and Cable and Wireless, our two sponsors, without whose contributions this edition of *Doing Business with China* would not have been possible.

Li Yong, Beijing
Jonathan Reuvid, London,
December 2002

China Association of International Trade

Who are we?

Established in Beijing in July 1981, China Association of International Trade (CAIT) is the first national research organisation in the field of international trade in the wake of China's opening up and economic reform. Under the direct leadership of the Ministry of International Trade and Economic Cooperation, CAIT's mission is to research and explore solutions, both in terms of theory and practice, to issues regarding China's development of foreign trade and economic cooperation. CAIT has members all over China. They include both business entities and research organisations. CAIT has a pool of top-level well-known experts, government officials, scholars, entrepreneurs and ex-diplomats on its directorate.

What do we do?

In addition to its professional research oriented towards filling gaps between trade and investment theories and practices, CAIT is committed to studying issues that have important implications for China's trade and investment policies. CAIT also undertakes other activities involving both its member and non-member organisations, such as the organisation of various kinds of workshops, seminars and training courses, market research and consulting, international academic exchanges, provision of information and research findings for governments and enterprises, the publication of magazines and books and business referral services.

How can we help you?

CAIT has an extensive network of members and good working relationships with both government at all levels and the business community at large in China. We can help you in a number of different ways. We can be a point of contact for anything where you think you would need someone to help. Speak to us about what help you need and we will come up with a solution.

Contact:

China Association of International Trade
2, Dong Chang An Street
Beijing 100731, China

Tel: +86-10-65197955 Fax: +86-10-6525 5899 E-mail: caitmoftec@mail.china.com

Preface: China, the EU and the WTO after Chinese accession

The Rt Hon The Lord Brittan of Spennithorne QC, Vice-Chairman of UBS Warburg and consultant to Herbert Smith, Former EU Commissioner for external trade relations and competition policy

There are three aspects to China's accession to the WTO and its impact on EU business. Firstly, the impact on the European Union; secondly, the business opportunities that arise for Europe in China as a result of its WTO membership; and thirdly China's role as a WTO member in the Doha Development Round and in the workings of the WTO more generally.

As far as China's access to the European market is concerned, it is important to stress that the new rights that China has, either vis-à-vis Europe or other members of the WTO, are now legally enforceable rights. Whether we are talking about China's access to the EU market or the EU's access to the Chinese market there are bound to be disagreements, which are not a reflection of the good faith of either side but rather of the fact that in any major agreement there are certain to be ambiguities and uncertainties. These should be resolved as far as possible by discussion and negotiation but if that is not possible then both China and the EU should not feel in any way inhibited in going to a dispute settlement procedure, because that is what it is there for. To use it is not to embark on a 'trade war', but is rather a sign of readiness to use the machinery that exists to deal with disputes and resolve ambiguities and I hope that both China and the European Union will look at it in that spirit.

In terms of the actual economic impact on the EU, there is a certain degree of phasing in but the most important opening up of the European market for China will consist of the ending of quotas by 2005 and the fact that it will probably be harder to apply safeguard measures, if anyone is inclined to do so, even before that period expires. The end of quotas is of considerable significance and European industry has to prepare for that. The biggest impact of China's membership in terms of access to the European market is likely to be in the area of textiles, where one can expect enhanced competition and increased exports from China. It is not clear how active China will be in seeking to enforce its rights with regards to Europe. China has focused more on the impact of WTO membership on its own market than on the opportunities it gives it in other markets such as Europe. But even if this is the case to begin with, it will change as membership gathers momentum. It is interesting for example to see that China itself is now taking an interest in imposing antidumping measures, which previously was not something that China did at all.

The other side of the equation is EU opportunities in China. To gauge what is actually going to happen it is enormously important to understand why China wanted to join the WTO. China's huge growth since 1979 has very much been associated with growth in trade. China's share of world trade grew five fold between 1978 and 1998, but more important (because we are talking about growth from a very low base) is the fact that exports as a proportion of China's GDP increased from 5 to nearly 25 per cent. Thus, the growth of the Chinese economy was associated with the growth in exports and the Chinese leadership understood very well that while this was beneficial, it was not sustainable without China opening up to the rest of the world and, moreover, that opening up would be beneficial. For the Chinese leadership, opening up the economy is not a favour to the rest of the world, nor is it even just a political gesture done in order to join the WTO because China wishes to participate actively in all international organizations. Rather it is a crucial part of the Chinese reform and modernization programme. The leadership believes that the spur of foreign competition, with foreign entry into the market, not only in terms of trade but also in terms of investment, will help the Chinese economy to modernize. As far as the leadership is concerned, this idea has been internalized. It is not just a question of reluctantly accepting obligations hardly negotiated in the discussions on the terms of Chinese membership of the WTO.

It is also important to note that, in spite of the far reaching nature of China's WTO commitments, it would be wrong to regard the results as just providing an opportunity for Europe, the United States or Japan to grab business. We can already see that the prospect of liberalization is having the effect that it is intended to have, namely to help strengthen the Chinese economy. Financial services are a good example. Foreign banks will be able to conduct local currency business with domestic corporate customers two years after accession and with any Chinese after five years. This process has led to the reform of the 'Big Four' state owned banks. This is a very painful process, but they are getting rid of non performing loans, introducing principles of corporate governance, hitherto unknown, and the Bank of China has restructured its Hong Kong operations and floated on the Hong Kong stock exchange. So what you are seeing is the strengthening of the Chinese economy to handle the new foreign access to it. We should not, therefore, assume that there will simply be rich pickings and that the Chinese will sit and wait to have their markets scooped up by foreigners.

The question sometimes asked, though, is: can China implement these reforms? It is a huge task and the results are bound to be patchy. We can't ignore the possibility of new barriers being erected if the going gets tough or if there is a strong political desire to resist in a particular area. That can be done in all sorts of ways which are difficult to penetrate through the WTO rules such as in the grant of state approvals for the setting up of banks. But I don't believe that this will be the norm.

I think that we will see the capacity as well as the intention to implement the reforms, and good faith in doing so.

Finally, a word about China's role as a member of the WTO. It is hugely important. It is a major player but it is not yet clear how China is going to play it in the WTO. I don't think China has made up its own mind yet. One thing I am quite sure about is that it is not right to assume that China is just going to be a cheerleader for the developing world. It has distinctive interests of its own which are often, but not always, the same as developing countries, and this was reflected in the negotiations. I was constantly being asked: is China a developing country? The answer is yes, in certain respects it is, but it is also a very large country and therefore it can't expect to be treated in exactly the same way as an ordinary developing country. By the same token it is not now going to behave as an ordinary developing country.

I hope that China will conclude that further liberalization of the world economy is in its interests. It is a great exporter and further liberalization must be in its interest. China will certainly be difficult if there are any excessive attempts to impose new environmental obligations, which do not at present operate in the world trading system. While we can expect China to resist that, I hope it will be a supporter of Europe in the belief that agreements on competition and investment are a legitimate part of the new round and that negotiations for these should be effectively launched in the review period. I do believe that the total impact, the net impact of China's presence, will be a positive one, but China, I suspect, will be feeling its way and I hope that those who have close contacts with and are friends of China will use their influence to try and help it see that the further liberalization of trade is in its interest and try to persuade those who are less sure that this is the right way forward.

おもてなしのエアライン

/With New Style, Club ANA you're in Business

ANA now flies daily from London Heathrow and 14 European connecting cities to Japan, Asia and the Pacific.

Relax with our in-seat massage and a selection of fine western and Japanese food. Catch up on your work with a personal laptop computer connection or be entertained with 58 audio-visual channels including games and the latest films. All followed by a good night's sleep on our flat-bed seat.

With New Style, Club ANA you really are in business.

50 million guests fly ANA

ANA ◢

A STAR ALLIANCE MEMBER ✧

Preface

Shen Jueren, Honorary Chairman, China Association of International Trade, Former Vice Minister of the Ministry of Foreign Trade and Economic Cooperation, People's Republic of China

This newly published fourth edition of *Doing Business with China* has been enriched with plenty of fresh content which will undoubtedly prove a useful guide to business people around the world.

China became an official member of the World Trade Organisation (WTO) on 11 December 2001. China's accession to the WTO not only represents a new era in its opening up to the outside world, but also marks the beginning of a new period of development for the economic exchanges between China and the rest of the world.

The Chinese government has solemnly pledged that it will fully implement all its commitments to the WTO and will abide by the various rules and protocols. To this end, China has made necessary amendments and revisions to the laws and regulations governing its foreign economic and trade activities. Some new laws and regulations have been legislated while those that are not in conformity with the WTO rules have been phased out. All of these will ensure that all WTO rules, treaties and protocols can be fully implemented.

In the meantime, we also request all other members of the WTO community to honour their respective commitments and implement the relevant rules in order to achieve balanced rights and obligations among members.

China's entry into the WTO will certainly provide more opportunities for foreign companies to trade with China, and it will also serve to create a better environment for foreign investments in China. Readers will be able to obtain a detailed understanding of China from this book.

It is my sincere wish that the publication of this book will help people from around the world to deepen their understanding of China's economic regime and foreign economic and trade realities, on the basis of which cooperation for mutual benefit between Chinese and foreign businesses will be further enhanced so as to contribute to the development of world economy and trade.

About the Editors

Jonathan Reuvid

Economist and international business strategist, Jonathan Reuvid has specialized in the development of joint ventures and technology transfers in Northern China since 1984. In 1993 he formed an association with Li Yong, then Managing Director of the Centre for Market and Trade Development (CMTD), to write and publish the first edition of *Doing Business with China*.

After graduating in PPE at Oxford and service in the Scots Guards, Jonathan Reuvid was employed as economist by the French national oil company, Total, for its newly formed UK subsidiary. From there he moved into investment banking, financial consultancy and corporate planning, focusing on the application of market research techniques to diversification and acquisition strategy.

There followed a series of appointments in industry including Director of European Operations for Associated Spring Barnes Group, the US multinational manufacturer of precision-engineered components.

Since 1989 Jonathan has embarked on a second career in business publishing, initially in trade magazines and then in the editing and writing of a series of international business books, and guides to management, financial practice and business start-ups, all for Kogan Page.

Currently Jonathan Reuvid is series editor for *Global Market Briefings*, a new Kogan Page series to be supported by websites, focused on the Central and East European States which are Accession Candidates for the EU in 2004. This fourth, expanded edition of *Doing Business with China* is published as a part of the new series.

Li Yong

Li Yong is a leading expert in market research and marketing in China. His present position is the Deputy Secretary General of China Association of International Trade, which is a national organization in China that advises governments on trade and investment policies, and companies on corporate development strategies. His responsibilities include business development, training of local and foreign business executives, research on key trade and investment issues and corporate development strategies.

After graduating from the University of International Business and Economics, the leading business school in China, in 1986 with a Master's Degree in economics, Li Yong joined the International Trade Research Institute (ITRI) as a researcher of international commodity markets. Between 1988 and 1992, he worked in China Intric Limited, Hong Kong, which was a company specializing in marketing services and research. He was the manager of its Marketing Services Department and was subsequently promoted to Assistant General Manager. His responsibilities encompassed a range of marketing services, including marketing and research services for foreign businesses with interests in China, the promotion of Chinese products to the overseas market and information services for both Chinese and foreign customers.

In October 1992, Li Yong came back to Beijing from Hong Kong and was appointed Deputy Director of the Centre for Market and Trade Development (CMTD), which is a consulting arm of the Chinese Academy of International Trade and Economic Cooperation (CAITEC) of China's Ministry of Foreign Trade and Economic Cooperation (MOFTEC). In 1995, he became CMTD's Director. During his eight-year leadership of CMTD, Li Yong developed CMTD into CAITEC's profit centre. His client base included many blue chip multinationals and international institutions. He has extensive hands-on experiences in a variety of industries and in providing advisory services with different consulting requirements. He joined the China Association of International Trade in 2001. He also holds management positions, as China Director of PMC Consulting, an American firm that specializes in business development strategies in the Asia Pacific area, and as Executive Director of Sino-World Sincerity Advertising.

With his English proficiency and years of working experience with western companies, Li Yong has developed a good understanding of western culture and mindsets, with which he has been successfully advising foreign companies in China on their corporate communications, joint venture negotiations, human resource management, marketing/advertizing campaigns and training programmes. As a part of his consulting effort to improve corporate performances of foreign businesses in China, Li Yong has developed his own set of methodologies in dealing with cultural differences and clashes in the context of joint venture negotiations and management.

In addition to his wide market research and consulting experience, which has generated a network of associates and contacts throughout the leading business centres in China, Li Yong has also been actively involved in seminars and corporate training venues both at home and abroad. At the same time, he is a guest professor at the University of International Business and Economics and the Institute of Economic Management. He has been invited to conduct lectures at Peking University, one of China's most renowned universities, for their executive MBA programmes. His recent lectures at those universities included a variety of subjects such as strategic considerations for Chinese companies investing outside China, changing marketing environments of the pharmaceutical industry after WTO, implications of WTO accession on corporate competitive landscape and strategies of multinational companies in China. For four consecutive years, Li Yong has been teaching business courses, 'Marketing in China' and 'Purchasing from China', at an executive training college that conducts training programmes for foreign business executives and students. One of the research projects he is now involved in is on sustainable foreign trade development strategy for China. Li Yong has been the co-editor and co-author of all four editions of this book *Doing Business with China*.

HONG KONG INTERNATIONAL AIRPORT

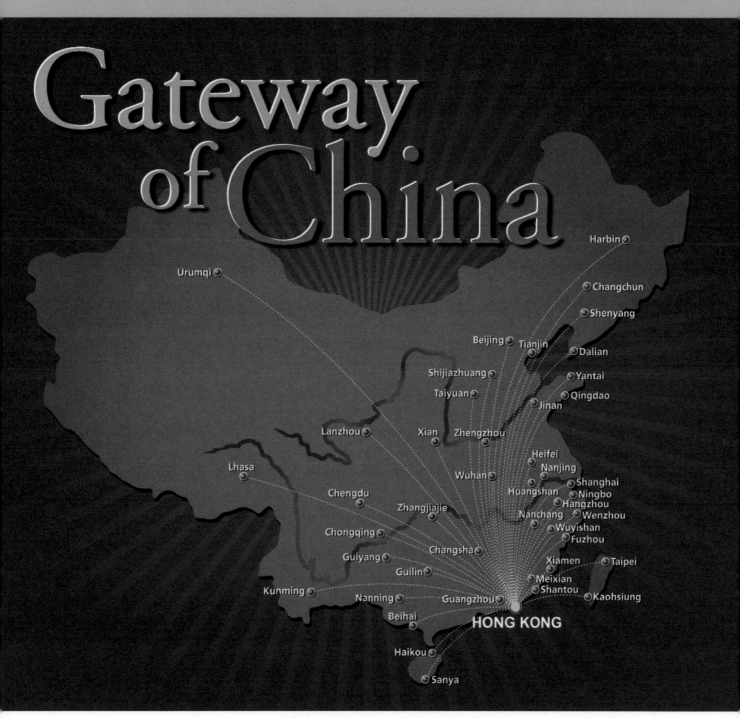

Gateway
of China

Hong Kong International Airport (HKIA) is one of the world's busiest international airports - some 76 airlines operate more than 3,900 flights every week to over 130 destinations worldwide, including 42 cities in the Mainland of China. With half of the world's population within 5 hours' flying time from Hong Kong, HKIA is indeed a prominent aviation hub for the region and the gateway of China.

香港 | AIRPORT
機場管理局 | AUTHORITY
| HONG KONG

AIRPORT AUTHORITY HONG KONG
I CHEONG YIP ROAD, HONG KONG INTERNATIONAL AIRPORT, LANTAU, HONG KONG
TELEPHONE (852) 2188 7111   FACSIMILE (852) 2824 0717   WEBSITE WWW.HONGKONGAIRPORT.COM

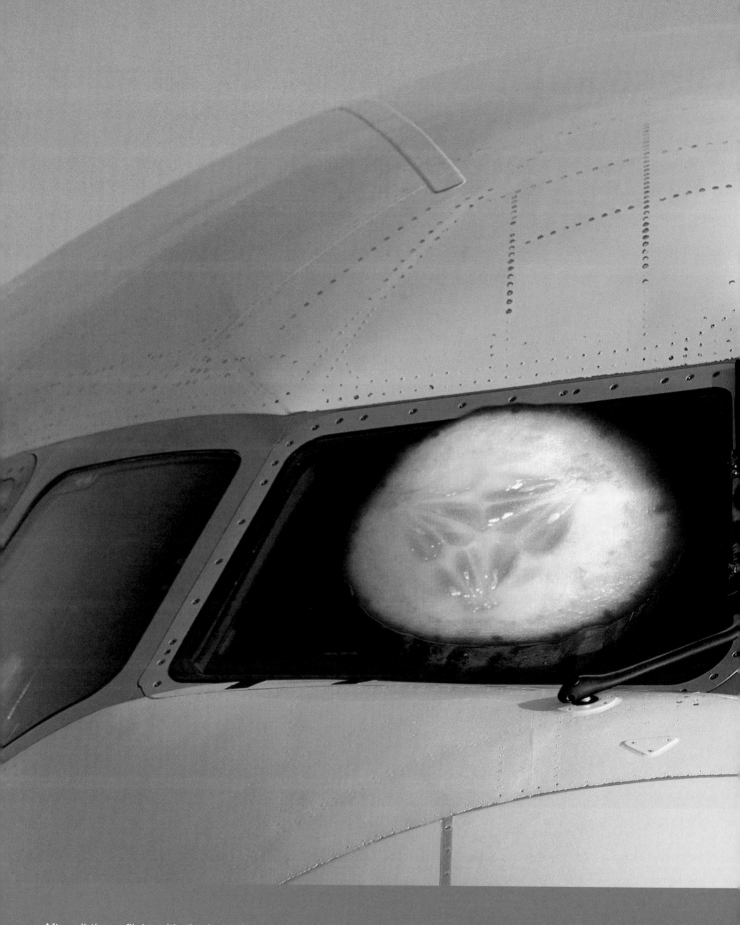

After all those flights, it's the least they deserve. And we, at KLM Engineering & Maintenance, know exactly how to indulge them. We have a global presence that delivers base, line, and heavy maintenance for airframes, engines and components, as well as modification programs for all Boeing 737 series (including Next Generation), 747, 767 and MD-11.

We handle all types of CF6 engines and we can repair and deliver over 12,000 components while handling everything from single shop order to Total Component Care®.

And all of this is available within a Total Aircraft Care® package, managing all your MRO requirements in an integrated program.

TLC from nose to tail

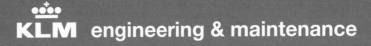

kem Total Aircraft Care®

From its location at Schiphol East, KLM Engineering & Maintenance offers, with approximately 5,000 employees, customers Total Aircraft Care. This includes Total Airframe-, Total Engine-, and Total Component maintenance or any other tailormade services. Heavy maintenance is performed on B747, -737, and -767, GE CF6 engines and all related components. CFM56 capabilities are added by 2004.

The maintenance services have been fully accredited by many aviation authorities, including the FAA, JAA and CAA-NL. All maintenance can be done on a basis of flight-hours 'time and material' and fixed fee. Line Maintenance capabilities at homebase and worldwide include Boeing 737, -747, -757, -767, -777, MD11, MD80, DC10, A300 through A600, A310, A320, A330 and A340. KLM E&M can also assist an airline in optimising its total engineering operation according to its own targets and specifications.

Total Engine Care

KLM Engineering & Maintenance has knowledge of and experience in maintaining and supporting CF6 engines, modules, parts and accessories, backed up by highly efficient line maintenance- and AOG support on a global and round-the-clock basis. KLM E&M has a well-equipped, 25,000 square meters overhaul centre and test facilities, where it is assured of high on-wing engine times combined with low visit costs. As a result, the maintenance costs per flighthour are amongst the lowest in the industry. In addition, its engine- and LRU inventory provides unique opportunities for solving the customer's problem of spares during shop visits and AOG requirements.

Being alert to the ever changing needs of the market, KLM E&M has introduced a range of options in terms of billing. These include power by the hour, fixed quotes, leasing and other arrangements, all of which can be tailored to the customer's specific requirements. To further enhance the engine service, a new and enlarged shop is being build while CFM56 overhaul will be added as from 2004.

Total Airframe Care

The airframe maintenance side of KLM E&M is split into two sections: line- and base maintenance. Line maintenance covers the ongoing maintenance of aircraft, such as the daily checks and the six-weekly A-checks. Base maintenance involves the more complex and time consuming C- and D-checks, as well as aircraft modifications.

Base maintenance to widebody aircraft can be done on Boeing 747-100 through -400 and Boeing 767). Modifications to ageing aircraft, corrosion prevention programmes, pylon to wing modifications, cabin- and cockpit upgrade programmes, and section 41 modifications are possible. Complete aircraft docking (including hydraulic floor spits) is available and operations are linked by a fully-integrated IT network.

Base maintenance to narrowbody aircraft can be done on Boeing 737. KLM E&M has the ability to deliver the expert, timely and economical completion of all regular maintenance checks (A, C and D) required by all Boeing 737 series, including the Next Generation. Available for all aircraft the state-of-the-art (re)decoration programmes are performed in a climate-controlled hangar. Unique movable platforms surround the aircraft, while revolutionary ventilation/extraction systems remove paint and dust particles to an underground technical waste system.

Line maintenance is, in addition to airframe, engines and components, the fourth structural branch of KLM. Working from some 120 stations around the world, KLM E&M is responsible for the transit maintenance and platform checks of the KLM fleet and other airlines. Line maintenance involves all inspections and resulting rectifications required on an aircraft while it is 'en route' – in other words, ensuring the aircraft is scheduled as operational.

Total Component Care

Component maintenance forms an integral part of KLM's Total Aircraft Care® package.

KLM E&M has in-house shop repair capabilities for more than 12,000 different components. KLM E&M Material Services is responsible for the repair and replacement of all aircraft rotables (line replaceable units. Once a component has been removed it is taken to one of the in-house 'repair shops'. These facilities cover a vast number of components for the Boeing 737 (current and next generation), Boeing 747, Boeing 767, MD11, DC10 and CF6, with specialised sections for hydraulics, electric controls, computers, airframe parts, rudders, flight controls, flaps and flap tracks. A successful venture has been the Loan/Lease programme, through which other companies can 'rent' components from KLM E&M on a temporary basis, such as AOG.

Editorial Associates

Mr. Shi Yonghai, a distinguished senior researcher in the field of international trade in China, is now the Chairman of China Association of International Trade. Previously, he was President of the Chinese Academy of International Trade and Economic Cooperation (CAITEC), the largest research organization under the Ministry of Foreign Trade and Economic Cooperation (MOFTEC). He was also the Minister Counsellor of the Economic and Commercial Section of the Chinese Embassy to Japan between 1990 and 1994.

Shi Yonghai has long been engaged in the research of international trade, particularly research and studies on the Japanese economy and issues regarding China's foreign trade and economic cooperation. He also participated as a leader in a number of important research projects, of which the latest included 'ISO 14000 and China's Foreign Trade', and environment- and trade-related issues in APEC countries. In addition, Shi Yonghai has been involved in researching key issues regarding China's effort to further open up and develop China's foreign trade and economic cooperation. Most recently, based on his research on the environment and trade issues, Shi Yonghai has initiated for the first time the concept of 'environmental competitiveness of products'. This concept has extended conventional theory on product competitiveness and has important implications both in theory and practice.

Liu Baocheng is an Associate Professor and Assistant Dean at the School of International Business Management of the University of International Business and Economics (UIBE), Beijing, China. He also serves as dean of the Sino-US School of International Management, which is a partnership between UIBE and the University of Maryland's Rober H. Smith School of Business. At the same time, Liu Baocheng also holds a deanship at the Sino-French School of International Business Management. His area of research and teaching covers a variety of disciplines including marketing, cross-cultural negotiation and business law. His most recent publications include the translation of the *Blackwell Encyclopedia of Business Ethics* and *English for Business Negotiations*.

Besides his research and teaching experiences, Liu Baocheng has worked in the management of London Export Corporation, Union Merchant Overseas Corporation and Cathay Trading Ltd. He is still in active business executive positions with Unigene Laboraroty Inc., Herborium Inc. and Novark Consulting. His hands-on business experiences cover international trade, joint venture management and marketing research. He worked as senior research fellow for the Institute of International Business at Seton Hall University in the United States for four years and served as an adjunct professor at Seton Hall and Montclair State University. He has been a speaker at various renowned academic and corporate institutions and in media. These include China Central Party University, China University of Central Administration, Citibank, BASF, OTIS, Schneider, Voice of America and China Central Television (CCTV).

Map of China Showing Provinces, Autonomous Regions, Municipalities, Coastal Cities and Special Economic Zones

XINJIANG UYGUR AUTONOMOUS REGION

GANSU

PAKISTAN

QINGHAI

TIBET
AUTONOMOUS REGION

NEPAL

SICHUAN

BHUTAN

INDIA

BANGLADESH

YUNNAN

BURMA

LAOS

THAILAND

staying interesting

{Good morning.
Welcome to Beijing!}

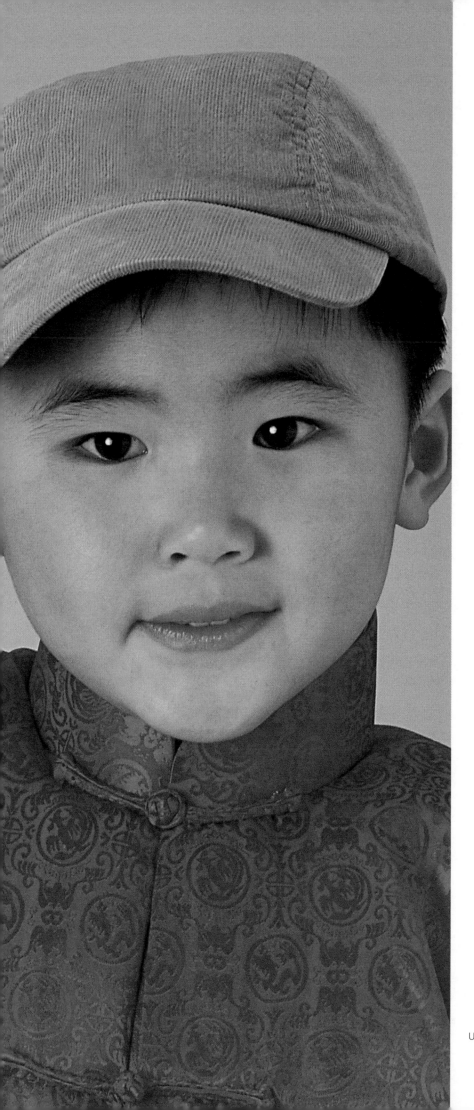

With the dawn,
a new beginning.
Renaissance Beijing Hotel
welcomes you to
China's capital.
The perfect blend of
Chinese tradition
and European elegance.
A fresh and exciting
new approach to
hospitality.
Superior personal service
in an exceptional
ambiance.

RENAISSANCE®
BEIJING HOTEL
BEIJING, CHINA
北 京 国 航 万 丽 酒 店

36 Xiao Yun Lu,
Chaoyang District, Beijing 100 027, PRC
Tel : (86 10) 6468 9999 Fax : (86 10) 6468 9913
United Kingdom Toll Free Reservations : 0800 221 222

www.renaissancehotels.com

to do business
in China
you need more...

...nonstopflights
to Beijing than any other airline

AIR CHINA
www.air-china.co.uk

World Freight Terminal - take a load off your mind.

Within Manchester Airport's purpose built **World Freight Terminal** we accommodate global logistics providers, global handling companies and world class airlines.

We have facilities for all types of cargo, from perishable to outsize.

And with over 90 airlines serving 180 destinations across five continents, our connections are excellent.

So come and offload at Manchester Airport's **World Freight Terminal**. We have all the cargo facilities you'll ever need.

**Logistics Services · Freight Forwarders · Perishable Cargo Facilities · Outsize Cargo Facilities
Temperature Controlled Transit Shed · Customs · Border Inspection Post · DEFRA
Environmental Health · Chamber Of Commerce**

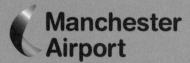

**Manchester
Airport**

www.manchesterairport.co.uk

Contact: Chris Walkden
Industry Affairs and Cargo Manager
Tel: 0161 489 3797
Fax: 0161 489 2703
Email: chris.walkden@manairport.co.uk

Part One

China's Economy and Administration System

China's Economic Performance and Outlook*

Li Shantong, Development Research Centre of the State Council

Since the beginning of China's economic reforms and its opening to the outside world, China's economy has achieved unprecedented rapid growth. From 1978 to 2000 average annual GDP growth was 9.5 per cent, thanks to China's stable environment for development and the deepening of global economic integration. China's fast growth can mainly be attributed to a rapid increase in capital investment and improved productivity. Five years from now the international political and economic situation may be volatile, but the general international environment and pattern of development will support China's continuing economic development. Although China faces a variety of developmental issues, the policy environment will continue to favour rapid economic growth. Based on the trend to changes in investment, productivity and labour supply, China's economy will still be able to maintain a relatively high growth rate, with annual average GDP growth above 7.5 per cent. The key to achieving such rapid economic growth is the continuation of the strategic restructuring of the economy. This is being driven, on the one hand, by reforms and the opening to the outside world and, on the other, by technological progress.

Taking a long-term perspective on economic growth, the momentum is determined by both quantitative and qualitative improvements in productivity, capital and labour. Before looking ahead at economic growth in five years, one must look back at the sources of China's economic growth over the past 20 years.

Since 1978, rapid capital accumulation and improvements in productivity are the major factors explaining China's rapid economic growth. Increases in the overall labour supply have played a relatively small role in fuelling economic growth, although the impact of the reallocation of labour resources should not be altogether ignored. A substantial body of research on China's economic growth from 1978 to 1997 confirms that capital input accounts for nearly 60 per cent of China's economic growth in this period; improvements in productivity represent 30 per cent of growth, while the expansion of aggregate labour supply represents only 12 per cent of growth.

This investment has been increasing at a high rate. Since the outset of reforms and opening to the outside world, China's investment rate has remained at around 35 per cent of GDP. The investment rate in about half of the years from 1978 to 2000 was close to or above 40 per cent. This high investment rate can be in part explained by the fast-growing income of the Chinese people and their high propensity to save. From 1980 to 2000, total bank savings rose from 160 billion renminbi to 12 trillion renminbi, of which private savings grew from 40 billion renminbi, or 25 per cent of total savings, to 6.4 trillion renminbi, or 52 per cent of total savings. Another factor supporting rising investment was the large inflow of foreign investment as a result of preferential foreign investment policies. From 1979 to 2000, China received a total of US$518.9 billion in foreign investment.

Productivity has also improved. In the past 20 years or so, China has been able to improve productivity largely as a result of the following factors:

- Technological progress has increased the output associated with a given amount of capital.

---

* This chapter was originally written in Chinese and translated by Li Yong.

- The rise in the level of education in the workforce has increased per capita output.
- Market reforms have contributed to a rational flow of resources, particularly of labour resources, across different sectors. At the micro level, this has made enterprises more profit-focused.
- The inflow of foreign investment has not only compensated for the limited domestic supply of capital and increased total investment, but has been accompanied by advanced foreign technologies and management expertise. All of these have helped Chinese enterprises to improve their competitiveness in both domestic and international markets.

Our research suggests that improvements in productivity since the beginning of reforms in the late 1970s can mostly be explained by two factors. The first of these factors, the more effective allocation of resources, is at the macro level. The second factor, which is at the micro level, is the increased efficiency of individual enterprises as a result of market reforms, technological progress and the spillover effect of foreign investment and foreign trade. Technological progress is, however, not the key contributing factor for improved productivity. The reallocation of labour across industrial sectors and different regions is considered a more important source of growth. Large-scale migration of labour from the agricultural sector to secondary and tertiary industries has fuelled the rapid growth of the economy, given the relatively higher level of efficiency of the industrial sector.

China's economic growth over the next five years hinges on whether the relatively high rate of investment can be sustained and productivity levels improved further. Our analysis of these factors supports the conclusion that China's economy will be able to maintain a relatively high rate of growth over the coming five years, despite signs of a decline in the rate of growth in recent years, from 14.2 per cent growth in 1992 down to 7.3 per cent in 2001.

Our research also confirms that China will maintain a relatively high investment rate and that productivity will be improved further. First, the investment rate in the next five years is expected to stay at the current level of between 35 to 40 per cent. There have been quite a few precedents of other regional economies sustaining both high levels of savings and investments. Taiwan Province, Japan and South Korea, for example, have experienced long periods of maintaining high savings and investment rates.

A sustained increase in household income will also contribute to a high rate of growth in household savings. Although the aging of the population will have some impact, the relatively strong propensity of Chinese households to save is not expected to change. Moreover, China's stable political and economic environment, as well as its huge market potential, will continue to remain attractive to foreign investors. The formalization and transparency of foreign investment policies after China's entry into the World Trade Organization will strengthen foreign investors' confidence in mainland China. Therefore, in the long run, the inflow of foreign investment will maintain the momentum of rapid growth.

Second, China's labour supply in the next five years is expected to grow on average by 1.2 per cent per year, which will satisfy the demand for labour implied by such levels of economic growth. With rising levels of education and urbanization, the quality of the labour force will be continuously improving. The accumulation of human capital will thus play a greater role in supporting economic growth than it has in the past.

Third, the implementation of the government strategy of 'transforming the country through science and education' will enhance the country's overall capacity for technological innovation while at the same time raising the general quality of the workforce. The policy of opening to the outside world will continue to attract foreign investment, encourage the inflow of advanced technology and introduce management expertise. As a developing and technologically backward country, China will, by embracing learning and innovation, unleash its huge potential for technological progress. The level by which technological progress will support economic growth is expected to maintain or exceed the levels of the past 20 years.

Fourth, China's industrialization is not yet complete. The 'dual structure' in the economy is still largely pervasive. The mobility of resources, especially human resources, across different sectors, such as labour migration from agricultural to non-agricultural industries, will lead to further improvements in productivity and to growth in aggregate national output. Fifth, the improvement in the market economy regime and the further expansion and deepening of the policy of opening to the outside world will result in fiercer competition among enterprises, and hence to improvements in all economic activity.

In an economy that not too long ago experienced product shortages and where product supply is now in relative surplus due to structural problems, changes on the demand side, in addition to those on the supply side, will have an influence on the rate of economic development. Our analysis of demand side factors indicates that China's high rate of growth in the coming five years will not be impeded by constraints on the demand side. However, the following priorities remain:

- First, the level of development and of people's standard of living in China needs to be greatly improved. According to the World Bank's *World Development Report 2002*, China's gross national income (GNI) per capita was US$840, which represents only about 16.3 per cent of the world average and 3.1 per cent of the average in high-income countries. Even by the measurement of purchasing power parity (PPP), China's per capita GNI in 2000 was only US$3,940 dollars, representing 53.6 per cent of the world average or 14.4 per cent of the average for high-income countries. In 1998, as measured by PPP, daily consumption for 18.5 per cent of China's population amounted to less than US$1, while for a further 53.7 per cent of the population it was less than US$2.

- Second, China needs to construct more large-scale infrastructure. The average rate of infrastructure per person (or the infrastructure per square kilometre) is far below the world average. In the next 15 years and beyond, a great deal of effort will be directed toward the development of infrastructure, such as roadways and railways, electric utilities and communications infrastructure. In 1997, Chinese people consumed the equivalent of 907 kilograms per person of petroleum, while the per capita consumption of electricity amounted to 714 kilowatt-hours. The world average consumption in these categories for the same year was 1,692 kilograms and 2,053 kilowatt-hours respectively.

- Third, traditional industries should be reformed and expanded. China's traditional industries are technologically backward and not competitive, and require reconstruction on the basis of new and high technologies. In terms of productivity per person, the output of some traditional industries, such as food processing, is not as high as it should be, and needs to be raised. Accordingly, the transformation of traditional industries should focus on the upgrading of existing projects with new and high technologies on the one hand, and on the construction of new projects employing new and high technologies on

the other. Both will require large-scale investment.

- Fourth, a great effort needs to be made to develop high-tech industries. In general, hi-tech industries are capital intensive, and the development of such industries will also require a large amount of investment.

- Fifth, urbanization needs to be further promoted and intensified. In 1999, the level of urbanization in China was 32 per cent, compared with a world average in the same year of 46 per cent urbanization. The average rate of urbanization in middle-income countries was 50 per cent and in high-income countries it was 77 per cent. The expected massive migration of agricultural population into urban areas will bring about a huge growth in aggregate demand. On the one hand, such migration will generate great demand for urban infrastructure, which will in turn drive the growth in the demand for investment. On the other hand, the migration of the farming population into urban areas will lead to urbanized consumer behaviour, which will also boost the growth in demand.

- Sixth, China needs to rapidly develop its service industry. Since the start of reforms and the opening of China to the outside world, the service industry has experienced rapid growth. However, the service industry is on the whole still quite backward. Traditional service industries that are quite mature in the developed countries, such as finance, insurance, accounting and legal services are insufficiently developed in China and are far from being able to satisfy the needs of economic development. Newer areas of the services industry in China are lagging even further behind. A rapid development of China's service industry will satisfy the population's growing demand for services arising from an improved standard of living. At the same time, this will address the requirements of structural changes to the economy and the upgrading of the industrial structure. As such, the development of the Chinese service sector may well be a new source of economic growth, generating a large number of job opportunities which will mitigate the pressures associated with structural changes to the workforce.

On the basis of the above analysis, we have elaborated two scenarios for the future growth of the Chinese economy in the next five years, employing a dynamic computable general equilibrium (CGE) model as a simulation tool. The first scenario assumes that past growth performance will be sustained to realise a relatively high rate of growth. The second scenario is of low growth, and emphasizes possible sources of a slowdown as a result of identified risks and challenges in the future course of China's economic development.

In the first or higher growth scenario, the average annual rate of growth in China's economy between 2001 to 2005 will be 8.1 per cent, whereas in the low growth scenario, the average annual rate of GDP growth will be 6.9 per cent in the same period. We contend that the current slowdown in the growth rate of China's economy is mainly the result of structural factors. To tap into China's growth potential, there are two critical issues that need to be solved from the demand side, one of which is how to raise people's spending in order to turn potential demand into real demand, and the other is how to eliminate bottlenecks in investment growth. From the supply side, however, the critical issue is how to raise the efficiency of resource allocation.

In the tenth Five Year Plan period China will adopt a series of policy measures aimed at facilitating strategic adjustments to the economic structure, increasing the growth in personal income and enabling the two driving forces of the economy: the policy of reform and opening to the outside world on the one hand and, on the other, technological progress. We have good reason to believe that China is able to realize rapid economic growth in the next five years.

Changes in the Laws and Regulations Regarding Foreign Investment in China*

Hu Jingyan, Director General, Department of Foreign Investment, Ministry of Foreign Trade and Economic Cooperation

China's absorption of foreign investment experienced a substantial increase in 2001. The actual utilization of foreign investment hit a record high of US$46.878 billion, an increase of 15.14 per cent year-on-year. China has been the largest recipient of foreign investment among developing countries for nine consecutive years. By the end of December 2001, the cumulative number of Foreign-Invested Enterprises (FIEs) was recorded at 390,025, with the cumulative contracted investment and actual utilization being US$745.29 billion and US$395.22 billion respectively.

Key changes in laws and regulations concerning foreign direct investment since 2001

Over the past two years, China has been revamping, adjusting and perfecting its existing laws, rules and regulations on foreign investment in order to prepare for the new dynamics that will prevail upon China's accession to the WTO. A complete, unified and transparent legal system that meets the needs of a socialist market economy and conforms to the rules and requirements of the WTO, as well as the conditions of the country, has been put into place. Since 2001, China has made the following efforts to amend and revise its laws and regulations concerning foreign investment in China:

- The foreign investment laws and regulations have been overhauled, with modifications or revisions made to parts that are in conflict with the rules of the WTO. A key step in this direction was the revision of the basic foreign investment laws, namely, *the Law*

of People's Republic of China on Sino-foreign Equity Joint Ventures, the Law of People's Republic of China on Sino-foreign Contractual Joint Ventures, the Law of People's Republic of China on Wholly Foreign-owned Enterprises and the detailed provisions or rules of implementation thereof. Clauses such as those pertaining to foreign exchange balance of FIEs, local content, export obligations and the filing requirements for FIEs' production plans have been abolished. Work on the revision and amendments have been completed, and the revised version of the pertinent laws and regulations has been promulgated for implementation.

- In order to catch up with the strategic restructuring of the national economy and the changes required by China's accession to the WTO, the State Council promulgated, on 11 February 2002, a revised version of the *Provisions on Guiding the Direction of Foreign Investment*, and, with the approval of the State Council, the State Development Planning Commission, the State Economic and Trade Commission and the Ministry of Foreign Trade and Economic Cooperation jointly announced, on 11 March 2002, a new version of the *Catalogue of Industries for the Guidance of Foreign Investment*. The new industrial policies as reflected in the Catalogue continue to observe the principle of active, rational and effective utilization of foreign investment. Both the new Provisions and the new Catalogue went into effect as of 1 April 2002.

- The new Catalogue consists of four categories of industries where foreign investments are encouraged,

---

* This chapter was originally written in Chinese and was translated by Li Yong.

allowed, restricted or forbidden. The Catalogue has greatly expanded the scope of industries that are open to foreign investments. First, the number of industries in which foreign investments are encouraged has increased from 186 to 262, whereas the number of industries to which foreign investments have restricted access has been reduced from 112 to 76. Second, the restrictions on the share holdings of foreign investors have been relaxed; for example, the requirement for a dominant Chinese share holding in jointly built and used dock facilities at a port has been abolished. Third, new areas of investment that previously forbade foreign involvement, such as telecommunications, urban piping facilities such as gas supply, heat supply, and water supply and drainage, are now opened up to foreign investments. Fourth, greater access to service sectors such as banking, insurance, commerce, foreign trade, tourism, telecommunications, transportation, accounting, auditing and legal services has been given to foreign investors. Fifth, foreign investments in the Western Area of China are encouraged and foreign investors investing in that area will enjoy even greater relaxation of the restrictions on foreign investors' share positions and access to industries. Finally, the Catalogue allows the mechanism of market competition full play, which is reflected in the inclusion of general industrial products in the category of industries in which foreign investments are allowed. The intention is to speed up the modernization of both industry and product structures through competition.

- A series of laws and regulations on foreign investment have been perfected and promulgated.
- The Ministry of Foreign Trade and Economic Co-operation, the Ministry of Science and Technology, and the State Administration of Industry and Commerce have jointly promulgated the *Provisional Regulations on the Establishment of Foreign-Invested Venture Capital Investment Enterprises*. This regulation has drawn from the venture capital mechanism in various countries and international practice in an attempt to regulate foreign-invested venture capital companies in terms of their equity investment in non-public, hi-tech enterprises and in related venture capital management services.
- China's Securities Regulatory Commission and the Ministry of Foreign Trade and Economic Cooperation jointly issued *Opinions on Issues Relating to the Involvement of Foreign Investment in Listed Companies*, which sets out the conditions and procedures

regarding Initial Public Offerings (IPOs) of foreign-invested enterprises on the A share and B share markets within the territory of China. According to the Opinions, foreign-invested enterprises are allowed, on the strength of the *Provisional Regulation on Domestic Investment by Foreign-invested Enterprises*, to acquire the unlisted shares of domestic listed companies, and foreign-invested joint-stock companies with B shares are allowed to float the non-tradable shares held by foreign investors on the B-share stock market.

- The Ministry of Foreign Trade and Economic Co-operation, the Ministry of Finance and the People's Bank of China jointly promulgated the *Interim Provisions on Financial Asset Management Companies Absorbing Foreign Capital to Participate in the Asset Restructuring and Disposal*, allowing foreign-invested companies to participate in asset restructuring and the disposal of the financial assets of management companies. At the same time, the provision has also legally defined the scope of the financial assets that can be transferred to foreign investors, the evaluation of their value and procedures for transfer.
- The Ministry of Foreign Trade and Economic Cooperation has also published *Supplementary Provisions (II) to the Interim Provisions on Foreign Investment Establishing Investment-type Companies*, on the strength of which foreign-invested investment companies are given greater scope of business. They are allowed, for example, to:
  - provide related technical training to domestic enterprises;
  - act as an initiator to establish foreign-invested joint-stock companies;
  - purchase both domestically and internationally manufactured components and semi-finished products for conversion into finished products for sale on the domestic market;
  - import, from their parent companies, small amounts of products that are not subject to the regulation of import quotas and are the same or similar to those being produced by their invested enterprises in China for trial sales in the domestic market.
- The Ministry of Foreign Trade and Economic Cooperation has revised and promulgated *Provisional Administrative Measures Regarding the Examination and Approval of Foreign-invested Leasing Companies*, and issued a *Notice on Issues Regarding the Expansion of Import and Export Rights by Foreign-Invested Enterprises*, which allows FIEs with annual export values

exceeding US$10 million to procure products from other enterprises for export, and foreign-invested research and development centres to import some hi-tech products for test-marketing in China. In addition, amendments have been made to the *Regulations on the Merger and Division of Foreign-Invested Enterprises*, which has further defined the practice of merger between FIEs and domestic enterprises.

- Laws and regulations on foreign investment in the service sector have been revamped. In order to facilitate the opening of the service sector to the outside world in a positive, smooth, appropriate and orderly manner, China has also promulgated laws and regulations regarding the service sector, including:
  - *Interim Measures on the Administration of Establishing Employment Agencies in the Form of Equity and Contractual Joint Venture;*
  - *The Rules of the People's Republic of China on International–Marine Transportation, Notice Regarding the Printing and Issuance of the Opinions on the Encouragement of the Township and Village Enterprises to Expedite the Structural Adjustment in their Utilization of Foreign Investment;*
  - *Regulations on the Administration of Travel Agencies (Revised);*
  - *Administrative Rules of the People's Republic of China on Foreign-invested Insurance Companies–Regulations on the Administration of Foreign-invested Telecommunications Enterprises;*
  - *Regulations on the Administration of Foreign Investment in Road Transportation Industry;*
  - *Rules and Regulations of the People's Republic of China on the Administration of Foreign-invested Financial Institutions;*
  - *Regulations on the Administration of Foreign Investment in International Freight Forwarding Sector;*
  - *Rules regarding the Administration of the Resident Representative Offices of Foreign Law Firms,*
  - *Provisional Regulations on Foreign Investment in Cinemas;*
  - *Administrative Measures Regarding the Contractual Joint Venture of Audiovisual Product Distribution;*
  - *The Decision of the State Council Regarding the Revision of the Rules and Regulations on Sino-foreign Cooperative Exploitation of Onshore Oil Resources;*
  - *The Decision of the State Council Regarding the Revision of the Rules and Regulations on Sino-foreign Co-operative Exploitation of Offshore Oil Resources–Interim Measures on the Administration of Sino-*

Foreign Equity and Contractual Joint Venture in Medical Institutions;
  - *Interim Measures on the Administration of the Examination and Approval of Foreign Wholly-owned Shipping Companies;*
  - *Provisional Regulations on the Establishment of Foreign-invested Printing Enterprises;*
  - *Provisions on the Administration of the Talent Market;*
  - *Rules and Regulations on the Administration of Publications,* etc.

Trends in China's foreign investment policies in 2002

The year 2002 has been the first year of China's official membership of the WTO. The development and changes in the economic situation both at home and internationally have created unprecedented opportunities for China while, at the same time, bringing forward rigorous challenges. China will take advantage of the opportunities to make efforts to improve the legal, policy, administrative and market environment for foreign investment. Such efforts will bring the influx of foreign investment to a new level. In 2002, emphasis will be placed on the following areas.

Striving to improve the legal and policy environments for foreign investment

The continuing review of the laws, regulations and rules relating to foreign investment will be the starting point for further improvements in the foreign investment environment. The legal system regarding foreign investment will be further improved in compliance with China's commitments to the WTO and the requirements arising from the new situation. The enactment of new laws will be expedited while administration based on the rule of law will be vigorously promoted. Efforts to rectify local laws, regulations and related policy measures concerning foreign investment will be redoubled, bringing them in line with national laws and regulations, WTO rules and China's commitments to the outside world. While existing laws and regulations are being revised, special attention will be paid to maintaining stability, consistency, predictability and workability in foreign investment policies and laws, thereby creating a sound and favourable policy and a legal environment for foreign investors.

Maintaining and perfecting a fair and open market environment

The on-going nationwide effort to rectify and normalize the functioning of an open and fair market economy will be given added momentum by:

- eradicating unapproved collection of fees, unauthorized inspections, unjustified allotment of expenses and groundless fines directed toward FIEs;
- dismantling the blockade of local protectionism and sectoral monopolies;
- dedicating a greater level of law enforcement resources to protect intellectual property and cracking down decisively on piracy and infringements of rights.

At the same time, further steps will be taken to perfect the environment for FIEs so that the rule of law prevails in the protection from infringement of legitimate rights and interests.

Further opening-up of the service sector to foreign investment

According to both the requirements of economic development and the commitments made to the WTO, China will actively, systematically and steadily open up the entire service sector to foreign involvement. Laws and regulations regarding foreign investment in construction, accounting services, education, commerce, foreign trade, civil aviation and medical services will be passed within the shortest possible time. Such efforts will help to build a complete, formalized and open market access system for foreign investors in the service sector. Foreign investment in logistics and distribution will be encouraged. FIEs will be encouraged to operate retail chains and establish foreign-invested export purchasing and commodity distribution centres. Investment in the service sector will be actively encouraged, as will the introduction of modern technologies as well as managerial and operational practices. All of this will help to improve both the structure and quality of China's entire service sector.

Encouraging foreign investors to go to Western China and striving to create favourable conditions for the western area to attract more foreign investments

In a proactive effort to implement the grand development strategy for the western area, China will push through foreign investment policies designed for the mid-western areas. For foreign investment in the mid-western area, foreign investment requirements in the service sector will be further relaxed, while at the same time foreign-invested projects in the area will also enjoy more relaxed financing requirements. Greater effort will be made to design an industrial policy biased in favour of the western area. In conjunction with the revision of the *Catalogue of Industries for the Guidance of Foreign Investment*, China will consider an appropriate expansion in the scope of the *Catalogue of Advantageous Industries for the Absorption of Foreign Investment in the Mid-western Area*, in order to encourage the flow of foreign investments in the region in projects such as infrastructure, development of mineral resources, tourism, bio-environmental protection, the processing of agricultural and livestock products and science and technology projects. Meanwhile, the necessary conditions will be created for FIEs in the coastal areas to reinvest in the mid-western area. In addition, foreign investors are encouraged to invest in the west-to-east gas pipeline project, the west-to-east power supply project and their ancillary projects.

Encouraging foreign investment in new and high technology industries, infrastructure and associated peripheral projects

FIEs are encouraged to bring in, develop and innovate technologies. Such encouragement is intended to promote foreign investment in capital and technology-intensive projects and to guide foreign investors in setting up more hi-tech projects. To enhance guidance in policy terms, restrictions on the ratio of registered capital and the requirements for capital contribution in the form of industrial properties will be relaxed at an appropriate time. Relevant regulations regarding venture capital will be further eased in order to create favourable conditions for the establishment and development of hi-tech enterprises. Meanwhile, favourable conditions will also be created for FIEs investing in industries that are in the lower reaches of the supply chain. They will be encouraged to source raw materials locally for their manufacturing. Medium-sized and small enterprises, including township and village enterprises, will be given external support and encouragement in introducing appropriate advanced technologies, in order to qualify themselves as competent suppliers to large FIEs and eventually to become established suppliers to multinationals.

Encouraging multinational companies to invest in China

Multinational companies (MNCs) are the leading force in the global economy. Efforts will be made to study possible policy measures aimed at attracting MNC investment and to encourage the establishment of MNC regional headquarters and to set up their international export purchasing centres in China. International experiences and practice in the area of mergers and acquisitions will be studied in the hope of quickly developing workable policies and regulations for foreign investment in the form of mergers and acquisitions. In doing so, the characteristics of the Chinese economic system and the unique conditions of Chinese enterprises will be taken into account. Regulations regarding foreign investment in investment-holding companies and joint-stock companies will be further reviewed and revised. The various rules and regulations regarding foreign investment in the form of build, operate and transfer (BOT), franchise transfers and the flotation of FIEs on domestic and foreign stock markets will continue to be enacted and improved. All these efforts will be directed at creating favourable conditions for MNCs to invest in China.

Accelerating the shift of government functions and enhancing the level of law-based administration

China is stepping up the transformation of government functions and work practices in an effort to build a government that is free from corruption, that is diligent, practical and highly efficient. Rationality, effectiveness, openness and responsibility are the basic principles that China will follow in its efforts to simplify examination and approval procedures. This will particularly be the case with the approval of contracts and articles of association. A formalized and standardized examination and approval system will be implemented. Civil servants in the government will be trained in enhanced awareness and recognition of the rule of law. They are expected to have a good knowledge and understanding of laws and to abide by the laws. Each should perform the correct duties and their conduct on behalf of the government should be open, fair and transparent. Random elements in the performance of government duties should be reduced. Continuous efforts will be made to raise the level of law-based administration in order to create a favourable administrative environment for foreign investment.

China officially became a member of the WTO in December 2001. The rules of the WTO will be strictly observed and China's commitments will be adhered to. China will proactively promote the comprehensive opening up of its economy at all levels, participating in the process of economic globalization in greater depth. With the sustained, rapid and healthy development of China's economy, the consolidated strength of the country and the gradual and steady advance in economic reform and opening-up to the outside world, foreign investment will have greater scope for development in China. Accordingly, the quality and overall level of foreign investment will reach new heights.

China as a WTO Member: Systemic Issues

Craig Pouncey and Lode van den Hende, Herbert Smith, Brussels

Introduction

On 11 December 2001 China finally became a WTO member, following a process of negotiation that took more than 15 years. Throughout the world this was considered a major achievement for China, for the WTO and for the global economy. Relatively little has been said, however, about the precise meaning of China's accession, which is described in more than 800 pages of highly technical legal documentation.

The purpose of this chapter and Chapter 2.2 on WTO accession is two-fold. In this chapter we explain what the WTO is, as well as the systemic consequences of China's WTO membership, both for China and for the WTO. Chapter 2.2 provides an overview of some of China's specific obligations in the area of 'market access', examining the extent to which China is obliged to allow foreign businesses, goods and services to trade or be traded in China.

What is the WTO?

The simplest way to describe the WTO is to compare it to the original European Economic Community (the predecessor of the European Union). The original EEC concentrated on opening markets via 'free movement' and non-discrimination disciplines that were legally enforceable on the Member States via a specialized international court. Those same principles underpin the WTO. In fact, some of the most important provisions of the EEC Treaty were inspired by provisions of the General Agreement on Tariffs and Trade (GATT), the predecessor of the WTO.

Not direct reciprocity but 'most favoured nation' treatment

On the other hand, there are significant differences between the WTO and the EEC/EU, the most important being that whilst in the EEC/EU all Member States have the same obligations, this is not the case in the WTO. The obligations of a WTO member are to a large extent determined by the commitments and concessions made by the country concerned in a specific sector or for a specific product. These commitments and concessions are set out in detail in 'Schedules' that each WTO Member has deposited with the WTO. It is important to note that once a WTO member makes a market access commitment the benefit of that market access commitment extends to all other WTO members (and of course their companies). This is referred to as the 'Most Favoured Nation' (or MFN) principle.

However, it is important to note that the commitments made by WTO members are not necessarily parallel between members: the fact that country X gives access to services sector Y does not mean that country Z also does. This is fundamentally because of the way in which market access commitments are negotiated in the WTO (ie 'trade-offs' are made as between market access 'offerings' across a wide range of services and products), with the result that access is not parallel across all sectors and products for all WTO members.

For instance, during the Olympic summer games in Australia in 2000 the EU based press agency Reuters was denied access to certain areas of the stadiums where only Australian and US news agencies were allowed to bring their cameras. The European Commission successfully intervened on behalf of Reuters pointing out that Australia had made relevant commitments in the relevant sector (ie the audio-visual sector). This is despite the fact that the EU itself has made no WTO commitments in that sector and that under WTO law the EU could lawfully apply such discriminatory measures against Australian press agencies.

This may seem awkward but the WTO should be looked at as a global deal whereby every member country has accepted that the market access level offered by all other countries is sufficient. This functions like an entrance fee that is different for all members but once the other members have accepted the entrance fee, the acceding country can come in and enjoy all the rights and benefits of the club.

An important consequence is that, whilst China's obligations in the WTO are determined by China's commitments and concessions in the WTO, China's rights as an exporter are largely determined by the commitments and concessions of the other WTO members. It is to be presumed that China has undertaken its obligations in full knowledge of the rights it obtains as a result of doing so.

Import and export of goods

Reduction of import tariffs, and abolition of 'non-tariff' barriers and disciplines for agricultural subsidies

The core objective of the WTO in the area of trade in goods is to replace all 'non-tariff' barriers such as quantitative import or export limits with customs duties that are 'bound' at a maximum level the country cannot exceed. Tariffs are transparent and easily identifiable whereas non-tariff barriers tend, by definition, to be more covert means of market protection. Through periodic negotiations these maximum levels are then reduced. The only exception is textiles where quantitative restrictions (quotas) can remain in place until 1 January 2005.

The Agreement on Technical Barriers to Trade and the Agreement on the Application of Sanitary and Phytosanitary Measures aim to prevent technical product and testing rules being abused to frustrate imports. The Hormones dispute between the EU and the US is the best-known example of this but there are also examples involving China. In early 2002, for instance, the EU banned the import of certain Chinese meat and seafood items said to be tainted with a banned antibiotic. In March 2002 the Chinese authorities reacted by prohibiting the sale of 177 items of perfume and

cosmetics from Europe said to contain substances causing 'mad cow' disease.

The Agreement on Agriculture obliges WTO members to reduce agriculture subsidies (both domestic support and export subsidies). China has agreed to abolish all export subsidies and to keep other trade distorting internal support under 8.5 per cent of the total value of agricultural production (this threshold applies both to general support and to each specific product). This cap on agricultural subsidies appears to raise considerable concern in China due to the lack of competitiveness of its agricultural sector. It has been suggested, however, that the WTO may also contribute to solving that competitiveness problem which appears to be related to a poor distribution and warehousing infrastructure rather than to the farm gate price (the price received by the farmers). This makes bulk commodities shipped from North or South America to processing plants on the Chinese coast cheaper at plant gate level than products grown in China. A liberalization of the distribution system, one of China's WTO obligations, could attract the necessary investment and foreign know-how to modernize the distribution system and, ultimately, improve the competitiveness of Chinese farm products at factory level.

Trade defence instruments such as antidumping

Finally, a number of agreements regulate and restrict the use of trade defence instruments such as anti-dumping, anti-subsidy and safeguard measures. All these instruments involve the temporary introduction of restrictions on imports in specific circumstances:

- anti-dumping duties are applied when a country 'dumps' products on export markets at cheaper prices than the 'normal price' charged on the home market;
- anti-subsidy measures are applied when a product is sold on export markets below a normal market price due to subsidies received by the producer in his home country;
- safeguard measures are emergency measure aimed to prevent 'serious injury' to domestic industry caused by increasing imports.

Such trade defence measures are of course, *prima facie*, a breach of normal market WTO access commitments and are highly regulated. Regulation of safeguard measures is particularly strict because, unlike anti-dumping and anti-subsidy measures, safeguard measures restrict imports that are not inherently 'unfair'. As a result the use of safeguard measures is relatively rare compared to the use of anti-subsidy and, in particular, anti-dumping measures.

China is one of the main targets of anti-dumping measures around the world and whilst it remained outside the WTO, it had no means of defending itself against such anti-dumping measures. That is clearly different following WTO accession. Indeed, China has already launched its first WTO challenge against the safeguard measures imposed by the US in March 2002 against imports of steel from, among others, China.

A major issue for China with regard to the application of anti-dumping rules is the extent to which it is treated as a 'non-market' economy. The latter allows other WTO members much more discretion when imposing anti-dumping duties than they have with regard to a market economy country (a status that almost all WTO members have). As long as China is treated as a 'non-market' economy a WTO member introducing anti-dumping duties can use data from another country, such as the US for instance, to calculate the 'fair' price. As costs in the US are normally much higher than those in China this can make it very easy to find 'dumping' when the Chinese export price is compared to a 'normal' American price. The terms of China's accession allow the application of this 'non-market' economy methodology for a period of 15 years. It is possible, however, for individual companies to escape from that disadvantaged status if they can prove that their company operates in a sector where 'market economy conditions prevail'. China's Protocol of Accession also provides for two specific safeguard clauses. A first one, which will be available for twelve years, allows WTO members to take safeguard measures only with respect to imports from China (safeguard measures are normally against all imports irrespective of their origin). A second one, which will be available for eight years, makes it easier than under the standard procedure to impose safeguard measures restricting imports of textiles.

Trade in services

The General Agreement on Trade in Services (GATS) regulates the way in which WTO members must open their services markets to each other. The real scope of a country's WTO obligations is determined, sector by sector, in its 'Schedule of Specific Commitments on

Services' on the basis of four different 'modes of supply' of services:

- cross-border supply (for instance via the Internet);
- consumption abroad (for instance Chinese tourists being able to 'consume' tourism services in France);
- commercial presence (for instance an EU bank operating from a commercial location in China);
- presence of natural persons (for instance EU building engineers providing their services 'on the spot' in China).

The scope of a country's GATS obligations depends entirely on the details of its schedule of commitments. It is perfectly possible, for example, for a WTO member to accept supply of certain services via commercial presence whilst not accepting cross-border supply. Chapter 2.2 provides a more detailed overview of some of China's services commitments.

It is important to note that, in practice, the distinction between trade in goods and trade in services is not a rigorous one. For instance, a country's WTO obligations in the area of trade in goods may allow a WTO member to maintain a so-called Tariff Rate Quota for a specific product (ie it may allow the importation of a product up to a certain volume at a lower tariff, whilst imposing a considerably higher tariff on imports above that volume). If a country uses such instruments it also needs to decide which companies can import the 'in-quota' volumes at the lower customs duty rates. This is important because the companies that can make use of this quota can make a profit that is considerably higher than the profits that will be made by those importing out-of-quota volumes at the higher duty rates. An unfair distribution of these import possibilities over Chinese and foreign companies can result in a violation of a WTO member's obligations in the field of distribution services. China is currently involved in such a debate with the US on the distribution of import licences for fertilizer.

Intellectual property

The Agreement on Trade Related Aspects of Intellectual Property Rights (TRIPS) obliges WTO members to guarantee a minimum level of protection for intellectual property rights such as copyright, trademarks and patents. To a large extent the TRIPS Agreement refers back to other international agreements in this area predating the WTO. However, this 'integration by reference' brings these pre-existing arrangements into the WTO system and gives them the same enforceability as other WTO obligations.

WTO dispute settlement and China as a litigant

The WTO has an internal dispute settlement system that has been described as the 'jewel in the crown' of the WTO. Many of the currently existing WTO rules on trade in goods already existed before the WTO entered into force in 1995, in the context of the GATT (which dates back to 1947). The rule of law, however, was much less prominently present in the GATT, where a country which lost a dispute settlement procedure could prevent such a ruling from becoming binding by simply voting against it. This option was removed when the WTO entered into force. The WTO incorporates a legal enforcement system with real teeth and this is one of the main reasons why the WTO has become a much more prominent international organization than the GATT ever was.

The dispute settlement system is used frequently. Since the WTO came into effect in 1995, 259 official complaints have been filed (figures up to date to May 2002). It is important to note that these are all disputes between countries. The WTO dispute settlement system is only open to countries, not for private parties (although these will often ask their country of origin to start a procedure on their behalf and support their government in doing that). This frequent use of the dispute settlement system and a number of acrimonious disputes between the EU and the US have triggered criticism that the WTO is too much focused on litigation and that the EU and the US could eventually undermine the WTO by taking too many disputes to WTO dispute settlement rather than finding a mutually satisfactory solution.

It is important to put some of this criticism of WTO dispute settlement in a proper context. The WTO comprises a very large body of complex rules and 144 member countries. In this context divergent opinions are unavoidable and it is a strength of the WTO, not a weakness, that there is a neutral arbitrator that can decide the precise meaning of a text in a specific case. If that were not possible, the parties to the dispute would simply stand by their own interpretation and the practical effect of the agreements would remain limited (as is so often the case in international cooperation). Without the WTO, trade disputes would still exist without

an effective way of resolution. Indeed, some of the disputes between the EU and the US (Bananas, Beef-Hormones and the FSC dispute) are considerably older than the WTO and it is only through WTO litigation that some real progress has been made.

A much more legitimate question is how China, which has no Western style litigation tradition, will function in such a context. Most observers seem to agree that it will be impossible for China to maintain a perfect implementation record and that disputes over the correct implementation of China's WTO obligations are inevitable. The question is how the other WTO members will react to this. There appears to be scope for a genuine avalanche of procedures against China as a number of trade disputes have already emerged (for the EU and the US only this includes the measures against European 'mad cow' cosmetics and American GMOs, the management of Tariff Rate Quotas, and restrictions in insurance, express delivery services and retail distribution services, ie supermarkets). However, at least the EU and the US seem to adopt the position that it would be counterproductive to make intensive use of dispute settlement vis-à-vis China and, at least in the initial stage, will only do this as a measure of last resort. On the other hand, this position will be influenced by the behaviour of China as a complainant in dispute settlement procedures. If China makes intensive use of dispute settlement the EU and the US will become less reluctant to use it against China. (In this context, we have already noted that China has recently started a procedure against the US in relation to the US safeguard measures on steel.)

Conclusion

WTO accession provides a legally binding roadmap to the further liberalization and modernization of the Chinese economy

The importance of China's WTO accession is that it provides a legally binding roadmap to the further liberalization and modernization of the Chinese economy over the next 15 years. This should not be interpreted as submission to an external power. On the contrary, China's WTO membership and the terms thereof are simply the next logical phase in a process of internal economic reform that was launched more than 20 years ago. People very close to the negotiations have pointed out that all the changes that China has agreed to make in the framework of its WTO accession are changes that

China wanted to make and would have been made in any event in the foreseeable future. Thus WTO accession is a useful tool to keep the internal reform agenda on target rather than an externally imposed obligation. There will certainly be short-term conflicts about specific issues, and companies affected by these short-term conflicts may find that they need to work hard to minimize damage and ensure correct implementation of China's WTO obligations. In the long term, however, there should be no doubt that China is committed to fulfilling its WTO obligations, if only because these reflect China's own policy choices.

China's Commitments to the WTO – a Chinese Perspective*

Shi Yonghai, Chairman, China Association of International Trade

Abiding by the non-discrimination principle

As the most basic principle of the WTO, non-discrimination includes most favoured nation treatment and national treatment. Before its accession to the WTO, most-favoured nation treatment was accorded to the countries with which China had signed bilateral preferential trade agreements. Now, according to the principles of most favoured nation treatment, China will eliminate or bring into conformity with the WTO Agreement all special trade arrangements, including barter trade arrangements, with third countries and separate customs territories, which are not in conformity with the WTO Agreement. Therefore, the non-discrimination principle in the accession documents refers mainly to national treatment of imported products.

The national treatment principle requires that the imported products be accorded treatment no less favourable in terms of tariffs and internal taxes than that accorded to the same kind of domestic products. In fact, national treatment, which is a principle that endorses the fair competition principle, is consistent with the target of China's reform and opening to the outside world and of establishing a socialist market economy. Except in a few cases, before its accession China had basically realized national treatment for imported products. China is committed to according treatments to forgeign products no less favourable in terms of tariffs and internal taxes than that accorded to the same kinds of domestic products. China is also making the necessary amendments and readjustments to practices and policies that are inconsistent with the national treatment principle to address issues such as the initial import registration of chemical products and the different treatment accorded to the sale of imported and domestic cigarettes.

China will notify the WTO of all the relevant laws, regulations and other measures relating to its special economic areas, where a special system has been established on tariffs, internal taxes and regulations. The non-discrimination principle shall also be fully observed within such special economic areas.

Uniform administration of trade policy

The WTO requires that its members implement uniform trade policies. According to the Law of the People's Republic of China on Foreign Trade approved by the People's Congress in 1994, a uniform trade policy has been established in China. As such, China has committed to implementing its uniform trade policy throughout the entire customs territory of China.

China's WTO accession protocol shall apply to the entire customs territory of China, including border trade regions and minority autonomous areas, Special Economic Zones (SEZ), open coastal cities, economic and technical development zones and other areas where special regimes for tariffs, taxes and regulations are established (collectively referred to as 'special economic areas'). China will apply and administer in a uniform, impartial and reasonable manner all its laws, regulations and other measures of the central government as well as local regulations, rules and other measures issued or applied at the sub-national level pertaining to or affecting trade in goods, services, trade-related aspects of

---

* This chapter was originally written in Chinese and was translated by Yu Jin.

intellectual property rights or the control of foreign exchange.

Transparency of trade policy

Transparency is another basic principle of the WTO, according to which all members shall publish all trade-related laws, regulations and other measures. The implementation and observation of the transparency principle is conducive to building an open and fair market environment for competition. In fact, since 1991, China has itself been gradually publishing its trade-related laws, regulations and other measures. As such, China has committed to observation of the WTO transparency principle.

All the laws, regulations and other measures related to foreign trade will be published before they are implemented. Laws and regulations pertinent to WTO agreements shall be reported by China to the WTO. Following accession to the WTO, China will establish or designate an enquiry point in the foreign trade administration, which shall provide a reasonable period for comment to the appropriate authorities before such measures are implemented. Replies to WTO members shall be complete and shall represent the authoritative view of the Chinese government. Accurate and reliable information will be provided to individuals and enterprises. Replies to requests for information shall generally be provided within 30-45 days after receipt of a request. Upon the request of WTO members, a translated version in formal WTO language shall be provided within 90 days after the publication of the laws and regulations.

Following its entry to the WTO, China has set up the WTO Notification and Consulting Bureau in MOFTEC. Since 14 January 2002, when it began offering consulting services to the public, the bureau has received hundreds of enquiries from foreign embassies in China, overseas and domestic enterprises and individuals. Most of the enquiries have been replied to in writing.

Providing opportunities for judicial review to the affected parties

The WTO requires all its members to provide opportunities for appealing, judicial review and reexamination. The opportunity for judicial review in the trade and investment field will help to improve the trade investment environment in China. China's Administrative Procedural Law has clear provisions on judicial review. Therefore, China has committed to fulfil the obligation of judicial reviews so long as it is not contradictory to the provisions in the Administrative Procedural Law.

China shall establish fair and independent judicial review tribunals to review all administrative actions relating to the implementation of laws, regulations, judicial decisions and administrative rulings of general application. So long as a case is not contradictory to China's Administrative Procedural Law, individuals or enterprises affected by administrative action shall have the right of appeal. If the initial right of appeal is to an administrative body, in all cases there shall be the opportunity to choose to appeal the decision to a judicial body.

Progressively liberalizing the right to trade

Availability of the right to trade (right to operate foreign trade) to enterprises in China has been subject to an examination and approval system. The common international practice is that enterprises shall be granted the right to trade so long as they are legally registered. According to China's WTO Protocol, China will abolish the examination and approval system of the right to trade within three years after accession. All enterprises in China shall have the right to trade in all goods throughout the customs territory of China, except for those goods that continue to be subject to state trading and designated trading. More details on the liberalization of trading rights are given in Chapter 2.3 – *The Deregulation of China's Foreign Trade within the WTO*.

Abiding by the WTO agreements on state trading

China has committed itself to abiding by the WTO agreement on state trading. Chinese state trading companies shall operate from commercial considerations and shall fulfill the notification obligations. China shall retain its system of state trading but at the same time non-state trading companies shall be allowed to take certain proportions of imports. In addition, China shall phase out state trading controls on vegetable oils (including soybean-oil, palm oil and colza oil) from 1 Jan 2006 onwards.

China has reserved the right of state pricing and government guidance pricing of some important products, services and public utilities, which are listed in Annex 4 to the agreement. China has also reserved the right to exercise government pricing on products such as tobacco, edible salt and pharmaceuticals, on public utilities such as gas for civil use, tap water, electricity, heating power and water supplied by irrigation works and on services such as posts and telecommunications, entrance fees for tourist sites and education services charges. Government guidance pricing will be applied to products such as grain, vegetable oil, processed oil, fertilizer, silkworm cocoons and cotton, services such as transport services charges, professional services charges, charges for commission agents' services, charges for ranks' settlement, clearing and transmission services, the selling prices and rents of residential apartments, and health related services.

Non-tariff measures

According to the WTO agreement, China is committed to eliminating non-tariff measures on more than 400 product items by 1 January 2005. China has also committed that no non-tariff measures shall be increased or expanded, nor shall any new measures be applied, unless in conformity with the provisions of the WTO Agreement. By 1 January 2005, China shall eliminate the current non-tariff measures on more than 400 tariff items, including import quotas, import licences and specific tendering requirements. The phase-out of non-tariff measures will involve products such as motor vehicles, natural rubber and colour photographic materials. During the phase-out period, China will implement the growth rates for quotas as indicated in Annex 3. The WTO Agreement on Import Licensing Procedures will be strictly observed in terms of quota allocation standards, timing of quota allocations, availability and extension of import licenses. More details may be found in Chapter 2.3 – *The Deregulation of China's Foreign trade within the WTO.*

Removing export subsidies

China is committed to abiding by the WTO Agreement on Subsidies and Countervailing Measures, eliminating export subsidies prohibited by the agreement and notifying the WTO on those subsidies allowed by the agreement.

China has committed itself to eliminating gradually the subsidies inconsistent with the WTO agreement, such as priority in obtaining loans and foreign currencies based on export performance. At the same time, China has reserved more than 20 subsidies that are consistent with the Agreement and they are listed in Annex 5 of the Protocol. The subsidies include: preferential policies for the SEZs, the economic and technology development areas, the special economic zone of the Pudong Area of Shanghai, and for foreign-invested enterprises, loans from the state policy banks, financial subsidies for poverty alleviation, funds for technology innovation, research and development, infrastructure construction funds for agricultural water conservancy and flood protection projects, tax and tariff refunds for export products, tariff and import duty reductions and exemption for enterprises, the provision of low-price inputs for special industrial sectors, subsidies to certain enterprises in the forestry industry, preferential income tax treatment to high-tech enterprises, to enterprises utilizing waste, to disaster stricken enterprises and to enterprises which provide job opportunities to the unemployed.

Implementing the agreement on trade-related investment measures

China has committed to implementing the Agreement on Trade-related Investment Measures after its accession to the WTO and eliminating trade-related investment measures such as foreign-exchange balancing and trade balancing requirements, local content or technology transfer requirements and export performance requirements. China has committed, according to the common practice of most WTO members, to not enforcing mandatory provisions on export performance in laws, regulations and rules. Such provisions in contracts shall be the result of commercial negotiations.

Following China's accession to the WTO, China's legislative authorities have revised the three basic laws governing foreign direct investment, the Law on Chinese-foreign Equity Joint Ventures, the Law on Chinese-Foreign Contractual Joint Ventures and the Law on Wholly Foreign-owned Enterprises. Their detailed rules of implementation have also been revised accordingly. The revisions have been made on the articles relating to balance of foreign exchange, local content, export performance and the filing of enterprises' production plans. China has unified the turnover tax system for both Chinese and foreign-invested enterprises, removed the collection of high charges on foreign-invested enterprises and eliminated the dual charge standards on foreigners' purchase of plane tickets, bus, train or steamer tickets, entrance tickets and fees on public utilities. In addition, the Catalogue of Industries for the Guidance of Foreign Investment and a new policy for the automobile industry have been published.

Accepting the transitional review mechanism

According to the WTO's trade policy review mechanism, China's trade policy will be reviewed every four years, the same as for those countries that have similar trade shares to China. At the same time, the Protocol has a provision on the transitional review mechanism, as the commitments made by China and other the WTO members in the negotiations will be mainly implemented within 10 years from China's accession. Within eight years after China's accession to the WTO, the relevant WTO committee will conduct annual reviews on China's implementation of WTO obligations and commitments, and annual reviews shall terminate in the 10th year.

Chinese Government Structure

Li Yong, Deputy Secretary General, China Association of International Trade

The government reform

The First Session of the Ninth National People's Congress held in Beijing between 5–19 March 1998 adopted a major organizational restructuring, as a result of which the number of ministries and commissions under the State Council was reduced from 40 to 29 and the total staff size halved.

Why reform?

Reform of the administrative system is crucial to deepening economic restructuring and promoting economic and social development. It is also an important part of the reform of the Party and government leadership regime.

Since the inception of reform and the opening-up of China to the outside world in late 1978, some progress has been made in government restructuring. However, multiple efforts in reforming government organizations have been unable to eradicate the problems, due to the constraints of historical conditions and the limitations of the macro-environment. The contradiction between the government organizational set-up and the development of a socialist market economy has been increasingly prominent. The key symptoms are:

- The framework of present government institutions has evolved from the environment of the planned economy. One increasingly apparent drawback of the regime is the lack of separation between government functions and enterprise management, which has resulted in direct government intervention in the production and operation of enterprises and the establishment of numerous specialized economic management departments. At the same time, unjust-

ified emphasis on the interplay between comprehensive and specialized departments gave rise to overlapping government functions, red tape and inefficiency. Nonetheless, the 20-year reforms have brought about significant changes in the forms of corporate entities, management and operational practices, all of which have identified that the current management of enterprise affairs by the government is inadequate for establishing a modern enterprise system.

- The principles against which the existing government structure was set up were formulated in the absence of a complete socialist legal system. The government resorted to administrative means in its efforts to manage economic and social affairs. Many problems that should have been solved by legal means, or through intermediary bodies, were dealt with by establishing specialized government departments. As a result, excessive social responsibilities and routine contradictions remain with the government. To achieve the objectives of regulating the socialist market economy by legal instruments and of standardizing market practices, the government should respond to the need to perfect the socialist legal system. It should also develop social intermediary bodies by reforming the principles of setting up government departments as well as the operational mechanism of the government.

- The existing government has many overlapping and overstaffed departments which have not only spawned red tape and bureaucracy, but have also given rise to corruption and unhealthy tendencies, and which constitute a heavy burden on the government budget. Currently, there are about 33 million administrative staff at all levels of governments funded by the state budget, which seriously erode the government's capability in carrying out socialist construction and in protecting public interests.

Targets and principles of the reform

The current government restructuring is designed to achieve the following targets:

- Establishment of a highly efficient, well co-ordinated and standardized administrative management system;
- Perfection of the public service system, thereby setting up a highly qualified and specialized administrative management team;
- Gradual formation of an administrative management system that has Chinese characteristics and is compatible with the socialist market economy.

Principles for restructuring

- Government functions need to be transformed and separated from enterprise management to respond to the requirements of developing the socialist market economy. Government functions shall be shifted to macro-control, social management and public service. Decision-making powers with respect to production and operation should be given entirely to enterprises.
- In accordance with the principles of being 'simple, unified and efficient', the structure of the government organizations shall be restructured to reduce redundant administration and staff size. The macro-economic control departments shall be strengthened. The specialized economic departments shall be readjusted and reduced. At the same time, social service departments shall be appropriately adjusted while strengthening law-enforcement and supervision departments. Intermediary organizations shall be developed.
- According to the principle that the level of power should be commensurate with the level of responsibilities, the power and responsibilities of government departments shall be readjusted to define a clear-cut division of government functions among various departments. Identical or similar functions will be delegated to one department only so as to eliminate the problems of overlapping management and policy making.
- To respond to the requirements of managing the country by legal means and exercising administration with legal instruments, the construction of a legal-based administrative system shall be strengthened.

Government structure streamlined

The emphasis of government reform is on the restructuring of the departments under the State Council. Some of the previous ministries, commissions and administrations have been removed, merged or reorganized.

1. The Commission for Economic Restructuring is removed.
2. Eleven ministries are removed. They include:
   - Ministry of Power Industry
   - Ministry of Coal Industry
   - Ministry of Metallurgical Industry
   - Ministry of Machine Building Industry
   - Ministry of Electronics Industry
   - Ministry of Chemical Industry
   - Ministry of Internal Trade
   - Ministry of Posts and Telecommunications
   - Ministry of Labour
   - Ministry of Forestry.

   The ministries removed from the State Council have been reorganized into industrial bureaux which are under the jurisdiction of the State Economic and Trade Commission.
3. Two national industrial councils have been removed and reorganized into bureaux under the State Economic and Trade Commission. They are:
   - National Council for the Textiles Industry
   - National Council for Light Industry
4. Two new departments have been set up:
   - Ministry of Information Industry, which is a merger of the former Ministry of Posts and Telecommunications and the Ministry of Electronics Industry.
   - The State Commission of Science and Technology for National Defence Industry
5. Two departments were renamed:
   - The State Commission of Science and Technology has been renamed the Ministry of Science and Technology
   - The State Commission of Education has been renamed the Ministry of Education
6. The Ministry of Labour and Social Security has been established on the basis of the former Ministry of Labour.
7. The Ministry of Land and Resources is formed to take over the responsibilities of the former Ministry of Geology and Mineral Resources, State Administration of Land, State Bureau of Oceanography and the State Bureau of Survey and Cartography.

8. The former Ministry of Radio, Film and Television is now a bureau under the State Council while part of its remit – the TV network – is given to the Ministry of Information Industry.

In 2000, a further reform effort was made resulting in the scrapping of nine bureaux and administrations. They include:

– State Internal Trade Bureau
– State Machine-Building Industrial Bureau
– State Metallurgical Industrial Bureau
– State Petrochemical Industrial Bureau
– State Light Industrial Bureau
– State Textile Industrial Bureau
– State Building Materials Industrial Bureau
– State Non-ferrous Metals Industrial Bureau
– State Coal Industrial Bureau.

These bureaux no longer assume government functions, having been turned into industry associations.

The new government structure

The central administrative system in the People's Republic of China includes: the central administrative organs under the system of the National People's Congress and the leadership of the central administrative organs over local administrative organs at various levels. The central administrative organ is the State Council of the People's Republic of China.

State Council

The State Council, or the Central People's Government, of the People's Republic of China is the executive body of the highest organ of state power and the highest organ of state administration. It exercises unified leadership over local state administrative organs at various levels throughout the country, regulates the specific division of power and function of the state administrative organs at the central level and at the provincial, autonomous regional and municipal levels. The head of the State Council is the Premier, who assumes overall responsibility for the work of the State Council and is responsible to the National People's Congress (NPC) and its Standing Committee on behalf of the State Council. The Premier is assisted by a Vice Premier and State Counsellors. The Premier has the following decision-making powers:

- The final decision-making power on all major issues in the work of the State Council.
- Power to propose to the NPC and its Standing Committee the appointment or removal of the Vice Premiers, State Counsellors, Ministers, the Auditor-general and the Secretary-general.
- Decisions, decrees and administrative rules and regulations promulgated by the State Council, and bills and proposals for appointments and removals submitted by the State Council to the NPC and its Standing Committee are legally valid only after the Premier has signed them.

The State Council consists of ministries, commissions, the People's Bank of China and administrations, who, under the unified leadership of the State Council, are in charge of directing and administering the administrative affairs in their respective areas and exercising prescribed state administrative powers. These government departments can be classified into the following categories by the nature of their function:

Macro-control organs

Such organs include:

– State Development Planning Commission
– State Economic and Trade Commission
– Ministry of Finance
– People's Bank of China

These organs, particularly the state commissions, co-ordinate at the national level and on a cross-industry basis and therefore have overruling decision-making power over the ministries and administrations.

Functional ministries

Functional ministries are mainly those which have a specified area of administrative interest and can be categorized into the following:

- Special economic administrative organs
  Such organs mainly consist of ministries that have an assigned industry-wide area of responsibilities, which are often reflected in the names of those ministries. The following is a list of such ministries:
  – Ministry of Railways
  – Ministry of Transport
  – Ministry of Construction

- Ministry of Agriculture
- Ministry of Water Conservancy
- Ministry of Foreign Trade and Economic Co-operation
- Ministry of Information Industry
- Commission of Science, Technology and Industry for National Defence

These ministries represent the State Council for decision-making on specific industries and exercise macro-administration over those industries.

- Social security organs
  - Ministry of Labour and Social Security
  - Ministry of Personnel
  - State Family Planning Commission
- Natural resource administrative organ
  - Ministry of Land and Resources
- Foreign affairs, internal affairs and security organs
  - Ministry of Foreign Affairs
  - State Commission of Ethnic Affairs
  - Ministry of Civil Affairs
  - Ministry of Justice
  - Ministry of Public Security
  - Ministry of State Security
  - Ministry of National Defence
  - Ministry of Supervision
  - National Audit Office
- Education, science, culture and health administrative organs
  - Ministry of Education
  - Ministry of Science and Technology
  - Ministry of Culture
  - Ministry of Health.

Administrations and Bureaux under the State Council

Most of the administrations and bureaux are sub- or semi-ministerial government agencies. They are more like supervisory and regulatory bodies on a cross-industry basis than sector-oriented decision-making departments. Such administrations and bureaux include the following:

- General Administration of Customs
- State Administration of Taxation
- State Environmental Protection Administration
- General Administration of Civil Aviation of China
- State Administration of Audio, Film and Television
- State Sports General Administration
- National Bureau of Statistics

- State Administration for Industry and Commerce
- General Administration of Press and Publication
- State Forestry Bureau
- General Administration of Quality Supervision, Inspection and Quarantine
- State Drug Administration
- State Intellectual Property Office
- National Tourism Administration
- State Administration of Religious affairs
- Counsellor's Office under the State Council
- Government Offices Administration of the State Council.

Offices directly under the State Council

These offices are designed to assist the Premier in dealing with matters in special areas. Generally, these organizations are at the vice-ministerial level in terms of their official ranking. They include:

- Hong Kong and Macao Affairs Office
- Legislative Affairs Office
- Office for Restructuring the Economic System
- Research Office
- Information Office
- Taiwan Affairs Office.

Institutions directly under the State Council

- Xinhua News Agency
- Chinese Academy of Sciences
- Chinese Academy of Social Sciences
- Chinese Academy of Engineering
- Development Research Centre
- China National School of Administration
- China Seismological Bureau
- China Meteorological Administration
- China Securities Regulatory Commission
- China Insurance Regulatory Commission.

State Bureaux under the supervision of ministries and commissions

- State Administration of Grain under the supervision of the State Development Planning Commission
- State Administration of Work Safety also known as the State Administration of Coal Mine Safety Supervision under the supervision of the State Economic and Trade Commission

- State Tobacco Monopoly Administration under the supervision of the State Economic and Trade Commission
- State Administration of Foreign Experts Affairs under the supervision of the Ministry of Personnel
- State Oceanic Administration under the supervision of the Ministry of Land and Resources
- State Bureau of Surveying and Mapping under the supervising of the Ministry of Land and Resources
- State Postal Bureau under the supervision of the Ministry of Information Industry
- State Administration of Cultural Heritage under the supervision of the Ministry of Culture
- State Administration of Traditional Chinese Medicine under the supervision of the Ministry of Health
- State Administration of Foreign Exchange under the supervision of the People's Bank of China.

Government hierarchy

Administrative hierarchy of the government system

The administrative hierarchy is quite complicated. The introduction to the government structure provided earlier attempted to explain the hierarchical ranking of those government departments. However, in some cases, it is very difficult for anyone to determine a ranking simply by looking at the position of an organization in the government structure, as some higher-ranking officials take positions in lower ranking organizations. To generalize, those ministries, commissions and administrations that constitute the main body of the State Council are at the ministerial level as shown in Fig.1.5.1.

Those bureaux, commissions, administrations and institutions that are under the supervision of the State Council are generally understood to be sub- or semi-ministerial level organizations.

Typical structure of a ministry

The management body of a ministry usually consists of a minister, several vice-ministers and assistant ministers. Under the ministry there are departments, under which there are divisions (see Figure 1.5.2). Normally, the divisions are the place where the first point of contact with the ministry starts. Parallel with the departments, there are in some cases also industry associations and other institutions such as information centres or research institutes, which are relatively independent in terms of operation, but organizationally affiliated.

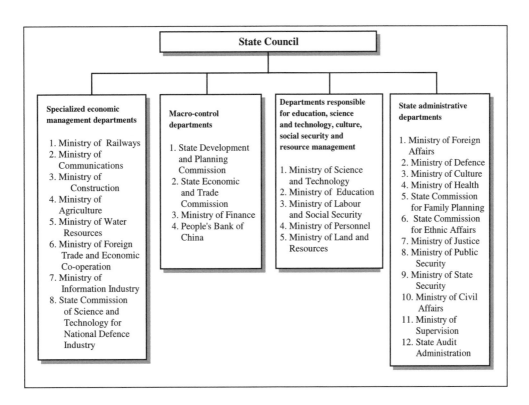

Figure 1.5.1   Ministries, Commissions and Administrations that constitute the main body of the State Council

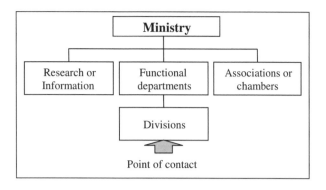

Figure 1.5.2 Departments within the Ministry

Before the government reforms, the ministries were responsible for business corporations and large state-owned enterprises, which are now independent as a result of the government reform in separating government functions from enterprise management.

Provincial level governments

The local governments that are immediately under the central government are provincial-level governments. China now has on its mainland 22 provinces, five autonomous regions and four municipalities under state jurisdiction. All the governments in those 31 locations are provincial level governments. The heads of those provincial stations are officials of ministerial level.

Provincial governments must accept the unified leadership of the State Council, which has the power to decide on the division of responsibilities between the central government and provincial administrative organs. The State Council also has the power to annul inappropriate decisions and orders of provincial governments. At the same time, provincial governments implement local laws, regulations and decisions of the provincial people's congresses and their standing committees, and are responsible to and report to those congresses and their standing committees. Provincial people's congresses and their standing committees have the power to supervise the work, change and annul inappropriate decisions of the provincial governments.

The structure of a provincial government resembles that of the central government. Under a provincial government, there are similar set-ups that correspond to the ministries and commissions at the central level. For example, there are provincial development planning commissions, bureaux of finance, bureaux of foreign trade and economic co-operation, bureaux of education, drug administration, etc., that correspond to the State Development Planning Commission, the

Ministry of Finance, the Ministry of Foreign Trade and Economic Co-operation, the Ministry of Education, State Drug Administration, etc. The heads of the local bureaux, commissions, administrations, etc. are appointed by and are responsible to the provincial governments, while at the same time executing the policies made both by the provincial governments and the central ministries. A typical reporting structure is described in Figure 1.5.3.

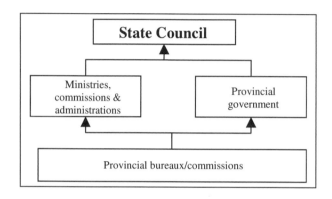

Figure 1.5.3 A typical reporting structure

Lower level governments

Chinese cities vary not only in size, but also in official ranking. Some provincial capitals and cities of key economic importance have different administrative status and a certain level of independence from the provinces where they are located. There are 15 cities that are called 'separately planned cities', which means that such cities have independent administrative status and are singled out to enjoy quasi-provincial status in national planning. In terms of reporting routes, the government functions such as bureaux, commissions and administration in these cities do not report to the corresponding provincial departments, but to those at the central level. The heads of those governments are referred to as vice-ministerial officials. Such cities include Shenyang, Dalian, Changchun, Harbin, Jinan, Qingdao, Nanjing, Ningbo, Hangzhou, Xiamen, Wuhan, Guangzhou, Shenzhen, Xian and Chengdu. Their reporting structure in relation to the central government is very much the same as described in Figure 1.5.3.

Most of the other cities such as prefectural cities are under the jurisdiction of the provincial government. To understand the reporting structure of such cities, it is important to clarify the position of a prefectural city in the administrative structure of a typical province (see Figure 1.5.4).

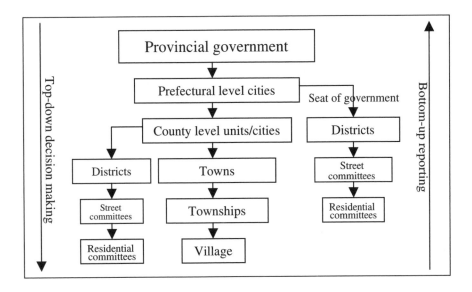

Figure 1.5.4   Administrative structure for a typical province

The reporting structure of a prefectural city and the county-level cities under a prefectural city is depicted in Figure 1.5.5.

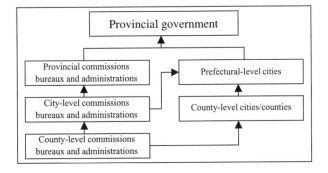

Figure 1.5.5   Reporting structure of a prefectural city

In terms of official ranking, the head of a prefectural city is equivalent to the heads of provincial bureaux, commissions and administrations; all are known as director-general level officials. The existing prefectural level cities are largely the heritage of the old administrative system of China. It is not a rigid hierarchical ladder now, because county-level cities can be promoted to prefectural level cities if the following criteria are met:

- over a quarter of a million non-farming population in total, with the place of a government seat having a population over 200,000;

- total industrial and agricultural output value at 1990 constant prices exceeding 3 billion renminbi, of which 80 per cent should be industrial output value;
- GDP over 2.5 billion renminbi;
- the share of the output value of tertiary industry at not less than 35 per cent of GDP and surpassing that of primary industry;
- annual budgetary fiscal revenue in excess of 200 million renminbi;
- the city becoming a centre of the neighbouring areas.

Official ranking

Official ranking is an important part of China's administrative hierarchy. There is a saying that 'the person in charge is more helpful than the person who supervises', which means that a person with no official ranking can be very important in handling government relations. Nevertheless, a better knowledge of the official may help you to understand the roles that the officials you are dealing with play in the decision making process. Figure 1.5.6 provides a comparison of the official rankings in different government structures.

As a result of the government effort to separate government functions from enterprise management, government at all levels are not supposed to be involved in business activities. The government reform effort has also removed the official rankings associated with the management of state-owned enterprises. Enterprises are mostly using corporate titles now with no implications of official ranking.

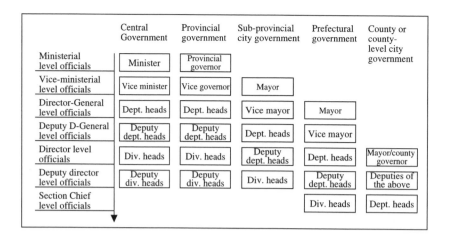

	Central Government	Provincial government	Sub-provincial city government	Prefectural government	County or county-level city government
Ministerial level officials	Minister	Provincial governor			
Vice-ministerial level officials	Vice minister	Vice governor	Mayor		
Director-General level officials	Dept. heads	Dept. heads	Vice mayor	Mayor	
Deputy D-General level officials	Deputy dept. heads	Deputy dept. heads	Dept. heads	Vice mayor	
Director level officials	Div. heads	Div. heads	Deputy dept. heads	Dept. heads	Mayor/county governor
Deputy director level officials	Deputy div. heads	Deputy div. heads	Div. heads	Deputy dept. heads	Deputies of the above
Section Chief level officials				Div. heads	Dept. heads

Figure 1.5.6   Comparison of the official rankings in different government structures

China's Prospering Private Sector*

Wang Chaoping, Senior Researcher, Director General, Policy Research Department of Central Committee of the Communist Party

At the end of the 1970s, a major change took place in China, which was the implementation of economic reforms and opening to the outside world. These policy initiatives represented an effort to build a socialist country with Chinese characteristics. The initial efforts at reform thereafter gradually led China to realize that it is still in the initial stage of socialism, which is going to be a long historical process. In this period, China must adhere to the basic economic system in which public ownership will remain dominant but in which other forms of ownership are allowed to develop. As a result, the pace of restructuring ownership was accelerated, which has greatly liberated and developed society's productivity, adding impetus to the rapid development of China's economy.

If one looks back at the statistical data from 1980, one notices that there was no separate entry for the non-state or private sector, meaning, in other words, that the private sector was so negligibly small at that time that it did not make sense to include it in the statistics. However, by the end of 2001, the total number of what is called *ge ti gong shang hu* (namely, individual industrial and commercial proprietors) had surged to 24.33 million, while *si ying qi ye* (privately-run enterprises) have developed to a total of 2.03 million. They employed 74.74 million workers and their total registered capital amounted to 2.2 trillion renminbi. The total value of output created by the private sector in 2001 reached 1.96 trillion renminbi, one fifth of China's GDP. The total retail sales of consumer products contributed by the private sector in the same year was 1.77 trillion renminbi, about half of the country's total. The private

sector also provided one quarter of China's employment opportunities. The non-state or private sector has thus become an important part of the economy, playing a positive role in China's economic operation and development.

China's non-state or private sector has been able to maintain a good trend of development, evidenced by the following statistics.

Steady growth in numbers and obvious strengthening

By the end of 2001, there were 24.33 million individual industrial and commercial proprietors employing 47.6 million people and their registered capital increased by 3.64 per cent to 343.58 billion renminbi.

The number of privately-run enterprises grew by 15.1 per cent to reach 2.03 million. Their registered capital increased by an even larger margin of 36.9 per cent, or 1.82 trillion renminbi. The average registered capital was 898,000 renminbi in 2001, a rise of 18.8 per cent year-on-year. There were 23,000 privately-run businesses whose registered capital was over 10 million renminbi, while those with registered capital of more than 100 million totalled 383. The number of investors involved in those privately-run enterprises was 4.61 million in 2001, 16.6 per cent more than the previous year.

The privately-run enterprises employed 27.13 million workers, an increase of 12.8 per cent over 2000. The average number of workers employed by privately-run enterprises was 11.1 persons. About 21,700 privately-run enterprises employed 100–500 workers and there

---

* This chapter was originally written in Chinese and was translated by Li Yong.

were 1,808 enterprises employing 500 to 1000 workers. 337 large privately-run enterprises employed over 1000 workers.

Larger concentration in eastern China and higher growth in western China

In eastern China, there were 11.62 million individual industrial and commercial proprietors, 47.4 per cent of the national total. They employ 22.62 million workers, 47.5 per cent of the total employment by individual industrial and commercial proprietors. Their registered capital accounted for 56.5 per cent of the total or 194.14 billion renminbi. There were 1.39 million privately-run enterprises in eastern China, representing 68.4 per cent of the total number of privately-run enterprises countrywide. There were six provinces or municipalities where the number of privately-run enterprises exceeded 100,000.

Table 1.6.1 Provinces/municipalities with more than 100,000 privately-run enterprises

Province/municipalities	Number of privately-run enterprises (thousands)
Jiangsu	226
Guangdong	211
Zhejiang	209
Shanghai	176
Shandong	145
Beijing	124
Total	1,091

These six locations are all in the eastern part of China and are the home of 53.8 per cent of China's total number of privately-run enterprises.

In the central part of China there were 8.04 million individual industrial and commercial proprietors, accounting for 33 per cent of the country's total. They employed 17.1 million workers, representing 35.9 per cent of the total employment offered by such proprietors nationwide. Their total registered capital amounted to 101.39 billion renminbi, 29.5 per cent of the total registered capital of individual industrial and commercial proprietors. There were 360,000 privately-run enterprises in the region in 2001, accounting for 17.8 per cent of the total number in the country.

In the western part of China the number of individual industrial and commercial proprietors reached 4.68 million, or 19.5 per cent of the national total. They

provided 7.88 million jobs, 16.6 per cent of the total job opportunities offered by such businesses countrywide. Their share of total registered capital was 14 per cent, amounting to 48.05 billion renminbi. The number of privately-run enterprises totalled 281,000, 13.8 per cent of the country's total. The rate of increase in the number of privately-run enterprises in the region was 18.8 per cent in 2001, higher than the average rate of growth.

Larger share of non-state business in cities and townships and faster growth in numbers

The number of individual industrial and commercial proprietors in urban China (cities and townships) was 11.27 million in 2001, which was 46.4 per cent of the national total. They offered 21.31 million jobs, 44.8 per cent of the total employment provided by such proprietors countrywide. The privately-run enterprises in the urban areas of China totalled 1.29 million in 2001, accounting for 63.6 per cent of the national total and representing an increase of 19.6 per cent year on year. At the same time, the registered capital also increased by 36.8 per cent to 1.26 trillion renminbi. The number of investors in privately-run enterprises grew by 21 per cent to a total of 2.99 million. In 2001 the total employment by privately-run enterprises in urban China was 12.28 million, 20.3 per cent more than in 2000.

In rural areas of China, the number of individual industrial and commercial proprietors in 2001 was 13.04 million, or 53.6 per cent of the country's total number of individual industrial and commercial proprietors. They provided jobs for 26.29 million people, which was 55.2 per cent of the total jobs provided by individual industrial and commercial proprietors in the country. Privately-run enterprises, on the other hand, reached a total of 737,000, 36.4 per cent of the country's total. This figure was an increase of 8 per cent over 2000. The registered capital of the privately-run enterprises in rural China saw an increase of 37.1 per cent over 2000, totalling 563.8 billion renminbi. There was an increase of 9.2 per cent in the number of investors (1.62 million) in rural privately-run enterprises in 2001. The number of jobs provided by rural privately-run enterprises increased by a moderate 3.5 per cent to a total of 10.25 million.

Industrial structure further adjusted and the share of the service industry on the rise

There were 907,000 individual industrial and commercial proprietors in primary industry, with a total registered capital of 12.97 billion renminbi, employing 1.94 million people. In secondary, or manufacturing, industry, the number of individual industrial and commercial proprietors was 2.852 million, with a total registered capital of 63.78 billion renminbi, employing 20.57 million people. The number of individual industrial and commercial proprietors in the tertiary, or service, industry was 20.571 million, having a total registered capital of 266.83 billion renminbi and employing 37.60 million. Their shares against the national total number of individual industrial and commercial proprietors, total employment and registered capital were 84.6 per cent, 79 per cent and 77.7 per cent respectively. It should be noted, however, that most of the indicators for individual industrial and commercial proprietors in the primary and secondary industries have been on the decline, while the indicators for those in the tertiary industry have been rising.

Those privately-run enterprises in the secondary and tertiary industries have enjoyed higher rates of growth, while those in the primary industry have decreased. In 2001, the number of privately-run enterprises in primary industry dropped by 5.8 per cent and there was a decrease of 6.7 per cent or 522,000 in the number of people employed. The registered capital of privately-run enterprises in primary industry had increased by 21.2 per cent to 33.32 billion renminbi. In secondary industry, privately-run enterprises increased by a total of 767,000, a rise of 10.4 per cent over 2000. Total employment was 14.03 million, 9.5 per cent more than in 2000. Total registered capital had also seen an increase of 34.1 per cent to 654.47 billion renminbi. Privately-run enterprises in the service industry have developed very rapidly in 2001, increasing in number by 19.1 per cent to 1.224 million, in the provision of jobs by 17.7 per cent to 12.59 million and in registered capital by 39.1 per cent to 1.134 trillion renminbi. The ratio for privately-run enterprises among primary, secondary and tertiary industries is 2:38:60.

Individual industrial and commercial proprietors are more concentrated in commerce and trade, privately-run enterprises in manufacturing

Among the individual industrial and commercial proprietors, 60.7 per cent or 14.76 million were engaged in wholesaling, retailing, food services and social services. Manufacturing proprietors accounted for only 12.8 per cent (3.12 million) of the total. 11.3 per cent

or 2.74 million were in the communications and transport businesses, while 2.38 million of them (9.8 per cent) operate in warehousing and storage businesses.

There were 685,000 privately-run enterprises in the manufacturing sector in 2001, accounting for 33.8 per cent of the total. They employed 12.21 million workers, representing 44.9 per cent of the total workforce in all privately-run enterprises. The registered capital of enterprises in the manufacturing sector was 500.09 billion renminbi, amounting to 27.5 per cent of the total registered capital. In the trade and food services sectors, there were 822,000 privately-run enterprises, which was 40.5 per cent of the total. They employed 8.76 million people, accounting for 32.3 per cent of the total jobs in all privately-run enterprises, and their registered capital was 645.92 billion renminbi, representing 35.5 per cent of the total registered capital of all privately-run enterprises.

The limited liability company is the main form of private businesses while sole proprietorship has grown very slowly

For the obvious reason that investors assume limited liabilities under the structure of a limited liability company while their liabilities are unlimited in the case of sole proprietorship, the owners of private businesses choose the limited liability company as the main form of business structure. As a result, the number of limited liability companies has increased for several years. By the end of 2001, there were 1.38 million limited liability companies in China, an increase of 26.9 per cent over the previous year. These private limited liability companies had a total registered capital of 1.61 trillion renminbi in 2001, a rise of 43 per cent against 2000. The number of investors involved in those companies in the same year was 3.654 million, 26.9 per cent more than in 2000. There was also an increase of 29.9 per cent in total employment to a total of 14.42 million people. Private joint-stock companies numbered 289, a drop of 8.3 per cent; however, their total registered capital surged by 68.2 per cent to a total of 12.77 billion renminbi.

Partnership enterprises experienced a drop of 24.9 per cent in 2001 to a total of 131,000. Their registered capital was 48.74 billion renminbi, down by 24.9 per cent. The number of investors in partnership enterprises shrank by 23.9 per cent to a total of 426,000. In addition, the number of jobs provided by partnership enterprises declined by 27.5 per cent to 1.94 million.

Solely owned proprietorships grew by 3.5 per cent in 2001 to a total of 517,000. Their registered capital reached 148.39 billion renminbi, an increase of 12.6 per cent, but the workforce employed by solely owned proprietorships dropped by 2.7 per cent to 6.153 million.

China's private sector has developed quite rapidly within a short span of 20 years or so from the late 1970s. The private sector has now reached a considerable scale and has injected vibrancy into the economy as whole, while maintaining a strong momentum. This has proved that the principles and policies regarding the private sector were correct. The achievements made in China's economy are only a start and there will be great potential for future development. Many private businesses have entered the high-tech sector and have launched export-oriented processing operations. In 2001, there were 164,000 exporting and foreign exchange earning private businesses, which generated 91.35 billion renminbi (roughly US$11 billion) worth of foreign exchange, an increase of 23.3 per cent over the previous year. The organizational structure of private businesses is also moving in the direction of standardized modern corporate governance. There are more and more private companies that have become joint-stock companies, publicly listed companies and joint ventures with foreign investors. Some of the large private enterprises have also extended their business presence in overseas markets. It is firmly believed by the Chinese people and the government that, as long as the principle of 'maintaining public ownership as the mainstay while allowing the development of diversified ownership' is adhered to in the long-term, China's economy will be full of vigour and energy. It will progress faster, in new and better ways, creating further economic achievements while at the same time contributing to world prosperity and development.

China's Consumer Market

Li Yong, Deputy Secretary General, China Association of International Trade, and
Liu Baocheng, Professor, University of International Business and Economics

Introduction

When one thinks globally in terms of market expansion, China is a market that no business would ignore. One simple reason is that China is the largest single market that has yet to be developed. The population size, increasing consumer affluence and a strong momentum of economic growth make China an attractive marketplace in which many foreign companies have attempted to gain a foothold. In fact, many have. Most Fortune 500 companies have had operations of one kind or another in the marketplace. 70 per cent of the world's top 50 retailers are already active in China. These facts demonstrate that China is of significant strategic value for corporate growth and globalization. Indeed, manufacturing in China should mean reduced costs and increased competitiveness. Marketing in China should mean new sources of profit and additional gains in global market share.

Often, people tend to think of China in terms of a simplistic arithmetic calculation – if each of the 1.3 billion people spent one dollar or used a product once in a year, what enormous sales that would bring. It does not hurt to generalize on the market size with such a calculation, but to approach the market in such an arithmetic manner would satisfy only the desires of wishful thinking. In fact, no one should be so naive as to think of the market in these terms. It is true, however, that many marketers in China have overestimated market prospects by underestimating the complexity of the market. This introductory chapter on China's consumer market does not intend to provide solutions for market success, but aims to paint a picture of what the market looks like, particularly for those who have not yet stepped out of their national boundaries but are already planning international strategies that include China.

Consumer demographics

Population

Population is a factor in market size. For some products whose consumers are potentially every walking person, the total population represents the customer base and a percentage of the population would be the target of sales efforts. For other products, the population size would need to have a denominator before a company can assess the market. In other words, the size of the population does not determine a market that a company can address economically and realistically reach. It is an onion of which the outer skins need to be peeled off.

At the end of 2001, China registered a population of 1,276.7 million (excluding Hong Kong, Macao, Taiwan and other southern islands). Evidently China is now the most populous country in the world, while India is catching up. Some experts predict that India will replace China as the world's largest country. One underlying reason for this expectation is that China's population growth has slowed and the family planning policy has been effective in controlling the once explosive population. Table 1.7.1 below depicts the trend of China's population growth over the last two decades or so and the slow growth trend is obvious. According to one estimate, by 2010 the population is expected to stay at 1.4 billion, and by the middle of this century the population growth will halt at a peak of 1.6 billion. Thereafter, the population is expected to decline.

Table 1.7.1 China's population changes (1978-2001)

Year	Total population (000)	Natural growth rate(%)
1978	96,2590	12.00
1979	97,5420	11.61
1980	98,7050	11.87
1981	1,000,720	14.55
1982	1,016,540	15.68
1983	1,030,080	13.29
1984	1,043,570	13.08
1985	1,058,510	14.26
1986	1,075,070	15.57
1987	1,093,000	16.61
1988	1,110,260	15.73
1989	1,127,040	15.04
1990	1,143,330	14.39
1991	1,158,230	12.98
1992	1,171,710	11.60
1993	1,185,170	11.45
1994	1,198,500	11.21
1995	1,211,210	10.55
1996	1,223,890	10.42
1997	1,236,260	10.06
1998	1,248,100	9.53
1999	1,259,090	8.77
2000	1,265,830	7.58
2001	1,276,270	6.95

Source: China Statistical Yearbook 2001 and China Statistical

Population distribution by administrative divisions

Geographically, the Chinese population is distributed over 31 administrative regions, excluding Taiwan, Hong Kong and Macao. On its mainland China has four provincial level municipalities under the direct jurisdiction of the central government (Beijing, Shanghai, Tianjin and Chongqing), 5 autonomous regions (Inner Mongolia, Guangxi, Tibet, Ningxia and Xinjiang) and 22 provinces.

The top ten most populous provinces are Henan, (95.55 million), Shandong (90.41 million), Sichuan (86.4 million), Jiangsu (73.55 million), Guangdong (77.83 million), Hebei (66.99 million), Hunan (65.96 million), Anhui (63.28 million), Hubei (59.75 million) and Guangxi (47.88 million). These ten most populous places account for 57 per cent of the total population (see Figure 1.7.1).

Urban and rural population distribution

China began to practise a residence control system in 1951. Migration from rural to urban residences has

Table 1.7.2 Population distribution by administrative divisions 2001

Region	Total population (000)	Natural growth rate (%)
Beijing	13,830	0.80
Tianjin	10,040	1.64
Hebei	66,990	4.98
Shanxi	32,720	7.16
Inner Mongolia	23,770	4.98
Liaoning	41,940	1.64
Jilin	26,910	3.38
Heilongjiang	38,110	2.99
Shanghai	16,140	-0.95
Jiangsu	73,550	2.41
Zhejiang	46,130	3.77
Anhui	63,280	6.61
Fujian	34,400	6.04
Jiangxi	41,860	9.38
Shandong	90,410	4.88
Henan	95,550	6.94
Hubei	59,750	2.44
Hunan	65,960	5.08
Guangdong	77,830	8.33
Guangxi	47,880	7.73
Hainan	7,960	9.47
Chongqing	30,970	2.80
Sichuan	86,400	4.37
Guizhou	37,990	11.3
Yunnan	42,870	10.94
Tibet	2,630	12.10
Shaanxi	36,590	4.16
Gansu	25,750	7.15
Qinghai	5,230	12.62
Ningxia	5,630	11.71
Xinjiang	18,760	11.13
National total	1,276,270	6.95

Source: China Statistical Abstract 2002

a) Military personnel were included in the national total population, but excluded from the regional total population.

b) The national total population excluded the populations of Hong Kong, Macao and Taiwan.

been under strict control, as a result of which the rural population has remained predominantly high. In 1978 the proportion of rural population was 82.08 per cent, against an urban population share of 17.92 per cent. With the progress of urbanization, the share of urban population has increased to 37.65 per cent. This is a remarkable progress compared vertically with the past, but it is still quite low if compared horizontally with the

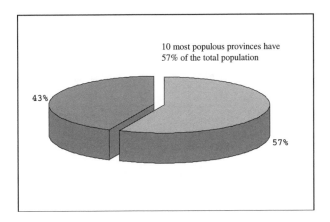

Figure 1.7.1 Share of the ten most populous provinces

Table 1.7.3 Urban vs rural population

Year	Urban population (million)	% of total	Rural population (million)	% of total
1978	172.45	17.92	790.14	82.08
1980	191.40	19.39	795.65	80.61
1985	250.94	23.71	807.57	76.29
1987	276.74	25.32	816.26	74.68
1988	286.61	25.81	823.65	74.19
1989	295.40	26.21	831.64	73.79
1990	301.91	26.41	841.42	73.59
1991	305.43	26.37	852.80	73.63
1992	323.72	27.63	847.99	72.37
1993	333.51	28.14	851.66	71.86
1994	343.01	28.62	855.49	71.38
1995	351.74	29.04	859.47	70.96
1996	359.50	29.37	864.39	70.63
1997	369.89	29.92	866.37	70.08
1998	379.42	30.40	868.68	69.60
1999	388.92	30.89	870.17	69.11
2000	458.44	36.22	807.39	63.78
2001	480.64	37.65	795.63	62.34

Source: China Statistical Yearbook 2001 and China Statistical Abstract 2002

world average of 47 per cent, not to mention a 70 per cent ratio of urban populations in developed countries.

Following China's accession to the WTO, agriculture is going to be one of the industries most impacted and labour migration from rural to urban areas is expected to increase. At the same time, the urbanization process will quicken in order to absorb the surplus labour from rural areas. There are indications that policies regarding control over the migration of the rural population into urban areas have been relaxed and rural residents are expected to receive 'national treatment'. Undoubtedly, urbanization is going to be vitally important in narrowing the gap between rural areas and urban districts, boosting China's economic growth and creating more jobs. According to a report by Guangming Daily in July 2002, the number of people living in Chinese cities is expected to reach 1.12 billion by 2050, accounting for 70 per cent of the country's total population. More than 600 million Chinese people will shift from rural areas to urban districts in the next 50 years. The same report says that the Chinese mainland now has more than 660 cities and 19,000 towns, and by 2050, 80 per cent of towns will have grown into small or medium-sized cities. By then, China will have 50 ultra-large cities, each with an urban population of more than 2 million, 150 big cities, 500 medium-sized cities and 1,500 small cities.

Population breakdown by gender
As shown in Table 1.7.4, the male population as a percentage of the total population has been higher than that of females. The Chinese Constitution and legislation give equal rights to both male and female in terms of social status and employment opportunities, but the culture's preference for masculinity is considered to be the key reason for a greater male population. This is particularly true in the less developed rural areas. In 2001 the female population reached a historical low of 48.31 per cent over the period from 1988 to 2001. Although the imbalance between the male and female populations is not so significant as to cause problems with social and economic implications, experts have expressed concerns for social stability if this trend continues.

Age distribution
According to China's Population Report, over 30 per cent of the population were under 20 years of age. On the other hand, the population segment of the people aged over 60 accounted for over 10 per cent, and those above 65 reached 6.95 per cent in the 2000 census. Population aging will become increasingly felt. By 2010 the people born in the baby boom period in the 1950s and 1960s will enter the elderly groupings and the elderly segment will experience the fastest growth. In the next 25 years the elderly population will be double today's count.

When studying the age distribution, marketers are invited to look into the two extremes of the population,

Table 1.7.4   Male vs female population

Year	Male		Female		Total
	Population (million)	% of total	Population (million)	% of total	population (million)
1988	572.01	51.52	538.25	48.48	1,110.26
1989	580.99	51.55	546.05	48.45	1,127.04
1990	589.04	51.52	554.29	48.48	1,143.33
1991	594.66	51.34	563.57	48.66	1,158.23
1992	598.11	51.05	573.60	48.95	1,171.71
1993	604.72	51.02	580.45	48.98	1,185.17
1994	612.46	51.10	586.04	48.90	1,198.50
1995	618.08	51.03	593.13	48.97	1,211.21
1996	622.00	50.82	601.89	49.18	1,223.89
1997	631.31	51.07	604.95	48.93	1,236.26
1998	636.29	50.98	611.81	49.02	1,248.10
1999	641.89	50.98	617.20	49.02	1,259.09
2000	653.55	51.63	612.28	48.37	1,265.83
2001	656.72	51.69	619.55	48.31	1,276.27

Source: China Statistical Yearbook 2001 and China Statistical Abstract 2002

one of which is the population of teenagers or what is called the 'little emperors' generation, and the other is the growing aging population. Marketers have already invested efforts to address the needs of the pampered little emperors but little attention has been given to the elderly population.

The little emperors have enjoyed higher living standards and better education and training than previous generations in China. But they have also displayed distortions in behaviour. Research indicates that the little emperors do not only represent a group of consumers, but also have increasing influence over parents' purchase decision-making. Over time, there will be more 'only' children joining the workforce. They will have better education as a result of their parents' investment in only children schooling. Considerable study effort is necessary to understand the behavioural characteristics of only children, as they will soon become the core of Chinese society.

Household structure

The average household size is getting smaller. In 2001 average household size in urban areas was 3.10 persons compared to 3.97 persons in 1990. One of the reasons for the decline in average family size is the low birth rate as a result of family planning. Social, economic and cultural factors have also contributed to the reduction in the average family size. There is an increasing number of DINK (double income no kids) families in urban areas, particularly among those who have higher education.

Urban households are characterized by high proportions of childless families while rural households average four-person families. The average size of rural households was 4.15 persons. Experts have commented that the urban household structure resembles that of developed countries and will not change much in the foreseeable future. With the continued family planning effort, the average size of rural households is expected to reduce.

China's family planning policy, which was designed to reduce the population, encourages late marriage and late childbearing. Better and fewer births are strongly advocated and a single-child family is promoted as state policy. The basic principle of family planning policy is to integrate the state instruction with individual consent. While respecting and safeguarding the individual's basic rights, the policy calls for individual's social responsibility and obligations. Health care institutions throughout the country are providing various kinds of services for mothers, children and couples at the childbearing age. However, at the same time, from 2003, most young people of marriageable age in urban areas will be only children. The one-child policy is expected to be relaxed. When two only children marry, they will be allowed to have more than one child.

Table 1.7.5 Age composition by region

Region	Population by age group (10,000)				% of total population		Total (10,000)
	Age 0–14	Age 15–64		Age 65+	Age 0–14	Age 15–64	Age 65+
Beijing	188	1,078	1,382	116	13.60	78.04	8.36
Tianjin	168	750	1,001	83	16.75	74.93	8.33
Hebei	1539	4,742	6,744	463	22.82	70.32	6.86
Shanxi	851	2,242	3,297	204	25.80	68.00	6.20
Inner Mongolia	506	1,743	2,376	127	21.28	73.37	5.35
Liaoning	749	3,157	4,238	332	17.68	74.49	7.83
Jilin	517	2,051	2,728	160	18.96	75.19	5.85
Heilongjiang	697	2,792	3,689	200	18.90	75.68	5.42
Shanghai	204	1,277	1,674	193	12.19	76.28	11.53
Jiangsu	1,462	5,325	7,438	651	19.65	71.59	8.76
Zhejiang	845	3,418	4,677	414	18.07	73.09	8.84
Anhui	1,528	4,012	5,986	446	25.52	67.03	7.45
Fujian	799	2,445	3,471	227	23.02	70.44	6.54
Jiangxi	1,076	2,811	4,140	253	25.99	67.90	6.11
Shandong	1,893	6,457	9,079	729	20.85	71.12	8.03
Henan	2,401	6,211	9,256	644	25.94	67.10	6.96
Hubei	1,379	4,269	6,028	380	22.87	70.82	6.31
Hunan	1,428	4,543	6,440	469	22.17	70.54	7.29
Guangdong	2,089	6,030	8,642	523	24.17	69.78	6.05
Guangxi	1,178	2,991	4,489	320	26.24	66.64	7.12
Hainan	216	519	787	52	27.47	65.95	6.58
Chongqing	678	2,168	3090	244	21.93	70.17	7.90
Sichuan	1,887	5,822	8329	620	22.65	69.90	7.45
Guizhou	1,068	2,253	3525	204	30.29	63.92	5.79
Yunnan	1,116	2,915	4,288	257	26.02	67.98	6.00
Tibet	82	168	262	12	31.20	64.30	4.50
Shaanxi	902	2,490	3,605	214	25.01	69.06	5.93
Gansu	692	1,742	2,562	128	27.00	68.00	5.00
Qinghai	138	358	518	22	26.62	69.05	4.33
Ningxia	160	377	562	25	28.38	67.15	4.47
Xinjiang	526	1312	1,925	87	27.30	68.17	4.53
National total	28,979	88,793	126,583	8,811	22.89	70.15	6.96

Notes: a) The national population total includes the number of service people in the Chinese People's Liberation Army, who are excluded from the regional population figures.

b) Data in this table are preliminary results of the 5th national population census as of zero hour 1 November 2000.

Source: China Statistical Yearbook 2001

Education

The proportion of the illiterate among adults has decreased from 182 million or 15.9 per cent of the population in 1990 to 84.81 million (6.7 per cent) in 2000.

The government education fund in proportion to GDP has increased from the historical average of 2.4 per cent to 3.1 per cent. However, it is still below the world average of 4.8 per cent. As shown in Figure 1.7.2, 69.7 per cent of the population have received primary and

Table 1.7.6 Number and size of households

Year	Number of households (000)	Average household size
1990	288,300	3.97
1991	294,580	4.01
1992	300,390	3.95
1993	305,740	3.92
1994	311,040	3.89
1995	316,580	3.70
1996	321,680	3.70
1997	326,630	3.64
1998	341,190	3.63
1999	336,512	3.58
2000	348,370	3.13
2001	n.a.	3.10

Source: China Populations Statistics Yearbook 1998, China Statistical Yearbook 2001 and China Statistical Abstract 2002

junior high school education while 11.1 per cent have had senior high school education. The percentage of population that has received education at college level or above was only 3.6 per cent.

There still exists a marked disparity in the levels of education received by urban and rural populations. The segment of rural population aged 15 and above has a predominant share of primary education, accounting for 43.29 per cent. The percentages of rural population having received junior high school, senior high school and college and above education were 28.2 per cent, 4.48 per cent and 0.27 per cent respectively. In contrast, a majority of the urban population has a higher level of education than the rural population.

The current education structure is such that urban education has shifted its focus to middle level education while rural education is still concentrating on primary education.

Per capita disposable income

Since the economic reforms and opening door policy adopted in 1978, China has made remarkable progress in the improvement of the national standard of living. The pattern of growth is moving from the former, simple quantitative expansion to quality enhancement. As a result the quality of people's lives has been improved.

Although Chinese people, both urban and rural, have more income, the income disparity between urban and rural households has widened in absolute terms. In 1991, the gap between rural income and urban disposable income was RMB992, which rose to RMB4493.2 in 2001. In the 10-year period from 1991 to 2001, the average growth of rural incomes was 12.82 per cent while that of urban was 14.97 per cent.

Urban household income

Apart from the disparity between rural and urban income, urban household income also varies among cities of different sizes. The per capita disposable income in extra-large cities is predominantly higher than all other cities of varying sizes. An interesting phenomenon is that the per capita disposable income in small cities is higher than both large and medium-sized cities.

Urban household incomes were unevenly distributed among different income groups and the gap between the highest income group and lowest income group has also widened. In 1997, for example, the gap between the

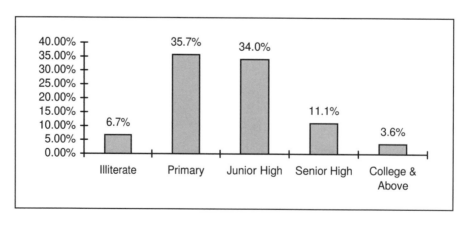

Source: State Statistical Yearbook 2001

Figure 1.7.2 Level of education by percentage of population in 2000

Table 1.7.7   Comparison of rural and urban incomes

Year	Per capita net income of rural residents (RMB)	Per capita disposable income of urban residents (RMB)
1978	133.6	343.4
1980	191.3	477.6
1985	397.6	739.1
1986	423.8	899.6
1987	462.6	1,002.2
1988	544.9	1,181.4
1989	601.5	1,375.7
1990	686.3	1,510.2
1991	708.6	1,700.6
1992	784.0	2,026.6
1993	921.6	2,577.4
1994	1,221.0	3,496.2
1995	1,577.7	4,283.0
1996	1,926.1	4,838.9
1997	2,090.1	5,160.3
1998	2,162.0	5,425.1
1999	2,210.3	5,854.0
2000	2,254.4	6,280.0
2001	2,366.4	6,859.6

Source: China Statistical Yearbook 2000, 2001 and China Statistical Abstract 2002

lowest and highest income group was RMB9758.09. In 2000, however, the disparity was RMB10712.17.

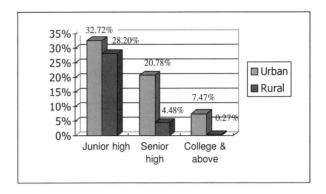

Source: State Statistical Bureau

Figure 1.7.3   Comparison of urban and rural education

Regional differences in urban per capita disposable income

Households in the relatively developed areas in Eastern China have the highest income compared with Middle and Western China. Guangdong, Shanghai and Beijing were the top three provinces (municipalities) having the highest per capita disposable income, while Henan, Jilin and Gansu, Shanxi, Ningxia and Inner Mongolia stayed at the bottom. Table 1.7.10 provides a picture of the regional differences in urban per capita disposable income and their changes over the last five years.

Rural household income and regional variations

With deepening of economic reform in the agricultural sector and development of the agricultural economy,

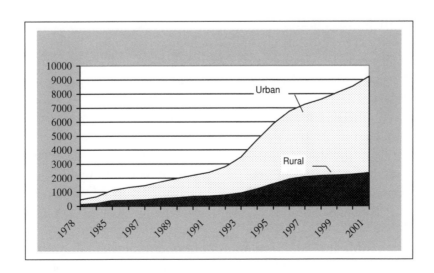

Source: China Statistical Yearbook 2000, 2001 and China Statistical Abstract 2002

Figure 1.7.4   Income disparity among urban and rural residents – a widening gap

Table 1.7.8 Per capita disposable income of urban households by city sizes

City size	Per capita disposable income (RMB)	
	1999	2000
All cities and county towns	5,854.02	6,279.98
Extra-large cities	7,667.78	8,371.66
Large cities	5,825.21	6,309.57
Medium-sized cities	5,449.25	5,860.92
Small cities	6,167.14	6,655.91
County towns	4,890.42	5,162.17

Source: China Statistical Yearbook 2000, 2001

Table 1.7.9 Income distribution among different income groups in urban areas

Income group	Per capita disposable income (RMB)	
	1997	2000
Lowest income households	2,325.70	2,678.32
Low income households	3,492.27	3,658.53
Lower middle income households	4,363.78	4,651.72
Middle income households	5,512.12	5,930.82
Upper middle income households	6,904.96	7,524.98
High income households	8,631.94	9,484.67
Highest income households	12,083.79	13,390.49

Source: China Statistical Yearbook 1998, 2001

rural household income has been increasing. In the period 1992–1997 per capita net income of rural households increased from RMB784 yuan to RMB2090 yuan (about US$251.8), with an annual average rate of increase of 21.7 per cent. However, the rate of growth between 1997 and 2001 slowed down considerably to an average annual growth rate of 3.1 per cent.

The regional differences in rural incomes resemble the pattern of urban income. The per capita net income of rural households in the developed eastern areas of China is higher than in the middle and western areas. In 2001 the per capita net income of rural households in Shanghai was the highest of all other provinces and municipalities, being RMB5870.87, followed by Beijing (RMB5025.5), Zhejiang (RMB4582.34), Tianjin (RMB3947.72), Jiangsu (RMB3784.71) and Guangdong (RMB3769.79).

Tibet 's rural per capita net income was the lowest, being RMB1404.01, followed by Guizhou (RMB11411.73), Shaanxi (RMB1490.8), Gansu (RMB11508.61) and Yunnan (RMB 1533.74).

Savings

The rate of saving in China has surpassed all other countries in the world since the 1970s. In 1978, the first year of China's economic reform and opening up, the total urban and rural household savings were only RMB21.06 billion yuan. Ten years later, the total household savings jumped to over RMB500 billion in 1989. Twenty years later, the savings by urban and rural households rocketed to RMB4627.98 billion yuan (about US$557.6 billion), with the rate of savings reaching over 30 per cent. By the end of 2001, the household savings further increased to RMB7.38 trillion (US$892.38 billion).

Although recently the saving rate has slowed down as a result of big-ticket consumption such as housing, the saving rate remains high. Although the government has introduced interest income tax, which has effectively reduced proceeds from bank savings, the rate of increase in savings is still rising. As shown in Figure 1.7.5, urban and rural household savings rose steeply from 1993, the first year after China's official adoption of the socialist market economy. The average annual rate of increase from 1991 to 2001 is 23.09 per cent.

Interestingly, however, the high savings rate is not motivated by the pursuit of monetary increments. The People's Bank of China (PBOC) conducted a survey on people's propensity to save in 34 cities in May 1998. The survey results indicated that 53.4 per cent of the respondents stated that they would continue to save when asked what they would do with their money if the interest rate remain unchanged. Nearly 70 per cent of the low and middle income residents interviewed stated that they are saving for long-term expenditures such as retirement, children's education, personal misfortunes and illnesses. The savings deposits tend to be mid-to-long term, and the interest earnings are regarded as an extra benefit. Even when the interest rate is low, the propensity to save would not be likely to change very much. Economic Daily explained that this unusually high propensity to save characterized the mentality of the Chinese people in the economic transition, which has increased uncertainty. Since the economic reform and opening up, factors of uncertainty have increased and people tend to choose to sacrifice today's consumption for the sake of future consumption. Housing, children's education, medical care and pension, which

Table 1.7.10   Per capita disposable income (1997–2001) (RMB)

Region	1997	1998	1999	2000	2001
Beijing	7,813.2	8,472.0	9,182.8	10,394.7	11,577.8
Tianjin	6,608.4	7,110.5	7,649.8	8,140.5	8,958.7
Hebei	4,958.7	5,084.6	5,365.0	5,661.2	5,984.8
Shanxi	3,989.9	4,098.7	4,342.6	4,724.1	5,391.1
Inner Mongolia	3,944.7	4,353.0	4,770.5	5,129.1	5,535.9
Liaoning	4,518.1	4,617.2	4,898.6	5,357.8	5,797.0
Jilin	4,190.6	4,206.6	4,480.0	4,810.0	5,340.5
Heilongjiang	4,090.7	4,268.5	4,595.1	4,912.9	5,425.9
Shanghai	8,438.9	8,773.1	10,931.6	11,718.0	12,883.5
Jiangsu	5,765.2	6,017.9	6,538.2	6,800.2	7,375.1
Zhejiang	7,358.7	7,836.8	8,428.0	9,279.2	10,464.7
Anhui	4,599.3	4,770.5	5,064.6	5,293.6	5,668.8
Fujian	6,143.6	6,485.6	6,859.8	7,432.3	8,313.1
Jiangxi	4,071.3	4,251.4	4,720.6	5,103.6	5,506.0
Shandong	5,190.8	5,380.1	5,809.0	6,490.0	7,101.1
Henan	4,093.6	4,219.4	4,532.4	4,766.3	5,267.4
Hubei	4,673.2	4,826.4	5,212.8	5,524.5	5,856.0
Hunan	5,209.7	5,434.3	5,815.4	6,218.7	6,780.6
Guangdong	8,561.7	8,839.7	9,125.9	9,761.6	10,415.2
Guangxi	5,110.3	5,412.2	5,619.5	5,834.4	6,665.7
Hainan	4,849.9	4,852.9	5,338.3	5,358.3	5,838.8
Chongqing	5,322.7	5,466.6	5,896.0	6,276.0	6,721.1
Sichuan	4,763.3	5,127.1	5,477.9	5,894.3	6,360.5
Guizhou	4,441.9	4,565.4	4,934.0	5,122.2	5,451.9
Yunnan	5,5583	6,042.8	6,178.7	6,324.6	6,797.7
Tibet			6,908.7	7,426.3	7,869.2
Shaanxi	4,001.3	4,220.2	4,654.1	5,124.2	5,483.7
Gansu	3,592.4	4,009.6	4,475.2	4,916.3	5,382.9
Qinghai	3,999.4	4,240.1	4,703.4	51,700.0	5,853.7
Ningxia	3,836.5	4,112.4	4,472.9	4,912.4	5,544.2
Xinjiang	4,844.7	5,000.8	5,319.8	5,644.9	6,395.0
National total	5,160.3	5,425.1	5,854.0	6,280.0	6,859.6

Source: China Statistical Abstract 2002

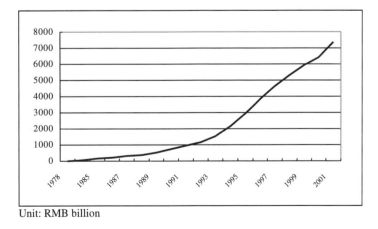

Unit: RMB billion

Source: China Statistical Yearbook 2001 and China Statistical Abstract 2002

Figure 1.7.5   The growth of urban and rural household savings (1978–2001)

were covered by the government in the past, are now increasingly paid by the Chinese people themselves. There are indications that even if inflation were to increase, the people's propensity to save would continue to rise, which is very different from the 'rules of the game' in Western economies and it reflects the unique features of the socialist market economy with such Chinese characteristics.

To sum up, the factors underlying such a persistently high saving rate are:

- household income has increased as a result of the sustained high GDP growth;
- consumer aspirations are dampened by the lack of new consumption lure;
- the expectation that future spending on housing, children's education and medical care will increase as a result of relevant reforms;
- an expectation of future uncertainties;
- cautious attitudes toward investment in financial products such as securities, bonds and funds.

According to the prediction of the State Information Centre, the savings rate will be about 12.2 per cent in the next five years.

Consumption pattern

Chinese consumers have had increasingly more disposable income to satisfy their basic needs of life as well as their aspirations for modern life styles. At the same time, the opening up and reforms have also benefited the Chinese consumers with the material abundance

that could not have been possible before. Consumer preferences, life styles and consumption patterns change over time, with the evolvement of the consumer market.

Declining Engel's coefficient in urban areas

With the increase in disposable income, spending on food as a percentage of the total consumption expenditure has been declining, which indicates that the standard of living in China has been improving. As shown in the following figure, the Engel's coefficient was relatively high before 1980 at above 55 per cent. From 1982 to 1993, the coefficient was within the range of 50–55 per cent although there were fluctuations. Starting in 1994, the Engel's coefficient has been below 50 per cent. By 2001 the Engel's coefficient had declined to 37.94 per cent compared to 39.18 per cent in 2000.

Continuously escalating consumer aspirations

With the declining Engel's coefficient, the Chinese people have more money to spend on non-staple items. The opening of the country to the outside world has also provided the Chinese people with an opportunity to realize their aspirations for what is called 'household modernization'. The changes are reflected in the durable items that the Chinese people hope to own. In the 1970s it was a symbol of wealth for people to own a bicycle, a watch and a sewing machine. They were regarded as fashionable for the then newly-married couples. In the 1980s the desired durable items became electrical household appliances, namely, television sets, washing machines, refrigerators and VCRs. Consumer aspirations continued to escalate in the 1990s, when

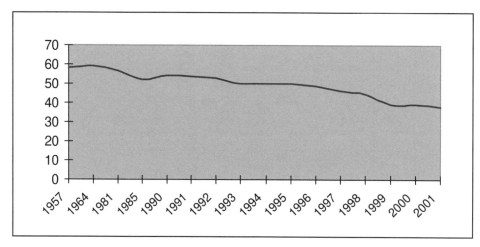

Source: Engel's Coefficient, China Development Report (1998), Cheng Xuebin, page 258, China Statistical Abstract 2002

Figure 1.7.6 Engel's coefficient for urban residents is declining

people shifted to video cameras, audio systems, telephones, motorcycles and modern furniture. The Chinese people are now hoping to realize their dream of owning a personal computer, a private car, an apartment and a modern home decor.

An average urban household now owns more than one bicycle and one television set. A majority of urban households have electrical household appliances such as washing machines, refrigerators and colour television sets. More and more households are acquiring air-conditioners, personal computers, cars and mobile phones (see Table 1.7.11). By the first quarter of 2002, the number of telephones subscribed has reached 350 million, among which 161.5 million are mobile phones.

Changing life style

The life styles of the Chinese have also changed greatly since the economic reform and opening up. The green or blue uniforms have been replaced by modern fashion products and western suits. Western suits are accepted as formal clothing on formal occasions. Hosting friends at restaurants is no longer a luxury. The tradition of family gatherings at home is increasingly replaced by more chances to dine out together. Processed or semi-processed foods are becoming part of the Chinese people's life as a result of increased income and preferences for more leisure time. Unbranded generic products are losing their footholds in the market as people are building their brand awareness in pursuit of better products.

Modern marketing has also contributed to the change in consumption habits. Supermarkets, chain convenience stores and membership club stores are attracting more customers, while direct mail and TV sales are gaining increasing acceptance. In addition, the decision making processes of Chinese consumers are becoming

more complex than formerly. The tradition of spending below earnings is now challenged by consumer credit.

It is not difficult now to see Western influences in people's life style. The great tea-drinking nation has now given way to coffee drinking. Chocolate sales will go up on Valentine's Day. Cognac has invaded the territory of the traditional Chinese liquor, making China one of the largest cognac consumers in the world. Coca-Cola and Pepsi-Cola penetrated the market with their 'herbal medicine tastes'. Marco Polo's mistaken imitation of Chinese-style stuffed pie – pizza, with its stuffing on top rather than inside – has made a successful inroad into the country of great food culture. Completely Western fast-food concepts such as McDonald's and Kentucky Fried Chicken are embraced by Chinese people, particularly the younger generation. Christmas has now been celebrated unofficially by young non-Christian Chinese as a fashionable event. Interestingly, dogs and cats are now not only delicacies on dinner tables, but also loved and cared home pets. As a result, there are increasing numbers of pet hospitals in large urban centres of China. Pet foods are now advertised on the TV and other media.

Recent trends in the composition of consumer spending

Although consumer spending on food is steadily declining, food still remains at the top of average consumer spending, followed by recreational, educational and cultural services, housing, clothing, etc. (see Table 1.7.12).

However, the consumption of food is no longer seen as satisfying basic needs. The composition of food consumption is shifting toward more nutritious pursuits, which was reflected in the significant declines in spending on food grains. The consumption of non-

Table 1.7.11 Average number of consumer durables owned per 100 Chinese urban households (1999 and 2001)

Description	1999	2001	Description	1999	2001
Motorcycle	15.12	20.4	Hi-fi system	19.66	23.8
Car	0.34	0.6	Video camera	1.06	1.6
Washing machine	91.44	92.2	Camera	38.11	39.8
Refrigerator	77.74	81.9	Microwave oven	12.15	22.3
Colour TV set	111.57	120.5	Air conditioner	24.48	35.8
VCD	24.71	42.6	Health equipment	3.83	4.0
VCR	21.73	19.9	Mobile phones	7.14	34.0
PC	5.91	13.3	Shower heater	45.49	52.0

Source: China Statistical Yearbook 2000 and China Statistical Abstract 2002

Table 1.7.12 Composition of consumer spending in urban areas (%)

Description	1999	2000	2001
Consumption expenditure			
1. Food	42.78	39.18	37.94
2. Clothing	10.68	10.01	10.05
3. Home equipment, items and services	8.57	8.79	8.27
4. Medical and health care	5.32	6.36	6.47
5. Transportation and communications	6.73	7.90	8.61
6. Recreational, educational and cultural services	12.3	12.56	13.00
7. Housing	9.84	10.01	10.32
8. Miscellaneous commodities and services	4.96	5.17	5.35

Source: China Statistical Yearbook 2000, 2001 and China Statistical Abstract 2002

Table 1.7.13 The food consumption pattern of urban households (per capita expenditure)

Item	1997	1998	1999	2000	2001
Grains	238.1	226.8	215.4	188.7	188.1
Oils and fats	70.7	75.3	73.7	66.5	58.9
Meat, poultry and their products	459.6	431.2	406.5	411.3	413.5
Aquatic products	141.0	142.5	144.0	143.5	152.0
Vegetables	203.9	197.0	194.6	192.3	194.3
Tobacco	92.2	93.6	94.8	100.9	103.8
Alcohol and drinks	91.0	91.6	95.3	103.2	103.9
Dried and fresh fruits	127.0	120.7	130.0	127.5	131.3
Dining out	203.4	227.0	249.6	287.8	314.2

Source: China Statistical Yearbook 2000 and China Statistical Abstract 2002

staple foods, such as meat/poultry and their processed products, aquatic products, dried and fresh fruits, milk and dairy products, has been on the rise. The pursuit of healthier foods has also resulted in the decline in per capita consumption of fine grains and pork.

The second largest category of spending is spending on recreational, educational and cultural services. The adoption of the 40-hour week and improved working conditions have given people more time for leisure activities and educational pursuits, and the related spending has been increasing. In 2001, 13 per cent of disposable income or RMB 690 per capita was spent on such services. In 1997 the figure was only RMB 448.4.

Housing reform has brought about increases in housing expenditure. The objective of the reform is to transform government-provided free housing into private housing ownership. Under such a scheme, apartments are sold to individuals or provided at cost. In 1997 the per capita spending on housing, including water, gas and electricity, was RMB358.6; by 2001 the

figure had risen to RMB548, an increase of 52.82 per cent. Spending on housing is expected to continue to increase in the years to come.

Per capita spending on clothing also registered an increase in 2001, and is 6.63 per cent up on 2000 but only 2.47 per cent above 1997. In fact, spending dipped to RMB 480.9 in 1998 from 1997's RMB520.9. In 2000, spending on clothing was still less than in 1997. In 2001 expenditure picked up and rose to RMB533.7.

With reform of the medical care system, medical expenses that used to be covered by the government are now increasingly paid by individuals. Per capita out-of-pocket expenditure on medical services and healthcare was RMB180 in 1997. In 2001 spending on this category had increased to 343.3 per capita. The deepening of medical care system reform will result in increased medical expenditure in the next few years.

Modern life demands convenient transportation and communications. Consumer spending on transportation and communications has been increasing at a high rate in the last few years. In 1997 per capita spending on transportation and communications was RMB233 yuan, an increase over the prior year of 17 per cent, while in 2001 the figure almost doubled to RMB 457, an increase of 15.7 per cent over 2000. The key drivers of the increase are increased interest in travel as a result of the increase in income and increased mobile telephone consumption.

The Chinese consumer market

Market dynamics

China's consumer market continues to expand at impressive speed. The State Development and Planning Commission has predicted that, in the tenth five year plan (2001–2005) period, China will continue to maintain a relatively high economic growth. The average annual increase rate of GDP is expected to be 7–8 per cent with consumption raised to a higher level and urban and rural markets expanding further. By the end of 2001, total consumer spending, as reflected by total retail sales of consumer goods, reached RMB3,759.5 billion yuan, which is 10.1 per cent higher than the previous year. In spite of the small proportion of the urban population, urban dwellers account for two-thirds of the purchasing power.

DRI-WEFA, an economics consulting firm in Lexington, Massachusetts, rated China among the three top emerging markets with fastest growth and expected its consumer spending to grow by 11 per cent in 2002 (Keenan, 2002). However, at the current level, the consumer market is still undergoing a stress test. The rate of increase in consumer spending had already dropped by 0.6 per cent in 2001. In July 2002 the State Statistics Bureau reported that total retail sales of consumer goods was RMB309.66 billion. Though 8.6 per cent higher than the same month last year, the rate of increase was 1.2 per cent lower than the average annual rate in 2001. At the same time, the level of consumer spending dropped by 0.9 per cent for the same period. Market price remained stable for most of 2001 (See Table 1.7.14), but has showed a clear sign of decline since the last quarter of the year.

While market prices continued to fall for the first nine months of 2002, the savings rate did not cease to rise. A fresh report by the People's Bank of China, the central bank, revealed that by the end of July aggregate bank deposits amounted to RMB8,300 billion yuan, an increase of 7.5 per cent over 2001. This is characteristic of an emerging market where, on the one hand, there is a glut of goods and service of inferior quality, and on the other hand, consumers continue to save. The total balance of bank deposits by Chinese residents topped

Table 1.7.14   China's consumer price index in 2001 over 2000 as the base year

Items	Whole country	Cities	Countryside
Consumer Price Index	100.7	100.7	100.8
Food	100.0	100.1	99.8
Grain	99.3	99.2	99.7
Meat	101.6	101.7	101.4
Eggs	106.0	106.3	105.3
Aquatic products	97.1	96.9	97.8
Vegetables	101.4	101.4	100.9
Dining out	100.2	100.4	99.6
Cigarettes and liquor	99.7	99.7	99.6
Clothing	98.1	97.8	98.9
Household appliances and services	97.7	97.5	98.4
Health care products	100.0	99.3	101.1
Transportation and communication	99.0	99.1	98.7
Entertainment, education and entertainment	106.6	106.7	106.4
Housing	101.2	101.7	100.3

Source: Statistical Report on PRC National and Social Development, 2001
State Statistics Bureau

RMB 7 trillion yuan (US$853.6 billion), also a record high, earlier in 2002. When basic subsistence items like food, clothing and shelter are not in contention, quality products and services as well as the support infrastructure become the major challenge to boost the consumption level. The consumption emphasis in the cities is placed on housing, private cars, education and personal communication. All of these, however, are curbed by the inadequate infrastructure in financial services and telecommunication networks.

In the short run, prices are expected to come under further pressure as some import tariff reductions begin to take effect, and increased competition from cheaper imports may spur more price wars within China.

Table 1.7.15 Market price changes in 2001

Item	Percentage change over 2000
Food	
Grain	−0.7
Meat	1.6
Vegetables	1.4
Eggs	6.0
Household appliances	−2.3
Transportation and communication	1.0
Education and entertainment	6.6
Housing	1.2
Industrial goods	−1.3
Raw materials and energy	−0.2
Capital investment	0.4

Source: Statistical Report on PRC National and Social Development, 2001 State Statistical Bureau

On the retail side, consumers' favourites are changing over time. A survey of 100 large department stores in December 2001 provides some insight into changing consumer preferences and priority of spending.

Table 1.7.17 shows the results of a survey of 200 supermarkets identifying 30 top sellers, which again reflects the changing consumption pattern of urban dwellers.

Selected markets in China

Automotive market

Now the fastest growing market lies in the private sector. According to a recent sample survey by North-West Information News, among 22,800 people in 57 Chinese cities, 12 per cent planned to buy a private car in 2002 and 29 per cent expressed their intentions to buy cars with bank loans. The State Development and Planning Commission expects private cars to account for 70 per cent of China's annual auto sales within the next 10 years. A detailed account of the expanding automobile market and opportunities for foreign companies to participate is given in Chapter 6.1.

Real estate market

Housing and home furnishing have become the top priority for Chinese people. At present, in China, the average urban dwelling space is 9.6 square metres per person. This figure varies in different regions. In some cities it is below 5 square metres. Economic growth is

Table 1.7.16 Growth rate of sales in December 2001

High Rollers		Slow climbers		Downhill walkers	
Articles	Growth rate (%)	Articles	Growth rate (%)	Articles	Growth rate (%)
Stationery	68.8	Footwear	14.0	Mini-metals and machine tools	−40.1
Electronic publications	55.3	Tobacco	10.5	Books and journals	−26.6
Construction and home-furnishing materials	54.5	Athletic and recreational products	10.3	Oil and petroleum products	−23.9
Caps	54.1	Liquor	8.6	Furniture	−14.6
Household electronics	45.2	Communication products	4.7	Audio-video equipment	−12.6

Source: China Economic Monitoring Centre 2002

46

Table 1.7.17 Top sellers in December 2001

TV sets above 64 cm	VCD/DVD players	Refrigerator
Household air-conditioner	Automatic washing machine	Cylinder washing machine
Gas burner	Cooking smoke disperser	Electric boiler
Electric rice cooker	Camera	Wrist watch
Vacuum cleaner	Leather shoes	Sports shoes
Men's suit	Men's shirt	Women's suit
Children's wear	Blue jeans	Leather clothes
Skin care products	Hair care products	Fruit juice
Grain wine	Grape wine	Beer
Lactic drinks	Carbonated drink	Bottled water

Source: China Economic Monitoring Centre 2002

the engine of real-estate development with demand geared-up for residences, office buildings and factory space. Huge market potential remains to be tapped as the real-estate industry accounts for only 3 per cent of China's GDP, compared with 10–20 per cent in developed countries. It is estimated that the annual expansion of the real-estate industry will exceed 10 percentage points. If China is aiming at a two-bedroom apartment for each family of three, it will mean the average dwelling space will be at least 10 square metres per person. By 2020 the urbanization level of China is expected to reach 51.4 per cent, which means that China's urban population will increase to 630 million. To meet this standard, China needs to build residential housing of 5.2 billion square meters within the next two decades.

The ratio of annual personal income to commercial house prices is 5.8:1. With the implementation of various state housing policies, and improvements in all kinds of housing systems such as low rent houses, economy dwellings, commercial housing, reforms policy houses, the ratio of personal incomes to house prices will drop down to 3:1. Since 1998 the sales revenue for commercial houses has been increasing at more than 20 per cent while in 2001 it exceeded 30 per cent.

Credit card market

The consumer market is experiencing restraint in credit card use. For example, in Shanghai, the most financially developed city, the use of debit and credit cards accounted for only 2.7 per cent of all consumer spending in 2001 and only 3 per cent of retailers will accept them (*Far Eastern Economic Review*, Hong Kong, 14 Feb 2002).

In major cities, average spending through the use of credit cards is 1,779RMB per family, which is 5.7 per

cent of total family expenditure. There are three likely reasons. First, the consumer may think that it is too difficult to obtain a credit card; second, the credit card may actually be a debit card; third, many places do not accept credit cards and overdrawing a debit card is simply impossible.

Communications market

In 2001 post and telecommunications registered total revenue of 437 billion yuan with 24 per cent increase over the previous year. Telecommunications is an area of exponential growth. The mother switchboards reached a total capacity of 200 million by the year-end. Of the 179 million handset users, 111 million were in the cities and 68 million in rural area. In terms of mobile phones, China overtook the United States and boasted the biggest market with 144.8 million users. These add up to present-day China having 26 phones per hundred people. The government continues to invest 84 million yuan each year for the installation of optical fibres. Therefore, this momentum will be maintained for quite a long time to come as the potential is realized. Handset users in China are expected to exceed 260 million by 2005, and mobile phone users will grow at more than 20 per cent annually.

The Internet is another nascent area of rapid growth. Internet users exceeded 30 million by the end of 2001. Internet application in business is surging. It is estimated by eMarketer, a firm specializing in Internet and e-business research, that business-to-business e-commerce revenues in China will grow from US$1.5 billion this year to US$21.8 billion by 2004.

In the telecom equipment market, foreign-funded enterprises now account for over 70 per cent of the country's total production capacity. There are more than 20 Sino-foreign joint ventures in the production of mobile phones, with Nokia, Motorola and Ericsson commanding more than 75 per cent of the Chinese market. The fibre-optic transmission equipment market is mainly dominated by joint ventures with investment from well-known foreign manufacturers. Satellite communications systems, facsimile machines and microwave communications equipment are mainly imported from abroad; very few joint ventures engage in the production of this equipment in China.

Cosmetic market

Being part of the fashion industry, the cosmetics market in China first took shape in the 1980s but its rapid development occurred in the 1990s, with growth at an annual rate of 35 per cent. The startling contrast: in 1980 people only spent RMB0.2 yuan on cosmetics, but in 1999, it had grown to RMB28 yuan. There are more than 3,000 factories and 600 organizations in the cosmetics market employing more than six million persons. At present, more than 1,000 kinds of cosmetics are displayed on shelves once a week. The sale of cosmetics has reached more than RMB16 billion yuan and continues to increase at the rate of 15 per cent every year. It is predicted that by 2010 total sales of this market will be RMB80 billion yuan. The concentrated market segment for cosmetics is the 6,850,000 women in cities within the age range of 20 to 40. If each woman in China spends 50 yuan per year on cosmetics, they can generate RMB13.3 billion yuan to the market. China's cosmetics market still has plenty of room for growth since annual consumption of cosmetics is only 10 per cent of the world's average level. At the same time, purchasing power is concentrated in the cities. It is estimated that there are more than 1.1 million consumers in Beijing and Shanghai, and 0.4 million in Guangzhou. The consumption level in Chinese rural area is only 10 per cent of the cities'.

Consumer confidence

Consumer confidence in the overall performance of the economy and their future income is very much an indicator of consumer willingness to spend. The Report on Economic Performance in China 2001 offered the following observations:

Compared with 2000, in terms of the economic performance in 2001:

45 per cent of consumers feel that the year's economy is better;
46 per cent of consumers feel that it is basically the same;
9 per cent of consumers feel that it is worse.

Compared with 2000, in terms of family income in 2001:

32.5 per cent of consumers felt that their family income increased;
47.5 per cent of consumers felt that their family income remained basically the same;
19.9 per cent of consumers felt that their family income dropped;
0.1 per cent did not respond.

Globalization of the Chinese consumer market

Pushed by the wave of globalization, China is moving away from an economic system in which national markets are distinct entities, isolated from foreign markets by barriers of distance, time, culture and government intervention. Increasingly its national market is converging into an integral part of the global marketplace. One characteristic of this convergence is the increasing participation of foreign product and service providers in China.

China's accession to the WTO accelerates the pace of market liberalization. As a result, international competition will internalize, exerting great pressure on domestic market players and the pattern of competition is expected to change. Internationalization of domestic competition is bound to take place. Foreseeable results of the globalization are increased efficiency and enhanced consumer benefits.

China's WTO entry also increases the possibilities of integrating the Chinese consumer market with the outside world. China is now regarded as a leading world manufacturing centre and Chinese producers are supplying not only the domestic market but also foreign markets. WTO rules are supposed to clear the obstacles that Chinese businesses used to have before China's accession. In this context, the consumer market is truly a global concept.

The Restructure and Development of China's State-owned Enterprises*

Dr Lu Chunshan, Deputy Division Chief, Economic Restructuring Office of the State Council

The institutional transformation of the state-owned enterprises and structural readjustment has entered a critical period and the reform efforts need to take new steps

The reform of the state-owned enterprises (SOEs) is an extensive and profound change and revolution. Years of efforts to reform the SOEs have been manifested in the profound changes that have taken place in the SOEs' management system and operating mechanism. As a result, the aggregate strength of the state-owned economy has further improved, and the state-owned sector continues to play a leading role in the national economy and has remained a main source of the country's fiscal revenue. In 2001 the SOEs and state-equity-controlled industrial enterprises achieved, amidst fierce competition, a total profit of 230 billion renminbi, which basically paralleled the total of the previous year. Quite a number of SOEs have grown and developed in competition and their technological capabilities have been significantly improved.

Doubtless the achievements in SOE reform have, by nature, only fulfilled the phase one objectives of the continuing reform efforts. SOE reform still stays in the centre of the overall effort to reform the whole economic regime. Under the circumstances of economic globalization and accelerated technological progress, SOEs face increasingly stiff market competition and some of the built-in contradictions and problems have now been exposed. A considerable number of SOEs are still unable to adapt themselves to the requirements of the market economy, sharing common problems such as rigid operating mechanisms, weak capability in technological innovation, heavy debts and social obligations, redundant workers, difficulties in production and operation, declining profits and the subsistence difficulties of some workers. The large- and medium-sized SOEs have basically realized the goals of reform and the target of 'getting out of difficulties'. However, small-sized state-owned industrial enterprises and other state-owned non-industrial enterprises are still facing accumulating problems. In the distribution area, for example, state-owned enterprises in material supply, grain supply and foreign trade are confronted with heavy tasks of reform. Therefore, pushing forward the SOE reform still remains an urgent and arduous challenge, and the pace of reform will have to be quickened in order to achieve new breakthroughs.

Strategic readjustment in the pattern of the state-owned sector presence in the economy will be made in order to propel the strategic reorganization of the state-owned enterprises

Since the economic reform and opening up, positive changes have taken place in the layout of the state-owned sector in the economy as well as in the SOE organizational structure. There remain irrationalities, however, which mainly include the over-extended presence of the state-owned sector in the economy, serious duplications in construction projects and in rational resource allocation. The overall competence of SOEs is not streamlined and, typically, large or small enterprises are set up as completely independent operations, which have hindered the formation of specialized production,

---

* This chapter was originally written in Chinese and was translated by Li Yong.

socialized coordination and cooperative system and economies of scale, leading to an overall lack of competitiveness of the state-owned sector. For a period of time, the market supply and demand balances in China have experienced historical changes and competitive industries have been made to face a buyers' market. The state treasury is unable, and it is no longer necessary for the treasury, to support such an extensive presence of state-owned sectors in industries in such huge numbers. It is therefore imperative to accelerate strategic readjustment and reorganization so as to achieve a relatively rational distribution and structure of the state-owned sector in the national economy.

Strategic readjustment follows the principle of discretionary entry and exit mechanism and prioritizing 'what to do and what not to do', focusing on enhancing dominant control by the state-owned sector. SOEs will only be present in key sectors and critical industrial territories that are of vital importance to the national economy. Dominant positions will be maintained in industries such as those that involve national security, have natural monopolies, provide critical public products and services, and in the back-bone enterprises in pillar industries and hi-tech development. In other sectors and industrial territories, the state-owned sector will gradually withdraw or reduce its presence in order to allow more room for the private economy and foreign invested enterprises (FIEs) to develop.

At different stages of economic development, the proportion of the state-owned economy can vary in different industries and for different regions, but the pattern of presence should be adjusted accordingly. The importance of the state-owned economy does not necessarily depend on its numerical size and proportion. The dominant control of the state-owned economy will not be impeded as long as the pattern of presence can be optimized and quality enhanced. The current status is that there are still too many state-owned and state-equity-controlled enterprises and the development of strategic readjustment in different industries and regions is not balanced, with some industries and regions lagging far behind. Therefore, the tasks of strategic readjustment will still be arduous.

The state-owned sector will mainly take the form of dominant share-holding or equity participation in enterprises. The state-owned sector will be able to attract and organize more social capital to amplify the function of state-owned capital by way of the joint-stock or shareholding mechanism, thus increasing its power of control, influence and leadership. Wholly state-owned enterprises can be transformed into shareholding enterprises by flotation on the stock market, joint venturing with foreign investors and mutual equity participation among enterprises. Such effort will help develop an economy of mixed ownership.

The path of advancing strategic readjustment is to 'keep hold of the large enterprises while freeing the small ones'. 'To keep hold of the large enterprises' is an effort to nurture and develop powerful and competitive enterprise giants and groups. The enterprise groups will be formed by way of capitalization and as a function of the market. They should be distinctive in their core businesses and competitive, and they will be the 'national team' in China's participation in international competition. 'To free the small enterprises' is to liberalize and rejuvenate the small- to medium-sized SOEs. Having regard to the practical conditions of the small- to medium-sized enterprises, asset rearrangement and structural readjustment can be carried out in various forms such as reorganization, alliance, merger, leasing, contract operation, joint-stock cooperatives and sell-off. Up until now, the reform has covered 81.4 per cent of the small- to medium-sized SOEs in the country.

For disadvantaged enterprises, the pace of their exit from the market will be accelerated. As a result of the structural problems inherited historically and from the rigid regime that has created enduring SOEs, there have accumulated a large number of enterprises that have neither the ability to survive nor the basic conditions for development. They should secede from the market. Enterprises with unmarketable products, long-term losses, little hope to turn around and exhausted resources should go bankrupt or be shut down. The same fate should be imposed on those small operations that are resource-wasting, technologically backward, inferior in quality and seriously polluting environmentally, such as small-scale coal mines, oil refineries, cement factories, glass factories and coal-fired power plants. In order to help such enterprises exit from the market, the central government took out a total of 208.6 billion renminbi for bad-debt write-offs between 1996 and 2000. In 2001, 50 billion renminbi were made available for that purpose. In 2002, the effort to write-off bad debt is focused on the shutdown, bankruptcy and orderly exit of SOEs in defence, nonferrous metal and coal mining industries.

Separation of government functions from enterprise management will be carried out at full swing, while efforts will be made to explore effective modes of managing state assets in seeking to construct a state asset core operating system

In recent years a great effort has been made to transform the government function. The Party organizations and government agencies at all levels have been successively 'unhooked', in terms of personnel relationships, financial links and material involvement, from the business entities they have established and the enterprises that have been under their direct management. Administrative affiliations of enterprises with the governments and the administrative rankings associated with enterprise management have been eliminated, all of which has greatly facilitated the severance of enterprise links from government. China's accession to the WTO will result in indiscriminate treatment of all enterprises and the government will no longer use its administrative power to intervene in the production and operation of SOEs. At the same time, SOEs will no longer receive special favours from the government. With the reform of the administrative examination and approval system as well as the reform of the investment and financing regime, the operating environment for SOEs will be more relaxed. The efforts aimed at breaking departmental and sectoral monopolies in areas such as civil aviation, power and telecommunications will catalyse the reform of the SOEs in those areas that were originally regarded as sectors of natural monopoly.

While the separation of government functions from enterprise management is being promoted, problems regarding the management of state assets have become increasingly prominent. The absence of an effective management system for the state assets will hinder the smooth execution of the SOE reform. In fact, the problems that have long troubled the SOE reform, such as ambiguity between government functions and enterprise responsibilities, absence of owners, insider control and pending legal-person status of the enterprise assets are all related to this vacuum. As a result, it is essential to establish a state asset management system. So far, a sequence of principles such as state ownership, management by different levels of authorities, authorized operation and supervision with designated division of responsibilities, have been established, aiming at the gradual establishment of a state asset management, supervision and operation system and mechanism. In

addition, a complete and rigorous responsibility system has also been established, which will gradually evolve into an institutional framework and a management mechanism that will reinforce the supervision of SOEs. The State Council represents the State in exercising a uniform right of ownership over state assets, while the central and local governments administer the state assets. Large enterprises, enterprise groups and state-equity-controlled corporations will be the authorized operators of state assets. Designated localities are allowed to carry out experiments in their effort to explore concrete modes of state asset management.

The establishment of a modern enterprise system needs to be advanced faster

The mechanism of market competition that determines the success of the efficient enterprises and elimination of the inefficient is the most important driving force for enterprise development. If SOEs are to win under intense competition, they will have to accelerate their convergence with international rules and establish advanced operating and management mechanisms. In view of this requirement, it is imperative for the SOEs to push forward, in line with the principles of clarity of ownership, clear division of power and responsibilities, breakaway of enterprises from government links and scientific management practices, and the establishment of a more complete modern enterprise system with a reinforcing system of decision-making, execution and supervision. This is a natural course of action in the development of socialized mass production and the market economy. It is also the future direction of SOE reform.

At present, a majority of the large- and medium-sized backbone SOEs has undergone incorporation and has established by law shareholder committees, boards of directors, supervisory boards and management teams. Among those enterprises that are undergoing debt-for-equity swaps are some that have set up new corporate entities by law and in accordance with the requirements of a modern enterprise system. Generally speaking, most of the enterprises have built up a modern corporate system framework, but a number of enterprises remain whose practices in shareholding transformation and actual operations are not up to standard. Therefore, there is still quite a distance to go towards a perfect, modern enterprise system.

In pushing further the establishment of a modern enterprise system, the focus will be placed on advancing the reform in the direction of a standardized corporate system. Reform and improvements will be made towards regulating capital contributors, reinforcing corporate surveillance, establishing incentive and disciplinary mechanisms for the selection and appointment of enterprise managers and formulating standardized corporate governance. Problems such as the irrational equity structure of publicly listed companies, single share holder dominance and difficulties in reducing the state-held share will need to be solved with due attention.

Improvement of the enterprise system will have to be based on the transition of an enterprise's operation system, and to achieve such a transition, other reinforcing mechanisms such as survival of the fittest enterprises, the opening of manager positions to competition, unchecked staff mobility and performance-related pay schemes, will need to be gradually established. Those enterprises that have run into extreme difficulties or are on the verge of bankruptcy are allowed by law to resort to job displacement. Factors of production such as capital and technology are allowed and encouraged to participate in the distribution of proceeds. Technical personnel are permitted to take equity positions in their critical technologies or to receive stock options or other forms of reward or incentives for their contributions to the enterprise. Distribution according to work is a principle that should be adhered to within an enterprise in designing the salary scheme, while allowing an appropriate level of disparity between the incomes of workers and management. The board of directors and members of the management team should be remunerated according to their respective responsibilities and contributions to the enterprise, whereas the salary level of the workers can be determined by the enterprise itself, taking into consideration the average local salary level and the economic efficiency of the enterprise. At present more than 7,400 enterprises have implemented annual salary packages for the managers on a trial basis. Another 10,000 plus enterprises are experimenting in collective consultation (or bargaining) for salaries. In addition, the test for post-specific salaries, an alternative reform measure, is steadily progressing.

Strengthening and improving enterprise management

Management is an eternal theme. Strengthening enterprise management and enhancing the level of scientific management is not only an inherent requirement for a modern enterprise system, but also an important avenue for the SOE to increase profitability and competitiveness. Following China's entry into the WTO, SOEs will directly face competition from multinational companies and their weak management will be made more apparent. In this situation the requirement for an overall improvement in enterprise management and enhancement of the level of scientific management has become increasingly pressing. Therefore, efforts will have to be made to remove the fundamental weaknesses in the current status of enterprise management, characterized by widespread random decision-making, loose governance and casual disciplines.

In order to strengthen enterprise management, the SOEs will adopt a series of measures of which the following are the most significant:

- The research effort in relation to enterprise development strategies will be strengthened so as to enable SOEs to adjust their strategies in a timely manner in order to respond to market changes;
- The rationale of decision-making will be improved by adopting scientific and democratic approaches in order to manage risks effectively;
- Various corporate rules and regulations will be instituted and strengthened at a very basic level in order to eradicate completely the phenomena of 'no rules to follow, rules in place but disregarded and violations of rules without punishment';
- A complete labour contract system will be established to ensure lawful operation and management;
- The weak points in enterprise management will be tackled with great emphasis and priority will be placed on improving the management of costs, capital and quality;
- The accounting system will be perfected and modern information technology will be employed in an effort to build a responsive and accurate information system that will truthfully reflect the condition of the business;
- Foreign intellectual resources will be introduced into SOEs to allow management experts to play a role in SOE management in order to take advantage of the advanced management methods of foreign enterprises.

Developing Statistics in China

Du Xishuang, Director, Senior Statistician, National Bureau of Statistics

Statistical work in China: origin and development

Efforts to initiate statistical activities and set up a statistical system in the new China started soon after the founding of the People's Republic. In October 1949, a Statistics Division was set up under the Commission of Finance and Economy of the central people's government. The National Bureau of Statistics was set up in August 1952. Subsequently, statistical structures and various statistical systems were established by localities, departments, enterprises and institutions across the country. During the 'Great Cultural Revolution' in the mid-and late-1960s, most statistical structures were either demolished or merged. Statistical work across the country suffered serious destruction with statistical activities in many organization plunged into virtual standstill.

After China adopted the policy of reform and opening-up in 1978, statistical work was soon resumed. By gradually being incorporated into the legal framework, statistical work has entered a new era of reform and development.

Since the 1980s, especially since the 1990s, with the deepening of economic restructuring and opening-up, profound reforms have been carried out to China's statistical system. Significant changes have occurred in the following major respects:

- With regard to statistical service, the long-standing self-enclosure of statistical work has been gradually replaced by the opening up to society and to the rest of the world. More and more statistical information is regularly disseminated to the general public both at home and abroad. Exchanges with other countries and relevant international organizations have been expanded. Necessary statistical data are regularly provided to international organizations including the World Bank, IMF, UN Statistical Division, FAO etc. Major aspects of statistical methods have been brought in line with international organizations' norms and can be used directly in international comparison.

- With regard to the accounting system, the long-standing material production system (MPS) is gradually being replaced by the new national economics accounting system (SNA). This new system, which enables systematic accounting and description of the national economy through production accounts, input-output accounts, flow of funds accounts, balance of payments accounts, assets-liabilities accounts and economic circulation accounts, has brought national accounting in conformity with international accounting practices.

- With regard to statistical indicators and standards, the traditional system suitable for the planned economy has been gradually replaced by new ones in compliance with the market economy. This effort has expedited the pace of compliance with international practice and elevated the standardization of statistical work to a new level.

- With regard to statistical methods, the long-standing unitary method of statistical survey has been gradually replaced by a relatively scientific method system of statistical survey. A new survey system has been established, integrating censuses, sampling surveys, thorough surveys and other means.

- With regard to the building of a legal system, the long-standing situation of no applicable legislation has come to an end. Efforts have been made to bring statistical work within a legal framework. The Statistics Law of the People's Republic of China and the Detailed Rules concerning the Implementation of the Statistics Law have been promulgated.

- With regard to statistical technology, the previous backward means of information transmission and processing has been transformed. A basic framework of statistics-related modern technology has taken shape. A nationwide statistical information network is basically built and in operation. A network links the National Bureau of Statistics and statistical agencies in all provinces, autonomous regions and municipalities directly under the central government, as well as those in some prefectures and cities. Online transmission of statistical information is now possible.

Functions of government statistics and the statistical system in China

Functions of government statistics

As an agency directly under the State Council, the National Bureau of Statistics is in charge of statistics and economic accounting in China. In accordance with the Statistics Law of the People's Republic of China and relevant regulations of the State Council, major functions of the National Bureau of Statistics include:

- To work out laws and regulations on statistical work, to formulate directive rules for statistical operation, to draw up plans for statistical modernization and nationwide statistical surveys, to organize, exercise leadership and supervision over statistical and economic accounting work in various localities and departments, and to supervise and inspect the enforcement of statistical laws and regulations.
- To set up and improve the national economic accounting system and statistical indicator system; to institute a unified basic statistical system for the whole country; to work out national statistical standards; to review and approve statistical standards by other government departments; to organize the administration of national statistical survey projects; to examine, approve and manage plans and schemes for statistical surveys by other departments.
- To organize the implementation of major censuses on the basic items relating to the state and strength of the country; to exercise unified administration over socio-economic surveys in various localities and departments, to collect, process and tabulate basic

statistical information from across the country; to carry out analyses, forecasts and supervision from a statistical perspective on the national economic and scientific progress and social development; to provide statistical information and relevant proposals for the State Council and government departments concerned.

- To act as the exclusive agency in verifying, approving, administering and publishing basic national statistical data and to disseminate regularly to the general public statistical information regarding national economic and social development.
- To build up and administer the national statistical information system and the national statistical database system; to formulate basic standards and operational rules for statistical database networks in various localities and departments.
- To exercise leadership over directly-affiliated surveying agencies in various localities; to exercise unified management over operating expenses of statistical activities for statistical agencies in local governments at and above county level; to assist in the management of directors and deputy directors of local statistical offices of provinces, autonomous regions and municipalities directly under the central government; to organize and administer qualification examinations and the evaluation of professional titles for statisticians across the country.

The statistical system in China

The official statistical system in China consists of the government statistical system and department statistical system.

The government statistical system
The institution of statistical agencies and employment of statisticians at all levels of the government constitute the government statistical system. The National Bureau of Statistics is established under the State Council while independent statistical agencies are set up in local government at and above county level. At the township level, either statistical stations are instituted or full-time or part-time statisticians are employed. In addition, the National Bureau of Statistics has also established, under its direct leadership and administration, three survey-taking institutions, namely, Organization of Rural Socio-economic Surveys, Organization of Urban Socio-economic Surveys and Organization of Enterprise Surveys across the country.

The major functions of the overall government statistical system include: to work out plans for statistical surveys, making arrangements for and inspecting statistical work and economic accounting work at national or local level; to organize the implementation of national and local statistical surveys, to collect, process and provide statistical data for the whole country or a particular region; to conduct statistical analysis on economic and social development and to exercise statistical supervision; to administer and coordinate statistical survey questionnaires designed by various departments.

The statistical agencies of local governments not only collect and provide statistical data for government agencies at higher levels but also collect and provide statistical information and submit statistical analysis reports for the local government.

Department statistical system

The institution of statistical agencies and employment of statisticians by various departments, both directly under the State Council and at the local levels, constitute the department statistical system. Its major responsibilities include: to organize and coordinate statistical work of the department concerned, accomplish the tasks in national and local statistical surveys, work out and implement department statistical survey programmes, and to collect, process and provide statistical data; to make statistical analysis of and exercise statistical supervision over the development of the department and sector concerned; to organize and coordinate statistical work of enterprises and institutions within the jurisdiction of the department concerned and manage statistical questionnaires to be used by the department.

Statistical surveys organized and implemented by the National Bureau of Statistics

Regular census system

In accordance with the provisions of the *Statistics Law of the People's Republic of China* and requirements set by the State Council for the establishment of the national census system and reform of the statistical survey system, the National Bureau of Statistics officially initiated the regular census system in 1994. Census items include population, agriculture, industry, tertiary industry and basic units. A census on population, the tertiary industry, industry and agriculture is conducted every 10 years in years ending with 0, 3, 5 and 7 respectively. A census

on basic units is held every five years in years ending with 1 and 6. The first round of regular censuses as legally required has been completed, culminating in the ending of the first nationwide agricultural census.

Commencing the second round of regular censuses, the National Bureau of Statistics conducted the second nationwide census on basic units in 2001. Respondents to this census were all legal entities and affiliated active industrial units across the country (excluding Taiwan Province, Hong Kong and Macao). The standard date for this census was 31 December 2001. The surveying year of the census data was 2001. Major contents of the census encompassed four aspects: basic information of units (code, name, address and communication numbers of the unit); major properties of the unit (industrial category, affiliation); basic economic activities of the unit (total employment, actual capital utilization, fixed assets and operating revenue); other information of the unit (type of accounting system, number of active industrial units).

The system of regular annual and monthly statistical survey

Statistical Survey on Basic Units

Basic unit statistics are an annual survey carried out by provincial statistical agencies in non-census years under the instruction of the National Bureau of Statistics in order to obtain data on the total number of basic units across the country and their changes. This survey is the base of the regular survey system, with which to ascertain the number of various units across the country and the distribution among various localities and economic sectors, and to prepare the framework for sampling surveys.

Statistical Survey on Population and Labour

The sample survey on population change is an annual event conducted between two population censuses to collect information on the yearly population change. Major contents of the survey include the number of births and deaths, education and employment of the population. Surveyors make visits to households to register information. The sample size is 1 per cent of the entire population. In years ending with 5, it is increased by 1 per cent, and new contents are added.

The system of survey on labour includes the Urban Labour Survey and the General Statistics Reporting System on Labour. The system of the Urban Labour Survey is a quarterly sample survey system launched by the National Bureau of Statistics in 1996. The survey covers urban populations across the country with respondents selected from the age group of persons age 15 and over, taking households as the unit; The General Statistics Reporting System on Labour is a general requirement with regard to labour statistics set by the National Bureau of Statistics for provincial-level statistical agencies. Provincial-level statistical agencies, as required by the National Bureau of Statistics, instruct prefecture and county statistical officers to collect, process and report various labour statistical data, and submit the processed data to the National Bureau of Statistics.

Agriculture and Rural Statistical Surveys

The Agriculture and Rural Statistical Surveys include the Agriculture Production Sample Survey System, the Rural Community Basic Conditions Survey System and the General Statistics Reporting System on Agricultural, Forestry, Animal Husbandry and Fishery. Of these the Agriculture Production Sample Survey is a quarterly survey, while others are annual surveys.

Statistical Survey on Industry and Transportation

The Statistical Survey System on Industry includes the Overall Statistics Reporting System, the Direct Reporting System of Key Industrial Enterprises and the Sample Survey System of Sub-scale Industrial Enterprises. Of these the Overall Statistics Reporting System is a general requirement with regard to industrial and energy statistics set by the National Bureau of Statistics for provincial-level statistical agencies and relevant departments under the State Council. It covers all industrial enterprises with an individual annual revenue of and above 5 million renminbi and greater. The total number of respondent enterprises is 160,000. Major contents of the survey include production, input, output and sales. The Direct Reporting System of Key Industrial Enterprises was initiated by the National Bureau of Statistics in 2000, based on the existing data communications network within the statistical system. The selection of key enterprises are made by the National Bureau of Statistics with balanced consideration of their sale revenue, total assets and pre-tax profits. Selected enterprises report monthly data via the network in accordance with the format and other requirements set by the National Bureau of Statistics. Major contents of the survey include basic conditions of enterprises, major economic indicators, production, marketing, inventory and ordering, investment in technological development

and labour conditions. The Sample Survey System of Sub-scale Industrial Enterprises is conducted twice every year to obtain data for the January-September period and the whole year respectively. The sub-scale industrial enterprises are selected from those industrial enterprises with an annual sales revenue below 5 million renminbi.

The Overall Statistics Reporting System on Transportation, Post and Telecommunications is a general requirement with regard to transportation, post and telecommunications statistics set by the National Bureau of Statistics for provincial-level statistical agencies and relevant departments under the State Council. Provincial-level agencies are required to report annually the total number of civil vehicles in the area of their respective jurisdiction. Departments under the State Council are required to report annually data on the total business volume, finance and energy consumption for highways, water traffic, ports, railways, aviation, pipeline transportation, post and telecommunications. They are also required to report monthly headline data for the foregoing statistics.

Statistical Survey on the Construction Industry, Real Estate and Fixed Assets Investment

This survey system includes the Overall Statistics Reporting System on the Construction Industry, the Overall Statistics Reporting System on Fixed Assets Investment, the Direct Network Reporting System of 3000 Key Real Estate Enterprises and the Sample Survey on Rural Fixed Assets Investment.

Statistical Survey on the Wholesale and Retail Trading and Catering Industry

The survey includes the Overall Statistic Reporting System on Wholesale and Retail Trading and Catering Industry, the Sample Survey on Sub-benchmark Wholesale and Retail Trading and the Catering Industry, and the Direct Reporting System on Key Wholesale and Retail Trading Enterprises.

Household Survey

The Household Survey includes the Rural Household Survey and the Urban Household Survey. Respondents of the Rural Household Survey are permanent households in the area with a residence of longer than a year. Major contents of the survey include basic information, per capita income and net income, daily consumption expenditure, the amount of major consumer goods consumption and the amount of durable goods. Taking the province as the universe, the method of multi-phase, random start and symmetrically equidistant sampling is applied. During the survey, sample households keep a record of their accounts and surveyors collect and report data monthly. The Urban Household Survey respondents are non-agricultural households in cities and county seats. Major contents of the survey include family members, employment details, cash income and expenditure, the amount of major goods purchased, housing conditions and the amount of durable goods. A total of 36,000 sample households are selected in 226 sample cities. During the survey, sample households keep a record of their accounts and surveyors collect and report data monthly.

Statistical Prices Survey

The Price Survey on Fixed Assets Investment, the Survey on Consumption Prices of Residents and the Survey on Prices of Industrial Goods together comprise the elements of the Prices Survey.

Besides these surveys, the National Bureau of Statistics also conducts other surveys, such as the Survey on Science and Technology, and the Enterprise Boom Cycle Survey, etc.

National Economic Accounting System

The National Economic Accounting System was formulated in conformity with the UN SNA.

The Gross Domestic Product Accounting System

China's gross domestic product and its components are calculated by the National Bureau of Statistics using different methods in light of characteristics and data sources in different departments. For some departments the accrued value is calculated using the production method. Some are calculated using the income method and obtained through aggregating the accruement of various departments. The gross domestic product accounting system is a general requirement with regard to GDP accounting set by the National Bureau of Statistics for provincial statistical agencies. It consists of annual and regular reports. Major contents of annual reports include total output, GDP at same-year prices, GDP at comparative prices, GDP calculated with expenditure methods, ultimate consumption and consumption level of residents. The regular report is the quarterly GDP.

Input-output Accounting System

The input-output survey is conducted every five years in China. National input-output sheets are compiled in years ending with 2 and 7. The extended input-output sheets are compiled in years ending with 0 and 5. In accordance with the requirements for the input-output survey and compilation plan, provincial-level statistical agencies and the National Bureau of Statistics compile their respective sheets in tandem. The input-output accounting system is a general requirement with regard to input-output accounting set by the National Bureau of Statistics and imposed on provincial-level statistical agencies. It consists of product sector input-output sheets, enterprises sector input (U tables) and enterprise sector output sheets (V tables). Provincial-level statistical agencies are only required to report product sector input-output sheets. The other two sheets are for reference.

The Funds Flow Accounting System

The National Bureau of Statistics and the Central Bank compile the funds flow table jointly. China's funds flow table is similar to internationally accepted forms. The table is divided into two parts. The upper part is goods transactions compiled by the National Bureau of Statistics; the lower part is financial transactions compiled by the Central Bank. The system is a general requirement for funds flow accounting set by the National Bureau of Statistics for provincial-level statistical agencies and the Central Bank. It includes funds flow tables (distribution of incomes) and funds flow tables (financial transactions), compiled respectively by provincial-level statistical agencies and provincial branches of the Central Bank. These data are reported annually.

Balance of Payments Accounting System

China started to establish its balance of payments system in 1980. The concept, principle and framework of the system derive from the Balance of Payments Manual compiled by the IMF. The State Administration of Foreign Exchange compiles the balance of payments sheet. Data needed for the compilation come mainly from business statistics and administrative records of relevant departments under the State Council.

The National Assets Accounting System

This system is a general requirement with regard to national assets accounting set by the National Bureau of Statistics and imposed on provincial-level statistical agencies. It consists of an assets-liabilities sheet and four sectors of assets-liabilities sheets for non-finance businesses, financial institutions, government departments and households. These data are reported annually.

The Economic Circulation Accounts System

This system is a general requirement with regard to economic circulation accounts set by the National Bureau of Statistics and required of provincial-level statistical agencies. It consists of 36 sheets in three categories, namely the overall economic account, sector accounts for institutions and comprehensive sector accounts for industries. These data are reported annually.

Publication and provision of statistical data

Chinese official statistical agencies provide information not only for governments and governmental organization at various levels for decision-making purposes, but also for the public and international exchanges. They publish and provide statistical information in various forms to cater for the needs of customers with different interests on a monthly, quarterly and annual basis.

Printed statistical publications

Many kinds of statistical yearbooks are available to the public, such as China Statistics Yearbook, all localities Statistics Yearbooks at and above county level, and some special-subject year books (such as China Industrial Statistics Yearbook, China Rural Statistics Yearbook, etc.).

China Development Report

This is an illustrated version of the previous yearbook. It describes both the trajectory of China's reform and opening-up and the forecasts made by experts from various fields. It is rich in content including review of the past year and prospects for the coming year. It also incorporates major documents and annuals of China's economic development.

Statistical newspapers and journals

Major newspapers and journals under the National Bureau of Statistics include: *China Information News* (published from Monday to Friday), *China Statistics* (monthly), *Statistical Research* (monthly), *China Economic Performance Monthly*, *China Conditions* (monthly).

These newspaper and journals have comprehensive statistical information content.

China statistical information network servers

Websites are established to disseminate statistical information. On the website there are detailed data on the nation's economy and development, such as census data on the state and the strength of the country, survey reports and statistical data for 160 counties and regions. Using the links on the website, users can visit statistical agencies at all provincial levels.

Statistical bulletins and statistical service

The National Bureau of Statistics and district government statistical agencies at various levels release statistical bulletins on the national economy and the social development situation each year, and they hold press conferences regularly. During festivals or historical anniversaries, the government statistical organs make use of their statistical data and compile series reports on various topics.

Statistical information international exchange

Regular exchanges of statistical information are arranged with international organizations and many national statistical offices; partnerships have been set up between Chinese statistical offices and international, regional and foreign institutions.

Statistical analysis

Government statistical agencies also carry out extensive in-depth statistical analysis and provide more and more statistical analysis reports to the government, companies and the public. The government statistical offices at different levels submit many analysis reports each year. These reports are an important foundation for government at various levels to understand the current economic and social aspects, draw up policies and plans and supervise their implementation. Governments at various levels are paying more attention to the analysis and research reports of the government statistical offices. In recent years, the National Bureau of Statistics has submitted many important analyses and suggestions on the operation of the country's macro economy and social development, and some have been adopted by the state council. Government statistical offices are increasingly playing a significant role in the process of governmental decision-making.

Objectives of future reform

The overall objective of China's statistics is to establish a new statistical system that conforms to the requirements of the socialist market economy and current Chinese conditions, and to international practice. Priorities for this objective are the establishment of a scientific and efficient national statistical system, a rationally structured organizational management system with coordinated operation, a modern national statistical information network system, well-developed statistical legislation and a rationally structured contingent of competent statisticians equipped with modern knowledge and technology. In relation to this objective, much needs to be done. Further deepening of reforms is required. Practical experiences since the launch of China's reform and opening-up policy will be adapted. In addition, exchanges and cooperation with other countries will be strengthened to learn from their successful practice and more advanced experiences.

Part Two

China's Foreign Trade Within the WTO

Key Issues in the Development of China's Foreign Trade*

Liu Xiangdong, Vice Ministerial Chair, Ministry of Foreign Trade and Economic Cooperation, PRC

Since the establishment of New China, especially after the adoption of reform and the open-door policy, rapid development has taken place in China's foreign trade. In 2001 the value of China's foreign trade amounted to US$509.77 billion, comprising US$266.15 billion in exports and $243.61 billion in imports. In a span of 22 years (1979–2001), the total value of foreign trade, exports and imports has been growing at rates of 15.7 per cent, 16.2 per cent and 15.2 per cent respectively. In the meantime China's trading status has surged from 32nd to sixth in the world. Foreign trade has proven to be an essential contributor to the development of our national economy. It is estimated that every 5 per cent of growth in exports contributes 1 per cent to growth in the national economy. At this rate China's exports have been accountable for over 2 per cent of the growth in the country's economy. Therefore, while invigorating domestic demand, a rapid, sustainable performance in foreign trade plays a pivotal role toward the grand goal of China's socialistic modernization.

We are aware that we shall encounter various obstacles en route, some of which may be unpredictable. We are confident, however, that the foundations for foreign trade development are well in place. First, we enjoy the advantage of our socialist system and the guidance from the Communist Party, as well as the evolving socialist market economy. All these combine to ensure national integrity and individual prosperity since they aim at mobilizing social commitment and maximizing the utility of all our available resources, which in turn will lead to enormous spiritual enhancement and material wealth. Second, our international competitiveness has

been improving on the basis of continuous economic growth and the implementation of education and technological progress strategies. Already, China ranks sixth in the world in terms of its GDP, and its economy is expected to continue growing by about 7 per cent over the coming years. This has provided a solid base for China's export increase as well as gearing up demand in the domestic market. Third, national unity and the traditions of the Chinese people have highlighted China as a market unique for its abundant, hardworking, high-quality and low-cost labour. The diversified market structure helps to give China a strong manoeuvrability in turning around market fluctuations across the world. In addition, China is rich in many types of natural resources, yielding a large potential for value creation and stable market prospect. Fourth, China is able to take advantage of the current international environment in which peace and development are the two predominant themes.

The world is poised for further diversification and every country is striving toward integrated competitive advantage. More and more countries begin to realize that scientific and technological progress is the primary motive behind economic development. They also begin to pay attention to renovating their national economic structures. At the same time, international cooperation and coordination in economic development have become increasingly prevalent. We are also cognizant that the world economy will continue to fluctuate, that it will take some time before a full recovery unfolds, and that economic recession in certain countries and regions will frequently surface. Nonetheless, the world econ-

---

* This chapter was originally written in Chinese and was translated by Professor Liu Baocheng of the University of International Business and Economics

omy is unlikely to plunge into an all-round depression and there will not be fundamental upheavals in the broad international spectrum. Therefore, there will be opportunities and additional room for China to expand its presence in the world market. Finally, through two decades of operating in the world economy, China has accumulated a wealth of experience, and a sizable pool of talents, to cope with sudden changes in the global economy and marketplace. Accession to the World Trade Organization (WTO) has brought China new opportunities for its foreign trade development, and the external operating environment will be greatly improved, providing an expanded platform for various Chinese industries to play more visible roles in the global market.

We cannot overlook the challenges before us. First and foremost, with the acceleration of economic global-ization, international trade will be further intertwined with international finance. The instability of financial markets definitely exerts a negative impact on trade expansion. Besides, we have noted that the onset of financial crisis occurs in a speedy and rampant manner, and the forces behind it are so complex that they are hard to predict. Our foreign trade system and mechan-ism are not responsive enough to the changes and, more often than not, the counter measures are lagging, thus rendering China vulnerable to financial exposure. The second challenge is directly related to the international economic environment. The general slowdown of the world economy and intensified competition underline the rise of trade protectionism. Quite a number of countries, developed countries in particular, are devis-ing numerous measures to erect a basket of tariff and non-tariff barriers. Technical and legal barriers, for example, in the name of environment and health con-servation, various types of anti-dumping and counter-vailing measures have been deployed for the protection of domestic markets and industries. All these move-ments pose a restraining force against the cultivation of the international market for Chinese businesses. The third challenge is generated from within. Chinese enterprises are still wrestling with the establishment of proper corporate governance and a fair market order that are compatible with the law of competition. The basic principles of a modern corporate system, for example, independent operation, company responsi-bility for its own loss and profit, self-sustained growth and self-discipline, will have to be revisited. Various chambers of commerce have been unable to function in their expected roles for internal regulation and coordin-ation. As a result, unfair competition has long been an overriding concern. Confronted with the harsh reality of today's rising protectionism, this tends to be no less harmful than suicide attempts.

The fourth challenge involves the concept of quality among Chinese enterprises. In spite of 'winning through quality' strategies, we observe considerable room for improvement in our perceptions of quality and brand management. Unethical or even illegal behaviour, such as counterfeiting and piracy, continue to undermine our reputation in the world market. Finally, the role of government in foreign trade administration has to be redefined. We have been accustomed to government intervention which dampens the motivation of market players. Now we have to learn more to lean on indirect measures for overall coordination so as to bring the market mechanism into full play.

To seize opportunities, and to preserve advantages while avoiding threats, the following key issues will have to be dealt with for the sake of achieving sustainable development in China's foreign trade.

To carry out the 'winning through quality' strategy for enhanced competitiveness in the world market

We are convinced that quality is the lifeline of a busi-ness, and it is also the passport to international markets. In a way, the world's general perception over a country's product quality hallmarks that country's national capa-bility, the level of its social progress, its national strength and, consequently, its international status. In a world of tense competition and rising trade protectionism, qual-ity products and services, on the one hand, are the toughest vehicles to combat trade barriers in the world market to achieve competitive advantage. On the other hand, quality products and services reflect the commit-ment by business communities to the imperative demand for an improved standard of living and quality of life in the home market. They further represent the most effective choice for businesses to grow at the junction of China's accession to WTO. A quality standard does not merely denote conformance to bottom-line per-formance requirements; it will have to ensure that the quality complies with safety and environmental protec-tion standards. In addition, quality must also reflect evolving market needs, eg appealing product design and packaging. Contract commitment and service are an indispensable part of quality. Quality standards will have to be recognized internationally, and we ought to aim at zero defects. Over a broad spectrum, education and training are the ultimate assurance of quality. Therefore, it is important to enhance a sense of responsibility among all members of society. We are resolved to build the right mechanism, strengthening the link between the individual's quality of performance and their own career development as well as the future of our nation. A moral atmosphere will have to be fostered where the attitude to quality becomes an integral part of social customs and personal habit. A quality assurance system requires a specified quality standard, quality control and assurance. A causal link will have to be put in place between the quality of output and benefits to the workers. Defective products will have to be blocked before they enter the market. A recall system will be established for defective products. Chinese enterprises should attach greater importance to quality accreditation by reputable international institutions. They have to further appreciate the value of brand awareness and brand loyalty.

In respect of the 'green barriers' encountered in the export of agricultural products, the idea of establishing a production base should be promoted while production against purchase orders should be adopted as a prevailing practice at production centres. Export companies should provide quality seeds and breeds and offer guidance in terms of quality standards and scientific processes, eg in farming and breeding. Product procurement processes should strictly observe the required quality standards before the products are processed for export. For industrial goods that already enjoy considerable recognition in the international market, OEM production and processing with systematic quality control and supervision should be encouraged in order to expand the scale of production. In doing so, more enterprises will be able to shorten their learning curve in improving the quality system, thereby cultivating their own ability to enter the world market. As a result the whole industry will be better equipped to compete in the global marketplace with superior quality.

Technological innovation drives quality improvement. As the world economy and technology move forward, consumer expectations over the quality of products and services escalate. Chinese enterprises must capture timely market information and predict market trends so as to guide their research and development. Continuous innovation and a steady flow of new products and services will ensure market compatibility and productivity, and ultimately contribute to international competitiveness.

Social quality supervision is another important dimension. Various levels of quality inspectors and administrations, industrial organizations and the media should fulfil the professional responsibilities in their respective positions over quality control and public awareness. The enforcement of ethical conduct and compliance with laws and regulations must be strengthened. Companies and individuals who commit severe misdemeanours in quality, particularly those who cause adverse impact both at home and abroad, will have to be duly punished. No mercy shall be spared in denunciation and penalty. Organizations and officials convicted with power abuse, for example, those who forge quality accreditations, will be deprived of professional qualification and severely punished. Quality is an issue that will have to receive serious attention, and comprehensive measures will have to be taken to prevent quality problems from arising. There will be no compromise in winning the campaign of quality enhancement.

To seriously renovate the operating environment for China's exports

Disorderly competition, particularly the race to undercut each other among Chinese exporters, remains a serious concern. Let's take the example of motorcycle exports, which have experienced a substantial growth in recent years. Total exports in 2001 amounted to three million units; however, their unit price had degenerated to half of the comparable price of 1998. Anti-dumping lawsuits were ignited and some countries are requesting China to exercise voluntary export constraint. Competitive pricing has been so devastating that 1) it deviates from the strategic goal of China's national export promotion programme; 2) it imposes losses on parts of the country and the entire industry; 3) it damages the overall reputation of Chinese products and thus reduces the confidence of clients and customers; 4) more profoundly, it causes the activation of anti-dumping measures with the effect that the target market turns its back on Chinese exports.

Since the 1990s there has been a sharp increase in anti-dumping lawsuits against Chinese exports with an average of 30.5 cases per annum. In the year 2001, as many as 43 anti-dumping lawsuits were lodged by 13 countries against Chinese exports, which involved an array of industries such as iron and steel, light industrial goods, chemicals, mechanical and electronic products, textiles and medicinal drugs. By the end of 2001, anti-dumping lawsuits against Chinese exports totaled 485 cases, over 60 per cent of which were adjudicated as violating anti-dumping legislation. The surtax rates levied ranged from 8 per cent to 1,005 per cent, which can be translated as a humongous loss of $10 billion over Chinese exports. To rub salt into the wound, Chinese companies are reluctant to defend themselves against anti-dumping allegations. Most companies chose to back off from defensive efforts for fear of the litigation cost, thus increasing the chances of loss. From a practical point of view, companies who were ready to defend stood a better chance over the outcome of the lawsuit. Even in cases of loss, the surtax levied would be far less than for those who chose to back off. We conclude that in order to eradicate disorderly competition, we must continue the restructuring endeavour and accelerate the establishment of a modern enterprise system so that companies will adopt as the basis of independent operation, full responsibility for loss and profit, self-growth and self-discipline. We must completely dismantle the stereotype in which state-owned enterprises are free from responsibility when losses occur. Corporate governance has to be changed to the extent that the responsibility of the board of directors is completely separated from the management. The board of directors should be restricted to the preservation and growth of state assets, and is vested with the role of effective supervision over management. The salary and benefits of the management and workers should be directly related to the performance of the business. In addition, public auditing by independent accounting firms will be promoted. Internal regulation within specific industries through chambers or associations formed by exporters will play a strengthened role in serving their members with information, coordination, facilitation and protection. The customs house can be involved in the assessment of import and export pricing schemes. Effective measures will be formulated to sanction unethical behaviour that inflicts harm on the whole market, such as competitive auctions. Administrative departments will strengthen their role in policy guidance and supervision over implementation. They will ensure that those who achieve outstanding performance through lawful and ethical means are rewarded, and that those who engage in malpractices that are detrimental to national interest will be duly punished. Economic and business attachés within Chinese embassies and consulates abroad will provide guidance, service and supervision to the local operations of Chinese business entities within their jurisdiction. They are vested with the responsibility to prevent vicious competition among Chinese firms, to protect the national interest and to maintain friendly cooperation with host countries.

To continue the reform in the administrative approval system so as to unleash the potential of various market players in the area of foreign trade

Along with the progress in market opening to the outside world and reform of the economic system, the list of projects subject to approval has been substantially compressed. This is not yet compatible, however, with the requirements for socialist market economics and active participation in international competition. The list, subject to administrative review, will need to be further streamlined before it can unleash the potential of various market players.

A primary target for reform is the approval and licensing system over the qualification of companies to engage in foreign trade business. The 15th plenary session of the central party congress clearly identified that a diversified ownership structure with state ownership as the backbone is the foundation of the Chinese economic system during the preliminary stage of socialism. A non-state owned economy is recognized as an essential part of the socialist market economy. However, not only the non-state owned firms, but also some state owned firms, are still under certain restrictions on engagement in foreign trade transactions. China has pledged to the world that, within the next three years, it will substitute a registration system for the rights to engage in foreign trade for the approval system, and that foreign companies will be able to enjoy identical treatment in this respect. We are working under the pressure of that timeline. The first step is to institute a registration system among various types of domestic firms so as to foster the core competence of domestic firms within the transitional period. In the meantime the Chinese government will take advantage of the transitional period to improve its administrative system so as to prepare for the wholesale rollout of the registration system. We understand a smooth transition is utterly important to ensure market order and fair competition. Practically speaking, for the sake of the healthy development of Chinese foreign trade, the registration system is both feasible and necessary. Already over 400,000 foreign invested enterprises (FIEs) have obtained the right to engage in foreign trade at the time of their inception. A positive result has been achieved over the first year of its implementation among firms of different ownership structures. Some firms that have not been granted the right to engage in foreign trade have long been renting licences from other companies, which poses considerable difficulty for administration and supervision. The infrastructure for foreign trade administration, such as digitalized government regulation, the 'Gold Pass' programme and the 'Gold Taxation' programme are well under way. These provide the necessary base for effective administration when the foreign trade registration system rolls out among various business entities. In terms of the need to expand China's foreign trade, it is necessary to optimize the trade composition and to reorganize and restructure the business community in order to be prepared for a new chapter in global competition. While harvesting and refocusing on existing markets, we need to cash in on new market segments. More flexible business models and entrepreneurship are required to explore new markets. These are the markets where small and medium-sized businesses can exercise a particular competitive advantage.

The next target for reform is administration over foreign trade products. Except for a limited number of products that are vital to the national economy and those that are subject to the commitments of international conventions, the remaining products that have been placed on the quota and licence control list will be gradually phased out. Firms will be placed on an equal footing for competition and growth. Products that need to be retained (or maintained for a certain period) on the control list, or those that have to be handled by designated companies, will be publicized, as much as possible, for competitive bids. Only companies which outperform competition on their own business strength will be awarded quotas and licences. This approach better reflects the policy initiative for quota and licence control, and is instrumental in boosting the integrated competitiveness of China's foreign trade.

The third target for reform is the macro-management mechanism of China's foreign trade. The government must learn to substitute for direct intervention through administrative measures with indirect methods such as economic and legal measures to coordinate and supervise. Government intervention in the market will be substantially reduced by the ongoing reform in the administrative approval system and installation of market economics. This does not imply that the government will play a lesser role in macro-management, but rather that it has to rely more on economic and legal measures to indirectly coordinate and supervise. Tariffs,

exchange rates, interest rates, credit, taxation and insurance are examples of the tools available to lead foreign trade on to the track of orderly competition and healthy development. Experience shows that under the open-door policy and market economics, economic measures are far more effective than administrative regulations. For example, in the early years of our open-door policy, although our export value surged, the amount of foreign exchange received dropped on a yearly basis. The results of the administrative orders for control were insignificant. In 1994 the government decided to eliminate dual track foreign exchange rates and set the exchange rate afloat as dictated by market supply and demand. This floating rate has been subject to management by the government through open market operations. The government buys and sells foreign exchange reserves to keep fluctuations within a tolerable range in line with its foreign trade and economic development objectives. Consequently firms were driven by the profit motive to call back their foreign currencies and have them exchanged in China. Almost automatically the inflow of foreign exchange by Chinese exporters increased and a reasonable level has been sustained up to the present. It is also worth noting that we have accumulated a certain experience in regulating foreign trade through interest rates, credit and taxation. The Import and Export Bank was established to provide credits to buyers or seller's credit for the purpose of supporting China's exports of machinery and electronic equipment. The Bank is especially instrumental in the support of export packages for equipment from China. We must be ready to learn both from our past experience and foreign practices so as to facilitate the transformation of our approach to foreign trade administration. At the same time, government offices in the foreign trade area must reinforce communication and coordination with other relevant government organs for concerted action. An information system responsible for the surveillance of foreign trade operations is of paramount importance for the government to make correct and prompt decisions.

To devise various international economic cooperation channels for the strategic promotion of foreign trade

At present, our international economic cooperation structure is multidimensional to include import and export trade, foreign investment, overseas project construction, labour service exports and foreign aid. These activities are interrelated and intra-facilitative.

International investment, piggy-backed by international trade, is one of the major elements in global economic activities. In retrospect, since the launch of China's open-door policy, and especially in the past ten years, foreign investment in China has been playing an increasingly important role in our foreign trade growth. The proportion of the import and export value generated by FIEs has far outweighed China's industrial output. Moreover, the contribution to the rate of growth both in import and export value, as well as foreign exchange surplus, has far exceeded that of domestic enterprises. FIEs stand out as an important force behind our export growth and a major source of the increase in foreign exchange reserves. Many FIEs are associated with multinational corporations that possess advanced technology, management expertise and established global marketing networks. Their products are perceived to be of superior quality with a higher technology content and added value, thus enjoying competitive advantage in overseas markets. They are ready examples for domestic Chinese firms to learn from in the implementation of the 'winning through quality' strategy and in their business and market diversification. China is in the process of conversion from a 'big' trading nation into a 'strong' trading nation. To that end, we have to open our arms to foreign direct investment and further integrate FIEs into the major efforts of the country's foreign trade development.

As China's economy and foreign trade develop, the 'stepping out' strategy, ie to invest abroad, becomes both imperative and feasible. We enjoy an abundance of labour supply and a considerable level of industrial capability. To cope with the limited per capita resources, we have to utilize both domestic and foreign resources synergistically. To tap overseas resources through investment abroad or production relocation can serve multiple purposes. It can compensate for the shortage of domestic resources while reducing the export costs. It is conducive to the balance of bilateral trade. It can facilitate the export of Chinese products and equipment. More realistically, it helps to penetrate protectionist barriers and to allow Chinese businesses to grow together with the host countries in terms of both economic development and technological progress. We also encourage Chinese firms to set up research and development centres in selected markets. This will improve our product compatibility through technological localization and market customization. Attention is also directed towards combining overseas investment promotion with our foreign aid programme. Through localized manufacturing, a showcase will be presented in the host country for the level of our technology and product quality. This is the most effective approach to market promotion and helps to facilitate ensuing exports, particularly export package of equipment, significantly. We have accumulated considerable strength in project construction overseas. If we are better able to integrate project consulting and design in constructing contracted projects, our exports, particularly export packages of equipment, will enjoy an enormous market. Success depends on concerted efforts from both government and the business community. With strategic integration of management and operation, our foreign trade will broaden its horizon.

The development of foreign trade is a highly complex system involving multi-faceted endeavours. Naturally, much remains to be considered and desired. Above all, we count on all our colleagues in the foreign trade arena to exercise their patriotic enthusiasm, to disregard difficulties, and always to move forward in the pursuit of excellence. As the popular proverb goes, 'wherever there is a will, there is a way'. Willpower is the driving force behind abundant material wealth, and it is also the most important guarantee for the sustainable, rapid and healthy development of China's foreign trade.

China as a WTO Member: the Opening-up of the Chinese Market

Craig Pouncey and Lode van den Hende, Herbert Smith, Brussels

This chapter provides an overview of China's specific obligations in the area of 'market access' in the principal commercial sectors in which China has allowed foreign businesses, goods and services to trade or be traded in China. We have outlined the type of liberalization commitments that China has made and the type of legal issues that can arise. However, China's accession to the WTO is set out in more than 800 pages of detailed legal documentation and it is obviously not possible to provide a complete and accurate explanation of these issues in this short contribution. For fully accurate information it is necessary to consult the original documents or take appropriate advice.

At the outset, it is important to note that China has made two types of commitments:

- Like all WTO members, China has submitted schedules of commitments and concessions on trade in goods and services. Broadly speaking these determine the customs tariffs that China can apply to imported products and the extent to which China is obliged to allow foreign services companies to operate on its territory.
- China has also made a number of special concessions on its current and planned investment regime and on a number of specific issues such as trading rights. These 'special' commitments reflect the fact that China is an economy in transition from a state-based system to a market-based system. Thus, certain issues that arise in the Chinese context do not arise in the context of a 'normal market economy' and, for that reason, are not dealt with by traditional WTO rules. These special rules can be found in the Protocol of Accession and in the WTO Working Party Report on China's accession. As China's transition towards

a market economy progresses, the practical significance of these special rules will diminish accordingly.

Trading rights

Before China's accession, the right to import and export goods was available only to some 35,000 Chinese enterprises and, on a restricted basis, to some foreign-invested enterprises. Within three years of accession all companies will have the right to import and export all goods throughout the customs territory of China. For a limited number of products (grain, vegetable oil, sugar, tobacco, cotton, oil and fertilizers) the right to import will remain reserved for state trading enterprises. Importation of oil and fertilizers will gradually be opened to non-state importers. The right to export will also be liberalized, although exports of the following products will remain subject to state trading: tea, rice, corn, soy bean, certain minerals, coal, oil, cotton and silk (the silk export monopoly will be gradually opened up for competition).

Abolition of discriminatory measures and practices

China has explicitly agreed to eliminate all measures and practices that discriminate against foreign companies including:

- all taxes and dual pricing systems that discriminate against foreign or foreign-invested companies;
- restrictions on after sales services for imported products;
- special pricing rules and profit ceilings imposed on imported pharmaceuticals;

- special licensing rules for retail outlets selling imported cigarettes;
- special rules for the distribution and sale of imported spirits;
- special registration procedures for imported chemicals;
- differences in certification and inspection procedures for imported boilers and pressure vessels.

Import tariff reductions and removal of quota restrictions

Like all WTO members, China has made commitments to remove or reduce 'border measures' such as import tariffs and import quotas. China's Schedule for goods provides details for this on a product-by-product basis for *thousands* of products. The table below provides an overview of these reductions in a number of specific sectors (which will themselves sometimes contain very many individual sub-products, each with separate and different tariff rates). The figures mentioned are averages calculated by the European Commission and the US authorities and need to be approached with some

care as it is not always clear how these averages have been calculated. Furthermore, the use of averages can obscure important differences. When negotiating with China the other WTO members have concentrated on specific product categories that are of interest to their own exporters. For instance, at the request of the EU China has reduced its tariffs on five particular types of footwear from 25 per cent to 10 per cent. These five specific product categories account for more than 70 per cent of EU footwear exports to China. Thus, this reduction will have an important market opening effect for EU exporters although the average tariff reduction for all footwear categories may appear relatively limited.

Table 2.2.1 nevertheless provides an indication of the scope of the tariff reductions and highlights the sectors where the impact will be very significant, such as automobiles and alcoholic beverages. Furthermore it is important to note that even for sectors where the reduction is limited WTO accession provides an important advantage because it imposes a legal obligation on China to maintain (or 'bind') import tariffs at a specific and often low level. It will not be possible for China to increase these tariffs beyond that rate when importers

Table 2.2.1 Target tariff rate reductions by sector

Products	Import tariffs and quota restrictions at the moment of WTO accession	Target reduction and target date
Agricultural equipment	Average of 8.2%	Average of 5.8% by 1 January 2003
Automobiles	80% to 100% Quotas in place	Reduction to 25% by 1 July 2006 Higher initial quota to be increased by 15% annually and phased out by 1 January 2005
Automobile parts	Average of 17.4%	Average of 9.5% by 1 July 2006
Beer	42%	Completely eliminated by 1 January 2005
Chemicals	Average of 8.8%	Average of 6.9% by 1 January 2008
Construction equipment	Average of 10.5%	Average of 6.5% by 1 January 2004
Cosmetics	Average of 23.5%	Average of 10.7% by 1 January 2008
Fish	Average of 16.6%	Average of 10.3%
Furniture	Average of 13.9%	Completely eliminated by 1 January 2005
Information technology Products	Average of 6.4%	Tariffs on three-quarters of information technology products will be eliminated by 1 January 2003. All tariffs will be eliminated by 1 January 2005
Medical equipment	Average of 6.5%	Average of 3.9% by 1 January 2005
Paper	Average of 15–25%	Average of 5.4% by 1 January 2006
Pharmaceuticals	Average of 7%	Average of 4.7% by 1 January 2004
Spirits	Average of 65%	Average of 10% by 1 January 2005

become increasingly successful (China will only be able to do that using trade defence instruments such as anti-dumping and safeguard measures, but these are subject to strict conditions and offer only temporary protection). Thus WTO accession greatly increases legal certainty for importers.

Telecommunications

Basic telecommunication services (ie relay of voice or data)

Foreign service suppliers are permitted to establish joint ventures in accordance with the following conditions:

- For mobile services foreign investment in the joint venture can amount to a maximum of 25 per cent upon accession, 35 per cent after one year and 49 per cent after three years. For fixed-line services the foreign investment in joint ventures is opened only three years after China's accession up to a maximum of 25 per cent. This is to be increased to 35 per cent after five years and 49 per cent after six years.
- Initially these joint ventures will be allowed to operate services in and between the cities of Shanghai, Guangzhou and Beijing. This would be expanded to include Chengdu, Chongqing, Dalian, Fuzhou, Hangzhou, Nanjing, Ningbo, Qingdao, Shenyang, Shenzen, Xiamen, Xian, Taiyuan and Wuhan.
- The commitment covers domestic and international voice and facsimile services, packet-switched and circuit-switched data transmission services. It also extends to domestic leased circuit services.

Problems are already reported to have arisen in the mobile services market since accession. Foreign companies looking to establish joint ventures have to wait almost a year for the Chinese authorities to process applications for a mobile telephony permit. Furthermore, new regulation has set the Chinese partner's required capital inputs, at a level that is well above what is conceivable for most potential Chinese partners. The Chinese authorities are also looking to reduce the number of joint venture partners available by reducing the number of domestic telecom companies from seven to four large state companies. The WTO-compatibility of some of the manoeuvres of the Chinese authorities is doubtful.

Value-added telecommunications services

This covers electronic mail, voice mail, on-line information and database retrieval, electronic data interchange, enhanced/value added facsimile services, code and protocol conversion, on-line information and/or data processing.

Foreign investment in a joint venture can amount to a maximum of 30 per cent upon accession, 49 per cent after one year and 50 per cent after two years. These joint ventures are allowed to operate services in and between the cities of Shanghai, Guangzhou and Beijing from the date of accession. This will be expanded to include Chengdu, Chongqing, Dalian, Fuzhou, Hangzhou, Nanjing, Ningbo, Qingdao, Shenyang, Shenzen, Xiamen, Xian, Taiyuan and Wuhan one year after accession. Two years after accession all geographic restrictions will be abolished.

Specific rules concerning anti-competitive behaviour in the telecommunications sector

China has also undertaken to respect the obligations contained in the so-called 'Reference Paper'. This WTO document defines a number of regulatory principles for the telecommunications sector and includes measures to prevent anti-competitive behaviour such as cross-subsidization and also sets out rules concerning licensing criteria, universal service, and the independence of the regulator.

Distribution services

Wholesale distribution services

No later than 11 December 2002, foreign service suppliers will be permitted to establish joint ventures and engage in the wholesale business of imported and domestically produced products. For books, newspapers, magazines, pharmaceutical products, pesticides and mulching film, the date is set at 11 December 2004. For chemical fertilizers, processed oil and crude oil that date is 11 December 2006.

No later than 11 December 2003, foreign majority ownership will be permitted and no geographic or quantitative restrictions will apply. As of 11 December 2004 all restrictions on equity and form of establishment should be abolished (except for chemical fertilizers, processed oil and crude oil for which the date is set at 11 December 2006).

Retail services

Upon accession foreign service suppliers will be permitted to participate in joint ventures in major cities and the five Special Economic Zones. As from 11 December 2004 there will be no geographic or quantitative restrictions or restrictions concerning equity or form of establishment. There are specific rules, however, for chain stores with more than 30 outlets.

The retail market is one of the sectors where the impact of WTO accession is expected to be greatest. That does not necessarily mean that it will be easy to enter the market. The experience of foreign retail chains like the French Carrefour and the US company Walmart is that Chinese domestic retail enterprises have woken up and are actively competing through mergers, acquisitions and reorganization. It also takes time for foreign retailers to get the necessary approvals for new stores from the central government. Carrefour was recently sanctioned for opening stores without the required central government permission.

Construction services

Upon accession it will be possible to provide construction services via joint ventures with a foreign majority. After three years, wholly foreign owned enterprises will be permitted to carry out foreign-financed projects (including projects funded by institutions such as the IMF and the World Bank) and Chinese-funded projects where Chinese construction firms can justify the need for international assistance.

Banking services

China will gradually abolish restrictions imposed on the operations of foreign banks in China. These will be allowed to offer renminbi banking services to Chinese corporations on 11 December 2003 and to Chinese individuals on 11 December 2006. As of the latter date, China will also issue banking licences solely on the basis of prudential criteria, without quantitative limits on licences and restrictions on ownership, operation and juridical form of foreign banks. There are no more geographic restrictions for foreign currency business, and geographic restrictions on local currency business will be phased out by 11 December 2006 (with additional areas opening up each year).

A new regulation introduced by the Chinese authorities since accession will make the practical consequences of these undertakings less effective. According to this regulation foreign banks would be allowed to open only one new branch per year. This will make it difficult for foreign banks to gain market share and the WTO compatibility of this measure is doubtful.

Courier services

Foreign companies may provide courier services (except those reserved for the Chinese postal services) through joint ventures that are up to 49 per cent foreign owned. By 11 December 2002 majority ownership will be allowed and by 11 December 2005 foreign courier service suppliers may establish wholly foreign-owned subsidiaries.

Insurance

As in the case of banking China has agreed to issue licences, solely on the basis of prudential criteria, without quantitative limits. Foreign insurance companies with a Chinese licence will be allowed to expand by opening branches in line with the phasing out of geographic restrictions. Foreign life insurers will be able to establish joint ventures with 50 per cent foreign ownership. Geographic restriction for these joint ventures will be removed by 11 December 2004. Foreign non-life insurers will be able to operate as wholly foreign-owned entities as of 11 December 2003 and without geographic restrictions as of 11 December 2004.

The need to tread carefully

The fact that China has accepted these and other obligations in the framework of the WTO does not necessarily mean that China will have an impeccable implementation record. As discussed in Chapter 1.3, China certainly has the political will to implement its obligations in a serious manner. At the same time, it is generally acknowledged that China has made ambitious commitments and that there will be short-term conflicts and difficulties.

The type of legal discussions that tend to occur in the WTO may well appear entirely novel to Chinese government circles. It has taken a number of EU Member States a long time to fulfil their EC obligations to set up an independent telecommunications regulator that effectively safeguards competition and curtails the incumbent operators. Clearly, one cannot expect such a process to run any smoother in China where the concept of pro-competitive regulation is entirely new.

The time it will take for China to implement its promises will also most certainly depend on the health of the Chinese economy. A blooming economy would give China the incentive to allow more foreign competition whereas an economic downturn would probably encourage further protectionism.

Consequently, business will need to remain careful and diligent when planning to make use of China's accession to the WTO. The impact on China and the potential for business are clearly enormous. It is rare, however, for such sweeping changes to take place entirely smoothly.

Craig Pouncey is experienced in all types of trade and WTO law as well as European Union and UK competition law, including Articles 81 and 82, State aids, monopolies and mergers. He deals regularly with the European Commission and the UK Competition authorities in major cases, including notifications of agreements and complaints about anti-competitive conduct.

Lode Van Den Hende was among the very first private lawyers who were allowed to appear in a WTO dispute settlement hearing and has been involved in a number of high-profile WTO disputes between the EU and the US. He has advised on all types of WTO law, and the General Agreement on Trade in Services in particular.

The Deregulation of Foreign Trade within the WTO*

Shi Yonghai, Chairman, China Association of International Trade (CAIT)

Eliminating the system of examination and approval of trading rights and applying the registration regime

As committed at the time of WTO accession, China will progressively lower the threshold for the availability of trading rights within the three-year transition period and eliminate its system of examination and approval of trading rights at the end of the transition period. All kinds of enterprises will have the right to trade upon registration.

During the transition period the Ministry of Foreign Trade and Economic Cooperation (MOFTEC) will make further efforts to reform the foreign trade system and will do its best to complete the following three areas of work:

- First, steps will be taken to reduce progressively the qualification requirements for obtaining trading rights;
- Second, a registration system will be implemented for enterprises to qualify for trading rights;
- Third, the restrictions on the business scope of production enterprises will be eventually lifted.

According to the Protocol and the Report of the Working Party on the accession of China, the specific procedure will be:

- China will eliminate its system of examination and approval of trading rights within three years after accession;
- Upon accession, China will eliminate any export performance, trade balancing, foreign exchange balancing and prior experience requirements;

- China will reduce the minimum registered capital requirement for wholly Chinese-invested enterprises to obtain trading rights to 5,000,000 renminbi for year one, 3,000,000 renminbi for year two, 1,000,000 renminbi for year three and will eliminate the examination and approval system for trading rights at the end of the phase-in period;
- China will progressively liberalize the scope and availability of trading rights for foreign-invested enterprises. Such enterprises will be granted new or additional trading rights based on the following schedule: beginning one year after accession, joint-venture enterprises with minority share foreign-investment will be granted full rights to trade; and, beginning two years after accession, majority share foreign-investment joint-ventures will be granted full rights to trade.

At the same time, MOFTEC will carry out reforms on the modes of foreign trade administration in accordance with the principle of 'lenient examination and approval, strict administration and facilitation of development', shifting the focus of administration to macro-supervision and maintenance of market order. In order to effect such a transformation of government administration, MOFTEC will coordinate with other concerned government departments to amend the *Foreign Trade Law of the People's Republic of China* and draft the rules regarding registration of import and export trading rights. Meanwhile, technical means of registration will be improved to achieve online electronic registration eventually. Coordination and cooperation with other government departments will be strengthened and a uniform code of administration over import and

---

* This chapter was originally written in Chinese and was translated by Li Yong.

export enterprises will be implemented. In this connection, all government departments will be electronically networked in order to establish a nationally unified network system for the surveillance and monitoring of import and export enterprises, which will also enable government departments to implement precautionary administration of those operating activities that have records of malpractice.

The deregulation of trading rights and the associated upsurge in the number of enterprises dealing in import and export have caused an urgent requirement for the government to transform the modes of administration and improve the level of administration. From now on, MOFTEC will shift its emphasis progressively from the administration of market access to macro-management in order to maintain market economy order and ensure that fairness, justice and order are maintained in competition.

Eliminating non-tariff measures progressively

In Chapter 1.4 on China's commitments upon accession to the WTO, it was stated that China would eliminate the non-tariff measures of more than 400 tariff headings by 1 January 2005. During the phase-out period, China will implement growth rates for quotas on relevant products. The criteria and timing for the grant of quota allocations, obtaining and extending licences should be implemented in strict conformity with the provisions of the Agreement on Import Licensing Procedures.

In order to perform the commitments, the categories of products subject to import licensing in 2002 have been reduced from 20 to 12.

Starting from 1 January 2002, China has already eliminated import licensing for the following 14 products: polyester fibre, acrylic fibres, polyester fillet, tobacco and its products, acetate tow, colour television sets and TV kinescope, radios, tape recorders and their main components, audio and video tape duplication equipment, refrigerators and their compressors, recording equipment and its key parts, air conditioners and their compressors, open-end spinning machines, wine and colour-sensitive material. Import licence restrictions on some of the products under the headings of motor vehicles, their key parts and vehicle tyres have also been removed.

The 12 categories of products subject to import licensing in 2002 include 170 eight-digit sub-categories. Products subject to import quota licensing are: pro-

cessed oil, natural rubber, vehicle tyres, motor vehicles and their key parts, motorcycles and their key parts, cameras and their bodies, watches, crane lorries and their chassis, totaling eight categories. Another four categories of products subject to import licensing are disc-producing equipment, controlled chemicals, chemicals that can be used to produce narcotics and ozone depleting substances.

The import quotas for machinery and electronics products in 2002 are: US\$7.935 billion for motor vehicles and their key parts, US\$380 million for motorcycles and their key parts; US\$120 million for crane trucks and their chassis, US\$133 million for cameras and US\$482 million for watches.

According to China's commitments upon WTO accession, China will completely eliminate import quotas and licensing on motor vehicles and their key parts, and motorcycles and their key parts by the year 2005. Moreover, China will increase the quota for motor vehicles and their key parts by 15 per cent every year from 2002. From now on, other products subject to import licensing would be reduced progressively.

Administration of the tariff rate quota regime

The Agreement on Agriculture provides that WTO members must offer minimum market access opportunities for agricultural products, which entails the application of a tariff rate quota regime. The amount of the tariff quota is just a market access opportunity but not an import obligation; the volume of imports is determined by the actual demand in the importing country. The amount of the tariff quota should be not less than the average import volume in the base period 1986–1988. If the import volume is less than 3 per cent of domestic consumption in the base period, it should extend to 3 per cent and, in addition, members should also be committed to certain increments of annual growth. For the applicants, the base period should be the latest three-year data available.

After the WTO accession, China will implement tariff quotas on agricultural products such as wheat, corn, rice, cotton, sugar, bean oil, palm oil, colza oil, wool and industrial products such as fertilizer, and wool top. The amount of the tariff quota for industrial products will be calculated against the base period 1995–1997. Specific commitments such as the tariff rate quotas quantities, in-quota and out-quota tariff rates, non-state-trading enterprises and implementation periods have been listed in Annex 8 of the protocol –

China's Schedule of Concessions and Commitments on Goods.

The administration of tariff rate quotas has also been defined in the Report of the Working Party and Annex 8. China will ensure that tariff rate quotas (TRQs) are administered on a transparent, predictable, uniform, fair and non-discriminatory basis using clearly specified timeframes for announcement, application and issuance; it will reflect consumer preferences and end-user demand, and will not inhibit the filling of each TRQ and will provide the opportunity for reallocation.

In addition to administration of the state-trading regime, China will also grant trading rights to non-state trading entities to import the TRQ allocations set aside for importation by such entities.

In February 2002 China's State Planning Development Commission (SPDC) promulgated and implemented *the Regulations on Administration of Import Tariff Quota for Agricultural Products, Provisional Regulations on Administration of Import Tariff Quota for Important Agricultural Products in 2002* and *the Detailed Rules of Implementation on the Administration of Import Tariff Quota for Wool and Wool Tops in 2002. Regulations on Administration of Import Tariff Quota for Fertilizer* and *Proclamation on Fertilizer Application in 2002* have also been promulgated.

Supplement 1 to Chapter 2.3

NON-TARIFF MEASURES FOR SELECTED KEY PRODUCTS SUBJECT TO PHASED ELIMINATION

(This table is adapted from Annex 3 of the Protocol. For standard interpretation of the commitments, please refer to the official text of Annex 3)

Quota Category	Unit	Initial Quota Volume/Value	Annual Growth Rate	Phasing-out Period (Calendar year 1 January)
1 Processed oil	million metric tons	16.58	15%	2004
2 Sodium cyanide	million metric tons	0.018	15%	2002
3 Chemical fertilizer	million metric tons	8.9	15%	2002 (parts upon accession)
4 Natural rubber	million metric tons	0.429	15%	2004
5 Rubber tyres used on automobiles	million pieces	0.81	15%	2002 (parts upon accession or 2004)
6 Motorcycles and key parts	US$ million	286	15%	motorcycles: 2004 key parts: 2003
7 Motor vehicles and key parts	US$ million	6,000	15%	automobiles: 2005 other motor vehicles: 2004 key parts: upon accession or 2003
8 Air conditioners and compressors	US$ million	286	15%	Upon accession or 2002
9 Recording apparatus and key parts	US$ million	293	15%	2002
10 Magnetic sound and video recording apparatus	US$ million	38	15%	Upon accession or 2002
11 Recorders and transport mechanisms	US$ million	387	15%	2002
12 Colour TV sets and TV tuners	US$ million	325	15%	Upon accession or 2002
13 Crane lorries and chassis	US$ million	88	15%	2004
14 Cameras	US$ million	14	15%	2003
15 Wrist watches	US$ million	33	15%	2003

Supplement 2 to Chapter 2.3

A LIST OF PRODUCTS SUBJECT TO TARIFF RATE QUOTAS

(This table is adapted from Annex 8 of the Protocol. For standard interpretation of the commitments, please refer to the official text of Annex 8)

Product Category	Product	Supervision Condition	Detailed Description
Food	Wheat	1. State-Trading Enterprises (STE)	STE share: 90%
		2. Tariff Rate Quotas	2002: 8,468,000 MT 2003: 9,052,000 MT 2004: 9,636,000 MT Implementation period: 2004 In-quota tariff rate: 1%–10% Out-quota tariff rate: decrease from 71% to 65%
	Corn	1. State-Trading Enterprises	STE share: decrease from 68% to 60%
		2. Tariff Rate Quotas	2002: 5,850,000 MT 2003: 6,525,000 MT 2004: 7,200,000 MT Implementation period: 2004 In-quota tariff rate: 1%–10% Out-quota tariff rate: decrease from 71% to 65%
	Rice	1. State-Trading Enterprises	STE share: Short and medium grain: 50% Long grain: 50%
		2. Tariff Rate Quotas	Short and medium grain 2002: 1,995,000 MT 2003: 2,327,500 MT 2004: 2,660,000 MT Long grain 2002: 1,995,000 MT 2003: 2,327,500 MT 2004: 2,660,000 MT Implementation period: 2004 In-quota tariff rate: 1%–9% Out-quota tariff rate: decrease from 71% to 65%

Product Category	Product	Supervision Condition	Detailed Description
Vegetable Oil	Soybean Oil	1. State-Trading Enterprises	STE share: decrease from 34% to 10%, eliminated on 1 January 2006
		2. Tariff Rate Quotas	2002: 2,518,000 MT 2003: 2,818,000 MT 2004: 3,118,000 MT 2005: 3,587,100 MT Implementation period: 2005 In-quota tariff rate: 9% Out-quota tariff rate: decrease from 52.4% to 19.9% 2006: 9% single tariff rate
	Palm Oil	1. State-Trading Enterprises	STE share: decrease from 34% to 10%, eliminated on 1 Jan 2006
		2. Tariff Rate Quotas	2002: 2,400,000 MT 2003: 2,600,000 MT 2004: 2,700,000 MT 2005: 3,168,000 MT Implementation period: 2005 In-quota tariff rate: 9% Out-quota tariff rate: decrease from 52.4% to 19.9% 2006: 9% single tariff rate
	Rape-seed Oil	1. State-Trading Enterprises	STE share: decrease from 34% to 10%, eliminated on 1,Jan 2006
		2. Tariff Rate Quotas	2002: 8,789,000 MT 2003: 1,018,600 MT 2004: 1,126,600 MT 2005: 1,243,000 MT Implementation period: 2005 In-quota tariff rate: 9% Out-quota tariff rate: decrease from 52.4% to 19.9% 2006: 9% single tariff rate
Sugar	Sugar	1. State-Trading Enterprises	STE share: 70%
		2. Tariff Rate Quotas	2002: 1,764,000 MT 2003: 1,852,000 MT 2004: 1,945,000 MT Implementation period: 2004 In-quota tariff rate: decrease from 20% to 15% Out-quota tariff rate: decrease from 60.4% to 50%
Cotton	Cotton	1. State-Trading Enterprises	STE share: 33%
		2. Tariff Rate Quotas	2002: 818,500 MT 2003: 856,250 MT 2004: 894,000 MT

Product Category	Product	Supervision Condition	Detailed Description
Wool	Wool	1. Designated trading	Implementation period: 2004 In-quota tariff rate: 1% Out-quota tariff rate: decrease from 54.4% to 40% Eliminated 3 years after accession
		2. Tariff Rate Quotas	2002: 264,500 MT 2003: 275,750 MT 2004: 287,000 MT Implementation period: 2004 In-quota tariff rate: 1% Out-quota tariff rate: 38%
	Wool tops	1. Designated trading	Eliminated 3 years after accession
		2. Tariff Rate Quotas	2002: 72,500 MT 2003: 76,250 MT 2004: 80,000 MT Implementation period: 2004 In-quota tariff rate: 3% Out-quota tariff rate: 38%
Fertilizer	– Diammonium hydrogenortho-phosphate (diammonium phosphate) – Urea – NPK	1. State-Trading Enterprises	STE share: Diammonium hydrogenorthophosphate (diammonium phosphate): decreasing 5 percentage points per year until reaching 51% in year 9. The tariff quota level will be increased by 5% annually Urea: 90% NPK: decreasing 5 percentage points per year until reaching 51% in year 8. The tariff quota level will be increased by 5% annually
		2. Tariff Rate Quotas	– Diammonium hydrogenorthophosphate (diammonium phosphate) (31,053,000) Initial quota quantity: 5,400,000 Final quota quantity: 6,900,000 Implementation period: 2006 In-quota tariff rate: 4% Out-quota tariff rate: 50% – Urea (31021000) Initial quota quantity: 1,300,000 Final quota quantity: 3,300,000 Implementation period: 2006 In-quota tariff rate: 4% Out-quota tariff rate: 50% – NPK (31052000) Initial quota quantity: 2,700,000 Annual growth rate: 5% Implementation period: 2006 In-quota tariff rate: 4% Out-quota tariff rate: 50%

China's External Cooperation of Agriculture after the Entry into WTO*

Ni Hongxing, Department of International Cooperation, Ministry of Agriculture

Remarkable achievements have been made in China's external cooperation in agriculture since the reform and opening up

Since the reform and opening up, remarkable achievements have been made in China's external cooperation in agriculture, which have played a positive role in promoting a sustained, rapid and healthy development of the industry as a whole and of the rural economy in particular. First, the utilization of foreign investment in the agricultural sector has grown rapidly. Since the early 1980s, there have been more than 10,000 foreign-invested agricultural projects with a total contracted investment of US$20 billion. The introduction of foreign investment has not only made up for China's insufficient input into agriculture, but also has mobilized additional funds raised from various sources including the central and local governments, collective entities and the farmers themselves.

Second, China has introduced numerous applicable agricultural technologies and quality varieties which have accelerated progress in China's agricultural technology. Through international cooperation, China has imported over 100,000 animal and plant germ plasma resources and a large number of advanced, applicable and economically efficient technologies. These technologies include: film mulching, dry nursery low density planting in rice cultivation, agricultural remote sensing, straw ammonification, comprehensive prevention and cure, mechanized chicken farming, fish culture in net pens and the preservation of processed fruits and vegetables. Notably, film mulching has been applied to nearly 100 crops, and dry nursery low density planting technology has been promoted in over 10 provinces. These two technologies alone have generated over 1 billion renminbi worth of benefits. In addition, the overall competence of China's agricultural research and development has been improved as a result of cooperative research, the import of scientific research equipment, the exchange of research people and training, all of which has contributed to the recent progress in China's agricultural science and technology.

Third, external cooperation has boosted the development of agriculture-related industries and undertakings. Typical examples are the following:

- the EU aid for dairy projects that have played an important role in boosting the development of China's dairy industry;
- China's agricultural technology popularization system that has been gradually established and developed through the trust fund aid programme of the United Nations Food and Agriculture Organization and aid from the United Nations Development Programme; and
- China's first agricultural census that was completed on the basis of groundwork in technology, staffing and equipment that was established with the assistance of aid from Italy and the United Nations Food and Agriculture Organization.

Fourth, external cooperation fostered the formation of a large number of modern agricultural enterprises. The utilization of foreign investment in agriculture has resulted in the establishment of a large number of modern joint ventures and wholly foreign-owned enter-

---

* This chapter was originally written in Chinese and was translated by Li Yong.

prises. At the same time this investment has introduced new concepts of modern agricultural management and operation, which have changed the conventional perception of agriculture as a simplistic sector of cultivation and farming into an understanding of agriculture as an industry that involves, in addition to cultivation and farming, processing, transportation and sales, with each element being closely linked, interacting and mutually reinforcing. This has exerted a profound influence over China's agricultural development. At present, foreign-invested agricultural enterprises are playing a very important role in China's industrialized agricultural operations and the export of agricultural products.

Fifth, various grant aid programmes have facilitated China's efforts to help the poor and provide disaster relief. The United Nations World Food Programme (WFP), for example, has been providing food and emergency aid since 1980. By implementing food-for-work initiatives, the aid programmes have helped establish comprehensive agricultural development and post-disaster rehabilitation projects in China. By the end of 2001, WFP had approved 66 food aid programmes, with a total value equivalent to US$900 million. Most of these projects are distributed among nationally or provincially designated poor counties and have benefited over 30 million people. In addition, the International Fund for Agricultural Development has provided 16 aid programmes for comprehensive agricultural development in China, involving total contracted loans of US$400 million, of which most are on highly preferential terms.

Opportunities and challenges for China's external cooperation of agriculture after the entry into the WTO

Having joined the WTO, China's agricultural market will be opened further and the levels of marketing and internationalization in China's agriculture will be increasingly enhanced. As a result, China's agriculture will face unprecedented opportunities and challenges in its external cooperation.

- China's entry into the WTO signals a new stage in China's opening up of agriculture. In the first place, China's entry into the WTO reflects the inherent requirements for deepening reform, expanding the opening up and establishing a socialist market economic system. It is also a natural selection process in China's effort to utilize markets and resources both

at home and abroad in its participation in the global economy. Indeed, it is another important milestone in China's opening up. For a long time, China had been scheduling its opening up according to its own timetable. However, after accession to the WTO, China's opening up will experience several changes, for example from the past opening to a limited extent in certain areas to an all-round opening up, or from policy-driven opening characterized by pilot programmes to predictable opening under the framework of the law, and lastly, from unilateral and voluntary opening to a mutual opening up between China and other members of WTO. In other words, China's economy will be integrated into the world economic system at a higher level and in greater depth. Thus the depth and width of China's opening up will increase, expanding the scope and areas for external cooperation, and external cooperation will be more stable.

- Second, China's entry into the WTO will help to improve the environment of agricultural cooperation. As the governance of the WTO has extended from the traditional areas of tariff and non-tariff measures regarding trade in goods to new areas such as investment measures, service trades and intellectual property. In this connection, international trade is not limited to traditional commodity trade but also includes trade in the factors of production. China's membership in the WTO will be conducive to establishing stable relations in trade, economic and technological cooperation with other countries. It will also greatly improve transparency and consistency in China's trade and investment policies. In the area of agriculture, China's entry into the WTO will improve the environment for the introduction of investment and technologies into agriculture, provide impetus for the optimal allocation of agricultural resources over a larger field and enhance the overall quality and efficiency of China's agricultural economy. Therefore, China's accession to the WTO will bring unprecedented opportunities for external cooperation in agriculture.

- New challenges for external cooperation in agriculture are arising with China's entry into the WTO.

China's entry into the WTO will mean an increasing integration of China into the global economy and liberalization of trade, particularly in agricultural products. As a result, the market for agricultural products will have to be gradually opened up and China will apply the international division of labour to the principle of comparative advantage, and allocate domestic resources accordingly. However, there are a number of factors that will pose grave challenges to China's agricultural industry under the WTO framework. One factor is that there still exists a considerable gap between the current agricultural regime and structure of industry in China and WTO requirements and the qualifications necessary to participate in international competition. The general quality of agricultural products, quality and safety standards are not compatible with the requirements of the international market. Another factor is that the farmers' entry into the market has been poorly organized and the marketing capabilities of agricultural enterprises have been inferior. Moreover, China's agricultural products have limited market channels outside China. All of these factors have combined to become constraints on China's agricultural products really benefiting from their comparative advantages, thereby circumscribing China's ability to utilize the opportunities that the WTO brings for China's near term agricultural development. In addition, the relatively high-level of openness in China's agricultural markets to which China has committed in the WTO negotiations is contrasted with the limited role of the WTO Agreement on Agriculture in opening up world agricultural markets, which in effect have a high level of protection. Therefore, substantial increases in the import of resource-intensive agricultural bulk goods such as grains, cotton and oils in which China does not have advantages will be seen in the immediate term following China's accession to the WTO, whereas the export of labour-intensive products in which China enjoys comparative advantages, such as small category cereals, livestock and horticultural products, will increase only to a limited extent. These developments will bring grave challenges to China's agriculture in the immediate term. There is important work to be done in further strengthening the international cooperation in agriculture to adapt to this new situation by expanding the opening up of agriculture to solve the problems that occur. As a part of this effort, the opportunities that the WTO brings to China, such as foreign investment in agriculture, introduction of technologies, agricultural varieties and management expertise, as well as the opportunity to optimize structurally and upgrade, will be fully exploited to boost the overall competitiveness of China's agricultural industry, on the one hand, and, on the other to actively implement the 'Going Out' strategy encouraging Chinese companies to operate

outside China in agriculture and agricultural products. Clearly, this has raised the requirements and brought new challenges for China's external cooperation in agriculture.

Firstly, after China's entry into the WTO and with the progressive opening up of China's agricultural markets, together with the increased internationalization of agriculture, the relations between China's and the world's agriculture will become closer and closer. At the same time, international friction and disputes will also increase. International treaties, agreements and codes of conduct, combined with the agricultural policies of individual countries will have more and more important impacts on the development of China's agriculture. All of these will require China to strengthen the function of international cooperation in agriculture, in order to strive for a better and more favourable international environment for China's agriculture. Second, following accession to the WTO, China will have to compete internationally according to the principle of comparative advantage. In order to utilize markets and resources both at home and abroad to best effect, China will have to make efforts to improve comprehensive competitive strength in its agriculture and quicken the pace of 'going out'. To this end, the content and scope of China's external cooperation in agriculture will have to be expanded, shifting the objectives from enhancement of agricultural production capabilities to enhancement of comprehensive competitiveness of agriculture. Meanwhile, the previous priority of 'bringing in' (ie introducing foreign investment, technologies, management expertise, etc into China) will be shifted to giving equal weight to both 'bringing in' and 'going out'. Third, China's efforts to learn from foreign experiences, participate in international multilateral negotiations and consultations on agriculture, settle agricultural disputes and provide information services for Chinese agriculture and agricultural products to 'go out' will all demand strengthened research into foreign agriculture and the construction of an information system. The level of investment in the construction of an international agricultural information system will have to be increased to integrate the international agricultural information resources with relevant domestic capabilities. Current multilateral and bilateral information sharing and rapid feedback mechanisms will be reinforced and substantiated. Direct channels for collecting international agricultural information will need to be established. Information analysis and publication efforts will be intensified.

Propositions regarding the strengthening of China's external cooperation and opening up of agriculture

Following entry into the WTO, work on the external cooperation of agriculture should shift from previous efforts to serve the needs of improving agricultural production capabilities to enhancing China's overall agricultural competitiveness, while the past emphasis on 'bringing in' should be shifted to giving equal importance to 'bringing in' and 'going out'. External cooperation in agriculture should concentrate on the core matters of agricultural and rural development. The introduction of foreign advanced agricultural technologies, new breeds of livestock and crop varieties, management expertise, talents and capital should be boosted and the 'going out' of agricultural industry and products be promoted. On the international front, China should participate actively in multilateral and bilateral consultations and other activities in the area of international food and agriculture. All efforts should be made to help gain a favourable international environment for China's agricultural development.

Transformed perceptions and enlarged external cooperation functions are needed to help create a favourable international economic environment for China's agricultural development

China's WTO membership and its progressive opening up of agricultural product markets require the strengthening and improvement of the three key functions of agricultural administration:

- providing effective protection, support and services for agriculture, rural areas and farmers' interests;
- maintaining and regulating the order of agricultural production and markets;
- striving to construct an international environment that is favourable for the development of agriculture in China.

These key functions are common to agricultural administration agencies in most countries worldwide and even more so in countries that have a higher degree of internationalization in their agricultural sector, such as the United States, France and the Netherlands. In the face of the various challenges and opportunities arising from the entry into the WTO, external cooperation needs to be re-conceptualized and given prominence with a view to participating in the improved circulation of the world economy. In order to create a favourable international environment for China's agricultural development, changes and improvements in the mechanism of bilateral cooperation should be made through the existing bilateral working groups, joint committees and mixed committees. While giving full play to the bridging role of working groups and joint committees, the content of cooperation should be adjusted so that emphasis is placed on combining the economic, scientific and trade elements in cooperation programmes in order to pave the way for all-round cooperation in agriculture. In addition, China should participate actively in the negotiations of multilateral international food and agricultural agencies, including the formulation of international standards for agricultural products initiated by the Codex Alimentarius Commission of the United Nations Food and Agriculture Organization and World Health Organization, the Code of Conduct on Prior Informed Consent for Certain Hazardous Chemicals and the revision of International Plant Protection Convention. Effort should be made to join, as soon as possible, the International Animal Health Organization (Office International des Epizooties or OIE) and participate in its activities. In order to gain and build a favourable international environment for the development of China's agricultural economy, China should be well prepared for participation in the new round of agricultural negotiations and work on policy reviews and possible trade dispute resolutions.

Efforts should be made to expand the scale of foreign investment in agriculture while the level and quality of investment utilization should continue to be improved

The task of utilizing foreign investment in agriculture is of outstanding importance in that foreign investment supplements the insufficient supply of domestic capital, facilitates the introduction of foreign advanced technologies, varieties and management expertise, helps the formation of modern agricultural enterprises and quickens the process of agricultural industrialization and trade development. However, the amount of foreign investment in agriculture only accounts for 1.7 per cent of total foreign investment in China, which is proof that a greater effort needs to be made to attract more foreign investment into agriculture through diversified channels and under different arrangements. Both soft and hard environments for foreign investment in agriculture should be improved. Proactive measures should be taken to encourage the use of domestic capital in relation to foreign investment. The developed areas should continue to step up their efforts to introduce foreign investment in the agricultural sector, employing various foreign investment vehicles such as equity joint ventures, contractual joint ventures and wholly foreign-owned enterprises. In the process of introducing foreign investment, a conscious effort should be made to foster large-scale 'leaders' enterprises and to align them with the farmers in the form of 'communities of common interests'. The poorer areas, especially those in the vast mid-western region, should, in addition to utilizing low-interest loans or grant aids for poverty reduction development, take advantage of their resources and the government preferential policies to improve the soft environment for agricultural investment and expand the size of foreign investment in agriculture. All in all, various localities should expand further the channels of foreign investment utilization to promote foreign direct investment. Focal attention should be given to the technological contents of foreign-invested projects while a strong endeavour should be made to introduce foreign equipment, talents, advanced technologies, quality varieties and modern management expertise. The size of foreign-invested projects should be increased as a part of the effort to foster 'leaders' enterprises in order to better promote the industrialised agricultural operations and the export of agricultural products.

Implementation of the 'going out' should be accelerated

'Going out' as a strategy is a natural choice for China's economic development as well as an integral part of the opening-up policy. 'Going out' and 'bringing in' are the two complementary parts of China's opening-up policy. To increase the power and momentum of China's economic growth, China will have to:

- utilize the 'two markets', both domestic and overseas markets, and the 'two kinds of resources', both local and foreign, in its effort to optimize resource allocation;
- actively participate in international competition and cooperation;
- bring into play China's comparative advantages in its effort to achieve mutual convergence and complementarity between the Chinese and the world economies.

In over 20 years of reform and opening up, 'bringing in' has been the mainstay. The practice of such a strategy has proved that 'bringing in' foreign capital, technologies, management expertise and talents is not only wholly necessary, but also highly effective. Without the process of 'bringing in', it would be hard for China to achieve its level of products, technology and management, and 'going out' would have been impossible. Therefore, active implementation of a 'going out' strategy for agriculture and agricultural products will have to be accompanied at the same time by a continued effort to boost the introduction of foreign advanced agricultural technologies, new varieties of crops and livestock, management expertise, talents and capital. In view of the fact that China's agriculture is characterized by small volume exports, a diverse range of export varieties and an overwhelming number of small- to medium-sized operators, green foods should be regarded as a point of breakthrough. In this connection, China should publicize green foods in the international market and promote international cooperation in the area of quality accreditation. China should also take advantage of the applicability of Chinese agricultural technologies in developing countries to pioneer the 'going out' of agricultural technologies. China should purposefully provide facilitation to those areas and enterprises that have necessary conditions to develop trade and economic cooperation. In the external cooperation of agriculture, the export of advantageous products such as horticultural products, fruits and vegetables should be promoted.

Research on foreign agriculture should be strengthened and a foreign agricultural information system should be established to provide public services regarding external cooperation in agriculture

Presently the lack of knowledge about supply and demand situations in foreign agricultural markets, unfamiliarity with trade policies, quality standards for agricultural products and investment environments in foreign countries and lack of clarity about the information needed for the resolution of possible trade disputes are the common problems that hamper different localities in their efforts to develop foreign economic and trade cooperation. Following China's entry into the WTO, it is of paramount importance for China to legislate, improve and adjust agricultural laws, regulations and policy measures with reference to the experiences of other countries. In this context China should intensify its effort to research the WTO rules, foreign agriculture and the countermeasures in relation to China's entry into the WTO. The tracking, collection and transmission of information on the dynamics of agricultural science, technology, economy and trade should be strengthened in order to achieve the objective of information resource sharing. A national-level window of information on economic and trade cooperation in agriculture should be established as soon as possible. Such a window should be able to provide information on both domestic and foreign policies, authoritative forecasts for market development and other important international information. Research into foreign agriculture should be carried out according to priorities, taking into consideration the reform of China's agricultural operating and management regime and the need to improve the overall competitiveness of China's agriculture. Using the existing platform, the sources of international agricultural information should be integrated with relevant domestic capabilities in order to speed up the construction of a foreign agricultural information system. Work on the analysis of foreign agricultural information should be strengthened and the current channels of bilateral agricultural cooperation should be utilized to improve bilateral information sharing and install a rapid feedback mechanism in order to provide effective public services for external cooperation in agriculture.

The Opening-up of the Service Sector in China*

Shi Yonghai, Chairman, China Association of International Trade

After China's accession to the WTO the service sector will be opened up conditionally in several stages in accordance with WTO regulations and the related laws of China.

Telecommunications

- Within the first year after China's accession to WTO, network services (mainly Internet Service Providers) shall be opened up as a first step.
- Starting from the second year after the WTO accession, geographical restrictions will be relaxed gradually on value-added services, such as cellular communication, wireless paging services and Internet.
- Starting from the third year after the accession, cable network and optical cable services will start to open up and there will be no geographical restrictions on value-added services. The tariff restrictions on semiconductors, computers, computer equipment, telecommunications equipment and other high-tech products will be eliminated.
- Starting from the fourth year after the accession, the restrictions on the share of foreign investment in basic telecommunication services will be raised from 25 per cent at the initial stage of accession to 49 per cent. In value-added service areas such as paging, data compression and forwarding, the maximum share of foreign investment will be increased to 50 per cent from 30 per cent in the initial stage of opening-up.
- Starting from the fifth year after the accession, geographical restrictions on the import of pagers and cellular phones as well as the services of the domestic

fixed line network will start to be phased out for complete network services.
- Starting from the sixth year after the accession, cable network and optical cable services will be completely opened up.

Banking

- The geographical restrictions on the renminbi services by foreign banks shall be eliminated. For foreign currency business, there will be no geographic restriction upon accession. For local currency business, the geographic restriction will be phased out as follows:
  - upon accession, Shanghai, Shenzhen, Tianjin and Dalian;
  - within one year after accession, Guangzhou, Zhuhai, Qingdao, Nanjing and Wuhan;
  - within two years after accession, Jinan, Fuzhou, Chengdu and Chongqing;
  - within three years after accession, Kunming, Beijing and Xiamen;
  - within four years after accession, Shantou, Ningbo, Shenyang and Xi'an;
  - within five years after accession, all geographic restrictions will be removed, after which foreign banks will be permitted to conduct renminbi business nationwide.
- The restrictions on renminbi business clients of foreign banks shall be eliminated. For foreign currency business upon accession, foreign financial institutions will be permitted to provide services in China without restriction as to clients. For local currency

---

* This chapter was originally written in Chinese and was translated by Li Yong.

business, within two years after accession, foreign financial institutions will be permitted to provide services to Chinese enterprises. Within five years after accession, foreign financial institutions will be permitted to provide services to all Chinese clients, which means that the renminbi retail business is open to foreign banks. Foreign financial institutions licensed for local currency business in one region of China may service clients in any other region that has been opened for such business. In addition, foreign banks and financial institutions are permitted to provide consumer credit for motor vehicles.

Insurance

- After China's accession to WTO, foreign life insurance companies are permitted to have business establishments only in the form of joint ventures in China and foreign ownership in the joint venture shall not exceed 50 per cent. Within three years after accession, the foreign equity share in a joint venture is allowed to increase to a dominant 51 per cent. However, such a foreign insurance company should have more than 30 years of established experience in a WTO member state with total assets of more than US$5 billion. In addition, the foreign insurance company should have had a representative office in China for two consecutive years.
- Upon approval, the formation of a branch network of an insurance company will be permitted consistent with the phase out of the geographical restrictions.
- After China's accession to WTO, three more cities (Dalian, Shenzhen and Foshan) will be opened up for foreign insurance companies in addition to Shanghai and Guangzhou where foreign insurance services have already been allowed. Within two years after the accession, another ten cities (Beijing, Chengdu, Chongqing, Fuzhou, Suzhou, Xiamen, Ningbo, Shenyang, Wuhan and Tianjin) will be added to the list of areas where foreign insurance companies are allowed to provide services. Within three years after China's accession, geographical restrictions will be completely removed.
- Within two years after China's accession, foreign non-life insurance companies will be permitted to establish wholly-owned subsidiaries in China. Within four years after China's accession, compulsory cession requirements will be removed. Within five years after China's accession, wholly-owned subsidiaries of foreign insurance brokers will be permitted.

- Foreign life insurance companies are permitted to provide individual life insurance services to both foreigners and Chinese citizens after China's accession to the WTO. Within three years after accession, they will be permitted to provide health insurance, group insurance and pension/annuities insurance to foreigners and Chinese.

Security industries

- Upon China's accession to the WTO, joint ventures in security investment fund management will be permitted in China. Within three years after the accession, the foreign equity share in such joint ventures will be permitted to increase to 49 per cent.
- Within three years after China's accession, joint-venture securities companies will be permitted where the foreign equity share does not exceed 33 per cent. They will be permitted to engage in underwriting A shares, B shares and H shares, as well as government and corporate debts and to launch funds.

Audio and video products

- Foreign companies will not be permitted to produce audio and video products in China.
- Without prejudice to China's right to examine the content of audio and video products, contractual joint ventures with Chinese partners to engage in the distribution of audiovisual products, excluding motion pictures, are permitted.
- Upon accession, China will allow the import of up to 20 motion pictures per annum on a revenue-sharing basis. Foreign investors are permitted to construct or renovate cinemas, but the percentage of foreign investment shall not exceed 49 per cent.

Distribution service

- Within three years after China's accession, the restrictions on geographical areas, equity shares, quantities in relation to foreign wholesale services (excluding tobacco and salt) and commission agents' services (excluding tobacco) will be removed. The restriction on the equity share of franchising operations will also be removed within three years after accession.
- Retail joint ventures will be allowed in the five Special Economic Zones (Shenzhen, Zhuhai, Shantou,

Xiamen and Hainan), as well as in Beijing, Shanghai, Tianjin, Guangzhou, Dalian, Qingdao, Zhengzhou and Wuhan. Four joint-venture retail enterprises shall be allowed in Beijing and Shanghai respectively. In each of the other places, no more than two will be permitted. Two among the four joint-venture retail enterprises in Beijing may set up branches in the same city.

- Within five years after China's accession, all restrictions on the field of distribution with foreign involvement will be removed.
- For those chain stores with more than 30 outlets selling products of different types and brands of multiple suppliers, foreign majority ownership is not permitted if such stores distribute grains, cotton, vegetable oils, sugar, books, magazines, pharmaceutical products, pesticides, mulching films, processed oil, fertilizers and other designated products.

Tourism

Travel service agencies

Upon accession, foreign service providers must meet certain qualifications before they can provide services in the form of joint ventures, such as:

- they must be professional tour operators or travel agencies
- annual world-wide turnover must exceed US$40 million
- registered capital not less than 40 million renminbi.

Within three years after accession, the required minimum registered capital for joint venture travel agencies/ tour operators will be reduced to RMB2.5 million and foreign majority ownership in a joint venture will be permitted. Within six years after accession, wholly foreign-owned travel agencies will be permitted in China, and the geographical restrictions and limitations on wholly foreign-owned subsidiaries will be removed.

Hotels

Upon China's accession, foreign investors shall be permitted to hold the majority ownership in joint-venture hotels. Within four years after accession, there will be no restrictions on market access and wholly foreign-owned subsidiaries will be permitted.

Transportation

- For maritime transport services, joint venture fleets are permitted, but the foreign equity share shall be no more than 49 per cent.
- Joint ventures for internal waterway transport, road transport and railway transport are permitted. But there are restrictions on equity shares.
- For aviation services, the foreign service providers are permitted to offer computer reservation services and aircraft repair and maintenance services subject to certain conditions.

The above is a summary of China's commitments to the WTO and its members in terms of the opening of services industries. For the detailed commitments, reference to relevant WTO documents is available at the website (http://www.moftec.gov.cn) of the Ministry of Foreign Trade and Economic Relations, People's Republic of China.

2.6

Foreign Trade Activity and its Administration

Li Yong, Deputy Secretary General, China Association of International Trade

Trade environment

Until now, market access for new entrants to China's foreign trade activities have been strictly controlled. Significant changes have taken place in more than two decades of reform and the foreign trade administration system has gradually been liberalized. Liberalization of foreign trade is mainly manifested in the relaxation of restrictions on import and export trading rights and reduction of import and export licence control. In the past, only a small number of companies and enterprises had legitimate trading rights and a large number of commodities whose import and export were subject to licence control. These control measures created monopolistic advantages for those who had the privileges of trading rights, and barriers to the free flow of import and export.

Relaxation of trading rights

Alongside the progress of economic reform and the opening up drive, economic development has advanced to the point where the present limited trading rights will need to be expanded in order to meet increasing import and export needs. Reform of the foreign trade system has responded to these needs by loosening the reins on trading rights control. As a result, trading rights are no longer the privilege only of professional trading companies (ie companies that used to be under the jurisdiction of the foreign trade and investment authorities), but are also available to other types of companies, such as industrial trading companies, manufacturing enterprises, manufacturing joint ventures (who have automatic trading rights for their exports of own products and imports of necessary equipment and materials), research institutions, private entities and Sino-foreign

joint venture trading companies, although the qualification requirements for some of these have been quite demanding. Even more encouraging is the fact that efforts to liberalize trading rights are ongoing and lowering the threshold to an eventual registration of trading rights (instead of approval) has been set as the final objective of the reformation process. Reform has been accelerated by China's commitment under the WTO to further open up trading rights within a specified period of time. On joining the WTO, China has agreed to grant full trading rights to joint-venture enterprises with minority share foreign investment in 2002 and to majority share foreign-invested joint-ventures in 2003. Within three years of accession, all enterprises in China would be granted full rights to trade.

Phase-out of non-tariff measures

At the same time, effort has also been made to reduce non-tariff measures such as the number of commodities that are subject to import and export licence controls. The reduction of non-tariff barriers was an ongoing process prior to WTO entry; by the end of 2001, for example, quotas and licensing requirements involved only 5 per cent of all imports compared with about 50 per cent little more than a decade ago. From 1 January 2002, the number of commodity categories further dropped from 33 to 12. China has pledged to eliminate the remaining import quota and licence restrictions by 2005 (for details, please refer to Chapter 2.3).

Tariff reduction

In addition to non-tariff measures, China has also committed to reduce the import tariff level. In fact, by

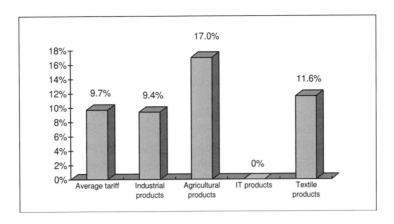

Figure 2.6.1 Average tariff by key categories of products by year 2005

the time it entered the WTO in 2001, the general tariff level had already fallen to an average of 15 per cent. In 2002, the first year of China's WTO accession, the average tariff has been further reduced to 12 per cent and by 2005 it will be reduced to 10 per cent (see Figure 2.6.1).

State trading

However, there are a number of products that are subject to state trading and designated trading. According to China's WTO protocol,

> without prejudice to China's right to regulate trade in a manner consistent with the WTO Agreement, China shall progressively liberalize the availability and scope of the right to trade, so that within three years of accession, all enterprises in China shall have the right to trade in all goods throughout the customs territory of China, except for those goods listed in Annex 2A which continue to be subject to state trading in accordance with this Protocol.

In Annex 2A are two separate lists that specify the types of commodities falling into the scope of state trading: state importation and state exportation (see Tables 2.6.1 and 2.6.2). These commodities are considered essential goods with an important bearing on national security and social stability.

In addition to state trading products are products subject to designated trading, including natural rubber (4 sub-categories), timber (28 sub-categories), plywood (3 sub-categories), wool (9 sub-categories), acrylic (18 sub-categories) and steel (183 sub-categories).

Price controls

While China is committed to allowing prices for traded goods and services in every sector to be determined by market forces, and multi-tier pricing practices for such

goods and services will be eliminated, China still maintains its control over the pricing of some categories of products and services.

Products that are subject to state pricing include tobacco (4 sub-categories) salt (1 category), natural gas (1 category) and pharmaceuticals (40 sub-categories).

Public utilities subject to government prices are gas for civil use, tap water, electricity, heating power and water supplied by irrigation works.

Services subject to state pricing include postal and telecommunication services charges (including postal services charges, national and trans-provincial telecommunication services charges), entrance fees for tourist sites (significant historical relics and natural landscape under protection) and education services charges.

Apart from government priced products and services, there are also products and services to which government guideline pricing will apply. Products that are subject to such guideline pricing include grain (14 sub-categories), vegetable oil (4 sub-categories), processed oil (7 sub-categories), chemical fertilizer (1 category), silkworm cocoons (2 sub-categories) and cotton (1 category). The services that fall into this category are listed in Table 2.6.2.

Types of players in the field

The granting of full trading rights to all enterprises registered in China will take place over time. Within the three-year transitional period, companies that deal in import and export will still need to have appropriate trading rights. Those who do not have rights to trade are not legally permitted to handle import or export contracts directly, although they can contract companies who have trading rights to carry out import or export on their behalf on a commission basis.

Table 2.6.1 Products subject to state importation

Vegetable oil (7 sub-categories)	1. China National Cereals, Oil & Foodstuff Import and Export Co.
	2. China National Native Products and Animal By-products Import & Export Co.
	3. China Resources Co.
	4. China Nam Kwong National Import & Export Co.
	5. China Liangfeng Cereals Import & Export Co.
	6. China Cereals, Oil & Foodstuff Co.(Group)
Sugar (6 sub-categories)	1. China National Cereals, Oil & Foodstuff Import and Export Co.
	2. China Export Commodities Base Construction Co.
	3. China Overseas Trade Co.
	4. China Sugar & Wine Co. (Group)
	5. China Commerce Foreign Trade Co.
Tobacco (6 sub-categories)	China National Tobacco Import & Export Co.
Crude oil (1 category) and Processed oil (7 sub-categories)	1. China National Chemical Import & Export Co.
	2. China International United Petroleum & Chemicals Co.
	3. China National United Oil Co.
	4. Zhuhai Zhenrong Company
Fertilizer	1. China National Chemical Import & Export Co.
	2. China National Agricultural Means of Production Group Co.
Cotton (2 sub-categories)	1. China National Textiles Import & Export Co.
	2. Beijing Jiuda Textiles Group Co.
	3. Tianjing Textiles Industry Supply and Marketing Co.
	4. Shanghai Textiles Raw Materials Co.

Source: Ministry of Foreign Trade and Economic Cooperation, available in detail at www.moftec.gov.cn/table/wto/law05.doc

Table 2.6.2 Products subject to state exportation

Products	State Trading Enterprises
Tea (4 sub-categories)	China National Native Products and Animal By-Products Import & Export Co.
Rice (4 sub-categories)	China National Cereals Oil and Foodstuffs Import & Export Corp.
Corn (3sub-categories)	
Soy bean (5 sub-categories)	Jilin Grain Import & Export Co. Ltd.
Tungsten ore (3 sub-categories)	1. China National Metals and Minerals Import & Export Co.
Ammonium paratungstates (2 sub-categories)	2. China National Non-ferrous Import & Export Co.
Tungstate products (8 sub-categories)	3. China Rare Earth and Metal Group Co.
	4. China National Chemical Import & Export Co.
Coal (5 sub-categories)	1. China National Coal Industry Import & Export Co.
	2. China National Metals and Minerals Import & Export Co.
	3. Shanxi Coal Import & Export Group Co.
	4. Shenhua Group Ltd.
Crude oil (1category)	1. China National Chemical Import & Export Co.
Processed oil (13 sub-categories)	2. China International United Petroleum & Chemicals Co.
	3. China National United Oil Co.
Silk (13 sub-categories)	China National Silk Import & Export Co.
Unbleached silk (4 sub-categories)	
Cotton (2 sub-categories)	1. China National Textiles Import & Export Co.
Cotton yarn (44 sub-categories)	2. Qingdao Textiles United Import & Export Co.
Woven cotton fabrics (13 sub-categories)	3. Beijing No.2 Cotton Mill
	4. Beijing No.3 Cotton Mill
	5. Tianjin No.1 Cotton Mill

Table 2.6.2 (Contd)

Products	State Trading Enterprises
	6. Shanghai Shenda Co. Ltd
	7. Shanghai Huashen Textiles and Dying Co. (Group)
	8. Dalian Huanqiu Textiles Group Co.
	9. Shijiazhuang Changshan Textiles Group
	10. Luoyang Cotton Mill, Henan Province
	11. Songyue Textiles Industry Group, Henan Province
	12. Dezhou Cotton Mill
	13. Wuxi No.1 Cotton Mill
	14. Puxin Textiles Mill, Hubei Province
	15. Northwest No.1 Cotton Mill
	16. Chengdu Jiuxing Textiles Group Co.
	17. Suzhou Sulun Textiles Joint Company (Group)
	18. Northwest No.7 Cotton Mill
	19. Xiangmian Group Co., Hubei Province
	20. Handan Lihua Textiles Group Co.
	21. Xinjiang Textiles Industry Co. (Group)
	22. Anqing Textiles Mill
	23. Jinan No.2 Cotton Mill
	24. Tianjin No.2 Cotton Mill
	25. Jinhua Textiles Mill, Shanxi Province
	26. Jinwei Group Co., Zhejiang Province
	27. Northwest No.5 Cotton Mill
	28. Baoding No.1 Cotton Mill
	29. Liaoyang Textiles Mill
	30. Changchun Textiles Mill
	31. Huaxin Cotton Mill, Henan Province
	32. Baotou Textiles Mill
	33. Ninbo Hefeng Textiles Group Co.
	34. Northwest No.4 Cotton Mill
	35. Xinjiang Shihezi Bayi Cotton Mill
Antimony ores (2 sub-categories)	1. China National Metals and Minerals Import & Export Co.
Antimony oxide (1 category)	2. China National Non-ferrous Import & Export Co.
Antimony products (3 sub-categories)	3. China Rare Earth and Metal Group Co.
Silver (3 sub-categories)	1. China Banknote Printing and Minting Corporation
	2. China Copper Lead Zinc Group

Source: Ministry of Foreign Trade and Economic Cooperation, available in detail at www.moftec.gov.cn/table/wto/law06.doc

Developing an understanding of the various types of business structure in China is important to firms looking for import/export opportunities in this market, and can be critical to the success or otherwise of a foreign company's China business plan. The following seeks to outline the kinds of companies that foreign companies may encounter.

National foreign trade companies

National foreign trade companies are companies that are set up at the national level and were once affiliated with government departments. At the beginning of China's economic reform and opening up, foreign trade was virtually monopolised by 12 national foreign trade corporations under the then Ministry of Foreign Trade (now the Ministry of Foreign Trade and Economic Cooperation). With the deepening economic reform, other ministries governing different industries successively set up their own foreign trade functions, specializing in their particular product fields and known as 'industrial foreign trade companies.' Further government reform has resulted in separation of those national

Table 2.6.3 Services subject to government guideline pricing

Service	Notes
Transport services charges	Including rail transport of both passenger and freight, air transport of freight, port services and pipeline transport.
Professional services charges	Including architectural and engineering services, legal services, assets assessment services, authentication, arbitration, notarization and inspection.
Charges for commission agents' services	Including commission for trademarks, advertisement taxation and bidding agents.
Charges for settlement, clearing and transmission services of banks	Including settlement, clearing and transmission services of the RMB, transaction fees and seat charges of national securities exchanges, as well as seat charges for China Foreign Exchange Centre
Selling price and renting fee of residential apartments	
Health related services	

Source: Ministry of Foreign Trade and Economic Co-operation, available in detail at www.moftec.gov.cn/table/wto/law09.doc

companies from their government affiliation and they have now become independent in their decision-making.

Being state-owned in nature, some have been publicly listed on the stock market. Although their role has been eroded by an increasing number of emerging companies that have acquired trading rights, they still enjoy the advantages of being close to central government decision-making and often act as the purchasing or selling agents of the government in the trade of products of national importance. Under the WTO arrangements, many of these companies are designated companies for products subject to state trading. On those non-state designated products (both import and export), they are now competing on most fronts with other forms of trading entities. Trading companies with 'China' or 'China National' in their business names are normally national (or state-level) foreign trade companies.

Provincial foreign trade companies

Provincial foreign trade companies were once subsidiaries of national foreign trade companies under the old foreign trade system. Even those companies set up by industrial ministries also had local representatives. Between 1988 and 1990, those provincial subsidiaries became independent of their national headquarters as part of government efforts to reform the foreign trade system. These companies have since assumed a leading role in the development of foreign trade in their respective localities.

Foreign trade companies at lower administrative level

Also at the city level are foreign trade companies with rights to trade internationally. They undertake the tasks of generating export earnings and act as import agents for both local government purchase and orders by local enterprises. At the county level, the foreign trade companies more often perform the role of export suppliers than independent import or export operators.

Large industrial enterprises with trading rights

In the late 1980s, the Chinese government decided to grant large state-owned enterprises trading rights limited to the export of their own products and import of products needed for their production. Many of these large enterprises have now become conglomerates or group companies under which are the trading functions of separate corporate entities. Some of those trading functions are no longer limited to import and export related to production, but dealing with a wider range of products in their import and export activities.

Foreign-invested enterprises

Foreign-invested enterprises include equity joint ventures, contractual joint ventures and wholly foreign-owned enterprises. At present, these foreign-invested enterprises are only allowed to import what is needed in their production and export what they produce. Three years after China's WTO accession, they will be permitted to deal in other products.

Research institutions

To encourage the export of locally developed technologies and development of local R & D capabilities, large research institutions that meet certain qualification requirements will be permitted to have trading rights, which were limited to their research-related imports and exports, but now are permitted to export products of not their own production.

Private enterprises

With the development of the private sector, many private enterprises have emerged as leading sources of export supply. In the late 1990s, the government decided to grant trading rights to private enterprises, again limited to imports and exports related to their production.

The impact of the WTO on China's foreign trade activities

The above categories of entities with various levels of trading rights constitute the body of China's exporting task force. Foreign-invested enterprises are becoming key contributors to China's export earnings and have held around a 50 per cent share in China's total export in recent years. Foreign trade companies, both at the national level and lower levels, are being disadvantaged by manufacturing enterprises with the trading rights for not having their own production capabilities. They are competing on the export resources from those who have not yet obtained the rights to trade.

The impact on patterns of foreign trade activities

With the situation described above, the advantages of traditional foreign trade companies are limited to light industrial products, textile products, bulk raw materials, crude oil and petrochemical products and those that fall under the category of monopolistic trading. These products are characterized either by high levels of concentration, such as crude oil and petrochemicals, or extreme fragmentation such as textiles and light industrial products.

Recent trends have shown a weakening in the role of professional foreign trade companies. At the same time, foreign-invested enterprises are gaining momentum with a share in the total trade volume of 49 per cent. The opening of trading rights to more companies will naturally lead to increased competition for the export of products from highly fragmented industries, one conse-

quence of which would be a reduction in the profitability of professional trading companies. Higher or stable profitability can only be achieved from the export of products of monopolistic trading. Obviously, such monopolistic trading rights are not available to every foreign trade company. As a result, larger foreign trade companies will be forced to move horizontally to invest in the production of products they have been exporting and vertically engage in the manufacturing of what they perceive will have export potential. Those smaller foreign trade companies will have to shift their focus on general trading to differentiated product trading in order to survive. The role of foreign trade companies as intermediaries of trade between China and the outside world will diminish.

Impact on the distribution of imported products

Together with the elimination of the restrictions on full trading rights, China has committed to opening up distribution rights to foreign participants. Before the WTO accession, foreign companies were not permitted to distribute their products (except those produced in China), nor were they allowed to own distribution establishments, wholesale channels or even warehousing network. The imports would have to be handled by foreign trade companies and the distribution was highly dependent on the importing foreign trade companies or distributor/wholesaler under separate arrangements. This has considerably weakened the competitiveness of imported products and efficiency of distribution. China's commitments to the WTO on the opening of the distribution sector will improve the situation. Foreign exporters will no longer be 'air-locked' out of the Chinese market and import activities will be more of an inherent part of distribution and under WTO commitments foreign exporters will be able to have hands-on control. Chinese foreign trade companies will face the situation of once-high import profitability falling as a result of the lifting of restrictions on foreign participation in the distribution process. Large foreign trade companies may move down the supply chain to expand their own distribution capabilities. In the distribution sector, they will have to meet competition from international distributors and retailers.

Impact on the flow of import and export

The impact of tariff reduction on China's foreign trade as a whole is twofold. On the import side, reductions in the average tariff level will lead to increased inflow of imports. Imports will put competitive pressure on those industries that are less efficient, less economical and technologically backward. The industries suffering the greatest impact will include agriculture, automobiles, petrochemicals, equipment manufacturing, pharmaceuticals and steel. For some imports, however, the effective rates of tariff have been significantly lower than official average rate of 15 per cent at the time of accession as a result of various tariff reductions, exemptions, rebates and evasions. In 1997, for example, the total tariff revenue was RMB35.14 billion, about US$4.28 billion. The total import value in the same year was US$142.36 billion. The effective tariff rate in 1997 was only 4 per cent. Therefore, the impact of tariff reductions on certain products is expected to be minimal. On the export side, the lowering of import tariffs will greatly improve the competitiveness of those export products that use imported materials. For example, the import tariff on chemical fibre will be reduced from the current 18 per cent to around 6 per cent by 2005. China's textile exports will benefit from the tariff reduction.

Conclusion

After China's WTO accession, most of the non-tariff barriers that used to provide protective shelter for domestic industries and foreign trade companies will be removed. Also removed are the subsidies for the purpose of encouraging exports. China's market will be opened up for foreign participation to a much greater extent, thereby offering significant market possibilities for foreign businesses to do business with China.

Generally, the pattern of China's foreign trade will be reshuffled and foreign trade companies will need to reposition themselves under the regime of the WTO. In the battlefield of imports, foreign businesses will be engaged in head-on competition with the Chinese enterprises in China and it is too early to conclude who will win.

In terms of exports, more Chinese companies will join the team of exporters and the role played by foreign trade companies as intermediaries will weaken as a result. Horizontal or vertical integration is likely to take place as alternative strategic options for foreign trade companies. Participation of foreign players in the field of foreign trade will lead to competition for export resources and foreign markets.

The Changing Role of China's State-owned Foreign Trade Enterprises*

Xuekun Wang, Director, Division of Economic Analysis, Department of Policy Research,
Ministry of Foreign Trade and Economic Cooperation

China's economy is currently navigating a course of strategic restructuring. Its entry into the World Trade Organization(WTO) has elevated China onto a new stage in its reform and opening policy. In view of these new circumstances the role of Chinese state foreign trade enterprises (SFTEs) has to be radically transformed in order to meet the demand for further development.

The SFTEs have made tremendous contributions to the vitality of China's foreign-related economy and trade

Since the adoption of the reform and open-door policy, Chinese foreign trade has experienced a remarkable growth in which the SFTEs have played a crucial role. In 1980 China's foreign trade value stood at US$38.14 billion with exports at US$18.12 billion and imports at US$20.04 billion. The export value in that year ranked 26th in the world. At that time virtually all foreign trade activities were conducted by SFTEs. In 2001 China's foreign trade value surged to US$509.77 billion with exports at US$266.15 billion and imports at US$243.61 billion. Its position reached sixth in the world in terms of both trade value and export value. Among these, SFTEs achieved an export value of US$113.23 billion and import value of US$103.55 billion. With regard to the export of general commodities in particular, SFTEs occupied a share above 60 per cent.

In the field of foreign economic cooperation, such as contract engineering projects and labour export, SFTEs still maintains a predominant position. By the end of 2001 China had committed to a total contract value of US$127.86 billion in its foreign economic cooperation projects, of which US$93.07 billion has been completed. In the meantime 6,610 enterprises for overseas direct investment had been approved with an outflow valued at US$8.36 billion.

To accelerate the reforms of SFTEs is an important step for the development of China's foreign-related economy and trade

Since the introduction of a socialistic market economy, China has been determined in achieving its goal of the foreign economic and trade system – consistent policy, equal competition, self-responsibility and open operation. Naturally the reform and strengthening of SFTEs became a strategic part in this endeavour. In September 1999 the central government reaffirmed its resolve for strategic adjustment in its national economic structure and emphasized the acceleration of reform and strengthening of the state-owned enterprises (SOEs). Regarding foreign trade it was made clear that SFTEs would have to meet the requirements of the modern enterprise system and speed up the system innovation process. Through reformation, reorganization and transformation, SFTEs expedited the pace of renovating their internal operation mechanism and pursued resource optimization. As a result they have basically attained the goal of transforming into independent operations with self-responsibility, self-development and self-discipline, thereby assuming the role of market players. SFTEs

* This chapter was originally written in Chinese and translated by Liu Baocheng, Professor, University of International Business and Economics.

have also engaged in various types of equity restructuring. Some have conducted employee buyout (EBO), and an increasing number of SFTEs are turning into public companies either inside or outside China. At present there are 20 SFTEs that have been listed on the stock exchanges in Shanghai and Shenzhen. As a result their internal management mechanism and operations began to come into alignment with the norms of modern enterprises. The road for the reforms of SFTEs is still paved with enormous tasks, and the future of China's foreign trade hinges heavily on the outcome of the reforms.

Further relaxation on trading rights

In 1978 there were only a dozen specialized companies that were engaged in foreign trade activities. In 1986 this number rose to over 1,200. In 1996 the number of companies vested with foreign trading rights surged to over 12,000, including over 5,000 which were specialized trading houses. Soon after, more and more production-based enterprises, research institutions, collective and private firms were granted permits to import and export. The ban on joint ventures to engage in foreign trade was lifted. The foreign trading rights are changing from an approval system to a registration system. By the end of 2001, 38,000 companies of various business lines and ownership structures were granted import and export trading rights.

The core of SFTE reform is to solve the problems in the operating mechanism

The problems plaguing SFTEs are multifold, among the most outstanding of which are: excessive government involvement, singular equity ownership, inadequate corporate governance, shortage of motivation, insufficient regulation and oversight. The modern enterprise system is the irreversible therapy to further reform of SFTEs. It is imperative for large and mid-sized SOEs to adopt proper corporate governance in order to take on the role of market players. The aim is to usher in a system with clear equity structure, specific rights and responsibilities, separation of government and enterprises as well as scientific management. Increased government support will be given to small and mid-sized SFTEs on a selective basis. A certain number will be chosen to launch the reform programme which includes reorganization, combination, acquisition, merger, leasing, contract operation, equity dispersion and displacement. These measures will be instrumental

to vitalize and substantially improve their performance. SFTEs should strengthen internal management, consolidate business portfolios and take full advantage of their business categories. Financial management, particularly capital management and investment, should be further strengthened. A collective approval system is one of the important solutions to combat faltering investment decisions.

Sorting out of historical problems is the prerequisite for further development

Many SFTEs are ridden with debts and a redundant workforce. These constitute a bottleneck in the way of enterprise reforms. According to statistics from the Ministry of Finance during the period when the initial reform of contract responsibility system was experimented on between 1988 and 1990, SFTEs were burdened with a debt of 9.89 billion renminbi. Coupled with other operating losses due to government directives, the accumulated debts for SFTEs topped 5.50 billion renminbi by the end of 1988, and their asset and liability ratio reached a low of 88.4 per cent. In 1988 alone 60.5 per cent of SFTEs across the country sustained an overall loss of 6.14 billion renminbi. Some of the debt burden resulted from the poor performance of SFTEs and some was caused by government policy disorientation. As a result it exacerbated the balance of debt and liability and weakened the competitiveness of SFTEs, thus adding to the difficulties of enterprise reform.

The state has increased its effort to offset the bad debts in the SOEs' reform process. Special attention has been given to the priority industries and businesses and the debt burden of a group of firms was resolved. In 2001 the state began to introduce the 'equity for debt' programme which alleviated some of the debt-ridden firms with promising products. Because of the so-called peculiarity of SFTEs, however, little has been achieved in their debt alleviation. The growth of some SFTEs has been undermined by their debt burden, and some stalling SFTEs will remain on the waiting list for bankruptcy.

To promote the reform and development of SFTEs through foreign investment

Encouraging and supporting SFTEs to devise various means to absorb foreign investment, and developing and bolstering the state economy are effective ways to revitalize the non-performing state assets and strengthen the control of state economy. The inflow of foreign investment, capital, advanced technology and management expertise is, therefore, an indispensable element. In the process of SOEs' reforms and continuous opening-up to the outside world, the state will permit the concession of certain assets to foreign parties by SFTEs. Restrictions over equity percentage to be held by foreign parties will be alleviated in identified industries. Various forms of participation by foreign investors are encouraged in the reorganization and restructuring of SOEs. These measures are believed to be important vehicles in pushing forward the transformation of SFTEs and improving their performance.

To promote the 'stepping out' strategy for SFTEs through offshore contract manufacturing

Offshore contract manufacturing (OCM) is an effective means to spur the reform and growth of SFTEs. At present over 80 SFTEs have obtained such licences to engage in OCM. The state has mapped out favourable measures in capital financing, taxation, foreign exchange and labour expatriation in support of these activities. Resourceful large and mid-sized SOEs are given priority to set up subsidiaries overseas to extract their market potential.

New environment for SFTEs after China's entry into the WTO

China's commitments to the WTO

Commitment over foreign trading rights
China is implementing an approval system for foreign trading licences. China has pledged, within the next three years after China's WTO entry, to gradually reduce the registered capital requirement over its applicants and speed up its approval process. China will also expand the foreign trade business scope for foreign invested enterprises (FIEs). After three years of its WTO entry, China will phase out its approval system and all Chinese enterprises will be eligible for foreign trading rights upon registration.

The system of state foreign trade
After entry into the WTO, China will continue the state system regarding the import of those commodities that are fundamental to its national economy. The eight big-ticket commodities, ie grain, cotton, vegetable oils, sugar, crude oil, refined oils, chemical fertilizers and tobacco, will still be retained in the hands of a few SFTEs appointed by the government. In the meantime

a certain portion will be set aside for non-SFTEs with a quantity restriction. The licensing restrictions for vegetable oils (soybean oil, palm oil and rapeseed oil, etc) will be lifted to enable free competition by 2006.

Tariff-rate quotas
Tariff-rate quotas are simply an opportunity for market access instead of an obligation to import. The size of import will be left to the discretion of the importing country. After WTO entry China will continue the tariff-rate quotas over those agricultural products such as wheat, corn, rice, cotton, sugar, soybean oil, palm oil, rapeseed oil and wool, as well as industrial products like chemical fertilizers and wool tops. The quantity of tariff-rate quotas, the rates of tariff within and without quotas, the percentage allocated to non-SFTEs and the implementation schedule have been specified. While the products under tariff-rate quotas are subject to the management of SFTEs, a certain portion is carved out to benefit the non-SFTEs.

In light of China's WTO commitments, therefore, SFTEs will have to face the challenges from both fronts. On the one hand, domestic competition will be intensified as a result of the shift from the foreign trade approval system to a registration system. Their disadvantages in management style, financial sources and operating cost will be further exposed. On the other hand, their monopolistic position in import quota allocation over the key commodities will be slackened when more private and FIEs earn their legitimacy. For those items (imports in particular) subject to state operation, however, SFTEs will continue to play a dominant role for some time to come. For example, 90 per cent of grain, 10 per cent of vegetable oils (which has been reduced from 34 per cent), 70 per cent of sugar and 33 per cent of cotton will still be vested in the hands of SFTEs.

SFTEs will face fierce competition over human talents

Relatively speaking, fixed assets are insignificant for foreign trade firms. Much of their success depends on the availability of the right people and their corporate reputation. In foreign trade firms only a small number of people are responsible for the bulk of business revenue and profit. The core competence of the SFTEs is generally based on their workforce talents that are specialized in management, trade practices, finance, foreign languages, laws, negotiation and market intelligence. As more and more different kinds of enterprises such as foreign-invested, shareholding, private and production based firms come into the field of foreign trade, their competitive advantage in management mechanism, financial flexibility and products becomes more visible. The salaries, other incentive packages and job satisfaction offered by these firms will entice more human talents from the uncompetitive SFTEs which are still impeded by their system and other burdens carried over time. Rivalry over human talents is the toughest challenge that SFTEs will encounter. Loss of talents means loss of market, and eventually, the capability for the survival of SFTEs. In order to maintain their competitiveness and momentum for expansion, SFTEs are left with no choice but to expedite their reform process, dismantle barriers and invigorate their management mechanism so as to retain and attract more expertise into their talent pool.

Conclusion

In conclusion, a flurry of changes will occur amongst the market players in China's foreign trade which represents one of the competitive sectors of the national economy. In compliance with the underlying principle of non-discrimination, SFTEs will be on an equal footing to compete with private firms and FIEs. Some SFTEs will be able to respond to the challenge through successful reorganization and restructuring. Some will rely on licences for the import and export of key commodities designated by the government. The rest of the SFTEs who are unable to achieve the necessary improvements in efficiency and productivity will be left behind.

China's Tariff Regime after WTO Accession*

Wu Naiwen, Vice Chairman, China Customs Research Society

China's accession to the WTO symbolizes a new phase of China's opening up. It has an important bearing on improving China's business and investment environment, and will bring about profound changes and impacts on China's foreign trade and economic cooperation. This article provides a brief introduction to China's tariff regime and tariff administration.

The tariff is an important policy measure that the WTO allows its members to use for the protection of their domestic industries. Compared with various other measures, the tariff has a high degree of transparency in discerning the level of protection, and therefore enables trade competition to take place on a clearer, fairer and foreseeable basis. For this reason the WTO holds that its members should use the tariff as the only means of protection. At the same time, the WTO requires that its members effectively reduce tariff and other trade barriers through mutually beneficial arrangements in order to eliminate discrimination in international trade, and thereby contribute to the realization of the common goal of development.

The 15 years of China's negotiations for the resumption of its status at GATT and subsequently its joining of the WTO have been a period in which China's socialist market economy was established and reforms and opening up were accelerated towards such a market economy. The rules of the WTO have been followed in carrying out a series of reforms. The tariff rate has been voluntarily lowered numerous times during this process. The arithmetic average of the tariff rate has been reduced from 43.2 per cent in 1992 to 15.3 per cent in 2001. At the time of China's WTO accession, the Chinese government made further reductions of previ-

ously voluntary tariff cuts. The commitment is that the general tariff level will be progressively lowered from 15.3 per cent in 2001 to about 10 per cent in 2005. Specifically, the tariff for manufactured products will be reduced from 14.8 per cent to 9.1 per cent while that for agricultural products will be lowered from 18.8 per cent to 15.3 per cent. Of the tariff items 98 per cent will be implemented by 2005 while four tariff items will not be implemented until 2010. During this period of tariff reduction, each of the tariff lines is bound by an annual tariff rate. China automatically entered into the Information Technology Agreement (ITA) at the time of WTO accession with the result that all products under ITA will enjoy a zero tariff by 2005 according to the schedule of concessions on tariff reductions. The tariff on exports is limited to 84 tariff headings such as lead, tin and copper, with the highest rate being 40 per cent.

After China's accession to the WTO, the Chinese government has been seriously performing its commitments regarding tariff reductions. The tariff schedule as of January 2002 has the following characteristics:

- The general level of tariff has decreased. The arithmetic average of the tariff rate is down from 15.3 per cent to 12 per cent, which is a reduction of 21.6 per cent.
- The tariff reduction affects a wide range of products. Among the 7,316 tariff items, the rates for 5,332 have been cut by varying amounts. This has effectively covered 73 per cent of all tariff items. The average rate of tariff for industrial products is now 11.6 per cent, while that for agricultural products (including aquatic products) is 15.6 per cent. After

---

* This chapter was originally written in Chinese and translated by Li Yong.

the reduction, the average tariff rates for the following products are:

- agricultural products (excluding aquatic products) 15.8 per cent;
- aquatic products 14.3 per cent;
- crude and processed oil 6.1 per cent;
- timber, paper and their products 8.9 per cent;
- textiles and garments 17.6 per cent;
- chemical products 7.9 per cent;
- communications vehicles 17.4 per cent;
- machinery 9.6 per cent;
- electronic products 10.7 per cent.

● The reductions on high tariff commodities are substantial. Examples of such reductions include: polypropylene from 16 per cent to 10 per cent, ceramic sanitary wares from 45 per cent to 27.5 per cent, large cylinder capacity sedan cars from 80 per cent to 50.7 per cent, and small cylinder capacity sedan cars from 70 per cent to 43.8 per cent.

● The terms of the ITA have been implemented. The average tariff rates for 251 items of IT products have been reduced from 12.5 per cent to 3.4 per cent. In fact, a zero tariff rate has already been applied to 122 items of IT products. The tariff revenue in the period from January to June 2002 has declined by 25.6 per cent compared with the corresponding period of 2001.

Customs valuation is an important link in the chain of correct tariff calculation and levy. As provided in the WTO Agreement on Customs Valuation, the customs value is the actual transaction value of the imported goods, which is, in other words, the price actually paid in the normal trade process under the condition of full competition. However, the invoice of a transaction may not truthfully reflect the 'payable or paid price' and, therefore, the import value needs to be adjusted, namely by means of a re-assessment by customs valuation. The Agreement on Customs Valuation has stipulated specific methods of valuation on the basis of different facts it has established in determining the declared value. The purpose of this process is to establish a fair, uniform and neutral system for the valuation of goods for customs purposes and to prevent the use of arbitrary or fictitious

customs values. China has committed that, upon accession, it will fully apply the Customs Valuation Agreement. Initially China amended the principles regarding customs valuation in the *Customs Law* and the *Regulations on Import and Export Duties* in order to comply with the WTO Agreement on Customs Valuation from a legal perspective. Major changes have been made to the specific methods of valuation practices. In exercising customs valuation, the key point, which is also a difficult point, is the countermeasures against price cheaters. However, with the gradual improvement in the environment of law enforcement by China Customs and increasing awareness of enterprises to abide by the laws, we believe that more targeted anti-price-cheater measures will be taken by China Customs to crack down effectively on price-cheating conduct, which will reduce the negative impact to a minimum following the implementation of the WTO Agreement on Customs Valuation.

Transparency and consistency are the basic principles of the WTO. China Customs will implement a fair and uniform tariff policy within its tariff territory in compliance with the principle of non-discrimination. Laws and regulations that are inconsistent with the rules of the WTO will be rectified. For example, the preferential tariff measures for sedan cars and video cameras in relation to local content requirements have been abolished. Those laws and regulations that will continue to be implemented will be publicly published. In the process of progressively lowering the tariff, tariff reduction and exemption policies will be cleared up. A mechanism for the appeal of tariff disputes and reconsideration will be established. All of these will promote a standardized, fair, transparent and highly-efficient Customs administration and tariff levy.

The tariff regime and its administration is an important policy measure of a country. China's implementation of tariff concessions upon its WTO accession will benefit China's efforts to establish a socialist market economy and to restructure its industrial structure, while at the same time offer new opportunities for the economic and trade cooperation between China and other countries in the world.

Import and Export Financing in China*

Export–Import Bank of China

China's import and export financing system

After more than two decades of reform and open-door policy, a complete trade system and finance system have basically taken shape. The two systems have been integrated into a reciprocal cycle – the trade system has expanded China's foreign trade, and the continuous increase of foreign trade in return has spurred the completion of the country's import and export finance system.

The major players of China's import and export financing

The major financial players in import and export finance comprise two segments in China: banking institutions and insurance institutions.

Banking institutions
In China, banks can devise various financial vehicles to provide many kinds of trade financing services to firms that meet their qualification standards. The major players in the banking industry comprise many banks with different functions. There are three policy banks, four solely state-owned banks, 10 small and mid-sized shareholding commercial banks, 100 small and mid-sized shareholding city commercial banks, and 191 foreign financial institutions. All of these are under the auspices of the central bank – People's Bank of China. More specifically:

- The Export–Import Bank of China (Eximbank) is the only policy-oriented bank;

- Bank of China, Construction Bank of China and Agriculture Bank of China are solely state-owned;
- Bank of Communication, Everbright Bank, CITIC Enterprise Bank, Huaxia Bank, Minsheng Bank, Merchant Bank, Shenzhen Development Bank, Guangdong Development Bank, Shanghai Pudong Development Bank and Fujian Xingye Bank are shareholding commercial banks.

Insurance institutions
The major Chinese insurance institutions related to foreign trade are Export Credit Insurance Company of China and People's Insurance Company of China.

Financing tools in import and export

Banking services
Among the various foreign trade financing services available, the export credit funded by the government is provided by Eximbank, whereas general commercial loans are provided by commercial banks. Their businesses cover:

- export seller's credit, export buyer's credit, forfeiting, factoring, discounting, project financing, syndicated loans and offshore construction loans;
- issuance, acceptance, negotiation and confirmation of letters of credit, bank guarantees, export lending, packing credit, import lending, delivery guarantee, import credit line service and entrusted collection.

In addition, the Eximbank also offers countermeasures against foreign exchange exposure, which include the

---

* This chapter was originally written in Chinese and was translated by Liu Baocheng, Professor, University of International Business and Economics.

forward contracts and other derivatives like currency and rate options, hedging, swapping, etc.

Insurance services

The Export Credit Insurance Company of China and People's Insurance Company of China provide insurance coverage over the following:

- short-term export credit;
- long and mid-term export credit;
- political risk for Chinese overseas investment;
- political risk for foreign investment in China;
- import and export cargo transportation;
- seaborne vessels;
- others.

Eximbank and China's foreign trade

Mission and organization of Eximbank

Eximbank was founded in 1994. It is an exclusively state-owned, policy-oriented bank under the direct leadership of the State Council. Its primary responsibility is to implement industrial, financial and trade policies set forth by the state. It provides policy-oriented financial support to the export of capital goods such as mechanical and electronic products, high-tech products and complete sets of equipment. It also offers other financial assistance to offshore engineering projects and overseas investment. It facilitates other types of international economic and technological cooperation and exchange.

Eximbank is headquartered in Beijing. At home it has two subsidiaries (in Beijing and Shanghai) and eight representative offices in major cities (Dalian, Qingdao, Xi'an, Nanjing, Chengdu, Wuhan, Fuzhou and Guangzhou). Outside China, Eximbank has one representative office in Cote D'Ivoire and another one in South Africa. In 2002 it set up another subsidiary in Shenzhen and an additional office in Harbin.

Business development and the role of Eximbank

As a state policy-oriented financial institution dedicated to China's export promotion, Eximbank follows closely its articles of association approved by the State Council since its opening on 1 July 1994. It has steadily built up an extensive business portfolio to include export seller's credit, export credit insurance, overseas guarantee, export buyer's credit, etc. Since 1995 the bank has

undertaken foreign government concessionary loans, foreign favourable loans and foreign trade development loans funded by the central government. Eximbank also provides other overseas investment support products, such as those in support of offshore contract manufacturing, overseas engineering projects, and has put together a relatively complete service package through its policy-oriented financial service network. At the end of 2001 the State Council decided to transfer the entire export credit insurance business to the newly established Export Credit Insurance Company of China.

By the end of June 2002 Eximbank had accumulated loans totaling close to 200 billion renminbi. Its export financing for mechanical, electronic, high-tech products and complete sets of equipment totaled over US$80 billion. Its market covers 31 provinces, cities and autonomous regions in China, and export markets supported by the bank extend to 85 countries globally. Hence Eximbank plays an increasingly important role in bolstering China's national economy in line with the 'stepping out' strategy.

The major lines of Eximbank

The business lines of Eximbank primarily include: export credit (seller's credit and buyer's credit), overseas guarantees, foreign favourable loans and foreign government concessionary loans.

Export seller's credit is the financial service provided to Chinese exporters which enables exporters to be in a position to accept deferred payment by foreign importers. This includes five different types of arrangement: project loans, short and mid-term credit lines, overseas engineering project loans, offshore contract manufacturing loans and overseas investment loans.

Export buyer's credit refers to the long and mid-term loans in favour of foreign borrowers. Its purpose is to enable foreign importers to be in a position to offer upfront payment to Chinese exporters. This is an option in support of China's exports of goods and technology services.

Overseas guarantees denote the promise to pay offered to overseas creditors or beneficiaries in the form of a letter of guarantee. In the event that the debtor fails to honour its commitment to pay under contract stipulations, the bank will undertake the payment responsibility specified in the letter of guarantee. Such guarantees include such items as borrowing, tendering, contract performance and contract deposit. They cover areas such as the export of mechanical and electronic products, high-tech products and complete sets of equipment, offshore engineering projects, international tenders by domestic financial organizations and foreign government loans.

Foreign favourable loans are long- and mid-term low-interest loans offered to other developing countries by the Chinese government in the nature of foreign aid. Beneficiaries of this type of loan are Chinese and foreign firms who are able to construct production facilities in the designated countries. These facilities must demonstrate the prospect of economic return and the capability to pay back. Such loans can also be granted for the construction of infrastructures and social welfare projects which demonstrate the capability to pay back. Eximbank is the only bank to underwrite this type of loan.

Foreign government concessionary loans are those favourable loans and mixed loans offered by foreign governments to the Chinese government. Eximbank acts as an agent under the mandate of the Chinese Ministry of Finance to dispense these loans. Mixed loans are a combination of favourable loans offered by foreign governments and commercial loans offered by foreign banks. Eximbank is the primary concessionary bank for the loans offered by foreign governments.

Among all the business lines mentioned above, export financing constitutes the most important part of Eximbank's business. In practice it generally requires a 15 per cent down payment by the foreign importer, with the balance of 85 per cent being undertaken by Eximbank in the form of an export credit.

Sources of finance for Eximbank and its world credit rating

Renminbi business

According to its articles of association, besides its capital reserves, Eximbank raises credit capital through the issuance of financial bonds in China. In the event of a shortage of reserve funds, provisional loans can be applied for from the People's Bank of China, or short-term funds can be borrowed in the inter-bank market. By the end of June 2002 Eximbank had raised over 100 billion renminbi through 19 rounds of financial bonds. Long-term bonds were issued through interest rate difference bidding and short-term bonds were raised through a combination of interest rate difference bidding and price bidding. At present capital operations are also procured through interbank credit transfers, transactions of national bonds and national bonds buybacks.

Foreign exchange business

Except for the reserve fund the foreign exchange capital of Eximbank is primarily raised in the financial markets at home and abroad. In July 1996 and October 1999 the bank issued *bushi* bonds of 20 billion yen in Japan and US$200 million debenture bonds in the European financial market. In the meantime the bank also conducted interbank short-term capital financing. Its capital operations include inter-bank financing, foreign exchange transaction, bond sales and purchase as well as hedging and options.

In 2001 Eximbank's credit rating was rated BBB by US Standard and Poor's and A by Japan Rating and Investment Information, Inc., which is consistent with the sovereign rating standard.

China's import and export financing after WTO entry

China's entry into the WTO will drive China's import and export financing towards the improvement of financing services, the reduction of financing cost and further opening of the financial market to foreign financial institutions.

The WTO entry has built a more solid stage for Eximbank to exercise its role of policy orientation. The bank will be better able to integrate those successful experiences of foreign export financing institutions with Chinese realities and further deepen its reform and speed up its development. Under these new circumstances, effective measures must be taken at Eximbank to further promote China's foreign trade strategies. While the size of loans will be increased, Eximbank must also improve its lending structure, enhance its capability to weather financial exposures and upgrade the quality of lending. To meet the need for business development the Eximbank will improve its banking facilities and raise the quality level of financial services.

With regard to the treatment to foreign banks China has pledged in the second article of Specific Concession List on Service Trade – List of Exemptions to Most Favoured Nations under Appendix 9 of the Entry Protocol of the People's Republic of China:

- to remove geographic restrictions on foreign exchange business after entry;
- to phase out geographical restrictions over local currency according to the following timetable:
  - to eliminate all restrictions within five years after entry;

– to permit foreign financial institutions to provide services in China with no client restrictions;
– to allow foreign financial institutions to provide services to Chinese enterprises in local currency within two years of entry;
– to allow foreign financial institutions to provide services to all Chinese clients within five years of entry.

With the opening of financial markets, the service quality in foreign trade financing will be improved through competition, which in turn will benefit both Chinese and foreign companies in their import and export business.

Supplement 1 to Chapter 2.9

Brief introduction to The Export–Import Bank of China

Approved by the State Council, The Export–Import Bank of China was founded 26 April 1994 and officially opened for business on 1 July of the same year.

A policy-oriented financial institution under the direct leadership of the State Council, the Bank adheres to independent, break-even operating principles and strictly follows the guideline of carrying out management as a business entity.

The main mandate of the bank is to carry out state industrial policy, foreign trade policy and financial policy, to promote the export of Chinese mechanical and electronic products, complete sets of equipment and high and new-tech products, and to enhance overseas economic and technological cooperation and exchanges by means of policy financial support.

The government of the People's Republic of China is the sole owner of the bank. The Ministry of Finance provided exclusively the bank's registered capital of 3.38 billion renminbi.

The bank mainly offers the following business services: export seller's credit , export buyer's credit, foreign exchange guarantees, Chinese Government concessionary loans, the on-lending of foreign government loans, the issuing of financial bonds in domestic markets and debentures in overseas markets (excluding stocks).

As a state-owned policy bank mainly engaged in global business, the Bank has developed broad business relations with international financial organizations and domestic and overseas banks. The Export–Import Bank of China is focused on establishing and strengthening mutual contacts with friends in financial and business circles both at home and abroad in order to develop business cooperation.

The Export–Import Bank of China Articles of Association

CHAPTER I GENERAL PROVISIONS

Article 1
The legal name of the bank is 'The Export–Import Bank of China', abbreviated to 'China Eximbank'.

Article 2
The Export–Import Bank of China, under the direct leadership of the State Council, is a policy-oriented financial institution. It adopts the principles of independent, break-even operation and management as a business enterprise. Its financial business shall be subject to the direction and supervision of the Ministry of Finance, the Ministry of Foreign Trade and Economic Cooperation and the People's Bank of China.

Article 3
The Export–Import Bank of China mainly provides policy-oriented financial support for the export and import of capital goods such as mechanical and electronic products and complete sets of equipment.

Article 4
The head office of the Export–Import Bank of China is located in Beijing.

Article 5

The registered capital of the Export–Import Bank of China is renminbi 3.38 billion yuan.

CHAPTER II SCOPE OF BUSINESS

Article 6

The main business of the Export–Import Bank of China is as follows:

1. Providing export and import credit, including seller's credit and buyer's credit, for the export and import of capital goods such as mechanical and electronic products and complete sets of equipment;
2. On lending foreign government loans, mixed credits, and export credits in connection with the export of mechanical and electronic products; extending government loans and mixed credits from the Chinese government to foreign countries;
3. Engaging in international inter-bank loans, organizing and participating in domestic and international syndicated loans;
4. Providing export credit insurance, export credit guarantees, import and export insurance and factoring service;
5. Issuing financial bonds at home and negotiable securities abroad (excluding stocks);
6. Undertaking foreign exchange business authorized by the relevant Chinese authorities;
7. Representing China in international organizations of export and import banks, po1icy-oriented financial institutions and insurance providers;
8. Providing advisory services in export and import business, project evaluation, and services in foreign economic and technological cooperation;
9. Undertaking any other business approved and entrusted to by the relevant Chinese authorities.

CHAPTER III ORGANIZATION

Article 7

There shall be a Board of Directors of The Export–Import Bank of China. The President of the bank shall be responsible for its overall management under the leadership of the Board of Directors. The President of the bank shall be its legal representative.

Article 8

The Board of Directors of the Export–Import Bank of China shall be the bank's supreme decision-making body, and it shall be directly responsible to the State Council; the Board of Directors shall consist of a Chairman, two Vice-Chairmen and a number of Directors. The Chairman and Vice-Chairmen shall be appointed by the State Council, while Directors shall be nominated by the relevant ministries and commissions and approved by the State Council.

Article 9

The main functions of the Board of Directors are as follows:

1. To examine and determine the bank's long and medium-term development programmes, operation policies and annual plans in accordance with the industrial policy and foreign trade policy of China;
2. To review and evaluate the President's reports on the bank's operations, and to supervise the bank's financial and accounting status and the efforts for maintaining and increasing the value of State-owned assets;
3. To examine and approve the bank's budget, financial statements and after-tax profit distribution scheme;
4. To discuss and decide on important issues concerning national policy for export credit, export credit guarantee and credit risks;
5. To consider and determine the establishment and removal of the bank's internal departments and the adjustment of their functions;
6. To examine and determine the important rules and regulations of financial management;
7. To examine the bank's policies and procedures with respect to personnel management and other important issues.

Article 10

Meetings of the Board of Directors of the Export–Import Bank of China shall be held regularly. Should any important issue arise, an interim meeting shall be convened. Board meetings shall be convened and presided over by the Chairman. Should the Chairman be absent from the meeting, he shall entrust one of the Vice-Chairmen to call and chair the meeting.

A board meeting requires a quorum of over two-thirds of the Directors. Resolutions of the Board meetings require adoption by over 50 per cent of the Directors.

Article 11

There shall be a President and several Vice-Presidents of The Export–Import Bank of China, who shall be appointed by the State Council. Other personnel shall be appointed or dismissed according to the bank's rules and procedures.

Article 12

The President of The Export–Import Bank of China shall be responsible for the overall business management of the Bank. The Vice-Presidents shall assist the President in his duties according to division of responsibility. The specific functions of the functions of the President are as follows:

1. Managing the overall operation of the bank;
2. Implementing the resolutions of the Board of Directors;
3. Reporting regularly to the Board of Directors on his work;
4. Overseeing the formulation of the bank's development programme, management policies and annual business plan;
5. Overseeing the formulation of the bank's budget, financial statements and after-tax profit distribution scheme;
6. Overseeing the development of the bank's policies and procedures with respect to personnel management and financial management;
7. Organizing and designing the bank's programmes for the establishment and discontinuation of its internal departments and adjustment of their functions;
8. Other duties designated by the Board of Directors.

CHAPTER IV BUSINESS MANAGEMENT, FINANCIAL ACCOUNTING AND SUPERVISION

Article 13

The Export–Import Bank of China shall adopt the principles of independent accounting, and management as a business enterprise. It shall pay taxes in accordance with laws of China.

Article 14

The Export–Import Bank of China shall formulate the bank's detailed rules and regulations regarding its own financial management and accounting practices in accordance with 'Accounting Law of the People's Republic of China', 'Standard Accounting Rules for Enterprises', 'General Provisions for Business Financing' and relevant financial and accounting rules of banking and insurance enterprises promulgated by the Ministry of Finance.

Article 15

The Export–Import Bank of China shall submit the bank's financial statements to the relevant government authorities, and subject itself to the supervision of the Ministry of Finance and the State Administration of Auditing.

Article 16

The Export–Import Bank of China shall establish an internal auditing system, which will govern the auditing of the bank's financial revenues and expenditures under the leadership of the bank's President.

Article 17

The Export–Import Bank of China shall be entitled to make decisions regarding the recruitment and dismissal of the bank's staff in accordance with relevant regulations and laws of China.

Article 18

The Export–Import Bank of China shall determine the compensation policies for its staff on the basis of the salary system for banking staff promulgated by the State Council as well as in accordance with the relevant laws and policies of China.

CHAPTER V SUPPLEMENTARY ARTICLES

Article 19

The right to interpret these Articles of Association is vested in The Export–Import Bank of China.

Article 20

These Articles of Association shall come into force upon approval by the State Council.

Courtesy of Export–Import Bank of China: www.exim bank.gov.cn/eximbank/english

China's Exchange Control System

Ma Shabo, Capital Account Administration Dept., State Administration of Foreign Exchange and Li Yong,
Deputy Secretary General, China Association of International Trade

China's foreign exchange control regime

Foreign exchange control is an administration policy on foreign exchange expenditure and receipts that a country adopts in a specific period of time for the purpose of maintaining the balance of international payments, stablizing its currency value and sustaining the development of the national economy. Foreign exchange control is directly correlated with the level of a country's external economic exchanges, the degree of maturity of its financial market and the level and ability of its financial control and administration. It is also directly related to the state of a country's macro-economic development as well as its international finance and foreign exchange situations. However, with enhancement in the level of a country's economic development, foreign exchange control will be gradually relaxed.

Since the opening up in 1979, China's foreign exchange control regime has experienced quite a number of reforms with the deepening of economic reform, development of the national economy and gradual convergence with the world economy. Such reforms can be divided into the following periods:

The pre-1994 period

In this period, China's economy was under a planned regime, which was reflected accordingly in rigorous foreign exchange control regulation characterized by the exercise of a principle of 'centralized administration and uniform operation'. All foreign exchange receipts, either by enterprises or an individual, had to be turned over to the State, while all foreign exchange expenditures had to be supplied by the State. The State controlled and adjusted foreign exchange receipts and expenditures through mandatory plans and directives.

Although the foreign exchange retention system and foreign exchange readjustment business were implemented in the period – an effort to gradually bring market mechanisms into the field of foreign exchange allocation, the foreign exchange control regime was still predominantly a function of the planned economy.

The period from 1994 to 1996

To match the systemic reforms that had taken place in the fields of foreign trade, taxation and finance, the State Administration of Foreign Exchange announced its major reform measures on 1 January 1994 which included the following key points:

- convergence of the exchange rates to implement a single market-based and managed floating exchange rate regime;
- abolition of foreign exchange retention and submission in favour of a system of selling foreign exchange through banks;
- establishment of a nationally uniform inter-bank foreign exchange market to improve the mechanism of exchange rate formation;
- elimination of mandatory plans and directives for foreign exchange receipts and payments and employment of economic and legal means to adjust the international balance of payments and foreign exchange revenue and expenditure;
- discontinuation of foreign exchange certificate issuance, the banning of foreign currency denominated pricing and settlements.

As a result of these reforms, China lifted the exchange restrictions regarding trade and non-trade payments under commercial arrangements, thereby realizing conditional convertibility of renminbi (RMB) under the current account.

Post-1996 period

Fruitful results had been achieved following the reforms to the foreign exchange regime in 1994. Foreign trade had grown rapidly, while utilization of foreign investment had drastically expanded. The international balance of payments was in equilibrium and the RMB exchange rate was steadily climbing. Under such circumstances another major reform was made to China's foreign exchange control regime.

- inclusion of foreign-invested enterprises into the system of selling foreign exchange through the banks;
- abolition of exchange restrictions on non-trade payments under non-commercial arrangements.

The above reform measure eliminated all exchange restrictions on current account payments, realizing the convertibility of RMB under the current account. At the same time, China officially accepted Article 8 of the International Monetary Fund on 1 December 1996, promising a foreign exchange control regime with convertibility under current account and necessary control over capital account.

Trends of development in China's foreign exchange control regime

The ultimate goal of reform in China's foreign exchange control is to realize convertibility of RMB under capital account and gradually achieve full RMB convertibility. Since 1996, although China has experienced the shock of the Asian financial crisis and now faces the challenges and opportunities of its WTO accession, China's goals for the reform of its foreign exchange control regime have not changed.

In July 1997, when the Asian financial crisis exploded from Thailand, China was considerably affected. In order to resist the impact of the Asian financial crisis and combat illegal business and financial activities within China, a series of interim measures were adopted. These measures were intended to reinforce, on the premise of convertibility under current account and regulation under capital account, verification of the authenticity of foreign exchange receipts and payments on current account, thereby plugging up the loopholes in currency management to prevent capital flight. After

a period of implementation, some adjustments were made in accordance with international practice and the level of impact made by such measures on the normal business activities of enterprises. Those measures that were in conformity with international practices and China's commitments and had not produced adverse effects on enterprise business activities were consolidated in the form of laws and regulations. Those that had had generated significant negative impacts were adjusted or abolished in a timely manner. All these efforts ensured that China's foreign exchange control regime evolved on a normal track of development.

China has joined the WTO, as a result of which it will further reduce tariffs, phase out non-tariff barriers and further open up the market. Accordingly, entities having foreign exchange receipts and payments will increase in number, leading to drastic increases in the total volume of foreign exchange transactions. China's foreign exchange control regime is facing greater opportunities as well as challenges. To comply with WTO agreement and rules, China will rectify and amend laws and regulations to meet the WTO accession requirements.

At the same time, China will also push ahead gradually and prudently the convertibility of the capital account based on the improvement and development of China's macro-economic situation.

Control over the foreign exchange of foreign resident organizations

Administration of foreign exchange accounts

Resident organizations should file with the competent Administration of Foreign Exchange by presenting the approval documents issued by relevant authorities and certificate of registration with the relevant Administration of Industry and Commerce. A Filing Form for Foreign Exchange Account by Foreign Resident Organization will be issued, against which the applicant can process the opening of the foreign exchange account at a designated bank.

The sources of foreign exchange receipt should be the remittance from outside China for operational outlays and the expenditures should be expenses that are related to office operations.

Administration of foreign exchange payments

Foreign exchange received by foreign resident organizations can be deposited into their bank accounts or sold to the designated banks or remitted/carried out of China against valid proofs.

Legitimate RMB income earned by foreign resident organizations may be converted into foreign currency and remitted out of China at designated banks upon presentation of valid proofs and fee lists.

Should resident organizations and their personnel sell their personal items, equipment or appliances brought into China from abroad or purchased in China, they may convert the RMB proceeds into foreign currency and remit them out of the country through designated banks by presenting their business registration certificate (issued by the Administration of Industry and Commerce) and pertinent sales proofs.

Control over the foreign exchange of foreign-invested enterprises

Foreign exchange registration

1. Foreign-invested enterprises (FIEs) should, within 30 days after the issuance of the business licence, process foreign exchange registration with the competent Administration of Foreign Exchange and obtain Certificate of Foreign Exchange Registration against presentation of the following documents: approval documents issued by examination and approval authorities, capital verification report, business licence and its copy and the approved contract and articles of association.
2. After foreign exchange registration, in the event of any changes in the name, address and scope of business, or ownership transfer, capital addition or merger, the foreign-invested enterprises should go to the pertinent Administration of Industry and Commerce to register the changes, after which the changes should be registered with the competent Administration of Foreign Exchange in the foreign exchange register.
3. FIEs upon expiry or accidental termination of the enterprise, should, with approval for dissolution from the original approval authorities, cancel the foreign exchange registration with the Administration of Foreign Exchange within 30 days after liquidation.
4. Foreign exchange registration certificates will be reviewed on an annual basis by the relevant authorities. Fabrication, lending, transfer or selling of a registration certificate are strictly forbidden.

Control over foreign exchange accounts

Categories of accounts and scope of receipts and payment:

- foreign exchange settlement account
- special account for foreign exchange capital
- temporary special account
- special loan account
- special debt service account
- 'B' share account
- special account for stocks.

The opening of foreign exchange accounts
FIEs can open foreign exchange accounts within and outside China and in different locations of China. In order to do so, they will have to meet the relevant requirements of exchange control.

The use of foreign exchange accounts
The Administration of Foreign Exchange will review and ratify the highest limit for the foreign exchange account based on the paid-up capital and the cash flow needs under the current account of the FIE. Foreign exchange receipts within the limit are allowed to be retained but the part in excess of the limit will have to be sold to the designated banks.

Deposits by FIEs in foreign exchange control accounts can be converted into time deposits, but they are still subject to the control of a maximum limit.

The close of the account
The closure of a foreign exchange account by a FIE should be processed with the Administration of Foreign Exchange within 10 days after the clearing of the account. The certificate of account closure by the opening bank and the certificate of foreign exchange registration should be presented for account closing procedures. After the foreign exchange bank account is closed, the amount belonging to the foreign investor can be transferred or remitted out of China, while the amount that goes to Chinese investors should be sold to the designated bank.

Control over foreign exchange receipts and payments

Control over exchange receipts and payments under current account
The exchange receipt on the current account of a FIE can be sold to the designated banks or retained in its

foreign exchange account if the exchange receipts are within the ratified limit.

The exchange payments under the current account of a FIE can be made from its own foreign exchange account or the required amount for payments may be purchased from the designated banks.

Control over international commercial loans
FIEs can use international commercial loans without the approval of the Administration of Foreign Exchange, however, they will need to go through the procedures of external debt registration. In addition, the cumulative amount of mid-term and long-term international borrowings by FIEs should not exceed the difference between the registered capital and the total investment.

Control over foreign currency bonds
The issuance of foreign currency bonds, convertible bonds, negotiable certificates of deposit and commercial documents by FIEs should be approved by the Administration of Foreign Exchange and undergo external debt registration.

Control over foreign exchange borrowings from domestic financial institutions
The borrowing of foreign exchange loans by FIEs from domestic financial institutions does not require approval by the Administration of Foreign Exchange, but FIEs will have to complete foreign exchange loan registration procedures.

Control over external guarantees
External guarantees within a period of less than a year provided by FIEs for domestic entities will need to be approved by the local administration of foreign exchange. The external guarantees for more than one year by FIEs for domestic or overseas entities will have to be approved by the State Administration of Foreign Exchange. External guarantees by wholly foreign-owned enterprises will not need approval by the Administration of Foreign Exchange. An external pledge or hypothecation with the assets of a FIE as its security will not require approval from the Administration of Foreign Exchange. However, all external guarantees will have to undergo registration procedures at the Administration of Foreign Exchange.

Control over renminbi borrowings from domestic Chinese-funded financial institutions against guarantees provided by external organizations
FIEs can use their own foreign exchange funds as pledges for their borrowing of renminbi from domestic Chinese-funded financial institutions. FIEs can accept guarantees from their foreign shareholders, overseas banks or foreign banks within the territory of China for their borrowing of renminbi loans from domestic Chinese-funded financial institutions. The renminbi loans borrowed by FIEs can be used for the purpose of making up shortages in cash flow or long-term investments in fixed assets. The maximum term of such loans should not exceed five years.

Control over the payments under capital account
A FIE should present proof of external debt registration, external debt contract, and notice by creditors for repayment of principal and interest to the Administration of Foreign Exchange when applying for repayment of principal and interest. Upon approval by the Administration of Foreign Exchange, the FIE may make payment through its foreign currency account or at designated banks against the approval documents.

For repayment of foreign exchange loan principal to domestic Chinese-funded financial institutions in China, the FIE will need to obtain approval from the Administration of Foreign Exchange. No approval is needed, however, for the payment of interest.

Approval by the Administration of Foreign Exchange will need to be obtained when FIEs perform the obligations of external guarantees.

Control over foreign exchange settlement and selling

The amount of current account foreign exchange receipts by FIEs in excess of the limit prescribed by the Administration of Foreign Exchange will have to be settled.

- Foreign exchange capital, borrowed international commercial loans, the revenues from the issuance of 'B' shares and overseas public offerings can be settled. The settlement of borrowed foreign exchange loans by FIEs from domestic Chinese-funded financial institutions are not allowed.
- All selling and payments of foreign exchange should be processed against presentation of valid proofs and commercial documents, or by filing forms issued by the Administration of Foreign Exchange, or through requisition of foreign exchange selling ratified by the

Administration of Foreign Exchange. All selling and payments of foreign exchange under capital account must be processed against the document of ratification issued by the Administration of Foreign Exchange. Those who are unable to produce valid certificates as prescribed by the Administration of Foreign Exchange and valid commercial documents will have to submit applications to the Administration of Foreign Exchange for approval, against which selling and payments of foreign exchange can be processed. For the selling and payments of foreign exchange against the presentation of the filing document, the designated bank will examine and verify the authenticity of such document in accordance with relevant regulations. Such examination and verification will not be carried out by the designated banks if no approval documents issued by the Administration of Foreign Exchange are presented. For the non-trade foreign exchange payments, the applicant needs to provide a taxation certificate in addition to other certificates and documents. Payments on capital account should be made with the applicant's own foreign exchange, and purchase of foreign exchange for payment purpose is only allowed when the applicant's own foreign exchange falls short of the amount required.

- Control over the purchase of foreign exchange for payment purposes under trade arrangements governs the following realms of administration:
  - Those who purchase foreign exchange for payments against prescribed valid certificates and valid commercial documents;
  - Those who purchase foreign exchange for payments against foreign exchange filing forms;
  - Those who purchase foreign exchange for payments against requisition of foreign exchange selling ratified and issued by the Administration of Foreign Exchange; classification of customs declaration;
  - administration of foreign exchange purchases for payments by bonded warehouses;
  - administration of foreign exchange purchases for payments under the arrangements to transfer goods for additional processing.
- Control over foreign exchange purchases for payments under non-trade arrangements.
- Control over foreign exchange purchases for payments on capital account. Advance purchases of foreign exchange for repayment of loans is forbidden.

Control over the investment profits and investment capital

Administration over profits repatriation

The legitimate profit earned by a FIE can be remitted out of China. In doing so, the FIE needs to present the following documents:

- Foreign exchange registration certificate;
- Capital verification report by an independent accounting firm;
- Board resolution on profit distribution;
- Tax payment certificate and tax declaration form;
- Audit report on current-year profits by an accounting firm.

Upon approval, the FIE can expatriate the profit from its own account or purchase foreign exchange from designated banks for profit repatriation.

Administration over reinvestment

The foreign investors in FIEs are allowed, upon approval by the Administration of Foreign Exchange, to make reinvestments with their after-tax profits or the funds available as a result of liquidation, equity transfer or anticipatory returns on their investment. Against reinvestment certificates issued by the Administration of Foreign Exchange, the FIEs can make foreign exchange payments from their foreign exchange accounts or purchase foreign exchange with the Renminbi they have earned to make the payments.

For reinvestment of profits, the following documents need to be examined and verified:

- Foreign exchange registration certificate;
- Capital verification report by a certified accounting firm;
- Annual audit report;
- Board resolution on profit distribution;
- Letter of confirmation on reinvestment by the foreign investors;
- Tax payment certificate.

For reinvestment with the proceeds from a liquidation, an equity transfer and anticipatory returns on investment, the following criteria should be met. Foreign investors should be able to produce proof that they have:

– legitimately paid-up capital in the original FIEs (for this purpose, documents such as the approval granted by trade and investment authority, contract, articles of association and capital verification report will be examined and verified.)

– Proof that the funds for reinvestment are authentically from the proceeds of liquidation, equity transfer or anticipatory returns on investments and the procedures of such liquidation, equity transfer and anticipatory returns on investment are legal and in conformity with relevant regulations (documents regarding liquidation, equity transfer, etc will be examined and verified.)

– The foreign investors making a reinvestment are at the same time a shareholder of the reinvested enterprise and have an obligation to make a capital contribution (such documents as the approval granted by competent trade and investment authorities for reinvestment, contract and articles of association will be examined and verified)

Administration over capital increases

With approval by the Administration of Foreign Exchange, the foreign investors of FIEs can increase their capital contributions from their profit, development funds or reserve funds. Such capital increases can be processed with approval documents issued by the Administration of Foreign Exchange.

Capital increase from profit

Examination and verification of the following documents will be required for a capital increase from profit:

● Foreign exchange registration certificate;
● Capital verification report by a certified accounting firm;
● Annual audit report;
● Board resolution on profit distribution;
● Letter of confirmation of capital increase by the foreign investors;
● Approval documents by the original approving authority;
● Tax payment certificate.

Capital increase with development funds and reserve funds

Examination and verification of the following documents will be required for capital increases with development funds and reserve funds:

● Foreign exchange registration certificate;
● Capital verification report by a certified accounting firm;
● Approval documents by the original approving authority;
● Board resolution on capital increase;
● Amended contract and articles of association;
● Tax payment certificate.

Administration of equity transfers

After a transfer of equity by the foreign investor in a FIE, the proceeds from such a transfer, upon approval by the Administration of Foreign Exchange, can be remitted out of China. The foreign investor can do so either from its foreign exchange account or by purchasing foreign exchange from the designated banks. However, the enterprise needs to submit an application to the Administration of Foreign Exchange with the following documents:

● An application report;
● Foreign exchange registration certificate;
● The agreement for equity transfer;
● Approval documents regarding the change of equity structure issued by the competent trade and investment authority:
  – Business licence after the equity changes, certificate of approval, approved and valid contract and articles of association;
  – The latest capital verification report and audit report (or valid asset valuation report);
  – Account statements of all the enterprise's foreign exchange accounts;
  – Tax payment certificate.

Administration of liquidation

When a FIE is legally liquidated, the portion of funds that belongs to foreign investors can be remitted out of China upon approval. The remittance can be made from the foreign exchange account of the FIEs or the foreign investor can purchase foreign exchange from the designated banks for the purpose of remittance. An application will have to be filed with the Administration of Foreign Exchange with the following documents, and remittance can be processed against approval of the Administration of Foreign Exchange:

● An application report;
● Foreign exchange registration certificate;

- Approval for liquidation and termination by competent trade and investment authority;
- Resolution of the liquidation committee;
- Capital verification report;
- Liquidation report prepared by an accounting firm;
- Advice of bank account;
- Account statements of the foreign exchange accounts;
- Cancellation certificate of Tax Registration.

Administration of the transfer of investment funds by investment holding companies

Investment holding companies need to obtain approvals from the Administration of Foreign Exchange before they can transfer investment funds within the territory of China. To obtain approval, the following documents need to be provided together with an application to the Administration of Foreign Exchange:

- Capital verification report by a certified accounting firm;
- Approval documents regarding the newly-invested enterprise and the business licence of industry and commerce, approved contract and articles of association;
- Resolution regarding the investment project in China by the Board of the investment holding company;
- Foreign exchange registration certificate.

China's foreign exchange regime after WTO accession

The impact of the WTO on China's foreign exchange control regime

As a part of China's effort to honour its commitments to the WTO, China's foreign exchange control regime will take an active stance in observing WTO rules. The State Administration of Foreign Exchange will gradually transform its functions in order to create favourable conditions for both foreign investors investing in China and Chinese enterprises doing business with the outside world. On the one hand, China has signed up to Article 8 of the IMF agreement, as a result of which the restrictions on convertibility of current accounts such as trade in goods and services have been removed. Renminbi is currently convertible under current account and China's foreign exchange control regime is generally in line with the requirements of the WTO. Therefore, foreign exchange control was not a critical point in the WTO negotiations. In addition, unlike the issues of market

access for service trade and tariff reduction, there have been no specific commitments regarding the timing and scope of the opening of foreign exchange control. On the other hand, although there are no requirements regarding the opening of foreign exchange control, the opening of the Chinese market, especially the opening up of the financial and service sectors, will inevitably bring profound influences to bear on China's foreign exchange control regime.

Joining the WTO does not require a country to give up its capital controls to realize full convertibility of its currency under capital account. In fact, many WTO members, developing or developed, are still maintaining control to varying degrees over their capital accounts. China has not made any commitment in relation to convertibility of RMB under the capital account to the WTO, although, the promotion of RMB convertibility under capital account and eventually full convertibility of RMB are China's ultimate goal. In effect China's accession to the WTO will expedite the process.

In response to WTO accession, China's foreign exchange control authorities have voluntarily made adjustments to the laws and regulations regarding foreign exchange control. Reform efforts are aimed at improving the manner of exchange control by streamlining the examination and approval procedures, putting emphasis on ex-post supervision and inspection while reducing ex-ante administration. Since last November, a series of measures has been staged to adapt the control measures to the new situation under the circumstances of the WTO. These measures include:

- simplification of the examination and verification procedures for applications for foreign exchange by family-financed students going abroad to study. The ceiling placed on the purchase of foreign exchange from the designated banks was raised from the previous US$2,000 to US$20,000. No approval from the Administration of Foreign Exchange is needed for purchase of foreign exchange within the limit.
- Implementation of trial reforms on the administration of domestic foreign exchange loans, aiming at reducing the examination and approval procedures. Six cities and provinces were chosen for the trial reform, where the requirements for case-by-case registration by debtors were replaced by requirements for regular registration by the creditors (ie the banks). When enterprises repay domestic foreign exchange loans with their own foreign exchange under a normal repayment schedule, the competent

banks designated by the Administration of Foreign Exchange will take the responsibility of reviewing the legitimacy and authenticity of the applications when processing the transactions, after which the banks are required to submit monthly statements to the Administration of Foreign Exchange in their domiciles. The designated banks can independently open or cancel the special accounts of domestic foreign exchange loans.

- Reduction of ex-ante examination and verification by giving trial authorization to banks in processing the settlement of foreign exchange capital funds of FIEs. The original responsibility of the Administration of Foreign Exchange to examine and approve the settlements of foreign exchange capital funds under foreign investment projects was delegated to qualified state-designated banks. FIEs can go directly to the designated banks with relevant documents to process the settlements. Ex-ante examination and verification by the Administration of Foreign Exchange is no longer needed. Eleven cities and provinces were chosen to carry out this experiment.

- Adjustment of the administrative measures for the purchase of foreign exchange under some items of the capital account and some restrictions have been lifted or relaxed. The background was that some interim measures were taken during the Asian financial crisis to restrict the purchase of foreign exchange in order to stabilize the foreign exchange market and prevent foreign exchange flight or arbitrage. The macro economy has now been in healthy operation and the international balance of payment has fared well, all of which have enabled China to readjust those measures. The adjustments included a) the lifting of the restrictions on the purchase of foreign exchange for the repayment of overdue domestic loans, which now allows enterprises to submit exchange purchase application to the Administration of Foreign Exchange for approval by stages and installments, b) relaxation of the restrictions on the purchase of foreign exchange for advance repayment

of domestic foreign exchange loans, the swap of external debts to loans and repayment of external debts and c) relaxation of the restrictions on the purchase of foreign exchange for the purpose of overseas investments.

- Relaxation of the criteria for Chinese-funded enterprises to open foreign exchange settlement accounts in order to facilitate their production and business activities. This measure allows all Chinese-funded enterprises that have a) annual foreign exchange earnings equivalent to US$2 million or above, b) annual spending of foreign exchange equivalent to US$200,000 or above, c) trading rights to import and export, d) sound financial performance and e) no past record of violation of foreign exchange control regulations, to open foreign exchange settlement accounts and retain a certain amount of foreign exchange.

- The annulment of the validity period for the use of 'the paper for verification and cancellation of foreign exchange receipts on export'[1] and relaxation of the limit imposed on the numbers of issuance of such paper. This effort was intended to simplify the procedures of verification and cancellation to encourage the expansion of exports. According to this measure, enterprises that have been granted credit awards for outstanding export receipts and those that have fulfilled export receipt quotas are allowed to possess as many such papers as required for their export needs. At the same time, they are also allowed to process verifications and cancellations of their export exchange receipts on a monthly basis, while the Administration of Foreign Exchange exercises memorandum examination on the balances.

New policy measures

In a continued effort to streamline the foreign exchange control system, the State Administration of Foreign Exchange has announced a series of new policy measures in 2002. These new measures include the following:

---

[1] Editor's note: Export foreign exchange verification and cancellation is an ex-post administrative measure designed to verify the foreign exchange receipts against the reported export value. The paper for verification and cancellation of foreign exchange receipts on export is a certificate produced and issued by the Administration of Foreign Exchange bearing uniform serial numbers with a specified validity period. The paper is used for the following purposes: customs declaration, collecting the forex receipts on export from the designated bank, processing verification and cancellation of the forex receipts with the Administration of Foreign Exchange, and applying to the tax authorities for export tax rebates. Such paper is available to those Chinese companies that have import and export qualifications and all foreign-invested enterprises upon completion of certain procedures. – LY

- to continue to promote reform of the administration of foreign exchange accounts to support enterprises in their effort to develop foreign trade while at the same time strengthening the monitoring of foreign exchange receipts and payments. Chinese-funded enterprises with the trading right of import and export are allowed, upon approval by the Administration of Foreign Exchange to open foreign exchange settlement accounts.[2] Account ceilings will be determined as a proportion of the foreign exchange receipts under the current account of the enterprises and therefore can be adjusted. Experiments on the use of information management systems to monitor the foreign exchange accounts will be expanded in an effort to eventually achieve real-time monitoring of such accounts.

- to further streamline the verification and cancellation procedures for both imports and exports in order to facilitate the business operations of enterprises while strengthening ex-post supervision. On the basis of last year's effort to implement various measures such as the introduction of a sub-system monitoring foreign exchange receipts on exports into the electronic law-enforcement system at ports of entry and exit and a memorandum examination system on foreign exchange receipt balances, new measures of verfication and cancellation have been introduced which include:

  - relaxation of the time limit imposed on the filing of forward foreign exchange receipts with the Administration of Foreign Exchange, extending the filing period from the previous 90 days to 180 days;

  - further streamlining of verification and cancellation procedures for those enterprises which have good records of verification and cancellation of foreign exchange receipts on export;

  - annulment of procedures for filing the registration of foreign exchange payments for some imports;

  - establishment of a memorandum examination mechanism regarding foreign exchange payments for imports;

  - implementation of a classified handling approach for overdue verification and cancellation of import payments.

- to promote information management systems on personal purchases of foreign exchange as an effort to provide facilitation for normal use of foreign exchange by individuals and improve the means of supervising personal purchase of foreign exchange. The pilot operations of the information management system on personal purchase of foreign exchange are basically normal and have effectively prevented repeated purchases of foreign exchange by individuals. Such exercises will be adopted on a nationwide basis. The key consideration of such a move is to establish uniform procedures and criteria for market access, allowing qualified state-designated banks to open private foreign exchange banking business in order to provide better financial services to individuals while at the same time encouraging fair competition among banks.

- to strengthen the exchange control over insurance businesses in an effort to normalize insurance operations involving foreign exchange and fill in the gaps in supervision and administration in the foreign insurance area. To adapt to the needs of rapidly developing insurance businesses after WTO accession, relevant regulations governing the exchange control of insurance businesses will be announced and implemented in the near future. Such regulations will exercise uniform control over foreign exchange transactions by both Chinese and foreign insurance agencies.

- to further promote the reform of the administration of capital fund settlements of FIEs and domestic foreign exchange loans. In this connection, examination and approval procedures will be reduced while emphasis will be placed on indirect administration. On the basis of previous experiments, uniform implementation plans will be established in order to delegate control responsibilities regarding the examination and verification of capital fund settlements under foreign investment projects, domestic foreign exchange loans and repayment of foreign exchange loans with own foreign exchange to qualified state-designated banks. The Administration of Foreign Exchange will exercise its control and regulation of foreign exchange receipts and payments activities through its supervision over banks' execution of relevant rules and regulations. Effective from 1 July 2002, FIEs can settle their capital accounts directly with the designated banks and foreign investors can complete all procedures at bank counters.

---

[2] Editor's note: Prior to this, only foreign-invested enterprises and Chinese-funded enterprises that meet certain qualification standards could have such accounts.

- to reinforce the work on the verification of capital contributions in FIEs in order to fully establish a registration system for the inflow of foreign investments. In compliance with the requirements of the *Notice on Further Strengthening the Work on the Verification of Capital Contributions of Foreign-invested Enterprises and Establishing a Complete Exchange Registration System for Foreign Investment*, certified public accounts are required, before the issuance of capital verification reports, to make validation enquiries to the Administration of Foreign Exchange, which will check authenticity and legitimacy of capital contributions against its examination and verification records and through the import declaration network enquiry system, and at the same time register the actual inflow of foreign capital.

- to liquidate and gradually solve the problems of foreign exchange advances under banks' letters of credit in order to improve the quality of banking assets. The banks are allowed, with the approval of the Administration of Foreign Exchange, to use renminbi funds repaid by enterprises or recovered by legal means from enterprises or by realization of enterprise property to purchase foreign exchange to offset foreign exchange advances under letters of credit incurred before the stipulated time line.

Freight Forwarding in China

Liu Baocheng, Professor, University of International Business and Economics

The task of freight forwarding involves a facilitation service for the physical movement of goods. The customer of the freight forwarder is technically called the 'shipper' or 'consignor.' Broadly speaking, the facilitation service for the movement of goods can be broken down into three dimensions: transportation, communication and documentation. The freight forwarder does not have to transport the goods by itself using its own facilities, because this is primarily the function of the carrier that possesses sea-borne vessels, railway wagons or airplanes. Frequently the freight forwarder offers short distance transportation, eg from the warehouse to the container yard or from the plant to the loading port with trucks. Briefly, the role of freight forwarding is to bridge the gap between the shipper and the carrier. The freight forwarder can act either as an agent for the shipper or as the receiver of the goods. See Figure 2.11.1.

Under the state's economy, professional distribution options were scarce because provinces and organizations were supposed to be self-reliant. Firms had little choice but to rely on state distribution networks, which were organized along rigid, vertical command-control lines. Since China adopted the opening policy at the end of 1978, transportation has been a burgeoning industry that has attracted the attention of both domestic and foreign freight forwarding firms. The underlying trend of the past 20 years is one of centrifugal force as trading volume has expanded and infrastructure improved.

The government regiment over the administration of transport industries inclusive of the vehicles, terminals, routes and services, is divided into the different modes of operation. The Ministry of Communications (MOC) is in charge of water and highway transport; the Ministry of Railways (MOR) is in charge of railway transport; and the Civil Administration Aviation of China (CAAC) is in charge of air transport. The freight forwarding industry, particularly those parts related to import and export, is under the supervision of the Ministry of Foreign Trade and Economic Cooperation (MOFTEC).

Traditionally, foreign forwarding services were completely under the monopoly of the China National Foreign Trade Transportation Company (Sinotrans),

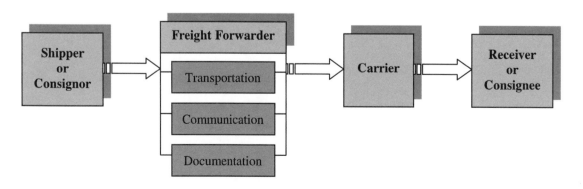

Figure 2.11.1 The position of a freight forwarder

itself under the administration of MOFTEC, since most of its direct clients are foreign trade corporations under MOFTEC's regime. The shipowner services were vested with China Ocean Shipping Agency (Penevico, an acronym derived from its former name – People's Navigation Company) with branches across Chinese coastal ports under MOC for the same reason. Since 1984 both Sinotrans and Penevico were given permission to step into each other's business. Soon the freight forwarding market was gradually liberalized for domestic companies. By the end of July 2002, according to the China International Freight Forwarders Association, the number of freight forwarders approved by MOFTEC that are eligible to conduct international business reached 3,216 (including subsidiaries) covering over 30 sectors of the national economy. Among them there is a 70:30 ratio, both in terms of ownership structure and geographic distribution – 70 per cent are state-owned and 30 per cent are joint ventures; 70 per cent are concentrated in the coastal regions and 30 per cent are spread out into the hinterland. So far, nearly 300,000 persons are employed in the freight forwarding industry.

In 1996 the State Council approved the establishment of the Shanghai Shipping Exchange under the auspices of the Ministry of Communications and Shanghai Municipal Government. The Exchange, being the first in China, was created to foster the development of China's shipping market and to help shape Shanghai into an international shipping centre. The Exchange has achieved great success in providing services to the shipping market, including organizing and procuring the filing of freight tariffs, coordinating freight rates, issuing shipping information, conducting research on shipping policies, publishing and issuing the Chinese freight rates index and establishing the Shanghai Shipping Service Center.

Freight traffic

Transportation correlates with the trade pattern and the level of infrastructure sophistication. For example, the surge of highway transport in the early 1990s was the result of port congestion and the boom of domestic trade. As China's trade volume continues to expand rapidly, the strain on China's transportation infrastructure will become greater. Recognizing this, China's national and regional governments have been investing in improvements to physical infrastructure. In addition, freight forwarding and document processing are crucial elements to addressing this demand.

In the view of experts, in order to capitalize on the potential growth of the cargo market, China must improve its transportation infrastructure, open its freight forwarding sector, improve service standards and streamline customs procedures.

Freight forwarding, in its professional sense, is still concentrated in the area of foreign trade where three-quarters of cargo volume is conducted via seaborne transport. In 2000 the leading ports in China registered an aggregate cargo throughput of 1.7 billion tons, an increase of 17.3 per cent year over year. Within the total

Table 2.11.1 Total cargo transport: volumes, turnovers and growth rates of different transport modes (units: million tons/billion ton-km)

Year	Waterways Cargo Volume	Turnover	Highways Cargo Volume	Turnover	Railways Cargo Volume	Turnover	Pipelines Cargo Volume	Turnover	Airways Cargo Volume	Turnover
1980	468	507.7	1,422	34.3	1,113	571.7	105	49.1	0.09	0.1
1985	633	772.9	5,381	190.3	1,307	812.6	137	60.3	0.20	0.4
1990	801	1,159.2	7,240	335.8	1,507	1,062.2	158	62.7	0.37	0.8
1995	1,132	1,755.2	9,404	469.5	1,659	1,287.0	153	59.0	1.01	2.2
1996	1,274	1,786.3	9,839	501.1	1,688	1,297.0	160	58.5	1.15	2.5
1997	1,134	1,923.5	9,765	527.2	1,697	1,309.7	160	57.9	1.25	2.9
1998	1,096	1,940.6	9,760	548.3	1,612	1,231.2	174	60.6	1.40	3.3
1999	1,146	2,126.3	9,904	572.4	1,569	1,261.6	202	62.8	2.00	4.2
2000	1,224	2,373.4	10,388	612.9	1,744	1,390.2	187	63.9	1.97	5.0
2000 growth (%)	6.8	11.6	4.9	7.1	11.2	10.2	–7.4	1.8	–1.5	19.0

Source: China Shipping Report 2001.

Table 2.11.2 Throughputs and growth rates of the leading Chinese ports from 1990 to 2000

Year	1990	1991	1992	1993	1994	1995	1996	1997	1998	1999	2000
Throughput (million tons)	716	778	877	956	1039	1116	1274	1310	1124	1450	1701
Growth (%)	−3.1	8.7	12.7	9.0	8.7	7.4	14.2	2.8	−14.2	29.0	17.3

Source: China Shipping Report 2001.

foreign trade cargo throughput amounted to 0.57 billion tons, up 33.2 per cent over 1999. Within the throughput of the leading ports, export cargo traffic is 46.5 per cent, and import cargo traffic is a little bit higher than export at 53.5 per cent.

Freight forwarding documentation

Documentation is an important part of the freight forwarding service. The most complex occurs with ocean shipping which involves liner transport and charter transport. Typical documents include:

Booking note

This is the document filed by the freight forwarder on behalf of the shipper for reservation of shipping space with the carrier. Before issuing the booking note, the freight forwarder has to examine carefully the shipper's contract and letter of credit stipulations for compliance with the shipping terms therein.

Shipping order

This is the document issued by the carrier or its shipping agent to the shipper, often represented by the freight forwarder, confirming the agreement for the shipping service. Upon the issuance of the shipping order, a transportation contract is established between the carrier and the shipper. The freight forwarder will be able to clear the goods with the customs on the strength of the shipping order.

Mate's receipt

After the goods are loaded on a vessel, for example, the chief mate of the carrier will issue the mate's receipt to the shipper represented by the freight forwarder to confirm receipt of the goods on board. The chief mate reserves the right to withhold this document if he finds discrepancies over the quantity and packages of the goods.

Tally report

A tallyman is a third party notary who can be hired by either the carrier or the freight forwarder to ascertain the quantity of goods actually loaded on board.

Bill of lading

Bill of lading is the most important shipping document issued by the carrier. It serves as the official receipt of goods on board substituting for the mate's receipt. More significantly it is regarded as a document of title to the goods.

Dangerous cargo list

If the goods are classified as dangerous cargoes, a separate dangerous cargo list must be tendered by the freight forwarder to the carrier. Loading and unloading a dangerous cargo have to be placed under strict supervision by the port superintendent to ensure conformity with the Port Dangerous Cargo Regulations.

Inspection certificates

Depending on the specialty nature of the goods and the sales contract requirements, the freight forwarder will help the shipper to obtain various types of inspection certificates such as quality certificates, sanitary certificates and quarantine certificates.

In addition, the weight list, packing list, GSP (General System of Preference) certificate and origin certificate are among the many further documents required to satisfy different modes of transport, contract stipulations and government regulations.

Large numbers of Chinese companies have neither strategic plans for freight forwarding arrangements nor maintain regular relations with a freight forwarder. Most of the foreign trading companies maintain their own freight forwarding department. To some firms, freight forwarding is a service readily available by a phone call, and can be shopped around for in case of

Table 2.11.3 Engagement with third party freight forwarding

Period of agreement	Percentage (%)	Number of freight forwarders used	Percentage (%)
Nil	35.85	Nil	0.00
Ad hoc	18.87	1	15.09
• 1 year	3.77	2	11.32
• 2 year	18.87	3	18.87
• 3 years	15.09	4	15.09
• 4 years	7.55	?4	39.62

Source: China Freight Forwarding Gazette, August 2002

need. Some focus on low-cost providers and particularly those who are creative enough to be able to help bypass the bureaucracies of inspection and customs administrations.

The market entry barrier is noticeably low for local firms in the freight forwarding sector, which explains why the average gross profit for handling one container has dropped below US$50 from US$200 previously. Only 70 per cent of the freight forwarders are able to earn a profit. The competitiveness of the freight forwarding business hinges heavily on the scale of operations. Most successful forwarders are those that are able to establish wholly owned, full-service operations with their own truck fleet, warehouses, container depot and connections with the various government agencies concerned.

Since transportation, particularly freight forwarding, is considered to be in the service sector, the Chinese government is cautious about opening this market to complete foreign competition. The concern is that many Chinese carriers and forwarders are likely to suffer because they lack the modern equipment and information technology that would allow them to keep up with foreign competitors. With entry into the World Trade Organization (WTO), China's liberalization process for foreign participation in various modes of transportation, warehousing, packing services and freight forwarding is finalized on a predictable timetable, albeit more slowly than in most other business sectors. In summary, the following specific commitments have been made:

- China shall allow private freight forwarding entities to provide services and information for pre-shipment inspection commencing from the day of WTO entry.
- China shall allow foreign firms to enter into joint ventures with Chinese firms in liner shipping and

tramp shipping. The equity share of the foreign firm shall not exceed 49 per cent. The chairman of the board and the general manager must be appointed by the Chinese party;

- While China imposes no restriction on the air transport services rendered by foreign firms, foreign firms are not permitted to operate independently in ocean-going freight forwarding, customs clearance and container depots in China unless they enter into joint ventures with a Chinese local counterpart, and the entire equity share of the foreign party shall not exceed 49 per cent;
- For highway transport, China permits majority equity ownership by foreign firms one year after its WTO entry and solely owned foreign entities are to be permitted three years after WTO entry;
- For railway transport, China will permit majority equity ownership by foreign firms three years after its WTO entry and solely owned foreign firms are to be permitted six years after WTO entry;
- For warehousing and other logistic services, China allows 49 per cent of the equity ownership by foreign firms. Majority ownership is permitted one year after WTO entry, and solely owned foreign entities are permitted three years after WTO entry;
- Freight forwarding firms who intend to set up joint ventures in China must show a minimum three-years' experience in this field and their equity share shall not exceed 50 per cent. One year after its WTO entry, China will permit the majority equity share to be held by the foreign party. Four years after its WTO entry, solely owned foreign operation shall be permitted in China;
- The registered capital of a freight forwarding joint venture shall be a minimum US$1 million. Within four years of China's WTO entry, national treatment shall apply. The term of such a joint venture is limited to 20 years;
- A joint venture freight forwarding firm which has operated in China for over one year is permitted to open subsidiaries. For each subsidiary set up, the registered capital of the firm shall be increased by US$120,000. Two years after China's entry to WTO, national treatment shall be applied to the registered capital requirement;
- A foreign freight forwarding firm that has entered into a joint venture for over five years in China is permitted to enter into a second joint venture with a Chinese partner. Two years after China's entry into WTO, this requirement shall be reduced to two years.

Part Three

Foreign Company Operations in China

Setting up Business in the People's Republic of China

Gary Lock and Brinton M. Scott, Herbert Smith, China

Introduction, commercial and legal framework

The People's Republic of China (PRC) has undergone major economic reforms since adopting its open door policy in 1978. Since 1978 China has encouraged foreign direct investment (FDI) to stimulate the economy, modernize the country, build infrastructure and obtain advanced technology. As a part of this China has made numerous economic changes, including decentralization of economic control from state management in certain sectors, creation of special economic zones and relaxation of state controlled production.

Development of the legal system

The Chinese government recognized early that a developed legal system would be necessary to support the planned economic reform. As a result the National People's Congress (NPC) revived and institutionalized the PRC legal system in 1982 by radically amending the PRC Constitution, and since then by rapidly developing a body of commercial law, including the 1993 *Company Law*, which unifies scores of regulations dealing with corporate governance.

Many of China's current laws are based on civil law systems, which are derived from general codes rather than judicial precedent as found in common law systems. Nevertheless, the Chinese also emulate the concepts and models of other legal systems.

World Trade Organization

China acceded into the World Trade Organization (WTO) on 11 December 2001. As a WTO member China must further revise its legal system to meet the WTO's three main principles of non-discrimination, uniform treatment for all, and a transparent legal system. China faces a six-year schedule, beginning in 2002, to formally integrate into the global trading system. As a lead up to its entry into the WTO, the PRC repealed and amended dozens of investment-related laws and regulations. The difficulties facing WTO compliance, however, are compounded where provincial and local interests are involved. Thus the process of modifying the PRC's commercial legal framework is certain to be lengthy.

Alternative business structures

Introduction, FIEs and alternative structures

The principal business vehicles for FDI in the PRC include cooperative joint ventures (CJV), equity joint ventures (EJV), wholly foreign-owned enterprises (WFOE), and limited stock enterprises. Collectively known as foreign invested enterprises (FIEs), these business vehicles are discussed in detail in the next chapter.

Foreign companies may also use other structures to conduct business in the PRC. These include representative offices, compensation trade, processing and assembly operations, management contracts, and agency, distribution, franchising and technology transfer arrangements.

Representative offices

Representative offices are a popular, low cost, alternative to FIEs. Representative offices allow foreign entities to explore the PRC market, search for investment opportunities and introduce their products and services to the PRC. Representative offices also offer certain advantages over FIEs. First, approvals are generally easier to obtain. Second, capital outlays are generally low. Finally, multiple offices may be established throughout China.

Legislation

The laws governing representative offices are found in the:

- PRC Interim Regulations Concerning the Control of Resident Representative Offices of Foreign Enterprises (October 1980);
- Circular Concerning the Registration of Resident Representative Offices of Foreign Enterprises (May 1981);
- Procedures of the PRC State Administration for Industry and Commerce (SAIC) for the Registration and Administration of Resident Representative Offices of Foreign Enterprises (March 1983); and
- Detailed Rules of the Ministry of Foreign Trade and Economic Cooperation (MOFTEC) for the Implementation of the Provisional Regulations Governing the Examination, Approval and Administration of Resident Representative Offices of Foreign Enterprises (February 1995).

The application process

In order to establish a PRC representative office, an applicant must apply (via an officially-sanctioned sponsoring agency) for formal approval to establish at MOFTEC or a delegate in specialized industries (the Approval Authority), and complete registration formalities with the SAIC. The Approval Authority will determine whether a 'genuine need' for a representative office exists and, if so, issue an approval certificate which the applicant must file with the SAIC within 30 days of receipt.

Scope of permitted activities

Although not allowed to engage in direct business operations, representative offices may:

- execute office and residential leases;
- obtain residence permits and multiple-entry visas for foreign staff;
- open foreign and local currency bank accounts in the company's name;
- display office signs and distribute business materials;
- employ local staff via government-sanctioned employment agencies;

- liase with contacts in the PRC on the parent company's behalf;
- coordinate the parent company's PRC business activities; and
- conduct market surveys and research.

Although there is no clear guidance on what constitutes 'direct business activities', the following activities are generally considered outside the scope of a representative office's lawful operations:

- directly engaging in revenue-generating activity;
- entering into commercial contracts in the parent company's name;
- buying property or importing production equipment;
- collecting or making payment in connection with sales and purchases; and
- providing services to entities other than the parent company.

Compensation trade (buchang maoyi)

Compensation trade is a barter transaction whereby a Chinese party obtains foreign machinery, equipment or technology from a foreign party who receives the product the Chinese party produces with the imported machinery, equipment or technology as its compensation.

Legislation

No single, comprehensive law governs this form of trade although it is actively encouraged. Rather, the applicable laws are found in the unified *Contract Law of the PRC* (the 'Contract Law'), licensing regulations, including the *PRC Measures for the Administration of Registration of Technology Import and Export Contracts* and the *PRC Administration of Technology Import & Export Regulations*, and various tax and customs laws.

Other considerations

Compensation trade, popular between Hong Kong companies and Chinese enterprises in Guangdong and Fujian provinces, has rapidly developed in the PRC in recent years. These arrangements usually involve fishery, agriculture, animal husbandry, natural resources, chemicals, light textiles and electronics.

Although product quality disputes are common, this form of trade is still frequently used. Incentives for using compensation trade include tax advantages, flexibility in structuring the agreement and no foreign party concern with labour issues.

Where possible, exporters will often obtain performance guarantees whereby a reliable financial institution will pay the purchase price if the importer fails to fulfil its obligations to deliver the products under the sales agreement. The Chinese party must be an enterprise or other economic organization with foreign trade authority (discussed in detail in the *Agency Relationships* section below) and cannot be an individual. This type of transaction does not produce a new or merged Chinese-foreign legal entity.

Processing and assembly agreements

Processing and assembly agreements exist where a Chinese party processes materials or assembles parts supplied by a foreign party. The foreign party usually also provides the manufacturing equipment. The Chinese party either earns a fee for services or retains a portion of the finished goods for on-sale as its compensation. Whether the Chinese party retains the equipment at the end of the term is negotiable.

Legislation

There are regulations governing processing and assembly at national and local levels. The early regulations governed the activities of domestic and foreign entities separately. This approach has been gradually abandoned and most laws now apply uniformly to domestic and foreign entities, such as the Contract Law. Some of the other major laws in this area include the:

- *Regulations of the General Administration of PRC Customs on Administration of Importation of Materials and Parts for Fulfilling Product Export Contracts by FIEs* (promulgated 24 November 1986);
- *Administrative Measures of the PRC Customs Governing Import and Export Commodities Involved in Import Processing* (promulgated 6 May 1999);
- *PRC Foreign Trade Law,* (adopted 12 May 1994); and
- *Provisional Measures on Administration of Examination and Approval of Processing Trade* (effective 1 June 1999).

Processing and assembly trade products are classified as prohibited, restricted, or permitted. The PRC Foreign Trade Law details the categorization of products, including those that are prohibited.

Restrictions

The relevant department in charge of foreign economics and trade at the local level has the right to approve all processing and assembly trade contracts. MOFTEC is responsible for nationwide examination and approval.

After completing processing or assembly, the end products must be exported within a specified time limit. This is specified in the Approval Certificate for Processing Trade Business and is, in principle, the same term as the export contract, which is generally not more than one year. Further permission must be obtained to make domestic sales of imported parts and materials and the completed end products.

Incentives

Various regulations provide incentives to encourage Chinese enterprises to undertake processing and assembly arrangements. Normally, imported goods are subject to customs duties, product tax or value-added tax. Imported parts and materials, which are used to produce end products and are then exported under a processing and assembly contract, however, are specifically exempt from these levies. Other incentives include waiver of import licence requirements, retention of a high proportion of the foreign exchange earned, other tax reductions and priority access to financing.

Management contracts

Foreign investors may cooperate with PRC enterprises through management contracts in certain locations and industries. Under such agreements the foreign party generally provides day-to-day management and training for a PRC enterprise in return for a share of revenues. As the PRC enterprise is generally responsible for providing the business facilities, equipment and staff, this type of business arrangement allows the foreign party to invest in a PRC without making a substantial capital contribution.

Legislation

MOFTEC promulgated the *Contract Management Regulations for Sino-foreign Joint Equity Enterprises* on 15 October 1990, to govern foreign management contracts.

Joint ventures

JVs may be contractually managed under certain conditions, such as when a JV is in financial trouble. The management contractor assumes all or part of the JV's operational and administrative rights and shares responsibility for the JV 's risks and liabilities. The board of directors must unanimously consent to be administered and the JV must submit proof of this to its original approval authorities, together with other documentation such as the management contractor's legal and financial status. The term may not exceed five years. In order to provide management under such an agreement, the contractor must demonstrate that it conducts business in the same industry as the JV and has at least three years of relevant management experience.

Agency relationships

A major point of discontent for foreign entities seeking to sell to PRC consumers has been market barriers put in place by the PRC government, which has generally restricted or prohibited the importation and distribution of foreign manufactured goods. As a result, foreign entities unwilling to establish FIEs have been forced to enter the PRC market via other avenues, the most common of which are agency and distribution agreements.

Foreign entities often appoint Chinese enterprises as agents or distributors. The local enterprises handle issues related to domestic sales on the foreign principal's behalf and assist with procuring export goods or materials. One positive aspect of the principal agent relationship is that, by utilizing an agent's knowledge of PRC markets, business contacts and distribution channels, foreign enterprises may achieve a certain degree of market penetration. However, market penetration often comes at a cost.

One important aspect of the principal/agent relationship is the concept of foreign trade authority (FTA). FTA is basically a government-sanctioned oligopoly. Under the *PRC Foreign Trade Law* only PRC enterprises with FTA may directly contract with foreign parties. This means that, unless the proposed agent has FTA (which is often not the case), the foreign entity must establish a contractual relationship with a third party, licensed PRC importer. This additional barrier to business relationships was a major obstacle in China's WTO negotiations and, as a result, all PRC entities should have FTA by 2005.

Franchising

A number of foreign entities have considered franchising as an alternate way to access the PRC market. However, the lack of a comprehensive and developed regulatory framework has limited the number of international franchise arrangements.

Legislation

The PRC laws governing franchising generally include:

- *The Rules for the Administration of Commercial Franchise Operations* (the Franchise Rules), promulgated on 17 November 1997 by the Ministry of Internal Trade;
- *The Circular Regarding the Response by the State Council To Questions Related to Foreign Investment in Domestic Trade*, issued by the State Council in 1992;
- *The Catalogue for the Guiding of Foreign Investment in Industry in the PRC* (the Foreign Investment Guidelines); and
- *The Measures for Pilot Projects for Commercial Enterprises with Foreign Investment*, issued by the SETC and MOFTEC in June 1999.

Practical considerations

China has yet to publish a definitive set of franchising regulations, although, at the time of this Chapter's publishing, new draft regulations have been circulated in the international community, and the MOFTEC is rumoured to be reviewing the draft language with an eye towards promulgation in late 2002 or early 2003. Today, however, most foreign enterprises franchise in the PRC through FIEs or licensing agreements.

Franchising through FIEs

The main issues under this type of arrangement are that FIEs are limited in their business scope so that franchising is normally not included and that investment in China is restricted by industry type by the Foreign Investment Guidelines. Nevertheless, certain foreign entities have established FIEs that execute franchise/licensing agreements with PRC domestic enterprises.

Franchising through licensing agreements

Considering the lack of legal clarity, foreign investors sometimes break down their franchise arrangements into a series of contracts that are more familiar within the PRC legal context. For example, instead of having a single franchise agreement, it may be desirable to conclude a trademark licensing agreement, a know-how transfer agreement and agreements for management consulting services. This increases transaction costs, but phrases the transaction terms in concepts more familiar to MOFTEC and other approval authorities. It also avoids some of the pitfalls associated with painting the arrangement as something entirely new.

Employment law for Chinese and foreign nationals

The Ministry of Labour and Social Security (the Ministry) formed in 1998 when the PRC Labour and Social Securities Ministries were merged. The Ministry is responsible for formulating national labour and social security policies. The labour and social security bureaus, which sit beneath the Ministry, are responsible for administering the national and local regulations.

Legislation

The *PRC Labour Law* (the Labour Law), effective from 1 January 1995, and the *PRC Trade Union Law*, promulgated on 28 June 1950 and revised on 3 April 1992 and 17 October 2001, are the principal Chinese labour laws. The laws, which apply to all enterprises and economic organizations, address most employment issues including recruitment, contracts, wages, work conditions, occupational health and safety, women in the workforce and dispute resolution.

Under the Labour Law all employers and employees must execute labour contracts that define the parties' rights and obligations and include the term, nature of the job, safety and working conditions, remuneration, discipline, and conditions for termination and breach of contract. Supplementary laws have also been issued for particular aspects of employment, including:

- *The Regulations on Labour Management in Foreign Investment Enterprises* (the Labour Management Regulations), adopted in 1994;
- *The Regulations of the State Council Governing Working Hours for Workers*, adopted in 1995; and
- *The Provisional Administrative Measures on Wage Incomes of FIEs*, adopted in 1997.

Labour practices also vary between regions as provincial and local labour departments have fairly wide discretion in handling local labour matters.

Recruitment

FIEs may recruit Chinese employees directly or through local employment service centres. Foreign nationals, however, require approval from the local labour bureau and the employer must demonstrate why local employees cannot fill the position or do not otherwise qualify.

Wages

The Labour Law provides a minimum wage requirement, which is determined at a provincial level. The 1993 *Regulations on Minimum Wages in Enterprises* (amended in October 1994) require all provinces, autonomous regions, and directly administered municipalities to set minimum wage standards and report them to the Ministry. Employers that fail to meet these standards may be ordered to compensate employees for the difference, pay other compensation, or both. Employers must also deduct and withhold employee individual income tax, social security and related payments.

Subsidies

Employers must pay living subsidies and provide medical treatment allowances for all PRC employees. Employers and employees must also participate in the PRC social insurance system for unemployment, old age pension, medical treatment, work-related injuries, and maternity care. In addition to these mandatory subsidies, employers may also introduce incentive schemes such as bonuses or allowances. These schemes must be paid out of an employee bonus and welfare fund which is created from the employer's after-tax profits.

Employment terms

The standard workweek is five, eight-hour days. Enterprises requiring different standards may, with approval from the local labour administration, adopt flexible work systems.

Overtime

Restrictions apply to overtime work. Overtime may not exceed one hour a day and 36 hours a month, although, under special circumstances and subject to agreement with trade unions and employees, this may be longer. Standard overtime wages are:

- 150 per cent of regular wage for overtime;
- 200 per cent of regular wage for work on rest days where alternative rest days cannot be found; and
- 300 per cent of regular wage for work on statutory holidays.

Annual leave

Employees are only entitled to annual leave after one year's service with the same employer. The amount of annual leave varies according to work obligations, qualifications, and other factors, but normally does not exceed two weeks a year. Employees are also entitled to home leave if they are required to live away from their spouse or parents. Employees visiting their spouse are entitled to 30 days home leave per year. Home leave to visit parents is either 20 days per year or 20 days per four years, depending on whether the employee is married.

Other restrictions

Special laws protect various aspects of female employees such as maternity benefits. 'Minor' employees between the ages of 16 and 18 years are also protected under special occupational health and safety measures, including special procedures for hiring minors. Hiring children less than 16 years of age is strictly prohibited. Employers must also implement occupational health and safety programmes in the workplace, and conduct regular physical examinations for employees in hazardous occupations.

Termination

Employment termination is complicated in the PRC and employers should exercise caution when sacking employees.

Termination by the employer

Employers may dismiss employees without notice only when the employee:

- is dismissed during the statutory probation period;
- has seriously violated workplace rules;
- causes great losses to the employer due to serious dereliction of duty, embezzlement or another criminal offence; or
- is being investigated for a criminal offence.

Employers may otherwise dismiss employees, by first giving 30 days' notice only when the employee:

- is unable to take up his original or any new work upon returning from non-work- related medical treatment for illness or injury;
- is unqualified for his job and remains unqualified even after receiving training or an adjustment to another work post; and
- is unable to agree with the employer, after mutual consultation, to modify his labour contract when the purpose for which he was originally hired has significantly changed or no longer exists.

Employers may not dismiss employees when they:

- suffer from a work-related sickness or injury that has been medically confirmed as having completely or partially caused the employee to lose the ability to work;
- suffer from an illness or injury for which medical treatment within a specified period is allowed; or
- are pregnant, on maternity leave or within the specified period for nursing.

The *Provisions Concerning Economic Redundancy in Enterprises* (effective 1 January 1995) allow employees to be laid-off or dismissed for economic reasons, such as when the employer:

- faces bankruptcy,
- undergoes statutory reorganization Court order, or
- falls into 'serious operational difficulty' as defined by the local government.

Employers, however, must give priority to laid-off employees if they recruit again within six months after a layoff.

Termination by the employee

Employees generally may resign at will, but generally must give at least 30 days' notice. No notice is required if an employee resigns:

- where the employer has 'coerced' workers with violence, threats or illegal restrictions on personal freedom;
- where the employer fails to pay wages or provide working conditions as agreed to in the labour contract; or
- at any time during his/her probation period.

Labour disputes

The *PRC Regulations Concerning the Handling of Labour Disputes in Enterprises* and the *Provisional Regulations on Handling of Personnel Disputes* establish the procedures for handling labour disputes. Under the dispute regulations, parties are encouraged to settle labour disputes by negotiation or mediation. If neither of these works, the parties must resort to compulsory arbitration before they may initiate legal proceedings.

Foreign employees

Foreign nationals may work in the PRC only after obtaining Employment Permits and Residence Certificates except where they:

- are a professional technician or management personnel employed directly by the Chinese Government;
- hold a Foreign Expert Certificate issued by the Foreign Expert Bureau and are employed by state authorities or public institutions;
- have specialized skills working in offshore petroleum operations without the need to go ashore and hold a Work Permit for Foreign Personnel Engaged in Offshore Petroleum Operations in the PRC; or
- engage in commercial activities with the approval of the Ministry of Culture and hold a permit to conduct temporary commercial activities.

Legislation

The *Administrative Regulations on the Employment of Foreign Nationals in the PRC* (the Provisions), promulgated on 22 January 1996, govern the employment of foreign nationals in the PRC (holders of Hong Kong, Taiwan and Macao travel documents are governed by separate regulations). The Provisions require that an employer must prove that a 'special need' (defined as where there are requirements for a position for which there is a temporary shortage of suitable local candidates) exists before employing a foreign national.

Foreigners without residency rights seeking employment in the PRC must:

- be at least 18 years of age and be in good health;
- have no criminal record;
- have a confirmed prospective employer;
- hold a valid passport or other international travel document; and
- be qualified for the position for which a 'special need' exists.

Representative offices

Registered representative offices are subject to different regulations. All Chinese staff hired by representative offices must be employed from Chinese organizations authorized by the State to provide services to foreign enterprises. Direct private hiring is prohibited.

Intellectual property: well-known trademarks

Legislation

Legislation relevant to the protection of well-known trademarks in the PRC includes:

- *Paris Convention for the Protection of Industrial Property* (the Paris Convention) 14 July 1967;
- *Agreement on Trade-related Aspects of Intellectual Property Rights* (the TRIPS Agreement) 15 April 1994;
- *Recognition and Administration of Well-known Trademarks Tentative Provisions* (the Tentative Provisions) 14 August 1996;
- *Trademark Office of the SAIC, Several Questions Concerning Applications for the Recognition of Well-known Trademarks Circular* (the Circular) 28 April 2000;
- *PRC Trademark Law, 2nd Revision* (the Trademark Law), 1 December 2001; and
- *Regulation for the Implementation of the PRC Trademark Law* (the Implementing Regulations), 15 September 2002.

Defined

Well-known trademarks are trademarks that enjoy a high reputation and are known through long-term use and which, due to their general recognition and reputation, cause the public to associate them immediately with certain commodities or services. Although not clearly defined under PRC law, the following factors are considered when well-known status is granted to a trademark:

- the trademark's degree of recognition among the relevant public;
- the length of continuous use of the trademark;
- the continuous length, degree and geographical scope of the publicity for the trademark;
- the record of protection of the trademark as a well-known trademark; and
- other factors associated with the trademark's being well-known.

Background

The concept of well-known trademarks originated under the Paris Convention. Article 6bis of the Paris Convention protects well-known trademarks, but the scope of protection is confined to the registration and use of trademarks identical with or similar to another person's well-known trademark for identical or similar goods. Under Article 16 of the TRIPS Agreement, however, protection of well-known trademarks includes the trademarks for goods or services of different classes from those for which an identical or similar trademark is used. China is a member of the Paris Convention, a signatory to the TRIPS Agreement, and now, a WTO member.

Under its WTO commitments, China must fully comply with the TRIPS Agreement standards for well-known trademarks. China's amendment of its Trademark Law is one way that it is trying to comply with its WTO commitments with respect to the TRIPS Agreement. Examples of such changes include stronger guidelines for authentication of a well-known trademark and judicial review of trademark office decisions.

Authentication under the revised Trademark Law

Before it was revised in 2001 the Trademark Law did not directly protect well-known trademarks. Instead, the Tentative Provisions protected well-known trademarks. Under the Tentative Provisions, authentication and protection of well-known trademarks were difficult to achieve and decisions, which were the exclusive domain of the Trademark Review and Adjudication Board, were not subject to review. In its WTO negotiations China promised to amend those parts of the Trademark Law that were not TRIPS Agreement compliant.

The revised Trademark Law provides that any mark that copies, imitates or translates a third party's well-known trademark covering identical or similar goods or services will not be registered, regardless of whether the well-known mark is registered in China. With respect to different and unrelated goods and services, the trademark will only be prohibited from use or registration if it is a copy, imitation or translation of a well-known registered mark in China.

Judicial review

Perhaps the most noteworthy change in the amended Trademark Law is the transfer of the power of final adjudication from administrative departments to judicial departments. In China, trademark rights established by the Trademark Review and Adjudication Board under the SAIC had always been final and the parties could not request judicial review. The amended Trademark Law rescinds the power of final adjudication of the Trademark Review and Adjudication Board and allows the parties to initiate legal proceedings at the people's court.

Scope of protection

The scope of protection of well-known trademarks is generally broader than that of ordinary trademarks because unauthorized usage may cause the public to mistake the ownership or origin of the goods or services, thereby impairing the well-known trademark owner's rights and interests. While the owners of ordinary registered trademarks may prohibit others from using trademarks that are identical with or similar to their registered trademark for identical or similar goods registered in the same class, the owners of well-known trademarks registered in the PRC may block a third party's use of the same mark for goods or services in different classes. Well-known trademarks that have not been registered in the PRC are eligible for protection against unauthorized use on similar products. This underscores a gap between PRC legislation and the Paris Convention in that, under the Paris Convention, well-known trademarks include registered and unregistered trademarks, so long as the unregistered trademarks are well-known. Under the PRC Trademark Law, however, if a well-known trademark is not registered in the PRC, it will only receive protection for the same class of goods or services.

Obtaining well-known status

Under the Implementing Regulations well-known status may be obtained in two ways:

- First, if a dispute arises during a trademark registration or appraisal, and any party believes its trademark is well-known, such party may ask the Trademark Office or Review and Adjudication Board to recognize it as well-known and to reject or cancel any other trademark registrations or applications that violate Article 13 of the Trademark Law; or
- Second, if a party requests the SAIC to prohibit the use of a trademark that it considers well-known (as provided under Article 13 of the Trademark Law), the party must first prove such claim by applying for well-known status for the trademark at the Trademark Office. The Trademark Office will review the application in accordance with Article 14 of the Trademark Law and determine whether such trademark qualifies as well-known.

Alternatively, the PRC courts have also determined that certain foreign-owned trademarks are well-known, and therefore subject to protection in accordance with the Trademark Law.

Commercial dispute resolution

Foreign investors should consider various aspects of their investment or commercial activity in the PRC in light of the dispute resolution options that are available should the need arise.

Legislation

The legal framework generally governing dispute resolution in the PRC consists of various laws including the:

- *New York Convention on the Recognition & Enforcement of Foreign Arbitral Awards* (the New York Convention);
- *PRC Civil Law*;
- *PRC Civil Procedure Law* (the Civil Procedure Law);
- *PRC Arbitration Law* (the Arbitration Law); and
- *PRC Contract Law*.

In specific cases, however, other laws may also impact on the choice of law and available dispute resolution options. These laws include the *Labour Law*, the *PRC Law on Sino-foreign CJVs*, and the *PRC Law on Sino-foreign EJVs*.

There are four general methods that parties use to resolve commercial disputes arising in the PRC: namely, negotiation (or 'friendly consultation'), mediation, arbitration and litigation.

Negotiation and mediation

Negotiation is often the first step in the PRC dispute resolution process. Foreign investors sometimes prefer negotiated settlements that are voluntarily accepted by their PRC counterparts in light of the difficulties associated with enforcing judgments in the PRC.

Mediation can provide the first formal step in dispute resolution if the parties are unable to negotiate. There are a number of mediation forums available in China, ranging from the People's Conciliation Committees (grassroots bodies that are generally called upon to mediate private disputes) to highly specialized commercial mediation centres. All mediation is voluntary and agreements reached through mediation are binding. Further action may be taken in the People's Courts where parties refuse to participate, decline to accept a mediated solution, or where one party fails to adhere to the terms of a mediated settlement.

China International Chamber of Commerce Conciliation Centres

The China International Chamber of Commerce (CICC) and the China Council for the Promotion of International Trade (CCPIT) have established more than 30 permanent commercial mediation centres within China. CCPIT Rules allow parties to appoint one or two mediators from a list of approved mediators with expertise in various fields including international trade, finance, intellectual property, technology transfers, construction and law.

Mediators are allowed wide latitude to conduct mediation and may exercise discretion over the admission and handling of evidence. Parties to CCPIT mediation may not refer to any information provided or offers made during the mediation in any future litigation or arbitration.

Conciliation conducted by the People's Courts

The People's Courts also conduct mediation, either as preliminary proceedings prior to litigation or later in the course of litigation. The Civil Procedure Law requires the People's Courts to conduct mediation between parties before commencing final litigation should mediation fail. If a mediated agreement is reached, it is signed by the judge, sealed by the Court and becomes enforceable upon execution by the opposing parties. Such a signed mediation agreement, formalized by the People's Court has the same legal effect as a final judgment and is subject to the same procedures for enforcement.

Arbitration

Arbitration is perhaps the most popular method of dispute resolution between PRC and foreign parties. Because China is a signatory to the New York Convention, most parties prefer to arbitrate outside the PRC, the most popular places being Hong Kong, Singapore and Stockholm.

Arbitration outside the PRC

As previously stated, most foreign parties prefer to resolve their disputes with PRC parties offshore. In certain contexts Chinese law allows parties to a foreign-related transaction to include dispute resolution clauses in agreements that provide for disputes to be submitted to arbitral tribunals outside the PRC. China acceded to the New York Convention in 1987, with two formal reservations: it only applies on the basis of reciprocity; and it only applies to disputes deemed commercial under PRC law.

Arbitration in the PRC

Although many disputes involving foreign parties are arbitrated offshore, where no previous agreement exists or PRC law forbids offshore resolution, it is also possible to arbitrate in China via PRC arbitral tribunals. The Arbitration Law establishes the standards for arbitrators and requirements for PRC arbitration commissions and the arbitration proceedings they conduct.

The Arbitration Law requires parties to agree voluntarily to submit to arbitration either before or after a dispute arises. Where a party attempts to litigate a dispute covered by a valid agreement to arbitrate, the People's Courts must dismiss the suit and refer the parties to arbitration. Most commercial disputes may be arbitrated.

The viability of arbitration as a means of dispute resolution is augmented by the Civil Procedure Law and relevant arbitration centre rules, that allow parties to seek injunctions to preserve property and evidence pending completion of an arbitration. The parties to the dispute may apply to the arbitration tribunal for injunctions, which may then be given full legal effect by the People's Courts.

The Arbitration Law requires arbitration tribunals to conduct mediation before rendering final decisions. When mediation is unsuccessful, the award made by the arbitration tribunal is binding upon the parties. The losing party has six months to appeal against a tribunal's decision. The Intermediate People's Courts retain powers to review and overturn awards where:

- there was no agreement to arbitrate;
- the issues arbitrated were not within the scope of the agreement to arbitrate;
- the dispute was outside the arbitration commission's jurisdiction;
- the composition of the arbitration tribunal or the arbitral proceedings did not conform to the tribunal's arbitration rules or other law;
- the arbitration decision was based upon fraudulent evidence;
- the arbitration tribunal clearly misapplied the law; or
- an arbitrator is guilty of misconduct, including the taking of bribes or otherwise acting out of self-interest.

Arbitration awards are also subject to cancellation by the Courts where they conflict with public policy.

The Arbitration Law contains special provisions for the arbitration of disputes that involve foreign investment and foreign trade (so called Foreign Affairs). Such arbitration may be handled by special Foreign Affairs arbitration tribunals (including CIETAC, discussed below) whose awards are subject to narrower review by the People's Courts. The People's Courts may consider cancelling such an arbitration award where a party did not receive meaningful notice and enforcement of the award would be contrary to public policy. However, awards are not subject to review due to the misapplication of law, insufficiency of evidence or misconduct by an arbitrator.

PRC arbitration tribunals

According to the *Notice of the Office of the State Council on Clarification of Several Issues Concerning the Implementation of the Arbitration Law of the PRC*, foreign-related disputes may be submitted to local arbitration tribunals where the parties have agreed. However, the parties may also select a Foreign Affairs arbitration forum.

The China International Economic and Trade Arbitration Commission

Although tainted by questionable decisions, the most popular alternative to offshore arbitration is the China International Economic and Trade Arbitration Commission (CIETAC). Established in Beijing in 1956, the CIETAC also has commissions in Shanghai and Shenzhen. CIETAC tribunals have jurisdiction to arbitrate disputes between:

- International or foreign-related enterprises (including those from Hong Kong, Macao and Taiwan);
- Separate FIEs; and
- FIEs and Chinese nationals.

CIETAC may also hear other types of disputes according to specific grants of jurisdiction pursuant to PRC law, such as Internet domain name disputes.

CIETAC maintains a list of approved arbitrators that includes professionals and experts from fields such as law, international business and trade, and science and technology. Presently there are a total of 492 arbitrators, 158 of whom are foreign nationals or residents of Hong Kong.

The CIETAC Arbitration Rules were amended by CCPIT and CICC, effective 1 October 2000. The Arbitration Rules set out the administrative guidelines for CIETAC and procedural rules for conducting the arbitration. Parties may appoint agents, including foreign lawyers, to represent them at arbitration. Parties may also nominate the language in which arbitration is to be conducted.

Where the dispute concerns less than 500,000 renminbi, or the parties otherwise agree, CIETAC can conduct streamlined summary arbitration proceedings. In summary proceedings, the arbitrators base their decisions on documentary evidence that the parties submit and must decide within 90 days of the formation of the tribunal, when necessary. The tribunal may also conduct hearings to receive testimony. Where hearings are conducted, the tribunal must issue its decision within 30 days of the conclusion.

Enforcement of arbitral awards in PRC Courts

PRC Courts must enforce foreign arbitration awards pursuant to the requirements of the New York Convention, except in limited circumstances. The execution of New York Convention obligations is embodied in the Code of Civil Procedure. The PRC Code of Civil Procedure provides that a party may sue to enforce an arbitral award in the Intermediate People's Court where one party fails to comply with such award. An action may be brought where the adverse party or the property subject to execution is located. PRC Courts are, however, often influenced and may refuse to enforce an arbitral award based on external considerations or law.

To counter this problem the Supreme People's Court issued a directive to the local People's Courts instituting procedural safeguards to encourage the enforcement of awards made in foreign arbitral tribunals and by foreign affairs tribunals within the PRC. The directive requires the Intermediate People's Courts to report their findings and reasoning to the Higher People's Courts where they refuse to enforce a foreign-related or foreign arbitral award. If the Higher People's Court affirms the lower Court's decision, they must in turn report their findings to the Supreme People's Court for final approval. Thus, no decision to bar enforcement of foreign or foreign affairs tribunal awards is final until the Supreme People's Court issues its approval. Awards rendered by domestic PRC arbitration tribunals, however, are not subject to the directive in cases that are not considered foreign-related under PRC law.

Hong Kong arbitral awards

Prior to Hong Kong's reunification with the mainland, PRC Courts were obligated to enforce arbitral awards issued by Hong Kong tribunals under the New York Convention. After Hong Kong's return, however, such awards could no longer be considered foreign and therefore the New York Convention could not apply.

On 24 January 2000 the PRC Supreme People's Court promulgated the *Arrangements of the Supreme People's Court on the Reciprocal Enforcement of Arbitral Awards by Mainland China and the Hong Kong SAR* (the Arrangements) to solve this problem. The arrangements require the Courts of the Hong Kong SAR (HKSAR) to enforce arbitral awards issued by mainland arbitration tribunals, subject to the Arbitration Law.

PRC Courts are similarly obligated to enforce arbitral awards issued by Hong Kong tribunals, pursuant to HKSAR law. When asked to enforce awards from the other jurisdiction, HKSAR and PRC Courts may refuse enforcement under circumstances very similar to those enumerated in the Arbitration Law and the New York Convention.

Litigation

Redress may also be sought in the People's Courts where mediation fails and the parties have not agreed to arbitrate their dispute. The PRC grants the right to sue and be sued to all aliens, foreign enterprises and foreign organizations based on reciprocity. PRC Courts will apply any restrictions placed on the rights of Chinese nationals when litigating in a foreign forum to the nationals of that forum.

In most civil claims the People's Court where the defendant is domiciled will have jurisdiction. In contract and tort claims, however, the People's Court in the jurisdiction where the contract was executed or tort was committed also has jurisdiction.

Appeals may be made to the appropriate Court of second instance, usually either the Intermediate or Higher People's Courts wherever a party objects to the ruling of the People's Courts. Courts of appeal must make their rulings within three months of the filing of the appeal, although extensions are granted in some cases. Rulings of the Courts of second instance are final and binding upon the parties.

Despite increased attempts at professionalism, PRC Courts are still susceptible to cronyism. Litigants are often subjected to prolonged delays even where Courts adhere to the letter of the law, especially when trying to enforce judgments. Nonetheless, the Code of Civil Procedure requires that judgments be timely executed and appeals to higher Courts allowed where execution is not rendered. In cases where property subject to execution is in the jurisdiction of another People's Court, that Court may be asked to execute the judgment within 15 days.

Gary Lock is a partner with Herbert Smith's corporate group and focuses on corporate finance, international capital raising exercises, and M&A in the PRC and Hong Kong. Gary has extensive experience in corporate finance and commercial transactions, including advising on Hong Kong and PRC securities regulations, mergers and acquisitions, corporate reorganizations, privatization and joint ventures.

Brinton M. Scott is a senior associate in Herbert Smith's corporate group where he focuses on M&A, IP, and general PRC foreign direct investment. His PRC legal experience exceeds six years and he has counselled an array of industries including, pharmaceutical, gas, automotive, high-tech, and entertainment. Josh Mandell and Kenneth Wong, research assistants in the Shanghai office of Herbert Smith's associate firm Gleiss Lutz Hirsch, assisted the authors.

Foreign Direct Investment Vehicles in China

Edward R. J. Neunuebel, Denton Wilde Sapte, China

Introduction and legislation

This chapter will introduce the reader to the alternative investment formats which are available in the PRC to foreign investors: equity joint ventures (EJV), cooperative joint ventures (CJV), Sino-foreign-invested joint stock companies (SFJSC), wholly foreign-owned enterprises (WFOE), and holding companies (also referred to as investment companies)(HC) and technology transfer. While technology transfer is not, strictly speaking, a separate investment vehicle, it is an investment of sorts and most foreign investments involve technology transfers. We will also look briefly at privatization, the use of stock exchanges as investment facilitators, and mergers and acquisitions as they are intimately related to FDI.

The doors to foreign direct investment (FDI) *via* the EJV and CJV formats were opened first in 1979 with the enactment of the *People's Republic of China Law on Chinese–Foreign Equity Joint Ventures.* WFOE investment became possible after the promulgation of the *Law of the People's Republic of China on Wholly Foreign-Owned Enterprises in 1986,* and the *Detailed Implementation Regulations for the Law of the People's Republic of China on Wholly Foreign-Owned Enterprises,* which became effective in 1986. FJSC investment became possible in 1985 with the *Provisional Regulations on the Establishment of Foreign Invested Joint Stock Companies.* HC investment was opened with the 1995 *Establishment of Companies with an Investment Nature by Foreign Investors Tentative Provisions.* Other important central governmental, as opposed to local, legislation for FDI vehicles and technology transfer are appended to this chapter.

In addition to the above, the 1999 *Contract Law of the People's Republic of China* and the 1993 *People's Republic of China Company Law* are also important pieces of legislation. The *Company Law* as well as the EJV law also apply to WFOEs where the WFOE laws do not cover a particular matter.

The recent accession of China to the WTO will have a massive impact on the economic scene in China and this includes foreign investment. For several years China has been enacting, repealing and amending its legislation to facilitate WTO entry. China has adopted the civil law system rather than the common law. As such its current practice is to adopt statutes and supplement them with implementing regulations and interpretations. While court precedent is somewhat influential, it is not binding law *per se.*

The goal of the WTO is to promote free and open trade among its member states. This does not directly include investment; however, WTO membership mandates the principle of national treatment and this affects foreign investments. As China is reshaping its laws to unify its bifurcated treatment of domestic and foreign interests, notably in regard to taxation and most contracts, it still treats FIEs separately from domestic investment in the areas of governance.

Regulation of FDI

The two primary governmental agencies involved in regulating, permitting and governing FIEs are the Ministry of Foreign Trade and Economic Cooperation and its local arm (MOFTEC and COFTEC) and the State Administration for Industry and Commerce and its local arm (SAIC and AIC). MOFTEC is the gatekeeper and all FDI and technology transfers are channeled through its processes and regulated by it. The SAIC is charged with licensing, corporate governance, trademark administration and fair trade. There are numerous other state, provincial, local and industrial agencies having their own local regulations that also impact on FDI.

Technology licensing/assignment to China

As a recipient of technology transfer, China has been seen as lagging behind the rest of the industrialized world by maintaining overly-protective regulations, and by affording insufficient IP protection, that, in fact, keep cutting edge technology out of the country. It made a great leap forward in 2001 with adoption of the following in order to comply with the WTO's *Trade-Related Aspects of Intellectual Property Rights* agreement: *Technology Import and Export Administrative Regulations, Tentative Procedures for the Administration of Trade in the Import and Export of Technology, Administrative Measures on Prohibited and Restrictive Technology Imports* and the *Catalogue of Technologies Prohibited and Restricted for Imports*. These laws and regulations govern the import of technology. The import of restricted technology must be approved by MOFTEC (for major projects) or by COFTEC (for projects not deemed major). The import of unrestricted technology must be registered with, but not approved by MOFTEC (except where the technology is to form part of a contribution to registered capital) or by COFTEC. While not completely satisfactory to technology providers, they are a significant improvement over the old system and bring China's black letter law closer to international standards.

Registration involves submission of documentation, and is supposed to take three days from the date of completed submission. The contract is effective when duly signed and before registration. Registration is required by law, however, and the resulting registration certificate is needed for purposes of banking, tax, customs and foreign exchange purposes.

Application for approval for the importation of restricted technology may take two paths:

1. The application is submitted to the approval authority and, if approved, a Proposal for Technology Import Licence is issued. With this document the parties may enter into a contract, which is then submitted for approval. On approval, an import licence is issued and only then does the contract take effect; or

2. A signed contract may be submitted with the import application for a decision by the authority, and, if approved, the import is licensed.

The new regulations are more lenient than the old regarding the content of the technology transfer contract. They contain fewer obligatory provisions and allow the parties to negotiate compensation amounts and forms, guarantees, usage after expiration of the contract, and the term of confidentiality obligations. They still prohibit provision for tie-ins, clauses restricting improvements or use of improvements by transferee, and clauses restricting the transferee from using competing technology. The new regulations will allow 'reasonable' clauses restricting the following: sources of equipment and raw materials, products produced with the technology and export channels. Under the new regulations, however, improvements made by the transferee belong to the transferee.

Cooperative joint ventures

CJVs provide a flexible joint venture format. The venture may be, but does not have to be, an incorporated legal person. The parties are free to distribute profit and recover investment capital as negotiated. For example, the parties may agree on a equal equity split but provide for a different profit allocation ratio. CJVs have been popular in projects involving large start-up development costs such as hotels and oil and gas projects.

A CJV must have either a Board of Directors with a Chairman and Deputy Chairman, or a Management Committee, with a Director and Deputy Director, as well as a managerial structure and these functions are similar to those of an EJV described below.

Equity joint ventures

EJVs represent a compromise of China's initial preference for technology licencing rather than investment and they have been allowed and regulated since 1979. An EJV is a limited liability company created pursuant to the EJV Law in which the investor parties share investment, control, risk and profit in accordance with the equity split. The Board of Directors plays the role of shareholder and board because, since no shares are issued, there are no shareholders. Equity interests are certified by qualified accountants.

The industrial sectors open to EJVs are more numerous than those open to WFOEs. The *Guideline Catalogue of Foreign Investment Industries* classifies sectors as encouraged, permitted, restricted and prohibited. With WTO accession these categories have all increased, except for the prohibited category. There are many sectors where EJVs are, but WFOEs are not, allowed. In some sectors the foreign equity is limited to a certain percentage.

EJVs are established via the following process:

- the parties negotiate and sign a Letter of Intent which, although not necessarily legally binding, is very important and should be treated seriously. The LOI should cover all important issues related to the project and be broad enough to allow a party to alter its position if necessary. It is wise to include exclusivity and confidentiality provisions in the LOI and to state that they are intended to be legally binding;
- the Chinese party prepares a project proposal report to be submitted to MOFTEC/COFTEC;
- the LOI is then submitted to the approval authorities for preliminary approval, which includes permission to negotiate the project;
- following preliminary approval, a joint feasibility study is undertaken. As the FS is the basis for formal project approval, it effectively defines the permitted project in the eyes of the Government. Again, while the FS is not necessarily legally binding it is extremely critical and should be treated as such. Although the Chinese investor may be willing to take charge of the FS work, the foreign investor should participate and be sure that it represents its views as well. Both parties must sign;
- while the FS is under way the parties negotiate the joint venture contract and its annexes which typically include the articles of association, technology licence, export agency agreements and other important contracts or documents;
- the FS, JVC and articles of association are then submitted to the approval authority (MOFTEC or COFTEC). The contracts take effect upon approval;
- the joint venture company registers with the Administration of Industry and Commerce and receives its business licence;
- within 30 days of the issuance of the business licence, the company must process registrations with customs, tax, the State Administration for Foreign Exchange and other government agencies.

Throughout the approval process it is a good idea for the foreign party to establish and maintain good relationships with government officials and departments rather than leave the matter to the Chinese partner. In general, approval levels for productive projects are: $100 million

of registered capital and greater – The State Council; US$30 million to US$100 million – MOFTEC; less than US$30 million – COFTEC. The local COFTEC approvals are seen as easier to obtain than MOFTEC approvals even though COFTEC is a branch of MOFTEC. Because of this the local partner might suggest the project be broken into parts within the limits allotted to COFTEC. This might work to the disadvantage of the foreign investor and should be avoided.

The Chairman of the Board is the legal representative of the company, and, as such, anything (ie anything which is within the legal scope of business of the company) he/she does in his/her capacity as Chairman binds the company *vis à vis* a third party. The chief executive officer of the company is the General Manager who is appointed by the Board along with other senior management. This person manages the day-to-day operations. The Chairman and the General Manager may be foreigners as well as Chinese and they are assisted by deputies. Usually, the Chairman is appointed from nominees of the PRC investor and the Deputy Chairman from nominees of the foreign investor. There is a provision in the law for one or more Deputy General Managers as well.

The Board meets at least once per year. Certain critical corporate decisions (amendments to the articles of association, assignment or increase in registered capital, dissolution and merger), by law require unanimous consent of the Board.

While EJVs are the FDI format most acceptable to MOFTEC, they are not allowed in every sector and, where allowed there may be limitations on the equity interest held by the foreign investor.

Wholly foreign-owned enterprises

WFOEs, companies owned by one or more foreign investors, are authorized under the *Wholly Foreign-owned Enterprise Law in 1986*, and the *Wholly Foreign-owned Enterprise Law Implementing Rules* of 1990, are seen as having fewer management and profitability problems and are now more popular among the foreign investment community than joint ventures because they do away with conflicting partner interests, corporate cultural differences and other control problems inherent in any joint venture.

WFOEs have become an important part of the investment scene. MOFTEC (COFTEC) regulates WFOEs more stringently than it does joint ventures. China currently bans WFOEs in key sectors such as publishing, telecommunications, some petrochemicals, some chemicals, pharmaceuticals and agriculture.

WFOE project proposals are submitted to MOF-TEC/COFTEC, depending on the registered capital of the project, and if approved, a formal application is made with the company's proposed articles of association and a feasibility study. Documents relevant to the investors are also required. If approved it takes the form of a limited liability company for a specified term, although a perpetual existence is theoretically possible. After approval the WFOE must go through the same AIC registrations as any other company. Laws, regulations and policies, which are passed for other FIEs often apply to WFOEs.

Where an investment project has begun as a joint venture limited liability company, it is often converted into a wholly foreign-owned company with the buyout of the PRC party's equity. This is accomplished by assignment of equity after approval of the Chinese partner and the original approval authority (MOFTEC or COFTEC) pursuant to the 1997 *Several Regulations Of The Ministry Of Foreign Trade And Economic Cooperation And The State Administration For Industry And Commerce Concerning Changes In The Equity Interest Of Investors In Foreign Invested Enterprises*. Considerable discretion is given to the local authorities in the actual conversion process.

Holding (investment) companies

HCs are governed by *The Provisional Regulations for the Investment and Operation of Investment Companies by Foreign Investors* and by the 1996–2001 explanations of and supplements to the *Provisional Regulations*. The impetus for this vehicle came from the foreign investment community which wanted a format that would allow certain facilities that were not present under the other formats. This investment format is a FIE limited liability company, either wholly-owned or joint ventured, without the right to manufacture. It allows integration and rationalization of a parent's China investment structure, direct hiring of PRC staff, centralization of PRC project shareholdings, human resources, sales, marketing and technical services and procurement. It does not allow direct intra-group lending or consolidated accounting.

Although having an HC raises the profile and prestige of the parent company within China, an HC has not been allowed to be engaged in trading services, production, or buying A shares (reserved for PRC legal persons)

of listed PRC companies. With WTO accession, HCs are expected to be utilized in trading and financing investments (without participation of the People's Bank of China) as it opens up to FIEs. Because of the trading restrictions, therefore, an HC is not a replacement for a representative office in locales employing a strict interpretation of the HC laws and regulations.

The requirements for establishing an HC are stringent: the foreign investor's asset value must be at least US$400 million; the parent must have established at least one FIE with at least US$10 million of the foreign investor's investment; and have at least three FIE projects which have received project approval (in this case, the *lixiang* approval) or have set up at least 10 manufacturing or construction FIEs in which it has invested at least US$30 million. Like many PRC regulations, the HC Regulations are selectively applied by MOFTEC, which is given the discretion to ignore certain requirements for establishing an HC.

MOFTEC retains control and supervision over HCs. The primary documentation to be submitted for HC application includes:

- proposal;
- feasibility study;
- joint venture contract, if applicable; or
- application form, if a WFOE;
- articles of association.

Foreign-invested joint stock companies

Also known as companies limited by shares, this format, unlike the other joint venture formats, issues stock. It was created in 1995 but has not been utilized extensively by foreign investors (Kodak is an exception) who are more familiar and comfortable with the EJV/CJV and WFOE laws, since the corporate governance burden placed on FSJCs is greater compared to that placed on other foreign invested joint ventures. As a vehicle for foreign investment, therefore, the FSJC has a short track record. This joint venture vehicle may be more appropriate now that FIEs are contemplating listing on the China stock exchanges to access capital. Most listed companies in China are joint stock companies. The investor's ownership interest in, and liability in relation to, the company is measured by shares of stock held rather than by registered capital. Joint venture companies may convert to FJSCs but it is not clear whether WFOEs may do so. On inquiry to MOFTEC, MOFTEC replied that since under Article 75 of the *Company Law* at least half of the five or more pro-moters of a FJSC must be domiciled in China, conversion of a WFOE into a FJSC was not possible. This explanation appears to conflict with Article 15 of the *Provisional Regulations of the Ministry of Foreign Trade and Economic Cooperation on Certain Issues Concerning the Establishment of Foreign Investment Companies Limited By Shares* which sets out the process for conversion of a foreign owned enterprise into a company limited by shares. Strict compliance with Article 75 and Article 15 is possible, therefore it is difficult to see their logic in this. But if this is MOFTEC's position, a conversion is not possible regardless of the logic used, as MOFTEC's approval is required.

Branches of foreign companies

Branches are allowed in theory by Chapter 9 of the *PRC Company Law*. In practice they are used only in construction and oil exploration, as approval is withheld.

Privatization, mergers and acquisitions of SOEs

The Government would like to see more acquisitions of State owned enterprises' (SOE) assets but few foreign companies are willing, without access to local stock exchanges and sources of equity, to assume the over-staffed SOEs with their attendant employee and social burdens. Additional deterrents include a well-founded fear, learned abroad, of trailing environmental remediation costs and liabilities, not to mention the poor state of a majority of the assets. Direct acquisitions of SOE company equity, of listed or unlisted companies, involve the additional problems of undisclosed liabilities and uncollectible accounts receivable; so this form of acquisition is even less likely in the medium term. Again, there would have to be a great deal of comfort regarding environmental liability before a foreign company would buy a site with the possibility of pre-existing environmental conditions and latent liability. Traditional merger and acquisition contract indemnification obligations and remedies would not provide such comfort, and it is doubtful that the buyer could negotiate a suitable escrow arrangement or a significant price reduction.

Indirect acquisition by foreign companies purchasing floated SOE shares has rarely been possible and requires MOFTEC approval, in consultation with other relevant agencies, on a case-by-case basis. To date only very small interests in companies like PetroChina, Sinopec and CNOOC have been floated allowing portfolio investment but no control benefits. Nevertheless, recent reports indicate that from 1 December 2002, foreigners will be allowed to acquire controlling interests in listed companies through the stock exchanges or through contract purchases. Until then take-overs are possible only by domestic companies. According to rules entitled the *Listed Company Takeover Rules,* a 30 per cent stake of a listed company is considered a controlling interest. There is no indication that these rules would apply to the strategic sector industries which include petrochemicals and chemicals, and case-by-case approval is required.

Additional matters

There are other matters that are relevant to FDI such as arbitration, tax, customs and termination. As they are covered in other chapters of this book, they are not included above. Finally, there are local regulations, policies and practices which apply to many issues discussed above and attention must also be paid to those when meeting with local officials.

Checklist for a joint venture contract:

- name and location of the JVC;
- business scope of the JVC;
- capital structure and contribution schedule;
- Board of Directors provisions: Chairman, members, powers, limitations and meetings;
- general management provisions: managerial structure, powers and limitations;
- land and facilities – offices, plant and factory;
- project schedule – construction and start-up;
- sales;
- financial provisions – tax, audit, accounting, finance management, bank accounts, profit allocation and distribution;
- investment incentives;
- labour – sourcing, hiring, probation, firing and unions;
- procurement of technology;
- procurement of raw materials for production;
- joint venture term, expiration and termination provisions;
- duties, powers and rights of the investors;
- liability of the investors;
- dispute resolution.

Annexes:

- articles of association;
- technology licence;
- export agency agreement;
- domestic sales agreement;
- form for proxy/power of attorney.

Mandatory provisions for technology licences:

- licensor's warranty that it is the legal owner or licensor/assignor of the technology rights with right to licence;
- licensor's warranty of quality, efficacy and completeness of the technology;
- licensor's agreement to be responsible for infringement claims of third parties;
- licensor's agreement to be responsible for harm to the legal interests of third parties;
- contract expiration date;
- definite licence price.

Prohibited provisions in technology licences:

- unnecessary terms requiring the purchase of products, raw materials, equipment, technology or services;
- restrictions on improvement or use of improvements of the licensed technology;
- restrictions on acquisition of competitive technology;
- terms requiring payments or obligations arising out of expired or invalidated patents;
- unreasonably restrictive terms concerning procurement, sales price, export channel and product type.

Major legislation relevant to FDI

CJVs

1. *Law of PRC on Sino-foreign Cooperative Enterprises* (Adopted 13 April 1988 by NPC, revised 31 October 2000);
2. *Detailed Rules for the Implementation of the Law of PRC on Sino-foreign Cooperative Enterprises* (Promulgated 20 September 1995 by MOFTEC);
3. *Interpretation of the Implementation of Certain Articles of the Detailed Rules for the Implementation of the Law of PRC on Sino-foreign Co-operative Enterprises* (Promulgated 22 October 1996 by MOFTEC);

4. *Certain Regulations on the Subscription of Capital by the Parties to Sino-foreign Equity Joint Ventures* (Jointly promulgated 1 January 1988 by MOFTEC and SAIC);
5. *Contract Management Regulations for Sino-foreign Equity Joint Ventures* (Promulgated 15 October 1990 by MOFTEC);
6. *Guideline Catalogue of Foreign Investment Industries* (Promulgated 31 December, 1997, jointly by the SPC, SETC, and MOFTEC).

EJVs

1. *Law of PRC on Sino-foreign Equity Joint Ventures* (Adopted 1 July 1979 by NPC, amended 4 April 1990 and 15 March 2001);
2. *Detailed Rules for the Implementation of the Law of PRC on Sino-foreign Equity Joint Ventures* (Promulgated 20 September 1983 by the State Council, amended 15 January 1986, 21 December 1987 and 22 July 2001);
3. *Provisional Regulations on the Duration of Sino-foreign Equity Joint Ventures* (Promulgated 22 October 1990 by MOFTEC);
4. *Provisional Regulations of SAIC on the Ratio between the Registered Capital and Total Investment of Sino-foreign Equity Joint Ventures* (Promulgated 1 March 1987 by SAIC);
5. *Certain Regulations on the Subscription of Capital by the Parties to Sino-foreign Equity Joint Ventures* (Jointly promulgated 1 January 1988 by MOFTEC and SAIC);
6. *Supplementary Regulations on the Certain Regulations on the Subscription of Capital by the Parties to Sino-foreign Equity Joint Ventures* (Jointly promulgated 29 September 1997 by MOFTEC and SAIC);
7. *Contract Management Regulations for Sino-foreign Equity Joint Ventures* (Promulgated 15 October 1990 by MOFTEC).

WFOEs

1. *The Law of PRC on Wholly Foreign-owned Enterprises* (Adopted 12 April 1996 by NPC, revised 31 October 2000);
2. *Detailed Rules for the Implementation of the Law of PRC on Wholly Foreign-owned Enterprises* (Promulgated 12 December 1990 by MOFTEC, revised 12 April 2001);

3. *An Explanation of Several Terms Used in the Detailed Rules for the Implementation of the Law of PRC on Wholly Foreign-owned Enterprises* (Issued 6 December 1991 by MOFTEC).

SFJSCs

1. *Provisional Regulations on Several Issues Concerning the Establishment of Foreign Investment Companies Limited by Shares* (Promulgated 10 January 1995 by MOFTEC);
2. *Notice of the General Office of MOFTEC on Issues Concerning Certain Questions Regarding Foreign Investment Companies Limited by Shares* (Promulgated 17 May 2001);
3. *PRC Company Law* (Adopted 29 December 1993 by NPC, effective 1 July 1994);
4. *Special Regulations of the State Council Concerning Floating and Listing of Shares Overseas by Companies Limited by Shares* (Promulgated 4 August 1994 by the State Council);
5. *Certain Opinions on Issues Concerning Listed Companies with Foreign Investment* (Jointly issued 8 November 2001 by MOFTEC and China Securities Regulatory Commission);
6. *The Supplementary Notice on Issues Relevant to Converting the Unlisted Foreign Investment Shares of Foreign Investment Companies Limited by Shares into B Shares and Making them Tradable* (Promulgated 16 August 2002 by MOFTEC).

Holding companies

1. *Provisional Regulations Governing the Establishment of Investment-type Companies by Foreign Business Investment* (Promulgated 4 April 1995 by MOFTEC);
2. *An Explanation of Several Issues Concerning the Provisional Regulations Governing the Establishment of Investment-type companies by Foreign Business Investment* (Promulgated 16 February 1996 by MOFTEC);
3. *Supplementary Regulations to the Provisional Regulations Governing the Establishment of Investment-type Companies by Foreign Business Investment* (Promulgated 24 August 1999 by MOFTEC);
4. *Supplementary Regulations (II) to the Provisional Regulations Governing the Establishment of Investment-type Companies by Foreign Business Investment* (Promulgated 31 May 2001 by MOFTEC);

5. *Interim Provisions for the Establishment of Foreign Venture Investment Enterprises* (Jointly promulgated 28 August 2001 by MOFTEC, Ministry of Science and Technology and SAIC).

Foreign invested joint stock companies

Provisional Regulations of the Ministry of Foreign Trade and Economic Cooperation on Certain Issues Concerning the Establishment of Foreign Investment Companies Limited By Shares (Promulgated by MOFTEC 10 January 1995).

Major regulations applicable to all forms of FIEs:

1. *Provisional Regulations of SAIC on the Ratio between the Registered Capital and Total Investment of Sino-foreign Equity Joint Ventures* (Promulgated 1 March 1987 by SAIC);
2. *PRC Company Law* (Adopted 29 December 1993 by NPC, effective 1 July 1994);
3. *Notice of MOFTEC and SAIC on Relevant Regulations and Procedures for Adjustment of Aggregate Investment and Registered Capital by Foreign Investment Enterprises* (Jointly issued 25 May 1995 by MOFTEC and SAIC);
4. *Measures on Liquidation Procedures for Foreign Investment Enterprises* (Issued 9 July 1996 by MOFTEC);
5. *Certain Regulations on Changes to Shareholders' Rights in Foreign Investment Enterprises* (Promulgated 28 May 1997 by MOFTEC and SAIC);
6. *Supplementary Regulations on the Certain Regulations on the Subscription of Capital by the Parties to Sino-foreign Equity Joint Ventures* (Jointly promulgated 29 September 1997 by MOFTEC and SAIC);
7. *Interim Provisions on Investment Inside China by Foreign Investment Enterprises* (Jointly promulgated 25 July 2000 by MOFTEC and SAIC);
8. *Provisions on Merger and Division of Foreign Investment Enterprises* (Jointly issued 23 September 1999 by MOFTEC and SAIC, revised 22 November 2001).

Technology transfer

1. *PRC Regulations of Administration of Technology Import and Export* (Promulgated 31 October 2001 by the State Council, effective 1 January 2002);
2. *Measures for Administration of the Registration of Technology Import/Export Contracts* (Issued by MOFTEC 16 November 2001, effective 1 January 2002);

3. *Interim Measures of Administration of Import Trade of Technology and Equipment* (Promulgated 22 March 1996 by MOFTEC);

4. *Measures of Administration of Prohibited and Limited Exports of Technology* (Jointly promulgated 30 December 2001 by MOFTEC and Ministry of Science and Technology, effective 1 January 2002);

5. *Measures of Administration of Prohibited and Limited Imports of Technology* (Jointly promulgated 30 December 2001 by MOFTEC and State Economic and Trade Commission, effective 1 January 2002);

6. *PRC Contract Law* (Adopted 15 March 1999 by NPC, effective 1 October 1999);

7. *PRC Patent Law* (Adopted 12 March 1984, amended 4 September 1992, 25 August 2000, recent version effective 1 July 2000);

8. *Detailed Implementation Rules of the PRC Patent Law* (Effective 1 July 2000);

9. *Notice of the Supreme People's Court Regarding Distribution of Nationwide Courts Intellectual Property Hearing Working Conference Summary Concerning Hearing of Cases Involving Technology Contract Disputes* (Issued 19 June 2001 by the Supreme People's Court).

Edward R.J. Neunuebel is the Head of China Practice (Hong Kong) for Denton Wilde Sapte. He formerly served The Dow Chemical Company as its Global Assistant General Counsel and General Counsel for the Pacific Region. A USA-qualified attorney and Mandarin speaker, Ed has been involved primarily in the chemical, plastics, mining, and steel industries over his 27 years as an international lawyer concentrating on M&A, joint ventures, corporate, commercial and intellectual property matters.

Accounting and Auditing Requirements and Practices in the People's Republic of China

PricewaterhouseCoopers

In this chapter the general framework governing the accounting and auditing requirements in the People's Republic of China (PRC) is introduced. Following an examination of the characteristics and features of different types of enterprises set up since China opened its door to the outside world, the accounting and auditing requirements as set out in the prevailing accounting 'regulations' and 'systems' are described.

Background and development

With the founding of PRC in 1949 all resources of production in the country came under State ownership and basically the only form of economic entity was the state-owned enterprise. The accounting rules and regulations, known as fund accounting, and characterized by their rigidity and uniformity, were used on the one hand primarily for establishing an information and reporting system for the implementation of State economic policies, and on the other hand for the maintenance of administrative control over assets of the State. To a greater extent accounting rules also served as a tool to strengthen the financial discipline of an enterprise and to safeguard State property.

Since the promulgation of the *Joint Venture Law* in 1979 a separate set of accounting rules was formulated to govern the preparation of financial statements by enterprises. This was undoubtedly the first step away from the fund accounting concept, which applies to state-owned enterprises and is used mainly for the purpose of resource allocation in a planned economy.

Alongside economic reform and the open-door policy adopted since the beginning of the 1980s, foreign investors were allowed to set up enterprises and conduct business in China. A separate set of accounting regula-

tions that is applicable to foreign investment enterprises only was developed and implemented. Although these regulations or principles are now much in line with the *International Accounting Standards* (IAS), the requirements are subservient more to the purpose of ascertaining the amount of tax an enterprise should pay rather than to the purpose of ascertaining the 'truthfulness and fairness' of the financial statements.

Concurrently China has undertaken a programme to restructure the form and structure of state-owned enterprises by transforming them into enterprises which issue shares and have limited liability – joint stock limited companies. Most of these enterprises will eventually go public. A third set of accounting regulations, intended specifically for joint stock limited companies, was formulated in the early 1990s and revised in 1998.

The rapid growth of the economy, the demand for foreign investment, the gradual maturity of China's securities market and the accession into the WTO have highlighted the need for a sound, reliable and transparent accounting system acceptable to foreign investors. The accounting regulations and systems designed to cater for tax regulations and state ownership under the communist system can no longer meet modern business management and funding requirements. To meet the demands of foreign investors and an increasing number of individual and institutional investors in the securities market, a series of regulations were issued. These include the *Accounting Law* which was issued in 1999, the *Regulations on Financial Reporting of Enterprises* issued in 2000 and finally the *Accounting Systems for Business Enterprises* (ASBE) issued in early 2001. The ASBE sets out the fundamental accounting framework and is more in line with IAS.

In 2001 joint stock limited companies offering shares to the public were the first to be made mandatory to adopt the ASBE. The *Accounting Regulations for Selected Joint Stock Limited Companies* were then abolished.

In 2002 foreign investment enterprises were the second to adopt the ASBE. The *Accounting Regulations for Foreign Investment Enterprises of the PRC* were replaced. Although not yet mandatory, State-owned enterprises and other domestic enterprises are encouraged to adopt these new rules. In essence the ASBE will become the primary set of basic accounting regulations applicable to different types of enterprises.

Throughout 1996 33 new exposure drafts were prepared on specific accounting issues. At the time of writing, 16 specific accounting standards have been issued, although not all of them are mandatory to foreign investment enterprises. Nevertheless the focus is clearly to steer the current systems and standards towards IAS.

Setting accounting standards

Unlike Western practice, setting authoritative accounting standards is not the responsibility of the Accounting Society of China (ASC) or the Chinese Institute of Certified Public Accountants (CICPA). Instead the Ministry of Finance (MOF) is responsible for formulating, promulgating and administering accounting regulations. ASC and CICPA are responsible for regulating, governing and monitoring the reform and development of the accounting profession in China. The CICPA also assumes administrative authority, delegated by MOF, to serve as a bridge between the government and practising accountants.

In China the government issues accounting regulations. They are rules and must be strictly adhered to. With the introduction of the ASBE, individual companies are allowed to exercise judgment in formulating their own accounting policies which will suit specific circumstances.

The conceptual framework

In Western countries, although amendments and revisions to accounting practices or standards do not have legal binding power, they are formulated according to an existing national legal framework which is provided in most cases by *Companies Ordinance* or *Acts*. *Companies Ordinance* or *Acts* together with other regulations applicable to individual industries, such as the *Banking Ordinance* for financial institutions and *Listing Rules* or *Securities Acts* for listed or public companies, provide a framework upon which accounting professional bodies formulate accounting and auditing standards. These standards form the basis for establishing accounting principles, and perhaps conventions, that allow enterprises flexibility in formulating their own accounting policies best suited to their individual circumstances. The ultimate objective, in a nutshell, is to produce a set of financial statements that are 'true and fair'.

Until 1994 China lacked a regulatory framework on which accounting and auditing standards could be set since the country's first national *Companies Laws* were not effective until 1 July 1994. The lack of such a framework also rendered the formulation of other regulations, such as the national *Securities Laws* and *Listing Regulations*, more difficult and time consuming.

Nevertheless, having realized the need for establishing acceptable accounting principles to enable PRC enterprises to attract foreign investment or have their stocks listed on overseas markets, the MOF promulgated a separate set of accounting regulations for selected joint stock companies in January 1992.

In addition, MOF made effective on 1 July 1993 the first set of accounting standards – *Accounting Standards for Enterprises* – applicable to all PRC enterprises. Although it might be confusing at times which accounting regulations or standards would apply, together with the then *Accounting Regulations for Foreign Investment Enterprises of the PRC,* they have provided relatively uniform accounting practices for enterprises to follow in preparing their financial statements. More importantly because of the lack of a complete regulatory and conceptual framework, these accounting rules or regulations are so comprehensive that they encompass accounting concepts, disclosure requirements, accounting entries, control procedures, record keeping and some aspects of auditing requirements and liquidation.

With the introduction of the *Accounting Law* in 1999, the *Regulations on Financial Reporting of Enterprises* in 2000 and the *Accounting Systems for Business Enterprises* in early 2001, which harmonizes the different accounting standards and regulations applicable to different enterprises, the framework of modern Chinese accounting has finally become clear.

Forms and contents of financial statements

Under the *Accounting Law*, the *Regulations on Financial Reporting of Enterprises* and the ASBE, financial statements or reports should comprise a balance sheet, profit and loss accounts, cash flow statements, notes to the accounts and a profit and loss appropriation account. The regulations also cover classification of assets and liabilities in the balance sheet.

Accounting concepts and bases

The general accounting principles or concepts employed in China's accounting regulations include accuracy, completeness, consistency, comparability, timeliness, materiality, accrual basis, matching, prudence, substance over form and going concern. By and large, the principles mirror those of IAS. Other major features of these regulations are as follows:

- The historical cost convention is prescribed. Assets are required to be recorded at purchase cost (less any necessary impairment provision) and revaluations are strictly prohibited except when allowed by other State provisions.
- The concept of fair market value is not commonly used due to the limited existence of open markets.
- These regulations also require companies to use the calendar year, that is 1 January to 31 December, as their financial year.
- The double-entry bookkeeping method should be adopted. Records in accounts and books have to be made in renminbi (yuan) (the lawful currency of the PRC). Transactions and balances denominated in foreign currencies have to be converted into renminbi (yuan) at the official rate, which may differ from the current market rate. All records and balances of transactions made in foreign currencies and the exchange rates used must be maintained for reference.
- A clause in these regulations specifically requires the appropriation of a collective Welfare Fund and a Statutory Reserve Fund from profit after tax.
- Due to the infancy of the new systems, certain footnote disclosures may not be as comprehensive as those acceptable elsewhere in the world. Yet, in certain areas, the Chinese standards are extremely stringent. This includes disclosing the corporate identity of related parties and commenting on the fairness of transactions conducted between related parties, and preparing the cash flow statements using both the direct and indirect methods.

The old standards are neither broad nor flexible enough to allow discussion or manoeuvrability on particular subjects. For the first time, ASBE gives management the authority to exercise professional experience and judgment. While the setting of the ASBE has in theory narrowed the gap between accounting issues in China and those of the Western world, the rigour of applying the ASBE may vary from province to province and from company to company.

Auditing requirements

In Western countries limited liability companies are generally subject to an annual audit carried out by independent external auditors whose role is to express an objective opinion on the truthfulness and fairness of the financial statements.

In China, auditing is not a legal requirement but is required under the regulations. Prior to the introduction of the ASBE, the primary objective of auditing in China was to carry out inspection on the financial records of a business to ascertain their accuracy and legality (ie whether the transactions conducted complied with relevant State laws and regulations). Auditors in China are concerned with protecting the legal interests of the company as well as the interests of the State. Only with the implementation of the ASBE were the concepts of true and fair presentation introduced.

Prior to 2000 financial statements of state-owned enterprises were not required to be audited annually by independent auditors, but periodical or special audits conducted for the purpose of ascertaining the enterprise's tax liabilities or other purposes might be conducted by the State Audit Bureau or Tax Bureau. Since 2002, except for a few types of specialized industries that have been explicitly exempted, all other State-owned enterprises must be audited at least annually. In addition, the regulations governing the accounting of joint stock companies and foreign investment enterprises require these companies to be subject to annual audit carried out by registered Chinese certified public accounting firms. When reporting on whether the financial statements of foreign investment enterprises are prepared in accordance with the relevant laws and regulations, auditors may make reference to the following main laws and regulations:

- The *PRC Sino-foreign Equity Joint Venture Law* (EJV Law) promulgated by the National People Congress

(NPC), effective 8 July 1979 and revised 15 March 2001;

- *Implementing Regulations* of the EJV Law promulgated by the State Council (SC), effective 20 September 1983 and revised 22 July 2001;
- *The PRC Sino-foreign Cooperative Joint Venture Law* (CJV Law) promulgated by NPC, effective 13 April 1988 and revised 31 October 2000;
- *The PRC Wholly Foreign-Owned Enterprises Law* (WFOE Law) promulgated by NPC, effective 12 April 1986 and revised 31 October 2000;
- *Implementing Rules* of the WFOE Law promulgated by SC, effective 12 December 1990 and revised 12 April 2001;
- *The PRC Small and Medium Enterprises Law* (SME Law) promulgated by NPC and effective 29 June 2002;.
- *The PRC Income Tax Law for Foreign Investment Enterprises and Foreign Enterprises* (FIEs Income Tax Law) promulgated by NPC and effective 1 July 1991;
- *Implementing Regulations* of FIEs Income Tax Law promulgated by SC and effective 1 July 1991.

Auditing profession, standards and forms of audit report

Only very recently has the impact of accountants or auditors on national economic activities become more apparent. By virtue of the PRC Accounting Law promulgated in January 1985, the function of certified public accountants in carrying out audits was established. This law has now been superseded by the PRC *Registered Accountant Law* which became effective 1 January 1994. Following the setting up of the Chinese Institute of Certified Public Accountants in 1988, the status of certified public accountants and professional accounting firms in society received a major boost. In China some accounting firms are direct functional units of certain government bureaus. Although other professional accounting firms are not direct functional units of any government departments, many of them are still financially dependent units and require approval from the State to conduct their business as certified public accountants. In 1998 the State Council set forth regulations that require certified public accountants to be independent from any government bureaus. Many professional accounting firms have transformed (or are

in the process of transforming) in order to operate in the form of sole proprietorship or partnership with unlimited liabilities.

In December 1988 the Ministry of Finance promulgated the *Auditing and Certification Regulations (Provisional)* which sets out the roles of certified public accountants, audit scope and procedures and the requirements for maintaining audit working papers. From 1995 to 1996 four *General Independent Auditing Standards – Basic Standards, Quality Control, Continuing Education and Ethics* were issued. New specific auditing standards applicable 1 January 1997 were also promulgated, which complete and clarify the provisional regulations and general standards. So far, twenty-seven specific auditing standards, ten practice bulletins and four practice guidelines have been issued.

The audit report normally contains a scope paragraph and an opinion paragraph. The scope paragraph sets out the areas covered, the principal audit work and procedures carried out and the results. The opinion paragraph sets out whether the accounts have been prepared in accordance with the relevant laws and regulations. Any reservations in the opinion need to be elaborated on.

In some instances different government bureaus may stipulate their own requirements as to what certified public accountants should opine on. Sometimes these additional requirements have not been agreed by the Ministry of Finance or the CICPA and fall beyond the expertise of what is normally expected of a certified public accountant. In some circumstances these requirements issued by other government bureaus have been retracted.

Conclusions

To cope with modern business management and funding requirements, the internationalization of accounting standards of principles is becoming more important as it facilitates the provision of reliable and comparable information to both domestic and overseas investors. A system of auditing will undoubtedly enhance the reliability of financial statements. In view of the rapid development of accounting reform in China, the above is only a representation of the latest information available at the time of writing and it is recommended that professional advice should be sought on the latest position before making any business commitments.

Taxation Issues

Becky Lai, PricewaterhouseCoopers

Corporate taxation in China

Introduction

The existing income tax laws which affect foreign companies doing business in China are discussed in this chapter. Since the Chinese taxation system is still in a developmental stage, attention should be paid to interpretations and practices of the local tax authorities.

Currently, domestic enterprises and foreign enterprises (FE) and foreign investment enterprises (FIE) are governed by two different sets of enterprise income tax legislation.

FIEs include Chinese-foreign equity joint ventures, Chinese-foreign contractual joint ventures and wholly foreign-owned enterprises established in China. FEs include foreign companies, enterprises and other economic organizations which have establishments in China and are engaged in production or business operations or which, although without establishments in China, have income from sources within China.

Establishments refer to management offices, business organizations, representative offices, factories, places where natural resources are exploited, places where contracted projects of construction, installation, assembly and exploration are carried out, places where labour services are provided and business agents.

FIEs are subject to income tax on their worldwide income whereas the FEs are generally liable to income tax in respect of their China-sourced income.

Income tax on resident enterprises

Generally the national income tax on FIEs and FEs with establishments is levied at 30 per cent while local income tax is 3 per cent on the net taxable profit. FIEs are eligible for various tax holidays and other tax reductions and exemptions under the tax law, depending on their locations and nature of operations.

The following are the preferential income tax rates for income derived from production and non-production operations carried on by FIEs and FEs located in various special tax regimes:

- Income from production or non-production businesses obtained by FIEs and FEs with establishments located in Special Economic Zones (SEZ) in Shenzhen, Zhuhai, Shantou, Xiamen and Hainan is subject to tax at 15 per cent.
- Income from production businesses obtained by FIEs located in the designated Economic and Technological Development Zones (ETDZ) is also subject to tax at 15 per cent.
- Income obtained by FIEs located in Coastal Economic Open Zones (CEOZ) and in the old urban districts of cities where the SEZs or ETDZs are located, and are engaged in production operations, is subject to tax at 24 per cent.
- Income obtained by FIEs located in Coastal Economic Open Zones and in the old urban districts of cities where the SEZs and ETDZs are located, and are engaged in the following projects, is subject to tax at 15 per cent:
  - technology-intensive or knowledge-intensive projects;
  - projects with a long investment return period with foreign investment of not less than US $30 million; and
  - energy, communications or port development projects.

- Income obtained by FIEs located in Shanghai Pudong New Area and engaged in productive operations, energy and transportation construction projects is subject to tax at 15 per cent.
- Financial institutions, such as foreign bank branches and Sino-foreign joint venture banks established in SEZs and other areas approved by the State Council, are subject to tax at 15 per cent if the registered capital from the foreign investor or operating fund transferred from the foreign head office is over US$10 million and the operation period is longer than 10 years. This applies to foreign currency business only. For renminbi currency business the normal income tax rate will continue to apply.
- Enterprises located in certain free trade zones and export processing zones and in certain Western and Central areas may also be subject to a 15 per cent reduced income tax rate.

Tax holidays and incentives

In addition to the preferential tax rates mentioned above, FIEs are entitled to the following tax holidays and incentives:

- Production FIEs scheduled to operate for a period of more than 10 years will be entitled to two years' tax exemption and three years' 50 per cent income tax rate reduction commencing from the first profit-making year.
- After the expiry the tax exemption and reduction period, a production FIE exporting 70 per cent or more of the value of its production output in a year may pay income tax at a 50 per cent reduction for that year subject to a minimum rate of 10 per cent.
- After the expiry of the tax exemption and reduction period, a 'technologically advanced FIE' may pay income tax at a 50 per cent reduction for a further three years subject, again, to a minimum rate of 10 per cent. The 'technologically advanced' status requires special certification from the local government.
- FIEs engaged in special projects, such as infrastructure projects with an operation period of 15 years or more, are entitled to five years' tax exemption followed by five years' 50 per cent income tax rate reduction.
- FIEs located in SEZs and engaged in service industries with foreign investment of more than US$5 million and operation period of more than 10 years,

with the approval of the SEZ tax bureau, may enjoy one year tax exemption followed by two years' 50 per cent income tax reduction commencing from the first profit-making year.

- Financial institutions such as foreign bank branches and Sino-foreign joint venture banks established in SEZs and other areas approved by the State Council, with the registered capital from the foreign investor or operation fund transferred from the foreign head office of over US $10 million and an operation period of longer than 10 years, may enjoy one year tax exemption followed by two years' 50 per cent tax reduction commencing from the first profit-making year. This tax holiday does not apply to renminbi currency business.
- In order to induce reinvestment of profits by foreign investors, a 40 per cent tax refund is granted to the foreign investor that reinvests its share of distributed profits in the same or a new FIE for a period of more than five years. Profits reinvested by the foreign investor in the same or in a new export-orientated enterprise or technologically advanced enterprise for a period of more than five years may be granted a 100 per cent tax refund.
- On repatriation of after-tax profits, no income tax is levied. In addition, dividend income received by FIEs in China is also tax exempt but any relevant loss or expenses incurred are non-deductible.
- For FIEs engaged in encouraged projects that purchase China-made equipment within the total investment or FIEs purchasing China-made equipment beyond the total investment but for the purpose of technological upgrading or for producing high-technology products, 40 per cent of the costs of the domestic equipment may be used as a credit to offset the increment in the enterprise income tax liability in the year of equipment purchase as compared with that of the previous year.
- If the expenditure on technology development of an FIE increases by 10 per cent or more over that of the previous year, the taxable income of that FIE for the current year, with the approval from the tax authority, will be offset by 50 per cent of the actual amount of the spending on technology development.
- Newly established software production enterprises will be eligible for two years of exemption and three years of 50 per cent reduction of Enterprise Income Tax (EIT) from the first year they make profits.
- Key software enterprises that fall within the state's planned arrangement that are not eligible for prefer-

ential tax exemption in a given year will have EIT levied at the reduced rate of 10 per cent.

- FIEs in the Central and Western areas and under the encouraged category of the Investment Guidelines will enjoy an extension of the normal tax holiday for three years. That is, on top of the normal tax holiday of two years' exemption and three years 50 per cent reduction of EIT, the reduced EIT rate of 15 per cent will be applicable for another three years after this five-year normal tax holiday. An extended 15 per cent reduced EIT rate will be available provided that the projects l fall within the key encouraged projects category and satisfy other conditions.

- Separate tax holidays will be available on the increased portion for FIEs engaged in encouraged projects for the increase of new registered capital of US $60 million or more, or increased by US $15 million which represents 50 per cent or more of the registered capital of the original FIE, subject to certain conditions and approval from the relevant tax authorities.

Local income tax

Local income tax is levied at three per cent of net taxable profit. Exemption or reduction in local income tax may be granted to FIEs located in SEZs, ETDZs and the old urban districts of cities where an SEZ is located, at the discretion of the local tax authorities.

Turnover taxes

Effective 1 January 1994 a turnover tax system consisting of value-added tax, consumption tax and business tax was introduced by the Chinese authorities. Value-added tax, consumption tax and business tax are indirect taxes charged on the gross turnover of businesses and enterprises operating in China.

Under the turnover tax system, FIEs will pay either value-added tax or business tax, depending on the nature of their businesses. Value-added tax is levied on the sales of tangible goods, provision of processing, repairs and replacement services and the importation of goods within PRC. The general value-added tax rate is 17 per cent on products and imports and a lower rate of 13 per cent is levied on certain specific products, mostly necessities.

Export sales are exempted under VAT rules and an exporter who incurs input VAT on purchase or manufacture of goods should be able to claim a refund from the tax authorities. However, due to a reduction in the VAT export refund rate of some goods, however,

exporters might bear part of the VAT they incurred in connection with the exported goods.

Business tax is applicable to enterprises in the service, transport and other non-production industries as well as the transfer of intangible assets or immovable properties. Business tax rates range from 3 per cent to 20 per cent, depending on the category of the business concerned.

Consumption tax is levied on the production in China of 11 categories of goods including cigarettes, alcohol, cosmetics, jewellery, gasoline and motor vehicles. Importation of taxable goods is also subject to consumption tax but export is exempt.

Turnover tax paid, except for value-added tax, is deductible for foreign enterprise income tax purposes, because both business tax and consumption tax are considered as costs to the business or enterprise concerned. Value-added tax, however, is a tax which is borne by the end-user of taxable products and services and would not be deductible for income tax purposes.

Computation of taxable income for corporate income tax purpose

Capital gains
Gains arising from the disposal of an FIE's assets are generally included as part of the FIE's taxable income. The capital gain is the difference between the book value and the selling price of the asset.

Treatment of dividends received
Dividends are to be included in taxable income but dividends received by an FIE in China are not taxable.

Depreciation of fixed assets
Wear and tear allowances are granted on fixed assets and other capital assets used in the production of income. Except where specially approved, only the straight-line method of depreciation is allowed. In applying the straight-line depreciation method, one should assume a residual value of not less than 10 per cent of the original cost. Depreciation in fixed assets should be computed starting from the month following that in which the fixed assets are put into use.

The minimum depreciation periods for different classes of fixed assets are as follows:

- premises, buildings and structures – 20 years;
- trains, ships, machinery and other production equipment – 10 years;
- means of transport (except for trains and ships), electronic facilities and equipment and

- other production-related tools, facilities, furniture, etc – five years.

Amortization of intangible assets

Intangible assets should be amortized by the straight-line method over a period of not less than ten years or the period as stipulated in an agreement relating to the said intangible asset.

Pre-operating expenses are to be amortized over a period of not less than five years.

Bad debts

FIEs engaged in the credit and leasing business may, upon approval of the local tax authorities, provide for doubtful debts at not more than 3 per cent of the year-end balances of their loans (not including interbank loans) or of their accounts receivable, bills receivable and other receivables. Such provision is allowed as a deduction for income tax purpose.

Bad debts actually written off by an FIE should be reported to the local tax authorities for examination and confirmation.

Accounts receivable may be written off as bad under the following circumstances:

- bankruptcy of the debtor;
- death of the debtor; or
- the debt has been outstanding for over two years.

Entertainment expenses

Entertainment expenses incurred in relation to the production and business operation of an FIE have to be backed up by reliable records or vouchers, and are deductible within the following limits:

- For FIEs engaging in production and retailing, where the annual net sales are 15 million renminbi or less, the entertainment expenses allowed as a deduction shall not exceed 0.5 per cent of the net sales, and for the portion above 15 million renminbi, the entertainment expenses allowed as deduction shall not exceed 0.3 per cent of such portion.
- For FIEs engaging in service businesses, where the annual business income is 5 million renminbi or less, the entertainment expenses allowed as a deduction shall not exceed 1 per cent of the total business income, and for the portion above 5 million renminbi, the entertainment expenses allowed as deduction shall not exceed 0.5 per cent of such portion.

Wages, benefits and allowances

Wages, benefits and allowances paid to employees may be listed as expenses, except foreign social insurance premiums paid for employees working inside China.

Fines

Fines and penalties paid are not allowed as deductible expenses.

Donations

Only donations to approved charitable organizations are allowed as deductible expenses.

Management fees

Management fees paid to related companies are not allowed as deductible expenses.

Loss carry-overs

In determining taxable income, losses incurred by an FIE in previous years may be used for set-off against future years' profits for a period not exceeding five years.

Other issues

Transactions between related parties

All FIEs are required to conduct revenue and capital transactions between related parties on an arm's length basis. Otherwise the tax authorities have the right to disregard, vary, or make adjustments to certain arrangements that are carried out for the purpose of tax avoidance and not for bona fide commercial reasons.

Consolidation of income

An FIE or FE which has two or more business establishments set up in China may elect one establishment for consolidated income tax filing and payment purposes, however, that establishment must meet the following requirements:

- It shall assume supervisory and management responsibility over the business of other establishments.
- It shall keep complete accounting records and vouchers that correctly reflect the income, expenses, profits and losses of other business establishments.

Tax periods

The tax year is the Gregorian calendar year starting from 1 January and ending on 31 December.

Currency

Currency

Income tax payable shall be computed in renminbi. Income in foreign currency shall be converted into renminbi according to the exchange rate quoted by the State exchange control authorities for purposes of tax payment.

Foreign tax relief

The Chinese taxation system provides for avoidance of double taxation and prevention of evasion for taxes incurred in territories outside China under tax treaties. Tax treaties or arrangements exist with 77 countries and regions including Japan, the USA, the UK, Belgium, France, Singapore, Malaysia, Norway, Denmark, Finland, Sweden, Canada, Thailand, Germany, New Zealand, Italy, Poland, Yugoslavia, Romania, Pakistan, Switzerland, Kuwait, the Netherlands, Korea, Vietnam, Mauritius, Hong Kong, etc.

FIEs are allowed to deduct from the amount of tax payable the foreign income tax already paid abroad in respect of the income derived from sources outside China; however, the deductible amount cannot exceed the amount of income tax otherwise payable in China in respect of the income derived from sources outside China.

Income tax on non-resident enterprises

Profit, dividend, interest, rental, royalty, gains from the disposal of buildings and structures and attached facilities located in China and gains from the assignment of land use rights within China and other China-sourced incomes, as specified by the Ministry of Finance derived by foreign enterprises with no establishment in China, are liable to a withholding tax of 20 per cent on the gross income (or amount of gain in the case of disposal of buildings or assignment of land use rights) so derived. Starting from 1 January 2000 the withholding tax rate on interest, rental, royalty and other income was reduced to 10 per cent by concession. In addition, exemption may be granted under the following circumstances:

- After-tax profits distributed to foreign investors of FIEs are exempt from withholding tax.
- Interest earned by international lending agencies from loans extended to the Chinese Government and Chinese state banks shall be exempt from withholding tax.
- Interest earned by foreign banks from loans extended to Chinese state banks at preferential rates shall be exempt from withholding tax.

- Where the terms are favourable and the technology transferred is advanced, royalty income may be exempted from withholding tax.

Individual income tax on foreign nationals

Individual income tax in China is levied on wages, salaries and other income of foreign nationals, depending on the length of their residence in China and the source of the income.

The Chinese tax year is from 1 January to 31 December. Individual income tax returns are required to be filed and the corresponding taxes paid on a monthly basis.

A foreign national should pay individual income tax on income derived from sources within the territory of China. The income chargeable to individual income tax includes the following categories:

- wages and salaries;
- production or business income derived from private industrial or commercial enterprise;
- income from subcontract operations;
- royalties;
- interest, dividends and bonuses from investments;
- property rentals;
- income from transfer of property;
- incidental income;
- other income specified as taxable by the Ministry of Finance.

Income taxes of foreign nationals and Chinese citizens are governed by one single income tax regime.

Foreign nationals who do not have PRC domicile are generally subject to PRC income tax only on those categories of income that are deemed to be China-sourced, unless the individual resides in China for over five years. For this purpose, residing for one year is defined as living inside China for 365 days. Leaving China for fewer than 30 days at a time or cumulatively fewer than 90 days in a taxable year shall not be deemed as absence from China for the purpose of determining whether a person has resided in China for one year.

Foreign nationals will be exempted from tax if they reside in China for fewer than 90 days cumulatively within a calendar year and their remuneration is borne by a foreign employer that does not have a permanent establishment in China. This 90-day period is extended to 183 days if the individual is a tax resident of a country which has signed a tax treaty with China.

Monthly income from wages and salaries is taxed according to a progressive nine-scale rate, ranging from 5 per cent to 45 per cent. There is a set allowable deduction on income from wages and salaries of 800 renminbi per month. Due to cost of living allowance and foreign exchange adjustments, foreign nationals are entitled to an additional monthly deduction of 3,200 renminbi. The monthly deduction amount for Chinese citizens varies according to location and may be adjusted annually.

A taxpayer who has paid foreign income taxes on income from sources outside China may apply for a tax credit against Chinese taxes provided that relevant supporting documentation is submitted. If an income tax treaty and domestic tax rules are both applicable to a transaction, the income tax treaty provision will override the domestic tax rules where the income tax treaty confers more favourable treatment.

If an individual is treated as resident of another country by the tax authorities in that country, he may qualify for a measure of relief or exemption from Chinese tax under the taxation agreement between that country and China. Most current agreements prescribe various tests to determine in which of the two countries an individual is resident for tax purposes. Most current agreements contain clauses that exempt a resident of one country from tax on employment income outside China and on employment income in China if such resident is present in China for fewer than 183 days in the tax year.

Comparison of Auditing Requirements and Practices in the People's Republic of China with International Accounting Standards

PricewaterhouseCoopers

Chapter 3.3 deals with the current accounting and auditing requirements in the People's Republic of China (PRC). Also highlighted are the development and features of the PRC Accounting Standards and Regulations which, due to the unique characteristics of the Chinese economy, are somewhat different from those adopted in the West. In this chapter the significance of the International Accounting Standards (IAS) in the Western accounting system will be discussed and a comparison made between the IAS and PRC accounting regulations. Because of the similarities between the IAS and standards issued by other professional accounting bodies, comparing the PRC accounting regulations with the IAS will highlight the major differences between the PRC accounting regulations and those of the West such as the US GAAP (General Accepted Accounting Principles in the United States of America), and the UK SSAP (Statements of Standard Accounting Practice in the United Kingdom) and FRS (Financial Reporting Standard).

Development of accounting regulations in China

To cope with the rapid growth of the country's economy and to facilitate a better understanding of the financial statements of a PRC enterprise, the PRC government has made significant changes and revisions to its accounting regulations. The Ministry of Finance (MOF) has recently promulgated new or revised accounting regulations. Chapter 3.3 includes a list of the regulations in use.

The *Accounting Systems for Business Enterprises* (ASBE), known to have been prepared after studying the accounting standards, guidelines and practices issued by the International Federation of Accountants (IFAC), International Accounting Standards Board (IASB) and other accounting bodies, are more in line with the IAS, and are similar to each other, although there are small differences regarding disclosure requirements and some accounting issues. In addition to the ASBE, the MOF prepared a set of new specific accounting standards (and exposure drafts) which were to be released into standards beginning in 1997 and which bring the accounting principles and regulations in the PRC further in line with IAS. So far only 16 of these exposure drafts have been formalized and made effective. They are shown in Table 3.5.1.

International Accounting Standards

The IAS has been chosen as the basis for comparison in this chapter because of its international acceptance and the similarities of its fundamental accounting concepts and principles with accounting standards published by other professional bodies.

The International Accounting Standards Board (IASB) (formerly known as the International Accounting Standards Committee (IASC)), the issuing body of the IAS, was founded on 29 June 1973 and as set out in its constitution its objectives are:

- to develop, in the public interest, a single set of high quality, understandable and enforceable global accounting standards that require high quality, transparent and comparable information in financial statements and other financial reporting to help participants in the world's capital markets and other users make economic decisions;

Table 3.5.1

Specific Accounting Standard	Applicable	Effective Date
Related party relationship and related party transactions disclosure	Listed companies only	1 January 1997
Cash flow statements (revised)	All types of enterprises	18 January 2001
Post balance sheet events	Listed companies only	1 January 1998
Debt restructuring (revised)	All types of enterprises	18 January 2001
Construction contracts	Listed companies only	1 January 1999
Investments (revised) [1]	Listed companies only	18 January 2001
Changes in accounting policy, estimates or fundamental errors (revised)	All types of enterprises	18 January 2001
Revenue	Listed companies only	1 January 1999
Non-monetary transactions (revised)	All types of enterprises	18 January 2001
Contingencies	All types of enterprises	1 July 2000
Intangible assets	Joint stock limited companies	1 January 2001
Borrowing costs	All types of enterprises	1 January 2001
Leases	All types of enterprises	1 January 2001
Interim reporting	Listed companies only	1 January 2002
Fixed assets [1]	Joint stock limited companies	1 January 2002
Inventories [1]	Joint stock limited companies	1 January 2002

[1] These standards are mandatory to listed companies and/or joint stock limited companies. All other types of companies, however, are encouraged to adopt.

- to promote the use and rigorous application of those standards; and
- to bring about convergence of national accounting standards and International Accounting Standards to high quality solutions.

The opening-up of China has attracted an influx of foreign investment. Foreign investors, before committing to an investment project, would like to know how the financial statements of the target enterprise would look if the statements were prepared under accounting standards used in their own countries. Prior to the issuance of the ASBE in 2001 and their mandatory adoption by FIEs in 2002, in the absence of a set of well-accepted accounting standards or practice in China, the IAS played an important role in assisting foreign investors in making their investment decisions.

It appears that there is now a set of more uniform accounting regulations governing the preparation of financial statements by PRC enterprises and that these accounting regulations are significantly closer to IAS compared to fund accounting which was used in the past. There are still a number of important areas in the PRC regulations, however, that are not in line with the IAS. A summary of the major differences between the PRC accounting standards and the IAS is provided in

Appendix V at the end of this book, using the latest information available at the time of writing. Where necessary, the US GAAP requirements have also been included. While the table serves as an easy reference, a few major differences for discussion are described below:

- Fair value is generally not recognized under PRC regulations due to the lack of open markets and the unavailability of fair values. In addition financial assets and liabilities that are realizable beyond one year are not discounted. Furthermore, the accounting for derivative instruments is not addressed.
- The accounting for special purpose entities is not addressed.
- The PRC regulations provide for the use of deferred taxation. In practice the use of deferred tax is not common due to the complexity of implementation.
- Expenses incurred during the pre-operational period are capitalized onto the balance sheet until such time that the company enters commercial operation. The expenses capitalized so far are expensed in the first month of commercial operation.
- Employer's accounting for post-retirement benefits, other than defined contribution plans, are not addressed.

Conclusion

It appears that there are not many material differences between the PRC accounting regulations and the IAS. As mentioned above, however, the PRC regulations are mandatory in nature and their coverage is not as broad as that of the IAS. While narrowing the gap between the two accounting standards may not be too difficult to achieve, the infancy of the new accounting system, the rigour of implementation by various companies and the extent of management that is capable of exercising fair judgment are practical difficulties to be surmounted in the PRC.

Trademark and Patent Application and Protection in China

Fan Weimin, Patent Attorney, CCPIT Patent & Trademark Law Office

In order to prepare for China's accession to the WTO and to improve intellectual property protection, China has revised its intellectual property laws and regulations in recent years. This chapter is intended to provide an overview of new trademark and patent application procedures and protection in China.

Trademark registration

Legislation

The Trademark Law of the PRC which had come into force 1 March 1983 was revised 22 February 1993, and came into force 1 July 1993. The Implementing Regulations of the Trademark Law of the PRC, which had come into force 13 January 1988, were revised 28 July 1993 and again 15 May 1995. On 27 October 2001 the 24th Session of the Standing Committee of the 9th National People's Congress approved the second revision of the Trademark Law and the revised Law came into force 1 December 2001. The Implementing Regulations of the Trademark Law of the PRC are being revised currently.

China has been a member of the World Intellectual Property Organization (WIPO) since 3 June 1980. On 19 March 1985 China acceded to the Paris Convention for the Protection of Industrial Property (Stockholm Act) and entered into the Madrid Agreement Concerning the International Registration of Marks on 4 October 1989. China also acceded to the Madrid Protocol on 1 December 1995.

Types of marks

Types of marks include trademarks, service marks, collective marks and certification marks.

Collective marks are defined as signs which are registered in the name of a group, an association or other organizations to be used by the members thereof in their commercial activities to indicate their membership in the organizations.

Certification marks describe the signs which are controlled by organizations capable of supervising certain goods or services and used by entities or individual persons outside the organization for their goods or services to certify the origin, material, mode of manufacture, quality or other characteristics of those goods or services.

Registrable marks

Registrable marks are any visually perceptible signs capable of distinguishing goods or services including words, devices, letters of an alphabet, numerals, three-dimensional signs and combinations of colours as well as the combination of such signs. Registrable marks shall be so distinctive as to be distinguishable, and shall not conflict with any prior right acquired by another person or entity.

Well-known trademarks

The Trademark Office is responsible for the determination and administration of well-known trademarks. The following factors shall be considered in determining a well-known trademark:

- reputation of the trademark in the relevant sector of the public;
- duration of use of the trademark;
- duration, degree and geographical scope of any publicity for the trademark;

- history of protection of the trademark as a well-known trademark;
- other factors contributing to the reputation of the trademark.

A trademark shall not be registered and its use shall be prohibited where the trademark constitutes a reproduction, an imitation, or a translation of a well-known trademark of another person not registered in China and is likely to:

- create confusion if the trademark is the subject of an application for registration regarding goods which are identical or similar to the goods to which the well-known trademark applies; or
- mislead the public and damage the interests of the owner of the registered well-known trademark, if the trademark is the subject of an application for registration regarding goods which are not identical or similar to the goods to which the well-known trademark applies.

Unregistrable marks

The following signs shall not be registered as trademarks:

- signs which consist exclusively of generic names, designs or models of the goods regarding which the trademark is used;
- signs which consist exclusively of direct indications of the quality, primary raw materials, functions, intended purposes, weight, quantity or other characteristics of the goods regarding which the trademark is used; or
- signs which are devoid of any distinctive character.

Signs mentioned in the preceding paragraphs may be registered as trademarks if they have acquired distinctive character through use and are capable of being readily identified and distinguished.

If a three-dimensional sign consists exclusively of the shape which results from the nature of the goods themselves, the shape of goods which is necessary to obtain a technical result, or the shape which gives substantial value to the goods, it shall not be registered as a trademark.

Other prohibited marks

The following signs shall not be used as trademarks:

- those identical with or similar to the State name, national flag, national emblem, military flag, or decorations, of the People's Republic of China, with names of the places where the Central and State organs are located, or with the names and designs of landmark buildings;
- those identical with or similar to the State names, national flags, national emblems or military flags of foreign countries, except where a foreign state's government agrees to their use;
- those identical with or similar to the names, flags or emblems or names, of international intergovernmental organizations, except where the organizations agree otherwise to their use or where it is not easy for their use to mislead the public;
- those identical with or similar to official signs and hallmarks, showing official control or warranty by them, except where their use is otherwise authorized;
- those identical with or similar to the symbols or names of the Red Cross or the Red Crescent;
- those of a discriminatory nature against any nationality;
- those of an exaggerative and fraudulent nature in advertising goods;
- those detrimental to socialist morals or customs, or having other unhealthy influences.

The geographical name of an administrative division at or above the county level or a foreign geographical name well-known to the public shall not be used as a trademark, unless the geographical name has another meaning or the geographical name is used as a component part of a collective mark or a certification mark. Previously registered trademarks consisting of or containing geographical names shall continue to be valid.

Classification

China adopted on 1 November 1988 the International Classification of Goods and Services formulated pursuant to the Nice Convention.

Conventional priority

Conventional priority may be claimed within six months from the date of filing outside China. Priority documents must be submitted to the Trademark Office within three months from the date of filing in China.

First-to-file rule

The Trademark Law adopts a strict first-to-file rule for obtaining trademark rights. The first applicant to file an application for registration of a mark will pre-empt all other later applications for the same mark in the same class. Where an application to register a mark has been rejected due to its identity or similarity to a previously registered mark, evidence of prior use will not be helpful for the purpose of challenging the registration, unless the mark is proved to be 'well-known' under the Paris Convention.

Filing requirement

It is important to note that each application shall cover only one trademark in one class and an official fee of about US$US12 is levied for each item in excess of 10 in each class. Each application must include the following documents:

- Application form;
- Power of Attorney, signed by the applicant (the notarization and legalization of the Power of Attorney is generally not required);
- Five prints of the label, not exceeding 10 centimetres or being less than five centimetres in length and breadth. If the mark is in colour, one black and white label shall be submitted in addition to the five colour prints;
- Priority document, if priority is claimed.

Examination

Applications are examined regarding the formality and substance. Examination regarding the formality will include the correctness of the document and classification. Examination regarding the substance will include the registrability of the mark and possible conflict with prior rights.

Amendment of application

Amendment is only possible when required by the Trademark Office. At the stage of examination in substance, amendment may lead to the deletion of a part of the mark or of the specification.

Failure to make an amendment required by the Trademark Office may lead to refusal of the application.

Provisional refusal

The Trademark Office may provisionally refuse an application if, after examination, it is found that the mark is devoid of distinctiveness or identical with or similar to prior marks regarding identical or similar goods or services.

Publication

Applications that have passed examination will be published in the Trademark Gazette, which is published weekly for purposes of dispute.

Registration/duration/renewal

A mark will become registered if within the period of three months following its publication no opposition is filed against its registration, or the opposition filed is decided not to be justifiable.

A registration is valid for 10 years starting from the date of registration and can be renewed indefinitely for further 10-year periods each time.

Renewal applications shall be made within the six months before the expiry date or, subject to payment of an additional fee (official fee: about US$61), within the six months after the expiry date. Each renewal application shall include an application for renewal of trademark registration, a Power of Attorney and a copy of the 'Certificate of Trademark Registration'.

Madrid registrations

An international registration in the PRC under the Madrid Agreement or Protocol can be effected by notifying the Madrid Union Office to add the PRC to the list of registration countries for a particular mark. Under the Madrid Agreement or Protocol the Trademark Office has the right to reject trademarks not conforming with the trademark law.

Scope of protection

A registered mark is protected regarding the goods or services registered. In particular any of the following acts shall be an infringement upon a registered mark:

- to use a trademark that is identical with or similar to a registered trademark in relation to identical or similar goods without the authorization of the owner of the registered trademark;
- to knowingly sell goods that are in infringement of the exclusive right to use a registered trademark;

- to counterfeit or make without authorization, representations of a registered trademark of another person or to sell such representations;
- to change a registered trademark and put goods bearing the changed trademark on the market without authorization of the owner of the registered trademark;
- to cause, in any other respect, prejudice to the exclusive right of another person to use a registered trademark.

Appeal

The provisional refusal of an application may be appealed against to the Trademark Review and Adjudication Board (TRAB) within 15 days from the receipt of notification.

Opposition

Within three months from the date of publication anyone can oppose an accepted trademark. The Trademark Office shall make a written decision, which can be appealed against to the Trademark Review and Adjudication Board, if any party is not satisfied with the decision.

Cancellation or dispute

Where a registered trademark belongs to the category of unregistrable marks or other prohibited marks, or has been acquired by fraud or any other unfair means, any other organization or individual may request the Trademark Review and Adjudication Board to make a judgment to cancel such a registered trademark.

Where a registered trademark:

- constitutes a reproduction, an imitation or a translation of a well-known trademark of another person not registered in China in respect of identical or similar goods, and is likely to create confusion;
- constitutes a reproduction, an imitation or a translation of a well-known trademark of another person already registered in China in respect of non-identical or dissimilar goods and is likely to mislead the public and damage the interests of the owner of the registered well-known trademark;
- has been acquired by the agent or representative of the original trademark owner without authorization where the owner objects;
- consists of or contains a geographical indication regarding goods not originating in the region indi-

cated to such an extent as to mislead the public (registrations made in good faith shall continue to be valid);
- infringes the existing earlier right of another person, with the intent of registering a trademark which is used by another person and enjoys a certain reputation;

the owner of the trademark or any interested party may, within five years from the date of registration, request the Trademark Review and Adjudication Board to make a judgment to cancel the registered trademark. Where the registration has been made in bad faith the owner of a well-known trademark shall not be bound by the five-year time limit for filing a request.

In addition to the situations defined in the preceding two paragraphs, any person disputing a registered trademark may, within five years from the date of registration, apply to the Trademark Review and Adjudication Board for adjudication.

Application for cancellation may be filed at any time where the registered trademark has ceased to be used for three consecutive years.

The power of the Board

Any party who is dissatisfied with the decision of the Trademark Review and Adjudication Board may, within 30 days from receipt of the notification, institute legal proceedings with the People's Court.

Recording change of name/address/assignment/licence

All changes in registration details including name and/or address shall be recorded with the Trademark Office.

When applying for the assignment of a registered trademark, both the assignor and assignee shall send jointly an 'Application for Assignment of Registered Trademark' to the Trademark Office accompanied by the original 'Certificate of Trademark Registration'. The assignee shall perform the formalities required in applying for the assignment of a registered trademark. An assignment is effective only when recorded with the Trademark Office.

A licence contract is to be recorded with the Trademark Office within three months following the execution of such a contract.

Use requirement

A registration is subject to cancellation if not in use for three consecutive years. Use of a trademark includes its use on goods, packages or containers, or in trading documents, and use in advertising, exhibition or other business activities.

Marking

Marking is compulsory for a registered trademark; however, false marking will result in a fine of up to 20 per cent of the sales income of such falsely marked products.

Status of unregistered marks

An unregistered mark can be used; however, an unregistered trademark is not protected unless it is recognized as well-known.

Registering the Chinese version for a Latin mark

Registering the Chinese version for a Latin mark is necessary if the Chinese version is to be used. Even if it is not to be used, registration of its Chinese version is also necessary if the Latin mark has *de facto* obtained its Chinese version that is well-accepted by consumers, especially when the mark was coined.

Representation

Any foreign nationals intending to apply for trademark registrations or to handle other trademark matters in China shall be represented by an agent licensed by the Chinese government.

Patent procurement

Legislation

On 1 April 1985 the Patent Law of the PRC and its Implementing Regulations came into effect. The Patent Law was revised on 4 September 1992 for the first time and became effective on 1 January 1993 together with its Implementing Regulations. On 25 August 2000 the 17th Session of the Standing Committee of the 9th National People's Congress approved the second revision of the Patent Law and the revised Law came into force on 1 July 2001.

China has been a member of the World Intellectual Property Organization (WIPO) since 3 June 1980. On 19 March 1985 China acceded to the Paris Convention for the Protection of Industrial Property (Stockholm Act). China became a member of the Patent Cooperation Treaty (PCT) on 1 January 1994 and has been a member of the Budapest Treaty for the Deposit of Micro-organisms since 1 July 1995. China entered into the Locarno Agreement Establishing an International Classification for Industrial Designs on 19 September 1996 and the Strasbourg Agreement Concerning International Patent Classification on 19 June 1997.

Language

All documents filed and formal communications with the State Intellectual Property Office of PRC (SIPO) and the Patent Re-examination Board must be in Chinese.

Types of patent

There are three types of patent: a patent for Invention, a patent for a utility model and a patent for design.

Duration

The duration of a patent for invention is 20 years, and the duration of a patent for utility model or design is 10 years, and runs from the filing date in China.

Definition of invention, utility model and design

- 'Invention' means any new technical solution relating to a product, a process or improvement thereof.
- 'Utility model' means any new technical solution relating to the shape, the structure, or their combination, of a product which is fit for practical use.
- 'Design' means any new design of the shape, the pattern or their combination, or the combination of the colour with shape or pattern, of a product which creates an aesthetic feeling and is fit for industrial application.

Unpatentable subject matters

No patent right shall be granted for any of the following:

- scientific discoveries;
- rules and methods for mental activities;
- methods for the diagnosis or the treatment of diseases;
- animal and plant varieties;
- substances obtained by means of nuclear transformation.

Patents may be granted for processes used in producing animal and plant varieties.

Biological material (Micro-organisms)

Biological material *per se* is a patentable subject matter.

Where an application for an invention concerns a new biological material which is not available and which cannot be described in the application in such a way as to enable the invention to be carried out by a person skilled in the art, the applicant shall deposit a sample of the biological material with an international depository authority (IDA) under the Budapest Treaty before the date of filing, or at the latest on the date of filing (or the priority date where priority is claimed) and submit, at the time of filing or at the latest within four months from the filing date, a receipt of deposit and proof of viability from the depository authority.

Computer software

Computer software *per se* is not patentable. Computer software is protected, however, under the Copyright Law and can be protected under Patent Law if it falls within a technical field, resolves a technical problem and achieves a technical result.

New plant varieties

New plant varieties *per se* are not patentable; however, since 1 October 1997 new plant varieties may be protected under the Regulations on the Protection of New Plant Varieties. China has been a member state of the International Convention for the Protection of New Plant Varieties since 23 April 1999. The term of protection of new plant varieties runs from the date of grant thereof, and shall be 20 years for vines, forest trees, fruit trees and ornamental plants and 15 years for other plants, subject to the payment of annual fees.

Novelty

An invention or utility model is novel if before the filing date no identical invention or utility model has been disclosed in publications anywhere in the world, or has been publicly used or made known to the public by any other means in China. Novelty is destroyed by an application filed earlier by another person that describes an identical invention or utility mode and is published after the filing date of the said invention or utility model.

Similarly, a design is novel if it is not identical with and similar to any design, which before the filing date has been publicly disclosed in publications anywhere in the world or has been publicly used in China, and must not be in conflict with any prior right of any other person.

Inventiveness

An invention possesses inventiveness if, compared with the technical solutions existing before the filing date, the invention has prominent substantive features representing a notable progress.

Likewise, a utility model possesses inventiveness if it has substantive features and represents progress.

Conventional priority

Conventional priority for invention applications and utility model applications can be claimed within 12 months from the date of first filing outside China. Conventional priority for design applications can be claimed within six months from the date of first filing outside China. Priority documents must be submitted to the SIPO within three months from the date of filing in China.

Domestic priority

Domestic priority for invention applications and utility model applications can be claimed within 12 months from the date of first filing in China. A domestic parent application on which the domestic priority claim is based should not claim any conventional or domestic priority, and the parent application will be deemed withdrawn when the new application claiming domestic priority is filed.

Late entry of PCT application

If an applicant under the PCT fails to go through the relevant formalities for entering the Chinese national phase within 20 or 30 months from the priority date, the applicant may, after paying a surcharge for the late entry (official fee: about US$121), go through these formalities before the expiration of the time limit of 22 months or 32 months, respectively, from the priority date.

First-to-file rule

The Patent Law, like the Trademark Law, adopts a first-to-file system.

Filing documents

Each application for an invention or utility model must include the following documents:

- power of attorney, signed by the applicant (without notarization);
- specification with claims and abstract;
- drawings, if any (two sets of formal drawings);
- certified copy of the priority application if priority is claimed (translation of the full text is only necessary when required by the SIPO);
- assignment of priority right is required to be provided only if the applicant of the Chinese application differs from that of the priority application.

Each application for a design must include the following documents:

- power of attorney, signed by the applicant (without notarization);
- drawings or photographs of the design, in triplicate (minimum 3 × 8 centimetres, maximum 15 × 22 centimetres);
- certified copy of the priority application if priority is claimed.

Claim format

The 'European' claim format, which contains a preamble portion indicating the technical field and the technical features of the prior art, and a characterizing portion stating the technical features of the invention, is highly recommended.

Publication

Patent applications for inventions are published promptly after the expiry of 18 months from the filing date or priority date, whichever is the earlier, after the preliminary examination.

Substantive examination

Patent applications for inventions are examined as to substance. In order to initiate the substantive examination procedure, applicants must submit a formal request within three years from the Chinese filing date or the priority date, whichever is earlier. Failure to do so will result in the application being deemed withdrawn.

Utility models and designs are not examined as to substance. Patents will be issued automatically after preliminary examination.

Duty of information disclosure

When the applicant of an invention application requests substantive examination, the applicant shall provide prefiling date reference materials concerning the invention. The SIPO may ask the applicant to furnish any search reports and examination results issued by foreign patent authorities such as the European Patent Office (EPO), The United States Patent Treaty Organization (USPTO) and the Japanese Patent Office (JPO) during the examination of the corresponding foreign applications.

Unity requirement

An application for an invention or utility model shall be limited to one invention or utility model. Two or more inventions or utility models belonging to a single general inventive concept, which may be filed in one application, shall be technically interrelated and contain one or more identical or corresponding special technical features. The expression 'special technical features' shall mean those technical features that define a contribution, which each of those inventions, considered as a whole, makes over the prior art.

An application for designs shall be limited to one design incorporated in one product. Two or more designs, which are incorporated in products belonging to the same class and are sold or used in sets, may be filed as one application. The expression 'the same class' means that the products incorporating the designs belong to the same sub-class in the classification of products for designs. The expression 'be sold or used in sets' means that the products incorporating the designs have the same designing concept and are customarily sold or used at the same time.

Filing of divisional application

A divisional application shall be filed by an applicant before the expiry of two months from the date of receipt of the notification in which a patent right is granted for the parent application. Where an application for patent has been rejected, withdrawn or is deemed to have been withdrawn, no divisional application may be filed.

Multiple dependent claim

Any multiple dependent claim that refers to two or more claims shall refer to the preceding one in the alternative only, and shall not serve as a basis for any other multiple dependent claim.

Amendment of applications

Amendments of applications are allowed but may not go beyond the scope of original disclosure in the initial description and claims.

Applicants may amend their applications on their own initiative at the same time as the examination request is submitted, or within three months from the date of receipt of the notification from the SIPO informing the entry of the application into the examination stage.

For utility models and designs, amendments can be made within two months from the filing date. Applicants may amend the applications on their own initiative. Amendments should not change the essential elements of the designs.

Final rejections and appeals (re-examination)

If an application is found to be unacceptable by the SIPO and the applicant has been given an opportunity to make a response, a final rejection can be made.

Appeals against rejections may be made to the Patent Re-examination Board (the official term for an appeal to the Board is 're-examination').

Invalidation

Anyone may request the Patent Re-examination Board to declare a patent invalid from the date of announcement of the grant of the patent right.

The power of the Board

The Board's decisions on the allowability of invention, utility model and design applications on the validity of invention, utility model and design patents are not final, and therefore, can be further appealed against to the court.

The scope of patent protection

The scope of patent protection for inventions and utility models is determined by the terms of the claims. The description and the appended drawings may be used to interpret the claims.

The scope of protection of designs is determined by the products incorporating the designs as shown in the drawings or photographs.

Patentees have the right to prevent others from making, using, offering to sell, selling or importing the patented products (or products incorporating patented designs), or using the patented processes, or offering to sell, selling or importing the products directly obtained by the patented processes, for production or business purposes.

Right of prior users

It is not an infringement if before the filing date of a patent application a person has already made an identical product, used an identical process, or made necessary preparations for its manufacture or use, and this person continues to make or use it within its original scope only, after the patent is issued.

Maintenance fees and annuities

Maintenance fees are to be paid within two months from the date of receipt of the notification to grant the patent right. From the third year after the filing of a patent application and before the patent right is granted, an applicant is required to pay the maintenance fee for the application.

The annuities shall also be paid within two months from the date of receipt of the notification to grant the patent right.

There is a grace period for paying the annuities of six months.

Representation

Foreign entities and individuals having no permanent residence or business office in China must be represented by an authorized Chinese patent firm in patent prosecutions and other proceedings before the Chinese Patent Office and the Patent Re-examination Board.

Assignment and licence contracts

Assignment of patents to foreigners by Chinese entities or individuals must be approved by the competent departments of the State Council. Assignment contracts come into force after they are recorded with the SIPO. Any licence contract shall, within three months from the date of coming into force, be submitted to the Chinese Patent Office for recording.

Marking

Marking is not compulsory but recommended. The number of the patent application or patent should be indicated.

Enforcement

A unique feature of China's intellectual property enforcement mechanism is the so-called double track (litigation in court or administrative resolution) system. Under this system one may bring an action against the infringer directly in a court or request the relevant administrative authority to handle the dispute. It is important that administrative resolution need not necessarily be a procedure prior to judicial resolution.

Court system

The court system in China under the Organic Law of Courts consists of the following four levels:

- Supreme People's Court;
- Higher courts: each province, autonomous region, as well as the municipalities directly under the central government, has one higher people's court;
- Intermediate courts: each major city has one or two intermediate people's courts;
- Basic courts: each county and each district of a major city has a basic people's court.

China has adopted a 'two instances' system for trial. At present a total of 43 intermediate people's courts are authorized as the first instance courts to deal with foreign-related trademark cases and patent cases.

Administrative authority for patent affairs

A distinct feature of the Chinese patent system is that administrative authorities for patent affairs are established as departments under the local governments in all the provinces, autonomous regions, municipalities directly under the central government, or cities which consist of districts. Each department has a large amount of patent administration work to attend to and the ability to deal with the matter. The function of the authorities is to administer patent affairs and handle patent disputes in the areas of their jurisdiction. The authorities are not branches of the Patent Office and do not accept patent applications.

Administration of Industry and Commerce (AIC)

Administration of Industry and Commerce is established as administration departments under central and local governments. Its branches extend nationwide and reach the lowest level of a township. The function of AIC is of enterprise registration, market supervision, etc.

Trademark enforcement

Infringement

A person shall be liable for trademark infringement if he/she commits any of the following acts:

- uses a trademark that is identical with or similar to a registered trademark in relation to identical or similar goods without the authorization of the owner of the registered trademark;
- knowingly sells goods that are in infringement of the exclusive right to use a registered trademark;
- counterfeits, or makes without authorization, representations of a registered trademark of another person or sells such representations;
- changes a registered trademark and puts the goods bearing the changed trademark on the market without authorization of the owner of the registered trademark;
- in other respects causes prejudice to the exclusive right of another person to use a registered trademark.

Preliminary injunction

Where the owner of a registered trademark or an interested party has evidence indicating that another person is engaged in or will soon engage in an act of infringement of the owner's exclusive right to use his/her registered trademark and that, unless the act is stopped in a timely manner, irreparable injury will be caused to the owner's legitimate rights and interests, the owner may, before instituting legal proceedings, apply to the people's court for an injunction prohibiting the act and preserving the owner's assets.

Preservation of evidence

To stop an act of infringement where evidence may be destroyed or lost or become difficult to obtain in the future, the owner of a registered trademark or an interested party, before instituting legal proceedings, may apply to the people's court to have the evidence preserved.

The people's court shall make a decision within 48 hours from receipt of the application. Where the people's court decides to provide the preservative measures, the decision shall be executed immediately.

The people's court may order the applicant to provide security. Where no security is provided, the people's court shall reject the application.

Where the applicant fails to institute legal proceedings within 15 days from the day on which the people's court takes the preservative measures, the people's court shall revoke the measures.

Compensation for damage

The amount of damages for infringement of the exclusive right to use a registered trademark shall be the profit that the infringer has earned through the infringement during the period of the infringement, or the losses that the infringee has suffered through the infringement during the period of the infringement, including any reasonable expenses the infringee has incurred in an effort to stop the infringement.

Where the profit earned by the infringer or losses suffered by the infringee through such an infringement cannot be determined, the people's court shall grant compensation not exceeding 500,000 renminbi yuan according to the circumstances of the act of infringement.

Where a party unknowingly offers for sale goods that are an infringement of the exclusive right of another person to use a registered trademark, but is able to prove that he/she has obtained the goods lawfully and identifies the supplier, such party shall not be held liable for damages.

Criminal sanction

Any person whose use, without the consent of the owner of a registered trademark, of a trademark that is identical to the registered trademark in relation to identical goods, commits a crime and shall be prosecuted according to law for his/her criminal liabilities in addition to compensation for the damages that the infringee suffers.

Any person who counterfeits, or without authorization makes, representations of a registered trademark of another person, or offers for sale such representations, shall be prosecuted according to law for his/her criminal liabilities if such actions constitute a crime.

Any person who knowingly sells goods that bear a counterfeited registered trademark, thereby committing a crime, shall be prosecuted according to law for his/her criminal liabilities in addition to compensation for the damages that the infringee suffers.

In any of these cases the infringer may be subject to a maximum of seven years imprisonment.

Administrative actions

A request for administrative actions may be filed with the AIC in the place of the infringement or the place of the infringer's residence. In trademark infringement cases administrative actions through the AIC are the most effective and most frequently chosen approach. AIC may take the following measures to halt the infringement:

- an order to stop immediately the sale of the goods;
- seize and destroy the representations of the trademark in question;
- an order to remove the infringing trademark from the remaining goods;
- seize such moulds, plates and any other tools of offence used directly and exclusively in the trademark infringement;
- an order to destroy the infringing articles, if it cannot sufficiently stop the infringing by taking the four previous measures, or if the infringing trademark and the goods involved cannot be separated from each other.

In comparison with court proceedings the administrative proceedings are both efficient and cost-effective. If damages are sought, however, judicial proceedings are highly recommended.

Juridical actions

A trademark infringement can be brought before court under whose jurisdiction the infringement takes place or where the infringer resides.

Statutory limitation

Administrative or court actions against trademark infringement must be brought within two years from date that the trademark owner knows or should have known that the counterfeiting and/or infringing acts were taking place.

For successive infringement acts, however, courts may accept cases filed after the two-year time limit expires and order the infringer to cease infringing and compensate the infringee for the damage. Such damages may not include those suffered by the infringee more than two years prior to the date of the suit.

Burden of proof

The person who initiates proceedings bears the burden of proof. Without appropriate evidence the court or the AIC will not take any action.

Any denial of the charge of infringement or counter-claim must also be supported by evidence.

Appeal

A party may request reconsideration of the decision of an AIC by the AIC at a higher level. The decision of the higher AIC may be appealed against to the court having jurisdiction.

In court proceedings a party may appeal to the court of second instance if it is not satisfied with the decision of the court of first instance. The decision of the court of second instance is final and binding.

Patent enforcement

Infringement

A person will be liable for patent infringement and actions may be brought against him/her if for business purposes and without authorization of a patentee, such person committed any of the following acts:

- making, using, offering for sale or selling the patented product;
- using the patented process;
- using, offering for sale or selling the product directly obtained by the patented process;
- importing the patented product; or
- importing the product directly obtained by the patented process.

Preliminary injunction

Where any patentee or interested party has evidence to prove that another person is infringing or will soon infringe his/her patent right and that, if such infringing act is not checked or prevented from occurring in time, it is likely to cause irreparable harm to such patentee,

the latter may, before any legal proceedings are instituted, request the people's court to adopt measures for ordering the suspension of relevant acts and the preservation of property.

Compensation for damages

The amount of compensation for the damages caused by the infringement of the patent right shall be assessed on the basis of the losses suffered by the patentee or the profits which the infringer has earned through the infringement. If it is difficult to determine the losses or the profits, the amount may be assessed by reference to the appropriate multiple (from one to three times) of the amount of the exploitation fee of that patent under contractual licence.

Criminal sanction

Passing off the patent of another person will be a criminal offence if the circumstances are serious. The infringer will be subject to a penalty or detainment or up to three year's imprisonment.

Judicial or administrative actions

A patentee or an interested party may bring an action against an infringer in a court having jurisdiction or seek to resolve the dispute through administrative action by making a request to the relevant administrative authority for patent affairs. The administrative authority is empowered to order the infringer to stop infringing acts and to mediate disputes on the claimed damages to the infringee. In cases of passing off, the administrative authority may order the confiscation of the illegal gains by the infringer, and impose on the infringer a penalty of up to three times the illegal gains, or 5,000 renminbi if there were no illegal gains.

A patent infringement should be brought before the court under whose jurisdiction the infringer is located or the infringement takes place, or the place where the infringing products are made or sold.

For administrative resolution the request should be filed with the administrative authority for patent affairs in the place where the infringement occurs.

Statutory limitation

An infringement suit must be initiated within two years from the date on which the patentee or any interested party obtains or should have obtained knowledge of the infringement act.

Burden of proof

The plaintiff has to submit evidence to prove his claim against infringement and to support his claim for damages. Any denial of the charge of infringement or counter claim must be also supported by evidence.

The burden of proof will be borne by the defendant if the litigation concerns a process patent for the manufacture of a new product filed after 1 January 1993. In the case of such a charge the defendant denying the charge should present evidence proving that his product is not manufactured using the patented process.

For a process patent filed before 1 January 1993, the burden of proof will be borne by the defendant regardless of whether the process is for the manufacture of a new product. The court or administrative authority may ask for a search report to be made by the patent office.

Appeal

The decision of the court of first instance can be appealed against to the higher level court whose decision is final and enforceable. The statutory time limit for an appeal is 15 days after the date on which the written judgment is served for domestic parties, or 30 days for foreign parties having no residence in China.

The decision of the administrative authority may be appealed against to the intermediate court having jurisdiction if a party is not satisfied with the decision. The judgment of the intermediate court may be appealed again to the higher level court.

Border enforcement by Customs

The Regulations of the People's Republic of China on the Customs' Protection of Intellectual Property Rights were promulgated by the State Council 5 July 1995 and entered into effect 1 October 1995.

Scope of application

The Customs Regulations forbid the import or export of goods protected by Chinese laws and regulations including trademark, patent and copyright. The trademark or patent owners or their agents are first required to record their intellectual property (IP) rights with Customs.

Record entry

IP rights owners must submit to the General Administration of Customs a written application including the following details:

- information about the applicant;
- information about the suspected infringing goods and the infringer (if possible);
- the Customs HS Code of suspected infringing products in the Customs declaration;
- certificate of intellectual property rights: a copy of the Chinese trademark registration certificate, patent certificate or copyright certificate;
- a copy of the applicant's business licence or business registration certificate;
- clear colour photographs of the authentic or suspected infringing goods;
- a concise description of the features of the suspected infringing goods;
- a statement on disputes and documents for current litigation, cancellation and revocation actions, etc;
- a list of other parties using the IP rights in a legitimate way including the licencee and the trustees.
- the Customs shall notify the applicant whether the application is admitted for entry in the records within 30 days after receiving all the application documents.

Period of validity

The period of validity shall be seven years counted from the day the record entry is admitted by the General Administration of Customs Office.

Subject to the validity of IP, the intellectual property owner may apply for a renewal of the record entry within six months before the period of validity of the record expires. The period of validity for each renewal of the record entry shall be seven years.

The record entry of the customs' protection shall expire when the period of validity of the registration for the trademark, patent or copyright recorded expires.

Application for protection measures

IP right owners whose rights have been entered in the record of the Customs General shall file an application with the customs, located in the place of import or export of the suspected infringing products, to detain the goods and submit the guarantees equal to the CIF value of the imported goods or the FOB value of the exported goods when they consider it necessary.

The customs may detain the suspected infringing goods based on the request of the intellectual property owner; it can also initiate *ex officio* action to detain suspected infringing goods and notify the IP owner in writing.

If the IP owner who applies to the customs to take protection measures has not recorded his right with the Customs General, he shall undertake the formalities of recording the IP in accordance with the Regulation at the same time as he applies to the Customs General for protection measures.

Protection measures

If the consignee or consignor of the detained goods does not file an objection with the customs on detention, the customs has the power to:

- confiscate infringing goods;
- destroy the goods infringing a trademark, unless the infringing trademark can be removed from the goods;
- fine the infringer who imports or exports the infringing goods intentionally;
- transfer proceedings against the offender, whose act of importing or exporting goods infringing IP rights

constitutes a crime, to the judicial authorities for investigation.

Rights of the suspected infringer and the IP rights owner

- The consignee or consignor of seized goods has seven days from the date of being served with a Customs Detaining Receipt to raise an objection to the customs' seizure.
- The IP owner has 15 days from the date of being served a written notification from the Customs Department to apply to the appropriate authorities handling IP for remedies or to commence action in the People's Court.
- A consignee or consignor of detained goods, who alleges that his goods do not infringe any IP rights, may apply for clearance of the goods. A bail bond in the amount equal to twice the CIF value of the imported goods or twice the FOB value of the exported goods shall be provided.

(Editor's note: Mr Fan Weimin can be contacted the following address at: 10/F,Ocean Plaza,158 Fuxingmennei Street, Beijing 100031, China.
Tel: 0086 10 6641 2345 Fax: 0086 10 6641 5678)

Part Four

Market Entry and Business Development in China

Discovering Chinese Cultural Roots

Liu Baocheng, Professor, University of International Business and Economics

China's foreign trade totalled US$509.77 billion in 2001. By the end of June 2002, total foreign investment in China amounted to US$419.8 billion with investment from over 180 countries and regions. Nearly four-fifths of the top multinational companies have set up their subsidiaries here. As the frequency of business communication with China grows, cultural differences and clashes present some significant challenges. One must remain constantly alert, not only to different business behaviours, but also to their underlying values and their history, in order to prevent unnecessary mishaps.

Cultural traits

Effective cross-cultural communication requires knowledge, attitude and tactics. Chinese people eat with chopsticks, they always have good excuses for you to drink more at the dinner table, they are reluctant to say no even if a proposal is unacceptable and so on. To present a long list of the differences in Chinese behaviour, one does not need to know an overwhelming amount about China. However, to understand and cope with these differences, it is necessary to go beyond this superficial level. As a matter of fact, behaviour is only the tip of the iceberg. Behind differences in behaviour lies attitude – attitudes towards oneself, time, the environment and the people around them. What is more profound and deeply embedded are different beliefs and values that are shaped by experience, history, tradition, family and society.

Table 4.1.1 is a broad summary of contrasting cultural traits between Chinese and Westerners in terms of different business methods. While considering the diversity and ongoing changes in the cultures under

Table 4.1.1 Summary of different cultural traits in Chinese and Western business methods

Cultural traits	Chinese	Westerner
Religion	Basically atheist	Basically Christian
Business relations	Highly interpersonal	'Business is business'
Planning	Incremental	Objective driven
Decision-making	Collective	Individualistic
Negotiation style	Friendly	Aggressive
Expression	Contextual	Explicit
Communication	Infrequent	Frequent
Organizational structure	Hierarchical	Horizontal
Logical reasoning	Deductive	Inductive

discussion, the author does not attempt to avoid charges of stereotyping.

Cultural roots

Chinese people on the whole are not fervent adherents to any religion. Most have a practical mindset and are more concerned with earthly happiness than any spiritual quest. However, with the long history of reverence for a supernatural power derived from early Chinese civilization, superstition and animism are still occasionally present and can cause social waves. A bewildering array and variety of gods – native, foreign, heroic and primitive – can be found in Chinese shrines. The Chinese have long been tolerant of all religions and customs and religious wars and persecutions are rare in Chinese history.

Though officially atheist, Chinese people have been strongly influenced by two prominent schools of thought – Taoism and Confucianism – and by the religion of Buddhism. Taoism and Confucianism, particularly the latter, are more philosophical schools of thought than religions and are devoted to social teachings. Buddhism and Islam are formal religions. The former is widespread across the country, whereas the latter is practised mostly in the north-western regions of the country.

As an officially atheist country, social customs are viewed more as part of the culture than as rigid rules of conduct and behaviour. The Chinese are known for their benevolence and tolerance. There are few taboos and sensitive topics and 'deviant' behaviour by foreigners are generally tolerated provided they are free from ill intention. They are generally considerate when dealing with foreigners: there is a Chinese saying that 'Ignorance is excusable'.

The influence of Taoism

Taoists believe that the world is constituted by the interplay of two interacting forces, *Yin* and *Yang*. The word *Tao* means 'the way' or 'the path'. Every object in the universe represents the process and outcome of interplay between these two forces, one passive, the other positive. These seemingly opposite forces can coexist, although one may prevail over the other at times. Moreover, even within *Yin*, there contains *Yang*, and vice versa. The state of *Yin* may over time shift to *Yang*.

Thanks to the Taoist influence, Chinese people are highly dialectical in their judgements. Expressions such as 'on one hand. . . but on the other hand. . .' or 'yes. . . but. . .' are part of their daily language. For example, if goods are returned because of inferior quality, it is not surprising to hear a manager remark that 'this is a good thing, on the other hand, because it helps us to dig deep to the root cause of the problem'. Balance, coexistence and harmony with people, time and environment both within and outside oneself are considered to be essential constituents of a good quality of life.

For some Chinese, the practice of *feng shui* (literally 'wind and water', which represent harmony with the physical environment) is popular when selecting building sites and arranging offices. Chinese people tend to be less enthusiastic to take initiative, be different or be confrontational. Drafting the contract or formulating the minutes of meetings is very likely to be the job of the foreign party. 'Let's meet halfway' is a typically proposed solution by the Chinese party during business negotiations.

The influence of Confucianism

Confucius was a pragmatic philosopher obsessed with defining specific personal relationships. Based on his central doctrine of *li* (proper conduct), Confucius expected every person strictly to observe his or her prescribed position in the different social strata in order to maintain the 'perfect social order' into perpetuity. In Confucianism, ruler and subject, father and son, husband and wife, elder and younger brother and senior and junior are specifically assigned proper rules of conduct in relation to each other. With good character and personal virtue displayed by every member of society, penal laws became unnecessary because acting contrary to *li* would result in the far graver moral and social sanction of shame. Without this sense of shame, however punitive the legislation may be, people would attempt to violate it.

Family is placed at the centre of society and in Confucianism, to conceal the wrongdoings of family members is righteous behaviour. *Li* is also addressed in dealing with friends. 'What a joy to have friends from afar!' Confucius declared. The impact of Confucianism on the Chinese mode of thinking and way of life is profound. As one author put it, China may espouse Marxist socialism, but the bedrock beneath the socialist topsoil is almost pure Confucianism. A patriarchal organizational structure, *mianzi* (face), reverence to seniority, unquestionable loyalty to the ruler, nepotism, hospitality and humility are all familiar terms in the Confucian vocabulary.

Geert Hofstede attributed 'Confucian Dynamism' to 'a society's search for virtue' rather than a search for truth. This explains why China has been short of solid scientific foundations despite its rich civilisation. Examinations for public offices were the only path for scholars to move into official rank, but these exams included no discipline of natural science; more attention was paid to conscience and social order. China maintained this tight superstructure throughout its history, but its foundations for natural science are weak.

In fact, the origin of Chinese scientific understanding largely lies in the Taoist alchemy: a superstitious pursuit of immortality, and the initial motivation for the grand overseas expeditions in the Ming Dynasty was neither adventure nor diplomacy but the search for the overthrown emperor who was thought to be hiding in exile. Missing out on the sweeping industrialization and renaissance in Europe, empiricism and scientific experimentation have been lacking in favour of abstract thinking and relativism. Take traditional Chinese medicine for example. Most formulas involve a compound of herbal ingredients validated by experience passed on through generations. Actual clinical studies, scientific processes, quality control and quality assurance are noticeably lacking.

The influence of Buddhism

Mahayana Buddhism was imported from India in the sixth century BC and soon became entwined with native faiths. The doctrine of *karma* denotes fate or destiny operating by the cyclical law of causation. The present life is the result of deeds in the past life and the future life is determined by actions in the present life. To many Chinese, the law of causation is interpreted in two ways, as with the tenets of native Chinese philosophies.

The passive interpretation conforms with the Taoist *wuwei* (let go, or do nothing); since every individual's destiny has been predetermined, and thereby all miseries, hardships and joys should be accepted as part of one's fate. Unlike Christianity, Buddhism calls on people to eradicate all desires and retreat from worldly affairs. The fact that Buddhist temples are secluded in high mountains and Christian churches are located in pre-eminent city areas is one manifestation of this contrast.

The positive interpretation is consistent with the Confucian insistence on active social service; good deeds in the present life will be rewarded in the next life. *Karma* is also used to supplement Confucianism, which is rendered futile if social forces fail to enforce conformity to the prescribed ethical standards. It is at least emotionally comforting for victims of wrongdoing to believe that these wrongdoers will eventually receive adequate retribution on the strength of *karmic* law, when they are unable or unwilling to take positive action against them.

The confluence of Buddhism and Taoism means the Chinese are more content with the state of being than of doing. Chinese people tend to enjoy indoor activities – playing poker games, mahjong, or simply spending hours cooking; they prefer to stay at home rather than travelling during their holidays. While none of these prevailing spiritual forces nurture entrepreneurship, they collectively breed impressive endurance during hardships or misfortunes. Chinese people have experi-

enced so many famines, disasters and military repression over their history that they find their own path to survival in forbearance and endurance. Despite the low level of disposable income, the savings rate in China is among the highest in the world, and a large body of the elaborate national cuisine is actually a reflection of the people's capability to live through famines by using whatever materials they could lay their hands on. Apart from all kinds of plants and vegetables, as the saying goes, 'Chinese people eat anything with two legs but a man, anything with wings but a chopper, anything with four legs but a table'.

Cultural attitudes

Hospitality

In China, gift exchange is an indispensable part of relationship building. This practice extends even to the family of the recipient. The context of gift exchange is believed to generate an expansion of human sympathy. Foreigners are cautioned to avoid admiring the possessions of a Chinese friend during a house visit as they will very likely be offered as gifts. Traditionally, it is impolite to unwrap the gifts in front of the giver.

Wining and dining is an important part of business dealings. Obstruction at a negotiation table may well be solved after a couple of toasts at dinner table. 'Going Dutch' is generally not acceptable. In paying the bill, initiative or even a friendly fight is expected. Splitting the bill may initially seem fair but Chinese people look at the long-term relationship. Friends or business counterparts do not only meet once in a lifetime so everyone has the opportunity to reciprocate. If only one party has to pay, the wealthier one, or one who will be reimbursed by his or her organization is expected to take the initiative.

Face-saving

Actually, the real purpose of humility, modesty or self-depreciation is to save or gain face. 'I am not well prepared due to the short notice or personal incompetence...' is often heard at the beginning of a speech. 'Due to limited knowledge, the author begs for criticism of the mistakes in the book' is often found at the end of the preface to a book. A positive result is more likely if parties have been paying attention to face-saving. On the contrary, an outright 'no', pointing to the face or banging on the table will definitely lead to hostility. Chinese people have suffered a long history of foreign oppression and the imposition of 'unequal treaties', which render them more sensitive to perceived power games by foreigners. An American friend doing business with China won immediate applause when he said 'my grandfather was a member of the "Eight Foreign Troops" who looted Beijing, and now I am here to find a way to compensate within my limited capacity.'

Most business contracts start with the words 'through friendly negotiation, both parties unanimously agree to the following terms and conditions in the spirit of equality and mutual benefit'. Executives would do well to keep the stated objectives in mind so that they can structure proposals in a manner acceptable to their Chinese counterparts. Price negotiation is usually regarded as the highlight of a business deal. Scope must be allowed in the price quotation for strenuous bargaining. A 'take-it-or-leave-it' position even when the price was structured at the bottom line is not perceived as sincere, because price reduction through bargaining is a necessary component of face-saving.

With regard to contract disputes, most contracts maintain a standard clause stipulating that amicable settlement through friendly negotiation or mutual consultation is a prerequisite before any other legal action, such as arbitration, takes place. One of the unique characteristics of Chinese arbitration is that before formal arbitration proceeds, disputants are in the first place referred to the Conciliation Centre for mediation. The goal of 'amicable settlement' – so different from the Western norm of compromise through adversarial negotiations – reflects the Chinese insistence on peaceful coexistence and harmony in all human endeavour, including business. In conflict resolution, a losing party is far more likely to agree to end a struggle if a way out of the situation is suggested that is not too embarrassing. Excessively driving the other side to admit a loss is an unwise approach. The recent announcement by Philips to withdraw the lawsuit against the accused unauthorized use of DVD technology by Chinese companies ended with more gains to Philips. If there is a creative way to frame the outcome of the dispute to the effect that all sides can claim at least some success, at least on the surface, it will make it much easier for the losing side to back down.

Forms of address and expressions

In addressing the elderly or senior, it is impolite to use the first name. It is advisable to include the job position of the senior person, for example 'Manager Wang',

'Teacher Liu' or 'Section Chief Zhao'. To the elderly with no senior position, one is advised to use *lao* (old), or *shifu* (master) (if he or she is a blue-collar worker) before the family name. To the younger, *xiao* (young) is often used before the family name to show cordiality. *Tongzhi* (Comrade) is a legacy of the communist revolutionary usage whose frequency of use has declined sharply except for some official occasions. There is a growing tendency to address white-collar workers with *teacher* before the family name. In the meantime, *xianshen* (Mr) and *xiaojie* (Miss) are increasingly popular in the cities. But while *taitai* (Mrs) is used behind the husband's family name, its popularity is limited since most Chinese women are socially and economically independent and their maiden names are retained after marriage. Women hold half the sky! They appear in equal positions with men both in the business and entertainment scenes.

Chinese people are good and careful listeners. Ample time is given to their counterparts to spell out their intention, proposal and solution. Most Chinese are not adept at body languages, but when they speak they demonstrate a clear line of logic. Exasperation or irritation is considered bad manners, however heated the discussion. A Minnesota magazine journalist, John Marshall, describes a businessman from a European company who had been pushed to his personal breaking point on the matter of price. The hot weather and the days of discussion over a fairly small price differential led him finally to rise from the table saying 'Obviously, we are not going to get an agreement. You've had everything I can offer you except the shirt off my back, and you can have that now'. With that, he got up, unbuttoned his sweaty shirt, tossed it on the table, and walked out of the room. After the embarrassed silence that followed, the Chinese told the leader of the company's negotiation team that they would prefer the group not to return as its representative had shown such bad manners. (Source: *Business strategy for the PRC*, Business International Asian Research Report, 1980, p 296)

Collectivism

It is not traditional for Chinese people to embrace collectivism. For the greater part of its, 2000-year history, China was ruled by an absolute monarchy. Unlike ancient Europe, where the basic unit of social production was the manor, the family was the basic unit of social production in traditional Chinese society. On this basis a series of ethical principles were developed that bound the Chinese tightly to their homes. In time, a mentality was formed among the Chinese, marked by heavy dependence on the collectives of family, clan and nation. This dependence inevitably produced inertia and a conservative attitude. People simply wanted to feel secure; they were afraid of change and lacked an enterprising spirit. Ironically, all such psychological needs were supposed to be met under the centralized system, in which everything from clothing to food, from housing to transportation, from cradle to grave was to be taken care of. People tended to look to the organisation or the government for a secure life.

Managers of an organization are expected in some ways to assume the role of parents. Today, particularly in state-owned organizations, employees can be found pestering their managers for better housing or even for settlements of family disputes. Individualism is not a welcome quality where collective decisions and responsibility are the accepted way of the world. Excessive numbers of meetings are an important part of the work routine, either for ascertaining public opinion or broadcasting directives from senior staff. In spite of all its merits, collectivism is also, for the executives, a shield against uncertainty. They do not have to delegate their power, but neither do they have to shoulder individual responsibility if things go wrong. When security prevails over efficiency, mediocrity finds a rich soil. In virtually all Chinese organizations, clear job descriptions and professionalism are still in a lax condition. This lack of clear job descriptions and professional responsibility necessitates collective discussions and layers of approval. Paradoxically, under this type of collectivism, it is usually on the top person who makes the final decision; collectivism is perfectly compatible with a hierarchical chain of command. It is not surprising that dozens of rubber stamps may be needed before a business licence can be obtained: it may take months to get contract approval and it would be foolish to expect decisions to be made on the spot.

Corruption

It may seem odd to relate contemporary corruption and abuse of power by government and corporate officials to the virtues advocated by Confucius. However, it not too far fetched to hold Confucius partly responsible for the prevailing corruption in China for the following reasons:

1. his condemnation of legislation;

2. his class distinction between the gentry and the petty;
3. his proposition that it is righteous for the son to help conceal the wrongdoings of the father.

Believing in the essential and original goodness of man, Confucius held that strict laws were unnecessary and that virtue was the root of civilization. 'If the ruler is virtuous,' he said, 'the people will also be virtuous'. Therefore, power should not need to be checked. Confucius took such a partial stance in favour of the gentry class that he contrived defences for their misconduct: 'Mistakes of the gentry are like eclipses of the sun and moon: they will not keep them from shining' he proclaimed. Officials are part of the learned and the learned constitute the gentry's class. The Confucian *li* applied, in reality, only within this class stratum. He focused on the importance of moral teaching and establishing exemplary models, but to many, the temptation of economic interest was irresistible without the threat of penalty. Active concealment by family members, relatives and other barriers built up by corrupt officials add further complication to legal enforcement.

Guanxi

Guanxi (connection) may be seen as a web of strong personal connections where the connection's official position may be utilized to extend personal favours and commitments. For example, if a friend helped my daughter to find a better job, I would be more inclined to grant him an import licence within my authority. The culture of *Guanxi* is based on binding social units: family, school, office or social networks. Though a controversial and subtle subject, *Guanxi* is so widespread and pervasive in Chinese culture that it is a subject of study – *Guanxiology*. It does not aim at direct exchange or immediate gratification. Chinese culture holds it of paramount important to reciprocate favours received. Even today, many families keep a record of the gifts for a wedding or funeral so that one day they will find a way to reciprocate. *Guanxi* is a strategic reserve, which takes time to accumulate but can be cashed in in case of need and convenience. Some conclude that 'to get things done in China, it is not important to know what, but to know who'. It is particularly useful in tapping benefits from bureaucrats who possess freewheeling authority.

Excessive gift giving and extensive use of *guanxi* can be a subject of anti-corruption scrutiny both along the

Communist Party line and on the strength of public law. However, the importance of *guanxi* and the pervasiveness of corruption tend to be generally exaggerated to many westerners to the point that it becomes misleading. Reform over the state-owned enterprises (SOEs) took the corporate management position out of the hands of former government officials and into those of business executives. The correlation between personal motivation and performance is being legitimized. While the burgeoning private enterprises are in no position to be bribed, they have the motivation to act as a source of corruption in dealing with government officials and corporate executives of SOEs, partly due to their flexibility when it comes to decision-making and distribution of cash.

Overall, the corruption situation in China is changing for the better. Incessant anti-corruption campaigning and legal changes have helped to restore bureaucratic reverence for, if not responsibility to, their duties. The ultimate driver lies in streamlined government functions, increased law enforcement, free market competition and free access to information. As China becomes an active member of the world community, especially by its entry into the WTO, wholesale changes have been taking place toward these objectives.

Today, the deep-rooted culture of *guanxi* still exists in China, but its importance is more restricted at the stage of 'knocking on the door'.

Tips for doing business with China

The Three 'P's

Conventional terms like the 3 'P's – patience, persistence and product – are still valid when doing business with China.

AT&T waited for eight years before being accepted as a partner in the telecom business. Under Chinese law, foreign companies are required to have at least three years' history of maintaining representative offices in China before becoming eligible to enter into joint ventures with a Chinese counterpart in the service sector. The Chinese premier Zhu Rongji once said at a press conference to foreign companies lining up to join the Chinese market, 'your patience will be duly rewarded'. Once a strategy to enter into Chinese market is validated, impatience is likely to end in disappointment.

After all, after 2,000 years of imperial dynasties, plus decades of isolation over the last century, China has only been open to the outside world for 23 years. Many things that are taken for granted in western countries are still new to the Chinese. They need time to catch up with the world. Two years ago, the author – representing a US firm – spent nearly an hour during a business negotiation with a Chinese partner explaining what NASDAQ and GAAP were. China has achieved remarkable success in its reform programmes. Compared with the Russian 'shock therapy', this incremental approach may proceed more slowly but has been effective. In the face of these realities, although power play can occasionally be effective, contempt and disgruntled attitudes can only lead to destructive confrontation.

The need for patience and persistence does not end when a business deal is signed. Patience and persistence are still necessary to ensure that the deal is implemented. Particularly in the case of technology transfer and other types of giant undertakings such as a turnkey project, more tutorial work and communication is needed to ensure the Chinese party really understand what is underway. Extra assistance is often required to pave the way for approval and foreign exchange allocation. Executive time and travel should be built into the initial phase of project budgeting. As competition grows and experience of the Chinese party increases, patience and persistence become a crucial element to stand out among business rivals. Those who are able to endure a considerable period of delays to allow the Chinese parties time for collective decision-making, coordinating with different stakeholders, comparing different bidders, going through adjustment and readjustment of business policies, will be the likely winners in the end. During such a critical period, the frontline executives must be prepared for the toughest challenges communicating with their headquarters while facing a black-box operation at the China end. However, perseverance despite these trials demonstrates the important quality of the will to succeed.

Finally, patience and persistence are not substitutes for high-quality products supported by sound technology and adequate service. Again, Chinese people are highly practical. Typically, their technical negotiators are very knowledgeable and often raise tough questions over materials, processes, patent validity, quality controls and assurances. The author once experienced a rather hard time putting to rest a request for the 'most advanced technology' through the addition of a number of conditional clauses such as 'at the time of delivery', 'to the best knowledge of the licensor' and 'by the standard set forth by the licensor' etc.

Self-reference criterion

As previously stated, effective cross-cultural communication requires knowledge, attitude and tactics. It is important to learn to shift positions to prevent cultural stereotyping and myopia. The self-reference criterion (SRC) (Lee, 1966) is a practical guide in getting along with the Chinese culture. Summarized by Keegan (1997), it is reflected in a four-step systematic framework:

1. Define the problem or goal in terms of home-country cultural traits, habits and norms.
2. Define the problem or goal in terms of host-country cultural traits, habits, and norms. Do not make value judgements.
3. Isolate the SRC influence and examine it carefully to see how it complicates the problem.
4. Redefine the problem without the SRC influence and solve for the host-country market situation.

Precautions

China is a vast country with over 1.3 billion people divided into 56 ethnic groups speaking hundreds of different dialects. Although 5,000 years of history has resulted in substantial cultural homogeneity, diversity has always been the counter force to any attempt at generalization. Democratic movements and socialism, and the Great Cultural Revolution in particular, have overturned traditional Chinese values and beliefs. Opening to the outside world and domestic reforms over the last two decades have ushered in an unprecedented flow of western ideas – some soon evaporated, some remain foreign, and some have been distilled into the native value system. In a nutshell, today's China, like its marketplace, is a cultural kaleidoscope and no statement about Chinese culture should be taken at face value or have universal validity. Nonetheless, the practical value of this chapter rests on the presumption that the roots of a culture shaped by its long history are generally resistant to change. It is the author's hope that when readers are presented with the 'roots and soil', they will be able to identify or predict the fruit of the tree.

Cultural Differences and Clashes in Communication

*Li Yong, Deputy Secretary General, China Association of International Trade, and
Liu Baocheng, Professor, University of International Business and Economics*

Games with familiar and unfamiliar rules

There is a story about a cross-cultural training session at a western company. The trainees were going to be expatriated to overseas positions. At one point in the training, the trainees were asked to take a break to play poker games. Very quickly, they agreed on the type of game they were going to play, and naturally they played one of the games they were familiar with, whose rules were clearly understood by all the players. After a while, the instructor interrupted their game and said, 'Now, you are not allowed to play the game with the familiar rules of your home country. Please continue the game.' The players' minds suddenly went blank. They looked at each other in silence with bewildered expressions on their faces, and no idea how the game should continue. The instructor then broke the silence by saying, 'The country you guys are going to be assigned to is one that has no rules, or you will be completely ignorant of the rules there are. Are you ready for that?'

Indeed, it is easy to play a game with rules understood by all players, and it is fun to play games with players who understand the rules. However, it is not fun at all to play a game without a rule and with players who have different sets of rules for the same game. These cultural differences can cause different understandings of the same thing. When each of the players is trying to play the game according to the rules that they are familiar with, differences in the understanding of these rules will lead to cultural clashes. Of course, cultural differences have much more profound roots than a simple game, and solving cultural clashes is much more complicated than simply setting up uniform rules, as has been done in sports such as the Olympic Games.

With the development of international trade and world economy moving towards what is termed globalization, people's interactions against different cultural backgrounds have become increasingly frequent and inevitable. The world is now called a 'global village', and like it or not, it is true that we are living in a multicultural 'village'. In transnational economic operations, it is difficult, if not impossible, to establish rules such as those of the Olympic Games that people from all cultures will abide by. Historical concepts of the 'game' such as beliefs, ethical standards, religions, codes of practice, institutions and behavioural patterns, as well as factors of inter- and intra-competition, language, approaches to a particular objective, interactions of cultural traits, conflicts of value, legal framework and social structures all come into play, and make the pursuit of a uniform cultural rule under a bicultural or multicultural environment difficult and practically impossible to achieve. In addition to this, 'cultural' games are a dynamic process and there is no one single rule that can apply to all situations. There is only one rule to remember when it comes to cultural differences – people may look at the same thing but they all see it differently, regardless of whether they come from the same or a different culture. This rule goes some way to explaining the diversity of the world.

Returning to the training story, no information is given about how the trainees were instructed to deal with a situation in which there were no rules, or rules that they were ignorant of. One criticism of the instructor's first comment – that there are no rules in the country concerned – is that he was using self-reference criteria (see Chapter 4.1), one of the sources of cultural clashes. However, his second comment that there might be rules that the trainees were completely ignorant about offers a chance of cultural understanding, if the trainees were encouraged to learn more about the rules in a foreign country and make an effort to bridge the gap of cultural differences.

China as a member of the international community

Since China opened up to the outside world in 1978, it has made unremitting efforts toward integration into the global economy. Import and export as a percentage of the GDP has surged from 14 per cent in the early 1980s to 44 per cent in 2000. China's foreign trade volume in 2000 accounted for 3.2 per cent of world trade, an almost fourfold increase on 1978. According to the WTO, China ranked seventh in export volume and eighth in import volume in 2000. China has been the largest recipient of foreign direct investment (FDI) among developing countries since 1993. By the end of December 2001, the cumulative number of foreign-invested enterprises (FIEs) stood at 390,025, with a cumulative contracted investment of US$745.29 billion and an actual utilization of US$395.22 billion. About 80 per cent of Fortune 500 companies have so far made investments in China. The accession to the WTO will greatly facilitate China's participation in globalization.

The above facts and figures clearly demonstrate that China is already an active, participating member of the international business community. With increased foreign investment in China, an understanding of Chinese culture from the perspective of tactics for striking a deal in business negotiations is no longer enough when tackling clashes between Chinese culture and other cultures in economic alliances or joint ventures. Indeed, the opening up of China has ushered in not only foreign investments, technologies and management expertise, but also foreign cultures that challenge the traditional thinking processes and behavioural patterns of the Chinese people. Differences exist and clashes remain. Many joint ventures run into problems and cultural clashes are often a key factor. Culture-led failures of joint ventures, mergers or acquisitions are not unique phenomena in China. There has been a great deal of research in the west indicating a high percentage (in the order of 50 per cent to as high as 75 per cent) of failures of joint ventures, mergers and acquisitions, and many of these failures are believed to have been caused by cultural conflicts.

Decisions to form joint ventures are usually made on economic grounds, as the pooling of the partners' resources are expected to be advantageous to both parties and lead to higher profitability. Stories of failures, however, have revealed a growing body of evidence that non-economic factors often set in and lead to poor joint venture performance. Because of the difficulties that exist in the effort to bridge cultural differences, there has been an increasing trend of solely owned overseas operations: an attempt to avoid cultural clashes, at least at the management level. The same is true in China. Since 1997 an increasing number of solely foreign-owned enterprises has been established in China. In addition, many foreign investors holding minority shares in joint ventures have increased their capital input to become majority share holders. All of these are efforts to gain management control and so reduce the chances of decision-making being held up by disagreements with local partners, but does not necessarily eliminate cultural differences and clashes, because the joint ventures are still operating in an environment dominated by Chinese culture and need to deal with people who think different things, in different ways.

Some concluded that as globalization develops and national boundaries become increasingly blurred, interest in joint venture would subside. However, in an era of great flux in the commercial world, strategic alliances work at all levels, and joint ventures are still a popular method of expanding businesses. The advantages of joint ventures are obvious. A joint venture can turn under-utilized resources into profit and create a new profit centre, help enter untapped markets quicker and at less cost than trying it alone and minimise the risk of a large investment undertaking. There are a number of successful joint ventures in China but it takes sensitivity to a range of cultural differences over styles of communication, attitudes, value judgements and social and managerial behaviours to achieve this success.

Anecdotal analysis of the differences between Chinese and western cultures

Chinese cultural roots and traits, the underlying drivers of the Chinese mental and behavioural patterns, were discussed in Chapter 4.1. When examining cultural differences, note should also be taken of the fact that China is moving towards a more open society and increased interaction of Chinese people with westerners has prepared the ground for acceptance of western management concepts and practices. Table 4.2.1 is a list

Table 4.2.1 Key differences between Chinese and western cultures

Chinese culture	Western culture
Large power distance	Small power distance
Reverence to rank and power	Equality among people
Bureaucracy	Authority of law
Strong tendency of risk avoidance	Strong tendency of risk taking
Dominance of group interest and values	Dominance of individualistic interest
Doctrine of the mean and ambiguity	Clarity in expression
Resistance to change	Acceptance of change
Lack of original creativity	Pro-innovation
Pursuit of moral accomplishments	Pursuit of objective being
Cultivation of personal virtue	Knowledge and skill learning
Despise material gains	Recognition of material gains
'Face' is important	'Face' is unimportant
Connotation and tolerance	Candour and rigidity

of key differences in the business context between Chinese and western cultures.

Of course, this list is not exhaustive and many others can be added to it from different perspectives and experiences. The differences identified here are more relevant to the business environment than to personal traits. They are not only key variables of Chinese 'collective mental programming' (Hofstede) process, but also the determinants of conflict management behaviour.

Power distance, one of Hofstede's measures of cultural difference, is one of the most prominent differences of Chinese culture compared to that of the west. The Confucian cultural and social traditions dictate a rigid social hierarchy – top-down control and distribution of power by rank, as a result of which bureaucracy is seldom challenged and reverence to rank and power is considered to be a virtue. The results of power distance are often manifested in a lack of efficient vertical communication, obedience in execution of the orders/instructions of the superior and avoidance of a direct challenge to power. The top-down control structure makes many Chinese organisations resemble the personal characteristics of the top leader.

In the context of a joint venture, power distance is also at play. Open argument with the management about, for example, corporate strategies, is rarely seen. Private, one-on-one meetings may encourage a Chinese manager to speak more freely about his opinion. Foreign managers should be careful with their mode of expression when challenging the ideas of Chinese managers who hold superior positions.

Power distance does not only exist within an organization. It is omnipresent in the web of the social hierarchy. The mental programming process in handling power distance is situational and involves complex considerations, among which 'face' is an important factor. Whether or not a person in an organisation will challenge the ideas of another person depends on his judgement of the 'face' element as well as the other person's rank in the hierarchy. He is less likely to challenge his superiors and likely to challenge others of the same rank. Face is less of an element of consideration when dealing with underlings, but face-giving is also a lubricant of power distance in a bottom-up direction. For example, the Chinese have a tendency to credit the successes of corporate achievements to the supervising authority or government departments, a face-giving effort to minimize obstacles resulting from power distance. This, amongst other things, often causes 'culture shock' in foreigners. A German engineer, leading a group of technicians to install the equipment contributed by the German partner in China, was bewildered when he heard at the opening ceremony of the joint venture, that the successful commissioning and operation of the equipment was credited to 'the correct leadership' of the supervising authority and his team's effort in making equipment running was not acknowledged. When he learned that it was a rhetoric formality to mention the supervising authority, he copied this exercise when the equipment failed and announced that the equipment went wrong due to the leadership of the supervising authority. Everyone present was taken aback.

The story of the German engineer reflects not only a lack of understanding of cultural context, but also the differences between Chinese and western culture in terms of the emphasis on group and individual contribution. China is generally a collectivist society. Individualism-collectivism, another of Hofstede's dimensions of culture, is an important parameter in measuring cultural variability, as it shows the norms and values that a culture attaches to social relationships and social exchanges. The Chinese people have a tendency of pursuing collective goals rather than individual interests, and this is a fundamental characteristic of the Chinese culture governing the relationship between organization and individuals. Collectivism is still emphasized in China as a virtue and a citizen's social responsibility. In the official doctrine of collectivism, individualism is regarded as egoism or a source of selfish desire and is therefore suppressed for the common well-being. However, over the past 24 years since China opened up to the outside world, the collectivism tendency has been exposed to western individualism, and its influence is clear among the younger generation, who have a stronger sense of self-importance.

In a business environment, collective consensus is often sought in the decision-making process, although power distance may block different opinions. Managers often speak of collective interests to hold back individual desire, whereas the individual aspirations are often achieved in the name of collectivist pursuit. In addition to this, collectivism underlies egalitarianism in welfare and income distribution. An extreme example of this egalitarianism is a Chinese scholar who won a prize for his remarkable achievements but divided his prize money between not only his leaders and team members, but also people irrelevant to his work such as drivers and cooks. He attributed his success to the leaders at the top of the organization for their support and those at the bottom of the structure for their logistical support. Although this egalitarianism is weakening following Deng Xiaoping's advocacy of 'let some people get rich first', this inclination towards egalitarianism driven by collectivism should be taken into consideration in managing employee relations.

Where collectivism seems to correlate with the western management practice of teamwork is that people of a collectivist culture prefer to work in groups rather than individually. Although the Chinese characteristic of collectivism prepares the ground of team spirit in some ways, it still represents a departure from what teamwork requires. The lack of horizontal communication, tend-

ency to work only with peers, reluctance to share knowledge and mistrust among co-workers arising from the lack of explicit expression need to be carefully handled before teamwork and team spirit can be established.

To fit the Chinese culture into Hofstede's uncertainty avoidance dimension is difficult, because the tendency of uncertainty avoidance in Chinese culture is high in some cases and low in others and so some researchers put China into the low category; others in the high. (The authors wish to avoid uncertainty by not making this judgement.) Typically, Chinese people have a tendency to avoid risks, resist changes, tolerate contradictions, accept ambiguities, pursue cultivation of virtue rather than truth, observe informal rules (affective) and compromise on formal rules (instrumental). In a business context, the tendency of risk avoidance often leads to a different understanding of change, while tolerance of contradictions leads to different paths of conflict resolution. Ambiguity in expression as a typical feature of a high-context culture often makes cross-cultural communication ineffective. Ambiguity in Chinese culture comes from the contextual and dialectical thinking which contrasts with the westerners' linear thinking patterns.

Let us take a look at a case of cultural differences in a joint venture, which will help understand how some of Hofstede's culture dimensions are at play in a corporate environment.

Case study

The company is a joint venture between an overseas Chinese and Western entrepreneur, operating in China with the Chinese holding the majority shares. After 10 years of development, the venture has become a multi-million dollar business and it is still growing. The company's marketing department consists of three teams. Interestingly, each team has the same function as the other, which is basically to solicit customers and provide 'tailor-made' services. To encourage teamwork, the company staged an incentive system that provides performance-related bonuses.

The outcome of the incentive system was both positive and negative. On the positive side, a competitive environment was established and sales increased. However, teams began to compete against each another for customers and hostility later arose among the teams. John, a marketing assistant, observed the development and communicated his concerns and observations to Robert, the company's western partner and vice-president with responsibility for marketing. This is a summary of his points:

- The three groups are competing against each another for clients and blocking client information
- There is an unwillingness to cooperate and consult with each other among the teams
- The teams undercut each other on prices in their fight for the same customer
- There has been a lack of coordination, which has resulted in separate marketing promotions running at the same time and targeting the same customer categories, leading to a waste of corporate resources and time.

Robert decided to have a meeting with the Chinese marketing manager, Mr Zhang, and the team leaders, to discuss these issues. During the meeting, Robert communicated his thoughts about the teamwork situation and invited the attendees to comment in the hope that the issues could be solved at the meeting. Much to Robert's surprise however, John appeared to be the only one who was concerned about the situation. After the meeting, Robert had a private conversation with Mr Zhang, who said that the current situation was satisfactory and that the competition had increased the total sales of the company. Robert accepted it as a fact, but still expressed his opinion that Mr Zhang should improve the teams' coordination and cooperation.

A couple of months later, the Chinese partner, Mr Wang, had a discussion about John's sales performance. Mr Wang said that John had fallen behind all other marketing assistants and had not been able to get a contract for about two months. Wang then asked Robert if John should be relocated from his present position to the administrative department, where more people were needed as the business expanded. Robert was unhappy about Wang's suggestion and said that John had been a good member of staff, and unlike other Chinese staff had been straightforward in communication, positive in his effort to develop corporate business, independent in his judgement and willing to speak out with his opinions and suggestions. Robert wanted to keep John in his marketing position as an independent source of understanding of what was really happening at the frontline of the corporate business. As Wang held management control as a majority shareholder, he insisted that Robert relocate John. Robert also heard from an informal source that Zhang had claimed that he would eliminate John from the scene because John had talked too much about his department's problems. John was removed from his marketing position.

In this case, the points of differences are as follows:

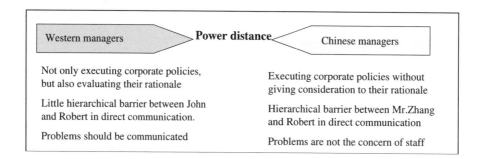

Figure 4.2.1 a. Power distance has determined different approaches in communication of problems.

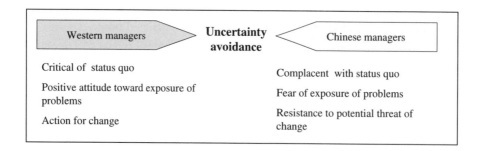

Figure 4.2.2 b. The varied degree of uncertainty avoidance led to attitudinal differences towards problems.

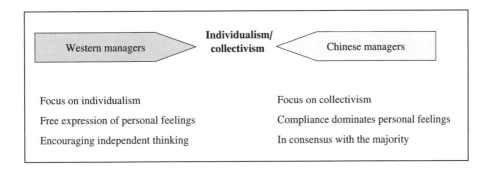

Figure 4.2.3 c. Collectivism-individualism predestined behavioural differences in response to problems

Table 4.2.2 Cross-cultural communication problems

Complaints from western managers	*Complaints from Chinese managers*
Marathon negotiations and decision-making	Lack of understanding of the unique local environment
Decisions reached by discussion instead of voting	Over-rigid in handling business affairs and lack of flexibility
Indirect expression of opinions	Impersonality and rule-orientation without giving consideration to circumstances
Great importance is given to 'face'	Lack of thrift in the use of corporate money
Dependent on *Guanxi* and personal emotions in business dealings	Disregard local management suggestions
Submissive and lack creativity	Individualistic and arbitrary in decision-making
Ambiguity in policies, laws and regulations	Money-making is the top priority
Bureaucracy	Lack of respect and care for staff/employees
Excessive government intervention	Ignore the interests of Chinese partners
Complicated and closely-knit interpersonal relations	Arrogance and conceit

All these differences are attributed to a failure in effectively communicating the problems.

Sources of cultural clashes in communication

Increased exposure of one culture to another in the context of economic globalisation is bound to lead to cultural clashes. It is unlikely that a person of one culture, entering a country of another culture, will completely forget his own culture and the familiar rules of his game, nor that he has a mission to achieve his corporate goals in the host country. It is impossible that he will be completely assimilated by the culture of the host country. The same is true for the people from the other culture. They cannot be expected completely to accept a foreign culture and to lose their own cultural identity. Given these cultural stances, the convenience of using self-reference criteria for people of both cultures will naturally come into play, and this is in fact the primary source of cultural clashes.

Cultural clashes can take many forms and it is impossible to produce an exhaustive list identifying all the sources of cultural clashes, because people interaction is a dynamic process. Table 4.2.2 summarizes the most common complaints by both westerners and Chinese about the problems they face in cross-cultural communications.

Two things can be done to bridge the communication gap. One is to learn to understand the Chinese way of communication and the other is to educate Chinese counterparts to understand the rationale of your way of doing things. Sometimes, an intermediary who understands both mindsets can be helpful in communicating the differences and achieving understanding.

Abrupt and forceful transplantation of western rules of management into a joint venture will only lead to conflict. In a Chinese-French joint venture, for example, the French brought, along with their equipment and technology, a complete set of French management rules, which were enforced without adaptation by the French managers who occupied all key managerial positions. Such an exercise aroused strong resentment from the workers and eventually triggered a strike, which was finally resolved by the mediation of the Chinese government and the French Consulate General. A staff of the joint venture commented later: 'If the French style management was executed by Chinese managers, it might perhaps be easier for us to accept. We just couldn't put up with the bullying and overbearing of the French.' This extreme case of cultural clash demonstrates the need for improved and effective communications to achieve mutual understanding and respect. Although the elements that should be taken into consideration for cross-cultural management are far more complicated than in a mono-cultural environment, readiness to understand and adapt to a foreign culture is certainly an effective means of improving efficiency. In the same Chinese-French joint venture, the Chinese managers suggested restricted use of the copying machines, which, at that time, were not popular office equipment. The French did not listen, and placed the machines in the corridor for free use as they did in France. The result was that the machines often went wrong because of wrong operation, and some Chinese staff used the machine to copy personal documents, all of which led to unnecessary increase in the cost of maintenance and paper. The French eventually adopted the Chinese suggestion and the cost related to the copying machines was brought under control. This example shows that people of different cultural backgrounds have different ways of thinking and behaving. The differences, if properly communicated, will complement one another as driving forces rather than barriers.

Education of the Chinese partners and workers at large is absolutely necessary. The objectives of education can be achieved through training, which should concentrate not only on skill improvements but also management understanding. A number of multinational companies have successfully implemented training programmes aimed at achieving trust and understanding. Hewlett Packard has successfully introduced its 'HP Way' into its China operations. Motorola has implemented training programmes, not only for its own staff, but also for its suppliers and customers. GE has established its core value of business ethics, honesty and credibility, by trying a number of different ways of communication including the distribution of booklets of corporate ethics to its staff. Chinese workers at Lucent Technologies are motivated to produce better quality products than their counterparts in Atlanta.

Apart from the purely cultural, there are other differences, such as the attitude towards and ability to handle market changes, corporate development strategies, conception of business management and management style. In addition, educational background and professional experiences vary among Chinese and western managers. All of this will lead to clashes in the communication of corporate strategies, development plans and so on. One elevator joint venture was once in serious confrontation on issues of corporate development strategy. The foreign partner suggested that the joint venture should improve services and provide maintenance to customers, while the Chinese management, whose average age was 58, put the emphasis on improvement of production. On accounting issues, the foreign partner proposed that unrecoverable accounts should be written off as bad debts, while the Chinese side expressed concerns that the joint venture would suffer an accounting deficit. Similar clashes as a result of differences in the conception of corporate development strategies were also seen in another joint venture, a Sino-American automobile manufacturing operation. In the early stages of the joint venture, the American partner suggested that the dividends should be reinvested into the joint venture to expand the scale of production. The response from the Chinese side was that the joint venture was comfortably well off, with annual sales of several hundred thousand cars, and the market demand was so strong that there was no need to invest in expansion and to divide the annual profit of RMB200–300 million would be the practical choice. The American partner made a concession by offering a unilateral increase in their capital contribution; this was declined by the Chinese side who calculated that the change in equity ratio would reduce their share of the dividend. By the mid-1990s, however, the market had begun to change and the old model quickly lost its market.

Managing cross-cultural differences for cross-cultural advantage

Culture is in itself a difference. Differences come from people. People can bridge differences. The effort to converge culture differences can turn these differences into cross-cultural advantages. Let us take a look at how this is achieved at a Sino-American food company.

This is a 50-50 joint venture. The American partner sent just one manager to represent the parent company, a Chinese American who had obtained an MBA degree in the US and had a good understanding of Chinese culture and history. His position in the joint venture was general manager. He implemented a typical American model of management in terms of business strategy, marketing and accounting practices, while at the same time making efforts to minimize the cultural differences at both inter- and intra-cultural levels. Among many management measures adopted by this individual, the following have the distinctive features of cultural convergence.

Hierarchical management ladder to offset the negative side of power distance

He understood that too many deputy positions in a typical Chinese organization would often lead to a shirking of responsibilities, so he established a middle management team without deputies. The managers at each level were held responsible for their own performances, good or bad, with no room for excuses. They were also delegated independent decision-making rights, such as reward and penalty of their subordinates, promotion and dismissal. Meanwhile, he made a strictly hierarchical reporting rule so that no one could circumvent their immediate supervisor. Management instructions were also required to follow through such a hierarchical ladder. This exercise incorporated the power distance characteristics of the Chinese culture, while assigning clearly defined responsibilities (job definition), decision-making (power definition) and reward (salary scheme according to positions held) to the managers.

Incentive system to encourage individualistic contributions without inflicting collectivist setbacks

To avoid the usual egalitarianism, a bonus system was established using a strict rating system. Bonuses were not part of the salary scheme as they are in other companies. The bonus amount was kept confidential in order to minimize the chances of negative impacts such as a loss of self-esteem, jealousy and comparison among the workers.

Requirements for teamwork expressed in a collectivist framework

The joint venture advocated team spirit in a slogan – 'Unity and Cooperation' – which has a typically collect-ivist feature. To encourage team cooperation and coordination, the general manager made a special rule that if one department failed to achieve its assigned targets, all other departments' rating scores would be reduced accordingly.

Respect for everyone to demonstrate American-style corporate culture

Inequality in the form of different treatment for people in different job positions is omnipresent and such inequality is tolerated by most Chinese people. To maintain order and management authority, such inequality is guarded by the hierarchical management ladder, but compensated for by equality in paid annual leave for non-management staff and workers.

Example set by the general manager in observing corporate rules

The general manager takes the lead in observing the rules he has established for the managers, staff and workers. A heart-warming scene was when the general manager was seen bending down to pick up a small piece of litter, which produced a strong psychological impact on the workers.

Informal communication with non-management staff and workers

To establish an effective channel of communication, the general manager uses his weekly breakfast meeting to interact informally with his staff and workers. This has shortened power distance.

Generosity only for the benefit of the joint venture

The general manager holds that the joint venture is a place of business operation, the ultimate goal of which is to profit from the market. Anything other than this will not be considered. He rejects the idea of an enterprise running redundant functions such as nurseries and schools. He refuses sponsorship requests that have nothing to do with the profit objectives, while being very generous in public events that increase corporate publicity and improve the corporate image. He also invests heavily in staff training, which has increased the sense of responsibility at all levels.

These approaches, together with other management measures, have turned a joint venture of cross-cultural differences into a harmonious enterprise of cross-cultural advantages. A year after the joint venture was put into operation, the Chinese side had recovered its investment with a marginal profit.

The above example illustrates the possibility of effectively managing cultural differences in the context of joint ventures. Analysis of this single success story is not intended to provide a universal reference point for all joint ventures in China, but it may provide insightful observations into how cultural differences can interact with each other to produce a positive rather than a zero result. One conclusion that can be drawn is that cultural differences are not written into the genes of human beings, be they from China or any other part of the world. A possible solution for cultural differences could come from the following:

- adapting to each other's culture
- building shared values
- adjusting decision making references
- forming a unique management style accommodating both cultures
- establishing effective interpersonal communications that are free from prejudiced assumptions.

Networking Practice in China

Wei-ping Wu, BA, MA, DPhil, MIEX, Assistant Professor, Department of Marketing and International Business, Lingnan University, Hong Kong and Li Yong, Deputy Secretary General, China Association of International Trade

In the study of Chinese business networks, a generally accepted conceptual framework which can give in-depth explanations to help understand the plentiful anecdotal evidence is still lacking. A sound approach should be able to analyse not only Chinese business networks in mainland China but also those in other Chinese communities such as Hong Kong, Taiwan and southeast Asian countries. As recent phenomena indicate, Chinese business networks have gone beyond the geographical, political and social boundaries (Kao 1993). In the rapid economic development in southern China may be recognised the workings of such business networks (East Asian Analytical Unit 1995).

This chapter intends to combine transaction cost theory, network theories and the key Chinese cultural values of different Chinese communities to present a new framework for analysing the Chinese business networks in mainland China, Hong Kong, Taiwan and other Chinese communities regardless of the different economic and social systems in which they operate. It also aims to provide foreign companies in China with some practical advice.

Business networks in China and overseas Chinese communities

One can often hear the word *guanxi* in any Chinese community, whether it is mainland China (Bian 1994; Wu 1995a), Hong Kong (Wong 1991), Singapore (Wong 1995) or Taiwan (Kao 1991; Numazaki 1985), though there may be some slight differences in pro-nunciation as a result of the distinctive Chinese dialects spoken in those communities.

Guanxi has been regarded as a special relationship two persons have with each other (Alston 1989), as a special kind of personal relationship in which long-term mutual benefit is more important than short-term indi-vidual gain (Zamet and Bovarnick 1986), and as having the status and intensity of an on-going relationship between two parties (Kirkbride et al 1991). Bian (1994) states that *guanxi* has two meanings attached to it: the indirect relationship between two people and the direct relationship between two people and a contact person. For the purpose of this study, *guanxi* can be defined as a special personal relationship in which long-term mutual benefit is more important than short-term indi-vidual gain and contains the key elements of indirect relationship between two people through proper intro-duction by a third party, and direct relationship between two people who trust each other and the contact person.

While *guanxi* operates on a dyadic level, *guanxiwang* (network)* certainly goes further than that. *Guanxiwang* refers to a network of exchanges or transactions between two parties and beyond. Goods and services such as physical products or favours exchanged can be anything of value and mutual benefit to the parties concerned, for example, raw materials, promotion, gifts, information, facilitation and so on. *Guanxiwang* obtains when one set of separate, personal and total relationships between two individuals, A and B, and another set of such relationships between B and C are interlinked through the common agent, B, acting as a witness and facilitator (see Figure 4.3.1). As a result, the originally 'total and personal relationship' (Alston 1989) transforms into a complex network of social exchanges with such inter-linkage extended into other sets through numerous

---

* Network and *guanxiwang* are interchangeable throughout this chapter.

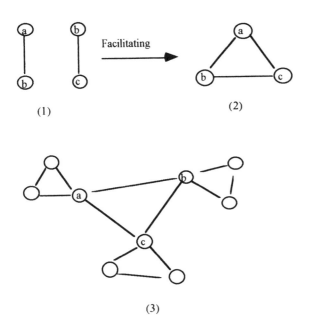

(1)   (2)

(3)

Figure 4.3.1   Guanxi and guanxiwang

common agents like A, B and C. Therefore, it can be concluded that *guanxi* is not simply, as many believe, one of the key features of Chinese culture (Lockett 1988) or one of the key 'themes' which depict core aspects of Chinese values (Kirkbride et al 1991); it is the mother of all relationships.

Although there are various kinds of *guanxiwang* in China and overseas Chinese communities, they can be divided into two main groups: social networks and business networks. It is important to understand the relationship between a social network and a business network. A social network can be broadly defined as a web of social relationships established within the sphere of core family members, extended family members, friends, classmates, fellow townsmen and so on. According to Redding (1990), the Chinese social network consists of lineage, village or neighbourhood, clan or collection of lineage and special interest associations. Their main function is to protect and help each other and to have an ethnic and/or unique identity in a wider social context. A business network can be defined as a web of business organisations to create or internalise a market for the purpose of profit maximisation or cost minimisation for all the members concerned.

There are four distinct types of such inter-firm networks:

1. ownership networks (firms linked though common ownership);
2. investment networks (firms linked by capital and investment;

3. production networks (firms linked by production sequences); and
4. distribution networks (firms linked by the distribution of commodities) (Hamilton et al 1990).

While a social network is not a business network per se, the former can reinforce and overlap with the latter (Omohundro 1983). It has been widely accepted that one needs a good personal relationship (*guanxi*) to do business successfully in the Chinese communities such as China, Taiwan and Singapore (Redding 1990). It is common practice for Chinese to do business with trusted friends. Johanson and Mattsson (1987) stress that it is individual actors that are the major players in an industrial or business network. Deglopper (1978: 297) says: 'Business relations are always, to some degree, personal relations.' Consequently, sometimes the difference between the two can become very blurred. There is an increasing body of research devoted to the study of the relationship between social/personal networks and business networks (Kao 1991; Numazaki 1985; Omohundro 1983).

There is a bias in the study of Chinese business networks. Although there exists much corruption among overseas Chinese (Redding 1990), very little has been mentioned in the study of overseas Chinese business networks. Yoshihara (1991) may be one of the few exceptions to echo indigenous peoples' view that Chinese businessmen in south-east Asia are not genuine entrepreneurs because they are basically successful by making the right political connections, favours and contracts. However, when it concerns mainland China, *guanxiwang* is immediately branded as corruption (Li and Wu 1993; Agelasto 1996; *The Economist* 1989:62). Many people often treat *guanxi* and *guanxiwang* as derogatory terms. *Guanxiwang* is regarded as an unhealthy social tendency. The truth is *guanxiwang* per se is purely a form of organisational governance. Nothing more, nothing less. It has nothing to do with corruption when a transaction is legal and does not infringe any public interests, but simply takes place between members within a business network. *Guanxiwang* only becomes corrupt when exchange or transaction taking place within a *guanxiwang* involves corrupt activities such as bribery. Because of the special characteristics of *guanxiwang* such as trust and bonding, corrupt deals are more likely to take place between members of a *guanxiwang* particularly when an adequate and effective legal and disciplinary system is lacking.

Networks are essential to overseas Chinese success in China. They allow access to the right officials at the township or village level. Benefits flow both ways through the networks (East Asia Analytical Unit 1995). Business networks existed throughout the history of the People's Republic of China (Bian 1994). During the period of the Cultural Revolution, the classic market was not allowed to exist. For example, there were campaigns to cut 'the tail of capitalism' in the countryside. With the failure of bureaucratic governance and non-existence of market, an alternative, the network, played a major role in social and industrial exchanges and transactions in China. In a recent empirical research on the relationship between *guanxi* and the allocation of urban jobs in China, Bian (1994) found that *guanxi* accounted for a considerable proportion of jobs in all historical periods between 1949 and 1988. The operation of network was suppressed by a tight and rigid bureaucratic control before the economic reform. It has been revealed that with the loosening of state control, *guanxi* had been widely used to substitute for the imperfect market (Bian 1994). Solinger (1989) discovered that the withdrawal of the planning system based on quotas and local government-directed input and output transactions gave rise to relational contracting in which many of the former business relationships were maintained.

Therefore, it can be concluded that with the shared legacies of social history and the key Chinese cultural values, there is no significant difference between business networks in China and their counterparts in overseas Chinese communities. The difference, if any, is diminishing rapidly with the ever increasing number of cross-border investments by overseas Chinese in China and the further deepening of Chinese economic reform.

The framework of Chinese business networks

However, to understand better the Chinese business network,* a theoretical framework is necessary. This can be accomplished by extending existing transaction cost theory and network theories.

When both markets and hierarchies fail, an intermediate mode of governance can be used to facilitate a transaction (Williamson 1979). Market failure can be caused by uncertainty and low volume conditions compounded by limited rationality and opportunism.

Uncertainty can be greatly reduced within a network. For example, the volume uncertainty, where there are few suppliers and many buyers and raw materials are in short supply, should not pose any serious problem for those buyers who have good *guanxi* with suppliers, because they have a greater chance of getting supplies than those who are not a member of the network. Furthermore, low volume conditions can also be dealt with effectively within a network. The network relationship is usually established through introduction and facilitation and is also witnessed by a third party. Contracting parties are less likely to behave opportunistically as the culprit will be penalized by the network codes/rules. Contrary to the conventional belief that the Chinese system of networked transactions is uncodified (Boisot and Child 1994), a network has its own rules and codes which are often 'invisible' but effective. An entrepreneur who behaves properly, in honouring verbal promises, repaying loans on time and caring for his family can be drawn into a Chinese business network (Wong 1995). It is fairly obvious that Chinese social networks such as clan associations, trade associations and dialect associations are established on the common values (codes) shared by members. For example, the foundation for a dialect association is the dialect which depicts shared values among members. Therefore, any opportunistic behaviour such as attempts to breach a contract or a 'gentleman's agreement' will be checked by potential penalties.

Another network mechanism is trust. Every single paper on network will mention trust as the key element of a network relationship. Without trust, there will be no network. Trust is regarded as confidence in the continuation of a mutually satisfying relationship (Thorelli 1986) or as 'glue' (Ouchi 1980). Trust is established on the positive feelings built by interacting with one another for a reasonable period of time. Therefore, trust can greatly reduce uncertainty which is usually faced by two contracting parties in a classic market. Network can also provide other effective means to deal with hazards in a market situation. Under a network relationship, opportunistic behaviour will be checked by the prospect of future business transactions, the need for reciprocity, reputation and the prospect of ostracism among peers (Williamson 1983; Maitland et al 1985; Macaulay 1963). These effects are in line with the key Chinese cultural values such as face, trust,

---

* Hereafter, the term Chinese business network refers to the business networks in all Chinese communities.

reciprocity and so on. This is one of the main reasons why the business network has been ubiquitous in Chinese communities. As a result, therefore, with checked opportunistic behaviour and reduced uncertainty, the business network lowers transaction costs. As Williamson (1975) argues, it is not uncertainty or low volumes, individually or together, that results in market failure, it is the joining of these factors with limited rationality on the one hand and opportunism on the other that gives rise to exchange difficulties. Solinger (1989) discovered the advantages that business networks could provide in an economic environment where uncertainty persisted with regard to the honouring of trading agreements, the assurance of quality in goods exchanged, the provision of working capital, and so forth. Chong (1994) argues that whether it is personal reputation or the firm's, reputation can often play an important role in reaching agreements in East Asia.

Nevertheless, existing discussions on whether to internalise an activity within a firm or to farm it out to other firms in a network (Walker and Weber 1984) are rather limited in scope. The advantage of network is far beyond this 'make or buy' decision. By networking with potential partners in another industry or another consumer market, firms can support each other and share know-how and information. As a result, firms in a network relationship will become more competitive than their competitors outside the network. The firm is frequently faced with many limitations such as lack of finance, technology and the regulations of local government. Owing to the lack of information, there is sometimes no market to internalize in the first place. By networking with other enterprises, a firm can have better access to much needed information which is likely to flow between members within a network. Transactions require the production and exchange of information (Boisot and Child 1988). Consequently, a market can be created with the availability of information within a network. Therefore, network relationship cannot provide only economies of scale (or whatever source of efficiency) (Jarillo 1988) and synergy, but also help to create a new market which does not exist in the classic market. The benefit of a network is that it has the best of both worlds: markets and hierarchies. It provides the merits of a quasi internalization, such as reduced transaction costs and the creation of new markets, as well as the advantages of a classic market such as economies of scale, wider choice than total internalization and the flow of information. In conclusion, the network can provide three key advantages:

1. reduced transaction cost;
2. creation of a new market; and
3. synergy and economies of scale.

The network is not only efficient but also effective (Jarillo 1988). It was found that those firms that relied solely on core family members were less successful than those that relied also on friends (Omohundro 1983). This finding indicates that the limited sphere of family business is a liability rather than an asset to the success of a firm. It is the business network which can offer a wider sphere of interactions which resemble a classic market of more choice and an internalization which can protect firms from the hazards, such as uncertainty, and opportunities attached to the classic market.

However, like other forms of transaction governance, business networks can fail (Thorelli 1986). That is when the transaction costs of using a business network outweigh the benefits. For example, if the need for reciprocity disappears, either party may feel it is too costly to keep up the unnecessary relationship. As a result, the *guanxi* relation lapses (Alston 1988). However, members of a business network may change, but the business network itself often survives and develops with the joining of new members. According to Johanson and Mattsson (1985, 1987), networks are stable and changing with new relationships being established and old relationships dissolved. Therefore, the business network is a dynamic organization.

In real life, a firm may belong to dozens of business networks at the same time. Therefore, to many firms, network relationships are three dimensional. A firm may have horizontal inter-organizational relationships as well as vertical business relationships such as the relationship between the firm and local government offices. Sometimes these networks may overlap with each other. Therefore, to be a credited member, firms have to abide by the codes which are shared by other members. These 'invisible' codes and values are, more often than not, the substitution for an insufficient legal system.

Business networks and Chinese cultural values

Boisot and Child (1988), among others, stress that there is a potential interplay of cultural, economic, and technological influences on transaction governance. Although *guanxiwang* is a transaction governance rather than a key feature of Chinese culture, it is inevitably influenced by Chinese cultural values such as trust, face, reciprocity, respect for age and authority, harmony and time. Most of these cultural values are interrelated; for example, making someone lose face will negatively affect an harmonious relationship. Hence, it is Chinese cultural values that make a major difference between *guanxiwang* and similar governance in western countries. The ubiquitous existence of business networks in China and overseas Chinese communities is determined by the fact that network codes overlap with the key Chinese cultural values (Figure 4.3.2). Chinese business networks are sustained by Chinese cultural values and tradition. When these values disappear, the networks will collapse (Wong 1995). The following values have been identified as the key Chinese cultural values:

- trust (Redding 1990; Wong 1995);
- mistrust (Redding 1990; Low 1995; Wu 1995a);
- reciprocity (Redding 1990; Kirkbride et al 1991);
- face (Yau 1994; Lockett 1988; Kirkbride et al 1991; Redding 1990)
- time (Yau 1994; Kirkbride *et al.* (1991);
- harmony (Yau 1988, 1994; Kirkbride et al 1991);
- hierarchy;
- power distance (Kirkbride et al 1991; Lockett 1988; Yau 1988, 1994); and
- long-term orientation (Bond 1987).

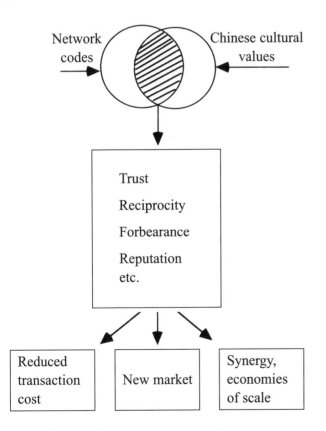

Figure 4.3.2   The research framework

These Chinese cultural values are the main representations of the seven core rituals of Confucianism: Benevolence, Harmony, Midway, Forbearance, Filial Piety, Trust and Cautious Words (Li and Wu 1993).

Trust/mistrust

In China, chronic suspicion prevails (Smith 1894). Chinese 'appear to be quite suspicious and cold towards strangers with whom relationships have not been established' (1988 Yau). Nobody could be trusted except one's kinfolk in the form of the extended family (Hofstede 1993). As Chinese do not trust outsiders, a social network consisting of family members, relatives, friends, classmates, colleagues etc is the immediate sphere on which trust can be established, reciprocated and developed. Such an obsession with trust is caused by another, often neglected, phenomenon in China, dishonesty. In business transactions, a great deal of adulteration of goods is practised, for example, weights and measures are juggled (Latourette 1972). To protect one's interest and ensure that opportunistic behaviours such as cheating are kept to a minimum, trust must be established before any serious business relationship can be cemented. Trust-based *guanxiwang* is the alternative to the market which is often riven by opportunistic behaviours.

Not coincidentally, for both transaction cost theory and network theory, trust has been also regarded as a critical component of the network (Thorelli 1986; Jarillo 1988; Williamson 1988). Williamson advocates that exchange relationships based on personal trust will survive greater stress and display greater adaptability. Thorelli observes that trust in Oriental cultures may even take the place of contractual arrangements.

Face, hierarchy and power distance

Face is a concept of central importance because of its pervasive influence in interpersonal relations among Chinese (Yau 1988). According to Hu (1944), Chinese face can be classified into two types, *lian* and *mian-zi*. *Lian* 'represents the confidence of society in the integrity of ego's moral character, loss of which makes it impossible for him to function properly within the community', while *mian-zi* 'stands for the kind of prestige that is emphasised. . . a reputation achieved through getting on in life, through success and ostentation'. When *lian* is lost, the person will feel that he/she can no longer live in the world.

Loss of *lian* within a *guanxiwang* as a consequence of opportunistic behaviour means that peers will no longer have confidence in the persons or firms concerned. As a result, their membership within a *guanxiwang* and in society will be untenable. Therefore, face can be another hostage which minimizes the possibility of opportunistic behaviour within a *guanxiwang*. This is another reason why *guanxiwang* cannot merely survive but can also develop in mainland China and overseas Chinese communities.

Mian-zi can also be used to form new *guanxiwang*. One of Confucius' virtues is to respect authority and the elderly. Someone with authority, often elderly and with a good reputation, can ask favours of others. The person may act as a common agent to start a new exchange relationship. Favours can also be asked between friends. It is an accepted norm that as 'old friends' one should give face to the other when favour is requested. Once again, it has been shown that the Chinese cultural values such as face, hierarchy, power distance are closely related to the creation and development of the business network.

Reciprocity

Guanxi cannot be sustained between two parties if there is no need of reciprocity. Like face, the principle of reciprocity is universal but, in the Chinese case, the concept has particular salience (Kirkbride et al 1991). When internalized in both parties, the norm obliges the one who has first received a benefit to repay it at a later time. Consequently, there may be less hesitancy in being the first and a greater facility with which the exchange and the social relation can get underway (Gouldner 1960). For most Chinese, a transaction or exchange will only take place when there is mutual benefit for both parties involved. As indicated earlier, reciprocity is a 'hostage' which sustains a network relationship. Without reciprocity, established *guanxi* will elapse.

Time/long term orientation

It was suggested in Yau (1994) that the time dimension for Chinese has two orientations: past-time orientation and continuity. This implies that for Chinese, once a relation is established it is hard to break and once a relation is broken, it is very difficult to re-establish (Yau 1988).

Continuity indicates that Chinese people are long-term oriented. Once a *guanxi* is established, both parties will try their best to keep this relationship by reciprocat-

ing benefits. Compromise is found to be the preferred solution by Chinese to an unsettled conflict (Kirkbride et al 1991). Future business opportunities also act as hostages to a business relationship. The benefits of establishing a long-term supplier and buyer relationship have been regarded as one of the pillars of Japanese management styles which is now being enthusiastically followed by western firms (Imrie and Morris 1992). Jarillo (1988) argues that an emphasis on long-term relationships is also essential to the development of trust which is considered as a critical component of network.

Harmony

The Confucian 'Doctrine of the Mean' urges individuals to avoid competition and conflict, and to maintain inner harmony (Hsu 1947). It has been found that traditional Chinese cultural values and cognitive orientations have influenced the Chinese people to preserve overt harmony by avoiding confrontation and to adopt a non-assertive approach to conflict resolution (Kirkbride et al 1991). *Guanxi* cannot survive without harmony between two parties in a relationship. Without harmonious relationships, trust cannot be established, face cannot be saved, reciprocity will not continue and no further *guanxi* can be established.

It is now evident that the key factors which help sustain and develop networks overlap with the key Chinese cultural values. This is why the network as a form of organizational governance is so widespread in both China and overseas Chinese communities.

Implications and recommendations

While an increasing number of western companies have entered the Chinese market, they are way behind firms from Hong Kong, Taiwan and southeast Asian countries. An estimated 80 per cent of all foreign investment came from overseas Chinese in Hong Kong, Taiwan and southeast Asian countries. The simple reason is that overseas Chinese share the common Chinese cultural values and they can either minimize or avoid problems by using their skills in understanding the Chinese cultural codes. In order to reduce these disadvantages, western firms are advised to pay attention to the following while operating in China.

Good personal relationship vs contract

As has been clearly demonstrated, the most important part of a business relationship is the building of personal relationships. Personal relationships often entwine with business relationships in China. Many foreign companies conduct business based on market situations without too much consideration of the personal feelings involved. They treat business impersonally while Chinese do the opposite. Foreigners tend to be contented with the signed contracts while the Chinese look beyond the contract for sincere commitment as in a good personal relationship. This does not mean that the Chinese will not abide by the signed contract without a good personal relationship. It denotes the general tendency of Chinese people to do business with a long-term orientation. When a deal is closed, you can expect the Chinese to perform their part of it. With good personal relationships, you can always rely on your Chinese partner to find a better solution when unexpected circumstances occur. In many cases, one can be better off with goodwill and friendship than one can be with a signed contract.

Guanxi and transaction costs

A well-established *guanxi*, however, can go beyond just business facilitation. In the Chinese business community, one can often hear people say, 'This is our old client, we should give them special terms' and 'We are old *guanxi*, therefore we can get better deals'. If someone chooses to ask why he or she is not treated on an equal footing, the answer is very likely, 'you are not our old client'. As a supplier, a good *guanxi* means that you can stay on the value chain of a manufacturer as long as you do not break the codes of *guanxi* even if you have competition from other suppliers. As a buyer, an old client can get better terms of payment or take delivery of goods on credit, all of which would be impossible without maintaining a good *guanxi*. A well-established *guanxi* is built on the basis of mutual trust, giving face to one another, a good track record of exchanges of favours, long-term non-opportunistic intimacy, obligation or gratitude from past help, etc. It cannot be overused and the favours will have to be reciprocated in one way or another.

Guanxi and consumer/customer loyalty

In a business-to-business relationship, *guanxi* is usually with individuals who are often the representatives of firms. Apart from consistent quality, timely delivery, attractive price and good after-sales services, a good *guanxi* should also be built into the business relations.

The obligation that a *guanxi* carries can be developed into a loyalty that ordinary business relations cannot achieve. Without *guanxi*, one can easily lose a customer simply because of an unavoidable human error. You will not even have recourse to remedy. With *guanxi*, you will be excused for future improvement and the business stays.

For a business that is serving the consumer market, *guanxi* or a relationship with the consumers shall be considered as an alternative perspective in approaching the objectives of brand image and brand loyalty. Many foreign companies are using a number of different ways to get publicity, secure more trials and create trust by consumers. Many of these efforts, although appealing and persuasive, still give people a feeling of distance, not being involved or directly related, and therefore cannot be translated into effective means of reinforcement. This also explains why people prefer, among many other means of promotion, discounts or give-away types of promotion. Obviously, price discount is not the best way to establish brand image and loyalty. But it will certainly help if you establish your image as a friend, communicate with the consumer on a friendly basis, provide favours to the consumer community, offer opportunities for consumer involvement and give consumers a privileged sense of belonging.

Reciprocity and long-term business relationship

In China, any business relationship should be considered from a long-term view. To maintain a long-term business relationship, one must reciprocate. One never knows when one will be in trouble and a friend in need is a friend indeed. This reflects the necessity of reciprocity. The experience of a joint venture in Beijing offers a typical example of reciprocity. In the early 1990s one of the suppliers of cashmere in Inner Mongolia had funding problems when planning its technical transformation. The joint venture, a producer of cashmere knitwear, was approached for help. Considering the long-term relationship, the joint venture decided to provide funding for the supplier. In the mid-1990s, the market for cashmere knitwear heated up and the price of cashmere raw material rocketed and, as a consequence, many cashmere knitwear producers had difficulties in absorbing the price rise and had to reduce production. The joint venture faced the same problem. However, the supplier in Inner Mongolia did not forget the help that the joint venture had given and offered to supply cashmere raw material at below market price. The joint venture not only survived the price rise in raw material, but also captured the market that their competitors left because of the price rise. The implication of this joint venture's experience is that the commitment to a good and long-term business relationship and the obligations arising from such a relationship will survive market changes.

Maintain *guanxi* when terminating business relationship

If a business is not meant to be long term, the way to end a business relationship should be properly selected. It is inappropriate to end a business relationship when a deal cannot be closed by complaining about the way the Chinese counterparts do things. This may not only cause loss of face by the Chinese counterpart, but also put an end to the *guanxi* that may otherwise have continued. Some foreigners who know very little about China even threaten to report the business failure to the boss or the supervising authority. This conduct is despised as lacking in ethics and is detrimental to the business relationship not only with the Chinese counterparts but also with the people in the network. As a result, many Chinese companies will avoid doing business with the foreign company.

Network codes and Chinese cultural values require that disputing parties solve problems through amicable means, ie solving the problem without damaging the harmonious business relations. This does not suggest that no litigation is used in setting problems through friendly discussions. It is advisable to exercise care and caution when taking court action. Litigation should be used as a last resort only when the future course of the business relationship has become clearly unpredictable.

Midway and bureaucracy

The Confucian philosophy, 'Doctrine of the Mean', governs the behaviour and mental actions of the Chinese people. The general tendency that Chinese people do not give answers upfront, saying '*yanjiu yanjiu*' (we will study it), instead of yes or no is often regarded as a sign of bureaucracy by foreign business people. While bureaucracy does exist in China, in business, however, it may have other implications. In China, when people say *yanjiu yanjiu*, it might indicate that he or she is not sure, has limited authority, does not see your proposal as viable, but does not want to disappoint you by saying no or that he or she wants to have a collective decision rather than an individual one. What frustrates foreign

business people is that the *yanjiu yanjiu* process could take a matter of weeks to months before they get an answer. If you can have a *yes* answer in a couple of weeks' time, it may imply that your proposal has been received positively. If it takes a couple of months to get a yes answer, there might have been a lot internal balancing and your proposal has cleared the way. Unfortunately, you will only have your assumptions to rely on when you cannot get either a positive or a negative answer, which may mean that your proposal is not going to work or it is not the right time to do it or there is internal disagreement which your Chinese partners do not want you to know of. To articulate your assumptions, it is recommended that foreigners enquire about the progress at appropriate and graceful intervals, which will help shape a reasonable answer.

Some foreigners who have had some experience in China might have found that negotiation may revert to things discussed and agreed. The reason, in many cases, is that the negotiator has received from his superiors instructions in principle, which often do not cover details which may be revealed in the course of discussion. This is again a reflection of the midway way of doing things and the in-built ambiguity of instructions in principle. This process can be easily observed if the superior happens to be present in the negotiation, during which the negotiator will be stopped, interrupted and corrected from time to time by the superior. The implication here may be that the subject brought up again is likely to be something that has caused internal disagreements or is perceived to have operational difficulties from the higher level of the decision-maker's point of view. Sometimes, it may be more to the benefit of foreigners to help them out than to insist on things agreed that the Chinese partners have or perceive having difficulties in executing.

Accessing business networks via recruiting contact persons

This aspect has a strong implication for foreign firms' recruitment policies. For those companies exploring the Chinese market, the advice is to recruit contacts, who can sometimes be life-saving. The contacts could be local residents having active business or social network or immigrants with business related work experiences or family background. The mistake is that, in many cases, foreign companies tend to employ Chinese in their home country for their operations in China, simply because they look Chinese. Those Chinese may not have the understanding of the market which you would require for making a successful entry.

As has been argued already, operational issues such as volume uncertainty can be best dealt with within a network. It is a well-known fact that foreign firms are usually not sure who the Chinese decision-makers are. These contact persons could not only find the decision-makers without too much difficulty, but can also help build the trust between the Chinese decision-makers and western companies. They can not only save western companies time and money but also future business deals because they have no trouble with cultural barriers, and they are fully aware of the Chinese ritual codes and protocols. The implication here is that foreign companies, while recruiting contacts, can at the same time gain access to a network in the Chinese market or become part of the existing network through the facilitation of those contacts.

However, although hiring a useful contact person is a good accomplishment as a start, retaining the contact person can sometimes be a daunting task. As the demand for contact persons or senior management is much higher than the market can supply, job hopping is becoming more and more a practice in the Chinese job market. One of the reasons is the difference in approach between Chinese and foreigners. As a business network is based on the linkage facilitated by trusted contact persons, this has determined that the way in which contact persons do things will have a distinctively different style from that of foreigners. In some cases, these different styles are not understood and supported by the foreign employers. Another reason could be a result of the general perception by foreigners that the average level of labour cost is low and that contact persons are therefore not properly remunerated in terms of salary package. This issue has to be handled sensibly. Losing them to one's competitors means loss of money and future business contracts. The possible solution to this problem is diversification and development of the new contact person. However, proper training and reward packages may be another alternative. While the importance of contact persons cannot be over-emphasized, the establishment of good business relationships with all important business clients, government offices and policy makers is a must for any business in the Chinese market to succeed.

To summarize, maintaining harmony is one of the key virtues of social behaviour. That is why in China even if one is in the right one should not treat the other party so harshly as to make him to lose face. Important here is that in doing business in China one should keep all relationships harmonious and long-term oriented whenever it is possible as one does not know when a seemingly useless relationship will one day save one's commercial life or business. Western companies should also have a long-term commitment in the Chinese market. To succeed in the Chinese market, foreign firms are advised to use mentors (contact persons) to start up a business relationship. Understanding of the ways things are done in China can be difficult for foreigners, but will be rewarding as well. Whenever possible, a harmonious relationship should be kept and favours must be reciprocated. A legal solution should be the last option for solving business problems. For readers who are interested in exploring how *guanxi* can be established and maintained, the chapter on effective public relations may provide some practical guidance.

It can be concluded that the Chinese business network is a 'dynamic organization' which has contributed a great deal to the recent economic transformation in China. This dynamism is embedded in the key Chinese cultural values as network codes overlap with the key Chinese cultural values. Networks are not only efficient but also effective. They can internalize an existing market as well as create a non-existent market.

References and bibliography

Agelasto, Michael (1996) 'Cellularism, Guanxiwang, and Corruption: a Microcosmic View from within a Chinese Educational Danwei', paper given at the annual meeting of the Association of Asian Studies, April, Honolulu.

Alston, Jon (1988) 'Wa, Guanxi, and Inhwa: Managerial Principles in Japan, China and Korea', *Business Horizon*, March/April, pp26–31.

Bian, Yanjie (1994) 'Guanxi and the Allocation of Urban Jobs in China', *The China Quarterly*, Vol. 4, 971–99.

Boisot, Max and Child, John (1988) 'The Iron Law of Fiefs: Bureaucratic Failure and the Problem of Governance in the Chinese Economic Reforms', *Administrative Science Quarterly*, 33: 507–27.

Boisot, Max and Child, John (1990) Efficiency, Ideology and Tradition in the Choice of Transactions Governance Structures: The Case of China as a Modernising Society, in Clegg, St and Redding, Gordon S. (eds), *Capitalism in Contrasting Cultures*, Berlin: Walter de Gruyter.

Boisot, Max and Child, John (1994) 'China's Emerging Economic Order: Modernisation through "Weak" Markets and Quasi-Capitalism?', paper given to the conference on 'Management Issues for China in the 1990s', March 23–25, Cambridge.

Bond, Michael (1987) 'Chinese Values and the Search for Culture-Free Dimensions of Culture: The Chinese Culture Connection', *Journal of Cross-Cultural Psychology*, 18/2: 143–164.

Chong, Ju Choi (1994) 'Contract Enforcement across Cultures', *Organisation Studies*, 15.5: 673–82.

Deglopper, D.R. (1978) *Doing Business in Lukang*, in Wolf, A.P. (ed.), *Studies in Chinese Society*, Stanford: Stanford University Press.

East Asia Analytical Unit (1995) *Overseas Chinese Business Networks in Asia*, Department of Foreign Affairs and Trade, Australia: AGPS Press.

The Economist (1989) Free Markets for Free People. 27 May; 62.

Gao, Gang (1994) 'The Fear of being Cheated: a Widespread Social Disease', *China News Digest*, an electronic Chinese magazine, No. 188.

Gouldner, Alvin W. (1960) 'The Norm of Reciprocity: A Preliminary Statement', *American Sociological Review*, 25/2:161–78.

Granovetter, M. (1985) 'Economic Action and Social Structure: The Problem of Embeddedness', *American Journal of Sociology*, 91: 481–510.

Hamilton, Garry G., Zeile, William and Kim, Wan-Jin (1990) *The Network Structures of East Asian Economics*, in Clegg, St and Redding, Gordon S. (eds), *Capitalism in Contrasting Cultures*, Berlin: Walter de Gruyter.

Hofstede, Geert (1993) 'Cultural Constraints in Management Theories', *Academy of Management Executive*, 7/1: 81–94.

Hsu, F.L.K. (1947) *Under the Ancestor's Shadow: Kingship, Personality, and Social Mobility in China*, Stanford: Stanford University Press.

Hu, H.C. (1944) 'Chinese Concept of Face', *American Anthropologist*, 46: 45–64.

Imrie, R. and Morris, J. (1992) 'A Review of Recent Changes in Buyer-Supplier Relations', *International Journal of Management Science*, 20, 5/6: 641–52.

Jarillo, Jose-Carlos (1988) 'On Strategic Networks', *Strategic Management Journal*, Vol. 9, 31–41.

Johanson, Jan and Mattsson, Lars-Gunnar (1985) 'Marketing Investments and Market Investments in Industrial Networks', *International Journal of Research in Marketing*, 2: 185–195.

Johanson, Jan and Mattsson, Lars-Gunnar (1987) 'Interorganisational Relations in Industrial Systems', *International Studies of Management and Organisation*, 17: 34–48.

Kao, Cheng-shu (1991) *'Personal Trust' in the Large Businesses in Taiwan: A Traditional Foundation for Contemporary Economic Activities*, in Hamilton, G. (ed.), *Business Networks and Economic Development in East and Southeast Asia*, Centre for Asian Studies, University of Hong Kong.

Kao, John (1993) 'The World-wide Web of Chinese Business', *Harvard Business Review*. March/April: 24–36.

Kirkbride, Paul S. *et al.* (1991) 'Chinese Conflict Preferences and Negotiating Behaviour: Cultural and Psychological Influence', *Organisation Studies*, 12/3: 365–386.

Latourette, Kenneth Scott (1972) *The Chinese: their History and Culture*, London: Collier-Macmillan Limited.

Li, Xiandong and Wu, Qinghua (1993) Theoretical chapter on guanxinology, in Zheng, Liang, Wen, 'Control of Unhealthy Tendencies should be Tightened up not Loosened', *Democracy and Law*, 168: 2–3.

Lockett, Martin (1988) 'Culture and the Problems of Chinese Management', *Organisation Studies*, 9/4: 475–496.

Low, Linda (1995) 'The Overseas Chinese Connection: An ASEAN Perspective', *Journal of Southeast Asian Studies*, 89–117.

Macauley, Stewart (1963) 'Non-contractual Relations in Business: A Preliminary Study', *American Sociological Review*, 28: 55–69.

Maitland, Ian *et al.* (1985) 'Sociologists, Economists, and Opportunism', *Academy of Management Review*, 10/1: 59–65.

Numazaki, Ichiro (1985) *The Role of Personal Networks in the Making of Taiwan's Guanxiquiye (Related Enterprises)*, in Hamilton, G. (ed.), *Business Networks and Economic Development in East and Southeast Asia*, Centre for Asian Studies, University of Hong Kong, 1991.

Omohundro, John T. (1983) *Social Networks and Business Success for the Philippine Chinese*, in Lim, L. and Gosling, L.A. Peter (eds), *The Chinese in Southeast Asia*, Vol. 1, *Ethnicity and Economic Activity*, Singapore: Maruzen Asia.

Ouchi, William G. (1980) 'Markets, Bureaucracies and Clans', *Administrative Science Quarterly*, 25: 129–141.

People's Daily overseas edition (1996) 28 June: 6.

Redding, S. Gordon (1990) *The Spirit of Chinese Capitalism*, Berlin: Walter de Gruyter.

Redding, S. Gordon (1991) *Weak Organisations and Strong Linkages: Managerial Ideology and Chinese Family Business Networks*, in Hamilton, G.G. (ed.) *Business Networks and Economic Development in East and South East Asia*, Centre for Asian Studies, University of Hong Kong.

Redding, S. Gordon (1995) 'Overseas Chinese Networks: Understanding the Enigma', *Long Range Planning*, 28:1, 61–9.

Smith, Arthur. H. (1894) *Chinese Characteristics*, London: Revell.

Solinger, D.J. (1989) 'Urban Reform and Relational Contracting in Post-Mao China. An Interpretation of the Transition from Plan to Market', *Studies in Comparative Communism*, 23: 171–85.

State Statistical Bureau, People's Republic of China (1995) *China Statistical Yearbook*, Beijing, China Statistical Publishing House.

Su Sijin (1994) *The Dynamics of Market-Oriented Growth of Chinese Firms in Post-Maoist China: An Institutional Approach*. Unpublished PhD thesis. Cornell University.

Thorelli, Hans B. (1986) 'Networks: Between Markets and Hierarchies', *Strategic Management Journal*, 7: 37–51.

Walker, Gordon, and Weber, David (1984) 'A Transaction Cost Approach to Make-or-Buy Decision', *Administrative Science Quarterly*, 29: 373–391.

Williamson, Oliver E. (1975) *Markets and Hierarchies*, New York: Free Press.

Williamson, Oliver E. (1979) 'Transaction Cost Economies: the Governance of Contractual Relations', *Journal of Law and Economics*, 22/2: 233–61.

Williamson, Oliver E. (1981) 'The Economics of Organisation', *American Journal of Sociology*, 87: 548–77.

Willamson, Oliver E. (1983) 'Credible Commitments: Using Hostages to Support Exchange', *American Economic Review*, 73: 519–40.

Wong, Gilbert (1991) *Business Groups in a Dynamic Environment: Hong Kong 1976–1986*, in Hamilton, G. (ed.) *Business Networks and Economic Development in East and South East Asia*, Centre for Asian Studies, University of Hong Kong.

Wong, Siu-lun (1995) *Business Networks, Cultural Values and the State in Hong Kong and Singapore*, in Brown, Rajeswary (ed.), *Chinese Business Enterprises in Asia*, New York: Routledge.

Wu, Wei-Ping (1995a) 'Towards a Definition of *guanxiwang* (network) and its Significance in Business Transactions in China', *Proceedings of Academy of International Business Southeast Asia Regional Conference*, Perth, Australia, 129–134.

Wu, Wei-Ping (1995b) 'Barriers in the Path of Chinese Firms' Internationalisation Efforts', *Journal of Chinese Political Science*, 2: 109–126.

Yau, Oliver H.M. (1988) 'Chinese Cultural Values: their Dimensions and Marketing Implications', *European Journal of Marketing*, 22/5: 44–57.

Yau, Oliver H.M. (1994) *Consumer Behaviour in China: Customer Satisfaction and Cultural Values*, London: Routledge.

Yoshihara, Kunio (1991) 'Ethnic Chinese and Ersatz Capitalism', paper given to the International Conference on Southeast Asian Chinese: Culture, Economy and Society, organized by the Singapore Society of Asian Studies, the Association of Nanyang University Graduates and the Singapore Federation of Chinese Clans Association, 12–13 January, Singapore.

Zamet, M. Jonathan, and Bovarnick, Murray E. (1986) 'Employee Relations for Multinational Companies in China', *Columbia Journal of World Business*, Spring: 13–19.

Zhang, Jian Hau and Yu Lin (1995) *Xiang Zhen Qi Ye Di Jue Qi Yu Fa Zhan Mo Shi*, Wuhan: Hu Bei Jiao Yu Chu Ban She.

Due Diligence for Market Entrants

Li Yong, Deputy Secretary General, China Association of International Trade, and Jonathan Reuvid

Introduction

Interest in the China market arises from different causes, but is often not the result of serious study and informed discussion. Imagining the size of this market would excite any CEO and the simple maths of tapping into a tiny fraction of it may prompt a visit to China. It might be thought that such a visit can only be beneficial to both sides, but unfortunately this is not always the case. If the homework has not been done to prepare for the visit, and the mission is not supported by experienced and honest advisers, the stage may well be set not for the jump-start of a successful new project in China but for a series of delays and disappointments based on false expectations and misunderstandings on both sides.

It is true that the China market presents many opportunities in terms of trade and investment. However, lack of understanding about the market is often the cause of failure and can thwart closely calculated business plans. Thorough due diligence is of crucial importance in shortening the learning curve and minimizing possible risks. In this book, there are many chapters that focus on the complexity and intricacies of doing business in China and provide insightful comments on how a company should approach the market. This chapter intends to provide for new market entrants an additional and different perspective on what due diligence is needed. These may be over-used clichés but an ounce of prevention is worth a pound of cure and a stitch in time does save nine. The point to emphasize is that due diligence is a much wider concept here than is generally realized. It is not a partner-specific investigation effort, but an endeavour to widen the scope of understanding about the market.

Where is the market?

This may seem an obvious question requiring no answer, as everybody knows that China has a population of 1.3 billion and that must be the market. However, the reality is not so simple. Only a few companies can really consider selling to 1.3 billion people, while most will be working on gaining a share of the market. Where this share of the market should come from is really a question of where the market is.

All too often, a foreign company would think first of large urban centres like Beijing, Shanghai and Guangzhou as points of entry, and many have been given advice by various kinds of advisers or consultants to attack these large urban markets because they have the most affluent consumers. It is true that these large urban centres are the most dynamic local economies where opportunities exist. However, they are crowded not only with domestic players but also with international competitors. The trend of internationalized competition is more pronounced in the large urban centres than in other areas. The benefits and costs of entering these markets need to be carefully weighed against other alternative entry strategies.

On China's mainland there are 31 administrative regions, each with its own development policy and plan, and each competing to develop its economy. Since the characteristics of all regions vary from the next, they can be regarded as separate markets. Due diligence investigation should concentrate on these regional differences and identify the most suitable entry market to attack. If a high level of competition exists in the market you are targeting, consider choosing a region that has a less high profile to establish your foothold in the market.

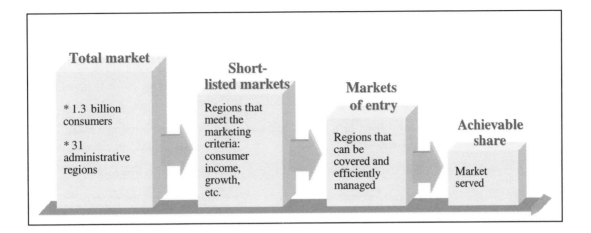

Figure 4.4.1   Roadmap to the market

How to approach the market

Figure 4.4.1 shows a generalized situation in which a company can eventually reach its final market. There are a number of different routes for a foreign company to make its approach:

- through a local foreign trade corporation;
- through Hong Kong for an agent, distributor or partner;
- establishing a representative office;
- exhibiting at trade fairs;
- appointing a distributor or agent in China;
- direct marketing;
- advertising in industry-specific trade journals or magazines;
- opening your own distributorship or retail stores;
- negotiating a joint venture with a local company;
- bidding on projects.

China's accession to the WTO will improve the trade environment over the next five years. Tariff reductions and the dismantling of non-tariff barriers will greatly increase opportunities for export to China. China's commitment to opening up the service sector to foreign-owned distribution will allow greater levels of participation in the market. China's promise to grant full trading rights to all enterprises, without discrimination against foreign players will offer a wider range of options for foreign businesses to tap into the development of the market. However, at the micro level, the possibility of failure still exists if the entry process is not carefully monitored. The alternative operating modes that are available now, and will be made available in the near future, have advantages and disadvantages which are compared in Table 4.4.1.

Identifying your business partner

China has millions of companies and enterprises and there are many different reasons for a foreign business to find a Chinese business partner: export and import from China, investment in China, contract manufacturing and so on. It is an arduous job to search among such a vast number of companies and enterprises for the right partner to work with. Market research will help to generate a list of potential business partners. If you do not wish to employ a consulting firm, there are other alternatives for identifying business partners.

Contact the overseas offices of Chinese companies

Many large Chinese companies have set up their own overseas offices. These offices are responsible for import and export of Chinese products. Working with these offices will save time, and communications with them are normally easier as they are run by people who understand the language of the host country. A list of such companies can be obtained from the Chinese embassies in the host country.

Approach the commercial section of the Chinese embassy in your location

Chinese embassies have a commercial function of responsibility for trade promotion. They normally maintain a database containing information on enterprises in different industries and this information is usually provided free of charge. In addition, they may also have information on important trade missions from China. Inviting Chinese trade missions to visit your company or production sites can be a convenient and cost-effective way of initiating contacts with potential business partners/buyers.

Table 4.4.1 Alternative modes of operation for market entry

Mode of operation	Strengths	Weaknesses
Use of own staff	Full control of the process	Long learning curve, frequent travel, long lead time
Representative office in China	In the market, help of local staff and hands-on control.	Very costly (minimum US$250K/year for a basic establishment), limited functionality
Having an office in Hong Kong	Close to the market	Higher costs, frequent travel
Agents	Low cost, network advantages	Little control, dependence
Consultants	Expert experience, cost effective, inside track (local consultants)	Part time service, no control
Joint venture	Have local partner, shared risk, understanding of local conditions	Limited to product/project, disagreement on corporate strategies and implementation
Wholly owned operation	Full control of the operation	Start-up difficulties due to limited understanding of the local conditions
Own distribution	Full control of the channels	Unfamiliarity with the channels, limited access at present

Visit industry associations or import and export chambers in China

If you are planning a trip to China, arrangements with relevant industry associations are a good way to gain an understanding of the industry in which you have a particular interest and at the same time you can procure a list of referrals from them. Normally, it would useful to employ a local contact to arrange such visits. Most industry associations and all import and export chambers are located in Beijing.

Hold technical seminars or product introduction meetings

This type of activity should be designed as a targeted exercise and requires the help of a local company such as a consulting firm, a public relations company or the consulting function of an industry association to arrange for the appropriate audience. Such services are available on a fee basis.

Attend trade fairs and exhibitions

Numerous trade fairs and exhibitions are held in China and attended by an array of Chinese companies. Guang-zhou Export Commodity Fair, for example, twice a year gathers together thousands of Chinese companies to demonstrate their products in sectioned areas of the exhibition compound. There are also professional trade industry-specific fairs or exhibitions in areas such as plastics, fine chemicals, auto, water treatment, electrical equipment and many more, held regularly or occasionally. These trade fairs and exhibitions are normally held in large cities such as Beijing, Shanghai and Guangzhou. Information on major trade fairs can be obtained from the commercial section of Chinese embassies, overseas offices of the China Council for the Promotion of International Trade (CCPIT), industry associations, and import and export chambers.

Advertise in professional newspapers, magazines and journals

For industrial products, another possibility for establishing contacts is to advertise in professional newspapers, magazines and journals. There are thousands of trade press publications that target professional readers or industry specialists, who may contact you with specific business propositions.

Purchase mailing lists from database companies and launch direct mail advertising

There are now a number of companies offering database search services for a fee. Armed with a mailing list, companies who wish to test end-user interest can launch direct mail campaigns. Such an exercise will generate a shortlist of companies that have an interest in working with you.

Join the trade missions organized by your government or industry associations

Foreign governments and industry associations often maintain bilateral relations with their Chinese counterparts. They frequently organize trade missions to China, some of which are coordinated with state or official visits. In all cases, there will be scheduled arrangements for business interactions with Chinese companies. This exercise encourages government attention which will be beneficial in China, as Chinese companies tend to be very careful with projects that have a governmental background or support.

Internet search

Many Chinese enterprises have websites, thanks to the government's encouragement of information technology, and many are in English.

How to assess your business partner

Checking the credit history of Chinese companies can be challenging, if not impossible. Credit agencies claim that they have special contacts that will ensure accuracy in their reporting of the credit status of Chinese companies. However, it is always advisable to check with different sources and to crosscheck the results, if having a good and thorough understanding of your partner's financial situation is essential. In cases of exporting to China, the best proof of a company's credibility is whether or not the Chinese company is able to open a letter of credit from the bank. If so, you can save the effort of checking the company's financial standing because the opening bank will have done the job.

If you want to establish a business relationship which goes further than simply exporting to China, you may need to understand more than the financial situation. Other elements such as the vision the company has for the market, the management team and its possible terms of service, corporate background and relationships with suppliers and distributors. In many cases, observation of interpersonal relationships, the manufacturing site and the office area will give you a reasonable level of intelligence for judgmental evaluation. Talking to suppliers and distributors/agents, and even a customer or two, can be very useful for gaining an understanding of your partner.

In some places, there is a system of misconduct blacklists erected for the purpose of establishing good business credibility. In Beijing, for example, the Beijing Administration of Industry and Commerce launched a Misconduct Record System in July 2001, blacklisting those who have been caught engaging in illegitimate economic activities or misconduct. Some banks also maintain a blacklist of companies or persons who fail to honour loan repayment contracts.

Key terms and conditions in an import contract

In China, importers tend to use standard form contracts in their import transactions. Foreign contracts are seldom accepted for fear of being trapped by contract stipulations with which they are not familiar. Adding special provisions to the contract form is normally acceptable. The key terms and conditions include the following:

Terms of price and shipment

In China's import businesses, many transactions are concluded at FOB prices in consideration for using Chinese shipping companies. C&F and CIF terms are accepted only if the freight is proved to be cost-effective.

Insurance

Commodities imported by China are normally in larger quantities and of a great many varieties. Some goods, due to transport reasons, need to be stored in foreign ports or wait for shipment or transhipment. It would be very complicated and troublesome to arrange insurance on a case by case basis. Therefore, companies that conduct frequent import businesses normally have 'open insurance' for their import cargoes, ie the importing companies submit their notifications of import cargo shipments and other relevant documents, which are acknowledged by the insurance company as insurance orders and against which the insurance premium will be settled with the insured.

Terms of payment

For most imports, payments are made by L/Cs (letters of credit). The opening of an L/C is based on the contract signed between the Chinese buyer and foreign seller. The L/Cs opened by Chinese banks, particularly reputable national banks, are accepted by foreign banks and there will be no problems of non-payment on the part of the Chinese banks if the requirements of the L/C are met. It should be noted, however, that the L/C, once effected by the bank, will become a contract independent of the purchase contract in the sense that the bank undertakes the responsibility of making payment provided that the documents submitted to it are in strict compliance with the stipulations of the L/C, regardless of the stipulations of the purchase contract. Conversely, if the documents submitted by the seller for negotiation of payment do not conform with the requirements of the L/C, the bank will reject payment regardless of the contract stipulations.

Therefore, it is always advisable for foreign exporters to check carefully the contents of the L/C against the terms agreed in the contract. If anything that is found in the L/C is not in conformity with the contract stipulations, the exporter should request amendments from the importer. As a matter of principle, Chinese importers and banks will not issue confirmed L/Cs.

Inspection

Certificates of quality and quantity or weight issued by manufacturers or public assessors are normally required as a part of the negotiating documents for payment under the relevant L/C. However, in cases where the quality, quantity or weight of the goods is found not to be in conformity with those stipulated in the contract after re-inspection by Chinese inspection authorities within the agreed period after arrival of the goods at the port of destination, the importer usually either returns the goods to the exporter or lodges claims against the seller for compensation of losses on the strength of inspection at the port of destination.

In the case of equipment imports, Chinese companies will often insert a clause in the contract withholding a portion of the payment, normally 5–10 per cent of the total contract value, which will be paid only when the equipment is installed and commissioned.

Dispute resolution

In cases of dispute, the formal contract has a provision that a solution must be sought through friendly consultation. If this does not produce a result, arbitration is then adopted to settle the disputes. Litigation is only a last resort.

How to manage sales and distribution effectively – selection of agents and distributors

As a starting point, companies should define an optimal mix of direct and wholesale accounts. The parameters should be first and foremost the cost-to-serve economics which determine optimal effectiveness in running one's own independent sales network versus alternative channels to market.

Markets can be divided into core and secondary by their level of importance to the company, location advantages and disadvantages and manageability. Generally, it is advisable to serve the core market with one's own sales force, while leaving secondary markets to agents and distributors.

To manage wholesalers properly, companies need to define their wholesaler selection criteria and performance measurement:

Selection criteria

Maturity

- company size
- age (history)
- previous experience
- technical capability (ability to lead technical personnel)
- management competence
- financial stability

Operating (serviced) area

- Local operator (servicing only one market)
- Regional operator (servicing several neighbouring/selected markets)
- National operator (servicing all key markets countrywide)

Terms and conditions

- payment terms
- volume commitment
- commitment to promotion and advertising

Other

- transportation
- feedback system
- warehousing
- after-sale service levels
- required skills of salespeople

When managing agent/distributor relationships, it is suggested that companies link performance with incentives and provide regular, scheduled training to the selected wholesalers in order to achieve optimal effectiveness.

How to source from China

Increased global competition requires marketers to lower their costs effectively in order to survive the competition. One of the options for achieving lower costs is to outsource parts, components or even the whole product. China is a low-cost outsourcing destination. There are basically two options when setting up your own production presence in China: direct import from China and/or contract manufacturing.

In both cases, two types of companies must be considered: export trading companies and manufacturing companies with export licences (licences are available to all enterprises within five years of China's accession to the WTO in November 2001). The advantages and disadvantages of both types are analysed in Table 4.4.2.

Caution must be exercised when choosing between the two types of vendor. The following provide some guidelines for foreign companies outsourcing in China.

Vendor maturity

Vendor maturity can be measured by several criteria including:

- company size (annual sales, total headcount, capacity);
- age (history);
- previous experience;
- export records;
- understanding of foreign customer concerns;
- financing capability for export sales;
- production capability (capacity to handle volume, equipment conditions, quality assurance system);
- management (professional backgrounds, understanding of export practices, language).

Factors to be considered if the vendor is a trading company:

- sourcing capabilities (financing, geographical coverage);
- experience (history, relationships with key suppliers and key ports, export records);
- staff (language proficiency, understanding of international trade practices, attitudes).

It is always worthwhile contacting several vendors to compare prices and quality before you decide with whom to contract. Even if you have chosen one that you think is satisfactory, start with a small order before you become totally dependent on the partner. It is also advisable to be aware that deliveries are often late because of infrastructure problems in some areas. Another factor that causes late delivery is over-commitment by producers to export orders. If you are to place an order, it is advisable to make time allowances for the expected delivery.

Dealing with language problems to achieve best possible communications

Apart from the differences of culture, history and politics, language is a significant barrier in business com-

Table 4.4.2 Comparative strengths and weaknesses of importing channels from China

	Strengths	*Weaknesses*
Export Trading Company	Export-oriented Handling variety of products More international exposure Professional trade staff Sourcing from different areas (order consolidation) Familiarity with trade practices	Lack of understanding about product Less control over quality Less control of production schedules Dependent on price mark-ups Insufficient understanding of the manufacturers by the buyers
Manufacturers	Understanding of product nature Technically competent Quality control Control over production schedules No mark-up on product costs Direct communication on product requirements	Lack of understanding about trade practices Less international exposure Operating in one area only Inability to consolidate orders Lack of experience in handling export-related matters

munications. It might be thought that the possibility of language problems would be high on the priority list of those entering the China market but evidence suggests that language difficulties are seldom given any serious thought.

Language problems in written communications

The work of organizing translations and the preparation of presentation materials are all too often delegated to a public relations department, which in turn passes the job on to someone whose experience they cannot judge. Worse still, foreign managers tend to take it for granted that the interpreter employed to do the job will carry it out. This may not be true. Frequently, mistakes in translations are made, even by large organizations which could easily afford to ensure that the bridge that they are trying to build into the China market gives them a good image as serious players, rather than making them a laughing stock. Smaller companies often use translation services in their home country or in Taiwan, Hong Kong and the mainland. Because of a lack of industry knowledge and reluctance to consult with industry people when translating, the poor quality of translation often results in non-professional language.

Despite the twenty-odd years which have elapsed since China opened its doors to foreign trade and investment, some companies are still having their brochures translated by translators from Taiwan or Hong Kong, whose style of language and technical terminology are different from that of the mainland. Take the name of President Bush, for example: in each of these three locations the Chinese translation is different, although the name is transliterated in all cases. Differences in translating President Bush's name do not really cost anything, but variations in translations of technical terms and marketing concepts will be more likely to cause misunderstandings or costly clarification efforts. In addition, Hong Kong and other non-mainland printers are still to be found using archaic, complex characters, instead of the simplified characters that the younger generation on the mainland now learns in school; indeed, many have difficulty recognizing complex Chinese characters.

In business correspondence, poor translation may well lead to misunderstanding or disregarded communications between the two sides of a business relationship. In such cases, the translator often takes the easy option of using familiar words rather than going deeper to convey the meaning and feeling vested in the wording.

Language problems in oral communications

The problems in written communications are easily identified since the evidence is on paper for all to see. But examples of interpretation problems in the spoken language are more difficult to document. It may be assumed however that the same people who are so ignorant and careless of written language are no less cavalier in their treatment of other aspects of the language problem. One of the authors of this chapter recently received a long-distance call from the manager of a joint venture which he helped to establish several years ago. They were having a board meeting to discuss the next steps in their marketing plan, but had problems understanding the foreign partner's proposition. He talked to the foreign manager for a while and found that it was in fact the interpreter who could not get the message across.

It is unfortunately true, broadly speaking, that the language barrier is seldom paid much attention by the business world and even if interpretation has been identified as a potential problem, sufficient resources may not be made available to find effective solutions.

The easygoing attitude that everything will be 'all right on the night' and the Chinese side will provide an interpreter is not safe. If the interpreter, particularly one who has won the job on the basis of a language qualification from a university, finds him/herself out of his/her depth and there is no one to help, there is a serious danger that he/she will be too embarrassed to admit to the difficulty and ask for clarification. Worse still, to cover up his/her ignorance and embarrassment, the interpreter may be tempted to make something up. Such cover-ups may lead to the loss of some vital point, or to major misunderstandings.

It is certainly unwise to rely on the Chinese side to find someone from within their own organization who will perform effectively as an interpreter on behalf of both sides. In a non-negotiation environment, particularly in daily management communications in a joint venture, one of the problems, unconnected to language, is that potential bias of the interpreter, conscious or otherwise, can easily lead to an interpretation which shades the meaning or to choosing 'doctored' language in order to please the audience.

It is also unrealistic to assume that any well-educated Chinese, who can speak understandable English, will be able to provide effective interpretation in complex negotiations. The foreigner's ignorance of the Chinese language will make it difficult to judge the quality of the interpretation; remembering that there is a huge difference between the ability to conduct a reasonable dialogue in a private situation and the ability to interpret in public, particularly when faced with new subject matter which may be highly technical, and will certainly have a strange vocabulary, idiom, accents, and personal idiosyncrasies. Even a practised, professional interpreter may have some difficulty with new specialist terms outside his/her general knowledge, or in understanding the idiosyncratic accents and idioms of strangers.

All these considerations apply whether the interpreter is from the Chinese or foreign side. The fundamental weakness is the same. It is perhaps surprising, in view of the number of occasions when this amateurish arrangement has been used, that so much business has eventually been negotiated. But the speed of negotiating could certainly have been much faster and many misunderstandings could have been avoided if proper arrangements for interpreting had been the rule, rather than the exception. We shall never know how many negotiations have failed and deals been aborted, because of failure to pay serious attention to overcoming the language barrier.

Advice for dealing with such language problems is:

1. A glossary of technical terms should be prepared before the negotiation takes place. This will enable the interpreter to understand the technical side of the business and facilitate a smooth conduct of the technical discussions.
2. Your own interpreter should be present. Whether or not he/she is going to play the role of interpreter, he/she should be assigned the additional role of picking up the points that have not been conveyed correctly in the process.
3. Before you engage an outside interpreter, you should make sure that the interpreter is able to perform the job. Do not risk using an interpreter who speaks only 'understandable' English. He should be given sufficient briefing about the background of the business.
4. The principal negotiator should be prepared to speak slowly with frequent pauses. In many cases, the principal negotiator will forget that he is talking to people who do not understand his/her language and keeps talking until he thinks he has finished his argument. But the interpreter may not be able to memorise your long speech. The longer you talk, the more likely you are to confuse your interpreter and the less you can put across effectively to your listeners.

5. Debrief the interpreter after each session to ensure he/she is able to keep up with your style of speech.

Building an in-house China team

Undertaking proper market research to gain a better understanding of the market is one aspect of the effort to prepare for entry into China. Another is the development of an in-house China team to use this understanding to penetrate the market. All too often, a company does not deploy sufficient resources to build a China team within its organization. This is entirely understandable for those companies which are only testing the water. But those who have established a firm interest will need to set up an in-house, expert capability before launching themselves into a campaign to tackle the market. Unfortunately, few organizations attempt to do this, and in many cases such responsibility is delegated to a department handling the Asian region market in general.

Those who do attempt to set up their own China department naturally have some difficulty in deciding the best way to find and recruit staff who can offer the appropriate qualifications, including linguistic and general communication skills.

Recently graduated language students are one obvious pool of potential talent, but only a most exceptional recruit from the field is likely to meet more than a part of the job requirements. Even their linguistic skills are likely to be limited unless the student has spent years in China, not only while at university. Also, unless the students are much older than normal first degree graduates, their general business experience can hardly be very wide. All these considerations may make it difficult for new recruits, coming straight from university, to perform initially as anything other than a student interpreter. This is not to say that good recruits cannot be found from this pool of talent, but they will need time before their skills are likely to meet total requirements.

On the other hand, the pool of foreigners available who are both experienced in the China market and linguistically qualified, is likely to be severely limited. Most of those who might meet the requirements will either already be retired, or still be gainfully employed. If such an experienced person can be found to act in the liaison role, and recruited as a part of the company team planning its China entry strategy and tactics, this is certainly a good solution to the problem, but mature people with experience of the Chinese market and Chinese language qualification are more likely to be successfully in mid-career, than in the job market.

Fortunately, there is a third, growing source of suitable talent: the pool of Chinese with good English and an understanding of western culture, who have either worked in western countries for years or been educated in western schools. These second-generation Chinese, born, brought up and educated in western countries, are known as 'bananas'. When recruiting these, companies should be careful not to make judgements based only on their Chinese appearance. Their understanding of Chinese culture, business experiences with and/or in China are just as crucial as when you recruit your own fellow countrymen. There is an increasing number of young elite who, after several years of experience working in China, are now studying in western schools. Their business experience can be valuable in building your China team's capability.

If you intend to set up an office in China, it is possible to recruit local Chinese talents with business experience and essential communication skills. Although they may have less understanding of the foreign culture, many will have worked with foreign companies and gained a reasonable understanding of western business norms and practices. They will bring with them a much broader and deeper knowledge of the Chinese language, and should have a greater understanding of Chinese culture and systems. They can certainly make very good members of a foreign business team. However, although a decision to recruit from the mainland immediately broadens the scope of the search, such a solution may well not commend itself to a company which has no Chinese experience, and therefore no criteria by which to judge the suitability of the candidates. The use of a professional head-hunter may help to solve the problem. Following China's WTO accession, foreign headhunting services in the form of joint ventures are now available.

Finally, since China is a country with a traditional respect for age, young graduates will have to overcome age prejudice, in addition to their lack of business and technical experience. Therefore, it is advisable to appoint a middle-aged manager to take charge of the China operation.

Using the services of advisers

Recruiting staff for an in-house China capability is difficult for companies which have decided to tackle the Chinese market and which, almost by definition, do not have any in-house expertise to enable them to judge the quality of outside advice, or the suitability of potential recruits on offer. Therefore, many companies entering the China market find themselves in uncharted waters and at the mercy of outside advisers and interpreters. The choice of reliable advisers and effective interpreters is crucial to the success of any initial operation, but there is no magic formula that can guarantee the right choice. The rule of thumb for businesses starting out in the China market is to take counsel from more than one adviser.

When seeking external advice, consulting firms can be valuable contacts, if they can provide a holistic evaluation of the market, knowledge about business practices and understanding of cultural background based on their hands-on experience. In many cases, consulting firms claiming expertise on China do not even have Chinese staff in the team and rely secondhand on lessons that they learnt from published literature. Being critical of everything Chinese seems to be a convincing tool for some consulting firms. However, being critical is also an effective tool for screening consulting firms. Of course, there are a number of good consulting firms that can be of great assistance in designing your entry strategy. Nevertheless, the fact remains that the quality of specialist advice available to a company addressing the China market for the first time is variable.

Frequently, companies will encounter overseas Chinese offering various kinds of advisory services, and proclaiming their advantages of having 'close contact' with government or governmental organisations at certain level. Sometimes they even produce some kind of a document – an agreement or Memorandum of Understanding (MOU) – to demonstrate their 'strong ties' with governmental organizations. Some of these claims are true, but many are not quite what they seem. The documents might have been obtained through cold contacts warmed up by the lure of offers of 'opportunities of cooperation' in exchange for cooperation agreements. It is all too easy for foreign businesspeople to be so impressed by the good English spoken by their newfound friend that they suspend their critical faculties. Such advisers will have a vested interest in maintaining the momentum of the China project; their instincts are likely to be to emphasise opportunity, not difficulty. The lesson from experience is that much damage has been caused by uncritical, careless acceptance by inexperienced foreign businesspeople of advice from goldentongued, plausible overseas Chinese. Of course, there are good candidates to be found amongst overseas Chinese, but foreign companies should beware of too ready an acceptance of specious claims that racial origins and good connections can by themselves solve every business problem.

There are other types of advisers in China who can be extremely useful, but whom many companies have ignored in their effort to seek outside assistance. They can be any of the following:

- retired government officials;
- those who previously worked with the government but are now running private consulting practices or are freelance consultants;
- researchers in leading research institutions;
- university professors;
- journalists who specialise in covering the dynamics of a particular industry.

Such people have a considerable understanding of the China market and also many contacts that few, if any foreign advisers might have in practice. They can be contracted under special arrangements to constitute part of your China team. Unfortunately, companies seldom take the time to seek out such local advisers.

Joint Venture Contract Negotiations and Approvals
Jonathan Reuvid

From MOU to joint venture agreement or draft contract

Initial discussions for a joint venture (JV) with a selected Chinese partner, if fruitful, will result in a Memorandum of Understanding (MOU) signed jointly. The MOU should contain a clear statement of intent to develop together a feasibility study for a joint venture (JV) and to negotiate the terms of the joint venture to the mutual benefit of the parties. The MOU must be filed by the Chinese party together with a 'pre-feasibility study' (in reality a checklist of the major parameters for the proposed JV) with the authorities to which it reports. More detailed negotiations cannot proceed until the reporting authorities have given a preliminary indication of approval to the project.

Formal MOUs in China, in a joint venture context, are not legally binding but are considered to be a commitment to continue discussions and to carry out a serious feasibility study. Therefore, it is considered to be a breach of good faith for a foreign company to enter into negotiations for the same project with another Chinese enterprise once a formal MOU has been signed, unless it is first terminated by the mutual consent of the two original parties. It follows that the initial choice of preferred partner is crucial. Signing an MOU in haste with an ill-chosen potential partner imposes a major impediment to further progress.

For this reason , it is important to carry out as much as possible of the due diligence discussed in Chapter 4.4 before signing any MOU. If in doubt, the foreign company should confine itself to a simple minute which records that discussions have taken place which will be reported to the boards of the two companies which will decide mutually within an agreed period of time whether or not to continue studying the project.

The pre-feasibility study

The pre-feasibility study usually takes the form of a standard checklist of the main parameters for the joint venture, some of which may be mentioned in the MOU but most of which are an expression of the initial 'ball-park' numbers which the parties may have discussed together. The checklist is not a joint declaration of the Chinese and foreign parties, but foreign partner input will certainly be requested. Key elements in the pre-feasibility checklist include:

- scope of business;
- total investment in the JV in US dollars;
- amount and shares of registered capital to be subscribed by the partners in US dollars;
- form of contribution for registered capital by each partner: cash, equipment, patented designs, technology, land use and buildings (proportions not usually quantified at this stage);
- nature of technology; must be to international standard, preferably advanced;
- planned production capacity (unit/volume output rather than value);
- proportion of output to be sold in export markets (normally not less than 20 per cent);
- surface area of facility and of covered factory space (existing or new building);
- in what proportions equipment is to be imported or sourced within China;
- workforce to be employed (provisional numbers);
- foreign partner's commitment to training and continuing technical support.

There is a 'chicken and egg' element in specifying these parameters at such an early stage, since most of this detail cannot be quantified with certainty in advance of a full-scale feasibility study. Indeed, it is advisable that the foreign party distances itself, as far as possible, from the pre-feasibility process so that responsibility for any major changes to the parameters which have to be identified to the authorities is limited.

The feasibility study

Assuming that the authorities' response to the pre-feasibility study and MOU is positive, the parties may now move forward jointly to a full-scale project feasibility study. It is quite possible that the authorities may reject one or more of the parameters in the pre-feasibility checklist – perhaps the form in which contributions to registered capital may be made, or a demand for a higher proportion of export sales. By this time, the relationship between the prospective partners should have advanced to the point where such obstacles are addressed together in the spirit of trying to find a solution which will satisfy the authorities and be acceptable to both sides.

The complexity of the feasibility study will be determined by the nature of the project, its technical content, procurement issues in respect of equipment, raw material and locally sourced components, quality assurance standards and sales potential. It is recommended that all phases of the study be carried out by a joint team and that the data provided by either side should have maximum transparency. In the course of the study, the Chinese members of the team will certainly want to visit the foreign partner's facilities and to inspect technology, equipment and manufacturing processes.

The amount of detail which the Chinese partner will require to complete the feasibility study for its purposes and the scope of the study will be broadly similar to the foreign partner's requirements. The Chinese side will focus particularly on the detailed specification and performance of any equipment and tooling to be imported, and if used equipment or tooling is involved will need to satisfy itself fully as to condition and market value.

Market studies are a necessary part of the overall feasibility study to satisfy both partners that the products which the JV is targeted to manufacture are saleable in both export and domestic markets in the proportions and at the prices planned. In the early days of JVs in China, Chinese partners were often content to rely on a commitment by the foreign partner to take full responsibility for exports with the amounts to be exported in the early years specified in the JV contract. Chinese partners increasingly demand a fully researched market study which demonstrates in which overseas markets and in what proportions the JV's products can be sold at the projected export sales price.

Conversely, foreign partners, seduced by the mirage of a billion-plus Chinese consumers, used to be content to rely upon government institutes' published statistics or projections and the Chinese partner's assurances of marketability. Increasingly today prospective foreign JV partners demand studies of key regional markets in China by professional research organisations, such as CMTD, or western market research firms operating in China with appropriate fieldwork capabilities.

The business plan

The feasibility study should culminate in the preparation of a business plan by the two parties jointly. This is not a formal requirement by the authorities to whom the feasibility study must be submitted with the JV agreement or draft JV contract, although the Chinese partner needs to include an income and expenditure plan showing profit projections for the first three to five years of the JV's life.

However, from the foreign partner's perspective, the addition to the feasibility study of a business plan (in the western sense) and a draft budget for the period from company registration through start-up is strongly recommended. In particular, the business plan should include a cash-flow statement, as well as a profit and loss statement, and operating statements including analyses of fixed and variable expense and a manpower plan which specifies maximum staffing at each stage of development in the JV. In this way, the business plan becomes a financial blueprint, subject to review and amendment by the board of the JV after the company is formed, but a clear reference point for management discussion.

Until the early 1990s the concept of medium-term cashflow planning (as opposed to income and expenditure projections) was foreign to most Chinese company managers, brought up in the traditions of command economy accounting. However, exposure to foreign investors and international accounting standards and procedures has effected considerable changes in Chinese corporate best practice, and the merits of 'market economy' business planning in the early stages of a joint venture are now well understood.

Negotiating the joint venture agreement, draft contract and articles of association

In the 1980s it was common for the designated JV partners to negotiate the detailed terms of the JV in the form of a non-binding joint venture agreement which was then submitted to the local reporting authorities for approval, together with the Chinese version feasibility study.

Following approval, possibly with some amendment, the two sides would then reconvene, convert the joint venture agreement into a draft joint venture contract and, at the same time, draft the articles of association (or 'statutes' as they were sometimes called) for the joint venture company. As the incidence of JV negotiations multiplied and the pace of joint venturing quickened, many local authorities, notably the Commissions of Foreign Trade and Economic Cooperation (COFTECs) in major cities, relaxed the procedure and permitted the partners to proceed direct to the drafting of the joint venture contract and articles of association. Today, use of the preliminary joint venture agreement is generally limited to very complex or contentious projects where some intermediary clarification is helpful or the parties prefer a more protracted negotiation. In the sections which follow, it is assumed that the parties proceed direct to the contract stage.

The use of advisers

At this point, the senior management of the foreign party entering into formal JV contract negotiations needs to select its negotiating and drafting team and to decide how it will conduct the negotiations within the framework of standard Chinese practice. Normally, the principal Chinese party (always referred to as 'Party A' in the documents) will prepare a first draft of the joint venture contract and the articles of association which it will submit, in advance of negotiation, to the principal foreign party (invariably referred to as 'Party B' in a bilateral agreement).

Perhaps the first issue to address is the force and practice of Joint Venture Law. The principal applicable law on equity joint ventures (and other forms of foreign investment also) is published in Chinese and in English in a single volume, entitled *Investment in China,* compiled jointly by the Foreign Investment Administration and China Economic and Trade Consultant Corporation of MOFTEC (see also the reference list of relevant laws at the end of Chapter 3.2 'Foreign Direct Investment Vehicles'). The laws set out clearly (and generally,

unambiguously) the content and principal clauses which must be included in both a joint venture contract and the articles of association. Many of the detailed clauses which appear in the first drafts submitted by Party A are culled direct from these laws, but the English language is usually not identical. One reason why the wording is often different is that copies of *Investment in China* with the official English translation are not generally in circulation among Chinese companies.

Variations of substance to the standard clauses of the Joint Venture Law, other than those dealing with the scope of the business, investment and registered capital contributions, scale of production, export content and the specific responsibilities of the parties, are not generally allowed by the authorities. Therefore, a commonsense approach to these secondary clauses is to incorporate them in the joint venture contract and articles of association as drafted, and translated, in the law unless either party has some major objection. Taking this approach to its logical conclusion, foreign companies negotiating a JV for the first time may be tempted to conduct the negotiations on a 'do it yourself' basis without external advisers, but such a course of action exposes the investor to unnecessary risk.

At the other extreme, the foreign investor may wish to engage a law firm to advise on the legal documents and to participate in the negotiations. There are a number of leading international law firms with offices in China, with experienced foreign and Chinese staff authorised to practise law in China. However, involvement of western law firms in joint venture negotiating sessions can be counter-productive and an 'offstage' involvement may be preferable. In most JV negotiations the Chinese party will not involve an external Chinese lawyer unless a western law firm is introduced. Mega-projects involving billion dollar investment, international financing or major infrastructure projects are a different matter where the contractual documents are susceptible to western legal drafting, but the routine equity joint venture does not involve international law and the contracts are rigidly controlled by the standard Chinese framework.

Joint venture contract negotiators are well advised to concentrate on substance rather than form. However forcefully they may seek to interpose tightly drafted clauses in western legal language, the final product will still contain wording through which the proverbial 'coach and horses' could be driven in a western court of law. Essentially, what matters is that the joint venture contract and articles of association are written in transparent business language, which is as unambiguous as possible to both parties.

The success of the JV will depend on a strong, enduring relationship between the partners. If mutual understanding and respect fail, the joint venturer should question what the remedies are. Chinese contracts always provide for 'the resolution of disputes through friendly consultation' and, if that fails, by arbitration. Arbitration in China has a good record with arbitrators often finding in favour of the foreign party. Under a judicial system such as China's where there are no formal case law precedents to which courts can refer, litigation is hazardous and an unattractive course of action. If the partnership relationship fails in China and becomes confrontational, the ultimate recourse is to walk away.

However, in the context of negotiating an acceptable joint venture contract and articles of association drafted in layman's language, the foreign partner can benefit from the services of external advisers in three respects:

- As noted at the initial discussion phase, competent translation both of the written word and through a skilled interpreter. (To achieve unambiguity it is crucial that the Chinese and English versions have the same meaning, particularly since the contract will specify that 'in the event of any discrepancy between the two versions the Chinese version shall prevail').
- As a member of the negotiating team, an experienced consultant or staff member who has been through the whole process of a Chinese JV negotiation and the start-up of operations, and can input from experience what problems are likely to arise from contract omissions, loose wording or inadequate provisions for the management of the JV.
- As an adviser, an experienced China consultant, preferably Chinese, having good working relationships with or connections to the relevant departments of the approval authorities concerned, who can check out the key points which arise in negotiation on ad hoc basis.

The third role cannot be performed in respect of sensitive issues without excellent connections. Foreign trade support groups having any foreign political association will not be effective in this field.

During the course of the negotiations, the foreign partner may also need to take advice on taxation or accountancy issues. The bigger international accountancy firms all have audit offices in China, mainly in

Beijing and Shanghai, and their expert advice is readily available.

The negotiation process

JV contract negotiations are best conducted in the same city as the approval authorities to whom the draft contract and articles of association have to be submitted for preliminary approval. Therefore, if the Chinese partner is part of a national corporation the negotiations are better held in Beijing where the relevant ministries are located so that informal opinion may be sought on the issues of substance. Whatever other ministry may be involved in the subsequent approval process, MOFTEC for major joint ventures or the appropriate local COFTEC will certainly be involved, since all foreign investment projects require ultimate MOFTEC endorsement.

Assuming that the foreign party has studied the draft contract and articles of association (and taken advice where appropriate) in advance of discussion, the actual negotiating sessions are likely to take less than seven days. The negotiating procedures are well defined. As for the original set of meetings, the representatives of the two parties will be ranged either side of a meeting room table with up to ten Chinese representatives present. The composition of the Chinese team may vary from day to day, but the same key members are likely to attend each session under the leadership of a designated chief negotiator.

In spite of the apparent formality, the climate of the discussions should be quite relaxed. If the parties have reached a high degree of unanimity on the structure and financing of the JV during the joint feasibility study work together, there will be a presumption on both sides that the JV will go ahead. This does not mean to say that no serious differences of opinion will emerge in the course of formal negotiation, but a conducive atmosphere of mutual sincerity and flexibility will have been created. On many points of detailed drafting, the focus of discussion is more likely to be on satisfying the legal requirements and state policy guidelines, rather than resolving differences between the parties.

The work of amending the draft documents will be carried out methodically, beginning with the recitals and clause 1 of the joint venture contract and proceeding to the end of the contract before turning to the articles of association. Discussion of the articles is generally more straightforward than negotiation of the contract for two reasons:

- many of the articles are a repetition of clauses in the contract; and
- the contract is effectively a partnership agreement involving the relative detailed responsibilities of the parties, while the articles are concerned more with the ground rules and procedures for the management of the JV company.

There are practical points of Chinese negotiating style, of which foreign party negotiators should be aware. First, there is no merit in allowing discussions to stall on any single point at issue; it is quite acceptable for either party to say: 'Let's come back to this subject tomorrow and go on now to the next point.' Provided that the foreign party has explained its point of view clearly and answered any questions on its stance, the delay is usually helpful. It gives both negotiating teams an opportunity to refer to their superiors for instruction or to develop an alternative to overcoming the obstacle. Where appropriate, it also allows time to take soundings from the relevant department authorities.

It is also perfectly acceptable for the foreign team, when faced with an unfamiliar point or doubt, to ask for an intermission in the discussions to caucus outside the meeting room. If this device is shown to be effective in removing roadblocks, it is possible that the Chinese team may employ the same expedient, although the 'common line' among the members of the Chinese negotiating group is likely to have been well rehearsed.

Understandably, the Chinese party will be concerned to broaden the scope and nature of Party B's responsibility, not only in terms of the export sales commitment but also in terms of training, continuing technical support and management expertise. As an argument for the provision of support at Party B's cost, Chinese negotiators are skilful at emphasising the superior nature of the foreign partner's 'advanced technology' and expertise which is always flattering and is usually effective in drawing out the maximum commitment which the foreign partner is prepared to make. The foreign negotiating team should take particular care to ensure that the scope of each responsibility is clearly defined in terms of quantifiable limits (eg maximum days, weeks, etc of management time in each specialised and general function).

As an important side issue, the foreign negotiating team should also be aware that the manager whom the Chinese partner intends to nominate as general manager of the JV will probably be a member of the Chinese negotiating team, very possibly the chief negotiator. The right to nominate the general manager lies with the majority shareholder in any JV and, in the case of a 50/50 JV, it is normal for the general manager designate to be Chinese, even if there is a temporary foreign general manager at the outset. The contract negotiations are therefore a test for prospective general managers and a first opportunity for the foreign partner to assess candidates in action. Although the nomination of general manager is not usually made until after registration of the joint venture company and before the first board meeting, the foreign negotiating team should be at pains to identify the likely candidate during negotiations and, if it considers him unsuitable as a general manager, to find a way of making more senior Chinese management aware of its concern after the successful conclusion of negotiations.

The formal negotiations continue until the joint venture contract and the articles of association have been drafted in both languages, and are signed by both parties. Of course, these documents are not yet legally binding as they lack the formal approval of the authorities; they may also be signed by both parties subject to the ratification of the boards of directors of both companies. It is also wise to draft and sign a further memorandum, to which the draft contract and articles are appended, which records the closing position and sets out the actions which each partner will take in the interval before approval and signature of final binding contracts.

The senior foreign negotiator must have his company's authority to sign the draft documents on the spot, with the understanding that there will be no provision for further negotiation, except in respect of amendments which the approval authorities wish to be made.

Contents of the joint venture contract and articles of association

A checklist of the contents of a standard equity joint venture contract is included at the end of Chapter 3.2. Expertise and guidance on interpretation of standard wording or drafting hints can be provided by an accredited joint venture consultant or professional adviser as discussed earlier in this chapter.

Certain specific issues relating to the commitments and responsibilities of the partners to the joint venture company, rather than to each other, are normally incorporated in separate agreements which are ratified by the JV board of directors at the first board meeting.

The substance of these agreements, if not the complete detail, is covered during the joint venture contract negotiations and the parties may prefer to include the draft agreements in an appendix to the joint venture contract. There is not usually an absolute requirement by the approval authorities that the supplementary draft agreements are annexed to the main contract. However, in the interests of banishing ambiguity or uncertainty there is merit in inclusion.

The supplementary agreements which are most common are:

- export sales agreement between the JV and Party B; (a domestic market sales agreement between the JV and Party A is less common, as the JV is usually responsible for the sales of its own products/services in the home market);
- technology, patent or copyright licence between Party B and the JV;
- training agreement between Party B and the JV, covering training outside China and subsequent on-site training in China;
- lease from Party A to the JV in cases where Party A retains the land use right and leases an existing facility to the JV; and
- consultancy agreement between Party B and the JV to cover the continuing provision of foreign experts and/or management support.

For identification purposes the joint venture contract may include schedules which provide technical process and product specifications and details of patent, copyright or other intellectual property registrations.

The joint venture articles of association are roughly similar to the memorandum and articles of association which are standard under English company law, although provisions for the operating management of the company are more detailed in the Chinese version.

One innovation in Chinese articles of association is provision for the formation of a preparatory group or preparation committee, whose members are drawn from both parties and whose function is to carry out the necessary preparatory work for the start-up of the JV following receipt of the formal certificate of registration from MOFTEC.

The approvals and registration process

As specified in the draft contract, it is the responsibility of the Chinese partner to submit the formal application documents to the relevant authorities and to lobby the departments involved within each reviewing body. This task is normally assigned to the Chinese chief negotiator personally.

The documents to be submitted to the approval authorities are listed in Detailed Rules for the Implementation of the Law of the People's Republic of China on Sino-foreign Equity Joint Ventures (promulgated on 20 September 1993 by the State Council and amended on 15 January 1986, 21 December 1987 and 22 July 2001), Article 9, and consist of the following:

- application for the establishment of an equity joint venture;
- the feasibility study report prepared by the parties to the venture;
- equity joint venture agreement (optional), contract and articles of association signed by representatives authorised by parties to the venture;
- list of candidates for chairman, deputy chairman and directors of the board appointed by parties to the venture; and
- written opinions of the department in charge and the people's government of the province, autonomous region or municipality directly under the central government where the equity joint venture is located with regard to the establishment of the equity joint venture.

All the documents submitted must be written in Chinese, but the second, third and fourth documents in this list may be written simultaneously in a foreign language agreed jointly by the parties.

The status of the Chinese partner, the nature and industrial classification of the project and the limits of authority of the municipality, province, autonomous region or city under whose jurisdiction the JV falls and the value of the total investment will together determine whether the authorities involved are at central government ministry level or at local level where ministry authority is entrusted to a local department, commission or bureau. At the appropriate level, the ministries involved will be the industry ministry to which the Chinese partner reports and, invariably, MOFTEC. In some cases, more than one industry ministry may be involved, and the approval process abounds with complexities (see chart in Chapter 1.5).

At central government level, each of the ministries involved has an effective right of veto over any joint venture application, but outright rejection is unlikely at this stage, particularly if a continuing dialogue with the authorities has been maintained during the negotiating phase.

Familiarity with the project and prior consultation will help to ease the approvals process, but it is likely that some amendments to the contract and articles will be demanded. Hopefully, these amendments will not be of substance and can be addressed by the parties between them at a distance. If not, then representatives of the parties will have to reconvene to determine whether an acceptable solution can be found. Reversals of ministry decisions are necessarily difficult to achieve, which underlines the value of consultation during the negotiation process.

Article 10 of the above law stipulates that the examination and approval authorities shall decide within three months whether or not to approve the documents submitted. If the documents are not approved, the authorities are obliged to demand any modifications, without which no approval shall be granted, within a limited period of time thereafter.

In practice, the decision and any modifications can often be completed within the specified three-month period. For smaller joint ventures, the approvals procedure can be much swifter. In Tianjin, for example, which has approval authority for projects up to US$30 million total investment, the municipality has located all of the relevant approvals departments in a single foreign investment service centre (FISC) under the leadership of Tianjin's Commission of Foreign Economic Relations and Trade.

As noted earlier, the establishment of all equity joint ventures in China is subject to examination and approval by MOFTEC. On approval, the certificate of registration for the joint venture is issued by MOFTEC. Within one month after receipt, the Chinese partner shall register the certificate of registration with the administrative bureau for industry and commerce of the province, autonomous region or municipality directly under the central government where the JV is located. The date on which the bureau (referred to as the registration and administration office) shall then issue its business licence for the JV is regarded as the date of formal establishment of the equity joint venture.

Employing Staff in China

Li Yong, Deputy Secretary General, China Association of International Trade

Since the economic reform and opening up, China's vast market potential and fast-growing economy have attracted the attention of foreign businesses. Having a presence in China is key to tapping into market opportunities. Foreign entry into the market takes a number of different forms such as representative offices, equity joint ventures, contractual joint ventures and wholly foreign-owned enterprises. Whatever the form of entry a business takes to establish its presence in China, employment of local staff is an unavoidable issue. However, not every kind of foreign establishment can legally employ Chinese staff on its own.

Employing staff in representative offices

Since the beginning of China's opening up to the outside world, representative offices have been frequently used and are the easiest and most convenient tool to explore the local market. A registration certificate must be obtained in order legally to employ Chinese nationals and this requires a series of formalities to be completed, such as opening a bank account for foreign exchange, applying for direct telecommunication lines and securing a multiple entry visa for expatriate managers. The business activities of the representative offices may only be within the range of business networking, product introduction, marketing, technology exchange and consulting services. They are not permitted to engage in direct profit-making activities.

Technically, representative offices do not have independent legal person status and they are not supposed to employ staff as joint ventures or wholly owned operations can. According to the relevant laws and regulations governing the establishment and operation of foreign representative offices in China, they must take on staff through designated employment agencies that provide specialised services for foreign representative offices.

Employment service providers

In the early days of the opening up, when most foreign representative offices were concentrated in Beijing, the provision of Chinese nationals to work in foreign representative offices was monopolised by Beijing Foreign Enterprise Services Corporation (known as FESCO). Its services were designed to help foreign representative offices handle practical issues of human resource management such as identification of qualified local staff, welfare, pensions, residency and mobility. This monopoly ended when other government sponsored 'foreign services' companies were established to compete with FESCO.

At present there are over 70 authorized foreign services companies providing local staff to representative offices in 25 provinces and municipalities. The leading ones include:

- FESCO;
- China Star Corporation for International Economic and Technical Cooperation (China Star Corporation);
- China International Intellectech Corporation (CIIC);
- China International Enterprises Cooperation Co (CIECCO);
- China International Talents Development Centre (CITDC).

The key functions of foreign employment service providers in China include, but are not limited to, the following:

- Providing assistance to customers setting up representative offices in China. This service is normally fee-based and designed to facilitate the process of application;
- Identifying and recommending local staff to foreign representative offices. This service is provided on the basis of different fee arrangements, which vary from place to place and from organization to organisation;
- Manage as proxy labour relations of the staff assigned to foreign representative offices. Normally, foreign employment service companies maintain contractual relationships with foreign representative offices regarding staff deployment;
- Providing welfare benefits to the deployed staff depending on the terms and conditions agreed between the service companies and foreign representative offices, although the latter can deal with welfare benefits on its own;
- Managing personnel logistics such as the management of personal archives (a record file containing information about staff's education, career achievements, professional qualifications etc); transferring archives from previous employers; residence permits when staff come from other parts of the country; passport applications; visa applications for foreign travel and subscriptions to social security where applicable;
- Organizing job fairs and arrange job advertisements for foreign representative offices and other foreign-related organisations;
- Head-hunting senior management staff according to customer requirements;
- Offering various other services related to expatriate staff, such as obtaining multi-entry visas, work permits and residence permits.

How to recruit?

Normal procedure requires a foreign representative office to enter into an employment service contract with a government authorized service agency. On the strength of this contract, the authorized employment service agency will recommend candidates to the representative office. The service agency will also sign contracts with candidates against its contract with the representative office.

Normally, staff will serve a probation period before official employment begins. According to the Labour Law of the People's Republic of China, the probation period should not exceed 15 days for a six month

contract, 30 days for a six to twelve month contract and 60 days for a one to two year contract. The maximum probation period should not exceed six months.

Relevant laws and regulations provide that the minimum ratio of Chinese staff in foreign representative offices is 1:1, which means that if you have one expatriate staff member in the office, there must be at least one local member of staff. If the recommended candidates do not meet requirements, the representative offices may look for suitable staff on their own. They can even agree on the terms and conditions regarding salaries, compensation packages and other benefits with the candidates they find by themselves. However, these staff must register with an authorized employment service agency before their employment is legal.

Dismissal of staff

Normally, there are two reasons for staff to leave the representative office. One is voluntary resignation and the other dismissal for reasons such as misconduct. In either case, 30 days advance notice is required from both the staff and the representative office. As the relationship between the staff and the representative office is based on an employment service contract between the representative office and the service agency, the service agency must be duly notified of the resignation or dismissal. In the case of voluntary resignation, the representative office is free of compensation obligations; in the case of dismissal these will have to be recognized. Normally, a staff member who is dismissed after less than six months' service will not receive any compensation. For members of staff who have worked for more than six months, there are varying degrees of compensation ranging from one month's to six months' pay.

It is illegal to dismiss an employee who is pregnant, nursing or on maternity leave, or any staff receiving prescribed treatment for illness or injury. In cases of misconduct by the Chinese staff, the dismissal should be accompanied with sufficient evidence of violation of Chinese laws and regulations or corporate regulations (which should be made known to the service agency). No compensation is required if the misconduct is recognized by the service agency.

Employment in joint ventures and wholly foreign-owned enterprises

Joint ventures and wholly foreign-owned enterprises have independent legal person status and therefore have much more autonomy in terms of employment. The supervising authority for the employment of labour in these circumstances is the labour and social security department in the venture's place of domicile. The supervising authority exercises supervision of the labour contracts to make sure that the legitimate rights and interests of workers are well protected. Joint ventures and wholly foreign-owned enterprises have complete autonomy in terms of their employment decisions. The relationship between the supervising authority and the joint venture is that the joint ventures or wholly foreign-owned enterprise needs to file their recruitment plans with the local labour authority, which in turn will provide assistance with sourcing employees and processing necessary documents to validate the employment. The joint venture or wholly foreign-owned enterprise has freedom to determine what criteria to apply when screening qualified staff.

Labour contract

It is a requirement of the Labour Law that employers sign an employment contract with their employees. In some places, the labour authority will encourage employers to use their standardised labour contract, which is considered to be neutral and trustworthy. Employers can draft their own labour contract, but it must be strictly in compliance with the labour law. An employer may also enter into a collective labour contract with its employees. Terms and conditions are negotiated by the trade union or by elected representatives of the workers.

In a labour contract, the rights and obligations of both the employer and employees should be clearly defined. Clauses such as job description, labour remuneration, insurance and welfare, labour protection, safety conditions, disciplinary requirements, probation and validity period and conditions under which the contract can be terminated or changed should be included in the contract. Employers must file the standard labour contract with the governing labour authority. Although there is no explicit stipulation regarding what language a labour contract should use, it is advisable for the employer to use the Chinese language, or at least to produce a bilingual document. In any case, the labour authority requires a Chinese language contract (or translation). All contracts signed between the employer and the employees must be verified by the labour authority. Such verification is intended not only to ensure it is signed on the basis of equality and free will, but also to check the different language versions are consistent. There have been cases in which the stipulation of rights and obligations varies greatly between different language versions.

Some foreign-invested enterprises sign a probationary contract before they engage themselves in a formal labour contract, which is not correct practice. According to relevant laws and regulations, the probationary period is the precondition of a formal labour contract. A probationary contract does not free employers from their responsibilities and obligations. In cases of labour disputes, a probationary contract will be regarded as a formal contract. Employers may require a probation period, but it is not mandatory. The probation period should not exceed the statutory length. the maximum of which is six months depending on the length of contract term. During the probation period, either contracted party may terminate the contract without compensation from the employers. No prior notice is needed.

There are two important elements that the employer should take into account in the labour contract: confidentiality and non-competition covenant. A non-disclosure agreement will help protect employers' trade secrets and a non-competition commitment may prevent competitors from taking advantage of the staff's experience and knowledge about the company.

Termination of labour contract and labour disputes

According to the Labour Law, employers are required to provide 30 days' notice prior to dismissal of employees or termination of labour contracts. Under PRC Labour Law, an employer cannot dismiss an employee without cause.

The employer can terminate the labour contract by giving the employee 30 days written notice if one of the following situations occurs:

1. If, after recovering from an illness or non-work-related injury, within a prescribed period of medical treatment, the employee is unable to perform the original duties or other alternative jobs arranged by the employer;

2. The employee is proved incapable of performing a job, even after receiving training or being transferred to another position;

3. Major changes in the circumstances based on which the labour contract was signed have led to the employer's inability to perform the original contract

and agreement to amend the contract can not be reached among parties of the contract.

However, employers can not dismiss employees under the following circumstances:

1. Employees who have been suffering from occupational diseases or work related injuries and have been proved to have completely or partially lost the ability to work;
2. Employees who have been suffering from illness or injuries but are still in the prescribed period of medical treatment;
3. Employees who are pregnant, nursing or on maternity leave;
4. Other circumstances as stipulated by pertinent laws and administrative regulations.

The employer has the right to terminate a labour contract with immediate effect if an employee

1. fails to satisfy requirements during the probation period;
2. has seriously violated the disciplinary rules or regulations of the work place;
3. has committed a serious abuse of duties or engaged in graft, causing serious damages to the employer;
4. is charged with a criminal offence.

Once a dispute arises, the case must first go to arbitration with the labour arbitration committee. This procedure is required by law before a lawsuit can be filed. Application for arbitration must be filed within 60 days after the dispute. If either party is not satisfied with the arbitral award, they may file a lawsuit within 15 days of receipt of the award.

Foreign participation in China's job market

According to its WTO commitments, China will allow foreign human resource service enterprises to enter its talent market. The Ministry of Labour and Social Security and State Administration for Industry and Commerce jointly promulgated the *Provisional Regulation on the Establishment and Administration of Job Referral Agencies of Sino-Foreign Joint Ventures and Cooperatives*, which was implemented as of 1 December, 2001. According to the regulation, foreign employment agencies can engage in the employment agency business in China through the establishment of equity or contractual joint ventures with qualified Chinese partners. The setting up of job referral agencies as Sino-foreign joint ventures and cooperatives must be approved by the provincial-level government labour and social security department and the provincial-level government foreign trade and economic cooperation department. The minimum capital requirement for such joint ventures is US$300,000. Wholly foreign-owned employment service companies are not allowed by the current regulation.

With the entry of foreign employment service companies, foreign-invested enterprises will receive services from local as well as foreign-invested employment service agencies. These latter will undoubtedly improve the overall quality of China's employment services industry.

Industrial and Commercial Market Research

Li Yong, Deputy Secretary General, China Association of International Trade

China is a country with unique socio-economic features. A sound business strategy will have to be based on careful market research, which will analyse the unique features of the marketplace and generate information for decision-making. There have been instances when foreign investors have failed to conduct effective market research after their entry into China; even worse, some companies do not appreciate the value of market research and simply believe that they have good products and so people in China will buy them. This has invariably varying degrees of failure.

When a company is established in China, continuing research efforts should be made in order to monitor the performance/position of the company in the changing marketplace against its competitors, changes in consumer/customer preferences and changes in market conditions likely to affect its sales volume or profitability.

Industrial market research

Is it possible to do industrial market research in China?

The intricacies of China's industrial operations and the complexities of its socio-economic environment have caused international market researchers to question of whether it is possible to conduct industrial market research in China. Lack of familiarity with the information systems has also make them feel sceptical about the prospect of doing industrial market research in China to answer questions in relation to their business decisions, such as:

- what factories could make the product?
- what kind of demand is there for it?
- what are the channels of distribution like?
- what impact do prices have on demand in an economy that only recently adopted a market mechanism?
- how will the product be marketed?
- how will the market evolve over the next five or ten years?
- what are the key market drivers?
- are there any entry restrictions?
- what are the unique characteristics of the local marketplace?

With the deepening of China's economic reform, once private information has become increasingly public, a result of China's efforts to increase transparency. China's accession to the WTO will create a much more open environment for information sharing. Up-to-date, systematic and comprehensive secondary information can be found in the massive compendia published by Chinese organizations. Apart from the *Statistical Yearbook* published by the State Statistical Bureau, many Chinese ministries now publish yearbooks and almanacs containing information about the development of their respective sectors. There are also around 3,500 technical journals for professionals in many specialized fields. Such journals often contain technical descriptions of a technology, product, or development trend of a particular sector. A careful observer of the Chinese market will also find an increasing number of professional newspapers featuring the dynamics of different industries.

However, collecting and studying secondary information, something many foreign companies are doing as part of their day-to-day research effort, may not be sufficient to support business decisions or delineate a complete picture of the market. Some of this information may have built-in discrepancies, such as incompleteness in ministry statistical releases which may have excluded the industrial operations that fall outside its administrative jurisdiction and inconsistencies in different statistical sources for the same industry because of the different statistical standards applied. Moreover, a legacy of the planned economy is that much of the secondary information depicts the picture on the production side and gives little insight into other critical information such as the demand dynamics of end-users and end-use segments, competitive environments, prevailing terms of sales and marketing practices, or the strengths and weaknesses of the existing distribution network.

The study of secondary information can achieve the following from the standpoint of information users:

- obtain a macro picture of the business environment;
- identify market opportunities before commitment is made to more costly field research;
- pinpoint specific factors that need to be investigated further
- locate the types of information to be collected through field research.

Given the insufficiencies and inadequacies of secondary information, it is necessary to carry out primary research in order to find first-hand information and remove the possible flaws that may exist in the secondary information. In some cases, primary data will have to be obtained simply because no systematic statistics have ever existed, or the product in question has been grouped into a very broad statistical entry. Even if there is an abundance of secondary data, some of them will have to be screened and validated via field interviews.

General practices and methodologies in industrial market research

In China, understanding of industrial market research varies among research providers of different types and backgrounds and this determines the methodologies used to carry out research. Generally speaking, there are two schools of methodology in China. One school is represented by research providers who understand industrial market research as industrial market intelligence. They boast their close links with government officials, industry associations, key suppliers or access to sources of information not available from published sources. As a result, much of the research effort is devoted to 'ploughing' insider information or statistics,

and the research conclusions are constructed on the basis of documenting the findings of the 'ploughing' efforts. The advantages of such methodology are that the information documented can be systematic in terms of time series and official in terms of information sources. They can be of good value as a benchmark study, or for the understanding of less dynamic markets, but may not be good enough for an assessment of market opportunities.

The second school concentrates on an interactive and cross-checking approach and obtains research findings through systematically designed research planning. This does not exclude 'ploughing' secondary information from both published and unpublished sources, but also builds into the research process a series of interactive and cross-checking interviews along the value chain of a particular market. Secondary information is used as a benchmark for the truth-seeking efforts and validated in the process of interviews. The interviews do not only focus on hard facts such as production, market size, terms of sales and logistical issues, but also on market dynamics such as general business mood, level of confidence in future outlook, comments on development targets set forth by supervising authorities, role of market specifiers in determining future market trends, the likely impact of inter-material competition and perceived market drivers. The interview process will demand highly skilled interviewers with sufficient understanding of the industry. Interview findings and conclusions drawn from them not only provide insights into the market, but also establish accountability in the assessment of market opportunities.

Consumer market research

Tools and techniques

Generally, the tools and techniques of consumer market research in China are much the same as for other countries. Although the application of the tools and techniques may vary a little, the basic principles of consumer market research do not change in the context of the Chinese market. The most frequently used techniques are:

1. quantitative interviews
   - face-to-face (in-home and central location intercept)
   - telephone
   - mail

– diary
2. qualitative interviews (in-depth interviews)
   – face-to-face
   – focus groups

Other international market research techniques are employed to meet specific information needs. However, costly and highly sophisticated techniques are unusual.

Selection of nationally representative locations for consumer research

Target locations for research are usually Beijing, Shanghai and Guangzhou. These cities are thought to be representative of China in terms of distinctive consumer characteristics and inferences on the population are established on the basis of findings there. These locations, however, may not be as representative as they are thought to be, because they are the most developed areas in China and have the highest living standards compared with other cities in the country. In addition, the behavioural characteristics, purchasing motivations and decision-making processes are not necessarily shared by consumers in other areas of China. Of course, many studies do not intend to be representative of China and the three cities are only used for benchmarking purposes, or establishing benchmark parameters. Many other researchers also focus on these cities because they are seen as points of entry, or targets of penetration.

If a research project is intended to achieve a representative picture of China, it is recommended that other geographical locations are considered, such as Chengdu/Chongqing, Xi'an, Wuhan, Shenyang/Dalian.

Sampling practices

Probability and non-probability sampling are common in Chinese consumer research. Probability sampling is more often used in quantitative research and non-probability in qualitative research. Typical probability sampling methods are stratified sampling and cluster sampling. Applications of sampling methods vary from organization to organization. Statistical organizations (ie those within the system of the State Statistical Bureau, such as the Organisation of Urban Socio-Economic Surveys and its local counterparts) claim that their sample bases are established by way of stratified sampling. Other research organizations tend to use cluster sampling methods, such as area sampling. A typical route to reach the households in the sampling process is described in Figure 4.7.1.

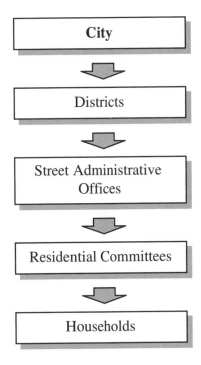

Figure 4.7.1 A typical route to reach the households in the sampling process

Normally, a city is divided into several districts. Under the district government, there are two levels of administrative bodies, street administrative offices and residential committees. A street administrative office usually exercises administrative responsibilities on behalf of the district government in a number of street blocks. Under each street administrative office are a varying number of residential committees. Residential committees are the basic elements of government administration.

Increasingly, however, many research organizations are using what is called street intercept, shopping centre or central location sampling, where samples are drawn by way of randomly intercepting people on the street, in shopping centres or in the central locations of a city. Although street intercept or shop intercept interviews have limitations, not least unrepresentative sampling, research organizations use this methodology to reduce costs, and because it is increasingly difficult to carry out in-home face-to-face interviews.

Fieldwork practices

In fieldwork, street administrative offices and residential committees may be contacted to obtain information on residential committees/households in order to establish sampling frames. Fieldworkers can have easy access to households with the assistance of the residential committees.

In order to regulate market research activities, the statistical authority has promulgated a regulation requiring market research organisations to obtain approval from statistical authorities before gaining access to households. In reality, however, this regulation has not been effectively enforced.

As quantitative consumer research involves a relatively large sample size, most research organizations regularly employ university students to carry out field interviews. While proper training is important to ensure the quality of the interviews, an appropriate monitoring mechanism such as random backcheck is even more important to ensure that the interviews are carried out in strict compliance with the designed methodology. Common problems with using student interviewers are questionnaires not being administered properly, sampling procedures not being strictly followed, interviewers faking questionnaires after repeated refusals or not-at-homes, and answers to open-ended questions not being properly probed and/or recorded.

The statistical organizations employ professional interviewers when carrying out field interviews. They are well trained and have routine contacts with residential committees, which will facilitate the interviews.

Differences in the research environment

Unfamiliarity with market differences often causes misunderstanding of the market and/or misinterpretation of the business environment, which may eventually lead to wrong decisions. It is important to note differences in the environment where the research is carried out. The following are generalizations of some of the major differences in the Chinese research environment. However, it is always advisable for researchers to analyse the research environment on a case by case basis before embarking on research planning and design.

Differences in the basic data

As is true in other countries, the statistical system in China has its own unique features. Some of the statistical information is collected and prepared in accordance with international standards, such as the Customs Statistics, which follows the Harmonious System (HS). Many other statistics still resemble the characteristics of the planned economy, although great efforts have been made by the statistical authority to improve the statistical system.

The State Statistical Bureau publishes a series of official statistics, including the most authoritative

China Statistical Yearbook. But these tend to be more macro than micro compared with the statistics compiled by different ministries. In some instances, there are also discrepancies between the statistics of state statistical publications and ministerial releases. Even ministerial releases on industries can be incomplete because enterprises of the same or similar nature may fall under different ministries. In some cases, statistics on certain industries simply do not exist.

Differences in reporting systems

While the incompleteness of the statistical system can be attributed to problems such as outdated classification and obsolete collection methods, complicated reporting systems are also at fault. Normally, industrial statistics are reported in a bottom-up manner: ie enterprises or business entities report to their supervising departments at city/county levels, who will then report to higher level authorities such as provincial departments. The statistics will be relayed to central government departments, such as ministries. Departments in cities with separate planning from the central government are independent of the provincial departments and report directly to the corresponding departments at central levels. As government departments at different levels may have their own statistical requirements for reporting purposes, the statistics kept at different levels may also vary. For example, the central departments may only be interested in knowing the performances of the enterprises at county level and above, while a city or county level department will also collect information on lower level enterprises, such as village enterprises.

Differences in the social environment

- Market research organizations tend to group people/families into different social classes for particular research purposes. In China, the doctrine of equality among different professions has determined that there is no standardized classification of social class;
- Moreover, the socialist welfare system has also determined that employers provide housing for their employees. Although this is being reformed, the residents in a building tend to be the staff of the same work unit and may share some common characteristics;
- Increased security-consciousness and awareness of privacy have made in-home interviews more difficult. Telephone owners still represent higher income

households and mail questionnaires may not find their way to targeted respondents because personal details such as home addresses are not easily available.

- Reported household expenditure on some commodities, such as soft drinks, beer, staple food (ie rice or wheat flour), edible oil, and tea etc may not reflect the actual consumption because some of these commodities are provided to employees of state-owned enterprises, government organizations and business corporations as a part of the welfare package and they are not counted as out-of-pocket expenditure.

Differences in reactions and length of interviews

The novelty of the structured questionnaire may arouse interest in the interviewee, but sophisticated and prolonged questioning may lead to a loss of interest or perfunctory answers. In most cases, respondents of a consumer study are open in their comments.

In industrial research, respondents tend to be very careful when giving comments. Respondents are easily alerted when being asked questions which they regard as probing into their commercial secrets. An offer to share the research findings at a later date is not regarded as a recompense for giving out information.

In qualitative research, in-depth interviews with respondents in senior positions will normally take longer than planned. The expense of being polite and showing respect, which is essential when carrying out in-depth interviews in China, is to allow divergence. In interactive focus groups, people with dominant personalities tend to lead opinion and they should be carefully managed.

A local research organization tends to have a better understanding of the local market and will be able to adapt to their client's research requirements, particularly when the research organization has working experience with and good understanding of the information needs of foreign companies.

The research industry and research organizations in China

The market research industry emerged as a result of China's open-door policy. The entry of foreign capital in China created a demand for market research. In the early 1980s, the International Trade Research Institute was one of the few primary contacts for market research. In 1984, a consultant arm of the Institute – the Centre for Market and Trade Development (CMTD) – was

established to provide a specialist research service for foreign companies. In 1986, the Opinion Research Institute of the People's University was founded. Later in 1987, two doctors of sociology set up the first commercial market research company. There is now a large number of research organizations in China who are involved in one way or another in market/marketing research. There are over 300 registered marketing research organizations and large advertising companies have market research functions. Professional research institutions and information centres also provide market research services of various kinds.

Foreign research organizations are also operating in China in different establishments. Gallup and AC Nielson are active in China. China's accession to the WTO will further open up the services industry and more foreign consulting and market research companies will establish their operations in China.

Recommendations for market research in China

To fully understand the Chinese market, it is necessary to consider the realities of the vast territory and regional differences. Breaking China down into a multitude of smaller markets and prioritising the research effort on the core market(s) would be a sensible strategy to begin with. In the planning stage of the research, it is important to understand the extremes of demography and geography. For consumer products, the key urban markets will be the natural place to start, while for industrial products, the layout of China's key industries will have to be taken into consideration. Market research should be able to find out, in addition to other critical information, where your core market is and what potential it can offer.

In choosing a research provider, it is important to test their understanding of the market and their understanding of how market research should be carried out to meet research objectives. Both within and outside of China, there are numerous research organisations and consulting firms that boast of their expertise on and special connections in China, but their understanding of market research in China varies greatly. Some understand market research as market intelligence. They build their advantage on their claimed special connections with China or access to insider information or statistics that are not publicly available. As a result, much of the research effort is devoted to 'ploughing' this information while neglecting changing dynamics. It is important to appreciate special connections or access to privately held information, but the capacity to be able to deploy an on-the-ground research force to explore first hand information is even more important.

In designing the research, it is highly recommended that a company planning to carry out research in China takes the following into account:

- Objectives should be clearly defined to exclude any possible ambiguity. The statement of research requirements or terms of reference should not only include the scope and problems to which answers are needed, but also precise specifications of the meaning of all words and terms;
- The disparity between what the company wants to find out and what the research provider can realistically do under the proposed budget and schedule should be recognized, while the limitations of carrying out research in China should be frankly discussed;
- Protection of the ownership of the research results should be made clear in the form of a confidentiality agreement. There have been instances where research providers infringed on the ownership of the research findings by publishing them in newspapers;
- Sources of information need to be detailed to justify the validity and reliability of the research findings;
- A face-to-face meeting with key researchers upon completion of the research is important to pick up opinions and observations that might not be included in the report.

Why employ local research organizations?

Because of the complexity and sensitivity of industrial market research, foreign research organizations often remain in the wings, consigning the job to local research organizations. Apart from the language barrier, which can make communications difficult or impossible, there are other considerations when employing local research providers, such as concerns about disclosing identity, culture and tradition that may influence the general willingness to respond, and distortion may arise from language and/or cultural differences when it comes to understanding questions and answers.

The general practice of foreign research organizations in conducting industrial market research in China is that local research providers are commissioned to carry out fieldwork in a way that should follow international practice, and submit the findings to the foreign research organization for analysis and interpretation. The drawback of this practice is that the interpretation of the research findings without involvement of the local resident researchers may build distorted understanding into the analytical process and lead to misinterpreted conclusions.

Growing Consumerism Strategies for the China Market

T S Chan and Wei-ping Wu, Department of Marketing and International Business,
Lingnan University, Hong Kong

Summary

Since China's 'Open Door' policy began in 1978, Chinese consumers have experienced an unprecedented consumer revolution. However, due to historical, economic and other related reasons, regional differences exist in the development of consumerism in China. This chapter investigates three key dimensions of growing consumerism in China: health consciousness, environmental consciousness and confidence in business ethics among the four major Chinese cities of Beijing, Guangzhou, Hangzhou and Xian. An ANOVA *post hoc* Scheffe test was employed for data analysis. Among the findings, it was revealed that consumers in Guangzhou were less environmentally conscious than their counterparts in the other three cities. It is concluded that firms should pay attention to existing regional differences in consumerism when formulating their marketing strategies for regional Chinese markets.

Introduction

With China's entry into the WTO, international firms are becoming excited about the lifting of the barriers to potentially the largest consumer market in the world. Since China's current economic reform launched in 1978, foreign firms have shown tremendous enthusiasm about the emerging China market. Thousands of foreign investors have entered the market in the last two decades. In the meantime, a new Cultural Revolution has taken place in China (Pollay et al 1990). Together with foreign investors, western goods, as well as marketing concepts and techniques, are flooding in. Consumers in China are quickly adopting new values and western ideas (Tai and Tam 1997, Wei and Pan 1999) because

of their increased exposure to global media and western lifestyles (Batra, 1997). Consequently, a new wave of consumerism is sweeping the mainland (Tong 1998).

For historical reasons, western China has been developing very slowly and the reason is thought to be the prevalent business philosophy (Sims and Schiff 2000). People in western China are generally more traditional and conservative than those in the east and south. However, little is currently known about whether there are significant differences between eastern, western, northern and southern regions of China in terms of the development of consumerism. By providing a better understanding of the different development stages of consumerism across China, this chapter aims to provide some valuable insights for MNCs designing their marketing strategies for the different Chinese regional markets.

We will specifically look at three extremely important and widespread phenomena resulting from growing consumerism in today's China: health consciousness, environmental consciousness and business ethics consciousness. Along with ongoing economic development, most Chinese people have experienced a significant improvement in living standards and as a result are paying more and more attention to their own health. Health consciousness is seen as one of the 'megatrends' to impact on the China market (Tong 1998) and Chinese women have been found to be more health conscious than their counterparts in Hong Kong and Taiwan (Tai and Tam 1997). The 'Open Door' policy has also brought about Chinese people's growing awareness of the importance of environmental protection. They have demonstrated much stronger environmental concern than their American counterparts (Chan 2000). Chinese female consumers were found to be more environmentally conscious than those in Hong Kong (Tai and Tam 1997). At the same time, consumerism has both bridged and exposed gaps in trust among entrepreneurs, government bureaucrats, and consumers (Veeck 2000). Chinese consumers are becoming increasingly conscious of business ethics. A survey of business people in eastern China revealed that business ethics has become a new and popular topic and business leaders have begun to realize its importance (Wu, 1999). These three issues are important to an understanding of China's growing consumerism.

Method

Sampling

A random sampling method was applied. Four major Chinese cities – Beijing, Hangzhou, Guangzhou and Xian – were selected, representing northern, eastern, southern and western China respectively. Data were collected by research assistants in local cities, using personal interview methods in key local shopping districts. These research assistants were mainland Chinese students recruited by referral and trained in the basic techniques of conducting personal interviews. Proper guidance and instruction were given before data collection started. Mall intercepts were carried out between December 1999 and February 2000 with every fifth person until a target of 200 was reached. Finally, 200 usable questionnaires each were collected from Beijing, Hangzhou and Xian. Some questionnaires from the Guangzhou group had a significant number of missing values resulting in only 196 usable cases. In the aggregate sample, there were 391 females and 402 males so the sample is evenly distributed between males and females.

40.2 per cent were aged 17–25, 24.8 per cent 26–35, 15.7 per cent 36–45, 15.9 per cent 46–55 and 3.4 per cent 56–68. These age groups represent those who are in active work and financially independent.

Measurement

After an extensive literature review, ten items related to trust in business ethics, environmental consciousness and health consciousness were selected to measure lifestyle dimensions. The questionnaire was initially developed in English, translated into Chinese and translated back into English following standard blind procedures to ensure the accuracy of translation. Finally, a Chinese version was used for data collection. A five-point Likert type scale was used for both lifestyle and marketing mix statements on consumers' post purchase perceptions of product quality, service quality and price, ranging from (1) 'strongly agree' to (5) 'strongly disagree'.

To ensure that all the measurements have good internal consistency, a Cronbach alpha test was applied to the three derived scales: trust in business ethics (a=0.68), environmental consciousness (a=0.62) and health consciousness (a=0.55). While alphas for two out of three scales are reasonably acceptable, alpha for the health consciousness construct is slightly lower than the threshold of a=0.60. However, from an exploratory perspective, a slightly lower alpha is still acceptable (Nunnally, 1978). To confirm the existence of three dimensions, a factor analysis was conducted. A principle component analysis was used as the extraction method. The rotation converged on four iterations, using the varimax method. It can be observed from Table 4.8.1 that three factors (Eigenvalue >1) were derived, resulting in an accumulated explained variance of 58.67 per cent.

Results

Data from four cities – Guangzhou, Beijing, Hangzhou, and Xian – were compared using a one-way ANOVA *post hoc* Scheffe test (see Table 4.8.2). There is no difference in consumers' health consciousness across the four cities and with all the arithmetic means below 2.02 ('1' strongly agree and '5' strongly disagree), indicating that Chinese consumers in all four cities are very health conscious.

Consumers in Guangzhou have a lower confidence in business ethics than those in Hangzhou and Xian. While there is no significant difference in consumers' confidence in business ethics between Guangzhou and Beijing, consumers in the latter turn out to be less confident than those in Hangzhou.

Consumers in Guangzhou are less environmentally conscious than in the other three cities. Interestingly, there is no difference between these three cities. Nevertheless, all the respondents indicated a fairly good environmental consciousness as all the arithmetic means are below 2.15.

Discussion and conclusion

Our goal was to explore the regional differences in China's growing consumerism. The results show that regional differences do exist.

Table 4.8.1 Factor analysis of lifestyle variables

	Factor 1	*Factor 2*	*Factor 3*
Trust in Business Ethics (a=0.69)			
You believe that product quality is improving	.721	117	–7.339E-02
You believe that firms are beginning to pay attention to customers' complaints	.721	4.763E	–6.228E-02
You believe that product trademarks start to follow rules and regulations	.720	159	7.097E-02
You believe that the dangers arising from using products are decreasing	.707	–9.076E-02	5.912E-02
Environmental Consciousness (a=.62)			
My country should invest in environmental protection	1.900E-02	.820	3.729E-02
The possibility of an energy crisis still exists	2.112E-02	.760	.188
From the country's point of view, the one child policy is necessary	.132	.666	1.006E-02
Health Consciousness (a=.55)			
Drinking is a bad hobby	3.293E-02	–3.172E-02	.865
Smoking can cause cancer	5.635E-02	.249	.768
Eigenvalue	2.081	1.805	1.394
Variance explained	23.126	20.057	15.491

Extraction Method: Principal Component Analysis.
Rotation Method: Varimax with Kaiser Normalization.
Rotation converged in 4 iterations.

Table 4.8.2 One-way ANOVA post hoc Scheffe Test of differences in lifestyles among Guangzhou, Beijing, Hangzhou and Xian

	Guangzhou (1)			*Beijing (2)*			*Hangzhou (3)*			*Xian (4)*		
	SD	*N*	*Mean*	*SD*	*N*	*Mean*	*SD*	*N*	*Mean*	*SD*	*N*	*Mean*
Health Consciousness	186	1.946	.930	198	1.980	.714	199	2.020	.763	198	1.846	.846
Confidence in Business Ethics	185	2.635	.607	195	2.542	.545	196	2.297	.515	196	2.431	.551
Environmental Consciousness	178	2.150	.906	195	1.670	.537	197	1.702	.457	195	1.622	.531

a Scales range from (1) 'Strongly Agree' to (5) 'Strongly Disagree'

Health consciousness

It is very interesting that no significant regional differences in consumers' health consciousness were found. The arithmetic means of this variable for all four cities are smaller than 2.02, indicating that Chinese consumers in all four cities are reasonably health conscious. A possible explanation is that Chinese people are historically health conscious. For example, many health-enhancing practices such as Tai Chi and Chi Kong are still very popular in today's China. Tong (1998) observed that one of the attractions for visitors to China is the number of people doing exercises such as Tai Chi, Chi Kung, social dances, or Kung Fu in public places in the mornings. As China makes the transition from a subsistence society to a *Xiao Kang* (comfortable) society, increasing attention is being given to personal health

(Tong, 1998). Chinese consumers are embracing a more casual and health conscious lifestyle (Geng et al 1996).

Environmental consciousness

The findings reveal that consumers in Guangzhou are less environmentally conscious than their counterparts in the other three cities. But there was no difference in environmental consciousness among the other three. Guangzhou is known to be a more market-oriented city than the other three, which are mainly tourist cities. Over-emphasis on economic growth through commercialization may have somewhat dampened consumers' environmental concerns in Guangzhou. According to CNN's *Asia Now* (1999), the World Bank listed Guangzhou, capital of the fastest growing province, Guangdong, and seven other Chinese cities among the ten most polluted cities in the world. Consumers in Guangzhou may have been too preoccupied with making money to pay attention to environmental issues. Beijing's bid for the 2000 Olympic Games and current successful bid for the 2008 Olympic Games may have contributed towards the increasing environmental awareness of its residents. Hangzhou is renowned for its natural beauty and is one of China's tourist cities while Xian is not a tourist city but is less industrialised than coastal cities such as Guangzhou. Nevertheless, respondents from the four cities had a relatively high environmental consciousness as the arithmetic means are below 2.15. This finding also lends further support to other studies that found Chinese consumers were more environmentally conscious than their western counterparts (Tai and Tam 1997; Chan 2000). However, what they do may not reflect what they say. Therefore, this finding should be treated with great caution.

Confidence in business ethics

Results show that consumers in Guangzhou and Beijing have less confidence in business ethics than those from Hangzhou and Xian. It is possible that with the increasing economic and commercial activities in Guangzhou, the number of illicit business practices is increasing. For example, in the Shenzhen Special Economic Zone, a model for China's economic reforms, one can buy cheaper Prada bags, pirated DVDs and even Louis Vuitton bags which are made in Guangdong (Perry 2001). Furthermore, as the political, economic and cultural centre, Beijing is exposed to a greater number of media reports of illegal and ethical practices throughout China than either Hangzhou or Xian.

Managerial implications

This study reveals no significant difference in consumers' health consciousness across all four cities and finds that consumers are fairly health conscious. MNCs should therefore develop non-differentiated marketing strategies for China's growing health and health related product market. As China prospers, people will live longer and be better taken care of. The traditional values of filial piety and respect for seniority will ensure that more resources are provided for health improvements and facilities for the aged. Therefore, there will be a substantial increase of consumption on health foods and health gadgets (Tong 1998) and more health and health related products will be needed throughout

China. Companies are advised to enter all four regional markets simultaneously.

For the green products market and 'green' consumers, MNCs should adopt a differentiated marketing strategy in China as the respondents in Guangzhou were found to be less environmentally conscious than their counterparts from other cities. Greater efforts may have to be made for Guangzhou. However, as it is understood that it is not so easy to be 'green' after all, firms should calculate carefully the costs and potential gains from being 'green'. For tourist cities such as Hangzhou and Xian, 'green' products may be more appealing to the local consumers. MNCs can put more emphasis on 'green' aspects of their products in these regional markets. Nevertheless, since all respondents demonstrated a positive environmental consciousness and consumers are also becoming more inclined to purchase eco-friendly products than before (Chan 2000), 'green' products will inevitably become more and more popular in China. MNCs should take advantage of being the first to produce and market products with an emphasis on 'green' features.

Respondents in Guangzhou were found to be less confident in business ethics than Hangzhou and Xian while Beijing consumers have even less confidence than in Xian. Therefore, MNCs should devote greater efforts in promoting consumers' confidence in their business operations in Guangzhou and Beijing. By promoting a positive corporate image throughout China, especially in cities such as Beijing, China's political, cultural and economic centre, MNCs can achieve a profound and far-reaching impact. Recent incidents of bad public relations by Toshiba notebooks and the Mitsubishi Jeep (Pajero) have seriously damaged both companies' images in China. Chinese consumers are now suing Toshiba for not compensating Chinese buyers (Smith 2000) while the government has banned the import of Pajero (Young 2001). MNCs, if they do not control their product quality properly, may find their development strategies for the China market severely handicapped.

Limitations and future research directions

One of the limitations of the study is that the data were only collected from four cities. Other equally representative cities were not included in the survey because of budget constraints. For instance, if different ethnic minorities had been surveyed, then the findings could have been more informative, possibly in terms of revealing more diversified consumerism resulting from regional differences in culture and ethnicity. Another limitation is that the reliability of the health consciousness scale is slightly lower than the threshold suggested by Nunnally (1978), even though the content validity seems reasonably high. Finally, the scope of the study is limited to the understanding of three key dimensions only of the growing consumerism in China.

Many more dimensions can be identified for future research. As Chinese consumers are maturing fast and the younger generation is becoming increasingly receptive to Western products, ideas and lifestyles, it is necessary to identify new emerging dimensions of consumerism. Furthermore, with China's entry into the WTO, Chinese markets will become more accessible to MNCs. Future studies could cover much wider geographical areas, particularly other parts of the Western China with more diversified ethnic cultures and lifestyles. Finally, as this study limited its scope to urban consumers, future studies could also look at the growing consumerism in rural areas and a comparison could be drawn between rural areas and urban cities. Although China is in the process of rapid industrialization, about 70 per cent of its population still lives in the countryside. Although no difference was found in consumers' health consciousness in the four cities, samples from the countryside in different regions might reveal a different picture.

References and bibliography

Batra, Rajeev (1997), Marketing Issues and Challenges in Transitional Economies, *Journal of International Marketing*, **5** (4), pp 95–114

Chan, Ricky R.K. (1999), Environmental Attitudes and Behavior of Consumers in China: Survey Findings and Implications, *Journal of International Consumer Marketing*, **11** (4), pp 25–52

Chan, Ricky Y.K. (2000), An Emerging Green Market in China: Myth or Reality? *Business Horizons*, March/April, pp 55–60

Child, John and Sally Stewart (1997), Regional Differences in China and their Implications for Sino-Foreign Joint Ventures, *Journal of General Management*, **23** (2), pp 65–86

CNN (1999), China's Industrial Growth Fuels Major Pollution Problems, *Asia Now*, September 26th

Cosmas, S (1982), Lifestyles and Consumption Patterns, *Journal of Consumer Research*, **8** (4), pp 453–455

Cui, Geng and Qiming Liu (2001), Emerging Market Segments in a Transitional Economy: A Study of

Urban Consumers in China, *Journal of International Marketing*, **9** (1), pp 84–106

Geng, Lizhong, Lockhart, B, Blakemore, C and Andrus, R (1996), Sports Marketing Strategy: A Consumer Behavior Case Analysis in China, *Multinational Business Review*, Spring, pp 147–154

Goldsmith, Ronald E, Freiden, Jon B. and Jacqueline C (1993), Social Values and Female Fashion Leadership: A Cross-cultural Study, *Psychology & Marketing*, **10** (5), pp 399–413

Harnett, Michael (1998), Expectation is the Key to Pricing, *Discount Store News*, September, pp 16 and 21

Hawkins, D., Best, R. and Coney, K. (1993), Consumer Behavior: Implications for Marketing Strategy, Plano, TX: Business Publications

Hui, Michael K. and David Tse (1996), What to Tell Consumers in Waits of Different Lengths: An Integrative Model of Service Evaluation, *Journal of Marketing*, **60** (April), pp 81–90

Lazer, W. (1963), Lifestyle Concepts and Marketing, in AMA *Proceedings on Scientific Marketing*, Chicago: American Marketing Association

Maslow, A. (1968), *Toward a Psychology of Being*, New York: Van Nostrand Co.

McGowan, Karen M. and Brenda J. Sternquist (1998), Dimensions of Price as a Marketing Universal: A Comparison of Japanese and U.S. Consumers, *Journal of International Marketing*, 6 (4), 49–65

Mitchell, A (1983), *The Nine American Lifestyles: Who We are and Where We Are Going*, New York: Warner Books

Nunnally, Ian (1978), *Psychometric Theory*, McGraw Hill

Perry, Alex (2001), Cross the Ling, *Time*, Asian Edition, May 7, 18–21

Shutte, Hellmut and Deannna Ciarlante (1998), *Consumer Behavior in Asia*, London: Macmillan

Sims, Thomas L. and Jonathan James Schiff (2000), Your Investment, *The China Business Review*, November and December, 44–49

Smith, Graign S. (2000), Miffed Chinese Sue Japan Companies, *The New York Times*, August 7, A.6

Tai, Susan H. C. and Jackie L. M. Tam (1997), A Lifestyle Analysis of Female Consumers in Greater China, *Psychology & Marketing*, 14 (3), 287–307

Thompson, Ann Marie and Peter F. Kaminski (1993), Psychographic and Lifestyle Antecedents of Service Quality Expectations, *Journal of Services Marketing*, 7 (4), 53–61

Tong, Louis (1998), Consumerism Sweeps the Mainland, *Marketing Management*, **6** (4), 32–3

Tse, David K., N. Zhou and Jonathan Zhu (1999), How They Spend their Money: An Empirical Investigation of Income Rise on Consumption Patterns for People's Republic of China Consumers, Working Paper, Chinese Management Centre, University of Hong Kong

Wei, Ran (1997), Emerging Lifestyles in China and Consequences for Perception of Advertising, Buying Behavior and Consumption Preferences, *International Journal of Advertising*, 16, 261–275

Marketing Consumer Products in China

Li Yong, Deputy Secretary General, China Association of International Trade

The concept of marketing has only recently been introduced to China. Initially, it was as a university course, not as a tool in supporting sales efforts. As a result of economic reforms, the government has ended the closed distribution system and allowed free market forces to develop mechanisms that respond to true market needs instead of bureaucratic wants. However, the immaturity of the market economy has contributed to irrational product composition, leading to over-supply of unmarketable commodities and piling up of inventories, while a buyer's market has eventually taken shape. In addition, the entry of foreign investment has further intensified the competition in the market. Marketers, both foreign and local, are racking their brains for marketing strategies that will attract more customers.

China has a booming consumer market. The gradual dispersion and decentralization of trading rights which has replaced top-down leadership, central authority and monopolistic positions, have allowed marketers to compete on almost all fronts. The marketing tools commonly used in western countries are also employed by Chinese marketers, although they may not be as integrated and holistic as they could be.

Pricing practices

Most Chinese consumers are sensitive to price and will usually choose less expensive products. Price competition is the practice most frequently employed by enterprises to compete for market share. There have been 'price wars' on VCRs, microwave ovens, television sets and food products such as packaged milk. Many Chinese companies believe in the strategy of *Bo Li Duo Xiao*, which means low profit margin and volume sales.

This belief has lead to a diverse range of pricing practices, including *Shi Dian Li* (10 per cent profit), ex-factory price, zero wholesale mark-up, etc. All of these tactics are based on the assumption that lower price will increase the speed of turnover and eventually generate high profit. This practice has led to vicious competition and culminated in the price of packaged milk in Shanghai being lower than the cost.

While low price strategy is widely adopted, some marketers use a high-price strategy, taking advantage of the conventional wisdom that *Pian Yi Wu Hao Huo* (cheap is no good) and *Yi Fen Qian Yi Fen Huo* (each additional cent paid is associated with additional value). This strategy is often associated with prestigious products or products that are intended to establish prestigious reputation. Foreign branded products or imported products are generally high-priced and perceived as superior products.

Other pricing strategies common to developed markets are also used by Chinese marketers including 'price lining', 'skim-the-oil' pricing, 'odd-even' pricing, 'was-is' pricing, 'special event' pricing and so on. It is interesting to observe the unique characteristics of psychological pricing practices in China, which go beyond the simple odd-even considerations. Some Chinese people have a superstitious belief in lucky numbers. Marketers price their products in such a way that the numbers denote good luck. For example, a piece of furniture may be priced at 1199 to indicate *Chang Chang Jiu Jiu* (long and lasting), or 4451 meaning *Shi Shi Ru Yi* (everything is as you wish). Other examples include: 518 (*Wo Yao Fa*, meaning I will have a fortune), 888 (*Fa Fa Fa*, meaning fortune, fortune and fortune), 1688 (*Yi Lu Fa Fa* – endless fortune down the road), etc.

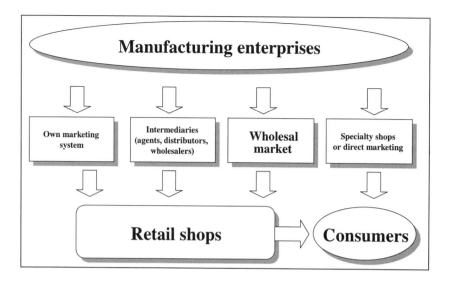

Figure 4.9.1 Typical marketing channels in China

Sales practices

The old days when products were produced and allocated according to government plans have gone. Companies will have to rely on their own sales or marketing teams to get their products to the market. They now face multiple choices of ways to market their products, including direct and indirect marketing.

Direct marketing can include such practices as soliciting direct orders from customers, setting up a retail outlet, door-to-door sales, telemarketing, TV sales, direct mail sales and internet marketing. Direct selling as a way of direct marketing used to be exercised by both domestic and foreign firms in China, the most notable being Amway and Avon. Unfortunately, criminals have also exploited direct selling systems and abuses such as price frauds, scams, sales of inferior/fake and smuggled products, seeking exorbitant wind-fall profits and tax evasions have been rife. All of these seriously impaired the interests of the consumers and derailed the normal economic order and so the Chinese government issued a ban on direct selling. Other direct marketing tools such as telemarketing, TV sales and Internet marketing are relatively new to Chinese consumers and there have been reports that these tools have not been very successful.

Indirect marketing channels as described in marketing textbooks are all used in China for marketing consumer products. There are over 1.36 million wholesalers and nearly 14 million retailers of consumer products in China. Manufacturing enterprises are using diversified channels of distribution to get their products to the consumers. Many set up regional branches to perform the function of wholesaler or distributor. To establish direct communication with consumers, an increasing number of manufacturing enterprises rent sales counters at retail outlets such as department stores and employ their own sales clerks. It is not rare to see special counters in department stores which are promoted as a factory outlet.

As a part of the sales effort, the old rule of 'goods sold are non-returnable' no longer holds and many marketers offer goods on a returnable basis if not satisfied. Warranties are also offered for durable goods. It has become common for heavy items to be delivered to the consumer's home free of charge.

As the government is allowing consumer credit to play a role in stimulating the consumption of valuable items, many enterprises and retailers are offering consumer credit either on its own or in cooperation with banks to consumers. Some marketers have begun to offer interest-free credit packages. According to an estimate, 10 per cent of urban households can afford consumer credit of over RMB100,000, 30 per cent between RMB50–100,000 and 20 per cent below RMB50,000.

It is worth noting that an increasing number of supermarkets, hypermarkets and chain stores have emerged in recent years, challenging conventional modes of retailing. They offer greater channel reach for manufacturers of consumer products. However, getting into supermarket chains is a costly exercise (see Figure 4.9.2).

Unconditional deduction: 45% of the total price of goods supplied for the first year
24% for the second year
Consulting service fee: Before 2001, 0.5% of the total price (including tax). Starting from 2002,
1% of the total price (including tax) to be deducted when settling payments in June, September
and December
Unconditional discount: 3.5% of of the total price (including tax) to be deducted from the
payment on monthly basis
Conditional discounts: 0.5% of the total price (including tax) when the annual sales is ≥
RMB700k, 1% of the total price (including tax) when the annual sales is ≥ RMB1 million
Order charge: 3% per store
Entry fee: RMB15,000 per store upon delivery of goods
Bar code fee: RMB1000 per product category

Shelf fee for new arrivals: RMB1,500 per store
Festival fee: RMB1,000 per store/time on five occasions – New Year, Spring Festival,
May Day, Mid-autumn Day and Christmas
Store anniversary fee: RMB1,500 per store/time, for two anniversary occasions –
international store anniversary and China store anniversary
POS poster fee: RMB2,500 per store/time, once in a year
Promotional stacking fee: RMB1,500 per store/time, three times in a year
Service charge for nationwide product recommendation: 1% of the total purchase price
(including tax) to be deducted on a monthly basis
Store renovation fee: RMB7,500 per store, to be charged at the location of the store
New store start-up fee: RMB20,000 per store, to be charged at the location of the new store
Penalties: a) all stores can only handle 5+1 categories as provided by the contract. Addition
of products or change of a product category will result in termination of contract and a fine
of RMB5,000. b) delivery of products should be made in three days including the date of
order. Suppliers are subject to a penalty of 0.3% of the contract value. A fine of RMB3,000
will be charged in case of failure to deliver.

Source: Beijing Evening Newspaper, 30 July 2002

Figure 4.9.2   The cost of entering the Carrefour chain

Advertising practices

Advertising is an important means of marketing. Many Chinese enterprises in one way or another believe that advertising will automatically generate sales. This belief has resulted in over-extended outlays on advertising and high prices. A recent example of exorbitant advertising expenditure is Qinchi liquor, who spent RMB320 million (US$38.55 million) in the open bidding for prime time advertising on CCTV (China Central Television Station), the only national television network. The only reward seemed to be the title of 'king of the bid', rather than the expected sales increase.

Terms such as gross rating point (GRP) or cost per thousand (CPT) in advertising theory seem to be unknown to most advertising decision-makers. Consequently, few have given thought to an integrated and holistic approach to communication. Interestingly, however, those foreign joint ventures that have been successful in advertising their products are rarely seen on the seething bidding floor. None has gone so far as to chase the title of 'king of the bid'.

For many years, most advertising dollars have gone to television media, as they are seen as the most effective channels of communication to create product awareness among potential consumers in China.

Over 50 per cent of the media have agency agreements with advertising companies and nearly half their business is given to advertising agencies as a result of the agency agreements. Advertising agents normally receive 15 per cent commission on advertising sales. The majority of the media requires advance payment, while advertisers are left with little recourse if the advertisement is not aired or published at agreed times. The lack of reliable ratings data is another problem that makes it difficult for advertisers to make decisions and evaluate the effectiveness of their advertising efforts.

Comparison advertising is not permitted under the Advertising Law, nor is the use of superlatives. All advertising copy must be reviewed and approved by the regulatory authority, the State Industrial and Commercial Administration, before going into media. Claims such as 'No 1' or 'Top selling' need to be supported by documentation, such as certificates issued by the relevant government agencies or authoritative survey organizations.

Higher prices used to be charged to foreign companies but this price discrimination has been removed and all companies, both foreign and local, now pay the same price. Advertising rates are reviewed and published on an annual basis.

Promotion practices

Both retailers and producers use consumer-oriented promotion techniques. These practices range from coupons, premiums and deals to prizes, lucky draws, contests and sweepstakes. The most common promotion methods are the following:

A) Buy one and get one or more free
- Open [the package] for a prize
- More product for the same price
- Discount coupons or token money coupons

B) Premiums
- Collecting labels or packages for prizes
- Numbered tickets for lucky draw
- VIP discount card for purchases reaching a certain value
- Prize winning contests
- Live radio broadcast of contests
- First-comer prize on live radio broadcast consulting on product attributes and usage
- Event-related price reduction or discount

C) Free samples slip
- On-site trials or demonstration
- Mail-back for lucky draw
- Turn in the old for a new one
- Membership privileges

D) Free products against advertisement slip
- Quantity discount
- Life time warranty
- Payment by instalments
- Consumer credit
- Shortage of one and compensation for ten[1]

E) Self-penalty for under-delivered quality[2]
- Trail use on marginal cost
- 100 per cent refund if not satisfied

The above list is not intended to be exhaustive. Obviously, these practices reflect the level of intensity in consumer market competition. When employing promotion techniques, either those listed above or others, it is important to develop appropriate consumer insights which are extremely critical in a market that is large in territory, diverse in consumer preferences across regions and rapid in its pace of change. Some research results have indicated that consumers are pragmatic in their attitudes toward promotion exercises. Buy one and get one free, price reduction or discount, discount coupons and premiums seem to be favoured by consumers.

However, marketers need to be very careful when designing promotion strategies and extreme situations should to be taken into consideration. The practice of free product offers against advertisement slips from newspapers has caused chaos in some instances when unexpected numbers of people besieged the site to claim free products that could not be offered. The guarantee of 100 per cent refund for unsatisfied consumers needs to be carefully thought out to prevent exploitation of the guarantee. Amway has run into situations where false consumers came to claim a refund with discarded or reclaimed empty bottles.

Branding practices

The lack of well-known brands is considered to be one of the weaknesses of Chinese consumer products manufacturers. A 'famous brand strategy' has been advocated by the government in a bid to improve the brand images and marketability of locally produced products. Painstaking efforts by local marketers has yielded some results, with some brands having established national recognition. The majority, however, have not yet made much progress in breaking away from the images of a local brand. Worse still, many brands are still unknown to their intended consumers.

Local marketers have a tendency, as they do with numbers, to favour brand names that convey goodness, luck, happiness, longevity and prosperity. In some cases,

---

[1] In China, some discredited factories do not deliver their promised products in terms of number or weight. To build consumer confidence, factories claim that they will compensate customers with ten times the amount of the shortage found.

[2] A similar practice where manufacturers assure customers that if the quality falls short of what is promised, they will penalize themselves to varying degrees.

brand names are associated with historical events. Few have tested their brand names before affixing them to their products. Because of the reputation of foreign products as premium quality, many local marketers even go so far as to give brand names that read and sound foreign. Local brands are often unrelated to product content or attributes, and therefore brand communications tend to be weak. In fact until recently, little effort was invested in developing a name or product image using integrated and holistic approaches. Clever marketers skipped brand name testing by putting out advertisements inviting consumers to give names for their products, but whether the arbitrarily chosen ones are liked by consumers is still unknown.

While some local marketers are trying to use brand names that have a foreign touch, foreign marketers are struggling to find a proper Chinese name for their brands. Indeed, it is often very difficult to translate a western brand name into Chinese. The usual approach is either to take on a new name and create new meaning, or give a similarly-sounding phonetic name. For example, P&G's Rejoice shampoo had a completely new name, Piao Rou, whose pronunciation is totally different, meaning 'softly wave to and fro', while its Pantene shampoo was transliterated as Pan Ting, which is phonetically similar and does not carry a specific meaning. Ideally, a brand should both have phonetic similarity and good meaning. A classical example of this is Coca-Cola, which is phonetically translated as Ke Kou Ke Le with the meanings of 'deliciously enjoyable' and 'bringing about happy laughter'. Asics sportswear has a Chinese name, Ai Shi Ke Si, which is again pronounced very similarly, but the meaning of 'love the world and overcome selfishness (or ego)' does not seem to be particularly well associated with the product.

Some foreign marketers, recognizing the difficulties in translating their brand names into Chinese, avoided the effort of associating the name with any particular Chinese meaning. Brands such as Philips, Nokia, Motorola, Electrolux and Sony are all using their transliterated names, and all have established brand recognition.

There are also instances where brand names already in use in Hong Kong are transplanted to the mainland. Some of the brands were a result of transliteration into Cantonese and read differently in Mandarin. McDonald's, Pizza Hut and Del Monte are typical examples.

Whichever way you go in adapting your brands to the local conditions, it is important that the Chinese brand names should be easy to read and to remember, and not too long. Brand names longer than four Chinese characters will be difficult both to read and remember. The name chosen should be commonly used words. Strange words will cause difficulties in brand recognition. For example, the last word of the two-Chinese-word brand for Del Monte is difficult to find in a regular dictionary. Another factor that should be taken into consideration when adopting a Chinese brand name is the diverse dialects. A brand name that reads well in Mandarin may be read very differently in different dialects meaning very different things. A normal exercise of brand name testing would cover at least three cities such as Guangzhou, Shanghai and Beijing to make sure that the name does not carry undesired meanings.

However, a good brand name does sell itself on the merit that it has a good meaning. Effective branding means more than Chinese labelling. A brand image manifests itself in many ways: in a memorable brand name and well-designed logo, attractive packaging, in the quality and services associated with the brand, and, importantly, in integrated marketing communications.

Developments in Chinese Logistics

Li Yong, Deputy Secretary General, China Association of International Trade

The 'dark continent' is still dark

As early as the 1960s, logistics was described by the American management guru Peter Drucker as 'the economy's dark continent' and 'the last frontier for competitive advantage'. Over the 40 years since then, logistics has been seen in the developed world as an effective means of optimizing corporate resources to reduce costs and achieve profit objectives. In the context of economic globalization, the 'last frontier' is exploited on a global basis.

In China, however, the concept was not introduced until the 1970s, when logistics was discussed only within the domain of material management and mostly at an academic level. It was not until the early 1990s that logistics was brought into standard practice. It has now become a buzzword in China; it is 'cool' for the managers to talk about logistics, particularly among those companies that have traditionally been in the transportation, warehousing and distribution businesses. The concept of logistics has also attracted the attention of the Chinese government, who have become convinced that logistics is a modern tool of supply chain management that will help turn around state assets and add impetus to reform efforts. As State Councilor Wu Yi commented in her letter to a symposium on logistics and e-commerce in 2000, '(logistics) will help realize the two fundamental transformations in China's economic structure and economic growth, and promote the sustainable and healthy growth of the Chinese economy', and 'Central government has decided that logistics and distribution will be a priority in the service industry for the country's tenth five year plan period between 2001 and 2005'.

Logistics has clearly been given significant strategic weight in the national plans as well as at the corporate level. But what is logistics all about? What standards will apply when delimiting the content and scope of logistics as an industry? While these questions, and many others, need to be answered, logistics has been seen as the holy grail that every business searches for, as a result of which thousands of companies – who may well be nothing more than transportation or warehousing companies – have registered themselves as logistics firms. In Beijing, there were more than 120 company registrations under 'logistics' in 2001. The number of logistics companies had exceeded 1000 in Shanghai by the end of 2001. In the past two years or so, over 70,000 companies have registered as logistics providers. Yet two years ago, the Chinese term for logistics wasn't even recognized by business registration authorities. Large enterprise groups, typically consumer electronics giants like TCL and Haier, who have painstakingly developed their distribution networks through years of marketing effort, have also announced plans to cash in on the logistics opportunities, taking advantage of their existing networks.

At a seminar on 'Challenges to the modernization of logistics in China' in September 2001, the attendees, consisting of government and association officials, reviewed the development of China's logistics and conclusion that logistics is not clearly enough defined in China. Logistics is translated in Chinese as *wu liu*, which literally means 'material flow', suggesting that logistics is related to movement of physical goods or physical distribution. Interestingly, however, the term *wu liu* was borrowed from the Japanese, who still use some Chinese characters. The convenience of importing the term from Japan has caused debate over whether this Chinese term can properly reflect the dimension of modern logistics. Academics who have learned more about the concept from western practices and theories, argued that *wu liu* had limitations in conveying logistics as a modern concept of management. Some suggested that *wu liu* should be changed in order to differentiate the term from conventional understandings of material management or physical distribution.

Since the term has been in use for nearly three decades, it was decided to retain it as it is, although it may sound misleading. The problem is not really how logistics should be translated or theoretically defined as a concept but more in the definition of what should go into the 'basket' of logistics and what policies should be implemented in relation to logistics as a burgeoning sector. In addition, there was an argument at the seminar that the WTO's General Agreement on Trade in Services has not singled out logistics as a separate sector, and China has not made commitments to logistics in its WTO concession arrangements. This argument does not really challenge China's commitments to the WTO in terms of opening up its service sector as logistics should fall into the scope of services. It is important, however, that logistics should be defined and recognized both legally and administratively, with a series of workable qualification standards and policy measures to support its development, as well as avoiding possible arbitrariness or conflicting rules and regulations in the administration of logistics businesses at both central government and local level.

Indeed, a multitude of government bodies are involved in decision-making on the development of logistics and there needs to be coordinated policy-making among them. On 1 March 2001, six central government departments – the State Economic and Trade Commission, the Ministry of Railways, Ministry of Communications, Ministry of the Information Industry, Ministry of Foreign Trade and Economic Co-operation and the General Administration of Civil Aviation of China – jointly issued a circular entitled 'Several Opinions on Expediting the Development of Modern Logistics in China'.

This is the first policy guidance related to and with explicit reference to logistics. It assessed the situation in logistics development and recognized it as a value-creating tool for economic development in China. Modern logistics is described by the circular as a new growth point for the Chinese economy. It calls for the provision of guarantees by government departments at all levels in terms of policies and laws/regulations in

order to promote the marketability of logistics. State Economic and Trade Commission will coordinate the policy-making and legislation of laws and regulations on logistics. Regarding the opening up of the logistics sector to foreign participation, the circular recommends synchronisation with the opening up of transport services and distribution and that the entry of foreign logistics providers into the Chinese market should be actively sought.

In fact, foreign-invested logistics providers are already operating in China. According to the 2002 White Paper on American Businesses in China, published by the American Chamber of Commerce-PRC, there are only four solely foreign-owned companies in China offering logistics outside the special economic zones. Licensing options include forming joint ventures with local agents or operating within special zones. In this context, the circular advocated that governments at all levels should speed up the pace of opening up the logistics sector and encourage hands-on cooperation with foreign logistics providers. With the quickening of economic globalization, increased participation by foreign logistics providers is inevitable.

Logistics infrastructure

China's logistics infrastructure has developed rapidly since the economic reform and opening up, although it is still insufficient to meet the growing demand of the developing economy and the needs of modern logistics. Table 4.10.1 provides a snapshot of the transport infrastructure over the period 1996–2000.

Railways

The railway is losing its position as the main method of freight transport. It once carried over 75 per cent of the country's freight but now takes only 13.1 per cent of total freight volume, of which 2.46 per cent is containerized traffic. The sector is heavily controlled by the state. The lack of flexibility in transport schedules and prices has contributed to the railway's shrinking market share.

Ports

By the end of 2000, China had 581 deep-water berths for vessels of 10,000 tons and above along its coasts and inland river ports, and a total 26.19 million tonnage of ocean-going vessels. According to Customs statistics, inbound and outbound containers totalled 25.46 mil-

Table 4.10.1 China's transport infrastructure: development 1996–2000 (thousand km)

Item	1996	1997	1998	1999	2000
Length of operating railways	56.7	57.6	57.6	57.9	58.7
Electrified Railways	*10.1*	*1.2.0*	*13.0*	*14.0*	*14.9*
Total length of highways	1,185.8	1,226.4	1,278.5	1,351.7	1,402.7
Length of navigable inland waterways	110.8	109.8	110.3	116.5	119.3
Total length of civil aviation routes	1,166.5	1,425.0	1,505.8	1,522.2	1,502.9
International routes	*386.3*	*504.4*	*504.4*	*523.3*	*508.4*
Petroleum and gas pipelines	19.3	20.4	23.1	24.9	24.7

Source: China Statistical Yearbook 2001

lion TEUs, among which 25 million TEUs were in ocean shipping containers. Apart from Hong Kong, Shanghai and Shenzhen Ports are among the 10 largest container ports in the world.

Airfreight

There are 139 civilian airports in China. In 2000, airfreight had a negligible share – only 1.97 million tons – of China's total volume of freight. However, it had been increased at an average annual rate of 14.36 per cent in the 1996-2000 period and it is expected that airfreight will increase at an average rate of 13 per cent over the next five to ten years. Currently, airfreight and air express services are mainly covered by passenger aircraft. Airfreight is rarely connected with other modes of transport and there is a lack of sufficient warehousing capabilities at most airports. Also, value-added services such as processing and consolidation are rarely available.

Highways

Highway transport plays an important role in the movement of goods in China. In 2000, 10.39 billion tons (76.49 per cent) of China's total freight was carried by trucks. The total size of the truck fleet in China was 7.16 million, 6.97 million of which were standard sized trucks. Long trailers are rarely seen on the roads. The level of containerization is low.

Warehousing

Another element of the logistics infrastructure is warehousing. A survey of the commerce sector, ie wholesale and retail, grain supply, industrial material supply, rural supply and marketing and foreign trade, revealed that there is a total warehousing capacity of more than 300 million square metres. The capacity is even larger if the warehousing capacities owned by the transport sector,

postal services and industrial operations are taken into account. However, most warehouses are simple and crude. Improvements and renovations are badly needed.

Information technology

In 2000, fibre optic networks exceeded a total length of 300,000 kilometres. Together with digital microwaves and satellites, China has a fairly sophisticated telecommunications network covering all the major cities and 90 per cent of the counties and townships. Internet services have developed rapidly. The total number of Internet users had reached 33.7 million by the end of 2001, an increase of 49.8 per cent. The application of broadband transmission technology has alleviated the bottleneck in Internet services.

Future plans

In an effort to further improve the logistics infrastructure, China will increase capital input to beef up the transport capabilities in the tenth five year plan period. RMB270 billion (roughly US$33 billion) will be invested in railroad construction and by 2005, the total length of operating railroad will be 75,000 kilometres. An additional 26,000 kilometres of trunk-line highway will be built, upon completion of which 99.5 per cent of the townships and 93 per cent of administrative villages will be connected by highways.

It is recognized that economic globalization and China's integration into the world will accelerate China's trade flows, which will require improved handling capabilities by major Chinese ports. The government will therefore intensify its efforts to improve port facilities. One such effort is the construction of the Shanghai port into an international shipping centre. Containerization of the key ports such as Shanghai, Ningbo, Dalian, Tianjin, Qingdao and Shenzhen will receive priority support from the government and fourth-generation or higher standard container docks will be constructed at those ports. By the year 2005, the container throughput capacity of China will reach 50 million TEUs. There are also plans to renovate or build 200 inland shipping berths, an addition of 25 million tons to the existing capacity.

Airfreight capabilities will also be improved. As mentioned above, total airfreight volume is expected to reach 2.8 million tons by 2005. To achieve this target, three major airfreight terminals will be constructed in Beijing, Shanghai and Guangzhou.

China has the necessary basic infrastructure to support reasonable growth in logistics, while recognizing the need to improve value-added service capabilities to meet the requirements of modern logistics.

Huge potential demand for logistics

China is now the seventh largest economy in the world and this means a huge demand for logistics. In 2001, China's GDP was RMB9.59 trillion (about US$1.16 trillion). According to World Bank estimates, logistics costs account for 16.7 per cent of China's GDP. Industry experts in China believed that the costs of logistics could be 20 per cent or even higher, twice as much as in developed countries. Based on this, total spending on logistics could amount to RMB1.92 trillion.

To understand the potential demand for logistics, it is worth taking a look at the levels of growth in some of the key industries where logistical opportunities lie.

Secondary industry

The value-added of secondary industry (see Table 4.10.2) hit a record high of RMB4.91 trillion in 2001, having

Table 4.10.2 Value-added of secondary industry (manufacturing and construction)

Year	Amount (RMB billion)
1996	3,361.29
1997	3,722.27
1998	3,861.93
1999	4,055.78
2000	4,548.78
2001*	4,906.90

Source: China Statistical Yearbook 2001
*2001 figure is a preliminary estimate by the China Statistical Bureau

grown at an average annual rate of 9.8 per cent within the ninth five year plan period. Total sales of industrial materials amounted to RMB5.5 trillion.

Retail

The retail sector has experienced sustained growth over recent years. Total retail sales of consumer products grew at an average annual rate of 10.6 per cent in the ninth five year plan period and 2001 saw a new high of RMB3,759.5 billion. The retail infrastructure has also undergone significant changes in the past few years and will require higher standards in logistics services.

Table 4.10.3 Total sales of consumer products 1995–2001

Year	Amount (RMB billion)
1995	2,477.4
1996	2,062.0
1997	2,684.3
1998	2,915.3
1999	3,113.5
2000	3,415.3
2001*	3,759.5

Source: China Statistical Yearbook 2001
*2001 figure is a preliminary estimate by the China Statistical Bureau

Agriculture

The efficient flow of agricultural products depends very much on the quality of the logistics. Products need to be moved from farming areas to the market for industrial and consumer consumption. They also need to be processed on their way to the markets for added value. In value terms, China's agricultural sector has been increasing at an average rate of 3.5 per cent in the period of the ninth five year plan (see Table 4.10.4).

Import and export trade

Imports and exports are economic power engines of China (see Table 4.10.5). In the period from 1996 to 2000, China's import and export trade increased at an annual rate of 11 per cent. Exports come from all over the country, are consolidated at the ports and go from there to other parts of the world. Likewise, imports arrive at Chinese ports for onward distribution into all parts of China. Both imports and exports need efficient

Table 4.10.4 Production of key agricultural products

Item	2000	2001*
Grains	462.18	452.62
Cotton	4.417	5.32
Oil bearing crops	29.548	28.72
Sugar cane and beet	76.353	87.90
Fruits	62.251	65.36
Aquatic products	42.784	43.75
Forestry products	2.623	
Meat	61.246	63.40
Poultry and eggs	22.433	

Source: China Statistical Yearbook 2001

*2001 figures are preliminary estimates by the State Statistical Bureau

Table 4.10.5 Import and export value, 1996–2001

Year	Total import and export value (US$ billion)
1995	280.9
1996	289.9
1997	325.1
1998	324.1
1999	360.6
2000	474.3
2001*	509.8

Source: China Statistical Yearbook 2001

*2001 figures are preliminary estimates by the State Statistical Bureau

logistics to deliver the right products to the right place in the right quantity and at the right time.

E-commerce

China's fledgling e-commerce industry has been developing rapidly over recent years. In 2000, B2B and B2C online transactions exceeded RMB700 million. Transactions from Internet 'matchmaking' reached RMB70 billion and it is reported that a proportion of the RMB60 billion government purchases in 2001 were also made via the Internet. According to an UNCTAD report, the total transaction value of e-commerce in China in 2001 was US$9.33 billion, 80 per cent of which was B2B. The Internet is emerging as an important mode of commerce and many Chinese enterprises use it as an alternative marketing channel. The statistics of the China Article Numbering Centre reveal that among those who have set up Internet sales capabilities,

13.5 per cent are in the manufacturing industry, 12.5 per cent in the wholesale sector and 17.9 per cent in retail. One bottleneck among others in the development of China's e-commerce is the lack of an efficient delivery system, a problem to which modern logistics can provide a solution.

Other sources of demand

Other sources of demand for logistics could include bonded zones, wholesale markets and the recuperation of recyclable resources.

According to a survey of China's 15 bonded zones in 2000, total imports and exports in those zones reached US$18.7 billion. The average import and export capacity of the bonded zones is US$1.25 billion. These zones are mostly located along the coastal areas and close to seaports. After China's WTO entry, the role of bonded zones may be challenged as a result of tariff concessions, but new opportunities lie in the existing warehousing and processing capabilities that can be developed into logistics and distribution capabilities. Bonded zones will allow third-party logistics providers to establish warehouse and distribution centres. Goods can be stored in bond until needed, delaying payment of customs duties and VAT, and keeping stocks of products closer to Chinese customers and consumers.

There are currently over 3,000 wholesale markets with a total transaction value of over RMB100 million. These markets play a very important role in the distribution of goods in China. The total value of transactions for these wholesale markets reached RMB1.64 trillion in 2000, equivalent to 20 per cent of the country's GDP and 47.8 per cent of total retail sales of consumer products. The flow of goods in and out of those wholesale markets will require efficient logistical support.

Recuperation of recyclable resources also offers logistics opportunities. There are large quantities of scrap materials sent for recycling each year: 3 million tons of scrap steel, 200,000 tons of scrap non-ferrous metals, 2 million tons of scrap paper, over 200,000 scrap cars, 800,000 tons of scrap plastics and 1 million tons of scrap glass.

Third-party logistics

The development of third party logistics with advanced warehousing, distribution and inventory management systems has been slow, although there has been a steady increase in the demand for third party logistics over the past few years. According to surveys commissioned by the China Association of Warehousing and Storage in 1999, 2000 and 2001, the share of third-party logistics in the distribution of finished products by manufacturing enterprises increased from 9.1 per cent in 1999 to 16.1 per cent in 2000, and to 21 per cent in 2001. The abundant supply of cost-effective labour and a lack of sophisticated logistics technology has in part hindered the demand for outsourcing logistics to third parties. Another reason is that the vestiges of the planned economy in the form of a fully fledged enterprise structure and self-sufficiency, resulting in a reluctance to hand over to stand-alone logistics.

Although the process of forming a modern third-party logistics system is slow, a structure has begun to take shape. There are four basic categories of third-party logistics providers in the market:

Logistics companies that have evolved from the traditional state-owned warehousing and transport enterprises

These logistics companies have inherited the state-owned logistics resources, such as infrastructure, customer base, operating networks and facilities, all of which have given them advantages in making the transformation towards becoming third-party logistics providers. They are taking a dominant position in the third-party logistics market, although they are still learning to extend their services beyond physical movements of goods. Such companies include COSCO and Sinotrans, who are developing intermodal and integrated service offerings and investing in port and infrastructure improvements.

Newly established logistics providers that are state-owned enterprises or state-equity-controlled enterprises

These logistics providers are the offspring of enterprise reform towards a modern corporate system. They have relatively complete corporate governance and operate independently of their parent companies. One such company is China Shipping Logistics, which is a state-owned company and was established in 1997. This company is now providing third-party logistics services such as warehousing, transportation, distribution and customs clearance to a number of multinational companies. Another example is Tsingtao Beer Merchants Logistics, which has been spun off from its parent Tsingtao Beer Group and merged with China Merchants Logistics to become an independent third-party logistics provider.

Private logistics providers

Although many of these logistics providers are small in terms of size of operation, they have the advantages of being flexible in their operating mechanisms and low in overhead costs. Many of these private logistics providers are locally based and there have been a small number able to offer cross-region services. One successful logistics provider in this category is PG Logistics Group. This company started by contracting a rail freight transit station in 1992. In 1994, the company began to provide logistics services to Procter and Gamble. It has now developed into a leading third-party logistics provider, with over 40 branches or offices in key Chinese cities. There are over 40 multinationals in its customer base.

International third-party logistics providers

These companies have the advantage of advanced business concepts, well-established business models and quality services and provide extensive logistics services for their international customers. Typically, they provide services in China to those companies that they have already been servicing at home. An example of such a company is Japan's Kintetsu World Express Co Ltd, which chiefly provides logistics services to Japanese companies in China. These international logistics companies have ambitious plans to expand their services in China's post-WTO era. Maersk Logistics, for example, have established their own National Distribution Centre in Shanghai, the first of its kind in China. In the airfreight arena, the big names such as FedEx, UPS and DHL have all made ambitious moves to expand and diversify their China operations to capture the growth in third-party logistics.

Despite the fact that third-party logistics needs to be fleshed out by adopting modern logistics concepts and technologies, it has developed at a high rate over the past few years. According to the China Federation of Logistics and Purchasing, third-party logistics is growing at an annual rate of 30 per cent. In addition, a research survey carried out by the China Association of Warehousing and Storage on China's logistics market indicated that there was great potential demand for third-party logistics. Among the enterprises interviewed, 57 per cent of the manufacturing enterprises and 38 per cent of the commercial enterprises stated that they are looking for new logistics agents.

Most third-party logistics is taking place in the more dynamic areas of China, such as Guangdong province and the Shanghai-Zhejiang-Jiangsu cluster, where many manufacturing and export-oriented processing operations are concentrated. The relatively small sizes of those manufacturing and processing operations have in part determined the fragmented structure of third-party logistics in those areas. In addition, the logistics services are mostly limited to basic warehousing and transport. Few third-party logistics providers offer value-added services such as processing, packaging, consolidation, distribution management and order processing. These deficiencies in third-party logistics development leave substantial room for improvements, while at the same time offering great potential for growth. Industry experts forecast that third-party logistics will grow by 25-30 per cent over the next four or five years. As a general observation, it is interesting to see that China's railways and postal services, which are facing competitive attacks from various fronts, are planning to play a significant role in the third-party logistics market. Their existing networks bring obvious advantages, but winning bureaucratic administration over to modern logistics management concepts remains a challenge.

Challenges ahead

The general belief that logistics is the 'third source of profit' and the central government's supportive approach to logistics development as a new area of economic growth have prompted more than 30 cities to put logistics at the top of their development agenda. Many have engaged a significant amount of capital in building 'logistics centres'. In a country such as China, macro leveraging by government policies does play an important role in terms of guiding development into the desired direction.

There has previously been no separate category in the national economic administration system for logistics. In other words, logistics cannot be fitted into any existing industrial sector and so government support is important to eliminate unnecessary administrative barriers. However, excessive government involvement in designing the development of logistics, regardless of economic rationale, may lead to distortion of the logistics market. Should logistics be demand-driven or supply-pushed? Or, should logistics be developed with the 'invisible hand' being the determinant? The answers

to these questions need to be supported by the fundamentals and not just by the government's goodwill. If everybody jumps on the bandwagon of the 'logistics economy', will an investment bubble be generated?

Inadequate technology and limited capacity to innovate are particular weaknesses of many industries in China. In many respects, logistics in China – both in-house and third party – fall short of the technological and management requirements of modern logistics. For example, in the case of data communications, although there have been growing electronic links between supply chain participants, there has also been an absence of logistics tools (ie software) to offer effective tracking systems. There is also a lack of IT specialists to take care of data communications on both sides of a logistics relationship – shippers and logistics providers. Shippers' general reluctance to share information with logistics providers is also an impediment to effective two-way data communication. As well as all this, the information infrastructure varies in quality from place to place, which causes real problems for electronic connections.

Regional blockades and departmental partition have remained a frontier to conquer before logistics services can effectively move goods around unchecked across different regions and industries. Rail, road and water transport are under the jurisdiction of different government departments, all of which have plans to develop logistics capabilities. Departmentalism may result in the patronage of the department's own logistics providers, driving others out of competition, while a regional blockade will check the free flow of goods and services, all of which will endanger the optimisation and integration of logistics resources. Effective coordination between different departments and regions is key to the healthy development of logistics in China.

The misconception of logistics by shippers as a 'third source of profit' has resulted in a reluctance to outsource logistics services. Many enterprises have in-house transport capabilities, which encourage decision-makers to take a step further by developing in-house logistics. In addition, there have also been fears that outsourcing logistics may lead to a loss of control over purchasing and sales, the additional lay-off of workers and disposal of transport assets at discounted values. Moreover, there is often a gap between what logistics can ideally do in terms of cost reduction, and logistics providers' actual ability to deliver on their claimed advantages. The lack of qualified personnel in logistics management has also been attributed to low levels of confidence in the quality of servicee offered by logistics providers. Third party logistics providers will need to take time and effort to educate buyers, while at the same time sharpening their skills to provide really cost-effective services.

Following accession to the WTO, China has pledged to offer national treatment to foreign logistics providers. The entry of foreign logistics providers will not only bring in modern logistics technology and management expertise, but also, more importantly, trigger off intense competition. Competition will lead naturally to the consolidation and integration of the existing logistics structure, and eventuallyvthe convergence of China's logistics services to international standards.

To conclude, the saying that has become popular when assessing competitive situations in China – 'challenges and opportunities co-exist' – may best describe the future trend of logistics development.

Brand Management and Publicity

Li Yong, Deputy Secretary General, China Association of International Trade

Brand management

Local brand vs foreign brand

Among many other things to consider in a venture investment in China, one key issue in the area of marketing is the branding of the product(s) that the venture will produce. In an equity joint venture with a Chinese partner, there is always a trade-off in terms of whose brand should be used in the marketing of the products. There are usually the following options:

Local brand
'Local brand' here refers to the brand(s) that have been used by the Chinese partner for marketing in China. In many cases the brand owned by the Chinese partner would be sold to the foreign partner as equity. Apart from the bargaining process, one key point of consideration would be whether a local brand has an advantage over other options such as the brand name owned by the foreign partner, or the creation of a new brand. The local brand may have the following attributes to attract it to the foreign partner:

- brand image already established;
- brand awareness, easy recognition and ready acceptance among customers/consumers;
- existing distribution network and market share.

However, a foreign partner may also have the following concerns about the pitfalls of using a local brand. These could include:

- poor brand image associated with poor quality products/services;

- low level of awareness, recognition and acceptance by customers/consumers;
- poor distribution and small market share.

It is a complicated process to find out whether or not a local brand has the necessary value. Careful market research is essential in determining whether a local brand should be adopted before commitment is made. Some joint ventures use a local brand to cash in on its expanded marketing efforts and improved product/service attributes. Some adopt local brands as part of their multi-branding strategy. All of these will have to be weighed against the cost and benefits of using a local brand.

Foreign brand
'Foreign brand' here refers to a brand that the foreign partner of a joint venture already owns and wants to introduce into the local market by way of investment. As a part of globalization, the introduction of foreign brands – particularly those that have been marketed internationally and gained worldwide recognition – is the preferred way of branding joint venture products. Using foreign brands is often perceived as a symbol of market presence and penetration.

However, promoting foreign brands in order to increase awareness and build a quality image will be a long-term engagement, resembling similar patterns of development as in the home country and entailing a strong financial commitment. The general perception by consumers in China that a foreign branded or a joint venture product is a synonym for good quality has encouraged many foreign companies entering into joint ventures in China to use their own brands. Chinese partners also welcome foreign brands for the conventional belief that a foreign brand will increase the marketability of the products. Increasingly, however, Chinese partners have learned from experience that there is a danger of losing their own established brand when they adopt a foreign brand from their foreign partner. Two examples are the microwave oven manufacturer and the colour film manufacturer who have refused a number of joint venture proposals because of the use of foreign brands.

Although some foreign manufacturers have been successful in using their own brands in China, others have experienced difficulties in keeping the quality image of the products and services that their brands represent. Factors associated with the brand image need to be considered and evaluated before a decision can be made to use your own brand. Among others, the following factors are considered to be critical:

- **Product quality**. When managing the brand in China, the brand owner will have be sure that the quality associated with the brand will be guaranteed in terms of raw materials and production. At the same time, the manufacturer's quality will have to be adapted to meet the standards set by local government. Otherwise, there may be quality problems subjecting the brand image to question;
- **Quality of services**. Service is an important part of the brand image. The brand owner will have to be sure that services will be provided to the consumer/customer in such a way that they satisfy the expectations of the brand. If quality services can not be guaranteed, it will threaten the brand image;
- **Effectiveness of distribution**. The effectiveness of the joint venture's distribution network will have to be assessed. If the distribution is such that the foreign branded products cannot reach the consumers/customers in time and there is little that can be done to improve it in the short term, the strengths that the brand may have will only be a theoretical advantage.

The solution to these problems hinges on how much control the brand owner could have over the joint venture operations. This control is not just a matter of majority holding but it can be achieved through good contract negotiation. If the Chinese management shares the same marketing concepts as the foreign partners, the above disadvantages can be transformed into strengths. However, things do not always happen as expected. When the owner of a foreign brand cannot be sure whether the operations will be such that the chances of damaging the brand image as well as the corporate image are minimized, it might be safer to create a new brand.

New brand

A new brand can be the result of compromises from both sides of the joint venture, or similarities in strategic thinking. Whatever it might appear to be, a new brand is the product of the union between the Chinese and foreign partners. The advantages of having a completely new brand are that agreement between both sides can be easily reached and there will be a common objective in promoting the brand. The shared interests in the brand will provide incentives for both sides to co-operate. The disadvantages could be that there may not be ready recognition if part of the production is intended for export markets. If export is an essential part of the joint venture agreement, a separate brand arrangement might be necessary.

Joint branding

Another compromise, or a strategy to circumvent the deadlock of branding, is joint branding, where the identities of both partners can be maintained and reflected in the brand. In fact, this is not a bad strategy for foreign firms to adopt at the early stage of joint venturing, avoiding risking their own brand image if product quality and related services are unstable. A joint brand gives consumers/customers a clear message that the product is made by a joint venture, whose quality is generally believed to be higher than that of local products.

The advantages of such exercise are:

- None of the partners of the joint venture need worry about losing their own brand identities;
- Promotion of the joint brand will increase awareness of both brands;
- Resources committed to promoting the joint brand will reflect the fair-deal principle;
- The image of foreign brands can be maintained as a separate brand;
- It is easy to create recognition in both domestic and overseas markets.

Selecting a good brand name

A good brand name may add value to the good quality and services associated with the brand. A bad brand name may already have given the consumer/customer an unpleasant impression, which may even have prevented them from trying the product. Goldlion, a brand for men's clothes and accessories, used to experience sluggish sales in Hong Kong, because the pronunciation of the literal translation of the brand in Cantonese was associated with the meaning 'willing loss', or 'lose always'. The Chinese translation was later changed to mean 'gold profit comes'; sales increased substantially and it has become a prestigious brand.

There are no hard and fast rules for picking a good brand name. When creating a new brand name or giving a foreign brand an appropriate Chinese name, it is advisable to consider the following principles:

- The brand name should use words that are within the vocabulary of most of the consumers. Unusual or difficult to pronounce words, or words that have more than one pronunciation should be avoided.
- The brand name should be short and easy to read, pronounce and remember. Most of the brand names in China are two or three words. Some, such as Coca-Cola and Pepsi-Cola, have four. There is hardly any brand that has five Chinese words.
- The pronunciation of the brand name should not carry any possible negative implications. The name of the beer brand 'Yunhu'(meaning cloud lake) also sounds like the words for 'dizzy' and 'muddleheaded' in Chinese.
- The brand name should carry positive implications with regard to the product's function, uses and features. Tylenol cold drug has a Chinese name – Tai Nuo – meaning 'safe' or 'peaceful' promise. The Chinese name of Signal toothpaste, Jie Nuo, means 'clean promise'.
- Of course, a brand name should not have the potential to cause legal problems.

A good name might result from a brainstorming session among the marketing people of a company. In order to eliminate possible negative connotations, references or associations, however, it will be safer to test the name or names among consumers/customers. China is a country of multiple dialects and so testing should be carried out in different places with different dialects. In practice, Beijing, Shanghai and Guangzhou are chosen to test brand names in order to make sure that the selected name does not have negative elements when pronounced in different dialects.

Brand protection

China has promulgated a series of laws and regulations to protect the rights of the owners of intellectual property. These are covered in more detail elsewhere in this book.

The government attaches great importance to its counter-faking efforts and several campaigns are waged each year to fight against counterfeits. China's crackdown on counterfeits checks illegal activities from both the production and distribution sides. The production of counterfeits is illegal and sales of counterfeits are also illegal. If retailers are found to be selling counterfeits, they are subject to penalties and the buyer of the counterfeits is compensated at twice the price at which the counterfeits are sold. Apart from government efforts, there are also non-governmental organisations and individuals engaged in the crackdown on counterfeits. All these have enhanced consumer awareness to reject and fight against counterfeit products.

Brand owners should properly register the brand with relevant authorities in China in order to protect the brand from the legal point of view. The Great Hall of the People, the place where national conferences are held, has registered its name, *'Ren Min Da Hui Tang'*, with the State Administration of Industry and Commerce for 288 varieties in 22 categories. This was intended to prevent manufacturers from taking advantage of the trust that people have in the name. Wahaha Group, a manufacturer of baby health food, has registered not only the brand name 'Wahaha', but also other similar names, such as Hahawa, Wahawa, Hawaha and Hawawa. While a brand can be protected from the legal perspective, manufacturers can also take measures to prevent their products from being copied. One of these measures is to affix anti-fake labels to the products or the packages, or to use counter-faking devices. Some manufacturers have designed their distribution in such a way that the distributors take on some of the counterfeit monitoring in each of the regional markets. There are also manufacturers who publicly offer cash or material awards for those who report and help obtain evidence on counterfeit production.

Towards brand loyalty

Brand loyalty is considered to be the most desirable objective of marketing. China has moved from a shortage economy into an economy of relative abundance. Many consumer products are in excessive supply. Increased consumerism and 'buyers' markets' will make brand management a delicate job. While most Chinese enterprises are still using mass marketing techniques in an attempt to maintain their market shares, some, particularly joint ventures, have started to study marketing alternatives in order to establish brand loyalty.

It is important for brand managers as well as marketing managers to realize that a brand will not be as much of an asset or equity as in the past or present if there is no loyalty from consumers/customers. Brand loyalty is the core target of brand management and marketing. When a product is adopted or accepted, trust can be established by meeting consumer/customer expectations and providing satisfaction. However, trust will have to be reinforced to gain loyalty. Building brand loyalty involves a process that can go far beyond the products' physical attributes and their invisible merits. Brand loyalty is more of a psychological reinforcement process than a process of persuasion by different means of promotion. This is particular true in China, where the legacy of 5,000 years of civilization governs a unique system of value judgement. When the marketing people are trying to formulate a strategy for brand loyalty marketing, Chinese cultural traits (see Chapters 4.1 and 4.2) should be exploited. To give consumers 'face' may result in consumer/customer loyalty. An appropriate use of the principle of reciprocity in personal relationships may create obligations/gratitude from the consumer/customer. Harmonious consumer/customer relations can be established by abiding by cultural codes.

Advertising

The advertising environment

Advertising is without doubt an effective means of communicating brand information to the consumer or customer. However, China is a very different country with distinctive features compared with the western world. For firms who either have a production presence in China, or who want to market their products directly in China, they are advised to design their marketing campaign, or more specifically advertising campaign, very carefully. The first thing they should do is to study the advertising environment.

In general, insufficient demand and excessive supply have characterized the consumer market. Lack of motivation to consume has resulted in an accumulation of cash savings in the hands of consumers, which the lowered interest rate has failed to release. As a result,

many advertisers are having sales problems and will have to reconsider their marketing strategies. Some have chosen to downsize their advertising input and increase sales efforts.

The conventional problem of a short supply of media seems to have been a problem. One of the reasons is that many media have expanded their resources to cash in on the fast-growing advertising market and competition for media has intensified. Apart from cross-medium competition, there is also inter-medium competition, typically the competition between terrestrial and cable television stations. As part of the effort to integrate television resources by the State Administration of Radio, Film and Television, most local terrestrial and cable television stations have undergone a merger process, bringing cable and terrestrial TV stations under one roof. It was reported that there are over 3,500 television channels, more than 1,000 newspapers and 7,000+ magazines. By the end of 2000, there were over 70,000 advertising-related entities employing 0.64 million workers.

Fragmentation of the advertising industry has remained a problem plaguing the growth of the industry. The trend of fragmentation seems to have continued over the last few years. The problems that come along with fragmentation are diseconomies of scale and fiercer competition. Fragmentation has also impeded the promotion of the advertising agency system and the relationships between advertisers, advertising companies and media are distorted.

The government has enhanced its monitoring and control of the advertizing industry, with the intention of disciplining the conduct and organisation of the advertising industry and protecting the interests of consumers and advertisers. The first attempt to regulate the advertising industry was made in 1987 and further key legislation on advertising censorship was implemented in 1993. In 1995, the Advertising Law was officially promulgated. A new version of the Advertising Law has been drafted and reviewed and will be promulgated in the latter half of 2002.

Brand communication

There are many options when it comes to communicating brand information in China. But it is important to recognize that consumer attitudes have been changing fast over the past two decades. It is no longer possible for a company like Nestlé, one of the few pioneers of advertising in the early days of China opening up, to establish brand awareness virtually overnight. Consumers in China are more complex and sophisticated in receiving product and brand information. Increased consumerism has made consumers more critical of marketers' efforts to communicate product and brand information. The frequent use of celebrities in TV commercials, for example, has been criticized by consumers who question whether these celebrities are communicating the brand and product information for the sake of money or in the interests of consumers. De Beers' decades old slogan 'a diamond is forever' has faced challenges from Chinese consumers who have different judgements on what values diamonds suggest. The kind of values that can be associated with diamonds, such as being symbolic of long-lasting love, gifts of love and purity of love, were all interpreted quite differently. One cause of the different reactions is deep-rooted cultural values which do not really recognize diamonds as an expression of love. In addition, the impact of western culture and associated changes in people's lifestyle has also had some influence on people's perception of love.

While taking cultural elements into consideration, marketers will also need to take a holistic approach in designing brand communications. Demographics are important in determining your target consumers and segmenting the market, but the complexities of the consumer world require more effort in the study of psychographics and geographics, which will help in establishing brand appeal. In a country as vast as China, people in different locations tend to have different consumption preferences. One example of this is that in north-eastern China, people tend to pursue common fashion values, while in southern China, for example Shanghai, consumers tend to be more individual and the emphasis is on personal taste.

Advertising congestion

Advertising congestion here does not mean that there are not enough media to carry advertisements, but rather refers to a phenomenon that almost all media are congested with advertisements to the extent that few could effectively catch the attention of viewers. Chinese firms seem to believe heavy advertising will help establish brand recognition and natural acceptance. There have been too many cases in which advertising created miracles, and almost all of them have ended up being closed down. However, people can still see enthusiastic advertisers lining up at CCTV's annual open bid and

the top bidders are always Chinese companies. Very rarely, if ever, does one see any joint ventures or foreign firms among them.

In this situation, it is advisable for foreign brands to take an integrated marketing communications approach. As the cultural preferences, eating habits and dialect can be differ substantially from region to region within China, any attempt at national promotion in the early stages of market development will be a costly exercise. Combined use of different media at different times in different target markets can be more effective than an effort to cover the national market. PR events in priority markets can add a special twist to the advertising efforts.

One encouraging fact is that Chinese people are increasingly brand-conscious. When they purchase, they not only take products as products, they look to value at the same time. They make comparison with using knowledge and information about the product before they are willing pay for it. Therefore, the 'advertising' on the product packages is also an important means to communicate brand information.

Rampant branding

In the mid-1990s, Chinese enterprises were prompted by the continued influx of foreign branded products to come to realise the importance of branding. They found that branding as a marketing strategy would not only create additional value, but also maintain a group of loyal customers. Academics began to study the branding strategies of these international companies and came to the conclusion that for China to survive in the world market, it would need a large number of globally recognized brands. Therefore, a 'famous brand strategy' approach was incubated and created great enthusiasm among Chinese enterprises who were eager to catch up with the lessons of branding strategy. This enthusiasm also found an echo in central government policies regarding improvement of product quality. At the central level was the China Council for the Promotion of Famous Brands, an organization that is responsible for 'uniform evaluation, management, publicity and cultivation' of brands. At the provincial level were 'leading groups' who drafted concrete plans to develop a certain number of 'national level famous brands' and 'provincial level famous brands'. The same process was copied at lower levels of government, all with plans to nurture their own famous brands.

Almost immediately, people found themselves besieged by brands, many of which had the label of 'famous brand' at county, city or provincial level. Some government departments were also involved in rating famous brands for enterprises that fell under their jurisdiction. Some foreign companies even found their way to milk the brand enthusiasm by offering foreign awards or accreditations to Chinese enterprises just for the money!

This desperate craving for famous brands has cooled down as a result of government efforts to stop various brand evaluation or rating exercises, which were regarded as misleading. But the sequel seems to be a rampant branding exercise. You can hardly buy a pair of shoes that do not bear a metal badge or an embroidered logo. The same is true with shirts: on the pocket of almost every shirt is an embroidered logo. You will be lucky if you can buy socks without an embroidered logo. Excessive branding has in effect caused problems for consumers, who are more prudent than before in selecting their preferred brands.

The above is intended to provide a portrait of the competitive situation is in China in terms of branding awareness by Chinese enterprises. The truth is that some enterprises did succeed in building their brands in the process, which helped them win over their foreign rivals. This is particularly true in the consumer electronics industry. The message here is that Chinese consumers have become buried in an onslaught of brands, and winning their trust and loyalty is not the job of advertising alone.

panding your reach in China

with Sino-World Sincerity

Sino-World Sincerity is a registered advertising company in Beijing, China. It offers not just advertising services!

Advertising

With various advertising media available, you may be wondering which ones are best for you. Sino-World Sincerity provides a wide range of advertising choices which allow your advertising dollar the ability to reach its maximum impact.

Research

With a market that is totally different from your own, you may be thinking of doing a research to base your business decision on. Sino-World Sincerity has a professional research team to offer you a tailored research service.

Consulting

More than research, you will probably need specialist consultants to assist you in entry strategies, business development planning, negotiation, marketing communications and so on. Sino-World Sincerity also advises on all those issues and other.

Training

Surprised? We have found that effective communications will have to be established with understanding of the local culture, social customs, mindset, etc. We do, and we want to share it with you. We have tailored training programmes to fit in your training needs.

We speak English.
We convert differences into differentiated strategies.
We expand your reach in China.

Contact us at: Rm 1517/1558, 5th Executive Office Floor, Ming Gong Hotel, No. 16 , Xi Ba He Xi Li, Beijing 100028, China. Tel: +86-10-6420 7782 Fax: 8316 7065
E-mail: sinoworld_ad@mail.china.com

Effective Public Relations

Li Yong, Deputy Secretary General, China Association of International Trade

Public relations in China shares some common characteristics with western concepts but has unique features, deeply ingrained as a legacy of its 5,000-year-old culture. An understanding of Chinese culture, related value judgements, codes and protocols is key to effective public relations. The business network discussed in Chapter 4.3 constitutes a part of this, but much of Chinese public relations is concerned with interpersonal relationships.

For the purposes of this chapter, the concept of public relations is divided into micro public relations, which involves interpersonal interactions, and macro, which involves communication with the public on a collective basis.

Micro public relations

Micro public relations here refers to relations with your Chinese colleagues, business partners, investment partners, government officials and people of different social functions. The discussion below is not intended to provide a panacea for dealing with various types of relationships, but rather the general rules that foreign business people should pay attention to in order to get along with the Chinese.

Your business partners

First impressions

It is important in the initial meeting to establish a good 'first impression'. Showing respect for local customs and habits is a good start, but adopting some of them may 'shorten the distance' in the first meeting and win recognition from the Chinese partners. For example, using two hands to present and receive business cards is considered to be good manners. Lightly knocking on the table with your forefinger and middle finger when you are served a cup of tea or drink will be taken as a sign of significant social experiences in southern coastal areas of China, particularly in Guangdong area. Proposing or accepting a toast at a dinner table with one hand holding the cup and the other the bottom of it is seen as respectful to the Chinese hosts. Neatly dressed and well organized businesspeople will always leave a good impression on their Chinese partners.

Nurturing your image

Apart from social rituals, foreign firms should also establish an image of professionalism and authoritativeness in order to gain the trust of their Chinese partners. For example, as an importer of Chinese products, the capability of your distribution network should be discussed in as much detail as possible to ensure trust and to assure the Chinese partner of the advantages of using the network you have outside of China. A bank reference will help eliminate possible doubts about your credibility.

As an exporter, you are expected to understand the products and technology you are trying to promote in China. If you are to make a presentation about your company, visual aids and properly translated brochures are extremely useful for a better understanding by your Chinese counterparts. Some foreign companies have Chinese version brochures, but the translation is almost as difficult to understand as the foreign language. Some reference of export acceptability will be helpful in building up confidence in trading your products in China. Sales into China also often involve many technical exchanges between the foreign sellers and the Chinese buyers and an important part of this effort is endorsements from relevant technical authorities in China. The endorsements can be explicit and implicit. Explicit endorsement usually take the form of technical certifications issued by relevant Chinese organizations, while implicit endorsements can be any type of public relations activity that you have had with well-known officials, technical experts or past projects in China. Evidence that your technology and products have gained endorsements and certifications elsewhere are also a plus. All of these should have a favourable impact on the decision making of the Chinese partners.

Dealing with hidden relations

When you are sure you have given your Chinese partners a good impression in your initial contact and that they are also impressed by your technology and products, you may then advance to the stage of business negotiation. In a business negotiation, you may expect to deal only with negotiators. In fact there could be other unknown decision-makers, particularly when the business involves decisions made by other organizations that are not directly participating in the negotiation. For example, if you are selling power plant equipment, the organizations involved in the decision making will include, among others, the State Power Corporation (previously the Ministry of Electric Power), the local power supply authority, design institute, environmental protection authority, banks providing the financing, and so on. These may not appear to be direct concerns in the negotiation but they are influencing the decision making process and will have to be dealt with appropriately to facilitate the decision-making process. It is recommended that foreign suppliers help the Chinese partners solve the problems arising from these hidden relations by giving understanding and patience to your counterpart in the first place and providing the necessary proofs to alleviate possible concerns. At the same time, some lobbying of these organizations by the foreign partners may be helpful. For this purpose, informal meetings, technical seminars and entertainment can be organized through a contact who knows when and where these activities will be appropriate. These negotiations could be very delicate, and making inappropriate proposals could be even worse than doing nothing.

Keeping a good track record

Business relations are a long-term commitment in China. Keeping a good track record will not only improve your position in the market, but also enhance your corporate image from a public relations perspective. Good track records with previous customers in terms of product quality, technology reliability and after-sales technical support will save the time for building trust in the products and technology with a new client. Even if you had not been able to gain publicity in the media, your good track record tends to generate good word-of-mouth publicity among the people in the industry. Good track records can accumulate into an impressive list of references, which will speak for itself in your promotional efforts.

Warm the threshold

Even if business with your Chinese partners is quite sporadic, keeping the relationship warm should be considered part of your long term strategy. A Christmas/ New Year card will remind them of your existence and tell them they are remembered. Occasional phone calls will give the relationship a personal touch. When you travel to China for unrelated business, having a chat over lunch/dinner would bring the relationship even closer. When the paths of your business do cross sometime in the future, you will still be treated as an old friend.

Your investment partner

Trust

While in business you can have alternative partners, in an investment venture you could not possibly do so unless you wished to terminate the venture prematurely. You will have to stay with your investment partner for a considerable period of time: identification and selection of a good partner is very important, and is discussed in detail in Chapter 4.5. Once you have chosen your partner and the contract has been signed, success depends very much on how well you co-operate with your partners. Trust is the basic element of successful cooperation in a joint venture.

The rules for building trust here differ little from elsewhere. Cultural clashes can be a cause of mistrust. In addition however, the fact that you and your Chinese colleagues represent the interests of two different organisations can be an obstacle to building trust. In the absence of trust, the Chinese colleagues may read some hidden purpose into what you do and vice versa. This is particularly hazardous to the development of the joint venture and eventually your own interest. While keeping good personal relations with the Chinese management, it is advisable for foreign executives to do things under the umbrella of mutual interests. When there is a disagreement, it will never lead you anywhere if you try to convince your Chinese partners that this is the way things are done in your company. Blaming your Chinese counterparts to cause loss of face is especially detrimental to the working relations. It is better, for example, to say that there is an alternative that may work. Any material efforts that you make for the mutual benefit of the two parties will bring you closer to gaining trust from your Chinese partner.

Educating your partner

Dealing with your Chinese partner is a learning process on both sides. One of the general perceptions of Chinese enterprises when introducing foreign elements into a venture is to learn what is called 'advanced managerial expertise'. One side of the education could be a kind of demonstration by which your partner can learn your management style on site. The other side is the formal training that can be conducted both on the job at the location of the joint venture and off the job at the foreign partner's factory. The training can enhance understanding of the Western management style and at the same time be conducive to gaining the support of local management. Once you have the understanding and support of the local partner, it will be much easier to carry out a business decision.

Communication with your partner

In an investment venture in China, communication between partners is a delicate matter. Mishandling communications may cause misunderstanding and eventually impede the efforts by both sides towards a harmonious relationship. Poor communications can lead to business failure. Establishing a good communications mechanism is a job for both partners. In many cases, foreign executives find that their Chinese colleagues remain silent at corporate meetings that are intended to solicit comments and suggestions from all managers; Chinese managers should be encouraged to talk openly about corporate decisions.

For the foreign partner, it is important to understand the reporting structure of the Chinese partner and the roles of the Chinese directors in the board. In the initial period of the joint venture, an appropriate channel of communication should be discussed with the Chinese partner in order to avoid possible misunderstanding in future communications. Routine meetings and internal circulation of corporate documents are the means of communication that are familiar to Chinese executives.

Internal organizations

Treat trade unions as a means of communication with employees

According to relevant laws and regulations, a joint venture in China must have a trade union in order to protect the rights and interests of employees. Apart from its role as a spokesperson on behalf of the employees, if a harmonious relationship can be established a trade union can also serve as an effective channel of communication with employees. Any effort to turn a trade union into a mere cipher will not help eliminate possible conflicts with employees. On the contrary, to delegate some responsibilities to the trade union may help improve relationships between the employer and employees. In a Chinese organization, a trade union also has an employment relations and welfare function. In a joint venture, it is advisable to have the trade union assume a similar function. The union can be used to increase awareness by employees that their well being is one of the primary interests of the venture. In furthering a better relationship with employees, the union can also be delegated the task of organizing employee activities, through which management can initiate closer, less formal and friendlier interactions with employees.

Party organizations are task forces

The Chinese communist party has over 60 million members active in different sectors and industries in China. In each Chinese organization there is a party committee or branch responsible for the organization of the communist party. There are also some party organisations active in many Sino-foreign joint ventures. Because of ideological differences, the foreign management of a joint venture may have a certain degree of reluctance in accepting such organizations in the joint venture. In reality, however, many foreign managers have found that such organizations play an important role in the execution of decisions made by the board. Party members are supposed to be people of excellence and the elite at all levels of an organization. Party principles require members to take the lead in the face of difficulties and to set examples for non-members through their work. They can always be referred to for help in critical situations. In dealing with the party organisations, respect should be given to party members and they should be encouraged to take proactive roles at different levels of management. Appropriate time should also be allocated to these organizations for their own activities. As an offshoot of a good relationship with the party organizations, they can be used as task forces to help the management realize management objectives and enhance employee communications.

Employees

In internal public relations, a good image of the management team is of pivotal importance in establishing the trust of employees. Trust can be established through candid communication. The following list of rules is not exhaustive but should be taken into account when dealing with employees:

- The first meeting with employees is very important in terms of building trust. Employees should be clearly briefed on corporate objectives and their association with the well-being of employees;
- When introducing 'western advanced management', communications should be understandable and free of ambiguity. On points that are particularly 'foreign', there should be clarity. To play safe, implementation of management policy on a trial basis will allow adjustments at later stages;
- Communications with employees should be regular and ongoing. Employees should be informed of the progress that the company is making both in good and bad times;
- Employee participation in the management process should be encouraged. If possible, a platform should be provided for employees' suggestions and comments;
- A sense of employee pride should be developed by creating a unique corporate culture. Employee contributions should be recognised and appreciated in the form of both spiritual and material rewards;
- A ladder of promotion should be established in order to encourage employees to be career-motivated. Promotion schemes should be designed to meet different career needs, such as promotion to management positions and technical skills. Pay schemes should be linked to promotions.

Government officials

Because of the pervasive red-tape and bureaucracy in almost every government across the world, companies outside China tend to employ or engage professional lobbyists to deal with governments and government officials. In China, however, lobbying is not a professional trade. Although there is an increasing number of public relations companies who claim to have special connections with Chinese government officials, no such organizations could realistically offer the service of dealing with government officials on behalf of the client on a regular basis. Like anywhere else, government functionaries can be very influential over corporate decisions or in business deals, and therefore maintaining a good relationship with them is imperative for foreign firms doing business in China. The advantages of having a good relationship with government officials are as follows:

- **Advice on corporate decisions.** Government officials are involved in policy making process of the governments at different levels. They are also well informed with regard to trends and policy orientation. Their judgement on corporate decisions can be extremely valuable;
- **Gaining government understanding.** Contacts with government officials on a good relationship basis will help a company to deliver or communicate the messages of corporate strategies/actions and gain government understanding of the corporate position;
- **Facilitation of government procedures.** Advice by government officials on how to meet reporting requirements will save a lot of time and effort to gain consent or approval from the government organizations;
- **Publicity for corporate image.** A formal meeting between the CEOs and high ranking officials such as ministers, provincial governors and city mayors will receive a lot of publicity in the local media. A meeting with central level officials will be covered by TV and newspapers;
- **De facto recognition.** The comments made by government officials during formal meetings and a picture taken with them may appear to be an indication of de facto recognition of your company by government organizations.

To the uninitiated, the Chinese government can appear to be an incomprehensible labyrinth. The reporting structure and its associated requirements are even more so. You will be very lucky if your business partners have strong relations with government organizations at different levels. With the help of contact people, consultant organizations and public relations companies, contact with government organizations and officials can also be initiated. Once the contact is initiated, a reasonably good relationship with government officials can be maintained by employing appropriate personal and public relations skills. Government officials can be invited to participate in the ribbon-cutting ceremonies, news conferences, major corporate events, inspection tours, seminars, exhibitions and so on. Sponsoring government-initiated community projects and public affairs can also be a good way of cementing closer relationships with government officials and generating positive publicity.

People of different social functions

Apart from the types of people mentioned above, there are others that cannot be ignored in corporate public relations: industry experts, research professionals, personnel of industry and commerce bureaux, tax bureaux, Customs offices and stars in the recreational industry. These are influential groups. They can be dealt with on a good personal basis with a view to creating external public relations effects. Of special significance are relations with journalists and reporters. Keeping a good relationship with them will always be useful.

Macro public relations

Macro public relations here refers to communications with the public on a collective basis. The target of macro public relations is to create among the public a favourable corporate or brand image that could not possibly be achieved on an interpersonal basis or by mere commercial advertising efforts.

Consumers

Consumers are the largest group with which a company deals. Increased consumerism has substantially improved consumers' awareness of their rights and made consumer relations more challenging to handle. The consumer no longer takes what is available and tolerates defective products, inadequate service or failures in quality and safety. The government has also invested significant effort in formulating laws and regulations to protect the rights of consumers and consumer activists have emerged in recent years. Newspapers and TV stations are more interested in protecting the rights of consumers. They evaluate products under the supervision of a public notary and publicise the results in newspapers and on TV. There are also individual consumer activists, who fight against counterfeits by making volume purchases to claim multiple compensation. Consumers are becoming increasingly sceptical of advertising information, which in turn has made public relations practitioners

more consumer-oriented than before. The task of public relations with consumers is to establish effective channels of communications with consumers on a non-advertising basis.

The community

The community in which a company operates can mean the survival and development or otherwise of the company. A construction site may encounter resistance from the residents of neighbouring areas because of noise problems. An office building with a glazed exterior may be blamed for light pollution. A factory may be sabotaged by neighbouring farmers for suspected pollution. It is the task of public relations people to work towards gaining an understanding from the community, if not its support.

To convince the community that your company is a good citizen and part of the community, you should deliver the message that the company benefits and cares about the community in terms of providing employment opportunities, generating other community businesses and contributing to the communal well-being. At the same time, the company should build an image of visible safety and clean production in order to eliminate possible concerns. To gain community acceptance and approval, you should also provide support for community development, such as opening the service facilities to the community, offering assistance in maintaining public security, participating in social welfare activities, sponsoring community campaigns to clean up the environment and so on.

Media

A good working relationship with the media in China is imperative for successful public relations. The Chinese media are not only the mouthpiece of the government, but also opinion leaders. They now play an increasingly important role in shaping opinions, benchmarking values and disseminating information and knowledge. Public media in China are owned by the government and therefore have a special position in the minds of the Chinese people. Getting favourable publicity in the media signifies official acceptance and recognition.

Because of the special status of public media, maintaining good relationships with it is a common practice of public relations people in China. The 'competition' for good relationships resulted in the practice of paying for news reports. At one time, paid news reports were rampant, which jeopardized the impartiality of public media and subjected the public audience to questionable or misleading advocacy. As a result, the government reinforced its rules against paid news and journalists/reporters are likely to be expelled from the profession if they are found to have engaged in such deals. Therefore, public relations practitioners are advised not to attempt to influence the independence of public media. However, this does not preclude efforts to maintain a good working relationship with them. Of course, it always pays to build good personal relationships with journalists and reporters.

Maintaining a good working relationship requires much understanding of the media business, its unique feature of decision making and its information needs. The needs for news by public media often corresponds to the political, economic and social themes of the time. It will make good news if your story coincides with these current themes. Good public relations practitioners should be able to identify opportunities for corporate publicity and translate a corporate event into a story with news value. Being responsive and cooperative is the key to a good media relationship.

Government organisations

As discussed above, maintaining good personal relationship with government officials will help a company gain support and facilitation from government organizations on the basis of personal understanding. In practice, however, it would be impossible for any company to know all the government officials on an interpersonal basis, so good government relations should receive additional strategic consideration in macro public relations.

The Chinese government consists of a large number of national government agencies as well as provincial and local government units. Each has a distinctive set of responsibilities and is charged with a mission that gives it a level of policy making. The government regulates the macro economy and also disciplines corporate behaviour.

When dealing with government relations, the first step is to understand policies, laws and regulations to ensure that corporate operations are in line with government requirements. At the same time, companies should minimize where possible the likely conflicts with government organizations at different levels, if such conflicts cannot be avoided. Possible sources of conflicts are unauthorized inspections and fines, illegitimate collec-

tion of fees, unjustified allocation of public spending funds and solicitation of sponsorships. Cooperation with government organizations is essential for harmonious government relations. Responding positively to government advocacy will not only result in appreciation from the government but also create positive public relations.

Issues management

Managing relations with the public is in effect an effort to minimize issues that may arise from possible conflicts. However, issues do arise. China has a unique political, economic and social system and issues management should be tailored to its unique features.

To avoid political issues, it is important for foreign companies to observe the rules of the political game in China: essentially to keep away from any political involvement. Corporate spokesmen should avoid commenting publicly on political issues. In business operations, foreign companies are advised to ensure there are no political associations in their products, brands and tradenames. A Japanese computer software company, for example, ran into a political issue by marketing in China a war game package featuring Japanese war criminals.

Economic and social issues are more manageable than political issues. Common issues, among others, are environmental pollution, product quality, health concerns, safety problems, employment disputes, advertising claims, intellectual property and consumer complaints. The extent to which these issues affect an organization varies depending on how they evolve in the process of corporate development in the context of China's economic and social environment. A company which does not have an issue now may well have one in the future. To manage issues that may arise in the future, a company should be able to anticipate emerging issues and plan their issues management. A tracking mechanism should be established to define and analyse existing and emerging issues. Possible sources of issues should be given priority tracking efforts.

Public media are one of the sources from which issues originate. For example, the media recently disclosed a research finding that air fresheners contain one kind of carcinogenic chemical. Soon after that, the media reported another research finding that dietary recipes marketed in China will not help to reduce weight and may be hazardous to health. All these reports will have negative impact on companies producing these products. Identifying issues that may exist is important to prevent an issue from developing into a crisis.

Publicity techniques

Media publicity

Unlike advertising, media publicity is not in the hands of a company's management. Because of this, it has the kind of objectivity that advertising can not possibly achieve. The Chinese media have developed very rapidly in recent years, particularly in technological terms. Transmission of news is as fast as in any other countries. Avenues of publicity include televisions (terrestrial and cable), radio, newspapers, magazines and increasingly the internet.

Television

Television is now the most influential medium and the most important source of information in China. Getting publicity on television is considered to be the best result of a public relations effort. To achieve national publicity, China Central Television (CCTV) is the 'one and only' choice. The most influential news programme is the evening news between 7:00 and 7:30pm each day. Other key news programmes include morning, noon and late night news.

Apart from CCTV, there are also local television stations. For publicity other than national coverage, provincial and provincial capitals and large cities' stations are the best media. Some provincial stations are also aired via satellite, which can be received by cable television subscribers in most parts of China.

It is the most challenging task for public relations people to get publicity on television. Practitioners are advised to make sure that the story you recommend will interest television people and that it has news value. An invitation should be sent to TV stations well in advance and be accompanied by an introduction of the story. Public relations people should prepare a copy of a new release for television editors. It should be clear and brief to suit the nature of television broadcasting. Supplementary materials should also be prepared in case the television editors need to understand more about the background to the story. You should also provide additional visual materials, if any, for the convenience of the editor to make a better visual presentation. Public relations people should always offer to provide transport for the camera crew, which will guarantee their punctual arrival on the scene.

Radio

Although the emergence of television as a key information disseminator has overwhelmed the role of radio, which was the key news medium 15 to 20 years ago, radio publicity still has characteristics that television cannot replace. For example, radio reception has less constraints in terms of time and place. People can listen to the radio even on the way to work on bikes and in buses and taxies from their walkmans or radio receivers. Almost all cars are equipped with a radio receiver. Radio can reach an audience that television cannot.

The system of radio broadcasting resembles that of television. There is a Central People's Broadcast Station (CPBS), which broadcasts throughout the country. There are also local broadcast stations. Most stations use middle wave and FM to reach their audience.

Radio journalists are relatively more receptive to the story ideas of public relations people, although getting publicity can be also be challenging. For news releases, public relations practitioners should prepare a write-up in advance for the journalists to refer to when producing the programme. Always send formal letters of invitation before the event takes place. In many cases, a news report may not need to involve direct participation by radio journalists. Public relations should not take it for granted that radio journalists do not have to be invited. Inviting them will offer good opportunities for interpersonal relations.

Newspapers

Newspapers provide more diversity and depth of coverage than either television or radio. There are thousands of newspapers in China, which fall into the following basic categories: national daily, local daily, evening, morning, professional, weekend and feature newspapers.

National daily newspapers are normally institutional papers of the government, which target institutional readers. The same is true of local daily newspapers. All such dailies carry reports on government policies, economic achievements, progress of social development, etc. Newspapers that fall into the category of evening and morning papers cover local interests and tend to be aligned to general interests. Professional newspapers normally cover special areas of interests, such as industry information and developments. Weekend newspapers and feature newspapers are more entertainment-oriented.

Gaining publicity in newspapers is relatively easy compared with television and radio. One way to do so is to write to the newspaper in which you wish to have your stories covered. To make sure that your contribution receives personal attention, it is advisable to write to a specific editor rather than an editor in general. For some story coverage, it is better to invite journalists to come to the scene, in which case a prepared news release with some details should be provided. For stronger impact, public relations people normally invite journalists/reporters not only from television and radio, but also several newspapers, to witness the event.

Magazines

Although there are thousands of magazines in China, they play a less important role in terms of creating corporate publicity. Most are published on a monthly or fortnightly basis; few are weekly. Magazines will not offer immediate publicity, but allow for more intense coverage of a corporate event. Publicity through magazines requires a different type of public relations strategy. Articles covering corporate stories should be structured with a featured style. Story-telling by independent writers can be a good strategy for objectivity.

Event publicity

This means publicizing a company or a brand by organizing an event that will catch public attention. Event publicity is also known as event marketing. Common events include:

- **Sports events**. Sports are gaining popularity in China. Sports events can create corporate publicity that can not be achieved by merely advertising. Successful events include Philips Football Association Cup, Pepsi Cola Football League Competition, Motorola Badminton Tour Competition, Toupai (a Chinese liquor brand) International Wushu (kungfu) Competition, and others;
- **Cultural events**, such as film festivals, fashion shows, art festivals and music concerts can also be an avenue of publicity. For example, Samsung sponsored a music event featuring original student music composition;
- **Social events** designed to correspond to social concerns. Such events include nature conservation,

protection of endangered species, relief funding of disaster stricken areas, aid to poverty-stricken children to allow them to return to school, sponsorship of tree planting in response to the government effort to reduce defenestration;
- Seminars/conferences that deal with issues of public concern, economic and social progress.

The above does not exhaust the possibilities of event publicity. All such events are intended to target the public at large. The purpose of organizing such events is to reinforce the image of a company as a corporate citizen, and hence the brand image of their products and services. For such events, public relations people are required to demonstrate their ability to capture points of public interest as well as their capabilities in planning and organizing the events. There is an increasing number of public relations companies providing such services in China.

The following tips might be useful for companies that intend to create publicity in China.

- The objective which the sponsoring organization wishes to achieve through the event should be clearly defined and justified;
- Understanding must be achieved between management and the public relations people that such an event will not bring immediate sales benefits;
- Understanding should also be achieved that event sponsoring should be a continuous effort. A one-off approach is not going to produce the expected publicity benefits;
- Careful planning for media coverage should be made well in advance with back-up plans for contingencies;
- The presence of government officials and celebrities can add special publicity impact;
- Excessive emphasis on the role of sponsor(s) should be avoided in order to prevent possible aversion by the public;
- Efforts should be made to create two-way communication with the public;
- Crisis prevention should be given due attention before the event.

Part Five

Banking, Foreign Exchange Transactions and the Regulation of Securities

Banking Services for Foreign Investment Enterprises (FIEs)
HSBC

Further opening for China's banking sector

China has revealed more details of its plans to expand the opening up of the banking sector to foreign participation upon entry to the WTO. Restrictions on the operation of foreign banks will be gradually reduced over the next few years and as a result foreign banks are stepping up their efforts to secure a firmer foothold in China's banking sector in expectation of increasing business opportunities. The pace of the search for foreign investment in China's banks has accelerated, providing an alternative channel to foreign participation in the Chinese banking sector.

Following China's formal accession to the WTO, more details on the opening of its banking sector have been released, covering both foreign exchange and renminbi business. The major changes to the restrictions are scheduled to be completed by 2007.

Schedule for easing of restrictions

1 January 2002

- Foreign exchange business permitted for foreign banks without geographic and client restrictions;
- Renminbi business permitted for foreign banks in four cities, with four additional cities permitted each year thereafter and nationwide access beginning on 1 January 2007. Foreign banks licensed to conduct renminbi business in one city may service clients in any other city that has been opened for such business;
- Foreign non-bank financial institutions permitted to provide auto financing without any market access or national treatment limitations.

1st January 2004

- Renminbi business with Chinese enterprises permitted for foreign banks.

1st January 2007

- Renminbi business with Chinese individuals permitted for foreign banks;
- Auto-financing to Chinese individuals permitted for foreign banks;
- Restrictions lifted on foreign banks' equity composition and form of establishment;
- Permission granted to set up branch networks within the same city, with approval on the same basis as domestic banks;
- Financial leasing permitted for foreign banks where permitted for domestic banks.

Foreign exchange business

According to the agreement, foreign banks are permitted to provide foreign exchange-related services in China without geographic and client restriction from 1 January 2002, one year earlier than the relevant terms of the Sino-US agreement.

As a result, foreign banks will be allowed to conduct foreign exchange business for Chinese enterprises and individuals in all locations within mainland China.

Renminbi business

Conducting renminbi business with foreign clients is permitted and will be expanded to include Chinese enterprise clients within two years and Chinese individuals within five years. Initially, foreign financial institutions will be restricted to Shanghai, Shenzhen, Tianjin and Dalian for renminbi business, with three to four cities added each year until all geographic restrictions are removed within five years.

Looking ahead, a new phase of banking development in China is imminent with competition intensifying in the wake of China's WTO entry. Hopefully a more efficient industry will result from the competitive interaction among a growing number of domestic and foreign banks. This will benefit the economy in general and both foreign invested and domestic enterprises in particular from the services of foreign banks.

Basic bank accounts in China

Capital account

The capital account is set up for receiving injection of capital, overseas loans and other funds under capital account items. Given that the renminbi is not yet fully convertible, restrictions apply to the exchange of capital account items involving foreign currency conversion.

The capital account is subject to State Administrative Foreign Exchange (SAFE) approval before it can be opened, and only one capital account is allowed per company. Generally, approval is given for the capital account to be opened in the same city in which the venture is registered.

Since 1 July 2002, some items under the capital account can be settled directly with authorized banks via SAFE. Prior to the reform, each settlement transaction for capital accounts first had to be approved by SAFE before being submitted to banks. Now authorized banks are responsible for checking settlements and SAFE oversees bank operations.

The banks involved should report data to SAFE on a daily basis and monthly reports must be submitted.

Current account

The current account is used for remitting and receiving foreign currency trading payments as well as for service charges and fees and dividends to foreign shareholders.

Frequently asked questions about current account items are:

Dividend payments: what is the process for paying a dividend and what documents are needed?
When a company opens for business in China, as part of its business licence application it must submit a capital injection schedule to the Ministry of Foreign Trade and Economic Cooperation (MOFTEC). Unless the amount of capital due to be injected within a given financial year has been paid up, dividends cannot be remitted abroad.

The remitting bank can arrange the payment upon receiving the following documents:

- Audited accounts to show profit has been made (compulsory reserves have been made);
- A tax report to show profit tax has been paid;
- A capital verification report to show capital investment has been injected according to the schedule;
- Board resolution to show the amount of funds to be remitted;
- Other documents required by the bank.

Trade payments: what approvals or documents are needed to pay for goods imported into China?
Settlement for imported goods invoiced in US dollars does not require prior approval from SAFE, although the remittance bank will have to be provided with the relevant documents. As standard practice, the overseas payment is made from the importer's (FIE's) account and the Renminbi account would only be debited to make up any shortfall. The documents to be provided are as follows:

- Import Payment Reconciliation Form (SAE document);
- Copy of sales (import) contract
- Commercial invoice
- Original bill of lading or air waybill
- Original customs declaration form (the paying bank needs to verify the declaration form online before effecting the payment)
- SAFE registration form
  - when the name of the remitter is not the same as the importer on the customs declaration form or
  - when the importer is not included in the SAFE 'approved importer list' or
  - when the payment is effected via a bank outside the city where the importer is registered
- Agent agreement, when the consignee name on the bill of lading is different from the importer's name on the customs declaration form, buyer of the sales contract and the applicant of the remittance.

Trade services in China

A wide range of import and export services is offered by banks operating in mainland China. The main import services offered include documentary credit issuing and the provision of shipping guarantees and clean import loans.

An extensive range of export services includes documentary collection, documentary credit confirmation and negotiation, as well as pre- and post-shipment finance. Export credit-backed facilities can be arranged through the various national export credit agencies to support the importation of capital goods into mainland China.

Import Services

DC issuing

A documentary credit (DC), also known as a letter of credit (LC), is a written undertaking by a bank, issued on the instructions of the buyer in favour of the seller, to effect payment under stated conditions.

A DC gives the seller the comfort of knowing that he can look to the importer's bank for payment and that the buyer will only be able to gain access to the goods (via the necessary documents) once they have complied with all the terms of the DC. The buyer has the comfort of knowing that he will not be required to pay for the goods before he has control of the documents.

Shipping guarantee

Sometimes goods arrive before the documents. In such cases 'shipping guarantees' can be used. A shipping guarantee is an application from the bank to authorize the release of goods by a shipping company against the bank's undertaking to deliver the original bill of lading in future. It is usually applicable under import DC transactions and allows prompt clearance of goods ahead of the arrival of documents. However, when taking the goods, protection against discrepant documents is lost.

Clean import loans

A working capital facility can be made available to pay for the goods imported under the DC. The finance will often be required to enable the buyer to turn the goods into manufactured items for onward sale. The advance will usually be made available for the manufacturing period on sight of original invoices and shipping documents only.

Export services

Documentary collection

Documentary Collection is a dedicated export bill collection service offered by banks to follow up on bill payments as agents of the exporter.

Documents are received by the local branch of the exporter's bank. These documents are then forwarded to the collecting bank (for non-DC transactions) or DC-issuing bank (for DC transactions) together with a collection order requesting payment.

DC confirmation

Documentary credit confirmation is a service offered by foreign banks to add an undertaking to pay in the event that the issuing bank is unable to, even though the documents submitted by the exporter are fully compliant.

An exporter's main concern is with receiving payment and it may be difficult to retrieve goods that have been shipped to the importer's country in the event that payment is not forthcoming and so an exporter may choose to seek the reassurance of DC confirmation in situations where the issuing bank is not well known, or in financial difficulties itself, or if the administration of the importer's country presents risks – real or perceived – with which the exporter is uncomfortable.

DC negotiation

Documentary credit negotiation is a service offered by banks which involves checking and making a payment advance against the documents presented by the exporter, upon shipment of goods under an export documentary credit.

The bank will check to ensure that the exporter's documents are in full compliance with the terms and conditions of the DC, and where possible, work with the exporter to make appropriate amendments to rectify any discrepancies. However, some discrepancies such as expired DCs or late shipment are not rectifiable.

Any discrepancy whatsoever could render the exporter's export DC inoperative as an undertaking of payment from the issuing bank.

Pre-shipment finance

Pre-shipment finance provided by a bank is generally termed 'loans against exports'. Loans must be supported by original irrevocable DCs. Facilities may also allow advances to be made against confirmed orders by specified reputable buyers of international standing.

Types of pre-shipment finance offered include packing credits, manufacturing advances and red clause credits.

Packing credits provide an exporter with finance after goods have been manufactured but before they are shipped. This helps to smooth the exporter's cash flow while the goods are being packed and waiting for shipment. The advance is repaid when the goods are shipped, if the documents were negotiated with the exporter's bank.

Manufacturing advances are provided to exporters to meet manufacturing costs such as the purchase of raw materials.

A red clause credit is a DC containing a clause from the issuing bank that authorises the advising bank to grant an advance to the exporter before documents are presented. Facilities are not required for this type of pre-shipment finance as the advising bank is relying on the issuing bank for reimbursement rather than the customer.

Post-shipment finance

Post-shipment finance occurs when an exporter asks its bank to advance funds against a shipment that has already been made. The exporter eases their cash flow by obtaining funds for their shipment without having to wait for the importer to pay.

Trade trends after WTO entry

China's WTO entry will change the way trade is conducted in the country, in terms of levels of trade, types of goods being traded, and associated financial and documentary arrangements.

Trading terms

The current trend of strongly growing imports into China is expected to continue. The growth in the import of primary and capital products has been particularly significant – the increase in primary goods being mainly due to the large jump in petroleum products which will remain a major item for the foreseeable future. Imports of raw materials including timber, pulp, minerals, chemicals and metals have also risen strongly (up 50 per cent in 2000 according to China Trade Roundtable), while within an overall increase in manufactured products, electrical, electronic and automotive products and instruments rose 40 per cent – a reflection of China's economic restructuring and upgrading.

The slowing of export growth through 2001 signalled the end of recovery-induced high growth and a slowing world economy. The depreciation of the currencies of China's trade partners weakened the country's export competitiveness and a shift towards high tech products like electronic components, electronics products and computers and their peripherals became apparent in China's export market. This shift in the pattern of trade is the inevitable outcome of foreign direct investment of US$330 billion, mostly through the establishment of some 350,000 foreign-funded firms in the five special economic zones (SEZs) along China's southern coast, which has helped to transform the economy from exporting primarily raw materials to becoming a large exporter of manufactured goods.

Payment terms

While the trade finance products available in China are largely generic, DCs remain prevalent in trade deals with foreign suppliers. However, there does appear to be an increasing number of requests to suppliers to offer open account terms, even for bulk commodities (raw materials).

On the export side, a greater percentage of transactions are on open account, and this number is growing. Estimates vary from 30–65 per cent, depending on the products involved and the location of the exporters. This growing trend will encourage trade banks to look at meeting the needs of the market quickly.

Cash management

Increased foreign investment in mainland China has inevitably led to a greater focus on cash management. Historically, corporate growth in China has been a fragmented affair, resulting in numerous legal entities with completely separate operations and administration. Under local regulations, a subsidiary's scope of business is tightly defined by its 'business licence' and this makes it impossible to create centralized treasury or cash management operations under a holding company structure. However, the position improved significantly in 1999 and 2001 when the Ministry of Foreign Trade and Economic Cooperation (MOFTEC) extended the business scope of holding companies. This enabled them (subject to certain conditions and approvals from MOFTEC) to act as principal in selling their subsidiaries' products, thereby centralizing sales and invoicing, to provide transporting and warehousing for their subsidiaries only, and to house a research and development centre.

The Payments infrastructure

A number of clearing systems and payment methods are commonly used in China. In-city payments are generally made by cheque whereas cross-city renminbi (RMB) payments are generally made by telegraphic transfer or demand draft.

The most commonly used payment instrument for RMB transfers within the same city is the local transfer cheque. Whereas company-issued cheques would be sent directly to the beneficiary and then presented through local clearing, local transfer cheques are delivered directly to the payer's bank, which then clears them through the local clearing house. The advantage here is that local transfer cheques do not need to be stamped with the company's finance chop and so the instruction can be sent electronically and the production of the local clearing cheque outsourced to the bank. An alternative payment method for in-city payments is the cashier's order which as a bank issued payment instrument can be credited to the beneficiary's account on sight.

Foreign companies operating in China face an additional challenge if their enterprise resource planning (ERP) systems do not produce Chinese language payments output files. This can result in significant manual intervention and rekeying to create payments files in Chinese. Banks can assist customers by building a link between the customer's ERP system and their electronic banking system if the latter has the ability to translate payment instructions into Chinese. HSBC's Hexagon system takes the instruction directly from customers' ERP systems and converts it into Chinese, at which point the payment is presented on screen for approval. The resulting SWIFT instruction is routed to the relevant partner bank for payment, reducing the end-to-end payment cycle to 24 hours.

For cross-city payments, there are multiple channels, including the central bank-administered China National Automated Payments System (CNAPS) which spans 800 cities and provides access to cleared funds in one to two working days for the larger cities. However, the larger domestic commercial banks have developed efficient in-house clearing to clear between their own branches. For example, HSBC's strategic alliances with the big four state commercial banks (Industrial and Commercial Bank of China, China Construction Bank, Bank of China and Agricultural Bank of China) give

customers access to over 26,000 branches via partner banks' real-time internal clearing. As a result, telegraphic transfers can now, in some cases, be cleared within two to three hours.

Receivables management

Given the complex range of clearing mechanisms described above, receivables management can present a challenge, especially if remote locations are involved. However, various solutions are available. If the collecting entity is based in an area (such as Shanghai and Guangzhou) where foreign banks are allowed to provide RMB services, alliances with domestic banks can be used to improve collection times. Any items that come in through the domestic banks' branches will be concentrated through the domestic banks' electronic systems and settled via a nostro account that the foreign bank maintains with a local bank.

Consolidated electronic reporting of these transactions is as important as the need to better manage the receivables cycle and this can be achieved via consolidated, timely electronic reporting of transactions via the foreign bank's electronic banking system. By assigning a unique transaction reference to each transaction and providing a file extract programme, banks can help customers to automate their reconciliation process within the customer's own ERP system.

Account and liquidity management

In the absence of a 'financial holding company' structure in China, transfers of funds between subsidiaries are subject to severe restrictions. Inter-company loans from the parent are subject to withholding tax. The interest rate environment is also regulated and margins charged or paid by banks are set by the central bank, resulting in wider spreads between deposit and lending rates than those found in more market regulated environments.

In early 2000, a system of 'entrusted loans' was introduced by the People's Bank of China for RMB funding. This has significantly improved opportunities for inter-company funding for groups with multiple operations in China. Entrusted loans allow related parties to lend and borrow from each other via a third party. An entity with surplus cash places a deposit with a bank and designates the company to whom the funds are to be lent. The rate is prescribed by the central bank by reference to the central banks' own lending rate and the intermediary bank is allowed to charge a fee within a specified range by the central bank. It is a central bank requirement that the credit risk is assumed by the lending entity. The ability to provide 'entrusted loans' was extended to foreign banks in November 2001.

Another regulation with cash management implications is the requirement for companies to hold only one RMB account. From an accounting perspective this can present issues for those corporates which normally use multiple accounts to handle divisional accounts or create separate accounting records for payables and receivables, often for ease of reconciliation.

Certain foreign banks have developed services which enable clients to monitor their consolidated account position via a central account. The different divisions would then have associated accounts enabling the over-seas parent (and the company financial controller), for example, to maintain separate records of payables and receivables.

Conclusion

Despite the market-specific requirements of cash management in China, significant opportunities exist for corporates to improve their payables and receivables and liquidity management practices. This is an area where extensive cooperation between foreign and domestic banks is likely to continue to develop services that meet the needs of multinational clients with multiple subsidiaries operating in China.

Foreign Exchange Administration Systems in China

Xin Liu, Director of Investment Division, State Administration of Foreign Exchange (SAFE)

Overview

China has maintained a healthy condition in terms of foreign exchange payments and balance of payments in recent years. All the statistical ratios show that its external debts are in a safe condition. 2001 saw China achieving a surplus in foreign exchange payments on both capital and current accounts for the first time. China maintains a healthy condition in the foreign exchange payment and the balance of payment and all the ratios of the external debt are in a safe condition. Foreign exchange reserves increased by US$46.6 billion in 2001, the highest in history, and the figure surged to US$227.6 billion at the end of March 2002. The foreign exchange rate of renminbi (RMB) remains stable.

All these achievements are owed to reform in the Chinese Foreign Exchange Administration accompanying the reform and opening up process in the country over more than a decade. The following changes are featured in the reforms, especially the two major reforms of 1994 and 1996:

- From centralized control and unified receipts and payments of foreign exchange before 1979 and from dual exchange rates and foreign exchange retention in the early stage of reform to single exchange rate and RMB convertibility on current account;
- From planned distribution of foreign exchange sources in combination with market demand to distribution based mainly on market demand;
- The current nationwide unified inter-bank trading market has developed from a non-existent foreign exchange market and separated swap centres.

China's present foreign exchange administration system may be summarized as RMB current accounts made convertible at a single, managed floating rate based on market demand and supply, while control is still exercised over most items on capital account.

Framework of China's foreign exchange administration system

China's foreign exchange administration system includes the following major elements:

- management of current account convertibility;
- control over capital accounts,
- the system of a single, managed floating RMB rate;
- a nationwide inter-bank market; and
- macro-management of balance of payments, as well as the supervision and control of foreign exchange operations in the financial institutions.

Management of convertibility of current account

On 1 December 1994, China adopted Clause 8 of the International Monetary Fund (IMF) and provided for convertibility of RMB current accounts. Since then, all transactions relating to bona fide trades in foreign exchange on current accounts can be effected without administrative control. However, this does not necessarily mean that domestic enterprises and individuals can purchase foreign currencies without any supervision. The foreign exchange administration authority (SAFE) still verifies authenticity for the receipts and payments of foreign exchange in accordance with international practice.

Management of foreign exchange account under current account

At present, there are two types of foreign exchange current accounts which should be inspected and approved by SAFE before opening: the settlement account and the foreign exchange account for special purposes. Foreign-funded enterprises (FFEs)[1] and those qualified enterprises funded by domestic capital can apply to SAFE to open settlement accounts in the designated banks which are domestically funded and qualified to transact business in foreign exchange. Amounts of foreign exchange within limitations may be kept on account.

Accounts in foreign exchange for a special purpose include those foreign exchange accounts opened for businesses such as importing in proxy, special trade, labour contracts, donations and assistance, special proxies, international shipments, international remittances, international travel and tourism agencies, duty-free goods and accounts for temporary receipt among others.

In order to open a foreign exchange account, the FFE should present to SAFE an application report and the FFE Registration Certificate. With the 'Notice of Opening Account' granted by SAFE and its Registration Certificate, the FEE may then open a foreign exchange account at a bank or financial institution. The bank or financial institution opening the account should enter the account number, type of foreign exchange and opening date in the corresponding columns of the Registration Certificate and stamp its seal on the Registration Certificate.

When an FFE needs to open foreign exchange accounts in other cities or areas than the city where it is registered, it should apply to the local SAFE office in its city of registration for the 'Notice of Opening Account' issued by that office, and then apply to the SAFE offices in the cities where it wishes to open the new account in order to file and receive verification to open accounts in the designated banks.

Upon submitting approval documents for setting up or a business licence, the resident office of a foreign organisation in China should register and file with SAFE, and procure the 'Registration and Filing Form of Foreign Exchange Account for Foreign Organization'. The resident office may then open its foreign exchange account with the Registration and Filing Form in a designated bank.

Domestic organizations (excluding FFEs) can open accounts in foreign exchange with the approval of SAFE branches to keep their receipts in foreign exchange on current account.

When a foreign exchange account has been opened, it is not permitted to change the opening bank during the first six months. After that, it is possible to apply to transfer the account to other banks due to relocation of offices, or any dissatisfaction with the service provided by the original opening bank.

When the foreign exchange account is no longer needed, due to a normal change in business circumstances, the enterprise can file with SAFE an explanation for closing the account, the approval document for opening account and the 'Certificate of Using Foreign Exchange Account'. SAFE will withdraw the Using Certificate and issue a 'Notice to Rescind Account'. With these supporting documents the enterprise can close the bank account. The enterprise should send documents relevant to the account closing to SAFE within 10 working days.

SAFE carries out annual inspections on all foreign exchange accounts from January to April. All enterprises with foreign exchange accounting should participate in the annual inspection. Specific inspections are implemented by accounting firms appointed by enterprises. SAFE will examine the list of authoritative accounting firms annually and re-publish the list from which an enterprise can select the accounting firm itself.

Any breach of rules found during the annual inspection and/or daily supervision will be punished according to the relevant regulations. Breaches include: opening a foreign exchange account without proper approval, letting, lending or transferring the account to others, changing the usage limitation without approval, exceeding the ceiling of the amount authorised or the valid duration of the account or any other misdemeanour.

When a serious breach of rules by an enterprise in the use of a foreign exchange account is found by SAFE during an annual or spot inspection, it may cause closure of the account. The opening bank will close the account upon the Notice to Rescind Account or other relevant documents issued by SAFE. The enterprise should nullify the account by submitting to SAFE the notice documents from the bank, the approval docu-

---

[1] Foreign-funded enterprises (FFEs) refer to joint-invested ventures, foreign cooperative joint ventures, and wholly foreign-owned enterprises registered within Chinese territory.

ment to open the account and the Using Certificate within 10 working days after receipt of certification from the bank of the account closure.

Payment in foreign currencies under current account

Under current accounts, RMB payments for imports may be converted into foreign currencies, as well as capital gains within China, for transfer abroad.

Only those importers which have been placed in the 'list of importers paying in foreign exchange' by SAFE and its local offices can make payments in foreign exchange directly through the designated banks. To be listed, the importers should submit to the local SAFE:

1. approval to carry out imports and exports by the local Foreign Trade and Economic Cooperation department;
2. business licence issued by the Industrial and Commercial Administration; and
3. Organization Coding Certificate issued by the Technology Supervision Bureau.

Payments for normal trade in goods may be effected directly from the foreign exchange accounts of importers and exporters without any approval from SAF. Alternatively, domestic entities can purchase foreign currencies as needed at the official rate under current account from the designated banks with the necessary supporting documents to pay foreign trade contracts.

- In cases where a purchase of foreign exchange is needed to open an L/C for goods imported under a documentary credit/payment guarantee, the import contract, Verification Certificate for Foreign Exchange Payment for Imports and the application to open an L/C shall be presented to the designated bank. When payment for a purchase is needed, valid commercial documents shall be presented if payment is made by L/C. For verification of imports, the original customs declaration form for import shall be presented.
- For goods imported under documentary collection, the import contract, 'Verification Certificate for Foreign Exchange Payment for Imports', payment notice and valid commercial documents under collection shall be presented. The original customs declaration form is also required for verification.

- For import by remittance payment, the import contract, Verification Certificate, invoices, original customs declaration form and original transport document shall be presented. In cases of a difference between the consignee of the bill of lading and the business unit on the customs declaration form, and the name of buyer on the import contract, a proxy agreement between the parties concerned is needed;
- For those goods in the above-mentioned categories subject to import quota or under import control, an import licence granted by the relevant government agency or import certificate shall be presented; for those under the registration system, a completed form of registration shall also be presented.
- Advance payment for imports below 15 per cent of contract value or exceeding 15 per cent but less than the equivalent of US$100,000 or a payment for commission that exceeds a certain amount or proportion can be effected through the designated banks against a certificate of authenticity by SAFE. Individual payments for private purposes can be made directly through the banks if the amount is within the authorized limit. For the payments that exceed the authorized amount, the relevant valid documents should be re-checked by SAFE before payment.

Payment for service trades in foreign exchanges is managed as follows. Transactions in foreign exchanges for payment and income generated from service trade are made through the designated banks upon submitting the necessary supporting documents as required.

Transportation

- Income in RMB from passenger services and goods transportation by offices of foreign airlines in China may be converted into foreign currencies upon presenting the Notice of Sales of Foreign Exchange issued by SAFE, a list of tickets sold and other relevant documents;
- Payment in foreign currencies for freight under import and export contracts may be effected from the importer/exporter's foreign exchange account or paid with foreign currencies purchased at banks against relevant documents;
- Payment for transportation expenses, equipment maintenance and port usage fees may be processed as stipulated above and be subject to verification afterwards.

Patent, trademark use/transfer and royalties

To effect payments in foreign exchange for the licence of or transfer of patent or knowhow, trademarks (with or without patents and knowhow), software, technical consultancy, technical services, co-operative design, co-operative research and development, and hardware maintenance,[2] domestic units should present to the designated bank the following documents:

- written application;
- contract or agreement;
- invoice or payment notice;
- registration and effect certificate for technology and equipment import contract granted by foreign trade department (or permission of technology import, or registration of technology import contract, or data-sheet of technology import contracts);
- tax voucher.

In addition, other documents are required according to the nature of the business such as:

1. Filing certificate issued by the State Bureau of Intellectual Property for implementation of a patent licence;
2. Copy of patent registration or verification of advertisement on patent issued by the administration agency of patents for transfer of the patent;
3. Copy of patent registration or verification of advertisement on Patent issued by administration agency of patents, and verification of transfer of a trademark issued by trademark administration agency;
4. For consent to software usage, the contract should be stamped additionally with the ' Seal of Registration of Copyright Contract' or approval of the contract granted by the copyright administration agency.

Advertisement and exhibition

Payment in foreign exchange for overseas advertising and exhibitions may be paid through the user's foreign exchange account or with foreign currency purchased at banks against the necessary documents such as contract, approval from relevant administration agencies, and invoices or notices of payment etc.

Remuneration, bonus and allowance for employees of foreign nationality

Individuals of foreign nationality may purchase foreign currencies at banks with the documents including: written application, valid passport or identification document, employment document,[3] and breakdown of income in RMB and tax payment receipt.

Outward remittance of profits, stock dividends and interest

According to international balance of payment statistics principles, the outward remittance of profits, receipts and payments of interest, dividends and rentals, as well as payments of interest on external debt, all fall under current account. The relevant rules for their management are as follows:

- Payments in this category may be paid through the concerned enterprise's foreign exchange account or with foreign exchange purchased at banks.
- To remit abroad the current year gains mentioned above, FFEs shall present documentary proof to the designated foreign exchange banks including: tax payments; any receipt and taxation declaration forms;[4] current year audit report issued by a CPA; the board of directors' resolution on the distribution of profits, stock dividends or stock bonuses; FEE's Foreign Exchange Registration Certificate; Capital Assessment Report issued by a CPA; and other documents required by SAFE.
- To remit previous year gains abroad, the foreign investors in FFEs and enterprises issuing stock abroad shall present the audit report issued by a CPA in addition to the documents prescribed above. The audit report must be for the relevant years when the profits, stock dividends or stock bonuses arose.
- Neither an FFE whose registered capital has not been fully paid up as provided by the articles of association nor an enterprise issuing stock abroad, whose foreign

---

[2] Including consultancy on hardware, maintenance of computer hardware and relevant external equipment etc.

[3] Such as: certificate of employment issued by the social security agency, certificate of expert issued by bureau of administration of foreign expert and employment contract etc.

[4] For enterprises enjoying tax reduction or exemption, certificate of tax reduction or exemption issued by domiciled taxation administration agency shall be provided.

exchange funds raised by the issuance of stock have not been fully repatriated, is allowed to remit profits, stock dividends or stock bonuses abroad.

- Interest on external debts payable by domestic units should be paid or the foreign exchange required may be purchased at banks against certificates of authenticity issued by SAFE.

Foreign exchange for resident individuals

Foreign exchange needed by resident individuals to go abroad on personal business may be purchased from banks against valid documents required to illustrate authenticity and validate the need for foreign exchange. Banks should sell foreign currencies to individuals at the current day quoted rates and according to SAFE regulations. Standards for amounts which may be purchased by individuals are set for various situations and purposes.

Foreign exchange remitted legally to resident individuals, or drafts in foreign exchange brought back personally by residents, can be kept in foreign exchange bill account. Convertible foreign currencies owned by resident individuals or brought back by them can be kept in a bank note account in foreign exchange.

Other payments

Other foreign exchange payments, such as those for education and the entertainment industry, will be reviewed and may be effected according to the corresponding regulations of the regulations on sale and purchase of and payment in foreign exchange.

Income in foreign currencies under current account should be remitted back through designated banks

The sale and purchase of foreign currencies in current accounts should be carried out through those designated banks with foreign exchange transaction licences, which are issued and supervised by SAFE.

All domestic entities must remit in a timely manner all their earnings in foreign currencies under current account back to China and sell them to the banks at the official rate. Only those incomes in foreign currencies with approval from SAFE may be kept in foreign exchange accounts.

Profits repatriated from abroad by Chinese investors, repayments in foreign currency under China's economic aid projects and incomes from property abroad (including dividends and interest on securities, interest

on loans to foreign borrowers and on deposits) must be wholly settled through the banks.

All FFEs are allowed to open current accounts in foreign exchange with a ceiling on the amount of income which may be kept in foreign currencies. Some qualified Chinese enterprises are also authorized to open foreign exchange accounts in the designated banks to keep their foreign exchange earnings up to a maximum value. The opening of foreign exchange accounts requires the approval of SAFE.

Verification of import payments and export proceeds (VIEP)

In order to standardize banking procedures and to prevent speculation and other illegal activities, a verification system for import payments and export proceeds was implemented. The VIEP system is an important means of retrospective supervision aimed at ensuring safe receipt of foreign exchange and preventing foreign exchange from draining away through illegal channels.

The verification of export proceeds took effect on 1 January 1991 and the verification of import payments on 1 August 1994. The verification of export proceeds requires that all export earnings in foreign exchange should be verified by SAFE within a stated period after the declaration of goods.

Verification of import payments requires SAFE to verify foreign exchange payments in the stated period after goods are delivered. The verification certificate of import payment in foreign exchange shall be completed by the importer and acts as proof document for the designated bank to make import payments in foreign exchange. The timing of verification varies according to the different terms of settlement. In the case of payment upon delivery, verification is made when the designated foreign exchange bank makes payment against the original customs declaration form. For other settlements, the importer shall apply to SAFE for verification by presenting the verification certificate, record form and original customs declaration forms (receipts verifying foreign exchange derived from entrepot trade surrendered in case of payment for entrepot trade)

The VIEP system is an important tool in supervising the inflow and outflow of foreign exchange through imports and exports, preventing illegal capital movements and the outflow of foreign exchange, as well as providing regular supervision of foreign exchange transactions on current account. Since 1 May 1999, regulation of the examination of receipts in foreign exchange has been implemented as a method to reward genuine and punish illegal exporters. The ratios of filed foreign exchange proceeds to submitted verification forms of export transactions are the main items under examination. Exporters are classified into groups according to examination results and are judged to deserve reward or punishment accordingly, as an incentive to promote exports and encourage export companies to collect export earnings fully in foreign exchange in a timely manner.

On 1 January 1999, a checking system for import and export declarations was put into operation through the SAFE network, the customs and the banks. The verification of import and export declarations may be effected through the online network checking system which makes the work much easier and more efficient, as well as more convenient for companies.

Control over capital accounts

China maintains a policy of actively encouraging FDI while guiding the direction of capital flows. According to the strategic long-term goal of foreign exchange administration in China, the basic principle of administering capital accounts is to perfect the administration system and to advance the convertibility of capital accounts in a progressive and planned manner.

Foreign exchange on capital account is controlled nowadays in the following ways:

- All foreign exchange gains on capital account should be repatriated from abroad except those cases specified by the State Council.
- All domestic entities should put their foreign exchange income on capital account into special accounts opened in the designated banks and approval from SAFE is required when foreign exchange needs to be converted into RMB.[5]
- All purchases of foreign exchange and payments on capital account to abroad must be checked by SAFE and the banks cannot process a payment without an approval document from SAFE.

At present, there are three major types of transaction on capital accounts in China: external debt, foreign direct investment and the Chinese investment abroad.

Administration of external debt and external guarantee

The general aim of external debt control is to limit the size of the external debt to a moderate level, to set up a rational debt structure and safe debt servicing sources.

China's control over external debt and external guarantees takes three major forms: management through planning, examination of financial qualifications and the registration system.

External debt includes:

- international financial institution loans;
- foreign government loans;
- foreign bank and financial institution loans;
- buyer's credits;
- foreign enterprise loans;
- foreign currency bonds;
- international financial leases;
- deferred payments;
- debts repaid directly in foreign exchange in compensation trade; and
- external debt in other forms.

Funds borrowed in foreign exchange by debtors from banks with foreign capital and Chinese and foreign joint banks registered in China are also regarded as external debt. Funds borrowed in foreign exchange from abroad by banks with foreign capital or by Chinese and foreign joint banks, which are registered in China, are not regarded as external debt.

Foreign borrowings by Chinese financial institutions and Chinese enterprises with a term longer than one year, excluding government loans, must be incorporated into the state external debt plan made by the State Development and Planning Committee (SDPC). SAFE gives case-by-case approval to the international commercial loans borrowed by all Chinese financial institutions except the state-owned commercial banks, which exercise management of the long and mid-term external debt. The People's Bank of China (PBC) controls the nationwide scale of short-term external commercial debt balances. Within the scale, SAFE allocates debt quotas to provincial financial institutions and/or enterprises. All financial institutions can borrow external loans with one-year maturity within the given quotas and quotas may be used repeatedly within their limits.

---

[5] All the foreign founded enterprises can convert their registered capital in the authorized banks without approval from SAFE since 1 July 2002.

Foreign-funded enterprises can borrow external loans without any advance approval.

China follows a policy of managing external debt by registration. The registration of external debt may be on a case-by-case or periodic basis. All domestic entities (including foreign-funded enterprises) are required, while borrowing, to register at and obtain a case-by-case registration certificate for their external debt from the local branch of SAFE by submitting a copy of the loan agreement within 15 days of signing the formal agreement.

For international financial institution loans, foreign government loans, external borrowing by the Bank of China or other authorized banks and financial institutions, the debtors concerned are required to register at and obtain periodic registration certificates for their external debt from a domiciled branch of SAFE. All repayments of principal and interest should be approved by SAFE (except for banks).

External debt inflows and outflows are managed by special accounts. External debt special accounts (including External Debt Special Accounts and Debt Service Special Accounts) shall be opened in the designated foreign exchange banks. Domestic foreign-funded banks can only open external debt special accounts for their own lending. External debt special accounts shall be opened upon the approval of SAFE and its branches.

Issuing bonds abroad (including convertible bonds, negotiable certificates of deposit and commercial paper) is under strict control. The qualifications to issue bonds abroad of all domestic entities, except the Ministry of Finance (MOF), are appraised biannually jointly by the SDPC, PBC and other relevant organizations and approved by the State Council. Before a qualified entity issues bonds, it should undergo an appraisal made by SDPC together with SAFE and receive approval of the State Council. The selection of target market, the timing for bond issues and other relevant conditions must be examined by SAFE. Local governments are forbidden to issue bonds abroad. The issuance of commercial bonds by domestic entities must be approved by SAFE and the amount of the issues should be deducted from their short-term external loans quotas. Convertible bonds issued in overseas markets by listed foreign-funded enterprises are exempt from qualification examination but must follow the same approval formalities as applied to domestic entities on issuing bonds abroad within their annual quotas.

An external guarantee is regarded and controlled as external debt in China. 'External guarantee' refers to guarantees in the forms of guarantee letters, stand-by letters of credit, promissory note, cheques and drafts, mortgages over properties, hypothecation of current assets, or by property rights as stipulated, provided by institutions within Chinese territory to institutions outside China. Guarantees provided to foreign-funded financial institutions inside China are also regarded as external guarantees.

Only financial institutions with authorized licences for external guarantees (excluding foreign-funded financial institutions) and non-financial institutions having the ability to repay the external debts they guarantee are permitted to provide external guarantees. Governmental institutions should not guarantee external debts except for the State-Council-approved utilization of foreign government loans or loans from international financial institutions. It is forbidden to guarantee overseas enterprises against loss.

SAFE examines and approves each external guarantee provided by a domestic entity case by case and all cases of external guarantee must be filed with SAFE. While examining and approving an external guarantee, SAFE will examine the amount and risk, the ratio between assets and debts, losses and benefits of the guarantees before appraising and deciding the guarantee ceiling.

External guarantees for up to and including one year can be examined and approved by the SAFE at province, autonomous region, municipality, listed city or special economic zone levels.

Those external guarantees for more than one year should be submitted to local branches of SAFE for initial examination and then to SAFE headquarter for examination and approval. Verification by SAFE is required when the warrantor will fulfil the guarantee liability.

Management of foreign direct investment (FDI)

Flexible management is adopted in foreign exchange payments and earnings under capital account of foreign-funded enterprises in China to encourage FDI.

The capital subscriptions of foreign investor(s) in an enterprise can be reserved in the form of foreign exchange under its foreign exchange account and can be converted into RMB upon approval by SAFE.

To open a capital account, temporary account or investment special account the FFE should apply to SAFE presenting the following documents:

1. Application form stamped with the seal of the enterprise which illustrates the basic situation of the enterprise, the reason for opening the account, and the potential bank where the account is to be opened;
2. Registration certificate of foreign exchange (to be returned after inspection);
3. Phased investment plan and investment contract to be provided by a foreign investor as a non-legal entity when applying to open an investment special account;
4. Certificate of credibility issued by the account opening bank of the foreign legal person or natural person;
5. Legally notarized proxy agreement when a domestic legal person or natural person applies to open an account on behalf of a foreign person;
6. Other documents required by SAFE when necessary (such as investment contract, or company constitution etc).

Foreign-funded enterprises can borrow foreign exchange loans and repay directly to overseas banks without approval in advance, while the transaction must be registered with the foreign exchange administration afterwards. The balance of mid-to-long term loans of the enterprise can not exceed the difference between total investment and the registered capital of the enterprise concerned.[6]

When a foreign investor in a foreign-funded enterprise terminates an investment legally, the foreign exchange received can be remitted abroad from its foreign exchange account or be paid at the bank upon approval.

Foreign exchange registration and the annual inspection system are applied to foreign-funded enterprises as means of supervision and management.

Within 30 days of receiving a business licence for legal person status in China, a FFE should carry out foreign exchange registration with the local branch of SAFE. SAFE will issue a Foreign Exchange Registration Certificate of Foreign-funded Enterprise after reviewing the documents including: approval for establishment issued by the relevant government agencies, business licence as legal person of the PRC issued by the State Administration of Commerce and Industry, approved and valid enterprise contract and constitution, and other documents required by SAFE. The enterprise can

open foreign exchange accounts at designated banks with the certificate; SAFE will inspect the registration certificate annually.

A foreign-funded enterprise is permitted to reinvest its profits in RMB and the reinvestment is treated the same as an investment in foreign exchange.

In order to reinvest its distributed foreign exchange or RMB profit domestically in a new FFE, the foreign party of an existing FFE shall apply for verification of authenticity with the local branch of SAFE by presenting the following documents:

1. Capital assessment report issued by CPA;
2. Annual financial audit report;
3. The board of directors' profit distribution resolution;
4. The re-investor's confirmation of its reinvestment of profits;
5. Foreign exchange registration certificate of the existing FFE;
6. Other documents required by SAFE.

At present, the opening of China's financial market is at a very early stage. Only a few kinds of listed stocks in foreign exchange are available to foreign investors such as B shares listed on the domestic stock exchanges, H shares on the Hong Kong Stock Exchange and N shares on the New York Stock Exchange. Possible investors in B shares include: natural persons, legal entities and other organizations in foreign countries, Hong Kong, Macao or Taiwan, and Chinese citizen residing abroad.

Management of investment abroad

Capital in China is far from sufficient and therefore, capital outflow is under strict administration. The term 'investment abroad' refers to a China-registered enterprise which sets up any kind of enterprise, purchases stocks, or participates in an overseas enterprise for the purpose of production and operation.

Currently, the SDPC and the Ministry of Foreign Trade and Economic Cooperation (MOFTEC) and their delegated agencies examine and approve all overseas investment projects. SAFE is responsible for examining the project in terms of foreign exchange flow. Before domestic entities submit their applications to SDPC and MOFTEC, SAFE must carry out its examination.

SAFE will review the following documents:

---

[6] Foreign holding companies are allowed to expand the difference up to 1:7.

- certificate of approval by the competent state department,
- official assessment of the investment risks and availability of foreign exchange sources;
- investment contract or any other documents testifying to the amount of foreign exchange funds to be remitted abroad. The purpose of the examination is to appraise the qualification of the domestic entity as an investor abroad, the foreign exchange risk for the investment and the capital resource to invest abroad.

SAFE offices at the provincial level are responsible for the review, and emphasis will be placed on three aspects: qualification of the domestic investors, assessment of investment risk and sources of foreign exchange.

Profits gained by Chinese investors should be wholly repatriated home.

When an enterprise abroad legally terminates its operation or disincorporates, the domestic investor must submit to SAFE for recording the relevant documents after liquidation including its balance sheet, asset inventory, and property valuation, etc. The property in foreign exchange belonging to the Chinese investors must be remitted back within 30 days after liquidation and can not defalcate or remain abroad without the approval of SAFE.

Except for authorized financial institutions and industry-trade integrated enterprises, no resident individuals are permitted to purchase securities abroad. Such purchases by authorized financial institutions are subject to SAFE's prior examination and approval. Foreign currency securities (except blue chips and government bonds) purchased by banks should not exceed 10 per cent of the total of their foreign exchange assets. The corresponding ratio for non-bank financial institutions is 25 per cent. Banks and non-bank financial institutions should present detailed reports to SAFE on a quarterly basis when trading securities in foreign currencies other than listed stocks on overseas stock exchanges.

Evolution of the RMB exchange Rate mechanism

The RMB exchange rate is a single, managed floating exchange rate based on market demand and supply which has been set up since RMB exchange rates were unified on 1 January 1994.

Before the 1994 reform, there were many foreign exchange swap centres across the country characterized by strong administration, regional segmentation, and fluctuating prices. In 1994, the China (Shanghai) Foreign Exchange Trading Centre was established linking 34 cities and neighbourhood regions through a computer network. A nationwide, unified inter-bank trading market was set up. The main trading bodies on the market include domestic-funded banks and their authorised branches, and authorized non-bank financial institutions. Following foreign-funded enterprises' participation in the market, foreign-invested banks are also permitted to operate in the market, so that the interbank trading market is further stimulated.

At present, four foreign currencies are tradable with the RMB at the Centre: the US dollar, the Japanese yen, the Hong Kong dollar and the euro. The daily weighted average exchange rate is published by the People's Bank of China (PBC) as a benchmark rate for the ensuing business day. On this base, floating limits of 0.3 per cent for the US dollar and 1 per cent for the Japanese yen and the Hong Kong dollar are permitted when banks trade. The designated foreign exchange trading banks can decide their exchange rates within fluctuating limits. The actual trading rate can not exceed the intermediate rate by more than 0.5 per cent, which is calculated according to the real price in the international foreign exchange market. The trading banks can negotiate the price with their clients within a regulated range for transactions up to US$1 million and more.

The single RMB exchange rate and unified inter-bank system has created more favourable conditions for China to participate in international competition on fair and equal terms. PBC exercises macro-control over the RMB exchange rate and intervenes when necessary to ensure the soundness and stability of the rate.

Macro-management system of balance of payments

The balance of payments is a comprehensive reflection of a nation's external economic activities. The balance sheet is an integrated record of a nation's external payments and earnings in a certain period of time and an important basis for macro-economic policy making. China began to compile its balance sheet in 1980 and has published it since 1982. A new method of declaring external payments and earnings was put into practice in 1996, and indirect declaration by financial institutions was carried out in the same year. Direct declaration of four types of business began in 1997 including direct investment, securities investment, external property and profit and loss of financial institutions, and foreign exchange payments and conversions. The balance of payments statistics and the relevant analysis and forecasting has played a very important role in the tuning and management system of the Chinese macro-economy.

According to the reporting system of balance of payments statistics, Chinese residents[7] must duly report their international receipts and payments accurately and comprehensively with effect from 1 January 1996. Reporting may be made mainly through financial institutions, item by item for each business day, for checking and verification by SAFE. If any problems are discovered, the bank concerned should rectify them without delay.

FFEs in China and Chinese enterprises with direct investment abroad should report directly to SAFE their direct investment statistics concerning the rights and interests of investors, liabilities as well as proportions of dividends.

Domestic securities registration agencies and dealers on domestic stock exchanges should report to SAFE on receipts and payments under transactions in securities investments made for their own account or for clients. Dealers trading in offshore securities for their own account or for domestic clients should complete and submit to SAFE a reporting form for offshore portfolio Investment.

Supervision and control of foreign exchange operations in the financial institutions

Following RMB convertibility on current account and formulation of the inter-bank market, most payments and earnings in foreign exchange on current account can be transacted directly in the designated banks with licences. Transactions on capital account should also be made after checking and/or approval in those banks with licences. In order to avoid the mixing of transactions on capital account with those on current account and to prevent fraudulent foreign exchange purchases, the licensed banks must inspect all approval certificates according to relevant regulations when processing sales and payments in foreign exchange. Since 1994, as

relevant managerial regulations and measures were formulated, supervision on compliance with foreign exchange regulations has been strengthened when financial institutions deal in foreign exchange operations and punishment of wrongdoings has been reinforced.

A foreign exchange system suitable for a socialist market economy

Since opening up and reform, especially the 1994 reform, distinct achievements have been made in the foreign exchange system. The convertibility of the RMB on current account was realized. A foreign exchange system suitable for a socialist market economy was set up, thereby boosting the healthy and sustainable development of the national economy and promoting the degree of opening up.

In December 1980, the *Provisional Ordinance of Foreign Exchange Control of P R China* was promulgated, and a series of regulations and measures were issued subsequently. Following the 1994 reform, the *Provisional Ordinance* was revised and then the *Ordinance of Foreign Exchange Control of P R China* was enacted in February of 1996. At the end of 1996, the Ordinance was adjusted after convertibility of the RMB on current account was realised. The Ordinance is one of the important and basic regulations in the legal system of foreign exchange administration in China. An across-the-board review and revision of regulations, measures and policies was carried out in recent years, and new regulations were formulated and promulgated. These new regulations embody outputs of the reforms since 1994. To sum up, it is important to enrich continuously and perfect the foreign exchange administration system, based on the country's situation and practical experience, and to establish gradually a scientific, rational and effective legal system of foreign exchange administration. All these efforts will form the legal safeguard to ensure real convertibility on current account and effective control of transactions on capital account, to strengthen the macro-management of external balances and to maintain a well-balanced foreign exchange market.

On the basis of the current administration system, China will continue to push forward foreign exchange

---

[7] Herein refers to: natural persons residing in China for over one year except students; people for medical care; foreign nationals working for foreign embassies and their dependants; Chinese people going abroad for short stays (residing abroad for less than one year); legal persons (including FFEs) set up in China according to law and missions of foreign legal people (except those of international organizations and foreign embassies and consulates); Chinese government organizations and establishments and army units.

administration reform step by step. The achievements gained in realizing convertibility on RMB current account will be maintained and amplified. Greater efforts will be exerted to achieve capital account convertibility gradually so that full RMB convertibility can be accomplished. The Chinese government will take a prudent and pragmatic attitude towards implementing convertibility of the RMB on capital account gradually. Reform of foreign exchange administration will be deepened in order to adapt to the new situation after China's entry into the WTO, providing better service to enterprises and investors and ensuring healthy and stable development of the national economy.

5.3

China's Securities Market*

China Securities Regulatory Commission

The current status of China's securities industry

China's securities market has evolved and developed gradually alongside the progress of China's opening up and economic reform. With the establishment of the Shanghai Stock Exchange in December 1990 and the Shenzhen Stock Exchange in June 1991, China's securities market has formally taken shape. In more than ten years of development, the securities industry has experienced a process of transition from virtually nothing to its present scale, from decentralization to centralization, from manual operation to the adoption of modern technologies, from a regional to a national market and from a domestically oriented to an internationally integrated market. Remarkable progress has been achieved in both the size of the market and the trading technology. China's securities market is now the third largest in Asia after Tokyo and Hong Kong and has formed a market structure that comprises A-share, B-share, H-share and a multitude of other financing options, which have played a vitally important role in improving financing structures, optimizing resource allocations and propelling the economic development.

By the end of June 2002, 1,188 companies were listed on the Shanghai and Shenzhen stock exchanges with a total market capitalization and float capitalization of RMB4.77 trillion and RMB1.56 trillion respectively. The number of investor accounts totalled RMB68.07 million. There were 51 close-ended contractual securities investment funds and five open-ended securities investment funds, with a total funding of about RMB100 billion. The futures market has reversed the continued downturn of the past few years

and begun to gather momentum for growth. In terms of securities trading technology, paperless systems have been applied to the issuance and trading of shares and funds, and all securities trading agencies have started to implement uniform technical standards.

While the securities market is developing rapidly, the securities regulatory mechanism is also gradually being perfected. Initially, the regulation and supervision of the securities market was dispersed among a number of central government departments such as the State Planning Commission (now the State Development Planning Commission), the Ministry of Finance and State Commission for the Restructuring of the Economic Structure (now the Office for Restructuring the Economy), and local government. A dual regulatory system evolved later, with the Securities Commission of the State Council being responsible for macro control and the China Securities Regulatory Commission (CSRC) exercising specific regulatory functions. The promulgation of the Securities Law in December 1998 firmly established China's securities regulatory regime with centralized and unified regulation and supervision of the securities market in the country by CSRC at the core, supported by self-disciplinary regulation by the stock exchanges and Securities Industry Association.

CSRC is an agency directly affiliated with the State Council. Within it are 13 functional departments and three subordinate institutions. CSRC is also represented regionally by nine securities regulatory offices, two offices directly affiliated with it and 25 special commissioner offices of securities regulation and supervision in key cities in China (see Figure 5.3.1). Self-regulating organizations in the industry include China

* This chapter was originally written in Chinese and was translated by Li Yong.

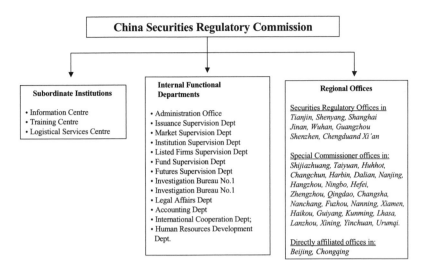

Figure 5.3.1 Breakdown of departments within the CSRC

Securities Industry Association, Shanghai and Shenzhen stock exchanges, China Association of Futures Industry and the commodity exchanges in Shanghai, Dalian and Zhengzhou. These organizations conduct self-regulation and supervision in accordance with relevant industry regulations. In a newly developing market such as China, the role of self-regulating organisations is still weak because of the immature market mechanism. With improvements in this and the levels of regulation and supervision, many regulatory and supervisory functions will gradually be transferred from the CSRC to self-regulating organisations.

The legal framework regarding the securities market is still in development. Under the principle of 'rule of law, regulation and supervision, self-discipline and standardisation', a legal framework of laws and regulations governing the securities market has taken shape. The core of this is the Corporations Law and Securities Law, supplemented by administrative regulations, and the key body is the departmental regulations and normative circulars, rules established by the stock exchanges and the rules and regulations introduced by self-regulating organisations such as the Securities Industry Association.

The Corporations Law and Securities Law are the two basic laws governing China's securities market. The administrative regulations by the State Council either fill in the legislative blanks in related areas or provide specific details on related legal regimes. The departmental regulations and normative circulars issued by the CSRC in accordance with relevant laws and administrative regulations are to provide particulars and supplements on relevant laws and regulations, thereby

constituting the important elements of China's legal systems governing the securities market.

Following China's accession to the WTO, the CSRC has rectified and amended all regulations and administrative approval procedures in order to comply with the commitments China has made in relation to the securities industry. Some new rules have been promulgated, such as the Rules for the Establishment of Securities Companies with Foreign Equity Participation and the Rules for the establishment of Fund Management Companies with Foreign Equity Participation. At the same time, both Shanghai and Shenzhen Stock Exchanges are revising their rules of management on memberships and on B-share trading seats, in compliance with China's WTO commitments.

New dynamics faced by China following WTO accession

On 11 December 2001, China officially joined the WTO. This marked a new phase in the opening up of the securities industry.

The main elements of China's opening up of the securities industry are the following:

1. Foreign securities institutions may engage directly (without a Chinese intermediary) in B share business.
2. Upon accession, representative offices of foreign securities institutions in China may become Special Members of all Chinese stock exchanges.
3. Upon accession, foreign service suppliers will be permitted to establish joint ventures with foreign investment of up to 33 per cent participation to

conduct domestic securities investment fund management business. Within three years of accession, the foreign investment participation limit will be increased to 49 per cent.

4. Within three years of accession, foreign securities institutions will be permitted to establish joint ventures, with foreign minority ownership not exceeding 1/3, to engage (without a Chinese intermediary) in underwriting A shares and in underwriting and trading of B and H shares as well as government and corporate debts and launching of funds.

Joining the WTO is necessary for the promotion of the sustained and healthy development of China's economy. It is an important milestone marking China's entry into a new phase of opening up and has also offered an opportunity of historic significance for the long-term and normal development of China's securities industry and market. Firstly, following WTO accession, China's economy will be integrated into the world economic system and WTO membership will provide new momentum for economic development, facilitating rapid economic growth which will in turn yield a better development of China's securities industry. Secondly, the opening up of insurance and banking industries will attract foreign investors to China, as a result of which there will be expanded sources of market funds and fund availability will be better than before. Thirdly, more intermediaries will come from mature markets to join China's securities industry. This will be conducive to adjusting the investor structure and elevating the professional level of securities agencies. Finally, participation in international competition will impel publicly listed companies to enhance the quality of their corporate performance and level of corporate governance.

While the securities industry has many opportunities, WTO accession has also brought great challenges. The first challenge is that the entry of foreign securities institutions will generate new tasks for China's securities regulation and supervision. International political and economic factors will have an increased impact on China's financial market, which will consequently increase the level of difficulty in regulating and supervising the securities market and therefore in handling possible crises.

The second challenge results from the great gap that has existed between Chinese securities institutions and their foreign counterparts in terms of size of capital, level of corporate governance and risk control. Although

foreign securities institutions can only enter China's securities market in the form of joint ventures at present, their direct entry into the securities market will inevitably become a reality with the acceleration of the opening up process. If domestic securities institutions are not able to mature quickly, they will eventually be eliminated by the market.

The third challenge is that domestic listed companies will be subject to the ordeal of the law of the market – survival of the fittest – when competing with international giants on the same stage. The performances of the listed companies will polarise and there is likely to be large annual fluctuations. Last but not least, China's securities market needs to converge with international practices, which will require major reforms in an effort to improve market transparency and crack down on illegal conduct. The process of reform is in itself a great challenge for China's securities industry.

Future development trends

The sustained development of China's economy has motivated a demand for financing by a large number of enterprises. Such demand alone will require that the capital market continues to maintain its trend of rapid development. At the same time, China's savings rate has been high and significant funds need to find diversified channels of investment. From the perspectives of both supply and demand, there will be greater development space for China's capital market, manifested specifically in the following:

1. There is still considerable room for the stock issuance market to develop. Stable growth of China's economy will increase enterprises' demands for financing, which will give impetus to the prosperity of the A-share market. With China's accelerating process of opening up and in order to meet the needs of foreign-invested enterprises for financing in China, CSRC has promulgated rules and regulations in relation to the financing of FIEs on the stock market in China. The issuance of shares and public listing of FIEs on the stock market has now entered the stage of actual operation, as a result of which China's securities market will quickly expand.
2. The general quality of publicly listed companies will improve. The CSRC will step up regulation and supervision of all publicly listed companies. This effort is, firstly, to improve the corporate governance structure of listed companies and guide them to

establish modern enterprise systems. Secondly, the CSRC will push forward the improvement of accounting standards and information disclosure in order to make them converge gradually with international accounting standards and international practices. Thirdly, China has implemented a classified system of regulation and supervision according to the quality of the publicly listed companies. The system has clarified the responsibilities of regulation and supervision, thereby forming a coordinating mechanism between the audit of share issuance and the regulation and supervision of listed companies. Finally, systems of appointing independent directors and delisting companies has been implemented. All these measures will help to improve the general quality and competitiveness of listed companies.

3. Institutional investors will increase. The outline tenth five year plan for the national economy has expressly pointed out that active effort will be made between 2001 and 2005 to foster institutional investors such as securities investment funds, pension funds and insurance funds. At present, insurance funds can enter the securities market indirectly by purchasing securities investment funds. Pension funds, on the other hand, are taking on an increasingly important role and will in the future become the largest institutional investor in the capital market. At the same time, the entry of foreign institutional investors will play a positive role in terms of facilitating capital inflow, introducing technology and management expertise and strengthening both co-operation and competition, all of which will be conducive to enhancing the level of maturity of China's securities market.

4. There will be diversified trading products available at the stock market. In recent years, China's funds and bonds markets have developed rapidly. T-bonds, corporate bonds and transferable bonds will expand further in terms of the size of issues, which will offer the investors more investment options. After WTO accession, the competitive advantages of foreign investors in the aspects of business competence, market experiences, risk management and fund size will correspondingly pose advance requirements for financial products on the securities market and prompt further diversity of trading products. With the increase in the depth and width of China's securities market, a pattern will develop characterized by domination of stock markets, rapid development of bonds and funds and further trials on financial derivatives.

5. Market transparency will increase further. With improvement of accounting rules and information disclosure standards, the authenticity and reliability of corporate financial and accounting information as well as the transparency of corporate operations will be further enhanced. The principle of transparency in WTO rules also require that regulatory bodies change their conception of regulation and supervision, reduce the items subject to examination and approval and simplify examination and approval procedures so that the formulation and implementation of laws and regulations conforms with international practices and is transparent. All of these will help increase market transparency, enhance the predictability and procedural guarantee of policies and regulations, heighten public credibility and strengthen investor confidence.

Under the conditions of rapid and sustained development of China's macro economy and accompanied by enhancement of the level of securities regulation and supervision, gradual improvement of securities laws and regulations, the increasing importance given to the protection of investors' interests and the maturity of equity culture, China's securities industry will follow the liberalization, globalization and securitization trends of the international financial market. China's securities market will be more open, fair, efficient and orderly.

Supplement 1 to Chapter 5.3

List of key laws and regulations concerning the securities and futures industry

Laws (three items of legislation)

1. *Company Law of the People's Republic of China*, adopted by the 5th Session of the Standing Committee of the 8th National People's Congress on 29 December 1993, amended in accordance with the *Decision Concerning Amending The Company Law of the People's Republic of China* by the 13th Session of the Standing Committee of the 9th National People's Congress on 25 December 1999, promulgated by Order No. 29 of the President of the People's Republic of China on 25 December 1999.

2. *Securities Law of the People's Republic of China*, adopted at the 6th Meeting of the Standing Committee of the 9th National People's Congress of the People's Republic of China on 29 December 1998, promulgated by Order No. 12 of the President of the People's Republic of China on 29 December 1998.

3. *Trust Law of the People's Republic of China*, adopted at the 21st session of the Standing Committee of the 9th National People's Congress, promulgated by Order No. 50 of the President of the People's Republic of China on 28 April 2001

Administrative regulations (18 sets)

1. *Notice of the State Council on Further Strengthening of the Macro Administration of the Securities Market*, promulgated on 17 December 1992. Guo Fa [1992] No. 68

2. *Provisional Regulations for Administration of the Issuance and Trading of Shares*, promulgated by Order No. 112 of the State Council of the People's Republic of China on 22 April 1993.

3. *Rules on the Administration of Enterprise Bonds*, promulgated by Order No. 121 of the State Council of the People's Republic of China on 2 August, 1993.

4. *Interim Measures on the Prevention of Securities Frauds*, approved by the State Council on 15 August 1993 and promulgated by the State Council Securities Committee on 2 September 1993.

5. *Special Regulations on Overseas Offering and Listing of Companies Limited by Shares*, promulgated by Order No. 160 of the State Council of the People's Republic of China on 4 August 1994.

6. *State Council Regulations on Domestic Listing of Foreign Shares by Companies Limited by Shares*, adopted at the 37th standing conference of the State Council and promulgated by Order No. 189 of the State Council of the People's Republic of China on 25 December 1995.

7. *Interim Measures on the Administration of Convertible Corporate Bonds*, approved by the State Council and promulgated by the State Council Securities Committee on 25 March 1997.

8. *State Council Notice on Further Strengthening of the Administration of Overseas Shares Issuance and Public Offering*, promulgated on 20 June 1997, Gua Fa [1997] No. 21.

9. *Interim Measures on the Administration of Securities Investment Funds*, approved by the State Council on 5 November 1997 and promulgated by the State Council Securities Committee on 14 November 1997

10. *Interim Measures on the Administration of Securities and Futures Investment Consultancy*, approved by

the State Council on 30 November, 1997 and promulgated by the State Council Securities Committee on 25 December 1997

11. *Measures on Penalising Illegal Financial Conducts*, promulgated by Order 260 of the State Council of the People's Republic of China on 22 February 1999

12. *Provisional Rules on the Administration of Futures Trading*, promulgated by Order 267 of the State Council of the People's Republic of China on 2 June 1999

13. *Rules of the Share Issuance Examination Committee of China Securities Regulatory Commission*, approved by the State Council on 19 August, 1999 and promulgated by China Securities Regulatory Commission on 16 September 1999.

14. *Guidance for the Regulation, Supervision, Examination and Approval of the Applications by Domestic Enterprises for Listing on Hong Kong's Growth Enterprise Market*, approved by the State Council on 6 September 1999 and promulgated by China Securities Regulatory Commission on 21 September 1999.

15. *Interim Measures on the Administration of Venture Capital Funds of the Securities Exchanges*, approved by the State Council on 31 January 2000 and promulgated by China Securities Regulatory Commission and the Ministry of Finance on 4 April, 2000.

16. *Interim Measures on the Administration of Securities Settlement of Venture Capital Funds*, approved by the State Council on 31 January 2000 and promulgated by China Securities Regulatory Commission and the Ministry of Finance on 4 April 2000.

17. *Procedures of Verification and Approval for Share Issuance*, approved by the State Council and promulgated by China Securities Regulatory Commission on 16 March 2000.

18. *Interim Measures on the Reduction of State-held Shares to Raise Social Security Funds*, promulgated on 6 June, 2001, *Guo Fa* [2001] No. 22

(Editor's note: The above list was provided by China Securities Regulatory Commission. There has been no official translation of the names of the laws and regulations, therefore they may vary in wording in other publications.)

Part Six

Sectors of Opportunity

Automobile and Motorcycle Industries

Mark Norcliffe, Society of Motor Manufacturers and Traders, and Jonathan Reuvid

Market growth

The China Association of Automobile Manufacturers has estimated that in the period from January to October 2002 overall vehicle sales reached 2.38 million units, matching total sales for the whole of 2001 and showing explosive year-on-year growth of 33 per cent. Within this total, car sales at 803,000 registered a significant increase of 53,000 in ten months over sales for the whole of 2001.

Since the beginning of the 1990s, the Chinese passenger car market has multiplied from a low base of fewer than 50,000 units in 1990 to 750,000 in 2001 and an estimated 950,000+ in 2002. By the end of 2000, the PARC (vehicle population on the road) of passenger vehicles (cars and buses) was estimated at 8.5 million.

As Figure 6.1.1 demonstrates, what was already strong growth has accelerated over the past two years. The market's main drivers for growth are

- a rapidly increasing percentage of private buyers;
- a large number of new models appearing in the market;
- continued targeting of the Chinese market by major global vehicle manufacturers;
- gaining of market share by new indigenous manufacturers.

Each of these market drivers is examined in more detail in this chapter.

By contrast, growth in the production and sale of motorcycles is modest. Sales rose from 8.9 million in

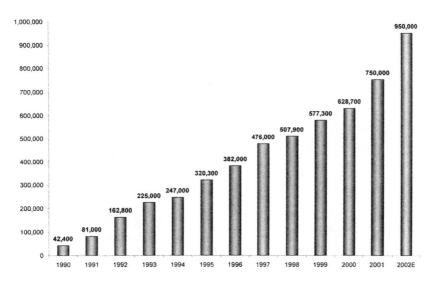

Notes: For local production only

Source: Automotive Resources Asia Ltd (ARA) Forecast

Figure 6.1.1 China's passenger car market 1990 to 2002

1998 to 11.5 million in 2000 and 5.7 million new two wheeled motorcycles were registered in the first six months of 2002, up 13.2 per cent year-on-year. Sales of the traditional Chinese three-wheelers fell 7.1 per cent year-on-year for the same period to 180,000 but at the end of 2000, 4,547 million of the 37,718 million motorcycles in use in China were still of the three-wheeled variety.

Segmentation of the passenger car market

The most striking aspect of the developing passenger car market in the past six years has been the growth in private ownership. As Figure 6.1.2 shows, the proportion of automobiles sold to individuals and private enterprises rose from 10 per cent in 1995 to an estimated 50 per cent in 2001. Private sales rose from approximately 32,000 to 375,000 units over this period, a more than eleven-fold increase.

The share of the taxi sector fell from 30 per cent in 1995 to 24 per cent in 2001. Sales growth potential has been constrained in many cities which have capped their taxi populations but the market of 180,000 units annually remains attractive.

At the other end of the market spectrum, the share of sales to state-owned enterprises and to central and local government have declined by two-thirds and one-third respectively to 10 per cent each (75,000 units in

2001). Automobile sales to joint ventures and wholly-foreign owned enterprises also declined by two-thirds, to 37,500 in 2001. It seems very likely that these sectors have declined further in 2002 in favour of the increasing private sector.

The current segmentation of the market in terms of units sold is reflected in a dispersed price segmentation. China lacks a significant middle class population and the demand for passenger cars is concentrated in two segments: compact automobiles priced at less than RMB150,000 (US$18,000) which account for 58 per cent of the market (24 per cent at less than US$11,000) and mid- to high-end cars priced over RMB250,000 (US$30,000) which account for a further 24 per cent market share.

Geographical dispersion of the market

The geographic dispersion by province of passenger vehicles in use at the end of 2000 casts further interesting light on the development of the market. Table 6.1.1 confirms that only 14 municipalities and provinces registered passenger vehicle PARCs of more than 2.5 million.

Together they account for 72 per cent of the total passenger vehicle PARC nationally and generally accurately reflect the GDP per head among the more developed areas of the Chinese economy.

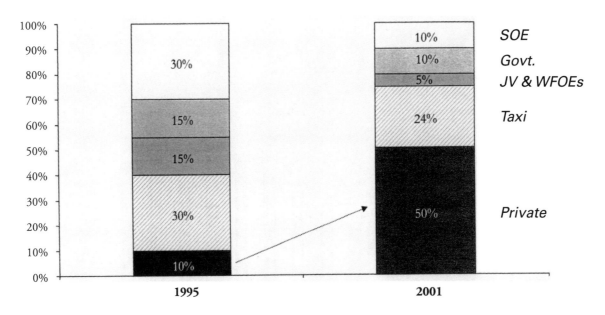

Source: ARA China National Car Market Survey

Figure 6.1.2 Customer segmentation: growth of private customers

Table 6.1.1 Passenger vehicles in use by leading provinces (end 2000)

Province	No of vehicles (million)
Beijing	8.2
Tianjin	2.5*
Hebei	5.0
Shanxi	2.5*
Liaoning	4.4
Heilongjiang	3.1
Shanghai	3.3*
Jiangsu	4.1
Zhejiang	3.2*
Shandong	5.3*
Henan	4.6
Guangdong	8.5*
Sichuan	4.4
Yunnan	2.8*
Total	61.9

*average <10 seats per vehicle
Source: China Association of Automobile Manufacturers

The motorcycle PARC is dispersed less evenly with higher than average usage in both urban and sparsely populated areas. Between 1990 and 2000, motorcycles in use per 1,000 head of population nationally multiplied tenfold from 3.0 to 29.8. Table 6.1.2 indicates the variation in popularization by listing the 10 municipalities and provinces where usage per 1,000 is above the national average of 29.8.

Automobile manufacturing

At present, there are over 100 vehicle assemblers in China, but the market is concentrated in the hands of a few. The Big Three auto companies, First Auto Works (FAW), Shanghai Auto Industry Corporation (SAIC) and Dong Feng Motors captured 47 per cent of the total market in 2001. However, a number of Chinese domestic producers – Chery, Geely and Qinchuan Flyer – have grabbed a significant share of the dynamic private car market from the multinational vehicle manufacturers by offering low priced basic cars.

These inroads into the market have been made possible by powerful backers. Chery is supported financially be the Anhui provincial government. The brothers Li, who own Geely, had made fortunes from the construction industry and motorcycle production, while the Qinchuan Flyer is ultimately an offshoot of NORINCO, the commercial arm of the People's Liberation Army.

Table 6.1.2 Above average popularization rate of motorcycles by province, 2000

Province	Units per 1,000 people
Tianjin	44.6
Hebei	37.3
Shanghai	32.1
Jiangsu	59.9
Zhejiang	39.4
Fujian	44.7
Shandong	54.4
Guangdong	78.7
Guangxi	35.7
Hainan	47.5

Source: China Association of Automobile Manufacturers

These newcomers do not intend to remain at the bottom end of the market. Chery have recently invested US$55 million in a new paint-shop, whilst Geely have plans for six new models in the design stage. They are now looking for outside expertise to help them move up to the next level.

Major vehicle assemblers

The geographical location of the major vehicle assemblers with multinational participation is illustrated in Figure 6.1.3. These include the Big Three, together with Guangzhou Honda, Changan Suzuki & Ford and Tianjin Toyota.

The current market shares of the major manufacturers and their models are profiled in Tables 6.1.3 which details unit production and sales of each model during June and for the six month period to June 2002. The table shows clearly that the two Volkswagen models of the FAW-VW joint venture and the three models of the Shanghai-VW joint venture no longer predominate.

Profiles of the top ten automobile assemblers

FAW (First Auto Works)

Location	Changchun
Joint venture partner	VW
Models	Jetta, Audi A6, Bora, Red Flag (re-styled Audi 100)

Comments
Long-established joint venture (1985).
FAW is also a leading commercial vehicle manufacturer. In mid-2002, concluded a new 50/50 joint venture with Toyota to produce cars under Lexus brand; Crown saloon will be first model (2005).

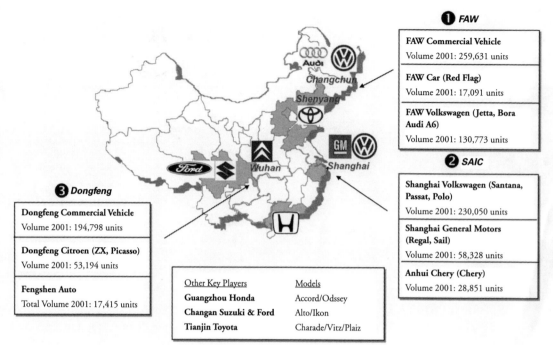

Source: ARA

Figure 6.1.3   Mapping of major vehicle assemblers

Table 6.1.3   Car production and sales by model, June 2002

In units

Manufacturer	Model	Production		Sales	
		June	**Accumulated**	**June**	**Accumulated**
FAW	Red Flag	2,932	16,178	2,918	16,163
Shanghai-VW	Santana 2000	7,711	29,849	7,655	29,653
	Passat	5,016	28,131	5,004	28,088
	POLO	3,004	8,975	3,016	8,817
Shanghai GM	Buick G	2,657	10,416	2,777	10,317
	Buick 3.0	728	3,839	901	3,743
	Buick GL8	1,280	5,844	1,420	5,912
	Sail	2,142	11,715	2,020	12,285
FAW-VW	Jetta	9,364	46,713	10,903	57,848
	Audi	2,649	16,092	3,525	15,053
Guangzhou Honda	Accord	5,582	25,417	5,379	25,364
TAIC	Xiali	8,950	39,523	6,731	46,442
DCAC	Fukang	5,124	26,975	5,289	30,216
	Elysee	2,354	2,354	2,255	2,255
Channa	Alto	5,187	26,617	3,925	26,829
BAIC	Cherokee	409	1,512	312	1,414
DFAC	Aeolus	3,133	14,037	1,776	12,866

Source: China Association of Automobile Manufacturers

Have recently taken control of Tianjin Auto.
Outlook: Winner

SAIC (Shanghai Auto Industry Corporation)
Location	Shangai
Joint venture partners	VW, GM (since 1998)
Models	Santana, Santana 2000, Passat, Polo, Buick Regal, Sail (Corsa, with boot)

Comments
Strongly supported by Shanghai Municipal Government.
Alliance with GM has caused tensions with long-time partner VW.
Actively purchasing shares in other regional manufacturers (eg Anhui Chery).
Outlook: Winner

Dong Feng Motors
Location	Wuhan
Joint venture partner	PSA Citroen
Models	Fukang (aka Citroen ZX), 988 (Fukang with boot), Picasso.

Comments
Hampered by limited model range.
In September 2002, concluded new JV with Nissan, with an ambitious target of 220,000 cars by 2006.
PSA poised to introduce 307 model.
Strong player on domestic CV market.
Outlook: Fortunes may improve with Nissan alliance.

Guangzhou Honda
Location	Guangzhou (Honda took over the facility when Peugeot abandoned earlier joint venture in mid 1990s)
Joint venture partner	Honda (Chinese partner), Denway (in background role)
Models	Accord, Odyssey

Comments
Accord is the best-selling 'prestige' car in China.
Only plant to be operating above 70 per cent capacity.
Outlook: Winner

Brilliance China
Location	Shenyang
Joint venture partner	Alliances with Toyota, BMW and MG Rover
Model	Zhonghua saloon

Comments
The 'mystery' company of the Chinese auto industry.
Privately owned and listed on New York Stock Exchange.
Was third most profitable auto company from manufacture of Jinbei van before profits slipped.
Chairman and major shareholder, Yang Rong, has been publicly ousted.
Only received car manufacturing licence in June 2002.
Outlook: Clouded. Timing when BMW 3-series production comes on stream may be critical.

TAIC (Tianjin Auto Industry Corp.)
Location	Tianjin
Joint venture partner	Daihatsu
Model	Daihatsu Charade

Comments
An early joint venture that stagnated. When Toyota decided to introduce the Vitz model, they built their own factory next door.
Recently announced that they are to be taken over by FAW in first big consolidation of the Chinese auto industry.
Outlook: New ownership may revive loser.

Changan Auto
Location	Chongqing
Joint venture partners	Suzuki, Ford
Models	Alto, Ikon (starts 2003)

Comments
Solid, local sales base; but remote from other main consumer markets.
Alto engine meets higher emission standards than competitors.
Outlook: Perception of Ikon as dated model casts doubt on market prospects. Early introduction of Mondeo would have positive impact.

Anhui Chery
Location	Wuhu
Joint venture partner	None
Models	Chery

Comments
Spectacular sales growth in 2001/2 with Chery saloon (similar to Jetta).
Strong support of local government has enabled undercut of competitors.
Part-owned by SAIC (see above).
Outlook: Winner

Geely Motors

Location   Ningbo
Joint venture partner   None
Models   Merrie (Daihatsu derivative)
Comments
Privately-owned company with background in construction and motorcycle industries.
Competitively priced entry-level car.
Achieved sales of 30,000 in 2001 from standing start.
Outlook: Short-term winner

BAIC (Beijing Automotive Industry Co)

Location   Beijing
Joint venture partner   Daimler Chrysler
Models   Cherokee Jeep
Comments
The first automotive joint venture in China, with track record of expensive mistakes. In particular, the wrong product led to very poor sales.
Daimler-Chrysler cannot afford to walk away from the market and has committed to another 30 years' co-operation.
In the short-term BAIC (and other Beijing-based companies) have contracted with Hyundai to build the Sonata, rumoured to become the official taxi for the Beijing Olympics

Outlook: Daimler-Chrysler will seek to revive fortunes with Mitsubishi-based SUVs. The Pajero model has been named.

Motorcycle manufacturing

Production and sales by engine size
The proportions of motorcycle production and sales by size of engine for two- and three-wheeler categories for the month and six months prior to June 2002 are detailed in Table 6.1.4. Among two-wheelers, there appears to be a marked shift toward higher-powered models in the 110 to 250 ml categories where current growth is strong. Conversely, both production and sales of smaller engine two-wheelers are in decline, although 100 ml models remain the second most popular size with a 29 per cent market share (125 ml models – 68 per cent).

Among three-wheelers, only sales of the very small engine models of 50 ml are growing. The most popular category, where sales year-on-year fell 8.5 per cent, remains the 50 to 250 ml category with an 88 per cent market share in the three-wheeled sector.

Exports of major motorcycle manufacturing enterprises
The unit exports of the top 15 motorcycle manufacturing enterprises in June 2002 are compared with June 2001 in Table 6.1.5. The two biggest exporters are

Table 6.1.4   Motorcycle production and sales by engine displacement (June 2002)

In units

Index	Production			Sales		
	June	Accumulated	Change, %	June	Accumulated	Change, %
Subtotal on 2Ws	**970,533**	**5,667,882**	**10.20**	**996,691**	**5,710,071**	**13.19**
50ml	86,018	399,623	−14.65	89,894	424,401	−8.63
60ml	707	2,257	−60.82	523	4,910	−36.21
70ml	9,140	57,834	−37.64	9,806	63,078	−31.34
80ml	8,483	22,363	−22.04	8,689	22,259	−36.10
90ml	25,773	177,147	−16.78	25,829	179,436	−13.02
100ml	199,836	1,197,043	−14.18	209,011	1,237,936	−9.56
110ml	72,964	487,990	42.18	75,954	493,238	45.62
125ml	480,323	2,919,342	24.92	488,296	2,879,009	25.96
150ml	79,660	344,706	47.25	80,837	347,822	55.83
250ml	7,129	57,248	121.87	7,532	56,135	141.60
Subtotal on 3Ws	**37,644**	**178,606**	**−8.55**	**38,549**	**180,306**	**−7.14**
50ml	2,507	15,295	21.98	3,100	15,471	31.03
>50ml	34,106	157,608	−9.52	34,442	159,159	−8.48
250ml	723	4,301	−24.50	628	4,220	−24.71
750ml	308	1,402	−51.49	379	1,456	−48.80
Total	**1,008,177**	**5,846,488**	**9,51**	**1,035,240**	**5,890,377**	**12.44**

Source: China Association of Automobile Manufacturers

Table 6.1.5 Volume of motorcycle export sales by key enterprises, June 2002

In units

Enterprise	June	The Same Period of Last Year
Total	**564,874**	**669,292**
Chongqing Loncin (Group) Co., Ltd.	91,998	120,895
Chongqing Lifan-Honda Industry (Group) Co., Ltd.	84,523	146,955
Jincheng (Group) Co., Ltd.	57,236	65,107
Qianjiang (Group) Co., Ltd.	41,345	42,335
China South Aviation Power Machine Company	35,515	29,784
Chongqing Zongshen Hailing Machine Vehicle Co., Ltd.	32,622	36,784
Jianshe Industrial (Group) Co., Ltd.	30,711	28,451
Jilong Motorcycle Co., Ltd.	27,611	46,914
MACAT Motorcycle Co., Ltd.	20,595	12,100
China Jialing Industry Share Co., Ltd.	18,019	26,940
China Qingqi (Group) Co., Ltd.	15,715	24,798
Guangdong Kingtown Group Guangzhou Tianma Motorcycle Co., Ltd.	11,152	6,320
Dachangjiang (Group) Co., Ltd	14,102	3,168
Fosti Motorcycle (Group) Co., Ltd.	10,418	1,060
Luoyang Northern Enterprises (Group) Co., Ltd.	9,893	16,039
Changchun Changling (Group) Co., Ltd.	2,904	6,631

Source: China Association of Automobile Manufacturers

Chongqing Loncin (Group) and Chongqing Lifan-Honda Industry (Group), accounting respectively for 16 per cent and 15 per cent in 1992, a reversal of their 1991 positions (18 per cent and 22 per cent). Overall, motorcycle exports slipped by 16 per cent in June alone, to 564,874 units.

Impact of China's WTO entry

Under the negotiated terms of China's entry to the WTO, import tariffs and localization requirements will be gradually reduced in stages. The progress of liberalization may be charted as shown in Table 6.1.6.

Table 6.1.6 Stages in the reduction of tariffs and local content requirements

Impact	Current	2003	2006
Tariff reductions	Import tariffs for autos: 80%–100%	Import tariff cuts phased in equally 15% each year	Import tariffs for autos will be reduced to 25%
	Import tariffs for auto parts: 40%		Auto parts tariffs will fall to average of 10%
Investment and technology transfer	Local content requirements for CBU will be restricted to 40% for Year 1, 60% (Year 2) and up to 80% (Year 3)	Will eliminate policies which restrict foreign automotive companies from importing inputs for production	Significant commitments in addressing concerns about the terms and conditions of investment in China, and the government's role in what should be commercial decisions
	Foreign ownership is allowed (up to 50%)	Will eliminate and cease enforcing trade and foreign exchange balancing requirements	

Whatever changes these relaxations in restrictions on foreign company operations bring to the structure and ownership of the industry and the reduction of prices, it is likely that local production will maintain the mainstream of the China automotive market. There is no precedent in the import experience of other Asian markets, ranging from Korea (1 per cent share) through Thailand (3 per cent) to Japan (5 per cent) for supposing that multinational auto-manufacturers will succeed in penetrating the China auto market, except for luxury cars, other than through foreign invested enterprises.

In the medium term there is some reason to question whether China will be able to sustain the tremendous market growth in passenger cars seen in 2002 and to question what might be done to keep the bandwagon rolling by stimulating demand. Possible measures could include the relaxation of import quotas, modernization of vehicle financing, improved vehicle servicing and recall facilities. There are certainly business opportunities in all these areas.

A more intriguing question is how long it will be before China begins to export automobiles. In other industrial sectors, such as white goods, computers and now communications, Chinese manufacturers have progressed from being backward domestic suppliers to global exporters in a very few years. In the automotive sector, King Long Buses have established a joint venture in India to build CKD bus kits supplied from China, and Honda have begun to talk openly about producing a derivative of the Fit/Jazz supermini for export from China. The prospect of China becoming an automotive exporter draws closer.

Automotive Components

Liu Baocheng, Professor, University of International Business and Economics, and Che Yanhua, Volkswagen, China

Market overview

China's automotive industry has enjoyed rapid development over the last two decades. Three large-scale automotive enterprises have been established: China First Automobile Group Corp (FAW), Dongfeng Motor Corp (DMC) and Shanghai Automotive Industry (Group) Corp (SAIC). They accounted for 44 per cent of the country's total vehicle production and over 70 per cent of the total number of cars. According to the Chinese State Economic and Trade Commission (SETC), over the last three quarters of 2002, these three groups produced a total output value of 231.2 billion yuan, an increase of 34.8 per cent. In the meantime, almost all the multinational OVMs (Original Vehicle Manufacturers) representative of the world '6+3' (ie, six groups: General Motors (GM), Daimler-Chrysler, Ford, Toyota, Volkswagen and Renault; and three independent companies: Honda, BMW and Peugeot) have established their presence in China primarily in the form of joint ventures with Chinese partners. There are more than 600 foreign invested automotive enterprises involving 20 countries and regions. Total committed foreign investment in the automotive sector amounted to US$21billion, with a total registered capital of US$10.6 billion and paid-up funds of US$4.5 billion. More than 300 OE and supplier technology projects are in place.

In 2000, total vehicle output reached 2.07 million with a value of 391.1 billion yuan, an increase of 80 per cent on 1995. Chinese domestic manufacturers still have a dominant role with over 95 per cent of the total market share. Car production rose by 86 per cent to 605,000 units, while motorcycle production rose by 45 per cent to 11.53 million units over the same period.

Demand for commercial vehicles >6t GVW exceeded 300,000 units, an increase of 14,000 units.

According to SETC's 2001 report, there were 2,391 automotive enterprises in China by the end of 1999, of which 118 were automobile manufacturers, 546 automotive converters, 136 motorcycle assemblers, 51 engine makers and 1,540 automotive/motorcycle parts and components companies.

Parts and components are the most crucial sector of the automotive industry. The major international suppliers, including Delphi, Alpine, Continental, Robert Bosch and Siemens, see China as one of their strategic target markets. Many have already found local partners in China in order to access local resources and the industry anticipates huge demand in the years following the country's entry to the WTO.

Market structure

The business of the automotive parts industry can broadly be categorized into two levels: the original vehicle manufacture (OVM) market and the after market. The OVM market means that the part/component manufacturers provide their products directly to the original vehicle manufacturers. For instance, Delphi Automotive Systems is the OVM supplier for General Motors and Volkswagen. The after market means that the part/component manufacturers distribute their products to the specified channels and the end users. Many part/component manufacturers are involved in both markets.

The OVM market

This is a regular and stable market with the following characteristics:

1. A B2B business model, where in most cases long-term contracts are maintained between the part/component suppliers and the OVMs.

2. Routine orders placement by the OVMs with the suppliers carrying a quantity of inventory for after-sales service. OVMs require the identification of their own brand names on the spare parts and their unique packaging to be distributed through their authorized service centres.

3. Transparent information flow between suppliers and clients, ie suppliers appoint account managers on the OVM's sites to understand their real-time demands and requirements.

4. The delivery system is shifting from the traditional single part delivery towards module delivery. Module suppliers are responsible for the whole process chain, from pre-development to the spare parts business.

5. The prerequisites to be an original supplier of the big automakers are:
   - competence of quality;
   - correct ratio between price and performance;
   - security of delivery;
   - flexibility.

6. The suppliers' performance review is based on:
   - client satisfaction;
   - flexibility; reactions to volume changes;
   - competitiveness;
   - reputation of delivery service;
   - client orientation;
   - innovative participation in the producer's R&D activities.

7. Massive investment in marketing is not needed. For example, there is no need to purchase a great deal of advertising space in auto magazines; most expenses are related to corporate image promotion.

8. The most valuable market information for suppliers is the producers' production plan, which forms the basis of the suppliers' sales, marketing and integrated business plans.

The after market is quite different:

1. The clients are distribution channels, business partners and end users and so the business model is much more dynamic and complex, and the products are considered consumer products. Therefore, the products need a unique brand identity and packaging. And the sellers have to segment their target markets and analyse the consumers' behaviour in order to establish a market differentiation strategy. For instance, some companies have developed a range of product portfolios with different prices, different brands and different packages to meet different markets.

2. More resources in marketing activities are required in order to improve brand awareness, recognition, preference and loyalty. An integrated marketing communication plan is needed, ranging from participation in auto shows, solo shows, brand launch events, technical seminars, dealer conferences, print ads, billboards, broadcasting, online promotion, POP etc.

3. The PARC, age information and the typical ownership of the vehicle are the most valuable marketing data for suppliers. The PARC data shows the total market scale, the age information indicates the product's lifespan and the ownership information shows the different consumer behaviour with regard to taxis, business and households.

4. The structure of the after market is more complex than for the OVMs and includes positions such as channel development manager; channel support manager; regional manager; brand manager; order processor; logistics manager and so on.

5. The market players are not only parts/components manufacturers: some are also trading companies. For example, General Motors' Service Parts Organization International (SPOI) sometimes purchases parts and components internationally, brands them 'AC Delco' and then sells them to after market channels.

6. Many OVM suppliers are involved in the after market business. However, OVMs do not generally encourage their OVM suppliers to serve the after market independently and therefore most suppliers have the role of 'purifying' the market for the OVMs who are, after all, the 'authentic' parts providers

7. Customer relations management (CRM) is increasingly important. The customer database is the backbone of the whole business operation, ranging from identifying ways of generating sales leads, qualifying sales prospects, segmenting sales leads, setting up dealer extranets, retaining existing customers and enticing competitors' customers to switch. And every detail of the whole value chain, from the supplier to the distribution channel and end users, calls for a specific strategy.

8. The competition is much fiercer than in the OVM market. The players have to enhance their overall

competitiveness, from product portfolio including packages and services, pricing policies and promotion mix to channel management.

The after market

Apart from imported products, three sectors currently serve the domestic automotive parts/components market in China. The first sector is the localized manufacturing facilities of global suppliers such as Delphi Automotive Systems, Bosch GmbH, Lucas Varity and GM Service Parts Organization International (SPOI), who are involved in both the OVM and after markets. The second sector comprises local suppliers such as Wangxiang Group, some of which have already been included in the worldwide purchasing systems of major multinational OVMs. The last is the counterfeit and fake parts/components manufacturers. The three sectors' business behaviours are quite different and they apply different market strategies and market mixes. The first sector and part of the second have set up an entire distribution network, warehousing and logistics network and have unique brand identities and packaging. The different distribution channel networks are illustrated in Figures 6.2.1 and 6.2.2

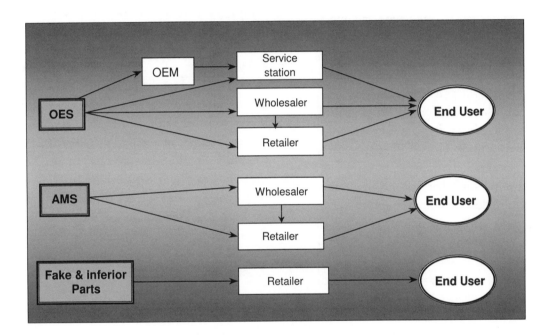

Figure 6.2.1   After market distribution channel (local parts)

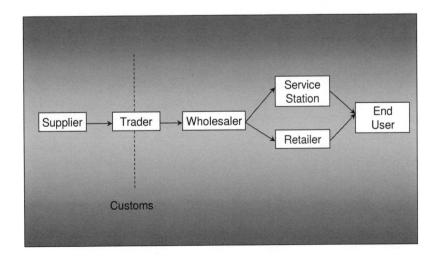

Figure 6.2.2   After market distribution channel (imported parts)

More and more suppliers are getting involved in the after market to extend their channel lengths. The after market potential is said to be worth around RMB50–60 billion (US$6-7.2 billion) and the PARC is RMB13–14 million, of which passenger cars account for a third.

Business is evenly divided among the service stations and the after market. This is why so many multinational automotive parts/components manufacturers and suppliers are involved in the after market business, especially in the car part sectors. The market is there, but how best to enter it and develop within it, how to realize the profit diversification and leverage the existing business models? The first step is to identify problems and obstacles.

Many multinational parts/components manufacturers are doing well in the OVM market, but it does not necessarily follow that they will be able to grab a sizeable share in the after market. The major OVMs are looking for new markets for growth and this is their reason for coming to China. They include Volkswagen, Audi, General Motors, Mitsubishi, Renault, Toyota, Volvo and BMW amongst others. The OVM suppliers pay close attention to localization requirements. In the past, the OVM projects in China that met the localization rate of 40 per cent in the first year were able to obtain government approval and so the original suppliers of OVMs set up manufacturing facilities, sales offices or service centres in China.

Suppliers normally establish joint ventures to produce different parts. Table 6.2.1 shows how this can work, using Robert Bosch as an example.

OVM business is the focus of multinational auto parts/components manufacturers and so their organizational behaviour and operations bear strong B2B characteristics, which eventually impact upon the after market.

1) Different marketable product portfolios and product re-engineering

Automotive parts and components include slow-moving and fast-moving products. Fast-moving products are marketable products in the after market, as are other consumer products. So companies that maintain wider product lines should select marketable products. For example, batteries, with a life span of around two years, fall into the fast-moving category, whereas steering columns are slow-moving and are not usually after market marketable products. In addition, the OVM business prefers module and systems supplies, while the after market treats modules and systems as the separate components and accessories. When something goes wrong with the fuel pump in the fuel pump modules, the consumer demands replacement of the exact part and is reluctant to pay extra money for the whole module, which includes the fuel pump, racks and filters. If the consumer is using the fuel pump assembly branded Bosch, you must know whether your fuel pump is fit to replace the Bosch or not. So, on your product catalogue, you must state that your product number XXXXXX is equivalent to Bosch product number XXXXXX. The engineering process is more complicated and requires engineers' expertise not only in the whole module, but also in the separate parts. Unlike OVM supplies, the after market business requires the installation manual in the package.

2) Support from the whole organization

Given the differences between the OVM market and the after market, the OVM business is, in most cases, paid more attention by management. Most financial and manpower resources are traditionally allocated to the OVM business. However, once management decides

Table 6.2.1   Bosch joint ventures

Name of venture	Major customers	Major products	Bosch ownership (%)	Sales revenue (US$ million)	Total investment (US$ million)
Bosch Braking Systems	DCAC, BJ Jeep	Brake	70	N/A	21
Nanjing Huade Spark Plugs	N/A	Spark plug	51	1.2	35
Wuxi Euro-Asia Diesel Injection	N/A	Diesel injection	26	4	322
United Automotive Electronic	DCAC, SVW; FAW-VW	EMS	50	48	322

to develop the after market and expects it to be a significant contributor to corporate revenue and profit diversification, the management must attach more importance to the after market. A complete and integrated team should be set up, which might range from 4 to 30 or even 60 people. Furthermore, marketing activities need considerable investment in order to improve brand awareness, to get brand recognition and build brand preference and loyalty. The after market needs support from every function, especially in the early stages when the business is small and low profile. It will take two or three years for the after market business to break even. So when the management conducts a performance review it must be remember that in the early stages profit alone is no indication of performance.

3) Differentiation strategy in terms of product, price and marketing activities is essential

In the OVM business, the same products are set at the same price and quality level but the after market business faces a dynamic environment and its customers cannot be treated as a homogenous group. Different sectors behave differently. Taxi drivers tend to buy the cheapest products; and are reluctant to pay a higher price. Private car owners are most concerned with the authenticity of the parts, and institution car owners will pay even more. Marketing intelligence must make a detailed study to support the different products strategies with appropriate brand names and promotion plans.

4) Channel development and management experiences are crucial to the business success

The OVM business requires the ability to deal with business partners and car manufacturers. If the whole organisation has very strong B2B experience, they will do well in dealing with business partners. After market products are sold through distribution channels, typically from the authorized exclusive distributors, authorized regional distributors, dealers, and wholesalers to retailers. So it is of utmost important to understand how to develop and manage the distribution channel, how to impact the channel with the organization culture, particularly in the current Chinese parts industry. The distributor selection procedures, price structures, warranty terms, channel support, distribution contracts and incentive programmes must be well established. Otherwise, the whole distribution channel will be in a mess. The distributor will fight for profits in the territory and will cut their price against others.

5) Brand building experience is valuable

OVM-oriented companies are typically engaged in corporate image building. While they promote their corporate identities through various marketing communications tools, they tend to ignore product brand promotion and so they need to learn the whole process of building product brand awareness, brand recognition, brand preference and brand loyalty. They will learn how to carry cross-promotion with their distribution channels. The pull and push strategies need to be applied simultaneously.

6) Quick response plays an important role in customer retention

The OVM business is comparably stable, since the business relationship between the OVM and its supplier is based on a long-term commitment, or the supplier carries over the OVM business from its overseas companies and so the suppliers are not worried about their business. In contrast, the after market is dynamic. In spite of the customer base available, if they are not treated properly (eg their purchase inquiry is not replied to), they will switch to competitors' brands; it is unlikely they will choose to wait. Meanwhile, even if customers are ready to buy, they can hardly be retained if the sellers cannot provide the right products or services in a timely fashion. Even worse, they will tell their friends and relations about their disappointment. Losing one customer can mean losing five or six business opportunities.

Internal record is different from that of OVM business

Normally, the marketing information system of OVM-oriented organizations is relatively simple. It usually includes the major customer books, macro economic environment, government policies, competitor intelligence and automotive production information. Most information can be obtained from internal records and key accounts. In contrast, the marketing information systems for the after market will be much more complex and should cover a broader area. Apart from the content mentioned above, it should include information about the distribution network, the end user profile and consumer behaviour analyses, vehicle population and product life span, all of which are crucial to the after market business. The intelligence is not easy to obtain and cannot be found internally; it will require a third party to conduct the research or the company might introduce successful marketing information systems from companies which manufacture or sell mass non-durable products.

Solving internal problems does not guarantee a bright future. The after market players must also understand what is going on within the industry and deal with the question of how to avoid the disadvantages, how to transcend the barriers and formulate their core competitiveness. The after market suppliers have to closely monitor the external environment.

Major issues in the auto-parts after market

The environment of the automotive parts/accessories after market in China is currently still in its infancy. A summary of the major problems follows:

Fragmented and complex distribution network

Using local distributors might in theory offer a cost advantage, but the distribution channels can be highly fragmented. Most foreign companies found that their Chinese joint venture partners have hundreds of direct distributors. For instance, a typical state-owned brewery in a large city has over 2,000 primary distributors, many of whom resell to hundreds of secondary wholesalers and thousand of independent 'street hawkers'. Many companies felt that their distributors were inadequate in terms of delivery, sales, merchandising, promotion

and collection. Few had the most basic customer tracking, customer care and credit rating systems.

Unfortunately, a better distribution system is unlikely to emerge soon, again because of government restrictions on foreign investment. Currently, with a few exceptions, joint ventures are strictly limited to distributing goods that they manufacture themselves.

With regard to the channel characteristics of the automotive industry at present, while the number of dealers in automotive parts/accessories amounts to 220,000 nationwide, few can achieve US$24 million sales revenue. Take Shanghai as an example, since it is the biggest OVM manufacturing site with Shanghai Volkswagen and Shanghai GM amongst others, and the biggest automotive parts/accessories warehouse. Many distributors from other regions order their products from Shanghai:

Figure 6.2.3 shows that it is not easy for after market suppliers to select the right distributors and manage the whole channel, vital to the success of the business.

Valuable after market-oriented information is hard to find

Information and intelligence for the OVM market are more complete and integrated than for the after market. Consulting companies can track monthly, quarterly and yearly production and sales by using their network around the country. While production and sales figures

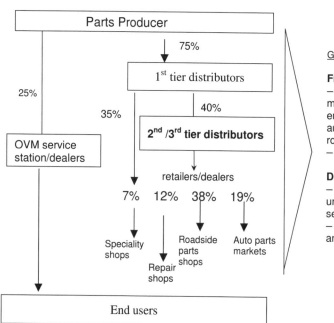

Figure 6.2.3   Shock absorber distribution map, volume flows

are not difficult to obtain through newspapers, automotive magazines and online services, there is not enough information for the after market that covers the vehicle population, vehicle utility purposes and the vehicle age.

The process of segmenting the market and evaluating market potential involves many challenges. Not all official vehicle management organizations in China have computer-aided statistical systems and this is even more a problem in remote areas. Furthermore, there is almost no way to assess the number of imported cars, because some cars are sold to China through illegal channels. Although there are some automotive consulting institutions who claim to have data to hand, they can only provide the vehicle population by general categories. These figures can only tell which car models have a larger market share, but not the car's life span and so the replacement rate of different car models must be identified.

Companies might choose regional distributors in some specific areas according to their product lines and current market circumstances and so a multi-dimensional survey showing the car population by purpose, brand and region is essential. Annual sales revenue, financial standing, management skills and industry reputation are the basic assessment criteria when selecting distributors.

Strong domestic and international competition is imminent

The competition in after market business is much more intensive than for OVM. Figure 6.2.4 shows how fierce the competition is in the automotive parts/accessories after market field.

The major OVMs do not expect OVM suppliers to develop their distribution channel independently

OVMs have different attitudes towards the fact that their suppliers are developing their after market business independently. Major OVMs do not encourage their suppliers to develop their distribution network independently and to sell their parts/accessories outside OVM service stations. When OVMs place orders with suppliers, they will order extra products for their service stations. They put their brand names on their unique packaging, display the price tag including their markups and distribute the parts to the authorized service stations. Most OVMs have their own complete service network, and some have adopted '4S' policies, which integrate car selling, part supply, car repairing and information feedback into one system. For instance, Shanghai Volkswagen suppliers have to follow the regulation that SVW supplier should provide service parts only to SVW. However, it has a dual supply system for each component purchase and the market is shared between two or three suppliers; sometimes the suppliers is not satisfied with their OVM business split share and looks elsewhere for markets to supply. Furthermore, SVW's prices for these parts are always higher, leading many suppliers to sell their cheaper parts via other channels. The suppliers have to promise that they will only supply parts to territories unoccupied by SVW, and that they will sell the parts at a higher price to the free market than to SVW. They state that their major function is to help the OVMs purify the market.

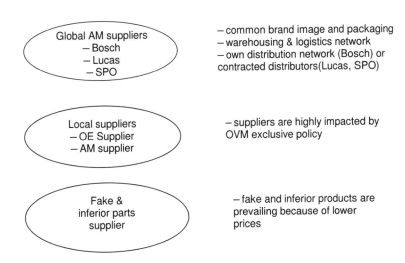

Figure 6.2.4 After market suppliers

Accounts receivable is another problem after market suppliers need to consider seriously

Not all the multinational players have enough experiences of dealing with accounts receivable. Products selling well or in huge volume does not necessarily mean the business has gained significant profit. After the products are sold, if the money cannot be collected, profit is lost.

As stated above, the distribution channel, consisting of authorized distributors, a dealer and wholesalers, is the mainstay of the after market. Whether the whole value chain is healthy or not will determine its business success. Therefore, selecting the distributors, financial status and credit must be the priority. Only with these in mind can the supplier initiate a payment policy according to the channel structure and characteristics (see Figure 6.2.5).

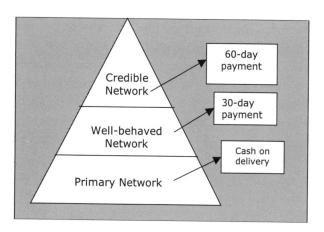

Figure 6.2.5 Payment terms

However, at the beginning of the business, if you tell customers that you require them to accept the 'Cash on Delivery' payment term, your customers might switch to other brands, and not come back again. So the suppliers are in a dilemma. They will certainly want to sell their products, but they must risk bad debts.

Fake and inferior products are prevailing in the markets.

Apart from original equipment suppliers (OES), there are some small local producers in the markets selling fake and inferior parts to the retailers and the end users. While family car and company car owners prefer authentic parts, many taxi drivers are willing to get their cars fixed at roadside shops whose prices are cheaper because they source their products from the small producers who duplicate OES technology or put the OES brand name on the products they make themselves.

Why are some consumers willing to buy those products? There are two reasons. Firstly, some drivers lack the knowledge to distinguish fake parts from authentic ones. Secondly, there is a significant price advantage against the original parts. Sometimes it is not only the roadside shops who sell the fake parts, but also a few authorised dealers. After the authorized dealers gain the title of 'Brand Authorized Distributors', they actually stock both authentic and fake parts. They will sell the cheaper parts to their price-sensitive buyers and so jeopardize the OES's interest.

Faced with counterfeiting and arbitrary pricing, some companies are using counterfeit-proof packaging. By printing retail prices on packages and marking production runs differently by channel, counterfeits should be easier to identify. Nevertheless, the sheer scale of these problems increases the level of complexity for managers in China.

Recommendations on market research and segmentation

- **Basic market analysis** will draw a map of the major car brands in the market covering the car population (PARC) by brand, replacement rates by product and after market size by product, car brand and region. It will also determine component life span by mileage or time, market volume by product portfolio and cross country analysis/cross check.
- **Geographic segmentation** will segment the market by region and major metropolitan area and prioritize market penetration region by market size, growth and competitive intensity.
- **End user segmentation** will categorize the end user into different consumer groups, understand their distinctive characteristics including expectations, preferences, drivers of product and channel choices. It will also uncover the best way to cater for the segmented targeted consumer groups.
- **Product analysis** reveals the strength and weakness of the major products/brands in the market and match channels and end user preferences.

The above analyses must be based on facts, and the following sources and methodology can be applied to gather the relevant information:

- **Desk research:** Government statistics and reports, industry materials from newspapers/magazines/internet/other domestic and international media, data published by automotive research institutions (DRI, Boston Consulting); the annual reports of the OVMs and the OES.
- **Internal marketing information:** The existing database or marketing information systems (MIS); the key account managers of major OVMs (remember, they always have good relations with OVM executives and are able to get first hand information very quickly); the clipping and monitoring systems of the PR department.
- **First hand interviews or surveys:** To delegate a third party survey service institution to conduct a focus group interview, consisting of distributors, wholesalers, dealers, retailers and end users, or a specified survey will help the company get the first hand materials. Nowadays, on-line survey on the Internet is another cost-effective way.
- **Industry events:** While enjoying auto shows, trade fairs, technical shows and other customer occasions, remember to attend the seminars where famous market players, government officials and industry authorities deliver speeches and distribute market information.

Market entry

Winning in China has become a top priority for the multinational automotive giants, many of which see the Chinese market as a once-in-a lifetime opportunity to catapult themselves into a position of global leadership. They make their mark on the Chinese market by setting up manufacturing facilities, transferring technologies and establishing service centres.

Tariffs and quotas

Currently, the country's import/export regulations are: Import tariff, VAT, Certificate:

Tariff

- Raw materials for manufacturing sites: approximately 5–15 per cent
- Spare parts or assemble parts using on whole vehicle: approximately 10–50 per cent
- Production machinery and test equipment: approximately 15–25 per cent

VAT

- Most imported commodities: 17 per cent
- Some commodities eg books: 13 per cent

Tariff and VAT formula

- Import Tariff = CIF x Tariff rate
- VAT=(CIF *Tariff rate) x 17 per cent

As China enters the WTO, tariffs on whole vehicles as well as parts and components will be significantly lowered. Import licences will gradually disappear. This will have various impacts on the automobile and supplier industry. For complete vehicles, the tariff will be gradually reduced from its current level of 70 per cent to 25 per cent by 2006 (from 50 per cent to 10 per cent for automotive components).

Of the different types of motor vehicle, the hardest hit will be passenger cars, high-tech engines, driving axles and key parts assemblies, with high-end heavy-duty trucks next. The impact on mini-vehicles, medium-sized trucks and large and medium-sized buses will be relatively small and the motorcycle industry will be the least affected. The effect of increased import quotas prior to the final disappearance of the quota and licence scheme will be much greater than the reduction of tariffs. It will create tremendous pressures on domestic OE assemblers because once the import licence is phased out there will be a major increase in the number of cars and components imported at reduced tariff rates. For the after market suppliers there will be new opportunities and challenges. The suppliers can import their products, manufactured globally at a lower cost, into the China market, or they can purchase their products from international manufacturing facilities, brand them and import them into China. However, they will be faced by fierce competition.

The liberalization of the automobile service industry

At present, only the Chinese Trading Company, joint ventures and wholly-owned companies are licensed to handle goods import and export. However, joint ventures and wholly-owned companies can only import the raw material/parts for their production and export their own products.

After joining the WTO, China will open its service trade up to overseas companies in the areas of vehicle and parts sales and distribution, automobile import and export, franchised dealership, shipping and transportation, automobile financing, car rental and leasing and financing for production. This will open up more channels for imports and seriously impact on China's market because the country lacks an established system of automobile service trade.

Competition

The after market business has vertical and horizontal distributors. The vertical distributors arrange their products by car models, for example Shanghai Longfeng Auto Parts Limited sells the various parts of Santana. The horizontal distributors arrange their goods by part categories, for example Liaoning Yejin Auto Parts Company sells batteries of different brands. It depends on the company's capabilities and on the market situation and it can of course begin with vertical distributors, and then expand to horizontal channels.

Competition in the after market will originate from both local and international companies. International competitors can be divided into two categories; one being the manufacturers who are also involved in the trading business, for example, Delphi Automotive Systems and Bosch. The second group restricts itself to trading and buying products from manufacturers, putting their own brand names on them and selling on, for example NAPA. Many Chinese local manufacturers are beginning to realize that they must set up their own brand names and distribution network, and that they are enjoying a lower price due to lower costs. Some, such as Hangzhou Wanxiang Group, are becoming strong competition with multinational companies in some market segments.

Table 6.2.2   Global tier one companies with presences in China

Name	*Locations*	*Activities*
Bosch	Shanghai	Eight JVs – EMS; Sparks, etc.
Delphi	Changchun	Fourteen JVs & WFOEs –
	Shanghai	electronics; chassis; harnesses;
	Wuhan	climate control
Valeo	Wuhan	Eight JVs & WFOEs – climate control; electrical products
Visteon	Changchun	Six JVs – interior;
	Shanghai	climate control;
	Wuhan	electronics
Allevard	Shanghai	
Brose	Shanghai	
Huchuson	Wuhan	
Magneti Marelli	Shanghai	
Pilkington	Changchun, Shanghai, Wuhan	
Sachs	Shanghai	
Siemens	Changchun, Shanghai	
ZF	Shanghai	

Source: ARA Research

Commercial Vehicles

Mark Norcliffe, Society of Motor Manufacturers and Traders, and Jonathan Reuvid

Market growth

The Chinese commercial vehicle industry consists of two main segments of buses and trucks, further divided into four categories of bus and four of truck. As Table 6.3.1 shows, overall growth in both these segments since 1998 has been strong, following a similar pattern in the expanding passenger car market.

Table 6.3.1 Commercial vehicle sales in China (units)

Year	Trucks	Buses
1998	867,648	436,719
1999	1,014931	511,291
2000	1,213,400	610.182
2001	1,424,151	717,403
2002 (estimated)	1,835,500	924,500

Source: Automotive Resources Asia Ltd. (ARA)

The Chinese bus market is currently the largest in the world and in 2001 truck sales accounted for 51 per cent of the total Asian truck market.

Segmentation

Within the bus and truck sectors, patterns of growth and the proportion of buses to trucks differ significantly. Figure 6.3.1 shows historical sales in the bus market and Figure 6.3.2 historical sales of each of the four categories of truck.

There is a significant contrast between the development of the bus and truck sectors in terms of their relative sophistication. While improved infrastructure and more long distance travel are drivers for the expansion of both markets, the bus sector is progressing more rapidly because of consumers' demands for greater comfort. In the truck sector, where a driver can be hired for a few dollars a day, comfort is not a factor and price remains king. As a result, the traditional Big Two domestic manufacturers, FAW and Dong Feng, continue to dominate the truck sector with very cheap, basic products. Not surprisingly, imported trucks account for less than 1.5 per cent of the Chinese market.

Buses

The minibus, defined as a passenger mini vehicle less than 3.5 metres long, remains the most popular category in the bus segment and accounts for two-thirds of the total bus market. Between 1998 and 2002 unit sales increased by a factor of 2.5. Built mostly on Japanese technology, typically single-box and powered by 800cc engines, minibuses are money-making tools for people in small and medium-sized towns and are purchased by single people or consortia of private buyers.

Light buses, 3.5–7 metres long and typically seating 11–25, account for 27 per cent of the bus market and their sales have grown by 38 per cent since 1998. The principal purchasers of small buses are local taxi companies, either private or state-owned, who operate for hire, and individual companies who use the vehicles to transport employees to/from the workplace.

Medium-sized buses are 7–10 metres long and include 'urban buses' used for inner city public transport; these account for a further 5 per cent market share. They comprise two distinct sub-sectors, with ownership of higher quality vehicles largely in the hands of State-Owned Enterprises (SOEs), while the 'urban' buses which provide local mass transportation are owned by local municipalities and cities. Outside the

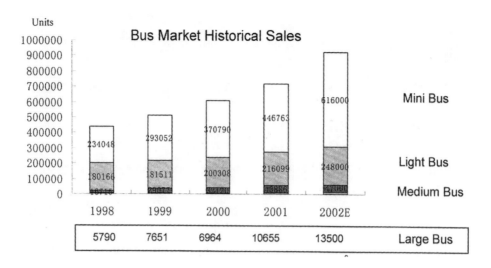

Source: Automotive Resources Asia Ltd (ARA)

Figure 6.3.1 Bus market historical sales (units)

most prosperous major cities, urban buses are normally poor quality products.

Large buses over 10 metres long, with projected sales of 13,500, represent less than 1.5 per cent. The majority of coaches used on inter-city transport routes and in the tourist trade are operated by SOEs. Previously, only SOEs have been able to access funds to make cash purchases. However, more private companies are likely to enter the market as bank loans for vehicle purchase become more readily available.

Any assessment of purchasing patterns should recognize the strong municipal and provincial ties existing in China, particularly in the business relations of SOEs who give preference to locally manufactured products (eg the TAIC Juali Minibus predominating in Tianjin).

Trucks

Light trucks (GW 1.8 to 6 tonnes) are the major sector of the truck market with a share of 37 per cent, and sales have grown 69 per cent since 1998. This includes the traditional Chinese 5 tonne medium truck.

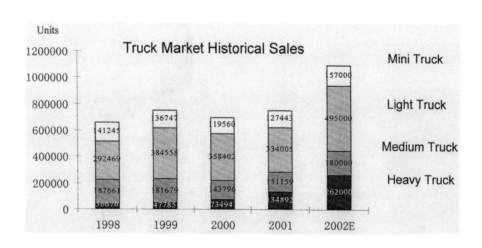

Source: Automotive Resources Asia Ltd. (ARA)

Figure 6.3.2 Truck market historical sales (units)

Sales in the medium truck sector (GW 6 to 14 tonnes) declined between 1998 and 2001 by 20 per cent but have revived in 2002 and are expected to gain almost 10 per cent of the market. By contrast, the mini truck sector (less than GW 1.8 tonnes) holds a dwindling share of the market, down from 16.3 per cent in 1998 to a projected 8.5 per cent in 2002.

However, the fastest growing sector is in heavy trucks (GW 14 tons or more), with a projected market share for 2002 of 14.2 per cent, where sales have grown by a factor of more than 4.2 since 1998 and are forecast to have almost doubled by the end of 2002.

While the percentage of heavy duty trucks in the total vehicle population is considered to be too small by industry commentators, five stimuli have been identified for the continued rapid development of China's heavy duty truck industry and market:

- Preferential monetary policies from central government to stimulate purchasing;
- Developing West Drive investment on infrastructure and flourishing real estate have increased demand (the officially backed policy to open up western China);
- Customer benefits from the greater efficiency of heavy trucks;
- Government crackdowns on the illegal overloading of transportation and illegal truck manufacture;
- The upgrading of truck makers and diversified product lineups to attract more customers.

A further factor in the increasing use of road freight, also favouring larger capacity trucks, is the steady increase in classified national highways. Since 1994, the total mileage of paved highway has increased from just under 1 million kilometres to 1.3 million in 2000, of which expressways and Class 1 to 3 roads now account for 466,000 kilometres.

Bus manufacturing

Leading light bus manufacturers

Shenyang Jinbei
Originally an FAW-owned enterprise to manufacture the Toyotas Hiace under licence, the company was taken over in 1993 by Hong Kong-based China Brilliance (see Chapter 6.1). Under the new management, sales increased dramatically from 8,700 in 1995 to a

projected 70,000 in 2001. A new production line was installed in 1997 and the model has been regularly updated. Currently in negotiation with Toyota to produce a fifth generation Hiace with plans to produce the 'Gran Via' van from 2002. Market share of 19.6 per cent (Jan–Jun 2002) but sales were reduced by 3 per cent.

Nanjing Yuejin Auto Group
A long-established (1994) joint venture with Iveco to produce the TurboDaily which has lost market share and is no longer among the top four light bus makers. The Chinese partner has been criticized for its lack of investment. Fiat is thought to be focusing on bringing a passenger car to the market, and recent Iveco investments have been in the heavy bus sector. Restriction on diesel-engine vehicles in Beijing have also impeded sales. Sales fell 22 per cent year-on-year in Jan-Jun 2002.

Anhui Jianghui Auto Co.
Originally a truck and chassis manufacturer, LJAC have successfully diversified into small buses in partnership with Hyundai, and produced 27,000 vehicles in 2000. Recently they acquired ownership of Anhui Ankai, a leading manufacturer in the large bus sector. Sales increased by 24 per cent year-on-year giving market share of 10.9 per cent (Jan-Jun 2002).

Fujian Southeast
A comparative newcomer, producing the Delica in partnership with Mitsubishi and Taiwanese investors. In 2000, sold 18,000 vehicles, a threefold increase year-on-year. Market share still rising to 11.5 per cent (Jan-Jun 2002) with sales increasing a further 38 per cent.

Zhejiang Haoqing Auto Manufacturing Co Ltd
A major manufacturer of buses located in south-west China with a low profile but registering a market share of 8.3 per cent (Jan-Jun 2002) in fourth place among the major light bus producers. In this period, sales rose by a more than healthy 69 per cent.

Beijing Automotive Industry Group Co (BAIC)
Manufacturers of the Hongye light bus. Based on Isuzu technology, the model still sells well in Beijing, but elsewhere is perceived as being out of date and in decline, with sales falling 17 per cent year-on-year (Jan–Jun 2002).

BAIC Beiqi Futian

Originally an agricultural vehicle builder under MAIC, Beiqi Futian have made rapid inroads into the light bus market with a derivative of Hiace. Sales in 2001 of 12,000 vehicles.

Jiangling Motors, Nanchang

Joint venture with Ford since 1997 to produce the Transit, which has failed to win a major share of the market after good initial sales, hampered by its late arrival and comparatively high price. Nevertheless, sales rose by 14 per cent in the first six months of 2002.

Sanjiang Aerospace Co

Established a joint venture with Renault in 1993 to produce the Trafic at Xiaogan, Hubei Province. Perceived as an expensive although high quality product, it suffers from poor local marketing. There are reports that Renault have bought out the Chinese partner.

Qingling Motor Group

Based in Chongqing, and manufacturer of the QL6470 light bus, based on Isuzu technology (Isuzu holds a minority 10 per cent stake only). Perceived as a technically good product, but poorly marketed.

In addition to these leading light bus manufacturers, each of the 'Big Four' vehicle manufacturers produces light buses in low volume, as follows:

First Auto Works (FAW)   Jiefang Light Bus
Shanghai Auto Industry Co   Feiling Light Bus
Tianjin Auto Industry Co   TJ 6480
Dong Feng Motors   Grand Motor
(in partnership with Hyundai and a Taiwanese investor)

Of these, the Dong Feng bus manufacturing operation registered the best performance in the first six months of 2002, achieving fifth place in the market with sales up 86 per cent.

There are also many small local producers such as Hebei Shengli Group (SL6400 model), Hebei Tianye (BQ6471 model) and some companies, listed as light bus manufacturers but whose products do not truly fall into the category such as Changfeng Group (whose principal vehicle is the Pajero Jeep).

Leading large/medium bus manufacturers

In the medium bus sector, the FAW Group maintained its market leadership. Although sales fell by 14.6 per cent, it held a market share of 26.2 per cent (Jan-Jun 2002). Dong Feng Auto (DFAC) retained second place with 22.8 per cent market share for the same period and its sales were only marginally (2.5 per cent) lower.

Jinlong Allied Auto (Souzhou) accounted for a further 12.7 per cent and Jiangsu Yaxing Motor Coach Group was in fourth place with a market share of 9.8 per cent and static sales (Jan-Jun 2002).

The clear market leaders in the large bus sector are Changzhou Changjiang Bus Group with a market share of 26.6 per cent and DFAC with 23.8 per cent. However, while the former's sales increased by 141 per cent (Jan-Jun 2002), DFMC's sales fell by 28 per cent over the same period. In third and fourth position of the large bus market are Ankai Auto group and Huanghai Auto Group with shares of 8.7 per cent and 8 per cent respectively.

Other leading domestic producers of large and medium buses are profiled in Table 6.3.2.

Table 6.3.2 Other domestic producers of large/medium buses in China

Name	Location	Output (2000)	Production capacity	Foreign partner
Yutong Bus Co	Zhengzhou	4,170	6,000	JV talks with MAN
Hunahghai Auto Group	Dandong	3,026	8,000	Talks with Renault
Zhongtong Bus Co	Liaocheng		4,000	BOVA Bus
Ankai Bus Group	Hefei	1,519	4,000	Kaisibor Bus
Shenwo Bus Co	Shanghai	957	3,000	Volvo
Shenyang Riye Auto Producing Co	Shenyang	1,787	5,000	HINO Motors
Chanjiang Bus	Changzou	5,288	6,000	Iveco
Xiamen King Long United Auto Ind. Co	Xiamen	6,339	7,700	Daimler Benz

Source: Society of Motor Manufacturers & Traders (SMMT)

Table 6.3.3 Production and sales of major truck manufacturers by type in June 2002

In units

Type	Manufacturer	Production			Sales		
		June	Accumulated	Change, %	June	Accumulated	Change %
Heavy Truck	FAW Group Corp.	11,884	72,202	76.84	10,665	68,994	91.93
	Dongfeng Motor Corp.	8,444	48,119	137.00	7,347	47,395	137.12
	China National Heavy Duty Truck Group Co. Ltd	1,459	7,418	151.80	1,331	7,442	162.41
	Chongqing Heavy Duty Auto (Group) Co., Ltd.	1,288	6,300	98.30	1,206	6,306	101.41
	Shannxi Auto (Group) Co., Ltd.	556	3,741	93.03	567	3,586	90.94
	Beijing Auto Industry Holding Co., Ltd.	169	716	–	182	700	–
	Shanxi Auto Industry (Group) Co., Ltd.	24	402	0.25	56	415	22.78
	North-Benz Heavy Duty Auto Co., Ltd.	28	379	18.07	65	342	9.97
Medium Truck	Dongfeng Motor Corp.	5,883	46,164	21.28	6,157	44,387	19.36
	FAW Group Corp.	5,883	46,164	21.28	6,157	44,387	19.36
	FAW Group Corp.	3,702	32,901	−28.73	3,538	33,207	−28.19
	Shaanxi Auto (Group) Co., Ltd.	438	5,211	66.91	451	5,132	65.92
	Nanjing Chunlan Auto Manufacturing Co., Ltd.	1,000	5,190	994.94	900	4,886	897.14
	Chengdu Wangpai Vehicle Holding Co., Ltd.	451	2,682	3,294.94	550	2,367	4,283.33
Light Truck	Beijing Auto Industry Holding., Ltd.	11,959	72,168	41.34	13,505	71,710	35.00
	Dongfeng Motor Corp.	5,490	37,154	29.76	5,394	34,911	26.69
	Nanjing Auto (Group) Co., Ltd.	2,766	21,135	30.88	3,122	20,472	25.12
	Jiangling Motors Group Corp.	4,418	20,969	33.70	3,341	21,196	32.99
	Anhui Jianghuai Auto (Group) Co., Ltd.	2,297	18,109	47.01	2,508	16,417	43.25
	FAW-Hongta Yunnan Automobile Manufacturing Co., Ltd.	3,094	15,370	23.76	3,005	14,200	38.92
	Qingling Motor (Group) Co., Ltd.	2,721	11,783	5.71	3,056	13,426	28.01
	FAW Group Corp.	2,751	10,401	13.04	2,002	8,411	5.01
	Sichuan Highway Machinery Works	945	9,120	17.12	1,136	8,743	11.22
	China National Bus & Coach Co., Ltd.	1,283	8,442	4.73	1,550	7,880	22.74
	Hebei Zhongxing Auto Manufacturing Co., Ltd.	1,206	4,773	21.64	775	4,831	29.41
	Zhengzhou Nissan Automobile Co., Ltd.	957	4,481	25.62	925	4,542	25.40
	Jinbei Auto Holding Co., Ltd.	1,165	4,183	−20.51	760	4,438	−29.60
Mini Truck	Liuzhou Wuling Automotive Co., Ltd.	2,411	36,124	19.20	3,250	35,867	17.09
	Chana Automobile (Group) Liability Co., Ltd.	284	21,070	−0.51	2,492	18,186	−11.61
	Changhe Aircraft Industries (Group) Co., Ltd	2,897	16,305	124.06	2,514	14,816	77.18
	Harbin Aircraft Manufacturing Corporation	1,231	11,416	128.46	1,592	8,975	50.23
	Nanjing Channa Auto Co., Ltd.	1,301	7,598	80.56	1,186	5,774	20.44

The last of the producers featured in Table 6.3.2, Xiamen King Long, is one of the most progressive companies in the sector. Originally using technology from Daimler Benz, they now have technical cooperation with MAN, Hino, Mitsubishi, Cummins and Alexander. They claim production of more than 40 models at three different sites, with export sales to south-east Asia, Middle East, Latin America and the USA. However, the company does not appear in official Chinese statistics because it is classified as a vehicle assembler rather than a manufacturer.

Truck manufacturing

The production and sales numbers of the major manufacturers of trucks for the first six months of 2002 are recorded by category in Table 6.3.3. Year-on-year percentage changes are also detailed.

Mini-trucks

Of the five mini-truck manufacturers listed, the three leaders – Liuzhou Wuling Auto (38.3 per cent), Chana Auto Group (22.4 per cent) and Changhe Aircraft Industries (17.3 per cent) – together accounted for 78

Table 6.3.4 Stages in the reduction of tariffs and local content requirements

Impact	Current	2003	2006
Tariff reductions	Import tariffs for autos: 80%–100%	Import tariff cuts phased in equally 15% each year	Import tariffs for autos will be reduced to 25%
	Import tariffs for auto parts: 40%		Auto parts tariffs will fall to average of 10%
Investment and technology transfer	Local content requirements for CBU will be restricted to 40% for Year 1, 60% (Year 2) and up to 80% (Year 3)	Will eliminate policies which restrict foreign automotive companies from importing inputs for production	Significant commitments in addressing concerns about the terms and conditions of investment in China, and the government's role in what should be commercial decisions
	Foreign ownership is allowed (up to 50%)	Will eliminate and cease enforcing trade and foreign exchange balancing requirements	

per cent of the market. In the first half of 2002, Changhe Aircraft Industries registered a 77 per cent increase in sales.

Light trucks

13 major manufacturers are listed in this category, of which the top four, each selling more than 40,000 units annually, account for 59.4 per cent of the market. Their individual market shares are BAIC (28.3 per cent), DFAC (14.6 per cent), Nanjing Auto Group (8.3 per cent) and Jiangling Motors (8.2 per cent). All four leaders recorded year-on-year sales increases of more than 25 per cent.

Medium trucks

The two industry leaders, DFAC (46.1 per cent) and FAW (32.8 per cent) dominate the medium truck segment, although the latter's sales slipped by 28 per cent in the first six months of 2002. Two smaller manufacturers, Nanjing Chunlan Auto. and Chengdu Wangpai, together accounting for about 8 per cent of the market, both advanced rapidly with nine-fold and forty-fold increases.

Heavy trucks

At the top end of the truck sector, FAW (50.5 per cent) and DFAC (33.6 per cent) again predominate. The next two heavy truck manufacturers, China National Heavy Duty Truck Corp (CNHTGC) and Chongqing Heavy Vehicle Group (CQHVC) account for market shares of 5.2 and 4.4 per cent respectively. All four, together with

the fifth ranking heavy truck manufacturer, Shaanxi Auto Industry, registered year-on-year sales growth above 90 per cent in the first six months of 2002.

Impact of China's WTO entry

The stages in which import tariffs and localisation requirements will be gradually reduced under the negotiated terms of China's entry to the WTO were summarised at the end of Chapter 6.1 and again in Table 6.3.4 The same comments offered in Chapter 6.1 in relation to the impact of the relaxation of restrictions in foreign company operations of automobile manufacture apply equally to the manufacture of buses and trucks. Whatever changes may be brought about to the structure and ownership of the industry and to prices, it is likely that local production will maintain the mainstream of the China markets.

Export success in developed markets for both trucks and buses will depend on the Chinese industry's capability to satisfy foreign technical specifications and safety and exhaust emission standards, in which further alliances with the leading foreign manufacturers will play a crucial role. To date, China has achieved some modest sales of trucks to developing markets in Africa and the Middle East, selling on cost. With buses, they have moved a stage further; for example King Long now have a joint venture in India to build CKJD kits supplied from China. However, penetration of developed markets will require greater product sophistication, especially in the truck sector.

The Engineering Plastics Industry

Editorial Department, China Chemical News and China Chemical Industry Yearbook

Overview[1]

In 2000, domestic consumption of engineering plastics came to 392,000 tons; 68,000 tons (21 per cent) higher than in 1999, and an increase of 148,000 tons over 1998.

Polyamides (PA)

Nylon 6

In 2000, there were nearly 40 sets of domestic polyamide (PA) polymerization facilities. The polymerization capacity exceeded 400,000 tons per annum, and actual output was 320,000 tons per annum.

Nylon 66

The domestic apparent consumption of nylon 66 in 2000 was 81,200t, and the output was over 100,000t.

Shenma Group plans to expand its output to 120,000 tons per annum, and its resin cutting capacity to 35,000 tons per annum, and to bring the facilities on stream at the end of 2003.

Other nylon products

The production of long carbon-chain nylon PA 11 and PA 12 for brake pipes and oil transmitting pipes has exceeded 2,000 tons per annum: the raw materials for these are all imported. In order to meet the require-

Table 6.4.1 Demand in recent years (thousand tons per annum)

	1998	1999	2000	2001 (estimated)	2005 (predicted)	Average growth
PA	62	67	83	92	165	23.7
PC	87	130	164	178	226	22.8
POM	66	82.4	96	98	130	13.8
PBT/PET	24	35.6	41	44	57	19.6
MPPO	5.7	9	8	8.8	10	10.7
ABS		1,434	1,490	1,520	1,600	
Total	244.7	324	392	426.8	590	20.0

---

[1] Editor's note: Generally speaking, China is dependent on imports of high value-added special-purpose engineering plastics. It is estimated that the rate of self-sufficiency will be around 40 per cent in the next five years or so. The current production of engineering plastics, basically low-end products, cannot meet the increasing demand for higher grade engineering plastics. The production of high-grade and high value-added products is quite limited in terms of domestic capacities. Interestingly, there do not seem to be many plans by domestic petrochemical giants to tap into the high-end market. Weak R&D is believed to be the reason. With the increase in end-use segments such as motor vehicles, machinery, consumer electronics and telecommunications, the opportunities for foreign exports to China will increase, particularly with the reduction of the tariff level after China's accession to the WTO. At the same time, options of strategic alliances such as joint ventures will also offer prospects of development in China's engineering market.

Table 6.4.2 Output of main Nylon 6 enterprises

Enterprise	Output (thousand tons per annum)
Guangdong Xinhui Meida Polyamide Fibre Co Ltd	66
Zhejiang Cixi Jinlun Co	60
Yueyang Petrochemical Plant	45
Yingshan Petrochemical Plant	13
Shijiazhuang Chemical Fibre Co	25
Kaiping Polyamide Fibre Plant	10
Yantai Huarun Co	5
Qingdao Zhongda Chemical Fibre Plant	6
Shunde Nylon 6 Plant	7
Gaoyao Nylon 6 Plant	13
Qingdao State-owned Cotton Plant	12
Zhangjiagang Junma Polyamide Plant	30
Qingjiang Synthetic Fibre Plant	4
Ji'nan Chemical Fibre Plant	4

Table 6.4.3 Output of main Nylon 66 cutting resin enterprises

Enterprise	Output (tons per annum)
Henan Shenma Group	1,700
Shanghai No.18 Plastics Plant	300
Heilongjiang Nylon Plant	5,000
Liaoyang Petrochemical Company	10,000
Shanghai Celluloid Plant	200
Haian Nylon Plant	800

ments of the domestic market, the National Planning Committee has approved the setting up of a PA 11 unit in Shanxi using the technology of North China Technological College, and the setting up of a PA1212 unit in Zhengzhou, He'nan. These units, together with the transformation of the PA1212 unit of the former Shandong Zibo Mining Bureau, currently under construction, will, when completed, certainly meet the domestic market requirements for long chain nylon.

The research achievements in star pattern nylon polymer made by East China University are comparable to those of advanced countries. Research into nano nylon plastics has been attracting the attention of manufacturers across the world. The total global sales volume of nano plastics in the world was 1,000 tons in 1999, all nano nylon plastics. It is predicted that in 2004 the global sales volume of nano plastics will be 125,000 tons, the majority of which will be nylon. The

cost of nano nylon plastic bearing pedestals jointly developed by Nanjing Julong Co and Longda Transmission Parts Co is 50 per cent lower than those made of stainless steel. Output of the product has come to 200,000 sets, and has generated US$4 million of exchange exports, having an increased output value of 35 million yuan.

Polycarbonates (PC)

Owing to the rapid development in electric/electronic appliances, computers, telecommunications and building materials, the domestic PC demand has been increasing year on year, exceeding that of nylon. PC is regarded as one of the largest categories of engineering plastics, but most of the supply still depends on imports.

Table 6.4.4 Imports of polycarbonates (thousand tons per annum)

Year	1997	1998	1999	2000	2001 (predicted)
Volume	81.8	108.8	160.5	180	200

Table 6.4.5 Polycarbonates consumption pattern by end-use (%)

End use	1997	1998	1999	2000
Optical medium	35	40	42	41
Sheet profile	1	2	2	4
Water bottles/package	12	10	11	9
Electric/electronic appliances	46	43	40	40
Others	6	5	5	6

In China, PC is mainly used for electric/electronic appliances, compact discs, packaging, textiles and building materials. In 2000, the domestic demand for building sheets increased significantly, because of the rapid development of the road building and construction sectors. The price of PC climbed to the highest level in recent years, and import prices approached 40,000 yuan per ton, 12,000 yuan higher than that in the previous two years.

It is expected that Teijin Chemical Co Ltd of Japan will set up a solely-owned, 50,000-100,000 tons per annum PC production line in China. Existing domestic PC facilities are also expected to expand. Lanxing

Company intends to use the transesterification process to build up a PC unit with an output of 10,000-50 000 tons per annum. The domestic PC market will face fierce competition in the future. It is forecast that PC price will probably be fixed at about 24,000 yuan per ton.

Polyoxymethylene (POM)

In 2000 there was no POM resin production. The new unit in Yuntianhua, using Polish technology, is still at the trial stage, and its 10,000 tons per annum capacity unit will be expanded to 15,000 tons per annum. Lanxing Co plans to resume operation of the 3,000 tons per annum unit at Shanghai Solvent Plant, and then to extend to 20,000 tons per annum. The programme by the Japanese Baoli Co in Nantong to build a 60,000 tons per annum POM unit has been approved by Jiangsu Province and is under active preparation. Among applications for construction submitted to the National Planning Committee, Daqing oil field methanol Plant and the Shanxi Province Lanhua Kechuang Group have been approved and entered the feasibility study stage.

In the domestic market, the demand in 2000 markedly increased, and the import volume was 10,000 tons more than the previous year: a growth rate of 9.26 per cent.

Table 6.4.6 POM import volume in recent years (thousand tons)

Year	Volume	Year	Volume
1994	19.4	1998	63.4
1995	26.4	1999	90.6
1996	39.4	2000	99.1
1997	57.1	2000	100.6 (predicted)

Table 6.4.7 POM domestic consumption pattern

End-use	Proportion (%)	End-use	Proportion (%)
Electric/electronic appliances	32	Machinery	15.5
Automobiles	9.6	Farming machinery	4.5
Light industry	24	Others	14.4

Thermoplastic polyester

PBT

China succeeded in developing PBT resin in the early 1980s. Up to now, capacity has exceeded 50,000 tons per annum. In 2000, output was about 20,000 tons, which represented at most 47 per cent of the total domestic demand. Among the five largest engineering plastics, PBT is considered to be the most successfully developed.

The average growth rate of domestic PBT market demand remains at about 17 per cent. Meanwhile, import volume increases year by year. PBT manufactured domestically can only meet the requirements of mid- or low-level products' market share. As supply exceeds demand, most manufacturers are operating under capacity, and price competition is fierce.

Table 6.4.8 Output of main PBT resin enterprises in 2000

Enterprise	Capacity (tons per annum)	Output (tons)
Yizheng Chemical Fibre Engineering Plastic Plant	20,000	8,000
Yuyao Fanwei Engineering Plastic Plant	10,000	
Jiangyin Sanfangxiang Group	8,000	4,000
Nantong Synthetic Material Plant	5,000	2,000
Nanjing Jiangning Chemical Fiber Plant	3,000	1,000
Yueyang Docron Plant	3,000	
Shanghai Docron Plant	1,000	
No.2 Film Factory of Lucky Group	3,000	
Suzhou Xiangxuehai Co	1,000	500
Zhangjiagang Additive Chemical Plant	2,000	1,000

Table 6.4.9 Domestic PBT consumption pattern by end-use

End-use	Proportion (%)
Electric/electronic appliances	62
Automobile and machinery	13
Telecommunication	4
Others	21

Other thermoplastic polyester varieties

In China, although the level of R&D of PET plastics is high, the level of industrialization remains low. So far, large-scale production has not been achieved, and only a few plants are operating, turning out small quantities of products to replace some of the imported goods. In 2000, Beijing Lianke Nano Co and Yanshan Petrochemical Corp, employing the technology of the Chemistry Institute of the Chinese Academy of Sciences, succeeded in developing PET modified with nano materials, and carrying out a test trial on production facilities, with development and application tests still under way. Some manufacturers plan to develop PEN, which is similar to PET, but since the supply of the raw material naphthalene dicarboxylic acid is pending, large-scale production cannot be formed in the short term.

Modified polyphenylene oxide (MPPO)

The domestic demand for MPPO is about 10,000 tons. In the early 1990s, China completed construction of two polymerization facilities, with 2000 tons per annum resin production capacity and 4000 tons per annum blending capacity. However, these plants have ceased production leaving a few blending plants with a capacity of about 4,000 tons per annum. At the end of the tenth Five Year Plan, domestic MPPO capacity will reach 1,000 tons.

Special engineering plastics

Polyphenylene sulphide

In 2000, the demand for PPS was 5,700 tons, of which 60–70 per cent were used to make parts for import. It is predicted that demand in 2005 will exceed 10,000 tons. Currently, some plants with a capacity of 100 tons per annum are still operating.

During the tenth Five Year Plan, several PPS expansion units will begin to operate, which should solve the problems of relying on imports. It is understood that Japan Ink Co intends to build PPS facilities in cooperation with China.

Polyimide

In 1962, China began to develop polyimide for use in mechanical and electrical instruments, the chemical industry, rockets and space projects and other advanced science and technology fields. At present, the domestic output exceeds 1,000 tons per annum, and it should go up to 1,700 tons per annum in 2005. The demand in 2000 was 4,000 tons. According to estimates, the demand will be 8,000–10,000 tons in 2010.

Polysulphone

It is reported that Shanghai Plastic Industry Co. has started to build a production facility.

Liquid crystal polymer

Beijing University, Zhejiang University, Tianjin Synthetic Material Institute, Wuhan Chemical Engineering College, the Chemistry Institute of the Chinese Academy of Sciences and Qinghua University are all working on the synthesis and application of liquid crystals.

Polyether ether ketone

The Special Engineering Material Plant attached to Jilin University was approved to set up a 500 tons per annum facility to manufacture PEEK, PES and other special engineering plastics.

The Food Additives Industry

Editorial Department, China Chemical News and China Chemical Industry Yearbook

Overview

There was a marked increase in the production of food additives in 2000 compared with 1999, with the exception of the restriction imposed by the government on the production and consumption of saccharin. The total output for the year reached 1.8 million tons, including products for the fermentation industry such

Table 6.5.1   Output of major food additives in 2000

Product	Output (thousand tons)
Monosodium glutamate	700
Citric acid	340
Enzyme preparations	250
Yeast	100
Flavouring essences and flavorants	35
Colourants	28
of which natural colouring matters	25
High-intensity sweeteners	44
of which saccharin	19.6
Sodium cyclamate	20
Stevioside	1.2
Aspartane	1.2
AK sugar	2
Nutritive sweeteners	112
of which xylose and xylitol	12
Sorbitol	100
	(and 70 imported)
Preservatives and antioxidants	80
Nutrition enhancers	58
of which vitamins	46
mineral elements	12
Emulsifiers, thickeners and quality ameliorants	60

as monosodium glutamate, citric acid, enzyme preparations, etc, a rise of 14 per cent over the preceding year. In 2000, production of several food additives increased significantly.

In order to prolong the quality guarantee period and shelf life of food, the output of preservatives and anti-staling agents rose sharply. In 2000, output of sodium benzoate came to about 70,000 tons; its domestic sale was around 50,000 tons, and over 10,000 tons were exported.

The catering business flourished in 2000. Its sales value was 263.8 billion yuan from January to September 2000 and was expected to exceed 370 billion yuan for the year. The domestic output of special flavourings based on sodium glutamate, guanylic acid (GMP) and inosinic acid (IMP) surged.

With improvements in quality of life, functional food additives (functional factors) and ingredients also increased.

It can be seen from Table 6.5.2 that the export of major food additives saw a substantial increase in 2000. Total export was 388,000 tons, 12.2 per cent more than the preceding year. Those with export volumes of over 10,000 tons and a large increase were: citric acid, with an increase of 12.3 per cent; citrates (12.2 per cent), benzoic acid and sodium benzoate (11.44 per cent), vitamin C (12 per cent) and monosodium glutamate (15.8 per cent), the highest increase.

Imports of major additives showed an increase of 5.9 per cent on 1999 (see Table 6.5.3).

Both import and export volume in 2000 were higher than the preceding year, but the FOB and CIF prices per unit of product were lowered. Competition in the global food additive market was very intense, and it was a case of survival of the fittest. Food additives companies

Table 6.5.2 Export of major food additives in 2000

Product	2000 Volume (tons)	Value (US$ million)	1999 Volume (tons)	Value (US$ million)
Citric acid	225,415.7	188.70	183,312	159.43
Citrates	32,762	27.80	26,740	22.89
Lactic acid and lactates	3,720	3.90	4,249	5.30
Tartaric acid	4,107.6	10.16	2,350	3.42
Gluconic acid and gluconates	3,509.4	18.02	2,394	13.01
Monosodium glutamate	21,238	25.52	13,432	17.38
Mannitol	1,221.9	1.56	697	1.17
Benzoic acid and sodium benzoate	16,133.6	22.15	14,098	36.31
Saccharin	14,818.3	36.42	14,914.6	36.31
Natural flavorants	9,716	60.96	11,192	67.44
Vitamin C	34,675.9	173.88	28,793	146.26
Vitamin E	8,595.7	69.30	6,471	85.78
Sodium cyclamate	6,508.5	8.62	4,384	5.53
Live yeast	5,767.7	11.41	4,878	8.69
Total	388,090.9	647.57	317,905	588.443

Table 6.5.3 Import of major food additives in 2000

Product	2000 Volume (tons)	Value (US$ million)	1999 Volume (tons)	Value (US$ million)
Sorbitol	79,187	30.04	72,600	26.87
Propionic acid	9,109	5.51	10,364	6.36
Glutamic acid	7,293	6.01	15,818	10.09
Other amino acids	2,777	22.23	2,239	18.37
Arabic gum	725	1.71	639.8	1.00
Locust bean and guar gum	3,207	4.87	6,687	6.65
Total	102,298	70.37	108,347	69.33

abroad were carrying out readjustments, mergers and intensive operations to improve their competitive power. With imminent entry to the WTO, the domestic food additives industry must face new challenges: make efforts to improve quality, increase product variety and lower costs.

The total output of domestic food additives (including products from the fermentation industry) in 1991 was 476,000 tons, with a value of 5.2 billion yuan. In 2000 these figures went up to over 1.8 million tons (abut 20 billion yuan), so that in ten years output increased by 3.78 times and output value by 3.85 times.

Table 6.5.4 Production growth of key food additives (thousand tons)

Product	1991	1995	2000	Factor increase between 1992 and 2000
Monosodium glutamate	250	522	700	2.88
Citric acid	65	154	320	4.92
Sodium benzoate	4		70	17.5
Dietary gourmet powder	13.9	13	35	1.84
Colourants	3.2	11	28	8.75
Xylose and xylitol	2.7	6	12	4.44
Sorbitol	20	50	100	5.00
Vitamins	4	20	38	4.75

Trends in product lines

Preservatives, antioxidants and antistaling agents

Sodium benzoate

The market price of sodium benzoate was 6,500-7,000 yuan per ton, but the internationally accepted price for low toxicity, high efficiency potassium sorbitate was more than 30,000 yuan per ton. The ten sodium benzoate producers had a capacity of 70,000 tons per annum, of which benzoic acid and sodium benzoate comprised 30,000 tons per annum at Wuhan Organic Chemical Industrial Co. In 2000 the actual output was over 60,000 tons nationwide, and exports more than 10,000 tons.

Potassium sorbitate

In the domestic market, cheap sodium benzoate was used in large quantities. The use of potassium sorbitate was limited and its production was mainly for export and developed quickly. Its global capacity was 36,000 tons per annum, and the US consumed 12,000 tons per annum at US$2 per pound. Producers in China increased in number from 20 up to about 50. In the fierce competition costs were lowered, and its price fell from 60,000 yuan per ton down to under 28,000 yuan per ton. Some producers ceased production, and those that remained expanded their production scale and were consolidated. Guangxi Nanning invested with Hoechst AG to enlarge its capacity from 1,000 to 4,000 tons per annum; Wuxi Daxin extended its capacity to over 3,000 tons per annum, and Nantong Acetic Acid Chemical Plant extended to 8,600 tons per annum, to become the largest domestic potassium sorbitate producer. As the export of domestic potassium sorbitate increased considerably, its price was low and it was fully competitive. Several large international companies, including Eastman announced that it would withdraw from the potassium sorbitate market, and Japan was in the process of closing down its potassium sorbitate enterprises.

Sodium isoascorbate

This was a biosynthetic antioxidant developed successfully in China in the 1990s and was able to replace the antioxidant vitamin C in meat products. The demand in the international market was about 120,000 tons: Japan consumed 800 tons per annum, and the domestic output was about 5,000 tons. Since the price of sodium isoascorbate was lower than for vitamin C, it tended to replace vitamin C in the food processing industry. With competition from foreign producers, the price of vitamin C abroad dropped from 120,000 to less than 60,000 yuan per ton, and if the price of sodium isoascorbate is not also reduced, it will be difficult for it to keep its foothold. The domestic price of sodium isoascorbate also fell due to competition, and its selling price decreased to 23,000 yuan per ton. Consequently, the number of domestic producers of sodium isoascorbate diminished from the original 20–30 down to 3–4, through selection of the superior and elimination of the inferior. The largest producer was Jiangxi Dexing Vitamin C Plant, which by continual improvement on technology and shortening of fermentation time, lowered its cost by a significant margin. Its mill price was less than 22,000 yuan per ton, and its output extended to 3,000 tons per annum. The next was Zhengzhou Biochemical Plant, with a yearly output of 1,000 tons.

Colourants

There were 56 varieties of colourant products by 1996, of which 10 were synthetic and 46 natural. China has approval of the largest number of natural pigments in the world besides Japan. The US and European Union had so far approved of 26 natural colouring matters. The total annual domestic output of colourants was 28,000 tons, of which 3,000 tons were synthetic and 25,000 tons natural.

Emulsifiers, thickeners and quality ameliorants

Xanthan gum

Among the producers of xanthan gum, the leaders are: Nanjing Jinhu, Shandong Zibo Zhongxuan and Shunda, Henan Tianguan, Qinyang and Xinhe, Shanghai Guoruun, Baoji Fuyang and Heilongjiang Gannan plants, whose capacity surpasses 6,000 tons per annum; their output was 4,000 tons in 2000.

A gap existed between the quality of domestic xanthan gum and that of foreign products, and the shortcomings were mainly yellowing of the colour, unevenness of the grains, high ash content, presence of moulds, and high yeast content. The domestic product was used chiefly at home, with a little for trial export, and the selling price at home was about 50,000 yuan per ton. Domestic production was on a small scale; the largest capacity was 2,000 tons per annum. National output was only 4,000 tons, a quarter of that of Kelco in the US, and therefore the sector lacked competitive power.

Monoglyceride

In the period of the ninth Five Year Plan, Guangzhou Light Industry Research Institute completed the key project of 'molecular distillation technology' for tackling its scientific and technological problems, put forward by the former State Science and Technology Commission, and a molecular distillation unit of 3,000 tons per annum has been constructed. The production of monoglyceride by molecular distillation progressed remarkably well in the latter part of the ninth Five Year Plan period, and there were already 10 domestic producers, four producing monoglyceride by molecular distillation, in Guangdong alone, in addition to the 5,000 tons per annum unit for monoglyceride by molecular distillation in Kunshan, owned by Danisk of Denmark.

In 2000 the output of monoglyceride by molecular distillation exceeded 10,000 tons, and with mutual competition its price fell from over 20,000 yuan per ton in 1997 to 15,000–17,000 yuan per ton. In this way, further reductions in cost and mill price became the chief means of competition in the production of monoglyceride by molecular distillation.

High intensity sweeteners

Aspartane

With the limitations imposed by the Chinese government on the production and use of saccharin in 1999, the market for aspartane was broadened, and at the same time the National Food Additive Standardization Technical Committee revised its remarks on hygienic standards for the use of aspartane to include L-phenylalanine content, thereby dispelling misgivings on its use in the food industry. In 2000 the aspartane market enlarged, and producers intended to extend their capacity further. Two producers in Zhejiang planned to extend to 1,000 tons per annum each, and Hangzhou also increased its capacity. In Zhejiang Province alone the capacity of three aspartane producers reached 2,000 tons per annum. Indiscriminate expansion of production should be avoided, because although saccharin was limited in its use, and other sweeteners were not yet restricted, the price of aspartane was the highest for a unit of sweetness. Producers paid attention to technical input, saved energy, reduced consumption, and the cost of the raw materials decreased. The price of imported product was US$30 per kilogram, while that of the domestic product was 250 yuan per kilogram: definitely competitive.

The main raw material for domestic aspartane was L-phenylalanine, which once depended on imports. In 2000, on the basis of tackling key problems in the ninth Five Year Plan period, various places in China could produce L-phenylalanine themselves, with its quality reaching the FCC grade. This meant that the cost dropped from the former 200,000 to 130,000 yuan per ton, and the cost for one or two producers came down to less than 100,000 yuan per ton. The other raw material aspartate was produced domestically, with a selling price of 8,000–9,000 yuan per ton. There was therefore the potential for further lowering the cost of domestic aspartane.

Stevioside

Total domestic output was slightly higher than in 1999, but the production was relatively contained. Its total capacity was 3,000 tons per annum, with an actual output of 1,100 tons and an export of 1,000 tons. In 2000 the largest stevioside producer was Shandong. Jining Huaxian Group purchased Lunan Stevioside Plant and capacity rose from 700 to 1000 tons per annum, becoming the largest stevioside producer in the world. This producer cultivated 150000 mu (1mu= 0.0667 hectares) of stevia and bred a new stevia variety, with a glucoside content of 18 per cent.

Nutritive sweeteners

Sorbitol

In 2000, Sorbitol was the edible sugar alcohol with the highest output and the widest use and 150,000 tons were consumed domestically in the year. In the past few years since the production of vitamin C increased, the demand for sorbitol increased, with an annual consumption of over 100,000 tons. It was also used as a humectant for toothpaste, with an annual consumption of 40,000 tons. The raw materials for the domestic sorbitol producers were expensive, and the producers were small, with an average output below 10,000 tons per annum, so their production costs were high. The domestic market price was 3,500-4,000 yuan per ton, but from the 1990s the import of sorbitol (mainly from France) increased year on year. In 1999 it came to 79,000 tons, and in 2000 it was 72,600 tons. The CIF price fell from US$500 per ton at the beginning of the year down to US$375 per ton. The production costs of most of the domestic sorbitol producers was over 3,500 yuan per ton. Due to lack of competitive power, although capacity was 300,000 tons per annum, the actual output was only 100,000. The domestic market consumed 160,000 tons of sorbitol, of which over 60,000 tons were imported.

Xylitol

50–60 domestic xylitol producers had a capacity of over 30,000 tons per annum, but in line with market demand only 12,000 tons were produced in a year. Large scale producers were Tangyin Xylose Plant (capacity: 3,000 tons per annum, output of 2,400 tons per annum), Baoding Xylitol Co (capacity of 1,500 tons per annum) and Shandong Yucheng Guangda Group Xylitol Plant (2,000 tons per annum).

Isomaltol and erythritol

As the raw material cane sugar for isomaltol was cheap, China mastered the production technology for isomal-

tose. The characteristics of erythritol were similar to those of isomaltol, but it was made by fermentation of starch, without hydrogenation of sugar, so its capital construction investment was expected to be lower than for other sugar alcohols. In the FIA-FIC exhibition in Shanghai, a French company and Mitsubishi exhibited their respective crystalline erythritol products. China began research and development into erythritol, but no production was reported. Zhejiang Haizheng Pharmaceutical Industry Group adopted the technology of Beijing University, carried out production on a pilot plant scale, and displayed erythritol samples in the exhibition.

Insurance

Liu Baocheng, Professor, University of International Business and Economics

Overview

With a population base of over 1.3 billion, steady economic growth for more than two decades, and now being a new member of the WTO and so committed to opening its financial service market, China has every reason to stand out as the new El Dorado for foreign insurance firms.

The growth rate of China's insurance industry has been exceptionally striking. Total income from premiums topped US$25.7 billion in 2001 compared with US$56 million in 1980 – an increase by a factor of 459 within a matter of 21 years.

A brief historical account may help to explain such a surge. Insurance, along with all other industries in China, was subject to government manipulation under command economy policies. The domestic insurance industry was completely eradicated following the resolution by the National Finance Conference in 1958 and only the part relating to overseas insurance was retained. It was not until 1979 when the State Council approved the proposal filed by China's central bank – the People's Bank of China (PBOC) – that it gradually resumed operation. Before 1986, when the Xinjiang Farm Production Insurance Company was established, the Chinese insurance market was a state monopoly operated by the People's Insurance Company (PICC) acting as an affiliate of PBOC. Initially, no more than 30 products were offered. In 1988, the Shenzhen Ping-An Insurance Company was formed – the first company with shareholders operating in south-eastern coastal regions. The founding of China Pacific Insurance Company with investment from China's Communication Bank and which was operating on a national level in 1991 symbolized the market's shift from a monopoly to an oli-

gopoly. In 1992, the first foreign insurance firm was permitted to begin operation in China. In 1995, the passage of PRC Insurance Law provided the first across-the-board regulatory structure over the insurance market.

Contributing to this dramatic growth rate is the process of liberalization in the insurance sector, although it has been far slower than it could have been, particularly in the eyes of foreign firms on the waiting list for approval to operate in China. In 1999, the state council permitted the expansion of insurance fund appropriation, ie indirect participation in the stock market through financing of a security investment fund. By the end of 2001, 52 insurance firms were in operation, among which five were state-owned, 15 were share-held, 19 were joint ventures with at least one foreign party, and 13 were wholly owned by foreign firms. The number of insurance entities almost doubled in two years. More interestingly, the number of foreign invested insurance firms exceeded the number of Chinese firms for the first time in history, although the major market share is still in the hands of state-owned domestic firms. (see Table 6.6.1.) Firms specializing in insurance brokerage emerged on the scene, with seven in operation and another seven under review. The number of insurance products offered exceeded 1,000.

Table 6.6.1 Number of insurance firms in China (1999 and 2001)

Year	State owned	Share-holding	Joint ventures	Foreign owned	Total
1999	4	9	4	11	28
2001	5	15	19	13	52

Most of the substantive increase took place during the latter half of the 1990s (see Figure 6.6.1)

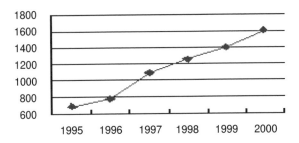

Figure 6.6.1 Increase in insurance revenue 1995–2000 (100 million RMB)

The total assets of China's insurance companies were US$56 billion in 2001. The industry turned over US$25.7 billion in premiums, accounting for 2.2 per cent of the country's GDP. It registered an increase of 32.2 per cent over the previous year, according to Yongwei Ma, chairman of the China Insurance Regulatory Commission (CIRC). Of this, US$17.37 billion, or 67.5 per cent of the total premium income came from life insurance. This marked a 42.8 per cent increase over 2000. A total of US$3.69 billion was paid out to insure property, or 51 per cent of property insurance premiums. Life insurance income increased by 14.4 per cent to US$12.07 billion, accounting for 62 per cent of the total premium income, and US$2.66 billion was paid out against life liabilities. (see Table 6.6.2)

Before the open-door policy in 1978, the number of people employed in the insurance sector was no more than 200. In 2000 there were 8,828 organizations engaged in the insurance industry. There were 166,602 full-time employees, nearly 50 per cent of whom were college-educated. This figure does not include the approximately 800,000 insurance representatives selling insurance across the country. The number of employees in Chinese insurance firms was 163,743, whereas those working for foreign insurance firms was 2,432, only 1.46 per cent of the industry's total workforce (see Table 6.6.3).

Legal and regulatory framework

The PRC Property Insurance Contract Act (1983) and Provisional Regulation on the Administration of Insurance Enterprises (1985) (both recently abolished) were the first two-pillar documents outlining the legal framework of the insurance market in China. The Insurance Law of China (consisting of eight chapters)

Table 6.6.2 Performance of China's insurance firms in 2000 (Billion RMB)

Insurance items	Insured amount	Premium	Indemnity & payout
Property Insurance Firms	**16,152.1**	**60.8**	**30.8**
Corporate Properties	6,960.3	11.8	5.1
Household Properties	582.9	1.3	0.4
Automobiles	3,404.1	37.3	20.3
Ships	983.4	1.1	0.9
Cargo	1,773.5	3.6	1.6
Satellites & Nuclear Energy	266.7	0.3	0.2
Construction and Installation	335.7	0.6	0.2
Risks & Liabilities	**1,845.5**	**4.8**	**2.1**
Liabilities	668.2	2.1	1.1
Warranties and Guarantees	54.1	0.2	0.1
Export Credits	38.8	0.3	0.1
Farming	49.9	0.4	0.3
Others	1,034.5	1.8	0.5
Life Insurance Firms	**34,705.8**	**99.0**	**21.8**
Life	6,928.2	88.2	17.4
Health	2,727.7	2.8	1.2
Third Party Liabilities	25,049.9	8.0	3.2
Total	**50857.9**	**159.8**	**52.6**

Table 6.6.3 Number of insurance companies and their staffing level, 2000

Insurance companies	Number	Number of staff	Number of women
Chinese insurance firms	13	164,170	60,534
(a) State-owned firms			
National head offices	4	1,047	415
Provincial level	63	6,960	2,284
Cities under separate fiscal plan	28	1,457	641
Outlets in provincial capital cities	24	2,865	1,111
Subsidiaries at prefecture level	910	34,675	12,811
Outlets in prefecture cities	103	1,720	747
Subsidiaries at county level	4,313	57,204	18,883
Outlets at county level	915	10,157	3,237
Out-placed offices and outlets	1,892	3,142	1,250
Insurance colleges	4	427	186
Other	29	586	198
(b) Private companies			
Head offices	9	3,000	1,231
First tier subsidiaries	86	24,522	10,897
Second tier subsidiaries	34	5,074	2,155
Branches	197	9,789	3,881
Out-placed offices and outlets	185	1,474	597
Other	11	71	28
Foreign firms	21	2,432	1,359
Joint ventures	7	688	409
Foreign subsidiaries	12	1,659	899
Foreign branches	2	85	51

Note: The number of employees does not include sales representatives.

was promulgated in May 1995 and took effect in October of that year and is the most comprehensive legislation regulating the expanding insurance industry so far. The recently promulgated Administrative Rules on Foreign Invested Insurance Companies (2001) is the only legislation defining foreign invested insurance companies operating in China. However, this legislation is most likely to be transitional as more and more foreign companies push into the Chinese market and new problems begin to appear over time. For example, the current harsh restrictions on both domestic and foreign insurance firms may eventually be eased. The following is a list of the major Chinese laws and regulations in connection with insurance.

- Insurance Law (1995)
- Contract Law (1999)
- Chapter 20 – Maritime Law (1993)
- Provisions on the Collection of Social Security Insurance Premium (1999)

- Provisions on Unemployment Insurance (1999)
- Company Law (1994)
- Administrative Rules on Foreign Invested Insurance Companies (2001)
- Administrative Rules on Insurance Brokerage Companies (2001)
- Administrative Rules on Insurance Agency (2001)
- Administrative Rules on Insurance Assessment Institutions (2001)
- Provisions on Executive Review by China Insurance Regulative Commission (2001)
- Notice Against Unfair Competition within the Insurance Industry (2001)
- Provisional Rules on Intra-firm Insurance Agency (2001)
- Administrative Rules on Insurance Assessors (2001).

Because China's insurance sector is still a young market, much of the legal framework remains to be consolidated. Old rules that cannot cope with the ongoing development are being phased out and a new wave of legislation phased in since the turn of the century. Most recently, a motion has been submitted to the People's National Congress, China's top legislature, to amend the Insurance Law. The proposed amendments include further liberalization of those areas such as insurance fund appropriation, the corporate structure and the regulatory process. Recent information reveals that it is highly likely the amendments will be approved.

1998 saw two dramatic restructuring events in the industry. Firstly, the People's Insurance Company of China (PICC), which dominated 80 per cent of the market, was split into four corporate entities with the parent company adopting the name of Chinese Insurance Group (CIG). Secondly, the government decided to separate the three financial industries of banking, securities and insurance and at the same time established government arms for their regulation and supervision. As a result, the Chinese Insurance Regulatory Commission (CIRC), a watchdog under the state council officially established in November 1998, is vested with the following responsibilities to regulate and supervise the insurance industry in China:

- To formulate national strategies, policies, rules and regulations in areas concerning the insurance industry;
- To conduct integrated supervision of the insurance market through a national network;
- To examine and approve the establishment and reorganization of various insurance entities;
- To examine and approve the appointment of senior executives in various insurance entities;
- To formulate qualification criteria for professional positions in the insurance industry;
- To formulate basic insurance terms and conditions as well as rates of premium for various lines of insurance operations, and to ensure conformance by the industry;
- To formulate financial accounting standards and ensure conformance
- To supervise the financial operation and indemnity capability of insurance entities;
- To administer the indemnity and warranty fund deposited by insurance entities;
- To conduct risk assessment and market surveillance through systematic analysis, scanning and forecasting in the insurance market;
- To conduct statistics and news updates in the industry;
- To be responsible for international exchanges and co-operation in the industry;

- To handle complaints and disputes;
- To administer industry associations and research institutions in the insurance field;
- To execute any other matters designated by the state council.

The CIRC has ten functional departments in Beijing and retains 31 representative offices in most capital cities of each province, autonomous regions and centrally administered municipalities.

Unfolding potential

Population size and income level are the two most important elements of any market. With a population of over 1.3 billion, China offers the world's largest insurance market. At present, most of this market is concentrated in the cities where there is a population of 460 million, particularly the coastal areas. An overview of China's insurance market reveals that a large potential market remains untapped. In 1999, only a fifth of the total population had purchased life insurance and as few as 3 per cent of the labour force is covered under a retirement insurance scheme. With regard to property insurance, 93 per cent of individuals and 85 per cent of businesses remain uncovered.

Depth and density are the two most popular indices to measure the sophistication of a country's effective insurance market demand and the status of insurance in the country's economy. Depth refers to the ratio of total premium revenue over GDP while density refers to per capita expenditure on insurance. Measured in this way, in 2000 China was ranked 61st and 73rd in the world. Its insurance depth was 1.8 per cent and its insurance density US$15.2. This was far below the global average of 7.84 per cent and US$385.4. While the total premium revenue was 2.2 per cent of the 2001 GDP, it still falls far below the world average.

Early in 2002, a Beijing-based firm – Chinese Mainland Marketing Research Co – conducted a survey among the residents of Beijing, Shanghai and 20 other cities across China in connection with insurance. This revealed that only 3 per cent held policies to protect their personal property, and only 1.7 per cent held car insurance policies. However, the survey also showed an encouraging increase in the number of families in the low and average income brackets who hold insurance policies. 38 per cent of families with a monthly income below US$120.77 and 40 per cent of families with monthly incomes from US$120.89 to US$241.55

bought insurance in 2000. 43 per cent of families with monthly incomes between US$241.67 and US$362.32 bought insurance, and the figure for families with monthly incomes above US$362.32 was 44 per cent.

According to Sigma, a reputable Swiss insurance source, China ranked 16th in the world in terms of insurance revenue in 1999. Although accounting only for 0.72 per cent of the world market share, its growth rate was highly promising and second only to Italy (see Table 6.6.4).

Table 6.6.4 China's position in the world insurance market (1999)

Rank	Country	Revenue (US$ million)	Actual growth rate (%)	World market share (%)
1	USA	795,188	5.1	34.22
2	Japan	494,885	–4.9	21.29
3	UK	204,893	12.9	8.82
4	Germany	138,829	5.3	5.97
5	France	123,113	9.6	5.30
6	Italy	66,649	18.5	2.87
7	South Korea	47,929	–8.4	2.06
8	Canada	41,882	5.3	1.80
9	Australia	38,712	5.9	1.67
10	Holland	37,985	4.1	1.63
16	China	16,830	13.3	0.72
World total		2,324,025	4.5	100.00

According to Mr Mingzhe Ma, Chairman and CEO of China Ping An Insurance Company, insurance will see the highest growth within the Chinese financial sector. The growth rate over the next five years will remain at between 20 and 30 per cent. Other experts believe that by 2005, the total value of insurance premium will reach US$33.82 billion, constituting 2.3 per cent of the total GDP. The average premium per person will increase to US$27.78. Currently, China's insurance industry constitutes only a small fraction of the entire economy (2.2 per cent), but by 2025 the aggregate premium revenue will reach 5 trillion RMB, equivalent to US$610 billion. This figure will place China among the top five largest insurance markets in the world.

Foreign insurance firms in China

American International Group (AIG) was the first foreign insurance firm permitted to operate in China, in 1992.

According to Xiaoping Wu, vice chairman of CIRC, 34 foreign insurance companies have been granted permission to operate some form of insurance business in China, while 112 foreign firms from 19 countries have set up 199 representative offices and are waiting for permission to establish their own insurance operations in China. The operation area was restricted to Shanghai and Guangzhou; now they are permitted to spread across coastal cities as far north as Dalian and some are permitted to penetrate inland cities such as Wuhan, Chongqing and Chengdu. In 2001, foreign insurance firms achieved a total premium revenue of US$39.02 billion.

Despite the restrictions, foreign insurance firms have experienced rapid growth. In 2001, they registered revenue of US$0.4 billion. In Shanghai, they have already seized a market share of 14.4 per cent of the life insurance market and 6.7 per cent of the property insurance market and in Guangzhou 11.8 per cent and 1.5 per cent respectively.

According to the Administrative Rules on Foreign Invested Insurance Companies (2001), foreign insurance firms can apply to CIRC for permission to set up either joint ventures or wholly owned entities in China. However, they must meet the following criteria:

- At least 30 years' history in the insurance market;
- Having had a representative office in China for at least two years;
- A minimum total asset base of US$5 billion at the year end before application;
- Their home country has a complete regulatory system over the insurance industry;
- Permission from home country regulatory body.

The following documents are required to be filed with CIRC:

- Application letter (to be countersigned by the Chinese partner in the case of a joint venture);
- Business licence and certificate for indemnity capability issued by the home country regulatory bodies;
- Articles of association and annual reports for the past three years;
- Application materials by Chinese party in the case of joint venture;
- Feasibility study and business plan;
- List of names and profiles of all persons responsible for the new entity;
- Other materials as requested by CIRC.

CIRC shall notify the applicant within six months from the date of full application after the due diligence review. Upon notification of initial approval, the applicant is given one year to prepare for the establishment of the insurance entity in China. Along with the completed standard application form, the applicant shall file the following documents with CIRC for approval:

- Summary report;
- Articles of association for the new entity;
- List of shareholders and intended capital contribution by each party;
- Certificate of capital contribution by official organisations;
- Power of attorney to nominated managers and introduction of their professional background;
- Business plan for the following three years;
- Intended insurance clauses, rate of premium and statement of liability reserve fund;
- Intended premises, facilities for business operation;
- Guarantee letter against liabilities of the subsidiary from parent company;
- Joint venture contract in the case of joint venture arrangement.

CIRC shall make a final decision within 60 days of the official application. If approved, a business licence to engage in insurance shall be issued. The business licence specifies the scope and geographical areas of business activities together with the target market segments to be served by the insurance entity.

In addition, new insurance entities set up in China are subject to the following restrictions:

- They are required to have a minimum paid-up registered capital of RMB200 million or equivalent. CIRC shall reserve the option to raise the bar for the requirement over the registered capital. After the business is established, 20 per cent of the registered capital will be deposited into an escrow account in China designated by CIRC as a warranty fund.
- They must arrange for 30 per cent of their business to be reinsured with designated Chinese insurance firms.
- A single entity is not permitted to engage in both property and life insurance.
- The currency unit of the account shall be in the Chinese local currency.

In spite of the difficulties in obtaining approval, foreign insurance firms do enjoy certain preferential treatments in China. For instance, while Chinese domestic firms have to pay income tax at a rate of 33 per cent, foreign firms pay only 15 per cent. In addition, foreign firms are permitted to engage in the stock market and purchase corporate bonds.

According to the Agreement reached between China and the USA as well as its commitment as a member of WTO, China will fully open its insurance market within the next five years. In the meantime, China is taking full advantage of the five years transitional period granted through the WTO negotiation to hold the pace of market liberalization. According to a recent paper published in the *People's Daily*, China intends to restrain the market share occupied by foreign insurance firms to 5 per cent within the next five-year transitional period and 10 per cent within the following 10 years.

In November 2001, the Fortis Group, a Benelux based giant with a market capitalization of 37.7 billion euros, invested US$88 million in 24.7 per cent of the equity interest in the TaiPing Life Insurance Company held by CIG and its subsidiary China Insurance International Holding Company(CIIH), thus became the first foreign company with the largest equity position in Chinese insurance companies.

Changes under the WTO commitments

In November 2001, China was officially admitted as a member of the World Trade Organization (WTO). Within the package deal to conform with the General Agreement on Trade in Service (GATS), China has entered into wholesale commitments with regard to market access, national treatment, most favoured nations treatment and transparency. The restrictions over all types of insurance and related services for foreign insurance firms which include geographic scope, equity limitation and business lines will be alleviated pursuant to the specified time table. They cover life, health and retirement pension insurance, non-life insurance and reinsurance. Reinsurance is now completely open, non-life insurance can be wholly foreign owned within two years, and life insurance allows for 50 per cent foreign ownership. All geographic limitations will be phased out within three years. The following is a reverse summary translation of China's commitments under WTO from the Chinese version. (For the official wording please refer to the original English version.)

1. China will permit foreign non-life insurance firms to set up subsidiaries in China and enter into joint ventures with Chinese partners with an equity share up to 51 per cent. Within two years of WTO membership, foreign non-life insurance firms will be permitted to set up solely-owned operations in China, and the form of corporate entity will be left to the decisions of business owners.

2. Immediately upon accession, the Chinese government would cease to dictate the terms and conditions of the joint venture between foreign insurance firms and Chinese partners, and the selection of the Chinese domestic partner will be the free decision of the foreign insurance firm.

3. Foreign firms engaged in insurance and reinsurance brokerage for the carriage of goods by sea, air and land would be permitted to enter into joint ventures with domestic partners for no more than 50 per cent of the equity share immediately upon China's membership. Foreign equity participation can be increased up to 51 per cent within three years of China's WTO membership. These restrictions will be completely phased out within five years of membership.

4. Foreign insurance firms operating in China will be gradually permitted to establish sub-branches as geographic restrictions are removed.

6. Upon accession to the WTO, China would open Shanghai, Guangzhou, Dalian, Shenzhen and Foshan for foreign life and non-life insurers and brokers. Within 2 years of WTO membership, China will further open a dozen other cities. These are Beijing, Chengdu, Dalian, Chongqing, Shenzhen, Fuzhou, Suzhou, Xiamen, Ningbo, Shenyang, Wuhan and Tianjin. A year later, all geographic restrictions are to be lifted.

7. Upon accession to the WTO, China will permit foreign non-life insurance firms to offer all kinds of products and services to overseas clients and to offer property, liability and credit insurance to foreign invested enterprises (FIEs) in China. Within another two years, these restrictions will be removed and domestic Chinese enterprises will be open to foreign non-life insurers.

8. Upon accession to the WTO, foreign insurance firms are permitted to provided master policy insurance and large-scale commercial risk insurance nationwide;

9. Upon accession to the WTO, China would permit foreign insurance firms to sell personal insurance to foreign and Chinese individual citizens, excluding groups. After another three years, they will be permitted to sell health and retirement pensions to both individuals and groups.

10. Upon accession to the WTO, foreign insurance firms would be approved to operate in China to offer reinsurance, and no geographic or quantitative restrictions will be imposed.

11. China will award licences for insurance business solely on the basis of prudence reviews, with no economic needs tests or quantitative limits on the number of licences issued provided they meet the following requirements:
    - The investor should have operated in a WTO member country for at least 30 years;
    - The investor should have had a representative office in China for at least two years;
    - The investor should have maintained US$5 billion of total assets at year-end before the application is filed (this restriction does not apply to brokerage firms);
    - Foreign brokerage firms, in order to qualify, should show total assets of US$500 million. After two years of China's WTO membership, they should have total assets of US$400 million, and two years after that, US$200 million.

Conclusion

The insurance market in China will undoubtedly continue to expand rapidly on the strength of large unsatisfied demand; steady economic growth; enhanced consumer awareness; continuous enterprise reform; improving market order and increased competition and committed market access to foreign participation by the government. However, excessive optimism must be tempered by the fact that, apart from market access, there are a host of other factors that will complicate the competitive situation – such as irregularities – that may occur along the road to open competition, resistance from the previous oligopolistic state-owned insurance companies and unique characteristics of local market conditions.

IT and the Internet

Li Yong, Deputy Secretary General, China Association of International Trade

IT industry

Telecommunications

China's telecommunications industry has experienced rapid growth in recent years. In the period of the ninth Five Year Plan, total telecommunications revenue increased at an average annual rate of 28.8 per cent, 3.2 times the GDP growth rate over the same period. However, the unit price went down across the board as a result of structural adjustment to the telecom tariff, and market competition became increasingly intense, triggering off price wars which led to a decline in the average revenue per user. The removal of the initial installation fee for fixed-line users and the network fee for mobile users also had an adverse impact on the rate of increase in total revenue. Despite these unfavourable changes, China's telecom industry still registered an increase of 25 per cent in 2001, with total traffic revenue of RMB361.2 billion, measured in 2000 unit prices. The total number of fixed-line users increased by 34.83 million to 179.03 million. There was a total of 59.55 million new mobile users in 2001, bringing the total to 144.81 million and making China the world's largest mobile communications market.

With the development of China's telecoms industry, demand for telecom facilities and telecom network equipment continues to grow. According to statistics from CCID Consulting, a corporatised research arm of the Ministry of Information Industry (MII), investment in fixed assets in 2001 was RMB277.95 billion, an increase of 25 per cent over 2000.

Reform of the telecom sector accelerated in 2001, driven largely by China's WTO accession. One historic event was the break-up of China Telecom, one of the few remaining monopolies. With the approval of the State Council, China Telecom has now been divided in two, one part of which retained the name China Telecom while the other became China Netcom.

In the next five years, the number of users of China's fixed-line and mobile phone network is expected to double, with the total number of subscribers reaching 500 million, while the national telephone penetration rate is expected to reach 40 per cent.

Table 6.7.1 Fixed asset investment by telecom industry 1997–2001

Year	Total investment in fixed assets		Size of telecom equipment market	
	Value (RMB billion)	*Growth (%)*	*Value (RMB billion)*	*Growth*
1997	105.595	15.9	74.375	12.0
1998	150.074	42.1	107.4	44.4
1999	160.522	7.0	110	2.4
2000	222.381	38.5	145	31.8
2001	277.95	25.0	169.46	16.9

Source: CCID Consulting

The PC market

Desktop PCs

The desktop PC market is typically demand driven because of the excess of desktop PCs on the market. In order to reduce the increasing inventory, manufacturers are making every effort to build a brand image in an attempt to gain consumer recognition and acceptance. Accompanying the brand-building effort, the battle for market share has also resulted in competitive price-cutting, which led to paper-thin profit margins. Industry participants have described competition in the desktop PC market in 2001 as 'unprecedented'.

Although competition in the desktop market was fierce, total sales value and volume have both registered impressive growth thanks to increasing consumer demand. According to CCID Consulting, total sales revenue from desktop increased by 12.3 per cent, while the number of desktops sold rose by 17.4 per cent (see Figure 6.7.1).

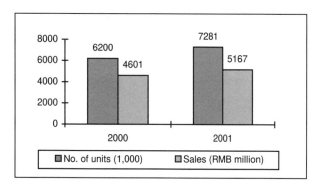

Source: CCID Consulting

Figure 6.7.1 Desktop PC sales in 2000 and 2001

The characteristics of China's desktop PC market are:

- Domestic brands have the advantage;
- It is a dynamic market with significant potential, while at the same time being a very competitive battlefield;
- Smaller brands are challenging traditional brands, while non-branded compatibles are making inroads into the branded market.

The market leader in 2001 was Legend, with 45.1 per cent of the desktop market. Competing brands such as Founder and TCL held 9.6 per cent and 8.5 per cent of the market respectively.

Of the total units sold in 2001, 2.89 million were home PCs, accounting for 39.7 per cent of the total desktop market. Industry experts warned that China's PC market faced tough challenges in 2002; the growth of the PC market is expected to have slowed down and an increase of 10 per cent, to reach 3.2 million units, is expected in 2002.

Laptop PCs

Because of the technological barriers, the laptop PC market is less crowded than the desktop market in terms of numbers of brands and players. However, price is still an important influence on the market pattern. With improvements in technology reducing the costs of manufacturing laptop computers, price competition became an effective means to gain market share. In the first half of 2001, a number of multinational IT giants such as Dell, Compaq, Toshiba, IBM and HP joined the price-cutting race, slashing prices by more than 10 per cent. Reasons for multinationals to join the competitive race include:

- the advantages of scale economics in mass production;
- closely calculated strategies based on the fast-growing potential of China's market;
- the enhanced development strength that the multinational enterprises have;
- anticipation of import tariff cuts following China's WTO accession that will lower the costs of laptop manufacturing across the board to the advantage of other laptop brands.

As a result of price competition, the best price for a laptop was RMB12,755, a significant reduction compared with RMB20,000–30,000 two or three years ago. In 2001, laptop sales reached a new high of 596,000 units and sales revenue was RMB9.03 billion.

Legend led the laptop market with a share of 21 per cent, followed by IBM (14.3 per cent), Toshiba (14.3 per cent), Dell (12.2 per cent) and Acer (7.6 per cent). In fact, there are three competing forces on the ground. One leading force consists of international brands such as IBM, Dell, Toshiba, HP and Compaq, whose combined market share clearly predominates. Another force is represented by local brands such as Legend, Founder, Uinsplendour and Winbook, with Legend the leader. The third source of competition comes from Taiwanese manufacturers, such as Acer, Asus, Compower and Twinhead, with Acer winning the largest market share of this group (see Figure 6.7.2).

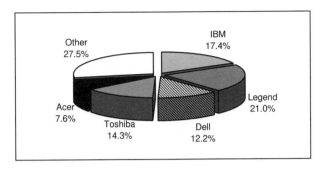

Source: CCID Consulting

Figure 6.7.2 Market share of the key laptop brands 2001

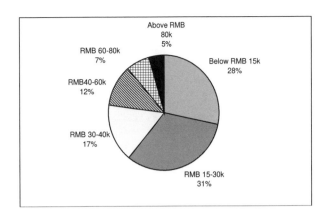

The market for laptops has continued to grow in 2002 and total sales are expected to exceed 800,000 units, which will be an increase of 35 per cent on 2001.

The server market

Driven by the global trend towards digitalization, Chinese organizations and businesses have stepped up their networking efforts and as a result the demand for servers has risen.

IA servers
According to CCW Research, the total sales of IA servers in 2001 reached RMB667,900 million, with the total number of units being 203,700 which, according to a separate source (*Internet Weekly*), represented an approximate 40 per cent increase over 2000. Many server manufacturers adjusted their marketing strategies to address the increasing market demand. The competition had become intense. In general, domestic brands are fighting at the lower-end of the market while international brands are competing at the higher-end. According to research by CCID Consulting, servers priced at under RMB30,000 accounted for about 60 per cent of the market, but their total sales revenue was less than one-third of total market sales (see Figure 6.7.3).

In sales value terms, HP took a leading share of 22.7 per cent in the 2001 server market in China. IBM were in second place, capturing 18.6 per cent of total market sales. Two domestic leaders, Legend and Langchao, ranked third and fourth, followed by Dell in fifth (see Figure 6.7.4)

It is predicted that the IA server market will maintain a growth of 20 per cent, to reach 245,000 units in 2002.

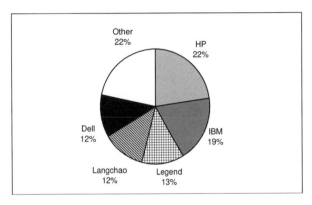

Source: CCW Research

Figure 6.7.4 IA server market shares by sales value of key brands, 2001

RISC servers
Sales of RISC servers in 2001 hit a total value of RMB684,000 million, an increase of 31.3 per cent on 2000. This section of the IT sector is dominated by international brands such as IBM, Sun, HP, Compaq and SGI, although domestic manufacturers have been trying to catch up. As Figure 6.7.5 shows, the combined share of the top three market leaders was 84.5 per cent.

The main markets for RISC servers are telecom enterprises, government organizations, financial institutions and large manufacturing enterprises. In 2001, these four categories of end-users accounted for 86.5 per cent of the total market. Growth for 2002 is projected to be around 25 per cent.

Computer peripherals

In 2001, the key computer peripheral products market experienced volume increases of varying degrees. The

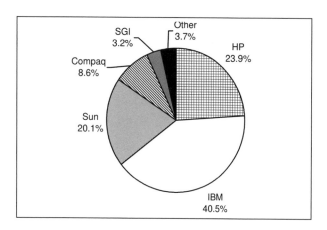

Source: CCW Research

Figure 6.7.5 RISC server market share by brand, 2001

monitors market saw another year of intensified competition. There were nearly 100 monitor brands, producing about 45 million monitors in 2001, or 37 per cent of the world's total monitor output. The leading producers of monitors in China are Samsung, Philips and LG, whose combined share of the market was 63.5 per cent. However, their dominance was eroded by other smaller brands and new entrants in the first half of 2002 when AOC took second position by gaining 15 per cent of the monitor market in the first six months.

Table 6.7.2 Market shares of leading brand monitors in China

	2000	*2001*	*Jan–June 2002*
Samsung	27.4%	29.9%	30%
Philips	24.1%	16.7%	10%
LG	11%	16.9%	13%
Total share	62.5%	63.5%	53.%

Source: eNews

While the CRT monitors market is engaged in a fierce battle, LCD monitors have been cultivating a growing market. Total sales of LCD monitors in 2001 were 170,000 units. Benq led the other brands by capturing a market share of 20.5 per cent. The second to fifth positions were taken by Samsung, Philips, LG and EMC and the total market share of the top five brands was 77.9 per cent.

The performance of the printers market was relatively stable and competition was less volatile. In the laser

printer category, HP dominated the market with 56.9 per cent. The competing laser printer brands were Legend, Canon, Epson and Founder. Total laser printer sales in 2001 were 735,000 units with a value of RMB3.05 billion. The inkjet printer market is quite concentrated and competition in 2001 was essentially restricted to the leading brands. Epson had a 30.3 per cent share of the market in 2001, but was under threat from Canon's 27.2 per cent market share. Close behind were Legend and HP, whose market share in 2001 were 16.7 per cent and 14.9 per cent respectively. Lexmark took fifth position with a share of 8.5 per cent. The combined share of the five largest brands in China's inkjet printers market in 2001 was 97.6 per cent and total sales amounted to 2.1 million units.

The performance of other computer peripherals in 2001 varied in terms of sales revenue and volume. Scanners and CD writers saw impressive increases in sales volume, although sales value had negative growth. Data projectors registered an increase of 40 per cent in volume terms, while disk memory systems grew at 111.4 per cent and network memory systems developed at explosive speed.

While the computer peripherals market in 2001 operated under the shadow of price competition, it still achieved total sales of RMB439 billion, an increase of 8.4 per cent over 2000.

Software market

Despite growing evidence that the US IT market slowdown was having a global impact, the software market in China has been growing steadily in value terms (RMB183 billion in 2001), although the rate of growth slowed down.

Table 6.7.3 Growth of the software market in China, 1999–2001

Year	*1999*	*2000*	*2001*
Software sales (RMB billion)	17.6	23.0	28.5
Rate of growth (%)	27.5	30.7	23.9

Source: CCID Consulting

In terms of software growth by category, platform software lost 2 percentage points of its share in the total software market in 2001, as a result of the slowdown in the growth of the hardware manufacturing sector. Intermediary software, largely used in network applications, gained 1.7 percentage points over 2000 in its share of the total software market. This gain was largely attributed to the rapid development of the internet in China. The rate of increase in the sales of intermediary software reached a phenomenal 59.6 per cent. Applications software maintained its growth trend in 2001 by recording a gain of 0.7 percentage point in total software market share. Its growth has been steady over the past few years and in 2001 sales of applications software increased by 25 per cent.

Table 6.7.4 Software sales and growth by types of software in 2001

Type of software	Sales (RMB billion)	Growth (%)
Platform software	85.9	16.4
Intermediary software	15.8	59.6
Applications software	183.3	25.3
Total	285	23.9

Source: CCID Consulting.

China's share of the world software market is about 1.2 per cent. The government has undertaken to increase this to 3 per cent by 2005. To achieve this, the country will focus its efforts on basic software and critical technologies, software for business management, social services and e-commerce and educational and home-use software. The software industry in China is generally fragmented and software development is dispersed among small software companies. China currently has over 10,000 businesses and 400,000 people engaged in software development and related services. There are another 1,023 higher education institutions in China with computer or software departments, recruiting a total of 586,000 students.

In response to the need to develop China into a major software country, the tenth Five Year Plan of 2001–2005 provides for a growth target for the software industry of more than 30 per cent annually. The government will continue to create a favourable environment for software industry development in an effort to achieve so-called 'hop-skip-and-jump' growth. Among various preferential policies, the most important is *the Notice of Certain Policies to Promote the Software and Integrated Circuit Industry,* promulgated by the State Council in June 2000. The Notice, clearly recognising the importance of these two industries in the development of China's information technology sector, sets out preferential policies such as VAT refunds to be used for R&D

and expanded production by software enterprises, preferential income tax relief and fast-track approval for overseas IPOs of software companies.

However, alongside policies encouraging the development of the software industry, there are challenges. The main ones include low domestic market share, shortage of capital availability, fragmentation characterized by small and non-competitive enterprises, lack of innovative ability, and insufficient protection of intellectual property rights. In another step to boost the development of China's software market, the government has geared up its efforts to crack down on software piracy.

IT services

Competition between hardware and software has become increasingly turbulent, and profit margins are becoming more and more squeezed. IT services has become a new leverage of market profit (see Figure 6.7.6). According to CCID Consulting, China's IT service market in 2001 was worth RMB40.16 billion.

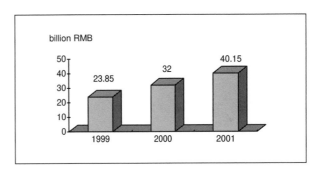

Source: CCID Consulting

Figure 6.7.6 Growth of the IT services market 1999–2001

In 2001, the markets of hardware support and maintenance, professional services and network services were valued at RMB9.07 billion, RMB21.102 billion and RMB6.995 billion respectively. Their shares in the total IT service market are shown in Figure 6.7.7.

Professional services captured the largest share of the IT services market. Systems integration was the main element of professional services, accounting for 83.4 per cent of the total professional services market. The demand for systems integration has increased over recent years (see Figure 6.7.8).

According to projections by CCID Consulting, the size of China's IT services market is expected to rise in

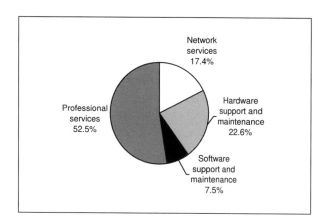

Source: CCID Consulting

Figure 6.7.7 Market share by IT services category, 2001

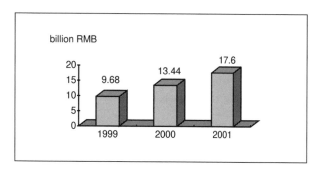

Source: CCID Consulting

Figure 6.7.8 Growth of the system integration market

2002 by 25.4 per cent to RMB50.4 billion. By 2006, the IT service market will be worth RMB 136.2 billion, with annual average growth at 27.7 per cent.

The Internet industry

Since 1994, when the Internet was introduced to China, it has developed at a rapid speed. According to the latest survey by China Internet Network Information Centre (CINIC), there were 45.8 million Internet users by the end of June 2002. A separate source from the Ministry of Information Industry (MII) reveals that the number of Internet users is increasing by 5–6 per cent each month, making China the fastest growing Internet market in the world.

Internet access

According to CINIC, by the end of June 2002, the number of computers in China with Internet access had

reached 16.13 million, of which 3.07 million (19 per cent) use leased lines, 12 million (74 per cent) use dial-up connection, and the remaining 1.06 million (7 per cent) employ other means.

Compared with the figure at the beginning of 2002, the number of computers with Internet access has increased by 3.59 million units over six months, an absolute increase of 28.6 per cent and an increase of 61 per cent year-on-year. Of this total, the number of computers using leased lines has grown by 0.73 million in the six months between January and June 2002, an increase of 31.2 per cent. The number of dial-up computers grew by 1.8 million in the same period, an increase of 17.6 per cent.

Number of Internet users

By June 30th 2002, the number of Internet users in China had reached 45.8 million, representing a net increase of 12.1 million users or an increase of 35.9 per cent over the previous six months. Among these, 9.46 million (21 per cent) use leased lines and 26.82 million (58 per cent) have dial-up connections. Dial-up users constitute the main part of Chinese Internet usage. It is estimated that 3.15 million users are using ISDN connection and 2 million are connected with broadband access.

Although the number of Internet users is growing fast, they represent only about 3.6 per cent of the total population. There still remains considerable room for further development. According to the State Development Planning Commission, the total number of Internet users is expected to reach 8 per cent of the total population.

Domain names registered under .cn and number of websites

By the end of June 2002, the number of domain names registered under .cn totalled 126,146: 1,173 less than six months before and 2,216 less than at the end of the same period in 2001. The reduction of domain names is believed to be associated with the bursting of the Internet bubble around the world. While the number of domain names had declined in the first half of 2002, the number of domains registered under .gov.cn increased by 822 to a total of 6,686. This increase is a result of government efforts to increase transparency.

Despite the decline in the number of domain names registered under .cn in the period, the number of worldwide web sites in China saw an increase of 16,113 (5.8

per cent) to 293,213 in six months. Most of these websites are distributed in the developed areas of northern, eastern and southern China and they constitute about 85 per cent of total websites. The less developed areas in the north-east, south-east and north-west of China only account for a small proportion. The same pattern is also reflected in the distribution of .cn domain names.

User composition

The results of the CINIC survey show that by the end of June, 2002, male Internet users accounted for 60.9 per cent of the market. Compared with the first survey in October 1997, the gender distribution of Internet users has changed as follows:

- female users increased from 12.3 per cent to 39.1 per cent;
- the proportion of male users has decreased from 87.7 per cent in 1997;
- there are currently 27.89 million male Internet users (51 times the number five years ago) and 17.91 million female users (236 times the number five years ago);
- 4.2 per cent of the total male population and 2.9 per cent of the total female population are Internet users.

58.9 per cent of Internet users are single and 41.1 per cent married. Single Internet users account for 5.7 per cent of the whole single population and married Internet users for 2.3 per cent of the whole married population.

Internet users are predominantly young. 82 per cent are under 35 years of age and 18 per cent above 35. Among users of all ages, young people in the age group of 18 to 24 account for the highest proportion (37.2 per cent), followed by those aged between 25 and 30 (16.9 per cent) and under 18 (16.3 per cent).

The breakdown of Internet users by level of education indicates that the largest group of internet users, accounting for 30.5 per cent, have senior high school education or equivalent. Those with college degrees constitute the second largest group, accounting for 29.2 per cent of total Internet users, followed by those with junior college education.

However, in general, the higher the income, the smaller the incidence of Internet users. The CINIC survey found that 86.6 per cent of Internet users have monthly incomes of less than RMB2,000. Those with higher incomes account for only 13.4 per cent. In terms of occupation, student users account for the highest proportion (26.2 per cent), followed by technical specialists (17.5 per cent), office assistants (13.2 per cent), and trade and service sector personnel (12 per cent). Internet users from the military forces and rural sector (agriculture, forestry, husbandry and fishing) account for the lowest proportion, each around 1 per cent.

E-commerce

Over recent years, the government of China has made a considerable effort to promote the development and use of information technologies at both government and business levels. As part of this effort, considerable investment has been made in improving the telecommunications infrastructure and this has laid the foundation for development of e-commerce. However, e-commerce cannot be developed solely by building hardware platforms. A host of other elements are required to make e-commerce work, the most important being customers, delivery systems and payment settlement systems. These also constitute the key obstacles to China's e-commerce development, however, as they are in an undeveloped state.

According to MII, the regulatory government authority, there were about 1,665 B2C online shopping sites at the beginning of 2000. By the end of 2000, only about 1,300 remained, and the number of sites reduced further to 1,188 by the end of 2001, a drop of almost 30 per cent over two years. This decline contrasted asymmetrically with the sharp increase in the total Internet population and number of websites.

The rapidly increasing Internet population has boosted revenue from Internet services, which grew from RMB 5.3 billion in 2000 to RMB7 billion in 2001, an increase of 32.08 per cent. It is believed that the trend of growth will continue to be dramatic for the next few years before it stabilises. The scenario for e-commerce looks as promising. While there are no new statistics for the total revenue of e-commerce in 2001, the decline in the number of online shopping sites during 2001 does not necessarily indicate future decline. In 2000, the total size of the e-commerce market was RMB77.16 billion, about US$9.3 billion. An overwhelming majority of e-commerce transactions were B2B, totalling RMB76.77 billion and accounting for 99.49 per cent of total e-commerce transactions. The remaining 0.51 per cent of B2C transactions only amount to RMB390 million, or about US$47.2 million. There were 667 B2C online shopping sites in 2000, and only 205 of these had been able to operate with a sustained stream of business. The number of B2B transaction sites was 370.

In this situation, it is not difficult to conclude that e-commerce in China is still in its infancy. Optimists anticipate a regrowth in e-commerce over the coming years. Pessimists argue that e-commerce at present still needs to struggle with fundamental problems such as the immaturity of its logistics and online payment issues, which will not be solved in the near future. However, the consensus is that China's entry into the WTO has injected a new development impetus and that e-commerce will experience major development.

In the process of its development there are still many obstacles to be overcome, such as infrastructure bottlenecks, lack of appropriate technology, disarticulation with the financial sector, logistical constraints, the small Internet population as a percentage of total population and relatively high cost of Internet access in terms of average disposable income. Together with other problems, China's e-commerce will still need time to reach maturity.

Mining

Li Yong, Deputy Secretary General, China Association of International Trade

An overview

China's mining industry plays an important role in social and economic development, providing 95 per cent of the country's energy needs, 80 per cent of its industrial raw materials and 70 per cent of production materials needed by agriculture.

A total of 171 different kinds of minerals have been discovered and reserves of 157 kinds have been proven in over 200,000 locations. Over 10,000 state-owned enterprises operate in the mining industry. In 2000, the total production of solid minerals reached 4.77 billion tons, crude oil 163 million tons, natural gas 27.7 billion cubic metres and coal 998 million tons. China is now the second largest mining economy in the world. Although China ranks third in total proven reserves of minerals, the per capita possession of minerals is only 58 per cent of the world average, ranking 53rd in the world and there are still shortages of key mineral resources. Although China exports about US$25 billion worth of mineral products per annum, it imports about US$30 billion worth, making the country the third largest importer of minerals in the world.

For a long time, the mining industry has been in a chaotic situation. Duplication of mining projects, uneconomical and poorly managed operations, slipshod mining decisions, rampantly increasing numbers of small mines, excessive mining, runaway exports, competitive price-cutting and low value-added exports are the high profile problems in the industry. In addition, the distribution of resources does not match the distribution of industries. A large number of the mining sites are operating on medium- to small-sized mineral beds and producing low-grade minerals.

Foreign investment in China's mining industry

Foreign investment in China's mining industry has experienced ups and downs since the adoption of the opening up policy in the late 1970s. In the early stages, only a few foreign investors came to invest in China's mining industry and they were there to test the water. The best known investment was a surface coal mine project funded by the US Occidental Petroleum Corporation. This was the largest investment project of the time, involving a total of US$344 million. In the period from 1989 to 1996, there was a surge of foreign participation in China's mining industry, the driving force of which was the deepening of China's economic reform and opening up policy.

Apart from investment in mining projects, foreign investors also entered into venture prospecting operations, a notable example of which was BHP's US$4.5 million prospecting venture to explore lead-zinc ores in China. However, foreign investment experienced a setback in the 1997-1998 period. The internal flaws in the investment environment of China's mining industry, together with the Asian financial crisis, the downturn of the world gold market and the impact of the Bre-X incident, had combined to cause the setback. A number of foreign mining companies left China, including Asia Minerals and Zen International. Since 1999, foreign investment has begun to pick up as improvements were made in the investment climate. In addition, China's growth potential in economic development and its imminent membership of the WTO have made many foreign mining companies revisit their China strategies and come to China to pursue new cooperative opportunities. Large international mining firms such as Billiton and Placer Dome have come to China, with the former investing in a lead-zinc mine project and the latter a gold mine project.

The following is a list of companies that have or have had a presence of some kind in China:

Anglo	King Bridge
Asia Minerals	Kores
AMR	Mevicar Minerals
Baja Gold	Minco
Barrick Gold	Minorco
Billiton	Naneco
Broadwater	New Mont Mining
Breckenridge	Pan Asia
Cameco	Pan-Pacific Peron
Carson Gold	Resources
China Gold	Placer Dome
Columbia Gold	Phelps Dodge
Cominco	Quantum
Cyprus Amax	Royal Oak
De Beers	RTZ
Donner Resources	Sino Mining
FMC Gold	Southwest Gold
Frontier Pacific	Spur Venture
Gen Corp	Teck
General Minerals	Technology
Global Pacific	Tri-a
Golden Pacific	Turnbul
Griffin Mining	West Mining
Inco	World Wide
International Skyline	XMP
Gold	Zen International
Iscon	

Source: Ishiung J Wu, Liu Yikang, *Mining climate improves in China*, Mining Engineering, September 2001, 19–24 'Mining Engineering' 2001.9 and China Gold Association

Impact of WTO accession on China's mining industry

One of the key impacts of China's WTO accession will be on the current institutions, operating modes and marketing practices of China's mining industry. The WTO rules require the establishment of new institutions and mechanisms for the Chinese mining industry, which will fundamentally change the relationship between enterprises and the government. Government support in terms of low interest government loans and debt-equity swaps will be under the scrutiny of the

WTO rules. Commercial loans will have to be provided under commercial arrangements, which means no bad debt write-offs will be possible. This will greatly impact on the old-fashioned state-owned mining enterprises which have relied heavily on government support. In addition, WTO-driven changes will also take place in the administrative systems and modes of management of China's mining industry.

WTO entry will also have an impact on the brain-drain, while the improvement of the investment environment will stimulate foreign interest in greater participation in the mining industry. One of the entry strategies will be localization, which means that foreign participants in the market will employ local specialists effectively to capture the local market. Retaining local talents in the state-owned mining operations will present a great challenge.

The reduction of entry barriers as a consequence of WTO entry will lead to an influx of foreign investment and import. The advantages of foreign mining companies, such as capital, technology, management, information and marketing networks will manifest themselves in the competition with local mining enterprises for advantageous mining resources. In fact, this competition has been ongoing since the 1990s and many local mining operations have collapsed as a result. The reduction of tariffs as an inevitable by-product of the post-WTO era will weaken the level of protection erected by tariffs. According to the projection by the China Exploration and Engineering Bureau, imports will increase as the level of tariff protection weakens (see Table 6.8.1 below).

Table 6.8.1   Forecast changes in the rate of tariff protection after China's WTO entry

Year	Rate
2000	4.7%
2002	4.1%
2004	3.5%
2006	3.2%
2010	3.2%

Source: China Exploration and Engineering Bureau

In addition, output, employment and foreign trade will also change (see Table 6.8.2)

Table 6.8.2 Forecast changes in China's mining industry

	Output	Employment	Import	Export
Metal mining	−2.5%	−1.7%	0.6%	−3.9%
Non-metal mining	1.6%	0.4%	6.7%	−2.2%

Challenges ahead

Apart from the impact of WTO entry described above, the mining industry also faces challenges from within China. One major challenge is that the industrialization process has put great pressure from the demand side on the development of China's mining industry. In the past ten years or so, demand for mineral products has been increasing rapidly with the fast-growing economic development, has which averaged at an annual rate of about 10 per cent. Disparities among the reserves, output level and demand have become increasingly noticeable. Take aluminium for example: the reserve has increased by only 1.1 per cent in the past 10 years, while production and demand have been growing at average annual rates of 11 and 17.3 per cent respectively. The industry's ability to supply the most needed minerals has weakened, leading to drastic increases in imports. Moreover, the proven reserves for some minerals can hardly meet the demand in the next 10 or 20 years. In the future, the demand for minerals will increase at speed along with the country's industrialization process. China will soon become the world's largest consumer of many key minerals.

The requirements for sustainable development of the mining industry are also a source of pressure. Currently, the rate of utilization of mineral resources has been low. The runaway exploration of mineral resources has inflicted both biological and environmental damage. The dilemma that the industry is facing is that resources of key minerals are in serious shortage while crude mining operations are wasting the precious resources, and the biological environments in many localities are already fragile and mining operations have further damaged them. To reverse the situation, it is imperative to increase exploration efforts to discover more reserves, improve the rate of resource utilization, promote resource-efficient production processes and technologies and, more importantly, maintain the balance of the biological environment. All of those, however, will require greatly enhanced technological input into the existing operations. Many of the local mining operations do not have the financial strength or technical capability to achieve the much needed technological advancements. It is a pressing issue for the industry to maintain a sustained mineral supply while keeping a sustainable social and economic development in the country.

Opportunities

Mining opportunities in China are obvious from the above analysis. China needs foreign capital, technologies and management to upgrade its mining industry. To achieve this, China has introduced policies to encourage foreign participation in non-petroleum and non-gas mineral projects. In the resource-rich western region of China, more preferential treatments are offered for foreign investment. As a recent change in the government stance on foreign investments in the mining industry, a new policy has been implemented from 1 July 2002, making geological information available to both Chinese and foreign concerns.

With the depletion of some key mineral resources, export opportunities for foreign mining companies will increase.

The Paints and Coatings Industry

Editorial Department, China Chemical News and China Chemical Industry Yearbook

Production

Upward trend for the total output of paints and coatings and prominence in coastal areas

According to data issued by the State Statistical Bureau, the domestic output of paints and coatings was 1.8394 million tons in 2000, up by 7.44 per cent on 1999 and an increase on the average growth of 2.09 per cent from 1997 to 2000. This excludes small producers with an annual output of of less than 5 million yuan, and if this amount was added, domestic output would top 2 million tons, ranking third in the world. Of the total, output of building coatings was 563,200 tons in 2000, an increase of of 9.25 per cent on 1999. These data show that the total domestic output of paints and coatings was basically stable and ascending year on year

In the coastal areas, total output was 1.3542 million tons in 2000, 73.62 per cent of the total domestic output and a rise of 16.08 per cent on 1999. Total output of building coatings was 97,700 tons, a gain of 48.06 per cent on 1999. It was evident that the coastal areas' increase in total output was much higher than the average domestic growth, and the growth of building coatings was unprecedented.

In the western regions, total output was 142,300 tons in 2000, constituting only 7.73 per cent of the total domestic output, and this total was 24.78 per cent less than in 1999, while the total output of building coatings was 34,200 tons, a fall of 61.36 per cent from 1999. This decrease in output was consistent with the economic gap between western and eastern regions.

Total output of paints and coatings in other regions (south-central, north-east, etc.) was 343,400 tons in 2000, accounting for 18.67 per cent of the total domestic output, which was a drop of 3.73 per cent from

1999. Total output of building coatings was 131,300 tons, a decrease of 11.11 per cent on 1999. Total output of paints and coatings and building coatings decreased compared with the previous year.

From the above analysis it is evident that the total domestic output of paints and coatings was effectively stable and increasing year on year, but development in various regions was uneven. The gap between western and eastern regions continued to widen, but the eastern regions' specialized production base for coatings and larger producers helped to accelerate its development so that the level of specialization in paint production rose constantly, raising the technical level of the paint industry and promoting product quality. From the market viewpoint, the strategic principle of developing the economy of the west central region and the implementation of state preferential policies, give the market in the west central region excellent prospects.

The shape of specialized paint production bases and the emergence of specialized paint producers

An analysis from the geographical point of view of the distribution of the total output of paints in 2000 would show that grouped paint production bases had taken shape and large-scale specialized paint producers are beginning to emerge.

In 2000 the production of paints and coatings was distributed mainly in the East China region, making up 41.56 per cent of the total domestic output, and the south central region (30.84 per cent of the total), with output concentrated in three places: Guangdong Province, Shanghai Municipality and Jiangsu Province. The total output of these three was 48.02 per cent, nearly half of the total.

Table 6.9.1 Regional distribution of total domestic output of paints and coatings

| | Total output | | | | Of which total output of building coatings | | | |
| | 1999 | | 2000 | | 1999 | | 2000 | |
Region	Total (kt)	Share (%)	Total (kt)	Share (%)	Total (kt)	Share(%)	Total (kt)	Share(%)
Nationwide	1,712.2	100	1,839.4	100	515.5	30.11	563.2	30.61
coastal areas	1,166.6	68.13	1,354.2	73.62	268.6	52.11	397.7	60.89
Guangdong	283.3	16.55	402.6	22.95	64.5	12.51	118.2	20.99
Fujian	25.4	1.48	25.5	1.39	7.2	1.40	7.1	1.26
Shandong	123.4	7.21	115.4	6.27	11.8	2.29	11.2	1.99
Zhejiang	96.1	5.62	114.1	6.20	7.8	1.51	18.9	3.36
Shanghai	217.9	12.73	255.6	13.90	89.8	17.42	114.3	20.30
Jiangsu	234.4	13.69	225.1	12.24	38.5	7.47	62.5	11.10
Tianjin	56.7	3.31	79.3	4.31	7.1	1.38	7.6	1.35
Hebei	87.4	5.11	108.3	5.89	25.7	4.99	47.7	8.47
Liaoning	42.0	2.45	28.3	1.54	16.2	3.14	10.2	1.81
Western regions	188.91	11.03	142.1	7.73	88.5	17.17	34.2	6.07
Shaanxi	27.1	1.58	28.9	1.57			0.3	0.05
Sichuan	14.0	0.82	15.0	0.82	0.7	0.14	0.9	0.16
Chongqing	50.0	2.92	49.1	2.67	16.8	3.26	16.8	2.93
Gansu	66.9	3.91	16.8	0.91	55.1	10.69	2.9	0.52
Ningxia	2.9	0.17	2.0	0.11	2.2	0.43	1.4	0.25
Xinjiang	20.3	11.86	25.2	1.37	10.0	1.94	10.2	1.81
Inner Mongolia	7.7	0.45	5.1	0.28	3.7	0.72	1.7	0.30
Other regions	356.7	20.83	343.4	18.67	158.4	30.73	131.3	23.31

Table 6.9.2 Distribution of total domestic output of paints and coatings in 1999 and 2000 (thousand tons)

| | Total output | | | Of which total output of building coatings | | |
Region	1999	2000	2000/1999 (%)	1999	2000	2000/1999(%)
Nationwide	1,712.2	1,839.4	7.43	515.5	563.2	9.25
North	278.6	303.2	8.83	146.3	143.3	−2.05
North-east	56.6	51.5	−9.01	16.9	14.6	−13.61
East	723.3	764.5	5.70	157.9	217.0	37.43
South Central	444.1	566.6	27.58	98.1	153.7	56.68
South-west	91.6	81.3	−11.24	28.9	19.8	−21.49
North-west	118.0	73.3	−37.88	67.4	14.8	−78.04

The growth rate in the three regions of the Zhujiang delta, Changjiang (Yangzi River) delta and the neighbouring regions of Beijing, was 18.02 per cent in 2000, and further increases are likely. The development tendency was particularly strong in Zhujiang delta, whose growth rate was 42.11 per cent.

The analysis of Table 6.9.2, with reference to the data of major producers in the paint industry, shows the number of producers of more than 20 000 tons' output was on the increase in 2000, and some even reached over 50,000 tons. Large-scale paint producers were also mainly grouped in these three regions. According to the

Table 6.9.3 Total output of three major paint production regions in 1999 and 2000 (thousand tons)

Region	Total output				Of which: total output of building coatings			
	1999		2000		1999		2000	
	Total (kt)	Share (%)	Total (kt)	Share (%)	Total (kt)	Share (%)	Total (kt)	Share (%)
Pearl River Delta	*283.3*	*16.55*	*402.6*	*21.89*	*64.5*	*12.51*	*118.2*	*20.99*
Guangdong	283.3	16.55	402.6	21.89	64.5	12.51	118.2	20.99
Yantze River Delta	*548.4*	*32.03*	*594.8*	*32.34*	*136.1*	*26.40*	*195.7*	*34.75*
Shanghai	217.9	12.73	255.6	13.90	89.8	17.42	114.3	20.29
Jiangsu	234.4	13.69	225.1	12.24	38.5	7.47	62.5	11.10
Zhejiang	96.1	5.61	114.1	6.20	7.8	1.51	18.9	3.36
Neighbouring Beijing areas	*257.6*	*15.05*	*288.2*	*15.67*	*136.5*	*26.48*	*140.8*	*25.00*
Beijing	113.5	6.63	100.6	5.47	103.7	20.12	85.5	15.18
Tianjin	56.7	3.31	79.3	4.31	7.1	1.38	7.6	1.35
Hebei	87.4	5.15	108.3	5.89	25.7	4.99	47.7	8.47

data from the State Statistical Bureau in 1999, more than 50 producers had proceeds from sale in excess of 100 million yuan, and 46 of these were distributed in these three major regions. It could be said that the three major domestic paint bases tentatively took shape (mainly grouped in a few provinces and cities), large specialized producers began to emerge, and an alliance of these producers could act as a counterweight to competition in the international paint market.

The buoyant trend in developing building coatings and a bright outlook

Statistics show domestic output of building coatings totalled 427,400 tons in 1997, 447,600 tons in 1998, 515,500 tons in 1999, 563,200 tons in 2000, although the actual output was far higher than this. There has been an average annual growth of 9.72 per cent, and there seems to be a trend towards further development. Geographically, the producers of building coatings were principally distributed in eastern, south-central and northern China, accounting for 38.53 per cent, 27.29 per centand 25.44 per cent respectively of total domestic output. These producers are mostly grouped in Gangdong, Shanghai, Beijing, Jiangsu and Hebei, amounting to 20.99 per cent, 20.29 per cent, 15.18 per cent, 11.10 per cent and 8.47 per cent respectively of the total, and the five provinces and municipalities made up 76.03 per cent of the total domestic output. This was consistent with the pattern of regional policies and the development of the regional building trade.

Table 6.9.4 Top 11 enterprises by output of paints and coatings in 2000

No	Company	Output (thousand tons)
1	Nippon (China) Co Ltd	78.0
2	China Huili Group Co Ltd	53.7
3	Guangzhou Zhuhua Group Co Ltd	43.5
4	Shandong Lehua Group Co Ltd	41.8
5	Shunde China Resouces Co Ltd	41.8
6	Shanghai Huasheng Co Ltd	34.3
7	Chongqing Sanxia Co	30.0
8	Langfang Nippon (China) Co Ltd	24.7
9	Tianjin Dengta Co Ltd	24.7
10	Shanghai Paint Co Ltd	24.1
11	Zhejiang Huanqiu Paint Manufacturing Co Ltd	21.1

Condition of producers

In 2000, the total industrial output value of the 42 fairly large scale producers was 5.858 billion yuan, a rise of 3.34 per cent on 1999, and their output was 576,900 tons, a gain of 1.59 per cent over 1999. The total sales volume of 40 producers was 572,700 tons, an increase of 2.19 per cent on 1999, and the proceeds from sale amounted to 5.550 billion yuan, up by 3.45 per cent on 1999.

Production and marketing of key paint producers were essentially satisfactory with a definite growth, but far below the average national growth rate. Growth in

Table 6.9.5 Top 10 enterprises by sales of paints and coatings in 2000

No.	Company	Sales (million yuan)
1	Nippon (China) Co Ltd	1,470
2	Shanghai Huasheng Co Ltd	441
3	Shanghai Huili Co Ltd	407
4	Shunde China Resources Co Ltd	403
5	Guangzhou Zhuhua Group Co Ltd	368
6	Tianjin Dengta Co Ltd	350
7	Shanghai Paint Co Ltd	300
8	Xiangjiang Group Co Ltd	285
9	Shandong Donghua Group Co Ltd	265
10	Chongqing Sanxia Co Ltd	256

output and sales volume was basically synchronized. In 1999 and 2000 the production/marketing ratio of paints and coatings was 1:1.01, indicating that the producers had retreated from the trend of production in excess of sales and going blindly after volume. Production and marketing in balance and inventory under control were more favourable to a rational distribution of business funds.

In spite of production and marketing taking a turn for the better, the economic benefits of the producers continued to diminish. In 2000, the added value tax turned over to the state by 36 producers totalled 251 million yuan, a fall of 5.65 per cent from 266 million yuan in 1999, and their profits declined by 2.37 per cent from 429 million yuan in 1999 to 419 million yuan.

Import and export trade

Paints imported in 2000 were mainly automobile paints, automobile patching coatings, high-grade building coatings, speciality coatings, furniture coatings, and other high-grade products, while those exported were mostly low-grade, solvent-based coatings. 180,000 tons of coatings were imported and 75,000 tons exported in 2000.

Problems and recommendations

Following entry into the WTO, China's paint industry will face a new challenge. Domestic producers are small-scale and scattered, the industrial structure is not rational enough, labour productive power is low, and technology is backward. All these are prominent problems in the paint industry, and in the 21st century producers should make special efforts to develop in the following three areas:

1. Handling the relationship between quantity and quality. The domestic paint industry output has already leapt to third place globally, but there remains a definite disparity in quality with advanced foreign countries. The focal point in the development of paints and coatings should be quality improvement, updating existing products and developing new ones.

2. Attaching more importance to promoting further environmental protection and developing environmental friendly coatings. People today are more aware and pay greater attention to environmental protection. The pollution of the environment by the paint industry is manifested in two ways: one being environmental pollution by production waste products; the other contamination by the volatilization of organic solvents or harmful materials in the application of coatings. So the direction of the development of paints and coatings in the 21st century lies in the production of water-based, powdered, high-curing and radiation-curing coatings.

3. Laying emphasis on the cultivation of a large number of qualified hi-tech personnel.

The Petrochemical Industry

Li Yong, Deputy Secretary General, China Association of International Trade

After 50 years of development, China has become one of the world's largest crude oil producers. For 13 consecutive years, China's crude oil production has ranked 5th after the US, Saudi Arabia, Russia and Iran and in 2001 its total output was 165 million tons. China has the largest refining capacity in Asia at 276 million tons, which makes it the third largest in the world after the US and Russia. China is also the third largest consumer of gasoline, diesel oil and kerosene after the US and Japan.

The petrochemical industry is basically dominated by three major groups; China National Petroleum Corporation (CNPC), China Petrochemical Corporation (Sinopec) and China National Offshore Oil Corporation, which was a result of the industry reshuffling in 1998. The total assets of the three groups amount to nearly RMB1 trillion, about 12 per cent of the total state-owned assets. Sinopec has the largest oil refining capacity in the country, accounting for 53 per cent of China's total refining capacity. CNPC takes the second position with 40 per cent, while the remaining 7 per cent is distributed among smaller local refineries. After years of effort to develop independent technological capabilities, China's crude refining technology can now meet the refining requirements of the country.

China's ethylene capacity ranks fifth in the world; sixth in synthetic resins; fourth in synthetic rubber and first in synthetic fibre. With the deepening of economic reform and opening up of the market, China introduced a number of petrochemical processing technologies, which have enhanced local R&D capabilities in developing local technologies for downstream processing. The once import-dependent catalysts, for example, are now mostly produced by local producers and the rate of localized production of catalysts is well over 85

per cent. Some catalysts have reached international quality standards and are exported to foreign countries, reversing the one-way import situation of the past.

However, with the growth of China's economy, the gap between the development of the petrochemical industry and the increasing demand for petrochemical products has been widened. The main problems in the petrochemical industry are the low levels of industry concentration and an inability to supply the necessary products. There are over 130 crude refineries spread over most of the provinces, autonomous regions and municipalities. Eighteen ethylene plants are scattered over 15 cities. This contrasts sharply with the high concentration level of petrochemical operations in more developed countries. At the same time, the average plant size is also much smaller than the world average. Fragmentation and poor plant economics have led to a small market share of the petrochemical products being produced at home such as synthetic resins, synthetic rubber, synthetic fibre and organic chemical raw material, which make up about 50 per cent of the market. The industry has also been troubled by the problem of fewer grade varieties, generally low quality and smaller product ranges. The required grades and products of high enough quality have to be imported in great quantities from abroad each year. In addition, the insufficient supply of organic raw material at home has also hindered the development of downstream fine chemicals, leading to a lack of coordination between the petrochemical and traditional chemical industries.

In the 1990s, the demand for ethylene in China grew at an average annual rate of 17 per cent, much higher than the average GDP growth in the same period. The growth in the production of ethylene in the period, however, averaged only 12 per cent per annum, leading

Table 6.10.1   The gap between supply and demand of three major synthetic materials

	Synthetic resins			Synthetic fibre			Synthetic rubber		
	1999	*2000*	*2001*	*1999*	*2000*	*2001*	*1999*	*2000*	*2001*
Production	8.417	10.80	12.03	5.487	6.15	7.599	0.684	0.836	1.045
Net imports	12.59	11.40	14.39	1.285	1.54	1.395	0.65	0.65	0.638
Apparent consumption	20.70	22.20	26.43	6.72	7.69	7.772	1.25	1.481	1.683
Rate of self-sufficiency (%)	39.2	48.6	46	81	80	82	48	56.5	62

to a widening gap between supply and demand. As a result, the import of petrochemical products has been increasing at an average annual rate of 32 per cent. Import of petrochemical raw materials as expressed in its ethylene equivalent accounts for about 50 per cent of China's total consumption of petrochemical products. For some petrochemical products such as polystyrene (PS) and ABS, the rate of dependence on import can be as high as 80 per cent.

As shown in Table 6.10.1, the self-sufficiency rates for synthetic fibre and rubber increased in 2001, while that for synthetic resins declined. This demonstrates the problem of a lagging supply of synthetic resins compared with rapid increasing demand.

The production pattern of China's petrochemical industry has the following characteristics:

- The production of ethylene, petrochemical raw materials and their products are largely concentrated in Sinopec and CNPC operations, whose total capacity now accounts for 90 per cent of the country's total. These two majors own 16 of China's 18 ethylene projects.
- State-owned enterprises at the local level, small- to medium-sized collectively-owned factories and private operators mainly operate in the downstream production of petrochemical products.
- Foreign-invested petrochemical enterprises produce those downstream products that are in short supply in China. Their products are typically concentrated in polymer and synthetic fibre categories and their production is based on imported feeds.

As shown in Table 6.10.2, Sinopec and CNPC have a dominant role in China's production of polyolefin resins. The two majors also own the majority of the production and capacity of synthetic rubber and synthetic fibre raw materials. In the case of PVC, production is dispersed among local operations as a legacy of

Table 6.10.2   Distribution of petrochemical production by player

Products	Sinopec share (%)	CNPC share (%)	Others' share (%)
Ethylene	61	32	7
Polyethylene	63	32	5
Polypropylene	67	22	11
PVC	8	1	91
PS	43	7	50
ABS	0	89	11
BR	77	23	0
SBR	34	34	32
PET chip	35	10	55
PTA	78	11	11
glycol	70	30	0
ACN	40	45	15
Hexanolactam	100	0	0
Terylene (polyester fibre)	17	3	80
Acrylic fibre	53	21	26
Polyamide fibre (nylon)	7	0	93
Polypropylene fibre	10	5	85

Source: Beijing Yigou Petrochemical Consulting

the historical distribution of production and diversification of raw material supplies. Styrenic resins such as PS and ABS are largely concentrated in joint venture operations. Synthetic fibres such as polyester, acrylic, polyamide and polypropylene fibres are produced by local enterprises.

China's ethylene industry will continue to develop over the next 10 years or so. The priority of development for domestic ethylene plants is on expansion of capacity to improve plant economics or increase economies of scale. Table 6.10.3 lists the 18 ethylene installations, their capacities and expansion plans.

According to the estimates in China's petrochemical industry's tenth Five Year Plan, the demand for ethylene

Table 6.10.3 China's ethylene capacity by plant and capacity expansion plans (thousand tons)

Company	Planned	Current	Expansion	Completion
Yanshan Petrochemical	300	660	660	2001
Shanghai Petrochemical Plant 1	300	400	700	2002
Shanghai Petrochemical Plant 2	110	145	145	
Yangtze Petrochemical	300	400	650	2002
Qilu Petrochemical	300	450	600	2003
Maoming Petrochemical	300	380	800	2004
Tianjin United Chemical	140	140	200	
Zhongyuan Ethylene	140	140	200	
Guangzhou Petrochemical	140	140	200	
Beijing Oriental Chemical Plant	140	140	200	
Daqing Petrochemical	300	480	600	2005
JilinPetrochemical Plant 1	300	300	400	
Jilin Petrochemical Plant 2	115	145	145	
Fushun Petrochemical	124	144	144	
Liaoyang Chemical Fibre	88	88	88	
Lanzhou Petrochemical	80	160	160	
Dushanzi Petrochemical	140	140	220	2002
Panjin Ethylene	130	160	160	
Total	3,447	4,612	6,272	

Source: Beijing Yigou Petrochemical Consulting

Table 6.10.4 Key foreign-invested ethylene projects

Project	Planned capacity (thousand tons)	Chinese investors	Foreign investors
1. Huizhou Nanhai ethylene project	800	CNPC and Guangdong province	Shell
2. BASF-YPC Integrated ethylene project	600	Sinopec and Yangtze Petrochemical	BASF
3. Shanghai BP ethylene project	900	Sinopec and Shanghai Petrochemical	BP
4. Fujian Ethylene project	600	Sinopec and Fujian province	Exxon and Saudi
Total	2,900		Arabian Petroleum

expressed in ethylene equivalent will grow at an annual rate of 8.5 per cent and reach 15 million tons of ethylene equivalent by 2005. To capture the growth, foreign investors have invested heavily in China's ethylene projects (see Table 6.10.4).

In the tenth Five Year Plan period (2001–2005), China's economy is predicted to grow by between 7 and 8 per cent, which will drive the demand for ethylene downstream products, particularly the five major synthetic resins PE, PP, PVC, PS and ABS. According to estimates by China Packaging Technology Association, the market for the five major synthetic resins will develop at a rate of 6.1 per cent in this period. By 2005, the total demand will reach 24.45 million tons. Another estimate indicates that the demand for the five major

synthetic resins will be between 25 and 27 million tons. However, it is important to observe the following trends in relation to the demand changes in the five major synthetic resins:

1. In the PE category, LLDPE will gradually gain greater market share over LDPE. As LLDPE technology improves, LLDPE will not only perform better, which will expand its application areas, but will also become competitive on price against LDPE. The demand for LDPE will gradually reduce while that for LLDPE will pick up and the consumption of LLDPE will eventually surpass that of LDPE. In addition, LLDPE and LDPE applications in agricultural films will subside against the trend of de-

mand for long-life, thinner, low unit-usage and multifunctional agricultural films. The rate of growth in the demand of LLDPE/LDPE will slow in the next five years. However, the applications of LLDPE and LDPE will increase in other industries such as wires and cables, whose development is largely driven by the prospering telecommunications industry.

2. The consumption pattern of HDPE will change little by the year 2005. With the increase in the usage volume of materials in the packaging industry and the shift of packaging operations from Japan and Europe to China and other south-east Asian countries, this growth in demand for HDPE will be sustained. HDPE films will remain the largest area of HDPE application. With the development towards diversification of HDPE applications in hollow products, production of HDPE products such as multi-layer extruded tubes, plastic bottles in pharmaceutical and food applications and large- to medium-sized plastic containers will increase, leading to a moderate increase in the share of HDPE application in hollow plastic part manufacturing.

3. The usage of high value-added PP is growing. In some applications, high value-added PP, with its improved properties, has replaced engineering plastics, as a result of which the share of PP consumption in the injection moulded products is expected to rise. At the same time, PP fibre will find an expanded area of application in the development of civil engineering materials. Rapid growth of PP application in the production of films for packaging purposes is also expected over the next five years, but the traditional application of PP in woven products will decline.

4. Driven by the development of so-called chemical construction materials, PVC has gained a strong momentum of growth over the past few years and will continue to be a key material for the production of door and window frames and pipes. Some large cities have formulated policies to encourage the use of plastic materials in property development projects, which will stimulate the growth of demand for rigid PVC products. PVC flexible products will face a mixed scenario, with increases of applications expected in the manufacturing of shoes and synthetic leather, while growth in film and cable applications will slow. PVC film will have to face the challenge posed by PE film.

5. Environmental concerns about white pollution have already had a negative impact on the demand for EPS in the applications of lunch boxes and fast-food containers, which has slowed in the last couple of years. Generally, the pattern of consumption for GPPS and HIPS will not see major changes and their applications will increase with the development of the end-use industries such as household electrical appliance and office automation. The negative impact of the ban on the use of EPS containers in the food service sector will be offset by the increase in the application of EPS in the building materials sector.

6. Under the pressure of increased application of PS in the household electrical appliances, ABS consumption in large electrical appliance items is expected to decline, while its application in small household appliances will increase. More importantly, the development of China's automobile industry will be the key driving force for future growth of demand for ABS.

As predicted in the petrochemical industry's tenth Five Year Plan, consumption of synthetic rubber between 2001 and 2005 is expected to grow at annual rate of 4 per cent to reach 1.1 million tons by 2005. Synthetic fibre, on the other hand, will experience a growth rate in the range of 5.4–8.3 per cent, with the total demand being between 10.8 and 12.6 million tons by 2005.

China's entry into the WTO will certainly impact by varying degrees on the development of its petrochemical industry. However, compared with other highly protected industries, the impact of the WTO will be less significant because protection has been gradually lifted since the 1980s and the majority of petrochemical products have been 'marketized', which means that the demand, production, purchase, sales and prices have been integrated with international market trends. However, it is speculated that the tariff reduction will stimulate the already large influx of imports, which will challenge the survival of low-efficiency petrochemical enterprises.

The expected increase in imports following China's accession to the WTO has caused concerns about further decline in the market share of domestically produced petrochemical products. The market share of imported synthetic resins rose from 33 per cent in 1990 to 52 per cent. The share of imported synthetic rubber has risen from only 9 per cent to the current 44 per cent and that of imported synthetic fibres is now 53 per cent.

Table 6.10.5 Committed petrochemical tariff rates post WTO entry

Product description	Tariff rate 2002 (%)	Committed at the accession date (%)	Final committed rate (%)	Implementation
Organic chemicals				
Ethylene	2.8	3.5	2.0	2003
Propylene	2.8	3.5	2.0	2003
Butylene	2.8	3.5	2.0	2003
Butadiene	2.8	3.5	2.0	2003
Isopentene	2.8	3.5	2.0	2003
Benzene	4.0	4.7	2.0	2005
Toluene	5.0	6.0	2.0	2005
Ethylbenzene	5.5	6.7	2.0	2005
Paraxylene	5.0	6.0	2.0	2005
Alkylbenzene	5.5	6.7	2.0	2005
Phenol	5.5	7.0	5.5	2002
Acetone	5.5	5.5	5.5	
Glacial acetic acid	5.5	5.5	5.5	
Phthalic Anhydride	6.6	8.3	6.5	2002
Synthetic fibre raw materials and polymers				
Glycol	8.8	10.5	5.5	2004
Acrylonitrile	6.5	6.5	6.5	
Hexanolactam	10.8	12.5	9.0	2003
PTA	12.8	13.9	6.5	2008
Polyester (other)	12.8	13.9	6.5	2008
Nylon 66 salt	6.5	6.5	6.5	
Synthetic resin				
LDPE	14.2	15.4	6.5	2008
HDPE	14.2	15.4	6.5	2008
Polypropylene	10.0	13.9	6.5	2008
PS	12.8	13.9	6.5	2008
ABS	12.8	13.9	6.5	2008
PVC	12.8	13.9	6.5	2008
Synthetic rubber				
SBR	7.5	7.5	7.5	
BR	7.5	7.5	7.5	
NBR	7.5	7.5	7.5	
IR	3.0	4.5	3.9	2002
EPR	7.5	7.5	7.5	
Synthetic fibre				
Polyester filament	11.4	14.6	5.0	2004
Polyester staple fibre	10.6	13.4	5.0	2004
Acrylic filament	8.3	10.0	5.0	2004
Acrylic staple fibre	8.3	10.0	5.0	2004
Acrylic top	8.3	10.0	5.0	2004
Nylon filament	9.8	12.2	5.0	2004
Nylon staple fibre	9.8	12.2	5.0	2004
PP staple fibre	9.8	12.2	5.0	2004

The increasing market share of imported petrochemical products puts a great deal of pressure on Chinese petrochemical enterprises in their competition with their foreign counterparts. The lifting of restrictions on trading rights and distribution within China will lead to head-on competition with foreign distributors of petrochemical products. Domestic companies will have to make further and greater efforts to reduce costs and enhance their ability to develop new products. As well as this, their marketing systems and adaptability to market changes will have to improve if they are to increase their chances of winning in the competition.

Pharmaceuticals

Liu Baocheng, Professor, University of International Business and Economics, and
Gao Chunping PhD, Shijiazhuang Pharmaceutical Group Company

The sheer size and growth rate of the Chinese pharmaceutical market cannot have gone unnoticed by pharmaceutical companies with ambitions to compete for global market share and lucrative margins. With an annual growth rate averaging around 15 per cent for the past 15 years, the aggregate value of pharmaceutical output in 2000 stood at US$29.2 billion, an increase of 22 per cent over the previous year. This is double the average growth in the entire national industrial sector (11 per cent). Moreover, it is expected that this industry will continue to grow at 12–13 per cent for the next five years, which will be almost double the targeted overall growth rate for China's GDP set forth in the new five year plan. Some analysts believe that China will become the largest pharmaceutical market in the world by 2020.

Backed by its large population and substantial increase in disposable income, it is estimated that the current customer base for pharmaceutical products is 400 million and that this will continue to expand by ten per cent per annum. In addition, increased life expectancy as well as the one child policy have boosted general awareness of health care.

In 2000, the total value of China's pharmaceutical market was equivalent to US$14.2 billion and per capita expenditure on health care was US$11. Shifts in the demographic pattern will have a significant impact on the pharmaceutical market. In 2000, China became an elderly nation with ten per cent of its population aged over 60. This figure is expected to rise to 11.52 per cent by 2005, 17 per cent by 2025 and 47 per cent by 2025 by 2050. Currently, 50 per cent of drug consumers are elderly. Even at the current average growth level, the market value of the elderly population will reach US$20 billion by 2005.

In the process of preparing for and now being a new member of the WTO, China has paved the way for far better access to foreign drugs. They can either be directly imported or manufactured by domestic foreign-invested pharmaceutical enterprises. China is committed to the reduction of import tariffs from the current 12 per cent to 5.5–6.5 per cent over the next five years. Likewise, the Chinese government has streamlined regulations both in pharmaceutical manufacturing and in the marketing process. Since 1997, following the inception of the Chinese State Drug Administration (SDA), in order to ensure the safety and quality of pharmaceutical products, a massive programme has been enforced on existing manufacturing facilities for Good Manufacturing Practice (GMP) inspection in different phases with specified deadlines. For new facilities, GMP is a prerequisite before they are permitted to manufacture. In a drive to modernize the production of Traditional Chinese Medicine (TCM) and ensure consistent quality, the government has also introduced the Good Agricultural Practice (GAP) standard for farms producing herbal plants.

Aside from diagnostic equipment, the pharmaceutical market in terms of access routes can be broken down into two sectors: the prescription drug market and the over-the-counter (OTC) drug market. Over the past 10 years, the Chinese government has made substantial efforts to distinguish between prescription drugs and OTC drugs. The Categorical Administration Act for Prescription and OTC Drugs was officially implemented on 1 January 2000. Most chemical drugs are treated as prescription drugs and are sold in the in-house pharmacies of hospitals and clinics. The share of OTC drugs has been increasing by 15 per cent per annum. Motivated by profit incentives and loose regulatory control, most drug stores continue to sell beyond the borders of the OTC classification.

China's health care market broadly consists of three major sectors: chemical and biological drugs (typically referred as western drugs), TCMs and overall health enhancement products (HEP). The market share of biological drugs is still negligible at US$1.5 billion in sales, although the potential is apparent. HEPs are further classified into pharmaceutical grade and health food grade and include both chemical and botanical extractions. At the end of 1996, of the 1,731 drugs approved in China, western drugs amounted to 61.78 per cent (1,071) and TCMs stood at 31.54 per cent (546).

Cultural differences do not support a significant bias against western drugs. The consumption pattern is chemical drugs at 68 per cent, TCMs 20 per cent and dietary supplements 12 per cent. As a matter of fact, most Chinese consumers, including the elderly, are highly receptive to western drugs, particularly as a solution to acute symptoms and infectious diseases. Competition from TCM is only noticeable in the prevention and health enhancement markets. It is ironic that the import value of foreign-made natural herbal medicines has exceeded China's TCM export.

There are nearly 7,000 pharmaceutical manufacturers in China with 5 per cent involving foreign investment. Although exceptionally numerous, most domestic manufacturers are small in size and their product portfolios are very similar. Due to the lack of scale production and barely any funding for R&D, most are only able to serve the market at arm's length, typically under the umbrella of local protection, and will have to rely on hefty subsidies if encouraged to compete across the country. The Chinese government has recognized the problem of inefficiency and decided to reduce their numbers firstly to encourage organizational integration through acquisition and merger by a recognized market leader and secondly to force companies to close down when they are unable to meet the GMP standard. This radical restructuring process with government intervention is expected to reduce the number of pharmaceutical companies by half over the next two to three years.

The trend towards concentration is already being felt. In the meantime, foreign invested manufacturers have begun to capture a larger share of the market. The top nine companies accounted for 12.5 per cent of the entire market in the chemical drug industry in 1999, five of which are foreign funded companies: Glaxo SK,

Johnson & Johnson, Pfizer Warner, Norvartis and United Pharm. The competitive advantage of foreign invested enterprises (FIEs) over domestic enterprises (DEs) in the pharmaceutical industry is reflected in their production efficiency, market promotion and profitability (see Table 6.11.1).

Table 6.11.1 Comparative profitability of pharmaceutical FIEs and DEs

Year	Cost of goods		Sales expenses		Other promotion costs		Profit	
	DEs	FIEs	DEs	FIEs	DEs	FIEs	DEs	FIEs
1994	77.0	56.6	4.0	16.7	10.3	4.0	8.7	22.7
1995	76.8	63.0	4.8	15.1	11.6	3.1	6.8	18.8
1996	77.4	56.4	5.7	20.4	9.7	0.0	7.2	23.2
1997	76.3	56.0	6.4	24.3	10.8	0.8	6.5	18.9

A recent sample survey conducted in early 2000 by China Pharmaceutical Distribution Association revealed the competitive pattern in the pharmaceutical market: – 57.22 per cent are manufactured by domestic companies, 29.33 per cent by foreign invested companies and the remaining 13.45 per cent consists of direct imports.

The distribution system for pharmaceutical products is probably unique to China. The retail market has for decades been dominated by the hospital sector. Unlike in western countries, hospitals are heavily reliant on sales of drugs as their primary income source, rather than diagnostic and medical treatment services. 71 per cent of all pharmaceutical products are sold through in-house pharmacies in hospitals and clinics, while 29 per cent are sold in drug stores. Each hospital and clinic runs its own in-house pharmacy. Mainstream wholesale channels are still monopolized by the hierarchical three-tier wholesalers – national, provincial and local. As a result, manufacturers are able to earn on average no more than 20 per cent of the retail price, with the rest being absorbed by the layers of distributors. Another unique problem derives from doctors. Since they are inadequately paid by the hospitals and clinics, doctors are tempted to solicit kickbacks from pharmaceutical companies for the drugs they prescribe. This can vary from 2 per cent to 20 per cent of the retail markup depending on the price level and popularity of the drugs. The Chinese government has recognized this as a serious social issue and since 2000 has been gradually disengaging pharmacies from hospitals. Now hospitals' income from diagnoses and treatment is beginning to grow at a faster rate than from sales of drugs.

Social medical health care is a fundamental factor in the health care market. For the past 500 years, China has maintained a policy to segregate urban residents from rural farmers in all areas of social welfare and health care is no exception. In cities, two-thirds of the population enjoys some kind of social medical insurance, while 83 per cent of farmers are not covered. While 70 per cent of the population is in the countryside, the per capita expenditure on health care is unevenly distributed between cities and countryside (see Table 6.11.2).

Table 6.11.2   Insurance cover by population

	Population (%)	
	Cities	*Countryside*
Labour Insurance	32	1
Public Insurance	28	3
Partial Labour Insurance	6	
Medical Insurance	3	2
General Insurance	1	
Co-operative Insurance	2	10
No Insurance	26	83
Other	2	1

The significance of medical insurance to pharmaceutical manufacturers lies in the fact that for a drug to be reimbursable, it must be included in the national Essential Drug List. Different regions tend to have different policies allowing them modify their own Reimbursement List depending on the prevalent diseases in their particular region as well as local government financial capabilities.

As discussed above, the sources of pharmaceutical products in are primarily foreign exporters, FIEs and domestic manufacturers. While Chinese domestic companies still have around 60 per cent market share, the quality difference, combined with pricing strategy and channel advantages mean that different sources have a distinctive market position in the cities and countryside. Imported products are concentrated in the cities (95 per cent), as are FIE products (65 per cent) whereas 70 per cent of all domestic products are positioned in the countryside (see Figure 6.11.1).

Over the past five years, Chinese domestic manufacturers have suffered a decline of 1.2 per cent in their

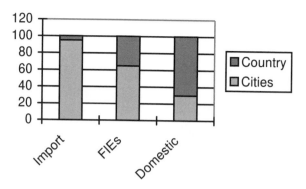

Figure 6.11.1   Market positions of pharmaceutical products in China by source

market share. It is estimated that FIEs will combine with foreign exporters to seize the majority market share by 2004.

China's reliance on international trade for pharmaceutical products is still on a small scale although the rate of growth has exceeded the country's average. According to customs statistics, the total international trade value of Chinese pharmaceutical products was US$6.4 billion in 2000, an increase of 16.4 per cent on the previous year. Total exports registered 13.8 per cent growth at US$3.8 billion and imports grew at 18.7 per cent to US$2.6 billion. However, China still has a trade surplus of US$1.2 billion. This is because most conventional chemical drugs have been successfully duplicated in China with a low cost advantage, thus reducing reliance on imports. On the other hand, the bulk of exports are in the form of industrial intermediaries, which mainly rely on low price leadership and have already taken 22 per cent of the world market. Finally, although China is the home of TCM products, barely any TCM products have been approved officially as preventative or treatment drugs by western regulatory authorities such as the US Food and Drug Administration (FDA) or European Medicinal Evaluation Agency (EMEA). Most TCM drugs can only be sold as dietary supplements in western food stores.

As living standards rise, particularly in the cities and coastal regions, a number of formerly common diseases and conditions associated with poverty – including many infectious diseases and certain types of malignant disease – have been almost entirely eliminated. However, problems associated with quality of life are beginning to emerge and as a result of reduced physical exercise and mismanaged diet, incidences of 'modern' diseases such as diabetes, cardiovascular disease and stress-related disorders are on the increase.

One serious issue that concerns western companies is the level of protection for foreign intellectual property rights in the area of pharmaceutical manufacturing. Unlike India, China does not enforce compulsory licensing. However, according to Chinese patent law, if a foreign company fails to file for patent protection in China within one year of its initial patent being granted in other countries, they will be barred from any protection in China. 97.4 per cent of all chemical drugs in China are duplicated from western technology. Given that a new drug development would cost US$400–1,000 million, and that even a licence would cost US$5–6 million, it is unrealistic to expect Chinese companies to pay the full price for industrial patents to foreign companies, despite the fact that the Chinese government has demonstrated a high level of commitment to the Paris Convention of Industrial Property Rights and the Uruguay Agreement on Trade-related Intellectual Properties (TRIPS). So a feasible solution, aside from direct import, would be for western companies to collaborate with local partners in a joint venture involving technology licensing.

Professional Services

Li Yong, Deputy Secretary General, China Association of International Trade

The liberation of the practice of professional services is an integral part of China's effort to open up its service sector to foreign participation. Before China's accession to the WTO, professional services were open to foreign service providers in varying degrees and with different levels of restrictions. The accession to the WTO has clarified the scenario of professional services opening, reflected in China's commitments to the WTO. These commitments were made with reference to international practices and the unique conditions that apply to China in the professional service area. The WTO definition of professional services includes the following services:

● Legal services
● Accounting, auditing and bookkeeping services
● Tax services
● Architectural services
● Engineering services
● Integrated engineering services
● Urban planning services (except general urban planning)
● Medical and dental services

The specific commitments with regard to the above professional services are as follows:

Legal services (CPC 861)

● Upon accession, foreign law firms can provide legal services in China, but only in the form of representative offices and in the following designated areas: Beijing, Shanghai, Guangzhou, Shenzhen, Haikou, Dalian, Qingdao, Ningbo, Yantai, Tianjin, Suzhou, Xiamen, Zhuhai, Hanghou, Fuzhou, Wuhan, Chengdu, Shenyang and Kunming.
● Representative offices in China shall be no less than the number established upon the date of accession. A foreign law firm can only establish one representative office in China.
● The above geographical and quantitative limitations will be eliminated within one year of China's accession to the WTO.
● Representative offices can engage in profit-making activities.
● The business scope of foreign representative offices is restricted to the following:
  – to provide clients with consultancy on the legislation of the country/region where the members of the law firm are permitted to engage in lawyer's professional work, and on international conventions and practices;
  – to handle the legal affairs of the country/region where the members of the law firm are permitted to engage in lawyer's professional work, when entrusted by clients or Chinese law firms;
  – to entrust Chinese law firms with Chinese legal affairs on behalf of foreign clients;
  – to enter into contracts to maintain long-term entrustment relations with Chinese law firms for legal affairs;
  – to provide information on the impact of the Chinese legal environment.

Entrustment allows the foreign representative office directly to instruct lawyers in the entrusted Chinese law firm, as agreed by both parties.

The representatives of a foreign law firm shall be practitioner lawyers who are members of the bar or law society in a WTO member country and have practised for no less than two years outside of China. The chief representative shall be a partner or equivalent of a law firm of a WTO member and have practised for no less than three years.

All representatives shall be resident in China for no less than six months of each year. The representative office shall not employ Chinese national registered lawyers outside of China.

Accounting, auditing and bookkeeping services (CPC 862)

Partnerships or incorporated accounting firms are limited to Certified Public Accountants (CPAs) licensed by the Chinese authorities.

- Foreign accounting firms are permitted to affiliate with Chinese firms and enter into contractual agreements with their affiliated firms in other WTO member countries;
- Upon accession to the WTO, issue of licenses to those foreigners who have passed the Chinese national CPA examination shall be accorded national treatment;
- Applicants will be informed of results in writing no later than 30 days after submission of their applications;
- Existing contractual joint venture accounting firms are not limited only to CPAs licensed by Chinese authorities;
- Accounting firms providing services in CPC 862 can engage in taxation and management consulting services. They will not be subject to requirements on the form of establishment in CPC 865 and 8630.

Taxation services (CPC 8630)

Upon accession to the WTO, foreign commercial presence shall only be in the form of joint ventures, with foreign majority ownership permitted. Within six years of the accession, foreign firms will be permitted to establish solely foreign-owned subsidiaries.

Architectural services (CPC 8671), engineering services (CPC 8672), integrated engineering services (CPC 8673) and urban planning services (except general urban planning) (CPC 8674)

- For cross-border supply there are no restrictions on scheme designs, but cooperation with Chinese professional organizations is required otherwise;

- Foreign commercial presence shall only be in the form of joint ventures upon accession to the WTO, with foreign majority ownership permitted. Within five years of China's accession, wholly foreign-owned enterprises will be permitted;
- Foreign service suppliers shall be registered architects/engineers, or enterprises engaged in architectural/engineering/urban planning services, in their home country.

Medical and dental services (CPC 9312)

- Foreign service suppliers are permitted to establish joint venture hospitals or clinics with Chinese partners with quantitative limitations in line with China's needs, and foreign majority ownership is permitted.
- Foreign doctors with professional certificates issued by their home country shall be permitted to provide short-term medical services in China after they obtain licences from the Ministry of Public Health. The term of service is six months and may be extended to one year.
- The majority of doctors and medical personnel of joint venture hospitals and clinics shall be of Chinese nationality.

Compared with its attitude towards the opening up of other service sectors such as telecommunications and financial sectors, the Chinese government has been relatively positive in opening up the professional services sector.

As early as 1992, China began to allow foreign legal service providers to operate in the country. By end of 1996, there were already 50 representative offices of foreign laws firms and 23 representative offices of Hong Kong law firms. At the time of writing, the number of representative offices of foreign law firms in China totalled 110. The commitments made in relation to legal services are based on this trial opening programme from the early 1990s. On the strength of these commitments, foreign law firms will face less restrictions than they used to in terms of service area and number of offices, except that the practice of Chinese laws remains a closed area.

In connection with its commitments on the opening of legal services to foreign law firms, China promulgated the Regulatory Rules on the Representative Offices of Foreign Law Firms in China on 27 December 2001. These regulatory rules further establish the details regarding the administration of the operations by the representative offices of foreign law firms. In addition to defining the scope of business, the rules also stipulate penalties for violation.

The opening up of accounting services also began in the early 1990s as an effort to promote the establishment and healthy development of China's certified public accountant system and to narrow the gaps between the Chinese accounting and auditing sector and its international counterpart. Although the opening up policy was on the basis of limited access in terms of commercial presence and qualifications, it resulted in the entry of the world's top six accounting firms (now five as a result of the merger between Price Waterhouse and Coopers Lybrand) in the form of joint ventures. Nine joint ventures have now been established and over 20 international accounting firms have established offices in China. Because of the unique position held by foreign accounting operations in China, they have captured about 80 per cent of the country's multinational clients. While their share in terms of the total number of accounting service providers in China is only estimated at about 1 per cent, their total revenue accounts for about 25 per cent of the total industry revenue. A significant number of Chinese companies listed on the stock exchanges overseas have been serviced by foreign accounting service providers.

With regard to the opening up of professional services other than legal and accounting services, China had allowed access of varying degrees before its accession to the WTO. China's commitments in relation to the opening up of those services have little restrictions in terms of service areas and number of operations except in the case of medical and dental services where the government will exercise quantity restrictions judgementally. The qualification requirements are largely associated with the qualifications that the foreign service providers have acquired in their home countries, except in the case of medical and dental services, which will require additional endorsement from the Chinese health authority. There are corresponding rules and regulations in China governing the operation of foreign professional service providers in some service areas, while such rules or regulations are absent from other areas, such as taxation services, for which there are no clearly defined qualification requirements. However, some of the existing rules and regulations need to be amended to reflect the new conditions under the WTO regime. It is expected that there will be amended and new rules and regulations in connection with China's commitments to the WTO on the opening of professional services to foreign participants. The promulgation of the Regulatory Rules mentioned above is part of the effort to respond to WTO requirements.

Promotional Advertising

Li Yong, Deputy Secretary General, China Association of International Trade

An overview

Advertising as an industry has developed in parallel with the opening up and economic reform in China since 1978. In the early stages of its development (1979–1981), advertising revenue totalled only RMB118 million. The increased awareness of modern marketing techniques and intensified competition in the domestic market have made advertisers spend increasing amounts on advertising, which has spurred the industry to develop at a dramatic pace. Over the last 20 years, the industry has been growing at an average annual rate of 38.49 per cent (see Table 6.13.1). By 2001, the total advertising spend had reached RMB79.5 billion, making China one of the 10 largest advertising markets in the world.

Table 6.13.1 China's advertising spend over the last two decades (RMB millions)

Year	Total spend	Year	Total spend
1979–1981	118	1992	6,787
1982	150	1993	13,409
1983	234	1994	20,026
1984	365	1995	27,327
1985	605	1996	36,663
1986	845	1997	46,196
1987	1,112	1998	53,783
1988	1,493	1999	62,205
1989	1,999	2000	71,266
1990	2,502	2001	79,488
1991	3,509	Jan–Jun 2002	37,965

It is clear that the average annual growth rate in China's advertising industry has well surpassed that of the GDP and of many other industries. It is also easy to see that such a high average growth rate is largely due to the development of the small denominator in the initial stage of the advertising industry. It is true that in the early 1990s the advertising industry hit a year-on-year growth rate as high as 97.57 per cent (1993). But the year-on-year growth rate started to slow down from there. The advertising spend in 2001 was only an increase of 11.54 per cent on 2000; however, the net gain was RMB8.22 billion.

Table 6.13.2 Year-on-year growth rate

Year	Advertising spend	Year-on-year growth
1991	3,509	
1992	6,787	93.42
1993	13,409	97.57
1994	20,026	49.35
1995	27,327	36.46
1996	36,663	34.16
1997	46,196	26.00
1998	53,783	16.42
1999	62,205	15.66
2000	71,266	14.57
2001	79,488	11.54

Although the growth rate has slowed, the increase in the advertising spend is still in double figures and has convinced more investors, particularly private investors, to enter the industry and cash in on this development. The number of advertising companies by 2001 reached a total of 78,339, an increase of 10.73 per cent. This increase was chiefly caused by the increase in the number of privately owned advertising agencies, which was 22.58 per cent up on 2000.

The advertising industry employed 709,076 people in 2001. With 78,339 advertising companies, the average staff size for each company was 11.59, a reflection of the fragmented nature of the industry.

The media

All media currently used to advertise in the developed world is also used in China. Traditional public media still play an important role in the transmission of advertising information. Television, radio, newspapers and magazines are considered to be the four pillars of the advertising media.

Television stations

Official statistics from the National Bureau of Statistics indicate that there were 362 television stations in China in 2001. This figure does not coincide with the number as given by the State Administration of Industry and Commerce, the supervising authority of China's advertising industry, whose statistics on advertising media shows that there were 3,076 TV stations. The difference may come from the application of different standards, with the latter calculating the number of stations engaging in advertising activities, regardless of whether or not they come under one umbrella.

In the last few years, however, the television industry has undergone reshuffling and consolidation. Many independent cable and satellite TV stations in key cities have merged with local stations such as municipal level or provincial level TV stations and operate under one name. In Beijing, for example, the four cable channels have now become part of Beijing TV (BTV) channels. Reasons for these mergers included avoiding vicious competition for advertising revenue and optimising channel resources.

In 2001, television coverage reached 94.2 per cent of the population. Cable television users in 2001 amounted to 90.91 million households. The increased coverage of television and its growing role as a key source of information and after-work leisure have made it a favourite medium for advertisers. In 2001, television stations received 22.57 per cent of total advertising revenue, which was RMB17.9 billion.

Radio

According to the same official statistics from the National Bureau of Statistics, there were a total of 300 radio stations in China. Again, this is contradicted by the State Administration of Industry and Commerce's figure of 711. In 2001, advertising revenue from radio stations amounted to RMB1.83 billion, a little over 10 per cent of the TV stations' revenue. Although radio coverage has been able to reach 92.9 per cent of the population, its role as a key source of information has been eroded by other competing media. Despite this, spending on radio advertising in 2001 grew by 2.3 per cent over 2000.

Newspapers

There were 2,007 newspapers by the end of 2000, according to official statistics. The figure from the State Administration of Industry and Commerce counted 2,182 in the year 2001. Advertising sales turnover stood at RMB15.8 billion in the same year. Unlike television and radio, which have a certain level of monopoly, newspapers are facing increasingly intense competition. Since many of the newspapers are of a local nature and carry information of local interest, many are used by advertisers to target consumers at a local level. National newspapers are often used to establish brand identity and image. In the battle for advertisers, newspapers still retain significant advantages, which explains their steady growth as a key medium of advertising, an impressive 19.84 per cent in 2001 as compared with 2000.

Magazines

Although there is a large number of magazines in China, a total of 8,725 in 2000, the advertising revenue was the smallest compared with other media. In 2001, the total advertising turnover was RMB1.19 billion, about 1.49 per cent of China's total advertising revenue. Interestingly, however, statistics by the State Administration of Industry and Commerce registered a total of 3,576 magazine publishing houses engaged in advertising sales. In the period from 1995 to 2000, there was a net increase of 1,142 magazines.

Advertising companies

These 'four pillars' of the public media attracted 46.13 per cent of the total advertising spend. The remainder went into the pockets of advertising companies. Reckoning in the advertising revenue by those advertising companies subordinate to non-advertising enterprises, the total share of the advertising companies would have been 52.1 per cent in 2001.

Clearly, advertising companies have played an important role in the advertising industry, as they should. What makes China's advertising industry different from other countries is that state-owned advertising companies have a dominant position in the industry who in 2001 accounted for only 22.67 per cent of the 78,339 advertising companies but took 54.94 per cent (RMB43.66 billion) of all advertising sales. However, a close look at the performance of those state-owned advertising companies reveals that the total number dropped by 2.4 per cent and the growth was a negative 8.3 per cent for state-owned advertising enterprises against a moderate increase of 3.1 per cent. Their dominant position seems to have been eroded by companies owned by private and foreign invested advertising bodies.

Private advertising companies dominated in terms of total number – 37906, or 48.39 per cent of the total number of advertising establishments. Their sales reached RMB13.95 billion in 2001, 17.55 per cent of the total advertising spend in China and a 35.44 per cent increase on 2000. However, the average advertising sales for each private advertising company was quite small at only RMB0.37 million.

Foreign companies have been active in China's advertising industry. Familiar names such as Saatchi & Saatchi, J. Walter Thompson, Ogilvy & Mather, Dentsu and McCann Erickson have all entered the battlefield of China's advertising industry. According to the State Administration of Industry and Commerce, the total number of foreign-invested advertising agencies was 329 in 2001, a drop of 13.42 per cent. However, the growth in their total advertising sales was a remarkable 64.02 per cent in 2001 and their share in the country's total advertising spending was 9.35 per cent. The average advertising revenue for these foreign-invested advertising firms was RMB22.6 million, which clearly demonstrates the competitive advantages of foreign-invested advertising firms over local ones.

Most advertised products and services

In 2001, the most advertised products were pharmaceutical products, foods, real estate, electrical household appliances and cosmetics. These five categories constituted an aggregate share of 48.3 per cent, almost half of China's total advertising outlay in 2001 (see Table 6.13.3).

In terms of growth, advertising spend on alcoholic products, foods and pharmaceutical products experienced strong growth in 2001, with respective growth rates of 69, 30 and 29 per cent. However, probably affected by a host of factors such as industry slowdown and market competition, advertising spend by motor vehicles, electrical household appliances and medical apparatus declined by 46, 11 and 16 per cent respectively compared with 2000.

The emergence of Internet advertising (e-advertising)

Development

When the first Internet advertisement appeared in March 1997 on Chinabyte.com, China was already three years behind the United States. However, this did

Table 6.13.3 2001 advertising spend by products/services

Category	Spending (RMB billion)	% of 2000	Share in total spending (%)
Pharmaceuticals	9,669	128.99	12.16
Foods	8,995	129.91	11.32
Real estate	6,948	116.6	8.47
Electrical appliances	6,588	89.62	8.29
Cosmetics	6,334	133.43	7.97
Alcoholic products	4,120	169.34	5.18
Medical services	3,261	106.88	4.10
Garments & accessories	2,427	114.54	3.05
Motor vehicles	2,286	53.79	2.88
Medical apparatus	1,873	86.63	2.36
Tourism	1,583	122.62	1.99
Tobacco	0,91	105.94	1.14
Other	24,495	108.27	30.82

mark the beginning of China's Internet advertising industry and played a critical role in the development of its Internet industry. From then on, Internet advertising has offered a new option in addition to conventional advertising modes for advertisers to establish a 'cyber communication' channel with their potential consumers/customers. According to WiseCast, in 1998, advertisers spent a total of RMB30 million on Internet advertising. In the next year, three times as much was spent, a total of RMB90 million. 2000 saw a dramatic increase of 289 per cent in Internet advertising spend, a total of RMB350 million. Although the advertisers' enthusiasm was dampened by the downturn in the IT industry and the general slowdown of the world economy in 2001, Internet advertising still managed a growth of 20 per cent to reach RMB420 million (see Figure 6.13.1).

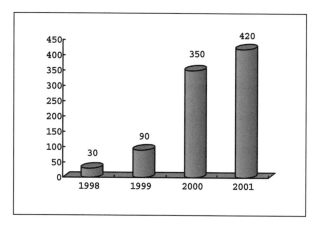

Source: WiseCast

Figure 6.13.1 Internet advertising spend in China (RMB million)

Advertisers

Many the advertisers still need time to recognize fully the role of Internet advertising and the popularity of the Internet will also take time to develop before there is a sufficient 'Internet population' to convince advertisers that advertising on the net will help them reach the target consumers/customers. According to a survey conducted by WiseCast, there was a total of 669 Internet advertisers in 2000 and the number increased to 1,004 in 2001, an encouraging increase of 50 per cent. However, a closer look at the composition of the advertisers will reveal that the advertisers were basically 'patrons' of the Internet or IT related businesses. In 2000, for example, the number of Internet medium advertisers

amounted to 220, 32.9 per cent of the total. There were also 101 advertisers of IT products and 23 from the telecommunications services sector. The same pattern continued in 2001, although the number of Internet medium advertisers declined to 193. This decline was offset by the increase in the number of advertisers from the IT and telecommunications sectors, which totalled 155 and 45 respectively.

Advertisers that use conventional media are still sceptical of the reach that Internet advertising can deliver. Few advertisers of fast-moving consumer products are using Internet advertising. A good sign in 2001, however, was that there were 45 advertisers from medical services and the health care sector posting their advertising on the Internet, although their total spend ranked last after Internet, IT products, real estate and home improvement products, financial services, consulting services for overseas students and emigration.

Internet users

On the other side of Internet advertising is the audience, ie Internet users. Since China began to build its Internet infrastructure in 1994, the size of the Internet population has been growing at a phenomenal speed. According to the latest survey conducted by China Internet Network Information Centre (CNNIC) the number of Internet users in China had reached 45.8 million by 30 June 2002, a net increase of 12.1 million (35.9 per cent) over the past six months. This is an increase by a factor of 75 compared with 0.62 million Internet users when CNNIC did the first survey in October 1997.

Internet users' attitudes to Internet advertising is critical to the success of the advertisers, and for this reason, CNNIC conducted two surveys in January and June of 2001. The responses to this appeared to be quite encouraging (see Figure 6.13.2), provided the surveys are representative.

The survey results suggest that Internet users are much happier to click on Internet ads than to receive e-mail advertisements, the latter being labelled junk mail and rejected by many foreign Internet portals.

The regulatory environment

The advertising industry is closely regulated by the government, as it is in many other countries. The basic law that governs the advertising industry in China is the *Advertising Law of the People's Republic of China*. There are also other bylaws that regulate the advertisement of

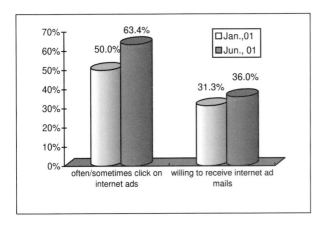

Source: China Internet Network Information Centre

Figure 6.13.2 Chinese Internet users' attitudes towards Internet advertising

specific lines of products such as tobacco, pharmaceutical products and medical equipment, amongst others. According to the Advertising Law, advertisements must not contain any of the following:

- the national flag, national emblem or national anthem of the People's Republic of China;
- the names of state organs or the names of staff of state organs;
- such words as 'state-level', 'highest-level' or 'best';
- matters hindering social stability or endangering the safety of life or property, or harming the public interest;
- matters hindering the public order or violating good social customs;
- pornographic, superstitious, offensive, violent or unpleasant matters;
- discrimination on the grounds of ethnicity, race, religion or sex;
- matters hindering environmental and natural resources protection;
- matters that are prohibited by laws and administrative regulations.

In addition, the law prohibits the use of comparison between competing products and also requires advertisers to submit advertisements for approval prior to publication to the 'competent administrative departments' – the Administration of Industry and Commerce in the domicile of the advertising agent.

There are also regulations regarding the maximum amount of tax-free advertising outlay. The tax authority issued a regulation in May 2000 providing that the advertising outlay of an enterprise within the designated limit of 2 per cent of its total sales can be deducted from its income as non-taxable expenses. This regulation has partly affected the willingness of enterprises to spend on advertising. In 8 May 2001, the tax authority issued another regulation that relaxed the controls on tax-free advertising outlay for certain industries, such as pharmaceuticals, foods (including health care products and drinks), household toiletries, electrical household appliances, telecommunications, software development, integrated circuits, property development, sports and cultural activities and shopping malls of furniture and building materials.

WTO commitments

In addition to the laws and regulations that govern advertising activities by businesses registered in China, there are also regulations regarding foreign entry into the advertising industry. After China's accession to the WTO, the restrictions in terms of equity ownership will be gradually phased out. Upon accession, foreign advertising companies can only enter China's advertising industry in the form of joint ventures and the foreign equity share in the joint venture should not exceed 49 per cent. Within two years after accession, foreign majority ownership will be permitted and within four years wholly foreign-owned subsidiaries will be permitted. In terms of cross-border supply and consumption abroad, foreign advertising services can only be provided through advertising agents registered in China and having the appropriate right to do so.

6.14

Retailing

Li Yong, Deputy Secretary General, China Association of International Trade, and Chen Congcong, Guanghua Management School, Peking University

Introduction

Since China initiated its reform and opening up drive in 1978, the Chinese retail sector has undergone an enormous transformation. Between 1978 and 2000, the sector grew at an annual average rate of 13.5 per cent. Since the 1990s in particular, developments have been more remarkable. Store ownership has diversified considerably. Today, individuals, private businesses and foreign-invested ventures are active players in China's retail sector. The entry of foreign investment has injected new dynamics of competition, while at the same time speeding up the retail revolution process that has totally altered the retail structure and competitive landscape in China. China's retail market has begun to reach a much more advanced stage of maturity in recent years in the main urban areas. Almost all the new retail formats that have been developed in western economies have been introduced including discount department stores, supermarkets, shopping centres/malls, franchise shops, factory outlets, warehouse stores/clubs and chain stores.

Market snapshots

Before China's accession to the WTO, the retail sector was sheltered by extreme protection, which is now being relaxed and the sector has been put on the 'fast track' of opening up. In three years' time, China will have to open up the retail sale sector across the board and eliminate the restrictions on region, amount and equity proportions of foreign wholesalers. Within five years, the country will open the wholesale sector. There will be an increase in the number of foreign retailers strategically entering the retail sector over the next few years.

Since the mid-1990s, total retail sales and consumption of consumer goods have been growing at a faster speed than that of the GDP. In 2001 for example, the rate of increase in the total retail sales of consumer goods was 10.1 per cent year on year, three percentage points higher than the rate of the GDP.

Driven by the fast-growing economy and increasing consumer affluence, China's retail market is expected to have great growth potential and should reach a total of RMB5.7 trillion by 2010.

The retail trade is highly fragmented and dominated by 'Mom-and-Pop' stores. According to a survey, the top 100 retailers in China have a share of less than five per cent of the retail market.

Retail formats have experienced great changes: chain stores have emerged as a significant force, growing at an annual rate of 48 per cent over the last few years. Correspondingly, sales by retail chains now account for more than eight per cent of the total retail market. There is a trend for independent stores to evolve into chains. According to a survey conducted by the State Economic and Trade Commission and the National Statistical Bureau, there were 1,138 retail chains in China by the middle of 2001, with a total of 25,119 outlets. The total sales of these retail chains in the first half of 2001 was RMB102.41 billion.

The total retail sales of consumer goods as a percentage of GDP has been on the rise in recent years. By 2001, its share of GDP approached 40 per cent. Compared with developed countries such as the United States, whose total retail sales accounts for over 60 per cent of its GDP, China's retail market still has a considerable room for growth, and as a result, the rate of growth in the foreseeable future is expected to be higher than that of the GDP.

There has been a disparity in terms of the ratio of consumption between urban and rural residents. According to one estimate, over 60 per cent of retail sales come from urban areas. The rural market has yet to be developed.

The generally oversupply of consumer goods has led to intense competition among retailers and profit margins for retailers are low. According to a survey by the Chinese Chain and Franchise Association of retail chains with a total turnover exceeding RMB100 million, the average net profit is only 1.33 per cent while gross profit averages 12.4 per cent. The low profit margin is in effect one of the key driving forces for Chinese retail chains to develop towards expansion in scale to compete with foreign-invested retailers, who are competing on volume orders in addition to having other advantages.

The rate of contribution by the domestic market to the development of China's economy is increasing steadily. But the pattern of growth that had originally been investment- and production-driven – has now begun to shift to consumption- and market-driven.

Key retail players

Although the total sales of the top 20 retail chains (see Table 6.14.1) as a percentage of total retail sales of consumer goods is relatively small at 2.6 per cent, the rate of growth was a phenomenal 43 per cent year on year, much higher than the 10.1 per cent increase in total retail sales of consumer goods. Equally impressive was the rate of increase in the expansion of retail outlets: 46.7 per cent over 2000.

Among the top 20 retail chains, four new chain store names made it into the top 20, while 16 remained in the top 20, albeit with different rankings. This ranking structure has led some analysts to believe that a group of retail chain enterprises with expanding scales, steady performance and some competitive advantages have started to emerge as a leading force of the retail market. However, there is a flaw in the ranking: some of the international retail chains operating in China such McDonald's and Carrefour, were not included because they registered under different company names in the

Table 6.14.1 Top 20 retail chains, 2001

Rank	Company name	Turnover (thousand RMB)	Increase on 2000 (%)	No. of outlets	Increase on 2000 (%)	Rank in first half of 2001
1	Lianhua Supermarket Co Ltd	14,063,410	26.24	1225	28.95	1
2	Hualian Supermarket Co Ltd	8,504,150	51.70	818	19.94	3
3	Beijing Hualian Comprehensive Supermarket Co Ltd	8,000,000	60.00	42	68.00	5
4	Shanghai Nonggongshang Supermarket Co Ltd	7,474,650	38.35	315	115.75	2
5	Sanlian Commercial Corp	7,026,000	32.28	177	98.87	2
6	Beijing Guomei Electrical Appliances Co Ltd	6,150,470	119.78	74	124.24	9
7	Suguo Supermarket Co Ltd	5,282,000	31.39	663	59.38	6
8	Yum! Brands China Investment Co Ltd (previously Tricon China Investment Co Ltd)	5,205,110	24.04	635	38.34	7
9	Shanghai Jinjiang Metro Co Ltd	4,949,220	32.20	15	87.50	8
10	China Resources Vanguard Co Ltd	4,647,660	34.94	344	42.15	13
11	Suning Electrical Appliances Chain Group Co Ltd	3,991,070	23.35	91	250.00	
12	Tianjin Home World Chain Commercial Group Co Ltd	3,266,680	47.76	28	40.00	11
13	Jiangsu Wenfengdashijie Chain Development Co Ltd	3,145,300	47.6	17	54.55	10
14	Jiangsu Five Star Appliances Co Ltd	2,546,000	74.38	66	26.92	12
15	Beijing Wumei Commercial Group Co Ltd	2,521,700	97.36	199	261.81	14
16	Beijing Jingkelong Commercial Mansion	1,893,310	33.94	57	5.56	15
17	Shenzhen Xinyijia Supermarket Co Ltd	1,890,000	148.36	16	128.57	
18	Shanghai Yongle Appliances Co Ltd	1,860,000	48.44	21	61.54	
19	Wuhan Zhongbai Group Co Ltd	1,784,010	41.55	84	1100.00	
20	Shanghai Jieqiang Tobacco Sugar and Wine (Group) Chain Co Ltd	1,717,570	19.88	240	20.00	17
	Total	95,918,310	42.99	5127	46.70	

Source: State Economic and Trade Commission

process of joint venturing and could not be regarded as chain operators.

Geographically, seven of the top 20 are headquartered in Shanghai, four each in Beijing and Jiangsu Province, two in Guangdong Province and one each in Tianjin, Shandong Province and Hubei Province. None is located in western China. Such a pattern of geographical distribution is determined by the gap that exists in the economic development between eastern and western China and this pattern is not expected to change very much.

In terms of retail formats, 13 of the top 20 are supermarket chains specializing mainly in fast-moving consumer products, with the rest being food chains such as Yum! Brands' Kentucky Fried Chicken and electrical appliance speciality chains such as Beijing Guomei and Jiangsu Suning.

In parallel with the release of the above list, China Chain and Franchise Association also announced its ranking of China's top 100 retailers for the year 2001. The accredited retailers reflected a wider spectrum of the retail sector to include not only the fast expanding supermarket (69), food service (12) and electrical appliance (8) chains, but also department store (4), drug store (4) and other retail chains such as hotel (1) and speciality chains (2) (see Table 6.14.2).

Retail chains have been expanding quickly and are becoming a dominant force in the retail sector. Accord-

ing to the Association, the total sales of the top 100 retail chains in 2001 was RMB162 billion, an increase of 48 per cent over 2000. The share of the top 100 in China's total retail sales of consumer goods was 4.3 per cent in 2001, 1.4 percentage points higher than in 2000. The total number of retail outlets owned by the top 100 chains was 13,117, a rise of 56 per cent compared with 2000.

Over the last five years, the trend of retail outlet expansion and increase of sales turnover by the top 100 retail chains has been strong and persistent. In 1997, the average number of retail outlets of the top 100 retail chains was 24.4 and in 2001 the number jumped to 131.2 (see Figure 6.14.1).

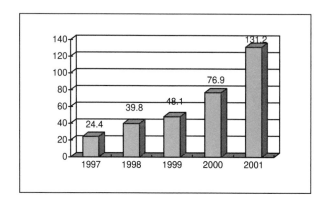

Source: China Chain and Franchise Association

Figure 6.14.1 Average number of retail outlets of the top 100 retail chains, 1997–2001

Table 6.14.2 Leading retail chains (excluding supermarket chains), 2001

Ranking	Company name	2001 turnover (thousand RMB)	Increase over 2000 (%)	No. of outlets	Increase over 2000(%)
Department store chains					
10	Beijing Wangfujing Group Co Ltd	4,887,300	9	8	0
36	Shenzhen Maoye Commercial Masion Co Ltd	1,238,650	20	4	33
41	Beijing SCITEC Commercial Development Co Ltd	1,014,020	42	11	120
42	Shenzhen Tianhong Shopping Centre Co Ltd	1,008,080	16	3	0
Drug store chains					
61	Chongqing Heping Pharmacy Chain Co Ltd	567,070	23	518	73
90	Dalian Meluo Pharmacy Chain Co Ltd	320,760	na	105	na
96		295,000	217	203	233
97	Jianmin Pharmacy Chain of Guangzhou Pharmaceutical Corp	289,560	3	100	69
Hotel chains					
57	Dalian Friendship Group	630,000		15	
Specialty chains					
19	Lengend (Beijing) Co Ltd (computer retailing)	2,092,940	107	565	117
87	Giant (China) Co Ltd (bicycle retailing)	343,540	75	1245	32

Source: China Chain and Franchise Association

Average sales of the top 100 retail chains have grown at an accelerated speed over the past five years. In 1997, for example, the average turnover of the 100 largest retail chains was only RMB240 million but leapt to RMB1.62 billion in 2001 (see Figure 6.14.2).

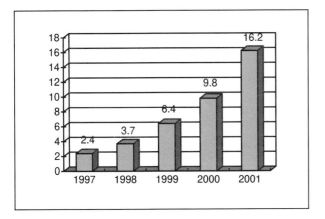

Source: Chinese Chain and Franchise Association

Figure 6.14.2   Average turnover of the top 100 retail chains 1997 to 2001 (RMB 100 million)

Interestingly, however, the survey of the top 100 retail chains for 2001 again missed out some of the major foreign retail players such as Carrefour, Wal-mart, Pricesmart, Makro Jusco, 7-Eleven, Roson, Parkson and McDonald's. Such omissions, for whatever reasons, have limited the representative nature of both this and the other survey of the top 20 retail chains conducted by the State Economic and Trade Commission. However, these surveys at least provide a picture of the local retail leaders and how they have been doing in their competition for a share of the market.

Foreign entry

Regardless of the fact that some of the international retail chains have been excluded from the top 20 and top 100 retail chains in China, it is undeniable that many foreign retail magnates have already established a presence in China and achieved success there. At present, 70 per cent of the top 50 largest retail chains in the world have a presence in China. From the time when China opened up the retail sector for foreign involvement on a trial basis in 1992 to the end of 2001, there were a total of 356 foreign-invested commercial enterprises operating in China, although only 40 of these were officially approved and the remaining 316 were operating without official licences.

Since the early 1990s, China's retail sector has been an international battlefield. The future competitive situation is expected to be even more aggressive as foreign retail chains start to penetrate deeper into the market.

Wal-mart, the magnate of the international retail community, entered China in 1996. Although it was relatively slow expanding its operations in the early stages, with only eight stores in the 4-5 years following its entry, it began a more aggressive expansion policy in 2001 and has now opened 20 stores in 9 cities with plans to open 50 stores over the next three years. Its first Beijing shop will be opened in 2002 and four more are planned over the next couple of years.

Carrefour, the first company to bring the huge retail store format to China in 1995, has spread all over the country, with 28 outlets in 15 big cities, making it the largest foreign retailer in China. It began to look at Chinese market opportunities in the early 1990s and opened its first premises in Beijing in a manner that circumvented the policy restrictions placed on the entry of foreign retailers to China. Along its road to expansion, Carrefour established some stores that did not have appropriate official approval and some that were virtually wholly-owned by Carrefour, which is against Chinese laws and regulations. It has been reported that Carrefour was requested to comply with government regulations by selling at least 35 per cent of its wholly-owned operations to local companies before its plan to open another 10 stores can be given the green light.

The German-based retail giant Metro has also been active in China. By 2000, it had established eight stores in the country. Since 2001, it has extended its operations to other parts of China, opening over 10 warehouse supermarkets in 11 cities including Hangzhou, Wuhan, Chengdu and Chongqing.

COSCO, the twelfth largest retailer in world, has also made progress in China's retail market. It is said that COSCO has engaged one of the leading Chinese retail chains in its plan to open ten large-scale warehouse supermarkets. New COSCO stores are expected to open in some of China's major urban centres.

Other international retail chains active in China include the Japan-based Ito-Yoado, Tesco, Auchan, B&Q, OBI and Ikea who all have aggressive plans to expand in China.

Taiwanese retail chains are also attempting to take a slice of the market. Instead of the crowded larger cities, Taiwanese retail chains began with medium-sized cities with a more regional oriented strategy. Trust-mart, for example, is concentrating its retail operations in the Pearl Delta River area, and developing from there into the west of China, where it has opened seven stores. So far, Trust-mart has opened 26 retail outlets in China, second only to Carrefour in terms of the number of outlets. Another Taiwanese retail chain, RT-mart, has successfully avoided direct competition with international retail chains in key cities by moving into cities such as Nanjing, Wuxi, Changzhou, Yangzhou, Suzhou, Changshu, Kunshan, Nantong and Jiaxing, all of which are on the flank of Shanghai.

Opportunities as a result of China's WTO accession

The regulatory environment will improve after WTO accession. China's commitments to the WTO in relation to the opening of the retail sector will eventually remove some of the restrictions that still limit market access to foreign retailers. In response to the WTO rules and in an effort to honour China's WTO commitments, the State Development Planning Commission, the State Economic and Trade Commission and the Ministry of Foreign Trade and Economic Cooperation promulgated a new Catalogue of Industrial Guidance for Foreign Investment on 31 March 2002. This sets out the schedule for the opening of the retail sector in line with China's WTO commitments. According to the Catalogue, restrictions on foreign participation in China's retail sector will be phased out as per the following schedule:

1. Foreign investment is permitted, except for books, newspapers, magazines, pharmaceuticals, pesticides, mulching films, fertilizers and processed oil.
2. A 50 per cent foreign equity share will be permitted and joint ventures will be permitted to deal in the retailing of books, newspapers and magazines no later than 11 December 2002.

3. Foreign majority ownership will be permitted no later than 11 December 2003.
4. Solely foreign-owned operations will be permitted and allowed to engage in the retailing of pharmaceuticals, pesticides, mulching film and processed oil no later than 11 December 2004.
5. Retailing of fertilizers by foreign-invested retailers will be permitted no later than 11 December 2006. Foreign majority ownership will not be permitted for those chain stores that engage in the following products and have over 30 outlets: motor vehicles (the restrictions on which will be removed no later than 11 December 2006), books, newspapers, magazines, pharmaceuticals, pesticides, mulching films, processed oil, fertilizers, grains, vegetable oils, sugar, tobacco and cotton.

The above schedule shows future opportunities for foreign investment in the retail sector. The macro opportunities are obvious – increasing consumer affluence in both urban and rural areas and the huge consumer base of 1.3 billion people. The micro opportunities are many – different options of entry such as joint venturing, merger, acquisition and wholly-owned subsidiary. A short-term option while the restrictions on wholly foreign-owned operations are still in force is to set up joint ventures in designated locations. This will offer immediate market access and incur minimal risk in terms of financial engagements. There are a number of Chinese retailers that have advantages such as retail sites, existing customer base, understanding of local conditions and brand recognition, while being disadvantaged by the lack of sufficient funding, management know-how, marketing expertise and retailing technology. These retailers can also be targets of mergers or acquisitions. For those who would prefer to have a solely-owned operation, the only option is to wait until 2004.

6.15

Synthetic Rubber

Editorial Department, China Chemical News and China Chemical Industry Yearbook

Production

In 2000, nitrile rubber capacity increased by 15,000 tons per annum, and the total capacity of synthetic rubber rose significantly. Currently, China has six varieties of synthetic rubber, and with the exception of isoprene rubber (IR), all other general purpose synthetic rubbers can be manufactured in China. At the end of 2000, there were 14 producers with 26 sets of facilities. The total capacity came to 1,044,000 tons per annum, of which the capacity of styrene butadiene rubber (SBR) by emulsion polymerization (E-SBR) was 360,000 tons per annum, and cis-butadiene rubber (BR) 425,000 tons per annum. These manufacturers produce not only general purpose synthetic rubber (excluding latex), but also SBS thermoplastic elastomers. China is still the fourth producer of synthetic rubber after the USA, Russia and Japan.

Latex is also a major product of the synthetic rubber industry. Styrene butadiene latex is the largest variety, with an output of 17–20 per cent of the synthetic rubber total. China currently owns five large-scale SBR latex production facilities, with a total output of about 140,000 tons per annum. However, there are only a few brands of SBR latex, and the products lack competitive power.

Table 6.15.1 Major domestic synthetic rubber producers and capacity in 2,000,000 tons per annum

Producer	BR	E-SBR	S-SBR	SBS	NBR	CR	EPR	IIR
Yanshan Petrochem. Co Rubber Plant	120		30	30				30
Qilu Petrochem.Co Rubber Plant	50	130						
50	50							
Yuehua Rubber Plant	30			50				
Shanghai Gaoqiao Petrochem. Co	15*							
	80							
Xinjiang Dushanzi Petrochem. Co	20							
Daqing Petrochem. Works	50							
Jihua Co Organic Synthesis Plant		90			10**		20	
Lanhua Co Organic Synthesis Plant		40			19			
Jiangsu Nantong Shenhua Co		100						
Ethylene Co,Maoming Petrochem Co	10		30	10				
Shanxi Synthesis Rubber Group						20		
Sichuan Changshou Chemical Plant						13		
Shandong Qingdao Chemical Plant						7***		
Total	425	360	60	90	29	40	20	30

*Production ceased in June 1998; **concurrent production on E-SBR unit not shown in total capacity; ***production ceased

Table 6.15.2 Major domestic SBR latex producers and capacity in 2,000 000 tons per annum

Producer	Capacity
Gaoqiao BASF Co	110
Qilu Petrochemical Co	10
Lanzhou Chemical Co	6
Yanshan Petrochemical Co	5
Zibo Heli Latex Co	5

In 2000, the total output of synthetic rubber in China (including SBS) was 703,000 tons, with only a slight increase of 1.4 per cent over 1999 (694 000 tons).SBS enjoyed the highest growth. Technical transformation allowed the SBS output of Yueyang Petrochemical Rubber Plant and Maoming Perochemical Ethylene Plant to surpass their designed capacity, and brought the rate of capacity utilisation to 148.4 per cent. In 2000, SBR decreased by a significant margin owing to the limitation imposed on output. The plant owned by Yanshan Petrochemical Group and intended to manufacture SBR by solvent polymerization (SSBR) did not go into production in 2000. Over recent years, several facilities for IIR, NBR and EPR have been set up, whose market capacities all surpass the total designed capacities of the existing domestic facilities. However, these newly built plants all have low capacity utilization of no more than 40 per cent. Their market share is also low at 9 per cent, 20 per cent and 25 per cent respectively.

Market supply and demand

In 2000, China continued to take action to stimulate the market, and to promote increased rubber consumption. Moreover, the rapid rise of the international crude oil price led to a continuous increase in the price of synthetic rubber, which to a certain extent prevented the price from going down further, and instead caused a slight increase. With China's imminent entrance into the WTO, import limitations are gradually being removed, including decreases in customs duty and increases in import allocation. As a result, imports in 2000 remained at a high level. Influenced by various factors, rubber prices continued to fluctuate in 2000, lacking motive force to push the price up and at the same time having only limited scope for it to slip down.

On the whole, the domestic price of synthetic rubber showed a general upward tendency, with two exceptions. The price of BR fluctuated throughout the year around 7,400 yuan/ton, with 8 per cent being the biggest margin. The average price was 7,395 yuan/ton in 2000, an increase of 16 per cent over the previous year. Meanwhile, the price of SBR showed a distinct upward trend in the first half year, when the margin went as high as 2,000 yuan/ton, while in the second half of the year the price stabilised and the average price was 7,790 yuan/ton, an increase of 25 per cent compared with 1999.

In China, the tyre industry is the largest consumer of synthetic rubber. With improvements in tyre performance, prolonged lifetimes and the popularity of radial tyres, rubber consumption of tyres is decreasing. The average annual growth rate of rubber consumption for tyres is about 5 per cent, of which synthetic rubber consumption is expected to increase from 40 per cent to 45-48 per cent. The world consumption of synthetic rubber in total rubber consumption remains steady at 60-61 per cent. It is predicted that China will reach the same level in 15 years.

According to forecasts, output and consumption of synthetic rubber will show a strong upward trend.

Table 6.15.3 Output and plant capacity utilization of major synthetic rubbers in 2,000 tons

Product	1999	2000	2000/1999(%)	Utilisation
BR	273952	313,441	14.4	73.8
E-SBR	275,102	196,512	−28.6	54.6
S-SBR	13,898	9,060	−34.8	15.1
NBR	8,987	8,559	−4.8	29.5
SBS	88,023	133,586	51.8	148.4
CR	26,156	30,525	16.7	76.3
EPR	7,328	7,257	1	36.3
IR		4,055		13.5
Total	693,446	702,995	1.4	67.3

Table 6.15.4   Rubber consumption and forecasts of the Chinese rubber industry in China (thousand tons)

	2000	*2005*	*2010*	*2015*
Tyre consumption	*1000*	*1250*	*1600*	*2000*
NR	580	650	850	1100
SR	420	600	750	900
SR proportion (%)	42	48	47	45
Non tyre consumption	*900*	*1100*	*1350*	*1700*
NR	350	400	400	400
SR	550	700	950	1300
SR proportion (%)	61	63	70	76
Rubber industry total	*1900*	*2350*	*2950*	*3700*
NR	930	1050	1250	1500
SR	970	1300	1700	2200
SR proportion (%)	51	55	57	59

Authoritative predictions show that the average annual growth rate demand for SBR and BR will be 5–7 per cent; for IIR, NBR (including hydro NBR) and EPR 8–10 per cent; and for CR 2–3 per cent.

Import and export trade

In 2000, the import volume of rubber continued to increase considerably from 1.08 million tons to 1.562 million tons, a 44 per cent increase on the previous year. Foreign exchange used for imports increased by 49 per cent, from US$0.88 billion the previous year to US$1.306 billion. Of the total, the import volume of synthetic rubber increased by 8.9 per cent, from 650,000 tons in 1999 to 710,000 tons in 2000, and the foreign exchange used grew by 20 per cent, from US$602 million to US$722 million. Import volume, of IIR, NBR and EPR all increased by over 30 per cent.

In 2000, the export volume of synthetic rubber was 64,000 tons, 8 per cent of the total output and an increase of 41.8 per cent on the previous year. Of this, BR accounted for 36,700 tons, SBR 14,800 tons and others 7,900 tons, all significant increases on 1999.

In 2000, synthetic rubbers were mainly imported from Taiwan, Japan, Korea and Russia; these constituting 77 per cent of the total.

The pattern of import trade changed considerably in 2000. The processing trade based on imported materials or on materials provided by customers still dominated, accounting for 54 per cent of the total trade; general trade volume surged from 89,000 tons in 1998 and 202,000 tons in 1999 up to 242,000 tons in 2000, a 20 per cent increase on the previous year and making up 34 per cent of the total import volume.

Table 6.15.5   Forecast demand for main synthetic rubbers in China (thousand tons)

	2000		*2005*		*2010*		*2015*	
	Demand	*%*	*Demand*	*%*	*Demand*	*%*	*Demand*	*%*
SBR	386–420	42.0	494–560	41.5	586–734	41.0	889–932	40.0
BR	277–290	29.0	340–385	28.5	400–500	28.0	610–641	27.5
IIR	60–65	6.5	83–95	7.0	107–134	7.5	77–186	8.0
EPR	55–60	6.0	77–88	6.5	93–116	6.5	155–163	7.0
CR	55–60	6.0	65–74	5.5	72–90	5.0	100–105	4.5
NBR	46–50	5.0	60–68	5.0	79–98	5.5	133–140	6.0
SBR latex	51–50	5.5	71–81	6.0	93–116	6.5	155–161	7.0
Total	930–1000	100	1190–1351	100	1430–1 788	100	2119–2 328	100

Table 6.15.6 Import and export of synthetic rubber in 2000 (tons)

Product	Import volume			Export volume		
	1999	2000	00/99 (%)	1999	2000	00/99 (%)
SBR and carboxylated SBR	140,322	126,166	10.1	13,896	14,835	6.8
BR	49,324	52,464	6.4	12,226	36,706	72.9
IIR*	30,120	39,286	30.5	212	1,037	389.1
CR	19,388	18,807	3.0	134	624	365.7
NBR	25,894	34,531	33.4	55	121	120.0
IR	11,266	18,105	60.7			
EPR	15,884	22,869	44.0	1,790	1,101	38.5
SBS		29,484				
Synthetic latex	109,149	132,828	21.7	1,100	1,551	41.0
Other synthetic rubber	246,659	228,981	7.2	6,740	7,908	17.3
Total of synthetic rubber and latex**	647,988	703,521	8.6	45,153	63,883	41.5

*Including halogenated butyl rubber; **Import and export including no-primary rubber.

Table 6.15.7 Main import sources

Origins	Volume (thousand tons)	Proportion (%)	Value (US$ million)	Proportion (%)
Taiwan	204.5	28.8	172.70	23.9
Korea	152.9	21.5	120.84	16.7
Japan	120.3	16.9	168.50	23.3
Russia	72.5	10.2	58.91	8.2
USA	41.2	5.8	62.27	8.6
Others	119.1	16.8	138.60	19.3
Total	710.5	100	721.82	100

Table 6.15.8 Import pattern of synthetic rubber, 2000

	Import volume (kt)		Proportion (%)	
	1999	2000	1999	2000
Total	652.2	710.5	100	100
Imports for processing purpose	274.3	276.2	42.1	38.9
General trade	202.2	242.3	31.0	34.1
Imports of customers' material for processing purpose	100.2	108.0	15.4	15.2
Small volume border trade	57.9	61.4	8.9	8.6
Goods in bonded warehouse*	17.3	22.6	2.7	3.0
Others	0.2	0	0	0

*Including transhipping in bonded zones

Currently 35 customs agencies are in charge of the declaration of the rubber import business in China. The import volumes and corresponding proportions in 2000 from different provinces are listed below. Synthetic rubber was mainly imported from Guangzhou, Fujian and Shanghai, the import volume accounting for up to 71 per cent of the total.

Capital construction and technical renovation

In April 2000, a 15,000 tons per annum NBR unit set up by Lanhua Rubber Plant began operation. Chengdu Fertilizer Plant also put an acrylate special synthetic rubber unit into production, which developed, designed and installed itself. The Rubber Plant of Qilu Petrochemical Co., based on the two new oil-extended rubbers, invested further to build another pilot unit of chlorinated BR, put successfully on stream in December 2000. Gaoqiao BASF Co. also expanded its SBR latex output from 50,000 to 110,000 tons per annum in March 2000, and prepared to make further expansion to 160,000 tons per annum in the future.

Dow Chemical Co, the world's largest latex producer, began in March 2000 to build a 45,000 tons per annum SBR latex plant in Zhangjiagang Economic Development Zone, Jiangsu Province, with an investment of 28.7 million yuan. The products made by the plant will be used for paper production. The French company invested US$30 million to set up a 100,000 tons per annum SBR plant in Zhenjiang Xinqu, Jiangsu Province, scheduled to be on stream in 2002, with 80 per cent of its products supplying a nearby large-scale paper mill.

The letter of intention to build a 20,000 tons per annum SBR latex plant was jointly signed by the Management Committee of the Economic Technology Development Zone, Nantong City and Shenhua Chemical Co Ltd. with an investment of US$15 million.

In addition, a project by China Petrochemical Co Ltd, to construct a 100,000 tons per annum S-SBR unit was approved by the State Planning Committee. It is intended to introduce capital and key equipment from foreign countries and has a total investment of 0.7 billion yuan and a construction cycle from 2002 to 2003. The main products and design capacity are 66,000 tons per annum cis-BR Asadene series and 34,000 tons per annum non-oil extended S-SBR 'Tufdene' series respectively. Also, a joint venture agreement to set up a 30,000-37,500 tons per annum CR unit using the calcium carbide acetylene process was reached by Shanxi Synthetic Rubber Group and the Ministry of Ecomony of Armenia.

During the overhaul in 2000, the Organic Synthetic Plant of Jilin Chemical Co completed the renovation of its SBR unit involving an additional condensation trough and a double line automatic package system line in line with a condensation system. Yueyang Petrochemical Rubber Plant, by exploiting its potential and optimizing processes, made the actual total output of the SBS unit surpass that of the design level by 1.4 times in 2000. The yearly output reached over 70,000 tons. In addition, Maoming Petrochemical Ethylene Plant, after the technical renovation of its synthetic rubber facilities, successfully produced cis-butadiene rubber (F-250) in April 2000. Yanshan Petrochemical Rubber Plant completed industrial tests on the use of hot pumps to recover low temperature waste heat from synthetic rubber production, and succeeded in reducing the cost of steam by 1.0–1.5 tons per ton of rubber. The plant also introduced a SBS after-treatment line to upgrade product quality and stability.

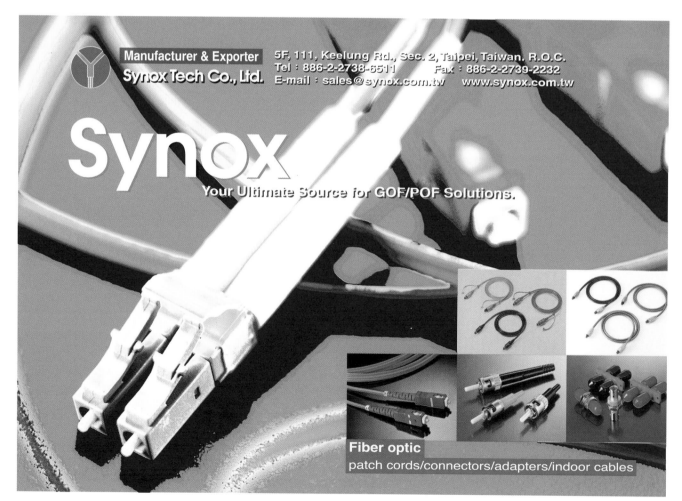

Telecommunications

Jonathan Sandbach and Michelle Ye, Cable & Wireless

This chapter has two purposes: firstly to give an overview of the development of the telecommunications services sector in China as it concerns overseas investors. Secondly, it suggests ways in which the sector may develop in future, particularly in terms of its regulatory oversight. We will concentrate on telecommunications service provision rather than telecommunications equipment manufacture.

Overview of China's telecommunications industry

China has six national operators providing a range of telecommunications services from fixed telephone to mobile, and from voice to data. These are China Telecom, China Unicom, China Mobile, China Netcom, China Railcom and China Satellite. China Unicom and China Mobile are public listed companies on the Hong Kong Stock Exchange market and China Telecom is planning its Initial Public Offering (IPO) in New York and Hong Kong in November 2002.

The following key facts give an idea of the magnitude of the Chinese telecommunication services' infrastructure and markets:

- China ranks **first** in the world in terms of numbers of both fixed and mobile telephone subscriptions, and consequent network capacity;
- China ranks **third** in the world in terms of the number of Internet users;
- China ranks **first** in the world in terms of number of mobile subscribers (180 million by September 2002).

On the basis of these facts alone, China would appear to be a market of huge interest to global telecommunications companies, given the opportunity to partner with such strong domestic players. Historically this has been difficult, but China's recent commitment to the WTO is providing some new and significant opportunities and it is to be hoped that further market development will follow.

WTO: China's telecommunications commitments

After 14 years of discussion, China joined the WTO in November 2001. As part of its commitment to membership, it has agreed to a phased liberalization of its telecommunications sector, as described in its Schedule of Specific Commitment relating to the World Trade Organization Basic Telecommunications Agreement.

China has adopted a deregulatory scheme, allowing foreign investment, subject to separate percentage caps on foreign ownership, according to service and geography. The timescale for commitments is as follows:

Value-added services (including Paging)

2002: Up to 40 per cent foreign ownership in Beijing, Guangzhou and Shanghai, and operations connecting these cities

2003: Up to 49 per cent foreign ownership in Beijing, Guangzhou and Shanghai as well as 14 other cities and operations connecting these cities (see list below)

2005: Up to 50 per cent foreign ownership with no geographic restrictions.

Mobile services

2002: Up to 25 per cent foreign ownership in Beijing, Guangzhou and Shanghai, and operations connecting these cities

2003: Up to 35 per cent foreign ownership in Beijing, Guangzhou and Shanghai as well as 14 other cities, and operations connecting these cities (see list below)

2005: Up to 49 per cent foreign ownership in Beijing, Guangzhou and Shanghai Shanghai as well as 14 other cities, and operations connecting these cities (see list below)

2007: Up to 49 per cent foreign ownership with no geographic limitations.

Domestic and international fixed wireline services

2005: Up to 25 per cent foreign ownership in Beijing, Guangzhou and Shanghai, and operations connecting these cities

2007: Up to 35 per cent foreign ownership in Beijing, Guangzhou and Shanghai as well as 14 other cities, and operations connecting these cities (see list below)

2008: Up to 49 per cent foreign ownership with no geographic limitations.

The 14 cities are:

Chengdu (Sichuan province)
Chongqing (central-reporting municipality)
Dalian (Liaoning province)
Fuzhou (Fujian province)
Hangzhou (Zhejiang province)
Nanjing (Jiangsu province)
Ningbo (Zhejiang province)
Qingdao (Shandong province)
Shenzhen (Guangdong province)
Shenyang (Liaoning province)
Taiyuan (Shanxi province)
Wuhan (Hubei province)
Xiamen (Fujian province)
Xi'an (Shaanxi province)

The AT&T Joint Venture

In 2001, AT&T became the first international carrier to form a joint venture (JV) since China joined the WTO, with a company called Shanghai Symphony Telecom. AT&T has a 25 per cent stake in the JV. Shanghai Symphony Telecom intends to offer broadband and IP services, such as Virtual Private Networks (VPNs), as well as managed hosting and other related professional services.

Historically, JVs in the telecommunications industry have not been universally successful and there are numer-

ous examples of failure. Of particular relevance, perhaps, is the failure of Concert, the JV between AT&T itself and British Telecom, aimed at providing global telecommunications services to multinational clients. The AT&T JV in the Shanghai Symphony Telecom project has yet to be tested. Both parties to the JV will need to demonstrate their commercial interest and commitment if success is to be assured. Nevertheless, it is to be hoped that the project is indicative of the opportunities that will exist in the future.

Future development

At first glance, it may be surprising that (other than Shanghai Symphony Telecom JV, which has yet to prove itself) there has been no rush of foreign capital or foreign operators to enter China's telecommunications sector following China's accession to the WTO, as many people had predicted before the event.

One explanation for this is that China's commitments in the liberalization scheme do not go far enough (essentially still preventing foreign companies from gaining management control), or are too slow in the lifting of foreign ownership limits.

However, apart from foreign ownership limits, there are other specific reasons that are holding back development in the sector. Both the external and internal environments have contributed to holding back overseas investment in the Chinese telecommunications sectors.

The external environment has been dominated by the global economic downturn which has particularly affected the worldwide telecommunications markets. The economic downturn in the market is compounded by over-supply of network capacity and accounting fraud within some of the newer international carriers. As a result, international capital has not favoured the telecommunications industry, and, in general, existing telecommunications companies are paring back their investment plans. Inevitably, this has led to limited financial and human resources being allocated to develop emerging markets such as China.

This external investment environment is largely beyond the control of Chinese policy makers. However, the following internal factors within China's own regulatory environment require policy attention if foreign investment in the Chinese telecommunications sector is to thrive. These issues are the ones on which future policy development should ideally take place:

- Lack of a transparent regulatory regime in China, adding insecurity to foreign carriers. Basic issues yet to be resolved include:
  - the status of telecommunications law;
  - lack of a truly independent and transparent regulator to implement the government's policy objectives (independent of both the industry players and political institutions);
  - detailed policies on universal service and interconnection (which will impact the cost base of companies), competition, and non-discrimination by vertically integrated dominant suppliers (for example, the availability of local network facilities to all parties on equal terms and conditions, including vertically integrated companies' own downstream operations).
- The state-owned nature of the current Chinese carriers results in protracted periods for partner selection and the building of mutual trust and corporate structures within JVs.
- Foreign carriers are naturally reluctant to initiate a JV when there is currently no possibility of them ever being able to gain management control.

6.17

Tourism

Li Yong, Deputy Secretary General, China Association of International Trade

China has abundant resources for tourism. The industry emerged with the adoption of the country's reform and opening up policy in late 1978. Since then, the industry has been developing rapidly; it is now a growth industry of a respectable magnitude with a maturing industrial composition and has become one of the fastest-developing industries of the national economy and a new economic growth point in the 21st century. Tourism is a 'smokeless' industry that will not only generate additional sources of revenue, but also create more employment opportunities. As a result, virtually every province, municipality and autonomous region has made tourism a priority industry.

According to National Tourism Administration (CNTA) statistics, China's tourist industry has developed rapidly over the last two decades. International tourist arrivals have been growing at an annual rate of 19 per cent (see Table 6.17.1).

The statistics from the World Tourism Organization (see Table 6.17.2) differ from those of the Chinese National Tourism Administration, although China ranked fifth in the world's top 15 tourism destinations in 2001. According to these figures, the total number of international tourist arrivals was 33.2 million in 2001, an increase of 6.2 per cent over 2000 and 4.8 per cent of the global total.

The World Tourism Organization also placed China in the fifth position in the world's top 15 tourism earners in 2001. The total international tourism receipts in the year hit a record high of US$17.8 billion, an increase of 9.7 per cent over the previous year and 3.8 per cent of the world's tourism receipts (see Table 6.17.3).

Table 6.17.1 International tourist arrivals between 1978 and 2000

Year	Total (thousands)	Foreigners	Overseas Chinese	Compatriots*	Taiwan
1990	2,746.18	1,747.3	91.1	25,623.4	948.0
1991	3,334.98	2,710.1	133.4	30,506.2	946.6
1992	3,811.49	4,006.4	165.1	33,943.4	1,317.8
1993	4,152.69	4,655.9	166.2	36,704.9	1,527.0
1994	4,368.45	5,182.1	115.2	38,387.2	1,390.2
1995	4,638.65	5,886.7	115.8	40,384.0	1,532.3
1996	5,112.75	6,744.3	154.6	44,228.6	1,733.9
1997	5,758.79	7,428.0	99.0	50,060.9	2,117.6
1998	6,347.84	7,107.7	120.7	56,250.0	2,174.6
1999	7,279.56	8,432.3	108.1	64,255.2	2,584.6
2000	8,348.09	10,196.9	76.0	73,208.0	3,108.6

Source: Chinese National Tourism Administration.

* The sum of visitors from Hong Kong and Macao.

Table 6.17.2 International tourist arrivals

Year	International tourist arrivals (million)
1990	10.5
1995	20.0
1998	25.1
1999	27.1
2000	31.2
2001	33.2

Source: 'International Tourist Arrivals by Country of Destination' and 'World's Top 15 Tourism Destinations', World Tourism Organization

Table 6.17.3 International tourism receipts

Year	Receipts (US$100 million)	Growth (%)
1990	22.18	19.2
1991	28.45	28.3
1992	39.47	38.7
1993	46.83	18.7
1994	73.23	56.4
1995	87.33	19.3
1996	102.00	16.8
1997	120.74	18.4
1998	126.02	4.4
1999	140.99	11.9
2000	162.31	15.1
2001*	178.00	

Source: Chinese National Tourism Administration.

*2001 figure is from the World Tourism Organization

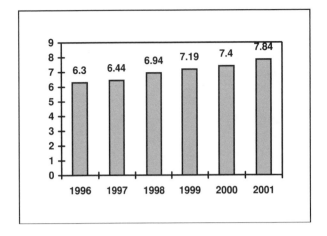

Figure 6.17.1 Growth of domestic tourists (100 million people)

At the same time, domestic tourism has also been developing rapidly as a result of improved standards of living and increased household incomes. People take advantage of the two seven-day holidays (International Labour Day on 1 May and the National Day on 1 October) to travel out of their hometowns to other parts of China. In 2000, for example, the number of people travelling for pleasure during the two holiday periods was 46 million and 59.8 million, generating 18.12 billion yuan and 23 billion yuan of revenue for the tourism industry. In 2001, domestic tourism revenue stood at RMB352.24 billion (about US$42.44 billion), causing the aggregate tourism revenue to reach RMB 499.5 billion, which was an increase of 10.5 per cent, 3.2 per cent higher than the GDP growth rate of the same year.

With the increased interaction of China with the outside world both economically and culturally, more people are travelling abroad for both business and pleasure. In recent years, the government has taken a series of measures to streamline the application procedures for private passports, which has facilitated the travels of Chinese people abroad. According to the Chinese National Tourism Administration, the top 10 destinations for Chinese travelling abroad were Hong Kong, Macao, Thailand, Russia, Japan, the Republic of Korea, the United States, Singapore, the Democratic Republic of Korea and Australia.

As can be seen in Table 6.17.4, the total number of trips abroad exceeded 10 million for the first time in 2000. In 2001, the number increased to 12.13 million, up by 15.9 per cent. Business travellers totalled 5.19 million trips, a rise of 7.2 per cent. Journeys for personal reasons increased by 23.3 per cent in 2001, a total of 6.95 million trips.

Since overseas tourist destinations opened up for Chinese people in 1989, the government has approved 23 destinations that Chinese people are allowed to visit as tourists. These include Thailand, Malaysia, Singapore, Hong Kong, Macao, the Philippines, Brunei, Burma, Vietnam, Japan, Korea, Laos, Cambodia, Australia, New Zealand, Indonesia, Turkey, Egypt, Malta, Germany, Nepal, South Africa and Greece. There will be no more tourism destination added to this list in the next few years. It is expected that there will be more leisure-oriented foreign tours and travels in the future.

As China's tourism market has thrived, foreign interest in participating in the growth of the market has been strong. Accor, American Express, Preussag and JTB have all been trying to pursue entry in one form or another. Since 1998, when China adopted the Measures on Implementation of Trials on Chinese-Foreign Joint

Table 6.17.4 Outbound travel of Chinese people in 2000

Destination	Number of trips	Percentage growth
Asia		
Hong Kong, CN	4,142,191	15.99
Macao, CN	1,644,421	6.04
Taiwan, CN	86,154	2.45
Japan	595,660	10.78
ROK	400,958	29.27
DPRK	194,970	10.81
Mongolia	63,044	24.58
Singapore	262,776	24.50
Philippines	33,647	−4.80
Malaysia	86,696	2.84
Thailand	707,456	−13.08
Indonesia	19,963	31.32
Kazakhstan	44,226	−10.53
Subtotal	*8,845,908*	*13.22*
America		
USA	395,107	19.15
Canada	100,178	31.03
Subtotal	*523,081*	*21.69*
Europe		
Germany	112,824	20.52
France	96,485	9.86
Britain	61,129	42.80
Russia	606,102	38.46
Subtotal	*1,079,089*	*31.03*
Oceania		
Australia	126,852	23.89
New Zealand	18,288	45.25
Subtotal	*150,231*	*26.08*
Africa	47,521	15.40
Other	3,625	−33.56
Total	10,649,455	15.35

Source: China National Tourism Administration.

Venture Travel Agencies, foreign travel agencies have begun to enter China's tourism market. With China's membership of the World Trade Organization, tourism will further open up for foreign participation. According to China's commitments to the WTO in relation to tourism and travel-related businesses, foreign tourism service providers who meet the following conditions are permitted to provide services in the form of joint venture travel agencies and tour operators in the holiday resorts designated by the Chinese government in the cities of Beijing, Shanghai, Guangzhou and Xi'an:

- a travel agency and tour operator mainly engaged in travel business;
- annual worldwide turnover in excess of US$40 million. The registered capital of joint venture travel agency/tour operators shall be no less than RMB4 million. Within three years of China's accession, the registered capital shall be no less than RMB2.5 million. Within three years of accession foreign majority ownership will be permitted. Within six years, solely foreign-owned subsidiaries will be permitted and geographical restrictions will be removed. The business scope of the travel agency/tour operator is defined as:
- travel and hotel accommodation services for foreign travellers which can be made directly with transportation and hotel operators in China covering such operations;
- travel services and hotel accommodation services for domestic travellers which can be made directly with transportation and hotel operators in China covering such operations;
- conducting of tours within China for both domestic and foreign travellers, and
- travellers cheque cashing services within China.

Within six years of accession, there will be no restrictions on the establishment of branches of joint venture travel agency/tour operators and the requirements on registered capital of foreign-invested travel agency/tour operators will be the same as for Chinese companies.

However, joint ventures or solely foreign-owned travel agencies and tour operators are not permitted to engage in the activities of Chinese travelling abroad and to Hong Kong China, Macao China and Chinese Taipei.

At present, 11 joint venture travel agencies have received operating licences, eight of which were approved before China's accession to the WTO. In addition to the opening up of the tourism sector to foreign participation, China has also vowed to open the sector to private entrants, an effort to demonstrate national treatment to the private sector, who complained about super-national treatment of foreign investments and sub-national treatment of the private sector.

The impact of China's WTO accession is generally regarded as positive. One reason for this was that China had already been exposed to and had the chance to become familiar with foreign competition before.

Although there are some concerns about the future of the smaller travel agencies under the pressure of foreign entrants, the opening is certain to take place. Chinese National Tourism Administration stated in late July 2002 that China would take active measures to open up the tourism sector, including:

- Allowing foreign investors to launch joint stock or wholly-owned travel services and break down the geographical barriers so as to attract more big name international travel agencies which are strong in financial capacity, solid in reputation and advanced in management practice;

- Energetically coordinating and standardizing the examination and approval procedures and principles for foreign-funded tourism projects, and improving laws and regulations;
- Improving investment guidance, giving more privileges to the central and western parts of the country in planning joint ventures;
- Deepening the reform of the tourism industry in line with the trend to improve tourism operations and management, upgrade the quality of tourism service and cultivate new growth.

Part Seven

Local Economies – the 49 Provinces, Autonomous Regions, Leading Cities and Special Administrative Regions

Beijing

Beijing, capital of the People's Republic of China, is situated in the northern part of the North China Plain and is the political, economic and cultural centre of the country. It is one of the four municipalities – the others being Shanghai, Tianjin and Chongqing – which are directly under the jurisdiction of the Central Government and have autonomy in economic, financial and administrative decisions. This ancient city has grown into one of the biggest industrial and commercial centres in the nation, covering an area of 16,808 square kilometres with a population of 13.8 million. Major economic indicators are shown in Table 7.1.1.

Resources

Minerals include iron, lead, zinc, molybdenum, copper and gold. There are also large reserves of coal, mostly high-quality anthracite and limestone, as well as building materials such as granite and marble. Oil has been discovered in the south-east.

Infrastructure

Beijing is the transportation hub of China. It has the best developed railway system in the country with direct railway services to all provincial capital cities. Since the Beijing West Railway Station began operating in January 1996, Beijing has had a total of four freight terminals and two passenger terminals. The road network has greatly improved in recent years and with the completion of the Beijing-Tianjin-Tangu Expressway, the ports in Tianjin can be reached from Beijing in two hours while the Beijing Capital International Airport is one of the largest in the country, providing access to

Table 7.1.1   Major economic indicators, Beijing

Item	2000	2001
Population (millions)	13.636	13.833
GDP (billion RMB)	247.876	281.8
GDP per capita (thousand RMB)	22.460	25.300
Disposable income per capita (thousand RMB)		
Urban residents	10.347	4.524
Rural residents	11.578	5.099
Savings (billion RMB)*	974.72	1,222.34
Investment in fixed assets (billion RMB)	128.046	153.1
Value-added of primary industry (billion RMB)	8.997	9.3
Value-added of secondary industry (billion RMB)	94.351	106.4
Value-added of tertiary industry (billion RMB)	144.528	166.09
Total retail sales of consumer goods (billion RMB)	144.3	159.4

Source: China Statistical Yearbook 2001 and State Statistical Bureau
*Both institutional and private savings

over 60 domestic cities and about 40 international destinations. The municipality also has a state-of-the-art telecommunication system. Beijing has successfully bid for the right to host the 2008 Olympic Games. To prepare for the Games, the Chinese government will invest over RMB 180 billion over the next five years in improving the city's infrastructure.

Foreign trade

In 2000, the total value of imports and exports increased by 38.8 per cent, from US$8.392 billion in the previous year to US$11.651 billion. The total value of exports increased by 41.8 per cent to US$4.627 billion (15.57 per cent of the city's GDP and 1.86 per cent of China's total export value). Export of primary products and manufactured products amounted to US$278 million and US$4348 million respectively, or 6 per cent and 94 per cent of China's total export value. Commodities were exported to 179 countries and regions. Changes in key export destinations over the last five years are shown in Table 7.1.2.

Import value totalled US$7.024 billion in 2000, up 36.8 per cent on US$5.181 billion in 1999. Import of primary products and manufactured products amounted to US$376 million and US$6.648 billion respectively; 5.4 per cent and 94.6 per cent of the total import value.

Imports came from 193 countries and regions. The changes in key import origins between 1995 and 2000 are as shown in Table 7.1.3.

Utilization of foreign capital

In 2000, foreign direct investment (FDI) had increased by 138.4 per cent in total approved contract value compared to 1999. A total of 1146 FDI contracts were approved that year. Of these projects, 409 were production-oriented while 737 were in non-manufacturing fields, the majority in social services.

Foreign direct investment came from 44 countries and regions. A breakdown of the major investors and the value of foreign capital involved is shown in Table 7.1.5.

By the end of 2000, 5082 foreign-invested enterprises (FIEs) had begun operation, employing a total of 454,000 people. The industrial output value by the operating FIEs in 2000 was RMB116.1 billion, an increase of 38.5 per cent on 1999, while total sales revenue reached RMB183.1 billion, an increase of 35.5 per cent. The total profit reported for the year 2000 was RMB5.44 billion, 3.7 times that of 1999, and the tax paid by the FIEs was RMB11.4 billion, up by 21.5 per cent.

Table 7.1.2 Top five export destinations, Beijing, 1995 and 2000

Country/region	Export value (US$ million)	% of total exports
1995		
Hong Kong	708.09	27.77
Japan	497.96	19.53
USA	317.92	12.47
Germany	151.34	5.94
Russia	70.61	3.83
Total	1,745.92	69.54
2000		
Japan	1,000.8	21.63
Hong Kong	806.45	17.43
USA	611.56	13.22
Germany	249.26	5.39
Russia	231.03	4.99
Total	2,899.1	62.66

Table 7.1.3 Top five import markets, Beijing, 1995 and 2000

Country/region	Import value (US$ million)	% of total export
1995		
Japan	784.22	42.61
USA	279.87	15.21
Hong Kong	239.11	12.99
Peru	120.65	5.56
UK	71.87	3.90
Total	1,685.13	91.56
2000		
Japan	1,434.11	20.42
Finland	1,378.82	19.63
USA	767.98	10.93
Germany	480.74	6.84
Sweden	443.74	6.32
Total	4,505.39	63.96

Table 7.1.4 Utilization of foreign capital, Beijing, 1995 and 2000

Type	Number	Approved contracts		Actual utilization	
		Total value (US$ million)	% over total value of previous year	Total value (US$ million)	% over total value of previous year
1995					
Direct foreign investment:	1,552	2,735.045	−39.66	1,402.770	−2.90
Equity joint ventures	982	1,334.989		915.050	
Contractual joint ventures	150	1,092.423		402.310	
Solely foreign-owned enterprises	420	307.633		85.370	
2000					
Direct foreign investment:	1146	433.08389	138.4	2,458.491	10.2
Equity joint ventures	428	1,356.8021	148.4	445.54	−16.7
Contractual joint ventures	144	494.4623	−21.5	485.718	−40.7
Solely foreign-owned enterprises	573	2,467.2382	330.3	1,527.219	61.6

Table 7.1.5 Key sources of foreign direct investment, Beijing

Source	No. of projects	Contract value (US$ million)
Hong Kong	285	1,321.4963
British Virgin Islands	222	1,239.8205
USA	201	624.2528
Republic of Korea	90	73.1886
Japan	52	222.283
Singapore	48	198.8752
Taiwan Province	47	25.8224
Cayman Islands	37	62.1801
UK	26	50.3055
Canada	25	17.8205
Germany	21	110.0517
Australia	11	57.9381
Western Samoa	5	5.3035
New Zealand	5	0.8608
Macao	4	4.7356
Thailand	4	3.2805
Italy	4	2.0073
Finland	4	34.6124
Malaysia	3	0.4702
Switzerland	3	5.15
Spain	2	3.1305
Russian Federation	2	1.192
Cuba	2	2.2628
Panama	2	0.3000

Tianjin

Tianjin municipality is directly under the jurisdiction of central government. In addition, it is one of the 14 coastal cities designated by the State Council to implement open policies to encourage foreign investment. Situated in the eastern part of the North China Plain, west of the Bohai Sea and south of the Yanshan Mountains, Tianjin is 137 kilometres south-east of Beijing and it is Beijing's gateway to the sea. Most of the land is flat and open. Tianjin has a total area of 11,305 square kilometres and a population of 10.01 million. Major economic indicators are shown in Table 7.2.1.

Resources

Because of its coastal location, Tianjin has abundant fisheries and high salt production. Tianjin's salt, with its high (96-98 per cent) sodium chloride content, is an important material for the marine chemicals industry. The Bohai Sea continental shelf has rich oil and natural gas deposits and has become one of China's major areas for oil exploration and production. The Dagang and Bohai Bay oilfields have plentiful reserves, and the Changlu salt field is the largest in China. More than 35 minerals, including coal, iron ore, copper, molybdenum, tungsten, barite, dolomite, manganese, china clay and marble, are found in Tianjin.

Infrastructure

Tianjin Port is one of the most important in north China and is capable of accommodating 'fifth generation' container vessels. It opens up to over 40 international shipping routes connecting with more than 300 ports in at least 160 countries and regions. There

Table 7.2.1   Major economic indicators, Tianjin

Item	2000	2001
Population (millions)	10.011	10.041
Gross domestic product (billion RMB)	163.936	182.7
GDP per capita (thousand RMB)	17.993	19.986
Disposable income per capita (thousand RMB)		
Urban residents	8.136	8.958
Rural residents	4.371	4.825
Savings (billion RMB)*	228.17	256.26
Investment in fixed assets (billion RMB)	61.094	70.5
Value-added of primary industry (billion RMB)	7.354	7.9
Value-added of secondary industry (billion RMB)	82.017	89.2
Value-added of tertiary industry (billion RMB)	74.565	85.66
Total retail sales of consumer goods (billion RMB)	73.7	83.8

Source: China Statistical Yearbook 2001 and State Statistical Bureau
*Both institutional and private savings

are eight container berths with an annual handling capacity of 1 million TEUs. Xingang (New Harbour) port has more than 62 berths and is one of China's largest container terminals with an annual handling capacity of 700,000 TEUs. The port also offers specialized handling facilities for coal, oil, grain and salt. With its convenient transport and communications facilities, the city is a major railway junction between northern and southern China. The airport, one of the largest in China, connects many cities in the country.

Foreign trade

In 2000, the total import and export value of Tianjin increased by 36.1 per cent, from US$12.601 billion in the previous year to US$17.157 billion.

The total export value hit a high of US$8.629 billion in 2000, which was an increase of 36.3 per cent over the 1999 figure of US$6.331 billion. It comprised 43.52 per cent of the municipal GDP, which stood at RMB163.941 billion (about US$19.824 billion), and accounted for 3.5 per cent of the total export of China.

The export of primary products amounted to US$1.361 billion, accounting for 15.78 per cent of total export value, while export of manufactured products came to US$7.265 billion, or 84.22 per cent of total export value. Exports were destined for 185 countries and regions and exports to the top five destinations (see Table 7.2.2) accounted for 66.6 per cent of the total.

Imports came to a total value of US$8.528 billion, an increase of 36 per cent compared with the 1999 import value of US$6.27 billion.

Import of primary products amounted to US$694 million, 8.14 per cent of total import value, while the value of manufactured products imported was US$7.834 billion, or 91.86 per cent of the total import value. Imports came from 179 countries and regions and the imports from the top five origins comprised 72.56 per cent of the total (see Table 7.2.3).

Utilization of foreign capital

Foreign direct investment increased by 27.1 per cent in 2000. However, the rate of increase in the total contract value of equity and contractual joint ventures was negative while the FDI in wholly foreign-owned enterprises increased sharply by 243.5 per cent.

Major sources of foreign direct investment (classified by amount) are shown in Table 7.2.5.

Table 7.2.2 Top five export markets: 1995 and 2000, Tianjin

Country/region	Export value (US$ million)	% of total exports
1995		
Japan	547.90	18.30
Hong Kong	547.59	18.26
USA	532.63	17.76
Republic of Korea	263.76	8.80
Germany	93.19	3.10
Total	1,985.07	66.22
2000		
USA	1,984	22.99
Japan	1,497	17.35
Hong Kong	828	9.60
Republic of Korea	797	9.24
Germany	640	7.42
Total	5,746	66.6

Table 7.2.3 Top five import markets: 1995 and 2000, Tianjin

Country/region	Import value (US$ million)	% of import total
1995		
Japan	1,118.49	31.53
Republic of Korea	562.13	15.85
USA	455.74	12.85
Hong Kong	372.25	10.49
Singapore	157.20	4.43
Total	4,660.81	75.15
2000		
Japan	2,096	24.58
Republic of Korea	1,902	22.30
USA	1,261	14.79
Taiwan Province	479	5.62
Hong Kong	449	5.27
Total	6,187	72.56

Distribution of FDI projects by sector is shown in Table 7.2.6.

The total value of foreign-invested enterprises in 2000 was RMB121.664 billion, an increase of 25.6 per cent on 1999. By the end of 2000, a total of 13,615 foreign-invested enterprises had been approved, involving a total contract value of US$39.272 billion, of which contractual foreign capital comprised US$31.346 billion, while the total of foreign capital actually used amounted to US$15.881 billion.

Table 7.2.4   Foreign direct investment in 1995 and 2000, Tianjin

Mode	Approved contracts			Actual utilization	
	Number	*Total value (US$ million)*	*% increase on previous year's total*	*Total value (US$ million)*	*% increase on previous year's total*
1995					
Direct foreign investment:	1,389	3,851.00	9.97	1,521.64	49.92
Equity joint ventures	476	1,846.00		867.55	
Contractual joint ventures	63	163.00		77.06	
2000					
Direct foreign investment:	626	4,600	27.1	2,560	1.1
Equity joint ventures	141	545	−37.4		
Contractual joint ventures	32	123	−92.4		
Solely foreign-owned enterprises	453	3932	243.5		

Table 7.2.5   Sources of foreign direct investment, Tianjin

Source	No. of projects	Contract value (US$ million)
USA	149	2,128
Hong Kong	94	1,652
Japan	47	188
Republic of Korea	162	120
Taiwan Province	51	45

Table 7.2.6   Distribution of FDI projects by sector, Tianjin

Sector	No. of projects	Value of foreign investment (US$)
Agriculture	12	3.34 million
Industrial and construction	398	3.981 billion
Real estate and public service	5	87 million
Communications and transportation	2	65 million
Retail, food services and material supplies	202	461 million
Other	7	1.31 million

Hebei Province

Hebei Province is situated in the northern part of the North China Plain, to the west of the Bohai Sea. It borders on Liaoning Province in the north-east and on Inner Mongolia in the north and north-west. Mountains account for 35 per cent of the total area, highlands north of the Great Wall for 12 per cent, and plains, hills and basins 50 per cent, and the coastline extends for about 500 kilometres. It has a total area of 187,700 square kilometres and has a population of 66.99 million. The provincial capital is Shijiazhuang. Major economic indicators are shown in Table 7.3.1.

Resources

The province is rich in mineral resources, and is a source of over 50 minerals, including oil, coal, iron, copper, lead, zinc, gold and petroleum. The province is advanced in agriculture, forestry, animal husbandry and fishing. Conditions for developing agricultural production are favourable. It is one of China's main cotton-producing areas.

Infrastructure

The transport facilities of the province are well developed and several trunk railway lines run through the area. Qinhuangdao is a major ice-free port in northern China which has 19 berths shipping routes to around ten countries and regions including Hong Kong, Japan and Singapore. Communications facilities are also good. Beidaihe is a well-known summer resort.

Table 7.3.1   Major economic indicators, Hebei Province

Item	2000	2001
Population (millions)	66.658	66.991
Gross domestic product (billion RMB)	508.896	557.8
GDP per capita (thousand RMB)	7.663	
Disposable income per capita (thousand RMB)		
Urban residents	5.662	2.479
Rural residents	5.984	2.603
Savings (billion RMB)*	552.43	612.45
Investment in fixed assets (billion RMB)	181.679	194.2
Value-added of primary industry (billion RMB)	82.455	91.4
Value-added of secondary industry (billion RMB)	255.996	274.4
Value-added of tertiary industry (billion RMB)	170.445	191.93
Total retail sales of consumer goods (billion RMB)	161.4	177.8

Source: China Statistical Yearbook 2001 and State Statistical Bureau
*Both institutional and private savings

Foreign trade

The total import and export value of Hebei stood at US$5.235 billion in 2000, an increase of 14.3 per cent on 1999.

The total export value was US$3.707 billion, a rise of 18.85 per cent on 1999. Its share in the national export value was 1.49 per cent. The export value was equal to 6.05 per cent of the provincial GDP, which stood at RMB507.631 billion (US$ 61.321 billion).

Export of primary products accounted for US$1.121 billion and of manufactured products US$2.586 billion, or 30.24 per cent and 69.76 per cent respectively of the total export value (see Table 7.3.2).

Total import value in 2000 was US$1.528 billion, an increase of 4.59 per cent on 1999. Import of primary products totalled US$554 million or 37 per cent of the total import value while that of manufactured products amounted to US$974 million, accounting for 64 per cent of the total import value (see Table 7.3.3).

Utilization of foreign capital

The total contract value of foreign direct investment in Hebei province in 2000 dropped by 20.4 per cent. 501 FDI contracts were approved, 83 per cent of which were manufacturing projects while the remaining 12 per cent were non-manufacturing projects (see Table 7.3.4).

Foreign direct investment came from 53 countries and regions. Major sources of FDI are listed in Table 7.3.5.

The majority (399) of these projects were in the manufacturing sector, with others in social services (23), agriculture, forestry, animal husbandry and fisheries (19) and construction (12).

By the end of 2000, a total of 9,749 foreign-invested projects had been approved and 1,599 foreign-invested enterprises were in operation, 24 more than in the previous year. The total output value by FIEs in 2000 reached RMB37.08 billion, an increase of 21.9 per cent on 1999. Total sales revenue was RMB36.46 billion, up by 32.3 per cent and profits amounted to RMB 1.47 billion, an increase of 540 per cent. The FIEs contributed RMB2.29 billion in tax revenue, up by 46.2 per cent. The export value of the operating FIEs was US$1 billion, up by 26.5 per cent, and accounted for 27.31 per cent of the total export value of Hebei Province.

Table 7.3.2 Top five export markets: 1995 and 2000, Hebei Province

Country/region	Export value (US$ million)	% of export total
1995		
Japan	942.98	30.98
Hong Kong	442.14	14.52
USA	341.81	11.23
Republic of Korea	239.95	7.88
Germany	159.21	5.32
Total	2,126.09	69.93
2000		
Japan	686.02	18.51
EU	636.59	17.17
Republic of Korea	495.84	13.38
USA	457.29	12.34
Hong Kong	249.79	6.74
Total	2,525.53	68.14

Table 7.3.3 Top five import markets: 1995 and 2000, Hebei Province

Country/region	Import value (US$ million)	% of import total
1995		
USA	199.98	21.95
Republic of Korea	122.18	13.41
Japan	120.87	13.27
Hong Kong	72.85	8.00
Germany	55.46	6.09
Total	571.34	62.72
2000		
EU	307.97	20.16
USA	238.38	15.60
Japan	211.14	13.82
Republic of Korea	173.46	11.35
ASEAN	88.88	5.82
Total	1,019.83	66.75

Table 7.3.4   Utilization of foreign capital in 1995 and 2000, Hebei Province

Type	Number	Approved contracts		Actually utilized	
		Total value (US$ million)	% over previous year's total value	Total value (US$ million)	% over previous year's total value
1995					
Direct foreign investment:	1,263	2,250.72	96.37	541.75	6.33
Equity joint ventures	992	1,687.99			
Contractual joint ventures	83	274.77			
Solely foreign-owned enterprises	188	287.96			
2000					
Direct foreign investment:	501	724.45	−20.4	1,023.76	−29.0
Equity joint ventures	317	373.07	−12.3	702.70	−37.0
Contractual joint ventures	53	167.68	−6.8	115.87	−30.4
Solely foreign-owned enterprises	131	183.70	−39.8	205.19	27.0

Table 7.3.5   Major sources of FDI, Hebei Province

Source	No. of projects	Contract value (US$ million)
British Virgin Islands	9	543.81
Hong Kong	55	254.48
Japan	41	74.02
USA	81	69.79
Singapore	15	62.48
Republic of Korea	62	41.96
Canada	16	35.76
Taiwan Province	47	31.67
Bahamas	1	20
Italy	8	10.54

7.4

Shanxi Province

Situated in the middle reaches of the Yellow River, on a plateau, Shanxi province is landlocked and borders on the Inner Mongolia Autonomous Region in the north and Henan Province in the south. Most of the area is more than 1,000 metres above sea level. Highlands and mountains in the eastern and western parts of the province account for almost three-quarters of the province's total area of 156,300 square kilometres and has a population of 32.72 million. The provincial capital is Taiyuan. Major economic indicators are shown in Table 7.4.1.

Resources

The province abounds in mineral resources, especially coal. The proven coal reserves account for approximately 203.5 billion tons, one third of the national

total. Major coal fields are located near Taiyuan and Datong. Taiyuan has developed a coal export system and become a major coal export base for the country. Other major minerals are iron, copper, cobalt, aluminium, molybdenum and titanium. Among the non-metal minerals are gypsum, limestone, pearlite and marble. Deposits of bauxite account for 45 per cent of the national total, amounting to 940 million tons.

Infrastructure

Shanxi's transportation relies heavily on railways. The railway network connects the province to all the major cities of the country and channels the coal supply to the main export ports. The province has completed seven double-track electric railways extending to coastal ports such as Qinghuandao, Qingdao, Yantai and Lianyun-

Table 7.4.1 Major economic indicators, Shanxi Province

Item	2000	2001
Population (millions)	32.478	32.716
Gross domestic product (billion RMB)	164.381	177.5
GDP per capita (thousand RMB)	5.137	5.444
Disposable income per capita (thousand RMB)		
Urban residents	4.725	1.906
Rural residents	5.391	1.956
Savings (billion RMB)*	262.71	309.07
Investment in fixed assets (billion RMB)	54.816	70.8
Value-added of primary products industry (billion RMB)	17.986	17.15
Value-added of secondary industry (billion RMB)	82.759	91.22
Value-added of tertiary industry (billion RMB)	63.636	69.09
Total retail sales of consumer goods (billion RMB)	62.9	68.0

Source: China Statistical Yearbook 2001 and State Statistical Bureau

*Both institutional and private savings

gang. The province has a good heavy industry base. Highways connect all the counties in the province. Civil aviation services offer direct flights to more than 28 major domestic cities including Beijing, Xian, Chengdu, Chongqing and overseas destinations such as Hong Kong, Singapore, Russia and Japan.

Foreign trade

In 2000, the import and export value of Shanxi Province came to US$1.764 billion, an increase of 37 per cent on 1999.

The total export value was US$1.237 billion, a 47 per cent increase over US$839 million in the previous year. This is equivalent to 6.24 per cent of the total GDP of the province and the province's share of the national total export value was 0.5 per cent (see Table 7.4.2).

The province exported US$691 million worth of primary products, which accounted for 55.86 per cent of its total export value. The export of manufactured products was 44.14 per cent of the total export amount (US$546 million).

Total import value was US$528 million, an increase of 17.75 per cent over 1999. The province imported

US$410 million worth of manufactured products, amounting to 77.7 per cent of the total import, while the imports of primary products accounted for a smaller share in the total import of US$118 million (see Table 7.4.3).

Utilization of foreign capital

Foreign direct investment in 2000 increased by 11.64 per cent over the previous year in terms of contracted FDIs. However, the FDI in wholly foreign-owned enterprises dropped sharply by a little over 90 per cent compared with 1999 (see Table 7.4.4).

Foreign direct investment came mainly from 39 countries and regions. The key sources of FDI are listed in Table 7.4.5.

Among FDI projects approved in 2000, 64 were production-related and 7 non-production. 57 projects were involved in the manufacturing industry, for example textiles, chemicals, pharmaceuticals, machinery, special equipment manufacturing, electronics and telecommunications equipment.

Table 7.4.2 Top five export markets, Shanxi Province

Country/region	Export value (US$ million)	% of export total
1995		
Hong Kong	220.11	18.22
Japan	181.80	15.00
Republic of Korea	179.20	14.83
USA	91.59	7.58
Germany	68.05	5.63
Total	740.75	61.26
2000		
Republic of Korea	207.35	16.76
Japan	189.63	15.33
USA	162.59	13.14
Netherlands	56.63	4.56
India	53.02	4.29
Total	669.22	54.08

Table 7.4.3 Top five import origins: 1995 and 2000, Shanxi Province

Country/Region	Import value (US$ million)	% of total imports
1995		
France	35.39	15.96
Hong Kong	33.72	15.20
Australia	29.48	13.29
USA	17.95	8.09
Germany	12.89	5.81
Total	129.43	58.35
2000		
USA	127.36	24.14
Germany	106.99	20.28
Australia	81.37	15.42
Republic of Korea	62.67	11.88
Belgium	23.36	4.43
Total	401.75	76.15

Table 7.4.4 Foreign direct investment in 1995 and 2000, Shanxi Province

Mode	Number	Approved contracts		Actual utilization	
		Total value (US$ million) year's total value	% change over previous year	Total value (US$ million) year's total value	% change over previous year
1995					
Direct foreign investment:	178	228.41	−6.35		99.58
Equity joint ventures	138	169.31			
Contractual joint ventures	14	27.04			
Solely foreign-owned enterprises	26	32.06			
2000					
Direct foreign investment:	71	261.74	11.64	224.720	−42.57
Equity joint ventures	48	150.28	146.64	23.75	−24.70
Contractual joint ventures	12	104.14	10.83	170.47	−32.64
Solely foreign-owned enterprises	11	7.32	−90.80	30.50	−71.41

Table 7.4.5 Main sources of FDI, Shanxi Province

Source	No. of projects	Contract value (US$ million)
Hong Kong	21	125.89
USA	17	84.02
Taiwan Province	10	17.00
Germany	5	0.78
British Virgin Islands	4	−11.95
Republic of Korea	3	0.66
Australia	2	6.72
Malaysia	1	7.17
India	1	4.82
France	1	2.58
Thailand	1	1.50
Switzerland	1	0.86
Hungary	1	0.70

Inner Mongolia Autonomous Region

The region is a long and narrow strip of land running from the north-east to the south-west along China's northern frontier and bordering on Mongolia and Russia in the north. It is comprised largely of a plateau some 1,000 metres above sea level. The total area is 1,183,000 square kilometres and the population is 22.32 million. The regional capital is Hohhot. Major economic indicators are shown in Table 7.5.1.

Resources

The region abounds in mineral reserves. It boasts 77 per cent of the world's deposits of rare earth and its coal deposits amount to 210 billion tons, a quarter of China's total. Its reserves of gold, mica, asbestos, chromium, iron, copper, zinc, lead and salt are among the largest in the country while its natural forests account for as much as a-sixth of China's timber reserves. There are also vast grasslands, making it China's leading livestock-breeding centre.

Infrastructure

The region's trunk railway lines are the Beijing-Hohhot, Beijing-Baotou, Hohhot-Hailar and Jining-Eren railways. Manzhouli and Erenhot stations, which connect the Trans-Siberian Railway in Russia and Mongolia, serve as important gateways between China and Europe. The highway network in the region is fairly well developed and the Hohhot-Baotou Expressway is the major highway in Inner Mongolia. Hohhot airport has around 50 air routes to major cities in China, Mongolia and

Table 7.5.1 Major economic indicators, Inner Mongolia Autonomous Region

Item	2000	2001
Population (millions)	23.724	23.774
Gross domestic product (billion RMB)	141.10	154.5
GDP per capita (thousand RMB)	5.872	na
Disposable income per capita (thousand RMB)		
Urban residents	5.129	1.908
Rural residents	5.536	1.950
Savings (billion RMB)*	126.78	149.88
Investment in fixed assets (billion RMB)	42.364	49.6
Value-added of primary industry (billion RMB)	35.08	36.1
Value-added of secondary industry (billion RMB)	55.628	62.4
Value-added of tertiary industry (billion RMB)	49.393	55.973
Total retail sales of consumer goods (billion RMB)	48.4	53.7

Source: China Statistical Yearbook 2001 and State Statistical Bureau

*Both institutional and private savings

Russia. Inner Mongolia has invested heavily to improve the telecommunications system and there is enough energy available to support the developing economy.

Foreign trade

The total value of import and export of Inner Mongolia Autonomous Region in 2000 was US$2.622 billion, up by 102.63 per cent on 1999. The total export value was US$970 million, up 81.31 per cent on 1999, equivalent to 5.73 per cent of the regional GDP and 0.39 per cent of the country's total export value.

The proportion of raw materials exported at a value of US$359 million amounted to 37 per cent of the region's total export value. The export of manufactured products accounted for the remaining 63 per cent and came to a value of US$611 million. The key export destinations were Japan, the Republic of Korea, Malaysia, Hong Kong, the USA., Mongolia, Italy and Thailand. These countries and regions imported US$740 million worth of commodities, accounting for 76.29 per cent of total exports.

The total import value was US$1.652 billion, up by 117.65 per cent over 1999. Import of raw materials amounted to US$619 million and the import of manufactured products amounted to US$1.033 billion, accounting for 37 per cent and 63 per cent respectively of the total value of import. The imports were mainly

from Russia, Mongolia, Germany, Australia, Italy, the USA, Japan and the Republic of Korea. The import value from these countries was US$1.601 billion, accounting for 96.91 per cent of the total import value.

Border trade, which is a popular mode of trade for provinces along the borders of China, also experienced substantial increases in 2000. The total value of border trade reached US$ 1.445 billion, up 117.62 per cent on 1999. The major exports included fruits, vegetables, miscellaneous articles for daily use and heavy duty trucks, while imports included mainly logs, aluminum products, PVC and copper concentrate powder.

Use of foreign capital

Foreign direct investment increased by 33 per cent in 2000 in terms of total FDI contract value, mainly in equity and contractual joint ventures. The contract value of wholly foreign-owned enterprises was reduced by 49 per cent (see Table 7.5.2).

Among the 95 FDI projects approved in 2000, 80 projects were in production and 15 in the service sectors. They were mainly in ten sectors, such as the manufacturing industry, agriculture, forestry, animal husbandry and social services.

The sources of FDI for Inner Mongolia came from 26 countries and regions. The leading investing countries and regions are listed in Table 7.5.3.

Table 7.5.2   Foreign direct investment in 1995 and 2000, Inner Mongolia Autonomous Region

Mode		Approved contracts			Actual utilization	
	Number	Total value (US$ million) of previous year	% over total value		Total value (US$ million) of previous year	% over total value
1995						
Direct foreign investment:	162	148.27	14.00		52.00	29.77
Equity joint ventures	130	120.19			41.60	
Contractual joint ventures	12	2.37			1.56	
Solely foreign-owned enterprises	20	25.71			8.84	
2000						
Direct foreign investment:	95	257.98	33		112.36	19
Equity joint ventures	52	107.72	60		64.07	
Contractual joint ventures	19	121.79	73		19.87	
Solely foreign-owned enterprises	24	2,847	−49		28.42	

Table 7.5.3   Key sources of investment, Inner Mongolia Autonomous Region

Source	No. of projects	Contract value (US$ million)
Hong Kong	22	29.47
Philippines	2	9.58
Singapore	3	3.86
Republic of Korea	9	2.52
South Africa	1	5.12
Germany	2	1.37
Italy	1	1.25
UK	2	6.70
British Virgin Islands	1	28.79
USA	24	132.27
Canada	5	4.38
Australia	7	28.86
Total	79	254.17

Investment priority and opportunities

The region is seizing the opportunity of the country's strategic shift of the development spearhead to the north-west and has begun a series of massive projects. Four central industries – metallurgy, energy, machinery and electronics and processing – and three key sectors – chemicals, building materials and forestry – will be intensively developed.

Areas ripe for cooperation with foreign companies include textiles, leather, fur and grassland development, amongst others.

Liaoning Province

Liaoning Province is situated in the southern part of north-east China, bordered by the Yellow Sea and the Bohai Sea in the south and facing Korea across the Yalu River. With a coastline extending 2,178 kilometres, some 62 per cent of its area consists of mountains and 30 per cent of plains. It has a total area of 145,740 square kilometres and a population of 41.94 million. The provincial capital is Shenyang. Major economic indicators are shown in Table 7.6.1.

Resources

The province is endowed with rich mineral resources. Its iron ore reserves rank first in the country, amounting to some 22 per cent of the nation's total. In addition, the province has many varieties of non-ferrous metals consisting mainly of manganese, copper, lead, zinc and magnesium. The province also boasts nearly 30 kinds of non-metallic ores, including coal, oil shale and talcum. The province abounds in such valuable medicinal items as ginseng and pilose antler. The Liaohe Oilfield is one of the largest oilfields in China, and there are rich salt resources along the province's coastline. The province's long coastline offers favourable conditions for fishery development. Luda is a famous fishery production base in China, supplying seafood for both the domestic and overseas markets.

Infrastructure

Liaoning has one of the densest railway networks in China. There are 39 trunk railway lines running through it. There are two international airports and four provincial airports. The province has five trading ports –

Table 7.6.1   Major economic indicators, Liaoning Province

Item	2000	2001
Population (millions)		41.94
Gross domestic product (billion RMB)	466.906	503.3
GDP per capita (thousand RMB)	11.104	12.070
Disposable income per capita (thousand RMB)		
Urban residents	5.358	2.355
Rural residents	5.797	2.558
Savings (billion RMB)*	592.4	659.14
Investment in fixed assets (billion RMB)	126.768	141.8
Value-added of primary industry (billion RMB)	50.344	54.5
Value-added of secondary industry (billion RMB)	234.44	244.4
Value-added of tertiary industry (billion RMB)	182.122	204.39
Total retail sales of consumer goods (billion RMB)	184.8	203.5

Source: China Statistical Yearbook 2001 and State Statistical Bureau

*Both institutional and private savings

Dalian, Yingkou, Huludao, Dandong and Jinzhou. Dalian is the fourth largest container port in terms of cargo handling tonnage in China. A new port in Panjin is now in operation, located at the Bohai Rim and handling commodities and oil products from the Liaohe Oilfield. Inland water transport is seasonal along the Liaohe and Yalujiang rivers. Liaoning has established one of the most developed electricity-supply networks within the country, which comprise the major part of the electricity-supply network in north-east China. The province has well-developed highways and telecommunications systems.

Foreign trade

The year 2000 saw a remarkable increase of 38.53 per cent in Liaoning's total import and export value, to US$19.022 billion, compared with the total value in 1999 of US$13.731 billion. Total export value was US$10.848 billion, up by 32.39 per cent against US$8.2 billion in 1999. This is equal to 19.2 per cent of the provincial GDP in that year, which was RMB466.83 billion (US$56.39 billion), ranking Liaoning seventh in the country in 2000.

The province exported US$3 billion worth of primary products, 27.6 per cent of the total export value. Export of manufactured products constituted the majority of these, amounting to US$7.85 billion and representing 72.4 per cent of the total value of export.

Table 7.6.2 Top five export markets: 1995 and 2000

Country/region	Export value (US$ million)	% of export total
1995		
Japan	3,360.99	40.70
USA	932.22	11.29
Hong Kong	869.58	10.53
Republic of Korea	719.99	8.72
Singapore	356.05	4.31
Total	6,238.83	75.55
2000		
Japan	444.426	40.97
USA	150.980	13.92
Republic of Korea	100.526	9.27
Netherlands	425.13	3.92
Singapore	385.40	3.55
Total	1,606.462	71.63

Although the province exported to 170 countries and regions, the top five export destinations (see Table 7.6.2) accounted for over 70 per cent of its total export value.

The growth of the province's import rate in 2000 surpassed that of its export. The total value of import registered a phenomenal growth of 47.79 per cent, totalling US$8.174 billion (US$5.531 billion in 1999). Import of primary products came to US$2.232 billion, accounting for 27.3 per cent of the total import value, while 72.7 per cent were manufactured products, the total value of these coming to US$5.942 billion. Imports originated from 110 countries and regions with 68 per cent of these coming from the top five markets (see Table 7.6.3).

Table 7.6.3 Top five import markets, Liaoning Province, 1995 and 2000

Country/region	Import value (US$ million)	% of import total
1995		
Japan	1,069.85	39.10
Republic of Korea	314.02	11.48
Hong Kong	310.12	11.34
USA	188.83	6.90
Singapore	131.09	4.79
Total	2,013.91	73.61
2000		
Japan	2,801.89	34.28
Republic of Korea	1,475.89	18.06
USA	530.53	6.49
Saudi Arabia	400.63	4.90
Iraq	378.50	4.63
Total	5,587.44	68.36

Utilization of foreign capital

In 2000, the province approved 867 FDI projects, involving a total contract value of US$5.17 billion, an increase of 16.5 per cent on the previous year (see Table 7.6.4). The contract value for contractual joint ventures more than doubled since 1999.

This FDI came from 19 countries and regions. Hong Kong and Macao topped all other sources of investment by investing US$1.354 billion in 287 projects. The second largest investor was the USA, investing nearly US$1 billion in 293 projects (see Table 7.6.5).

Table 7.6.4 Foreign direct investment, Liaoning Province, 1995 and 2000

Mode	Number	Approved contracts		Actual utilization	
		Total value (US$ million) year's total value	% change over previous year	Total value (US$ million) year's total value	% change over previous year
1995					
Direct foreign investment:	2,406	3,970.00	−11.55	1,430.00	0.03
Equity joint ventures	1,700	2,410.00		858.00	
Contractual joint ventures	249	430.00		185.00	
Solely foreign-owned enterprises	457	1,130.00		387.00	51
2000					
Direct foreign investment:	867	5,170	16.5	2,552	23.64
Equity joint ventures	967	2,390	4.0	1,429	11.46
Contractual joint ventures	160	1,370	114.5	229	6.02
Solely foreign-owned enterprises	740	1,370	−4.5	761	57.23

The FDIs were mainly concentrated in secondary and tertiary industries, which attracted US$2.782 billion (53.81 per cent of the total FDI for that year) and US$2.14 billion (41.39 per cent) respectively. 4.80 per cent of the FDI(US$248 million) went to primary industry.

By the end of 2000, 8310 FDI projects had started operation. The total production of these projects was valued at RMB112.8 billion, representing 25.3 per cent of the provincial GDP and a 27.78 per cent increase on 1999. The foreign exchange income generated from the exports by these operations reached US$6.24 billion in 2000, or 57.5 per cent of the total provincial export value and an increase of 43.09 per cent over 1999. Taxes from FDI companies amounted to RMB9.64 billion, an increase of 67.07 per cent on 1999 and 16.2 per cent of the total provincial tax revenue in 2000.

Table 7.6.5 Key sources of FDI in 2000

Source	No. of projects	Contract value (US$ million)
Hong Kong and Macao	287	1,354
USA	293	939
Japan	279	636
Republic of Korea	567	577
Taiwan Province	145	297
Canada	51	90
Australia	33	82
Singapore	33	77
Thailand	10	38
Netherlands	5	32
Germany	17	25

7.7

Jilin Province

The province is situated in the central part of north-east China, bordered by Russia in the north-east and the People's Democratic Republic of Korea across the Tumen and Yalu rivers in the south-east. Mountains, hills and flat land range from east to west. The total area of the province is 187,400 square kilometres with a population of 27 million. The provincial capital is Changchun. Major economic indicators are shown in Table 7.7.1.

Resources

The province has more than 70 kinds of verified mineral resources, mainly iron, copper, molybdenum, nickel and gold, as well as coal, oil shale and petroleum. Jilin is a grain-producing centre where fertile soil and plentiful rainfall provide favourable conditions for growing grain and beans. 38 per cent of the total land surface is

covered by forest and the Changbai Mountains are one of the country's major forest areas, teeming with ginseng, pilose antler, tussah silk and medicinal herbs. Changbai Mountain Forest Zone is one of the most important timber production bases in China and its annual output is the highest in the country, while the Jilin Oilfield is one of China's major oilfields.

Infrastructure

The province has a fairly well-developed transport and communications network. Jilin has four airports – in Changchun, Jilin, Yanji and Liuhe – offering links to domestic and international air routes. There are more than 120 rivers in the province, including Songhua, Liaohe and the Yalu river systems. Inland water transport is available between April and November along the

Table 7.7.1 Major economic indicators, Jilin Province

Item	2000	2001
Population (millions)		26.908
Gross domestic product (billion RMB)	182.119	203.2
GDP per capita (thousand RMB)	6.847	7.640
Disposable income per capita (thousand RMB)		
Urban residents	4.811	5.340
Rural residents	2.022	2.182
Savings (billion RMB)*	223.23	248.42
Investment in fixed assets (billion RMB)	60.351	68.0
Value-added of primary industry (billion RMB)	39.873	40.96
Value-added of secondary industry (billion RMB)	80.028	88.084
Value-added of tertiary industry (billion RMB)	62.218	74.204
Total retail sales of consumer goods (billion RMB)	81.11	90.7

*Both institutional and private savings
Source: China Statistical Yearbook 2001 and State Statistical Bureau.

Songhuajiang River. The Jingha railway line (Beijing to Harbin) is the most important trunk line in the province and the railway system handles more than two thirds of the province's cargo transport. The CIS and Europe are also accessible by railway via Harbin and Manzhoul. Jilin also has a number of scientific research institutions, colleges and universities.

Foreign trade

Jilin province achieved an increase of 15.99 per cent in its import and export value in 2000, which grew from US$2.21698 billion in 1999 to US$2.5714 billion.

Total export value increased from US$1.01956 billion in 1999 to US$1.25783 billion in 2000, up by 23.4 per cent. Export value comprised 5.7 per cent of the province's GDP (RMB182 billion) and accounted for 0.5 per cent of the entire country's total export value in 2000.

The province exported US$597.99 million worth of primary products in 2000 and export of manufactured products amounted to US$659.86 million. Exports were destined for 131 countries and regions and the top five export markets accounted for nearly 70 per cent of all exports (see Table 7.7.2).

Import value totalled US$1.31357 billion, up by 9.7 per cent over US$1.19741 billion in 1999.

Table 7.7.2 Top five export markets, Jilin Province, 1995 and 2000

Country/region	Export value (US$ million)	% of export total
1995		
Japan	371.11	26.14
Hong Kong	223.64	15.76
Republic of Korea	189.51	13.35
Democratic People's Republic of Korea	98.95	6.97
Total	967.95	68.19
2000		
Republic of Korea	362.75	28.8
Japan	256.01	20.4
Democratic People's Republic of Korea	98.20	7.8
USA	88.41	7.0
Malaysia	65.02	5.2
Total	870.39	69.2

Import of primary products and manufactured products amounted to US$259.79 million and US$1.05372 billion respectively, making up 19.8 per cent and 80.2 per cent of total import value.

Imports originated from 66 countries and regions. The massive production of automotive products in the province resulted in Germany being the biggest import market, taking 44.7 per cent of the province's imports (see Table 7.7.3).

Table 7.7.3 Top five import markets, Jilin Province, 1995 and 2000

Country/region	Import value (US$ million)	% of import total
1995		
Germany	533.56	35.34
Republic of Korea	153.92	10.19
USA	146.97	9.37
Japan	110.87	7.34
Russia	89.88	5.95
Total	1,035.2	68.19
2000		
Germany	587.66	44.7
Japan	149.58	11.4
USA	146.58	11.2
Republic of Korea	65.88	5.0
Russia	58.59	4.5
Total	1,008.29	76.8

Utilization of foreign direct investment

Foreign direct investment in the province increased by 32.3 per cent in terms of total contract value in 2000. 363 FDI projects were approved in that year (see Table 7.7.4).

Foreign direct investment came from 53 countries and regions. South Korea ranked first in terms of the total number of projects while Hong Kong invested the most (see Table 7.6.5).

By the end of 2000, 3,782 foreign-funded enterprises had been approved in Jilin province. Among these enterprises, 2966 were in production. To classify by sector, 137 were in agriculture, forestry, animal husbandry and fisheries, 30 in the mining industry, 2,589 in the manufacturing industry, 15 in power, gas and water producing and supplying, 195 in the construction industry, 153 in wholesale, retail and food services and 396 in social services. In 2000, the total sales revenue from foreign-invested enterprises came to RMB31.71 billion.

Table 7.7.4   Utilization of foreign capital, Jilin Province, 1995 and 2000

Mode	Number	Approved contracts		Actual utilization	
		Total value (US$ million) year's total value	*% change over previous year*	*Total value (US$ million) year's total value*	*% change over previous year*
1995					
Direct foreign investment:	667	857.34	3.8	398.76	25.3
Equity joint ventures	375	629.39		354.59	
Contractual joint ventures	53	59.53		17.76	
Solely foreign-owned enterprises	239	168.42		26.41	
2000					
Direct foreign investment:	363	596.15	32.3	337.01	11.89
Equity joint ventures	121	192.38	−24.3	224.31	10.69
Contractual joint ventures	24	143.08	150.6	44.37	196.80
Solely foreign-owned enterprises	218	260.69	87.0	68.33	−18.70

Table 7.6.5   Key sources of FDI, Jilin Province, 2000

Source	No. of projects	Contract value (million US$)
Republic of Korea	194	83.48
Hong Kong	56	181.94
Japan	24	20.46
USA	30	95.61
Taiwan Province	16	40.64
Singapore	6	22.16

7.8

Heilongjiang Province

Heilongjiang is in the northernmost part of China, bordered by Russia to the north and east. Some 60 per cent of its area consists of mountains and 30 per cent of plains. The topography of the province is characterized by dense forests and concentrated areas of plain. The total area is 469,000 square kilometres with a population of 38.110 million. The provincial capital is Harbin. Major economic indicators are shown in Table 7.8.1.

Resources

Richly endowed with mineral resources, the province ranks high in reserves of copper, lead, zinc, gold and silver. Other significant mineral and metal deposits include aluminium, tungsten, molybdenum, crude oil, coal, wood, soda, quartz, marble and mica. The province's deposits of gold and graphite are among the largest in China. It has the richest oil reserves in China, and Daqing Oilfield is the earliest and largest oil field in China supplying a third of the country's crude oil. The province's coal reserves amount to around 10 billion tons. It leads the country in timber reserves with a total of 1.8 billion cubic metres. It produces 90 per cent of the national annual production of flax. It is a major centre for the cultivation of sugar beet. Major crops in the province are soya beans, maize, wheat, sorghum, sugar beet and cured tobacco. Its milk production is the highest in China.

Infrastructure

The province has 22 state-level ports, the second highest number in China after Guangdong. The port of Harbin is the province's largest inland transport centre on the

Table 7.8.1   Major economic indicators, Heilongjiang Province

Item	2000	2001
Population (millions)	36.89	38.110
Gross domestic product (billion RMB)	325.3	356.1
GDP (thousand RMB)	8.577	9.349
Disposable income per capita (thousand RMB)		
Urban residents	4.915	3.825
Rural residents	5.426	4.192
Savings (billion RMB)*	333.16	374.21
Investment in fixed assets (billion RMB)	83.264	99.4
Value-added of primary industry (billion RMB)	35.7	40.89
Value-added of secondary industry (billion RMB)	186.855	199.87
Value-added of tertiary industry (billion RMB)	102.745	115.34
Total retail sales of consumer goods (billion RMB)	109.4	119.9

Source: China Statistical Yearbook 2001 and State Statistical Bureau.
*Both institutional and private savings

Songhua River. The province has a well-developed transport network centred around Harbin There are frequent train services to the ports of Dalian in Liaoning and Vladivostok in Russia. The key rail link is the Jingha (Beijing-Harbin) railway line. Harbin Taipin Airport has regular flights to other key domestic destinations as well as places like Hong Kong and Russia. Other major airports are located at Jiamusi, Mudanjiang, Heihe, and Qiqihar.

Foreign trade

In 2000, a total of US$2.986 billion in goods, an increase of 36.28 per cent compared with US$2.19 billion in 1999, were exported from and imported into Heilongjiang Province.

Total export was US$ 1.451 billion, up by 52.70 per cent over US$ 950 million in 1999. It equates to 3.70 per cent of the provincial GDP, which was RMB325.5 billion (US$39.216 billion) and 0.58 per cent of the total export value of the whole country. Primary products constituted 30.32 per cent of total export while manufactured products made up 69.68 per cent.

Exports were destined for 150 countries and regions and the top five markets (see Table 7.8.2) took over 70 per cent of exports. Russia was the province's leading trading partner, but its share in the market declined from 40.79 per cent in 1995 to 31.94 per cent in 2000.

Import value totalled US$1.535 billion, up by 23.7 per cent over US$1.24 billion in 1999. Import of primary products and manufactured products amounted to US$619 million and US$915 million, constituting 40.33 per cent and 59.67 per cent of total import value.

Imports originated from 55 countries and regions. Nearly 60 per cent of the province's total imports were from Russia and the top five import markets (see Table 7.8.3) accounted for just over 80 per cent of total imports.

Utilization of foreign capital

Foreign direct investment in the province experienced negative growth in 2000. 260 FDI projects were approved, with the total FDI contract value of US$812.83 million, less than in 1995 (see Table 7.8.4).

Table 7.8.2 Top five export markets, Heilongjiang Province, 1995 and 2000

Country/region	Export value (US$ million)	% of export total
1995		
Russia	855.11	40.79
Hong Kong	279.68	13.34
Republic of Korea	234.30	11.17
Japan	227.05	10.83
USA	82.72	3.94
Total	1,678.86	80.07
2000		
Russia	463.39	31.94
Japan	213.62	14.72
Republic of Korea	202.63	13.96
Hong Kong	93.60	6.45
USA	67.48	4.65
Total	1,040.72	71.72

Table 7.8.3 Top five import markets, Heilongjiang Province, 2000

Country/region	Import value (US$ million)	% of import total
Russia	908.38	59.17
Republic of Korea	127.07	8.27
USA	77.91	5.07
Japan	68.09	4.43
Hong Kong	53.22	3.47
Total	1,234.67	80.41

Of the 260 FDI projects, 187 projects were production-oriented while 73 were in non-production activities. Among these, 11 projects were in agriculture, forestry, animal husbandry, fishery and water conservation and the FDI contract value involved was US$10.61 million; A total of 187 projects were in the manufacturing industry with a contract value of US$149.86 million. Key sources of foreign direct investment are shown in Table 7.8.5.

Table 7.8.4 Utilization of foreign capital, Heilongjiang Province, 1995 and 2000

Mode	Number	Approved contracts		Actual utilization	
		Total value (US$ million) year's total value	*% change over previous year*	*Total value (US$ million) year's total value*	*% change over previous year*
1995					
Direct foreign investment:	844	987.99	37.2	448.68	32.1
Equity joint ventures	513	557.76		327.39	
Contractual joint ventures	49	208.06		31.76	
Solely foreign-owned enterprises	282	221.17		89.53	
2000					
Direct foreign investment:	260	812.83	−12.80	830.85	1.50
Equity joint ventures	139	138.23	−64.60	208.32	−40.70
Contractual joint ventures	16	64.12	−32.10	19.73	−49.20
Solely foreign-owned enterprises	105	100.48	−23.50	92.80	−17.80

Table 7.8.5 Key sources of foreign direct investment, Heilongjiang Province

Source	*No. of projects*	*Contract value (million US$)*
Hong Kong	53	165.77
Republic of Korea	73	24.94
USA	36	22.75
Japan	23	18.29
Taiwan Province	24	16.68

Jiangsu Province

Jiangsu Province borders on the Yellow Sea in the east and the lower reaches of the Yangtze River and Huaihe River in eastern China. Its terrain is the lowest in China with part of it lying 50 metres below the sea level. Plains cover 68 per cent of the province, hills 15 per cent and rivers and lakes 7 per cent. Jiangsu has a total area of 102,600 square kilometres and a population of 73.54 million, making it the most densely populated province in China. Jiangsu was the second strongest economy in China after Guangdong in terms of GDP. The main economic centres are Nanjing (the capital city of Jiangsu), the coastal port cities of Lianyungang, Nantong and Xuzhou, as well as the fast-growing industrial belt of Suzhou-Wuxi-Changzhou in the south. Major economic indicators are shown in Table 7.9.1.

Resources

Proven mineral resources in Jiangsu include manganese, copper, iron, phosphorus, coal, petroleum, limestone, pottery clay, serpentine, gypsum and marble. Rice and wheat are the main food crops, while cotton, rapeseed and peanuts are important cash crops. Its cotton accounts for a quarter of China's total output. With a coastline of over 1,000 kilometres and wide expanses of fresh water, the province is highly suitable for the development of fisheries and aquaculture.

Infrastructure

Jiangsu enjoys the most advanced and convenient inland water transportation system in the country. The Yangtze

Table 7.9.1 Major economic indicators, Jiangsu Province

Description	2000	2001
Population (millions)	73.25	73.54
Gross domestic product (billion RMB)	858.273	951.46
GDP (thousand RMB)	11.773	12.925
Disposable income per capita (thousand RMB)	6.800	3.594
Urban residents		
Rural residents	7.375	3.785
Savings (billion RMB)*	839.89	970.07
Investment in fixed assets (billion RMB)	256.997	330.3
Value-added of primary industry (billion RMB)	103.117	108.84
Value-added of secondary industry (billion RMB)	443.589	491.37
Value-added of tertiary industry (billion RMB)	311.567	351.25
Total retail sales of consumer goods (billion RMB)	260.41	286.90

Source: China Statistical Yearbook 2001 and State Statistical Bureau

*Both institutional and private savings

River flows through the province from the west to the east and the Grand Canal links Jiangsu with other provinces in the north and south. The ports of Lianyungang, Nantong, Zhangjiagang, Nanjing, Zhenjiang, Yangzhou and Jiangyin constitue a cluster of ports along the lower reach of the Yangtze River, all of which are open to foreign vessels. There are direct shipping routes linking the province to major international ports in Hong Kong, Japan, Southeast Asia, Australia and Europe. The province has a well-developed railway transportation network and several major railway lines pass through the province. The Longhai Line is an important part of the New Asia-Europe Continent Bridge, linking Lianyungang with the Siberia Railways to Europe. Highway development has been rapid and a web of highways networks all parts of the province. Currently, there are eight airports (located in Nanjing, Suzhou, Changzhou, Xuzhou, Wuxi, Nantong, Lianyungang and Yancheng) in Jiangsu offering flights to other parts of the country. The Nanjing Lukou International Airport is the main airport offering flights to Hong Kong, Japan, South Korea, the US and some European countries.

Foreign trade

In 2000, the flow of import and export in Jiangsu province hit a record high of US$45.638 billion, a remarkable increase of 46 per cent over the 1999 total of US$31.258 billion.

Total export value increased by 40.8 per cent, from US$18.307 billion in 1999 to US$25.769 billion in 2000. Exports played an important role in the provincial economy: total export value was equivalent to 24.8 per cent of Jiangsu's GDP. Jiangsu is the second largest exporting province in China and its share in the country's total export in 2000 was 10.34 per cent.

The province's key export market was Japan. About a quarter of the province's exports were destined for Japan in 2000. The second largest export destination was the USA, who took nearly 20 per cent of the province's exports. Exports to Japan and the USA combined took up about 45 per cent of Jiangsu's total export. Hong Kong's role as a stepping stone for the province's export declined, with its share in the province's total export shrinking from 23.46 per cent in 1995 to 7.9 per cent. In terms of value, exports to Hong Kong also dropped between 1995 to 2000 (see Table 7.9.2 below).

In 2000, the province imported US$19.870 billion worth of goods, an increase of 53.41 per cent over

Table 7.9.2 Top five export markets, Jiangsu Province, 1995 and 2000

Country/region	Export value (US$ million)	% of export total
1995		
Japan	3,097.61	26.27
Hong Kong	2,766.88	23.46
USA	1,755.35	14.89
EU	1,470.58	12.47
ASEAN	623.47	5.29
Total	9,713.89	82.38
2000		
Japan	6,361.07	24.69
USA	5,009.53	19.44
Hong Kong	2,034.63	7.90
Republic of Korea	1,058.88	4.11
Netherlands	1,058.63	4.11
Total	15,522.74	60.25

US$12.952 billion in 1999. Only 12.25 per cent of this (US$2.43306 billion) was spent on primary products, while 87.75 per cent, or US$17.43645 billion, went on manufactured goods.

Japan was again the largest single source of import. In 2000, imports to the province from Japan accounted for 25.4 per cent of the total. Over 60 per cent of imports came from the top five markets (see Table 7.9.3)

Table 7.9.3 Top five import markets, Jiangsu Province, 1995 and 2000

Country/region	Import value (US$ million)	% of import total
1995		
Japan	1,401.24	28.01
Hong Kong	932.14	18.64
EU	760.86	15.21
USA	613.02	12.26
Republic of Korea	387.79	7.75
Total	4,095.05	81.87
2000		
Japan	5,047.83	25.40
Taiwan Province	2,654.39	13.36
Republic of Korea	2,341.90	11.79
USA	1,516.58	7.63
Sweden	1,052.35	5.30
Total	12,613.05	63.48

Table 7.9.4 Utilization of foreign capital, Jiangsu Province, 1995 and 2000

Mode	Number	Approved contracts		Actual utilization	
		Total value (US$ million) year's total value	*% change over previous year*	*Total value (US$ million) year's total value*	*% change over previous year*
1995					
Direct foreign investment:	4,086	12,411.29	55.08	4844.57	15.02
Equity joint ventures	2,907	6,115.10		3,191.18	
Contractual joint ventures	272	713.30		363.14	
Solely foreign-owned enterprises	907	5,582.89		1,290.25	
2000					
Direct foreign investment:	2,645	10,613.01	52.3	6,264.69	0.3
Equity joint ventures	1,115	3,437.34		2,268.21	
Contractual joint ventures	117	569.66		343.46	
Solely foreign-owned enterprises	1,413	6,605.71		3,810.14	

Utilization of foreign capital

As one of the most dynamic local economies in China, Jiangsu province has maintained its attraction to foreign investors. In 2000, the province approved 2,645 FDI projects with a total contract value of US$10.6 billion, an increase of 52.3 per cent on 1999 (see Table 7.9.4).

Among the FDI projects approved in 2000, 2,329 were production-oriented while 316 were for service-oriented projects. Distribution of the FDI projects by sector is shown in Table 7.9.5.

Hong Kong and Taiwan were the key sources of FDI in the province in 2000. Hong Kong was first both in terms of the number of projects and total contract value. A list of FDI origins is provided in Table 7.9.6.

By the end of 2000, there were over 18,000 foreign-invested enterprises in Jiangsu province, with a total investment of over US$75 billion.

Table 7.9.5 Distribution of FDI project by sector, Jiangsu Province

Sector	Number of projects
Garment	316
Electronics and telecommunications	279
Textile	163
Metallic products	163
Chemical raw materials & chemical products	154
Electronic machinery & equipment	133
General machinery	118
Special-purpose equipment	112
Plastic products	103
Non-metallic mineral products	96
Transportation equipment	96
Cultural, education & sports products	88
Food processing	85
Property development	56
Computer application	50
Other	633

Table 7.9.6 Key sources of FDI, Jiangsu Province

Source	Number of projects	Contract value (US$ million)
Hong Kong	589	2,192
Taiwan	588	1,014
USA	343	910
Japan	259	800
Republic of Korea	151	237
Virgin Islands	144	1,422
Singapore	81	378
Germany	49	1,346
Cayman Islands	24	420
Samoa	30	252
UK	37	238
Italy	17	228

Shanghai

Shanghai, China's largest city, is situated on the estuary of the Yangtze River in the East China Sea and bordered by Jiangsu and Zhejiang provinces. It is one of the four municipalities that are under the direct jurisdiction of the central government. It has a total area of 6,341 square kilometres and a population of 13.27 million. Major economic indicators are shown in Table 7.10.1.

Resources

The Shanghai area is known for its rich water resources, with many rivers and lakes. Most of the rivers are tributaries of the Huangpu River. Originating from the Taihu Lake, this 113-kilometre-long ice-free river winds through the downtown area of the city. It is about 300 to 770 metres wide with an average width of 360 metres and is the main waterway in the Shanghai area. There is a copper mine in Zhangyan and attempts have been made to discover oil and gas reserves along the offshore areas of Shanghai, with some success. Pinhu Oilfield in the south-east of Shanghai has begun to turn out crude oil and gas, which are mainly supplied to the Shanghai area.

Infrastructure

Shanghai is a transportation hub of central China. It is a well-known international city conveniently connected by land, air and water to other parts of the country and to more than 160 countries and regions throughout the world. The port of Shanghai is the largest in China, having over 19 international container shipping lines. Shanghai is linked to the inland provinces via the Yangtze River, which reaches as far as Chongqing.

Table 7.10.1 Major economic indicators, Shanghai

Item	2000	2001
Population (millions)	13.64	13.27
Gross domestic product (billion RMB)	455.115	495.084
GDP per capita(thousand RMB)	34.547	37.3
Disposable income per capita (thousand RMB)		
Urban residents	11.718	5.566
Rural residents	12.883	5.850
Savings (billion RMB)	252.404	300.189
Investment in fixed assets (billion RMB)	186.938	198.431
Value-added of primary industry (billion RMB)	8.320	8.55
Value-added of secondary industry (billion RMB)	216.368	235.553
Value-added of tertiary industry (billion RMB)	230.427	2,509.81
Total retail sales of consumer goods (billion RMB)	172.23	186.13

Source: China Statistical Yearbook 2001 and State Statistical Bureau

Shanghai port has more than 100 berths, half of which are deep-water berths for ships of 10,000 tons and above. It runs regular routes to Western Europe, the United States, Japan, Australia, New Zealand, Singapore and Hong Kong and other less frequent routes to more than 400 ports around the globe. The railway network consists of trunk lines connecting Beijing, Hangzhou and other major cities in the country. Shanghai is China's aviation centre, having two airports – Hongqiao and Pudong – in the city. The two airports have 300 air routes and provide flight services to 88 domestic and overseas destinations. Shanghai has well-developed telecommunications services connecting it with over 100 cities in China and many cities abroad. There are more than 50 institutions of higher learning and 700 research institutes. The city has well-developed banking, insurance and commercial services, many of which are owned by foreign institutions.

Foreign trade

2000 saw a sharp increase in Shanghai's total trade, which came to US$54.710 billion, up by 47.72 per cent on 1999 (US$38.604 billion).

Total export rose by 34.97 per cent, from US$18.785 billion in 1999 to US$25.354 billion in 2000. Export was the main contributor to Shanghai's economy and its value in 2000 was equal to 46.2 per cent of Shanghai's GDP. Shanghai's export also contributed 10.2 per cent of the country's total export value, ranking it third in the nation.

Among the key export markets, Japan came first while the USA took the second place in 2000. Over 46 per cent of the city's export went to Japan and the USA in the year. The top five export markets (see Table 7.10.2) contributed 63.3 per cent of the total export earnings.

Shanghai's import increased by a rate of 48.12 per cent in 2000, registering a total value of US$29.356 billion (US$19.818 billion in 1999). Imports were largely manufactured products, totalling US$25.875 billion, or 88.14 per cent of the total import value. Import of primary products accounted for only 11.86 per cent of the city's total import, with a value of US$3.481 billion.

The level of dependence on the top five import markets was reduced from 72.17 per cent in 1995 to 60.6 per cent in 2000. However, Japan remained the city's largest supplier of imports, with the USA second.

Table 7.10.2 Top five export markets, Shanghai, 1995 and 2000

Country/region	Export value (US$ million)	% of export total
1995		
Japan	3,524.35	26.73
Hong Kong	2,326.36	17.64
USA	1,936.71	14.69
Republic of Korea	518.28	3.93
Germany	476.26	3.61
Total	8,781.96	66.6
2000		
Japan	6,081	24.0
USA	5,625	22.2
Hong Kong	2,302	9.1
Republic of Korea	1,059	4.2
Germany	948	3.8
Total	16,015	63.3

Table 7.10.3 Top five import markets, Shanghai, 1995 and 2000

Country/region	Import value (US$ million)	% of total import
1995		
Japan	2,324.18	31.28
Hong Kong	1,194.71	16.08
USA	764.20	10.29
Germany	735.80	9.90
Republic of Korea	342.99	4.62
Total	5,361.88	72.17
2000		
Japan	7,043	24.0
USA	4,011	13.7
Germany	2,659	9.1
Republic of Korea	2,062	7.1
Taiwan Province	1,944	6.7
Total	17,719	60.6

These two countries supplied 37.7 per cent of the city's imports in 2000 (see Table 7.10.3).

Utilization of foreign capital

In 2000, Shanghai approved 1814 FDI projects, involving a total contract value of nearly US$6.4 billion. The number of solely foreign-owned ventures accounted for

Table 7.10.4 Utilization of foreign capital, Shanghai, 1995 and 2000

Mode	Number	Approved contracts		Actual utilization	
		Total value (US$ million)	% increase over previous year's total value	Total value (US$ million)	% increase over previous year's total value
1995					
Direct foreign investment:	2,845	10,539.64	5.13	3,249.94	3.61
Equity joint ventures	1,373	4,636.39		1,753.87	
Contractual joint ventures	664	2,072.30		1,088.03	
Solely foreign-owned enterprises	799	3,725.98		363.44	
2000					
Direct foreign investment:	1,814	6,389.72	55.70	3,260.29	3.7
Equity joint ventures	441	1,385.58	−8.27	1,294.24	−14.7
Contractual joint ventures	226	585.75	21.03	298.91	−14.2
Solely foreign-owned enterprises	1,146	4,414.22	128.85	1,566.64	38.4

63 per cent of the projects approved in the year. The amount of capital that went into enterprises had more than doubled that of 1999. In contrast, the total investment in equity joint ventures fell by 8.27 per cent in terms of contract value (see Table 7.10.4).

Among the FDI projects approved in 2000, 944 projects were production-related while 870 projects were service orientated. Direct foreign investment came from 57 countries and regions. The ten countries and regions with the highest investment value are shown in Table 7.10.5.

By the end of 2000, over 15,930 foreign-invested enterprises were in operation. The total sales revenue of these enterprises reached RMB397.790 billion in 2000, an increase of 47.3 per cent over the previous year. Total profit by those FIEs reached RMB21.779 billion, up by 166.9 per cent, creating a total tax revenue of RMB15.893 billion, an increase of 28.1 per cent. The export revenue created by FIEs totalled US$14.261 million in 2000, up by 37.8 per cent over 1999.

Table 7.10.5 Key investment sources, Shanghai

Sources of FDI	No. of projects	Contract value (US$ million)
Cayman Islands	61	2,249
Hong Kong	419	944
Japan	237	705
USA	256	578
British Virgin Islands	152	544
Germany	47	276
Singapore	97	213
Taiwan	225	165
Netherlands	28	115
UK	32	100

7.11

Zhejiang Province

Zhejiang is a coastal province in east China, covering an area of 101,800 square kilometres, 70 per cent of which are mountainous, 23 per cent plains and 6 per cent rivers and lakes. There are over 2,000 offshore islands. Zhejiang has a population of 46.134 million and the provincial capital is Hangzhou. Major economic indicators are shown in Table 7.11.1.

Resources

Zhejiang has abundant non-metal mineral reserves, including fluorite, alunite, limestone and bentonite. Among the minerals, its fluorite and alunite reserves rank first and second respectively in China. Good soil and moderate rainfall provide favourable conditions for the growth of rice, tea, broad beans, hemp, oranges and angora. Raw silk and Longjing tea are well known at home and abroad. The Zhoushan Islands are one of the four major fishing grounds in China. Zhejiang's seaboard also has rich reserve of petroleum and natural gas.

Infrastructure

There are more than 50 ports along the coastline of Zhejing province, of which Ningbao, Wenzhou, Shenjiamen and Haimen are open to foreign ships. The port of Ningbo is the largest of the four. Zhejiang has a dense network of rivers and canals, serving as a key means of inland water transportation. The province is networked with the national and regional railway systems. New railways are planned to improve further the province's rail transport capability. Zhejiang has a good highway

Table 7.11.1 Major economic indicators, Zhejiang Province

Item	2000	2001
Population (millions)	45.950	46.134
Gross domestic product (billion RMB)	603.634	670.0
GDP (thousand RMB)	13.270	14.550
Disposable income per capita (thousand RMB)		
Urban residents	9.279	4.286
Rural residents	10.465	4.582
Savings (billion RMB)*	729.57	882.31
Investment in fixed assets (billion RMB)	234.995	276.9
Value-added of primary industry (billion RMB)	66.42	69.0
Value-added of secondary industry (billion RMB)	318.347	344
Value-added of tertiary industry (billion RMB)	218.871	257
Total retail sales of consumer goods (billion RMB)	229.88	255.55

Source: China Statistical Yearbook 2001 and State Statistical Bureau

*Both institutional and private savings

system and seven civil airports, of which Hangzhou, Ningbo and Wenzhou are international. Hangzhou airport can accommodate large jet planes such as Boeing 747s and there are direct flights to international destinations.

Foreign trade

Zhejiang province recorded a significant increase of 52.05 per cent in total trade in the year 2000, during which year import and export value grew from US$18.305 billion in 1999 to US$27.834 billion.

The province's total export value hit a high of US$19.444 billion, an increase of 51.06 per cent from US$12.871 in 1999. This was equal to 26.7 per cent of Zhejiang's GDP, which amounted to RMB603.0 billion (US$72.823 billion), and to 7.8 per cent of the total export value of the country.

Of the total export earnings, 10.06 per cent, or US$1.955 billion, came from the export of primary goods, while the remaining 89.94 per cent (US$17.488 billion), was generated from the export of manufactured goods. The USA and Japan were the province's largest export destinations and had a combined share of 35.72 per cent in the total export value. The total share of the top five export markets (see Table 7.11.2) dropped from 66.83 per cent in 1995 to less than 50 per cent, an indication that the province has a more diversified structure of trade partners than in the past.

Table 7.11.2 Top five export markets, Zhejiang Province, 1995 and 2000

Country/region	Export value (US$ million)	% of export total
1995		
Hong Kong	1,981.32	23.46
Japan	1,840.57	21.79
USA	1,115.94	13.21
Germany	384.06	4.55
Republic of Korea	322.93	3.82
Total	5,644.82	66.83
2000		
USA	3,626.03	18.65
Japan	3,319.33	17.07
Hong Kong	1,198.61	6.16
Germany	872.20	4.49
Republic of Korea	652.22	3.35
Total	9,668.39	49.72

The increase in import in 2000 was as impressive as for export. Import value totalled US$8.390 billion in 2000, up by 54.39 per cent over US$5.434 billion in 1999. Of the total import value, 24.21 per cent came from primary goods, which amounted to US$2.031 billion, and 75.79 per cent (US$6.359 billion) came from manufactured goods. Japan remained the biggest supplier of the province's import needs, accounting for a little over 20 per cent of total import. The top five import origins (see Table 7.11.3) played a significant role in the province's import, comprising 61.49 per cent of total import, although this was down on the 1995 total of 67.04 per cent.

Table 7.11.3 Top five import market, Zhejiang Province, 1995 and 2000

Country/region	Import value (US$ million)	% of import total
1995		
Japan	612.17	19.87
Hong Kong	599.24	19.45
Republic of Korea	388.42	12.61
USA	316.26	10.27
Indonesia	149.14	4.84
Total	2,065.23	67.04
2000		
Japan	1,740.13	20.74
Taiwan Province	1,016.16	12.11
USA	979.99	11.68
Republic of Korea	922.20	10.99
Germany	500.49	5.97
Total	5,158.97	61.49

Utilization of foreign capital

In 2000, Zhejiang province approved 1,642 FDI projects, with a total contract value of US$2.5 billion, a 16.8 per cent increase on 1999. The FDI in equity joint venture, however, decreased by 14.6 per cent. Solely owned foreign-owned enterprise increased by an impressive 47.1 per cent (see Table 7.11.4).

Most of these FDI projects were in the manufacturing industry. Among the 1,642 foreign-invested projects, 31 were in primary industry, 1,413 in secondary industry and 198 in tertiary industry. Hong Kong invested the most: US$665.85 million in 452 projects. A list of key sources of FDI is shown in Table 7.11.5.

Table 7.11.4 Foreign direct investment in 1995 and 2000, Zhejiang Province

Mode	Number	Approved contracts		Actual utilization	
		Total value (US$ million)	% over previous year's total value	Total value (US$ million)	% over previous year's total value
1995					
Direct foreign investment:	1,836	3,250.31	12.34	1,257.75	9.90
Equity joint ventures	1,334	1,046.41	17.84	870.88	7.15
Contractual joint ventures	113	362.36	50.46	93	86.07
Solely foreign-owned enterprises	389	841.45	−7.71	293.87	4.29
2000					
Direct foreign investment:	1,642	2,509.48	16.8	1,612.66	5.2
Equity joint ventures	973	823.18	−14.6	674.59	−21.1
Contractual joint ventures	55	254.55	21.0	194.09	19.2
Solely foreign-owned enterprises	614	1431.75	47.1	743.98	44.5

Table 7.11.5 Key sources of direct foreign investment, Zhejiang Province

Source	No. of projects	Contract value in million US$
Hong Kong	452	665.85
Taiwan Province	299	322.41
United States	265	305.78
Virgin Islands	44	225.31
Japan	147	176.05

By the end of 2000, 6,864 foreign-invested enterprises were in operation. These registered total annual sales of up to RMB169.4 billion (US$20.42 billion), 23 per cent more than in 1999. Of the total sales, US$5.573 billion came from export. Total profit of the operating FIEs was RMB12.85 billion, up by 48 per cent on 1999.

Anhui Province

Anhui is situated in the lower middle reaches of the Yangtze and Huaihe Rivers. In the southern part of the province is the famous Mount Huangshan, while the Yangtze and Huaihe rivers cut across central Anhui, dividing it into three zones: Huibei (north of the Huaihe River), Jianghuai (between the Yangtze and Huaihe) and Jiangnan (south of the Yangtze). Huibei is a vast plain, Jianghuai consists mostly of rolling hills, and Jiangnan is mountainous. The total area of the province is 139,427 square kilometres and it has a population of 63.28 million. The provincial capital is Hefei. Major economic indicators are shown in Table 7.12.1.

Resources

The province abounds in around 40 types of minerals including coal, iron, copper, manganese, molybdenum, lead, zinc, sulphur, phosphorus, alum, gypsum, limestone, and rock salt. The proven reserves of coal total 22,300 million tons, half of that in eastern China. The reserves of iron total 2.4 million tons, ranking the Province in first place in eastern China. Fishery and forest resources are abundant in the areas of the province lying along the bank of Yangtze River and around Lake Chaohu.

Infrastructure

Transport and communications are convenient. Anhui has a well-connected network of railways which provide easy transport to different parts of the country. The Beijing-Shanghai, Beijing-Kowloon and Longhai railways run through the province. The airport in Hefei provides direct air services to Shanghai, Beijing and

Table 7.12.1   Major economic indicators, Anhui Province

Description	2000	2001
Population (millions)	62.86	63.28
Gross domestic product (billion RMB)	303.824	329.01
GDP (thousand RMB)	4.867	
Disposable income per capita (thousand RMB)		
Urban residents	5.2936	1.931
Rural residents	5.669	2.020
Savings (billion RMB)*	248.55	290.73
Investment in fixed assets (billion RMB)	80.397	96.26
Value-added of primary industry (billion RMB)	73.219	75.42
Value-added of secondary industry (billion RMB)	129.63	141.52
Value-added of tertiary industry (billion RMB)	100.973	112.07
Total retail sales of consumer goods (billion RMB)	105.43	114.28

Source: China Statistical Yearbook 2001 and State Statistical Bureau

*Both institutional and private savings.

other cities in China. 400 kilometres of the Yangtze river flow through the province, allowing the passage of large ships all year round. Ports at Anqing, Wuhu, Tongling and Maanshan along the Yangtze River are open to foreign vessels. Vessels of 5,000 tonnes can sail through the rivers all year round and shipping services to Hong Kong, Japan, Russia and other south-east Asian countries are available. Major highways include the Hefei-Nanjing and the Hefei-Wuhu Expressways. Anhui's telecommunications networks have improved rapidly over the past few years and modern means of telecommunication are available in the province

Foreign trade

The total trade of Anhui Province reached US$3.33 billion in value in 2000, up by 25.7 per cent over US$2.65 billion in 1999. Export contributed to nearly 65 per cent of the province's foreign trade and the total export value was US$2.16 billion, up by 29 per cent over US$1.68 billion in 1999. However, export had less weight in terms of its contribution to the province's GDP. Export earnings in 2000 were equivalent to 5.9 per cent of the province's GDP and accounted for 0.87 per cent of the country's total export value.

Export of primary products amounted to US$290 million, accounting for 13.4 per cent of the total export value; the export of manufactured products was US$1.87 billion, accounting for 86.6 per cent of total export value (see Table 7.12.2).

Table 7.12.2 Top five export markets, Anhui Province, 1995 and 2000

Country/region	Export value (US$ million)	% of export total
1995		
Hong Kong & Macao	342	21.7
Japan	277	17.5
EU	238	15.1
USA	211	13.4
Total	1,068	67.7
2000		
North America	421.66	19.5
EU	360.63	16.7
Japan	279.97	12.9
ASEAN	165.18	7.6
Republic of Korea	146.92	6.8
Total	1,374.36	63.5

Total import value was US$1.17 billion, up by 20.1 per cent over US$970 million in 1999. Import of primary products accounted for US$450 million, or 38.9 per cent of the total import value, while import of manufactured products came to US$710 million, 61.1 per cent of the total. The European Union as a whole supplied 18.2 per cent of the province's import needs, a little more than Japan, which provided 18 per cent of the province's total import (see Table 7.12.3).

Table 7.12.3 Top five import origins, Anhui Province, 1995 and 2000

Country/region	Import value (US$ million)	% of import total
1995		
EU	144	19.7
USA & Canada	125	17.1
Japan	123	16.8
Hong Kong & Macao	91	12.4
EU	144	19.7
Total	627	85.7
2000		
EU	213.02	18.2
Japan	210.35	18
Republic of Korea	113.05	9.7
North America	112.42	9.7
ASEAN	81.94	7
Total	730.78	62.6

Utilization of foreign capital

Anhui province received US$636.02 million of foreign direct investment in 247 projects in 2000. Equity joint ventures sharply decreased while contractual and solely foreign-owned ventures recorded significant increases in terms of total contract value (see Table 7.12.4).

Among the foreign direct investment projects approved in 2000, 182 were production-orientated with a total contract value of US$429.95 million, while 65 were in service industries and had a contract value of US$206.07 million. China's Hong Kong and Taiwan provinces were the two largest sources of investment in terms of total contract value (see Table 7.12.5).

In 2000, the export value of FIEs reached US$400 million, up by 37.1 per cent over US$291 million in 1999. Their share in the province's total export value rose from 17.4 per cent in 1999 to 18.5 per cent.

Table 7.12.4 Utilization of foreign capital, Anhui Province, 1995 and 2000

Mode	Number	Approved contracts		Actual utilization	
		Total value (US$ million)	% over previous year's total value	Total value (US$ million)	% over previous year's total value
1995					
Direct foreign investment:	753	1,206		482.56	30.4
Equity joint ventures	538	778		311.12	
Contractual joint ventures	43	40		16.19	
Solely foreign-owned enterprises	172	388		155.25	
2000					
Direct foreign investment:	247	636.02	13.84	318.47	−11.86
Equity joint ventures	106	59.74	−80.30	119.21	−59.53
Contractual joint ventures	27	207.84	73.94	69.65	145.68
Solely foreign-owned enterprises	114	368.44	171.05	129.61	237.70

Table 7.12.5 Sources of direct foreign investment, Anhui Province, 2000

Source	Number of projects	Contract value (US$ million)
Hong Kong	69	116.21
Taiwan Province	52	75.80
Virgin Islands	11	75.22
USA	43	70.94
Germany	1	46.70
Singapore	6	28.05
Switzerland	2	27.14
Indonesia	2	21.75

Fujian Province

Fujian Province is situated on the south-eastern coast of China, facing Taiwan across the Taiwan Straits. Hills and rolling land account for 80 per cent of the province's territory. Along its 3,324 kilometre coastline are river estuaries, most of which form good natural harbours. It has a total area of 136,000 square kilometres and a population of 34.40 million. The provincial capital is Fuzhou. Major economic indicators are shown in Table 7.13.1.

Resources

The province abounds in mineral deposits, over 120 of which have been verified. Ferrous metals include iron and manganese, and non-ferrous metals include copper, tungsten and aluminium. The province's reserves of iron ores are among the highest in the country. There

are also deposits of coal, limestone and china clay. With an area of 50,000 hectares under forest, the province is rich in timber reserves, estimated at 400 million cubic metres. The province has ample supplies of sub-tropical products such as sugar cane, peanuts and oranges. Fujian's long coastline offers favourable conditions for fishing and aquaculture.

Infrastructure

The coastal ports in Fujian have a combined annual throughput of over 69 million tonnes. Fuzhou's Mawei, Xiamen's Dongdu and Meizhou Bay are the most important ports, with berths that can accommodate 10,000 to 50,000-tonne class vessels. Xiamen port has opened overseas shipping routes to Europe, America, Japan, Singapore, Hong Kong and the Republic of

Table 7.13.1 Major economic indicators, Fujian Province

Item	2000	2001
Population (millions)	34.10	34.40
Gross domestic products (billion RMB)	392.007	425.837
GDP (thousand RMB)	11.508	12.375
Disposable income per capita (thousand RMB)		
Urban residents	7.43226	3.222
Rural residents	8.313	3.381
Savings (billion RMB)*	311.431	361.426
Investment in fixed assets (billion RMB)	111.220	112.301
Value-added of primary industry (billion RMB)	64.057	65.24
Value-added of secondary industry (billion RMB)	171.116	190.42
Value-added of tertiary industry (billion RMB)	156.834	170.18
Total retail sales of consumer goods (billion RMB)	137.28	149.946

Source: China Statistical Yearbook 2001 and State Statistical Bureau
*Both institutional and private savings.

Korea. Passenger trains leave daily for Beijing, Shanghai, Guangzhou and other cities. The highway links up all cities in the province. The Changle International Airport in Fuzhou, the Xiamen International Airport and the airport in Wuyishan operate more than 90 domestic and international routes, linking the province with more than 40 domestic cities, as well as Hong Kong, Japan and the Philippines. The province is rich in hydropower resources, estimated at 10 million kilowatts.

Foreign trade

In 2000, the import and export value of Fujian Province totalled US$21.224 billion, a growth of 20.28 per cent over US$17.645 billion in 1999.

Total export value was US$12.909 billion, a growth of 24.41 per cent against US$10.376 billion in 1999 and equalling 27.26 per cent of the province's GDP of RMB392 billion (US$47.354 billion) and 5.18 per cent of the nation's total export value. Fujian was the sixth largest exporting province in China.

Export of primary products and manufactured products accounted for US$1.367 billion and US$11.541 billion respectively, or 10.59 per cent and 89.40 per cent in the total export. Hong Kong, which used to be the province's largest export market, with a share of nearly 50 per cent in 1995, became the third largest behind the USA and Japan (see Table 7.13.2). Over the previous six years, the province considerably reduced its dependence on the top five export markets, from nearly 95 per cent in 1995 to 61.67 per cent in 2000.

Import value totalled US$8.315 billion, up by 14.39 per cent on US$7.269 billion in 1999. This money was mainly spent on manufactured products. The split between the import of primary products and manufactured products was US$1.021 billion and US$7.293 billion respectively, accounting for 12.28 per cent and 87.71 per cent of total import value.

As in the case of export, Hong Kong moved from its position as the leading supplier of the province's imports down to the fifth (see Table 7.13.3). Taiwan, partly because of its geographical proximity to Fujian and also because of the many 'family ties' between the two provinces, took the first place in 2000. However, the province's dependence on one single source of import was not as high as it was in 1995. Taiwan's position as the leading supplier of the province's import in 2000 was far less significant than Hong Kong's had

Table 7.13.2 Top five export destinations: 1995 and 2000

Country/region	Export value (US$ million)	% of export total
1995		
Hong Kong	4,084	49.49
Japan	1,743	21.12
USA	1,131	13.70
Taiwan Province	650	7.89
Germany	228	2.76
Total	7,836	94.96
2000		
USA	3,189	24.70
Japan	2,356	18.25
Hong Kong	1,509	11.69
Germany	503	3.90
Taiwan Province	404	3.13
Total	7,961	61.67

Table 7.13.3 Top five import markets, Fujian Province, 1995 and 2000

Country/region	Import value (US$ million)	% of import total
1995		
Hong Kong	2,989	59.19
Taiwan Province	836	16.55
Japan	493	9.76
USA	186	3.68
Malaysia	168	3.33
Total	4,672	92.51
2000		
Taiwan Province	2,421	29.12
Japan	1,315	15.82
Republic of Korea	1,060	12.75
USA	799	9.61
Hong Kong	283	3.40
Total	5,878	70.7

been; the latter's share in the province's import in 1995 was as high as 59.19 per cent.

Utilization of foreign capital

In 2000, the province's use of foreign direct investment dropped by 11.96 per cent in contract value compared

Table 7.13.4 Utilization of foreign capital, Fujian Province, 1995 and 2000

Mode	Number	Approved contracts		Actual utilization	
		Total value (US$ million) year's total value	% change over previous year	Total value (US$ million) year's total value	% change over previous year
1995					
Direct foreign investment	2,728	8,906.47	24.05	4,038.81	
Equity joint ventures	858	1,735.84		1,248.72	
Contractual joint ventures	147	1,001.47		540.73	
Solely foreign-owned enterprises	1,723	6,141.16		2,249.36	
2000					
Direct foreign investment	1,463	4,313.73	−11.96	3,803.86	−5.47
Equity joint ventures	281	512.42	−50.43	745.48	−25.11
Contractual joint ventures	27	99.71	−73.31	132.63	−68.51
Solely foreign-owned enterprises	1,155	3,701.60	5.98	2,923.65	11.99

with 1999. Negative growth occurred in both equity and contractual joint ventures, while solely foreign-owned enterprises saw a slight increase of 5.98 per cent in total contract value (see Table 7.13.4).

Of the FDI projects approved in 2000, 1236 were production-orientated and 227 non-production.

At the beginning of 2000, 728 FIEs were in operation and by the end of the year an accumulative 15,887 had gone into production. FIEs played an important role in the local economy. The total industrial output value of the operating FIEs reached RMB153.865 billion in 2000, up 14.3 per cent over the previous year. Exports by FIEs totalled US$7.597 billion, up by 29.01 per cent over the previous year and accounting for 58.85 per cent of the total export value of the province.

Table 7.13.5 Key sources of foreign direct investment, Fujian Province

Source	Number of projects	Contract value (US$ million)
Hong Kong	602	2,125
Taiwan Province	213	321
British Virgin Islands	23	238
USA	79	210
The Philippines	60	176
Japan	72	169
UK	20	155
Singapore	58	102
Macao	28	49.58
Malaysia	14	46.43

Jiangxi Province

The province lies in the middle reaches of the Yangtze River. It is surrounded by mountains, with the Wuyi and Huaiyau mountains on the east and the Mufu and Luoxiao mountains on the west. There are many rivers and streams in the province. Poyang Lake is the largest fresh-water lake in China. The total area is 166,900 square kilometres and the population is 41.40 million by the end of 2000. The provincial capital is Nanchang. Major economic indicators are shown in Table 7.14.1.

Resources

The province is underlain with rich non-ferrous metals and rare metal deposits. Of the more than 140 mineral reserves in the world, 126 are found in Jiangxi, of which 73 have been verified. Its copper and silver deposits rank first in China. The total copper reserves amount to 12

million tonnes. Tungsten deposits rank second in the province and output is the highest in the country. The province's deposits of heavy rare-earth metals are well known, and its tantalum, niobium and uranium reserves occupy important positions in the country's total reserves. The province ranks third in the country in terms of timber reserves and it also has ample geothermal energy resources and mineral water.

Infrastructure

Jiujiang is the only city with a port in the province. With its advantageous geographical location at the intersection of the Yangtze River and the Beijing-Kowloon Railway, it has become a major distribution centre for Jiangxi, Anhui, Hubei and Hunan provinces. Jiujiang is also a major inland water-transportation

Table 7.14.1 Major economic indicators, Jiangxi Province

Description	2000	2001
Population (millions)	41.40	
Gross domestic product (billion RMB)	200.307	217.934
GDP (thousand RMB)	4.851	
Disposable income per capita (thousand RMB)		
Urban residents	5.104	2.135
Rural residents	5.506	2.232
Savings (billion RMB)*	196.71	228.67
Investment in fixed assets (billion RMB)	51.608	na
Value-added of primary industry (billion RMB)	48.514	50.503
Value-added of secondary industry (billion RMB)	70.076	78.765
Value-added of tertiary industry (billion RMB)	81.717	88.581
Total retail sales of consumer goods (billion RMB)	70.49	76.334

Source: China Statistical Yearbook 2001 and State Statistical Bureau

*Both institutional and private savings

centre at the middle reaches of the Yangtze River. The Jiujiang Port, now open to foreign trade, has a cargo-handling capacity of more than 3 million tonnes per annum. It can accommodate 5,000-tonne freighters and has shipping routes to Hong Kong, Japan and other south-east Asian countries. The province has several trunk railways that connect it with other parts of China. The five airports, in Nanchang, Jiujiang, Jingdezhen, Ji'an and Ganzhou, link the province to Shanghai, Beijing and Guangzhou and other cities in the country.

Foreign trade

In 2000, the total import and export value of Jiangxi Province was US$1.624 billion, an increase of 23.61 per cent over US$1.314 billion in 1999.

74 per cent of the province's trade came from its export. Total export value was US$1.197 billion, up 32.15 per cent from US$906 million in 1999. It was equivalent to 4.96 per cent of the province's total GDP, which amounted to RMB200 billion (US$24.162 billion). It also made up 0.48 per cent of the total country's total export value.

The export value of primary goods was US$220.02 million, accounting for 18.38 per cent of the total export value. The export value of manufactured goods was US$977.34 million, accounting for 81.62 per cent of the total export value (see Table 7.14.2).

Table 7.14.2 Top five export markets, Jiangxi Province, 1995 and 2000

Country/region	Export value (US$ million)	% of export total
1995		
Hong Kong	750.78	52.50
Japan	133.70	9.35
USA	88.91	6.22
Republic of Korea	54.12	3.78
Germany	40.62	2.82
Total	1,068.13	74.67
2000		
Hong Kong	160.46	13.40
Japan	134.52	11.23
USA	119.96	10.01
Republic of Korea	81.22	6.78
Cote d'Ivoire	59.80	4.99
Total	555.96	46.41

Total import value was US$426.64 million, up by 4.63 per cent from US$407.76 million in 1999, and accounting for 0.19 per cent of the total import value of the country.

Import of primary goods was US$137.02 million, accounting for 32.12 per cent of total import value. The import of manufactured goods was US$289.62 million, accounting for 67.88 per cent of total import value (see Table 7.14.3).

Table 7.14.3 Top five import markets, Jiangxi Province, 1995 and 2000

Country/region	Import value (US$ million)	% of import total
1995		
Hong Kong	53.09	22.78
Japan	27.73	11.90
Switzerland	27.27	11.70
USA	21.59	9.26
UK	19.15	8.21
Total	148.83	63.85
2000		
Japan	75.61	17.72
Hong Kong	60.06	14.08
USA	40.35	9.46
Chile	35.05	8.22
UK	32.69	7.66
Total	243.76	57.14

Utilization of foreign capital

Jiangxi province approved 272 FDI projects in 2000, with a total contract value of US$264.78 million, a 24.64 per cent decline against 1999. Apart from a moderate increase in the contract value of contractual joint ventures, both equity joint ventures and solely foreign-owned enterprises had experienced negative rates of growth (see Table 7.14.4).

Of the FDI projects approved in 2000, 195 were production-oriented, accounting for 71.69 per cent, and 77 (28.31 per cent) were non-production related.

Contracted foreign direct investment came from 33 countries and regions. The top six investors were Hong Kong (US$145.82 million), which accounted for 55.07 per cent of the total investment value; Taiwan (US$36.60 million), USA (US$23.32 million), Macao (US$9.61 million), Japan (US$8.35 million) and Republic of Korea (US$5.48 million).

Table 7.14.4 Utilization of foreign capital, Jiangxi Province, 1995 and 2000

Mode	Number	Approved contracts		Actual utilization	
		Total value (US$ million) year's total value	*% change over previous year*	*Total value (US$ million) year's total value*	*% change over previous year*
1995					
Direct foreign investment:	522	539.66	37.82	288.18	10.13
Equity joint ventures	295	274.05		176.52	
Contractual joint ventures	33	57.37		30.36	
Solely foreign-owned enterprises	194	208.04		81.30	
2000					
Direct foreign investment:	272	264.78	−24.64	227.24	−29.16
Equity joint ventures	111	96.90	−17.03	98.18	−14.27
Contractual joint ventures	21	37.49	5.49	22.00	−65.32
Solely foreign-owned enterprises	140	130.39	−26.97	107.06	−25.05

In 2000, 85 foreign-financed enterprises had begun operation. By the end of the year, 5,217 FIEs had been approved, of which 1,541 were in operation. These FIEs generated US$162.98 million export earnings, an increase of 63.16 per cent over US$99.89 million in 1999. Their percentage in terms of total provincial export value rose from 11.02 per cent in 1999 to 13.61 per cent in 2000.

7.15

Shandong Province

Shandong Province lies in the lower reaches of the Yellow River on China's eastern coast. The province covers a peninsula and hinterland. The peninsula stretches between the Bohai Gulf and Yellow Sea and faces Liaodong Peninsula in the north. Mountains and hilly land in the central and southern parts of the province and on the peninsula account for 35 per cent of the province's total area. The province has a coastline of more than 3,200 kilometres and a number of fine ports. Its total area is 156,700 square kilometres and its population is 90.41 million. The provincial capital is Jinan. Major economic indicators are shown in Table 7.15.1.

Resources

Shandong abounds in mineral resources. More than 90 kinds of minerals have been verified or are being mined, including coal, petroleum, natural gas, iron, copper, aluminium, diamond and magnetite. The province has large deposits of gold: eastern Shandong's gold production ranks first in China. Shandong is also rich in non-metallic ores, such as graphite, marble, granite, gypsum, sulphur and talc. The province is one of the four largest salt production bases in China. With a 3,200 kilometre-long coastline, one-sixth of China's total, Shandong has a strong fishing and aquaculture industry. The province

Table 7.15.1 Major economic indicators, Shandong Province

Item	2000	2001
Population (millions)	86.20	90.41
Gross domestic product (billion RMB)	854.244	943.83
GDP per capita (thousand RMB)	9.555	10.465
Disposable income per capita (thousand RMB)		
Urban residents	6.489	2.659
Rural residents	7.101	2.805
Savings (billion RMB)*	742.2	850.17
Investment in fixed assets (billion RMB)	253.110	277.84
Value-added of primary industry (billion RMB)	126.857	135.95
Value-added of secondary industry (billion RMB)	424.440	465.45
Value-added of tertiary industry (billion RMB)	302.947	342.43
Total retail sales of consumer goods (billion RMB)	254.59	283.49

Source: China Statistical Yearbook 2001 and State Statistical Bureau
*Both institutional and private savings

is the country's largest exporter of marine products such as prawns, crabs, scallops, shellfish, algae, abalone, sea cucumbers and sea urchins.

Infrastructure

Along the coastline of the Shandong Peninsula, there are 26 large and small ports with a cargo handling capacity of over 100 million tonnes per annum. Qingdao, Yantai and Weihai are the major cargo and passenger ports, while Rizhao is one of China's most important specialized coal transportation ports. Other ports include Dongying, Longkou, Shidao and Lanshan, who together with the above ports have been approved as first-class open ports. Qingdao is the fourth largest port in China. Qingdao port's container handling capacity is second only to Shanghai's. Several major railways run through the province offering rail connections to all major cities around China. A new rail development programme will further strengthen the province's links to other localities. Shandong has the best developed highway network in the country. The highway development has contributed greatly to the province's economic development and its effort to develop its highway network has been a model for other provinces and localities. Shandong has nine civil airports and the two international airports, at Jinan and Qingdao, offer air routes to domestic and international cities.

Foreign trade

2000 saw a growth of 36.8 per cent in Shandong's total trade value. Import and export value rose from US$18.271 billion in 1999 to US$24.99 billion.

Total export was US$15.53 billion in value, up by 34.1 per cent over US$11.58 billion in 1999. This figure was equivalent to 15.1 per cent of the Province's GDP, which was RMB854.24 billion (US$103.04 billion). The province's export contributed 6.2 per cent to the country's total export value, ranking it fifth in China.

Export of primary products generated 22.8 per cent of the export earnings (US$2.64 billion). Export of manufactured products amounted to US$8.94 billion, accounting for 77.2 per cent of the province's total export value.

Japan has been an important export market for Shandong over the last few years. In 2000, Japan was first among the province's five major export markets (see Table 7.15.2), taking 28.1 per cent of the total export.

Table 7.15.2 Top five export markets, Shandong Province, 1995 and 2000

Country/region	Export value (US$ million)	% of export total
1995		
Japan	2,857.31	29.6
Republic of Korea	1,690.51	17.5
Hong Kong	1,558.23	16.2
USA	1,265.36	13.1
Germany	327.28	3.4
Total	7,698.69	79.8
2000		
Japan	4,362.72	28.1
USA	2,899.06	18.7
Republic of Korea	2,272.08	14.6
European Union	2,047.01	13.2
Hong Kong	813.24	5.2
Total	12,394.11	79.8

The USA took the second position, with a share of 18.7 per cent.

Import accounted for 37.9 per cent of Shandong's total trade, with the total value being US$9.46 billion, an increase of 41.4 per cent over US$6.69 billion in 1999 (see Table 7.15.3).

Table 7.15.3 Top five import markets, Shandong Province, 1995 and 2000

Country/region	Import value (US$ million)	% of import total
1995		
Japan	683.80	22.5
Republic of Korea	664.50	21.8
USA	506.62	16.6
Hong Kong	266.74	8.8
Germany	119.35	3.9
Total	2,241.01	73.6
2000		
Republic of Korea	3,393.03	35.9
Japan	1,602.14	16.9
European Union	1,011.12	10.7
USA	883.10	9.3
Australia	228.91	2.4
Total	7,118.3	75.2

Utilization of foreign capital

Shandong province approved 2,728 foreign direct investment projects in 2000 with a total contract value of US$5.074 billion, an increase of 63 per cent over 1999 (see Table 7.15.4).

Among the FDI projects approved in 2000, 107 were in primary industry, 2334 in secondary industry and 278 in tertiary industry. Hong Kong was the largest source of investment in 2000, investing US$1.43 billion in 472 projects. Korea ranked second, with a total investment of US$980 million in 1,012 projects. The main sources of FDI are provided in Table 7.15.5.

Table 7.15.4 Utilization of foreign capital, Shandong Province, 1995 and 2000

Mode	Approved contracts		% change over previous year	Actual utilization	% change over previous year
	Number	Total value (US$ million) year's total value		Total value (US$ million) year's total value	
1995					
Direct foreign investment:	2,709	4,625.21	−12.1	2,607.19	2.8
Equity joint ventures	1,692	2,665.00		1,814.93	
Contractual joint ventures	141	373.74		83.64	
Solely foreign-owned enterprises	876	1,585.67		708.62	
2000					
Direct foreign investment:	72, 728	5, 074.35	63	2,971.19	20
Equity joint ventures	1, 101	1, 710.98	38	1,173.42	27
Contractual joint ventures	145	566.93	30	520.47	21
Solely foreign-owned enterprises	1, 495	2, 781.73	95	1,261.18	46

Table 7.15.5 Key sources of FDI, Shandong Province

Source	Number of projects	Contract value (US$ million)
Hong Kong	472	1,430
Republic of Korea	1,012	980
USA	282	830
Taiwan Province	267	420
Japan	250	280
British Virgin Islands	33	250

Henan Province

Henan Province is situated in the central plain on the middle and lower reaches of the Yellow River. It slopes from the north-west to the south-east. Mountains and hills constitute respectively 26.6 per cent and 17.76 per cent of the total area, plains and basins make up 55.7 per cent and the vast plain in the east is part of the North China Plain. The province has a total area of 167,000 square kilometres with a population of 95.55 million and the provincial capital is Zhengzhou. Major economic indicators are shown in Table 7.16.1.

Resources

Henan's reserves of molybdenum, marble, trona, asbestos, aluminium, natural gas, cesium, bauxite, coal, perlite and refractory clay are among the largest in

China. The province's coal output ranks third in China, after Shanxi and Shandong. The rich oil and gas reserves in the Nanyang Basin are currently being exploited. Zhongyuan oilfield is one of the largest oilfields in the country. Half of China's aluminium oxide output comes from Henan. Henan's bauxite reserves are the second largest in China. Henan is an agricultural province, with grain production ranking second only to Shandong. Major agricultural products include wheat, beans, ramie, oil and cotton.

Infrastructure

River transportation is available with easy access to the Yellow River, Huaihe, Weihe and Hanshui Rivers, all of which run through the province. Zhengzhou, the pro-

Table 7.16.1 Major economic indicators, Henan Province

Item	2000	2001
Population (millions)	94.88	95.55
Gross domestic product (billion RMB)	513.766	564.502
GDP per capita (thousand RMB)	5.444	
Disposable income per capita (thousand RMB)		
Urban residents	4.76626	1.848
Rural residents	5.267	1.968
Savings (billion RMB)*	473.766	553.016
Investment in fixed assets (billion RMB)	137.774	162.776
Value-added of primary industry (billion RMB)	116.158	123.4
Value-added of secondary industry (billion RMB)	241.378	266.2
Value-added of tertiary industry (billion RMB)	156.230	174.87
Total retail sales of consumer goods (billion RMB)	178.67	197.98

Source: China Statistical Yearbook 2001 and State Statistical Bureau
*Both institutional and private savings

vincial capital, is one of the most important railway transportation hubs in China and Asia itself. The railways are the main means of transport. Three trunk lines cross the province. Henan has airports in Zhengzhou, Luoyang and Nanyang and international flight services are available from Zhengzhou. All the towns and cities in the province are linked by highways.

Foreign trade

The total value of Henan's foreign trade in 2000 was US$2.274 billion, up by 29.9 per cent over US$1.752 billion in 1999. Export accounted for 65.7 per cent of the province's trade flow, with total export value standing at US$1.493 billion. This was a rise of 32.1 per cent over US$1.130 billion in 1999, and equivalent to 2.4 per cent of the provincial GDP (about US$512.6 billion) and 0.6 per cent of the country's total export value (see Table 7.16.2).

Table 7.16.2 Top five export markets, Henan Province, 1995 and 2000

Country/region	Export value (US$ million)	% of export total
1995		
Hong Kong	596.59	32.60
Japan	256.42	14.01
USA	179.56	9.81
Russia	135.65	7.41
Republic of Korea	89.59	4.90
Total	1,322.16	68.73
2000		
USA	303.78	20.34
European Union	204.10	13.67
Japan	178.81	11.97
Hong Kong	170.63	11.43
ASEAN	161.20	10.79
Total	1,018.52	68.2

Although Henan is largely an agricultural province, exports of manufactured products generated 85.3 per cent of the province's export earnings, totalling US$1.274 billion. Export of primary products took a much smaller share of US$220 million, or 14.7 per cent of the total export value.

Among the top five export markets (see Table 7.16.2), the USA imported the most: 20.34 per cent of the

province's export. The European Union as a whole ranked second, followed by Japan, Hong Kong and ASEAN countries. South Korea, although not appearing in the top five, had a significant share of 7.54 per cent of the province's export.

Import value totalled US$781 million, an increase of 25.7 per cent over US$545 million in 1999.

Import value of primary products came to US$251 million, accounting for 32.1 per cent of total import value, while the import value of manufactured products was US$531 million, 67.9 per cent of total import value.

The province's imports originated from 65 places, but the top five markets (see Table 7.16.3) supplied over 75 per cent of all imports. The USA exported the most to the province: 24.23 per cent of the total.

Table 7.16.3 Top five import markets: 1995 and 2000

Country/region	Import value (US$ million)	% of import total
1995		
Japan	78.10	16.86
Hong Kong	71.12	15.35
USA	65.96	14.24
Germany	50.59	10.92
Australia	40.15	8.67
Total	305.92	66.04
2000		
USA	189.33	24.23
European Union	151.61	19.40
Japan	127.32	16.29
Australia	71.54	9.15
ASEAN	46.95	6.00
Total	586.75	75.07

Utilization of foreign capital

There was a moderate increase of 8.1 per cent in the value of foreign direct investment in Henan province in 2000. 237 FDI projects were approved in that year, with a total contract value of US$699.21 million. The increase in the FDI contract value was attributed to the increase in equity joint ventures, which offset the negative growth in both contractual joint ventures and solely foreign owned enterprises (see Table 7.16.4).

The FDI projects approved in 2000 covered more than 40 different sectors. There were 197 production

Table 7.16.4 Utilisation of foreign capital, Henan Province, 1995 and 2000

Mode	Approved contracts			Actual utilization	
	Number	*Total value (US$ million) year's total value*	*% change over previous year*	*Total value (US$ million) year's total value*	*% change over previous year*
1995					
Direct foreign investment	805	915.67	16.43	476.22	23.47
Equity joint ventures	60	519.12			
Contractual joint ventures	61	279.89			
Solely foreign-owned enterprises	144	116.66			
2000					
Direct foreign investment	237	699.21	8.1	564.03	6.2
Equity joint ventures	139	457.57	22.8	412.18	67.7
Contractual joint ventures	26	149.68	–11.6	81.85	–42.8
Solely foreign-owned enterprises	72	91.78	–12.4	70.00	–47.2

projects with a total contract value of US$570.09 million, accounting for 81.53 per cent of the total. The remaining 40 projects were service-related. The FDI came from 37 countries and regions; the key sources of the province's FDI are shown in Table 7.16.5.

A total of 6,413 foreign-invested enterprises had been approved by the end of 2000 and more than 2,000 of these had begun production, employing a total workforce of over 300,000. Exports from foreign-invested enterprises in 2000 came to US$308.36 million, an increase of 29.8 per cent on 1999 and accounting for 20.65 per cent of the province's total export value.

Table 7.16.5 Key sources of FDI, Henan Province

Source	*Number of projects*	*Actual utilization (US$ million)*
Hong Kong	89	371.35
UK	6	114.55
Singapore	10	30.45
Thailand	5	24.85
USA	41	18.76
British Virgin Islands	7	15.85

Hubei Province

Hubei is situated in the middle reaches of the Yangtze River in central China. Topographically it is an incomplete basin with heights on the eastern, western and northern fringes forming a horseshoe round the central and southern regions. The central area is dotted with lakes and the western part is formed by a chain of mountains including Wudang. The total area is 185,900 square kilometres and the population is 59.75 million. The provincial capital is Wuhan. Major economic indicators are shown in Table 7.17.1.

Resources

Mineral resources currently being developed include iron, copper, phosphorus, manganese, gypsum and rutile. The province produces the most gypsum in the country. Deposits of phosphate, salt, silica, garnet and marlstone are among the highest in China. The province has a hydroelectric power potential of 14 million kilowatts and is also rich in forest reserves and aquatic resources.

Infrastructure

Hubei has good communications and transport facilities. The Yangtze river comes down from Sichuan and runs through the province. Wuhan and Huangshi harbours have the facilities to handle export goods and freighters of 5,000 tonnes can sail direct to Hong Kong and Japan. Highways link all parts of the province. There are eight inter-province highways and 118 intra-province highways covering all cities, counties and most villages and towns in the province. There are seven airports in Hubei including the Wuhan, Yichang, Sanxia,

Table 7.17.1   Major economic indicators

Item	2000	2001
Population (millions)	59.60	59.7456
Gross domestic product (billion RMB)	427.632	466.228
GDP per capita (thousand RMB)	7.188	
Disposable income per capita (thousand RMB)		
Urban residents	5.52454	2.269
Rural residents	5.856	2.352
Savings (billion RMB)*	355.719	423.847
Investment in fixed assets (billion RMB)	133.920	155.175
Value-added of primary industry (billion RMB)	66.230	69.217
Value-added of secondary industry (billion RMB)	212.370	231.37
Value-added of tertiary industry (billion RMB)	149.032	165.65
Total retail sales of consumer goods (billion RMB)	178.94	197.516

Source: China Statistical Yearbook 2001 and State Statistical Bureau
*Both institutional and private savings

Xiangfan and Shashi airports. International flights are available from Wuhan Tianhe Airport. Gezhouba, the largest hydro project in China, is now in operation.

Foreign trade

In 2000, Hubei province reported a growth of 20.4 per cent in its total foreign trade value, which rose to US$3.223 billion from US$2.677 billion in 1999. Total export value was US$1.936 billion, up by 28 per cent over US$1.512 billion in 1999 and equalling 3.75 per cent of the provincial GDP of RMB427.632 billion (US$51.56 billion).

Table 7.17.2   Top five export markets, Hubei Province, 1995 and 2000

Country/region	Export value (US$ million)	% of export total
1995		
Hong Kong	1,080.74	46.4
Japan	251.71	10.8
USA	144.69	6.2
Republic of Korea	142.73	6.1
Germany	72.13	3.1
Total	1,692	72.6
2000		
Japan	311.02	16.07
Hong Kong	265.97	13.74
USA	191.27	9.88
Taiwan Province	133.70	6.91
Germany	96.94	5.01
Total	998.9	51.61

Export of primary products amounted to US$194 million, accounting for 10 per cent of the total export value. Export of manufactured products was US$1.742 billion, accounting for 90 per cent of the total export value.

The top five export destinations played a less important role than 1995, when the top five took 70 per cent of the province's total export. This figure dropped to a little over 50 per cent in 2000.

Total import value was US$1.287 billion, up by 10.5 per cent over US$1.167 billion in 1999. Import of pri-

mary products amounted to US$322 million, accounting for 24.99 per cent of the value of all imports. The import value of manufactured products was US$966 million, or 75.01 per cent of the total import value.

Table 7.17.3   Top five import markets, Hubei Province, 1995 and 2000

Country/region	Import value (US$ million)	% of import total
1995		
Hong Kong	390	28.49
France	162	11.83
Japan	160	11.69
Germany	91	6.65
USA	74	5.41
Total	877	64.07
2000		
Japan	242.76	18.86
USA	151.24	11.75
France	127.3	9.89
German	108.4	8.42
Taiwan Province	81.71	6.35
Total	711.41	55.27

Imports came from 68 countries and regions, while the top five import markets (see Table 7.17.3) supplied over 55 per cent of the province's imports.

Utilization of foreign capital

Hubei province approved 331 foreign direct investment projects with a total contract value of US$1.065 billion in 2000, an increase of nearly 30 per cent over 1999. FDI for solely foreign-owned projects had declined by 43.9 per cent in terms of contract value (see Table 7.17.4).

Among the FDI projects approved in 2000, 246 were production-orientated and 88 non-production related. FDI originated from 36 countries and regions. The key sources of FDI are listed in Table 7.17.5.

The export value of FIEs in 2000 was US$430 million, up by 36.9 per cent, accounting for 22.2 per cent of the province's total export value. The processing trade was the driving force behind both import and export.

Table 7.17.4 Utilization of foreign capital, Hubei Province, 1995 and 2000

Mode	Number	Approved contracts		Actual utilization	
		Total value (US$ million) year's total value	% change over previous year	Total value (US$ million) year's total value	% change over previous year
1995					
Direct foreign investment:	881	1,088.47			
Equity joint ventures	583				
Contractual joint ventures	45				
Solely foreign-owned enterprises	253				
2000					
Direct foreign investment:	331	1,065.83	29.70	943.68	3.15
Equity joint ventures	156	279.36	14.89	598.79	1.23
Contractual joint ventures	16	487.11	97.15	27.80	−59.23
Solely foreign-owned enterprises	158	299.36	−43.90	317.00	24.59

Table 7.17.5 Key sources of FDI, Hubei Province

Source	Number of projects	Actually utilised (US$ million)
France	2	360.23
Hong Kong	126	252.12
USA	30	64.34
UK	18	53.35
Singapore	9	47.43
Germany	9	32.00
Japan	15	31.01
Taiwan Province	56	30.44
The Netherlands	2	28.00
Thailand	4	17.06
Macao	10	7.59

Hunan Province

Hunan is situated in the southern part of the middle reaches of the Yangtze River, south of Dongting Lake. Topographically, it is a U-shaped basin of rolling plains, with mountains rising in the east, south and west and flat lands extending northward. The total area is 212,000 square kilometres and it has a population of 65.95 million. The provincial capital is Changsha. Major economic indicators are shown in Table 7.18.1.

Resources

The province is rich in natural resources. Non-ferrous minerals have been found in many places and it has the largest deposits of tungsten, bismuth and antimony in China. Non-metallic minerals such as coal, realgar, marble, granite, fluorite are present in large quantities. The province produces more lead, zinc, hard alloy, salt fluorite and ramie textile products than any other part of the country, and its production of tungsten, electric aluminium, electric zinc, mercury and pottery ranks second. The province also has a water power resource potential of 13 million kilowatts. The timber reserves amount to 180 million cubic metres. Hunan is the fifth largest grain producer in China. It is also the largest producer of tea and the third largest producer of oranges.

Infrastructure

Major railways include the Beijing-Guangzhou line, Zhicheng-Liuzhou, Zhejiang-Jiangxi, Hunan-Guizhou and Hunan-Guangxi lines. The water transport network centres around the Dongting Lake. Highways link all counties and most of the rural townships in the province. Several trunk lines run across the province.

Table 7.18.1 Major economic indicators, Hunan Province

Item	2000	2001
Population (millions)	65.61	65.95
Gross domestic product (billion RMB)	369.188	398.3
GDP per capita (thousand RMB)	5.639	
Disposable income per capita (thousand RMB)		
Urban residents	6.22	2.158
Rural residents	6.78	2.26
Savings (billion RMB)*	287.0	334.2
Investment in fixed assets (billion RMB)	101.224	120.9
Value-added of primary industry (billion RMB)	78.492	82.6
Value-added of secondary industry (billion RMB)	146.186	157
Value-added of tertiary industry (billion RMB)	144.510	158.7
Total retail sales of consumer goods (billion RMB)	136.5	151.1

Source: China Statistical Yearbook 2001 and State Statistical Bureau

*Both institutional and private savings

The international Huanghua Airport in Changsha operates regular services to major domestic and international cities.

Foreign trade

The total import and export value of Hunan Province reached US$2.512 billion in 2000, an increase of 28.45 per cent over US$1.956 billion in 1999. The total export value was US$1.653 billion, up by 28.93 per cent compared with US$1.282 billion in 1999 and equal to 5.08 per cent of the province's GDP of RMB269.188 billion (US$32.55 billion) and 0.66 per cent of the country's total export value (see Table 7.18.2).

Table 7.18.2 Top five export markets, Hunan Province, 1995 and 2000

Country/region	Export value (US$ million)	% of export total
1995		
Hong Kong & Macao	1,013.19	48.23
Japan	228.92	10.92
EU	221.07	10.54
USA	169.65	8.09
ASEAN	101.65	4.85
Total	1,734.48	82.63
2000		
USA	239.61	14.50
Hong Kong	224.87	13.61
Japan	159.24	9.63
Republic of Korea	132.56	8.02
Germany	91.52	5.54
Total	847.8	51.3

Export of primary products was US$187.59 million, making up 11.35 per cent of total export value. Export of manufactured goods totalled US$1.465 billion, accounting for 88.65 per cent of the total export value.

Total import value was US$859.51 million, up by 27.52 per cent compared with US$673.94 million in 1999. Import of primary products accounted for US$167.35 million, or 19.47 per cent of total import value. Import of manufactured goods was US$692.16 million, accounting for 80.53 per cent of the total import value. Among the imports of manufactured products, mechanical and electronic products totalled US$515.12 million, accounting for 59.53 per cent of total import value (see Table 7.18.3).

Table 7.18.3 Top five import markets, Hunan Province, 1995 and 2000

Country/region	Import value (US$ million)	% of import total
1995		
Hong Kong & Macao	206.61	25.18
USA	85.66	10.44
Japan	76.95	9.38
Republic of Korea	70.54	8.60
Taiwan Province	53.33	6.50
Total	493.09	60.1
2000		
Republic of Korea	182.26	21.21
Japan	173.67	20.21
USA	80.22	9.33
UK	56.44	6.57
Taiwan Province	45.27	5.27
Total	537.86	62.59

Utilization of foreign capital

There were 320 foreign direct investment projects approved in Hunan in 2000, involving a total FDI contract value of US$667.09 million, an increase of 32.89 per cent over 1999. The contracted investments in equity joint ventures and wholly foreign-owned enterprises grew by 39.84 per cent and 46.69 per cent respectively while investment in contractual joint ventures shrank by 7.58 per cent (see Table 7.18.4).

Of 320 projects with foreign direct investment, 262 were production-orientated with a total contract value of US$502.41 million and 58 were non-production related, with a contract value of US$164.68 million.

Foreign direct investments came from 31 countries and regions. The main sources of FDI are shown in Table 7.18.5.

By the end of 2000, a total of 5,712 foreign-invested enterprises had been approved in the province. These contracts involved US$7.406 billion and the actual utilisation was US$5.238 billion. Over 2,000 of the approved FIEs had opened for business or started operation by the end of the year, employing about 250,000 workers. In 2000, the total sales revenue by the operating FIEs was RMB23.7 billion and the tax contribution was RMB1.17 billion. In 2000, FIEs generated US$182.50 million of export earnings, and purchased US$294.67 million worth of goods from overseas, accounting for 11.04 per cent and 34.28 per cent respectively in terms of the province's total export and import.

Table 7.18.4 Utilization of foreign capital, Hunan Province, 1995 and 2000

Mode	Number	Approved contracts		Actual utilization	
		Total value (US$ million) year's total value	*% change over previous year*	*Total value (US$ million) year's total value*	*% change over previous year*
1995					
Direct foreign investment:	574	1,354.62	97.50	488.02	50.11
Equity joint ventures	343	358.05		342.57	
Contractual joint ventures	48	446/27		42.07	
Solely foreign-owned enterprises	183	550.30		103.38	
2000					
Direct foreign investment:	320	667.09	32.89	681.82	4.30
Equity joint ventures	123	185.56	39.84	326.71	7.00
Contractual joint ventures	36	106.32	−7.58	73.28	−10.93
Solely foreign-owned enterprises	163	372.96	46.69	279.40	4.99

Table 7.18.5 Key sources of FDI, Hunan Province

Source of FDI	No. of projects	Contract value (US$ million)	Actual utilization (US$ million)
Hong Kong	150	298.06	323.81
Taiwan Province	69	65.37	69.50
The Philippines	6	57.65	4.12
UK	2	29.23	4.02
USA	28	29.11	55.37
Republic of Korea	7	28.71	73.29
Germany	5	23.12	49.45
Macao	7	21.72	18.26
Singapore	6	21.56	12.37
Australia	9	18.06	18.07

Guangdong Province

Bordering the South China Sea, Guangdong is one of the southernmost provinces in China. Mountains cover 33 per cent of the entire territory, hilly areas 25 per cent, plains 23 per cent and tableland 19 per cent. It has a coastline of more than 4,300 kilometres and a total area of 179,756 square kilometres. The population is 77.83 million and the provincial capital is Guangzhou. Major economic indicators are shown in Table 7.19.1.

Resources

Guangdong is rich in mineral resources with more than 50 kinds of proven mineral ores, mostly non-ferrous metals, including tungsten, tin, antimony, molybdenum, copper, lead, zinc and gold. Rare metals include monazite, niobium and zircon. At the Beibu Bay and in the shallow waters of Leizhou Peninsula in the west of Guangdong, oil has been discovered and exploited. The province also abounds in oil shale.

Infrastructure

Transportation and communications are convenient, with Guangzhou as a hub of water, land and air transport. Air services link Guangzhou with many cities within and outside Guangdong and Guangzhou Baiyun Airport offers international flights. The province has the Beijing-Kowloon and Beijing-Guangzhou railways as its trunk lines. Highways are widely used for transportation. Major ports include Guangzhou Huangpu, Zhanjiang, Shantou and Haikou.

Table 7.19.1 Major economic indicators

Item	2000	2001
Population (millions)	77.068	77.8341
Gross domestic products (billion RMB)	966.223	1055.647
GDP per capita (thousand RMB)	12.885	
Disposable income per capita (thousand RMB)		
Urban residents	9.679	3.642
Rural residents	10.415	3.770
Savings (billion RMB)*	168.503	194.2849
Investment in fixed assets (billion RMB)	314.513	354.729
Value-added of primary industry (billion RMB)	100.006	100.453
Value-added of secondary industry (billion RMB)	486.875	530.40
Value-added of tertiary industry (billion RMB)	379.342	424.80
Total retail sales of consumer goods (billion RMB)	407.149	451.528

Source: China Statistical Yearbook 2001 and State Statistical Bureau.

*Both institutional and private savings

Foreign trade

Guangdong province is China's largest exporting province. In 2000, it registered a total foreign trade value of US$170.106 billion, a robust increase of 21.2 per cent over US$140.34 billion in 1999.

Export contributed to slightly more than 54 per cent of the province's total trade. Total export value was US$91.92 billion, up by 18.3 per cent over US$77.675 billion in 1999, accounting for 36.9 per cent of the country's total export value. The province's exports in 2000 were largely manufactured goods, totalling US$88.474 billion, about 96.3 per cent of the total export value. Export of primary products was US$3.446 billion, accounting for 3.7 per cent of total export value.

Exports were destined for 214 countries and regions, though the top five export markets took about 87 per cent of the province's exports. The most significant change in the constitution of the top five markets is the reduction of Hong Kong's share in the province's export (see Table 7.19.2). In 1995, Hong Kong was a gateway for Guangdong's exports and took as much as 87.03 per cent of its exports. By 2000, however, its share in Guangdong's total export value had dropped to 34.3 per cent. The USA's share in the province's export increased from about 3 per cent in 1995 to 25.7 per cent in 2000, as did those of the European Union and Japan, whose shares in Guangdong's total export increased quite dramatically in those six years.

Table 7.19.2 Top five export markets, Guangdong Province, 1995 and 2000

Country/region	Export value (US$ million)	% of export total
1995		
Hong Kong	48,449.77	87.03
USA	1,708.22	3.07
Japan	1,085.72	1.95
European Union	1,073.03	1.93
Taiwan Province	1,059.48	1.90
Total	53,376.22	95.88
2000		
Hong Kong	31,528.71	34.30
USA	23,627.27	25.70
European Union	12,580.84	13.69
Japan	7,747.64	8.43
ASEAN	4,507.66	4.90
Total	79,992.12	87.02

The province's total import value hit a high of US$78.185 billion in 2000, an increase of 24.8 per cent over US$62.665 billion in 1999. The province imported more manufactured products than primary products in terms of total value: US$68.323 billion compared with US$9.692 billion worth. The split was 87.6 per cent and 12.4 per cent. Import commodities came from 166 countries and regions. As with export, the province's dependence on Hong Kong for imports has greatly reduced (see Table 7.19.3). Hong Kong ranked seventh in 2000 as a supplier of the province's imports, with its share in the total import value falling from 79.51 per cent in 1995 to 6.71 per cent in 2000.

Table 7.19.3 Top five import markets, Guangdong Province, 1995 and 2000

Country/region	Import value (US$ million)	% of import total
1995		
Hong Kong	30,346.82	79.51
Taiwan Province	3,994.91	10.47
Japan	1,155.29	3.03
European Union	857.03	2.25
USA	475.78	1.25
Total	36,829.83	96.51
2000		
Taiwan Province	15,126.53	19.35
Japan	14,013.19	17.92
ASEAN	9,178.82	11.74
EU	7,001.90	8.96
Republic of Korea	6,854.94	8.77
Total	74,886.04	66.74

Utilization of foreign capital

Foreign direct investment in the province increased by 40.64 per cent in 2000 (see Table 7.19.4). The total number of contracts approved in the year was 4245, involving a total contracted investment of US$8.68 billion. 67.42 per cent of the approved contracts were for solely foreign-owned enterprises, while their contracted investment comprised 66.64 per cent of the total contracted investment.

Of the 4,245 newly approved foreign direct investment projects, over 80 per cent were intended for production-related projects. Foreign direct investment came from 50 countries and regions, among which

Table 7.19.4 Utilization of foreign capital, Guangdong Province, 1995 and 2000

Mode	Number	Approved contracts		Actual utilization	
		Total value (US$ million) year's total value	% change over previous year	Total value (US$ million) year's total value	% change over previous year
1995					
Direct foreign investment:	8,177	24,832.44	4.23	10,180.28	8/33
Equity joint ventures	3,071	8,165.54		3,573.36	
Contractual joint ventures	2,416	9,641.46		4,064.61	
Solely foreign-owned enterprises	2,690	7,025.44		2,254.31	
2000					
Direct foreign investment:	4,245	8,683.93	40.64	12,237.20	0.28
Equity joint ventures	956	1,530.69	41.07	3,137.85	−23.17
Contractual joint ventures	426	1,312.93	−1.22	3,763.71	−2.97
Solely foreign-owned enterprises	2 862	5,787.05	54.42	5,280.16	26.40

Hong Kong was first in terms of aggregate contract value (see Table 7.19.5).

By the end of 2000, the number of approved foreign-invested enterprises in the province had reached 83,800. In 2000, the total export value of foreign-invested enterprises was US$49.55 billion, accounting for 53.9 per cent of the total export value of the province.

Table 7.19.5 Key sources of FDI, Guangdong Province

Source of FDI	No. of projects	Contract value (US$ million)
Hong Kong	2474	4122.19
British Virgin Islands	380	1816.92
Taiwan Province	482	483.54
Singapore	76	465.16
United States	193	443.89
Cayman Islands	26	205.78
Japan	51	196.08
Western Samoa	52	161.51
Macao	304	128.63
Republic of Korea	52	81.43
Australia	31	75.07
UK	18	71.58
Netherlands	14	59.48
France	7	56.70

Guangxi Zhuang Autonomous Region

With Beibu Gulf to its south and Vietnam to its southwest, Guangxi is situated in the western part of south China. Mountains and hilly areas account for 25 per cent, plains 25 per cent and rocky terrain about 50 per cent of the total area. With rivers criss-crossing the land and numerous underground streams, the scenery of Guilin is known as 'the best under heaven'. The total area is 230,000 square kilometres with a population of 47.88 million. The regional capital is Nanning. Major economic indicators are shown in Table 7.20.1.

Resources

Among the rich mineral resources of the region, tin ranks first in the country and zinc second. There are also sizeable reserves of antimony, aluminium, tungsten and lead. The region has the nation's largest reserves of manganese and crystal. Guangxi has a forested area extending to 5.5 million hectares with more than 5,000 species of plants. With a sub-tropical climate and fertile soil, Guangxi produces a large number of cash crops, including sugar cane, palm-oil seeds, bananas, pineapples and rosin. Among these, the amount of sugarcane and fruits produced is the largest in the country. The Beibu Bay is one of the most important tropical fishing grounds in China and abundant aquatic produce such as shrimp, shellfish, squid, pearl and oyster can be found along its 1,595 kilometre coastline. Beihai and Hepu are Guangxi's major fishing ports. Guangxi also produces some of the best pearls in the world.

Table 7.20.1 Major economic indicators, Guangxi Ahuang Autonomous Region

Item	2000	2001
Population (millions)	47.51	47.88
Gross domestic product (billion RMB)	205.014	223.119
GDP per capita (thousand RMB)	4.319	4.697
Disposable income per capita (thousand RMB)		
Urban residents	5.832	1.864
Rural residents	6.666	1.944
Savings (billion RMB)*	201.559	251.894
Investment in fixed assets (billion RMB)	58.334	73.125
Value-added of primary industry (billion RMB)	53.869	55.621
Value-added of secondary industry (billion RMB)	74.80	81.69
Value-added of tertiary industry (billion RMB)	76.345	85.81
Total retail sales of consumer goods (billion RMB)	85.939	93.588

Source: China Statistical Yearbook2001 and State Statistical Bureau.

*Both institutional and private savings

Infrastructure

Beihai, Qinzhou and Fangcheng are Guangxi's major ports with more than 23 berths for 10,000-tonne vessels. Inland river ports such as Nanning, Wuzhou and Guigang also play a significant role in the region's inland water transport system. The navigation channel of the Xijiang River is linked with Zhujiang in Guangdong Province from where ships can reach Whampoo port as well as Hong Kong and Macao. Five airports are located in Guilin, Nanning, Liuzhou, Beihai and Wuzhou and air services link Nanning and Gulin with Beijing, Shanghai, Guangzhou, Hong Kong and many other cities. Guilin and Lijiang are popular tourist centres. The region has several trunk railway lines, with Liuzhou as the hub. Over 98 per cent of rural towns are accessible by bus. The telecommunications system has been greatly improved as a result of heavy investment.

Foreign trade

Guangxi Zhuang Autonomous Region achieved 16.2 per cent growth in its total foreign trade value, from US$1.753 billion in 1999 to US$2.038 billion in 2000. The total export value reached US$1.493 billion, an increase of 19.7 per cent over US$1.247 billion in 1999. Export trade was responsible for 6.1 per cent of the region's GDP and accounted for 0.6 per cent of the whole country's total export value.

Export of primary products amounted to US$236 million and export of manufactured products came to US$1257 million, accounting for 15.81 per cent and 84.19 per cent respectively of the region's total export value.

Exports were destined for 222 countries and regions, while the top five destinations (see Table 7.20.2) took a share of 63.3 per cent in the region's total export value. The province's geographical proximity to Vietnam accounts for its high position in the top five.

Total import value was US$545 million, up by 7.6 per cent over US$506 million in 1999. Import of primary products amounted to US$170 million and import of manufactured products US$375 million, accounting for 31.19 per cent and 68.81 per cent respectively of the region's total import value. The top five import markets (see Table 7.20.3) had a collective share of 49.12 per cent in the region's total import, down from 67.85 per cent in 1995.

Table 7.20.2 Top five export markets, Guangxi Zhuang Autonomous Region, 1995 and 2000

Country/region	Export value (US$ million)	% of export total
1995		
Hong Kong	1,196.40	53.27
Vietnam	237.36	10.57
Japan	155.73	6.93
USA	138.88	6.18
Netherlands	72.68	3.24
Total	1,801.05	80.19
2000		
USA	233.39	15.6
Vietnam	222.14	14.9
Hong Kong	219.78	14.8
Netherlands	141.63	9.5
Japan	128.53	8.5
Total	945.47	63.3

Table 7.20.3 Top five import origins, Guangxi Zhuang Autonomous Region, 1995 and 2000

Country/region	Import value (US$ million)	% of import total
1995		
Hong Kong	229.00	28.21
Vietnam	141.45	17.43
Thailand	113.23	13.95
USA	33.97	4.18
Russia	33.08	4.08
Total	550.73	67.85
2000		
Taiwan Province	80.59	14.79
Vietnam	69.48	12.75
Japan	38.57	7.08
Republic of Korea	42.83	7.85
USA	36.27	6.65
Total	267.74	49.12

Utilization of foreign capital

The total number of FDI contracts approved by Guangxi in 2000 was 246, with a total contract value of US$715.49 million. This represented a moderate increase of 6.2 per cent over 1999. Investment in equity and contractual joint ventures experienced negative growth rates of 35.3 per cent and 17 per cent respectively but the contract

Table 7.20.4 Utilization of foreign capital, Guangxi Zhuang Autonomous Region, 1995 and 2000

Mode	Number	Approved contracts		Actual utilization	
		Total value (US$ million) year's total value	*% change over previous year*	*Total value (US$ million) year's total value*	*% change over previous year*
1995					
Direct foreign investment	571	1,041.77	−10.35	669.52	−17.86
Equity joint ventures	323	538.70		413.67	
Contractual joint ventures	76	186.91		104.22	
Solely foreign-owned enterprises	172	316.16	−44.26	151.63	
2000					
Direct foreign investment	246	715.49	6.2	527.66	−16.9
Equity joint ventures	100	101.57	−35.3	164.13	−30.0
Contractual joint ventures	42	279.63	−17.0	154.77	66.9
Solely foreign-owned enterprises	104	329.36	83.1	184.76	−40.0

value of solely foreign-owned enterprises increased by 83.1 per cent in 2000 (see Table 7.20.4).

In 2000, FDI came from more diversified sources. The percentage of direct investments from Taiwan Province, Hong Kong and Macao declined from 55 per cent in 1999 to 39 per cent, while investments from North America and Latin America were up from 5 per cent and 2 per cent respectively in 1999 to 27 per cent and 17 per cent. The top ten investing countries and regions are listed in Table 7.20.5.

Table 7.20.5 Key sources of FDI, Guangxi Zhuang Autonomous Region

Source of FDI	No. of projects	Contract value (US$ million)
Hong Kong	134	238.54
Canada	2	110.69
Cayman Islands	0	87.95
USA	24	81.28
Singapore	7	61.79
Taiwan Province	39	36.61
British Virgin Islands	3	34.97
Malaysia	4	31.17
The Philippines	1	28.00
Republic of Korea	5	15.15

Hainan Province

Hainan is an island province situated in the southernmost part of China. It is located 18 nautical-miles off Guangdong's Leizhou Peninsula in southern China. Hainan province is composed of the Hainan Island, Xisha Islands, Nansha Islands and Zhongsha Islands. Hainan Island is the second largest island in China, after Taiwan Island. It is an arch, high in the middle and low all around. Mountains account for 25.4 per cent, hills 13.3 per cent, tableland 32.6 per cent and plains 28.7 per cent. The province has a total area of over 33,920 square kilometres with a population of 7.9555 million. The island has a total of 1,528 kilometres of coastline. The provincial capital is Haikou. Major economic indicators are shown in Table 7.21.1.

Resources

The island is rich in natural resources. Its inland and offshore deposits of oil and natural gas rank are among the largest in China. Hainan has potential gas reserves of 5.8 trillion cubic metres and oil reserves of 29.1 billion tons in the main basins of the sea including the Yingge Sea and Beibu Bay. There are six oil and gas fields in operation, including Yacheng 13–1, Dongfang 1–1, Ledong 22–1 and Ledong 15–1. Since the beginning of 1996, Hainan has provided gas to Hong Kong through a 770-kilometre pipeline, annually supplying 2.9 billion cubic metres. Deposits of some 50 minerals have been discovered and more than 200 ore deposits

Table 7.21.1 Major economic indicators, Hainan Province

Item	2000	2001
Population (million)	7.8806	7.9555
Gross domestic product (billion RMB)	51.848	56.605
GDP per capita (thousand RMB)	6.894	n.a
Disposable income per capita (thousand RMB)		
Urban residents	5.3568	2.923
Rural residents	5.839	2.993
Savings (billion RMB)	84.337	87.31
Investment in fixed assets (billion RMB)	19.887	20.6
Value-added of primary industry (billion RMB)	19.656	20.028
Value-added of secondary industry (billion RMB)	10.245	13.12
Value-added of tertiary industry (billion RMB)	21.947	23.46
Total retail sales of consumer goods (billion RMB)	17.25	18.75

Source: China Statistical Yearbook 2001 and State Statistical Bureau.
*Both institutional and private savings

have been found, including iron, copper, cobalt, lead, zinc, tungsten, tin, cement limestone, barite and lignite. Its reserves of titanium amount to about 70 per cent of the national total. Hainan island has rich aquatic resources, with 800 types of fish and 25,000 hectares of shallow water suited to raising fish.

Infrastructure

Major ports in Hainan include Haikou Port, Basuo Port and Sanya Port. There are 28 berths in total, of which 22 can take over 10,000 tonnes. Air services link Haikao with major cities in China. Highways connect towns and cities in the province. The construction of Guangdong-Hainan railway linking Zhanjiang in Guangdong to Sanya – the first cross-sea railway in China – has recently been completed. This railway connects Hainan with the mainland railway network.

Foreign trade

In 2000, the total value of import and export for Hainan Province reached US$1.29 billion, a moderate increase of 5.68 per cent over US$1.22 billion in 1999. The total value of export was US$802.89 million, up by 7.25 per cent over US$748.6 million in 1999. It was 12.82 per cent of the provincial GDP of RMB51.9 billion (US$6.263 billion) and 0.32 per cent of the total export value of the whole country.

Export of primary products amounted to US$322.68 million, accounting for 40.19 per cent of total export value; the export of manufactured products totalled US$480.21 million, or 59.81 per cent.

Hong Kong was again the biggest export market for the province (see Table 7.21.2). In 2000, the province exported US$353.46 million worth of goods to Hong Kong, 44.02 per cent of the province's total export. Other major export destinations include Japan, USA, Korea and Taiwan Province.

The import total of Hainan Province increased by 3.17 per cent in total, a rise from US$470.07 million in 1999 to US$484.95 million in 2000.

Import of primary products amounted to US$138.65 million, making up 28.9 per cent of the total value, and that of manufactured products stood at US$346 million, or 72.08 per cent.

Hong Kong was again the largest import source for the province (see Table 7.21.3), supplying US$175.77 million worth of goods to the province. Japan ranked

Table 7.21.2 Top five export markets, Hainan Province, 1995 and 2000

Country/region	Export value (US$ million)	% of export total
1995		
Hong Kong	443.86	53.48
Japan	142.33	17.15
USA	57.33	6.91
Republic of Korea	52.74	6.35
The Netherlands	27.74	3.34
Total	724	87.23
2000		
Hong Kong	353.46	44.02
Japan	82.24	10.24
USA	80.94	10.08
Republic of Korea	29.77	3.7
Taiwan Province	20.45	2.55
Total	566.86	70.59

Table 7.21.3 Top five import markets, Hainan Province, 1995 and 2000

Country/region	Import value (US$ million)	% of import total
1995		
Hong Kong	658.62	46.19
Japan	153.17	10.47
USA	146.62	10.26
Vietnam	97.69	6.85
Singapore	70.13	4.92
Total	1,126.23	78.69
2000		
Hong Kong	175.77	36.25
Japan	67.29	13.89
USA	44.03	9.08
Republic of Korea	30.85	6.36
Thailand	20.75	4.28
Total	338.69	69.86

second with 13.89 per cent of the province's import value.

Utilization of foreign capital

Hainan province approved 184 FDI contracts with a total contracted investment of US$137.05 million, a

Table 7.21.4   Utilization of foreign capital, Hainan Province, 1995 and 2000

Mode	Number	Approved contracts		Actual utilization	
		Total value (US$ million) year's total value	% change over previous year	Total value (US$ million) year's total value	% change over previous year
1995					
Direct foreign investment:	389	2,780.77	127.05	1,062.07	21.46
Equity joint ventures	133	329.78	−5.35	235.30	−3.89
Contractual joint ventures	15	82.84	−39.18	90.43	311.79
Solely foreign-owned enterprises	241	2,368.15	220.02	736.34	21.18
2000					
Direct foreign investment:	184	137.05	−82.69	430.80	−11.08
Equity joint ventures	50	49.46	−26.15	172.87	9.74
Contractual joint ventures	2	5.17	−90.42	27.62	572.02
Solely foreign-owned enterprises	132	82.42	−87.64	229.10	−23.24

fall of 82.69 per cent against 1999. All three forms of FDI had experienced declines of various degrees (see Table 7.21.4).

Hong Kong was the most significant investor in the province (see Table 7.21.5). 88 Hong Kong-invested projects were approved in 2000, with a total contracted investment of US$47.37 million. Second to Hong Kong was Taiwan, who invested US$19.21 million in contract value in 45 projects.

Major foreign-invested projects were mainly engaged in tourism and hotels, agriculture, manufacturing and property development. Multinational companies such as Siemens, Dupont, BASF, Benz and Mitsubishi have also set up operations on the island. The province will place a priority on projects connected with power generation, transport, farm product processing, environmental protection and tourism in its future efforts to attracting foreign direct investment.

Table 7.21.5   Key sources of FDI, Hainan Province

Source of FDI	No. of projects	Contract value (US$million)
Hong Kong	88	47.37
Taiwan Province	45	19.21
Japan	8	3.92
Republic of Korea	5	4.28
UK	3	11.71

Chongqing

Chongqing is located at the upper reaches of the Yangtze River and crossed by the Jialing River in south-west China. It was part of Sichuan province until 1997, when it become the fourth municipality after Beijing, Shanghai and Tianjin to be directly under the jurisdiction of the central government. The administrative jurisdiction of the Chongqing government was expanded to include the neighbouring Fuling and Wanxian cities and the Qianjiang region. Chongqing covers a total area of 82,403 square kilometres. Major economic indicators are shown in Table 7.22.1.

Resources

Chongqing is rich in natural resources with more than 40 kinds of minerals. Its coal reserve is 4.8 billion tons. The Chuandong Natural Gas Field in Chongqing is China's largest inland production base of natural gas, with deposits of 270 billion cubic metres, more than a fifth of China's total. Chongqing also contains China's largest reserve of strontium.

Infrastructure

Chongqing is a major trading port on the upper Yangtze River. The Jialing and Minjiang rivers are the two major rivers flowing into the Yangtze. Upon completion of the Three Gorges Dam project, vessels of up to 10,000 tonnes will be able to enter Chongqing's Chaotianmen Port. Chongqing is also a major railway hub in southwest China, with three major railway lines that connect the city with the national railway network and China's major cities and ports. Currently, Chongqing has direct air routes to about 50 domestic and international desti-

Table 7.22.1 Major economic indicators, Chongqing

Item	2000	2001
Population (millions)	30.92	30.97
Gross domestic product (billion RMB)	158.934	175
GDP per capita (thousand RMB)	5.157	5.655
Disposable income per capita (thousand RMB)		
Urban residents	6.276	1.892
Rural residents	6.721	1.971
Savings (billion RMB)*	190.536	229.405
Investment in fixed assets (billion RMB)	57.259	80.182
Value-added of primary industry (billion RMB)	28.30	29.3
Value-added of secondary industry (billion RMB)	65.751	72.7
Value-added of tertiary industry (billion RMB)	64.883	73
Total retail sales of consumer goods (billion RMB)	64.336	69.933

Source: China Statistical Yearbook2001 and State Statistical Bureau.

*Both institutional and private savings

nations including Hong Kong, Macao, Bangkok, Munich and Nagoya. The city has mature telecommunication systems.

Foreign trade

In 2000, the import and export value of Chongqing Municipality increased by 47.53 per cent, from US$1.21 billion in 1999 to US$1.785 billion. Total export value doubled from US$490 million in 1999 to US$995 million in 2000. Export was equivalent to 5.18 per cent of the municipal GDP of RMB 159 billion (US$19.2 billion) and 0.4 per cent of the total export value of the whole country.

Very small amounts of primary goods, US$41.78 million or 4.2 per cent of the total export value, were exported from the city in 2000. Export of manufactured products, on the other hand, comprised 95.8 per cent of the total export value, amounting to US$953.44 million.

Interestingly, Vietnam was first among the top five major export destinations, taking 27.84 per cent of the city's export (see Table 7.22.2). This was largely attributed to the export of motorcycles to the country; Chongqing is a leading motorcycle producer in China.

Import experienced a moderate increase of 9.75 per cent to US$790 million. Total import in 1999 was US$720 million. The composition of imports resem-

bled the pattern of export, with the import of primary products taking a small share of 5.68 per cent or US$44.88 million, whereas the import of manufactured products took a share as high as 94.32 per cent (US$745.37 million).

The top five import markets (see Table 7.22.3) supplied 83.27 per cent of the import total, and over 58 per cent of the city's import came from Japan.

Table 7.22.3 Top five import markets, Chongqing, 1995 and 2000

Country/region	Export value (US$ million)	% of export total
1995		
Japan	241.43	38.67
Hong Kong	142.22	22.78
Sweden	45.25	7.25
Britain	36.17	5.79
USA	29.88	4.79
Total	494.95	79.28
2000		
Japan	459.25	58.11
Republic of Korea	90.57	11.46
Hong Kong	54.92	6.95
USA	28.41	3.59
Australia	24.95	3.16
Total	658.1	83.27

Utilization of foreign capital

In 2000, Chongqing approved 190 foreign-invested projects, an increase of 12.4 per cent over 1999, with contracted foreign investment dropping by 29.5 per cent against 1999 (see Table 7.22.4). The foreign investment actually utilised achieved a fractional increase of 2.3 per cent, to US$244.4 million.

Among these FDI projects, 111 were engaged in production activities, and 79 projects were in other operations.

Foreign direct investments came from 35 countries and regions. The top five investors and the value of the foreign capital involved were as follows:

The total export value of the operating FIEs reached US$97.94 million, up by 57.56 per cent over 1999. Total profit and tax reached a combined RMB1.160 billion, up by 21.96 per cent. Foreign-related tax revenue totalled RMB2.19 billion, accounting for 23.57 per cent of the municipality's total tax revenue.

Table 7.22.2 Top five export markets, Chongqing, 1995 and 2000

Country/region	Export value (US$ million)	% of export total
1995		
Hong Kong	348.42	40.71
Japan	90.44	10.57
USA	72.58	8.48
Korea	67.16	7.85
Germany	46.42	5.43
Total	625.02	73.04
2000		
Vietnam	277.02	27.84
Indonesia	109.66	11.02
USA	84.88	8.53
Japan	73.88	7.42
Hong Kong	60.88	6.11
Total	606.32	60.92

Table 7.22.4   Utilization of foreign capital, Chongqing, 2000

Mode	Number	Approved contracts		Actual utilization	
		Total value (US$ million) year's total value	*% change over previous year*	*Total value (US$ million) year's total value*	*% change over previous year*
2000					
Direct foreign investment:	190	357.16	−29.54	244.36	2.27
Equity joint ventures	80	77.31	−72.29	158.73	−3.83
Contractual joint ventures	19	65.42	−48.72	24.24	101.83
Solely foreign-owned enterprises	91	213.85	113.08	61.39	−0.78

Table 7.22.5   Key sources of FDI, Chongqing, 2000

Source	No. of projects	Contract value (US$ million)
Hong Kong	82	227.64
British Virgin Islands	6	29.18
Taiwan Province	32	28.04
Bahamas	2	12.96
USA	17	9.72

Sichuan Province

Sichuan Province is situated along the upper reaches of the Yangtze River. The eastern part of the province is a basin, surrounded by the Daliang, Qionglai, Daba, Wuahan and Emei mountains. The west of the province consists of snow-capped mountains. Mountains account for 49.8 per cent of the total area of the province, plateaux 29 per cent, hilly areas 18.6 per cent and plains 2.6 per cent. The total area is 485,000 square kilometres and the population is 86.396 million. The provincial capital is Chengdu. Major economic indicators are shown in Table 7.23.1.

Resources

More than 132 kinds of mineral resources have been found in the province and its deposits of natural gas are the second largest in the country. Reserves of 11 mineral resources such as vanadium, titanium and lithium are the largest in China. The Panxi region alone possesses 13.3 per cent of the national reserves of iron, 93 per cent of titanium, 69 per cent of vanadium and 83 per cent of cobalt. Other mineral sources include coal, phosphate rocks, symbiotic iron ores, well salt, mirabilite, asbestos, mica and marble. With more than seven million hectares of forest cover, the province is a leading producer of tung oil. Water resources are especially rich with more than 1.370 rivers criss-crossing the province. Sichuan is one of the major agricultural production bases in China. Cash crops include rapeseed, citrus fruits, peaches, sugar canes and sweet potatoes. Sichuan also has the highest output of pork and the second largest output of silkworm cocoons in China.

Table 7.23.1 Major economic indicators, Sichuan Province

Item	*2000*	*2001*
Population (millions)	86.02	86.396
Gross domestic product (billion RMB)	401.025	442.18
GDP per capita (thousand RMB)	4.784	
Disposable income per capita (thousand RMB)		
Urban residents	5.894	1.914
Rural residents	6.360	1.987
Savings (billion RMB)*	451.227	525.68
Investment in fixed assets (billion RMB)	141.804	157.38
Value-added of primary industry (billion RMB)	945.58	98.17
Value-added of secondary industry (billion RMB)	170.049	175.69
Value-added of tertiary industry (billion RMB)	136.418	168.32
Total retail sales of consumer goods (billion RMB)	152.348	168.04

Source: China Statistical Yearbook 2001 and State Statistical Bureau.
*Both institutional and private savings

Infrastructure

Chengdu, the provincial capital, is the railway hub of the province, with main lines extending to Yunna, Guizhou and Hunan provinces. By the end of 2000, the total length of highways in Sichuan had reached 1,000 kilometres, the longest in western China. Trunk roads lead to Sha'anxi and elsewhere. Sichuan has one of the best inland waterway transportation systems in China, with the Yangtze as the main traffic artery. Air services link Chengdu with major Chinese cities and there are regular international flights to Hong Kong, Bangkok, Singapore, Japan and the Republic of Korea. The province is a tourist centre, with beautiful mountains and rivers.

Foreign trade

Sichuan's total foreign trade in 2000 was valued at US$2.545 billion, fractionally higher (3.01 per cent) than 1999's figure of US$2.471 billion. Export, however, experienced quite a significant increase of 22.23 per cent from 1999's US$1.141 billion to US$1.394 billion in 2000. Total export value in 2000 was equivalent to 2.87 per cent of the provincial GDP for that year and 0.56 per cent of the total export value of China as a whole.

Export of primary products amounted to US$232 million and export of manufactured products came to US$1162 million, accounting for 16.6 per cent and 83.4 per cent respectively of the province's total export value (see Table 7.23.2).

Hong Kong was the biggest export market for the province in 2000, followed by Japan, the United States, Thailand and Korea.

The province reported a decrease in its total import value in 2000: US$1.151 billion, down by 13.5 per cent against US$1.330 billion in 1999. Import of primary products amounted to US$142 million and import of manufactured products came to US$1.009 billion, accounting for 12.3 per cent and 87.7 per cent respectively of the total import value.

Japan was the largest supplier of Sichuan's imports, followed by the United States, Korea, Germany and Taiwan province (see Table 7.23.3).

Utilization of foreign capital

Sichuan approved 293 FDI contracts in 2000, with the contracted investment totalling US$604.82 million, an

Table 7.23.2 Top five export markets, Sichuan Province, 1995 and 2000

Country/region	Export value (US$ million)	% of export total
1995		
Hong Kong	822.97	30.10
Japan	426.89	15.61
USA	206.80	7.56
Republic of Korea	182.62	6.68
Germany	129.63	4.74
Total	3,763.91	64.69
2000		
Hong Kong	236.75	16.98
Japan	199.80	14.33
USA	167.99	11.98
Thailand	82.94	5.95
Republic of Korea	71.02	5.10
Total	758.5	54.34

Note: 1995 figures are not comparable to 2000 figures because Chongqing city, which was part of Sichuan province in 1995, became a separate administrative region in 1997.

Table 7.23.3 Top five import markets, Sichuan Province, 1995 and 2000

Country/region	Import value (US$ million)	% of import total
1995		
Hong Kong	425.25	26.61
Japan	390.16	24.42
USA	172.03	10.77
Germany	95.11	5.95
UK	59.77	3.74
Total	1,142.32	71.49
2000		
Japan	254.04	22.07
USA	211.69	18.39
Republic of Korea	106.35	9.24
Germany	75.94	6.60
Taiwan Province	65.07	5.65
Total	713.09	61.95

Note: 1995 figures are not comparable to 2000 figures because Chongqing city, which was part of Sichuan province in 1995, became a separate administrative region in 1997.

increase of 2 per cent on 1999. FDI in equity joint ventures dropped by 2 per cent while investment in the form of contractual joint ventures and solely foreign-

Table 7.23.4   Utilization of foreign capital, Sichuan Province, 1995 and 2000

Mode	Number	Approved contracts		Actual utilization	
		Total value (US$ million) year's total value	*% change over previous year*	*Total value (US$ million) year's total value*	*% change over previous year*
1995					
Direct foreign investment:	826	1,206.82	−19.71	539.40	128.55
Equity joint ventures	519	744.97		383.91	
Contractual joint ventures	53	128.09		74.58	
Solely foreign-owned enterprises	254	333.76		80.91	
2000					
Direct foreign investment:	293	604.84	2.0	436.94	28.1
Equity joint ventures	156	265.03	−2.0	290.46	56.3
Contractual joint ventures	25	103.89	21.0	27.19	−44.8
Solely foreign-owned enterprises	112	235.92	112.0	119.29	12.6

owned enterprises increased by 21 per cent and 112 per cent respectively (see Table 7.23.4).

The FDI was distributed in a wide range of industries, such as manufacturing (60.79 per cent), real estate (11.77 per cent), services (10.7 per cent), power, gas and water supply (5.01 per cent), and the construction industry (3.53 per cent). Among the 293 FDI projects approved in 2000, 209 were production-related purposes with the remaining 84 for other projects.

Foreign direct investment mainly came from 51 countries and regions in 2000. The main sources of FDI are provided in Table 7.23.5.

By the end of 2000, 5,481 foreign investors had invested in Sichuan, with the accumulated contractual and utilised foreign investment reaching US$14.0 billion and US$7.3 billion respectively. The total value of import and export of the operating FIEs in 2000 was US$615.24 million, up by 43.06 per cent, of which the export value reached US$245.17 million, up by 54.9 per cent.

Table 7.23.5   Key sources of FDI, Sichuan Province, 2000

Sources of FDI	No. of projects	Contract value (US$ million)
USA	39	111.45
British Virgin Islands	17	89.00
Hong Kong	110	88.63
Singapore	14	33.53
Japan	11	21.93
Taiwan Province	46	13.84
UK	5	9.63
Norway	4	9.8
France	4	6.48
Germany	6	5.13
Bermuda	1	5

7.24

Guizhou Province

Guizhou is situated on the eastern part of Yunnan-Guizhou Plateau, criss-crossed by high mountains and rolling hills. The whole province is known as the Guizhou Plateau. Topographically, it is divided into three zones: the western plateau, the central hilly highland and the northern mountainous area. Guizhou's total area is 176,167 square kilometres and the population is 37.9851 million. The provincial capital is Guiyang. Major economic indicators are shown in Table 7.24.1.

Resources

Guizhou is abundant in coal, phosphorus, mercury, aluminium, manganese, antimony and zinc reserves. Phosphorus and aluminium deposits are the third largest in the country. Mercury deposits total 38,000 tons, ranking first in China. Guizhou has a strong agricultural sector and is one of the main producers of tobacco. It is also well known for its tea products and large varieties of traditional Chinese medicinal herbs.

Infrastructure

Four trunk railway lines lead to Yunnan, Sichuan, Guangxi and Hunan provinces. There are 2,800 kilometres of navigable inland waterways, of which 1,200 kilometres allow the passage of motorised boats. There are five state highways. Air services link Guiyang with Guangzhou, Chengdu, Chongqing, Kunming and other cities in China and there is a direct flight to Hong Kong. Several new airports are being planned and built. With exploitable water resources ranking sixth in the country, over one hundred hydroelectric power stations have been or are being built in the province.

Table 7.24.1   Major economic indicators, Guizhou Province

Item	2000	2001
Population (millions)	37.5572	37.9851
Gross domestic product (billion RMB)	99.353	108.219
GDP per capita (thousand RMB)	2.662	
Disposable income per capita (thousand RMB)		
Urban residents	5.247	1.357
Rural residents	5.452	1.412
Savings (billion RMB)*	110.664	134.111
Investment in fixed assets (billion RMB)	39.698	50.531
Value-added of primary industry (billion RMB)	27.099	27.426
Value-added of secondary industry (billion RMB)	38.785	42.16
Value-added of tertiary industry (billion RMB)	33.469	38.61
Total retail sales of consumer goods (billion RMB)	34.365	37.801

Source: China Statistical Yearbook 2001 and State Statistical Bureau.

*Both institutional and private savings

Foreign trade

In 2000, Guizhou Province's total import and export value came to US$660.02 million, an increase of 21 per cent over US$547.61 million in 1999.

Total export value was US$420.60 million, up by 18 per cent over US$357.79 million in 1999, equivalent to 3.5 per cent of the provincial GDP of RMB99.353 billion (US$12.001 billion) and 0.2 per cent of the total export value of the whole country.

Export of primary and manufactured products amounted to US$106.73 million and US$313.83 million respectively, or 25 per cent and 75 per cent of the total export value.

The top five export markets (see Table 7.24.2) took 47.51 per cent of the total export, with Japan first, followed by Korea, the United States, Hong Kong and India.

Table 7.24.2 Top five export destinations, Guizhou Province, 1995 and 2000

Country/region	Export value (US$ million)	% of export total
1995		
Hong Kong	116.15	27
Japan	70.52	16.39
USA	30.55	7.3
Republic of Korea	30.1	7
Netherlands	23.87	5.55
Total	271.19	63.24
2000		
Japan	50.74	12.06
Republic of Korea	45.18	10.74
USA	44.38	10.55
Hong Kong	37.41	8.89
India	22.17	5.27
Total	199.88	47.51

Import value totalled US$239.42 million, up by 26 per cent over US$189.82 million in 1999.

Import of primary and manufactured products amounted to US$125.03 million and US$114.39 million respectively, or 52.22 per cent and 47.78 per cent of the total import value.

Table 7.24.3 Top five import markets, Guizhou Province, 1995 and 2000

Country/region	Import value (US$ million)	% of import total
1995		
Hong Kong	40.42	16.03
Germany	37.38	14.82
USA	32.37	12.84
Japan	11.01	4.37
Netherlands	9.63	3.82
Total	130.81	51.88
2000		
USA	37.45	15.64
Australia	25.49	10.65
Japan	23.84	9.96
India	22.78	9.52
Germany	18.40	7.69
Total	127.96	53.46

The United States ranked first among the top five import markets (see Table 7.24.3), supplying 15.64 per cent of the province's import needs. Australia took the second position, followed by Japan, India and Germany.

Utilization of foreign capital

In 2000, Guizhou approved a total of 55 FDI contracts, involving a total investment of US$67.38 million. Contracted investment in 2000 increased by less than 1 per cent, only a little more than in 1999. The FDI in solely foreign-owned enterprises more than tripled while investment in contractual joint ventures dropped by 66.7 per cent on a year-on-year basis (see Table 7.24.4).

Among the 55 FDI projects approved in 2000, 44 were production-orientated while 11 projects were service-related. Foreign direct investments came from 18 countries and regions, with the main ones being Singapore with contracted investment of US$1.01 million, Hong Kong (US$27.40 million), the USA (US$13.09 million), Taiwan Province (US$1.63 million), the British Virgin Islands (US$480,000), France (US$540,000) and Canada (US$5.71 million).

The total export and import value of the operating FIEs in 2000 amounted to US$40.12 million and US$16.78 million respectively.

Table 7.24.4 Utilization of foreign capital, Guizhou Province, 1995 and 2000

Mode	Number	Approved contracts		Actual utilization	
		Total value (US$ million) year's total value	*% change over previous year*	*Total value (US$ million) year's total value*	*% change over previous year*
1995					
Direct foreign investment:	103	86.26		39.54	
Equity joint ventures	59	43.9		57.03	
Contractual joint ventures	4	4.28			
Solely foreign-owned enterprises	40	38.08			
2000					
Direct foreign investment:	55	67.38	0.79	25.01	−38.85
Equity joint ventures	26	30.58	80.84	16.30	−48.81
Contractual joint ventures	9	14.90	−66.70	1.21	−82.83
Solely foreign-owned enterprises	20	21.90	321.97	7.50	280.71

Yunnan Province

Yunnan is on China's southern border, facing Myanmar to the west and south-west and Laos and Vietnam to the south. The border of the country extends 4,000 kilometres. Hills and mountains account for 94 per cent of the total area and plains for 6 per cent. The province has a population of 42.874 million and the provincial capital is Kunming. Major economic indicators are shown in Table 7.25.1.

Resources

The province boasts more than 100 kinds of proven mineral resources. Reserves of lead, zinc and germanium rank first in China; tin second, copper, platinum and nickel third, and antimony, mercury, silver and bismuth fourth. The province is one of the five largest phosphorus ore producers. There are sizeable reserves of rock salt. Resources of quartz sand and gaoling clay are abundant. Forests cover more than 9.5 million hectares, accounting for 24 per cent of the country's total area and there are many rare species of plants and trees. Yunnan is also an important base for aromatic plants and flora with more than 300 varieties of essential oil-bearing plants and 2,500 kinds of ornamental plants and flowers.

Infrastructure

There are three major trunk railway lines connecting the province with other parts of China. Main roads in service cover more than 46,000 kilometres. The province has nine civil airports and air services link the

Table 7.25.1 Major economic indicators, Yunnan Province

Item	2000	2001
Population (millions)	42.408	42.874
Gross domestic product (billion RMB)	195.509	207.747
GDP per capita (thousand RMB)	4.637	
Disposable income per capita (thousand RMB)		
Urban residents	6.32345	1.471
Rural residents	6.798	1.534
Savings (billion RMB)*	246.482	277.971
Investment in fixed assets (billion RMB)	68.396	72.499
Value-added of primary industry (billion RMB)	43. 63	45.054
Value-added of secondary industry (billion RMB)	84.324	88.054
Value-added of tertiary industry (billion RMB)	67.559	74.639
Total retail sales of consumer goods (billion RMB)	58.308	64.08

Source: China Statistical Yearbook 2001 and State Statistical Bureau.
*Both institutional and private savings

province to Beijing, Shanghai, Guangzhou and other cities. The international airport offers direct flights to Hong Kong, Japan, Bangkok, Singapore, Rangoon, and Chiang Mai. There are also regular flights to Hong Kong. There are more than 600 rivers, with total water power resources of up to 104 million kilowatts, ranking the province second in the country.

Foreign trade

Yunnan's import and export value totalled US$1.81 billion in 2000, up by 9.2 per cent over US$1.66 billion in 1999.

Total export value was US$1.12 billion, up by 13.6 per cent over US$1.03 billion in 1999. It was equivalent to 4.99 per cent and 0.47 per cent of the provincial GDP and the total export value of the nation respectively. Export of primary products amounted to US$219.75 million and for manufactured products US$955.41, accounting for 18.7 per cent and 81.3 per cent respectively of total export value.

Export commodities were sold to 102 countries and regions. Myanmar, on Yunnan's border took the highest value of Yunnan's exports, followed by Hong Kong, Japan, Vietnam and the USA. However, the top five

Table 7.25.2   Top five export markets, Yunnan Province, 1995 and 2000

Country/region	Export value (US$ million)	% of export total
1995		
Hong Kong	410.07	30.81
Myanmar	392.10	29.46
Japan	134.29	10.09
Vietnam	53.24	4.00
USA	42.72	3.21
Total	1,032.42	77.57
2000		
Myanmar	293.06	26.17
Hong Kong	210.86	18.83
Japan	117.29	10.47
Vietnam	92.64	8.27
USA	61.72	5.51
Total	775.57	69.25

markets of the province took a smaller share of the total in 2000 than in 1999 (see Table 7.25.2).

In 2000, import value totalled US$637.67 million, up by 2 per cent over US$625.25 million in 1999. Import of primary manufactured commodities reached US$367.94 million and US$269.73 million, accounting for 57.7 per cent and 42.3 per cent of the total import value respectively.

Hong Kong was the biggest supplier of Yunnan's imports with 21.8 per cent of the province's total import. Australia took 17.04 per cent of Yunnan's import, ranking second, followed by Myanmar, Canada and Germany (see Table 7.25.3).

Table 7.25.3   Top five import markets, Yunnan Province, 1995 and 2000

Country/region	Import value (US$ million)	% of import total
1995		
USA	126.13	15.95
Germany	125.70	15.91
Myanmar	97.99	12.40
Hong Kong	84.03	10.64
Italy	73.98	9.36
Total	507.83	64.26
2000		
Hong Kong	139.04	21.80
Australia	108.68	17.04
Myanmar	69.93	10.97
Canada	42.92	6.73
Germany	36.68	5.75
Total	397.25	62.29

Utilization of foreign capital

In 2000, Yunnan approved 106 FDI contracts, with a total contracted investment of US$297.49 million. This was a fall of 10.45 per cent compared with 1999 (see Table 7.25.4).

Among the 106 FDI projects approved in 2000, 71 were production-orientated and 35 non-production-related. Foreign direct investment came from 21 countries and regions. The top ten sources of FDI and their contracted investment amount are listed in Table 7.25.5.

Table 7.25.4 Utilization of foreign capital, Yunnan Province, 1995 and 2000

Mode (US$ million) year's total value	Approved contracts			Actual utilisation	
	Number previous	Total value (US$ million) year's total value	% change over previous year	Total value	% change over previous year
1995					
Direct foreign investment:	269	374.59	31.52	235.02	15.77
Equity joint ventures	176	240.91		173.42	
Contractual joint ventures	8	30.79		8.94	
Solely foreign-owned enterprises	85	102.89		52.66	
2000					
Direct foreign investment:	106	297.49	−10.45	128.12	−16.72
Equity joint ventures	38	73.81		72.04	
Contractual joint ventures	20	101.15		23.71	
Solely foreign-owned enterprises	48	122.53		32.37	

Table 7.25.5 Key sources of FDI, Yunnan Province

Source	No. of projects	Contract value (US$ million)
Hong Kong	41	169.63
USA	16	98.05
Taiwan Province	18	6.92
Netherlands	1	5
Germany	1	4.07
Republic of Korea	2	3.7
Thailand	4	3.45
Australia	3	3.24
Singapore	5	2.78
Japan	5	2.4

Tibet Autonomous Region

Situated in south-western China, the Tibet Autonomous Region is bounded on the south by Nepal, Sikkim, Bhutan, India and Myanmar. Surrounded by the Himalayas, the Kunlun Mountauns and Tanggula Range, the region forms the main part of the Qinghai-Tibetan Plateau, which, with its average elevation of 4,000 metres, is known as the 'roof of the world'. The total area is over 1.2 million square kilometres and the population is 2.63 million. The regional capital is Lhasa. Major economic indicators are shown in Table 7.26.1.

Resources

Major mineral resources include chromium, iron, copper, lead, zinc, borax, mica and gypsum. The deposits of borax and chromium rank first in the country and copper third. The region is also rich in geothermal resources. Tibet's water power potential is estimated at 200 million kilowatts, or about 29.3 per cent of the nation's total.

Infrastructure

As yet there is still no railway line in the region, but the construction of the Qingzang Railway, specifically the section from Golmud to Lhasa, will change this. The region has more than 22,000 kilometres of highway, connecting it with other parts of the country. Air services offer more than 25 domestic and international air routes to Chengdu, Chongqing, Beijing, Xi'an, Qinghai and Katmandu in Nepal, amongst others. A new air route to Shanghai has been in service since April 2000. Telecommunications have been developing rapidly and

Table 7.26.1 Major economic indicators, Tibet Autonomous Region

Item	2000	2001
Population (millions)	2.5983	2.6295
Gross domestic product (billion RMB)	11.746	13.860
GDP per capita (thousand RMB)	4.559	
Disposable income per capita (thousand RMB)		
Urban residents	6.448	1.331
Rural residents	7.119	1.404
Savings (billion RMB)*	14.493	21.29
Investment in fixed assets (billion RMB)	6.405	8.577
Value-added of primary industry (billion RMB)	3.632	3.747
Value-added of secondary industry (billion RMB)	2.721	3.218
Value-added of tertiary industry (billion RMB)	5.393	6.895
Total retail sales of consumer goods (billion RMB)	4.287	4.904

Source: China Statistical Yearbook2001 and State Statistical Bureau.

*Both institutional and private savings

mobile phone and Internet services are available in all major cities of Tibet.

Foreign trade

In 2000, Tibet's total foreign trade value reached US$130.31 million, down by 21.6 per cent from US$166.22 million in 1999.

Total export value was US$113.34 million, up by 31.71 per cent on US$86.05 million in 1999 and equivalent to 8.02 per cent of the region's GDP of RMB11.65 billion.

Primary goods accounted for 8.27 per cent of the total, or US$9.37 million, while manufactured products accounted for 91.73 per cent, a total value of US$103.97 million.

Tibet is heavily dependent on its top five export markets (see Table 7.26.2). In 1995, 92.69 per cent of the export earnings were from these and in 2000 this percentage increased to 97.2 per cent. Nepal absorbed 92.37 per cent of Tibet's total exports.

Table 7.26.2   Top five export markets, Tibet Autonomous Region, 1995 and 2000

Country/region	Export value (US$ million)	% of export total
1995		
Japan	16.69	47.78
Republic of Korea	5.29	15.16
Nepal	4.88	13.98
Hong Kong	3.96	11.34
USA	1.54	4.43
Total	32.36	92.69
2000		
Nepal	104.687	92.37
Hong Kong	2.12	1.87
USA	1.562	1.38
Japan	1.48	1.31
Malaysia	0.3	0.27
Total	110.149	97.2

Total import value was US$16.97 million, down by 78.83 per cent from US$80.17 million in 1999. Import of primary and manufactured products amounted to US$175,000 and US$16.795 million, accounting for

Table 7.26.3   Top five import markets, Tibet Autonomous Region, 1995 and 2000

Country/region	Import value (US$ million)	% of import total
Hong Kong	12.32	34.63
Japan	14.34	40.31
USA	7.30	20.51
Nepal	0.90	2.52
Total	34.86	97.97
2000		
Japan	9.07	53.45
Nepal	6.72	39.61
Republic of Korea	0.39	2.3
UK	0.37	2.18
France	0.14	0.82
Total	16.69	98.36

1.03 per cent and 98.97 per cent respectively of the total import value. Import commodities came mainly from Japan (see Table 7.26.3), who supplied US$9.07 million worth of goods to Tibet, accounting for 53.45 per cent of the total import value. Nepal ranked second with US$6.72 million, a share of 39.61 per cent. Japan and Nepal had a combined share of 93.61 per cent in Tibet's total import value.

Utilization of foreign capital

In 2000, 11 FDI contracts were approved in Tibet Autonomous Region, with a total contractual foreign investment of US$68.6876 million, up by 90.4 per cent over US$6.84 million in 1999. Among these were nine equity joint ventures, with contractual foreign investment of US$13.6876 million and two solely foreign-owned enterprises, with a contractual foreign investment of US$55 million. Of the FDI projects, one was production-related and ten were in the service sector.

The FDI came from six countries and regions: Nepal (five projects and investment value of US$101800); Hong Kong (two projects and investment value of US$11.943 million) the USA (one project and investment value of US$50 million); Singapore (one project and investment value of US$1.6368 million); France (one project and investment value of US$6,000) and Republic of Korea (one project and investment value of US$5 million).

Shaanxi Province

Shaanxi Province is situated in north-western China in the middle reaches of the Yellow River. The province has a river valley in the centre and highlands in the north and south. A plateau lies in the north and the Qinling Range in the south. Xi'an is one of China's most famous tourist attractions with many historical sites and scenic spots, including the life-size pottery army (terracotta warriors and horses). The total area is 205,800 square kilometres and the population is 36.586 million. The provincial capital is Xi'an. Major economic indicators are shown in Table 7.27.1.

Resources

More than 100 mineral deposits have been discovered in the province, including iron, manganese, molybdenum, chromium, aluminium, copper, cobalt, vanadium, lead, nickel, mercury and gold. Shaanxi's asbestos reserves are the third largest in China, and its coal deposits rank fourth in the country. The northern part of Shaanxi has abundant reserves of coal, natural gas and petroleum. The waterpower potential is 12.74 million kilowatts.

Infrastructure

Xi'an, the capital of Shaanxi province, is known as the gateway to north-western China. Several trunk railways run through the province and Xi'an is one of the key railway hubs linking north-western China with other parts of the country. A network of highways has been established while the provincial government has committed additional investment to develop road transport capabilities further. Xi'an Xianyang International Air-

Table 7.27.1   Major economic indicators, Shaanxi Province

Item	2000	2001
Population (millions)	36.44	36.586
Gross domestic product (billion RMB)	1660.92	1841.24
GDP per capita (thousand RMB)	4.549	5.015
Disposable income per capita (thousand RMB)		
Urban residents	5.142	1.470
Rural residents	5.484	1.520
Savings (billion RMB)*	266.169	320.5
Investment in fixed assets (billion RMB)	65.367	85.022
Value-added of primary industry (billion RMB)	27.912	28.052
Value-added of secondary industry (billion RMB)	73.190	81.569
Value-added of tertiary industry (billion RMB)	64.990	74.503
Total retail sales of consumer goods (billion RMB)	60.740	66.51

Source: China Statistical Yearbook2001 and State Statistical Bureau.

*Both institutional and private savings

port operates more than 95 domestic lines to major cities in China and international air routes to Hong Kong, Macao, Japan, Thailand, Singapore, South Korea, Saudi Arabia and Europe. By the end of 2000, the number of fixed-line telephone subscribers, pager users and mobile phone users totalled 6.5 million. There are nearly 200,000 Internet users.

Foreign trade

Shaanxi's total import and export value increased by 5.94 per cent from US$2.008 billion in 1999 to US$2.128 billion in 2000.

The total export was US$1.310 billion in value, up by 11.3 per cent over US$1.177 billion in 1999. The province's export value was equivalent to 6.52 per cent of the provincial GDP of RMB166.1 billion (US$20.085 billion) and contributed 0.53 per cent to the country's total export value.

Export of primary products came to US$118 million, accounting for 9 per cent of total export value, while export of manufactured products totalled US$1.192 billion, or 91 per cent of total export value.

Shaanxi is not as dependent on its top five export markets (see Table 7.27.2) as other provinces. In 2000, the top five export markets contributed 46.3 per cent of the province's total export earnings. The United States and Hong Kong, who were first and second, had

Table 7.27.2   Top five export markets, Shaanxi Province, 1995 and 2000

Country/region	Export value (US$ million)	% of export total
1995		
Hong Kong	316.30	24.67
Japan	146.58	11.43
Republic of Korea	78.82	6.15
USA	49.07	3.83
Netherlands	45.84	3.58
Total	636.61	49.66
2000		
USA	167.93	12.82
Hong Kong	163.36	12.44
Japan	120.20	9.16
Republic of Korea	91.32	6.95
UK	61.17	4.66
Total	603.98	46.03

similar shares in the province's total export, 12.82 per cent and 12.44 per cent respectively.

In 2000, the province's import value dropped slightly by 4.44 per cent, from US$856 million in 1999 to US$818 million. Import of primary products came to US$190 million, accounting for 23.23 per cent of total import value, and import of manufactured products totalled US$628 million, or 76.77 per cent of total import value.

Japan was the largest exporter to the province, having a share of 21.39 per cent in the province's total import. The top five import markets (see Table 7.27.3) captured a share of 64.37 per cent of Shaanxi's import.

Table 7.27.3   Top five import markets, Shaanxi Province, 1995 and 2000

Country/region	Import value (US$ million)	% of import total
1995		
Japan	130.90	29.05
Hong Kong	40.98	9.09
Belgium	28.99	6.43
USA	13.33	2.96
Australia	12.50	2.77
Total	226.7	50.3
2000		
Japan	175.34	21.39
USA	128.80	15.77
France	111.24	13.57
Belgium	58.99	7.21
Germany	52.65	6.43
Total	527.02	64.37

Utilization of foreign capital

In 2000, Shaanxi province approved 215 FDI contracts with a total contracted investment of US$499.31 million (see Table 7.27.4). This was a slight increase on 1999, attributed to the sharp increase (+144 per cent) in the investment in solely foreign-owned enterprises. The FDI in equity and contractual joint ventures had declined by 43.29 per cent and 11.94 per cent respectively.

Of the 215 FDI projects approved in 2000, 145 were production-orientated and 70 were non-production-related. The foreign direct investment came mainly from 23 countries and regions. Key sources of FDI are listed in Table 7.27.5.

Table 7.27.4 Utilization of foreign capital, Shaanxi Province, 1995 and 2000

Mode	Approved contracts			Actual utilization	
	Number	Total value (US$ million)	% over previous year's total value	Total value (US$ million)	% over previous year's total value
1995					
Foreign direct investment:	272	415.21	0.92	324.07	36
Equity joint ventures	207	302.07		224.40	
Contractual joint ventures	26	57.09		43.49	
Solely foreign-owned enterprises	39	56.05		56.18	
2000					
Foreign direct investment:	215	499.31	17.00	288.42	19.00
Equity joint ventures	123	160.77	−43.29	158.02	10.01
Contractual joint ventures	31	224.54	−11.94	91.16	68.85
Solely foreign-owned enterprises	61	114.00	144.00	51.24	15.54

Table 7.27.5 Key sources of FDI, Shaanxi Province

Source	No. of projects	Amount utilised (US$ million)
Hong Kong	79	134.86
EU	9	26.16
Singapore	7	23.75
Japan	9	23.31
ASEAN	16	14.27
Taiwan	20	8.15
Thailand	7	4.10
Republic of Korea	9	3.72

Gansu Province

Gansu Province in north-western China is situated in the upper reaches of Yellow River. It shares a border with the People's Republic of Mongolia. The province is situated at the juncture of the Qinghai-Tibet Plateau, Neimonggu (Inner Mongolia) Plateau and the lower highlands, all more than 1,000 metres above sea level. The total area is 454,430 square kilometres and the population 25.752 million. The provincial capital is Lanzhou. Major economic indicators are shown in Table 7.28.1.

Resources

The province is richly endowed with mineral resources, of which about 60 kinds have been verified, including metals such as iron, copper, lead, zinc, nickel and cobalt

and non-metals such as coal, petroleum, salt, mirabilite, gypsum and limestone. The largest nickel deposit in China is at Jinchuan in Gansu.

Infrastructure

Lanzhou, the capital city of Gansu province, is a major transport hub in China. It is the intersection point of four trunk railway lines. The international railway between Asia and Europe also crosses the province. The Lanzhou Western Goods Station (the largest station for freight transport in north-western China) serves as the main transit and consolidation hub of containers on the New Asia-Europe Continental Bridge. There are five national truck highways leading to other provinces including Xinjiang and Sichuan. Lanzhou international

Table 7.28.1 Major economic indicators, Gansu Province

Item	2000	2001
Population (millions)	25.568	25.752
Gross domestic product (billion RMB)	98.336	107.3
GDP per capita (thousand RMB)	3.838	4.173
Disposable income per capita (thousand RMB)		
Urban residents	4.916	1.429
Rural residents	5.383	1.509
Savings (billion RMB)*		161.573
Investment in fixed assets (billion RMB)	39.540	50.542
Value-added of primary industry (billion RMB)	19.336	20.7
Value-added of secondary industry (billion RMB)	43.988	48.1
Value-added of tertiary industry (billion RMB)	35.012	38.5
Total retail sales of consumer goods (billion RMB)	36.27	39.543

Source: China Statistical Yearbook 2001 and State Statistical Bureau.
*Both institutional and private savings

airport offers flights to 37 domestic and overseas destinations.

Foreign trade

Total import and export value of Gansu Province in 2000 was US$570 million, up by 40 per cent over US$406 million in 1999.

Total export value was US$415 million, up by 31 per cent over US$317 million in 1999, equivalent to 3.5 per cent to the province's GDP of RMB 98.3 billion (US$11.9 billion) and 0.17 per cent of the total export value of the country. Export of primary goods was US$48.39 million, 12 per cent of the total export value, while the export of manufactured products amounted to US$366.56 million, or 88 per cent of the total export value (see Table 7.28.2).

Table 7.28.2 Top five export markets, Gansu Province, 1995 and 2000

Country/region	Export value (US$ million)	% of export total
1995		
Hong Kong, Macao and Taiwan Province	141.68	36.41
Japan	68.08	17.55
Western and Northern Europe	67.20	17.27
Republic of Korea	29.03	7.46
Oceania	10.93	2.81
Total	316.92	
2000		
Japan	153.68	37.0
Republic of Korea	44.01	10.6
USA	38.95	9.4
Singapore	27.58	6.6
Taiwan Province	23.08	5.6
Total		287.3

Total import value was US$155 million, up by 73 per cent over US$83 million in 1999. Import of primary goods came to US$80.93 million, accounting for 52 per cent of the total import value. Import value of manufactured products reached US$73.65 million, or 48 per cent of the total import value (see Table 7.28.3).

Table 7.28.3 Top five import markets, Gansu Province, 1995 and 2000

Country/region	Import value (US$ million)	% of import total
1995		
Hong Kong	28.81	19.24
Republic of Korea	19.71	13.16
Belgium	24.45	16.32
Taiwan Province	10.07	6.72
Germany	10.18	6.80
Total	93.22	
2000		
Australia	46.95	30.3
USA	20.01	12.9
Japan	16.35	10.5
Germany	10.76	6.9
Italy	5.45	3.5
Total	99.52	64.2

Utilization of foreign capital

Among the foreign direct investment projects, 64 were production-orientated and 14 were non-production-related. The main sources of FDI are provided in Table 7.28.5.

By the end of 2000, the 465 foreign-funded enterprises in production had yielded a total output of US$8.6 billion, a total profit of US$240 million and export value of US$38.7 million.

Table 7.28.4 Utilization of foreign capital, Gansu Province, 1995 and 2000

Mode		Approved contracts		Actual utilization	
	Number	*Total value (US$ million) year's total value*	*% change over previous year*	*Total value (US$ million) year's total value*	*% change over previous year*
1995					
Direct foreign investment:	156	199.76	140.67	99.59	14.78
Equity joint ventures	82	154.57	226.92	77.60	5.64
Contractual joint ventures	7	5.55	−24.69	2.76	−61.77
Solely foreign-owned enterprises	67	39.64	39.82	19.77	−39.24
2000					
Direct foreign investment:	78	123.92	50	6235	78
Equity joint ventures	42	70.36	490	4880	470
Contractual joint ventures	7	22.09	−54	659	−76
Solely foreign-owned enterprises	29	31.47	29	696	43

Table 7.28.5 Key sources of FDI, Gansu Province

Source	No. of projects	Contract value (US$ million)
Hong Kong	21	20.40
Thailand	1	5.78
Singapore	2	6.5
Japan	8	0.74
Republic of Korea	4	18.23
Israel	2	8.06
Canada	4	3.99

Qinghai Province

Situated in the southern part of north-western China, on the north-east of the Qinghai Tibet Plateau, Qinghai is named after its famous Qinghai Lake. The Qaidam Basin in the north-west of the province is surrounded by the Kunlun, Altun and Qilian mountain ranges. A significant part of the province lies more than 3,000 metres above sea level. The Yangtze and Yellow rivers rise in the highlands. The province's total area is 722,300 square kilometres and it has a population of 5.231 million. The provincial capital is Xining. Major economic indicators are shown in Table 7.29.1.

Resources

More than 60 kinds of minerals are found in Qinghai. Deposits of lake salt, sylvites, magnesites, lithium, iodine, natural sulphur, bromine, limestone for the chemical industries, quartzite and asbestos are the largest in the country. Potassium reserves account for 97 per cent of the country's total. The province has abundant reserves of oil and natural gas at the Qaidam Basin. Qinghai Oil Field is one of the four largest natural gas fields in China. The province has about 19 million kilowatts of electric power resources.

Infrastructure

Major railways include the Lanzhou-Qinghai, Qinghai-Xinjiang, Yangpingguan-Xining and Xining-Zhangxe lines. The province has three highway trunk roads. Golmud airport and Caojiabao airport in Xining city provide air services to major cities in China. Telecom-

Table 7.29.1 Major economic indicators, Qinghai Province

Item	2000	2001
Population (millions)	4.6	5.231
Gross domestic products (billion RMB)	26.359	30.083
GDP per capita (thousand RMB)	5.087	5.732
Disposable income per capita (thousand RMB)		
Urban residents	5.2	1.5
Rural residents	5.854	1.611
Savings (billion RMB)*	30.834	39.106
Investment in fixed assets (billion RMB)	15.114	20.161
Value-added of primary industry (billion RMB)	3.853	4.279
Value-added of secondary industry (billion RMB)	11.40	13.231
Value-added of tertiary industry (billion RMB)	11.106	12.573
Total retail sales of consumer goods (billion RMB)	8.2	9.035

Source: China Statistical Yearbook2001 and State Statistical Bureau.

*Both institutional and private savings

munications system have made remarkable progress. Apart from fixed-line telephone services, mobile tele-communications and internet services are available in the province's major cities.

Foreign trade

In 2000, Qinghai's import and export value came to US$159.75 million, an increase of 48.11 per cent over US$107.85 million in 1999. Total export value was US$112 million, up by 28.94 per cent over US$86.86 million in 1999 and equivalent to 3.52 per cent of the provincial GDP of RMB26.3 billion(US$3.18 billion) and 0.05 per cent of the country's total export value. Export of primary and manufactured products amounted to US$17.47 million and US$94.53 million respectively, or 15.6 per cent and 84.4 per cent of the total export value (see Table 7.29.2).

Table 7.29.2 Top five export markets, Qinghai Province, 1995 and 2000

Country/region	Export value (US$ million)	% of export total
1995		
Japan	43.57	31.56
Hong Kong	35.20	25.49
USA	13.78	9.98
Republic of Korea	7.70	5.58
Singapore	6.93	5.02
Total	107.18	77.63
2000		
Republic of Korea	35.52	31.71
Japan	28.63	25.56
USA	14.25	12.72
Singapore	5.45	4.87
Kazakhstan	4.60	4.11
Total	88.45	78.97

Table 7.29.3 Top five import markets, Qinghai Province, 1995 and 2000

Country/region	Import value (US$ million)	% of import total
1995		
Australia	6.85	28.32
Singapore	6.17	25.51
Japan	3.96	16.37
Hong Kong	2.54	10.50
Pakistan	1.38	5.70
Total	20.9	
2000		
Australia	28.77	60.26
India	6.01	12.59
USA	2.12	4.44
Japan	1.96	4.11
Hong Kong	1.85	3.88
Total	40.71	

Import value totalled US$47.74 million, up by 127.44 per cent over US$20.99 million in 1999. Import of primary products and manufactured products amounted to US$33.83 million and US$13.91 million respectively, making up 70.86 per cent and 29.14 per cent separately of the total import value.

Utilization of foreign capital

Among all the FDI projects, 28 were production-orientated and 12 were non-production related. Four were in the energy industry, four in agriculture, four in real estate, eight in the service industry, four in the building industry, twelve in manufacturinge industry and three in the excavation industry. Key sources of FDI are shown in Table 7.29.5.

Table 7.29.4 Utilization of foreign capital, Qinghai Province, 1995 and 2000

Mode	Number	Approved contracts		Actual utilization	
		Total value (US$ million) year's total value	% change over previous year	Total value (US$ million) year's total value	% change over previous year
1995					
Direct foreign investment:	28	28.10	131.93		
Equity joint ventures	23	24.46	116.34		
Contractual joint ventures	1	221.65			
Solely foreign-owned enterprises	4	0.50	328.43		
2000					
Direct foreign investment:	40	1.10202	67.5	0.3967	266
Equity joint ventures	20	0.111931	96	0.0481	323
Contractual joint ventures	6	0.4466	1745	0.1583	195
Solely foreign-owned enterprises	14	0.5436	793	0.1903	281

Table 7.29.5 Key sources of FDI

Source	No. of projects	Contract value (US$ million)
Hong Kong	18	48.63
USA	2	38.65
Australia	2	8.36
Canada	5	7.05
Taiwan	3	1.27
Singapore	1	4.82

7.30

Ningxia Hui Autonomous Region

The Ningxia Hui Autonomous Region is situated in the northern part of north-western China, covering the middle and upper reaches of the Yellow River. The land ranges from south to north with an elevation of over 1,000 metres above sea level. The total area is 66,400 square kilometres and the population is 5.6 million. The Hui ethnic group accounts for a third of the region's total population. The region's capital is Yinchuan. Major economic indicators are shown in Table 7.30.1.

Resources

The region boasts rich mineral resources, consisting mainly of coal, iron, phosphorus, petroleum, asbestos and limestone. Coal reserves are plentiful and estimated at 8.5 billion tonnes.

Infrastructure

The Yellow River is the only inland river for water transportation in Ningxia and it mainly provides short distance transport. Ningxia is connected with other parts of the country by several railway lines. New railways are currently being constructed and there are plans for more railways to improve the province's rail transportation capability. The so-called New Asia-Europe Continental Bridge, a railway that links Asia to Europe, runs through the province, offering the region access to the European continent. The region has a fairly well developed highway network centring on Yinchuan, which provides access to all counties, cities, key mining and industrial production bases in the region. Ningxia has eight air routes connecting the region with major cities in China.

Table 7.30.1 Major economic indicators, Ningxia Hui Autonomous Region

Item	2000	2001
Population (millions)	5.6	
Gross domestic product (billion RMB)	26.557	29.83
GDP per capita (thousand RMB)	4.839	
Disposable income per capita (thousand RMB)		
Urban residents	4.9	1.7
Rural residents	5.544	1.823
Savings (billion RMB)	39.649	46.887
Investment in fixed assets (billion RMB)	15.752	19.58
Value-added of primary industry (billion RMB)	4.595	4.95
Value-added of secondary industry (billion RMB)	12.004	13.5
Value-added of tertiary industry (billion RMB)	9.958	11.38
Total retail sales of consumer goods (billion RMB)	9.0	9.89

Source: China Statistical Yearbook 2001 and State Statistical Bureau.

*Both institutional and private savings

Foreign trade

In 2000, the total import and export value of the region came to US$439.82 million, a rise of 39 per cent over US$316.49 million in 1999.

Total export value was US$326.95 million, an increase of 32.6 per cent over US$246.58 million in 1999, equivalent to 10.2 per cent of the region's GDP of RMB26.5 billion (US$3.2 billion) and 0.13 per cent of the total export value for the whole country.

Export of primary and manufactured products amounted to US$28.48 million and US$298.89 million respectively, accounting for 8.71 per cent and 91.4 per cent of the total export value.

The United States became the biggest buyer of the region's exports in 2000, while Japan ranked the second (see Table 7.30.2). These two markets took over 40 per cent of the region's total exports.

Table 7.30.2 Top five export markets, Ningxia Hui Autonomous Region, 1995 and 2000

Country/region	Export value (US$ million)	% of export total
1995		
Japan	58.41	24.30
Hong Kong	50.03	20.84
France	22.55	9.39
USA	21.65	9.02
Italy	13.00	5.41
Total	165.64	68.96
2000		
USA	72.40	23.14
Japan	56.17	17.18
Republic of Korea	33.39	10.21
Israel	24.88	7.61
UK	18.73	5.73
Total	205.57	63.87

The region recorded an increase of 65.28 per cent in its import value from US$69.91 million in 1999 to US$115.55 million in 2000. Import of primary products took a share of 60.29 per cent of the import total, or US$69.67 million. Manufactured products amounted to US$45.89 million, accounting for 39.71 per cent of the total import value.

More than 42 per cent of the imports in value terms came from Australia and the USA. The top five sources of the region's imports (see Table 7.30.3) accounted for over 60 per cent of the total import value.

Table 7.30.3 Top five import markets, Ningxia Hui Autonomous Region, 1995 and 2000

Country/region	Import value (US$ million)	% of import total
1995		
Germany	5.04	13.27
Hungary	5.04	13.27
UK	4.65	12.24
Hong Kong	3.30	8.69
Russia	2.68	7.06
Total	25.84	68.04
2000		
Australia	28.75	24.88
USA	19.92	17.24
Japan	9.84	8.52
Germany	7.48	6.47
Republic of Korea	5.43	4.70
Total	71.42	61.81

Utilization of foreign investment

In 2000, 32 FDI contracts were approved in the region. The contracted investment totalled US$99.27 million, an increase of 59.4 per cent over 1999. FDI in contractual joint ventures dropped by 81.4 per cent, while investment in equity joint ventures and wholly foreign-owned enterprises experienced increased by 121.8 per cent and 36.75 per cent respectively (see Table 7.30.4).

Of all these FDI projects, 29 were production-orientated and 3 projects were non-production-related. Foreign direct investments came from 11 countries and regions (see Table 7.30.5).

In 2000, the FIEs in the region had generated US$42.89 million, which made up 13 per cent of the region's total export value.

Table 7.30.4 Utilization of foreign capital, Ningxia Hui Autonomous Region, 1995

Mode	Number	Approved contracts		Actual utilization	
		Total value (US$ million) year's total value	% change over previous year	Total value (US$ million) year's total value	% change over previous year
1995					
Direct foreign investment:	42	28.78	20	4.20	−42.15
Equity joint ventures	31	18.51		2.70	
Contractual joint ventures	2	1.27			
Solely foreign-owned enterprises	9	9.00		1.50	
2000					
Direct foreign investment:	32	99.27	59.4	17.41	68.9
Equity joint ventures	17	17.12	121.8	6.02	−2.4
Contractual joint ventures	4	10.11	−81.4	4.64	52.6
Solely foreign-owned enterprises	11	72.04	36.75	6.74	518.4

Table 7.30.5 Key sources of FDI, Ningxia Hui Autonomous Region

Source	No. of projects	Contract value (US$ million)
Hong Kong	13	29.59
USA	8	16.28
Taiwan Province	2	12.12
British Virgin Islands	1	25
Singapore	1	10
Canada	2	0.8

Xinjiang Uygur Autonomous Region

Xinjiang, situated on the north-western border of China, covers a sixth of the country's total area and is the largest region in China. It extends 2,000 kilometres from east to west and 1,500 kilometres from north to south. It has a 5,000 kilometre common border with the former Soviet Union, the People's Republic of Mongolia, Afghanistan, Pakistan and India. The region has many mountains, averaging 3,000 metres above sea level. Its total area is 1.65 million square kilometres and the population is 18.76 million. There are 13 nationalities in Xinjiang, of which the Uygur nationality is the largest ethnic group, accounting for 47 per cent of the population. The regional capital is Urumqi. Major economic indicators are shown in Table 7.31.1

Resources

Xinjiang possesses huge deposits of ferrous and non-ferrous metals, iron and chromium. It is rich in gold, mica, petroleum and coal. Jade is a specialist product of the region. Xinjiang has the largest reserves of oil, natural gas and coal in the country. The huge deposits of petroleum and natural gas in Tarim and Junggar basins and the coal reserves in other areas make the region a potential energy base. There are 100 locations with a total of over 1 billion cubic metres of proven granite reserves.

Table 7.31.1 Major economic indicators, Xinjiang Uygur Autonomous Region

Item	2000	2001
Population (millions)	18.49	18.7619
Gross domestic product (billion RMB)	136.436	148.5
GDP per capita (thousand RMB)	7.470	7.898
Disposable income per capita (thousand RMB)		
Urban residents	5.816	1618
Rural residents	6.590	1.710
Savings (billion RMB)*	183.143	197.255
Investment in fixed assets (billion RMB)	61.039	70.182
Value-added of primary industry (billion RMB)	28.818	28.7
Value-added of secondary industry (billion RMB)	58.684	64
Value-added of tertiary industry (billion RMB)	48.934	55.8
Total retail sales of consumer goods (billion RMB)	37.5	40.635

Source: China Statistical Yearbook 2001 and State Statistical Bureau.

*Both institutional and private savings

Infrastructure

Xinjiang has a railway line connecting it with the neighbouring province of Gansu and other parts of the country. The highway system is well developed and covers 99 per cent of the region. The Urumqi Airport has flights to 59 international and domestic destinations.

Foreign trade

The total foreign trade value of the region reached US$2.264 billion in 2000, an increase of 28.27 per cent over US$1.765 billion in 1999. 53.18 per cent of the foreign trade value of US$1.20409 billion came from export, an increase of 17.19 per cent over US$1.02743 billion in 1999.

Total export value in 2000 was equivalent to 7.3 per cent of the region's GDP and 0.48 per cent of the total national export value.

Export of primary products was worth US$360.03 million, making up 29.9 per cent of total export value, while for manufactured goods the figures were US$844.06 million or for 70.01 per cent

Export goods were destined for 99 countries and regions in 2000, though, the top five export markets (see Table 7.31.2) took 72.18 per cent of the total export value, with Kazakhstan being the largest buyer of the region's exports.

Table 7.31.2 Top five export destinations, Xinjiang Uygur Autonomous Region, 1995 and 2000

Country/region	Export value (US$ million)	% of export total
1995		
Hong Kong	139.86	18.19
Kazakhstan	121.40	15.79
Kirghizstan	99.02	12.88
Japan	66.35	8.63
Uzbekistan	26.40	3.43
Total	453.03	58.92
2000		
Kazakhstan	508.87	42.26
Hong Kong	104.98	8.72
Kirgizstan	104.37	8.67
Republic of Korea	89.37	7.42
Indonesia	61.53	5.11
Total	869.12	72.18

Total import value rose by 43.64 per cent from US$737.91 million in 1999 to US$1.05991 billion in 2000. Of the total spend on import, 43.87 per cent or US$465.02 million went on primary products, while 56.13 per cent or US$594.88 million was spent on the import of manufactured goods.

As with export, there was a high level of concentration on the top five trading partners (see Table 7.31.3). The top five import markets took 85.8 per cent of the region's total import dollars, with Kazakhstan again ranking first with a dominant share of 63.26 per cent.

Table 7.31.3 Top five import markets, Xinjiang Uygur Autonomous Region, 1995 and 2000

Country/region	Import value (US$ million)	% of import total
1995		
Kazakhstan	285.96	43.38
Kirghizstan	92.20	13.98
Hong Kong	64.31	9.75
Italy	49.17	7.46
Japan	31.73	4.81
Total	606.51	91.99
2000		
Kazakhstan	670.46	63.26
Italy	70.83	6.68
Kirgizstan	66.99	6.32
USA	51.88	4.89
Russia	49.32	4.65
Total	909.48	85.8

Utilization of foreign capital

Xinjiang approved 58 FDI contracts in 2000, with a total contracted investment of US$92.12 million, an increase of 49.76 per cent over 1999. The FDI actually utilized in the year, however, dropped by 20 per cent compared with 1999 (see Table 7.31.4).

Among the 58 FDI contracts, 42 were production-related, accounting for 72.41 per cent, and 16 were non-production-orientated projects, accounting for 27.59 per cent.

Foreign direct investment came from 18 countries and regions (see Table 7.31.5)

In 2000, FIEs generated a total foreign exchange earning of US$103.17 million through export, down 12.40 per cent compared with US$117.77 million in 1999 and accounting for 16.23 per cent of the total export earnings of the region.

Table 7.31.4 Utilization of foreign capital, Xinjiang Uygur Autonomous Region, 1995

Mode		Approved contracts		Actual utilization	
	Number	Total value (US$ million) year's total value	% change over previous year	Total value (US$ million) year's total value	% change over previous year
1995					
Direct foreign investment:	114	91.72	6.79		13.66
Equity joint ventures	91	55.47		54.90	
Contractual joint ventures	8	1.24		29.87	
Solely foreign-owned enterprises	15	34.56		18.28	
2000					
Direct foreign investment:	58	92.12	49.76	19.23	−20
Equity joint ventures	34	31.20		15.58	
Contractual joint ventures	5	25.36		0.69	
Solely foreign-owned enterprises	19	35.56		296	

Table 7.31.5 Key sources of FDI, Xinjiang Uygur Autonomous Region

Source	No. of projects	Contract value (US$ million)
Hong Kong	23	58.04
Taiwan Province	4	3.56
Thailand	1	1.55
Malaysia	1	0.55
Japan	3	1.71
Turkey	1	0.13
Republic of Korea	2	5.22
Germany	1	6.13
UK	1	0.08
Sweden	1	0.35
Switzerland	1	0.07
Russia	1	0.15
British Virgin Islands	2	1.96
Kazakhstan	2	0.16
Kirgizstan	1	0.02
Canada	3	10.2
USA	8	2.08
Australia	3	0.16

Dalian City

Dalian, one of the largest cities in Liaoning province, is located at the southern end of Liaodong peninsula in north-eastern China. It faces the Yellow Sea to the east and the Bohai Sea to the west. The Shandong peninsula is to the south. The port of Dalian is the trade gateway to the sea and provides access to and outlets for the three provinces in north-eastern China (Liaoning, Jilin and Heilongjiang) and also the eastern part of Inner Mongolia. Dalian covers an area of 12,574 square kilometres and has a population of 5.5 million. Major economic indicators are shown in Table 7.32.1.

Resources

Dalian has a sea surface of over 30,000 square kilometres and the coastline stretches for 1,906 kilometres.

The city teems with marine aquatic products. The shallow water along the Dalian coast is particularly suitable for breeding seaweed. Over 40 different kinds of mineral resources, scattered over 500 sites, have already been verified in the region. Diamond reserves rank first in the country, and their quality is amongst the best in the world. Mineral deposits include limestone, dolomite, asbestos, quartzite, coal, iron and copper.

Infrastructure

Dalian harbour is now the third largest in China, and the largest export harbour in the country. There are 65 berths especially for crude oil, other oil products, coal, steel, timber, grain, containers and general cargo. Among

Table 7.32.1 Major economic indicators, Dalian City

Item	2000	2001
Population (millions)	5.515	5.546
Gross domestic product (billion RMB)	104.712	12.356
GDP per capita (thousand US$)	2,447	2700
Disposable income per capita (thousand RMB)		
Urban residents	6.862	3.739
Rural residents	7.418	3.900
Savings (billion RMB)*	137.06	156.39
Investment in fixed assets (billion RMB)	26.86	30.51
Value-added of primary industry (billion RMB)	10.60	11.14
Value-added of secondary industry (billion RMB)	51.04	57.42
Value-added of tertiary industry (billion RMB)	488.45	55.0
Total retail sales of consumer goods (billion RMB)	49.70	53.42

Source: Dalian Statistical Bureau.

*Both institutional and private savings

these, 35 berths are for ships above 10,000 tonnes. The annual handling capacity of Dalian harbour is over 80 million tonnes and it has established shipping relationships with over 150 countries and territories worldwide. Forty-nine air routes have been established connecting Dalian with 47 cities in China and around the world. Railways from Dalian join the rail network of northeastern and northern China. The total length of roads and highways in Dalian is now 4,091 kilometres.

Foreign trade

In 2000, Dalian's foreign trade value totalled US$10.21 billion, an increase of 46.4 per cent over US$6.97 billion in 1999. Export accounted for a little more than 50 per cent of the total trade value at US$5.214 billion, up by 28.4 per cent over US$4.06 billion in 1999. Export plays an important role in the city's economy and is the driving force of local economic growth. Export value in 2000 was equivalent to 39 per cent of the municipal GDP of RMB111.08 billion (US$13.383 billion). Its share in the total export value of the whole country was 2.1 per cent in 2000. Export of primary products contributed 20 per cent of the city's export earnings (US$1.04 billion), while the export of manufactured products generated 80 per cent or US$4.17 billion.

The city exported to 147 countries and regions in 2000, the top five of which (see Table 7.32.2) contributed more than 80 per cent of the city's total export revenue. Japan ranked first among the top five export markets with a dominant share of 50 per cent in the city's total export value.

Import value totalled US$4.995 billion, up by 71.4 per cent over US$2.913 billion 1999. The import value of primary and manufactured products amounted to US$1.4 billion and US$3.59 billion respectively, or 28.1 per cent and 71.9 per cent of the total import value.

Imports came from 92 countries and regions. Japan, again, topped the other 4 among the top five import markets (see Table 7.32.3) by capturing a share of over 40 per cent of the city's import value.

Utilization of foreign capital

Dalian approved 697 FDI contracts in 2000, with a total contracted investment of US$2.386 billion, a slight decrease by 3 per cent as compared with 1999.

Table 7.32.2 Top five export markets, Dalian City, 1995 and 2000

Country/region	Export value (US$ million)	% of export total
1995		
Japan	1,423.32	56.31
Hong Kong	265.08	10.52
Singapore	220.83	8.74
USA	160.33	6.34
Republic of Korea	111.23	4.40
Total	2,180.79	86.31
2000		
Japan	2,584.44	50.0
USA	576.35	11.0
Republic of Korea	416.03	7.9
Singapore	317.52	6.1
Hong Kong	277.18	5.3
Total	4,171.52	80.3

Table 7.32.3 Top five import markets, Dalian City, 1995 and 2000

Country/region	Import value (US$ million)	% of import total
1995		
Japan	927.59	57.33
Republic of Korea	208.16	12.87
Hong Kong	154.81	9.57
Singapore	81.93	5.06
USA	65.41	4.04
Total	1,437.9	88.87
2000		
Japan	2,105.93	40.3
Republic of Korea	631.52	12.1
Iraq	378.50	7.2
USA	273.64	5.3
Germany	131.81	2.5
Total	3,521.4	67.4

The city's FDI in 2000 was characterized by a dominant number of solely foreign-owned enterprises (see Table 7.32.4).

Among the FDI projects approved in 2000, 485 projects were of production-orientated and 212 projects were non-production-related. FDI came from 32 countries and regions. The main investing countries and regions are set out in Table 7.32.5.

Table 7.32.4   Utilization of foreign capital, Dalian City, 1995 and 2000

Mode	Number	Approved contracts Total value (US$ million) year's total value	% change over previous year	Actual utilization Total value (US$ million) year's total value	% change over previous year
1995					
Direct foreign investment:	1,073	2,203.28	2.42	709.62	−12.91
Equity joint ventures	663	1,040.01		440.80	
Contractual joint ventures	175	328.34		81.24	
Solely foreign-owned enterprises	235	834.93		187.58	
2000					
Direct foreign investment:	697	2,386	−3	1,112	38
Equity joint ventures	34	1,217	−7.0	565	38
Contractual joint ventures	60	153	−4.1	95	12
Solely foreign-owned enterprises	603	1,015	9.8	452	70

By the end of 2000, 3930 foreign-invested enterprises had begun operation. The output value of the operating FIEs totalled RMB59 billion, an increase of 30 per cent, while profit totalled RMB3.5 billion, up by 600 per cent. Export value came to US$4.12 billion, up by 36.3 per cent.

Table 7.32.5   Key sources of FDI, Dalian City, 2000

Source	No. of projects	Total value (US$ million)
Japan	185	538
Republic of Korea	139	200
USA	115	476
Hong Kong and Macao	104	540
Taiwan Province	49	160

Qinhuangdao

Situated at the north-eastern end of Hebei Province, with the Yanshan Mountain to the north, the Bohai Sea to the south and Liaoning Province to the east, Qinhuangdao has a coastline of 113 kilometres, a total area of 7,523 kilometres, of which the city proper makes up 363 square kilometres. Its population is 2.69 million. It is one of the 14 open coastal cities designated by the State Council in 1984. Major economic indicators are shown in Table 7.33.1.

Resources

Qinhuangdao is rich in natural resources including gold, coal, iron, lead and zinc. Sand and limestone are available in abundance and reserves of granite and marble are sizeable. The major produce is apples, haws, grapes, peaches, pears, walnuts, chestnuts and apricots.

Infrastructure

There are 2,858 kilometres of road in the city. The No. 102 and No 205 state highways run through the city, giving access to all parts of China. Three trunk lines – Beijing-Shenyang, Beijing-Qinhuangdao and Datong-Qinhuangdao – run through it. There are 21 train stations of which Shanhaiguan station is one of the China's 12 marshalling yards. Qinhuangdao Airport is of international 4C standard, offering regular flights to all over 20 major cities of China, including Shanghai, Dalian, Xi'an and Kmning. Qinhuangdao is one of the largest natural seaports of North China, it is ice- and silt-free, with an annual cargo handling capacity of over 90 million tonnes, Qinhuangdao port has business relations with 130 countries and regions in the world as well as 30 domestic ports. The port has shipping lines connecting the city with more than 150 international ports.

Table 7.33.1 Major economic indicators, Qinhuangdao City

Item	2000	2001
Population (millions)	2.66	2.69
Gross domestic products (billion RMB)	28.72	30.7
GDP per capita (thousand RMB)	10.755	11.5
Disposable income per capita (thousand RMB)		
Urban residents	6.733	3.000
Rural residents	7.029	3.288
Savings (billion RMB)	23.065	24.957
Investment in fixed assets (billion RMB)	8.268	8.99
Value-added of primary industry (billion RMB)	3.901	4.03
Value-added of secondary industry (billion RMB)	10.39	10.94
Value-added of tertiary industry (billion RMB)		
Total retail sales of consumer goods (billion RMB)	8.548	9.488

Source: Qinghuangdao Euro-Industrial Park

Foreign trade

In 2000, the city's total foreign trade value came to US$638.96 million, up by 32.08 per cent against US$483.77 million in 1999.

Total export value was US$233.95 million, up by 21.84 per cent over US$192.07 million in 1999, an equivalent of 6.8 per cent of the city's GDP (RMB28.719 billion or about US$3.46 billion) and 7.14 per cent of the total export value of Hebei province.

Export of primary products amounted to US$104.66 million, accounting for 44.74 per cent of total export value, and for manufactured products US$174.76 million, or 74.7 per cent.

Exports were destined for 78 countries and regions, mainly in Asia and Europe. Japan was first among the top five export markets (see Table 7.33.2) by taking US$190.9 million worth of goods from the city, which was 38.85 per cent of the city's total export value. The city was fairly dependent on its key export markets and 76.01 per cent of its export revenue came from the top five.

Table 7.33.2 Top five export markets, Qinhuangdao City, 2000

Country/region	Export value (US$ million)	% of export total
Japan	190.90	38.85
Republic of Korea	24.25	10.36
Germany	22.41	9.58
USA	22.18	9.48
Hong Kong	18.08	7.74
Total	277.82	76.01

Import value increased by 38.82 per cent, from US$291.76 million in 1999 to US$405.52 million in 2000. Import of primary goods amounted to US$175.01 million and of manufactured products US$230 million, accounting for 43.16 per cent and 56.72 per cent respectively of the city's total value of import.

Imports came from 25 countries and regions. South Korea and the USA ranked first and second in the city's top five import markets (see Table 7.33.3). Interestingly, Ecuador and the Philippines took the third and fourth positions; this is believed to be because of the large quantity of bananas imported by the city.

Table 7.33.3 Top five import markets, Qinhuangdao City, 2000

Country/region	Import value (US$ million)	% of import total
Republic of Korea	62.47	15.85
USA	54.81	13.52
Ecuador	41.10	10.14
Philippines	36.60	9.03
Germany	28.66	7.07
Total	223.64	55.61

Utilization of foreign capital

The city approved 64 foreign direct investment projects in 2000, with a total contracted investment of US$197.83 million, a drop of 53.4 per cent compared with 1999. A little over half of the investment dollars went into equity joint ventures (see Table 7.33.4). Nearly all of the projects were production-related.

Foreign direct investment came from 44 countries and regions. Key sources of investment are provided in Table 7.33.5.

By the end of 2000, 244 FIEs were in operation. Their total output amounted to RMB6.493 billion, while sales revenue reached RMB6.744 billion. Foreign exchange income generated from exports by the operating FIEs was US$174.76 million, accounting for 74.7 per cent of the city's total export value and up by 7.72 per cent on 1999.

Euro-Industrial Park

As part of its efforts to attract investment from Europe, the city launched the Euro-Industrial Park (EIP) project in 2001, the first of its kind in China, to target European business. The Park is designed to offer a manufacturing base for European companies, particularly SMEs. Complete with all the necessary infrastructures including supplies of electric power, gas, water, heating, sewage, telephones etc, the Park offers competitive investment packages for European investors, one of which is a competitive land use fee (see Table 7.33.6).

With EIP's location at the juncture of north-eastern and northern China and in the vicinity of northern China's industrial base, EIP has easy access to a market of about 200 million people within a 500 kilometre radius and a wealth of cost-efficient manufacturing capabilities to meet investors' outsourcing needs.

Table 7.33.4 Utilization of foreign capital, Qinhuangdao City, 1995 and 2000

Mode	Number	Approved contracts		Actual utilization	
		Total value (US$ million) year's total value	*% change over previous year*	*Total value (US$ million) year's total value*	*% change over previous year*
1995					
Direct foreign investment:	138	299.49	115.32	97.24	
Equity joint ventures	103	235.37			
Contractual joint ventures	8	34.15			
Solely foreign-owned enterprises	27	29.97			
2000					
Direct foreign investment:	64	197.83	−53.4	115.14	−12.9
Equity joint ventures	35	100.09			
Contractual joint ventures	9	63.06			
Solely foreign-owned enterprises	20	45.75			

Table 7.33.5 Key sources of FDI, Qinhuangdao City

Source	No. of projects	Contract value (US$ million)
Hong Kong	9	7, 923
Singapore	4	3, 595
Republic of Korea	19	3, 285
USA	10	2, 108
Bahamas	1	2, 000
Brazil	1	700
France	2	555
Taiwan Province	2	301
Thailand	3	83
Cambodia	1	145

Geographical proximity to Nagasaki Port in Japan (1200km) and Seoul in Korea (688km) gives the Park a unique position as a springboard to other Asian markets.

The initial four square kilometre development area is fully equipped with import and export functions including a customs office, and bonded warehouses are available in the neighbouring export processing zone. Greenfield sites are available for options such as build-to-suit. The management body of the Park, CASSAN Euro-Industrial Park Co. Ltd., is committed to providing strong logistical and administrative support.

Table 7.33.6 EIP land use fee comparison with Chinese coastal regions (For 50 years' industrial use: RMB/m²)

	EIP	*Yantai Economic & Technological Development*	*Tianjin Economic & Technological Development*	*Guangzhou Export Processing*	*Beijing Economic & Technological Development*
Zone	Zone	Zone	Zone		
Price	75	167	280	450	525
Factor	1	2.23	3.73	6	7

Note: for other details, please visit the Park's website at www.eip.org.cn

Yantai

Yantai is one of the coastal cities of Shandong Province and is a key city on the Economic Ring around the Bohai Sea, a priority area of development in China. Located in the eastern part of the Shandong Peninsula, Yantai faces the Liaodong Peninsula across the Bohai Straits to the north. It administers four districts, one county and seven county-level cities with a total area of 13,700 square kilometres and has a population of 6.45 million. Major economic indicators are shown in Table 7.34.1.

Resources

With a coastline of 909 kilometres, Yantai is one of the key bases of the fishing industry, producing many offshore aquatic products, including prawns, sea cucumbers, abalone and scallops. It is also one of the key fruit producers in northern China. Peanuts, Yantai apple and Laiyang pears are famous in China and abroad. In addition, 36 minerals have been discovered, 20 of which have been exploited. The city supplies 25 per cent of China's gold and 20 per cent of its talcum.

Infrastructure

The city has a very good port and road and railway ties with the rest of Shandong and other parts of the country. Currently there are nine ports, four of which host foreign vessels. The total capacity of the nine ports is 24.74 million tons. The city has shipping relations with over 100 countries and regions in the world. Yantai Airport is a Class A port and is open to foreign flights, and now has 26 domestic and international routes.

Table 7.34.1   Major economic indicators, Yantai City

Item	2000	2001
Population (millions)	6.4582	6.4599
Gross domestic product (billion RMB)	88	98
GDP per capita (thousand RMB)	1,3626	
Disposable income per capita (thousand RMB)		
Urban residents	7.317	3,455
Rural residents	8.261	3.635
Savings (billion RMB)*	90.88	101.9
Investment in fixed assets (billion RMB)	21.92	28.364
Gross output value of agriculture (billion RMB)	24.23	24.445
Industrial value-added (billion RMB)	41.96	46.15
Total retail sales of consumer goods (billion RMB)	25.61	28.3

*Both institutional and private savings
Source: Yantai Statistical Bulletin 2000 and 2001
Note: The figures are preliminary and unadjusted

Foreign trade

In 2000, Yantai City reported an increase of 37.2 per cent in its total foreign trade value, which was US$3.139 billion over US$2.288 billion in 1999.

Total export value was US$1.966 billion, up 34.2 per cent over US$1.466 billion in 1999, and equivalent to 18.5 per cent of the City's GDP of RMB88 billion (US$10.6 billion). It also contributed 12.66 per cent to the total export value of Shandong province.

Export of primary and manufactured products totalled US$649 million and US$1.317 billion respectively, accounting for 33 per cent and 67 per cent of total export value.

The city's exports were destined for 136 countries and regions, 11 more than in 1999. The top five export markets are shown in Table 7.34.2.

Table 7.34.2   Top five export markets, Yantai City, 1995 and 2000

Country/region	Export value (US$ million)	% of export total
1995		
Japan	374.10	26.49
Hong Kong	255.20	18.07
Republic of Korea	247.54	17.53
USA	183.57	13.00
Taiwan Province	61.34	4.34
Total	1,121.75	79.43
2000		
Japan	673.37	34.2
USA	397.55	20.2
Republic of Korea	295.41	15.0
European Union	204.56	10.4
Hong Kong	69.17	3.5
Total	1,640.06	83.3

Import value totalled US$1.173 billion, an increase of 42.6 per cent over US$820 million in 1999. Import of primary and manufactured products amounted to US$306 million and US$867 million respectively, or 26.1 per cent and 73.9 per cent of the total import value.

Table 7.34.3   Top five import markets, Yantai City, 1995 and 2000

Country/region	Import value (US$ million)	% of import total
1995		
Hong Kong	67.39	20.74
Japan	54.31	16.71
Republic of Korea	41.05	12.63
Singapore	37.70	11.60
USA	34.13	10.50
Total	234.58	72.18
2000		
Republic of Korea	491.42	41.9
Japan	194.25	15.6
EU	179.78	15.3
USA	75.04	6.4
Australia	53.97	4.6
Total	994.46	83.8

Imports came from 74 countries and regions, though Korea took an overwhelming share of 41.9 per cent of the total (see Table 7.34.3).

Utilization of foreign capital

Yantai's total value of contracted FDI more than doubled in 2000 compared with 1999. A total of 371 contracts were approved in the year with total contracted investment being US$694.67 million (see Table 7.34.4). FDI in the form of solely foreign-owned enterprises more than doubled.

Of 371 FDI projects, 340 were production-orientated and 42 were non production-related. 14 were in agriculture and 340 in industry.

Foreign direct investment came from 27 countries and regions (see Table 7.34.5).

An additional 30 foreign-invested enterprises (FIEs) went into business during 2000. By the end of the year, 1900 FIEs had been in operation in the city. In 2000, the total sales revenue amounted to RMB23.77 billion with profits totalling RMB1.168 billion, and a tax contribution of RMB940 million. The FIEs also had a total export value of US$1.36 billion in 2000.

Table 7.34.4 Utilization of foreign capital, Yantai City, 1995 and 2000

Mode	Number	Approved contracts		Actual utilization	
		Total value (US$ million) year's total value	% change over previous year	Total value (US$ million) year's total value	% change over previous year
1995					
Direct foreign investment:	402	589.02	−38.19	532.08	−9.79
Equity joint ventures	271	344.65		4,315.28	
Contractual joint ventures	21	47.67		10.13	
Solely foreign-owned enterprises	110	196.70		106.67	
2000					
Direct foreign investment:	371	694.67	113.7		
Equity joint ventures	178	324.00	66.5		
Contractual joint ventures	16	39.20	36.1		
Solely foreign-owned enterprises	177	331.47	225.8		

Table 7.34.5 Key sources of FDI, Yantai City

Source	No. of projects	Contract value (US$ million)
Hong Kong	69	240.55
USA	40	145.04
Republic of Korea	128	142.54
Japan	35	47.53
Taiwan Province	38	39.17

Qingdao City

Qingdao is a major economic centre in Shandong Province. Situated on the eastern tip of the Shandong Peninsula, in Jiaozhou Bay in the Yellow Sea, Qingdao is one of China's principal ports with a coastline of 870 kilometres. The city has a total area of 10,654 square kilometres and the city proper covers 1,102 square kilometres. The population is 7.1049 million. Major economic indicators are shown in Table 7.35.1.

Resources

Qingdao is abundant in agricultural, aquatic and mineral resources. It has 7.52 million mu cultivated land, and 1.86 million mu forest land. The main aquatic products include salt, shrimp, sea cucumbers, abalone, scallops and seaweed. 30 kinds of mineral have been verified.

Natural resources such as gold, graphite, marble, granite and diamond are abundant. The province is China's major production base for cereals, peanuts, cotton, oil-bearing grain, fruit, silk and aquatic products.

Infrastructure

Qingdao Port is one of China's major trading ports and one of the top 1,500-million-tonne ports in the world. The port consists of docks for containers, ore, petroleum and coal. The annual cargo handling capacity in 2000 exceeded 86 million tonnes and 2.1 million TEUs. There are over 300 flights a week on 42 national and international air routes from Qingdao, including nine international routes with 40 flights a week. There are freight and passenger trains to many large cities in

Table 7.35.1   Major economic indicators, Qingdao City

Item	2000	2001
Population (millions)	7.0665	7.1049
Gross domestic product (billion RMB)	115.7	131.6
GDP per capita (thousand RMB)	15.41	18.6
Disposable income per capita (thousand RMB)		
Urban residents	8.016	3.637
Rural residents	8.731	3.901
Savings (billion RMB)*	107.31	123.24
Investment in fixed assets (billion RMB)	32.1	38.44
Value-added of primary industry (billion RMB)	13.99	14.32
Value-added of secondary industry (billion RMB)	56.00	64.88
Value-added of tertiary industry (billion RMB)	45.02	52.4
Total retail sales of consumer goods (billion RMB)	30.77	35.29

*Both institutional and private savings
Source: Qingdao Statistical Bureau.

China. As a sub-provincial-level city, Qingdao ranks first in terms of expressway traffic mileage in the country.

Foreign trade

Qingdao recorded a hefty increase in its total foreign trade value in 2000, from US$7.756 billion in 1999 to US$10.831 billion, an increase of 39.8 per cent.

Over 60 per cent of the trade was contributed by the city's robust exports, which were valued at US$6.114 billion, a rise of 37.3 per cent from US$4.463 billion in 1999. Total export value was equivalent to 43.97 per cent of the total GDP of Qingdao, which stood at RMB115.12 billion (US$13.906 billion), and accounted for 39.37 per cent of the total export value of the province.

The city exported US$805 million worth of primary goods, 13.2 per cent of the total export value. Export of manufactured products amounted to US$5.307 billion, or 86.8 per cent of the total export value.

Exports were destined for 179 countries and regions (see Table 7.35.2). The two largest export markets, Japan and the USA, had a combined share of over 50 per cent of the city's total exports.

Table 7.35.2   Top five export markets, Qingdao City, 1995 and 2000

Country/region	Export value (US$ million)	% of export total
1995		
Japan	709.05	28.93
Republic of Korea	515.92	21.05
Hong Kong	461.91	17.01
USA	342.47	13.97
Singapore	67.33	2.74
Total	2,096.68	85.9
2000		
Japan	1,575.76	25.8
USA	1,556.14	25.5
Republic of Korea	808.37	13.2
Hong Kong	301.87	4.9
Germany	280.16	4.6
Total	4,522.3	74

Total import in 2000 increased by 43.3 per cent from US$3.292 billion in 1999 to US$4.717 billion. Import of primary commodities came to US$843 million, accounting for 17.9 per cent of the total import value, and import of manufactured products was US$3.868 billion, or 82.1 per cent of the total import value.

The two largest suppliers of Qingdao's imports were Korea and Japan (see Table 7.35.3), who had a combined share of 61.8 per cent in Qingdao's total import value.

Table 7.35.3   Top five import markets, Qingdao City, 1995 and 2000

Country/region	Import value (US$ million)	% of import total
1995		
Japan	449.73	34.4
Republic of Korea	344.25	26.2
USA	201.05	15.3
Taiwan Province	45.69	3.5
Total	1,040.72	79.4
2000		
Republic of Korea	2,025.38	42.9
Japan	839.74	18.9
USA	435.59	9.2
Italy	119.47	2.5
Germany	109.84	2.3
Total	3,530.02	75.8

Utilization of foreign capital

The total of contracted foreign investment in 2000 went up by 54.12 per cent over 1999 to US$2,662.21 million. This amount was spread over 1128 investment projects (see Table 7.35.4). Solely foreign-owned enterprises outnumbered the other two forms of FDI in terms of both the number of FDI contracts and contracted value of investment.

In 2000, foreign investment came from 54 countries and regions. The top ten investors are shown in Table 7.35.5:

A total of 3328 foreign investment enterprises were put into operation in the city, employing a total of 330,000 people. The export value of these enterprises was US$4.438 billion in 2000.

Table 7.35.4 Utilization of foreign capital, Qingdao City, 1995 and 2000

Mode	Number	Approved contracts		Actual utilization	
		Total value (US$ million) year's total value	% change over previous year	Total value (US$ million) year's total value	% change over previous year
1995					
Direct foreign investment	718	1,467.34	22	593.08	13
Equity joint ventures	260	399.98		182.79	
Contractual joint ventures	45	147.74		36.83	
Solely foreign-owned enterprises	412	798.42		367.24	
2000					
Direct foreign investment	1,128	2,662.21	54.12	1,307.97	42.57
Equity joint ventures	303	698.89	26.42	451.34	64.78
Contractual joint ventures	57	268.35	38.59	74.52	28.26
Solely foreign-owned enterprises	767	1,693.70	72.64	782.11	33.60

Table 7.35.5 Key sources of FDI

Source	No. of projects	Contract value (US$ million)
Republic of Korea	560	664.78
Hong Kong	132	581.57
USA	82	411.75
Taiwan Province	92	201.05
Canada	23	164.3
Japan	106	153.6
British Virgin Islands	14	147.16
Mauritius	3	93.79
Germany	19	72.16
Spain	1	25.3

Lianyungang City

Lianyungang lies at the middle point of the China's long coastline and in the north-east region of Jiangsu Province. It faces the Yellow Sea in the east, overlooking Korea and Japan on the other side of the sea, and connects to the Economic Belt of Longhai Lanxin in the west. Built on a vast plain with Yuntai Mountain in the centre, the city has a total area of 6,317 square kilometres and a total population of 4.5561 million. Major economic indicators are shown in Table 7.36.1.

Resources

More than 40 types of mineral deposits have been verified including moroxite, pizardite, quartz, rock crystal, marble and placer. The Jinping Phosphate Mine is one of the six largest phosphate mines in China. Its major product, phosphate oxide, is rated as one of the nation's highest quality chemical products. The Zhunbei Salt Field, covering an area of 720 square kilometres, is one of the four salt-producing centres in China. Major salt by-products are potassium chloride, magnesium chloride and bromide.

Infrastructure

The city is one of China's biggest seaports. It has 35 berths of 10,000 tonnes with an annual handling capacity of 35 million tonnes. It has opened up nearly 70 international lines of container shipping. The port has established trade relations with over 1000 ports in nearly 160 countries and regions. On land, the New Eurasian Continental Bridge connects the city with western Asia and European countries. The railway links the city to all major centres of China. Lianyungang is

Table 7.36.1   Major economic indicators, Lianyungang City

Item	2000	2001
Population (millions)	4.5561	
Gross domestic product (billion RMB)	29.11	31.6
GDP per capita (thousand RMB)	6.488	
Disposable income per capita (thousand RMB)		
Urban residents	6.456	2.597
Rural residents	6.981	2.763
Savings (billion RMB)*	19.289	21.46
Investment in fixed assets (billion RMB)	12.793	15.1
Value-added of primary industry (billion RMB)	7. 58	7.78
Value-added of secondary industry (billion RMB)	12.58	13.73
Value-added of tertiary industry (billion RMB)	9.179	10.11
Total retail sales of consumer goods (billion RMB)	9.557	10.29

*Both institutional and private savings
Source: Liangyuangang Statistical Bulletin for 2000 and 2001

one of the 46 highway hubs in China. The Lianhuai, Lianxu and Tongsan expressways pass through the city. The inland waterway link directly to the Great Canal of Jing Hang and the Yangtzi River. Civil aviation lines have been opened up to major cities such as Beijing, Shanghai, Guangzhou, Xiamen and Kunming.

Foreign trade

In 2000, the import and export value of Lianyungang totalled US$485.10 million, an increase of 16 per cent over US$418.72 million in 1999. Total export value was US$388.31 million, up by 21 per cent over US$320.52 million in 1999. Export was equivalent to 10.97 per cent of the city's GDP of RMB29.3 billion (US$3.540 billion).

Export of primary and manufactured products amounted to US$110 million and US$278.31 million respectively, or 28 per cent and 72 per cent of the total export value.

Export commodities went to more than 100 countries and regions in the world. Japan was the largest buyer of the city's exports (see Table 7.36.2).

Table 7.36.2 Top five export markets, Lianyungang City, 1995 and 2000

Country/region	Export value (US$ million)	% of export total
1995		
Japan	38.59	28.73
USA	18.01	13.41
Republic of Korea	14.53	10.82
Hong Kong	11.28	8.40
Italy	6.97	5.20
Total	89.38	66.56
2000		
Japan	139.94	36
USA	50.30	13
Republic of Korea	47.50	12
Germany	20.40	5
Thailand	12.02	3
Total	270.16	69

Import value fell by 1 per cent from US$98.20 million in 1999 to US$96.08 million in 2000. Total import value of primary and manufactured products was 23 per cent and 77 per cent respectively, or US$22.42 million and US$74.38 million.

Japan ranked first among the top five import markets, with sales of US$36.69 million in 2000. See Table 7.35.3.

Table 7.35.3 Top five import markets, Lianyungang City, 1995 and 2000

Country/region	Import value (US$ million)	% of import total
USA	10.16	33.29
Japan	9.08	29.75
Hong Kong	2.94	9.63
Republic of Korea	2.75	9.01
Singapore	1.53	5.01
Total	26.46	86.69
2000		
Japan	36.69	38
Republic of Korea	19.37	20
Canada	8.16	8
USA	7.09	7
Taiwan Province	4.91	5
Total	76.22	78

Utilization of foreign capital

The city attracted less foreign investment in 2000 than in 1999. Contracted investment was down by 7 per cent to US$102.2 million. A total of 116 contracts were approved in the year (see Table 7.36.3).

Among the FDI projects, 103 projects were production-orientated and 13 were non-production-related. Foreign investment came from 17 countries and regions. Key sources are shown in Table 7.36.4.

In 2000, an additional 52 foreign-funded enterprises were in production. The total value of foreign earnings generated by FIEs in 2000 reached US$102.27 million, up by 11 per cent over US$91.90 million in 1999 and accounting for 26 per cent of the city's total export value.

Table 7.36.4 Utilization of foreign capital, Lianyungang City, 1995 and 2000

Mode		Approved contracts		Actual utilization	
	Number	Total value (US$ million) year's total value	% change over previous year	Total value (US$ million) year's total value	% change over previous year
1995					
Direct foreign investment:	279	261.12	93.21	69.74	20.14
Equity joint ventures	27	158.38			
Contractual joint ventures	11	8.97			
Solely foreign-owned enterprises	51	98.77			
2000					
Direct foreign investment:	116	102.2	−7	47.7	2
Equity joint ventures	53	34.12		25.61	
Contractual joint ventures	3	13.52		1.44	
Solely foreign-owned enterprises	60	54.38		20.65	

Table 7.36.5 Key sources of FDI, Lianyungang City

Source of FDI	No. of projects	Contract value (US$million)
Hong Kong	25	15.86
Japan	16	6.61
Taiwan Province	14	3.78
Republic of Korea	23	2.99
USA	19	2.57
Germany	2	2.04

Nantong City

Nantong is situated in the south of Jiangsu Province on the north bank of the Yangtze River estuary, facing Shanghai across the Yangtze River. It is 128 kilometres from Shanghai. Nantong is criss-crossed by rivers and canals and has a 430km coastline. It has a total area of 8,000 square kilometres and a population of 7.85 million. Major economic indicators are shown in Table 7.37.1.

Resources

A fertile soil and genial climate make Nantong one of China's major commodity grain producers. It also produces a rich assortment of farm and sideline produce, with its output of mulberry silk, peppermint and jute taking up a large percentage of the national total. The city has a well-developed fishery and aquaculture business as well as more than 120,000 hectares of beaches replete with marine resources.

Infrastructure

Nantong has well-developed port facilities. Cargo transhipment is undertaken for the provinces and cities along the Yangtze River and its tributaries and shipping lines link the port with Japan, Korea, Australia, Europe, Russia and Africa and a direct shipping service has been set up with Europe. A communications network consisting of water, land and air routes has been developed. Nantong Harbour is one of China's top 10 ports and

Table 7.37.1 Major economic indicators, Nantong City

Item	2000	2001
Population (millions)	7.845	
Gross domestic product (billion RMB)	74.28	80.94
GDP per capita (thousand RMB)		
Disposable income per capita (thousand RMB)		
Urban residents	7.911	3.710
Rural residents	8.485	3926
Savings (billion RMB)*	77.34	87.27
Investment in fixed assets (billion RMB)	23.95	25.81
Value-added of primary industry (billion RMB)	13.22	13.49
Value-added of secondary industry (billion RMB)	35.6	39.27
Value-added of tertiary industry (billion RMB)	25.46	28.18
Total retail sales of consumer goods (billion RMB)	25.01	27.1

*Both institutional and private savings.

Note: The above figures are preliminary and are unadjusted for errors and omissions

Source: Nantong Statistical Bulletin 2000 and 2001

Nantong Xindong Airport has flights to both domestic and international destinations. The city is also well connected to other parts of the province by high quality highways. A railway running through the city is currently being built to improve the city's land transportation capabilities.

Foreign trade

In 2000, Nantong City's foreign trade value totalled US$3.156 billion, an increase of 30.9 per cent over US$2.411 billion in 1999. Total export value was US$2.035 billion, a 27.5 per cent increase over US$1.596 billion in 1999 and equivalent to 22.67 per cent of the city's total GDP of RMB74.3 billion (US$8.977 billion), and 7.9 per cent of the total provincial export value.

Export value of primary goods and manufactured goods reached US$83 million and US$1.952 billion respectively, accounting for 4.08 per cent and 95.92 per cent of the total export value.

144 countries and regions imported from the city. However, the top five export markets (see Table 7.37.2) took a dominant share of 70.38 per cent of the city's total export. Japan alone had taken 43.48 per cent of the city's exports in value terms.

Total import value was US$1.121 billion, an increase of 37.4 per cent over US$816 million in 1999. The import value of primary goods and manufactured pro-

ducts amounted to US$143 million and US$978 million respectively, making up 4.72 per cent and 95.28 per cent of the total imports. The city's imports came from 61 countries and regions, 21 more than 1999. Although the sources of imports were more diversified, the top five markets (see Table 7.37.3) still had a dominant share in the city's total imports.

Table 7.37.3 Top five import markets, Nantong City, 1995 and 2000

Country/region	Import value (US$ million)	% of import total
1995		
Japan	123.93	38.49
USA	63.41	19.69
Republic of Korea	37.95	11.79
Hong Kong	27.79	8.63
Malaysia	13.20	4.09
Total	290.74	90.29
2000		
Japan	475.23	42.39
Republic of Korea	191.59	17.09
USA	106.48	9.5
Taiwan Province	103.58	9.24
Hong Kong	28.61	2.55
Total	905.49	80.77

Utilization of foreign capital

Contracted foreign direct investment amounted to US$329.38 million in 2000. This was a slight drop of 3.17 per cent compared with 1999. The decline in the total contracted FDI was attributed to the decrease in the total investment in equity joint ventures (see Table 7.37.4).

Among the 229 projects with direct foreign investment, 217 were production-related and the remaining 12 were non-production-orientated. Foreign direct investment came from 31 countries and regions. Key sources of FDI are shown in Table 7.37.5.

In Nantong, 1065 foreign-invested enterprises had gone into production. According to the statements of operations submitted by 901 enterprises, total business revenue reached RMB22.687 billion; foreign exchange earned through export went up to US$1.31 billion, an increase of 30.3 per cent on 1999; profit/tax totalled RMB2.258 billion, and net profit was RMB1.110

Table 7.37.2 Top five export markets, Nantong City, 1995 and 2000

Country/region	Export value (US$ million)	% of export total
1995		
Japan	655.65	48.00
Hong Kong	209.29	15.32
USA	179.83	13.16
Republic of Korea	92.67	6.78
UK	45.36	3.32
Total	1,182.8	86.58
2000		
Japan	882.72	43.48
USA	224.55	11.03
Hong Kong	156.78	7.7
Panama	90.24	4.43
Republic of Korea	76.08	3.74
Total	1,430.37	70.38

Table 7.37.4   Utilization of foreign capital, Nantong City, 1995 and 2000

Mode	Number	Approved contracts		Actual utilization	
		Total value (US$ million) year's total value	% change over previous year	Total value (US$ million) year's total value	% change over previous year
1995					
Direct foreign investment:	498	1,256.17	220.75	307.63	34.48
Equity joint ventures	408	491.44		177.38	
Contractual joint ventures	20	32.12		57.72	
Solely foreign-owned enterprises	70	732.61		72.53	
2000					
Direct foreign investment:	229	329.38	–3.17	142.92	–49.54
Equity joint ventures	140	97.48	–55.22	57.26	–75.89
Contractual joint ventures	7	40.11	204.32	10.10	72.35
Solely foreign-owned enterprises	82	119.19	75.5	75.56	89.71

Table 7.37.5   Key sources of FDI, Nantong City, 2000

Source	No. of projects	Contract value (US$ million)
Japan	69	111.72
Hong Kong	39	51.69
USA	30	46.51
Taiwan Province	22	8.47
Republic of Korea	14	5.22
Singapore	6	5.07
Australia	5	9.77
British Virgin Islands	2	29.90
Bermuda	2	25.05
UK	2	8.70
Italy	2	8.56

billion. There were 34 enterprises altogether, each of which had a total profit and tax of over RMB10 million. Among these, 21 achieved net profit of over RMB10 million, nine more than in 1999.

Ningbo City

Ningbo is situated on the eastern coast of China in the north-east of Zhejiang Province. Its north-east and centre sit in an alluvial plain criss-crossed by rivers. The total area of Ningbo is 9,365 square kilometres, of which 5,021 square kilometres are mountainous areas. The population is 5.4335 million. Major economic indicators are shown in Table 7.38.1.

Resources

The mountainous areas are rich in bamboo, mulberries, tea, fruits and mineral resources. 35 types of minerals have been found, including lead, zinc, iron, salt, fluorspar, silicon marble rocks and granites.

Infrastructure

The Port of Ningbo is one of the few ports in the world with 100 million tonnes of cargo throughput every year. It is also one of the few that can host ships of up to 300,000 tonnes. There are 132 berths of over 500 tonnes including 17 of over 50,000 tonnes. Among these are a 50,000 tonne berth for liquid chemicals, a dedicated container berth for fourth and fifth generation container vessels, an ore transhipment berth for 200,000 tonne vessels (also for vessels of 300,000 tonnes) and the 250,000 tonne terminal for crude oil. These are the largest berths in China at present. Ningbo is well connected by railway systems to other parts of the

Table 7.38.1   Major economic indicators, Ningbo City

Item	2000	2001
Population (millions)	5.4095	5.4335
Gross domestic product (billion RMB)	119.15	131.058
GDP per capita (thousand RMB)	22.078	24.121
Disposable income per capita (thousand RMB)		
Urban residents	10.841	5.044
Rural residents	11.991	5.362
Savings (billion RMB)*	116.8689	144.45
Investment in fixed assets (billion RMB)	36.06442	47.028
Gross output of agriculture (billion RMB)	14.736	15.643
Industrial value-added (billion RMB)	57.66	65.1
Total retail sales of consumer goods (billion RMB)	36.33	41.42

*Both institutional and private savings
Source: Ningbo Statistical Bulletin 2000 and 2001

province and from there to the rest of China. The Greater Ningbo area has 5,155 kilometres of highway and highway density is 55 kilometres per square kilometre.

Foreign trade

Ningbo city's total foreign trade value in 2000 was US$7.541 billion, up by 50.68 per cent over US$5.004 billion in 1999. The split between import and export was 31.5 per cent and 68.5 per cent, as the city's foreign trade is largely export-driven.

Total export value was US$5.168 billion, up by 48.61 per cent on US$3.477 billion in 1999. It was equivalent to 36 per cent of the city's GDP, which was RMB119.15 billion (US$14.355 billion).

Export of primary products amounted to US$395 million, 7.64 per cent of the total export value. Export of manufactured products came to US$4.77252 billion, or 92.36 per cent of the total export value.

Goods were exported to 183 countries and regions. The city was less dependent on the top five export markets (see Table 7.38.2) than before. These markets accounted for less than 50 per cent of the total export value, while in 1995 the figure had been nearer 70 per cent.

Total import value increased by 55.41 per cent from US$1.527 billion in 1999 to US$2.3731 billion in 2000. Import of primary products amounted to US$779.94 million, 32.87 per cent of total import value. The import

Table 7.38.2 Top five export markets, Ningbo City, 1995 and 2000

Country/region	Export value (US$ million)	% of export total
1995		
Hong Kong	624.51	26.36
Japan	490.25	20.69
USA	201.69	8.51
Republic of Korea	182.11	7.69
Germany	89.40	3.77
Total	1,587.96	67.02
2000		
Japan	973.19	18.83
USA	785.21	15.19
Hong Kong	309.79	5.99
Germany	234.52	4.54
UK	174.28	3.37
Total	2,476.99	47.92

value of manufactured products was US$1.59316 billion, or 67.13 per cent of the total import value.

Imports came from 91 countries and regions, of which 25 sold over US$10 million worth of goods to the city. The aggregate of the top 25 import markets came to a total of US$2.26158 billion, 95.3 per cent of the city's total import value. The top five markets (see Table 7.38.3) played an even greater role as they captured about 64 per cent of the city's import spending. Japan had again replaced Hong Kong at the top, with 16.48 per cent of the city's total import value.

Table 7.38.3 Top five import markets, Ningbo City, 1995 and 2000

Country/region	Import value (US$ million)	% of import total
1995		
Hong Kong	202.87	18.26
Republic of Korea	152.88	13.70
Indonesia	129.64	11.67
Japan	116.52	10.49
USA	71.49	6.43
Total	673.4	60.55
2000		
Japan	390.99	16.48
Taiwan Province	348.06	14.67
Republic of Korea	312.98	13.19
USA	283.32	11.94
Indonesia	183.93	7.75
Total	1519.28	64.03

Utilization of foreign capital

Ningbo attracted US$959.51 million worth of foreign direct investment in 2000, which was an increase of 44.91 per cent over 1999 (see Table 7.38.4). A total of 550 FDI contracts were approved in the year.

Among the foreign direct investment projects, 444 were production-orientated and 106 non-production-related. Foreign direct investment came from 40 countries and regions. The top five investors are shown in Table 7.38.5.

By the end of 2000, a total of 1813 foreign invested enterprises had been put into operation. These FIEs employed around 226,100 people and their sales revenue reached RMB41.734 billion, of which an equivalent of US$1.35335 billion was generated through independent export. Reported profit was RMB295,500.

Table 7.38.4 Utilization of foreign capital, Ningbo City, 1995 and 2000

Mode	Number	Approved contracts		Actual utilization	
		Total value (US$ million) year's total value	% change over previous year	Total value (US$ million) year's total value	% change over previous year
1995					
Direct foreign investment:	496	1,146.30	48.58	339.09	11.44
Equity joint ventures	327	805.68		235.13	
Contractual joint ventures	41	71.13		37.96	
Solely foreign-owned enterprises	128	269.49		126.00	
2000					
Direct foreign investment:	550	959.51	44.91	621.86	19.51
Equity joint ventures	280	191.37	−13.19	239.32	−10.57
Contractual joint ventures	20	123.65	113.37	107.46	56.65
Solely foreign-owned enterprises	250	636.49	68.29	275.08	49.39

Table 7.38.5 Key sources of FDI, Ningbo City, 2000

Source of FDI	No. of Projects	Contract value (US$ million)
Hong Kong	152	228.65
Taiwan Province	108	110.76
USA	95	110.17
British Virgin Islands	23	92.51
Japan	55	80.43

Wenzhou City

Located in the south-east of Zhejiang Province on China's south-eastern seaboard, Wenzhou faces the East China Sea in the east and has a coastline of 355 kilometres. With its location at the north of the Oujiang River, Wenzhou is a natural harbour. It has a total area of 11,784 kilometres and a population of 7.558 million. Major economic indicators are shown in Table 7.39.1.

Resources

More than 40 mineral deposits have been verified along the Oujiang River including iron, manganese, lead, zinc, molybdenum, alum and porcelain clay. Reserves of alum amount to 300 million tonnes.

Infrastructure

As the second largest port in Zhejiang Province, Wenzhou offers cargo shipping services to more than 80 domestic ports and the lower and middle reaches of the Yangtse River. It also has established trade-shipping ties with 113 ports in 26 countries and regions throughout the world. Wenzhou has a highly developed highway network. The 104 and 330 state trunk roads run through the city from east to west. The city has 151 long-distance bus lines to major cities in China such as Beijing, Guangzhou and Xi 'an. The railway line to Jinhua links Wenzhou with Hangzhou, Shanghai, Nanjing and Beijing . Wenzhou has 57 domestic air routes flying to Beijing, Shanghai, Shenzhen, Chengdu and

Table 7.39.1   Major economic indicators, Wenzhou City

Item	2000	2001
Population (millions)	7.558	
Gross domestic product (billion RMB)	83.1	93.322
GDP per capita (thousand RMB)	11.358	12.653
Disposable income per capita (thousand RMB)		
Urban residents	12.055	4.296
Rural residents	13.2	4.683
Savings (billion RMB)*	92.77	112.9
Investment in fixed assets (billion RMB)	26.53	32.87
Value-added of primary industry (billion RMB)	5.53	5.72
Value-added of secondary industry (billion RMB)	47	52.83
Value-added of tertiary industry (billion RMB)	30.56	34.77
Total retail sales of consumer goods (billion RMB)	39.79	43.85

* Both institutional and private savings

Source: Wenzhou Statistical Bulletin on National Economy and Social Development, 2000 and 2001

Note: Figures are preliminary and unadjusted.

Harbin, and two regional air routes to Hongkong and Macao.

Foreign trade

In 2000, Wenzhou's foreign trade value was US$2.02 billion, up by 64.3 per cent over US$1.227 billion in 1999. Export, in aggregate, surged by 82.1 per cent to US$1.5 billion in 2000, from US$823 million in 1999. Export of primary products amounted to US$28.43 million, 1 per cent of the total export, while industrial manufactured products stood at US$1.47160 billion, or 99 per cent of the total.

Wenzhou had a diversified export market of 169 countries and regions in 2000. The top five export destinations (see Table 7.39.2) had only 36.8 per cent of the total export value.

Import value stood at US$520million, an increase of 27.9 per cent over US$403 million in 1999. Of the total imports, primary products brought in US$118.60 million, or 22.8 per cent of the total, while industrial manufactured products stood at US$401.40 million, accounting for 77.2 per cent of the total.

The city's imports came from 66 countries and regions. The top five import markets (see Table 7.39.3) took up 71 per cent of the city's total import.

Utilization of foreign capital

Wenzhou reported an increase of 44.4 per cent in the inflow of FDI in 2000, with the total contracted investment coming to US$67.06 million. A total of 84 FDI contracts were approved, up 20 per cent on 1999. See Table 7.39.4.

Table 7.39.2   Top five export markets, Wenzhou City, 1995 and 2000

Country/region	Export value (US$ million)	% of export total
1995		
Hong Kong	80.05	29.0
Hungary	27.23	9.9
Japan	20.15	7.3
USA	17.75	6.4
France	15.37	5.6
Total	160.55	58.2
2000		
USA	143.02	9.5
Hungary	123.36	8.2
Hong Kong	103.44	6.9
Russia	103.27	6.9
Japan	79.29	5.3
Total	552.38	36.8

Table 7.39.3   Top five import markets, Wenzhou City, 1995 and 2000

Country/region	Import value (US$ million)	% of import total
1995		
Hong Kong	16.10	29
Japan	13.72	24.7
Switzerland	5.57	10
USA	4.85	8.7
Taiwan Province	4.77	8.6
Total	45.01	81
2000		
Republic of Korea	133.93	26
Japan	86.92	17
USA	69.27	13
Taiwan Province	53.62	10
Germany	25.11	5
Total	368.85	71

Table 7.39.4   Utilization of foreign capital, Wenzhou City, 1995 and 2000

Mode	Number	Approved contracts		Actual utilization	
		Total value (US$ million) year's total value	*% change over previous year*	*Total value (US$ million) year's total value*	*% change over previous year*
1995					
Direct foreign investment:	159	114.49	−51.72	73.52	20.17
Equity joint ventures	122	77.52		57.45	
Contractual joint ventures	13	17.15		1.60	
Solely foreign-owned enterprises	24	19.82		14.47	
2000					
Direct foreign investment:	84	67.06	44.4	72.02	35.89
Equity joint ventures	60	38.85	35.3	25.91	12.2
Contractual joint ventures	2	2.55	264	29.44	77.8
Solely foreign-owned enterprises	22	25.66	50.7	16.67	64.4

Foreign investment came from 29 countries and regions. The main sources of FDI are shown in Table 7.39.5.

Up to the end of 2000, a total number of 1475 foreign-funded enterprises had begun operation with a total output value of US$3.10006 billion. Sales income reached US$8.935 billion, an increase of 42.6 per cent compared with 1999 and total profits amounted to US$382 million.

Table 7.39.5   Key sources of FDI, Wenzhou City, 2000

Source	No. of projects	Contract value (US$ million)
Taiwan Province	15	6.02
France	13	20.44
USA	11	3.8
Hong Kong	9	14.09
Italy	9	2.1
Brazil	4	1.24
Netherlands	3	4.16
Romania	2	1.18

Fuzhou City

Fuzhou is a coastal city in south-eastern China, on the lower reaches of the Minjiang River. The terrain slopes from north-west to south-east. The Taiwan Straits separate Fuzhou from Taiwan Province, which is only 68 nautical miles away at the shortest distance. Fuzhou is a famous historic and cultural city and an open coastal port city. Its coastline of 1137 kilometres is one-third of that of the whole province. The Minjiang River flows through the city. Fuzhou is the provincial capital of Fujian, occupying a total area of 11,968 square kilometres and has a population of 5.89 million. Major economic indicators are shown in Table 7.40.1.

Table 7.40.1   Major economic indicators, Fuzhou City

Item	2000
Population (millions)	5.8923
Gross domestic product (billion RMB)	100.327
GDP per capita (thousand RMB)	
Disposable income per capita (thousand RMB)	
Urban residents	7.944
Rural residents	3.86
Savings (billion RMB)*	103.385
Investment in fixed assets (billion RMB)	10.88
Gross output of agriculture (billion RMB)	27.742
Industrial value-added (billion RMB)	75.01
Total retail sales of consumer goods (billion RMB)	35.117

* Both institutional and private savings.
Source: Fuzhou Statistical Bulletin on National Economy and Social Development 2000
Note: Figures are preliminary and unadjusted

Resources

Mineral resources in Fuzhou are rich, with around 30 different kinds of proven underground reserves. It is particularly rich in pyrophyllite, alumstone, granite, kaolin and quartz sand. There are sizeable proven reserves of non-ferrous minerals. There are over 500 types of marine life, 120 types of freshwater fish and 50 kinds of minerals. Fuzhou has exceptional terrestrial advantages including abundant hot springs. Key agricultural products include paddy rice, tea, sugar cane, cotton, hemp, tobacco, rape, longan, citrus, lychees, pineapples and shaddock.

Infrastructure

Fuzhou Port is one of the hub ports of China. It is 149 nautical miles to Keelung in Taiwan and 420 nautical miles to Hong Kong. There are 50 berths, including 13 deep-water berths over 10,000 tonnes. The sea routes extend to all major ports in China and to over 40 countries and regions around the world including Europe, America, Japan, the Philippines, Singapore, Hong Kong, Taiwan and Thailand. Railway transportation continues to play an important role. Ten trains go to Beijing and Shanghai daily. A regional highway network has been formed which radiates to all counties of the Fujian province. Air services offer connections with all major centres of the country and some international cities. Fuzhou has an international-standard telecommunications system.

Foreign trade

In 2000, the total import and export value of Fuzhou was US $5.07664 billion, an increase of 47.94 per cent over US $3.68424 billion in 1999. Total export value was US$2.70345 billion, an increase of 33.43 per cent over US $2.02617 billion in 1999, equivalent to 22.3 per cent of Fuzhou's GDP. The top five export markets are shown in Table 7.40.2.

Import value was US$2.37319 billion, an increase of 43.13 per cent over US $1.65807 billion in 1999. Imports came mainly from countries and regions such

Table 7.40.2 Top five export markets, Fuzhou City, 1995 and 2000

Country/region	Export value (US$ million)	% of export total
1995		
Hong Kong	858.06	54.75
USA	340.62	21.73
Japan	196.06	12.51
Taiwan Province	57.10	3.60
Germany	14.99	1.00
Total	1,466.83	93.59
2000		
Hong Kong	735.01	27.19
USA	656.75	24.29
Japan	312.86	11.57
Germany	130.84	4.84
Taiwan province	101.94	3.77
Total	1,937.40	71.66

as Hong Kong, Japan, Taiwan Province, USA, Republic of Korea, Italy, Germany, France and Malaysia.

Utilization of foreign capital

A total of 295 FIE contracts were signed in 2000, down 12.7 per cent over 338 projects in 1999. The contracted foreign capital was US$954.79 million, up 2.2 per cent over US$934.26 million in 1999. Of all the FDI projects approved in 2000 were 80 equity joint ventures with a foreign capital of US$156.52 million, six contractual joint ventures with US$11.71 million and 209 solely foreign-owned enterprises with US$786.56 million. The foreign capital actually utilized in the whole year amounted to US$800.87 million, an increase of 9.65 per cent over US$730.36 million in 1999. 93.94 per cent of the projects were production- or export-orientated.

In 2000, an additional 125 foreign-funded enterprises went into production. By the end of 2000, 3087 foreign-invested enterprises were in operation, with an industrial output value of RMB53.25 billion, or 53.1 per cent of Fuzhou's total municipal industrial output value in the same period. The foreign exchange generated through export by these enterprises came to US$2.35038 billion, an increase of 24.49 per cent over 1999's US$1.84360 billion, or 86.94 per cent of the city's total export value.

7.41

Guangzhou City

Situated in the Pearl River Delta near the South China Sea and adjacent to Hong Kong and Macao, Guangzhou is the capital of Guangdong Province. Surrounding hills, tableland and plains range from north to south and there are mountains nearby. Guangzhou is 182 kilometres from Hong Kong, and is China's largest and most prosperous southern city, an important seaport for foreign trade and a famous historical and cultural city over 2,000 years old. It hosts annual spring and autumn export trade fairs. The total area is 7,434 square kilometres and the population is 7.13 million. Major economic indicators are shown in Table 7.41.1.

Resources

With a sub-tropical climate and ample rainfall, Guangzhou is suitable for year-round farming. Agriculture, livestock breeding and sideline production are well developed and grain, oil-bearing crops and a rich variety of vegetables and fruits are grown. Guangzhou is also known as a 'City of Flowers'. At present there are 52 varieties of mineral deposits, including coal, lead, zinc, niobium, gold and other ferrous, non-ferrous, rare, and precious metals, at 396 locations. There are also raw materials for the chemical industry and building

Table 7.41.1 Major economic indicators, Guangzhou City

Item	2000	2001
Population (millions)	7.0069	7.126
Gross domestic product (billion RMB)	238.307	268.483
GDP per capita (thousand RMB)	34.389	38.000
Disposable income per capita (thousand RMB)		
Urban residents	13.967	6.068
Rural residents	14.694	6.446
Savings (billion RMB)*	554.519	622.804
Investment in fixed assets (billion RMB)	92.419	96.408
Value-added of primary industry (billion RMB)	16.3	16.705
Value-added of secondary industry (billion RMB)	100.84	113.651
Value-added of tertiary industry (billion RMB)	127.98	145.259
Total retail sales of consumer goods (billion RMB)	112.097	124.39

* Both institutional and private savings.
Source: Guangzhou Statistical Bureau
Note: 2001 figures are preliminary and unadjusted

materials. There are several thousand plant species and about 210 kinds of wild animals. Guangzhou's water area covers 74,400 hectares, accounting for 10 per cent of Guangzhou's total area.

Infrastructure

Guangzhou port, the third largest in China, is a distribution centre for goods and materials and a hub of international trade for the Pearl River Delta area and southern China. The port maintains trade relations with over 170 countries and regions and over 500 international ports. Guangzhou is also one of the key railway hubs in southern China. Guangzhou Baiyun Airport is the third largest international airport in China, with 60 domestic and 12 international air routes. The city boasts 3788.2 kilometres of highway network, offering access to over 97 per cent of the places in Guangdong province and major cites of China. Postal services reach over 190 countries and regions. The city has a sophisticated modern telecommunications system. DDD can reach more than 1,700 cities and townships in China while IDD connects the city with over 200 countries and region in the world.

Foreign trade

The total trade value of Guangzhou city in 2000 stood at US$17.641 billion, up by 21.60 per cent on US$14.507 billion in 1999. Over half of the foreign trade value was contributed by the city's export, which was worth US$9.176 billion, up by 16.77 per cent over US$7.858 billion in 1999. Total export compared to 30.82 per cent of the city's GDP, RMB238.3 billion, and contributed 9.98 per cent to the total export value of Guangdong Province. Export of primary and manufactured products stood at US$0.32 billion and US$8.856 billion respectively, or 3.49 per cent and 96.51 per cent of the total export value.

In 2000, commodities were exported to 196 countries and regions, among which the top five (see Table 7.41.2) accounted for 75.5 per cent of total export value. The two largest export destinations had a combined share of 62.87 per cent in the city's total export revenue.

Import value totalled US$8.465 billion, an increase of 27.32 per cent over US$6.585 billion in 1999. Import of primary and manufactured products amounted to US$620 million and US$7.845 billion respectively, making up 7.23 per cent and 92.67 per cent of the total

Table 7.41.2 Top five export markets, Guangzhou City, 1995 and 2000

Country/region	Export value (US$ million)	% of export total
1995		
Hong Kong	2,435.95	39.0
USA	253.57	4.1
Germany	88.52	1.4
Japan	79.43	0.9
UK	55.04	0.5
Total	2,912.51	45.9
2000		
Hong Kong	3,414.56	37.21
USA	2,355.10	25.66
Japan	731.5	7.97
Germany	241.80	2.48
Belgium	228.35	2.18
Total	6,971.31	75.5

Table 7.41.3 Top five import markets, Guangzhou City, 1995 and 2000

Country/region	Import value (US$ million)	% of import total
1995		
Hong Kong	734.47	21.4
Japan	81.56	2.4
USA	50.03	1.5
Republic of Korea	29.39	0.9
Taiwan Province	15.04	0.4
Total	910.49	26.6
2000		
Japan	1,648.69	19.46
Taiwan Province	1,269.76	14.99
USA	1,011.42	11.94
Hong Kong	806.11	9.52
Republic of Korea	604.07	7.13
Total	5,340.05	63.04

import value. Import commodities came from 123 countries and regions (see Table 7.41.3).

Utilization of foreign capital

In 2000, Guangzhou recorded an increase of 8.1 per cent as a result of its efforts to attract foreign direct

Table 7.41.4 Utilization of foreign capital, Guangzhou City, 1995 and 2000

Mode	Number	Approved contracts		Actual utilization	
		Total value (US$ million) year's total value	% change over previous year	Total value (US$ million) year's total value	% change over previous year
1995					
Direct foreign investment:	1.774	6,731.01	−1.85	2,144.44	18.21
Equity joint ventures	439	1,408.26		498.68	
Contractual joint ventures	852	4,390.22		1,386.09	
Solely foreign-owned enterprises	483	932.22		259.67	
2000					
Direct foreign investment:	647	1,527.59	8.1	2,989.23	0.1
Equity joint ventures	135	284.92	5.1	470.85	−61.2
Contractual joint ventures	124	565.38	4.3	1,779.77	48.2
Solely foreign-owned enterprises	388	677.29	12.8	738.61	29.2

investment. A total of 647 contracts were approved in the year, a total investment of US$1.53 billion. FDI in the form of wholly foreign-owned enterprises outnumbered both equity and contractual joint ventures (see Table 7.41.4).

Foreign investment came from 46 countries and regions which can be broadly divided into three categories: a) from overseas Chinese in Hong Kong, Taiwan Province, Macau and Singapore; b) international capital from developed countries such as Japan, the USA and Western Europe; and c) international floating capital from the British Virgin Islands. Detailed information on the key sources of investment is provided in Table 7.41.5.

By the end of 2000, the accumulated number of registered enterprises with foreign investment had reached 12,608 in Guangzhou. 5,541 of these had already gone into production. Foreign investment actually utilised amounted to US$20.669 billion. Total export value of enterprises with foreign investment reached US$6.01 billion, accounting for 65.44 per cent of the city's total export value.

Table 7.41.5 Key sources of FDI, Guangzhou City

Source	No. of projects	Contract value (US$ million)	Actual utilization (US$ million)
Hong Kong	359	637.87	1,957.47
British Virgin Islands	67	371.15	393.90
Taiwan Province	95	92.75	72.98
Japan	7	81.33	63.00
Singapore	18	77.19	104.63
USA	45	66.69	135.87
Cayman Islands	4	39.27	5.84
Netherlands	4	30.40	11.24
Samoa	6	23.53	6.12
Macao	8	16.45	63.40
Belize	1	10.00	2.75

Zhanjiang City

Located on the north-eastern Leizhou Peninsula in western Guangdong Province, Zhejiang is the southernmost port city on the mainland. Under its jurisdiction are three county level cities, two counties, four districts, a State-Level Economic and Technological Development Zone (ZETDZ) and five Provincial-Level Economic Development Test Zones (EDTZ). It has a total area of 12470.5 square kilometres and a population of 7 million. Major economic indicators are shown in Table 7.42.1.

Resources

Lying in the sub-tropics, the city has a mild climate, plenty of rainfall and a coastline of 467 kilometres with ample tropical and marine resources. It produces sugar cane, jute, pineapple, pepper and coffee. It is also one of China's major rubber producers. Aquatic products include lobster, prawn, grouper, abalone and jellyfish. The Leizhou Peninsula is rich in petroleum reserves. At present, Zhanjiang ranks first in the province in deep-sea fishing, aquaculture, salt production, offshore petroleum and gas.

Infrastructure

Sea transportation networks have been formed in Zhanjiang with 22 ports of a total of 174 berths, whose annual throughput exceeds 30 million tonnes. Zhanjiang port is the main entrepot in China with 33 berths, 25 of which can hold 10,000 to 50,000-tonne ships. Zhanjiang Port has commercial transactions with more

Table 7.42.1 Major economic indicators, Zhanjiang City

Item	2000	2001
Population (million)		7.0071
Gross domestic product (billion RMB)	40.1542	43.487
GDP per capita (thousand RMB)		
Disposable income per capita (thousand RMB)		
Urban residents	7.094	3.251
Rural residents	7.520	3.443
Savings (billion RMB)*	39.22	43.143
Investment in fixed assets (billion RMB)	7.68	8.486
Value-added of primary industry (billion RMB)	10.75	11.415
Value-added of secondary industry (billion RMB)	14.99	16.294
Value-added of tertiary industry	14.44	15.778
Total retail sales of consumer goods (billion RMB)	17.48	18.9

*Both institutional and private savings.
Source: Zhanjiang Statistical Bulletin 2000 and 2001
Note: Figures are preliminary and unadjusted

than 100 countries and regions in the world. It has developed into a multi-functioning harbour with a handling capacity of 18 million tonnes. The railways from Zhanjiang to Litang and from Zhanjiang to Guangzhou connect Zhanjiang with national rail networks. Highways are available to every village and town and the expressway from Guangzhou to Zhanjiang is under construction. Currently 18 airliners with 110 flights per week are scheduled for Hong Kong and other large cities.

Foreign trade

In 2000, the total foreign trade value of Zhanjiang City was US$1.16746 billion, an increase of 56.23 per cent over US$747.25 million in 1999. The contribution of export to this total was 32.42 per cent, although the total export value (US$378.43 million) experienced a substantial increase of 48.45 per cent in 2000 against 1999's US$254.92 million, equivalent to 7.72 per cent of city's total GDP (RMB40.59 billion or about US$4.902 billion) and 0.41 per cent of the total export value of Guangdong Province.

Export of primary goods came to US$84.12 million, accounting for 22.23 per cent of the total export value.

Table 7.42.2 Top five export markets, Zhanjiang City, 1995 and 2000

Country/region	Export value (US$ million)	% of export total
1995		
Hong Kong	280.56	77.46
Japan	28.06	7.75
Taiwan Province	13.08	3.61
USA	10.56	2.92
Thailand	6.03	1.66
Total	338.29	93.4
2000		
Hong Kong	78.47	20.74
USA	74.07	19.57
Japan	50.90	13.45
Vietnam	24.98	6.60
Taiwan Province	21.24	5.61
Total	249.66	65.97

Export of manufactured goods reached US$294.31 million, 77.77 per cent of the total export value. Exports were destined for 166 countries and regions (see Table 7.42.2).

The increase in the total import value was even greater than for export: a total of 60.27 per cent growth from US$492.38 million in 1999 to US$789.08 million. The import value of primary goods and manufactured products amounted to US$555.84 million and US$233.19 million respectively, 70.45 per cent and 29.55 per cent of the total imports.

Imports came from 56 countries and regions (see Table 7.42.3). The key imports were crude oil, fertiliser, potassium chloride, raw cotton and steel scraps.

Table 7.42.3 Major import markets, Zhanjiang City, 1995 and 2000

Country/region	Import value (US$ million)	% of import total
1995		
Hong Kong	65.19	70.90
Japan	14.40	15.66
USA	6.85	7.45
Thailand	2.88	3.13
Total	89.32	97.14
2000		
Australia	177.15	22.45
Malaysia	138.48	17.55
Papua New Guinea	76.95	9.75
USA	43.52	5.52
Yemen	43.48	5.51
Total	479.58	60.78

Utilization of foreign capital

The city approved 38 foreign direct investment projects in 2000 with a contracted investment of US$95.69 million, an increase of 36.14 per cent year on year. The FDI in equity and contractual joint ventures dropped while that in solely foreign-owned enterprises rose by 174.07 per cent (see Table 7.42.4).

Foreign investment came from eight countries and regions (see Table 7.42.5)

Table 7.42.4 Utilization of foreign capital, Zhanjiang City, 1995 and 2000

Mode	Number	Approved contracts		Actual utilization	
		Total value (US$ million) year's total value	% change over previous year	Total value (US$ million) year's total value	% change over previous year
1995					
Direct foreign investment:	145	515.15		185.29	
Equity joint ventures					
Contractual joint ventures					
Solely foreign-owned enterprises					
2000					
Direct foreign investment:	38	95.69	36.14	89.61	19.32
Equity joint ventures	12	17.30	−8.13	22.01	−35.77
Contractual joint ventures	7	8.94	−65.77	21.82	63.94
Solely foreign-owned enterprises	19	69.45	174.07	45.78	66.35

Table 7.42.5 Key sources of FDI, Zhanjiang City

Source	No. of projects	Contract value (US$ million)
Hong Kong	20	73.46
Singapore	3	13.06
Taiwan Province	6	5.48
Canada	2	3.15
USA	3	1.11
Australia	2	1.06
British Virgin Islands	1	1.05
Israel	1	0.3

Beihai City

Beihai is situated on the southern tip of the Guangxi Zhuang Autonomous Region, facing the Beibu Gulf and bordered by the sea on three sides. It has a total area of 3,337 square kilometres and a population of 1.45 million. In April 1984, Beihai was approved by the State Council as one of the 14 coastal cities to implement further opening policies to the outside world. Major economic indicators are shown in Table 7.43.1.

Resources

Beihai has ample natural resources. The waters of the Beibu Gulf are replete with marine products, including hairtail, cuttlefish, prawn, crab, squid and seahorse. In addition, the area contains rich deposits of ilmenite and quartz sand as well as oil. The Beibu Gulf is one of the six largest oil and gas basins in China. Proven reserves of petroleum amount to 22.56 million tonnes and reserves of natural gas are 35 billion cubic metres. The Beibu Gulf on the border of Beihai is one of the four well-known fishing grounds in China. The city benefits from the sea not only in fishing but also in pearl farming. It is the hometown of the world-famous Southern Pearls. For the tourism industry, Beihai has beautiful beaches, islands and mangrove forests. Beihai Silver Beach has been approved by the State Council as one of 11 State Tourism and Holiday Zones.

Table 7.43.1   Major economic indicators, Beihai City

Item	2000	2001
Population (millions)	1.430648	1.4471
Gross domestic product (billion RMB)	11.37956	12.472
GDP per capita (thousand RMB)		
Disposable income per capita (thousand RMB)		
Urban residents	6.167	2.155
Rural residents	7.013	2.265
Savings (billion RMB)*	10.371	11.347
Investment in fixed assets (billion RMB)	2.18	1.99
Value-added of primary industry (billion RMB)	3.612	3.735
Value-added of secondary industry (billion RMB)	3.06	3.45
Value-added of tertiary industry (billion RMB)	47.11	5.29
Total retail sales of consumer goods (billion RMB)	3.401	3.737

* Both institutional and private savings.
Source: Beihai Statistical Bulletin 2000 and Beihai Government Work Report 2001
Note: Figures are preliminary and unadjusted

Infrastructure

Beihai is one of the closest ports from China's mainland to the port cities in south-east Asia, West Asia, Africa and Europe and thus is a convenient gateway to the sea for Beihai's south-western region and part of southern and central China. Beihai has a coastline of 500 kilometres, with several gulfs and port areas. The city has three major ports: Beihai old port, Shibuling New Port and Tieshan Port. There are six berths of 10,000 tonnes and over, and 16 berths of under 5,000 tons. Beihai Airport operates over 20 domestic and international flights. Railway and highway construction have developed rapidly and the city is connected with other parts of the Guangxi province and the country. Beihai has high quality air and has one of the highest living standards in China.

Table 7.43.2 Top five export markets, Beihai City, 1995 and 2000

Country/region	Export value (US$ million)	% of export total
1995		
Hong Kong	31.02	51.74
Taiwan Province	8.60	14.35
Japan	5.99	9.99
Finland	2.98	4.97
Republic of Korea	2.10	3.50
Total	52.28	87.21
2000		
USA	22.45	46.06
Hong Kong	10.90	22.36
Germany	3.54	7.26
Japan	2.52	5.17
Vietnam	2.52	5.17
Total	41.93	86.02

Foreign trade

In 2000, the total import and export value of Beihai City was US$74.03 million, down by 37.93 per cent from US$119.26 million in 1999. Total export value was US$48.74 million, down 43.1 per cent from US$85.67 million in 1999, equivalent to 3.55 per cent of the city's GDP of RMB11.37 billion (US$1.37372 billion) and 3.26 per cent the total export value of the region. Export of primary and manufactured products amounted to US$2.28 million and US$46.46 million respectively, 4.68 per cent and 95.32 per cent of the total export value of the city. The top five export markets are shown in Table 7.43.2.

Beihai also reported a decline in its import value, from US$33.59 million in 1999 to US$25.28 million in 2000, down by 24.7 per cent. Import of primary products, primarily livestock, amounted to US$15.38 million, 60.84 per cent of the total import value. Import of manufactured products totalled US$9.90 million, 39.16 per cent of the total imports. Key import markets are shown in Table 7.43.3.

Table 7.43.3 Key import markets, Beihai City, 2000

Country/region	Import value (US$ million)	% of total import
2000		
Hong Kong	21.53	85.17
USA	0.45	1.78
Total	21.98	86.95

Utilization of foreign capital

Foreign direct investment came mainly from nine countries and regions across Asia, Oceania, Latin America and North America, the details of which are shown in Table 7.43.5.

Table 7.43.4 Utilization of foreign capital, Beihai City, 1995 and 2000

Mode	Number	Approved contracts		Actual utilization	
		Total value (US$ million) year's total value	*% change over previous year*	*Total value (US$ million) year's total value*	*% change over previous year*
1995					
Direct foreign investment:	56	101.55	−82.09		
Equity joint ventures	28	52.45	−82.73		
Contractual joint ventures	9	19.25	68.71		
Solely foreign-owned enterprises	19	29.85	−88.15		
2000					
Direct foreign investment:	17	6.03	−86.51	36.29	−16.38
Equity joint ventures	6	6.03	−47.57		
Contractual joint ventures	1	0.06	−		
Solely foreign-owned enterprises	10	6.92	−86.52		

Table 7.43.5 Key sources of FDI, Beihai City, 2000

Source	No. of contracts	Contracted value (US$ million)	Actually utilized (US$ million)
Hong Kong	6	3.37	7.84
Macao			2.2
Taiwan Province		1.32	0.8
ASEAN	3	0.62	3.65
Singapore	2	0.26	3.65
Japan	1	0.1	0.32
British Virgin Islands	1	2.60	3.74
USA	2	0.44	1.91

Shenzhen City

Located in Guangdong Province's coastal region, Shenzhen is the country's first Special Economical Zone (SEZ), established in 1979. The city consists of six districts, of which four are within the SEZ. Shenzhen is bordered by the New Territories of Hong Kong in the south, Wutong Mountain in the north, Dapeng Bay in the east and Houhai Bay in the west and it has a total area of 2,035 square kilometres. The population is 4.6876 million. Over 20 years of rapid economic growth have brought Shenzhen to the forefront of the major Chinese cities in terms of overall economic strength. The city is the fastest developing in China. Between 1980 to 2001, its annual increase in GDP averaged 29.5 per cent, in industrial output value 45.4 per cent, and in import and export value 39.1 per cent. Major economic indicators are shown in Table 7.44.1.

Resources

Shenzhen has abundant natural resources and products, particularly fresh vegetables, poultry and livestock, aquatic products and fruits. The coastal area teems with over 30 species of famous and rare fish including the golden thread fish, the 'big-eye' porgy, sea bass, shrimps, crabs, shells and algae. The city also abounds with oysters and coastal shrimps, which are renowned both in China and abroad. The city is Hong Kong's largest supplier of fresh milk. 15 metallic and 12 non-metallic minerals have been prospected and there are over 900 mineral deposits, of which building material minerals such as freshwater sand, marble, granite and limestone have abundant reserves.

Table 7.44.1 Major economic indicators, Shenzhen City

Item	2000	2001
Population (millions)	124.92	4.6876
Gross domestic products (billion RMB)	166.524	195.417
GDP per capita (thousand RMB)		43.344
Disposable income per capita (thousand RMB)		
Urban residents 21.626 9.27		
Rural residents	23.544	9.869
Savings (billion RMB)*	316.762	409.257
Investment in fixed assets (billion RMB)	61.625	67.337
Value-added of primary industry (billion RMB)	1.689	1.811
Value-added of secondary industry (billion RMB)	93.245	105.646
Value-added of tertiary industry (billion RMB)	77.703	87.960
Total retail sales of consumer goods (billion RMB)	53.82	60.926

* Both institutional and private savings.

Source: Shenzhen Statistical Bulletin 2000 and 2001

Note: Figures are preliminary and unadjusted

Infrastructure

The Guangzhou-Kowloon, and Guangzhou-Meizhou-Shantou Railways run through the central part of the Shenzhen SEZ. The section from Beijing to Shenzhen of the Beijing Kowloon Railway is open to traffic. Shenzhen Northern Rail Freight Station boasts 52 freight rails, 366 piers and 190,000 square metres of freight depot. Of the 17 cross-border facilities, Luohu checkpoint is the largest passenger port while Huanggang is the largest vehicular link and Yantian the second largest container seaport in the Chinese mainland. The Huangtian International Airport is the fourth largest in the nation. A modern transportation network is in place with highways, expressways and railways reaching out in all directions. Two trunk rail links – Beijing-Canton Railway and Beijing-Kowloon Railway – converge in Shenzhen. The city boasts eight ports and twelve cargo docks. With a handling capacity in 1999 of 2.98 million TEUs, Shenzhen has the second largest container terminal in China.

Foreign trade

Shenzhen's total foreign trade increased by 26.80 per cent in 2000, from US$50.428 billion in 1999 to US$63.943 billion. 68.53 per cent of the total trade value came from exports, the total value of which was US$34.557 billion, up by 22.51 per cent over US$28.208

Table 7.44.2 Top five export markets, Shenzhen City, 1995 and 2000

Country/region	Export value (US$ million)	% of export total
1995		
Hong Kong	18,870.06	91.93
Japan	197.56	0.96
USA	183.49	0.89
Germany	54.92	0.27
Singapore	54.36	0.26
Total	19,360.39	94.31
2000		
Hong Kong	11,368.29	32.9
USA	9878.28	28.59
EU	4602.73	13.32
Japan	3076.03	8.90
ASEAN	2126.11	6.15
Total	31,051.44	89.86

billion in 1999. Total export value was equivalent to 171.34 per cent of the city's total GDP (RMB166.524 billion or US$20.136 billion), accounting for 37.59 per cent of the total export value of Guangdong Province (US$91.920 billion) and 13.87 per cent of the total export value of the country (US$249.200 billion). Shenzhen ranked first among large- to medium-sized cities in China.

Export of primary goods came to US $ 1.399 billion, 4.05 per cent of the total export value. Export of manufactured goods was worth US$33.158 billion, or 95.96 per cent.

Total import value was US$29,386 billion, an increase of 32.25 per cent over 22.219 billion in 1999. The key import category was telecommunications equipment and devices, which accounted for 35.79 per cent of the city's total import value. Other key imports and their respective shares in the total import value were: plastics (9.48 per cent), machinery (6.76 per cent), ferrous metal (5.92 per cent), paper and paper products (4.44 per cent), textiles (2.46 per cent) and industrial chemicals (2.24 per cent). Japan was the largest supplier of Shenzhen's imports (see Table 7.44.3).

Table 7.44.3 Top five import markets, Shenzhen City, 1995 and 2000

Country/region	Import value (US$ million)	% of import total
1995		
Hong Kong	13,373.33	77.09
Taiwan Province	3,375.76	19.46
Japan	114.14	0.66
USA	113.92	0.65
Singapore	61.42	0.34
Total	17,038.57	98.2
2000		
Japan	6,199.47	21.10
Taiwan Province	5,097.57	17.35
Republic of Korea	2,278.10	7.75
USA	2,067.59	7.04
Hong Kong	1,611.60	5.48
Total	17,254.33	58.72

Utilization of foreign capital

In 2000, Shenzhen approved 1130 FDI projects with a total contracted investment of US$1.74 billion. The increase in the contracted value of investment was 43.6 per cent year on year (see Table 7.44.4).

Table 7.44.4   Utilization of foreign capital, Shenzhen City, 1995 and 2000

Mode	Number	Approved contracts		Actual utilization	
		Total value (US$ million) year's total value	*% change over previous year*	*Total value (US$ million) year's total value*	*% change over previous year*
1995					
Direct foreign investment:	1,633	3,463.07	22.31	1,309.89	4.75
Equity joint ventures	764	1,255.89		331.20	
Contractual joint ventures	109	635.61		280.03	
Solely foreign-owned enterprises	760	1,571.57		698.66	
2000					
Direct foreign investment:	1130	1,738.13	43.6	1,961.45	10.29
Equity joint ventures	339	283.74	73.5	717.89	−4.09
Contractual joint ventures	24	119.26	64.6	191.02	0.78
Solely foreign-owned enterprises	766	1,287.39	33.2	1,030.61	24.84

7.45

Zhuhai City

Zhuhai is one of the five Special Economic Zones approved by the State Council of the Chinese government. Zhuhai is located at the south of Guangdong province, by the western and southern banks of the Pearl River estuary. It is bordered by Macao to the south, and overlooks Hong Kong across the South China Sea to the east. Zhuhai covers an area of 7,555 square kilometres and its population is 1.25 million. Major economic indicators are shown in Table 7.45.1.

Resources

Minerals with sizeable reserves include porcelain clay, kaolin, feldspar and quartz. Glass-quality sand has

estimated reserves of about 5.18 million cubic metres. In Doumen County, there is a rich store of granite, magnet, red ochre, manganese ore, tungsten, tin, beryllium, peat, feldspar and quartz sand. The Pearl River has rich resources of many different fish.

Infrastructure

Zhuhai's transport system is well developed. Zhuhai port, a major port in southern China, has a 75-kilometre shore, which provides over 100 berths from 10,000 to 250,000 tonnes and has an annual throughput of 150 million tonnes. There are also about 100 berths of over 500 tonnes capacity in Jiouzhou, Xiang-

Table 7.45.1   Major economic indicators, Zhuhai City

Item	2000	2001
Population (millions)		1.253
Gross domestic product (billion RMB)	32.76	36.72
GDP per capita (thousand RMB)	26.34	29.100
Disposable income per capita (thousand RMB)		
Urban residents	15.115	4.398
Rural residents	15.871	4.75
Savings (billion RMB)*	44.32	49.42
Investment in fixed assets (billion RMB)	9.49	10.47
Gross output of agriculture (billion RMB)	2.26	2.39
Value-added of industry (billion RMB)	15.43	17.4
Value-added of tertiary industry (billion RMB)		
Total retail sales of consumer goods (billion RMB)	11.52	12.84

* Both institutional and private savings

Source: Zhuhai Statistical Bulletin 2000 and 2001, Zhuhai Statistical Bureau

Note: Figures are preliminary and unadjusted

zhou, Qianshan, Wanshan, Jing'an and Doumen ports. Zhuhai airport, built according to international standards, covers four million square metres with a runway of 4,000 metres. It has over 30 domestic airlines and around 130 scheduled flights every week. The road network, extending in all directions, connects Zhuhai with the rest of the country.

Foreign trade

Zhuhai's total foreign trade value in 2000 was US$9.164 billion ,up by 45.79 per cent over US$6.286 billion in 1999. Total export value was US$3.645 billion, up by 35.07 per cent over US$2.699 billion in 1999 and equivalent to 92 per cent of the city's total GDP (about US$3.966 billion) and 4 per cent of Guangdong's total export value.

Export of primary commodities was US$173 million, 5 per cent of the total export value. Export of manufactured products reached US$3.472 billion, or 95 per cent of the total export value.

The city's exports were destined for 140 countries and regions (see Table 7.45.2). Hong Kong remained the city's biggest supplier of imported goods and Hong Kong and Macao had a combined share of nearly 70 per cent of Zhuhai's total import.

Total import value was US$5.518 billion, up by 52.86 per cent over US$3.587 billion in 1999. Import of primary goods was worth US$274 million, 5 per cent

Table 7.45.2 Top five export markets, Zhuhai City, 1995 and 2000

Country/region	Export value (US$ million)	% of export total
1995		
Hong Kong	1,465.89	69.30
Macao	196.72	9.30
Japan	105.76	5.00
USA	27.50	1.30
Singapore	12.69	0.60
Total	1,808.56	85.5
2000		
Hong Kong	591.49	58.1
Macao	102.51	10.1
USA	58.80	5.8
Japan	29.75	2.9
Saudi Arabia	15.26	1.5
Total	797.81	78.4

of the total import value. The remaining 95 per cent went on manufactured products: US$5.244 billion.

Among the top five import markets (see Table 7.45.3), Iran ranked first with a share of 48.91 per cent of the city's total import value. This was due to the heavy import of processed petroleum products. The city's import of oil and related products, chemical material, various kinds of machines, telecommunication equipment and devices totalled US$2.12 billion.

Table 7.45.3 Top five import markets, Zhuhai City, 1995 and 2000

Country/region	Import value (US$ million)	% of import total
1995		
Hong Kong	997.24	59.10
Japan	313.85	18.60
Macao	141.74	8.40
USA	96.18	5.70
Taiwan Province	54.00	3.20
Total	1,603.01	95
2000		
Iran	1,467.51	48.91
Hong Kong	871.14	29.00
Republic of Korea	172.70	5.82
Iraq	160.88	5.40
Macao	118.75	4.0
Total	2,790.98	93.13

Utilization of foreign capital

Zhuhai registered an impressive increase of 75.02 per cent in its use of foreign direct investment in 2000. Contracted investment was worth US$554.9 million and 554 FDI contracts were approved (see Table 7.45.4).

FDI came from 25 countries and regions in 2000, 10 more than in the previous year. Investment came mainly from Hong Kong, the USA and Macao. There were 167 Hong Kong-invested projects with a contractual investment of US$198 million, 36.4 per cent of the total for the city. The USA and Macao also invested significant amounts. Investment came from Greece, Belize and Bermuda for the first time in 2000. 343 of these projects were production-related and 211 non-production orientated. 325 projects were in the manufacturing industry, with a total amount of contract value of US$407 million, or 74.68 per cent of the total foreign direct investment. Of the 211 non-production projects,

Table 7.45.4   Utilization of foreign capital, Zhuhai City, 1995 and 2000

Mode	Number	Approved contracts		Actual utilization	
		Total value (US$ million) year's total value	*% change over previous year*	*Total value (US$ million) year's total value*	*% change over previous year*
1995					
Direct foreign investment:	425	1,499.72	46.60	539.29	5.10
Equity joint ventures	187	622.83		172.09	
Contractual joint ventures	97	303.92		172.79	
Solely foreign-owned enterprises	141	572.97		194.41	
2000					
Direct foreign investment:	554	554.90	75.02	815.18	8.46
Equity joint ventures	96	81.64	−0.62	130.22	16.14
Contractual joint ventures	23	62.64	149.56	252.71	−29.46
Solely foreign-owned enterprises	435	400.62	100.79	432.25	69.91

165 were in the service industry, with a contracted investment of US$83.70, or 15.36 per cent of the total. There were 85 projects in computer applications and services, with a contractual value amounting to US$25.01 million.

7.46

Shantou City

Shantou is situated in the south-eastern part of Guang-dong Province. It is 161 kilometres from east to west and 148 kilometres from north to south. Shantou has a coastline of 389 kilometres, starting in the east at Shang-dong Village in Raoping County and ending in the west in Huilai County. Shantou Special Economic Zone was established in 1981. In 1991 the Zone was enlarged from 52.6 square kilometres to 234 square kilometres. Shantou administrates five districts (Longhu, Jinyuan, Shengping, Dahao and Hepu), one county (Nan'ao) and two county-level cities (Chaoyang and Chenghai). Major economic indicators are shown in Table 7.46.1.

Resources

Thirty-eight mineral deposits have been verified, includ-ing aluminium, zinc, silver, tungsten, tin, titanium and zircon. Plant resources include cereal and oil crops, cash crops, vegetables, medicinal herbs, fruits and wood.

Infrastructure

A great number of key infrastructure projects have been completed over the last two decades, including Guang-zhou-Meizhou-Shantou Railway, Shenzhen-Shantou Expressway, Across-Bay Bridge, Queshi Bridge, the International Container Dock, a 500-kilovolt Power Transmission and Transformation Project, the Eastern Guangdong Information Building and Shantou Inter-national Cable Landing Station. Shantou Harbour has grown into one of the twenty biggest hubs in the coun-try. Modern transport links, power supply and advanced telecommunications are in place.

Table 7.46.1   Major economic indicators, Shantou City

Description	2000	2001
Population (millions)	4.59	4.62
Gross domestic product (billion RMB)	47.79	460.99
GDP per capita (thousand RMB)	10.529	10.017
Disposable income per capita (thousand RMB)		
Urban residents	8.706	4.343
Rural residents	8.951	4.089
Savings (billion RMB)*	52.614	57.823
Investment in fixed assets (billion RMB)	11.152	10.184
Value-added of primary industry (billion RMB)	4.59	4.443
Value-added of secondary industry (billion RMB)	22.382	21.135
Value-added of tertiary industry (billion RMB)	19.98	20.521
Total retail sales of consumer goods (billion RMB)	21.9	22.416

Foreign trade

In 2000, Shantou's foreign trade value totalled US$4.213 billion, down by 4.6 per cent from US$4.391 billion in 1999. Total export value was US$2.596 billion, a drop of 3.6 per cent from US$2.694 billion in 1999. The city's export value was equivalent to 44.87 per cent of Shantou's GDP of RMB47.79 billion (US$57.86 billion), contributing 2.82 per cent to the total export value of Guangdong Province. Of the city's total export earnings, US$1.866 billion came from general export, down by 1.4 per cent on the previous year; the remaining US$729 million came from the outbound processing trade, a drop of 8.5 per cent.

The city exported to 151 countries and regions in 2000 and the top five markets (see Table 7.46.2) took a dominant share of 77.2 per cent of the total export value.

Table 7.46.2 Top five export markets, Shantou City, 1995 and 2000

Country/region	Export value (US$ million)	% of export total
1995		
Hong Kong	1,101.94	80.67
Japan	57.59	4.20
Singapore	41.89	3.10
USA	36.68	2.70
Malaysia	15.08	1.10
Total	1,253.18	91.77
2000		
Hong Kong	1,345.96	51.8
USA	304.68	11.7
Japan	196.48	7.6
Singapore	89.79	3.5
Panama	66.73	2.6
Total	2,003.64	77.2

Import value totalled US$1.617 billion in 2000, 4.7 per cent less than US$1.697 billion in 1999. Electromechanical products; plastics, industrial chemical products and petroleum gas were the key imports, each having a total import value over US$100 million. Imports came from 72 countries and regions and the

Table 7.46.3 Top five import markets, Shantou City, 1995 and 2000

Country/region	Import value (US$ million)	% of import total
1995		
Republic of Korea	415.08	18.49
Japan	305.96	13.63
Hong Kong	285.51	12.72
Taiwan Province	236.80	10.55
Russia	201.29	8.97
Total	1,444.64	64.36
2000		
Australia	177.15	22.45
Malaysia	138.48	17.55
Papua New Guinea	76.95	9.75
USA	43.52	5.52
Republic of Yemen	43.48	5.51
Total	479.58	60.78

top five markets combined (see Table 7.46.3) had a 60.78 per cent share of the city's total import value. Australia was the largest supplier of the city's imports, with Malaysia second.

Utilization of foreign capital

Foreign direct investment in the city dropped by 5.1 per cent in 2000. Total contracted investment was US$269.93 million and there were 81 approved FDI projects (see Table 7.46.4).

Foreign investment came from 13 countries and regions. The leading sources were: Hong Kong (US$116.26 million in 50 projects), Taiwan Province (US$11.07 million in 10 projects), Singapore (US$72.90 million in 5 projects), British Virgin Islands (US$45.31 million in 4 projects) and Australia (US$1.03 million in 3 projects)

In 2000, foreign-invested enterprises (FIEs) had a total output value of RMB15.244 billion, up by 11.9 per cent on 1999 and contributing 18.7 per cent to Shantou's gross industrial output value. The sales/business revenue was RMB14.76 billion, a growth of 11 per cent and export value totalled US$710 million, up by 5.7 per cent from that of the previous year.

Table 7.46.4   Utilization of foreign capital, Shantou City, 1995 and 2000

Mode	Number	Approved contracts		Actual utilization	
		Total value (US$ million) year's total value	% change over previous year	Total value (US$ million) year's total value	% change over previous year
1995					
Direct foreign investment:	393	1,264.67	3.58	802.92	15.08
Equity joint ventures	96	290.52		158.11	
Contractual joint ventures	138	533.26		315.68	
Solely foreign-owned enterprises	159	440.89		329.13	
2000					
Direct foreign investment:	81	269.93	−5.1	165.61	−75.1
Equity joint ventures	17	29.87	−27.2	47.43	−87.5
Contractual joint ventures	8	64.97	−44.2	39.58	−75.0
Solely foreign-owned enterprises	56	175.08	38.1	78.60	−37.4

Xiamen City

Xiamen is a port city on China's south-eastern coast in the Fujian province. It is only 120 nautical miles from Taiwan across the Taiwan Straits. It covers an area of 1,516 square kilometres, of which Xiamen Island is 127 square kilometres. It has a population of 1.29 million. Xiamen city is one of China's first four Special Economic Zones, and has been granted the right to manage its own economic affairs while offering preferential investment policies to foreign companies. Major economic indicators are shown in Table 7.47.1.

Infrastructure

Xiamen is China's sixth largest container port, with a handling volume of over 1 million TEUs in 2000. Xiamen is open to navigation with around 50 ports servicing over 30 countries and regions including Australia, Japan, Singapore, the USA, Canada and Hong

Kong. Xiamen Gaoji International Airport has 33 airlines flying to all major cities in China as well as Bangkok, Hong Kong, Kuala Lumpur, Macao, Manila, Osaka, Penang and Singapore. Xiamen is well connected to all parts of the country through the Yingtan-Xiamen Railway, which is linked up with the national rail network. Direct passenger services via rail are available between Xiamen and Shanghai, Nanjing, Hefei, Fuzhou, Nanchang and Yingtan. The Fuzhou-Xiamen and Zhangzhou-Xiamen Highways link Xiamen with every part of the Fujian Province and the provinces of Guangdong, Jiangxi and Zhejiang. Xiamen boasts a diversified highway transportation system with state-owned, Sino-foreign funded and Sino-foreign cooperative passenger and freight enterprises. Passenger services are provided daily between Xiamen and Fuzhou, Quanzhou, Zhangzhou, Longyan,Shantou, Shenzhen and Guangzhou, with deluxe limousines and light buses.

Table 7.47.1 Major economic indicators, Xiamen City

Description	2000	2001
Population (millions)		1.29
Gross domestic product (billion RMB)	49.68	55.64
GDP per capita (thousand RMB)	10.813	40.968
Disposable income per capita (thousand RMB)		
Urban residents	10.494	3.879
Rural residents	11.365	4.322
Savings (billion RMB)	46.216	64.237
Investment in fixed assets (billion RMB)	17.518	19.189
Value-added of primary industry (billion RMB)	2.061	2.251
Value-added of secondary industry (billion RMB)	26.233	29.696
Value-added of tertiary industry (billion RMB)	21.402	23.692
Total retail sales of consumer goods (billion RMB)	17.23	18.655

Container freight services are also available between Xiamen and Shenzhen and Hong Kong.

Foreign trade

In 2000, Xiamen's total import and export value increased by 26.20 per cent, rising to US$10.049 billion from US$7.963 billion in 1999. 58.5 per cent of the total trade came from exports, the total value of which in 2000 amounted to US$5.879 billion, up by 32.54 per cent over US$4.436 million in 1999. Export value was equivalent to 96.9 per cent of the city's GDP (RMB50.115 billion or about US$6.067 billion) and 45.54 per cent the total export value of the Fujian Province. Export commodities were sold to 151 countries and regions (see Table 7.47.2).

Total import value was US$4.170 billion, an increase of 18.23 per cent on US$3.527 billion in 1999. The top five markets (see Table 7.47.3) captured a share of 69.1 per cent of the city's total import spending.

Table 7.47.2 Top five export markets, Xiamen City, 2000

Country/region	Export value (US$ million)	% of export total
USA	1,446.16	24.94
Japan	1,037.77	17.65
Hong Kong	764.3	12.98
Taiwan Province	196.67	3.35
Germany	194.76	3.31
Total	3,639.66	62.23

Table 7.47.3 Top five import markets, Xiamen City, 1995 and 2000

Country/region	Import value (US$ million)	% of import total
1995		
Hong Kong	545	21.34
Japan	142	5.55
Republic of Korea	98	3.83
Russia	77	3.01
UK	46	1.8
Total	908	35.53
2000		
Taiwan Province	994.64	23.86
Japan	693.45	16.63
USA	524.41	12.57
Republic of Korea	474.59	11.38
Hong Kong	194.13	4.66
Total	2,881.22	69.1

Utilization of foreign capital

A total of 259 FDI contracts were approved by Xiamen in 2000, with a total contracted investment of US$1.004 billion, a drop of 21.96 per cent against 1999. This drop was attributed to the sharp decline in the FDI in equity and contractual joint ventures. FDI in solely foreign-owned enterprises, in contrast, increased by 21.66 per cent (see Table 7.47.4). See Table 7.47.5 for a list of key sources of foreign capital.

Table 7.47.4   Utilization of foreign capital, Xiamen City, 1995 and 2000

Mode		Approved contracts			Actual utilization	
	Number	Total value (US$ million) year's total value	% change over previous year		Total value (US$ million) year's total value	% change over previous year
1995						
Direct foreign investment:	505	2,062	10.56		1322	6.44
Equity joint ventures	130					
Contractual joint ventures	29					
Solely foreign-owned enterprises	346					
2000						
Direct foreign investment:	259	1,004.00	−21.96		10,3150	−23.13
Equity joint ventures	52	143.63	−70.02		3,6956	−10.69
Contractual joint ventures	5	10.09	−90.70		4595	−85.14
Solely foreign-owned enterprises	202	850.28	21.66		6,1599	0.46

Table 7.47.5   Key sources of FDI, Xiamen City

Source	No. of projects	Total value (US$ million)
Hong Kong	45	367.02
Taiwan Province	105	148.01
Singapore	16	32.08
Philippines	7	6.60
Japan	11	54.01
Malaysia	6	26.07
Macao	3	13.83
Republic of Korea	6	8.52
Indonesia	1	2.59
UK	11	146.98
Total	211	805.71

Macao: a Second Window to China

Chen Duo, Senior Researcher and Director General, Hong Kong and Macao Research Institute
Translated by Li Yong

At the turn of the new century, Macao was returned to China after over 400 years of colonization. Macao has now become the jewel in southern China's crown, a famous, modern, international and metropolitan city where history and culture merge.

In the past few decades, Macao has had many outstanding achievements which have brought about profound changes in its economy, society and culture and laid good foundations for further developments in the new century. Macao is one of the few free trade ports and independent tariff zones in the Far East.

Transport

As a relatively independent and open small island economy, Macao has long been restrained by the lack of natural conditions such as deep-water ports, and so has not been able to play a role compatible with its position as a free port. In order to rebuild its advantages, Macao has recently planned and successfully built a three-dimensional comprehensive transport system consisting of seaports, airport and an express highway.

Macao International Airport was completed in 1995, which has given the city a fast and convenient method of transport to reach the outside world. The airport has, to a certain extent, helped Macao rejuvenate its function as a free port. Macao is actively planning port facilities to accommodate even larger tonnage.

A modern land transportation system connecting Macao with the hinterland of the Pearl River Delta by rail and express highways is being planned. With the construction of the Guangzhou-Zhuhai-Macao express highway, Guangzhou-Zhuhai-Macao railway and the Lingdingyang Bridge connecting Hong Kong, Shenzhen, Zhuhai and Macao across the harbour, Macao's transportation system will be greatly improved. Such improvements will bring Macao closer to the western part of the Pearl River Delta area and the mainland of China and expedite the process of integration between Guangdong, Hong Kong and Macao.

With its advantages as a transportation hub consisting of sea, air and land and an integrated river-to-sea transport system upon completion of the construction of the passage connecting the Xijiang River to the sea, the constraints that have limited Macao's role as a free port for over 100 years will be completed eliminated in the not too distant future. Macao will rediscover its role as a free port and the economic, trade and investment ties between Macao and the mainland will be strengthened further, enhancing Macao's role as a 'bridge' and 'window' to China.

Industries

Looking to the future, Macao will have unprecedented opportunities for development along with the fast growth of the mainland economy and the flourishing of neighbouring Hong Kong. The growth of Macao's modern economy has been driven by export processing, a combined result of the opportunities available in this particular historic period and Macao's peculiar advantages. This kind of labour-intensive export-oriented processing had experienced rapid growth before, in the 1970s and 80s. Entering the 1990s, however, the manufacturing industry was largely in a state of decline, and little was done to upgrade and transform the industry. As a result, Macao's industrial structure and its whole economy has since entered a prolonged period of adjustment. A striking contrast with this is the significant growth achieved in Macao's service sector since the

1980s, the structure of which has diversified. Tourism, real estate, trade, telecommunications, finance and consulting have enjoyed an increasing trend of development and, at present, the percentage of tertiary industry in the GDP is well over 80 per cent, and it has become the most significant element in the local economy.

Tourism

Casinos and tourism will play an important part in Macao's economic development. The model of casino-driven tourism development has been a product of Macao's history and is also one of the important features of Macao's tourism industry. In the future, the development of tourism will continue to rely on casino-related tourism, and the future direction of it will involve the development of casinos towards mass recreation, reforms of the present system regarding the management and operation of casinos and an effort to innovate new casino technologies and improve the quality of services. In addition, Macao will expand its modern tourism and casino industries by fully utilizing its unique and rich historical and cultural heritage and facilitating the development of large-scale tourism attractions, in order to target more diverse sources of customers. To pursue a model of comprehensive tourism development, priority will be given to the development of a diversified range of tourism products related to interests such as sightseeing, conference, business, culture, sports, religion and holidaying, all of which will enhance the Macao's attractiveness as a tourism destination. As a joint effort to develop a greater 'triangle' tourism area consisting of Hong Kong, Macao and Guangdong, Macao will also reinforce its cooperation in tourism with these adjacent regions.

Finance

Sectors such as trade, finance, real estate, shipping and information will become Macao's cornerstone industries. The future of Macao's financial sector will focus on developing offshore financial services while strengthening and developing its local business of savings and loans. Macao will fully utilize its advantages of being a free port, such as free inflow and outflow of capital, no restrictions on foreign exchange, convertibility of Macao currency and its direct ties with other international financial centres, to develop its offshore financial businesses. By providing financing services to and deepening financial cooperation with the Pearl River Delta areas, Macao will gradually become an offshore financial centre servicing the neighbouring areas. It is foreseeable that with the prosperity of the economies in its neighbourhood, large-scale infrastructure constructions within the city combined with the economic recovery will give impetus to further development of Macao's financial sector.

Construction and real estate

Construction and real estate industries were once an important part of Macao's economy. In recent years, however, these industries have experienced a decline from prosperity to recession, which has had a negative impact on the whole of the city's economy. In the future development of the real estate industry, Macao will strengthen its urban planning and administration and combine the real estate development with the overall construction plans of urban facilities, matching up the division of urban functions with social services facilities. Secondly, the property market needs to be further regulated in order effectively to suppress excessive speculative manipulation of property prices. Finally, planning permission will be better controlled, which should improve the extent of land development and utilization. At the same time, the land area will be expanded through land reclamation efforts and offshore isle development will also be expedited. The prosperity of Macao's future economy requires a parallel development of the real estate industry. As long as development rules are respected, it is believed that the construction and real estate industries will, after a few years of adjustments, enter a new round of prosperous development.

Information technology

With the revolution of information technology and the global transition from an industrial society to an information society, industrialization of the information industry and 'informationization' of industry are the irresistible trends of the modern world. Macao is equipped with advanced facilities for international communications, and as early as 1991, Macao Telecom Company (Companhia de Telecomunicacoes de Macau S.A.R.L, CTM) adopted a digital control system. Macao now has access to over 100 countries and regions by direct dial and other dual-means of communication such as telegraph, facsimile and satellite television services. In effect, the information industry has already taken off and shown excellent development prospects.

Other industries

Commercial services, including warehousing, shipping, accounting, legal, commercial consulting, advertising and market research will all play increasingly important roles in Macao's economy.

For a considerable period of time, the export processing industry will remain an important part of Macao's economy. With agreements reached at the Uruguay Round regarding textiles and garments coming into effect and the gradual phasing out of the export quotas and other preferential treatments enjoyed by Macao, the labour-intensive industries will face stringent challenges. Macao's only choice is to guide and promote industrial transition by fostering the transformation of the existing industries. The future path to development for Macao's industries should be to enhance knowledge and technology for products in the export processing industry and the industries must move towards a high value-added, superior quality and well-established brand awareness, and must be highly responsive to market changes.

The future

Historically, Macao was an international trade centre and shipping hub connecting China with Europe, America, Africa and Latin countries. In over 400 years of peaks and troughs, Macao has always existed as an international city. It is for this reason that it has maintained extensive international economic, trade and cultural ties with the outside world. After its return to China on 20 December 1999, Macao's position as a special channel, connecting East and West economically and culturally, has been preserved and developed further under new conditions. It will continue to be the 'bridge' and 'window' for China's opening up, playing multiple intermediary roles that are both indispensable and irreplaceable.

Macao has maintained extensive economic and trade relations with over 100 countries and regions around the world, and is at the same time an independent signatory or participant in international treaties and organisations. Meanwhile, the fact that Macao enjoys preferential treatment from European countries and the United States, plus its unique culture and history that meld eastern and western cultures, as well as its position as a highly open port, all reinforce its function as a point of exchange, communications and contact with the outside world.

Macao's extensive international ties and marketing networks serve not only as an important gateway for China's exports and the development of the world market, but also as an important channel through which the Chinese mainland can obtain foreign capital, technology and equipment. Macao's frequent international exchanges, responsive reactions to information and advanced telecommunications systems will continue to be an important window for the mainland to acquire knowledge about the international economy, technology, information and management.

Macao's culture and history, converging both eastern and western cultures, will offer greater space for China to expand its economic and cultural exchanges between east and west. In particular, Macao's traditional ties over several hundred years with Portugal and other Latin countries will be an important bridge linking China to the European Union in terms of economic and cultural exchange, as well as an indispensable medium for China to further develop economic and cultural relations with these countries. Its unique position will offer the city a realistic opportunity to play the role of intermediary in the future.

On the one hand, Macao opens up a convenient passage for the ties between the mainland and Taiwan province. On the other, its ties with EU countries will also serve as a bridge for Taiwanese businesses to develop in the European market. The future role that Macao will play in China's external economic exchanges is going to be unique and irreplaceable. In this process, Macao will demonstrate its own value and earn valuable opportunities for its own economic development.

Hong Kong: China's Special Administrative Region

Chen Dou, Senior Researcher and Director General, Hong Kong and Macao Research Institute
Translated by Li Yong

In recent years, Hong Kong's economy has been besieged by serious recession and sustained depression. There are external as well as internal reasons for this. External factors mainly include the aftermath of the Asian financial crisis, the impact of the September 11th terrorist attacks and the overall slowdown of the world economy.

Internally, there are three key factors:

1. **The bursting of Hong Kong's economy's pre-1997 'bubble'.** In the mid-1980s, following clarification of its political future and the speedy development of economic and trade relations between Hong Kong and the mainland, Hong Kong's economy entered the ascending period of a new cycle which reached its peak in 1997. However, behind its flourishing appearance, a 'bubble economy' took shape in Hong Kong's property and stock markets, the two important pillars of its economy. The unusual rise had in effect prepared for the unusual fall that has taken place since the last quarter of 1997.

2. **'Hollowing' of Hong Kong's industrial structure.** Hong Kong has been in a 'post-industrial' period since the mid-1980s. Its manufacturing industry, another of its economic pillars, was under pressure caused by increasingly scarce land and labour resources and sharp rises in production costs, which prompted a large-scale relocation of the industry into Southern China, typically the Guangdong Pearl River Delta area. In the process, for reasons such as the generally small sizes of manufacturing enterprises, weak technological capability and the non-intervention policies of the then British government of Hong Kong, the region's manufacturing industry

failed to upgrade and transform its structure, which was manifested in the trend of 'hollowing'.

3. Structural unemployment as a result of industrial relocation, together with the negative assets and northward consumption shift caused by the aftermath of the Asian financial crisis, has led to a sustained weakness in consumer spending, which in turn has seriously deterred the recovery of the territory's economy.

During the Asian financial storm, Hong Kong's economy was hit hard. Although the pegged exchange rate of Hong Kong dollars was maintained, laying a foundation for economic recovery, the pressure of the expensive costs, particularly the adverse effects of the currency depreciation on neighbouring Asian countries and regions, made the upgrading and transformation of Hong Kong's industrial structure increasingly important and imperative, not only for the SAR government, but also for the business community and Hong Kong society as a whole. In fact, the SAR government, after China's takeover of the territory, corrected the short-sighted and short-term behaviour of the Hong Kong British government and began to look at Hong Kong's economic transformation from a strategic point of view. In his first Policy Address delivered in October 1997, the Chief Executive of Hong Kong, Tung Chee Hwa, explicitly stated that, with the northward relocation of Hong Kong industries, 'the invisible hand of market forces has already pointed the way forward: to develop high value-added industries and services'. In the new historic period, the upgrading and restructuring of Hong Kong economy in this direction is in effect a natural course of development. Such an effort involves two important and interrelated issues, the repositioning of Hong Kong's economy and the upgrading and restructuring of its industrial structure.

After the return of Hong Kong, Tung Chee Hwa confirmed in his second and third Policy Addresses, the positioning of Hong Kong as an important city. He said 'Hong Kong has the potential to become not only a major city within one country but also the most cosmopolitan city in Asia, enjoying a status similar to that of New York in America and London in Europe.' He pointed out that:

> Hong Kong already possesses many of the key features common to New York and London. For example, we are already an international centre of finance and a popular tourist destination, and hold leading positions in trade and transportation. These are all pillars of our economy. If we can consolidate our existing economic pillars and continue to build on our strengths, we should be able to become world-class. Then, like New York and London, we will play a pivotal role in the global economy, be home to a host of multinational companies and provide services to the entire region.

This positioning has received support and affirmation from the general public.

Closely related to the repositioning of Hong Kong's economy is the upgrading and restructuring of its industries. The Commission on Strategic Development, chaired by Tung Chee Hwa, issued a report entitled *Bringing the Vision to Life: Hong Kong's Long-Term Development Needs and Goals* which concluded that if Hong Kong is to achieve its goal of becoming the most cosmopolitan city in Asia and a major city in China in the next 30 years, several sectors and areas are key to its long-term development and its likelihood of maintaining its strong regional and international competitive advantage. These include sectors such as financial and business services, tourism, multinational corporations (MNC) regional headquarters, information services and telecommunications, innovation and technology, trade, transportation and logistics and creative and cultural activities. Among these, innovation and technology will undoubtedly be the new emerging industry in the economy, which will in turn equip other industries in Hong Kong.

Since globalization and the knowledge-based economy have become major trends in the development of the world economy, it is inevitable that Hong Kong, if it is to elevate its position in the Asia Pacific region and the global economy and to become the New York of Asia, must shift its whole economy to a high value-added one, pivoting on the development of a knowledge economy driven by innovation and information technology. In fact, under the active auspices of the SAR government following the Asian financial storm, Hong Kong's economy had begun such a transitional shift, one proof of which was the 'one-after-another' investment in information technologies by large enterprises and publicly listed companies in Hong Kong.

It should be recognized, however, that there is still a considerable way to go before Hong Kong can truly become 'the most cosmopolitan city in Asia'. Hong Kong is facing strong competition from powerful Tokyo, aggressive Singapore and rapidly emerging Shanghai within Asia. From a global perspective, only one country – the USA – has succeeded in transforming its post-industrial society into a knowledge-based economy. Japan has put 10 years of effort into that aim but is now struggling on the fringe of economic recession. The four Asian Dragons, including Hong Kong, Singapore, Chinese Taiwan and Korea, are lingering in the shadow of sluggish economies. The underlying reasons for this are manifested in their consequences. In terms of Hong Kong, the generally small sizes of the enterprises, the investment culture's preference for short-term high returns, weaknesses in science and technology, a shortage of talents in research and development and a narrow market, combined with a long-practised tradition of non-intervention by the former Hong Kong British government, all these have made Hong Kong's successful transition into a knowledge-based economy driven by innovation and information technology a difficult task, and there is a long road ahead before Hong Kong can reach this goal. The burst of Hong Kong's network technology bubble in 2000 has underlined the severity of the challenge.

Hong Kong's economy now seems to be experiencing a period of painful structural readjustments. In the short term, no industry has been able to play a driving role in the economy. This is why Hong Kong's economy has not been able to emerge from the bottom of its economic recession. For this reason, the recovery of its economy or the return of its prosperity need organic coordination of short-term, mid-term and long-term development strategies. However, cooperation between Hong Kong and its economic hinterland, Guangdong Pearl River Delta area is essential, whether a short- to mid-term effort to stimulate investment and consumption, or a mid- to long-term effort to elevate its base of innovation and technology.

Since the economic reform and opening up of the mainland, economic cooperation between Hong Kong and Guangdong has resulted in world-renowned achievements which have proved an important element in supporting the sustained development of Hong Kong's economy.

At the beginning of the 1990s, however, this cooperation came to a state of logjam, indicating that its foundation was weakened. This weakness was manifested in two ways. The first was the way in which the limitations of cooperation have gradually become apparent. After China's accession to the WTO, the implementation of 'national treatment' will be expedited, which will gradually reduce the preferential treatment that Hong Kong investors enjoyed in the past. At the same time, large numbers of foreign companies and products have flooded the mainland of China and Chinese enterprises have also gone into overseas markets. This means that products made by Hong Kong-invested enterprises are subjected to fierce competition from imported products in the mainland market, while in the overseas markets they are to face the threat of products made by mainland enterprises. In the face of such changes, labour-intensive manufacturing operations by Hong Kong investors will inevitably encounter pressure from capital- and technology-intensive industries. If Hong Kong investors fail to achieve a successful transformation of the region's manufacturing industry, the cooperative model of 'store in the front with factory in the back' between Hong Kong and Guangdong is likely to be challenged.

The second aspect of the weakening Hong Kong-Guangdong cooperation is the further shift in Hong Kong from entrepôt to offshore trade. China's accession to the WTO will stimulate sharp increases in its foreign trade, which will bring more trade opportunities. But, challenges still exist. As explained in the report by the Research Department of Hong Kong Trade Development Council, 'in the face of the changes in China and the rest of the world, Hong Kong's role as the mainland's trade hub will undoubtedly undergo fundamental changes'. With the reforms in China's trade system, and the opening up of the country, foreign companies will have complete access to trading and distribution rights. They will be more inclined to consider direct entry into or direct purchase from China. As a result, Hong Kong's entrepôt trade will further shift to offshore trade, and the traditional role of Hong Kong as an entrepôt port will be diluted.

However, there have been signs since the beginning of the 21st century that a new period of cooperation has begun and has quickly gathered pace, thanks to proactive efforts by the governments of Hong Kong SAR and Guangdong and their respective business communities. This new round of cooperation has occurred against various macro-economic backgrounds. Internationally, economic globalization and regionalization have become the leading trends of world economic development, and regional competition is becoming a key feature of modern times. Domestically, China's entry into the WTO will lead the country into a new era of all-round opening up, expedited economic reforms and gradual integration with the world economy. In this way, trade and investment interactions between China and the rest of the world will be speeded up and the flow of materials, capital and information will be accelerated. In addition, the rapid emergence of southeast China, centring on Shanghai and the beginning of a grand development programme for western China have made both Hong Kong and Guangdong aware of the absolute necessity of strengthening their cooperation in this new historic period.

With this new macro-economic background, and within the general framework of the WTO, new territories have emerged for the economic co-operation between Hong Kong and Guangdong. In particular, China's accession to the WTO will further accelerate the pace of opening-up of the service sector, which will undoubtedly bring a new round of development opportunities for Hong Kong's service sector. Those who stand to benefit the most, among others, are financial services, telecom and Internet services, freight forwarding and logistics, wholesale and retail, professional services, advertising and tourism. Of course, the level of benefit for different sectors will vary according to their different situations. Moreover, they will also confront fierce competition from multinationals coming from overseas.

Three sectors have strategic implications:

Logistics

After the accession to the WTO, China will for the first time open up distribution rights to foreign companies in areas such as wholesale, retail, transportation and repair services. All restrictions relating to the service sector, such as leasing, express delivery, freight handling, warehousing, technical inspection and testing and distribution and packaging services, will gradually be lifted. Large multinational logistics enterprises will quickly enter the Chinese market. This will offer new opportunities for the cooperation between Hong Kong and Guangdong. The problem here could be that, if Hong Kong is to be the key regional logistics centre, it will face competition from other central cities such as Shenzhen and Guangzhou., The essential question, therefore, is how Hong Kong can integrate its resources. If Hong Kong is able to establish itself as the most important logistics centre in the region, and to strengthen its position as such, it will undoubtedly be conducive to reinforcing the region's links with the Guangdong Pearl River Delta area, which has the reputation of 'world plant'. This will in turn advance the 'store-in-the-front-with-factory-at-the-back' mode of co-operation into a new period.

The financial sector and intermediary commercial services

Hong Kong, as a financial centre in the Asia Pacific region, has a complete and developed financial system and a large pool of industry talent. It is an important channel for international capital to enter China, as well as for Chinese enterprises with regards to financing and stock floatation. With China's accession to the WTO, Hong Kong's financial institutions, for historical and geographical reasons, may well capture the Guangdong market. If the financial services corridor that consists of Hong Kong, Shenzhen and Guangzhou can be extended to the whole of Guangdong, the level of economic integration between Hong Kong and Guangdong will be greatly enhanced. In addition to this, other intermediary services such as accounting, surveying and consultancy will also find promising development prospects in Guangdong.

Cooperation and coordination between the industries of Hong Kong and Guangdong will result in the upgrading and transformation of the current industrial structure into high value-added and hi-tech industries. Since the mid-1990s and into the 20th century, hi-tech industries in Shenzhen have rapidly expanded, laying a solid foundation for the coordination of industrial upgrading and transformation between the two places. If Shenzhen could learn from the experiences of the San Francisco Bay area and rely on the well-known universities and research institutions in northern China to retain a large number of hi-tech talents in the area, while at the same time taking advantage of Hong Kong's position as an international financial centre to intro-

duce international venture capital institutions to the area, Shenzhen would become a powerhouse for co-ordinated industrial upgrading and transformation between Hong Kong and Guangdong. Establishing a Hong Kong-Shenzhen science and technology corridor will help form a Hong Kong-Pearl River Delta hi-tech industrial belt.

Under the new conditions, particularly within the framework of the WTO, Hong Kong and Guangdong are likely to cooperate on a new basis. The economic integration of Hong Kong, Macao and the Guangdong Pearl River Delta Area will be greatly accelerated and become an important driving force for the recovery and sustained development of Hong Kong's economy.

Of course, challenges and opportunities co-exist in the cooperation between the two sides, and competition is also embedded in this cooperation. The key issues that should receive special attention are:

1. Hong Kong and Guangdong should actively promote regional economic integration and accelerate the process of establishing an unrestricted two-way flow of production factors, including capital and people, within the region. By doing this, Hong Kong will be able to strengthen its position as the most important service centre in southern China.

2. The barrier of an economic border between the two places should be reduced as far as possible in order to lower transaction costs in the cooperation of the two sides. Since the 1990s, along with the overall development of economic and trade relations between Hong Kong and Guangdong and increasing exchanges of people between the two sides, the checkpoints at the border have become a transportation bottleneck. Serious congestion of vehicles and people has become a major hindrance for economic co-operation between the two regions. Indeed, with the principle of 'one country two systems' and Hong Kong being China's special administrative region and an independent tariff zone, the border in its political sense should be respected and protected. At the same time, however, effort should be made to reduce the barrier of the economic border between the two places, in order to lower the expensive transaction costs arising from the border barrier. Recently, both Hong Kong and Guangdong have extended the opening hours of the border crossing. 24-hour border crossing is being considered by both sides and a proposal for the construction of a sea bridge linking Hong Kong, Macao and Guangdong

has been revisited. These areas are aware of the level of urgency required to solve the problem.

3. A multi-level and regular coordination mechanism should be established. In the past 20 years, economic cooperation between Hong Kong and Guangdong was mainly market-driven and promoted at an unofficial level. In the present climate of increasing economic integration in the region, however, policy coordination and institutional arrangements between the governments of the two places will be critical. Although Hong Kong and Guangzhou have now established a coordination mechanism of high-level joint meetings, the practice of such a mechanism in the last few years has proved that as it exists it is a long way from meeting the objective demands of economic cooperation between both sides. The two governments should consider setting up standing coordination agencies which, with the authorization of the central government, will coordinate all key issues regarding the regional cooperation between the two places. By doing this, problems arising from cooperation may be practically and effectively solved, thereby facilitating the process of economic integration.

Appendices

China's Top 500 Foreign-Invested Enterprises (2000–2001)

Published by the Ministry of Foreign Trade and Economic Cooperation, 3 December 2001

Rank	Enterprise	Sales revenue (million RMB)
1	Motorola (Tianjin) Electronics Ltd	31,288.88
2	Shanghai Volkswagen Automotive Company Ltd	28,697.51
3	Guangdong Mobile Technology Co Ltd	25,513.43
4	China Offshore Petroleum (China) Ltd	18,909.55
5	SAIC-Volkswagen Sales Co Ltd	15,866.69
6	FAW-Volkswagen Automotive Company Ltd	15,796.87
7	Dalian West Pacific Petrochemical Co Ltd	13,000.00
8	Nanjing Ericsson Communications Co Ltd	9,873.05
9	Zhejiang Mobile Telecommunications Co Ltd	9,718.02
10	Konka Group Co Ltd	9,016.55
11	China International Marine Container Co Ltd	8,954.27
12	Shanghai GM Automobile Co Ltd	8,846.78
13	Top Victory Electronics (Fujian)Co Ltd	7,790.86
14	Shanghai Siemens Mobile Communication Co Ltd	7,717.01
15	Guangzhou Honda Automobile Co Ltd	7,545.01
16	Great Wall International Information Products (Shenzhen) Co Ltd	7,224.05
17	Guangdong Nuclear Power Joint Venture Co Ltd	6,973.62
18	Shandong International Power Development Co Ltd	6,862.54
19	TCL King Electronic Co Ltd(Huizhou)	6,859.72
20	Dongguan Nokia Mobile Phones Co Ltd	6,828.91
21	Shanghai Bell Telephone Equipment Manufacturing Co Ltd	6,496.63
22	Jinguang Paper (Xishan) Co Ltd	6,250.80

Rank	Enterprise	Sales revenue (million RMB)
23	Shenyang Jinbei Passenger Vehicle Manufacturing Co Ltd	6,164.56
24	Philips Consumer Electronics Co Ltd Of Suzhou	6,143.84
25	Dongfeng-Citroën Automobile Company	6,136.16
26	Fujian Mobile Telecommunication Co Ltd	5,503.05
27	Seagate Technology International (Wuxi) Co Ltd	5,142.51
28	Dongguan Samsung Electro-Mechanics Co Ltd	5,136.16
29	Guangdong Guanghe Power Co Ltd	5,132.43
30	Shanghai Vacuum Electronic Company	5,055.65
31	Solectron(Suzhou)Technology Co Ltd	5,039.73
32	Shenzhen Seagate Technology Co Ltd	4,935.97
33	Epson Engineering (Shenzhen) Ltd	4,917.98
34	Henan Mobile Telecommunication Co Ltd	4,862.42
35	Hangzhou Wahaha Food Co Ltd	4,828.21
36	Yanzhou Coal Mining Co Ltd	4,780.58
37	Qingling (Isuzu) Automobile Co Ltd	4,683.16
38	Shunde Shunda Computer Co Ltd	4,516.18
39	Jiangsu Jindong Paper Co Ltd	4,,508.07
40	Shanghai Novel Color Picture Tube Co Ltd	4,440.45
41	Huafei Color Display Systems Co Ltd	4,418.29
42	Shanghai Hewlett Packard Co Ltd	4,208.85
43	Guangdong Nortel Telecommunications Equipment Co Ltd	4,021.80
44	Dell Computer (China) Limited	3,989.98
45	Shenzhen Skyworth-RGB Electronics Co Ltd	3,938.47
46	Shenzhen Kaifa Technology Co Ltd	3,864.11
47	LG Electronics (Huizhou) Co Ltd	3,848.18
48	Tianjin Samsung Electro-Mechanics Co Ltd	3,823.65
49	Cannon (Zhuhai) Co Ltd	3,790.40
50	Proctor & Gamble (G.Z.)Co Ltd	3,768.63
51	Epson (Suzhou) Co Ltd	3,768.31
52	Benq China Corp.	3,722.90
53	Chongqing Iron And Steel Co Ltd	3,722.76

Rank	Enterprise	Sales revenue (million RMB)
54	Shanghai Shangling Electronics Co Ltd	3,628.28
55	Zhanjiang Dongxing Oil Enterprises Co Ltd	3,560.11
56	Shenyang Xingyuandong Auto Components Co Ltd	3,553.88
57	Uniden Electronics Products (Shenzhen) Co Ltd	3,548.87
58	Tianjin Capital Environmental Protection Co Ltd	3,500.74
59	Robust (Guangdong) Bottled Water Co Ltd	3,478.54
60	Xiamen Overseas Chinese Electronics Co Ltd	3,447.91
61	Sharp Office Equipment (Changshu) Co Ltd	3,383.13
62	Shanghai Sony-SVA Electronics Co Ltd	3,345.51
63	Kodak (China) Holdings Co Ltd	3,339.43
64	Beijing Nokia Hangxing Telecommunication System Co Ltd	3,337.37
65	Harbin Hafei Motor Co Ltd	3,334.02
66	Dongguan Fuan Textiles Printing and Dyeing Limited	3,309.15
67	Lg Electronics Tianjin Appliance Co Ltd	3,307.76
68	CNOOC Development Shareholding Co Ltd	3,271.43
69	Shanghai Metro Jinjiang Shopping Center Co Ltd	3,215.76
70	Dalian Toshiba Television Co Ltd	3,200.00
71	Huayuan Kama Machinery Equipment Co Ltd	3,179.36
72	Shunde Galanz Electric Appliance Industrial Co Ltd	3,178.84
73	Shanghai Huizhong Automotive Manufacturing Co Ltd	3,160.11
74	Beijing International Exchange System Co Ltd	3,143.90
75	Shenzhen Hailiang Storage Products Co Ltd	3,128.45
76	Shanghai Suoguan Film Co Ltd	3,108.61
77	Tianjin Samsung Electronic Display Co Ltd	3,092.21
78	Zhangjiagang Bonded-zone East Ocean Oils & Grains Industries Co Ltd	3,086.06
79	Shaoguan Steel and Iron Co Ltd	3,057.68
80	Five-Ram Honda Motorcycle (Guangzhou) Co Ltd	3,047.16
81	Unilever Services (Shanghai) Co Ltd	3,040.29
82	Nokia (Suzhou) Telecommunications Co Ltd	3,011.23
83	Goldencard Trade (Shanghai)Co Ltd	2,995.37
84	Hewlett-Packard Computer Products (Shanghai) Co Ltd	2,993.80

Rank	Enterprise	Sales revenue (million RMB)
85	Shenzhen Sanyo Huaqiang Optical Technology Co Ltd	2,947.01
86	Shanghai Chloric Alkali Chemicals Ltd	2,942.37
87	Lucent Technologies (Qingdao) Co Ltd	2,918.47
88	China Merchants Shekou Holdings Co Ltd	2,917.23
89	Xianglu Fibres (Xiamen) Co Ltd	2,910.17
90	Xinhua Precision Machinery Co Ltd	2,907.25
91	Guangdong Fortune Technology Co Ltd	2,906.70
92	Beijing Matsushita Color Display Co Ltd	2,901.39
93	Hangzhou Motorola Cellular Equipment Co Ltd	2,884.72
94	Flextronics Industrial (Shenzhen) Co Ltd	2,849.76
95	Henan Anyang Color Picture Tube Glass Bulb Co Ltd	2,831.26
96	Jiangling Motors Co Ltd	2,825.16
97	First International Computer (Shenzhen) Co Ltd	2,820.55
98	Tianjin Samsung Electronic Tube Co Ltd	2,813.42
99	Nanjing Iveco Automobile Co Ltd	2,758.82
100	Southeast (Fujian) Motors Industrial Co Ltd	2,714.26
101	Shanghai Tyre Rubber (Group)Shareholding Co Ltd	2,702.88
102	Trigem Computer (Shenyang) Co Ltd	2,699.82
103	Suzhou Logitech Electronic Co Ltd	2,698.81
104	Philips Sangda Consumer Telecommunication (Shenzhen) Co Ltd	2,698.62
105	Shanghai Mitsubishi Elevator Co Ltd	2,697.21
106	Ningbo Zhonghua Paper Co Ltd	2,693.48
107	UT Starcom (China) Co Ltd	2,663.94
108	Chinachem Shuanghui Industry (Group) Co Ltd	2,641.02
109	Jilin Deda Co Ltd	2,604.38
110	Qingdao Haier Air-Conditioning Electronics Co Ltd	2,577.09
111	Hangzhou Eastcom Cellular Phone Co Ltd	2,564.44
112	Proview Technology (Shenzhen) Co Ltd	2,545.40
113	Compaq Computer Industry (China) Co Ltd	2,521.84
114	Xiamen Tsann Kuen Industrial Co Ltd	2,506.14
114	Amway China Co Ltd	2,474.43

Rank	Enterprise	Sales revenue (million RMB)
116	Zhangjiagang Pohang Stainless Steel Co Ltd	2,461.94
117	Shanghai Nestle Products Service Co Ltd	2,460.59
118	Shenzhen Samsung Digital Display Co Ltd	2,453.14
119	Sanyo Electric (Shekou) Co Ltd	2,448.86
120	Guangzhou Iron and Steel Co Ltd	2,444.73
121	Lucent Technologies Shanghai Co Ltd	2,427.17
122	Philips Electronics (Shanghai) Co Ltd	2,416.50
123	Shandong Chenming Paper Holdings Ltd	2,411.47
124	Matsushita Electric (China) Co Ltd	2,403.61
125	Ricoh (Shenzhen) Industrial Development Co Ltd	2,395.65
126	Flextronics Technology (Zhuhai) Co Ltd	2,390.86
127	Zhuhai Jiufeng Arco Energy Co Ltd	2,382.50
128	Zhejiang Eagle Household Cleaning Products Co Ltd	2,372.54
129	Legend (Shanghai) Co Ltd	2,368.74
130	Shanghai Carhua Supermarket Limited	2,352.69
131	Nanjing Ericsson Panda Mobile Terminal Co Ltd	2,302.92
132	Chongqing Changan Isuzu Motors Co Ltd	2,295.26
133	Beijing Matsushita Telecommunications Equipment Co Ltd	2,293.37
134	Shanghai Bright Dairy Co Ltd	2,279.83
135	Southsea Oils and Fats Industrial (Chiwan) Co Ltd	2,262.41
136	Dongfeng Honda Engine Co Ltd	2,261.72
137	Guangzhou Shipyard International Co Ltd	2,222.27
138	Antaibao Open Coal Mine	2,202.02
139	Huizhou Samsung Electronics Co Ltd	2,193.07
140	Xi'an Jassen Pharmaceutical Co Ltd	2,183.79
141	UT Starcom (Hangzhou) Telecommunications Co Ltd	2,179.33
142	Guangdong Kelong Refrigerator Co Ltd	2,161.07
143	Foshan Premier Camera Co Ltd	2,137.60
144	Matsushita Electric (Shenzhen) Co Ltd	2,134.02
145	Shenzhen Huaan LPG Co Ltd	2,111.49
146	LG Shuguang Electronic Co Ltd	2,067.60

Rank	Enterprise	Sales revenue (million RMB)
147	Shenzhen Southern CIMC Containers Manufacturing Co Ltd	2,064.36
148	Jinlong Copper Co Ltd	2,042.68
149	Hewlett-Packard Trading (Shanghai) Co Ltd	2,034.46
150	Shandong Huaneng Power Generation Co Ltd	2,010.68
151	Unilever Shareholding Co Ltd	2,006.50
152	Shenzhen Fujin Precision Industry Co Ltd	2,005.16
153	Shenzhen IBM Technology Product Co Ltd	2,005.04
154	Beijing Jeep Co Ltd	2,001.43
155	Shenzhen Seg-Hitachi Color Display Devices Co Ltd	1,992.52
156	Henan Philco Electrical Appliance Co Ltd	1,981.98
157	Hongfujin Precison Industry (Shenzhen) Co Ltd	1,981.00
158	Shenzhen Huawei Information Technology Co Ltd	1,966.45
159	Shenzhen GKI Electronics Co Ltd	1,963.78
160	Dongguan Pulse Electronics Co Ltd	1,943.51
161	Shanghai Yichang Steel Strip Co Ltd	1,938.88
162	Shanghai Sharp Electronics Co Ltd	1,924.94
163	Shenzhen Sanjiu Pharmaceutical Co Ltd	1,912.44
164	Jiangsu Ligang Electric Power Co Ltd	1,912.10
165	Shenzhen Mawan Power Co Ltd	1,893.26
166	Shunde Midea Air Conditioner Manufacturing Co Ltd	1,870.39
167	Shanghai Asa Electric Glass Co Ltd	1,854.29
168	BECKBURY International Co Ltd	1,843.68
169	Tangshan Guofeng Iron & Steel Co Ltd	1,830.73
170	Inner Mongolia Erdos Cashmere Products Co Ltd	1,827.82
171	Minebea Electronics & Hi-Tech Components Shanghai Ltd	1,826.49
172	Ericsson (China) Co Ltd	1,825.02
173	Arrow Electronics (Shanghai) Co Ltd	1,820.49
174	Tsingtao Brewery Company Limited	1,818.07
175	Zhejiang Meikeda Motorcycle Ltd	1,783.78
176	Siemens International Trading (Shanghai) Co Ltd	1,783.58
177	Shanghai Huahong NEC Electronics Co Ltd	1,772.96

Rank	Enterprise	Sales revenue (million RMB)
178	Zhangjiagang Shatai Steel Complex Ltd	1,756.82
179	Shanghai Refrigerator Compressor Co Ltd	1,756.77
180	Shanghai Hitachi Electrical Appliance Co Ltd	1,740.98
181	Guang-Shen-Zhu Expressway Ltd	1,732.53
182	Guangzhou Colgate Palmolive Co Ltd	1,723.52
183	Shanghai Bell Alcatel Mobile Communication System Co Ltd	1,712.86
184	Tianjin Mitsumi Electric Co Ltd	1,711.71
185	Toshiba Copying Machine (Shenzhen) Co Ltd	1,699.44
186	Shannxi Weihe Power Plant Co Ltd	1,677.13
187	Changfei Optic Fiber & Cable Co Ltd	1,672.69
188	Shanghai Ricoh Office Equipment Co Ltd	1,670.65
189	Hangzhou Zongce Rubber Co Ltd	1,665.13
190	Nanjing Walsin Wire & Cable Co Ltd	1,664.45
191	Jiangling Isuzu Automobile Co Ltd	1,660.40
192	Huaiyin Chiatai Co Ltd	1,657.50
193	Changzhou Kinyuan Copper Co Ltd	1,631.69
194	Shanghai Dajiang (Group) Corporation	1,620.43
195	Astec Electronics Co Ltd	1,618.67
196	Benxi North Dragon Iron And Smelting Co Ltd	1,616.76
197	Anhui Grandtour Tyre Co Ltd	1,613.29
198	LG Electronic Shenyang Co Ltd	1,588.10
199	Dongguan Elcoteq Electronics Co Ltd	1,582.82
200	Guangdong Kelon Air Conditioner Co Ltd	1,574.49
201	Benxi North Dragon Iron And Steel Group Co Ltd	1,563.93
202	UPM-Kymmene (Suzhou) Paper Co Ltd	1,552.01
203	Shanghai Sigma Metals Inc.	1,550.46
204	Shanghai RT-Mart Co Ltd	1,549.33
205	Guangdong Kelon Appliances Co Ltd	1,546.70
206	Qingdao Hisense Air-conditioner Co Ltd	1,538.14
207	Thomson (Dongguan) Co Ltd	1,530.02
208	Shanghai EK Chor Distribution Co Ltd	1,524.24

Rank	Enterprise	Sales revenue (million RMB)
209	Kaiping Zhonghui Synthetic Fiber Grains Co Ltd	1,519.14
210	Shanghai JVC Electric Co Ltd	1,517.11
211	Nantai Electronics (Shenzhen) Co Ltd	1,496.46
212	Xiamen Jinwoong Enterprise Company Co Ltd	1,487.40
213	Hewlett-Packard (China) Co Ltd	1,480.74
214	Huiyang Legend Computer Co Ltd	1,479.51
215	Shanghai Worldbest Shareholding Ltd	1,474.44
216	Guangzhou Hualing Air Conditioning Equipment Co Ltd	1,458.15
217	Guangdong Zhuhai Power Plant Co Ltd	1,456.77
218	NPG Monitor (Dongguan) Co Ltd	1,448.83
219	Jiangxi Changhe-Suzuki Automobile Co Ltd	1,446.99
220	Suzhou Samsung Electronics Co Ltd	1,444.32
221	Thomson OKM (Shenzhen) Co Ltd	1,436.09
222	Yantian International Container Wharf Co Ltd	1,430.67
223	Shijiangzhuang Baoshi NEG Glass Co Ltd	1,428.80
224	Zhangjiagang Runzhong Steel Complex	1,427.10
225	Wuxi Sharp Electronic Components Co Ltd	1,416.60
226	Ningbo Baoxin Stainless Steel Co Ltd	1,414.64
227	Robust (Guangdong) Food and Beverage Co Ltd	1,412.02
228	Jinzhou Donggang Power Ltd	1,409.96
229	Jiangmen Great Yangtse Motorcycle Ltd	1,406.09
230	Canon Office Equipment Dalian Co Ltd	1,400.00
231	Nidec (Dalian) Ltd	1,400.00
232	Shanghai Matsuoka Co Ltd	1,394.24
233	Yangtse BASF Styrene Co Ltd	1,382.49
234	Far East Textile Industry(Shanghai)Co Ltd	1,381.54
235	Nanjin LG Toptry Color Display System Co Ltd	1,377.38
236	Shanghai White Cat Co Ltd	1,351.41
237	Dazhong Transportation (Group) Co Ltd	1,349.82
238	Shanghai JHJ International Transportation Co Ltd	1,348.82
239	Shuangcheng Nestlé Co Ltd	1,346.59

Rank	Enterprise	Sales revenue (million RMB)
240	Siemens (China) Ltd	1,343.23
241	Itochu Shanghai Ltd	1,339.35
242	Hefei Meiling Shareholding Co Ltd	1,339.02
243	Hitachi Semi-Conductor (Suzhou) Co Ltd	1,336.03
244	Jinagyin Xingcheng Special Steel Co Ltd	1,333.67
245	Shanghai Mitsubishi Shangling Air-conditioning Appliances Co Ltd	1,326.89
246	Beijing Dafa Chia Tai Co Ltd	1,318.73
247	Shanghai Container Wharf Co Ltd	1,311.49
248	Cheng Shin Rubber (Xiamen) Industry Co Ltd	1,308.52
249	Zhuhai Mitsumi Electric Co Ltd	1,308.46
250	Shenzhen Advance Micro-Electronic Technology Co Ltd	1,303.28
251	China Hualu Matsushita Electronic Information Co Ltd	1,300.00
252	Guangdong Jianlibao Group Co Ltd	1,293.50
253	Tianjin Samsung Electronics Co Ltd	1,293.43
254	Coca-Cola (China) Beverage Co Ltd	1,289.50
255	Shenzhen Sanyo Huaqiang Energy Co Ltd	1,277.14
256	Wrigley Chewing Gum Co Ltd	1,275.78
257	Dongguan Huaqiang Sanyo Motor Co Ltd	1,273.97
258	CTS (Tianjin) Electronics Co Ltd	1,268.33
259	Shanghai Materials Trading Center Co Ltd	1,266.32
260	Fujito General (Shanghai) Co Ltd	1,266.10
261	Shanghai Diesel Engine Co Ltd	1,262.44
262	Guangzhou Dongfang Power Co Ltd	1,259.46
263	Guangzhou Zhujiang Electric Power Co Ltd	1,254.36
264	Shanghai Yanfeng Visteon Automotive Trim System Co Ltd	1,252.03
265	Guangzhou Paper Co Ltd	1,250.41
266	Huizhou TCL Computer Technology Co Ltd	1,243.59
267	Guangdong Power Development Co Ltd	1,243.41
268	Ramaxel Technology (Shenzhen) Co Ltd	1,238.61
269	Foshan Shiwan Eagle Brand Ceramics Co Ltd	1,238.20
270	Mitsubishi Stone Integrated Circuit Co Ltd	1,233.45

Rank	Enterprise	Sales revenue (million RMB)
271	Xinjiang Guanghui Property Development Co Ltd	1,226.46
272	Makita (China) Co Ltd	1,225.85
273	Tianjin Smithkline and French Co Ltd	1,224.10
274	Guangdong Midea Group Wuhu Refrigerating Equipment Co Ltd	1,213.82
275	Xiamen TDK Co Ltd	1,208.52
276	Guangzhou Jinpeng Mobile Communication Systems Co Ltd	1,206.18
277	Foxconn Precision Components (Shenzhen) Co Ltd	1,204.99
278	Gold Huasheng Paper (Suzhou Industrial Park) Co Ltd	1,203.19
279	Nantong Acetate Fiber Co Ltd	1,201.63
280	Dalian Alpine Electronics Co Ltd	1,200.00
281	Guangdong Esquel Textile Co Ltd	1,199.82
282	Anhui Huainan Pingyu Power Co Ltd	1,194.04
283	Compaq Computer (Shanghai) Co Ltd	1,193.21
284	P & G (China) Co Ltd	1,188.78
285	Budweiser (Wuhan) International Beer Co Ltd	1,179.81
286	Livzon Pharmaceutical Group Shareholding Ltd	1,178.55
287	Hunan Xianggang Huaguang Wire Products Co Ltd	1,176.18
288	Xinhui CIMC Container Co Ltd	1,170.99
289	Beijing Dragon States Properties Co Ltd	1,161.00
290	Adomax Electronic Enterprises (Zhaoqing) Co Ltd	1,157.40
291	Tianjin Tingyi International Food Co Ltd	1,152.07
292	Anhui Konka Electronic Co Ltd	1,151.43
293	Pingdingshan Yaomeng Power Co Ltd	1,143.83
294	Beijing zhong Hong Tian Real Estate Co Ltd	1,140.24
295	Guangzhou Hitachi Elevator Co Ltd	1,139.46
296	Marubeni (Shanghai) Co Ltd	1,137.54
297	Shunde Whirlpool Electrical Appliances Co Ltd	1,130.78
298	Guangdong Meizhi Compressor Co Ltd	1,129.54
299	Hangzhou Tingyi International Food Co Ltd	1,129.52
300	Nantong CIMC Shunda Container Co Ltd	1,121.75
301	Giant (China) Co Ltd	1,118.14

Rank	Enterprise	Sales revenue (million RMB)
302	Kunshan Uni-President Food Co Ltd	1,117.22
303	China South Glass Holding Co Ltd	1,116.43
304	J.W. Thomson-Zhongqiao Advertising Co Ltd	1,115.35
305	Acer Computer (Zhongshan) Co Ltd	1,114.87
306	Shenyang Neu-Alpine Software Co Ltd	1,109.00
307	National-Wanbao (Guangzhou) Compressor Co Ltd	1,105.80
308	Ningbo Youngor Garment Co Ltd	1,097.84
309	Qinghuangdao Chia Tai Co Ltd	1,094.43
310	Dongguan Zhili Computer Co Ltd	1,094.35
311	Guangdong Yuegang Water Supply Co Ltd	1,094.27
312	United Automotive Electronics Co Ltd	1,094.01
313	Nanjing Sharp Electronics Co Ltd	1,090.63
314	Qingdao Taiguang Footwear Co Ltd	1,083.69
315	Epson (Shanghai) Information Products Co Ltd	1,081.64
316	Shanghai LG SAV Electronic Co Ltd	1,079.59
317	Guangzhou Panyu Clifford Estates Co Ltd	1,078.24
318	Olympus (Shenzhen) Industrial Co Ltd	1,077.77
319	China Otis Elevator (Tianjin) Co Ltd	1,076.93
320	Shanghai Lucent Technologies International Trading Co Ltd	1,074.15
321	Shanghai Hitachi Home Appliance Co Ltd	1,073.49
322	Qingdao Chia Tai Co Ltd	1,071.15
323	Xinlong Enterprise (Shenzhen) Co Ltd	1,061.70
324	Zhangjiagang Baixiu Garment and Headgear Co Ltd	1,059.65
325	Shanghai Minolta Optical Products Co Ltd	1,056.59
326	Yangzhou Fengxiang Commercial Co Ltd	1,055.27
327	K-tronics Electronic (Suzhou) Co Ltd	1,054.42
328	Sony Precision Components (Huizhou) Co Ltd	1,051.90
329	Qiandao Kohap Co Ltd	1,047.32
330	Shandong Xinhua Pharmaceuticals Co Ltd	1,044.07
331	Shanghai Kerry Oils & Grains Industrial Co Ltd	1,043.97
332	Huayang Electricity Industrial Co Ltd	1,042.92

Rank	Enterprise	Sales revenue (million RMB)
333	Zhejiang Yipeng Engine Components Co Ltd	1,042.26
334	Shandong Airlines Co Ltd	1,041.98
335	Nanjin Jincheng Machinery Co Ltd	1,040.77
336	Tianjin TCB Samsung Electronic Co Ltd	1,038.64
337	Shantou Ocean No.1 Polystyrene Resin Co Ltd	1,038.17
338	Guangzhou Haoyoudou Department Store Commercial Plaza Co Ltd	1,037.95
339	Jintong Petrochemical Co Ltd	1,030.44
340	Intex Plastics (Fujian) Co Ltd	1,024.22
341	Shanghai Shenmei Beverage And Food Co Ltd	1,019.33
342	Chengdu Chenggang Steel Co Ltd	1,015.78
343	Henan TCL-Meile Electronic Co Ltd	1,015.47
344	Flextronics Enterprise (Zhuhai) Co Ltd	1,014.60
345	Shanghai CIMC Far East Container Co Ltd	1,009.05
346	Hefei Hitachi Excavators Co Ltd	1,006.98
347	Shenzhou Nanyou (Group) Co Ltd	1,006.39
348	Xiamen Huaxia International Power Development Co Ltd	1,002.89
349	Tianjin LG Dagu Chemicals Co Ltd	1,001.51
350	Zhuhai SEZ Hongta Yanlord Paper Co Ltd	1,001.24
351	Johnson & Johnson (China)Co Ltd	1,000.47
352	Zhuhai Matsushita Motor Co Ltd	998.76
353	Dachan Foods (Dalian) Co Ltd	997.82
354	Guangdong Hyundai Container Manufacturing Co Ltd	993.50
355	Qinhuangdao Shougang Plate Mill Co Ltd	992.06
356	Dongguan Shengyi Technology Co Ltd	988.68
357	Shenzhen Xerox High-Tech Co Ltd	986.71
358	Caltex Ocean Gas Energy Co Ltd	985.50
359	Beijing Hi-tech Wealth Electronic Products Co Ltd	983.31
360	Shenzhen Wal-Mart Zhujiang General Store Co Ltd	982.22
361	Guangzhou Friendship Baleno Garments And Attire Co Ltd	981.21
362	Toshiba (Dalian) Co Ltd	980.00
363	Bohai Aluminium Industries Ltd	979.18

Rank	Enterprise	Sales revenue (million RMB)
364	Shougang NEC Co Ltd	977.73
365	Xiamen King Long United Automobile Industry Co Ltd	976.84
366	Heilongjiang Chia Tai Industrial Co Ltd	975.46
367	Shanghai Yanfeng Johnson Controls Seating Co Ltd	974.14
368	DuPont Suzhou Polyester Company Limited	964.76
369	Umax Computer(China)Co Ltd	967.30
370	Alcatel (Suzhou) Communications Co Ltd	966.16
371	Hangzhou Jinguang Paper Product Service Co Ltd	965.92
372	Dalian Shide Plastic Building Materials Co Ltd	961.15
373	Dalian Pujin Coated Steel Plate Co Ltd	960.00
374	Hefei Jianghuai Automobile Co Ltd	957.44
375	Huatong Computer (Huizhou) Co Ltd	956.15
376	Philips Electronics Trading & Services (Shanghai) Co Ltd	953.26
377	Shanghai CIMC Refrigerated Container Co Ltd	952.21
378	GE Hangwei Medical Systems Co Ltd	947.14
379	Brightpoint International Trade (Shanghai) Co Ltd	946.66
380	Topsearch Printed Circuits (Shenzhen) Co Ltd	939.98
381	Beijing Lufthansa Youyi Shopping City Co Ltd	936.48
382	Wuhan Plaza Management Co Ltd	935.38
383	Black & Decker (Suzhou) Power Tools Co Ltd	935.04
384	Schitech Group Company Limited	933.22
385	Shanghai Ek Chor General Machinery Co Ltd	932.92
386	Shanghai No.1 Yaohan Co Ltd	930.81
387	Faw-Kelsey Hayes Automobile Chassis System Co Ltd	928.45
388	Heilongjiang China Resources Jinyu Enterprise Co Ltd	926.97
389	Xuzhou VV Food And Beverage Co Ltd	929.26
390	Shanghai Industrial United Co Ltd	921.44
391	Matsuoka Enterprise (Group) Co Ltd	919.34
392	Shanghai Ogilvy and Mather Advertising Co Ltd	915.84
393	Tianjin Pacific (Group) Co Ltd	914.55
394	Haian Mobile Communications Co Ltd	913.20

Rank	Enterprise	Sales revenue (million RMB)
395	Shenzhen Ata Jewelry Co Ltd	912.71
396	Harbin Longxing Chemical Fiber Co Ltd	912.68
397	Chia Tai Group(Tianjin) Industrial Co Ltd	911.26
398	Delta Electronics (Dongguan) Co Ltd	911.15
399	Suzhou Stora Enso Paper Industry Co Ltd	909.17
400	Philco Air-conditioner (Hefei) Industrial Co Ltd	907.47
401	Guangdong Swire-Cola Co Ltd	902.67
402	Shanghai Golden Phillips Petrochemical Co Ltd	902.10
403	Jiangsu Fujitsu Telecommunication Technology Co Ltd	900.04
404	Sino-America Shanghai Squib Pharmaceutical Co Ltd	899.98
405	Rongcheng Guotai Tyre Co Ltd	899.73
406	Daewoo Heavy Industry Yantai Co Ltd	897.45
407	Foxconn Precision Industry (Shenzhen) Co Ltd	896.90
408	Tangshan Yinfeng Iron & Steel Co Ltd	892.61
409	Shanghai Dongfang Commercial Building Co Ltd	894.18
410	Sanshui Jianlibao FTB Packaging Ltd	892.61
411	Casio Electronics (Shenzhen) Co Ltd	897.10
412	Shenzhen Nanshan Thermal-Power Co Ltd	889.71
413	Luoyang North Ek Chor Motorcycle Co Ltd	887.40
414	Shanghai Mingtai Property Development Co Ltd	887.13
415	Hangzhou Plaza Co Ltd	886.73
416	Hubei C-Bond Co Ltd	885.81
417	Shenzhen Chuanghua Cooperation Co Ltd	885.37
418	Huludao Oriental Copper Co Ltd	885.28
419	Thomson Foshan Color Picture Tube Co Ltd	883.97
420	Yizheng Chemical Foshan Polyester Co Ltd	881.33
421	Tianjin Mobile Communications Co Ltd	876.89
422	Guilin Daewoo Passenger Vehicle Co Ltd	876.17
423	Shenzhen Nantian Oil Pulp Co Ltd	875.04
424	Qingyuan City Rowa Electronic Co Ltd	873.75
425	Changyuan (Shanghai) International Trade Co Ltd	869.16

Rank	Enterprise	Sales revenue (million RMB)
426	Shanghai Lianji Synthetic Fiber Co Ltd	869.07
427	China Nanshan Development (Group) Incorporation	868.62
428	Fujian Huaxing Petrochemical Co Ltd	868.48
429	Guangdong Teem (Holdings) Co Ltd	867.50
430	Tatung Electronic Technology (Jiangsu) Co Ltd	867.22
431	Shanghai Yaohua Pilkington Glass Co Ltd	866.87
432	JD Metal Industry (Shenzhen) Co Ltd	866.46
433	Shanghai Sanrong Electric Appliance Co Ltd	865.51
434	Liaoning Qinghe Power Generation Co Ltd	865.28
435	Guangzhou P & G Paper Products Co Ltd	864.89
436	Foshan Shakou Power Plant Co Ltd	863.95
437	Ever-Splendor Electronics (Shenzhen) Co Ltd	862.91
438	Tianjin Yamaha Electronic Keyboard Co Ltd	861.94
439	Qingdao Haier Refrigerator (International) Co Ltd	861.49
440	WUS Printed Circuit (Kunshan) Co Ltd	860.34
441	Legend Computer (Shenzhen) Co Ltd	858.95
442	GE Plastics (China) Co Ltd	858.85
443	Sony Style Electronics (Zhuhai) Co Ltd	858.54
444	Xiamen FDK Co Ltd	855.51
445	Beihai Cereals & Oils Industry (Tianjin) Co Ltd	854.93
446	Shandong Fengxiang-L.D.C Co Ltd	854.54
447	Shanghai Pioneer Electrical Audio Equipment Co Ltd	851.32
448	IBM (China) Co Ltd	850.60
449	Star Precision (Dalian) Co Ltd	850.25
450	United Carrier (Shanghai) Engineering Services Co Ltd	850.21
451	Chongqing Loncin Gasoline Engine Manufacturing Co Ltd	848.84
452	Jilin Qifeng Chemical Fiber Co Ltd	848.29
453	Xuzhou China Resources Power Co Ltd	847.31
454	Shanghai New Construction Development Co Ltd	843.77
455	Beijing Parkson Light Industry Development Co Ltd	841.10
456	Inner Mongolia Yitai Coal Co Ltd	832.91

Rank	Enterprise	Sales revenue (million RMB)
457	Xerox Of Shanghai Limited	831.21
458	Jingyuan No. 2 Power Co Ltd	830.15
459	Fujian Sanfeng Footwear Co Ltd	829.85
460	Nike (Suzhou) Sports Goods Co Ltd	828.32
461	Intex Plastics(Xiamen)Co Ltd	822.52
462	Zhongshan Kawa Electronics (Group) Co Ltd	820.64
463	Wanwei Telecommunication Shenzhen Inc	817.61
464	Shanghai Waigaoqiao Bonded Zone Lansheng Daewoo Corporation	816.10
465	Guangdong Matsunichi Electronics Co Ltd	815.58
466	China-Arab Chemical Fertilizer Co Ltd	812.40
467	DuPont China Group Co Ltd	811.12
468	Ningbo LG Yongxing Chemical Co Ltd	809.60
469	Jilian (Jilin) Petrochemical Co Ltd	807.73
470	Cheng Shin Rubber (China) Co Ltd	804.88
471	Shanghai Delphi Packard Electric Co Ltd	804.17
472	Qingdao Haier Refrigerator Corporation	802.75
473	Shanghai Zijiang Enterprise Group Co Ltd	802.52
474	Yellow Dragon Food Industry Co Ltd	802.15
475	Shandong Mastushita Display Industry Co Ltd	801.15
476	Jiangyin Xingcheng Iron and Steel Co Ltd	800.36
477	Shanghai Pacific International Container Co Ltd	800.35
478	Shanghai BASF Colorants and Auxiliaries Co Ltd	800.06
479	Jingwei Textile Machinery Co Ltd	798.12
480	Chiaphua Appliances (Shenzhen) Co Ltd	795.71
481	Shanghai Dachang Copper Industry Co Ltd	795.33
482	Shanghai Brilliant Timber Co Ltd	794.66
483	Shanghai Pepsi-Cola Beverage Co Ltd	793.25
484	Dalian Hitachi Baoyuan Machinery and Equipment Co Ltd	789.20
485	Zhangjiagang United Copper Co Ltd	786.87
486	Shanghai Yanlord Property Co Ltd	786.49
487	Hangzhou Matsushita Home Appliances Co Ltd	785.42

Rank	Enterprise	Sales revenue (million RMB)
488	Toray Synthetic Fiber (Nantong) Co Ltd	785.24
489	Elec & Eltek (Guangzhou) Electronic Co Ltd	785.19
490	Qingdao Sanhu Footwear Co Ltd	784.75
491	Shenyang Aerospace Mitsubishi Motors Engine Manufacturing Co Ltd	781.30
492	Nokia (China) Investment Co Ltd	781.07
493	Shanghai Lucent Technologies Optical Fiber Co Ltd	780.04
494	Shanghai Lingyun Curtain Wall Science & Technology Co Ltd	779.41
495	Qingdao Mitsumi Electric Co Ltd	777.63
496	Conti Chia Tai (Shekou) Co Ltd	776.72
497	Shanghai East China Computer Digiland International Trade Co Ltd	769.83
498	Gemplus Tianjin New Technology Co Ltd	773.22
499	Sony Industrial (Shenzhen) Co Ltd	769.83
500	Beijing Chongwen-New World Real Estate Development Co Ltd	769.10

China's Top 100 Largest State-designated Companies for Liaison with the State Economic and Trade Commission in 2000

Provided by the State Economic and Trade Commission

Rank (2000)	Rank (1999)	Name of enterprise	Sales revenue (RMB million)
1	2	China Petrochemical Corporation	375,389.80
2	3	State Power Corporation of China	356,051.10
3	1	China National Petroleum Corporation	345,071.80
4	4	China Telecom Corporation	172,295.80
5	11	China Mobile Communications Corporation	124,551.13
6	5	China National Cereals, Oils & Foodstuffs Import & Export Corporation	103,890.80
7	6	Shanghai Baoshan Iron and Steel Company Ltd	70,856.28
8	7	Guangdong Electric Power Group Corporation	57,251.18
9	9	China Ocean Shipping (Group) Company	46,319.28
10	13	China State Construction ENGRG. Corporation	43,564.58
11	18	Haier Group Company	40,628.22
12	8	FAW Group Corporation of China	39,048.34
13	17	China North Industries Group Corporation	29,806.74
14	19	Legend Holding Group	28,441.42
15	24	China National Offshore Oil Corporation	28,354.07
16	78	China United Telecommunications Corporation	26,629.61
17	14	Dongfeng Motor Corporation	25,803.13
18	10	Shanghai Automotive Industry Corporation (Group)	25,801.19
19	15	*Shanghai Electrics (Group) Corporation	22,912.41
20	20	Shougang Group	21,026.48
21	33	China Aviation Industry Corporation	20,924.66

Rank (2000)	Rank (1999)	Name of enterprise	Sales revenue (RMB million)
22	23	Anshan Iron and Steel Group Corporation	20,589.09
23	21	China South Industries Group Corporation	20,047.72
24	32	China Aviation Industry II Corporation	19,532.70
25	25	*Orient International (Group) Co Ltd	19,394.54
26	39	*Beijing Telecom Supplies Group	18,108.01
27	28	TCL Holdings Co Ltd	17,754.13
28	27	Wuhan Iron and Steel Group Ltd Co	17,672.23
29	59	*Benxi Iron & Steel (Group) Co Ltd	17,636.69
30	22	Yunxi Hongta Tobacco (Group) Co Ltd	17,100.63
31	26	China Southern Airlines Company Limited	16,337.50
32	34	China Great Wall Computer Shenzhen Co Ltd	16,228.03
33	46	Panda Electronics Group Co Ltd	15,443.32
34	44	China Shipping (Group) Company	14,931.33
35	37	Air China	13,795.32
36	31	China State Shipbuilding Corporation	13,739.48
37	42	Hisense Group Corporation	13,473.36
38	52	CHINA National Machinery & Equipment Corporation (Group (CNME)	12,709.50
39	35	*Shanghai Pharmaceutical (Group) Corporation	12,425.58
40	45	China Port Construction Company	12,110.66
41	41	*Shanghai Construction (Group) Corporation	11,688.28
42	29	Konka Group Co Ltd	11,500.46
43	48	*Taiyuan Iron & Steel (Group)Corporation	11,391.83
44	40	*Guangzhou Railway (Group)Corporation	11,377.55
45	30	*Beidahuang Agriculture Group Co Ltd	11,182.73
46	38	China Shipbuilding Industry Corporation	11,072.16
47	43	China Eastern Airlines Corporation Limited	10,815.73
48	36	Changhong Electric Co Ltd	10,767.09
49	76	*China International Trade & Transportation (Group) Corporation	10,293.74
50	50	Beijing Peking University Founder Group Corporation	10,061.62
51	47	*Panzhihua Iron & Steel (Group) Co	10,034.30
52	116	Etsong Tobacco Group	9,951.33

Rank (2000)	Rank (1999)	Name of enterprise	Sales revenue (RMB million)
53	68	Chunlan (Group) Corporation	9,462.31
54	100	Guangzhou Iron & Steel Enterprises Group	9,244.91
55	60	Nanjing Iron & Steel Group Co Ltd	9,018.90
56	66	Handan Iron & Steel Group Co Ltd	8,969.13
57	96	China International Marine Containers (Group) Co Ltd	8,954.27
58	61	Eastern Communications Co Ltd	8,923.63
59	51	Baotou Iron & Steel Group Co Ltd	8,854.91
60	53	China Road And Bridge Group	8,778.45
61	79	Qianjiang Motor Group Co Ltd	8,648.06
62	85	Jiangsu Shagang Group	8,334.23
63	75	China National Nuclear Corporation	8,186.04
64	73	Maanshan Iron & Steel Co Ltd	8,185.69
65	65	SVA (Group) Co Ltd	8,129.96
66	57	*Beijing Municipal Construction Co Ltd	8,083.24
67	62	Shanghai Tobacco (Group) Limited	8,074.97
68	64	Macat Group	8,035.26
69	49	Shanghai Bell Co Ltd	7,729.29
70	56	*Beitai Iron & Steel Group Co Ltd	7,624.94
71	87	China National Pharmaceutical Group Corporation	7,600.88
72	82	China North Industries Corporation (NORINC)	7,600.57
73	77	China National Aero-Technology Import & Export Corporation	7,555.86
74	83	Yankuang Group Co Ltd	7,484.26
75	97	China Aerospace Machine and Electric Corporation	7,428.68
76	69	Hunan Valin Iron & Steel Group Co Ltd	7,425.57
77	103	China General Technology (Group) Holding Co Ltd	7,288.60
78	80	Tangshan Iron & Steel Group Co Ltd	7,121.44
79	74	Tianjin Bohai Chemical Industry (Group) Co Ltd	7,073.33
80	88	Union Developing Group Of China	6,991.58
81	55	Kelon Group	6,959.62
82	94	*Yibin Wuliangye Group Co Ltd	6,805.23
83	67	Guangdong Nuclear Power Group Co Ltd	6,792.00

Rank (2000)	Rank (1999)	Name of enterprise	Sales revenue (RMB million)
84	111	Wanxiang Group	6,775.01
85	71	Changsha BaiSha Group	6,765.64
86	157	*China Hengtian Group Co Ltd	6,738.68
87	106	Harbin Pharmaceutical Group Co Ltd,	6,653.74
88	81	Jinan Jigang Group	6,344.54
89	93	*China CSC (Group) Corporation	6,278.17
90	90	Tianjin Pharmaceutical Holdings Group	6,252.67
91	123	Henan Shineway Industrial Co Ltd	6,228.03
92	72	Kunming Tobacco Manufacturing Corporation	6,089.00
93	108	Laiwu Steel Group, Ltd	6,018.30
94	105	Anyang Iron & Steel Group Co Ltd	5,893.64
95	91	*Inner Mongolia Power (Group)	5,776.98
96	86	Guangzhou Municipal Construction Group Co Ltd	5,730.99
97	114	Dalian Daxian Group Co Ltd	5,716.48
98	89	*Najing Eastern China Electrics Group Co	5,668.72
99	112	*Xiamen Overseas Chinese Electronic Co Ltd (Xocec)	5,501.66
100	109	China National Textiles Import & Export Corporation	5,498.11

Appendix 1.3

China's Top 500 Private Enterprises (2000)

Published by the All China Federation of Industry and Commerce, October 2001

Unit: RMB million

Rank	Name of enterprise	Sales revenue (RMB million)
1	Legend Group Holdings Co Ltd	2,844,142
2	Hope Group Co Ltd	1,136,200
3	Wanxiang Group Co	677,501
4	Lantian Co Ltd	635,055
5	China Group Corporation	617,839
6	Delixi Group Co Ltd	520,887
7	Xingaochao Group Co Ltd	500,982
8	Xinjiang Guanghui (Group) Co Ltd	424,108
9	Suning Group Co	398,617
10	Jinluo Enterprise Group Co	378,000
11	Stone Group Co	339,269
12	Orient Group Industry Co Ltd	319,000
13	Jiangsu Suning Construction Group Co	291,300
14	Dawncom Group Co Ltd	287,020
15	Tongwei Group Co Ltd	277,887.56
16	Red Star Group Co Ltd	276,087.02
17	Holley Group Co Ltd	265,601
18	Chongqing Zongshen Motorcycle Group	262,220
19	Chongqing Lifan Industry Group Co Ltd	260,152
20	Shandong Huiye Group Co Ltd	231,030
21	Hubei Blue Star Group Co Ltd	225,837
22	Hongdou Group Co	223,800

Rank	Name of enterprise	Sales revenue (RMB million)
23	Xi'an Sea Star Technology Industry Group Co Ltd	220,556.13
24	Top Group Technology Co Ltd	208,639
25	Nanjing Yurun Meat Co Ltd	204,664
26	Heibei Xuri Group Co Ltd	200,153
27	Changchun Zhongdong Group Co Ltd	200,000
28	Tengen Group Co Ltd	181,518
29	Panpan Group Co Ltd	178,000
30	Shanxi Tongda Group Co Ltd	164,652
31	Shandong Qilu Industry Group Co Ltd	163,792
32	Guangdong Wen's Foodstuffs Group Co Ltd	161,006
33	Hongtaok Group Co Ltd	160,000
34	Shanxi Haixin (Group) Co Ltd	152,206
35	Feiyue Sewing Machinery Group Co	151,300
36	Nanchang Kerui Group Co Ltd	150,459
37	Geely Group	148,024.1
38	Baoji Dongling Group	140,200
39	Ningbo Shenzhou Textile Co Ltd	130,428
40	Guangdong Esquel Textile Co Ltd	130,000
41	Jilin Zhengye Group Co Ltd	127,210
42	Zhongda Group	124,875
43	Beijing Huiyuan Fruit Beverage Group Co	124,516
44	People Electrical Appliance Group Co Ltd	121,873
45	Hangzhou Futong Group Co Ltd	120,500
46	Tianjin Tjtheleader Group Co Ltd	120,463
47	Shiyanrong Dongfeng Automobile Exclusive Distribution Co Ltd	117,000
48	Shandong Longda Enterprise Group Co Ltd	115,220
49	Beijing Huapu Industry Group Co Ltd	107,579.5
50	Zhejiang Shuaikang	106,380
51	Tianjin Yinzuo Group Co Ltd	106,000
52	Chengdu Guoteng Communication Group Co Ltd	104,611
53	Jilin Henghe Enterprise Group Co Ltd	103,022

Rank	Name of enterprise	Sales revenue (RMB million)
54	Shanghai New Giant Biology Tech. Co Ltd	102,600
55	Zhejiang Fuchunjiang Communication Group Co Ltd	102,539
56	Anhui Anweiwang Wine Group	100,088
57	Shenyang Yuanda Aluminium Industry Group Co Ltd	100,078
58	Jiangxi Sanyuan Group Co Ltd	100,000
59	Changchun Jigang Group Co	99,859
60	Shenzhen Zhongkezhi Investment Developing Co Ltd	98,185
61	Gansu Guofang Gongmao Co Ltd	98,000
62	Hubei Jiaxing Group Co Ltd	96,870
63	Shandong Continent Enterprise Group Co Ltd	95,087.3
64	Guangdong Fegnyuan Grain & Oil Industry Co Ltd	90,000
65	Ningbo Luomeng Group Co Ltd	89,515.7
66	Tangshanshi Banbidian Steel Co Ltd	89,358.08
67	Jiangxi Huiren Group Medicine Research & Marketing Co	88,269
68	Tianjin Zihai Management Center	86,300
69	Zhejiang Shangfeng Group Co	86,006
70	Shanxi Antai Group Co Ltd	85,000
71	Jiangsu Feida Tools Group Co Ltd	83,849
72	Ningbo Haitian Co Ltd	82,622
73	Sany Heavy Industry Group Co Ltd	81,026
74	Yellow Dragon Food Industry Co Ltd	80,215
75	Shenyang Dongyu Group Co Ltd	80,156
76	Yingkou Donglin Group Co Ltd	80,000
77	Eastide Group	79,160.55
78	Shunde Biguiyuan Property Development Co Ltd	78,346
79	Shandong Sanwei Oil Co Ltd	76,313
80	Zunhua Jianlong Steel Plant	76,010
81	Zhejiang Zongheng Light Textile Group Co Ltd	76,000
82	Hualun Group Co Ltd	75,969
83	Ningbo Huaxing Group Co Ltd	74,047
84	Xiaoshan Rongsheng Textile Co Ltd	73,433

Rank	Name of enterprise	Sales revenue (RMB million)
85	Guangming Group	72,916
86	Zhejiang Shengda Packing Group Co Ltd	72,675.89
87	Changzhou Laosan Group	72,273
88	Hong Run Construction Group Co Ltd	72,199
89	Zhejiang Runtu Chemical Industry Group Co Ltd	72,000
90	Zhejiang Sunshine Group Co	71,692
91	Chengde Dixian Textile Co Ltd	71,649
92	Shandong Sanlong Industry Co Ltd	70,016
93	Lubao Jiaohua Coke Industry Co	69,579
94	Ma'anshan Dahan Resources Co Ltd	68,302.3
95	Success Holdings Group Co Ltd	68,200
96	Longkou Tianlong Tongen Chemical Co Ltd	68,095
97	Wenzhou Lucheng Foreign Trade Co Ltd	68,048
98	Zhejiang Wolong Hi-tech Group Co	68,000
99	Zhejiang 001 Ele. Group Co Ltd	67,680
100	Xizi Elevator Group Co Ltd	67,106
101	Huaqiao Phoenix Group Co	67,000
102	Zhejiang Deren Group	66,812
103	Zhejiang Huada Communication Equipment Group Co	66,000
104	Zhejiang Chunhui Group Corporation	65,610
105	China Aokang Group	65,214
106	Qinghua Group Co	65,006
107	Shanghai Heping Automobile Sales Co Ltd	64,605
108	Haci Group Co	64,308
109	Zhejiang Feihong Communication Equipment Group Co	63,759
110	Aiyimei Garment Co Ltd	63,499
111	China Junyao Group Co Ltd	62,135
112	Transfar Group	62,000
113	Shangdong Huaxia Group Co	62,000
114	Zhejiang Xingxing Group.	61,013.1
114	Anhui Quanli Group	61,000

Rank	Name of enterprise	Sales revenue (RMB million)
116	Weixing Group	61,000
117	Xiaoshan Liuqiao Feather & Down Products Co Ltd	60,545
118	Zhejiang Forlong Group	60,000
119	Beijing Jiaming Investment (Group) Co Ltd	60,000
120	Zhejiang Xingpeng Copper Material Group Corp.	59,823
121	Yixing Hengtong Copper Co Ltd	59,402
122	Yixing Oxygenated Copper Factory	59,146
123	Yimeng Dongfang (Industrial) Group	59,016
124	Liaoning Xiangwei Construction Group Co Ltd	58,200
125	Xiamen Huierkang Food Co Ltd	58,050
126	Qiaoxing Universal Telephone Inc	57,356.4
127	Xiuzheng Pharmaceutical Group Stock Co Ltd	56,030
128	Shanxi Yiwu (Group) Co Ltd	56,000
129	Shuangmei Group Co Ltd	55,090
130	Mingliu Material Group Co Ltd	55,038
131	Harbin Peace Metal Material Co Ltd	55,000
132	Jiangsu Yalu Industrial Group Co Ltd	54,865.21
133	Haicheng Quartz & Magnesite Group Co Ltd	54,319
134	Shanxi Meijin Coal Gasification Group Co Ltd	53,856
135	Powerise Group	53,729
136	Zhejiang Lianfeng Group Co	53,665.8
137	Wenzhou Jierda Shoes Co Ltd	53,462
138	Baoxiniao LTD	53,378
139	Hangzhou Dawn Communication Group Cable Co Ltd	53,346
140	Kaifeng Tractor Manufactory	53,320
141	Tengda Construction Group Co Ltd	52,336
142	Linqing Xinglong Industrial Group Co Ltd	52,228
143	Beijing City Light Commercial Co Ltd	52,061
144	Jiangsu Shenghui Decoration & Construction Industrial Co Ltd	52,000
145	Anhui Sanlian Group	51,788
146	Shangdong Huanghe Group Co Ltd	51,354

Rank	Name of enterprise	Sales revenue (RMB million)
147	Yunnan Huafeng Group Co Ltd	51,283
148	Xiaoshan Daodao Plastic Chemical Co Ltd	51,234
149	Wuhan Pengling Group Co Ltd	51,027
150	Zhejiang Fukoda Leather Group Co Ltd	51,000
151	Guangdong Welsun Group Co Ltd	50,770
152	China Judger Group	50,619
153	Harbin Shuangtai Electrics Industrial Co Ltd	50,468
154	Dankong Industry & Trade Group Co Ltd	50,368
155	Sichuan Great Wall Telecom Development Group Co Ltd	50,000
156	Dandong Shuguang Axle Joint Stock Co Ltd	49,283
157	Ningbo Tianan Group Co Ltd	48,823
158	Huanchi Bearing Group Co Ltd	48,500
159	Wenzhou Qimei Chemical Co Ltd	48,341.5
160	Jinlian Enterprise Group Co Ltd	48,326
161	Liaoning Xinglong Business & Trade Group Co Ltd	48,000
162	Shanghai Jiaoda Onlly Co Ltd	47,936
163	Guangdong Evergreen Group Co Ltd	47,631
164	Buchang Pharmaceutical Group Co Ltd	46,645
165	Strong Group Co Ltd	46,000
166	Tianjin Baocheng Group Co Ltd	46,000
167	Bright Oceans Corporation	45,975
168	Fuyang 512 Copper Industrial Co Ltd	45,100
169	Xinao Group	45,000
170	Beijing Li-Ning Company	44,861
171	Shandong Longji Group Co Ltd	44,070
172	Shunde Tianren Dongke Co Ltd	43,747.57
173	Yangzhou Happy Group Company	43,600
174	Chongqing Nanfang Group Co Ltd	43,506
175	Chongqing Nanchuan Mine Group Co Ltd	43,475.86
176	Guizhou Shenqi Group	43,401.2
177	Shanxi Zhenxing Group Co Ltd	43,362

Rank	Name of enterprise	Sales revenue (RMB million)
178	Jingyi Electric Appliance Group	43,299
179	Fuchengyangzhong Group	43,000
180	Desheng Steel & Iron Group Co Ltd	42,891
181	Nanjing Fuzhong Information Industry Group Co Ltd	42,800
182	Jiangsu Yuexing Furniture Group Co Ltd	42,601.13
183	Beijing Yuxing Electric Technologies Co Ltd	42,520
184	Shanxi Huanghai Group Co Ltd	42,338
185	Sichuan Mianyang Fulin Enterprise Group Co Ltd	42,260
186	Shanghai Genius Advanced Material Co Ltd	41,850
187	Shenyang Liaoshen Aluminum Plastic Group Co Ltd	41,722
188	Fubang Garments Co Ltd	41,400
189	Guangdong No.7 Construction Group Ltd	41,201
190	Zhejiang Half Earth Group Co Ltd	40,451
191	Liaoning Gongyuan Cement Group Co Ltd	40,088
192	Ningbo Feixiang Group Co Ltd	39,907
193	Zhejiang Maohua Industrial Group Co Ltd	39,767.6
194	Jiangsu Shenghong Printing & Dyeing Co Ltd	39,568
195	Ningbo Yunhuan Electronics Group Corp.	39,325
196	Shanghai Longyu Petrochemical Co Ltd	39,176
197	Ningbo Xingye Group Co Ltd	39,157.42
198	Zhejiang Zhongnan Motorcycle Company Co Ltd	38,943
199	Shenli Group Co Ltd	38,784
200	Henan Sida Technology Group Co Ltd	38,745
201	Zhejiang Shengshi Industrial Group Co Ltd	38,618
202	Yunnan Shengda Industrial Group Co Ltd	38,440
203	Taian jingwei Oil Group Co Ltd	38,392.67
204	Shandong Jinchao Group Co Ltd	38,000
205	Shanxi Huangwei Industrial Group Co Ltd	37,959.32
206	WenZhou Dongyi Shoes Co Ltd	37,801
207	Zhejiang New Asia-Pacific Machine & Electric Group Co Ltd	37,603
208	Zhejiang Hengyi Group Co Ltd	37,241

Rank	Name of enterprise	Sales revenue (RMB million)
209	Zhongzhi Enterprise Group Co Ltd	37,077
210	Yuncheng Shengda Industrial Group Co Ltd	37,000
211	Shenyang Jiying Group Co Ltd	36,300
212	Guangdong Zhanda Group Co Ltd	36,299
213	Shandong Hongda Construction & Engineering Group Co Ltd	36,282.2
214	Shanghai Xiang Sheng Group Co Ltd (SXSGC)	36,154.29
215	Huzhou Zhenxingaxiang Group Co Ltd	36,082
216	Shanghai Yinli Industrial Group Co Ltd	36,000
217	Tongling Zhongnan Industrial Group Co Ltd	36,000
218	Shanghai Zhaolin Co Ltd	36,000
219	Sichuan Dingtian Group Co Ltd	35,936
220	Yixing Huaya Chemical Fibre Co Ltd	35,772
221	Wujiang Zhengda Cable Manufactory	35,600
222	Zhejiang Shangfeng Packaging Group Co Ltd	35,505
223	Zhenhua Industrial Group Corporation	35,400
224	Keda Group Co Ltd	35,287
225	Zhejiang Wanli Tools & Furniture Co Ltd	35,159
226	Shunde Guangda Group Co Ltd	35,045
227	Zhejiang Linya Group	35,000
228	Shandong Luzhou Food Group Co Ltd	35,000
229	Sichuan Jiahe Industrial Group Co Ltd	34,587
230	Shandong Daqiang Industrial Group Co Ltd	34,500
231	Chengdu Tianyou Development Co Ltd	34,493
232	Hangzhou Jinfuchun Silk& Chemical Fibre Co Ltd	34,434
233	Ningbo Peacebird Group Co Ltd	34,259
234	Hangzhou Qianjiang Electric Appliance Group Co Ltd	34,245.25
235	Zhejiang Southeastern Network Construction Co Ltd	34,045
236	Anhui Jingzhong Group Co	34,000
237	Shanghai ShenTeng Information Tech. Co Ltd	34,000
238	Ningbo Yixiu Garment Group Co Ltd	34,000
239	Tianshui Great Wall Electric Group Co Ltd	33,837

Rank	Name of enterprise	Sales revenue (RMB million)
240	Zhuzhou Times Electric Group	33,693
241	Duojia Co Ltd, Hubei, China	33,602
242	Xinhua Electric Group Co Ltd	33,286
243	Jiangsu Zhonglian Technologies Group	33,166
244	Yingkou Huachen (Group) Co Ltd	33,000
245	Gongzhuling Huajiao Power Co Ltd	32,955
246	Jinshuangxi Industrial Development Group Co Ltd	32,700
247	Emeishan Aluminium Industry Group Co Ltd	32,500
248	Shenyang Beitai Group Co Ltd	32,211
249	Shandong Huale Industrial Group Co Ltd	32,180
250	Chongqing Meixin Group Co Ltd	32,156
251	Beijing Sound Environmental Industry Group Limited	32,000
252	Daqing Jitai Industrial Group Co Ltd	32,000
253	Shenyang Huaxin International Industrial Group Co Ltd	32,000
254	Ningbo Rouse Group Co Ltd	31,949
255	Jiangsu AB Group Co Ltd	31,926
256	Hunan Wangwang Food Co Ltd	31,749
257	Zhejiang Jingfa Industrial Group Co Ltd	31,700
258	Jiangsu Xiangtang Group Co Ltd	31,649.61
259	Zhejiang Huangyanzhou Industrial Co Ltd	31,287
260	Chongqing Juxin Business Group Co Ltd	31,041
261	Ningxia Qinyi Industrial Group Co Ltd	31,000
262	Gansu Jianxin Industrial Group Co Ltd	30,935
263	Ningbo Lishi Rubber & Plastic Co Ltd	30,900
264	Zhejiang Shunyu Group Co Ltd	30,884
265	Chongqing Bescar Automobile Co Ltd	30,834
266	Zhejiang Zhuguang Electric Group Co Ltd	30,819.72
267	Inner Mongolia Dongda Mongolia King Wool Group Co	30,532
268	Sichuan Tongwei Co Ltd	30,300
269	Shanghai Huahai Computer Co Ltd	30,295.1
270	Hangzhou Dikai Chemical Industry Co Ltd	30,158

Rank	Name of enterprise	Sales revenue (RMB million)
271	Zhejiang Weiling Metal Group Co Ltd	30,129
272	Hubei Duorenduo Development Industrial Group Co Ltd	30,100
273	Shaoxing TianRan FeiYue Printing Co Ltd	30,026.27
274	Daqing Xinchao Group Co Ltd	30,000
275	Zhejiang Jinyi Group Co Ltd	30,000
276	Nanning Zhengda	30,000
277	Tanshan Liguo Industrial Group Co Ltd	30,000
278	Fujian Sunner Industrial Co Ltd	30,000
279	Nantong	30,000
280	Xiajinjinhua Group Co Ltd	29,743
281	Changsha Wangwang Food Co Ltd	29,723
282	Huangyan Fruit Co	29,600
283	Hainan Yangshengtang Pharmaceutical Co Ltd	29,496
284	Hefei Zhongjian Engineering Machine Co Ltd	29,468
285	Jiaxing Zhonghua Chemical Group Co Ltd	29,432
286	Hangzhou Xiaohong Municipal Engineering Co Ltd	29,421
287	Jiaxing Longyuan Textile Co Ltd	29,336
288	China Dunan Group	29,224
289	Zhejiang Sanhong International Down & Feather Co Ltd	29,132
290	Liuzhou Jiayong Industrial Co Ltd	28,910
291	Beijing Haicheng Information Tech. Co Ltd	28,727
292	Xiamen Yongquan Group Co Ltd	28,629
293	Shanghai Weilong Co Ltd	28,622
294	Suzhou Changrong Lamp Co Ltd	28,410
295	Yuyao Union Textile Co Ltd	28,306
296	Zhejiang Xinzhongyi Business & Trade Co Ltd	28,265.68
297	Hunan Changhai Digital Development Co Ltd	28,250
298	Shanghai New Century	28,148
299	Kunshan Three-oxen Industrial Group Co Ltd	28,087.18
300	(Yinlu Group) Xiamen Tongmao Canned Food Co Ltd	28,050
301	Hejin Yumenkou Industrial Co	28,000

Rank	Name of enterprise	Sales revenue (RMB million)
302	Hubei Yuli Sand Cincture Co Ltd	28,000
303	Chendu Deep Blue Industrial Development Co Ltd	28,000
304	Yuyao Cable & Electric Manufacturer	28,000
305	Hangzhou Paradise Umbrella Group	28,,000
306	Jinan Yongjun Material Co Ltd	28,000
307	Pinghu Duoling Garment Co Ltd	28,000
308	Zhejiang Wanlun Vehicle Group Co Ltd	27,779
309	Anhui Guozhen Group Co Ltd	27,672.39
310	Shanghai Changfeng Real Estate Development Co	27,639
311	Zhejiang Yongtai Paper Group Co Ltd	27,621
312	Zhejiang Busen Group	27,,595
313	Wenzhou Semir Co	27,501
314	Sichuan Fanhua Construction Group Co Ltd	27,500
315	Ningbo Orient Copper Industry Corporation	27,478.65
316	Hangzhou Changhe Group	27,369
317	Changsha Jingge Group	27,251
318	Zhejiang Jiuzhou Pharmaceutical Co Ltd	27,129
319	Liaoyang High-frequency Weld Pipe Manufactory	27,041
320	Tongcheng Hongrun Group	27,000
321	Nantong Zhengda Co Ltd	26,999
322	Harbin Black Swan Housing Appliance Co Ltd	26,938
323	Zhejiang Pinghu Xinchengda Garment Co	26,,900
324	Hangzhou Hangxiao Steel Structure Co Ltd	26,859
325	Chengdu Enwei Group	26,746.74
326	Zhejiang Yunsen Spun Co Ltd	26,693
327	Jiangsu Zhongtian Technologies Co Ltd	26,591
328	Hebei Rongsheng Construction & Installation Co Ltd	26,575
329	Xinjiang Hongda Group	26,502.5
330	Sichuan Yihe Group Co Ltd	26,350
331	Jiangsu Fusite Arts & Crafts Group Co Ltd	26,143
332	Jiangsu Caihua Packaging Group Co Ltd	26,000

Rank	Name of enterprise	Sales revenue (RMB million)
333	Beijing Yeshi Group Co Ltd	26,000
334	Jiangsu Shangli Industrial Group Co Ltd	26,000
335	Shanxi Ruifulai	25,977
336	Zhejiang Huatong Wool Co Ltd	25,550
337	Laiwu Shuangfeng Material Co Ltd	25,443
338	Shanghai Sanming Foodstuff Co Ltd	25,365
339	Taizhou Jiaoguang Machinery & Electric Co Ltd	25,207
340	Zhejiang Tiantong Electric Co Ltd	25,184
341	Harbin Storage Battery Group Company	25,087
342	Chongqing Kuayue Group Co Ltd	25,000
343	Beijing Huabang Beverage Co Ltd	25,000
344	Gansu Shengda Industrial Group Co Ltd	25,000
345	Zhejiang Huangyan Canned Food Co	24,801
346	Shenyang Huihualou Gold & Bijouterie Co Ltd	24,112
347	China Ningbo Shuanglin Group Incorporation	24,000
348	Zhongyi Real Estate Development Co Ltd	24,000
349	Shangdong Guanxian Guanxing Textile Co Ltd	24,000
350	Wenzhou Jinglong Group Co Ltd	23,895
351	Xiaoshan Chemical Fibre Co Ltd	23,866
352	Tonglu Zhongqiao Industrial Co Ltd	23,800
353	Xuzhou Guohua Industry & Trade Co Ltd	23,752
354	Chongqing Yipin Construction Group Co Ltd	23,690
355	Zhejiang Himax Furniture Industry Corp. Ltd	23,654
356	Ningbo Rongan Real Estate Co Ltd	23,615
357	Zhejiang Xi Linmen Fitment Group	23,606
358	Cixing Co Ltd	23,527.14
359	Hunan Zengshi Enterprise Co Ltd	23,521
360	Shanghai Antarctica Enterprise Co Ltd	23,404
361	China Wanyu Group Co Ltd	23,365
362	Kunming Nuoshida Enterprise Co Ltd	23,360
363	Shandong Guanzhou Co Ltd	23,236

Rank	Name of enterprise	Sales revenue (RMB million)
364	Shaoxing Fuling Plastic & Textile Co Ltd	23,169.07
365	Shanghai Huatong Electromechanical Group	23,095.05
366	Tsinghua Tellhow Tech Co Ltd	23,003.7
367	Ningbo MOS Group Co Ltd	23,000
368	Zaozhuang Haiyang Textile Co Ltd	23,000
369	Xiamen Shuyou Sea Food Restaurant Co Ltd	22,980
370	Ningbo Progen Co Ltd	22,837.3
371	Changchun Xinyu Industrial Co Ltd	22,812.5
372	Liuzhou Liunan District Automobile Accessories Co Ltd	22,723
373	Zhejiang Hongxiang Construction Co Ltd	22,700
374	Zhejiang Jinda Enterprise Co Ltd	22,684
375	Hebei Electric & Machine Co Ltd	22,621
376	Guangdong Shanhe Group Co Ltd	22,548
377	Chengdu Kanghong Technology (Group) Co Ltd	22,542.51
378	Haiyan Spun Silk Industrial Co Ltd	22,509.1
379	Xiamen Zhonglong Export & Import Co Ltd	22,400
380	Zhejiang Yuanzhou Group Co Ltd	22,363.19
381	Zhejiang Gem Satorius Industrial Co Ltd	22,326
382	Zhejiang Yongxiang Group Co Ltd	22,212
383	Guanxi Huadian Group Co Ltd	22,191
384	Shantou Nanmei Electric Industrial Co Ltd	22,134
385	Xinjiang Industry & Trade (Group)Co Ltd	22,071
386	Jilin Fareast Pharmaceutical Group Co Ltd	22,024
387	Pinghu Yanxin Co Ltd	22,000
388	Chengdu Jinmali Group Co Ltd	22,000
389	Guangdong Mingjing Industrial Group Co Ltd	22,000
390	Changsha Southern Oversea Chinese Trade Co	21,800
391	Zhuzhou Sunrise Industrial	21,783
392	Ningbo Huikang Group Co Ltd	21,724.08
393	China Huarui Chemical Fibre Co Ltd	21,720
394	Zhejiang Shuangyang Group Co Ltd	21,600

Rank	Name of enterprise	Sales revenue (RMB million)
395	Guangzhou Panyu Iron & Steel Co Ltd	21,596
396	Haikong Haiwang Investment Co Ltd	21,551
397	ChongQing Cygnet Group Company	21,356
398	Beijing Honggao Architectural Design & Engineering Co Ltd	21,300
399	Ufsoft Co Ltd	21,288.5
400	Chongqing Sincere Industrial Group Co Ltd	21,282
401	Sichuan Kelun Industry Group Co Ltd	21,072
402	Kunming Fengchi Star Info. Co Ltd	21,053
403	Zhejiang Gonggao Plastic Co Ltd	21,000
404	Sichuan Dongneng Group Co Ltd	21,000
405	Shandong Dechang Group Co Ltd	21,000
406	Shenyang Fengxiang Group Co Ltd	21,000
407	Yunnan Nanlin Group Co Ltd	20,910
408	Zhejiang Shiliang Wine Co Ltd	20,729
409	Ningbo Yongnan Knitting Co Ltd	20,666
410	Hangzhou Chuangyuan Feather Co Ltd	20,508
411	Zhejiang Qinghe Biochemistry Co Ltd	20,490
412	Changchun Dongda Group Co Ltd	20,466
413	Hebei Dingsheng Construction Group Co Ltd	20,414
414	Shenyang Euro-Asian Industry & Trade Co Ltd	20,302
415	Jilin Shunfeng Group	20,243
416	Hangzhou Sunburge Electric Co Ltd	20,211
417	Cixi Hongyi Electronics Co Ltd	20,127
418	Zhanjiang Rongli Rubber Products	20,100
419	Zhejiang Haili Electric Technologies Co Ltd	20,100
420	Guangzhou Xinlin Air-Conditioning Co Ltd	20,072
421	Ningbo Shenma Children's Goods Co Ltd	20,063.27
422	Beijing Hisun Jinxin Info-Technologies Co Ltd	20,000
423	Zhongxi Group	20,000
424	Xinxiang Goldlion Shopping Center	20,000
425	Guangxi Yuanantang Pharmacy Manufactory	20,000

Rank	Name of enterprise	Sales revenue (RMB million)
426	Shanghai Good Future Garment Co Ltd	20,000
427	Beijing Dadi Feedingstuff Tech. Co Ltd	19,955.31
428	Huayi Elec. Apparatus Group Co Ltd	19,947.7
429	Beijing Bohua Cable Co Ltd	19,900
430	Shunde Taiming Metal-ware Co Ltd	19,874
431	Tianjin Wenguang Group Co Ltd	19,840
432	Rose Garment Group Co Ltd	19,779
433	Anhui Joy Senses Cable Co Ltd	19,778
434	Hefei Anlian Computer Group	19,707.29
435	Xinjiang Hongjing Investment Co Ltd	19,700
436	Zhejing Taizhou Hisoar Pharm. & Chem. Co Ltd	19,597.9
437	Zhejiang Junli Spun Co Ltd	19,595
438	Wuxi Sanxin Chemical Fibre Co Ltd	19,500
439	Shandong Jilong Industrial Group Co Ltd	19,463
440	Tangshan Dacheng Wire General Factory	19,444
441	Fujian Jianou Jianzhou Material Co Ltd	19,400
442	Zhanjiang Wanxiang Real Estate Co Ltd	19,188
443	Xiamen Ideal Foods Co Ltd	19,146
444	Shandong Tianfu Group	19,111
445	Tangshan Shuguang Industrial Group Co Ltd	19,103
446	Hangzhou Youwang Electric Co Ltd	19,007
447	Shenyang Minan Enterprise Group	18,980
448	Zhejiang Lianhua Group Co Ltd	18,912
449	Lanzhou Huafu Group	18,900
450	Yingkou Dazheng Group Co Ltd	18,858
451	Zhejiang Tiannv	18,852
452	Tangshan Hongwen Industrial Group Co Ltd	18,847
453	Zhejiang Huahai Pharmaceutical Co Ltd	18,834
454	Xuzhou Jiulong Group Co Ltd	18,809
455	Harbin Liantong Industry & Trade Co Ltd	18,776
456	Sanajon Pharmaceutical Group	18,757

Rank	Name of enterprise	Sales revenue (RMB million)
457	Chongqing Lidan Group Co Ltd	18,700
458	Gansu XinkaiyuanTechnologies Co Ltd	18,600
459	Jiangsu Chunxing Alloy Group Co Ltd	18,532
460	Wenzhou Yuetu Electric Co Ltd	18,491
461	Shangyu Tianlong Enterprise Co Ltd	18,449
462	Ningbo Kaibo Group Co Ltd	18,398.83
463	Zoje Sewing Machine Co Ltd	18,336
464	Pucheng Chia Tai Biochemistry Co Ltd	18,226
465	Zhejiang Yufeng Industrial Group Co Ltd	18,153
466	Zhejiang Chunjiang Spun Co Ltd	18,105
467	Zhejiang Aidier Packaging Co Ltd	18,069
468	Zhanjiang Jishideye Co Ltd	18,024.72
469	Zhejiang Hongda Co Ltd	18,010
470	Hebei Wuxin Chemical Group Co Ltd	18,000
471	Shandong Lurun Jingjiu Petrochemical Co Ltd	18,000
472	Daqing Zhenfu Group	18,000
473	Rizhao Xingye Imp.&Exp. Co Ltd	18,000
474	Liyang Dongni Group Co Ltd	18,000
475	Shanghai Geer Industrial Co Ltd	18,000
476	Zigong Huarun Meat Product Co Ltd	18,000
477	Sichuan Jingyan Food Co Ltd	18,000
478	Shenyang Qiangfeng Group Co Ltd	17,997
479	Zhejiang Futian Group Co Ltd	17,800
480	Shanxi Changzhi Zhegdong Industrial Co Ltd	17,800
481	Yongshengxu Real Estate Co Ltd	17,698.62
482	Liaoning Weihua Group Co Ltd	17,600
483	Ningbo Hongli Group Co Ltd	17,557.24
484	Wenzhou Zhenan Machinery & Electrical Equipment Co Ltd	17,557
485	Shanghai Junhai Industry Development Co Ltd	17,547
486	Wen Zhou Meters Bonwe Co Ltd	17,500
487	Shanghai Hongquan Investment Co Ltd	17,500

Rank	Name of enterprise	Sales revenue (RMB million)
488	Zhejiang Quartz Crystal Electronics Group Co Ltd	17,423
489	Rugao Diesel Engine CO,LTD	17,377
490	Wellsun Electric Meters	17,356.57
491	Shanghai Kaiquan Pump Group Co Ltd	17,200
492	Harbin Tongyi Enterprise Co Ltd	17,186
493	China Double-Doves Group Co Ltd	17,011
494	Zhejiang Jiaxing Banyu Group Co Ltd	17,000
495	Chengdu Baiwan Group Co Ltd	17,000
496	Zhejiang Xingge Group	17,000
497	Shangxi Lihai Group Co Ltd	17,000
498	Shanghai Longyuan Real Estate Co Ltd	16,944
499	Wenzhou Imitation Leather Co Ltd	16,933
500	Shanghai Sinocan Lianxing Printing Container Co Ltd	16,800

Savings by Residents in Urban and Rural Areas (100 million yuan)

	Year-end balance			Increased amount		
	Total	*Time deposits*	*Demand deposits*	*Total*	*Time deposits*	*Demand deposits*
1978	210.6	128.9	81.7	29.0	17.2	11.8
1979	281.0	166.4	114.6	70.4	37.5	32.9
1980	399.5	304.9	94.6	118.5	138.5	−20.0
1981	523.7	396.4	127.3	124.2	91.5	32.7
1982	675.4	519.3	156.1	151.7	122.9	28.8
1983	892.5	682.3	210.2	217.1	163.0	54.1
1984	1,214.7	900.9	313.8	322.2	218.6	103.6
1985	1,622.6	1,225.2	397.4	407.9	324.3	83.6
1986	2,238.5	1,729.7	508.8	615.9	504.5	111.4
1987	3,081.4	2,361.3	720.1	842.9	631.6	211.3
1988	3,822.2	2,848.5	973.7	740.8	487.2	253.6
1989	5,196.4	4,215.4	981.0	1,374.2	1,366.9	7.3
1990	7,119.8	5,911.2	1,208.6	1,923.4	1,695.8	227.6
1991	9,241.6	7,691.7	1,549.9	2,121.8	1,780.5	341.3
1992	11,759.4	9,425.2	2,334.2	2,517.8	1,733.5	784.3
1993	15,203.5	11,971.0	3,232.5	3,444.1	2,545.8	898.3
1994	21,518.8	16,838.7	4,680.1	6,315.3	4,867.7	1,447.6
1995	29,662.3	23,778.2	5,884.1	8,143.5	6,939.5	1,204.0
1996	38,520.8	30,873.4	7,647.4	8,858.5	7,095.2	1,763.3
1997	46,279.8	36,226.7	10,053.1	7,759.0	5,353.3	2,405.7
1998	53,407.5	41,791.6	11,615.9	7,615.4	5,473.7	2,141.7
1999	59,621.8	44,955.1	14,666.7	6,253.0	3,198.5	3,054.5
2000	64,332.4	46,141.7	18,190.7	4,976.7	1,310.3	3,666.4
2001	73,762.4	51,434.9	22,327.6	9,457.6	4,144.5	5,313.2

Source: China Statistical Yearbook 2001 and China Statistical Abstract 2002

Appendix 1.5

Gross Domestic Product

Data in value terms in this table are calculated at current prices.

(100 million yuan)

Year	Gross National Product	Gross Domestic Product	Primary Industry	Secondary Industry	Industry	Construction	Tertiary Industry	Transport, Post and Telecom- munication Services	Wholesale, Retail Trade & Catering Services	Per Capita GDP (yuan)
1978	3,624.1	3,624.1	1,018.4	1,745.2	1,607.0	138.2	860.5	172.8	265.5	379
1979	4,038.2	4,038.2	1,258.9	1,913.5	1,769.7	143.8	865.8	184.2	220.2	417
1980	4,517.8	4,517.8	1,359.4	2,192.0	1,996.5	195.5	966.4	205.0	213.6	460
1981	4,860.3	4,862.4	1,545.6	2,255.5	2,048.4	207.1	1,061.3	211.1	255.7	489
1982	5,301.8	5,294.7	1,761.6	2,383.0	2,162.3	220.7	1,150.1	236.7	198.6	526
1983	5,957.4	5,934.5	1,960.8	2,646.2	2,375.6	270.6	1,327.5	264.9	231.4	582
1984	7,206.7	7,171.0	2,295.5	3,105.7	2,789.0	316.7	1,769.8	327.1	412.4	695
1985	8,989.1	8,964.4	2,541.6	3,866.6	3,448.7	417.9	2,556.2	406.9	878.4	855
1986	10,201.4	10,202.2	2,763.9	4,492.7	3,967.0	525.7	2,945.6	475.6	943.2	956
1987	11,954.5	11,962.5	3,204.3	5,251.6	4,585.8	665.8	3,506.6	544.9	1,159.3	1,103
1988	14,922.3	14,928.3	3,831.0	6,587.2	5,777.2	810.0	4,510.1	661.0	1,618.0	1,355
1989	16,917.8	16,909.2	4,228.0	7,278.0	6,484.0	794.0	5,403.2	786.0	1,687.0	1,512
1990	18,598.4	18,547.9	5,017.0	7,717.4	6,858.0	859.4	5,813.5	1,147.5	1,419.7	1,634
1991	21,662.5	21,617.8	5,288.6	9,102.2	8,087.1	1,015.1	7,227.0	1,409.7	2,087.0	1,879
1992	26,651.9	26,638.1	5,800.0	11,699.5	10,284.5	1,415.0	9,138.6	1,681.8	2,735.0	2,287
1993	34,560.5	34,634.4	6,882.1	16,428.5	14,143.8	2,284.7	11,323.8	2,123.2	3,090.7	2,939
1994	46,670.0	46,759.4	9,457.2	22,372.2	19,359.6	3,012.6	14,930.0	2,685.9	4,050.4	3,923
1995	57,494.9	58,478.1	11,993.0	28,537.9	24,718.3	3,819.6	17,947.2	3,054.7	4,932.3	4,854
1996	66,850.5	67,884.6	13,844.2	33,612.9	29,082.6	4,530.5	20,427.5	3,494.0	5,560.3	5,576
1997	73,142.7	74,462.6	14,211.2	37,222.7	32,412.1	4,810.6	23,028.7	3,797.2	6,159.9	6,054
1998	76,967.2	78,345.2	14,552.4	38,619.3	33,387.9	5,231.4	25,173.5	4,121.3	6,579.1	6,307
1999	80,579.4	82,067.5	14,472.0	40,557.8	35,087.2	5,470.6	27,037.7	4,460.3	6,910.3	6,547
2000	88,189.6	89,403.6	14,212.0	45,487.8	39,570.3	5,917.5	29,703.8	4,918.6	7,306.9	7,078
2001	94,346.4	95,933.3	14,609.9	49,069.1	42,607.1	6,462.0	32,254.3	5,222.1	7,823.5	7,543.0

Since 1980, the difference between the total of primary, secondary & tertiary industries and the gross national product has been the net factor income from abroad.

Source: China Statistical Yearbook 2001 and China Statistical Abstract 2002

Appendix 1.6

Gross Domestic Product by Region

Absolute figures in this table are calculated at current prices

	Gross Domestic Product (100 million yuan)				
Region	1997	1998	1999	2000	2001
Beijing	1,810.09	2,011.31	2,174.46	2,478.76	2,817.6
Tianjin	1,235.28	1,336.38	1,450.06	1,639.36	1,826.7
Hebei	3,953.78	4,256.01	4,569.19	5,088.96	5,577.7
Shanxi	1,480.13	1,486.08	1,506.78	1,643.81	1,774.6
Inner Mongolia	1,099.77	1,192.29	1,268.20	1,401.01	1,545.5
Liaoning	3,582.46	3,881.73	4,171.69	4,669.06	5,033.1
Jilin	1,446.91	1,557.78	1,660.91	1,821.19	2,032.5
Heilongjiang	2,708.46	2,798.89	2,897.41	3,253.00	3,561.0
Shanghai	3,360.21	3,688.20	4,034.96	4,551.15	4,950.8
Jiangsu	6,680.34	7,199.95	7,697.82	8,582.73	9,514.6
Zhejiang	4,638.24	4,987.50	5,364.89	6,036.34	6,700.0
Anhui	2,669.95	2,805.45	2,908.58	3,038.24	3,290.1
Fujian	3,000.36	3,286.56	3,550.24	3,920.07	4,258.4
Jiangxi	1,715.18	1,851.98	1,853.65	2,003.07	2,173.8
Shandong	6,650.02	7,162.20	7,662.10	8,542.44	9,438.3
Henan	4,079.26	4,356.60	4,576.10	5,137.66	5,645.0
Hubei	3,450.24	3,704.21	3,857.99	4,276.32	4,662.3
Hunan	2,993.00	3,118.09	3,326.75	3,691.88	3,983.0
Guangdong	7,315.51	7,919.12	8,464.31	9,662.23	10,556.3
Guangxi	1,817.25	1,903.04	1,953.27	2,050.14	2,231.2
Hainan	409.86	438.92	471.23	518.48	545.3
Chongqing	1,350.10	1,429.26	1,479.71	1,589.34	1,749.8
Sichuan	3,320.11	3,580.26	3,711.61	4,010.25	4,421.8
Guizhou	792.98	841.88	911.86	993.53	1,082.2
Yunnan	1,644.23	1,793.90	1,855.74	1,955.09	20,775.0
Tibet	76.98	91.18	105.61	117.46	na
Shaanxi	1,300.03	1,381.53	1,487.61	1,660.92	1,841.2
Gansu	781.34	869.75	931.98	983.36	1,074.9
Qinghai	202.05	220.16	238.39	263.59	300.8
Ningxia	210.92	227.46	,241.49	265.57	298.1
Xinjiang	1,050.14	1,116.67	1,168.55	1,364.36	1,483.5

Source: China Statistical Yearbook 2001 and China Statistical Abstract 2002

Utilization of Foreign Capital

(US$100 million)

Year	Total Number of Projects	Value	Foreign Loans Number of Projects	Value	Direct Foreign Investments Number of Projects	Value	Other Foreign Investments
Total Amount of Contracted Value of Foreign Capital							
1979–1983	1,471	239.78	79	150.62	1392	77.42	11.74
1984	1,894	47.91	38	19.16	1856	26.51	2.24
1985	3,145	98.67	72	35.34	3073	59.32	4.01
1986	1,551	117.37	53	84.07	1498	28.34	4.96
1987	2,289	121.36	56	78.17	2233	37.09	6.10
1988	6,063	160.04	118	98.13	5945	52.97	8.94
1989	5,909	114.79	130	51.85	5779	56.00	6.94
1990	7,371	120.86	98	50.99	7273	65.96	3.91
1991	13,086	195.83	108	71.61	12978	119.77	4.45
1992	48,858	694.39	94	107.03	48764	581.24	6.12
1993	83,595	1,232.73	158	113.06	83437	1114.36	5.31
1994	47,646	937.56	97	106.68	47549	826.80	4.08
1995	37,184	1,032.05	173	112.88	37011	912.82	6.35
1996	24,673	816.10	117	79.62	24556	732.77	3.71
1997	21,138	610.58	137	58.72	21001	510.04	41.82
1998	19,850	632.01	51	83.85	19799	521.02	27.14
1999	17,022	520.09	104	83.60	16918	412.23	24.26
2000	22,347			711.3	22347	623.80	87.50
2001	26,140			719.8	26140	692.00	27.8
Total Amount of Foreign Capital Actually Used							
1979–1983		144.38		117.55		18.02	8.81
1984		27.05		12.86		12.58	1.61
1985		46.47		26.88		16.61	2.98
1986		72.58		50.14		18.74	3.70
1987		84.52		58.05		23.14	3.33
1988		102.26		64.87		31.94	5.45
1989		100.59		62.86		33.92	3.81
1990		102.89		65.34		34.87	2.68
1991		115.54		68.88		43.66	3.00
1992		192.02		79.11		110.07	2.84
1993		389.60		111.89		275.15	2.56
1994		432.13		92.67		337.67	1.79

Year	Total Number of Projects	Value	Foreign Loans Number of Projects	Value	Direct Foreign Investments Number of Projects	Value	Other Foreign Investments
1995		481.33		103.27		375.21	2.85
1996		548.04		126.69		417.25	4.10
1997		644.08		120.21		452.57	71.30
1998		585.57		110.00		454.63	20.94
1999	526.59	102.12				403.19	21.28
2000	593.56	100.00				407.15	86.41
2001	496.80	468.80				28.00	

Source: China Statistical Yearbook 2001 and China Statistical Abstract 2002

Appendix 1.8

Total Value of Imports and Exports

Data before 1979 were obtained from the Ministry of Foreign Trade, and the data since 1980 have been obtained from the customs statistics.

Year	*100 million Yuan*				*US$100 million*			
	Total Imports & Exports	*Total Exports*	*Total Imports*	*Balance*	*Total Imports & Exports*	*Total Exports*	*Total Imports*	*Balance*
1978	355.0	167.6	187.4	−19.8	206.4	97.5	108.9	−11.4
1979	454.6	211.7	242.9	−31.2	293.3	136.6	156.7	−20.1
1980	570.0	271.2	298.8	−27.6	381.4	181.2	200.2	−19.0
1981	735.3	367.6	367.7	−0.1	440.3	220.1	220.2	−0.1
1982	771.3	413.8	357.5	56.3	416.1	223.2	192.9	30.3
1983	860.1	438.3	421.8	16.5	436.2	222.3	213.9	8.4
1984	1,201.0	580.5	620.5	−40.0	535.5	261.4	274.1	−12.7
1985	2,066.7	808.9	1,257.8	−448.9	696.0	273.5	422.5	−149.0
1986	2,580.4	1,082.1	1,498.3	−416.2	738.5	309.4	429.1	−119.7
1987	3,084.2	1,470.0	1,614.2	−144.2	826.5	394.4	432.1	−37.7
1988	3,821.8	1,766.7	2,055.1	−288.4	1,027.9	475.2	552.7	−77.5
1989	4,155.9	1,956.0	2,199.9	−243.9	1,116.8	525.4	591.4	−66.0
1990	5,560.1	2,985.8	2,574.3	411.5	1,154.4	620.9	533.5	87.4
1991	7,225.8	3,827.1	3,398.7	428.4	1,356.3	718.4	637.9	80.5
1992	9,119.6	4,676.3	4,443.3	233.0	1,655.3	849.4	805.9	43.5
1993	11,271.0	5,284.8	5,986.2	−7,01.4	1,957.0	917.4	1,039.6	−122.2
1994	20,381.9	10,421.8	9,960.1	4,61.7	2,366.2	1,210.1	1,156.1	54.0
1995	23,499.9	12,451.8	11,048.1	1,403.7	2,808.6	1,487.8	1,320.8	167.0
1996	24,133.8	12,576.4	11,557.4	1,019.0	2,898.8	1,510.5	1,388.3	122.2
1997	26,967.2	15,160.7	11,806.5	3,354.2	3,251.6	1,827.9	1,423.7	404.2
1998	26,857.7	15,231.6	11,626.1	3,605.5	3,239.5	1,837.1	1,402.4	434.7
1999	29,896.3	16,159.8	13,736.5	2,423.3	3,606.3	1,949.3	1,657.0	292.3
2000	39,274.2	20,635.2	18,639.0	1,996.2	4,742.9	2,492.0	2,250.9	241.1
2001	42,193.3	22,029.1	20,164.2		5,097.7	2,661.6	2,436.1	

Note: A negative balance indicates an unfavourable balance of foreign trade.

Appendix 1.9

Balance of Foreign Debts

Type of Debts	1995	1996	1997	1998	1999	2000	2001
Total (US$100 million)	**1,065.90**	**1,162.75**	**1,309.60**	**1,460.43**	**1,518.30**	**1,457.30**	**1,701.1**
By Type of Debt							
Loans from Foreign Governments	220.58	221.64	207.82	224.06	265.60	246.10	237.0
Loans from International Financial Institutions	147.99	167.39	192.12	229.54	251.39	263.50	275.7 972.3
International Commercial Loans	526.27	569.44	647.68	682.22	653.80	947.70	216.1
Others	171.06	204.28	261.98	324.61	347.51		
By Repayment Terms							
Balance of Long-term Debts	946.74	1,021.67	1,128.20	1,287.00	1,366.50	1,326.50	1,195.3
Balance of Short-term Debts	119.16	141.08	181.40	173.40	151.80	130.80	505.8

Source: China Statistical Yearbook 2001 and China Statistical Abstract 2002

Appendix 1.10

Gold and Foreign Exchange Reserves

Year	Gold Reserve (10,000 Ounces)	Foreign Exchange Reserve (US$100 million)
1978	1,280	1.67
1979	1,280	8.40
1980	1,280	−12.96
1981	1,267	27.08
1982	1,267	69.86
1983	1,267	89.01
1984	1,267	82.20
1985	1,267	26.44
1986	1,267	20.72
1987	1,267	29.23
1988	1,267	33.72
1989	1,267	55.50
1990	1,267	110.93
1991	1,267	217.12
1992	1,267	194.43
1993	1,267	211.99
1994	1,267	516.20
1995	1,267	735.97
1996	1,267	1,050.49
1997	1,267	1,398.90
1998	1,267	1,449.60
1999	1,267	1,546.75
2000	1,267	1,655.74
2001	1,267	2,121.70

Source: China Statistical Yearbook 2001 and China Statistical Abstract 2002

Appendix 1.11

Total Investment in Fixed Assets

Item	1999	2000	Increase Rate in 2000 over 1999 (%)
Total Investment (100 million yuan)	29854.71	32917.73	10.3
Grouped by Ownership			
State-owned Units	15,947.76	16,504.44	3.5
Collective-owned Units	4,338.55	4,801.45	10.7
Rural	3,343.13	3,791.62	13.4
Individuals Economy	4,195.70	4,709.36	12.2
Rural	2,779.59	2,904.26	4.5
Joint Ownership Economic Units	97.90	94.73	−3.2
Share Holding Economic Units	2,478.88	4,061.88	63.9
Foreign Funded Economic Units	1,433.40	1,313.21	−8.4
Economic Units with Funds from Hong Kong, Macao and Taiwan	1,218.07	1,293.05	6.2
Others	144.44	139.61	−3.3
Grouped by Channel of Management			
Capital Construction	12,455.28	13,427.27	7.8
Innovation	4,485.08	5,107.60	13.9
Real Estate Development	4,103.20	4,984.05	21.5
Others	8,811.15	9,398.81	6.7
Grouped by Source of Funds			
State Budgetary Appropriation	1,852.14	2,109.45	13.9
Domestic Loans	5,725.93	6,727.27	17.5
Foreign Investment	2,006.78	1,696.24	−15.5
Fundraising	15,885.26	17,270.28	8.7
Others	4284.54	5,306.86	23.9
Grouped by Use of Funds			
Construction and Installation	18,795.93	20,536.26	9.3
Purchase of Equipment and Instruments	7,053.04	7,785.62	10.4
Others	4,005.74	4,595.85	14.7
Floor Space of Buildings (10,000 sq.m)			
Floor Space under Construction	263,294.25	265,293.53	0.8
Floor Space Completed	187,357.07	181,974.44	−2.9
Residential Buildings	139,305.93	134,528.83	−3.4

a) Total investment grouped by source of funds refers to financial appropriation, and the subentry figures do not add up to the total.
b) The growth rates are calculated without removing the factor of price.
Source: China Statistical Yearbook 2001

Money Supply at the Year-end

(100 million yuan)

Year	Money and Quasi-Money (M2)	Money (M1)	Currency in Circulation (M0)
1990	1,5293.4	6,950.7	2,644.4
1991	1,9349.9	8,633.3	3,177.8
1992	2,5402.2	11,731.5	4,336.0
1993	3,4879.8	16,280.4	5,864.7
1994	4,6923.5	20,540.7	7,288.6
1995	6,0750.5	23,987.1	7,885.3
1996	7,6094.9	28,514.8	8,802.0
1997	9,0995.3	34,826.3	10,177.6
1998	10,4498.5	38,953.7	11,204.2
1999	11,9897.9	45,837.2	13,455.5
2000	13,4610.3	53,147.2	14,652.7
2001	15,8301.9	59,871.6	15,688.8

a) The statistics coverage is according to China National Bank and Rural Credit Union before 1992.

b) The statistics coverage is according to *Banking Survey* since 1992.

Source: China Statistical Yearbook 2001 and China Statistical Abstract 2002

Appendix 1.13

Basic Statistics of National Population Censuses since the Founding of the People's Republic of China

Data in this table excluded the population of Hong Kong , Macao and Taiwan.

(10,000 persons)

Item	1953	1964	1982	1990	2000
Total Population (10,000 persons)	59,435	69,458	100,818	113,368	126,583
Male	30,799	35,652	51,944	58,495	65,355
Female	28,636	33,806	48,874	54,873	61,228
Sex ratio	107.56	105.46	106.30	106.60	106.74
Average Family Size (person/household)	4.33	4.43	4.41	3.96	3.44
Population by Age Group (%)					
Age 0–14	36.28	40.69	33.59	27.69	22.89
Age 15–64	59.31	55.75	61.50	66.74	70.15
Age 65 and Over	4.41	3.56	4.91	5.57	6.96
Nationality Population (10,000 persons, %)					
Han Nationality	54,728	65,456	94,088	104,248	115,940
% of Total Population	93.94	94.24	93.32	91.96	91.59
Minority Nationalities	3,532	4,002	6,730	9,120	10,643
% of Total Population	6.06	5.76	6.68	8.04	8.41
Population with Various Education Attainment					
Per 100 000 from Population Censuses (person)					
Junior College and Above		416	615	1,422	3,611
Senior Secondary/Secondary Technical School		1,319	6,779	8,039	11,146
Junior Secondary School		4,680	17,892	23,344	33,961
Primary School		28,330	35,237	37,057	35,701
Illiterate Population and Illiterate Rate					
Illiterate Population (10 000 persons)		23,327	22,996	18,003	8,507
Illiterate Rate (%)		33.58	22.81	15.88	6.72
Population By Residence (10,000 persons)					
Urban Population	7,726	12,710	21,082	29,971	45,844
Rural Population	50,534	56,748	79,736	83,397	80,739

a) Total population from population censuses included the military personnel. Military personnel were listed in urban population in population by residence.

b) Total population of 1953 census included the population from indirect survey, but excluded in the nationality population and urban/rural population.

c) Illiterate population of 1964 census referred to people of 13 years old and over who could not read. Illiterate population of 1982, 1990 and 2000 censuses referred to people of 15 years old and over who could not read or could read very little.

Source: China Statistical Yearbook 2001

Appendix 1.14

Employment

Item	1996	1997	1998	1999	2000
Total Number of Employed Persons (10,000 persons)	**68,850**	**69,600**	**69,957**	**70,586**	**71,150**
Primary Industry	34,769	34,730	34,838	35,364	35,575
Secondary Industry	16,180	16,495	16,440	16,235	16,009
Tertiary Industry	17,901	18,375	18,679	18,987	19,566
Composition of Employed Persons (total=100)					
Primary Industry	50.5	49.9	49.8	50.1	50.0
Secondary Industry	23.5	23.7	23.5	23.0	22.5
Tertiary Industry	26.0	26.4	26.7	26.9	27.5
Number of Employed Persons by Urban and					
Rural Areas (10,000 persons)					
Urban Employed Persons	19,815	20,207	20,678	21,014	21,274
State-owned Units	11,244	11,044	9,058	8,572	8102
Urban Collective-owned Units	3,016	2,883	1,963	1,712	1,499
Cooperative Units	–	–	136	144	155
Joint Ownership Units	49	43	48	46	42
Limited Liability Corporations	–	–	484	603	687
Share-holding Corporations Ltd.	363	468	410	420	457
Private Enterprises	620	750	973	1,053	1,268
Units with Funds from Hong Kong, Macao & Taiwan	265	281	294	306	310
Foreign Funded Units	275	300	293	306	332
Self-employed Individuals	1,709	1,919	2,259	2,414	2136
Rural Employed Persons	49,035	49,393	49,279	49,572	49,876
Township and Village Enterprises	13,508	13,050	12,537	12,704	12,820
Private Enterprises	551	600	737	969	1,139
Self-employed Individuals	3308	3,522	3,855	3,827	2,934
Number of Staff and Workers (10,000 persons)	**14,845**	**14,668**	**12,337**	**11,773**	**11,259**
State-owned Units	10,949	10,766	8,809	8,336	7,878
Urban Collective-owned Units	2,954	2,817	1,900	1,652	1,447
Units of Other Types of Ownership	942	1,085	1,628	1,785	1,935
Number of Female Employment	–	–	–	4,613	4,411
in Urban Units (10,000 persons)					
Number of Registered Unemployed Persons	553	570	571	575	595
in Urban Areas (10,000 persons)					
Registered Unemployment Rate in Urban Areas (%)	**3.0**	**3.1**	**3.1**	**3.1**	**3.1**

a) Since 1990 data on economically active population, the total employed persons and the sub-total of employed persons in urban and rural areas have been adjusted in accordance with the data obtained from the sample surveys on population changes. As a result, the sum of the data by region, by ownership or by sector is not equal to the total. The same as in the following tables.

b) Statistical coverage of staff and workers employed in urban units has adjusted since 1998.

Source: China Statistical Yearbook 2001

Appendix 1.15

Population and Its Composition

Data in this table include the military personnel, but exclude the population of Hong Kong, Macao and Taiwan.

(10,000 persons)

Year	Total Population (year-end)	By Sex				By Residence			
		Male		Female		Urban		Rural	
		Population	Proportion	Population	Proportion	Population	Proportion	Population	Proportion
1978	96,259	49,567	51.49	46,692	48.51	17,245	17.92	79,014	82.08
1979	97,542	50,192	51.46	47,350	48.54	18,495	18.96	79,047	81.04
1980	98,705	50,785	51.45	47,920	48.55	19,140	19.39	79,565	80.61
1981	100,072	51,519	51.48	48,553	48.52	20,171	20.16	79,901	79.84
1982	101,654	52,352	51.50	49,302	48.50	21,480	21.13	80,174	78.87
1983	103,008	53,152	51.60	49,856	48.40	22,274	21.62	80,734	78.38
1984	104,357	53,848	51.60	50,509	48.40	24,017	23.01	80,340	76.99
1985	105,851	54,725	51.70	51,126	48.30	25,094	23.71	80,757	76.29
1986	107,507	55,581	51.70	51,926	48.30	26,366	24.52	81,141	75.48
1987	109,300	56,290	51.50	53,010	48.50	27,674	25.32	81,626	74.68
1988	111,026	57,201	51.52	53,825	48.48	28,661	25.81	82,365	74.19
1989	112,704	58,099	51.55	54,605	48.45	29,540	26.21	83,164	73.79
1990	114,333	58,904	51.52	55,429	48.48	30,191	26.41	84,142	73.59
1991	115,823	59,466	51.34	56,357	48.66	30,543	26.37	85,280	73.63
1992	117,171	59,811	51.05	57,360	48.95	32,372	27.63	84,799	72.37
1993	118,517	60,472	51.02	58,045	48.98	33,351	28.14	85,166	71.86
1994	119,850	61,246	51.10	58,604	48.90	34,301	28.62	85,549	71.38
1995	121,121	61,808	51.03	59,313	48.97	35,174	29.04	85,947	70.96
1996	122,389	62,200	50.82	60,189	49.18	35,950	29.37	86,439	70.63
1997	123,626	63,131	51.07	60,495	48.93	36,989	29.92	86,637	70.08
1998	124,810	63,629	50.98	61,181	49.02	37,942	30.40	86,868	69.60
1999	125,909	64,189	50.98	61,720	49.02	38,892	30.89	87,017	69.11
2000	126,583	65,355	51.63	61,228	48.37	45,844	36.22	80,739	63.78
2001	127,627	65,672	51.46	61,955	48.54	48,064	37.66	79,563	62.34

a) Data before 1982 were taken from the annual reports of the Ministry of Public Security. Data in 1982-1989 were adjusted on the basis of the 1982 and 1990 national population censuses. Data in 1990-1999 have been estimated on the basis of the annual national sample surveys on population changes. Data of 2000 are obtained from the advance tabulation of the 5th national population census, with zero hour of 1 November 2000 as the reference time.
b) Urban Population figures include the military personnel.
Source: China Statistical Yearbook 2001 and China Statistical Abstract 2002

Population Distribution by Urban, Rural Residence and Region

Data in this table are obtained from the advance tabulation of the 5th national population census, with zero hour of 1 November 2000 as the reference time.

(10,000 persons)

Region	Total Population	Urban Population	Rural Population	% Total Urban	Rural
National Total	**126,583**	**45844**	**80,739**	**36.22**	**63.78**
Beijing	1,382	1,072	310	77.54	22.46
Tianjin	1,001	721	280	71.99	28.01
Hebei	6,744	1,759	4,985	26.08	73.92
Shanxi	3,297	1,151	2,146	34.91	65.09
Inner Mongolia	2,376	1,014	1,362	42.68	57.32
Liaoning	4,238	2,299	1,939	54.24	45.76
Jilin	2,728	1,355	1,373	49.68	50.32
Heilongjiang	3,689	1,901	1,788	51.54	48.46
Shanghai	1,674	1,478	196	88.31	11.69
Jiangsu	7,438	3,086	4,352	41.49	58.51
Zhejiang	4,677	2,277	2,400	48.67	51.33
Anhui	5,986	1,665	4,321	27.81	72.19
Fujian	3,471	1,443	2,028	41.57	58.43
Jiangxi	4,140	1,146	2,994	27.67	72.33
Shandong	9,079	3,450	5,629	38.00	62.00
Henan	9,256	2,147	7,109	23.20	76.80
Hubei	6,028	2,424	3,604	40.22	59.78
Hunan	6,440	1,916	4,524	29.75	70.25
Guangdong	8,642	4,753	3,889	55.00	45.00
Guangxi	4,489	1,264	3,225	28.15	71.85
Hainan	787	316	471	40.11	59.89
Chongqing	3,090	1,023	2,067	33.09	66.91
Sichuan	8,329	2,223	6,106	26.69	73.31
Guizhou	3,525	841	2,684	23.87	76.13
Yunnan	4,288	1,002	3,286	23.36	76.64
Tibet	262	50	212	18.93	81.07
Shaanxi	3,605	1,163	2,442	32.26	67.74
Gansu	2,562	615	1,947	24.01	75.99
Qinghai	518	180	338	34.76	65.24
Ningxia	562	182	380	32.43	67.57
Xinjiang	1,925	651	1,274	33.82	66.18

a) National total population and urban population include the Chinese People's Liberation Army, but population by regions exclude that.
Source: China Statistical Yearbook 2001

Appendix 1.17

Savings by Residents in Urban and Rural Areas (Year-end)

(100 million yuan)

Year	Year-end Balance			Increased Amount		
	Total	Time Deposits	Demand Deposits	Total	Time Deposits	Demand Deposits
1978	210.6	128.9	81.7	29.0	17.2	11.8
1979	281.0	166.4	114.6	70.4	37.5	32.9
1980	399.5	304.9	94.6	118.5	138.5	−20.0
1981	523.7	396.4	127.3	124.2	91.5	32.7
1982	675.4	519.3	156.1	151.7	122.9	28.8
1983	892.5	682.3	210.2	217.1	163.0	54.1
1984	1214.7	900.9	313.8	322.2	218.6	103.6
1985	1622.6	1,225.2	397.4	407.9	324.3	83.6
1986	2238.5	1,729.7	508.8	615.9	504.5	111.4
1987	3081.4	2,361.3	720.1	842.9	631.6	211.3
1988	3822.2	2,848.5	973.7	740.8	487.2	253.6
1989	5196.4	4,215.4	981.0	1,374.2	1,366.9	7.3
1990	7119.8	5,911.2	1208.6	1,923.4	1,695.8	227.6
1991	9241.6	7,691.7	1549.9	2,121.8	1,780.5	341.3
1992	11,759.4	9,425.2	2334.2	2,517.8	1,733.5	784.3
1993	15,203.5	11,971.0	3232.5	3,444.1	2,545.8	898.3
1994	21,518.8	16,838.7	4680.1	6,315.3	4,867.7	1,447.6
1995	29,662.3	23,778.2	5884.1	8,143.5	6,939.5	1,204.0
1996	38,520.8	30,873.4	7647.4	8,858.5	7,095.2	1,763.3
1997	46,279.8	36,226.7	10,053.1	7,759.0	5,353.3	2,405.7
1998	53,407.5	41,791.6	11,615.9	7,615.4	5,473.7	2,141.7
1999	59,621.8	44,955.1	14,666.7	6,253.0	3,198.5	3,054.5
2000	64,332.4	46,141.7	18,190.7	4,976.7	1,310.3	3,666.4
2001	73,762.4	51,434.9	22,327.6	9,457.6	4,144.5	5,313.2

Source: China Statistical Yearbook 2001 and China Statistical Abstract 2002

Basic Conditions of Urban Households

Item	1985	1990	1995	1999	2000	2001
Number of Households Surveyed (household)	24,338	35,660	35,520	40,044	42,220	43,840
Average Household Size (person)	3.89	3.50	3.23	3.14	3.13	3.1
Average Number of Employed Persons per Household	2.15	1.98	1.87	1.77	1.68	1.65
Percentage of Employment per Household (%)	55.27	56.57	57.89	56.43	53.67	53.23
Number of Persons Supported by Each Employee (including the employee himself or herself) (person)	1.81	1.77	1.73	1.77	1.86	1.88
Per Capita Annual Income (yuan)	748.92	1,522.79	4,288.09	5,888.77	6,316.81	6,907.08
Disposable Income	739.08	1,510.16	4,283.00	5,854.02	6,279.98	6,859.58
Per Capita Annual Living Expenditures for Consumption (yuan)	673.20	1,278.89	3,537.57	4,615.91	4,998.00	5,309.0
Food	351.72	693.77	1,766.02	1,932.10	1,958.31	2,014.0
Clothing	98.04	170.90	479.20	482.37	500.46	533.7
Household Facilities, Articles and Service	57.87	108.45	296.94	395.48	439.29	438.9
Medicine and Medical Service	16.71	25.67	110.11	245.59	318.07	343.3
Transport, Post and Communication Services	14.39	40.51	171.01	310.55	395.01	457.0
Recreation, Education and Cultural Services	55.01	112.26	312.71	567.05	627.82	690.0
Residence	32.23	60.86	250.18	453.99	500.49	548.0
Miscellaneous Commodities and Services	47.23	66.57	151.39	228.79	258.54	284.1

a) Data in the table are obtained from the sample survey on income and expenditures of urban households.

b) Since 1997, other income of staff and workers from their working units was cancelled and its value was divided in the wages of staff and workers in state-owned units or in collective owned units.

c) Since 1992, special income was cancelled. Its main value was divided between transfer income and other income.

Source: China Statistical Yearbook 2001 and China Statistical Abstract 2002

Appendix 1.19

Average Exchange Rate of RMB Yuan Against Main Convertible Currencies (Middle Rate)

(RMB yuan)

Year	100 US Dollars	100 Japanese Yen	100 Hong Kong Dollars
1981	170.50	0.7735	30.41
1982	189.25	0.7607	31.15
1983	197.57	0.8318	27.36
1984	232.70	0.9780	29.71
1985	293.66	1.2457	37.57
1986	345.28	2.0694	44.22
1987	372.21	2.5799	47.74
1988	372.21	2.9082	47.70
1989	376.51	2.7360	48.28
1990	478.32	3.3233	61.39
1991	532.33	3.9602	68.45
1992	551.46	4.3608	71.24
1993	576.20	5.2020	74.41
1994	861.87	8.4370	111.53
1995	835.10	8.9225	107.96
1996	831.42	7.6352	107.51
1997	828.98	6.8600	107.09
1998	827.91	6.3488	106.88
1999	827.83	7.2932	106.66
2000	827.84	7.6864	106.18
2001	827.70	6.8075	106.08

Source: China Statistical Yearbook 2001 and China Statistical Abstract 2002

Appendix 2.1

China's Top 100 Import and Export Enterprises by Value

Published by the Ministry of Foreign Trade and Economic Cooperation, 27 May 2002

Rank	Name of company	Export value (US$ million)	Import value (US$ million)	Total import & export value (US$ million)
1	China Petroleum & Chemical International Affairs Corporation	1,232.50	8,661.69	9,894.19
2	China National Chemicals Import & Export Corporation	1,634.51	4,285.78	5,920.29
3	SVA (Group) Co Ltd	1,747.97	2,096.09	3,844.06
4	China Putian Corporation	1,637.75	2,171.21	3,808.96
5	Motorola (China) Electronics Ltd	1,613.00	2,061.68	3,674.68
6	Orient International Group Corp	2,138.80	1,480.22	3,619.03
7	Hongfujin Fine Industry (Shenzhen) Co Ltd	2,031.78	1,222.90	3,254.69
8	China National Petroleum Corporation	1,183.49	1,876.55	3,060.04
9	China General Technologies (Group) Co Ltd	527.67	2,372.73	2,900.40
10	China Minmetals Group	640.77	2,133.28	2,774.05
11	China National Cereals, Oils & Foodstuffs Import & Export Corporation	850.13	1,426.72	2,276.85
12	Zhuhai Zhenrong Corp	0	2,052.58	2,052.58
13	China National Electrics Import & Export Corp	965.76	1,059.94	2,025.70
14	China State Shipbuilding Corporation	1,376.33	599.49	1,975.82
15	China National Coal Industry I/E (Group) Corp	1,688.09	208.83	1,896.92
16	China National Are-Technology Import & Export Corporation	748.37	1,122.49	1,870.85
17	China Aviation Supplies Imp.&Exp. Corporation	66.76	1,729.01	1,795.77
18	China National Machinery & Equipment Corp (Group) (CNMEG)	1,126.51	612.38	1,738.89
19	Shanghai Basin Iron and Steel Company Ltd	578.27	1,052.73	1,631.00

Rank	Name of company	Export value (US$ million)	Import value (US$ million)	Total import & export value (US$ million)
20	Shanghai Textile Holding (Group) Co	1,321.31	269.34	1,590.65
21	Shanghai Automotive Industry Corporation (Group)	152.17	1,436.53	1,588.70
22	Shanghai Light Industry Holding Company (Group)	867.34	667.73	1,535.07
23	China International Marine Containers (Group) Co Ltd	958.00	468.98	1,426.99
24	Shunde Shunda Computer Co Ltd	755.03	666.85	1,421.88
25	Seagate International (Shenzhen) Technologies Co Ltd	721.75	671.44	1,393.18
26	Seagate International (Wuxi) Technologies Co Ltd	661.10	710.68	1,371.79
27	TPV Technology Limited	752.95	597.04	1,349.98
28	Epson (Suzhou) Co Ltd	667.05	647.57	1,314.62
29	Epson Technologies (Shenzhen) Co Ltd	677.43	585.90	1,263.32
30	LG Electrics (Huizhou) Co Ltd	789.02	473.48	1,262.50
31	West Pacific Petrochemical Co Ltd Dalian	462.93	795.16	1,258.09
32	Dongguan Nokia Mobile Co Ltd	832.55	405.63	1,238.18
33	FAW Group Corporation of China	79.59	1,106.32	1,185.90
34	China National Offshore Oil Corp	893.03	274.03	1,167.06
35	Shanghai Instrumentation & Electrics Holding Group Company	610.63	537.24	1,147.88
36	Legend Import & Export Corp	3.18	1,094.75	1,097.93
37	China National Arts & Crafts Import & Export Corporation	701.47	377.26	1,078.74
38	Shenhua Group Co Ltd	833.56	233.62	1,067.18
39	China National Tobacco Import and Export Corporation (CNTIEC)	373.76	692.08	1,065.83
40	Great Wall International Information Co Ltd	1,028.82	00.7	1028.88
41	Philips Electronic Components (Shanghai) Company Limited	548.62	446.61	995.23
42	Guangdong Silk (Group) Co Ltd	770.48	218.32	988.79
43	Shanghai Electric(Group) Co Ltd	480.30	501.78	982.08
44	Dongguan Machinery Import & Export Company of Guangdong	567.59	393.95	961.54
45	Zhejiang Rongda Group Co Ltd	829.85	122.30	952.16
46	State Power Corporation of China	83.82	849.55	933.38
47	Canon (Zhuhai) Co Ltd	642.41	272.85	915.27
48	Shenzhen Mass Storage Equipment Co Ltd	452.17	455.93	908.11

Rank	Name of company	Export value (US$ million)	Import value (US$ million)	Total import & export value (US$ million)
49	Zhejiang Zhongda Group Co Ltd	562.84	312.06	874.90
50	Jinpeng (Shanghai) Co Ltd	363.54	495.31	858.85
51	Haier Group Company	401.52	450.63	852.15
52	Zhenjiang Orient Group Co Ltd	732.65	108.60	841.25
53	Shenzhen Kaifa Technology Co Ltd	438.72	386.52	825.24
54	Intel Technologies (China) Co Ltd	398.75	422.73	821.48
55	China Iron & Steel Industry & Trade Group	355.69	465.12	820.82
56	China North Industries Corporation (NORINCO)	624.34	190.90	815.23
57	Mingshuo Computer (Suzhou) Co Ltd	411.88	397.03	808.91
58	Guangdong Nuclear Power Group Co Ltd	639.07	154.05	793.11
59	Xinmao Technologies (Shenzhen) Co Ltd	481.42	300.39	781.80
60	Jiangsu Kaiyuan Light Industrial Products Import & Export Group Co Ltd	626.22	143.42	769.63
61	Jiangsu Guotai International Group	639.04	118.72	757.75
62	Jiangsu Overseas Group Co Ltd	248.37	503.84	752.21
63	Zhonggu Cereals, Oils & Foodstuffs Group Co	6.14	740.86	746.99
64	Huawei Technologies Co Ltd	124.79	610.46	735.25
65	China Native & Livestock Product Import & Export Co Ltd	439.86	291.45	731.31
66	Jiangsu Shuntian International Group Co Ltd	551.79	177.26	729.05
67	Dongguan International Trade &Development Group Co Ltd	372.59	349.35	721.95
68	Benq Diantong Information Technologies Co Ltd	361.96	324.69	686.64
69	China Worldbest Group Co Ltd	481.92	200.43	682.35
70	Shanghai Light Industrial International (Group) Limited	408.41	271.25	679.67
71	Ericsson & Panda Communication (Nanjing) Co Ltd	147.68	527.21	674.89
72	China National Textiles Import & Export Corp	282.67	387.84	670.51
73	Samsung (Dongguan) Electric & Machinery Co Ltd	415.03	250.24	665.27
74	China Nuclear Energy Industry Corporation	41.26	623.99	665.25
75	Xiamen C&D Corp Ltd	380.60	238.79	619.38
76	Shanghai Donghao International Service Co Ltd	432.24	158.46	590.70
77	Solectron Technology Co Ltd	129.17	459.80	588.96

Rank	Name of company	Export value (US$ million)	Import value (US$ million)	Total import & export value (US$ million)
78	Shanghai Industrial Investment (Group) Co Ltd	184.48	398.69	583.16
79	Dalian Toshiba TV Co Ltd	278.58	302.37	580.95
80	Lucent Technologies Qingdao Telecommunications Systems Ltd	69.46	509.953	578.98
81	Shenzhen Sanyo Huaqiang Laser Electrics Co Ltd	320.73	250.95	571.68
82	Caizhong Computer (Shenzhen) Co Ltd	313.71	250.89	564.60
83	China Great Wall Industry Corporation	263.48	291.07	554.54
84	China National Chemical Industry & Trade Co Ltd	30.48	522.41	552.89
85	Dongfeng Motor Corp	37.68	514.13	551.81
86	Advanced Micro Devices (Suzhou) Ltd	163.15	387.87	551.01
87	Youlidian Electrics (Shenzhen) Co Ltd	314.28	233.29	547.57
88	Tianjing Samsung Electromech. Co Ltd	315.38	231.51	546.88
89	Semiconductor Manufacturing International Corporation	0	546.35	546.35
90	Renbao Computer Industry (China) Co Ltd	310.75	233.76	544.51
91	Beijing Great Wall	0.08	541.19	541.27
92	IBM Shenzhen Co Ltd	273.39	254.55	527.94
93	China National Chemical Construction Corporation	278.10	248.72	526.83
94	China National Agricultural Goods Group Co	8.58	503.73	512.30
95	Foshan Pulihua Technologies Co Ltd	270.31	227.63	497.94
96	Nortel Guangdong Exchange System Co Ltd	10.49	486.48	496.97
97	Nokia Beijing Hangxing Communications System Co Ltd	72.24	419.55	491.79
98	Philips Consumer Electronics Company of Suzhou Ltd	284.99	206.44	491.44
99	China Hengtian Group Co Ltd	151.99	327.45	479.44
100	Jiangsu Sohu International Group Corporation	391.16	82.52	473.68

Appendix 2.2

Official Holidays and Traditional Festivals in China

Li Yong, Deputy Secretary General, China Association of International Trade

Chinese festivals can be divided into two categories. Official festivals commemorate major events such as National Day, which marks the founding of the People's Republic of China, and Youth Day on 4 May, commemorating a major student movement of 80 years ago. The second category is traditional festivals such as Spring Festival, Moon Festival etc. Traditional festivals are part of Chinese culture and have been handed down over thousands of years of history.

Holidays and festivals offer businesses the opportunity to socialize with clients and carry out marketing and public relations campaigns.

Official Chinese festivals

New Year's Day (1 January)
The first day of the Gregorian calendar is not widely celebrated in China as it is overshadowed by the anticipation of Chinese New Year. In business, it is the start of a new financial year. There is a one-day public holiday.

International Women's Day (8 March)
This is a festival for women in China: a time for women to celebrate and advocate sexual equality. Female staff receive a whole or half paid day's leave. There are activities recognizing the contributions made by the Chinese women to the social and economic development of China and marketers also take advantage of this festival to promote their female-orientated products.

Chinese Arbour Day (12 March)
Arbour Day is a relatively recent official day initiated by the central government in 1979. It is not a day off; instead, people are encouraged to plant trees. It is, in effect, an effort to plant more. It is a day to promote awareness of environmental protection, and so now receives more attention than it used to.

International Labour Day (1 May)
Also called May Day. This is a festival commemorating a workers' movement fighting for an eight-hour working day which began in Chicago on 1 May 1886. The working class is seen as the leading force of historical advancement and the Communist Party of China regards itself as part of the working class; therefore this is one of the most celebrated official festivals in China. The government sponsors activities in recognition of the role of workers in constructing the national economy. In September 1999, the State Council decided to extend public holidays for the National Day on 1 October and May Day on 1 May from one to three days. The two weekends before and after May Day are consolidated to make it a week-long holiday. May Day has now become an important holiday and inevitably many marketers have begun to cash in on it.

Chinese Youth Day (4 May)
A day in memory of the first mass student movement in 1919, which protested against the Paris Peace Convention in which the Japanese invasion of Shandong Province was endorsed by Germany. It developed into a political and cultural movement against imperialism and feudalism, embracing western scientific and democratic ideas. This festival is celebrated by young people (normally aged 14–28) and there are government sponsored activities but there is no statutory holiday on this day. Marketers often take this opportunity to launch PR or marketing events targeting young people.

Children's Day (1 June)

The day most celebrated by Chinese children all over the country. Places such as cinemas, parks and children's museums and palaces are open free or at a discount to children and their parents. Parents are often given a half day off to accompany their children. This day is also exploited by marketers as an opportunity to launch campaigns targeted at children. PR events often include donations to primary schools and nurseries.

Anniversary of the founding of the Chinese Communist Party (1 July)

Commemorates the founding of the Chinese Communist Party in 1921 in Shanghai. It is largely a political festival and often a time when important decisions are released.

Army Day (1 August)

Marks the founding of the People's Liberation Army. Non-military bodies often celebrate this day by providing voluntary services to promote donations to the Army. Some marketers take this opportunity to increase the visibility of their corporate image by organising celebration activities which are likely to receive media coverage.

Teacher's Day (10 September)

Started in 1985 as an effort to re-establish the social status of teachers and recognise their contribution to education. On this day, teachers often enjoy special discounts on products and services.

National Day (1 October)

A day that marks the anniversary of the founding of the People's Republic of China in 1949. There is a tradition of grand celebrations every tenth anniversary and lesser ones every fifth anniversary. Years other than the fifth and tenth are usually marked by simple celebrations such as symbolic public gatherings and parties. All government and business organisations have a statutory three-day holiday, which again combines the two weekends before and after the holiday to make the National Holiday last a week. Like May Day, the National Day is the second long holiday in the year seen by marketers as an important opportunity to promote their products and services.

Traditional festivals

The Chinese traditional festivals follow a unique lunar-calendar system, which differs from the Gregorian Calendar.

Spring Festival (the first day of the first lunar month)

The Spring Festival is also known as the Chinese New Year or Lunar New Year. To Chinese people, the Spring Festival is the most important festive occasion of all, comparable to Christmas Day in the west. The Spring Festival is considered to be the real start of the New Year. It symbolizes the arrival of spring and a fresh start. Members of a family, no matter where they are, will come home on the eve of the Lunar New Year and get together around the dinner table to enjoy the richest last meal of the year, the 'family reunion dinner'. It is also an occasion on which people visit friends and relatives giving greetings of the new year, and giving gifts. As with the National Day and May Day, there is a three-day statutory holiday, made into a week long holiday by swapping the two weekends before and after the Spring Festival. Some businesses may allow longer holidays for their staff depending on circumstances. Marketers at this time often target gift-giving requirements.

Lantern Festival (15th day of the first lunar month)

Also known as Yuanxiao Festival. It is commonly celebrated, although the type of celebration varies from place to place. Lantern exhibits, lion and dragon dances and flower fairs are just some examples. Instead of the dumplings eaten during Spring Festival, people typically eat Yuan Xiao in Northern China, or Tang Yuan in the south – ball-shaped sticky rice dumplings with a delicious stuffing. The round shape of Yuan Xiao or Tang Yuan is a symbol of perfection and of the union of family members. The Spring Festival atmosphere does not really come to an end until this day.

Qing Ming Festival (fifth day of the fourth lunar month)

A day when families commemorate their departed members or ancestors as part of the Chinese filial custom. Cleaning up tombs and presenting tributes (normally fruit and the favourite food of the departed) are the key events of the day.

Duan Wu (Dragon Boat) Festival (fifth day of the fifth lunar month)

This festival commemorates a great patriotic poet, Qu Yuan (340–278 BC), who drowned himself in protest at the corrupt emperor who sent him into exile and eventually caused the perdition of the State of Chu, Qu Yuan's beloved country. People who adored Qu Yuan went out on the boat in search of his body and threw Zongzi (sticky rice dumplings wrapped in reed or bamboo leaves) into the river in an attempt to protect his body from being eaten by fish. In some places there is a dragon boat contest to commemorate the day and Zongzi is eaten.

Mid-Autumn Festival (15th day of the eighth lunar month)
The mid-autumn festival takes place at a time when the moon is at its fullest. There are several fairy tales about the origin of the festival. People now celebrate the day as a time for family reunion. Those who cannot get together on the day will meet by looking at the moon. Eating moon cake and appreciating the roundness and clarity of the moon is the main event of the festival. Again, the round shape of moon cake indicates perfection and family union. Moon cakes are frequently given as presents during the festival: the gift of moon cake has been a custom for thousands of years.

Appendix 3.1

Contract Law of the People's Republic of China

Effective Date: 1 October 1999

Chapter 1: General Provisions

Article 1 This Law is formulated with a view to protecting the lawful rights and interests of the parties to contracts, maintaining the social economic order and promoting the progress of the socialist modernization drive.

Article 2 A contract in this Law refers to an agreement establishing, modifying and terminating the civil rights and obligations between subjects of equal footing, that is, between natural persons, legal persons or other organizations.

Agreements involving personal status relationship such as on matrimony, adoption, guardianship etc shall apply the provisions of other Laws.

Article 3 The parties to a contract shall have equal legal status. No party may impose its will on the other party.

Article 4 The parties shall have the rights to be voluntary to enter into a contract in accordance with the law. No unit or individual may illegally interfere.

Article 5 The parties shall abide by the principle of fairness in defining the rights and obligations of each party.

Article 6 The parties must act in accordance with the principle of good faith, no matter in exercising rights or in performing obligations.

Article 7 In concluding and performing a contract, the parties shall abide by the laws and administrative regulations, observe social ethics. Neither party may disrupt the socio-economic order or damage the public interests.

Article 8 As soon as a contract is established in accordance with the law, it shall be legally binding on the parties. The parties shall perform their respective obligations in accordance with the terms of the contract. Neither party may unilaterally modify or rescind the contract.

The contract established according to law shall be under the protection of law.

Chapter 2: Conclusion Of Contracts

Article 9 In concluding a contract, the parties shall have appropriate civil capacity of right and civil capacity of conduct.

The parties may conclude a contract through an agent in accordance with the law.

Article 10 The parties may conclude a contract in written, oral or other forms.

Where the laws or administrative regulations require a contract to be concluded in written form, the contract shall be in written form. If the parties agree to do so, the contract shall be concluded in written form.

Article 11 The written forms mean the forms which can show the described contents visibly, such as a written contractual agreement, letters and data-telex (including telegram, telex, fax, EDI and e-mails).

Article 12 The contents of a contract shall be agreed upon by the parties, and shall contain the following clauses in general:

1. title or name and domicile of the parties;
2. contract object;
3. quantity;
4. quality;
5. price or remuneration;
6. time limit, place and method of performance;
7. liability for breach of contract; and
8. methods to settle disputes.

The parties may conclude a contract by reference to the model text of each kind of contract.

Article 13 The parties shall conclude a contract in the form of an offer and acceptance.

Article 14 An offer is a proposal hoping to enter into a contract with other parties. The proposal shall comply with the following stipulations:

1. Its contents shall be detailed and definite;
2. It indicates the proposal of the offeror to be bound in case of acceptance.

Article 15 An invitation for offer is a proposal for requesting other parties to make offers to the principal. Price forms mailed, public notices of auction and tender, prospectuses and commercial advertisements, etc are invitations for offer.

Where the contents of a commercial advertisement comply with the terms of the offer, it may be regarded as an offer.

Article 16 An offer becomes effective when it reaches the offeree.

If a contract is concluded by means of data-telex, and a recipient appoints a specific system to receive the data-telex, the time when the data-telex enters the system shall be the time of arrival; if no specific system is appointed, the time when the data-telex first enters any of the recipient's systems shall be regarded as the time of arrival.

Article 17 An offer may be withdrawn, if the withdrawal notice reaches the offeree before or at the same time when the offer arrives.

Article 18 An offer may be revoked, if the revocation reaches the offeree before it has dispatched an acceptance.

Article 19 An offer may not be revoked, if

1. the offeror indicates a fixed time for acceptance or otherwise explicitly states that the offer is irrevocable; or
2. the offeree has reasons to rely on the offer as being irrevocable and has made preparation for performing the contract.

Article 20 An offer shall be null and void under any of the following circumstances:

1. The notice of rejection reaches the offeror;
2. The offeror revokes its offer in accordance with the law;
3. The offeree fails to make an acceptance at the time when the time limit for acceptance expires;
4. The offeree substantially alters the contents of the offer.

Article 21 An acceptance is a statement made by the offeree indicating assent to an offer.

Article 22 Except that it is based on transaction practices or that the offer indicates an acceptance may be made by performing an act, the acceptance shall be made by means of notice.

Article 23 An acceptance shall reach the offeror within the time limit fixed in the offer.

Where no time limit is fixed in the offer, the acceptance shall arrive in accordance with the following provisions:

1. If the offer is made in dialogues, the acceptance shall be made immediately except as otherwise agreed upon by the parties;
2. If the offer is made in forms other than a dialogue, the acceptance shall arrive within a reasonable period of time.

Article 24 Where the offer is made in a letter or a telegram, the time limit for acceptance commences from the date shown in the letter or from the moment the telegram is handed in for dispatch. If no such date is shown in the letter, it commences from the date shown on the envelope. Where an offer is made by means of instantaneous communication, such as telephone or facsimile, the time limit for acceptance commences from the moment that the offer reaches the offeree.

Article 25 A contract is established when the acceptance becomes effective.

Article 26 An acceptance becomes effective when its notice reaches the offeror. If an acceptance needn't be notified, it becomes effective when an act of acceptance is performed in accordance with transaction practices or as required in the offer.

Where a contract is concluded in the form of data-telex, the time when an acceptance arrives shall apply the provisions of Paragraph 2, Article 16 of this Law.

Article 27 An acceptance may be withdrawn, but a notice of withdrawal shall reach the offeror before the notice of acceptance reaches the offeror or at the same time when the acceptance reaches the offeror.

Article 28 Where an offeree makes an acceptance beyond the time limit for acceptance, the acceptance shall be a new offer except that the offeror informs the offeree of the effectiveness of the said acceptance promptly.

Article 29 If the offeree dispatches the acceptance within the time limit for acceptance which can reach the offeror in due time under normal circumstances, but the acceptance reaches the offeror beyond the time limit because of other reasons, the acceptance shall be effective, except that, the offeror informs the offeree promptly that it does not accept the acceptance because it exceeds the time limit for acceptance.

Article 30 The contents of an acceptance shall comply with those of the offer. If the offeree substantially modifies the contents of the offer, it shall constitute a new offer. The modification relating to the contract object, quality, quantity, price or remuneration, time or place or method of performance, liabilities for breach of contract and the settlement of disputes, etc, shall constitute the substantial modification of an offer.

Article 31 If the acceptance does not substantially modifies the contents of the offer, it shall be effective, and the contents of the contract shall be subject to those of the acceptance, except as rejected promptly by the offeror or indicated in the offer that an acceptance may not modify the offer at all.

Article 32 Where the parties conclude a contract in written form, the contract is established when both parties sign or affix a seal on it.

Article 33 Where the parties conclude the contract in the form of a letter or data-telex, etc, one party may request to sign a letter of confirmation before the conclusion of the contract. The contract shall be established at the time when the letter of confirmation is signed.

Article 34 The place of effectiveness of an acceptance shall be the place of the establishment of the contract.

If the contract is concluded in the form of data-telex, the main business place of the recipient shall be the place of establishment. If no main business place, its habitual residence shall be considered to be the place of establishment. Where the parties agree otherwise, the place of establishment shall be subject to that agreement.

Article 35 Where the parties conclude a contract in written form, the place where both parties sign or affix a seal shall be the place where the contract is established.

Article 36 A contract, which shall be concluded in written form as provided for by the laws and administrative regulations or as agreed upon by the parties, shall be established, as the parties do not use the written form, but one party has performed the principal obligation and the other party has received it.

Article 37 A contract, which is concluded in written form, shall be eslablished, if one party has performed its principal obligation and the other party has received it before signature or affixing with a seal.

Article 38 In case the State issues a mandatory plan or a State purchasing order task based on necessity, the relevant legal persons or other organizations shall conclude contracts between them in accordance with the rights and obligations as stipulated by the relevant laws and administrative regulations.

Article 39 Where standard terms are adopted in concluding a contract, the party which supplies the standard terms shall define the rights and obligations between the parties abiding by the principle of fairness, request the other party to note the exclusion or restriction of its liabilities in reasonable ways, and explain the standard terms according to the requirement of the other party.

Standard terms are clauses which are prepared in advance for general and repeated use by one party and which are not negotiatied with the other party in concluding a contract.

Article 40 When standard terms are under the circumstances stipulated in Article 52 and Article 53 of this Law, or the party which supplies the standard terms exempts itself from its liabilities, weights the liabilities of the other party, and excludes the rights of the other party, the terms shall be null and void.

Article 41 If a dispute over the understanding of the standard terms occurs, it shall be interpreted according to general understanding. Where there are two or more kinds of interpretation, an interpretation unfavourable to the party supplying the standard terms shall be preferred. Where the standard terms are inconsistent with non-standard terms, the latter shall be adopted.

Article 42 The party shall be liable for damages if it is under one of the following circumstances in concluding a contract and thus causing losses to the other party:

1. disguising and pretending to conclude a contract, and negotiating in bad faith;
2. concealing deliberately the important facts relating to the conclusion of the contract or providing deliberately false information;
3. performing other acts which violate the principle of good faith.

Article 43 A business secret the parties learn in concluding a contract shall not be disclosed or unfairly used, no matter the contract is established or not. The party who causes the other party to suffer from losses due to disclosing or unfairly using the business secret shall be liable for damages.

Chapter 3: Effectiveness Of Contracts

Article 44 The contract established according to law becomes effective when it is established.

With regard to contracts which are subject to approval or registration as provided for by the laws or administrative regulations, the provisions thereof shall be followed.

Article 45 The parties may agree on some collateral conditions relating to the effectiveness of a contract. The contract with entry-into-force conditions shall be effective when such conditions are accomplished. The contract with dissolving conditions shall be null and void when such conditions are accomplished.

To unfairly prevent the conditions from being accomplished by one party for its own interests shall be regarded as those conditions have been accomplished. To unfairly promoting the accomplishment of such conditions by one party shall be regarded as non-accomplishment.

Article 46 The parties may agree on a conditional time period as to the effectiveness of the contract. A contract subject to an effective time period shall come into force when the period expires. A contract with termination time period shall become invalid when the period expires.

Article 47 A contract concluded by a person with limited civil capacity of conduct shall be effective after being ratified afterwards by the person's statutory agent, but a pure profit-making contract or a contract concluded which is appropriate to the person's age, intelligence or mental health conditions need not be ratified by the person's statutory agent.

The counterpart may urge the statutory agent to ratify the contract within one month. It shall be regarded as a refusal of ratification that the statutory agent does not make any expression. A bona fide counterpart has the right to withdraw it before the contract is ratified. The withdrawal shall be made by means of notice.

Article 48 A contract concluded by an actor who has no power of agency, who oversteps the power of agency, or whose power of agency has expired and yet concludes it on behalf of the principal, shall have no legally binding force on the principal without ratification by the principal, and the actor shall be held liable.

The counterpart may urge the principal to ratify it within one month. It shall be regarded as a refusal of ratification that the principal does not make any expression. A bona fide counterpart has the right to withdraw it before the contract is ratified. The withdrawal shall be made by means of notice.

Article 49 If an actor has no power of agency, oversteps the power of agency, or the power of agency has expired and yet concludes a contract in the principal's name, and the counterpart has reasons to trust that the actor has the power of agency, the act of agency shall be effective.

Article 50 Where a statutory representative or a responsible person of a legal person or other organization oversteps his/her power and concludes a contract, the representative act shall be effective except that the counterpart knows or ought to know that he/she is overstepping his/her powers.

Article 51 Where a person having no right to disposal of property disposes of other persons' properties, and the principal ratifies the act afterwards or the person without power of disposal has obtained the power after concluding a contract, the contract shall be valid.

Article 52 A contract shall be null and void under any of the following circumstances:

1. A contract is concluded through the use of fraud or coercion by one party to damage the interests of the State;
2. Malicious collusion is conducted to damage the interests of the State, a collective or a third party;
3. An illegitimate purpose is concealed under the guise of legitimate acts;
4. Damaging the public interests;
5. Violating the compulsory provisions of the laws and administrative regulations.

Article 53 The following immunity clauses in a contract shall be null and void:

1. those that cause personal injury to the other party;
2. those that cause property damages to the other party as a result of deliberate intent or gross fault.

Article 54 A party shall have the right to request the people's court or an arbitration institution to modify or revoke the following contracts:

1. those concluded as a result of serious misunderstanding;
2. those that are obviously unfair at the time when concluding the contract.

If a contract is concluded by one party against the other party's true intentions through the use of fraud, coercion or exploitation of the other party's unfavourable position, the injured party shall have the right to request the people's court or an arbitration institution to modify or revoke it.

Where a party requests for modification, the people's court or the arbitration institution may not revoke the contract.

Article 55 The right to revoke a contract shall extinguish under any of the following circumstances:

1. A party having the right to revoke the contract fails to exercise the right within one year from the day that it knows or ought to know the revoking causes;
2. A party having the right to revoke the contract explicitly expresses or conducts an act to waive the right after it knows the revoking causes.

Article 56 A contract that is null and void or revoked shall have no legally binding force ever from the very beginning. If part of a contract is null and void without affecting the validity of the other parts, the other parts shall still be valid.

Article 57 If a contract is null and void, revoked or terminated, it shall not affect the validity of the dispute settlement clause which is independently existing in the contract.

Article 58 The property acquired as a result of a contract shall be returned after the contract is confirmed to be null and void or has been revoked; where the property can not be returned or the return is unnecessary, it shall be reimbursed at its estimated price. The party at fault shall compensate the other party for losses incurred as a result therefrom. If both parties are at fault, each party shall respectively be liable.

Article 59 If the parties have maliciously conducted collusion to damage the interests of the State, a collective or a third party, the property thus acquired shall be turned over to the State or returned to the collective or the third party.

Chapter 4: Performance Of Contracts

Article 60 The parties shall perform their obligations thoroughly according to the terms of the contract.

The parties shall abide by the principle of good faith and perform the obligations of notice, assistance and maintaining confidentiality, etc based on the character and purpose of the contract or the transaction practices.

Article 61 Where, after the contract becomes effective, there is no agreement in the contract between the parties on the terms regarding quality, price or remuneration and place of performance, etc or such agreement is unclear, the parties may agree upon supplementary terms through consultation. In case of a failure in doing so, the terms shall be determined from the context of relevant clauses of the contract or by transaction practices.

Article 62 If the relevant terms of a contract are unclear, nor can it be determined according to the provisions of Article 61 of this Law, the provisions below shall be applied:

1. If quality requirements are unclear, the State standards or trade standards shall be applied; if there are no State standards or trade standards, generally held standards or specific standards in conformity with the purpose of the contract shall be applied.
2. If the price or remuneration is unclear, the market price of the place of performance at the time concluding the contract shall be applied; if the government-fixed price or government-directed price shall be followed in accordance with the law, the provisions of the law shall be applied.
3. If the place of performance is unclear, and the payment is currency, the performance shall be effected at the place of location of the party receiving the payment; if real estate is to be delivered, the performance shall be effected at the place of location of the real estate; in case of other contract objects, the performance shall be effected at the place of location of the party fulfilling the obligations.
4. If the time limit for performance is unclear, the obligor may at any time fulfil the obligations towards the obligee; the obligee may also demand at any time that the obligor performs the obligations, but a time period for necessary preparation shall be given to the obligor.
5. If the method of performance is unclear, the method which is advantageous to realize the purpose of the contract shall be adopted.
6. If the burden of the expenses of performance is unclear, the cost shall be assumed by the obligor.

Article 63 In cases where the government-fixed price or government- directed price is followed in a contract, if the said price is readjusted within the time limit for delivery as stipulated in the contract, the payment shall be calculated according to the price at the time of delivery. If the delivery of the object is delayed and the price has risen, the original price shall be adopted; while the price has dropped, the new price shall be adopted. In the event of delay in taking delivery of the object or late payment, if the price has risen, the new price shall be adopted; while the price has dropped, the original price shall be adopted.

Article 64 Where the parties agree that the obligor performs the obligations to a third party, and the obligor fails to perform the obligations to the third party or the performance does not meet the terms of the contract, the obligor shall be liable to the obligee for the breach of contract.

Article 65 Where the parties agree that a third party performs the obligations to the obligee, and the third party fails to perform the obligations or the performance does not meet the terms of the contract, the obligor shall be liable to the obligee for the breach of contract.

Article 66 If both parties have obligations towards each other and there is no order of priority in respect of the performance of obligations, the parties shall perform the obligations simultaneously. One party has the right to reject the other party's request for performance before the other party's performance. One party has the right to reject the other party's corresponding request for performance if the other party's performance does not meet the terms of the contract.

Article 67 Where both parties have obligations towards each other and there has been an order of priority in respect of the performance, and the party which shall render its performance first has not rendered the performance, the party which may render its performance lately has the right to reject the other party's request for performance. Where the party which shall render its performance first violates the terms of a contract while fulfilling the obligations, the party which may render its performance lately has the right to reject the other party's corresponding request for performance.

Article 68 One party, which shall render its performance first, may suspend its performance, if it has conclusive evidence that the other party is under any of the following circumstances:

1. Its business conditions are seriously deteriorating;
2. It moves away its property and takes out its capital secretly to evade debt;
3. It loses its commercial credibility;
4. Other circumstances showing that it loses or is possible to lose the capacity of credit.

Where a party suspends performance of a contract without conclusive evidence, it shall be liable for the breach of contract.

Article 69 One party to a contract which suspends its performance of the contract in accordance with the provisions of Article 68 of this Law, shall promptly inform the other party of such suspension. It shall resume its performance of the contract when the other party provides a sure guarantee. After the suspension of the performance, if the other party does not reinstate its capacity of performance and does not provide with a sure guarantee, the party suspending performance of the contract may rescind the contract.

Article 70 If the obligee does not notify the obligor its separation, merger or a change of its domicile so as to make it difficult for the obligor to perform the obligations, the obligor may suspend the performance of the contract or have the object deposited.

Article 71 The obligee may reject an advance performance of the contract by the obligor, except that the advance performance does not damage the interests of the obligee.

Additional expenses caused to the obligee by advance performance shall be borne by the obligor.

Article 72 The obligee may reject the partial performance of the contract by the obligor, except that the partial performance does not damage the interests of the obligee.

Additional expenses caused to the obligee by partial performance shall be borne by the obligor.

Article 73 If the obligor is indolent in exercising its due creditor's right, thus damaging the interests of the obligee, the obligee may request the people's court for subrogation in its own name, except that the creditor's right exclusively belongs to the obligor.

The subrogation shall be exercised within the scope of the creditor's right of the obligee. The necessary expenses caused to the obligee by exercising subrogation shall be borne by the obligor.

Article 74 If the obligor renounces its due creditor's right or transfers its property gratis, thus damaging the interests of the obligee, the obligee may request the people's court to revoke the obligor's act. If the obligor transfers its property at an obviously unreasonable low price, thus damaging the interests of the obligee, and the transferee knows such situation, the obligee may request the people's court to revoke the obligor's act.

The right of revocation shall be exercised within the scope of the creditor's right of the obligee. The necessary expenses caused to the obligee by exercising the right of revocation shall be borne by the obligor.

Article 75 The time limit for exercising the right of revocation shall be one year, commencing from the day when the obligee is aware or ought to be aware of the causes of revocation. If the right of revocation has not been exercised within five years from the day when the act of the obligor takes place, the right of revocation shall be extinguished.

Article 76 After a contract becomes effective, the parties may not reject to perform the obligations of the contract because of modification of the title or name of the parties, or change of the statutory representative, the responsible person or the executive person of the parties.

Chapter 5: Modification And Assignment Of Contracts

Article 77 A contract may be modified if the parties reach a consensus through consultation.

If the laws or administrative regulations stipulate that a contract shall be modified through the procedures of approval or registration, such provisions shall be followed.

Article 78 If the contents of the modified contract agreed by the parties are unclear, it shall be presumed that the contract is not modified.

Article 79 The obligee may assign, wholly or in part, its rights under the contract to a third party, except for the following circumstances:

1. The rights under the contract may not be assigned according to the character of the contract;
2. The rights under the contract may not be assigned according to the agreement between the parties;
3. The rights under the contract may not be assigned according to the provisions of the laws.

Article 80 An obligee assigning its rights shall notify the obligor. Without notifying the obligor, the assignment shall not become effective to the obligor.

The notice of assignment of rights may not be revoked, unless the assignee agrees thereupon.

Article 81 If the obligee assigns its rights, the assignee shall acquire the collateral rights relating to the principal rights, except that the collateral rights exclusively belong to the obligee.

Article 82 After the obligor receives the notice of assignment of the creditor's rights, it may claim its demur in respect of the assignor to the assignee.

Article 83 When the obligor receives the notice of assignment of the creditor's rights, and the obligor has due creditor's rights to the assign or, and the creditor's rights of the obligor are due in priority to the assigned creditor's rights or due at the same time, the obligor may claim to offset each other to the assignee.

Article 84 If the obligor assigns its obligations, wholly or in part, to a third party, it shall obtain consent from the obligee first.

Article 85 If the obligor assigns its obligations to a third party, the new obligor may claim the demur belonging to the original obligor in respect of the obligee.

Article 86 If the obligor assigns its obligations to a third party, the new obligor shall assume the collateral obligations relating to the principal obligations, except that the obligations exclusively belong to the original obligor.

Article 87 Where the laws or administrative regulations stipulate that the assignment of rights or transfer of obligations shall go through approval or registration procedures, such provisions shall be followed.

Article 88 One party to a contract may assign its rights and obligations under the contract together to a third party with the consent of the other party.

Article 89 If one party to a contract assigns its rights and obligations under the contract together to a third party, the provisions of Article 79, Articles 81 to 83, and Articles 85 to 87 of this Law shall be applied.

Article 90 If one party to a contract is merged after the contract has been concluded, the legal person or other organization established after the merger shall exercise the contract rights and perform the contract obligations. If one party is separated after the contract has been concluded, the legal persons or other organizations thus established after the separation shall exercise the contract rights or assume the contract obligations jointly and severally.

Chapter 6: Termination Of The Rights And Obligations Of Contracts

Article 91 The rights and obligations of contracts shall be terminated under any of the following circumstances:

1. The debt obligations have been performed in accordance with the terms of the contract;
2. The contract has been rescinded;
3. The debts have been offset against each other;
4. The obligor has deposited the object according to law;
5. The debt obligations have been exempted by the obligee;
6. The creditor's rights and debt obligations are assumed by the same person; or
7. Other circumstances for termination as stipulated by the laws or agreed upon by the parties in the contract.

Article 92 When the rights and obligations of contracts are terminated, the parties to a contract shall, abiding by the principle of good faith, perform such obligations as making a notice, providing assistance and maintaining confidentiality according to transaction practices.

Article 93 A contract may be rescinded if the parties to the contract reach a consensus through consultation.

The parties to a contract may agree upon the conditions to rescind the contract by one party. When such conditions are accompanied, the party entitled to rescind the contract may rescind it.

Article 94 The parties to a contract may rescind the contract under any of the following circumstances:

1. The purpose of the contract is not able to be realized because of force majeure;
2. One party to the contract expresses explicitly or indicates through its acts, before the expiry of the performance period, that it will not perform the principal debt obligations;
3. One party to the contract delays in performing the principal debt obligations and fails, after being urged, to perform them within a reasonable time period;
4. One party to the contract delays in performing the debt obligations or commits other acts in breach of the contract so that the purpose of the contract is not able to be realized; or

5. Other circumstances as stipulated by law.

Article 95 Where the laws stipulate or the parties agree upon the time limit to exercise the right to rescind the contract, and no party exercises it when the time limit expires, the said right shall be extinguished.

Where the law does not stipulate or the parties make no agreement upon the time limit to exercise the right to rescind the contract, and no party exercises it within a reasonable time period after being urged, the said right shall be extinguished.

Article 96 One party to a contract shall make a notice to the other party if it advances to rescind the contract according to the provisions of Paragraph 2, Article 93 and Article 94 of this Law. The contract shall be rescinded upon the arrival of the notice at the other party. The party may, if the other party disagrees therewith, request the people's court or an arbitration institution to confirm the effectiveness of rescinding the contract.

Where the laws or administrative regulations stipulate that the rescinding of a contract shall go through the formalities of approval and registration, the provisions thereof shall be followed.

Article 97 If a contract has not yet been performed, its performance shall be terminated after the rescission. If it has been performed, a party to the contract may, in light of the performance and the character of the contract, request that the original status be restored or other remedial measures be taken.

Article 98 The termination of the rights and obligations of a contract may not affect the force of the settlement and clearance clauses in the contract.

Article 99 Where the parties to a contract have debts due mutually and the category and character of the debts are the same, any party may offset his debt against the other's one, except that the debts may not be offset according to the provisions of the laws or to the character of the contract.

Any party advancing to offset the debts shall make a notice to the other party. Such notice shall be effective upon the arrival at the other party. The offset may not be accompanied by any conditions or time limit.

Article 100 Where the parties to a contract have debts due mutually and the category and character of the debts are different, the debts may be offset against each other if both parties have reached a consensus through consultation.

Article 101 The obligor may deposit the object if the debt obligations are difficult to be performed under any of the following circumstances:

1. The obligee refuses to accept them without justified reasons;
2. The obligee is missing;
3. The obligee is deceased and the heir is not yet determined, or the obligee has lost his conduct capacity and the guardian is not yet determined; or
4. Other circumstances as stipulated by law.

If the object is not fit to be deposited or the deposit expenses are excessively high, the obligor may, according to law, auction or sell the object and deposit the money obtained therefrom.

Article 102 After the object is deposited, the obligor shall, except that the obligee is missing, make a notice promptly to the obligee or the obligee's heir or guardian.

Article 103 The risk of damage to and missing of the object after being deposited shall be borne by the obligee. During the period of depositing, the fruits generated by the object shall belong to the obligee. The deposit expenses shall be borne by the obligee.

Article 104 The obligee may claim the deposited object at any time. However, if the obligee is under a debt due to the obligor the deposit authorities shall refuse him to claim the deposited object at the request of the obligor, before the obligee has performed his debt obligations or provides a guaranty.

The right to claim the deposited object by the obligee shall be extinguished if it has not been exercised within five years as of the date of deposit. The deposited object shall be owned by the State with deduction of the deposit expenses.

Article 105 If the obligee exempts the obligor from the debt obligations wholly or in part, the whole or part of the rights and obligations of a contract shall be terminated.

Article 106 If the creditor's rights and debt obligations are assumed by the same person, the rights and obliga-

tions of a contract shall be terminated, except for those involving the interests of a third party.

Chapter 7: Liability For Breach Of Contracts

Article 107 Where one party to a contract fails to perform the contract obligations or its performance fails to satisfy the terms of the contract, the party shall bear such liabilities for breach of contract as to continue to perform its obligations, to take remedial measures, or to compensate for losses.

Article 108 Where one party to a contract expresses explicitly or indicates through its acts that it will not perform the contract, the other party may demand it to bear the liability for the breach of contract before the expiry of the performance period.

Article 109 If one party to a contract fails to pay the price or remuneration, the other party may request it to make the payment.

Article 110 Where one party to a contract fails to perform the non- monetary debt or its performance of non-monetary debt fails to satisfy the terms of the contract, the other party may request it to perform it except under any of the following circumstances:

1. It is unable to be performed in law or in fact;
2. The object of the debt is unfit for compulsory performance or the performance expenses are excessively high; or
3. The creditor fails to request for the performance within a reasonable time period.

Article 111 If the quality fails to satisfy the terms of the contract, the breach of contract damages shall be borne according to the terms of the contract agreed upon by the parties. If there is no agreement in the contract on the liability for breach of contract or such agreement is unclear, nor can it be determined in accordance with the provisions of Article 61 of this Law, the damaged party may, in light of the character of the object and the degree of losses, reasonably choose to request the other party to bear the liabilities for the breach of contract such as repairing, substituting, reworking, returning the goods, or reducing the price or remuneration.

Article 112 Where one party to a contract fails to perform the contract obligations or its performance fails to satisfy the terms of the contract, the party shall, after performing its obligations or taking remedial measures, compensate for the losses, if the other party suffers from other losses.

Article 113 Where one party to a contract fails to perform the contract obligations or its performance fails to satisfy the terms of the contract and causes losses to the other party, the amount of compensation for losses shall be equal to the losses caused by the breach of contract, including the interests receivable after the performance of the contract, provided not exceeding the probable losses caused by the breach of contract which has been foreseen or ought to be foreseen when the party in breach concludes the contract.

The business operator who commits default activities in providing to the consumer any goods or service shall be liable for paying compensation for damages in accordance with the Law of the People's Republic of China on the Protection of Consumer Rights and Interests.

Article 114 The parties to a contract may agree that one party shall, when violating the contract, pay breach of contract damages of a certain amount in light of the breach, or may agree upon the calculating method of compensation for losses resulting from the breach of contract.

If the agreed breach of contract damages are lower than the losses caused, any party may request the people's court or an arbitration institution to increase it; if it is excessively higher than the losses caused, any party may request the people's court or an arbitration institution to make an appropriate reduction.

If the parties to a contract agree upon breach of contract damages in respect to the delay in performance, the party in breach shall perform the debt obligations after paying the breach of contract damages.

Article 115 The parties to a contract may, according to the Guaranty Law of the People's Republic of China, agree that one party pays a deposit to the other party as the guaranty for the creditor's rights. After the debt obligations are performed by the obligor, the deposit shall be returned or offset against the price. If the party that pays the deposit fails to perform the agreed debt obligations, it shall have no right to reclaim the deposit. If the party that receives the deposit fails to perform the agreed debt obligations, it shall return twice the amount of the deposit.

Article 116 Where the parties to a contract agree on both breach of contract damages and a deposit, when one party violates the contract, the other party may choose to apply the breach of contract damages clause or the deposit clause.

Article 117 In case that a contract is not able to be performed because of force majeure, the liabilities shall be exempted in part or wholly in light of the effects of force majeure, except as otherwise stipulated by law. If the force majeure occurs after one party has delayed in performance, the liability may not be exempted.

Force majeure as referred to in this Law means the objective circumstances that are unforeseeable, unavoidable and insurmountable.

Article 118 One party to a contract that is not able to perform the contract because of force majeure shall make a notice to the other party promptly so as to reduce the probable losses to the other party and provide evidence within a reasonable time limit.

Article 119 After one party violates a contract, the other party shall take proper measures to prevent from the enlargement of losses; if the other party fails to take proper measures so that the losses are enlarged, it may not claim any compensation as to the enlarged losses.

The reasonable expenses paid by the party to prevent the enlargement of losses shall be borne by the party in breach.

Article 120 In case that both parties violate a contract, they shall bear the liabilities respectively.

Article 121 One party that violates the contract because of a third party shall be liable for the breach of contract to the other party. The disputes between the said party and the third party shall be settled according to law or their agreement.

Article 122 In case that the breach of contract by one party infringes upon the other party's personal or property rights, the aggrieved party shall be entitled to choose to claim the assumption by the violating and infringing party of liabilities for breach of contract according to this Law, or to claim the assumption by the violating and infringing party of liabilities for infringement according to other laws.

Chapter 8: Miscellaneous Provisions

Article 123 If there are provisions as otherwise stipulated in respect to contracts in other laws, such provisions shall be followed.

Article 124 Any contract which is not addressed explicitly in the Specific Provisions of this Law or in other laws shall apply the provisions of the General Provisions of this Law. The most similar provisions in the Specific Provisions of this Law or in other laws may be applied mutatis mutandis.

Article 125 With regard to disputes between the parties to a contract arising from the understanding of any clause of the contract, the true intention of such clause shall be determined according to the terms and expressions used in the contract, the contents of the relevant clauses of the contract, the purpose for concluding the contract, the transaction practices and the principle of good faith.

Where two or more languages are adopted in the text of a contract and it is agreed that both texts are equally authentic, it shall be presumed that the terms and expressions in various versions have the same meaning. In case that the terms and expressions in different versions are inconsistent, they shall be interpreted according to the purpose of the contract.

Article 126 The parties to a contract involving foreign interests may choose the law applicable to the settlement of their contract disputes, except as otherwise stipulated by law. If the parties to a contract involving foreign interests have not made a choice, the law of the country to which the contract is most closely connected shall be applied.

The contracts for Chinese-foreign equity joint ventures, for Chinese-foreign contractual joint ventures and for Chinese-foreign cooperative exploration and development of natural resources to be performed within the territory of the People's Republic of China shall apply the laws of the People's Republic of China.

Article 127 The departments of administration for industry and commerce and other competent departments shall, within the scope of their respective competence and functions, be responsible for supervision over and dealing with illegal acts in taking advantage of contracts to endanger and harm the State interests and public interests. In case that a crime is constituted, criminal responsibility shall be investigated.

Article 128 The parties may settle their disputes relevant to the contract through conciliation or mediation.

The parties may, if unwilling to settle their disputes through conciliation or mediation or failing in the conciliation or mediation, apply to an arbitration institution for arbitration according to their arbitration agreement. The parties to a contract involving foreign interests may, according to their arbitration agreement, apply for arbitration to a Chinese arbitration institution or other arbitration institutions. If there is no arbitration agreement between the parties or the arbitration agreement is null and void, they may bring a lawsuit before the people's court. The parties shall perform the court judgements, arbitration awards or mediation documents with legal effectiveness. In case any refusal in respect to the performance, the other party may request the people's court for execution.

Article 129 The time limit for action before the people's court or for arbitration before an arbitration institution regarding disputes relating to contracts for international sales of goods and contracts for technology import and export shall be four years, calculating from the date on which the party knows or ought to know the infringement on its rights. The time limits for action before the people's court or for arbitration before an arbitration institution regarding other contracts disputes shall be in accordance with the provisions of the relevant laws.

Article 130 A sales contract is a contract whereby the seller transfers the ownership of an object to the buyer and the buyer pays the price for it.

Article 131 Other than those as stipulated in Article 12 of this Law, a sales contract may also contain such clauses as package manner, inspection standards and method, method of settlement and clearance, language adopted in the contract and its authenticity.

Article 132 An object to be sold shall be owned by the seller or of that the seller is entitled to dispose.

Where the transfer of an object is prohibited or restricted by the laws and administrative regulations, the provisions thereof shall be followed.

Article 133 The ownership of an object shall be transferred upon the delivery of the object, except as otherwise stipulated by law or agreed upon by the parties.

Article 134 The parties to a sales contract may agree that the ownership shall belong to the seller if the buyer fails to pay the price or perform other obligations.

Article 135 The seller shall perform the obligation to deliver to the buyer the object or the documents to take delivery of the object, and to transfer the ownership of the object.

Article 136 The seller shall, according to the terms of the contract or transaction practices, deliver to the buyer relevant documents and materials other than the documents to take delivery of the object.

Article 137 When an object such as computer software with intellectual property rights is sold, the intellectual property rights of such object shall not belong to the buyer except as otherwise stipulated by law or agreed upon by the parties.

Article 138 The seller shall deliver the object according to the agreed time limit. If a time limit of delivery is agreed upon, the seller may deliver at any time within the said time limit.

Article 139 Where there is no agreement in the contract between the parties as to the time limit to deliver the object or such agreement is unclear, the provisions of Article 61 and Sub-Paragraph (4), Article 62 of this Law shall be applied.

Article 140 If an object has been possessed by the buyer before the contract is concluded, the delivery time shall be the time when the contract goes into effect.

Article 141 The seller shall deliver the object according to the agreed place. Where there is no agreement in the contract between the parties as to the place to deliver the object or such agreement is unclear, nor can it be determined according to the provisions of Article 61 of this Law, the following provisions shall be applied:

1. In case the object needs carriage, the seller shall deliver the object to the first carrier so as to hand it over to the buyer; or
2. In case the object does not need carriage, and the seller and buyer know the place of the object when concluding the contract, the seller shall deliver the object at such place; if the place is unknown, the object shall be delivered at the business place of the seller when concluding the contract.

Article 142 The risk of damage to or missing of an object shall be borne by the seller before the delivery of the object and by the buyer after the delivery, except as otherwise stipulated by law or agreed upon by the parties.

Article 143 Where the object cannot be delivered according to the agreed time limit due to causes of the buyer, the buyer shall bear the risk of damage to or missing of the object as of the agreed date of delivery.

Article 144 Where the seller sells an object delivered to a carrier for carriage and en route of carriage, the risk of damage to or missing of the object shall be borne by the buyer as of the time of establishment of the contract, except as otherwise agreed upon by the parties.

Article 145 Where there is no agreement in the contract between the parties as to the place of delivery or such agreement is unclear, and the object needs carriage according to the provisions of Sub-paragraph (1), Paragraph 2, Article 141 of this Law, the risk of damage to or missing of the object shall be borne by the buyer after the seller has delivered the object to the first carrier.

Article 146 Where the seller has put an object at the place of delivery according to the provisions of Sub-paragraph (2), Paragraph 2, Article 141 of this Law, while the buyer fails to take delivery of the object by violating the terms of the contract, the risk of damage to or missing of the object shall be borne by the buyer as of the date of breach.

Article 147 The buyer's failure in delivering the documents and materials relating to the object according to the terms of the contract may not affect the risk transfer of the damage to or missing of the object.

Article 148 Where it is not able to realize the purpose of a contract because the quality of the object has not satisfied the quality requirements, the buyer may refuse to accept the object or may rescind the contract. Where the buyer refuses to accept the object or rescinds the contract, the seller shall bear the risk of damage to or missing of the object.

Article 149 In case that the buyer bears the risk of damage to or missing of the object, the buyer's right may not be affected to claim the assumption by the seller of the liabilities for breach of contract because of the seller's performance failing to conform with the terms of the contract.

Article 150 The seller shall, in respect of the object delivered, assume the obligation to guarantee that no third party may claim any right to the buyer, except as otherwise stipulated by law.

Article 151 Where the buyer knows or ought to know, when concluding the contract, that a third party has rights on the object to be sold, the seller may assume no obligation as stipulated in Article 150 of this Law.

Article 152 Where the buyer has conclusive evidence to demonstrate that a third party may probably claim rights on the object, the buyer may suspend to pay the corresponding price, unless the seller provides a proper guaranty.

Article 153 The seller shall deliver the object according to the agreed quality requirements. In case that the seller provides with the quality specifications concerning the object, the delivered object shall satisfy the quality requirements in such specifications.

Article 154 Where there is no agreement between the parties in the contract on the object quality requirements or such agreement is unclear, nor can it be determined according to the provisions of Article 61 of this Law, the provisions of Sub-paragraph (1), Article 62 of this Law shall be applied.

Article 155 Where the object delivered by the seller fails to conform with the quality requirements, the buyer may claim the assumption by the seller of the liabilities for breach of contract according to the provisions of Article 111 of this Law.

Article 156 The seller shall deliver the object in the agreed package manner. Where there is no agreement on package manner in the contract or the agreement is unclear, nor can it be determined according to the provisions of Article 61 of this Law, the object shall be packed in a general manner, and if no general manner, a package manner enough to protect the object shall be adopted.

Article 157 The buyer shall inspect the object within the agreed inspection period after receiving the object. In case there is no such period agreed upon in the contract, the inspection shall be made in time.

Article 158 Where the parties have agreed upon the inspection period in the contract, the buyer shall, within the period for inspection, make a notice to the seller that the object quantity or quality fails to conform with the terms of the contract. If the buyer is indolent in making such a notice, it shall be deemed that the object quantity or quality has conformed with the terms of the contract.

Where there is no agreement between the parties in the contract on the inspection period, the buyer shall make a notice to the seller within a reasonable time period after it finds or ought to find that the object quantity or quality fails to conform with the terms of the contract. If the buyer fails in making a notice within such reasonable time period or within two years as of the date of receiving the object, it shall be deemed that the object quantity or quality has conformed with the terms of the contract. However, if there is a quality guarantee period on the object, the said quality guarantee period shall be applied instead of the above said two years.

Where the seller knows or ought to know the object to be supplied does not conform with the terms of the contract, the buyer may not be restricted by the time limit as stipulated in the preceding paragraph.

Article 159 The buyer shall pay the price according to the agreed amount in the contract. If there is no agreement in the contract on the price or such agreement is unclear, the provisions of Article 61 and Sub-paragraph (2), Article 62 of this Law shall be applied.

Article 160 The buyer shall pay the price at the agreed place. If there is no agreement in the contract on the place of payment or the agreement is unclear, nor can it be determined according to the provisions of Article 61 of this Law, the buyer shall pay at the seller's business place. However, if it is agreed that the delivery of the object or the documents to take delivery of the object is set as a prerequisite to the payment of the price, the payment shall be made at the place where the object or the documents to take delivery of the object are delivered.

Article 161 The buyer shall pay the price at the agreed time. If there is no agreement in the contract on the time of payment or such agreement is unclear, nor can it be determined according to the provisions of Article 61 of this Law, the buyer shall pay at the same time when receiving the object or the documents to take delivery of the object.

Article 162 Where the seller delivers excessive objects, the buyer may accept or refuse to accept the excess part. In case the buyer accepts the excess part, the buyer shall pay for it at the price in the original contract; if he refuses to accept the excess part, the buyer shall make a notice to the seller promptly.

Article 163 Any fruits generated by the object before delivery shall be owned by the seller, while those generated after delivery shall be owned by the buyer.

Article 164 If a contract is rescinded resulting from that the principal part of the object fails to satisfy the terms of the contract, the effectiveness of rescinding the contract shall extend to the collateral part. Where the collateral part of the object fails to satisfy the terms of the contract so that it has been rescinded, the effectiveness of its rescinding may not extend to the principal part.

Article 165 Where the object contains several items and one of them fails to satisfy the terms of the contract, the buyer may rescind the contract with respect to such item. However, if its separation from other items will damage the object value obviously, the parties may rescind the contract with respect to such several items.

Article 166 Where the seller delivers the object in batches, if the seller fails to deliver one batch of the object or the delivery fails to satisfy the terms of the contract so that the said batch can not realize the contract purpose, the buyer may rescind the contract with respect to such batch of object.

If the seller fails to deliver one batch of object or the delivery fails to satisfy the terms of the contract so that the delivery of the subsequent batches of objects can not realize the contract purpose, the buyer may rescind the contract with respect to such batch and the subsequent batches of objects.

If the buyer has rescinded the contract with respect to one batch of object and such batch of object is indispensable to other batches of the objects, the buyer may rescind the contract with respect to the various batches of objects delivered and undelivered.

Article 167 Where the buyer making payment by installments fails to pay the price due and the amount unpaid accounts for one fifth of the whole price, the seller may request the buyer to pay the whole price or may rescind the contract.

Where the seller rescinds the contract, the seller may request the buyer to pay for the use of such object.

Article 168 The parties to a sales transaction based upon the sample shall seal up the sample, and may make specifications on the sample quality. The object delivered by the seller shall have the same quality as the sample and the specifications.

Article 169 Where the buyer to a sales transaction based upon the sample does not know that the sample has a hidden defect, even if the object delivered is the same as the sample, the object delivered by the seller shall still meet the normal standards of the kind.

Article 170 The parties to a sales transaction on trial use may agree on the period of trial use of the object. If there is no agreement in the contract on such period or such agreement is unclear, nor can it be determined according to the provisions of Article 61 of this Law, it shall be determined by the seller.

Article 171 The buyer to a sales transaction on trial use may, during the period of trial use, buy the object or refuse to buy it. Upon the expiry of the period of trial use, if the buyer fails to express whether or not to buy the object, the purchase shall be deemed.

Article 172 The rights and obligations of the parties to a sales transaction in the form of inviting and making tenders and the procedures therefor, shall be in accordance with the provisions of relevant laws and administrative regulations.

Article 173 The rights and obligations of the parties to an auction and the procedures therefor, shall be in accordance with the provisions of relevant laws and administrative regulations.

Article 174 Where there is any provision on other non-gratuitous contracts in the laws, such provisions shall be followed; if no such provisions, the relevant provisions on sales contracts shall be applied mutatis mutandis.

Article 175 Where the parties make an agreement on a barter trade, and the ownership of the object is to be transferred, the relevant provisions on sales contracts shall be applied mutatis mutandis.

Chapter 10: Contracts For Supply And Use Of Electricity, Water, Gas Or Heating

Article 176 A contract for supply and use of electricity refers to a contract whereby the supplier of electricity supplies electricity to the user of electricity, and the user pays the electric fee.

Article 177 The contents of a contract for supply and use of electricity shall contain such clauses as the manner, quality, and time of supplying electricity, quantity of use, address and character of use, method of measurement, method of settlement and clearance of electricity price and fees, and the responsibility for maintaining the facilities for supply and use of electricity.

Article 178 The place where a contract for supply and use of electricity is to be performed shall be agreed upon by the parties. Where there is no such agreement between the parties in the contract or such agreement is unclear, the place where the property rights of the electricity supply facilities are demarcated shall be the place of performance.

Article 179 The supplier of electricity shall safely supply electricity in accordance with the standards for the supply of electricity stipulated by the State and the terms of the contract. Where the supplier of electricity fails to safely supply electricity in accordance with the standards for the supply of electricity as stipulated by the State and the terms of the contract, and causes losses to the user of electricity, it shall be liable for damages.

Article 180 When the supplier of electricity needs to suspend the supply of electricity due to such reasons as planned or ad hoc inspection and repair of the facilities for supply of electricity, restriction on electricity according to law or use of electricity in violating the law on the part of the user, it shall notify the user of electricity in advance in accordance with the relevant provisions of the State. Where it suspends the supply without notifying the user in advance and causes losses to the user, the supplier of electricity shall be liable for damages.

Article 181 Where the supplier of electricity suspends the supply of electricity due to such reasons as natural disasters, it shall make prompt repairs in accordance with the relevant provisions of the State. Where it fails to make prompt repairs and causes losses to the user, it shall be liable for damages.

Article 182 The user of electricity shall pay the electricity fees as scheduled in accordance with the relevant provisions of the State and the terms of the contract. If the user of electricity does not pay the electricity fees within the time limit, it shall pay breach of contract damages in accordance with the terms of the contract. If the user still does not pay the electricity fees and the breach of contract damages, the supplier may suspend the supply of electricity in accordance with the procedures stipulated by the State.

Article 183 The user of electricity shall use the electricity in accordance with the relevant provisions of the State and the terms of the contract. Where the user of electricity fails to use the electricity safely according to the relevant provisions of the State and the terms of the contract and causes losses to the supplier of electricity, it shall be liable for damages.

Article 184 Contracts for supply and use of water, gas or heating shall apply mutatis mutandis the provisions on contracts for supply and use of electricity.

Chapter 11: Contracts For Donation

Article 185 A donation contract refers to a contract whereby the donator presents gratis its property to the donee, and the donee expresses the acception of the donation.

Article 186 The donator may rescind the donation before transferring of the rights of the donated property.

Where the donation contract is of such nature as for public welfare or moral obligation in providing disaster or poverty relief, or the donation contract is notarized, the provisions of the preceding paragraph shall not be applied.

Article 187 If the donated property needs to go through such formalities as registration according to law, the relevant formalities shall be completed.

Article 188 In case of a donation contract being of such nature as for public welfare or moral obligation in providing disaster or poverty relief, or that the donation contract is notarized, if the donator does not deliver the donated property, the donee may request for the delivery.

Article 189 Where, due to the deliberate intention or gross fault of the donator, destruction or losses are caused to the donated property, the donator shall be liable for damages.

Article 190 The donation may be subject to collateral obligations.

Where the donation is subject to collateral obligations, the donee shall perform the obligations in accordance with the terms of the contract.

Article 191 Where the donated property has defects, the donator shall not bear any liability. In case of a donation subject to collateral obligations, if the donated property has defects, the donator shall bear the same liability as a seller within the limit of the collateral obligations.

Where the donator does not inform of the defects intentionally or insures that there is no defect, thus causing losses to the donee, the donator shall be liable for damages.

Article 192 Where the donee is under any of the following circumstances, the donator may rescind the donation:

1. seriously infringing upon the donator or his/her close relatives;
2. not performing the obligation in respect of supporting the donator;
3. not performing the obligation agreed upon in the donation contract.

The right of the donator to rescission shall be exercised within one year as of the date when he knows or ought to know the rescission reasons.

Article 193 In case of the donee's illegal acts resulting in the death of the donator or the loss of the donator's civil of capacity conduct, the heir or statutory agent of the donator may rescind the donation.

The right to rescission of the heir or statutory agent of the donator shall be exercised within six months as of the date when he knows or ought to know the rescission reasons.

Article 194 Where a person having the right to rescission rescinds the donation, the person may request the donee to return the donated property.

Article 195 Where economic conditions of the donator is strikingly deteriorating, which seriously affects his/

her production and business operations or the family life, the donator may no longer perform the donation obligation.

Article 196 A loan contract refers to a contract whereby the borrower raises a loan from the lender, and repays the loan with interest thereof when it becomes due.

Article 197 Loan contracts shall be in written form, except as otherwise agreed upon by natural persons in respect of loans between them.

The contents of a loan contract shall contain such clauses as the category of loans, the kind of currency, the purpose of use, the amount, the interest rate, the term and the method for returning the loan.

Article 198 In concluding a loan contract, the lender may require the borrower to provide a guaranty. The guaranty shall abide by the provisions of the Guaranty Law of the People's Republic of China.

Article 199 In concluding a loan contract, the borrower shall provide with the truthful information about the business activities and financial conditions relating to the loan according to the requirements of the lender.

Article 200 The interest of the loan shall not be deducted from the principal in advance. Where the interest is deducted in advance from the principal, the loan shall be repaid and the amount of the interest calculated according to the actual amount of the loan.

Article 201 Where the lender fails to extend the loan in accordance with the agreed date and amount and causes losses to the borrower, the lender shall compensate for the losses.

Where the borrower fails to accept the loan in accordance with the agreed date and amount, the borrower shall pay the interest according to the agreed date and amount.

Article 202 The lender may inspect and supervise the use of the loan in accordance with the terms of the contract. The borrower shall provide regularly the relevant financial statements and other materials to the lender in accordance with the terms of the contract.

Article 203 Where the borrower fails to use the loan in accordance with the agreed usage of the loan, the lender may cease in extending the loan, recall the loan ahead of time or rescind the contract.

Article 204 Loan interest rates of the financial institutions conducting loan business shall be determined according to the upper limit and lower limit of loan interest rates stipulated by the People's Bank of China.

Article 205 The borrower shall pay the interest in accordance with the agreed time limit. Where there is no agreement in the contract as to the time limit for payment of interest or such agreement is unclear, nor can it be determined according to the provisions of Article 61 of this Law, the interest shall be paid at the time when the loan is returned for loans under a term of less than one year; as for loans under a term of more than one year, the interest shall be paid at the time when every one full year expires, and if the remaining term is less than one year, the interest thereof shall be paid at the time when the loan is returned.

Article 206 The borrower shall return the loan in accordance with the agreed time limit in the contract. Where there is no agreement in the contract as to the loan term or such agreement is unclear, nor can it be determined according to the provisions of Article 61 of this Law, the borrower may return the loan at any time, and the lender may urge the borrower to return the loan within a reasonable time limit.

Article 207 Where the borrower fails to return the loan in accordance with the agreed time limit, the borrower shall pay overdue interest according to the terms of the contract or the relevant provisions of the State.

Article 208 Where the borrower returns the loan ahead of time, except as otherwise agreed upon between the parties, the interest thereof shall be calculated according to the actual term of the loan.

Article 209 The borrower may apply to the lender for an extension of the loan return term before the loan term expires. If the lender consents, the term may be extended.

Article 210 A loan contract between natural persons shall come into force as of the time when the lender extends the loan.

Article 211 If there is no agreement in a loan contract between natural persons as to the payment of interest or such agreement is unclear, it shall be deemed as non-payment of interest.

If the payment of interest is agreed in a loan contract between natural persons, the loan interest rates shall not violate the provisions of the State on the restriction on loan interest rates.

Article 212 A lease contract refers to a contract whereby the lessor shall deliver the leased property to the lessee for the latter's use or obtaining proceeds through the use, and the lessee pays the rent.

Article 213 The contents of a lease contract shall contain such clauses as the name, quantity, purpose for use, term of the lease, rent as well as time limit and method for its payment, maintenance of the leased property.

Article 214 The term of a lease may not exceed 20 years; in case of a term exceeding 20 years, the exceeding part shall be invalid.

At the expiry of the term of the lease, the parties may extend the lease contract; however, the extended term of the lease agreed upon shall not exceed 20 years as of the date of extending the contract.

Article 215 Where the lease term is above 6 months, the lease contract shall be in written form. If the parties do not conclude it in written form, it shall be deemed an unfixed lease.

Article 216 The lessor shall deliver the leased property to the lessee and keep it being fit for the use according to the terms of the contract during the term of the lease.

Article 217 The lessee shall use the leased property in accordance with the methods agreed upon in the contract. Where there is no agreement in the contract on the methods for using the leased property or such agreement is unclear, nor can it be determined according to the provisions of Article 61 of this Law, the leased property shall be used in a manner in light of its nature.

Article 218 Where the lessee uses the leased property in accordance with the methods agreed upon in the contract or the nature of the leased property and causes losses to the leased property, the lessee shall not bear the liability for damages.

Article 219 Where the lessee uses the leased property not in accordance with the methods agreed upon in the contract or the nature of the leased property and causes losses to the leased property, the lessor may rescind the contract and claim compensation for losses.

Article 220 The lessor shall perform the obligation of maintenance of the leased property, except as otherwise agreed upon by the parties.

Article 221 The lessee may request the lessor to maintain and repair the leased property within a reasonable time limit when the leased property needs maintenance and repair. Where the lessor fails to perform the obligation of maintaining and repairing the leased property, the lessee may maintain it by itself, and the expenses for the maintenance shall be borne by the lessor. Where the maintenance affects the use of the leased property, the rent shall be reduced or the lease term shall be extended correspondingly.

Article 222 The lessee shall keep the leased property in proper storage. In case that improper storage causes destruction of, damage to or lost of the leased property, the lessee shall bear the liability for damages.

Article 223 With the consent of the lessor, the lessee may improve or add other items to the leased property.

Where the lessee improves or adds other items to the leased property without the consent of the lessor, the lessor may request the lessee to restore it to the original conditions or compensate for the losses.

Article 224 With the consent of the lessor, the lessee may sublet the leased property to a third party. In case of subletting by the lessee, the lease contract between the lessee and lessor shall continue to be effective, and the lessee shall compensate for the losses if the third party causes losses to the leased property.

Where the lessee sublets the leased property without the consent of the lessor, the lessor may rescind the contract.

Article 225 The proceeds gained due to possession or use of the leased property shall belong to the lessee, except as otherwise agreed upon by the parties.

Article 226 The lessee shall pay the rent according to the time limit agreed upon in the contract. Where there is no agreement in the contract as to the time limit for payment or such agreement is unclear, nor can it be determined according to the provisions of Article 61 of this Law, the rent shall be paid at the expiry of the lease term if the lease term is less than one year, or shall be paid at the expiry of every one full year if the lease term is more than one year, the rest of rent shall be paid at the expiry of the lease term if the remaining lease term is less than one year.

Article 227 Where the lessee fails to pay or delays the payment of the rent without justified reasons, the lessor may require it to pay the rent within a reasonable time limit. If the lessee fails to pay the rent according to the time limit, the lessor may rescind the contract.

Article 228 Where a third party claims rights and makes it impossible for the lessee to use or obtain proceeds from the leased property, the lessee may request a reduction of rent or not to pay the rent.

Where rights are claimed by a third party, the lessee shall notify the lessor promptly.

Article 229 In case of a change with regard to the ownership of the leased property, the effectiveness of the contract shall not be affected.

Article 230 If the lessor sells out a leased house, it shall, within a reasonable time limit before the sale, notify the lessee and the lessee shall have the right to priority to buy the leased house on equal conditions.

Article 231 If, due to causes which are not attributable to the lessee, part or all of the leased property is damaged, destroyed or lost, the lessee may request for a reduction of the rent or not to pay the rent. If the damage to or destruction or loss of part or all of the leased property makes it impossible to realise the purpose of the contract, the lessee may rescind the contract.

Article 232 Where there is no agreement between the parties in the contract as to the term of the lease or such agreement is unclear, nor can it be determined according to the provisions of Article 61 of this Law, such lease shall be considered to be an unfixed lease. The parties may rescind the contract at any time, but the lessor shall, at the rescission of the contract, notify the lessee before a reasonable time limit.

Article 233 Where the leased property endangers the safety or health of the lessee, even if the lessee knows the leased property does not meet the quality requirements when concluding the contract, the lessee may rescind the contract at any time.

Article 234 Where the lessee is deceased during the term of a house lease, the persons who live together with the deceased may lease the house in accordance with the original lease contract.

Article 235 The lessee shall return the leased property at the expiry of the lease term. The property returned shall be in conformity with the conditions after use according to the terms of the contract or the nature of the leased property.

Article 236 Where the lessee continues to use the leased property after the expiry of the lease term, and the lessor does not raise objection, the original lease contract shall continue to be effective, but the lease term is not fixed.

Chapter 14: Contracts For Financial Lease

Article 237 A financial lease contract refers to a contract whereby the lessor buys the leased property from the seller based on the lessee's choice of the seller and the leased property, and supplies it to the lessee for the latter's use, and the lessee pays the rent.

Article 238 The contents of a financial lease contract shall contain such clauses as the title, quantity, specifications, technical performance and inspection methods of the leased property, the term of the lease, the rent composition and the time limit and kinds of currencies for payment of the rent, and the attribution of the leased property at the expiry of the lease term.

A financial lease contract shall be in written form.

Article 239 With regard to the sales contract concluded by the lessor based on the lessees' choice of the seller and the leased property, the seller shall deliver the object to the lessee according to the terms of the contract, and the lessee shall enjoy the rights of a buyer relating to the received object.

Article 240 The lessor, seller and lessee may agree that, where the sellor fails to perform the sales contract, the lessee shall exercise the right to claims. Where the lessee exercises the right, the lessor shall provide assistance.

Article 241 The sales contract concluded by the lessor based on the lessee's choice of the seller and the leased property, shall not be modified in respect of the contents of the contract relating to the lessee without the consent of the lessee.

Article 242 The lessor shall be entitled to the ownership of the leased property. In case of bankruptcy of the lessee, the leased property does not belong to the bankrupt property.

Article 243 The rent under a financial lease contract shall be determined according to the major part or whole of the cost for purchasing the leased property and reasonable profits of the lessor, except as otherwise agreed upon by the parties.

Article 244 Where the leased property does not conform to the terms of the contract or the purpose of its use, the lessor shall not bear any liability, except that the lessee decides on the choice of the leased property depending on the skills of the lessor or the lessor interferes with the choice of the leased property.

Article 245 The lessor shall insure the lessee's possession and use of the leased property.

Article 246 Where the leased property causes personal injury or property damage to a third party during the period wherein the lessee possesses the leased property, the lessor does not bear liability.

Article 247 The lessee shall keep the leased property in a proper storage and use it properly.

The lessee shall perform the obligation for maintenance of the leased property during the period wherein the lessee possesses the leased property.

Article 248 The lessee shall pay the rent according to the terms of the contract. If the lessee still does not pay the rent within a reasonable time limit after being urged, the lessor may request it to pay all the rent, or rescind the contract and take back the leased property.

Article 249 Where the parties agree in the contract that the leased property shall belong to the lessee at the expiry of the lease term, the lessee has paid the majority of the rent but is unable to pay the remaining rent, and the lessor rescinds the contract for this reason and takes back the leased property, the lessee may request the lessor to return a certain part if the value of the leased property taken back exceeds the rent and other expenses which the lessee owes to the lessor.

Article 250 The lessor and lessee may agree upon the attribution of the leased property at the expiry of the lease term. Where there is no agreement in the contract as to the attribution of the leased property or such agreement is unclear, nor can it be determined according to the provisions of Article 61 of this Law, the ownership of the leased property shall belong to the lessor.

Article 251 A work contract refers to a contract whereby the contractor shall, in light of the requirements of the ordering party, complete the work and deliver the results therefrom, and the ordering party pays the remuneration therefor.

Work includes processing, ordering, repairing, duplicating, testing, inspecting, etc.

Article 252 The contents of a work contract shall contain such clauses as the object, quantity, quality, remuneration and method of the work, supply of materials, term of performance, standards and method of inspection.

Article 253 The contractor shall use its own equipment, technology and labour force to complete the principal part of the work, except as otherwise agreed upon by the parties.

Where the contractor assigns the contracted work to a third party for completion, the contractor shall be responsible to the ordering party in respect of the work results completed by the third party. Where the assignment is without the consent by the ordering party, the ordering party may rescind the contract.

Article 254 The contractor may assign some auxiliary work contracted to a third party for completion. The contractor shall be responsible to the ordering party for the work results completed by a third party if the contractor assigns the auxiliary work to the third party.

Article 255 Where the contractor provides with materials, the contractor shall select and use the materials according to the terms of the contract and accept inspection by the ordering party.

Article 256 Where the ordering party supplies materials, the ordering party shall supply the materials according to the terms of the contract. The contractor shall promptly inspect the materials supplied by the ordering party and, if it discovers that they do not conform to the agreement in the contract, it shall promptly notify the ordering party to replace them or supply what is lacking or take other remedial measures.

The contractor may not unilaterally replace any materials supplied by the ordering party, and may not replace the components which do not need to be repaired.

Article 257 Where the contractor discovers that the drawings supplied by the ordering party or the technical requirements are unreasonable, it shall promptly notify the ordering party. If, due to the indolent reply of the ordering party and other reasons, losses are caused to the contractor, the ordering party shall be liable for making compensation.

Article 258 Where the ordering party changes the requirements of the contracted work midway and causes losses to the contractor, the ordering party shall be liable for making compensation.

Article 259 If the contracted work needs the assistance of the ordering party, the ordering party shall have the obligation to provide assistance Where the ordering party does not perform the assistance obligation and causes the contracted work unable to be completed, the contractor may urge the ordering party to perform its obligation within a reasonable time limit and may prolong the term of performance; the contractor may rescind the contract if the ordering party does not perform such obligation within the time limit.

Article 260 The contractor shall, during the period of working, accept the necessary supervision over and inspection of the work by the ordering party. The ordering party may not obstruct the contractor's normal work with the supervision and inspection.

Article 261 Where the contractor completes the work, it shall deliver the results of the work to the ordering party, and submit necessary technical materials and the relevant quality certificates. The ordering party shall examine and accept the results of the work.

Article 262 Where the results of the work delivered by the contractor do not conform to the quality requirements, the ordering party may request the contractor to bear such liabilities for the breach of contract as repairing, reprocessing, reducing remuneration and making compensation.

Article 263 The ordering party shall pay remuneration according to the time limit agreed by the parties in the contract. Where there is no agreement in the contract as to the time limit for payment of remuneration or such agreement is unclear, nor can it be determined according to the provisions of Article 61 of this Law, the ordering party shall pay it at the same time when the results of the work are delivered; where only part of the work results is delivered, the ordering party shall make corresponding payment.

Article 264 Where the ordering party fails to pay the remuneration or the price for the materials and etc, the contractor shall have the right to lien upon the results of the work, except as otherwise agreed upon by the parties.

Article 265 The contractor shall keep in a proper storage the materials supplied by the ordering party and the work results completed, and the contractor shall be liable for damages if they are destroyed, damaged or lost due to improper storage.

Article 266 The contractor shall maintain confidentiality according to the requirements of the ordering party and may not, without permission thereby, withhold and preserve the duplicates or technical materials.

Article 267 Co-contractors shall bear joint and several liability to the ordering party, except as otherwise agreed upon by the parties.

Article 268 The ordering party may rescind the contract at any time, but it shall bear the liability for making compensation for losses, if the contractor suffers losses therefrom.

Chapter 16: Contracts For Construction Projects

Article 269 A construction project contract refers to a contract whereby the contractor undertakes the construction of the project and the contract letting party pays the cost and remuneration.

Construction project contracts include project survey contracts, project design contracts and project construction contracts.

Article 270 Construction project contracts shall be in written form.

Article 271 The invitation and submission of tenders to a construction project shall be proceeded openly, equally and fairly according to the provisions of relevant laws.

Article 272 The contract letting party may enter into a construction project contract with a general contractor, or enter into a survey contract, design contract or construction contract with a surveyor, designer or constructor respectively.

The contract letting party may not divide the construction project that should be fulfilled by one contractor into several parts so as to be finished by several contractors.

With the consent of the contract letting party, the general contractor or the contractors for survey, design or construction may assign part of the contracted work to a third party. The third party shall assume joint and several liability to the contract letting party together with the general contractor or the contractors for survey, design or construction in respect of its work achievements. A contractor may not assign the whole contracted project to a third party or divide the whole contracted construction project into several parts and assign them respectively to third parties in the name of subletting.

The contractors are forbidden to sublet the project to any unit not having corresponding qualifications. The sub-contractor is forbidden to sublet its contracted work once again. The construction of the main body of the construction project must be completed by the general contractor.

Article 273 Contracts for major construction projects of the State shall be concluded in accordance with the procedures prescribed by the State and the investment plans, feasibility study reports and other documents approved by the State.

Article 274 The contents of a survey or design contract shall contain such clauses as the time limit for submission of the relevant basic materials and documents (including estimated budgets), the quality requirements, the expenses and other terms for cooperation.

Article 275 The contents of a construction contract shall contain such clauses as the scope of the construction, time period for the construction, the time for beginning and completing the intermediate construction projects, the quality of the construction, the cost of the construction, the time for submission of technical data, the responsibility for supply of materials and equipment, the allocation of funds and settlement of accounts, the inspection and acceptance of the project upon completion, the scope for guaranteed maintenance and repair and the quality guaranty period, the mutual cooperation of the two parties.

Article 276 Where supervision is practised in respect of a construction project, the contract letting party shall enter into a written supervision commission contract with a supervisor. The rights, obligations and legal liabilities of the contract letting party and the supervisor shall be in accordance with the provisions on commission contracts of this Law and other relevant laws and administrative regulations.

Article 277 The contract letting party may inspect the operation progress and quality at any time provided it does not hamper the contractor from normal operation.

Article 278 Before covering a project which needs to be covered, the contractor shall notify the contract letting party to inspect the project. If the contract letting party fails to inspect it in time, the contractor may prolong the construction period, and shall have the right to request the contract letting party for compensation for losses caused by work stoppages and idling of the labour force, etc

Article 279 Upon completion of a construction project, the contract letting party shall inspect and accept the projects in time according to the construction drawings and specifications as well as the construction inspection rules and quality standards issued by the State. If qualified, the contract letting party shall pay the costs and remuneration and accept the construction project according to the terms of the contract. A construction project may not be delivered for use until it is qualified through inspection and acceptance. A construction project may not be delivered for use without inspection and acceptance or proved to be unqualified through inspection and acceptance.

Article 280 Where the quality of survey or design work is not in conformity with the requirements, or the survey or design documents are not submitted in due time, thus delaying the construction period and causing losses to the contract letting party, the surveyor or designer shall continue to complete the survey or design,

reduce or do not charge the survey and design fees, and make compensation for the losses.

Article 281 If, due to the causes of the constructor, the construction quality does not conform to the terms of the contract, the contract letting party shall have the right to request the constructor to repair or reconstruct within a reasonable time limit free of charge. If such repair or reconstruction results in overdue delivery of the project, the constructor shall be liable for the breach of contract.

Article 282 If, due to the causes of the contractor, personal injury and property losses have occurred within the period of reasonable use of the construction project, the contractor shall be liable for damages.

Article 283 If the contract letting party has not supplied the raw materials, equipment, sites, funds or technical data according to the agreed time and requirements in the contract, the contractor may prolong the construction period and shall have the right to request for compensation for the losses caused by work stoppages and idling of the labour force, etc

Article 284 If, due to the causes of the contract letting party, a construction project pauses or is postponed in the course, the contract letting party shall adopt measures to offset or reduce the losses and compensate the contractor for losses and actual expenses incurred as a result of work stoppages, idling of the labour force, changes in transportation, transfer and move of machinery and equipment, overstocking of materials and components, etc

Article 285 If, due to modification of the plan, or inaccuracy of the data supplied or a failure in providing the necessary conditions for survey and design work according to the time limit by the contract letting party, the survey and design work has to be redone or stopped, or the design revised, the contract letting party shall pay additional expenses for the amount of work actually rendered by the surveyor or designer.

Article 286 If the contract letting party fails to pay the costs and remuneration in accordance with the terms of the contract, the contractor may urge the contract letting party to pay the money within a reasonable time limit. If the contract letting party fails to pay within the time limit, except that it is not appropriate to convert the construction project into money or auction it due to its characters, the contractor may consult with the contract letting party to convert the project into money, or apply to the people's court to auction the project according to law. The costs and remuneration of the construction project shall be compensated in priority by the money derived from the conversion or auction.

Article 287 Matters not addressed in this chapter shall apply the relevant provisions on contracts for work.

Chapter 17: Contracts For Transportation

Section 1: General Rules

Article 288 A transportation contract refers to a contract whereby the carrier carries passengers or goods from the starting place of carriage to the agreed destination, and the passenger or the shipper or the consignee pays for the ticket-fare or freight.

Article 289 A carrier engaged in public transportation may not refuse the normal and reasonable carriage request of a passenger or shipper.

Article 290 A carrier shall carry the passenger or goods safely to the agreed destination within the agreed time period or within a reasonable time period.

Article 291 A carrier shall carry the passenger or goods to the agreed destination via the agreed or customary carriage route.

Article 292 A passenger or a shipper or a consignee shall pay for the ticket-fare or for the freight. Where a carrier has not taken the agreed route or a customary carriage route, and consequently increased the ticket-fare or the freight, the passenger or the shipper or the consignee may refuse to pay for the increased part of the ticket-fare or the freight.

Section 2: Contracts For Passenger Transportation

Article 293 A passenger transportation contract shall be established at the time when the carrier delivers the ticket to the passenger except as otherwise agreed upon in the contract by the parties or there are other transaction practices.

Article 294 A passenger on board shall hold a valid ticket. A passenger on board without a ticket or exceeds the distance paid for or takes a higher class or higher berth than booked or holds an invalid ticket, shall make up the payment for an appropriate ticket. The carrier may charge an additional payment according to the rules. Where the passenger refuses to make such a payment, the carrier may refuse to undertake the carriage.

Article 295 A passenger unable to embark on the time stated on the ticket due to his/her own fault, shall go through ticket cancellation and refund formalities or ticket modification formalities within the agreed time period. Where the passenger fails to do so within the time period, the carrier may refuse to make the refund and shall no longer assume the obligation of carriage.

Article 296 A passenger shall bring with him/her luggage within the agreed limit of quantity. A passenger takes luggage exceeding the limit shall check in the luggage.

Article 297 A passenger may not bring with him/her or pack in the luggage such dangerous articles as are inflammable, explosive, corrosive or radioactive as well as those that might endanger the safety of life and property on board the transportation vehicle or other contraband articles.

Where a passenger violates the provisions of the preceding paragraph, the carrier may discharge the contraband articles, destroy them or hand them over to relevant departments. Where the passenger insists on bringing or packing in the luggage the contraband articles, the carrier shall refuse the carriage.

Article 298 A carrier shall inform the passengers in time of the important causes which hinders the normal carriage and the matters which shall be noted for purpose of safety carriage.

Article 299 A carrier shall carry passengers in conformity with the time and the carriage schedule stated on the ticket. A carrier delaying the carriage shall arrange the passengers to take other flights or numbers, or refund the tickets as requested by the passengers.

Article 300 A carrier unilaterally changing the carriage vehicle and consequently lowering the standards of service shall refund the ticket or lower the price of the ticket as requested by the passenger. A carrier unilaterally raising the standards of service, shall not charge additional ticket-fare.

Article 301 A carrier shall, during the period of carriage, render whatever help and assistance as it can to a passenger who is seriously ill, or who is giving birth to a child or whose life is at risk.

Article 302 A carrier shall be liable for damages for the death of or personal injury to passengers during the period of carriage, unless the death or personal injury results from the health conditions of the passenger himself/herself, or the carrier proves that the death or personal injury is caused by the deliberate intention or gross fault of the passenger.

The preceding paragraph shall be applicable to a passenger who is exempted from buying the ticket according to relevant rules, or who is holding a preferential ticket, or who is permitted by the carrier to be on board without a ticket.

Article 303 Where an article that the passenger takes with him/her on board is damaged or destroyed during the period of carriage, the carrier shall be liable for the damage if it has committed fault.

Where a check-in luggage of a passenger is damaged or destroyed, the relevant rules for the carriage of goods shall be applied.

Section 3: Contracts For Goods Transportation

Article 304 A shipper, when handling the formalities for goods carriage, shall precisely indicate to the carrier, the title or name of the consignee or consignee by order, the name, nature, weight, amount and the place for taking delivery of the goods, and other information necessary for goods carriage.

Where a carrier suffers from damage due to untrue declaration or omission of important information by the shipper, the shipper shall be liable for damages.

Article 305 Where such formalities as examination and approval or inspection are required for goods carriage, the shipper shall submit the documents of fulfilment of the relevant formalities to the carrier.

Article 306 A shipper shall pack the goods in the agreed manner. Where there is no agreement in the contract as to the manner of packing or such agreement is unclear, the provisions of Article 156 of this Law shall be applied.

Where a shipper violates the provisions of the preceding paragraph, the carrier may refuse to undertake the carriage.

Article 307 When shipping such dangerous Articles as are inflammable, explosive, corrosive or radioactive, a shipper shall appropriately pack the Articles in conformity with the rules of the State governing the carriage of dangerous Articles, and put on the marks and labels for dangerous Articles and submit the written papers relating to the nature and measures of precaution to the carrier.

Where a shipper violates the provisions of the preceding paragraph, the carrier may refuse to undertake the carriage, or take corresponding measures to avoid damage. Expenses thus caused shall be borne by the shipper.

Article 308 Prior to the delivery of goods to the consignee by the carrier, the shipper may request the carrier to suspend the carriage, to return the goods, to alter the destination or to deliver the goods to another consignee. The shipper shall compensate the carrier for losses thus caused.

Article 309 After the goods carriage is completed, if the carrier has the knowledge of the consignee, it shall notify the consignee promptly and the consignee shall claim the goods promptly. Where the consignee claims the goods exceeding the time limit, it shall pay to the carrier for such expenses as storage of the goods, etc

Article 310 When claiming the goods, a consignee shall inspect the goods within the agreed time limit in the contract. Where there is no agreement in the contract on the time limit or such agreement is unclear, nor can it be determined according to Article 61 of this Law, the consignee shall inspect the goods within a reasonable time limit. The failure of the consignee to make any claims on the amount, damage or losses of the goods within the agreed time limit or within a reasonable time limit, shall be deemed as the preliminary evidence that the carrier has delivered the goods in conformity with the statements indicated on the carriage documents.

Article 311 A carrier shall be liable for damages for the damage to or destruction of goods during the period of carriage unless the carrier proves that the damage to or destruction of goods is caused by force majeure, by inherent natural characters of the goods, by reasonable loss, or by the fault on the part of the shipper or consignee.

Article 312 The amount of damages for the damage to or destruction of the goods shall be the amount as agreed on in the contract by the parties where there is such an agreement. Where there is no such an agreement or such agreement is unclear, nor can it be determined according to the provisions of Article 61 of this Law, the market price at the place where the goods are delivered at the time of delivery or at the time when the goods should be delivered shall be applied. Where the laws or administrative regulations stipulate otherwise on the method of calculation of damages and on the ceiling of the amount of damages, those provisions shall be followed.

Article 313 Where more than one carriers take a connect carriage in the same manner of transportation, the carrier who concludes the contract with the shipper shall bear the liability for the entire transport. Where loss of goods occurred in a specific section, the carrier who concludes the contract with the shipper and the carrier who is responsible for the specific section shall bear joint and several liability.

Article 314 Where the goods are destroyed due to force majeure during the period of carriage and the freight has not been collected, the carrier may not request the payment of the freight. Where the freight has been collected, the shipper may request the refund of the freight.

Article 315 Where the shipper or the consignee fails to pay the freight, storage expense and other carriage expenses, the carrier is entitled to lien on the relevant carried goods except as otherwise agreed upon in the contract.

Article 316 Where the consignee is unclear or the consignee refuses to claim the goods without justified reasons, the carrier may have the goods deposited according to the provisions of Article 101 of this law.

Section 4: Contracts For Multi-Modal Transportation

Article 317 A multi-modal transportation business operator shall be responsible for the performance or the organising of performance of the multi-modal transportation contract, enjoy the rights and assume the obligations of the carrier for the entire transport.

Article 318 A multi-modal transportation business operator may enter into agreements with the carriers participating in the multi-modal transportation in different sections of the transport on their respective responsibilities for different sections under the multi-modal transportation contract.

Article 319 A multi-modal transportation business operator shall issue multi-modal transportation documents upon receiving the goods from the shipper. The multi-modal transportation documents may be negotiable or non-negotiable, as requested by the shipper.

Article 320 Where a multi-modal transportation business operator suffers losses due to the fault of the shipper when shipping the goods, the shipper shall bear the liability for damages even if the shipper has transferred the multi-modal transportation documents to other parties.

Article 321 Where the damage to, destruction or loss of goods occurs in a specific section of the multi-modal transportation, the liability of the multi-modal transportation business operator for damages and the limit thereof shall be governed by the relevant laws on the specific model of transportation used in the specific section. Where the section of transportation in which the damage or destruction or loss occurred can not be identified, the liability for damages shall be governed by the provisions of this Chapter.

Chapter 18: Contracts For Technology

Section 1: General Rules

Article 322 A technology contract refers to a contract that the parties conclude for purpose of establishing rights and obligations of the parties regarding technology development, technology transfer, technical consultancy and technical services.

Article 323 The conclusion of a technology contract must facilitate the progress of science and technology, accelerate the commercialisation, application and dissemination of the achievements of science and technology.

Article 324 The contents of a technology contract shall be agreed upon by the parties, and shall contain the following clauses in general:

1. title of the project;
2. contents, scope and requirements of the targeted object;
3. plan, schedule, time period, place, areas covered and manner of performance;
4. maintenance of confidentiality of technical information and materials;
5. sharing of liability for risks;
6. ownership of technological achievements and method of sharing proceeds;
7. standards and method of inspection and acceptance;
8. price, remuneration or royalties and method of payment;
9. damages for breach of contract or method for calculating the amount of compensation for losses;
10. methods for settlement of disputes; and
11. interpretation of technical terms and expressions.

Background materials on the technology, reports on feasibility studies and technological appraisals, project descriptions and plans, technological standards, technological specifications, original designs and documents on technological processes, as well as other technology files relevant to the performance of the contract may be deemed as an integral part of the contract as agreed upon by the parties in the contract.

Where a technology contract involves patents, the title of the invention or creation, the patent applicant and the patentee, the date and number of application, the patent number as well as the valid time period of patent rights shall be indicated.

Article 325 The method of payment of price, remuneration or royalties in the technology contract shall be agreed upon by the parties. The parties may agree on the method of an overall calculation and one time payment, or of an overall calculation and payment by instalment. They may also agree on the method of proportionate payment or such payment plus an advance payment of entrance fee.

Where the method of proportionate payment is agreed upon in the contract, the payment may be made according to a specific proportion to the price of the product, to the increased value of output derived from exploitation of the patent or from use of the know-how, to the profit or to the sales. They may also agree on other methods of calculation. The proportion may be a fixed proportion, or a proportion with yearly progressive increase or decrease.

Where the proportionate payment is agreed upon, the parties shall agree in the contract on the methods of checking on the relevant accounting books.

Article 326 Where the right to use or to transfer a job-related technological achievement belongs to the legal person or other organization, the legal person or other organization may conclude technology contracts with regard to the job-related technological achievement. The legal person or other organisation shall extract a certain proportion from the proceeds acquired from the use and transfer of such job-related technological achievement to reward or remunerate the individual who accomplished this technological achievement. Where a legal person other organization concludes a technology contract to transfer the job-related technological achievement, the individual who accomplished this technological achievement shall have the priority to be the transferee on equal conditions.

A job-related technological achievement refers to a technological achievement accomplished in the process of carrying out the task of the legal person, or other organisation, or mainly through using the materials and technological means thereof.

Article 327 The right to use or transfer a non-job-related technological achievement belongs to the individual who accomplished it. The individual may conclude a technology contract on such non-job-related technological achievement.

Article 328 An individual who has accomplished a technological achievement shall have the right to be named as such in the documents related to the technological achievement and the right to receive certificates of honour and awards.

Article 329 A technology contract which monopolises the technology or impedes the technological progress, or which infringes upon the technological achievement of others shall be null and void.

Section 2: Contracts For Technology Development

Article 330 A technology development contract refers to a contract concluded between the parties for purpose of conducting research in and development of new technologies, new products, new processes and new materials as well as their systems.

Technology development contracts include commissioned development contracts and cooperative development contracts.

A technology development contract shall be in written form.

A contract concluded between the parties for purpose of application or commercialisation of certain technological achievement which has potential value for industrial application shall apply the provisions concerning technology development contracts mutatis mutandis.

Article 331 The commissioning party to a commissioned development contract shall pay for the research and development expenses and the remuneration, supply technological materials and original data, accomplish coordinating tasks and accept the result of research and development on time according to the terms of the contract.

Article 332 The party responsible for research and development shall, according to the terms of the contract, formulate and implement a research and development plan, use the research and development budget in a reasonable way, complete the research and development on time, deliver the achievement according to the schedule, provide relevant technological materials and necessary technical guidance and assist the commissioning party in mastering the achievement of the research and development.

Article 333 Where the commissioning party violates the contract and causes a standstill, delay or failure in the research and development work, such party shall be liable for the breach of contract.

Article 334 Where the party responsible for research and development violates the contract and causes a standstill, delay or failure in the research and development work, such party shall be liable for the breach of contract.

Article 335 Parties to a cooperative development contract shall, make the investment according to the terms of the contract including making investment by way of technology contribution, taking part in the research and development in light of the division of labor according to the terms of the contract, and cooperating with other parties to the contract in the research and development work.

Article 336 Where a party to a cooperative development contract violates the contract and causes a standstill, delay or failure in the research and development work, such party shall be liable for the breach of contract.

Article 337 Where the targeted technology in a technology development contract has been made public by others, which makes the performance of this technology development contract meaningless, the parties may rescind the contract.

Article 338 The liability for risks involved in a failure or partial failure in the research and development resulting from insurmountable technical difficulties occurring in the process of performing a technology development contract shall be agreed upon by the parties to the contract. In the absence of such an agreement in the contract or in case of ambiguity of such agreement, nor can it be determined according to the provisions of Article 61 of this Law, such risk liability shall be shared reasonably by the parties.

Where one party discovers that the situation stipulated in the preceding paragraph is likely to result in a failure or partial failure in the research and development, the party shall promptly inform the other party of the situation and take appropriate measures to reduce losses. Where the party fails in making the notice and taking appropriate measures, and thus enlarging the losses, it shall be liable for the enlarged losses.

Article 339 With respect to inventions and creations achieved in the performance of a commissioned development, the right to apply for a patent belongs to the party that undertakes the research and development, except as otherwise agreed upon by the parties. Where the party that undertakes the research and development is granted a patent right, the commissioning party may exploit the patent for free.

Where the party undertaking the research and development transfers the right to apply for a patent, the commissioning party shall have the right to priority in acquiring such right on equal conditions.

Article 340 With respect to inventions and creations in cooperative development, the right to apply for a patent shall be jointly owned by the parties who participated in the cooperative development, except as otherwise agreed upon by the parties. Where one party transfers its part of the jointly owned right to apply for a patent, the other party or parties may have the right to priority in acquiring such right on equal conditions.

Where one party to the cooperative development contract declares that it renounces its part of the shared right to apply for a patent, the other party may apply for it alone or the other parties may apply for it jointly. Where a patent is granted to the applicant, the party that renounced its right to apply for a patent may exploit the patent for free.

Where one party to a cooperative development contract does not agree to apply for a patent, the other party or parties may not apply for it.

Article 341 The right to use or to transfer the know-how achieved in the commissioned development or cooperative development, and the method of distributing the proceeds derived shall be agreed upon by the parties in the contract. In the absence of such agreement or in case of ambiguity of such agreement, nor can it be determined according to the provisions of Article 61 of this law, either party has the right to use and transfer it. However, the party undertaking the research and development under a commissioned development contract may not transfer the result of the research and development to a third party before delivering them to the commissioning party.

Section 3: Contracts For Technology Transfer

Article 342 Technology transfer contracts include contracts on patent transfer, contracts on transfer of the right to apply for a patent, contracts on transfer of know-how and contracts on the licensing of patent exploitation.

A technology transfer contract shall be in written form.

Article 343 The scope of the exploitation of a patent or the use of the know-how by the transferor and the transferee may be agreed upon in a technology transfer contract provided that no restriction may be imposed on technological competition and technological development.

Article 344 A contract for the licensing of patent exploitation shall be valid only within the valid period of the patent right. Once the patent right expires or it is declared as invalid, the patentee may not conclude any contract with others for licensing of the exploitation of the said patent.

Article 345 The transferor of a patent exploitation licensing contract shall, according to the terms of the contract, permit the transferee to exploit the patent, submit the technological materials relevant to the exploitation of the patent and provide necessary technical guidance.

Article 346 The transferee of a patent exploitation licensing contract shall exploit the patent according to the terms of the contract, and may not permit any third party other than as provided for in the contract to exploit such patent, and shall pay the royalties according to the terms of the contract.

Article 347 The transferor of a know-how transfer contract shall, as agreed upon in the contract, supply technological materials, conduct technical guidance and ensure the practical applicability and reliability of the know-how as well as undertake the obligation of maintaining confidentiality.

Article 348 The transferee of a know-how transfer contract shall use the know-how, pay the royalties and undertake the obligation of maintaining confidentiality according to the terms of the contract.

Article 349 The transferor of a technology transfer contract shall guarantee that he/she is the lawful owner of the supplied technology and that the supplied technology is complete, without mistakes, effective and able to accomplish the agreed goal.

Article 350 The transferee of a technology transfer contract shall, in conformity with the scope and the time period as agreed upon in the contract, assume the obligation of maintaining confidentiality for the undisclosed part of the technology supplied by the transferor.

Article 351 A transferor failing to transfer the technology according to the terms of the contract, shall return part or total of the royalties and be liable for the breach of contract. The party exploiting the patent or know-how exceeding the agreed scope, or unilaterally permit a third party to exploit the patent or use the know-how in violation of the contract, shall cease the act of breach of contract and be liable for the breach of contract. A party violating the agreed obligation of maintaining confidentiality shall be liable for the breach of contract.

Article 352 A transferee failing to pay the royalties according to the terms of the contract shall, make up such payment and pay the breach of contract damages as agreed upon. The transferee refusing to pay the overdue royalties or the breach of contract damages, shall cease the exploitation of the patent or the use of the know-how, return the technological materials and be liable for the breach of contract. A transferee exploiting the patent or using the know-how in a way exceeding the scope as agreed upon in the contract, or permitting a third party to exploit the patent or use the know-how without the consent of the transferor, shall cease the act of breach of contract and be liable for the breach of contract. A transferee violating the agreed obligation for maintaining confidentiality shall be liable for the breach of contract.

Article 353 Where the exploitation of a patent or the use of know-how by a transferee in accordance with the terms of the contract infringes upon the legitimate rights and interests of others, the transferor shall be liable, except as otherwise agreed upon by the parties.

Article 354 The parties may stipulate in a technology transfer contract, the method of sharing technological achievements obtained from the follow-up improvements made in the exploitation of a patent or the use of know-how in light of the principle of mutual benefit. Where there is no such agreement in the contract or such agreement is unclear, nor can it be determined according to the provisions of Article 61 of this Law, the other parties shall have no right to share the technological achievements made by one party in the follow-up improvement.

Article 355 Where the laws and administrative regulations stipulate otherwise on the technology import and export contracts, or patent contracts or contracts on application for patents, such provisions shall be followed.

Section 4: Contracts For Technical Consultancy And Technical Service

Article 356 Technical consultancy contracts include contracts whereby feasibility studies, technological forecasts, technical investigations and analytical evaluation reports shall be provided in respect of specific projects.

Technical service contracts refer to contracts whereby one party undertakes to solve specific technical problems by using its technical expertise for the other party, excluding contracts for construction projects and contracts for work.

Article 357 The commissioning party of a technical consultancy contract shall, as agreed upon in the contract, state clearly the questions raised for consultancy, supply technological background information and relevant technical materials and data, accept from the commissioned party the result of its work and pay the remuneration.

Article 358 The commissioned party of a technical consultancy contract shall complete the consultancy report or answer the questions raised by the commissioning party according to the agreed time limit. The consultancy report thus submitted shall meet the requirements as agreed upon in the contract.

Article 359 Where the commissioning party of a technical consultancy contract fails to supply the necessary materials and data according to the terms of the contract which consequently affects the progress and quality of the consultancy work, or does not accept the result of the work or accepts it beyond the time limit, the remuneration already paid may not be refunded, and the remuneration unpaid shall be paid in due amount.

Where the commissioned party of a technical consultancy contract fails to submit the consultancy report on time or the report thus submitted does not meet the requirements as agreed upon in the contract, the said party shall bear such liabilities for breach of contract as reducing or waiving the remuneration, etc

The losses resulting from decisions made by the commissioning party of a technical consultancy contract on the basis of the consultancy report and of the advice of the commissioned party that meet the requirements as agreed upon in the contract shall be borne by the commissioning party, except as otherwise agreed upon by the parties in the contract.

Article 360 The commissioning party of a technical service contract shall supply the work facilities and accomplish cooperative undertakings according to the terms of the contract, and accept the result of the work and pay the remuneration.

Article 361 The commissioned party of a technical service contract shall complete the services, solve the technical problems, guarantee the quality of its work and convey to the other party the knowledge on the solving of technical problems according to the terms of the contract.

Article 362 Where the commissioning party of a technical service contract fails to perform the contract or the performance is not in conformity with the terms of the contract, which consequently affects the progress and the quality of the work, or does not accept the result of the work or accepts it beyond the time limit, the remuneration already paid may not be refunded, and the remuneration unpaid shall be paid in due amount.

Where the commissioned party fails to complete the service work in conformity with the terms of the contract, the said party shall bear such liabilities for breach of contract as waiving the remuneration, etc.

Article 363 Any new technological achievement accomplished by the commissioned party in the performance of a technical consultancy contract or a technical service contract using the technological materials and work facilities supplied by the commissioning party, shall belong to the commissioned party, while any new technological achievement accomplished by the commissioning party using the results of the work of the commissioned party, shall belong to the commissioning party, except as otherwise agreed upon by the parties in the contract.

Article 364 Where the laws and regulations stipulate otherwise on technical intermediation contracts and technical training contracts, such provisions shall be followed.

Article 365 A storage contract refers to a contract whereby the safekeeping party keeps in store the article handed over by the storing party, and returns the said article.

Article 366 The storing party shall, according to the terms of the contract, pay to the safekeeping party the storage fee.

Where there is no agreement in the contract regarding the storage fee, or such agreement is unclear, nor can it be determined according to the provisions of Article 61 of this law, the storage shall be for free.

Article 367 A storage contract is established at the time when the article to be stored is handed over, except as otherwise agreed upon by the parties.

Article 368 When the storing party hands over the article to be stored to the safekeeping party, the safekeeping party shall issue a storage certificate, except as otherwise practised in transactions.

Article 369 The safekeeping party shall keep in appropriate store the articles to be stored.

The parties may agree on the site or method of storage. The site or method of storage may not be unilaterally changed except in case of emergency or for the purpose of protecting the interests of the storing party.

Article 370 Where an article handed over by the storing party for storage has defects, or special measures need to be taken due to the character of the article, the storing party shall inform the safekeeping party of such matters. Where the storing party fails to inform the safekeeping party of such matters and consequently causes damage to the stored article, the safekeeping party shall not be liable for damages. Where the safekeeping party suffers losses therefrom as a consequence, the storing party shall be liable for damages, except in the event the safekeeping party knows the situation or ought to know it but fails to take any remedial measures.

Article 371 The safekeeping party may not turn the article to be stored over to a third party for storage, except as otherwise agreed upon by the parties in the contract.

Where the safekeeping party violates the provisions of the preceding paragraph and turns the article to be stored over to a third party for storage, thus causing damage to the article, the said party shall be liable for damages.

Article 372 The safekeeping party may not use or permit a third party to use the stored article, except as otherwise agreed upon by the parties.

Article 373 Where a third party claims rights on the stored article, the safekeeping party shall perform the obligation to return the article to the storing party, except that a preservative measure or executive measure is taken according to law with regard to the stored article.

Where a third party brings a lawsuit against the safekeeping party or applies for a seizure by the stored article, the safekeeping party shall promptly inform the storing party of the case.

Article 374 Where during the period of storage, the stored article is damaged, destroyed or lost due to improper storage by the safekeeping party, the safekeeping party shall be liable for damages. However, where the storage is provided for free, and the safekeeping party proves that it has not acted with gross fault, it shall not be liable for damages.

Article 375 A storing party depositing currency, securities or other precious articles shall, declare the case to the safekeeping party, and the safekeeping party shall inspect and seal up the article for storage. Where the storing party fails to declare as such and the article is damaged, destroyed or lost afterwards, the safekeeping party may compensate for it as it is an ordinary article.

Article 376 A storing party may claim and get back the stored article at any time.

Where there is no agreement between the parties in the contract as to the time period of the storage, the safekeeping party may request the storing party to get back the stored article at any time. Where there is such agreement on the time period of the storage, the safekeeping party may not request the storing party to get back the stored article before the time period expires without special causes.

Article 377 On the expiry of the storage time period or when the storing party claims and gets back the article before the expiry, the safekeeping party shall return to the storing party the original article and the fruits generated therefrom.

Article 378 A safekeeping party keeping in store currency may return the currency of the same kind and in the same amount. In case of storing other replaceable articles, the safekeeping party may return to the storing party articles of the same category, quality and quantity according to the terms of the contract.

Article 379 With regard to non-gratuitous storage contracts, the storing party shall pay to the safekeeping party the storage fee according to the time limit as agreed upon by the parties.

Where there is no agreement as to the time limit for the payment in the contract or such agreement is unclear, nor can it be determined according to the provisions of Article 61 of this Law, the storage fee shall be paid at the same time when the stored article is claimed and taken back.

Article 380 Where a storing party fails to pay the storage fee and other expenses according to the terms of the contract, the safekeeping party is entitled to lien on the stored article, except as otherwise agreed upon by the parties.

Chapter 20: Contracts For Warehousing

Article 381 A warehousing contract refers to a contract whereby the safekeeping party keeps in store the goods handed over by the storing party, while the storing party pays the warehousing fee.

Article 382 A warehousing contract comes into effect at the time of its establishment.

Article 383 Where inflammable, explosive, poisonous, corrosive, radioactive and other dangerous or perishable articles are to be kept in store, the storing party shall indicate the character of the goods and provide relevant documents and materials thereof.

Where a storing party violates the provisions of the preceding paragraph, the safekeeping party may refuse to receive the goods, or may take appropriate measures to avoid losses. The cost consequently incurred shall be borne by the storing party.

The safekeeping party shall have appropriate safekeeping facilities for the storage of inflammable, explosive, poisonous, corrosive, radioactive and other dangerous articles.

Article 384 The safekeeping party shall inspect, before letting in, the warehousing goods in conformity with the terms of the contract. A safekeeping party discovering in the inspection that the goods are not in conformity with the terms of the contract shall inform the storing party of the case promptly. After the inspection and acceptance by the safekeeping party, the safekeeping party shall be liable for damages if it is discovered that the category, quantity or quality of the warehousing goods are not in conformity with the terms of the contract.

Article 385 Upon handing over the goods by the storing party, the safekeeping party shall issue a warehouse voucher.

Article 386 The safekeeping party shall sign on the warehouse voucher or affix a seal on it. A warehouse voucher shall contain the following items:

1. title or name and domicile of the storing party;
2. category, quantity, quality, package, number of pieces and marks of the warehousing goods;
3. standards of spoilage of the warehousing goods;
4. place of storage;
5. time period of storage;
6. warehousing fee;
7. where the warehousing goods have been insured, the amount and time period of the insurance and the title of the insurance company; and
8. name of the person who issues the warehouse voucher, the place and the date of issuance.

Article 387 A warehouse voucher is the certificate for claiming the warehousing goods. The right to claim the warehousing goods may be transferred when the warehouse voucher is endorsed by the storing party or the person who holds the warehouse voucher, and signed or affixed with a seal by the safekeeping party.

Article 388 At the request of the storing party or the person who holds the warehouse voucher, the safekeeping party shall permit the person to check the warehousing goods or take samples.

Article 389 In the event that the safekeeping party discovers that the warehousing goods are deteriorated or otherwise damaged, the said party shall inform the storing party or the holder of the warehouse voucher of the case promptly.

Article 390 In the event that the safekeeping party discovers that the letting in warehousing goods are deteriorated or otherwise damaged, thus endangering the safety and the normal storage of other warehousing goods, the said party shall notify and urge the storing party or the holder of the warehouse voucher to make necessary disposal. In case of emergency, the safekeeping party may make the necessary disposal, but shall inform the storing party or the holder of the warehouse voucher of the case promptly afterwards.

Article 391 Where there is no agreement in the contract between the parties as to the time period of the storage or such agreement is unclear, the storing party or the person who holds the warehouse voucher may claim and get back the warehousing goods at any time, the safekeeping party may also at any time request the storing party to claim the warehousing goods, provided that a time period necessary for preparation shall be given.

Article 392 When the storage time period expires, the storing party or the holder of the warehouse voucher shall claim and get back the warehousing goods. Where the storing party or the holder of the warehouse voucher fails to claim the goods on time, an additional warehouse fee shall be paid. Where the goods are claimed before the time period expires, the warehouse storage fee shall not be reduced.

Article 393 Where the storing party or the holder of the warehouse voucher does not claim the warehoused goods when the time period expires, the safekeeping party may urge the holder to claim the goods within a reasonable time period. After this additional time period expires, the safekeeping party may have the goods deposited.

Article 394 If, during the time period of storage, the warehousing goods are damaged, destroyed or lost due to improper storage by the safekeeping party, the safekeeping party shall be liable for damages. Where the warehousing goods are perished or damaged due to unconformity of the character of the warehousing goods or of the packing with the terms of the contract, or the fact that the goods exceed the valid storage period, the safekeeping party shall not be liable.

Article 395 Matters not addressed in this chapter shall apply the relevant provisions governing storage contracts.

Chapter 21: Contracts For Commission

Article 396 A commission contract refers to a contract whereby the principal and the agent agree that the agent shall handle the matters of the principal.

Article 397 A principal may specially entrust an agent to handle one or several items of matters, or generally entrust the agent to handle all matters.

Article 398 The principal shall pay the expenses for handling the entrusted matters in advance. In case that the agent has prepaid the necessary expenses for handling the entrusted matters, the principal shall reimburse the expenses and the interest thereof.

Article 399 The agent shall handle the entrusted matters according to the instruction of the principal. Where the instructions of the principal need to be modified, consent of the principal shall be obtained; in case of such emergency that it is difficult to contact the principal, the agent shall handle the entrusted matters properly and report to the principal the case promptly afterwards.

Article 400 The agent shall handle the entrusted matters himself/herself. With the consent of the principal, the agent may sub- entrust the matter. If the sub-entrustment has obtained consent, the principal may directly give instructions to the sub-entrusted third party, and the agent shall be liable only for the selection of the third party and his own instructions to the third party. If the sub- entrustment has not obtained the consent, the agent shall be liable for the third party's acts, except that in an emergency the sub-entrustment is necessary for the protection of the interests of the principal.

Article 401 The agent shall report the handling of the entrusted matters according to the requirements of the principal. The agent shall report the result of the entrusted matters when the commission contract is terminated.

Article 402 If within the scope of the power delegated by the principal, the agent, in his/her own name, concludes a contract with a third party, and the third party knows the proxy relationship between the agent and principal at the time of concluding the contract, the contract shall directly bind the principal and the third party, unless there are conclusive evidences to prove that the said contract only binds the agent and the third party.

Article 403 When an agent concludes a contract in his/her own name with a third party, and the third party does not know the proxy relationship between the agent and principal, and if the agent does not perform the obligation in respect of the principal due to causes of the third party, the agent shall disclose the third party to the principal. The principal hence may exercise the agent's rights against the third party, except that the third party will not conclude the contract with the agent if he knows the principal at the time of concluding the contract.

If the agent does not perform the obligations in respect of the third party due to causes of the principal, the agent shall disclose the principal to the third party. The third party hence may choose the agent or the principal as the counterpart to claim its rights, but the third party may not change the chosen counterpart.

Where the principal exercises the agent's rights against the third party, the third party may claim its demur in respect of the agent against the principal. Where the third party chooses the principal as its counterpart, the principal may claim its demur in respect of the agent as well as the demur of the agent in respect of the third party against the third party.

Article 404 The agent shall hand over to the principal the property obtained from handling the entrusted matters.

Article 405 When the agent has finished the entrusted matters, the principal shall pay remuneration to it. If, due to causes not attributable to the agent, the commission contract is rescinded or the entrusted matters cannot be finished, the principal shall pay the agent corresponding remuneration. If otherwise agreed upon in the contract, the terms of the contract shall be applied.

Article 406 In respect of a non-gratuitous commission contract, where the principal suffers from losses due to the fault of the agent, the principal may claim compensation for the losses. In respect of a gratuitous commission contract, where the principal suffers from losses due to the deliberate intention or gross fault of the agent, the principal may claim compensation for the losses.

Where the agent is ultra vires and causes losses to the principal, the agent shall compensate for the losses.

Article 407 If, in handling the entrusted matters, the agent suffers from losses due to causes not attributable to its own, the agent may request the principal to compensate for the losses.

Article 408 With the consent of the agent, the principal may entrust a third party other than the agent to handle the entrusted matters. In respect of losses thus incurred to the agent, the agent may request the principal to compensate for the losses.

Article 409 Where two or more agents jointly handle the entrusted matters, they shall assume joint and several liabilities to the principal.

Article 410 The principal or agent may rescind the commission contract at any time. The party who causes losses to the other party due to the rescission of the commission contract shall compensate for the losses, except for causes not attributable to the said party.

Article 411 A commission contract shall be terminated when the decease of the principal or agent occurs, or the principal or agent loses civil capacity of conduct or goes into bankrupcy, except as otherwise agreed upon by the parties in the contract or except that it is inappropriate to terminate the contract according to the characters of the entrusted matters.

Article 412 If the termination of a commission contract due to the principal's decease, loss of civil capacity of conduct or bankruptcy will harm the principal's interests, the agent shall continue to handle the entrusted matters before the principal's heir, statutory agent or liquidation group take over these matters.

Article 413 If a commission contract is terminated due to the agent's decease, loss of civil capacity of conduct or bankruptcy, the agent's heir, statutory agent or liquidation group shall notify the principal promptly. If the termination of the commission contract will harm the principal's interests, the agent's heir, statutory agent or liquidation group shall take necessary measures before the principal makes appropriate arrangements in dealing with the situation.

Chapter 22: Contracts For Brokerage

Article 414 A brokerage contract refers to a contract whereby the broker is, in his/her own name, engaged in trade activities for the benefit of the principal, and the principal pays the remuneration.

Article 415 The expenses of the broker occurred in handling the entrusted matters shall be borne by the broker except as otherwise agreed upon by the parties in the contract.

Article 416 When possessing the entrusted articles, the broker shall keep in appropriate store the said articles.

Article 417 If the entrusted articles have defects or are perishable or have deteriorated when they are delivered to the broker, the broker may dispose of these articles with the consent of the principal. Where the principal cannot be contacted in time, the broker may dispose of these articles in a reasonable manner.

Article 418 Where the broker sells at a lower price or buys at a higher price than the price fixed by the principal, consent shall be obtained from the principal. Without the principal's consent, the transaction shall be effective to the principal if the broker makes up the price difference.

Where the broker sells at a higher price or buys at a lower price than the price fixed by the principal, remuneration may be raised according to the terms of the contract. Where there is no such agreement in the contract or such agreement is unclear, nor can it be determined according to the provisions of Article 61 of this Law, the benefits shall belong to the principal.

Where the principal has special instructions on price, the broker may not buy or sell violating these instructions.

Article 419 When selling or buying commodities of market fixed price, the broker may act as a buyer or seller, unless the principal expresses oppositely.

The broker may still request the principal under the circumstances stipulated in the preceding paragraph to pay the remuneration.

Article 420 Where the broker buys in the entrusted articles according to the terms of the contract, the principal shall accept the said articles in time. If, after the broker's urging with a notice, the principal refuses to accept the articles without justified reasons, the broker may deposit the entrusted articles according to the provisions of Article 101 of this Law.

If the entrusted articles cannot be sold out or the principal revokes the sale, and the principal does not take back or dispose of the goods after the broker's urging with a notice, the broker may have the entrusted articles deposited according to the provisions of Article 101 of this law.

Article 421 Where a contract is concluded between a broker and a third party, the broker shall directly have the rights and assume obligations under the contract.

If the third party fails in performing its obligations and causes losses to the principal, the broker shall be liable for damages, except as otherwise agreed upon by the parties.

Article 422 The principal shall pay to the broker corresponding remuneration when the broker has finished the whole or part of the entrusted matters. Where the principal fails to pay the remuneration in due time, the broker shall have the right to lien on the entrusted articles, except as otherwise agreed upon by the parties.

Article 423 Matters not addressed in this chapter shall apply the relevant provisions governing commission contracts.

Chapter 23: Contracts For Intermediation

Article 424 An intermediation contract refers to a contract whereby the intermediator reports to the principal the opportunity for concluding a contract or provides intermediate service for concluding a contract, and the principal pays the remuneration.

Article 425 The intermediator shall report truthfully to the principal the matters related to the conclusion of a contract.

Where the intermediator intentionally conceals the important facts relating to the conclusion of the contract or provides false information and harms the interests of the principal, the said party may not claim the payment of remuneration and shall be liable for damages.

Article 426 The principal shall pay the intermediator remuneration according to the terms of the contract if the intermediator has facilitated the establishment of the contract. Where there is no such agreement in the contract on remuneration or such agreement is unclear,

nor can it be determined according to the provisions of Article 61 of this Law, the remuneration shall be determined reasonably according to the service rendered by the intermediator. If the establishment of a contract has been facilitated by the intermediate service rendered by the intermediator, the remuneration shall be borne equally by the parties to the contract.

Where the intermediator has facilitated the conclusion of the contract, the expenses for the intermediate service shall be borne by the intermediator.

Article 427 Where the intermediator fails in facilitating the conclusion of a contract, the intermediator may not request for the payment of remuneration, but may request the principal to pay the necessary expenses for the intermediate service.

Article 428 This Law shall come into force as of 1 October, 1999. The Economic Contract Law of the People's Republic of China, the Law of the People's Republic of China on Economic Contracts Involving Foreign Interests and the Law of the People's Republic of China on Technology Contracts shall be invalidated simultaneously.

(Note: In case of discrepancies in terms of interpretation and understanding of this contract in the translation, the Chinese version shall prevail.)

Appendix 3.2

Basic Commercial Transactions

He Jiang, Centre for Market and Trade Development (CMTD)

Use of cheques in China

Types of cheques

There are two types of cheques commonly used by Chinese business entities and government institutions – cash cheques (for withdrawing cash and transferring funds) and transfer cheques (for bank transfer only).

Validity of cheques

Both types of cheques shall be made to the order of the issuer. The minimum amount payable by cheque is 100 yuan. The effective period of payment is five working days (starting from the date of issue). The cheque is invalid after expiry.

Issuing cheques

The cheque must be written out in black or carbon ink. The use of pencil or ball pen is not accepted. In case of a false claim as a result of writing the cheque with an unacceptable writing instrument, the issuer of the cheque will be responsible for the consequences.

When issuing a cheque, the name of payee, date of issue, amount in both Arabic numbers and Chinese numerical characters and a description of payment must be clearly written on the cheque. For payment by a transfer cheque for an amount that cannot be decided at the time of payment, it is permissible to leave the amount blank. Alteration of the amount (in both Arabic numbers and the Chinese numerical characters) or the name of payee is not allowed. If changes are to be made to other details on a cheque, they must be validated by additional stamping of the issuer's company seal which the bank will check against sample seals in their files.

The issuer of a cheque should make payment within the limit of its bank balance. It is not allowed to overdraw on the bank account. The cheque must be signed with a valid signature matching the bank's records. The issued cheque should bear all the required stamps which shall conform to the samples filed at the bank. Cheques issued in violation of the bank's rules and regulations will be rejected and the issuer subject to a fine of 5 per cent of the issued amount or a minimum of 50 yuan in case the issued amount is less than 1,000 yuan.

The cheque books made available to corporate or institutional users are confined to the exclusive use of authorised issuers only. Transfer of the cheque or cheque book to any unauthorised user in any form is illegal.

Receipt of cheques

The recipient should examine the cheque to make sure that all items of the cheque are correct. When receiving payment by a transfer cheque, the recipient has the right to request the holder of the cheque to produce documents that will sufficiently prove the identity of the holder such as ID card, and record the details of the supporting documents on the back of the cheque.

The cheque should be properly back-endorsed by the recipient when negotiating payment at the payer's bank. The bank may request documents of proof to verify the identity of the drawer before release of payment.

Loss of cheques

If an issued cash cheque is lost, the issuer should report the loss to the bank and apply for suspension of payment. A letter of reference or relevant document of proof bearing stamps which conform to the samples filed at the bank must be produced when reporting.

For lost bank transfer cheques either signed or blank, the banks do not accept reports for losses. The issuer may request assistance from the intended payee. The banks assume no responsibility for economic damages resulting from loss of cheques.

In Beijing there is a telephone enquiry service for reporting lost cheques or verifying if a received cheque is a reported lost cheque. The telephone number is 185.

Application for and use of a credit card in China

There are two types of credit cards classified by type of holder, namely the corporate card (for any company or institute recognized as a legal entity) and the private card (for individuals over 18 years of age with permanent residency at the place of application).

Application procedures for the corporate card

An applicant for a corporate credit card must appoint a specific person as the card holder. At the same time, a copy of the ID card of the cardholder needs to be submitted. Applicants should go to the card issuing bank, a branch or subbranch to obtain and fill out application forms.

Upon receipt of the application forms, the bank will start investigations on the credit status of the applicant. Qualified applicants will be advised of the bank's acceptance.

Upon receipt of the bank's acceptance advice, the applicant needs to make a deposit by cash or cheque before the card is issued.

If, for some reason, a corporation wants to change its official cardholder, advance notice needs to be given to the card issuing bank and, at the same time, the applicant should go to the bank and process the changes in accordance with the bank's requirements. Any losses resulting from an applicant's failure in claiming and processing the changes shall be borne by the applicant.

Application procedures for a private card

The applicant needs a guarantor. The application form shall be accompanied at the time of submission by copies of the applicant's ID card and the guarantor's ID card.

Preliminary examination will be carried out by the bank staff handling the application and approval will be given by department managers.

Qualified applicants will be notified of the bank's acceptance and an advance deposit needs to be made before the card is made available to the applicant.

How to use a credit card in China

When using the card to make a cash withdrawal or payment, the holder must show his ID card, and sign his name on the receipt.

Cross-city cash withdrawal is subject to a surcharge. Cardholders must pay an annual fee.

An overdraft is allowed for emergency situations and on a short-term basis. The overdrawn amount is repaid with interest to the bank within the designated period. The interest on the overdrawn amount will be doubled for an overdue overdraft. The card will be cancelled in the case of a seriously overdue overdraft.

If the credit card is lost or stolen, the holder should immediately report the loss to the issuing bank. All losses incurred before and within 24 hours from the time of reporting shall be borne by the cardholder. The bank charges a handling fee for reporting of lost cards.

Renting a car in Beijing

Reservations

Reservations shall be made with car rental companies. The documents required for car rental reservations normally include an ID card or other valid identification documents, a valid driving licence and a deposit (ranging from RMB2,000 to RMB10,000). Some car rental companies require a letter of guarantee issued by the company to which the lessee belongs.

Picking up the car

The car can be picked up at the agreed time. The car is examined by both sides and written confirmation of the state of the car at the time of renting shall be confirmed. The lessee shall leave his ID card or other valid identification documents with the company as a pledge.

Returning the car

The car will have to be returned at the designated premises of the car rental company. The car should be re-examined by both sides at the time of return. If damages are found, the costs of repair under RMB300 shall be paid completely by the lessee. Where the cost of repair is over RMB300, the lessee shall pay the balance of the insurance premium. If the car needs to be sent to a garage for the repair of severe damages, the lessee shall also compensate for losses resulting from non-availability of the car (normally 60–100 per cent of the daily rental).

Reservation cancellations

Cancellation of a reservation must be made 24 hours in advance, otherwise the lessee will be subject to a fine equivalent to 30 per cent of the daily rental. Those wishing to extend the rent must similarly notify the car rental company 24 hours in advance. The extension can only be made valid by approval from the car rental company. Otherwise, the extension will be regarded as a delay which will be subject to a fine (20 per cent of the daily rental for each hour overdue).

Maximum mileage

Each car rental company has a limit on maximum mileage per day of rental, normally between 120 to 150 kilometres a day. Additional kilometres will be subject to extra charges.

Breakdown

In case of breakdown, contact the car rental company immediately. Free on-site rescue services are normally provided.

Important points of attention when signing a contract

A contract specifically defines a cooperative relationship between two parties. When the parties' rights and obligations are not clearly stated, disputes often result. To avoid misunderstandings, it is advisable to pay attention to the following points when signing a contract.

The signed contract should be a written document

Although oral contracts are legally binding in Chinese law, signed documentation provides clear and concrete guidelines in case of dispute.

Both parties must thoroughly understand the contract's terms and conditions

The contract should be signed only when each side thoroughly understands each item. In certain circumstances, there are special procedures.

Review the contract with the other party carefully
If some part of the contract is vague – common with foreign contracts due to language and time restraints – review it with the other party to clarify the content.

Add applicable terms and conditions to the printed form contract
With contracts of a fixed form (ie real estate sales or rental), type or print applicable additional items when necessary. The addendum will be legally binding when both sides sign beside it. Each additional page should be numbered.

Signatures are needed to validate revision or deletion of terms in a contract
Signatures are needed when the complete deletion of a term in a contract is made. Partial revisions also require signatures from both sides.

Mark the blank spaces in a contract properly
When blank spaces are left in the contract, the notation 'blank below' should be printed to prevent unauthorised revision by either side.

The contract's terms should guard against future disputes

The contract's terms should be clear, specific and concrete to avoid future disputes. Its clauses should state the stipulations, bases and remedies for future disputes.

Appendix 4.1

'A' Shares Listed on Shanghai Stock Exchange

Stock Code	Company Name	Address	Postcode	Tel	Fax	Legal representative
600000	Shanghai Pudong Development Bank Co Ltd	12, Zhong Shan Dong Yi Lu, Shanghai, China	200002	86-21-63611226 86-21-63296188	86-21-63230249	Shen Si
600001	Handan Iron & Steel Co Ltd	232, Fu Xing Road, Handan, Hebei, China	056015	86-310-6074191	86-310-6074190	Li Bohai
600002	Qilu Petrochemical Company Ltd	Hi-tech Industries Development Zone, Zibo, Shandong, China	255086	86-533-3583728	86-533-3583718	Zheng Jiansheng
600003	Northeast Expressway Company Ltd	84, Jie Fang Road, Changchun, Jilin, China	130021	86-431-5679038 86-431-5673111-91810	86-431-5679038 86-431-5679058	Xu Peng
600005	Wuhan Steel Processing Co Ltd	3, Yan Gang Road, Qing Shan District, Wuhan, China	430080	86-27-86306023 86-27-86807873	86-27-86807873	Shi Jun
600006	Dongfeng Automobile Co Ltd	1, Che Cheng Road, Xiangfan, Hubei, China	441004	86-710-3396805	86-710-3396809	Lu Feng
600007	China World Trade Center Company Ltd	1, Jian Guo Men Wai Street, Beijing, China	100004	86-10-65052288	86-10-65051002	Jiao Ying
600008	Beijing Capital Co Ltd	7 Floor of Jingan Center, No.8, Bei San Huan Dong Lu, Chao Yang District, Beijing, China	100028	86-10-64689035	86-10-64689030	Zhang Yang
600009	Shanghai International Airport Co Ltd	2550, Hong Qiao Road, Shanghai, China	200335	86-21-62688899-44169	86-21-62681737	Jia Ruijun
600010	Inner Mongolian Baotou Steel Union Co Ltd	85, Iron & Steel Street, Kun District, Baotou, China	014010	86-472-2105037	86-472-2105006	Guo Jinglong
600011	Huaneng Power International, Inc	Bing 2, Fu Xing Men Nan Da Jie, Xi Cheng District, Beijing, China C Duan Xi District of Tianyin Building	100031	010-66491999	010-66491888	Huang Long
600016	China Minsheng Banking Corporation Ltd	4, Zheng Yi Road, Dong Cheng District, Beijing, China	100006	86-10-65269592	86-10-65229104	Gao Feng
600018	Shanghai Port Container Co Ltd	Ji Fa Building, 4049, Jun Gong Road, Shanghai, China	200432	86-21-56443578	86-21-56441469	Lu Weiguo
600019	Baoshan Iron & Steel Co Ltd	Guo Yuan, Fu Jin Road, Bao Shan District, Shanghai, China	201900	86-21-26647000	86-21-26646999	Zhou Zhuping
600026	China Shipping Development Co Ltd	168, Yuan Dong Shen Lu, Pudong New District, Shanghai, China		86-21-65966865	86-21-65966160	Ye Yumang

Code	Company	Address	Postal code	Phone 1	Phone 2	Contact
600028	China Petroleum & Chemical Corporation	A6, East Hui Xin Street, Chao Yang District, Beijing, China	100029	86-10-64990022	86-10-64990060	Zhang Honglin
600033	Fujian Expressway Development Company Limited.	19 Floor, No. 2 Building, Hong Yang Xin Cheng, 118, Yang Qiao Dong Lu, Fuzhou, China	350001	86-0591-7601476	86-0591-7612847	Jiang Jianxin
600036	China Merchants Bank Co Ltd	7088, Shen Nan Da Dao, Fu Tian District, Shenzhen, Guangdong, China	518040	86-755-83195200	86-755-83198888 83195883	Shao Zuosheng
600037	Beijing Gehua CATV Network Co Ltd	Dong Men, 35, Hua Yuan Bei Lu, Hai Dian District, Beijing, China	100083	86-10-62035573	86-10-62035573	Liao Ying
600038	Hafei Aviation Industry Co Ltd	15, You Xie Street, Ping Fang District, Haerbin, China	150066	86-451-6528350	86-451-6528350	Zhao Anli
600051	Ningbo United Group Co Ltd	Lian He Building, 1, Dong Hai Lu, Ningbo Development Zone, China	315803	86-574-86221320	86-574-86221609	He Xiaolu
600052	Zhejiang Guangsha Co Ltd	1, Zhen Xing Lu, Dongyang, Zhejiang, China	322100	86-0571-85125355	86-0571-8796998	Xu Xiaolin
600053	Jiangxi Paper Industry Co Ltd	112, Dong Jia Yao, Nanchang, Jiangxi, China	330006	86-791-8632392	86-791-8621141-2515	Huang Zhuozhen
600054	Huangshan Tourism Development Co Ltd	Wen Quan, Huang Shan Feng Jing Qu, Huangshan, Anhui, China	242709	86-559-5561110	86-559-5561113	He Jie
600055	Beijing Wandong Medical Equipment Co Ltd	6, Lang Jia Yuan, Jian Guo Men Wai, Chao Yang District, Beijing, China	100022	86-10-65682598	86-10-65682598	Zhang Danshi
600056	CNTIC Trading Co Ltd	3 Floor, Jiu Ling Gong Yu, 21, Xi San Huan Bei Lu, Hai Dian District, Beijing, China	100089	86-010-68404766	86-010-68404720	Qi Jianxi
600057	Amoisonic Electronics Co Ltd	45-47,Ti Yu Lu, Xiamen,China	361012	86-592-5051631	86-592-5058123-3500	Lv Dong
600058	Minmetals Townlord Technology Co Ltd	Block B, 5, San Li He Lu, Hai Dian District, Beijing, China	100044	86-10-68494207	86-10-68494208	Gao Yong
600059	Zhejiang Guyuelongshan Shaoxing Wine Co Ltd	Bei Hai Bridge, Shaoxing, Zhejiang, China	312000	86-575-5166884	86-575-5158435	Zhou Juanying
600060	Hisense Electirc Co Ltd	18, Tuan Jie Road, Economic & Technological Development Zone, Qingdao,China	266071	86-0532-3888515	86-0532-3863463	Sheng Qiang
600061	Sinotex Investment & Development Co Ltd	Room 1804, Sheng Kang Liao Shi Building, 738, Shang Cheng Lu, Pu Dong, Shanghai, China	200120	86-10-64958201	86-10-64958201	Bao Qinfei

Stock Code	Company Name	Address	Postcode	Tel	Fax	Legal representative
600062	Beijing Double-Crane Pharmaceutical Co Ltd	9, Guang Hua Lu, Chao Yang District, Beijing, China	100020	86-10-65060077-2190	86-10-6585578	Ni Jun
600063	Anhui Wanwei Updated Hich-Tech Material Industry Co Ltd	56, Chao Wei Lu, Chao Hu, An Hui, China	238002	86-565-2317280	86-565-2317447	Tang Huazhang
600064	Nanjing Xingang High-Tech Co Ltd	100, Xin Gang Da Dao, Nanjing Economic & Technological Development Zone, China	210038	86-25-5800942	86-25-5800941	Guo Zhao
600065	Daqing Lianyi Petrochemical Co Ltd	5, Lin Yuan Nan Jie, Da Tong District, Daqing, Heilongjiang, China	163852	86-459-6717944	86-459-6717944	Chai Ming
600066	Zhengzhou Yutong Coach Manufacturing Co Ltd	Shi Ba Li He, Nan Jiao, Zhengzhou, Henan, China	450061	86-371-6339748	86-371-6316894	Qi Jiangang
600067	Fuzhou Dartong M&E Co Ltd	81, Fu Ma Lu, Fuzhou, Fujian, China	350011	86-591-3660701	86-591-3660592	Lin Zhennan
600068	Gezhouba Co Ltd	3, Shi Zi Ling Lu, Yichang, Hubei, China	443002	86-717-6746439	86-717-6746470	Wu Hanming
600069	Henan Yinge Industrial Investment Holding Co Ltd	95, Ren Min Dong Lu, Yan Xian Luo He City, Henan, China	46200	86-0395-2355611	86-0395-2355460	Zhang Junli
600070	Zhejiang Furun Co Ltd	42, An Ping Lu, Zhuji, Zhejiang, China	311800	86-575-7222043	86-575-7223018	Chen Liwei
600071	Phenix Optical Co Ltd	1, Guang Xue Lu, Shangrao, Jiangxi, China	334000	86-793-8259547	86-793-8259547	Zou Jianwei
600072	Jiangnan Heavy Industry Co Ltd	18, Gao Xiong Lu, Shanghai, China	200011	86-21-63151818-4554	86-21-63141103	Shi Weidong
600073	Shanghai Maling Aquarius Co Ltd	400, Tong Bei Lu, Shanghai, China	200082	86-21-65419725	86-21-65123609	Zhong Yao
600074	Nanjing Zhongda Film (Group) Co Ltd	C, 20 Fl., Jin Ying Guo Ji Shang Cheng, 89, Han Zhong Lu, Nanjing, China	210029	86-25-4711201 / 86-25-4718467	86-25-4718465	He Zuyuan
600075	Xinjiang Tianye Co Ltd	Company Office Building, 94, Bei Yi Lu, Shihezi, Xinjiang, China	832000	86-0993-2866164	86-0993-2864515	Shen Ming
600076	Weifang Beida Jade Bird Huaguang Technology Co Ltd	272, Dong Feng Dong Jie, Kui Wen District, Weifang, Shandong, China	261041	86-536-8222888-8265	86-536-8264859	Ren Songguo
600077	Liaoning Guoneng Group Joint-Stock Co Ltd	108, Qing Nian Da Jie, Shen He District, Shenyang, Liaoning, China	110014	86-10-62047335	86-10-62047329	Lu Yongmin
600078	Jiangsu Chengxing Phosph-Chemicals Co Ltd	208, Hua Shan Lu, Jiangyin, Jiangsu, China	214432	86-510-6281316-431 / 86-510-6281316-432	86-510-6281884	Chen Yongqin
600079	Wuhan Humanwell Hi-Tech Industry Company Limited	369, Guan Shan Jie Lu Mo Lu, Hong Shan District, Wuhan, China	430074	86-27-87484718-8019	86-27-87484393	Du Xiaoling

Code	Company	Address	Postcode	Phone 1	Phone 2	Contact
600080	Ginwa Enterprise Group Inc	1, Zhen Xing Lu, Xi'an, China	710068	86-29-8404099	86-29-8404468	Qin Chuan
600081	Dongfeng Electronic Technology Co Ltd	No.22 Building, 2000, Zhong Shan Bei Lu, Shanghai, China	200063	86-21-62033003-21	86-21-62032133	Tian Ya
600082	Tianjin Hi-Tech Development Co Ltd	Block C, Hai Tai Huo Ju Chuang Ye Yuan, 2, Wu Hua Dao, Hua Yuan Industries Zone, Tianjin New-tech Industries Park, Tianjin, China	300384	86-022-23078880-205	86-022-23078889	Wen Jian
600083	Chengdu Fortune Science & Technology Co Ltd	12 Floor, Science and Technology Building, Shi Zhu Lu ,Central District, Xincheng, Dongwan, Guangdong, China	523071	86-769-2423114	86-769-2423119	Song Jingyuan
600084	Suntime International Economic-Trading Co Ltd	40, Hong Shan Lu, Urumuqi, Xinjiang Weiwuer Municipality, China	830002	86-991-2312439	86-991-2312439	Gao Xinshan
600085	Beijing Tongrentang Co Ltd	52, Dong Xing Long Street, Chong Wen District, Beijing, China	100062	86-10-67020018	86-10-67020018	Li Lianying
600086	Hubei Duojia Co Ltd	71, Feng Huang Bei Lu, Ezhou, Hubei, China	436000	86-711-3869107	86-711-3853712	Chen Ruifeng
600087	Nanjing Water Transport Industry Co Ltd	10 Floor, Jiangsu Huaqiao Building, 241, Zhong Shan Bei Lu, Nanjing, China	210009	86-25-3720378	86-25-3709524	Zeng Shanzhu
600088	China Television Media Ltd	Tang Cheng, 1, Qitang, Wuxi, Jiangsu, China	214081	86-510-5555168	86-510-5555168	Lu Fang
600089	Xinjiang Tebian Electric Apparatus Stock Co Ltd	52, Yanan Nan Lu, Changji, Xinjiang, China	831100	86-994-2724766	86-994-2724766	Guo Junxiang
600090	Xin Jiang Hops Co Ltd	Jiu Hua Building, 17, Jie Fang Bei Lu, Urumuqi, China	830002	86-991-2835219	86-991-2835219	Shu Qun
600091	Baotou Tomorrow Technology Co Ltd	Baotou Tomorrow Technology Co Ltd Office Building, 2 Km South to Baotou Railway Station	014013	86-472-5980190	86-472-5980275	Guan Ming
600092	Sha'anxi Precision Alloy Co Ltd	2, Zao Yuan Dong Lu, Lian Hu District, Xian, China	710077	86-29-4610536	86-29-4620414	Ge Xifu
600093	Sichuan Hejia Co Ltd	14, Gao Peng Dong Lu, Hi-tech Development Zone, Chengdu, Sichuan, China	610041	86-28-5155498	86-28-5155498	Fan Ping
600094	Shanghai Worldbest Co Ltd	31 Floor, Zhao Shang Ju Building, 161, Lu Jia Zui Dong Lu, Pudong District, Shanghai, China	200120	86-21-58823020	86-21-58825887	Zhang Lesheng

Stock Code	Company Name	Address	Postcode	Tel	Fax	Legal representative
600095	Harbin High-Tech (Group) Co Ltd	Building 26, Hi-tech Development Industries Zone, Haerbin, China	150090	86-451-2308164	86-451-2301029	Liu Haitao
600096	Yunnan Yuntianhua Co Ltd	Yunfu Town, Shuifu County, Yunnan, China	657800	86-870-8664318	86-870-8664319	Liu Gang
600097	Zhejiang Holley Technology Co Ltd	18, Xi Men Dou Lu, Hangzhou, Zhejiang, China	310012	86-571-88471777	86-571-88471666	Ma Sanguang
600098	Guangzhou Development Industry (Holdings) Co Ltd	27 Floor, Jianyin Building, 509, Dong Feng Zhong Lu, Guangzhou, China	510045	86-20-83606539	86-20-83606693	Li Hongmei
600099	Linhai Co Ltd	14, Tai Jiu Lu, Taizhou, Jiangsu	225300	86-523-6551888	86-523-6551403	Luan Yueming
600100	Tsinghua Tongfang Co Ltd	Tsinghua Tongfang Building, Beijing, China	100084	86-10-62789888	86-10-62789765	Sun Mang
600101	Sichuan Mingxing Electric Power Co Ltd	18, Da Dong Jie, Suining, Sichuan, China	629000	86-825-2227626	86-825-2210017	Jiang Qing
600102	Laiwu Steel Corporation	Gang Cheng District, Laiwu, Shandong, China	271104	86-634-6820601 86-634-6820011	86-634-6821094	Ding Zhigang
600103	Fujian Qingshan Paper Industry Co Ltd	Qingzhou Town, Sha County, Fijian, China	365506	86-591-7591043	86-591-7588745	Chen Bingsheng
600104	Shanghai Automotive Co Ltd	Building 18, East, 755, Huaihai Zhong Lu, Shanghai, China	200020	86-21-64158999	86-21-64730567	Zhang Jingen
600105	Jiangsu Yongding Co Ltd	Fenhu Economic & Technological Development Zone, Luxu Town, Wujiang, Jiangsu, China	215211	86-0512-3272395	86-0512-3271866	Zhu Qizhen
600106	Chongqing Road & Bridge Co Ltd	1, Dan Long Lu, Nanping Economic & Technological Development Zone, Chongqing, China	400060	86-23-62803632	86-23-62909387	Zhang Man
600107	Hubei Mailyard Share Co Ltd	Meierya Industrial Part, Tuanchengshan Development Zone, Huangshi, Hubei, China	435003	86-714-6360298	86-714-6360219	Hu Gang
600108	Gansu Yasheng Industrial Group Co Ltd	20 Floor, Jilong Building, 219, Zhang Ye Lu, Lanzhou, China	730030	86-931-8471961	86-931-8483195	Zhou Wenping
600109	Chengdu Commodities Co Ltd Group	83, Da Ci Si Lu, Chengdu, Sichuan, China	610016	86-28-6652215	86-28-6666775	Li Yong
600110	China-Kinwa High Technology Co Ltd	159, Ren Min Street, Changchun, Jilin, China	130022	86-431-5694024	86-431-5689715	Cai Hong

600111	Inner Mongolia Baotou Steel Rare-Earth Hi-Tech Co Ltd	West to Zhangjia Yingzi, Kun District, Baotou, Neimenggu, China	014030	86-472-5139097 86-472-5139079	86-472-5139079	Zhao Zhanbin
600112	Guizhou Changzhen Electrical Apparatus Co Ltd	100, Shanghai Lu, Zunyi, Guizhou, China	563002	86-852-8622952	86-852-8626701	Xing Yanyan
600113	Zhejiang Dong Ri Limited Company	92, Aideng Bridge, Wenzhou, Zhejiang, China	325003	86-577-88835216	86-577-88842287	Zhang Chengdong
600115	China Eastern Airlines Corporation Limited	2550, Hong Bridge, Shanghai, China	200335	86-21-62686268	86-21-62686116	Luo Zhuping
600116	Chongqing Three Gorges Water Conservancy Andelectric Power Co Ltd	72, Gezi Gou, Wanzhou District, Chongqing, China	404000	86-23-58234759	86-23-58251153	Chen Lijuan
600117	Xining Special Steel Co Ltd	Xining, Qinghai, China	810005	86-971-5299089	86-971-5218389	Yang Kai
600118	China Spacesat Technology Co Ltd	16, Fu Cheng Lu, Hai Dian District, Beijing, China	100037	86-010-68768890 68371188	86-010-68768891	Li Shifeng
600119	Y.U.D Yangtze River Investment Industry Co Ltd	1500, Shi Ji Da Dao, Pudong New District, Shanghai, China	200122	86-21-68407009	86-21-68407009	Zhu Lian
600120	Zhejiang Orient Holdings Co Ltd	199, Qing Chun Lu, Hangzhou, China	310006	86-571-87215009	86-571-87215000	Rao Minjie
600121	Zhengzhou Coal Industry & Electric Power Co Ltd	30, Da Xue Lu, Er Qi District, Zhengzhou, Henan, China	450052	86-371-6950227	86-371-6950227	Fu Shenglong
600122	Jiangsu Hongtu High Technology Co Ltd	83, Hubei Lu, Nanjing, China	210009	86-25-3300922	86-25-3300230	Zhang Wei
600123	Shanxi Lanhua Sci-Tech Venture Co Ltd.	181, Ze Zhou Lu, Jincheng, Shanxi, China	048000	86-356-2040123	86-356-2033799	Wang Liyin
600125	Dalian Tielong Industry Co Ltd	1, Xin'an Street, Zhong Shan District, Dalian, China	116001	86-411-2810881	86-411-2816639	Chang Xiaodong
600126	Hang Zhou Iron & Steel Co Ltd	Ban Shan Town, Gong Shu District, Hangzhou, Zhejiang, China	310022	86-571-88132917 86-571-88144301-2235	86-571-88132919	Han Xiaotong
600127	Hunan Jinjian Cereals Industry Co Ltd	37, Wuling Da Dao, Changde, China	415000	86-736-7258043	86-736-7251888	Liu Congyou
600128	Jiangsu Holly Corporation	Hongye Building, 50, Zhong Hua Lu, Nanjing, China	210001	86-25-2308738 86-25-2301288 -7908	86-25-2307117	Jiang Lin
600129	Chongqing Taiji Industry (Group) Co Ltd	68, Jian She Lu, Fu Ling District, Chongqing, China	408000	86-23-72800072	86-23-72800072	Xia Xue
600130	Ningbo Bird Co Ltd	99, Chengshan Lu, Fenghua, Zhejiang, China	315500	86-574-88918855	86-574-88929054	Ma Sitian

Stock Code	Company Name	Address	Postcode	Tel	Fax	Legal representative
600131	Sichuan Minjiang Hydropower Co Ltd	Xia Suo Bridge, Wen Chuan County, Sichuan, China	623007	86-28-7731485	86-28-7764010	Pu Hexiang
600132	Chong Qing Brewery CoLtd	16, Shi Qiao Pu Shi Yang Lu, Jiu Long Po District, Chongqing, China	400039	86-23-68629476	86-23-68629476	Su Fuyu
600133	Wuhan Eastlake High Technology Groupe Co Ltd	Donghu Hi-tech Building, Guandong Science & Technology Industries Part, Hong Shan District, Wuhan, China	430074	86-27-87561433	86-27-87561866	Shu Chunping
600135	Lucky Film Co Ltd	1, Jian She Nan Lu, Baoding, Hebei, China	071054	86-312-3227901-2899	86-312-3217937	Li Jianxin
600136	Wuhan Double Co Ltd	45 Floor, Jiali Square, 818, Hankou Zhong Shan Da Dao, Wuhan, Hubei, China	430020	86-27-82702848	86-27-82702818	Wu Xiaolin
600137	Sichuanchangjiang Packaging Holding Co Ltd	Ma An Shi, Yibin, Sichuan, China	644004	86-28-3189111	86-28-3189111	Fu Xianglin
600138	China CYTS Tours Holding Co Ltd	Bing 23, Dong Jiao Min Xiang, Beijing, China	100006	86-10-65243388-2210 / &2211	86-10-65282284	Zhang Lijun
600139	Dingtian Science & Technology Inc	114, Huashan Bei Lu, Deyang, Sichuan, China	618000	86-28-5181012	86-28-5181740	Huang Xiaojun
600141	Hubei Xingfa Chemicals Group Co Ltd	99, Min Zhu Street, Gaoyang Town, Xingshan County, Hubei, China	443700	86-717-2527022	86-717-2522917	Sun Weidong
600145	Chongqing Swell Ceramics Industry Co Ltd	Jiangjin Youxi Town, Chongqing, China	402285	86-23-47881756 86-23-68820484	86-23-47881756 86-23-68820484	Qiao Changzhi
600146	Ningxia Dayuan Chemical Co Ltd	Wen Chang Nan Lu, New District, Yinchuan, Ningxia, China	750021	86-951-2060021-6427	86-951-2060016	Zhang Hongbin
600148	Changchun Yidong Clutch Co Ltd	17-1, Fanrong Lu, Chao Yang District, Changchun, China	130012	86-431-5173591-224	86-431-5174234	Wang Younian
600149	Xingtai Mill Roll Co Ltd	1, Xin Xing Xi Lu, Xingtai, Hebei, China	054025	86-0319-2116168	86-0319-2022061	Jin Dianru
600150	Hudong Heavy Machinery Co Ltd	2851, Pudong Da Dao, Shanghai, China	200129	86-21-58461891	86-21-38710103	Wang Huiliang
600151	Shanghai Aerospace Automobile Electromechanical Co Ltd	South Wing of Hangtian Building, 222, Cao Xi Lu, Shanghai, China	200235	86-021-64827176	86-021-64827177	Chen Pingping
600152	Ningbo Veken Elite Group Co Ltd	99, He Yi Lu, Ningbo, China	315000	86-574-87341480	86-574-87253691	Nie Linhong
600153	Xiamen C&D Inc	7th Floor, Hai Bin Building, Lu Jiang Dao, Xiamen, China	361001	86-592-2132319	86-592-2132319	Lin Mao

Code	Company Name	Address	Postal Code	Phone		Contact
600155	Hebei Baoshuo Co Ltd	175, Chao Yang Bei Lu, Baoding National Hi-tech Industries Development Zone, Hebei, China	071051	86-312-3109607	86-312-3109605	He Shengli
600156	Hunan Huasheng Yixintai Co Ltd	7th Floor, Huasheng Building, 257, Fu Rong Nan Lu, Changsha, Hunan	410015	86-0731-5215526	86-0731-5217081	Hao Limin
600157	Taian Lurun Co Ltd	111, Qing Nian Lu, Taian, Shandong, China	271000	86-538-8201817	86-538-8226885	Shang Fuping
600158	China Sports Industry Co Ltd	285, Chao Wai Street, Chao Yang District, Beijing, China	100020	86-10-65536158	86-10-65515338	Wang Wuyi
600159	Neimenggu Ningchenglaojiao Biology Technology Co Ltd	Ba Li Han Town, Ning Cheng County, Inner-Mongolia , China	024231	86-476-4800807	86-476-4800131	Xing Fengyi
600160	Zhejiang Juhua Co Ltd	Ke Cheng District, Quzhou, Zhejiang, China	324004	86-570-3091704 86-570-3091688	86-570-3091777	Yu Jiemin
600161	Beijing Tiantan Biological Products Corporation Limited	4, San Jian Fang Nan Li, Chao Yang District, Beijing, China	100024	86-10-65772354 86-10-65772357 86-10-65724045	86-10-65792747	Zhang Yi
600162	Shandong Linyi Engineering Machinery Stock Co Ltd	18, Jin Que Shan Lu, Linyi, Shandong, China	276004	86-539-8308809	86-539-8109193	Gao Shujian
600163	Nanzhi Co Ltd Fujian	177, Bin Jiang Bei Lu, Nanping, Fjian, China	353000	86-599-8808806	86-599-8801260	Li Gongran
600165	Ning Xia Heng Li Steel Wire Rope Co Ltd	He Bin Street, Shi Zui Shan District, Shizuishan, Ningxia, China	753202	86-952-3671240	86-952-3671799	Zhang Wenbin
600166	Beiqi Futian Vehicle Co Ltd	Sha Yang Lu, Shahe Town, Chang Ping District, Beijing, China	102206	86-10-80717181	86-10-20717180	Gong Min
600167	Development And Construction Stocklimited Company In Shenyang New District	Floor 2, 35, San Hao Street, He Ping District, Shenyang, China	110032	86-024-23904434	86-0240-23993579	Nie Jing
600168	Wuhan Sanzhen Industry Holding Co Ltd	Floor 5, Dong Fang Shang Du, Fa Zhan Da Dao, Wuhan, China	430023	86-27-85600546	86-27-85877108	Zeng Mu
600169	Taiyuan Heavy Industry Co Ltd	53, Yu He Street, Wan Bo Lin District, Taiyuan, China	030024	86-351-6361154	86-351-6362554	Li Yingkui
600170	Shanghai Construction Co Ltd	33, Fu Shan Lu, Pudong New District, Shanghai, China	200120	86-21-68872178	86-21-58795500	You Weiping
600171	Shanghai Belling Co Ltd	810, Yi Shan Lu, Cao He Jing Development Zone, Shanghai, China	200233	86-21-64850700-157	86-21-64854424	Dong Qian

Stock Code	Company Name	Address	Postcode	Tel	Fax	Legal representative
600172	Henan Huanghe Xuanfeng Co Ltd	200, Ren Min Lu, Changge, Henan, China	461500	86-374-6165530	86-374-6128688	Li Jianzhong
600173	Heilongjiang Province Mudanjiang New Materials Technology Co Ltd	Wenchun Town Company Building, Xi'an District, Mudanjiang, Heilongjiang, China	157041	86-0453-6497558	86-0453-6497515 86-0453-6499002	Chen Genxiang
600175	Hainan Baohua Industry Share Co Ltd	6 Floor, 69, Bin Hai Da Dao, Haikou, Hainan, China	570105	86-898-68536699-6633	86-898-68550995	Zhou Yi
600176	China Chemical Building Materials Co Ltd	2, Zi Zhu Yuan Nan Lu, Beijing, China	100044	86-10-68434863	86-10-88411072 -828	Dang Yu
600177	Youngor Group Co Ltd	2, Jin Xian Da Dao Xi Duan, Ningbo, Zhejiang, China	315153	86-574-87425136	86-574-87425390	Lin Yan
600178	Harbin Dongan Auto Engine Co Ltd	51, Bao Guo Street, Ping Fang District, Haerbin, China	150066	86-451-6528172 86-451-6528173	86-451-6505502	Jiang Junqi
600179	Heilongjiang Heihua Co Ltd	2, Xiang Yang Street, Fu La Er Ji District, Qiqihaer, Heilongjiang, China	161041	86-452-6817411	86-452-6817998	Wang Hongwei
600180	Shandong Jiufa Edible Fungus Co Ltd	Floor 28, Jindu Building, 9, Nan Street, Yantai, Shandong, China	264001	86-535-6623880	86-535-6623798	Xu Aimin
600181	Unida Co Ltd	59, Ke Yi Lu, National Hi-tech Development Industies Zone, Kunming, China	650106	86-871-8315883	86-871-8315072	Hong Fang
600182	Hualin Tyre Co Ltd	Hualin Town, Mudanjiang, Heilongjiang, China	157032	86-453-6306948	86-453-6304100	Zhang Yuchen
600183	Guangdong Shengyi Sci.Tech Co Ltd	411, Wan Sui Da Dao, Dongwan, Guangdong, China	523039	86-769-2271828-8225	86-769-2271854	Wen Shilong
600185	Xi'an Seastar Modern-Tech Co Ltd	2 Floor, Haixing Aptitude Buiding, Jia 3, Xi Xin Street, Xi'an, China	710004	86-29-7274643	86-29-7286470	Qiu Shengping
600186	Henan Lianhua Gourmet Powder Co Ltd	18, Lian Hua Da Dao, Xiangcheng, Henan, China	466200	86-0394-4298666	86-0394-4298899	Li Guojian
600187	Heilongjiang Black Dragon Co Ltd	27, Chang Qing Lu, Long Sha District, Qiqihaer, Heilongjiang, China	161005	86-452-2816277	86-452-2816277	Li Guomin
600188	Yanzhou Coal Mining Company Limited	40, Fu Shan Lu, Zoucheng, Shandong, China	273500	86-537-5383310	86-537-5383311	Chen Guangshui

ID	Company	Address	Postal	Phone 1	Phone 2	Contact
600189	Jilin Forest Industry Co Ltd	114, Ren Min Street, Changchun, China	130021	86-431-8912969	86-431-8930595	Li Weiming
600190	Jinzhou Port Co Ltd	1, 1st Part of Jin Gang Street, Jinzhou Economic & Technological Development Zone, Liaoning, China	121007	86-416-3586372	86-416-3582841	Yu Jianping
600191	Baotou Huazi Industry Co Ltd	Baotou Huazi Industry Co Ltd, Hedong District, Baotou, Inner Mongolia, China	014045	86-472-4193885	86-472-4193504	Xiao Jun
600192	Lanzhou Greatwall Electrical Co Ltd	125, Nong Min Xiang, Lanzhou, Gansu, China	730000	86-931-8415001-2422	86-931-8414606	He Shimin
600193	Xiamen Prosolar Technology Development Co Ltd	9 Floor, Yangming Building, 18, Jianye Lu, Xiamen, China	361012	86-592-5311857 86-592-5311831	86-592-5311821 86-592-5311955	Li Xiaoling
600195	China Animal Husbandry Industry Co Ltd	Floor 11&12, Xinhua Insurance Building, 8, Lian Hua Chi Xi Li, Feng Tai District, Bejing, China	100073	86-10-63903309	86-10-63903308	Wang Ping
600196	Shanghai Fortune Industrial Co Ltd	1289, Yi Shang Lu, Shanghai, China	200233	86-21-64958682	86-21-64953655	Qin Xuetang
600197	Xinjiang Yilite Industry Co Ltd	Xiao Er Bu La Ke, Xinyuan County, Xinjiang, China	835811	86-999-8028819	86-999-8028819	Hong Yuzhou
600198	Datang Telecom Technology Co Ltd	40, Xue Yuan Lu, Hai Dian District, Bejing, China	100083	86-10-62303607	86-10-62303607	Jiang Yong
600199	Anhui Golden Cattle Co Ltd	259, Lian Hua Lu, Fuyang, Anhui, China	236023	86-558-2212836-2279	86-558-2212666	Chen Xuehui
600200	Jiangsu Wuzhong Industrial Co Ltd	388, Bao Dai Dong Lu, Wu Zhong District, Suzhou, Jiangsu, China	215128	86-512-5272131 86-512-5618665	86-512-5270086	Jin Jianping
600201	Inner Mongolia Jinyu Group Co Ltd	26, Nuo He Mu Le Street, Huhehaote, Neimenggu, China	010020	86-471-5972266-259	86-471-5972931	Li Shujian
600202	Harbin Air Conditioning Co Ltd	193, You Yi Lu, Dao Li District, Haerbin, China	150018	86-451-4644521	86-451-4676205	Wang Zuohai
600203	Fujian Furi Electronics Co Ltd	169, Wu Yi Bei Lu, Fuzhou, China	350005	86-591-3315984 86-591-3318998	86-591-3319978	Bian Zhihang
600205	Shandong Aluminium Industry Co Ltd	Bei Shou, Liu Quan Lu, Zibo Hi-tech Development Industries Zone, Zibo, Shandong, China	255086	86-533-2943467 86-533-2930136	86-533-2985999	Wang Guozhong
600206	GRINM Semiconductor Materials Co Ltd	2, Xin Jie Kou Wai Street, Beijing, China	100088	86-10-62355380	86-10-62355381	Tao Seng
600207	Henan Ancai Hi-Tech Co Ltd	Nan Duan, Zhong Zhou Lu, Anyang, Henan, China	450000	86-372-3932916-2533 / 2249	86-372-3938035	Xu Yingzhong

647

Stock Code	Company Name	Address	Postcode	Tel	Fax	Legal representative
600208	Zhong Bao Ke Kong Investment Co Ltd	11 Floor, 23, Jin Rong Street, Xi Cheng District, Beijing, China	314000	86-010-66214200	86-010-66214186	Qian Chun
600209	Lawton Development Co Ltd	68 Ren Min Da Dao, Haikou, Hainan, China	570208	86-898-66258868	86-898-66254868	Wei Shenghang
600210	Shanghai Zi Jiang Enterprise Group Co Ltd	5481,Hu Min Lu, Shanghai, China	201100	86-21-5415165-602	86-21-5415165-602	Gao Jun
600211	Tibet Rhodiola Pharmaceutical Holding Co	93, Beijing Zhong Lu, Lasa, China	850000	86-891-6837756	86-891-6837749	Gao Zili
600212	Shandong Jiang Quan Industry Co Ltd	Jiangquan Commercial Building, Shuang Yue Men Bei; Luo Zhuang District, Linyi, Shandong, China	276017	86-539-8246243	86-539-8241427	Li Jianren
600213	Yangzhou Yaxing Motor Coach Co Ltd	188, Yang Zi Jiang Zhong Lu, Economic Development Zone, Yangzhou, China	225009	86-514-7850400	86-514-7852329	Zhang Rongsen
600215	Changchun Economic & Technical Development Zone, Development And Construction (Group) Co Ltd	118, Zi You Da Lu, Changchu, Jilin, China	130031	86-431-4644225	86-431-4630035	Yang Yongxue
600216	Zhejiang Medicine Co Ltd	60, Ma Du Xiang, Zhong He Lu Si, Hangzhou, Zhejiang, China	310003	86-0571-87213883	86-0571-87213883	Zhang Guojun
600217	Sha'anxi Qinling Cement Group Co Ltd	East Suburb of Yao County, Sha'anxi, China	727100	86-919-6231630	86-919-6233344	Han Baoping
600218	Anhui Quanchai Engine Co Ltd	70, Jian She Dong Lu, Xianghe Town, Quanjiao County, Anhui, China	239500	86-550-5018888-2289	86-550-5015888 86-550-5011156	Ma Guoyou
600219	Shandong Nanshan Industry & Commerce Co Ltd	Dongjiang Town, Longkou, Shandong, China	265718	86-535-8616188	86-535-8616188	Kou Yu
600220	Jiangsu Sunshine Co Ltd	Masi Bridge, Xinqiao Town, Jiangyin City, Jiangsu Prov.	214426	86-510-6121688	86-510-6121188	Chen Hao
600221	Hainan Airlines Co Ltd	Haihang Development Building, 29, Haixiu Road, Haikou, Hainan	570206	86-898-66739961	86-898-66739960	Zhang Shanghui
600222	Henan Joyline & Joysun Pharmaceutical Stock Co Ltd	8, Jinsuo Road, High-tech Industries Development Zone, Zhengzhou, Henan	450001	86-371-7982194	86-371-7982194	Sun Xuezhi
600223	Shandong Wanjie High-Tech Co Ltd	Boshan Econ&Tech Development Zone, Zibo, Shandong	255213	86-533-4651082	86-533-4650151	Sun Feng

Code	Company	Address	Postal Code	Phone 1	Phone 2	Contact
600225	Hua Tong Tian Xiang Group Co Ltd	17th Floor, Huachen Group Building, Ningbo Road, Huangpu District, Shanghai	200002	86-0591-7525343	86-0591-7557949	Wu Tangqing
600226	Zhejiang Shenghua Biok Biology Co Ltd	Zhongguan Industry Zone, Deqing County, Zhejiang Prov.	313220	86-572-8402738	86-572-8402738	Chen Junbiao
600227	Guizhou Chitianhua Corp.	3rd Floor, Huoju Building, Xintian Street, Guiyang, Guizhou	550001	86-852-2878874	86-852-2878332	Yang Chengxiang
600228	Daheng Epoch Technology Co Ltd	11th Floor, Zhongke Building, 22, Zhongguancun Street, Haidian District, Beijing	100080	86-10-62628443	86-10-62628384	Yan Hongshen
600229	Qingdao Soda Ash Industrial Company Ltd	78, Siliu Bei Road, Qingdao	266043	86-532-4822574	86-532-4815402	Ding Zhaoyuan
600230	Hebei Cangzhou Dahua Co Ltd	Cangzhou Dahua Office Building, 66, Beihuan Zhong Road, Cangzhou, Hebei	061000	86-317-2046143	86-317-3025065	Wang Lu
600231	Lingyuan Iron Steel Co Ltd	3, Gangtie Road, Lingyuan City, Liaoning Prov.	122500	86-421-6834429	86-421-6831910	He Dongsheng
600232	Zhejiang Golden Eagle Co Ltd	Xiaosha Town, Dinghai District, Zhoushan, Zhejiang	316051	86-580-8021228	86-580-8020228	Jiao Kangtao
600233	Dalian Dayang Trends Share Co Ltd	23, Harbin Road, Econ&Tech Development Zone, Dalian	116600	86-411-7610778	86-411-7613354	Sun Changli
600234	Tai Yuan Tianlong Group CoLtd	291, Yingze Street, Taiyuan	030001	86-351-4043568	86-351-4810073	Song Yiqing
600235	Minfeng Special Paper Co Ltd	70, Yongli Street, Jiaxing, Zhejiang	314000	86-573-2070391	86-573-2070391	Zheng Jian
600236	Guangxi Guiguan Electric Power Co Ltd	3, Wangxian Po Yili, Minzhu Road, Nanning, Guangxi, P.R.C.	530023	86-771-5640918	86-771-5620664	Zhang Yun
600237	Anhui Tongfeng Electronics Company Limited	168, Shicheng Road, Tongling City, Anhui	244000	86-562-2819178	86-562-2831965	Zhou Xiaoping
600238	Hainan Yedao Company Limited	F Building of World Trade Centre, Hankou, Hainan	570125	86-898-68520319	86-898-68520851	Wang Guangxin
600239	Yunnan Honghe Guangming Co Ltd	120, Xinan Road, Kaiyuan City, Yunnan Prov.	661600	86-873-7123420	86-873-7122528	Ma Yupeng
600240	Inner Mongolia Shiqi Industrial Co Ltd	54, Nuo He Mu Le Street, Huhehaote	010020	86-471-5920334	86-471-5920337	Liu Haifeng
600241	Liaoning Times Garments I/E Inc	Times Building, 7, Gangwan Street, Zhongshan District, Dalian	116001	86-411-2798001-1160 86-411-2798317	86-411-2798000	Zou Minggang
600242	Guangdong Hualong Groups Limited Company	21st Floor, Wuyang Xincheng Square, 111, Siyou Xinma Road, Guangzhou	510600	86-662-3235645	86-662-3221747	Wang Xiao

Stock Code	Company Name	Address	Postcode	Tel	Fax	Legal representative
600243	Qinghai Huading Industrial Co Ltd	21, Nanchuan Dong Road, Qinghai	810021	86-971-6258124	86-971-6258774	Liu Wenzhong
600246	Beijing Pioneer Food & Agriculture Co Ltd	Pioneer Commercial Building, 277, Zhaodengyu Road, Xicheng District, Beijing	100034	86-10-66128936	86-10-66128935	Cheng Xiao
600247	Jilin Wuhua Group Co Ltd	29,Huaide Street, Jilin City, Jilin Prov.	132001	86-432-2485305	86-432-2452677	Gao Guansheng
600248	Yangling Qingfeng Agri.Sci.& Tech.Co Ltd	6, Fengcheng Er Lu, Econ&Tech Development Zone, XI'an	710016	86-29-6522221-8407	86-29-6522826	Li Ying
600250	Nanjing Textiles Import & Export Corp. Ltd	77, Yunnan Bei Road, Gulou District, Nanjing	210009	86-25-3306789	86-25-3300518	Ding Jie
600252	Guangxi Wuzhou Zhongheng Group Co Ltd	3, Dieshan Yi Road, Wuzhou City, Guangxi	543002	86-774-5830828	86-774-5830900 86-774-5833090	Li Chengyu
600253	Henan Topfond Pharmaceutical Co Ltd	2, Guangming Road, Zhumadian City, Henan Prov.	463003	86-396-3813379-3096	86-396-3815761	Liang Yaowu
600255	Anhui Xinke New Materials Co Ltd	23,Zhujiang Road, Econ&Tech Development Zone, Wuhu, Anhui	241009	86-553-5847323	86-553-5847423	Jiang Bin
600256	Xin Jiang Guanghui Industry Co Ltd	3,Shanghai Road, Econ&Tech Development Zone , Urumuqi, Xinjiang	830026	86-991-2851134	86-991-2851134	Yan Jinsheng
600257	Hunan Dongting Aquaculture Co Ltd	6th Floor, Hua Du Hotel,358, Renmin Zhong Road,Chang'de, Hunan	415000	86-736-7223888 -3688	86-736-7266736	Huang Xinyuan
600258	Beijing Capital Tourism Co Ltd	51,Fu Xing Men Nei Street, Xicheng District,Beijing (4th Floor, Minzu Hotel)	100031	86-10-66014466 -446	86-10-66019471	Wang Zhiqiang
600259	Hainan Xingye Polyester Co Ltd	19,Xing Ye Road, HK&Macao Industry Zone,Haikou,Hainan	570314	86-898-68669470	86-898-68664045	Ou Datan
600260	Kaile New Material Science And Technology Co Ltd Hubei	Chengguan,Hudi Town, Gong'an County, Hubei	434300	86-716-5237491	86-716-5224433	Chen Jie
600261	Zhejiang Yankon Group Co Ltd	Yangguan Building, 129, Fengshan Road, Shangyu City, Zhejiang	312300	86-575-2027721	86-575-2027720	Xu Guorong
600262	Inner Mongolia Northhauler Joint Stock Company Limited	Qingshan District, Baotou, Inner-Mongolia	014030	86-0472-3331144	86-0472-3335742	Zhang Yong
600263	CRBC International Co Ltd	8th Floor,Office Building A, Donghuan Square, 9, Dongzhong Street, Dongcheng District, Beijing	100027	86-10-64181166	86-10-64182080	Lin Chengxin

Code	Company Name	Address	Postal Code	Phone 1	Phone 2	Contact
600265	Yunnan Jingu Forestry Co Ltd	47, Weiyuan Road, Jinggu Dai Zu &Yi Zu Autonomous County, Yunnan, China	666400	86-879-5226908	86-879-5228008	Qiu Haitao
600266	Beijing Urban Construction Investment & Development Co Ltd	New City Tech-Building,11, Tucheng Xi Road,Chaoyang District, Beijing	100029	86-10-62035969-60 86-10-62260806	86-10-62223073	Yang Yuncheng
600267	Zhejiang Hisun Pharmaceutical Co Ltd	46,Waisha Road,Jiaojiang District, Taizhou City, Zhejiang	318000	86-571-85278141 86-576-8827809	86-571-85270053	Zhang Wei
600268	Guodian Nanjing Automation Co Ltd	38, Xin Mofan Road, Nanjing, Jiangsu	210003	86-25-3410173	86-25-3418700-3021	Zou Feng
600269	Jiangxi Ganyue Expressway Co Ltd	5&6th Floor, Fangxing Building, 508, Hongcheng Road, Nanchang	330025	86-791-6504265	86-791-6507178	Xiong Changshui
600270	Sinotrans Air Transportation Development Co Ltd	Jiuling Building, 21, Sanhuan Bei Road, Haidian District ,Beijing	100089	86-010-68405635	86-010-68405629	Zhou Bo
600272	Shanghai Kaikai Industry Company Limited	24th Floor, 888,Wanhangdu Road, Shanghai	200042	86-21-62127558	86-21-62125575	Xu Xiaobai
600275	Hubei Wuchangyu Co Ltd	1, Nanpu nan Road, Echeng District, Ezhou City, Hubei	436000	86-711-3200331	86-711-3200331	Xiong Guosheng
600276	Jiangsu Hengrui Medicine Co Ltd	145,Renmin Dong Road, Xinpu District, Lianyungang	222002	86-518-5457194	86-518-5452340	Xhen Xuemin
600277	Inner Mongolia Yili Science And Technology Industry Co Ltd	Yili Science And Technology Building, E'erduosi Xi Street, Dongsheng City, Inner-Mongolia, China	017000	86-477-8372777	86-477-8371744	Wang Jingsheng
600278	Orient International Enterprise, Ltd	Block A ,85,Loushanguan Road, Shanghai	200233	86-21-62785521	86-21-62784020	Huang Dayu
600279	Chongqing Gangjiu Co Ltd	113–13,Panlongwu Village, Panlong Town, Jiulongpo District, Chongqing	400051	86-23-63725685	86-23-63801564	Li Yujian
600280	Nanjin Central Emporium Co Ltd	79, Zhongshan Nan Road, Nanjing, Jiangsu	210005	86-25-4728470	86-25-4707466	Tao Hua
600281	Taiyuan Chemical Industry Co Ltd	15, Wenyuan Xiang, Yingze District, Taiyuan, Shanxi	030001	86-351-4181612	86-351-4180791	Wu Hongshan
600282	Nanjing Iron & Steel Co Ltd	Xiejia Dian, Dachang District, Nanjing, Jiangsu	210035	86-25-7056780	86-25-7052184	Xu Lin
600283	Qianjiang Water Resources Development Co Ltd	Investment Building,166, Tianmushan Road, Hangzhou, Zhejiang	310007	86-571-88805888 -1088	86-571-88822250	Wang Linjiang

Stock Code	Company Name	Address	Postcode	Tel	Fax	Legal representative
600285	Henan Lingrui Pharmaceutical Co Ltd	232,Xiangyang Road, Xin County , Henan	465550	86-0397-2987888	86-0397-2987888	Du Qiang
600286	Hunan Guoguang Ceramic Group Co Ltd	270, Huayuan An, Liling City, Hunan	412200	86-733-3232923	86-733-3247684	Duan Jun
600287	Jiangsu Sainty Corp Ltd	Shuntian Building, 98, Jianye Road, Nanjing, Jiangsu	210004	86-25-4208688 -82068	86-25-4201927	Yang Qingfeng
600289	Bright Oceans Inter-Telecom Corporation	Building 1,Harbin High-tech Industry Development Zone, Harbin, China	150090	86-451-2326789	86-451-2320579	Guo Shibin
		19, Haidian Nan Road, Zhongguancun, Beijing, China	100080	86-10-82666789	86-10-82666332	
600290	Sufoma Co Ltd	57, Xi Dayingmen, Suzhou, Jiangsu	215003	86-512-7513621	86-512-7513633	Hu Qixin
600291	Xishui Strong Year Co Ltd Inner Mongolia	Hannan District, Wuhai City, Inner-Mongolia	016032	86-473-4661666	86-473-4663855	Bai Xuefeng
600292	Chongqing Jiulong Electric Power Co Ltd	37,Yuzhou Road, Jiulong Po, Chongqing	400051	86-23-68637303	86-23-68635244	Zhang Qi
600293	Hubei Sanxia New Building Material Co Ltd	Econ &Tech Development Zone, Dangyang, Hubei	444105	86-717-3280108	86-717-8934018	Zhang Guangchun
600295	Inner Mongolia Eerduosi Cashmere Products Co Ltd	102, Da'te Nan Road, Dongsheng, Inner-Mongolia	017000	86-477-8346294	86-477-8336699	Li Chengjun
600296	Lanzhou Aluminium Co Ltd	375, Shandan Street, Xigu District, Lanzhou, Gansu	730060	86-931-7567057	86-931-7558888	Li Zhiyong
600297	Dalian Merro Pharmaceutical Co Ltd	112, Zhongshan Road, Zhongshan District , Dalian	116001	86-411-3631991 -905	86-411-3606084	Tang Dayong
600298	Hubei Angel Yeast Co Ltd	24, Zhongnan Road, Yichang , Hubei	443003	86-717-6352865	86-717-6352865	Zhou Bangjun
600299	Blue Star New Chemial Material Co Ltd	Commercial Assembly Hall, 30, Huayuan Dong Road, Haidian District, Beijing	100083	86-10-82070614	86-10-82070735	Wang Xiaodong
600300	Xuzhou V V Food & Beverage Co Ltd	Headquarter of Weiwei Group, Chengnan Development Zone, Xuzhou, Jiangsu	221111	86-516-3290169	86-516-2704888	Ding Jinli
600301	Nanning Chemical Industry Co Ltd	80, Tinghong Road, Nanning, Guangxi	530031	86-771-4835135	86-771-4821093	Gao Youzhi

Code	Company	Address	Postal	Phone 1	Phone 2	Contact
600302	Xi'an Typical Industries Co Ltd	9th Floor, Financial Building,42, Gaoxin Road, High-tech Industry Development Zone, Xi'an	710075	86-29-8313626	86-29-8329701	Li Jianping
600303	Dandong Shuguang Vehicle Axle Co Ltd	50, Shuguan Road, Zhen'an District, Dandong City, Liaoning	118001	86-0415-4146825	86-0415-4142821	Na Tao
600305	Jiangsu Hengshun Vinegar Co Ltd	84, Zhongshan Xi Road, Zhenjiang	212004	86-511-5233758	86-511-5230209	Wang Mingfa
600306	Shen Yang Commercial City Co Ltd	212, Zhongjie Road, Shenhe District, Shenyang	110011	86-24-24865832	86-24-24865832	Zhang Liming
600307	Gan Su Jiu Steel Group Hong Xing Iron & Steel Co Ltd	12, Xiongguan Dong Road, Jiayuguan City, Gansu	735100	86-937-6712325	86-937-6715507	Liu Yanqi
600308	Shandong Huatai Paper Co Ltd	Dawang Town, Guangrao County, Dongying City, Shandong Prov.	257335	86-546-6871957	86-546-6871957	Li Gang
600309	Yantai Wanhua Polyurethane Co Ltd	7, Xingfu Nan Road, Yantai	264002	86-535-6837888-537 86-535-6837894	86-535-6837894	Guo Xingtian
600310	Guangxi Guidong Electric Power Co Ltd	12, Ping'an Xi Road, Hezhou City, Guangxi	542800	86-774-5297881 86-774-5273622	86-774-5283343 86-774-5285255	Liu Shisheng
600311	Gansu Ronghua Industry Group Co Ltd	1, Ronghua Road,Dongguan Street, Wuwei City, Gansu	733000	86-935-2292183	86-935-2292328	Liu Yong
600312	Henan Pinggao Electric Co Ltd	22, Nanhuan Dong Road, Pingding Shan City, Henan Prov.	467001	86-375-3804061	86-375-3887040	Liu Wei
600313	Zhongken Agricultural Resource Development Co Ltd	C501, Yuetan Building, Yuetan Bei Street, Xicheng District, Beijing	100045	86-10-68082492	86-10-68083262	Chen Jiansheng
600315	Shanghai Jahwa United Co Ltd	527, Baoding Road, Shanghai	200082	86-21-65456400 -3725	86-21-65458990	Mr. Feng
600316	Jiangxi Hongdu Aviation Industry Co Ltd	Xinxi Bridge, Nanchang	330024	86-791-8467844	86-791-8467844	Chen Wenhao
600317	Yingkou Port Liability Co Ltd	1, Xin'gang Great Road, Boyuquan District, Yingkou City, Liaoning	115007	86-417-6268507	86-417-6268506	Yang Huijun
600318	Anhui Chaodong Cement Co Ltd	269, Changjiang Xi Road, Chaohu City, Anhui	238001	86-565-2391720	86-565-2391918	Qian Yeyin
600319	Weifang Yaxing Chemical Co Ltd	899, Yuanfei Road, Kuiwen District, Weifang City, Shandong	261031	86-536-8667941	86-536-8666877	Wang Bo
600320	Shanghai Zhenhua Port Machinery Co Ltd	3470, Pudong Nan Road, Shanghai	200125	86-21-58396666	86-21-58399555	Gao Lijuan
600321	Sichuan Guodong Construction Co Ltd	Shuangliuban Bridge, Chengdu, Sichuan	610206	86-28-5805811	86-28-5804146	Wang Xiaoming
600322	Tianjin Reality Development (Group) Co Ltd	80, Changde Road, Heping District, Tianjin	300050	86-22-23317185	86-22-23316822	Chen Changlai

Stock Code	Company Name	Address	Postcode	Tel	Fax	Legal representative
600323	Nanhai Development Co Ltd	3rd Floor, 43, Nangui Dong Road, Nanhai City, Guangdong Prov.	528200	86-0757-6280996	86-0757-6236551	Guo Zhanquan
600326	Tibet Tianlu Communications Co Ltd	14, Duodi Road, Lahsa City, Tibet	850000	86-891-6322208	86-891-6333071	Rao Bangji
600327	Wuxi Commercial Mansion Corp Ltd	343, Zhongshan Road, Wuxi, Jiangsu	214001	86-510-2702093	86-510-2700159	Zhang Bin
600328	Inner Mongolia Lantai Industrial Co Ltd	Jilantai Town, Anlashanzuo Qi, Inner-Mongolia	750333	86-483-8838608	86-483-8838735	Ren Fen
600329	Tianjin Zhongxin Pharmaceutical Group Corporation Limited	Jin wan Building, 358, Nanjing Road, Nankai District , Tianjin	300100	86-22-27500227	86-22-27500227	Mo Hao
600330	Zhejiang Tiantong Electronic Co Ltd	18th Floor, Longxiang Office Building, Haining City, Zhejiang Prov.	314400	86-573-7230878	86-573-7230228	Xu Lixiu
600331	Sichuan Hongda Chemical Industry Co Ltd	Minzhu Town, Shifang City, Sichuan Prov.	610041	86-28-86141081	86-28-86140372	Wang Yanjun
600332	Guangzhou Pharmaceutical Company Limited	45, Shamian Bei Street, Guangzhou, Guangdong Prov., P.R.C.	510130	86-20-81218117	86-20-81876408	He Shuhua
600333	Changchun Gas Co Ltd	48, Tongzhi Street, Changchun	130021	86-431-5668756	86-431-5668761	Sun Shuhuai
600335	China Construction International Development Co Ltd	156, Jintang Road, Hedong District, Tianjin	300180	86-22-24935580	86-22-24935580	Feng Xiaoyu
600336	Qingdao Aucma Company Limited	315, Qianwangang Road, Econ& Tech Development Zone, Qingdao	266510	86-532-6765129	86-532-6765166	Sun Wu
600337	Markor Furniture International Co Ltd	15, Yingbin Nan Road, Econ& Tech Development Zone, Urumuqi, Xinjiang	830014	86-991-3836028	86-991-3828180 86-991-3836028	Huang Xin
600338	Tibet Summit Industrial Co Ltd	Tibet Zhufeng Building, 161, 1st West Block,Yihuan Road, Chengdu, Sichuan	610072	86-28-7030618	86-28-7042657	Zhao Qiyun
600339	Xinjiang Dushanzi Tianli High & Newtech Co Ltd P.R.C.	3, Beijing Road, Dushanzi District, Kelamayi City, Xinjiang	833600	86-992-3680703 86 -992-3872308 86-992-3872045	86-992-3680651	Ma Xinhai
600345	Wuhan Yangtze,Communication Industry Group Co Ltd	11th Floor, Management Building, Donghu New-tech Development Zone, 200-1, Luoyu Road, Wuchang	430070	86-27-87411083	86-27-87411083	Hu Xiangjian
600346	Dalian Bingshan Rubber & Plastics Co Ltd	1, Zhoushuizi Square, Ganjingzi District, Dalian	116033	86-411-6641861	86-411-6641645	Xie Like

600350	Shandong Infrastructure Company Limited	Shandong University Technical Garden, Chuangye Centre, 71, Jingshi Road, Jinan, Shandong	250061	0531-2662952	0531-2662950	Wang Dawei
600355	Wuhan Jinglun Electronic Co Ltd	Miaoshan Community, Donghu Development Zone, Wuhan	430223	027-87921111-3221	027-87921111-3223	Jin Jiaming
600356	Mudanjiang Hengfeng Paper Co Ltd	11, Zaozhi Road, Yangming District, Mudanjiang City, Heilongjiang Prov.	157013	86-453-6331111-6451	86-453-6330989	Li Rongwei
600358	China United Travel Company Ltd	18th Floor, Building A, Jinying International Commercial City, 89, Hanzhong Road, Nanjing	210029	86-25-4711182	86-25-4702099	Li Li
600359	Xinjiang Talimu Agriculture Development Co Ltd	5th Floor, Social Security Building, 3, Jiankang Road, Akesu City, Xinjiang	843000	86-0997-2134083	86-0997-2130840	Li XInhai
600360	Jilin Sino-Microelectronics Co Ltd	100, Changjiang Street, Fengman District, Jilin	132013	86-432-4662099	86-432-4665812	Ding Dayue
600361	Beijing Hualian Hypermarket Co Ltd	5th Floor, Saite Square, 22, Jianwai Da Jie, Beijing	100037	010-88363718	010-68364733	Niu Xiaohua
600362	Jiangxi Copper Company Limited	15, Yejin Da Dao, Guixi, Jiangxi	335424	0701-3777735	0701-3777013	Huang Dongfeng
600363	Jiangxi Lianchuang Optoelectronic Science And Technology Co Ltd	125,Huoju Da Jie, High-tech Industry Development Zone, Nanchang	330029	86-0791-8108479	86-0791-8105326	Yao Weibiao
600365	Tonghua Grape Wine Co Ltd	28,Qianxing Road, Tonghua, Jilin	134002	86-0435-3948012	86-0435-3949616	Gao Zhencai
600366	Ningbo Yunsheng Group Co Ltd	348,Dongmin an Road, Ningbo, Zhejiang	315040	86-574-87776804	86-574-87776466	Ying Xinyi
600367	Guizhou Redstar Developing Co Ltd	Dingqi Town, Zhenning County, Anshun City, Guizhou Prov.	561206	86-853-6780066	86-853-6780074	Wen Xia
600368	Guangxi Wuzguangxi Wuzhou Communications Co Lrdhou	48, Xinmin Road, Nanning City, Guangxi	530012	86-771-2838485	86-771-2838485	Chen Shiyue
600369	Chongqing Changjiang River Water Transport Co Ltd	2, Zhongshan Dong Road, Fuling District, Chongqing	408000	86-23-63727484-201	86-23-63703361	Rao Zhengli
600372	Jiangxi Changhe Automobile Co Ltd	Dong Jiao, Jingdezhen, Jiangxi	333002	86-798-8448974	86-798-8448974	Wu Dequan
600373	Jiangxi Xinxin Industrial C0., Ltd	2, Nanhuan Road, Shangrao, Jiangxi	334000	0793-8238282-6178	0973-8222255	Peng Zhen
600376	Beijing Tianhong Baoye Real Estate Co Ltd	2nd, Jingbao Garden, 183, Andingmen Wai Da Jie, Dongcheng District, Beijing	100011	86-10-6425268	86-10-6425258	Gong Qianwei

Stock Code	Company Name	Address	Postcode	Tel	Fax	Legal representative
600377	Jiangsu Expressway Company Limited	Jiangsu Transport Building, 69, Shigu Road, Nanjing, Jiangsu	210004	86-25-4469332	86-25-4466643	Yao Yongjia
600378	Sichuan Tianyi Science Technology Co Ltd	455 Letter Box, Jichang Road, Chengdu, Suchuan	610225	86-28-5964616-3006-3168	86-28-5881997	Yang Zhongyi
600379	Shaanxi Baoguang Vacuum Electronic Apparatus Co Ltd	5,Yingda Road, High-tech Industry Development Zone, Baoji, Shaanxi	710006	86-917-6788528	86-917-6788528	Jin Baochang
600380	Shenzhen Taitai Pharmaceutical Company Limited	23F, Diwang Commercial Building, Shennan Dong Road, Luohu District, Shenzhen	518008	86-755-2478966	86-755-2478967	Qiu Qingfeng
600381	Qinghai Baichunlu Company Limited	36, Xiaoqiao Da Jie, Xining, Qinghai	810003	86-971-5130792	86-971-5134240	Li Zhe
600382	Guangdong Mingzhu Ball Valve Group Co Ltd	Chigang kou, Xingcheng Town, Xingning City, Guangdong Prov.	514500	86-753-3338549	86-753-3324118	Ou Yang Jin
600383	Goldfield Industries Inc	Goldfield Building, Fuqiang Road, Futian District, Shenzhen	518048	86-755-3303333	86-755-3844555	Yan Bing
600385	Shandong Jintai Group Co Ltd	29,Honglou Xi Road, Jinan, Shandong	250100	86-531-8902341	86-531-8902341	Fan Zhisheng
600386	Beijing Bashi Co Ltd	32, Zizhuyuan Road, Haidian District, Beijing	100044	86-10-68477383	86-10-68731430	Fu Shixue
600388	Fujin Longking Co Ltd	81, Xin Luolinyuan Road, Longyan, Fujian	364000	86-597-2210288	86-597-2290903	Chen Peimin
600389	Nantong Jiangshan Agrochemical Chemical Co Ltd	35, Yangang Road, Nantong City, Jiangsu	226006	86-0513-3517961	86-0513-3521807	Tao Kunshan
600390	Kingray New Materials Science Technology Co Ltd	1, Lushan Nan Road, Yuelu District, Changsha, Hunan	410012	86-731-8657382	86-731-8829998	Du Weiwu
600391	Sichuan Chengfa Aero-Science Technology Co Ltd	Shuangqiaozi, Chengdu, Sichuan	610067	86-28-84509005	86-28-84506406	Yang Guang
600393	Guangzhou Donghua Enterprise Co Ltd	30 Building, Si youxinma Road, Dongshan District, Guangzhou	510600	86-20-87393888-8339	86-20-87371634	Cai Jinlu
600395	Guizhou Panjiang Refined Coal Co Ltd	Gan Gou Bridge, Hongguo Economic Development Zone, Liupanshui, Guizhou, China	553536	86-858-3703046	86-858-3700328	Wu Zhengbin
600396	Shenyang Jinshan Thermoelectric Co Ltd	68, He Ping Bei Da Jie, Shenyang, China	110002	86-24-22871446	86-24-22872718	Wang Wei
600397	Anyuan Industrial Co Ltd	3, Zhaoping Dong Lu, Pingxiang, Jiangxi, China	337003	86-799-6581363	86-799-6581171	Chen Songliu

Code	Company	Address	Postcode	Phone 1	Phone 2	Contact
600398	Canal Scientific And Technological Co Ltd	Xinqiao Town, Jiangyin, Jiangsu, China	214426	86-510-6121388	86-510-6126877	Zhao Zhiqiang
600399	Fushun Special Steel Co Ltd	56, He Ping Lu Dong Duan, Wanghua District, Fushun, Liaoning, China	113001	86-413-6678441	86-413-6679476	Wang Yenong
600400	Jiangsu Hongdou Industry Co Ltd	Gangxia Town, Xishan, Jiangsu, China	214199	86-510-8761888-278	86-510-8350139	Jiang Weixiong
600415	Zhejiang China Commodities City Group Co Ltd	158, Binwang Lu, Yiwu, Zhejiang, China	32000	86-579-5544933	86-579-5546226	Chen Ronggen
600416	Xiangtan Electric Manufacturing Co Ltd	302, Zhuo Xia She Si Jie, Xiangtan, Hunan, China	411101	86-732-8595089 8595320	86-732-8595732 8610767	Tang Honghui
600418	Anhui Jianghuai Automotive Chassis Co Ltd	176, Dong Liu Lu, Hefei, Anhui, China	230022	86-551-3415133-6835	86-551-3425437	Wang Min
600419	Xinjiang Tianhong Papermaking Co Ltd	Xi San Lu, Shihezi, Xinjiang, China (Xinjiang Tianhong Papermaking Co Ltd Office Building)	832009	86-993-2515661-5555	86-993-2511714	Wang Qiaoling
600422	Kunming Pharmaceutical Group Ltd Corp.	7 Km to West Suburb, Kunming, Yunnan, China	650100	86-871-8101631	86-871-8101631	Xu Zhaoneng
600426	Shandong Hualu Desheng Chemical Co Ltd	24, Tianqu Xi Lu, Dezhou, Shandong, China	253024	86-534-2460426	86-534-2462421	Song Jie
600428	COSCO Shipping Co Ltd	Building 5, 412, Huan Shi Dong Lu, Guangzhou, Guangdong, China	510061	020-87766288	020-87625402	Lin Jingwei
600448	Huafang Company Limited By Shares	819, Huang He Er Lu, Binzhou, Shandong, China	256617	86-543-3288255	86-543-3288520	Cui Jianhua
600456	Baoji Titanium Industry Co Ltd	1, Tai Cheng Lu, Baoji, Shanxi, China	721014	86-917-3382026	86-917-3382132	Zheng Haishan
600466	Sichuan Dikang Sci & Tech Pharmaceutical Industry Co Ltd	PO Box 404, 1, Ke Yuan Er Lu, Hi-tech Zone, Chengdu, China	610041	86-28-5195555-8300	86-28-5184149	Liu Ming
600468	Tianjin Tejing Hydraulic Co Ltd	63, Nan Kai San Wei Lu, Tianjin, China	300100	86-22-27386320	86-22-27386320	Liang Yan
600486	Jiangsu Yangnong Chemical Co Ltd	39, Wen Feng Lu, Yangzhou, Jiangsu, China	225009	86-514-7813243-486	86-514-7815486	Lu Ximing
600488	Tianjin Tianyao Pharmaceutical Co Ltd	91, Cheng Lin Zhuang Lu, He Dong District, Tianjin	300161	86-22-24564837	86-22-24564837	Wang Jie
600496	Anhui Changjiang Agriculture Equipment Co Ltd	28, Jiang Huai Lu, Liuan, Anhui, China	237009	86-564-3321848	86-564-3325237	Yu Xiaoping

Stock Code	Company Name	Address	Postcode	Tel	Fax	Legal representative
600498	Fiberhome Telecommunication Technologies Co Ltd	88, You Ke Yuan Lu, Hongshan District, Wuhan, China	430074	86-27-87693885	86-27-87691704	Xiong Xiangfeng
600500	Sinochem International Company Limited	18 Floor, Jin Mao Building San Qu, 88, Shiji Da Dao, Pudong New District, Shanghai, China	200121	86-21-50495988	86-21-50490909	Wang Keming
600501	Nanjing Chenguang Aerospace Applying Technology Co Ltd	1, Zheng Xue Lu, Qin Huai District, Nanjing, China	210006	86-25-2413078-2028	86-25-2410226	Wu Daoqin
600503	Wholewise Sci Tech. Co Ltd	2 Floor, Min Dong Building, 57, Wuyi Zhong Lu, Fuzhou, Fujian, China	350005	86-591-3368240	86-591-3321996-572	Yang Yun
600505	Sichuan Xichang Power Jointstock Co Ltd	13, Lao Xi Men Jie, Xichang, Sichuan, China	615000	86-834-3830007	86-834-3830169	Xu Yuanyu
600506	Xinjiang Koerle Pear Co Ltd	Tuan Jie Lu Lan Gan Lu Kou, Kuerle, Xinjiang, China	841000	86-996-2204656	86-996-2204878	Deng Xiaotian
600508	Shanghai Datun Energy Resourses Co Ltd	18, Tao Lin Lu, Pudong New District, Shanghai, China	200135	86-21-58218560	86-21-58215101	Qi Houqin
600509	Xinjiang Tianfu Thermoelectric Co Ltd	54, Hongxin Lu, Shihezi, Xinjiang, China	832000	86-993-2902860 2901128	86-993-2901121 2901128	Xu Ruimin
600510	Black Peony Group Co Ltd	47, He Ping Nan Lu, Changzhou, Jiangsu, China	213001	86-519-8166510	86-519-8109996	Ge Yafang
600515	Hainan First Investment Merchant Co Ltd	15 Floor, Nan Yang Building, Bin Hai Da Dao, Haikou, Hainan	570105	86-898-68530096	86-898-68513887	Zhang Fengshan
600518	Guangdong Kangmei Pharmaceutical Co Ltd	Chang Chun Lu, Puni ng, Guangdong, China	515300	86-0663-2917777-8009	86-0663-2916111	Qiu Xiwei
600519	Kweichow Moutai Co Ltd	Maotai Town, Renhuai, Guizhou, China	564501	86-852-2386002	86-852-2386005	Fan Ningping
600520	Tongling Sanjia Mould Co Ltd	Shi Cheng Lu Electric Industries Part, Tongling, Anhui, China	244000	0562-2627520	0562-2627555	Xie Leping
600523	Guizhou Guihang Automotive Components Co Ltd	14 Floor, Wujiang Building, 9, Xin Hua Lu, Guiyang, Guizhou, China	550002	0851-5815780	0851-5870544	Zhu Huabing
600526	Zhejiang Feida Environmental Science & Technology Co Ltd	88, Wang Yun Lu, Zhuji, Zhejiang	311800	0575-7385602	0575-7214695	Tu Tianyun
600528	China Railway Brju Co Ltd	Zhong Tie Er Ju Building, Tongjin, Chengdu, China	610032	86-028-7684612	86-028-7683980	Deng Aimin
600529	Shandong Pharmaceutical Glass Co Ltd	8, Er Lang Shan Lu, YI Yuan County, Zibo, Shandong, China	256100	86-533-324231.22028	86-533-3249700	Zhou Shiyong

Code	Company	Address	Postal	Phone	Contact
600530	Shanghai Jiaoda Onlly Co Ltd	811, Hong Bridge, Shanghai, China	200030	86-21-62810808-111	Zhang Panhong
600531	Henan Yuguang Gold Lead Co Ltd	525, Ji Shui Da Jie Zhong Duan, Jiyuan, Henan, China	454650	86-391-6665836	Ren Wenyi
600536	Chinasoft Network Technology Company Limited	6 Floor, Building 1, Zhong Ruan Building, 55, Xue Yuan Nan Lu, Haidian District, Beijing, China	100081	86-10-62186577	Cheng Shuguang
600539	Taiyuan Lion-Head Cement Co Ltd	1, Kaicheng Jie, Wan Bo Lin District, Taiyuan, Shanxi, China	030056	86-351-6127621	Hao Ying
600548	Shenzhen Expressway Company Limited	Floor19, Building A, Lianhe Sqare, 5022, Bin He Lu Bei, Shenzhen, China	518026	86-0755-2910588-208	Zhang Rongxing
600550	Baoding Tianwei Baobian Electric Co Ltd	318, Jiang Cheng Lu, Baoding, Hebei	071056	86-312-3252455	Bian Haiqing
600555	Shanghai Matsuoka Co Ltd	Building 8, 841, Yanan Zhong Lu, Shanghai, China	200040	86-21-62893080	Wang Weimin
600556	Guangxi Beisheng Pharmaceutical Co Ltd	Building 88, Haiyu Community, Bai Hu Tou Lu, Beihai, Guangxi,China	536000	86-779-3216669	Yan Dan
600558	Sichuan Atlantic Welding Consumable Co Ltd	2, Chongkou Jie, Da An District, Zigong, Sichuan, China	643010	86-81-35100549	Guo Wancheng
600561	Jiangxi Changyun Co Ltd	118, Guanchang Nan Lu, Nanchang, Jiangxi, China	330003	86-791-6298107	Haung Hongyuan
600565	Chongqing Dima Industry Co Ltd	23 Floor, Zhenglian Building, 199, Nancheng Da Dao, Nan'an District, Chongqing, China	400060	86-23-69021877 69021876	Huang Lijin
600566	Hubei Hongcheng General Machinery Co Ltd	3, Hong Men LU, Jinzhou, Hubei, China	434000	86-716-8221198	Wang Sujian
600567	An Hui Shan Ying Paper Industry Co Ltd	3, Qin Jian Lu, Maan, Anhui, China	243021	86-555-2826369	Yang Yizhuan
600568	Hubei Qianjiang Pharmaceutical Co Ltd	T18, Heng Di Lu, Qianjiang, Hubei, China	433100	86-27-87300388	Wang Kai
600569	Anyang Iron& Steel Inc	Mei Yuan Zhuang, Tie Xi District, Anyang, Henan, China	455004	86-372-3120175	Sun Junbei
600578	Beijing Jingneng Thermal Power Co Ltd	10, Guang Ning Lu, Shi Jing Shan District, Beijing, China	100041	86-10-88992758	Wang Bin
600580	Zhejiang Wolong Hi?Tech Co Ltd	Economic Development Zone, Shangyu, Zhejiang, China	312300	86-575-2129895	Gong Hongwu
600582	Tian Di Science Technology Co Ltd	5, He Ping Li Qing Nian Gou Lu, Chao Yang District, Beijing, China	100013	86-10-84262803	Zhao Guodong

Stock Code	Company Name	Address	Postcode	Tel	Fax	Legal representative
600583	Offshore Oil Engineering Co, Ltd	3, Zha Bei Lu, Tang Gu District, Tianjin, China	300452	86-22-25807793 25801800	86-22-25801810	Liu Lianju
600585	Anhui Conch Cement Company Limited	209, Beijing Dong Lu, Wuhu, Anhui, China	241000	86-553-3115338	86-553-3114550	Zhang Minging
600588	Beijing Ufsoft Co Ltd	15, Kai Tuo Lu, Shangdi Information Industry Base, Haidian District, Bejing, China	100085	86-10-62986688	86-10-62971426	Zhang Ke
600589	Guangdong Rongtai Industry Co Ltd	1, Xin Xing Dong Er Lu, Rong Cheng District, Jieyang , Gnangdong, China	522000	86-663-8676616	86-663-8676899	Lin Yuejin
600590	Tsinghua Tellhow Sci-Tech Co Ltd	Taihao Building, Hi-tech Development Zone, Nanchang, Jiangxi, China	330029	86-791-8110590	86-791-8106688	Yang Jun
600592	Fujian Longxi Bearing Co Ltd	Yan'an Bei Lu, Zhangzhou, Fujian, China	363000	86-596-2072091	86-596-2051934	He Qiuyong
600593	Dalian Shengya Ocean World Co Ltd	608-6, Zhong Shan Lu, Sha Kou He District, Dalian, Liaoning, China	116023	86-411-4685225	86-411-4685217	Xiao Feng
600595	Henan Zhongfu Industry Co Ltd	31, Xinhua Lu, Gongyi, Henan, China	451200	86-371-4381551	86-371-4399595	He Huaiqin
600596	Zhejiang Xinan Chemical Industrial Group Co Ltd	93, Da Qiao Lu, Xin An Jiang Town, Jiande, Zhejiang, China	311600	86-571-64723891	86-571-64721344	Jiang Yongping
600598	Heilongjiang Agriculture Company Limited	35, Wenping Street, Haerbin, Heilongjiang, China	150001	86-451-2619838	86-451-2624107	Shi Xiaodan
600599	Hunan Liuyang Fireworks Co Ltd	369, Jin Sha Bei Lu, Liuyan, Hunan, China	410300	86-731-3620966	86-731-3611670	Tang Heping
600600	Tsingtao Brewery Company Limited	Qing Pi Building, Wu Si Square, Hongkong Zhong Lu, Tsingdao, China	266071	86-0531-5713831	86-0531-5713240	Yuan Lu
600601	Shanghai Founder Yanzhong Science & Technology Group Co Ltd	Building 9, Jiali Center, 1515, Nanjing Xi Lu, Shanghai, China	200040	86-21-52986118-9017	86-21-52985038	Hou Yubo
600602	Sva Electron Co Ltd	26 Floor, Century commercial Building, 97, Chang Shou Lu shanghai, China	200060	86-21-62980202-646 86-21-62980202-647	86-21-62982121	Hu Zhikui
600603	Shanghai Xingye Housing Co Ltd	333, Chang Le Lu, Shanghai, China	200031	86-21-54042455	86-21-54045488	Qi Yong
600604	Shanghai Erfangji Co Ltd	687, Chang Zhong Lu, Shanghai, China	200434	86-21-65318888-3981	86-21-65421963	Zhu Jianzhong

600605	Shanghai Light Industry Machinery Co Ltd	1576, Nanjing Xi Lu, Shanghai, China	200040	86-21-62560000-147	86-21-62566022	Shen Jun
600606	Shanghai Jinfeng Investment Co Ltd	17 Floor, Huaqiao Building, 129, Yan'an Xi Lu, Shanghai, China	200040	86-21-62496858	86-21-62496860	Wang Nan
600607	Shanghai Industrial United Holdings Co Ltd	5 Floor, Bao Qing Building, 8, Taojiang Lu, Shanghai, China	200031	86-21-64331098 86-21-64319966	86-21-64337533	Shi Zuqi
600608	Shanghai Broadband Technology Co Ltd	Building 1, 777, Zhong Shan Nan Er Lu, Shanghai, China	200032	86-21-64569832	86-21-64568423	Hu Xingtang
600609	Shenyang Jinbei Auto Motive Company Limited	Building A, 21 Century Building, 1, Shi Ji Lu, Hunnan Industries Development Zone, Hi-tech Development Zone, Shenyang, Liaoning, China	110179	86-24-24823002	86-24-24823284	Du Hongpu
600610	China Textile Machinery Stock Ltd	1687, Chang Yang Lu, Shanghai	200090	86-21-65432970	86-21-65455130	Shi Lifen
600611	Dazhong Transportion (Group) Co Ltd	12 Floor, Folks Building, 1515, Zhong Shan Xi Lu, Shanghai, China	200235	86-21-64289122	86-21-64288660	Gu Hua
600612	China First Pencil Co Ltd	Building 24, 550, Xu Jia Hui Lu, Shanghai, China	200025	86-21-64453300	86-21-64720802	Zhou Fuliang
600613	Shanghai Wingsung Data Technology Co Ltd	Building 11, 2669, Xie Tu Lu, Shanghai, China	200030	86-21-64397553 86-21-64399900	86-21-54590737	Lu Zhengzhi
600614	Shanghai Rubber Belt Co Ltd	630, Hai Men Lu, Shanghai, China	200086	86-21-65415210-234 86-21-235021-65123957	86-21-65123671	Yu Binghan
600615	Shanghai Fenghwa Group Co Ltd	3601, Dong Fang Lu, Pudong New District, Shanghai, China	200125	85-21-58811688	85-21-58702762	Wang Jiegen
600616	Shanghai First Provisions Store Company Limited.	720, Nanjing Dong Lu, Shanghai, China	200001	86-21-63529086 86-63222777-433421	86-21-63517595	Kuang Zhiqiang
600617	Shanghai Lian Hua Fibre Corporation	4290, Hu Yi Road, Jiading District, Shanghai, China	201800	86-21-59528713	86-21-59528433	Li Shou
600618	Shanghai Chlor Alkali Chemical Co Ltd	4747, Longwu Road, Shanghai	200241	86-21-64342640	86-21-64341341	Xu Peiwen
600619	Shanghai Highly (Group) Co Ltd	2555,Changyang Road, Shanghai, P.R.C.	200090	86-21-65660000	86-21-65670941	Zhong Lei
600620	Shanghai Tianchen Co Ltd	15th Floor, Xujiahui Road, Shanghai	200025	86-21-64453550-1520	86-21-64456910	Lv Nan
600621	Shanghai Jinling Co Ltd	26th Floor, 666, Fuzhou Road, Shanghai	200001	86-21-63222658 86-21-63226000-221	86-21-63502688	Chen Bingliang
600622	Shanghai Jiabao Industry & Commerce (Group) Co Ltd	6-7F, Jiabao Commercial Building, 55,Qinghe Road, Jiading District, Shanghai	201800	86-21-59529711	86-21-59536931	Sun Hongliang

Stock Code	Company Name	Address	Postcode	Tel	Fax	Legal representative
600623	Shanghai Tyre & Rubber Co Ltd	560, Xujiahui Road, Shanghai	200025	86-21-64735577	86-21-64735921	Zhou Jianhui
600624	Shanghai Fudan Forward Science & Technology Co Ltd	525, Guoquan Road, Shanghai	200433	86-21-65103021 86-21-63872288	86-21-65107402 86-21-63869700	Xu Wenyi
600626	Shanghai Shenda Co Ltd	Shenda Building,448, Wuning Nan Road,Shanghai	200042	86-21-62319898	86-21-62317250	Ma Tianyu
600627	Shanghai Electrical Apparatus Co Ltd	89, Fuzhou Road, Shanghai	200002	86-21-63216717	86-21-63297808	Cheng Liaomin
600628	Shanghai New World Co Ltd	2-68, Nanjing Xi Road, Shanghai	200003	86-21-63588888-3322	86-21-63583331	Ma Bingfang
600629	Shanghai Lengguang Industrial Co Ltd	4900, Jiuwu Road, Shanghai	200241	86-21-64348289	86-21-64345664	Li Hengguang
600630	Shanghai Dragon Corporation	736, Zhaojiabang Road, Shanghai	200030	86-21-34061116	86-21-54666630	Yuan Mei
600631	Shanghai 1 Department Store Co Ltd	18th Floor, Xin Yibai Building, Nanjing Dong Road, Shanghai	200001	86-21-63223344	86-21-6351744 7	Zhang Xiyuan
600632	Shanghai Hua Lian Co Ltd	635, Nanjing Dong Road, Shanghai	200001	86-21-63224466-7666	86-21-63226105	Xu Bo
600633	Shanghai Whitecat Shareholding Co Ltd	1829, Jinshajiang Road, Shanghai	200333	86-21-54097633	86-21-54096025	Ding Yixin
600634	Shanghai Hainiao Enterprise Development Co Ltd	9th Floor, 485, Xiangyang Nan Road, Shanghai	200031	86-21-64458259	86-21-64454222	Wu Yuqin
600635	Shanghai Dazhong Enterprises Of Science And Technology Ltd	8th Floor, Dazhong Building, ZhongshanXI Road, Shanghai	200235	86-21-64288888-5609	86-21-64288727	Chen Jingfeng
600636	Shanghai 3f New Materials Company Limited	6A, 20, Hengshan Road, Shanghai	200031	86-21-64310558	86-21-64310700	Zhang Jingyi
600637	Sva Information Industry Co Ltd	1646, Xietu Road, Shanghai	200032	86-21-64038833	86-21-64189828	Dai Jinbao
600638	Shanghai New Huang Pu Real Estate Co Ltd	6th, West Buiding, 668, Beijing Dong Road, Shanghai	200001	86-21-63238888	86-21-63237777	Li Weijie
600639	Shanghai New Huang Pu Real Estate Co Ltd	28, Xinjinqiao Road, Pudong, Shanghai	201206	86-21-58991818	86-21-58991533 86-21-58991812	Chen Enhua
600640	Shanghai Jinqiao Export Processing Zone Development Co Ltd	Guomai Building, 1207, Jiangning Road,Shanghai	200060	86-21-62763321	86-21-62763321	Zhao Yilei
600641	Unicom Guomai Communications Co Ltd	702, Pudong Street, Shanghai	200120	86-21-50367878-6805	86-21-50366858	Li Lan
600642	Shenergy Company Limited	22nd Floor, 1, Fuxing Zhong Road, Shanghai	200021	86-21-63900145	86-21-63900119	Wang Minwen
600643	Shanghai Aj Corporation	14th Floor, 583, Lingling Road, Shanghai	200030	86-21-64396600	86-21-64392118	Zhou Haokui
600644	Leshan Electric Power Co Ltd	46, Jiading Bei Road, Shizhong District, Leshan City, Sichuan Prov.	614000	86-833-2445800	86-833-2445900	Li Jiang

Code	Company	Address	Postal	Phone 1	Phone 2	Contact
600645	Shanghai Met Group Corporation	1168, Beizhai Road, Shanghai	200335	86-21-52171679	86-21-52600580	Liu Cheng
600646	Shanghai Zhongli Electric & Communication Medium & Transmition Co Ltd	32nd Floor, Zhonghuan Square, Huaihai Zhong Road, Shanghai	200020	86-21-63916888	86-21-63916555	Zhang Xiaoming
600647	Shanghai Tongda Venture Capital Co Ltd	25th Floor, Yinqiao Building, Jinxin Road, Pudong New District, Shanghai	201206	86-21-58545898	86-21-58541001	Hu Jiajie
600648	Shanghai Wai Gaoqiao Free Trade Zone Development Co Ltd	889, Yanggao Bei Road, Pudong, Shanghai, P.R.C.	200131	86-21-58669217	86-21-58680808	Gao Haiming
600649	Shanghai Municipal Raw Water Co Ltd	5th Floor, 818, Sichuan Bei Road, Shanghai	200085	86-21-63564899	86-21-63564880	Wang Chunjin
600650	Shanghai Jin Jiang Tower Co Ltd	161, Changle Road, Shangahi	200020	86-21-64151188-653	86-21-64726815	Wang Junxing
600651	Feilo Acoustics Co Ltd Shanghai	9th Floor, A building, Zhonghuan Commercial Office Building, 468, Changshou Road, Shanghai	200060	86-21-62770068-1833	86-21-62982217	Shi Zhengming
600652	Shanghai Ace Co Ltd	666, Zhaojiabang Road, Shanghai	200031	86-21-64710022-8818	86-21-64717222	Xu Hanzhang
600653	Shanghai Brilliance Holdings Co Ltd	1, Ningbo Road, Shanghai	200002	86-21-63372010	86-21-63372000	Tang Qi
600654	Shanghai Feilo Co Ltd	54, Shaohua Road, Shanghai	200050	86-21-62512629	86-21-62517323	Liu Renren
600655	Shanghai Yuyuan Tourist Mart Co Ltd	269, Fangbang Zhong Road, Shanghai, P.R.C.	200010	86-21-63559999	86-21-63550558	Cao Youyuan
600656	Shanghai Worldbest Pharmaceuticals Co Ltd	25th Floor, Huayuan World Square, 1958, Zhongshan Bei Road, Shanghai	200063	86-21-62030205	86-21-62030205	Wang Changhong
600657	Beijing Tianqiao Beida Jade Bird Sci-Tech Co Ltd	14th Floor, Pacific Technological Development Centre, Peking University, Haidian Road, Haidian District, Beijing	100080	86-10-62526688-660	86-10-62526688-656	Yu Ming
600658	Beijing C&W Technology Co Ltd	14, Jiuxianqiao Road, Chaoyang District, Beijing	100016	86-10-84567920	86-10-84567917	Yao Cheng
600659	Fujian Shenlong Development Co Ltd	15th Floor, Aviation Buiding, 123, East Street, Gulou District, Fuzhou, Fujian	350001	86-591-7503366	86-591-7503068	He Jia
600660	Fuyao Group Glass Industry Co Ltd	Fuyao Industry Village, Fuqing City	350301	86-591-5383777	86-591-5383666 / 86-591-5382719	Chen Yuedan
600661	Shanghai Jiaoda Nan Yang Co Ltd	6th Floor, 667, Fanyu Road, Shanghai	200030	86-21-62814035-20	86-21-62801900	Wu Wei
600662	Shanghai Qiangsheng Holding Co Ltd	18th Floor, 920, Nanjing Xi Road, Shanghai, P.R.C.	200041	86-21-62151181	86-21-62538782	Wu Benchu

Stock Code	Company Name	Address	Postcode	Tel	Fax	Legal representative
600663	Shanghai Lujiazui Finance & Trade Zone Development Co Ltd	981, Pudong Street, Shanghai	200135	86-21-58878888	86-21-58877100	Zhu Wei
600664	Harbin Pharmaceutical Group Co Ltd	431, Youyi Road, Daoli District, Harbin	150018	86-0451-4604688	86-0451-4604688	Liu Bensong
600665	Shanghai Hu Chang Special Steel Co Ltd	1988, Baoyang Road, Shanghai	200940	86-21-56126920	86-21-56128176	Shi Meijian
600666	Southwest Pharmaceutical Co Ltd	21, Tianxing Bridge, Shapingba District, Chongqing	400038	86-23-65313118-5027	86-23-65311721	Zhang Xinli
600667	Wuxi Taiji Industry Limited Corporation	Nan wan, Xiadian Bridge, Lucun, Wuxi	214041	86-510-5425660	86-510-5423742	Zhu Juxiong
600668	Zhejiang Jianfeng Group Co Ltd	88, Wujiang Dong Road, Jinhua City, Zhejiang	321000	86-579-2326868-3907	86-579-2324666	Xu Fei
600669	Anshan Co-Operation Group Co Ltd	168, Liuxi Street, Tiexi District, Anshan, Liaoning	114011	86-412-8840781	86-412-8813178	Wang Yuehong
600670	Changchun Goldenstar Biotech Group Co Ltd	62, Jiefang Avenue, Changchun	130022	86-431-8931333	86-431-8931333	Wang Weiwei
600671	Hangzhou Tian-Mu-Shan Pharmaceutical Enterprise Co Ltd	3, Ange Long, Jincheng Town, Lin'an, Zhejiang	311300	86-571-63722229	86-571-63715401	Zhou Qunlin
600672	Guangdongyinghao Science-Technology & Education Investment Co Ltd	3rd Floor, Yinghao Hotel, New Spring Tour&Vacation Section, Conghua, Guangzhou	510960	86-20-38791916	86-20-38791920	Yu Yi
600673	Chengdu Measuring & Cutting Tools. Co Ltd	14, East Block 1, Erhuan Road, Chengdu, Sichuan	610056	86-28-3241923-2425	86-28-3242494	Tang Xiaolin
600674	Sichuan Chuantou Holding Stock Co Ltd	Jiuli Town, Emeishan City, Sichuan	614222	86-833-5576179	86-833-5576490	Xu Keyi
600675	China Enterprise Company Ltd	Chinese Enterprise Building, 2, Huashan Road, Shanghai	200040	86-21-62170088-2701	86-21-62179197	Yin Xueqing
600676	Shanghai Jiao Yun Co Ltd	704, Yan'an Xi Road, Shanghai	200050	86-21-62520140-203	86-21-62525274	Li Lude
600677	Aerospace Zhonghui Group Co Ltd	138, Jiefang Road, Hangzhou, Zhejiang	310009	86-571-87075755	86-571-87077662	Cong Peiyu
600678	Sichuan Golden Summit (Group) Jotnt-Stock Co Ltd	East Block, Mingshan Road, Emeishan City, Sichuan	614200	86-833-5521267	86-833-5521244	Xu Yigang
600679	Phoenix Co Ltd	168, Gaoyang Road, Shanghai	200080	86-21-65954641 86-21-65950100-611	86-21-65952565 86-21-65956731	Cong QI
600680	Shanghai Posts & Telecommunications Equipment Co Ltd	700, Yishan Road, Shanghai	200233	86-21-64834310	86-21-64333435	Yang Jialin

Code	Company	Address	Postal	Phone	Phone	Contact
600681	Wuhan Cheng Cheng Investment In Culture Group Co Ltd	55, Minyi Si Road, Hankou, Wuhan	430022	86-27-85426963	86-27-85863470	Zou Yisheng
600682	Nanjing Xinjiekou Department Store Co Ltd	3, Zhongshan Nan Road, Nanjing	210005	86-25-4721819	86-25-4724722	Ling Zexing
600683	Ningbo Hualian Group Co Ltd	8th Floor, Hualian Building 55 Dongdu Road, Ningbo	315000	86-574-87092006 86-574-87092007	86-574-87092059	Zhong Haiming
600684	Guangzhou Pearl River Indusrial Development Co Ltd	2nd Floor, Huale Building, 49, Huale Road, Guangzhou	510060	86-20-83838056	86-20-83808469	Huang Yuwen
600685	Guangzhou Shipyard International Company Limited	South 40, Fangcun Avenue, Guangzhou, Guangdong, China	510832	86-20-81896411	86-20-81891575	Li Zhidong
600686	Xiamen Motor Co Ltd	27–28th Floor, Dihao Building, 820, Xiahe Road, Xiamen	361004	86-592-2962988	86-592-2960686	Yao Yongning
600687	Xiamen Newsky Software Co Ltd	30th Floor, Building A of Atlantic Sea-scenic City, Hubin Xi Road, Xiamen	361003	86-592-2397368	86-592-2397338	Xu Mingxing
600688	Sinopec Shanghai Petrochemical Company Limited	48, Jinyi Road, Jinshan District, Shanghai	200540	86-21-57943143	86-21-57940050	Zhang Jingming
600689	Shanghai Sanmao Textile Co Ltd	1150, Xuchang Road, Shanghai	200082	86-21-65121377	86-21-65453247	Zhang Lifang
600690	Qingdao Haier Co Ltd	99, Chongqing Nan Road, Qingdao	266032	86-532-8938138	86-532-8938313	Cui Shaohua
600691	Dongxin Electrical Carbon Co Ltd	22, Zhuozi Shan, Dongguang Road, Liujing Area, Zigong, Sichuan	643000	86-81-32600361	86-81-32600861	Du Donghai
600692	Shang Hai Ya Tong Co Ltd	9, Bayi Road, Chongming County, Shanghai	202150	86-21-69612714	86-21-69612782	Cai Fusheng
600693	Fujian Dongbai (Group) Co Ltd	18th Dongbai Building, 84, North Road of 817, Fuzhou, Fujian	350001	86-591-7531724	86-591-7531804	Chen Ling
600694	Dashang Group Co Ltd	1, Qingsan Street, Zhongshan District, Dalian	116001	86-0411-3643215	86-0411-3630358	Jiang Fude
600695	Shanghai Dajiang Group Stock Co Ltd	26, Guyang Nan Road , Songjiang District, Shanghai	201600	86-21-57817566 86-21-57817571	86-21-57820072	Gu Deming
600696	Linca Fujian Ltd	25, Dalijia City, 169, Wuyi Zhong Road, Quanzhou, Fujian	362000	86-0591-7114433	86-0591-7114466	Chen Yong
600697	Chang Chun Eurasia Group Co Ltd	14, Industry & Agriculture Avenue, Changchun	130021	86-431-5620053	86-431-5666517	Xi Luzhen
600698	Jinan Qingqi Motorcycle Co , Ltd	34, Heping Road, Lixia District, Jinan, Shandong	250014	86-531-6414419	86-531-6960676	Han Jinke
600699	Liaoyuan Deheng Company Limited.	3, Fuxing Road, Liaoyuan, Jilin	136200	86-437-3512077	86-437-3520181	You Chunling
600700	Shaanxi Meihang Digital Surveying (Group) Co Ltd	28, Nanxin Street, Xi'an	710004	86-29-7216331-259	86-29-7215541	Mu Yao

Stock Code	Company Name	Address	Postcode	Tel	Fax	Legal representative
600701	Harbin Gong Da High-Tech Enterprise Development Co Ltd	118, Hujun Street, Nangang District, Harbin	150006	86-451-6219247	86-451-6253555	Zhang Haiying
600702	Tuopai Yeast Liquor Co Ltd	149, Zhong Street, Liushu Town, Shehong County, Sichuan	629209	86-825-6766322 86-825-6766322	86-825-6766318 86-825-6766322	Xie Changrong
600703	Hubei Tianyi Science & Technology Co Ltd	1, Sanwan Road, High-tech Industry Development Zone, Shashi District, Jingzhou, Hubei	434000	86-716-8328443	86-716-8328443	Yi Shengze
600704	Zhejiang Zhongda Group Co Ltd	Building A, Zhongda Square, Hangzhou	310003	86-571-85777029	86-571-85777050	Qiu Yijun
600705	Beiya Industrial(Group)Co Ltd	26, Hongjun Street, Nangang District, Harbin	150001	86-451-3600764	86-451-3600764	Chen Dong
600706	Chang An Information Industry Group Co Ltd	41, Youyi Dong Road, Xi'an, Shaanxi	710054	86-29-2214266	86-29-2233943	Zhang Anping
600707	Irico Display Devices Co Ltd	16,Gaoxin Yi Road, West Area of High-tech Industry Development Zone, Xi'an	710075	86-29-8214865	86-29-8214864	Lu Xiliang
600708	Shanghai Donghai Co Ltd	11F, Yintong North Building, 1016, Dingxi Road, Shanghai	200050	86-21-52551620	86-21-62526043	Wang Zhongda
600709	Hu Bei Jianghu Ecology Co Ltd	18, Tangcheng Avenue, Zhaijiawan Development Zone, Honghu, Hubei	433228	86-716-2742181	86-716-2742275	Wang Yiling
600710	Changlin Company Limited	10, Changlin Road, Changzhou, Jiangsu	213002	86-519-6751888-3119	86-519-6750025	Gao Zhimin
600711	Xiamen Eagle Group Co Ltd	6-8 Depart. 17th Floor, Bank Centre, 189, Xiahe Road, Xiamen	361003	86-592-2394735	86-592-2394706	Ding Xiao
600712	Nanning Department Store Co Ltd	39–41, 45, Chaoyang Road, Nanning, Guangxi	530012	86-0771-2610906	86-0771-2810261	Zhang Yanhui
600713	Nanjing Medical Company Limited	486, Zhongshan Dong Road, Nanjing	210002	86-25-4453856	86-25-4523033	Wang Yongli
600714	Qinghai Shanchuan Ferroalloy Co Ltd	112, Chaoyang Xi Road, Xining, Qingdao	810028	86-971-5509464	86-971-5507586	Zhang Guangzhou
600715	Song Liao Automobile Co;Ltd	227, Qingnian Avenue, Shenhe District, Shenyang	110015	86-24-23985558	86-24-23985559	Sun Huadong
600716	Qinhuangdao Yaohua Glass Co Ltd	Xigang Road, Qinhuangdao, Hebei	066013	86-335-3028173	86-335-3028173	Song Yingli
600717	Tianjin Port (Group)Co Ltd	35, Road 2, Xin Gang, Tanggu District, Tianjin	300456	86-22-25706615	86-22-25706615	Li Quanyong

Code	Company	Address	Postal Code	Phone	Phone	Contact
600718	Shenyang Neusoft Co Ltd	Great Software Garden, Hunnan Industry Zone, Shenyang High-tech Industries Development Zone	110179	86-24-23783000	86-24-23783375	Wang Zidong
600719	Dalian Thermal Power Co Ltd	90, Yanhai Street, Xigang District, Dalian, China	116021	86-411-4422999-8290	86-411-4438670	Zhang Yaohe
600720	Gansu Qilianshan Cement Co Ltd	Zhongpu Town, Yongdeng County, Lanzhou, Gansu, China	730301	86-931-6479298 86-931-6476501	86-931-6476538	Wang Yunpeng
600721	Xin Jiang Bai Hua Cun CoLtd	141, Zhong Shan Lu, Urumuqi, Xinjiang, China	830002	86-991-2311642	86-991-2815307	Miao Jun
600722	Cangzhou Chemical Industrial Co Ltd	18, Nan Huan Zhong Lu, Cangzhou, Hebei, China	061000	86-317-3030719	86-317-3042321	Li Longhai
600723	Beijing Xidan Market Company Limited Bjxm Co Ltd	120, Xidan Bei Street, Xi Cheng District, Beijing, China	100031	86-10-66024984	86-10-66014196	Wang Jian
600724	Ningbo Fuda Electric Appliance Co Ltd	355, Yang Ming Xi Lu, Yuyao, Zhejiang, China	315400	86-574-62814275	86-574-62813915	Chen Jianxin
600725	Yunnan Yunwei Company Limited	Huashan, Town, Zhanyi County, Qujing, Yunnan, China	655338	0874-3064350	0874-3068590	Li Bin
600726	Heilongjiang Electric Power Company Limited	209, Da Cheng Street, Nangang District, Haerbin, China	150001	86-451-2525998	86-451-2525878	Mei Junchao
600727	Shandong Lubei Chemical Co Ltd	Chengkou Town, Wudi County, Shandong, China	251909	86-0543-645-1265	86-0543-6451057	Tian Yuxin
600728	Suntek Technology Co Ltd	51–53, Jianzhong Lu, Tianhe Hi-tech Industries development Zone, Guangzhou, Guangdong, China	116113	86-411-7125455	86-411-7600329	Pan Jiufu
600729	Chongqing Department Store Co Ltd	2, Min Quan Lu, Yu Zhong District, Chongqing, China	400010	86-23-63822594	86-23-63822594	Zhang Yong
600730	China Hi-Tech Group Co Ltd	17 Floor, Zhao Shang Ju Square South Building, 333, Chengdu Bei Lu, Shanghai, China	200041	86-21-52980810	85-21-52980816	Liu Danxu
600731	Hunan Haili Chemical Industry Co Ltd	399, Furong Zhong Lu, Changsha, Hunan, China	410007	86-731-5552484	86-731-5540475	Xiao Guangpu
600732	Shanghai Port Machinery Co Ltd	3500, Pudong Nan Lu, Shanghai, China	200125	86-21-58395139-6665	86-21-58398836	Cai Aiguo
600733	Chengdu Qingfeng Electronics Co Ltd	16 Floor, Jiaoyin Building, 211, Yulong Street, Chengdu, Sichuan	610015	86-28-6525719	86-28-6525725	Jiang Jiufu

Stock Code	Company Name	Address	Postcode	Tel	Fax	Legal representative
600734	Fujian Start Computer Group Co Ltd	Shida Technological City, Fu 2 Industry Part, Fuzhou, Fujian, China	350002	86-591-3708108	86-591-3708128	Mu Changyin
600735	Shandong Lanling Chenxiang Jiuye Co Ltd	426, Yimeng Lu, Liyi, Shandong, China	276004	86-539-8322568-3068	86-539-8315880	Chen Donghui
600736	Suzhou New District Hi-Tech Industrial Co Ltd	6 Floor, New Zone Management Center,8, Yun He Lu,New District, Suzhou, Jiangsu, China	215011	86-512-8251888-8636	86-512-8099281	Xu Liangzhi
600737	Xinjiang Tunhe Investment Co Ltd	33, Wuyi Dong Lu, Changji, Xinjiang, China	831100	86-994-2350079	86-994-2337689	Liu Tao
600738	Lanzhou Minbai Shareholding (Group) Co Ltd	8–10 Floor, Asian-Europe Commercial Building, 368, Zhong Shan Lu, Lanzhou, China	730030	86-931-8488329	86-931-8473891	Gan Peiwan
600739	Liaoning Chengda Co Ltd	71, Ren Min Lu, Dalian, China	116001	86-411-2803736	86-411-2656051	Luo Qiku
600740	Shan Xi Coking Co Ltd	Guang Sheng Si Town, Hongtong County, Shanxi, China	041606	86-357-6626012	86-357-6625045	Xi Guowang
600741	Shanghai Bashi Industrial (Group) Co Ltd	Bus Building, 525, Jianguo Dong Lu, Shanghai, China	200025	86-21-63848484	86-21-63863118	Wang Guojun
600742	Chang-Chun Faw-Sihuan Automobile Co Ltd	99, Puyang Street, Changchun, Jilin, China	130011	86-431-7629105	86-431-7629113	Fan Xijun
600743	Hubei Xingfu Industry Co Ltd	1, Xingfu Bei Lu, Zhangjin Town, Quianjiang, Hubei, China	433140	86-728-6641566	86-728-6641999	Li Jun
600744	Hunan Huayin Electric Power Co Ltd	428, Shaoshan Bei Lu, Changsha, Hunan, China	410007	86-731-5543400	86-731-5521259	Jin Yujiang
600745	Huangshi Kangsai Section Limited	512, Huangshi Da Dao, Huangshi, Hubei, China	435000	86-714-6226987	86-714-6226987	Wu Nianyou
600746	Jiangsu Sopo Chemical CoLtd	50, Yuehe Street, Jianbi Town, Zhenjiang, Jiangsu, China	212006	86-511-3366244	86-511-3362036	Xu Yizhong
600747	Dalian Daxian Co Ltd	Ge Zhen Pu, Jingzi District, Dalian, China	116035	86-411-6428612	86-411-6428328	Wang Zhongquan
600748	Shanghai Pudong Stainless Sheet Co Ltd	300, Budong Shangnan Lu, Shanghai, China	200126	86-21-58723089	86-21-68630598	Kan Zhaosen
600749	Tibet Shendi Co Ltd	6, Linguo Dong Lu, Lasa, Xizang, China	850000	86-891-6339150	86-891-6339041	Xie Qingjing
600750	Jiangxi Jiangzhong Pharmaceutical Co Ltd	15, Dongfeng Lu, Leping, Jiangxi, China	333300	86-798-6803483	86-798-6803406	Yang Renyan

Code	Company	Address	Postal	Phone	Contact
600751	Tianjin Marine Shipping Co Ltd	207, Ma Chang Dao, He Xi District, Tianjin, China	300204	86-22-23288000	86-22-23286115	Song Tao
600752	Haci Company Limited	169, Tong Xiang Street, Dong Li District, Haerbin, China	150046	86-451-2688688	86-451-5672268	Zhang Wenbo
600753	Henan Bingxiong Fresh-Preser Vation Equipmenis Co Ltd	22, Fu Hou Street, Min Quan County, Henan, China	476800	86-370-8551431 86-370-8522789-2026	86-370-8526256	Han Fei
600754	Shanghai New Asia (Group) Co Ltd	4 Floor, 285, Tian Mu Xi Lu, Shanghai, China	200070	86-21-63536304	86-21-63533021	Kang Ming
600755	Xiamen International Trade Group Corp., Ltd	8–18 Floor, National Trade Building, Hu Bin Nan Lu, Xiamen, China	361004	86-592-5161888	86-592-5160280	Xiao Wei
600756	Shandong Langchao Cheeloosoft Co Ltd	224, Shan Da Lu, Jinan, Shandong, China	250013	86-531-8932888-8668	86-531-8522334	Luo Wanli
600757	Shanghai Worldbest Industry Development Co Ltd	21 Floor, Lekai Building, 660, Commercial City Road, Pudong New District, Shanghai, China	200120	86-021-58792716	86-021-58792223	Yang Linfeng
600758	Liaoning Jindi Construction Consortium Co Ltd	118, Qingnian Street, Shen He District, Shenyang, China	110014	86-24-22870330	86-24-22855430	Zhu Danshi
600759	Hainan Overseas Chinese Investment Co Ltd	B8, Qiao Qi building, 28, Nan Hang Dong Lu, Haikou, Hainan	570206	86-898-66787220	86-898-66757661	Song Yang
600760	Shandong Heibao Co Ltd	107, Long Shan Lu, Wendeng, Shandong, China	264400	86-631-8352083	86-631-8352228	Sun Junfang
600761	Anhui Heli Co Ltd	15, Wang Jiang Xi Lu, Hefei, Anhui, China	230022	86-551-3648005-6498	86-551-3633431	Xu Lin
600762	Hunan Hengyang Jinli Technology (Agricultural) Co Ltd	168, Yan Jiang Bei Lu, Hengyang, China	421001	86-734-8709868	86-734-8709892	Ou Yangshuan
600763	Beijing Zhongyan Tango Down Products Share Co Ltd	East Part of 12 Floor, B, Yuan Da Center, 5, Hui Zhong Lu, Chaoyang District, Beijing, China	100101	86-10-84891867	86-10-84891805	Jin Tao
600764	Gansu Tristar Petrochemical (Group) Co Ltd	10, Yu Men Street, Xi Gu District, Lanzhou, Gansu, China	730060	86-931-7933055 86-931-7557333	86-931-7551922	Wang Chun
600765	Guizhou Liyuan Hydraulic Components Co Ltd	Xin Chang Xiang, Wu Dang District, Guiyang, Guizhou, China	550202	86-851-6132002	86-851-6132590	Shu Daiyou
600766	Yantai Hualian Development Group Co Ltd	26 Floor, Jin Du Building, 9, Nan Street, Yantai, Shandong, China	264001	86-535-6624347	86-535-6603260	Yang Jianbo
600767	Winsan Shanghai Industrial Corporation Ltd	Room 3108–3112, 31 Floor, Heng Long Square, 1266, Nanjing Xi Lu, Shanghai, China	350001	86-0591-7609998	86-0591-62880901	Li Wei

Stock Code	Company Name	Address	Postcode	Tel	Fax	Legal representative
600768	Ningbo Fubang Jingye Group Co Ltd	336, Zhong Shan Dong Lu, Ningbo, China	315040	86-574-87725920	86-574-87375767	Ma Xiaoyong
600769	Wuhan Xianglong Power Industry Co Ltd	31, Ge Hua Street Chemical Road, Hong Shan District, Wuhan, China	430078	86-27-87600367	86-27-87600367	Yang Sibing
600770	Jiangsu Zongyi Co Ltd	Huangjin Village, Xingdong Town, Tongzhou City, Jiangsu Prov.	226376	86-513-6639999	86-513-6563501	Ji Fenghua
600771	Topsun Science And Technology Co Ltd	Yong'an Buildign, 9, West Block of Nan'erhuan, Xi'an, Shaanxi	710068	86-29-8378949-8085	86-29-8378953	Tian Hong
600772	Petroleum Long Champ (Group) Co Ltd	158, Aimin Dong Road, Langfang City, Hebei Prov.	065000	86-316-2075875	86-316-2077066	Zhao Weiwen
600773	Tibet Jinzhu Co Ltd	182, Beijing Zhong Road, Lahsa, Tibet	850000	86-891-6833922	86-891-6824804	Cirren Duoji
600774	Wuhan Hanshang Group Co Ltd	134, Wuyang Avenue, Wuhan, Hubei	430050	86-27-84773750	86-27-84843197	Zhang Qing
600775	Nanjing Panda Electronics Company Limited	301, Zhongshan Dong Road, Nanjing, Jiangsu, China	210002	86-25-4801144	86-25-4820729	Shi Qiusheng
600776	Eastern Communications Co Ltd	398, Wensan Road, Hangzhou, Zhejiang	310013	86-571-88865242 86-571-88865228	86-571-88865243	Guo Ruirui
600777	Yantai Xinchao Industry Co Ltd	98, Moushan Road, Yantai, Shandon	264100	86-535-4259777 86-535-4259550	86-535-4225688 86-535-4211592	Yu Dehai
600778	Xinjiang Friendship (Group) Co Ltd	14, Youhao Bei Road, Urumuqi	830000	86-991-4841698	86-991-4815090	Wang Jianping
600779	Sichuan Quanxing Co Ltd	68, Block 2, Renmin Zhong Road, Chengdu	610031	86-28-6252847	86-28-6695460	Zhang Guangqian
600780	Top Energy Company Ltd Shanxi	Zone V-6, Xuefu Industrial Park, Taiyuan High-tech Industry Development Area, Shanxi	030006	86-351-7021827	86-351-7021857	Ye Ninghua
600781	Shanghai Minfeng Holding Group Co Ltd	13F, Technology Building, 285, Jianguo Xi Road, Shanghai	200031	86-21-64458811-33	86-21-64456611	Dai Haixiong
600782	Xinhua Metal Products Co Ltd	Chengdong Economic Development Zone, Xinyu, Jiangxi	338004	86-790-6460888	86-790-6460089	You Shaocheng
600783	Sisha Co Ltd	69, Nanding Bus-stop Street, Zhangdian District, Zibo, Shandong	255055	86-10-64106140	86-533-2981033	Li Jing
600784	Luyin Investment Group Co Ltd	128, Jingshi Road, Jinan, Shandong	250001	86-531-2024156	86-531-2024179	Liu Fangran
600785	Yinchuan Xinhua Department Store Co Ltd	29, Xinhua Dong Street, Yinchuan, Ningxia	750004	86-951-4010058	86-951-6041983	Ma Weihong

Code	Company	Address	Postcode	Phone	Phone	Contact
600786	Dongfang Boiler Group Co Ltd	150, Huangjiaoping Road, Five-star Street, Zigong, Sichuan	643001	86-813-4735000	86-813-2203200	He Jianqiang
600787	Zhongchu Development Stock Co Ltd	19, Youyi Road, Hexi District, Tianjin	300201	86-22-28010734	86-22-28010722	Xue Bin
600788	Xi'An Diamond Co Ltd	19, Jiangong Road, XI'an	710043	86-29-2238824	86-29-2244503	Wang Quansheng
600789	Shandong Lukang Pharmaceutical Co Ltd	173, West Road of Taibai Building, Jining, Shandong	272021	86-537-2213961-3324	86-537-2278572	Tian Lixin
600790	Zhejiang China Light & Textile Industrial City Group Co Ltd	Zhongqing Building, 6, Jianhu Road, Keqiao Town, Shaoxing, Zhejiang	312030	86-575-4119963-8008 86-575-4116158	86-575-4116045	Tang Guocan
600791	Tianchuang Property Co Ltd	16th Floor, Foreign Trade Food & Grease Building, 8, Shengfu Road, Guiyang, Guizhou	550001	86-851-5804482 86-10-66413762	86-851-5804482 010-66413760	Jiang Fan
600792	Yunnan Malong Chemicals & Construction Co Ltd	Wangjiazhuang Town, Malong County, Qujing, Yunan	655102	86-874-8010050	86-874-8010036	Xian Silin
600793	Yibin Paper Industry Co Ltd	54, Minjiangxi Road, Yibin, Sichuan	644007	86-831-3551975	86-831-3551965	Lu Biao
600794	Yunnan Freetrade Science And Technology CoLtd	A1506, 15th, Security Building, Chuncheng Road, Kunming, Yunnan	650011	86-871-3186316	86-871-3186312	Xiao Gongwei
600795	Sp Power Development Co Ltd	9th Floor, Gaoxin Building, Nanbinhe Road, Xuanwu District, Beijing	100055	86-10-63423555	86-10-63428555	Chen Jingdong
600796	Zhejiang Qianjiang Biochemical Co Ltd	598, Xishan Road, Xiash Town, Haining City, Zhejiang Prov.	314400	86-573-7042800	86-573-7035640	Hu Ming
600797	Zhejian Guniver-Sity Innovation Technology Co Ltd	17, Shengli Dong Road, Shaoxing	312000	86-0571-87950500	86-0571-87988110	Dong Danqing
600798	Ningbo Marine Company Limited	202, Zhongma Road, Ningbo	315020	86-574-87356271	86-574-87355051	Wu Mingyue
600799	Heilong Jiang Clever Net Corp.Ltd	Clever Network Building, 33, Chuangye Dong Road, Shangdi Info. Industry Base, Haidian District, Beijing	100084	86-10-82899729	86-10-82899731	Sun Bin
600800	Tian Jin Global Magnetic Card Co Ltd	325, Jiefang Nan Road, Hexi District, Tianjin	300202	86-22-23266601-2038	86-22-23269333	Wan Xiaoyan
600801	Huaxin Cement Co Ltd	897, Huangshi Avenue, Huangshi, Hubei	435002	86-714-6224971	86-714-6235204	Wang Ximing
600802	Fujian Cement Inc	Fujian Building, Hongyang New City, 118, Yangqiao Road, Fuzhou, Fujian	350001	86-591-7527300	86-591-7527300	Lin Chengchao
600803	Hebei Weiyuan Bio-Chemical Co Ltd	166, XinshiBei Road, Shijiazhuang, Hebei	050091	86-0311-3834233-8016	86-0311-3833524	Bai Yan

Stock Code	Company Name	Address	Postcode	Tel	Fax	Legal representative
600804	Chengdu Drpengtechnology Co Ltd	3, Jinghua Nan Road, Chengdu, Sichuan	610069	86-28-4550710	86-28-4407189	He Bin
600805	Jiangsu Yueda Investment Co Ltd	36, Tongyu Zhong Road, Yancheng, Jiangsu	224002	86-515-8222278	86-515-8334601 86-515-8227190	Gao Yishan
600806	Jiaoda Kunji High-Tech Company Limited	23, Ciba Road, Kunming, Yunan, China	650203	86-871-5212410 86-871-5212411	86-871-5150317	Feng Sizhong
600807	Shandong Jinan Department Stort (Group) Stock Co Ltd	264, Quancheng Road, Jinan, Shandong, China	250011	86-531-6030094	86-531-6914416	Zhao Chuanhui
600808	Maanshan Iron & Steel Company Limited	8, Hongqi Zhong Road, Maanshan, Anhui	243003	86-555-2888158	86-555-2887284	Wang Dapeng
600809	Shanxi Xinghuacun Fen Wine Factory Co Ltd	Xinghua Village, Fenyang, Shanxi	032205	86-358-7229381 86-358-7220255	86-358-7220394	Guo Zhihong
600810	Shen Ma Industry Co Ltd	63, Jianshe Zhong Road, Pingdingshan City, Henan Prov.	467000	86-375-3921231	86-375-3921500	Liu Zhen
600811	Orient Group Incorporatian	235, Huayuan Street, Nangang District, Harbin	150001	86-451-3666028	86-451-3666030 86-451-3643214	Guan Zhuohua
600812	North China Pharmaceutical Co Ltd	56, Tiyu Bei Avenue, Shijiazhuang, Hebei	050015	86-311-6678491	86-311-6060942	Li Yanru
600813	Anshan No.1 Construction Machinery Co Ltd	30, Hongqi Road, Lishan District, Anshan, Liaoning	114042	86-412-6213727	86-412-6211644	Tan Hong
600814	Hangzhou Jiebai Group Co Limited.	251, Jiefang Road, Shangcheng District, Hangzhou	310001	86-571-87016888-5015	86-571-87012247	Xu Xueqiang
600815	Xiamen Engineering Machinery Co Ltd	668, Xiahe Road, Xiamen	361004	86-592-2115449	86-592-2036720	Wang Zhiyong
600816	Anshan Trust &Investment Co Ltd	55, Five-block Street, Tiedong District, Anshan	114001	86-412-2234351	86-412-2217080	Liang Qingde
600817	Shanghai Hongsheng Technology Co Ltd	618, Shangcheng Road, Pudong New District, Shanghai	200120	86-21-58822100	86-21-58870670	Huang Defeng
600818	Shanghai Forever Co..Ltd	209, Liaoyuan Xi Road, Shanghai	200092	86-21-65136974	86-21-65139966	Yuan Zhijian
600819	Shanghai Yaohua Pilkington Glass Company Ltd	100, Jiyang Road, Pudong New District, Shanghai	200126	86-21-58839305	86-21-58801554	Jin Minli
600820	Shanghai Tunnel Engineering Co Ltd	239, Zhao Jia Bang Lu, Shanghai	200032	86-21-64312461	86-21-54520596	Jin Bo
600821	Tianjin Quanye Bazaar Group Company Limited	290, He Ping Lu, He Ping District, Tianjin	300022	86-22-27307227	86-22-27305348	Zhao Xizhen
600822	Shanghai Material Trading Centre Co Ltd	2550, Zhong Shan Bei Lu, Shanghai, China	200063	86-21-62570000-8522	86-21-62168718	Cai Jiade

	Company	Address	Postal Code	Tel	Fax	Contact
600823	Shanghai Shimao Co Ltd	Building 6, 358, Jin Ling Dong Lu, Shanghai	200021	86-21-63745428	86-21-63260888	Zhu Muying
600824	Shanghai Yimin Department Stores Company Ltd	Building 6, 645-659, Huai Hai Zhong Lu, Shanghai	200020	86-21-53067597	86-21-53066576	Shao Zhenyao
600825	Hualian Supermarket CoLtd	609, Long Chang Lu, Shanghai	200090	86-21-65705873	86-21-65432001	Dong Xiaochun
600826	Shanghai Lansheng Corporation	1230, Zhong Shan Bei Yi Lu, Shanghai	200437	86-21-65445880-2041	86-21-65446061	Zhang Zhu
600827	Shanghai Friendship Group Incorporated Company	Building 10, 518, Commercial City Road, Shanghai	200120	86-21-58799358	86-21-58883303	Wang Longsheng
600828	Chengdu People's Department Store Group Co Ltd	19, Dong Yu Street, Chengdu, Sichuan	610011	86-28-86660965	86-28-86651176	Zhang Xueqin
600829	Harbin Swan Industry Company Limited	182, Gong Le Street, Dao Li District, Haerbin	150076	86-451-4624124	86-451-4624142	Qiao Kerong
600830	Ningbo Da-Hongying Industry & Investment Co Ltd	48, 130 Nong, Kai Ming Street, Ningbo	315000	86-574-87315310	86-574-87294676	Lin Weiqing
600831	Shaanxi Broadcast & TV Network Intermediary Co Ltd	21, Xing Fu Bei Lu, Xian	710043	86-29-2526902	86-29-2525966	Li Daoguang
600832	Shanghai Oriental Pearl Co Ltd	1, Century Road, Pudong, Shanghai	200120	86-21-58791888	86-21-58792222	Cao Zhiyong
600833	Shanghai Commercial Real Estate Development Industry Co Ltd	Building 5, 974, Wai Ma Lu, Shanghai	200011	86-21-63136517	86-21-63135518	Lin Ankang
600834	Shanghai Shentong Metro Co Ltd	489,Pu Dian Lu, Shanghai	200122	86-21-58308595	86-21-58308595	Zhong Hui
600835	Shanghai Shangling Electric Appliances Co Ltd	2, Jian Ping Lu, Shanghai	200135	86-021-58857888-3436	86-021-58858624	Cao Jun
600836	Shanghai Jielong Industry Corporation Limited	7111, Chuan Zhou Gong Lu, Pudong New District, Shanghai	201205	86-21-63746888	86-21-63732586	Long Fuliang
600837	Shanghai Urban Agro-Business Co Ltd	8 Floor, Yong Hui Building, 765, Xizang Nan Lu, Shanghai	200011	86-21-63787858	86-21-63788881	Wang Peiyi
600838	Shanghai Join Buy Co Ltd	9 Floor, Jingan New Times building, 873-881, Nanjing Xi Lu, Shanghai	200041	86-21-62729898-838	86-21-62175212	Feng Yousun
600839	Sichuan Changhong Electric Co Ltd	35, Mian Xi Dong Lu, Hi-tech Zone, Mianyang, Sichuan	621000	86-816-2418486	86-816-2418158	Tan Mingxian
600840	Zhejiang Anping Venture Investment Co Ltd	Building 7, 479, Ti Yu Chang Lu, Hangzhou	310007	86-571-87055977 86-571-87055978	86-571-87055977 86-571-87055978	Lin Junbo
600841	Shanghai Diesel Engine Company Limited	2636, Jun Gong Lu, Shanghai	200432	86-21-65745656-2207	86-21-65749845	Liang Baoquan
600842	Shanghai Zhong Xi Pharmaceutical Co Ltd	1515, Jiao Tong Lu, Shanghai	200065	86-21-56082188	86-21-56083743	Zhu Gongzheng

Stock Code	Company Name	Address	Postcode	Tel	Fax	Legal representative
600843	Shanggong Co Ltd	12 Floor, Dong Fang Building, 1500, Century Road, Pudong New District, Shanghai	200122	86-21-68407700-617	86-21-63302939	Zhang Yifan
600844	Daying Moden Agricultural Co Ltd	127, Qi Lina Shan Lu, Shanghai	200331	86-21-62509596	86-21-62506181	Jiang Wei
600845	Shanghai Baosight Software Co Ltd	515, Guo Shou Jing Lu, Zhang Jiang Hi-tech Zone, Pudong New District, Shanghai	201203	86-21-50801155-1353	86-21-38953436	Chen Jian
600846	Shanghai Tongji Science & Technology Industrial Co Ltd	83, Chi Feng Lu, Shanghai	200092	86-21-65985860	86-21-65983325	Lin Xueyan
600847	Chong Qing Wan Li Storage Batteries Co Ltd	31, Ku Zhu Ba, Ba Nan District, Chongqing	400054	86-23-62597905	86-23-62591155	Zhu Maopei
600848	Shanghai Automation Instrumentation Co Ltd	7F, Yi Xiang Building, 1599, Yanan Xi Lu, Shanghai	200050	86-62800705	86-62801680	Huang Dingfa
600849	Shanghai Pharmaceutical Co Ltd	1399, Jin Qiao lu, Pudong New District, Shanghai	201206	86-21-58999802	86-21-58995835	Cao Weirong
600850	Shanghai East-China Computer Co Ltd	418, Guilin Lu, Shanghai	200233	86-21-64362789	86-21-64700357	Wu Zhiming
600851	Shanghai Haixin Group Co Ltd	19 Floor, Jin Ling Hai Xin Building, 666, Fuzhou Lu, Shanghai	200001	86-21-63917000	86-21-63917678	Chen Mouliang
600852	China Sichuan International Cooperation Co Ltd	24 Floor, Si Chuan International Building, 206, Shuncheng Street, Chengdu, Sichuan	610016	86-28-6520852	86-28-6520852	Chen Pu
600853	Long Jian Road Bridge Co Ltd	7, Hong An Street, Fu La Er District, Qiqihaer	161041	86-452-6802291	86-452-6801662	LIu Xiaodong
600854	Jiangsu Chunlan Refrigerating Equipment Stock Co Ltd	1, Chun Lan Lu, Chunlan Industries Part, Taizhou, Jiangsu	225300	86-523-6663663	86-523-6663839	Chen Zhen
600855	Beijing Aerospace Chengfeng Co Ltd	Spaceflight Numerical-control Building, 51, Yong Ding Lu, Hai Dian District, Beijing	100854	86-10-88271805	86-10-88525734	Zhang Jinkui
600856	Changchun Department Jituan Store Company, Limited	77, Ren Min Street, Changchun	130061	86-431-8965414	86-431-8920704	Gen Wenxi

Code	Company	Address	Postal	Phone 1	Phone 2	Contact
600857	HIT Shouchuang Technology Co Ltd	45, He Yi Lu, Ningbo	315000	86-574-87347621	86-574-87367996	Ha Ning
600858	Bohai Group Co Ltd	20 Floor, Zhong Yin Building, Luoyuan Street, Jinauan Street, Jinan, Shandong	250063	86-531-6960688	86-531-6966666	Li Lu
600859	Beijing Wangfujing Department Store (Group) Co Ltd	255, Wangfujing Street, Beijing, China	100006	86-10-65126677 / 86-10-65125960	86-10-65133133	Liu bing
600860	Beiren Printing Machinery Holdings Limited	44, South on Guan Qu Lu, Chaoyang District, Beijing, China	100022	86-10-67748470	86-10-67714086	Jie Peimin
600861	Beijing Urban-Rural Trade Centre Co Ltd	Jia 23, Fu Xing Lu, Hai Dian District, Beijing	100036	86-10-68296595	86-10-68216933	Zhao Lei
600862	Tonmac International Co Ltd	23, Ren Gang Lu, Nantong, Jiangsu	226006	86-0513-5516141	86-0513-5512271	Cheng Zhiping
600863	Inner Mongolia Mengdian Huaneng Thermal Power Corporation Limited	218, Xi Lin Nan Lu, Huhehaote, Neimenggu	010020	86-471-6942388	86-471-6926658	Zhang Tong
600864	Harbin Shirble Electric-Heat Co Ltd	27, Kunlun Commercial City Longshun Street, Nangang District, Haerbin	150090	86-451-2333238	86-451-2332228	Xu Jianwei
600865	Baida Group Co Ltd	546, Yanan Lu, Hangzhou	310006	86-571-85109129	86-571-85150586	He Meiyun
600866	Star Lake Bioscience Co, Inc Zhaoqing Guangdong	67, Gong Nong Bei Lu, Zhaoqing, Guangdong	526060	86-758-2290079	86-758-2286478	Chen Ming
600867	Tonghua Dongbao Medicines Co Ltd	Dongbao New Village, Tonghua County, Jilin	134123	86-435-5858025	86-435-5858025	Wang Junye
600868	Guang Dong Mei Yan Enterprise Group Co Ltd	Wan Shui Tang, Meizhou, Guangdong	514011	86-753-2218286	86-753-2232983	Li Haiming
600869	Qinghai Sunshine And People Pharmaceutical Industry Co Ltd	88, Jian Guo Lu, Xining, Qinghai, China	810007	86-971-8166017	86-971-8144025	LI Haijun
600870	Xiamen Overseas Chinese Electronic Co Ltd	22, Hu Li Road, Xiamen	361006	86-592-6021091-203	86-592-6021331	Jia Hua
600871	Sinopec Yizheng Chemical Fibre Company Limited	Yizheng, Jiangsu, China	211900	86-514-3231888	86-514-3235880	Wu Zhaoyang
600872	Jonjee Hi-Tech Industrial & Commercial Holding Co Ltd	Huo Ju Building, Zhong Shan Huo Ju HI-tech Industries Development Zone, Zhongshan, Guangdong	528437	86-760-5596818	86-760-5596877	Peng Haihong

Stock Code	Company Name	Address	Postcode	Tel	Fax	Legal representative
600873	Tibet Pearl Star Co Ltd	88, Chang Shun Zhong Jie, Chengdu, Sichuan	610031	86-28-6600798	86-28-6600928	Yu Sheng
600874	Tianjin Capital Environmental Protection Company Limited	45, Guizhou Lu, He Ping District, Tianjin	300051	86-22-23523036	86-22-23523100	Fu Yana
600875	Dongfang Electrical Machinery Company Limited	188, Huanghe Xi Lu, Deyang, Sichuan	618000	86-838-2409358 86-838-2410789	86-838-2402125	Gong Dan
600876	Luoyang Glass Company Limited	9, Tang Gong Zhong Lu, Xi Gong District, Henan, China	471009	86-379-3908588 86-379-3908560	86-379-3251984	Wang Jie
600877	China Jialing Industrial Co Ltd (Group)	Shuangbei, Sha Ping Ba District, Chongqing	400032	86-23-65194095	86-23-65196666	Haung Jingyu
600878	Dalian Beeda Technology (Group) Co Ltd	18F, Wantai Building, 7, Ren Min Lu, Zhong Shan District, Dalian	116001	86-411-2801226	86-411-2801696	Guo Yingli
600879	Long March Launch Technology Co Ltd	B21, Rui Tong Square, 847, Jian She Road, Wuhan	430015	86-27-85487719	86-27-85487727	Lv Fan
600880	Chengdu B-Ray Media Co Ltd	185, Hua Pai Fang Street, Chengdu	610031	86-28-7651183	86-28-7651183	Zhang Yueming
600881	Jilin Yatai (Group) Co Ltd	281, Jilin Road, Changchun	130031	86-431-4956688	86-431-4951400	Sun Xiaofeng
600882	Shandong Dacheng Pesticide Co Ltd	25, Hong Gou Lu, Zhang Dian District, Zibo, Shandong	255009	86-533-2111999-6358	86-533-2113511	Yu Ning
600883	Yunnan Fortune Science& Technology Industry Co Ltd	52, Xia Xiang Street, Baoshan, Yunnan	678000	86-10-62187958	86-10-62186807	Zhang Chundong
600884	Ningbo Shanshan Co Ltd	1133, Tiantong Bei Lu, Ningbo	315192	86-574-88208358 86-574-88203333-3033	86-574-88208333	Chen Zhengliang
600885	Wuhan Linuo Industry Co Ltd	9 Floor, Xinhe Building, Jian She Road, Hankou, Wuhan	430015	86-027-85497163	86-027-85497085	Yang Chuan
600886	Sinopec Hubei Xinghua Company Ltd	63, Bai Miao Lu, Jinmen, Hubei	448002	86-724-2210632	86-724-2271727	Zhao Guoping
600887	Inner Mongolia Yili Industrial Group Co Ltd	8, Jin Si Lu, Jinchuan Development Zone, Huhehaote, Neimenggu	010080	86-471-3601621 86-471-3602351	86-471-3601615	Yang Guiqin
600888	Xinjiang Joinworld Co Ltd	18, Ke Shi Dong Lu, Urumuqi, Xinjiang	830013	86-991-6635306-2933	86-991-6637493	Cui Lixin
600889	Nanjing Chemical Fibre CoLtd	Fu Jia Chang, Zhong Yang Men Wai, Nanjing	210038	86-25-5561011-3685	86-25-5562809	Chen Tong

600890	Changchun Chanlin Industry & Commerce Co Ltd	230, Lin He Street, Economic & Technological Development Zone, Changchun	130031	86-431-4647632	86-431-4647622	Liu Xiangyun
600891	Harbin Churin Group Jointstock Co Ltd	319, Dong Da Zhi Street, Nan Gang District, Haerbin	150001	86-451-3644632	86-451-3649282	Yi Guoqiang
600892	Huda Technology & Education Developement Co Ltd	Office on 4 Floor, 51, Zhongshan Dong Lu, Shijiazhuang	050000	86-311-6033034	86-311-6033718	Ma Xinwei
600893	Jilin Province Jifa Agricultural Development Group Co Ltd	113-1, Ren Min Street, Changchun, Jilin	130021	86-431-5646 655-183303	86-431-5630485	Tang Zhao
600894	Guangzhou Iron And Steel Co Ltd	Bai He Cavity, Fang Cun District, Guangzhou	510381	86-20-81809182	86-20-81809182	Huang Lizhuan
600895	Shanghai Zhangjiang Hi-Tech Park Development Co Ltd	200, Long Dong Road, Pudong New District, Shanghai	201203	86-21-50803686	86-21-50800492	Zhang Xi
600896	China Shipping Haisheng Co Ltd	25 Floor, Dihao Building, Zhujiang Square, 2, Long Kun Bei Lu, Haikou, Hainan	570125	86-898-66717985 86-66764777-307	86-898-66717486	Hui Xiaobo
600897	Xiamen Airport Development Co Ltd	On the West of Airport Lounge 3, Gaoqi International Airport, Xiamen	361006	86-592-6022936-6005	86-592-60229 36-8888	Wang Jiangang
600898	Zhengzhou Baiwen Co Ltd (Group)	2, Nanyang Lu, Zhengzhou, Henan	450053	86-371-3935993-3165	86-371-3935819	Qi Anping
600899	Zhejiang Xinlian Co Ltd	68, Shang Tang Lu, Hangzhou	310014	86-571-85454614	86-571-85454526	Cao Zhiyuan

Appendix 4.2

'A' Shares Listed on Shenzhen Stock Exchange

Stock Code	Company Name	Address	Postcode	Tel	Fax	Legal representative
000001	Shenzhen Development Bank Co Ltd	Shenzhen Development Bank Edifice, 178, Shennan Dong Road, Luohu District, Shenzhen, Guangdong	518001	86-755-2080387	86-755-2080386	Lei Ming
000002	China Vanke Co Ltd	27, Shuibei Road 2, Luohu District, Shenzhen	518020	86-755-5606666	86-755-5601764	Xiao Li
000003	Gintian Industry (Group) Co Ltd	23-26th Floor, Jintian Edifice, 1199, Heping Road, Shenzhen	518010	86-755-5573548	86-755-5592045 86-755-5591994	Peng Wei
000004	Shenzhen PKU High-Tech Co Ltd	A-D, 27th Floor, New Times Square, Shekou, Shenzhen	518067	86-0755-6826732	86-0755-6826779	Jiang Weicheng
000005	Shenzhen Fountain Corporation	13th, Development Centre Edifice, Renmin Nan Road, Shenzhen	518001	86-755-2208888	86-755-2207055	Luo Xiaochun
000006	Shenzhen Zhenye (Group) Co Ltd	29-32nd Floor, Zhenye Edifice, Baoan Nan Road, Shenzhen	518008	86-755-5863061	86-755-5863012	Li Fuchuan
000007	Shenzhen SEG. DASHENG Co Ltd	5th Floor, Saige Industry Building, Huaqiang Bei Road, Shenzhen	518031	86-755-3239242	86-755-3780408	Li Hongwei
000008	Yorkpoint S & T Co Ltd Guangdong	Room 3111–3115, News Building, Shennan Zhong Road, Futian District, Shenzhen	518027	86-755-82092131	86-755-82090850	Qiu Daqing
000009	China Baoan Group Co Ltd	28–29th Floor, Bao'an Square, Sungang Dong Road, Shenzhen	518020	86-755-5170296	86-755-5170300	Lou Bing
000010	Shenzhen Huaxin Co Ltd	10th Floor, Hualian Edifice, Shennan Zhong Road, Futian District, Shenzhen	518031	86-755-3668745	86-755-3668696	Liu Changqing
000011	Shenzhen Properties & Resources Development (Group) Ltd	39&42nd Floor, Foreign Trade Building, Renmin Nan Road, Shenzhen	518014	86-755-2253020	86-755-2251997	Guo Yumei
000012	Csg Technology Holding Co Ltd	Nanbo Edifice, 1, Gongye Road 6, Shekou , Shenzhen	518067	86-755-6695970	86-755-6675733	Wu Guobin
000013	Shenzhen Petrochemical Industry (Group) Co Ltd	Petrifaction Edifice, Hongli Xi Road, Shenzhen	518028	86-755-3344355	86-755-3324057	Cai Jianping
000014	Shahe Industry Co Ltd	7th Floor, Shahe Commercial Building, Baishi Zhou, Shahe, Shenzhen	518053	86-755-6902828 86-755-6900498	86-755-6608488	Wang Fan
000015	Shenzhen Zhonghao (Group) Ltd	98&10th Floor, Zhonghao Edifice, Bagua Si Road, Shenzhen	518029	86-755-2260864	86-755-2262272	Jiang Yonglin

No.	Company	Address	Postal Code	Phone 1	Phone 2	Contact
000016	Konka Group Company, Ltd	Eastern Industry Zone, Huaqiao Town, Shenzhen	518053	86-755-6600082	86-755-6608866	Chen Xuri
000017	Shenzhen China Bicycle Company (Holdings) Ltd	3008, Buxin Road, Shenzhen, Guangdong	518019	86-755-5516620	86-755-5516998	Li Hai
000018	Shenzhen Victor Onward Textile Industrial Co Ltd	18th Floor, Huangchuang Centre, 889, Chashawan Avenue, Jiulong, H.K.	518001	86-755-2339100 / 86-852-24805666	86-755-2320942 / 86-852-24281823	Ren Yuanwei
000019	Shenzhen Shenbao Industrial Co Ltd	1058, Wenjin Bei Road, Luohu District, Shenzhen	518020	86-755-5507480	86-755-5507480	Xu Yuqiao
000020	Shenzhen Huafa Electronics Co Ltd	6th Floor, Building 411, Huafa Bei Road, Futian District, Shenzhen	518031	86-755-3352207	86-755-3352207	Hu Jianping
000021	Shenzhen Kaifa Technology Co Ltd	7006, Caitian Road, Futian District, Shenzhen	518035	86-755-3275997 / 86-755-3275075	86-755-3275000-33187	Chen Yanming
000022	Shenzhen Chiwan Wharf Holdings Ltd (Cwh)	11–12th Floor, Chiwan Oil Building, Chiwan Gang, Shenzhen, China	518068	86-755-6694297	86-755-6694620	Pei Jiangyuan
000023	Shenzhen Universe (Group) Co Ltd	2–3rd Floor, Tiandi Edifice, Bao'an Nan Road, Shenzhen	518008	86-755-5590169	86-755-5566317	Li Weicheng
000024	China Merchants Shekou Holdings Co Ltd	30th Floor, New Times Square, Shekou Industry Zone, Nanshan District, Shenzhen	518067	86-755-6819680	86-755-6819610	Chen Ken
000025	Shenzhen Tellus Holding Co Ltd	3rd Floor, Teli Edifice, 56, Shuibei Er Road, Luohu District, Shenzhen	518020	86-755-5536658	86-755-5536888-315	Li Shengchang
000026	Shenzhen Fiyta Holdings Ltd	Feiyada Edifice, 163, Zhenhua Road, Shenzehn	518041	86-755-3348369	86-755-3217888-8218	Hao Huiwen
000027	Shenzhen Energy Investment Co Ltd	33rd Floor, 2068, Shennan Zhong Road, Futian District, Shenzhen	518031	86-755-3684248	86-755-3684356	Hu Jian
000028	Shenzhen Accord Pharmaceutical Co Ltd	11th Floor, Inter-Trade Centre Building, Renmin Nan Road, Shenzhen, Guangdong	518014	86-755-2222353	86-755-2251782	Chen Changbing
000029	Shenzhen Special Economic Zone Real Estate & Properties (Group) Co Ltd	45-48th Floor, Shenfang Square, 3005, Renmin Nan Road, Shenzhen	518001	86-755-2294024	86-755-2293000-4718 / 86-755-2293000-4715 / 86-755-2293000-4719	Ye Huanbao
000030	Guangdong Sunrise Holdings Co Ltd	Jiahua Edifice, Huaqiang Bei Road, Shenzhen	518031	86-755-3361777	86-755-3361666-255	Pan Shiming
000031	Shenzhen Baoheng (Group) Co Ltd	Baoheng Edifice, 5, Hubin Road, Bao'an District, Shenzhen	518101	86-755-7789701	86-755-7754322	Zhu Haibin
000032	Shenzhen Sed Industry Co Ltd	2nd Floor, 78 West, Zhenhua Road, Futian District, Shenzhen	518031	86-755-3200639	86-755-3200636	Jin Tao

Stock Code	Company Name	Address	Postcode	Tel	Fax	Legal representative
000033	Shenzhen Century Plaza Hotel Co Ltd	Room 316, Xindu Hotel, 1, Chunfeng Road, Shenzhen	518001	86-755-2320888-382	86-755-2344699	Dong Xiaoli
000034	Shenzhen Shenxin Taifeng Group Co Ltd	19th Floor, Custom Building, 28, Bao'an Road 3, Area 23 of Baocheng, Bao'an District, Shenzhen	518101	86-755-7849181	86-755-7849232	Liu Xiangyang
000035	China Kejian Co Ltd	6th Floor, Building B, Unity Square, Shenzhen	518026	86-755-2551050	86-755-2710095	Dong Zhigang
000036	Shenzhen Union China Holdings Co Ltd	17th Floor, Hualian Edifice, 2008, Shennan Zhong Road, Shenzhen	518031	86-755-3667257	86-755-3667583	Kong Qingfu
000037	Shenzhen Nanshan Power Station Co Ltd	18, Yueliang wan Avenue, Nanshan District, Shenzhen, Guangdong	518052	86-755-6072818-208 86-755-6650052-208	86-755-6650642	Fu Bo
000038	Shenzhen Capstone Industrial Co Ltd	Eastern Industry Zone, Huaqiao Town, Shenzhen	518053	86-755-6931038	86-755-6600398	Wu Bin
000039	China International Marine Containers Group Co Ltd	5th Floor, Financial Centre, Shekou Industry Zone, Shenzhen, Guangdong	518067	86-755-6691130	86-755-6826579	Wu Fapei
000040	Shenzhen Hongkal (Group) Co Ltd	25–27th Floor, Hongji Edifice, 1011, Dongmen Zhong Road, Luohu District, Shenzhen	518001	86-755-2367726	86-755-2367780	Deng Yougao
000042	Shenzhen Changcheng Real Estate (Group) Holdings Co Ltd	Group Building, East Depart. Of Changxing Edifice (Shengtingyuan Hotel), 2010, Hongli Road, Futian District, Shenzhen	518028	86-755-3789776	86-755-3789776	Liu Li
000043	Shenzhen Nan-Guang (Group) Plc	32nd Floor, Aviation Building, 68, Shennan Zhong Road, Futian District, Shenzhen	518031	86-0755-3689888-13253	86-0755-3688903	Huo Wufei
000045	Shenzhen Textile (Holdings) Co Ltd	6th Floor, Shenfang Edifice, 3, Huaqiang Bei Road, Futian District, Shenzhen	518031	86-755-3776043	86-755-3776139	Chao Jin
000046	Guangcai Construction Group Co Ltd	3rd Floor, Building A of Huifang Community, 8, Xuefu Road, Nanshan District, Shenzhen	518052	86-755-6406604	86-755-6072025	Chen Jiahua
000047	Shenzhen Overglobe Development Co Ltd	3rd Floor, Xihu Garden, Bao'an Nan Road, Luohu District, Shenzhen	518008	86-755-5894572	86-755-5566222	Yang Yumei

ID	Company	Address	Postal Code	Phone	Fax	Contact
000048	Shenzhen Kondarl Group Co Ltd	2–3rd Floor, Jihao Edifice, 1086, Shennan Zhong Road, Luohu District, Shenzhen	518003	86-755-5425020-288	86-755-5420155	Zhu Quxiu
000049	Shenzhen Worldsun Enterprise Co Ltd	M Floor, Building A of Guihua Edifice, 28,Guiyuan Road, Luohu District, Shenzhen	518001	86-755-2131400	86-755-2131400	He Bingjie
000050	Shenzhen Tianma Microelectronics Co Ltd	22nd Floor, Hangdu Edifice, Zhonghang Yuan, Shennan Zhong Road, Futian District, Shenzhen	518041	86-755-3793863	86-755-3790431	Liu Changqing
000055	China Fangda Group Co Ltd	Fangjing Lilong Dacheng Technology Building, Nanshan District, Shenzhen	518055	86-755-6788571-6622	86-755-6788353	Lu Weiwei
000056	Shen Zhen International Enterprise Co Ltd	23rd Floor, Development Centre Building, Renmin Nan Road, Shenzhen	518001	86-755-2285564	86-755-2285573	Xie Wei
000058	Shenzhen Seg Co Ltd	16th Floor, Baohua Edifice, Huaiqiang Bei Road, Futian District, Shenzhen	518031	86-755-3675060	86-755-3779770	Zheng Dan
000059	Liaoning Hujin Tongda Chemicals Company Limited	Liaoning	124021	86-755-2275565	86-755-2275575	Lu Feng
000060	Shenzhen Zhongjin Linnan Nonfemet Company Ltd	12 Floor, Pacific Commercial Trade Building, 4028, Jia Bin Lu, Shenzhen	518001	86-755-2138819	86-755-2138929	Peng Ling
000061	Shenzhen Agricultural Products Co, Ltd	22 Floor, Tian Le Building, 1021, Bu Ji Lu, Shenzhen	518019	86-755-5850936 86-755-5850688-2203	86-755-5850936	Chren Xiaohua
000062	Shenzhen Huaqiang Industry Co. Ltd	7 Floor, Company Headquarters, Shen Nan Zhong Lu Huaqiang Lu Kou, Shenzhen	518043	86-755-3216296	86-755-3368414	Zhou Hongbin
000063	ZTE Corporation	Zhongxing Communication Building, South Technology Road, Nanshan Hi-tech Industries Zone, Shenzhen	518057	86-755-6790282	86-755-6790286	Feng Jianxiong
000065	Norinco International Cooperation Ltd	Jia 12, Guang An Men Nan Jie, Baocheng District 34, Baoan District Shenzhen	518133	86-755-3279933 86-755-7809810	86-755-3279777 86-755-7808357	Haung Qianhua
000066	China Greatwall Computer Shenzhen Co Ltd	Great Wall Computer Building, Nanshan Technology & Industries Zone, Shenzhen, China	518057	86-755-6634759	86-755-6631106	Li Tian

Stock Code	Company Name	Address	Postcode	Tel	Fax	Legal representative
000068	Shenzhen Seg Samsung Glass Co Ltd	Factory 101, Shanghai Lin Industries Part, Fu Tian District, Shenzhen	518049	86-755-3311988-1810	86-755-3112656	Wang Kefu
000069	Shenzhen Overseas Chinese Town Holdings Company	Hua Qiao Cheng Jian She Headquarters Building, Nan Shan District, Shenzhen	518053	86-755-6909069	86-755-6600517	Xiao Dezhong
000070	Shenzhen Sdg Information Co Ltd	Building 1 Behind West Pubulic House of Xiangmihu Holiday Village, Futian District, Shenzhen	518034	86-755-3711473	86-755-3710133	Zhang Dajun
000078	Shenzhen Neptunus Bioengineering Co Ltd	26 Floor, Haiwang Building, Nanyou Road, Nanshan District, Shenzhen	518054	86-755-6416065 86-755-6649838-2671	86-755-6416053	Feng Jiaxin
000088	Shenzhen Yan Tian Port Holdings Co Ltd	18-20 Floor, Seaport Building, Yantian Port, Yantian District, Shenzhen	518081	86-755-5290180	86-755-5290932	Hua Xiang
000089	Shenzhen Airport Co Ltd	Office 1, Huangtian International Airport, Baoan District, Shenzhen	518128	86-755-7776018	86-755-7776327	Xie Ailong
000090	Shenzhen Tonge (Group) Co Ltd	Municipal Building, 7058, Hong Li Xi Lu, Futian District, Shenzhen	518034	86-755-3928130	86-755-3915736	Xu Zhaosong
000096	Shenzhen Guangju Energy Go., Ltd	6 Floor, She Kou Building, She Kou New Street, Shenzhen	518067	86-755-6690988	86-755-6690998	Ji Yuanhong
000099	CITIC Offshore Helicopter Co Ltd	188, Jiefang Xi Lu, Luohu District, Shenzhen	518001	86-755-5590755	86-755-5590755	Yan Qi
000150	Macat Optics & Electronics Co Ltd	15 Floor, Mai Ke Te Center, 63, Maidi Lu, Huizhou, Guangdong	516001	86-752-2119664	86-752-2118071	Liu Yongqing
000151	China National Complete Plant Import & Export Co Ltd	9, Bin He Lu, West to An Ding Men, Bejing	100011	86-10-64218520	86-10-64251026	Jie Bei
000153	Auhui Xinli Pharmaceutical Co Ltd	258, Wu Hu Lu, Hefei, Anhui	230061	86-551-2886567 86-551-2888062	86-551-2888056	Zhang Jun
000155	Sichuan Chemical Company Ltd	311,Tuan Jie Lu, Da Wan Town, Qing Bai Jiang District, Chengdu, Sichuan	610301	86-28-3308291	86-28-3308290	Yi Qianli
000156	Hunan Anplas Co Ltd	He Xi Wang Cheng Po, Changsha	410205	86-731-8861888-8065	86-731-8815299	Tao Yangbo
000157	Changsha Zoomlion Heavy Industry Science And Technology Development Co Ltd	307, Yinpen Nan Lu, Changsha, Hunan	410013	86-731-8923779 86-731-8923908	86-731-8923906	Cheng Xuhui
000158	Shijiazhuang Changshan Textile Co Ltd	183, Heping Dong Lu, Shijiazhuang, Hebei	050011	86-311-6673856	86-311-6673929	Li Jingchao

ID	Company	Address	Postal code	Phone 1	Phone 2	Contact
000159	Xinjiang International Industry Co Ltd	International Building, 45, Tuanjie Lu, Urumuqi	830001	86-991-2886434	86-991-2861579	Zhang yueqi
000301	Wujiang Silk Co Ltd	39, Shun Xin Zhong Lu, Shengze Town, Wujiang, Jiangsu	215228	86-512-3558328	86-512-3552272	Shen Zhixiang
000400	Xj Electric Co Ltd	178, Jianshe Lu, Xuchang, Henan	461000	86-374-3212348	86-374-3363549	Tu Dongming
000401	Tangshan Jidong Cement Company Ltd	Lin Yin Lu, New District, Tangshan, Hebei	063031	86-315?3244005	86-315-3244005	Zhang Shijiang
000402	Finance Street Holding Co Ltd	B8, Tongtai Building, 33, Jin Rong Street, Xicheng District, Beijing	100032	86-10-88086184	86-10-88086186	Xu Qunfeng
000403	Sanjiu Yigong Biopharmaceutical And Chemical Inc	A35, Lianhe Square, Futian District, Shenzhen	518026	86-755-2711988	86-755-2710777	Huang Hongwwei
000404	Huayi Compressor Corporation Ltd	28, Xin Chang Dong Lu, Jingdezhen, Jiangxi	333001	86-798-8470227	86-798-8441779	Jian Jiafeng
000405	Zhuhai Shining Metals Group Inc	Jinyuan Building, Jida Haizhou Lu, Zhuhai, Guangdong	519015	86-756-3338333-8103 8962-8034	86-756-3338123	Xia Wenshu
000406	Sinopec Shengli Oil Field Dynamic Group Co Ltd	228, Daming Building, Jinan Lu, Dongying, Shandong	257000	86-546-8556533	86-546-8556533	Xi Jingjie
000407	Shandong Shengli Co Ltd	Sheng Li building, 139, Heihu Spring Xi Lu, Jinan, Shandong	250011	86-531-6920495	86-531-6018518	Yu Xiaofeng
000408	Hebei Huayu Company Ltd	21, Pengxin Lu, Fengfeng Kuang District, Handan, Hebei	056200	86-10-64275193 86-310-5023927	86-10-64275193 86-310-5023067	Guo Baogui
000409	Stone Group Hi-Tech Co Ltd	Investment Building, 4009, Shennan Road, Futian Center District, Shenzhen, Guangdong	518026	86-755-2712233	86-755-2712266	Ke Jianhua
000410	Shenyang Machine Tool Co Ltd	10-1, Bei Er Dong Lu, Tie Xi District, Shenyang	110025	86-24-25876185	86-24-25878762	Mou Jixun
000411	Hang Zhou Kaidi Silk Co Ltd	508, Yanan Lu, Hangzhou, Zhejiang	310006	86-0571-85068752	86-0571-85068752	Bao Zhihu
000412	Changchun North China Wuhuan Co Ltd	15, Puyang Street, Lv Yuan District, Changchun, Jilin	130051	86-0431-7822218-8188	86-0431-7828282	Zhou Gang
000413	Shijiazhuang Baoshi Electronic Glass Company Ltd	9, Huanghe Road, Shijiazhuang Hi-tech Industries Development Zone, Hebei	050035	86-311-6044705	86-311-6041503	Luo Lina
000415	Xin Jiang Hui Tong (Group) Co Ltd	22, Huanghe Road, Urumuqi, Xinjiang	830000	86-991-5835644 86-991-5852082	86-991-5852082	Hu Minhui
000416	Qingdao Jiante Biological Investment Co Ltd	12, Taiping Jiao Liu Lu, Qingdao	266071	86-532-3884366	86-532-3876171	Chen Bo
000417	Hefei Department Store Group Co Ltd	150, Changjiang Zhong Lu, Hefei, Anhui	230001	86-551-2647133-3034 86-551-2640803	86-551-2652936	Zhao Wenwu

Stock Code	Company Name	Address	Postcode	Tel	Fax	Legal representative
000418	Wuxi Little Swan Company Ltd	67, Huiqian Lu, Wuxi, Jiangsu	214035	86-510-3704003-2192	86-510-3704031	Qiao Li
000419	Changsha Tongcheng Holdings Co Ltd	2, Laodong Lu, Changsha, Hunan	410007	86-731-5534994	86-731-5535588	Su Qianli
000420	Jilin Chemical Fibre Co Ltd	516-1, Jiuzhan street, Changyi District, Jilin	132101	86-432-3502331	86-432-3058453	Tang Jiawei
000421	Nanjing Zhongbei (Group) Co Ltd	81, Han Zhong Men Street, Nanjing	210029	86-25-6650169	86-25-6522634	Li Qingliang
000422	Hubei Yihua Chemical Industry Co Ltd	399, Xiaoting Road, Yichang, Hubei	443007	86-717-6517249 86-717-6516477	86-717-6516477	Yu Chenyang
000423	Shan Dong Dong E E Jiao Co Ltd	78, Ejiao Street, Dong E County, Shandong	252201	86-635-3264069	86-635-3260786	Wu Huaifeng
000425	Xugong Science & Technology Co Ltd	5, Su Di Bei Lu, Xuzhou, Jiangsu	221006	86-516-5756044-2528	86-516-5753151	Fei Guangsheng
000426	Chifeng Fulong Heating Co Ltd	Fulong Building, 8, Zhao Wu Da Lu, Chifeng, Neimenggu	024000	86-476-8240042	86-476-8231734	Zhang Chunshui
000428	Hunan Huatian Great Hotel Co Ltd	8 Floor, Company Compositive Building, 380, Jiefang Dong Lu, Changsha	410001	86-731-4442888-80928	86-731-4442270	Zou Changui
000429	Guangdong Provincial Expressway Development Co Ltd	85, Baiyun Lu, Guangzhou, Guangdong	510100	86-20-83731365 86-20-83731388-230	86-20-83731384	Huo Yanbin
000430	Zhang Jia Jie Tourism Development Co Ltd	Garden 1, Nan Zhuang Ping, Zhangjiajie, Hunan	427000	86-731-2233129	86-731-2233129	Yan Xiaoping
000488	Shandong Chenming Paper Holdings Ltd	595, Shengcheng Street, Shouguang, Shandong	262700	86-536-5280011	86-536-5228900	Hao Jun
000498	Dandong Chemical Fibre Co Ltd	58, Xianwei Street, Zhenxing Lu, Dandong, Liaoning	118002	86-415-6192271 86-415-6193718	86-415-6191684	Zhang Jie
000501	Wuhan Department Store Group Co Ltd	688, Jiefang Road, Hankou, Wuhan	430022	86-27-85714295	86-27-85714295	Li Xuan
000502	Hainan New Energy Co Ltd	24 Floor, Huayin Building, 38, Longkun Bei Lu, Haikou, Hainan	570105	86-898-66713081	86-898-66713216	Xu Dezhi
000503	Searainbow Holding Corp.	7 Floor, Wenhua Public House, Binhai Road, Haikou	570105	86-898-68510496	86-898-68510669	Shangguan Yongqiang
000504	Beijing Ccid Media Investments Co Ltd	Room 278, Youyi Hotel Suyuan Write Building, 1, Zhongguancun Street, Haidian District, Beijing	100873	86-10-68710712 86-10-68710713	86-10-68710711	Liu Xuli
000505	Hainan Pearl River Holdings Co Ltd	29 Floor, Dihao Building, Zhujiang Square, Binhai Road, Haikou	570125	86-898-6763723 86-898-6717888	86-898-6776026	Feng Pai

000506	Sichuan Dong Tai Industry Holdings Co Ltd	41, Nan'an Lu, Center District, Leshan, Sichuan	614000	86-833-2421473	86-833-2421473	Yan Shu
000507	Fuhua Group Co Ltd Zhuhai S. E. Z.	Fuhua Group Co Ltd Zhuhai S. E. Z., Gongbei Beiling Industries Zone, Zhuahai, Guangdong	519070	86-756-8886218	86-756-8888148	Xue Nan
000509	Sichuan Tiange Technology Group Co Ltd	Tiange Technological Building, Yi Huan Lu Nan Er Duan, Chengdu, Sichuan	610041	86-28-5435719	86-28-5445907	Shi Duying
000510	Sichuan Jinlu Group Co Ltd	Directorate Office	618000	86-838-2207936	86-838-2204384	Peng Lang
000511	Shenyang Ingenious Development Co Ltd	82, 11 Wei Lu, Heping District, Shenyang	110003	86-24-22857819	86-24-22846927	Wang Liqun
000513	Livzon Pharmaceutical Croup Inc.	Gongbei Guihua Bei Lu, Zhuhai, Guangdong	519020	86-756-8135888	86-756-8886002	Wang Wuping
000514	Chongqing Yukaifa Co Ltd	Fu 1 Hao, 1, Zengjiayan, Yu Zhong District, Chongqing	400015	86-23-63626484	86-23-63852638	Xia Guangming
000515	Chongqing Yu-Gang Tioxide Co Ltd	51, Zouma Er Cun, Ba Nan District, Chongqing	400055	86-23-62551281-388	86-23-62551279	Xiang Yuanping
000516	Xi'An Jiefang Group Co Ltd	6, Jiefang Market, Xi'an	710001	86-29-7217854	86-29-7217705	Liu Jiansuo
000517	Ningbo Success Information Industry Co Ltd	12AF, Ningbo Jinrong Building, 138, Jiang Dong Bei Lu, Ningbo	315040	86-574-87730360	86-574-87374078	Fu Biebiao
000518	Jiangsu Sihuan Bioengineering Co Ltd	Xinqiao Town, Jiangyin, Jiangsu	214426	86-510-6121071	86-510-6121071	Gao Lixin
000519	Chengdu Yinhe Innovation Technology Co Ltd	B25B, Wangfujing Commercial Building, 5, Huaxing Zheng Street, Chengdu, Sichuan	610016	86-28-6626418 86-28-6629638	86-28-2903003	Gao Bin
000520	Sinopec Wuhan Phoenix Co, Ltd	Changqing Lu, Qingshan District, Wuhan	430082	86-27-86516722	86-27-86515968	Xiong Kejin
000521	Hefei Meiling Co Ltd	48, Wuhu Lu, Hefei	230001	86-551-2884961-394	86-551-2885502	Xue Hui
000522	Guangzhou Baiyunshan Pharmaceutical Stock Co Ltd	Tonghe, Baiyun District, Guangzhou, Guangdong	510515	86-20-87706688-3513	86-20-87705599	Chen Ying
000523	Lonkey Industrial Co Ltd, Guangzhou	128, East of Huangpu Road Tianhe District, Guangzhou	510660	86-20-82305933 86-20-82305694-228	86-20-82305104	Li Jin
000524	Guangzhou Dong Fang Hotel Co Ltd	120, Liuhua Lu, Guangzhou	510016	86-20-86669900-3103 86-20-86662791	86-20-86669900-3102	Chen Cong
000525	Nanjing Red Sun Co Ltd	1606, 16 Floor, Jiangsu Commercial Building, 28, Zhongshan Bei Lu, Nanjing	210008	86-25-3315888-8211	86-25-3317828	Bao Jinjun
000526	Xiamen Sunrise Industrial Co Ltd	1, Changle Lu, Zhaishang, Huli District, Xiamen	361006	86-592-5651889 86-755-2496116	86-592-5652638	Li Houyang

Stock Code	Company Name	Address	Postcode	Tel	Fax	Legal representative
000527	Gd Midea Holding Co Ltd	Penglai Lu, Bei Town, Shunde, Guagdong	528311	86-765-6338779 86-765-6338807	86-765-6651991	Li Jinawei
000528	Guangxi Liugong Machinery Co Ltd	1, Liutai Lu, Liuzhou, Guangxi	545007	86-779-3886509-6510	86-779-3886509	Wang Zuguang
000529	Guangdong Meiya Group Co Ltd	40, Ren Min Xi Lu, Heshan, Guangdong	529700	86-750-8888888	86-750-8889240	Feng Wei
000530	Dalian Refrigeration Co Ltd	888, Xi Nan Lu, Shahekou District, Dalian	116033	86-411-6653081-8100	86-411-6641470	Lv Lianzhen
000531	Guangzhou Hengyun Enterprises Holdings Co Ltd	8, Xi Ji Lu, Economic & Technic Development Zone, Guangzhou	510730	86-20-82098330	86-20-82098658	Lin Guoding
000532	Zhuhai Huadian Co Ltd	33 Floor, Guangda International Economic & Trade Center, Hai Bin Nan Lu, Zhuhai	519015	86-756-3329623	86-756-3329828	Cao Haixia
000533	Guangdong Macro Co Ltd	38, Huanshi Bei Lu, Daliang District, Shunde, Guangdong	528300	86-765-2330206	86-765-2330200	He Jianxiong
000534	Shantou Electric Power Development Co Ltd	6 Floor, Jinfeng Cheng Long Zuo, Jinsha Dong Lu, Shantou, Guangdong	515041	86-754-8628249 86-754-8611172	86-754-8628249	Huang Manhua
000535	KMK Co Ltd	304, Yiling Lu, Yichang, Hubei	443003	86-717-6359775	86-717-6351835	Li Benlin
000536	Mindong Electric Group Co Ltd	12, Dou Dong Lu, Fuzhou, Fujian	350005	86-591-3348228	86-591-3326201	Huang Jinqiu
000537	Tianjin Nankai Guard Co Ltd	A24 Floor, Yinfeng Garden, Youyi Bei Lu, Hexi District, Tianjin	300211	86-22-28010550	86-22-28010599	Liu Yan
000538	Yunnan Baiyao Group Co Ltd	51, Xi Ba Lu, Kunming, Yunnan	650032	86-871-4179814	86-871-4144960	Haug Ainong
000539	Guangdong Electric Power Development Co Ltd	10 Floor, Guangfa Garden Boli Commercial Center, 498, Huan Shi Dong Lu, Guangzhou, Guangdong	510075	86-20-87609276	86-20-87609909	Zhang Dewei
000540	Zhong Tian Enterprise Joint Stock Co Ltd	5 Floor, Zhaiji Building, 1, Jixiang Lu, Yunyan District, Guiyang	550004	86-851-6809072 86-10-64425993	86-851-6809115 86-10-64425948	Zhao Hong
000541	Foshan Electrical And Lighting Co Ltd	15, Fenjiang Bei Lu, Foshan, Guangdong	528000	86-0757-2813838-282 86-0757-2814805	86-0757-2816276	Li Yihui
000542	TCL Communication Equipment Co Ltd	TCL Building, 10, Shangpai Daling Lu, Huizhou, Guangdong	516001	86-752-2288898	86-752-2261868	Lin Shengzhong
000543	An Hui Wenergy Company Ltd	Huanneng Building, 99, Ma An Shan Lu, Hefen, Anhui	230011	86-0551-4668888-701	86-0551-4672679	Zhou Qingxia
000544	White Dove (Group) Co Ltd	78, Huashan Lu, Zhengzhou, Henan	450006	86-371-7635588-2530	86-371-7628013	Cao Changling
000545	Jilin Henghe Pharmaceutical Ltd Company	99, Changchu Lu, Jilin City	132012	86-432-4809008	86-432-4841728	Wen Cheng

ID	Company	Address	Postcode	Phone	Fax	Contact
000546	Jilin Light Industrial Group Co Ltd	81, Jianshe Street, Changchun, Jilin	130061	86-431-8540236 86-431-8522149	86-431-8523476	Sun Zhenjiang
000547	Fujian Fufa Company Ltd	14 Floor, Wu Yi Branch of Industrial & Commercial Bank, 67, Wu Yi Nan Lu, Fuzhou, Fujian	350009	86-591-3296358	86-591-3260868	Lin Jie
000548	Hunan Investment Group Co Ltd	8, Youse Building, 177, Lao Dong Xi Lu, Changsha	410015	86-731-5500354	86-731-5518565	Huang Manchi
000549	Torch Investment Co. Ltd	3, Hongqi Bei Lu, Zhuzhou, Hunan	412001	86-733-8450019	86-733-8450105 86-733-8450019	Zhang Yingzi
000550	Jiangling Motors Corporation Co Ltd	Yingbin Bei Road, Nanchang Jiangxi	330001	86-791-5232839	86-791-5232888-6178	Xiong Zhongping
000551	Create Technology & Science Co Ltd	4, Nan Men Dong Er Lu, Suzhou	215007	86-512-5300551	86-512-5300551	Chen Xiaolin
000552	Gansu Changfeng Special Electronics & Appliances Co Ltd	270, Anning Xi Lu, Anning District, Lanzhou, Gansu	730070	86-931-7667172	86-931-7666251 86-931-7616756	Hu Huibin
000553	Hubei Sanonda Co Ltd	93, Beijing Dong Lu, Jinzhou,.. Hubei	434001	86-716-8316796	86-716-8314802	Li Zhongxi
000554	SINOPEC Shandong Taishan Pectroleum Co Ltd	104, Dongyue Street, Taian, Shandong	271000		86-538-8265456 86-538-8265450	Li Jianwen
000555	Shenzhen Techo Telecom. Ltd	Room A2, 4 Floor, Tianji Building, Tian'an Shuma City, Futian District, Shenzhen	518040	86-755-3892839	86-755-3892829	Chen Huaizhi
000556	Nanyang Shipping Group Stock Holding Co Ltd	7&8 Floor, Dong Fang Yang Building, 288, Binhai Road, Haikou	570311	86-898-66752989	86-898-66775208 86-898-68666999	Li Qian
000557	Guangxia (Yinchuan) Industry Co Ltd	8, Park Street, Yinchuan, Ningxia	750001	86-951-5054518	86-951-5054693	Yu Wanming
000558	Lander Real Estate Co Ltd	6 Floor, Bolong Building, 192, Nanjing Nan Street, Heping District, Shenyang, Liaoning	110005	86-24-23327946	86-24-23327948	Liu Feng
000559	Wanxiang Qianchao Co Ltd	Xiaoshan District, Hangzhou, Zhejiang	311215	86-571-82602132	86-571-82832999	Guan Dayuan
000560	Kunming Department Store (Group) Co Ltd	99, Dongfeng Xi Lu, Kunming Yunnan	650021	86-871-3623414	86-871-3621681	Wu Mengbing
000561	Chang Ling Group Co Ltd	75, Qingjiang Lu, Baoji, Shanxi, China	721006	86-917-3622392	86-917-3624433-5041	Wang Wangxuan
000562	Hong Yuan Securities Co Ltd	8 Floor, Hongyuan Building, Jianshe Lu, Urumuqi, Xinjiang	830002	86-991-2301779	86-991-2301870	Yu Fan
000563	Shaanxi International Trust & Investment Corp., Ltd	8, South of Huan Cheng Dong Lu, Xi'an, Shanxi	710048	86-29-3239456	86-29-3239354 86-29-3224277	Hu Mengqi
000564	Xi'An Minsheng Group Co Ltd	103, Jiefang Lu, Xi'an	710005	86-29-7481871	86-29-7481961	Ma Mingqing

Stock Code	Company Name	Address	Postcode	Tel	Fax	Legal representative
000565	Chongqing Sanxia Paints Co Ltd	121, Shi Ping Qiao Zheng Street, Jiulongpo District, Chongqing	400051	86-23-68825420-3100	86-23-68820710	Jie Luming
000566	Hainan Qingqihaiyao Co Ltd	7 Floor, Hongyuan Paper Building, 30, Longkun Bei Lu, Haikou, Hainan	570105	86-898-66785861	86-898-66705316	Li Ying
000567	Hainan Haide Textile Industrial Co Ltd	11 Floor, Huangjin Haijing Public House, 67, Binhai Road, Haikou	570106	86-898-68535653	86-898-68535942	Xu Ling
000568	Luzhou Lao Jiao Co. Ltd	46, Guihua Street, Luzhou, Sichuan	646000	86-830-2292023	86-830-2391774	Cai Ququan
000569	Sichuan Chuantou Changcheng Special Steel Co Ltd	195, Jiangdong Lu, Jiangyou, Sichuan	621701	86-816-3650392	86-816-3651872	Shen Qingfeng
000570	Changchai Company,Lrd	123, Huaide Zhong Lu, Changzhou, Jiangsu, China	213002	86-519-6600448 86-519-6603656-3155	86-519-6630954	Zhang Jianhe
000571	Hainan Sundiro Motorcycle Co Ltd	26 Floor, Dihao Building, Zhujiang Square, Haikou, Hainan	570125	86-0898-6858 3966-333-222	86-898-66715518	Lin Fan
000572	Hainan Jinpan Enterprise Co Ltd	12-8 Jinpan Lu, Jinpan Industries Part, Haikou	570216	86-898-66822672	86-898-66816370	Zhang Qian
000573	Dongguan Winnerway Industrial Zone Ltd	16 Floor, Hongyuan Building, Hongyuan Industries Zone, Dongwan, Guangdong	523087	86-769-2412655	86-769-2813341	Li Junyin
000576	The Jiangmen Sugarcane Chemical Factory Group Co Ltd	1, Ganhua Lu, Jiangmen, Guangdong	529075	86-750-3365000	86-750-3361973	Sha Wei
000578	Qinghai Digital Net Investment Share Holding Group Co Ltd	39, Wusi Street, Xining, Qinghai	810001	86-971-6138725	86-971-6144887	Sun Rongfang
000581	Weifu High-Technology Co Ltd	107 Renmin Xi Lu, Wuxi	214031	86-510-2719579	86-510-2751025	Liu Yonglin
000582	Beihai Xinli Industrial Co Ltd	145, Haijiao Lu, Beihai, Guangxi	536000	86-779-3922254	86-779-3906393	Yang Yanhua
000583	Sichuan Topsoft Investment Co Ltd	Tuopu Group Customer Center, 24, Jinxianqiao Lu, Chengdu, Sichuan	610031	86-28-7675467	86-28-7675753	Zhou Tao
000584	Chengdu Shudu Mansion Co Ltd	20, Shu Wa Bei San Street, Shudu Road, Chengdu	610016	86-28-6752215	86-28-6741677	Luo Yidi
000585	Northeast Electrical Transmission & Transformation Machinery Manufacturing Company Ltd	189, Taiyuan Nan Street, Heping District, Shenyang, Liaoning, China	110001	86-24-23527080	86-24-23527081	Li Bin
000586	Sichuan Changjiang Business Enterprise (Group) Co Ltd	34, Fuqing Lu YI Duan, Chengdu, Sichuan	610082	86-28-3324561	86-28-3333896	Buo Lihong
000587	Guangming Group Furniture Co Ltd	118, Qingshan Xi Lu, Yichun District, Yichun, Heilongjiang	153000	86-458-3667158	86-458-3660588	Zhang Falun

ID	Company	Address	Postal	Phone	Phone	Contact
000589	Gui Zhou Tyre Co Ltd	41, Baihua Road, Guiyang, Guizhou	550008	86-851-4843651	86-851-4844248	Li Shangwu
000590	Tsinghua Unisplendour Guhan Bio-Pharmaceutical Corporation Ltd	54, Xianfeng Lu, Hengyang, Hunan	421001	86-734-8239335	86-734-8239335	Liao Delin
000591	Chongqing Tong Jun Ge Co Ltd	120, Jiefang Xi Lu, Yuzhong District, Chongqing	400012	86-23-63843398	86-23-63843398	Zou Sha
000592	Fujian Cfc Industries Co Ltd	21 Floor, New World Building, 157, Wusi Lu, Fuzhou, Fujian	350003	86-591-7815650	86-591-7815622	Dong Lianghao
000593	Chengdu Hualian Business Building Co Ltd	55, Jianshe Lu, Chengdu, Sichuan	610051	86-28-4312393 / 86-28-4310018-20172	86-28-4299233	Li Nengfa
000594	Neimenggu Hongfeng Industry Company Ltd	B908, Study & Research Building, Tsinghua Technological Part, Haidian District, Beijing	100084	86-010-62795080	86-010-62795077	Lu Chunxiang
000595	Xibei Bearing Co Ltd	Beijing Xi Lu, Yinchuan	750021	86-951-2020394	86-951-2013747	Nie Limao
000596	Anhui Gujing Distillery Company Ltd.	Gujing Town, Haozhou, Anhui	236820	86-558-5710085	86-558-5710006	Wang Feng
000597	Northeast Pharmaceutical Group Co Ltd	37, North Heavy Industries Street, Tie Xi District, Shenyang	110026	86-24-25806662	86-24-25806664	Liu Yaying
000598	Blue Star Cleaning Co Ltd	9, Bei Tu Cheng Xi Lu, Chaoyang District, Beijing	100029	86-10-62376645	86-10-62376625	Ke Wei
000599	Qingdao Doublestar Shoe Manufacturing Co Ltd	Doublestar Industries Part, Qingdao	266229	86-532-2657986	86-532-2657986	Guo Weishun
000600	Shijiazhuang International Building Group Co Ltd	1, Guang'an street, Shijiazhuang, Hebei	050011	86-311-6672224	86-311-6672254	Han Jinping
000601	Guang Dong Shaoneng Group Co Ltd	148, Huimin Nan Lu, Shaoguan	512026	86-751-153162	86-751-535226	Hu Qijin
000602	Guangdong Golden Horse Tourism Group Stock Co Ltd	4 Floor, Lvyou Building, Chaofeng Lu, Chaozhou, Guangdong	521000	86-768-2268969	86-768-2297613	Liang Maohui
000603	Weida Medical Applied Technology Co Ltd	221, Lindu Road, Jiexi County	515400	86-663-5583675	86-663-5582865	Cheng Hongdong
000605	Sihuan Pharmaceutical Co Ltd	6 Floor, Dongrun Times Building, 3, Fu Wai Street, Xi Cheng District, Beijing	100037	86-10-68003377-8819	86-10-68001816	Li Jinzhu
000606	Qinghai Gelatin Company Ltd	13, Fu Dong Lu, Xining, Qinghai	810015	86-971-8013495	86-971-8012106	Zhang Haicang
000607	Chongqing Holley Share Co Ltd	No.76, Jianxin Bei Road, Jiangbei District, Chongqing	400020	86-23-67758090	86-23-67755788	Yuan ZIli
000608	Super Shine Co Ltd	No.2018, Futong Building, 2-1, Chegongzhuang Avenue, Xicheng District, Beijing	100044	86-10-68342951	86-10-68343211	Xiao Hu

Stock Code	Company Name	Address	Postcode	Tel	Fax	Legal representative
000609	Beijing Yanhua Up-Dated Hi-Tech. Co Ltd	No.2, Yanshan Yingfeng Er Li, Fangshan District, Beijing	102500	86-10-69347433	86-10-69345895	Shen Wenhui
000610	Xi' An Tourism Group Co Ltd	No.16, Huancheng Nan Road, XI'an	710054	86-29-7858883	86-29-7854296	Liu Jianli
000611	The Inner Mongolia Minzu Industry & Commerce Group Co Ltd	No.69,Zhongshan XI Road, Huhehaote, Inner-Mongolia	010020	86-471-6968822-2313	86-471-6962236	Na Sen Ba Ya'er
000612	Jiaozuo Wanfang Aluminum Manufacturing Co Ltd	Daiwang Town, Macun District, Jiaozuo City, Henan Prov.	454003	86-391-3903848 86-391-3903796	86-391-3903796	Jia Dongyan
000613	Hainan Dadonghai Tourism Centre (Holdings) Co Ltd	Great East Sea, Sanya City	572021	86-898-88219888-8264	86-898-88212298	Liu Juntao
000615	Hubei Golden Ring Co Ltd	Chenjia Lake, Xiangyang County, Hubei	441133	86-710-2108234	86-710-2108233	Tan Guangmin
000616	Dalian Bohan Hotel (Group) Co Ltd	No.27, Rongsheng, Zhongshan District, Dalian	116001	86-411-3633671-381	86-411-3642706	Zheng Liqi
000617	Jinan Diesel Engine Co Ltd	No.14, Wenhua Xi Road, Jinan, Shandong	250063	86-531-2965971-2716	86-531-2961241	Zhang Qianti
000618	Jilin Chemical Industrial Company Ltd	No.9, Longtan Avenue, Jilin City, Jilin Prov.	132021	86-432-3903651	86-432-3028126	Zhang Liyan
000619	Wuhu Conch Profiles And Science Co Ltd	Gangwan Road 2, Wuhu Econ & Tech Development Zone, Anhui Prov.	241009	86-553-5840158 86-553-5840151	86-553-5840118	Ming Zhangchun
000620	Heilongjiang Sunfield Science & Technology Co Ltd	8th Floor, Zhonghang Building, No.15, Gaoxin Road 1, Hi-tech Industry Development Zone, XI'an , Shaanxi	710075	86-029-8223129	86-029-8233538	Hu XIaodong
000621	Bit Technology Holding Co Ltd	8th Floor,Building A, Donghuan Square, No.9, Dongzhong Street, Dongcheng District, Beijing	100027	86-10-64181481 86-10-64181482 86-10-64181483	86-10-64181185	Zhang Jian
000622	Yueyang Hengli Air-Cooling Equipment Inc.	Qingnian Zhong Road, Yueyang City, Hunan Prov.	414000	86-730-8245198	86-730-8221311	Yu Fengting
000623	Jilin Aodong Medicine Industry Groups Co Ltd	No.88, Shengli Nan Avenue, Dunhua City, Jilin Prov.	133700	86-433-6224462	86-433-6224462	Guo Rong
000625	Chongqing Changan Automobile Company Ltd	No.260, Jianxin Dong Road, Jiangbei District, Chongqing	400023	86-23-67591249 86-23-67591568	86-23-67866055 86-23-67870261	Cui Yunjiang

No.	Company	Address	Postal Code	Phone 1	Phone 2	Contact
000626	Lianyungang Ideal Group Co Ltd	No.6, Xin Pubeijiao Road, Lianyungang, Jiangsu	222006	86-518-5150105	86-518-5153595	Liu Bin
000627	Hubei Biocause Pharmaceutical Co Ltd	No.132, Yangwan Road, Jingmen City, Hubei Prov.	448000	86-724-2217652	86-724-2211003-6218	Ding Zhenrong
000628	Chengdu Brilliant Development Group Inc	Chengdu Hi-tech Industry Development Zone, Sichuan, China	610041	86-28-5532288	86-28-5536633	Xie Ye
000629	Panzhihua New Steel & Vanadium Company Ltd	No.55,Dadukou Street, Panzhihua City, Sichuan Prov.	617067	86-812-2226014	86-812-2236281 86-812-2236280	Li Qiming
000630	Anhui Tongdu Copper Stock Co Ltd	West Building, Colored Yard, Changjiang XI Road, Tongling City, Anhui Prov.	244001	86-562-2825082	86-562-2825029	Wu Guozhong
000631	Lan Bao Technology Information Co. Ltd	No.158, Lingdong Road, Erdao District, Changchun	130031	86-431-4639948	86-431-4641596	Cao Zhiwei
000632	Fujian Sanmu Group Co Ltd	No.141, Guangda Road, Taijiang District, Fuzhou, Fujian	350004	86-591-3341504	86-591-3341509	Peng Dongming
000633	Shenyang Hejin Holding Co Ltd	24th Floor, A Zuo, Huayang International Building, No.386, Qingnian Avenue, Heping District, Shenyang	110004	86-24-23180061	86-24-23180414	Ren Suixin
000635	Ningxai Ninghe National Chemicals Co Ltd	Kangle Road, Shizuishan District, Shizuishan City, Ningxia	753200	86-952-3312333	86-952-3312333	Dong Haitao
000636	Fenghua Advanced Technology (Holding) Co.,Ltd	Fenghua Electronic Industry City, No.18, Fenghua Road, Zhaoqing City, Guangdong Prov.	526020	86-758-2849045	86-758-2844724	Liao Yongzhong
000637	Maoming Petrochemical Shihua Co. Ltd	No.162, Guandu Road, Maoming City, Guangdong Prov.	525000	86-668-2281965	86-668-2276176	Liang Jie
000638	China Liaoning International Cooperation (Group) Holdings Lrd	No.126, Zhonghua Road, Heping District, Shenyang	110001	86-24-23862853	86-24-23271740	Wang Tiemin
000639	Hunan Ginde Development Co Ltd	7–8th Floor, Zhuzhou Custom Building, Hexi Tiantai Road, Zhuzhou, Hunan	412000	86-733-8826307	86-733-8826301-20	Chen Xiaoping
000650	Jiujiang Chemical Fibre Co Ltd	Chemical Fibre Plant, Jiujiang	332017	86-792-8234629	86-792-8234601-5675	Yu Shuanheng
000651	Gree Electric Appliances, Inc of Zhuhai	No.6, Post-Shanjinji Xi Road, Zhuhai	519070	86-756-8622581	86-756-8614883-2416	Liu Xinghao
000652	Tianjin Economic-Technological Development Area Co Ltd	Yinhe Nan Road, Beichen District, Tianjin	300400	86-22-26828217	86-22-26828217 86-22-26397997-3183	Wang Pingfen
000653	Fujian Jiuzhou Group Co Ltd	5th Floor, Huguang Building, Hubin Dong Road, Xiamen, Fujian	361004	86-592-5365613	86-592-5365688	Lin XI

Stock Code	Company Name	Address	Postcode	Tel	Fax	Legal representative
000655	Shandong Zibo Huaguang Ceramics Co Ltd	No.6, Huguang Road, Hutian Town, Zhangdian District, Zibo, Shandong	255076	86-533-2061798	86-533-2061404	Liu Yuguang
000656	Chongqing Dongyuan Steel Co Ltd	Room 1216, A Zuo, City Square, No.39, Wusi Road, Yuzhong District, Chongqing	400010	86-23-63782974	86-23-63782974	Tao Xucheng
000657	China Tungsten And High Tech Materials Co Ltd	18th Floor, Didu Building, Zhujiang Square, No.2, Longkun Bei Road, Haikou, Hainan	570125	86-898-66777324	86-898-66779318	Feng Xiaoyuan
000658	Qidi Group Co Ltd	3F-A2, Building2, Siming Software Garden, Xiamen	361005	86-592-2516999	86-592-2513899	Tai Zhiqiang
000659	Zhuhai Zhongfu Enterprise Co Ltd	First Plant, Wanzai Town, Zhuhai, Guangdong	519030	86-756-8821350 86-756-8821449	86-756-8821103	Li Xiang
000660	Guangzhou Nanhuaxi Industrial Co Ltd	16th Floor, Chinese Oil Southern Building, No.111,Jiangnan Xi Road, Guangzhou	510240	86-20-84423292	86-20-84408033	Zhang DI
000661	Cchangchun High New Technology Industries (Group) Inc.	5th Floor, Huoju Building, No.64, Tongzhi Street, Changchun, JILin	130021	86-431-5631926	86-431-5675390	Zhou Weiqun
000662	Guangxi Hongri Co Ltd	No.137, Xinxing Road 2, Wuzhou City, Guangxi	543002	86-0774-3863686	86-0774-3863582	Li Bo
000663	Fujian Yongan Forestry Group Joint -Stock Co Ltd	No.12, Yanjiang Dong Road, Yong'an City, Fujian Prov.	366000	86-598-3614875	86-598-3633415	Huang Zhongming
000665	Wuhan Plastics Industrial Group Co Ltd	11–12th Floor, A zuo, Wuhan International Building, Special No.1, Dandong Road, Jiefang Avenue, Wuhan	430022	86-27-85425727	86-27-85891746	Zhan Dahu
000666	Jingwei Textile Machinery Company Ltd	7th Floor, First Shanghai Centre, NO.39, Liangmaqiao Road, Chaoyang District, Beijing, P.R.C.	100016	86-10-84534132 86-10-84534078-8188	86-8610-84534135	Ye Xuehua
000667	Yunnan Huayi Investment Group Co Ltd	No.19, Dongfeng Xi Road, Kunming, Yunnan	650031	86-871-3610134	86-871-3625615	Zhao Ankun
000668	Sinopec Wuhan Petroleum Group Co. Ltd	Building 18, Wansong Community, Wuhan	430022	86-27-85781439	86-27-85757897	Meng Hong
000669	Jilin Sinosinic Technology Development Co Ltd	No.38, Changjiang Street, Fengman District, Jilin City, Jilin Prov.	132013	86-432-4672831	86-432-4680646	Li Linxuan

ID	Company Name	Address	Postal Code	Phone 1	Phone 2	Contact
000670	Hubei Tianfa Co Ltd	Tianfa Building, NO.106, Jianghan Road, Jingzhou, Hubei	434000	86-716-8560320	86-716-8566160	Zhang Jinbin
000671	Fujian Shishi Xinfa Co Ltd	4th Floor, Shishi New Eden Great Hotel, NO.208,Minsheng Road, Shishi, Fujian	362700	86-595-8880671	86-595-8880410	Pan Shaohua
000672	Baiyin Copper Comercial Building (Group) Co Ltd	4th Floor, Tongcheng Commercial Building, No.8,Wuyi Street, Baiyin District, Baiyin City	730900	86-943-8224981	86-943-8224981	Ren Min
000673	Datong Cement Co Ltd	NO.1, Wufa Road, Mine Area, Datong, Shanxi	037001	86-352-4062400 86-352-4042623	86-352-4042623	Liu Gang
000675	Sichuan Yinshan Chemical Industry (Group) Co Ltd	Yinshan Town, Zizhong County, Neijiang City, Sichuan Prov.	641201	86-8325452216	86-832?5452216	Shi Han
000676	Henan Star Hi-Tech Co Ltd	No.31, Agriculture Road, Zhengzhou City, Henan	450053	86-371-3946860	86-371-3826929	Wang Xilin
000677	Weifang Sea Dragon Co Ltd, Shandong	No.555, North Road, Wei County, Hanting District, Weifang City, Shandong Prov.	261100	86-536-7275007	86-536-7252140	Niu Haiping
000678	Xiangyang Automobile Bearing Share Company, Ltd	No.1, Zhoucheng Road, Xiangcheng District, Xiangfan City, Hubei Prov.	441022	86-710-3564101-82205	86-710-3564019	Jiang Yuesheng
000679	Dalian Friendship Group Co Ltd	No.1, Qiyi Street, Zhongshan District, Dalian, Liaoning	116001	86-411-2691471	86-411-2650892	Zhang Baosen
000680	Shandong Shantui Construction Machinery Co Ltd	No.58, East Road of Taibai Building, Jining City, Shandong Prov.	272035	86-537-2909616	86-537-2340411	Liang Xuewen
000681	Far East Industrial Stock Co Ltd	11th Floor, Xinqu Building, No.446, Tongjiang Avenue, Changzhou City, Jiangsu Prov.	213022	86-519-5131666	86-519-5132666	Jiang Shunsheng
000682	Yantai Dongfang Electronics Information Industry Co Ltd	No.228, Shihuiyao Road, Yantai, Shandong	264000	86-535-6627308	86-535-6627537	Liu Yaojie
000683	Inner Mongolian Yuan Xing Natural Alkali Company Ltd	No.6 E'erduosi West Street, Dongsheng City, Inner-Mongolia	017000	86-477-8539874	86-477-8521747	Huang Jiang
000685	Zhongshan Public Utilities Science & Technology Co Ltd	2nd Floor, Caixing Building, No.18, Xingzhong Road, Zhongshan City, Guangdong Prov.	528403	86-760-3321168	86-760-3321111	Chen Qiuxia
000686	The Liulu Industrial Co Ltd Of Jinzhou Economic & Technology Development Zone	No.9, Hongxing LI, Guta District, Jinzhou, Liaoning	121001	86-416-4561247	86-416-4561377	Xiao Aidong
000687	Bao Ding Swan Co Ltd	No.1, Zhichang Road, Baoding, Hebei	071055	86-312-3137941-2261	86-312-3131755	Gao Zhiqiang

Stock Code	Company Name	Address	Postcode	Tel	Fax	Legal representative
000688	Zhaohua Science & Technology (Group) Co Ltd	3rd Floor, Jinhe Hotel, No.108, Yuzhou Road, Chongqing	400041	86-23-68638134	86-23-6880562	Zhang Guanghua
000689	Shantou Hongye (Group) Co Ltd	Hongye Building, Tianshan Road, Shantou City, Guangdong	515041	86-754-8893332	86-754-8895312	Zhou Yingqi
000690	Guangdong Baolihua Industry Stock Co Ltd	Baolihua Complex Building, Hongkong Garden, Huaqiao Town, Mei County, Meizhou Ciyt, Guangdong	514788	86-753-2511298	86-753-2511398	Zhou Jilai
000691	Hainan Huandao Industry Co Ltd	No.25, Renmin Avenue, Haikou, Hainan	570208	86-898-66255909	86-898-66254684	Kong Yan
000692	Shenyang Huitian Thermal Power Co Ltd	No.47, Renao Road, Shenhe District, Shenyang	110014	86-24-22928062	86-24-22939480	Zuo Xiaoming
000693	Chengdu Unionfriend Taikang Network Co Ltd	11th Floor, Shunji Building, No.252, Shuncheng Avenue, Chengdu	610015	86-28-6624176	86-28-6615233	Luo Hong
000695	Tianjin Beacon Paint & Coatings Co. Ltd	Nancang Road,Beichen District, Tianjin	300400	86-22-26345536	86-22-26340776	Shen Hongxin
000697	Xianyang Planzhuan Co Ltd	No70, Weiyang Xi Road, Xianyang City, Shaanxi Prov.	712021	86-910-3320567	86-910-3320066	Zhao Weijun
000698	Shenyang Chemical Industry Co Ltd	No.46, Weigong Bei Street, Tiexi District, Shenyang, Liaoning	110026	86-24-25820516-3506	86-24-25740956	Sun Jiaqing
000699	Jiamusi Paper Co Ltd	No.306, Guangfu Road, Jiamusi City, Heilongjiang Prov.	154005	86-454-8379070	86-454-8391258	Zhang Shejia
000700	Jiangnan Mould & Plastic Technology Co Ltd	No.8,Changqing Road, Zhouzhuang Town, Jiangyin City, Jiangsu Prov.	214423	86-510-6242802	86-510-6242818	Xu Jian
000701	Xiamen Xinde Co Ltd	2nd Floor, Xinhong Building, Huli District, Xiamen	361006	86-592-6021666-1718	86-592-6021391	Fan Dan
000702	Hunan Zhenghong Science And Technology Develop Co Ltd	Yingtian Town, Quyuan Administrative Zone, Yueyang, Hunan	414418	86-730-5728010	86-730-5728011	Cao Guoqing
000703	Centennial Brilliance Science & Technology Co. Ltd	16th Floor, Longtai Building, No187, Jianshe Xi Road, Zhengzhou, Henan	450007	86-371-7422266	86-371-7422233	Wang Zhijie
000705	Zhejiang Zhenyuan Co Ltd	No.289, Jiefang Bei Road, Shaoxing, Zhejiang	312000	86-575-5144161	86-575-5148805	Huang Jiming
000707	Hubei Shuanghuan Science And Technology Stock Co Ltd	No.26, Tuanjie Avenue, Mafang, Yingcheng City, Hubei Prov.	432407	86-712-3591199	86-712-3591099	Chen Zhuoping

No.	Company	Address	Postal Code			Contact
000708	Daye Special Steel Co Ltd	No.316, Huangshi Avenue, Huangshi City, Hubei Prov.	435001	86-714-6293836 / 86-714-6294678	86-714-6457917 / 86-714-6294678	Wang Pingguo
000709	Tangshan Iron And Steel Co. Ltd	No.9, Binhe Road, Tangshan, Hebei	063016	86-312-2702941	86-312-2702198	Yang Wanchen
000710	Chengdu Tianxing Instrument And Meter Co Ltd	Company Office Building, Wai Dongshiling Town, Chengdu	610106	86-28-4600583	86-28-4600581	Wu Chenghui
000711	Heilongjiang Long Far Inc.	No.68, Tianshun Street, Harbin Econ&Tech Development Zone	150090	86-451-2335442	86-451-2334782	Zhao Runtao
000712	Guangdong Golden Dragon Development Inc	Water Supply Building, Fangzheng Street 2, Area8 of New City, Qingyuan City, Guangdong Prov.	511515	86-763-3369393	86-763-3362693	Liu Guangmang
000713	Hefei Fengle Seed Co Ltd	No.8, Fangwa Road, Xi Qili Tang, Hefei City, Anhui Prov.	230031	86-551-5577479	86-551-5577479	Xu Jiping
000715	Citic Development Shenyang Commercial Building (Group) Co Ltd	No.86, Taiyuan Bei Street, Heping District, Shenyang, Liaoning	110001	86-24-23836008	86-24-23836008	Sun Guoliang
000716	Guangxi Strong Co Ltd	Sizhuang Building, No.8, Minzhu Road, Nanning, Guangxi	530023	86-771-5631973	86-771-5631879	Guan Zili
000717	Sgis Songshan Co Ltd	Company Office Building, Maba, Qujiang County, Shaoguan City, Guangdong Prov.	512123	86-751-8787265	86-751-8787676	Pang Dachun
000718	Jilin Paper Manufacturing Co Ltd	No.9, Linyin Road, Jilin City, Jinlin Prov.	132002	86-432-2702181	86-432-2773695	Guan Linghan
000719	Jiaozuo Xin'An Science & Technology Co Ltd	No.28, Huangcheng Bei Road, Jiefang District, Jiaozuo City, Henan Prov.	454000	86-391-2925951-288	86-391-2919211	Qin Haiyuan
000720	Shandong Luneng Taishan Cable Co Ltd	No.99, Jindou Road, Xintai City, Shandong Prov.	271200	86-538-7223012-262	86-538-7222439	Chu Jun
000721	Xi'an Catering & Service (Group) Co Ltd	No.298, East Avenue, Xi'an	710001	86-29-7232416	86-29-7232416	Tao Guangzhong
000722	Hengyang Gold Fruit Agriculture Industry And Commerce Co Ltd	No.15, Jinguo Road, Hengyang City, Hunan Prov.	421001	86-734-8229258	86-734-8250038	Deng Zhaohui
000723	Fuzhou Tianyu Electric Co Ltd	Tianyu Technology Building, Xindian Nanping Road, Fuzhou	350012	86-591-7916470	86-591-7916449	Zhu Qinghua
000725	Boe Technology Group Co Ltd	No.10, Jiuxianqiao Road, Chaoyang District, Beijing	100016	86-10-64370756	86-10-64366264	Chen Yanshun
000726	Luthai Textile Co. Ltd	No.81, Songling Dong Road, Zichuan District, Zibo, Shandong	255100	86-533-5185166	86-533-5182188	Qin Guiling

Stock Code	Company Name	Address	Postcode	Tel	Fax	Legal representative
000727	Nanjing Huadong Electronics Information & Technology Co Ltd	26th Floor, Jinying International Commercial Tower, No.89, Hanzhong Road, Nanjing	210029	86-25-470090-658 86-25-798 86-25-5311050-2231	86-25-4702989 86-25-5319623	Wu Hualin
000728	Beijing Huaer Company	Dajiao Ting, Chaoyang, Beijing	100022	86-10-67758106	86-10-67781459	Li Chonghua
000729	Beijing Yanjing Brewery Co Ltd	No.9, Shuanghe Road, Shunyi District, Beijing	101300	86-10-89490729	86-10-89495569	Li Yingjuan
000730	Shenyang Special Environmental Protection Equipment Manufact Co Ltd	No.118, Renao Road, Shenhe District, Shenyang	110011	86-24-24811162	86-24-24811162	Chen Haifeng
000731	Sichuan Meifeng Chemical Industry Co Ltd	No.87, Xinyang Street, Taihe Town, Shehong County, Sichuan	629200	86-838-2680243	86-838-2680243	Dong Guozheng
000732	Fujian Sannong Group Co. Ltd	Fujian Sannong Agency, 5th Floor, Yifada Building, No.298, Hudong Road, Fuzhou	365000	86-591-7840852 86-591-7801056	86-591-7810369	Jiang Binghua
000733	China Zhenhua (Group) Science & Technology Co Ltd	No.150, Xintian Avenue, National Hi-tech Industry Development Zone, Guiyang, Guizhou	550018	86-851-6302675 86-851-6301078	86-851-6302674	Yang Xuezheng
000735	Haikou Agriculture & Industry & Trade (Luoniushan) Co Ltd	9th Floor, Dihao Building, Zhujiang Square, Haikou	570125	86-898-66772221	86-898-66717830	Mao Yaoting
000736	Chongqing International Enterprise Investment Co Ltd	No.76, Yanghe Village 1, Jiangbei District, Chongqing	400020	86-23-67868187	86-23-67868390	Xi Minghua
000737	Nafine Chemical Industry Group Co Ltd	No.294, Jiefang Road, Yuncheng, Shanxi	044000	86-359-2017035	86-359-2023302	Zhu Qili
000738	Nan Fang Motor Co Ltd	Nanmo Office Building, Dongjia Duan, Zhuzhou, Hunan	412002	86-733-8559515	86-733-8559714	Liu Shaoxiong
000739	Qingdao Dongfang Group Co Ltd	No.140, Jiaozhou Road, Qingdao, China	266011	86-532-2829999-1698	86-532-2833885	Yan Guoqiang
000748	Hunan Computer Co Ltd	No.161, Yuhua Road, Changsha, Hunan	410007	86-731-5554610-588	86-731-5514776	Yang Lin
000750	Guilinjiqi Pharmaceutical Co Ltd	No.55, Yucai Road, Guilin, Guangxi	541004	86-773-5818066	86-773-5815328	Fu Wolong
000751	Huludao Zinc Industry Co Ltd	No.24, Xinchang Road, Longgang District, Huludao City, Liaoning Prov.	125003	86-429-2024121	86-429-2104084	Qu Luxin
000752	Tibet Galaxy Science & Technology Development Co Ltd	No.36, Sela Road, Lahsa, Tibet	850001	86-891-6329377	86-891-6329377	Mou Chunhua

Code	Company	Address	Postal	Phone 1	Phone 2	Contact
000753	Fujian Minnan Zhangzhou Economy Dvelopment Co Ltd	Donghuan Road, Zhangzhou, Fujian	363000	86-596-2951030-23507	86-596-2952023	Lin Xuebin
000755	Shanxi Sanwei Group Co Ltd	Shanxi Three Dimensions Company, Zhaocheng, Hongdong County, Shanxi	041603	86-357-6662666	86-357-6663423	Zhang Yaping
000756	Shandong Xinhua Pharmaceutical Company Ltd	No.14, East Road 1, Zhangdian District, Zibo, Shandong, China	255005	86-533-2184223	86-533-2287508	Cao Changqiu
000757	Sichuan Direction Photoelectricity Co Ltd	Photoelectricity Technology Garden, Tiancheng Avenue, Neijiang City, Sichuan Prov.	641113	86-832-2411301	86-832-2411301	Xu Lin
000758	China Nonferrous Metal Industry Foreign Engineering And Co	5th Floor, Enfei Technology Building, No.6–12, Fuxing Road, Haidian District, Beijing	100038	86-10-63955911	86-10-63965364	Wang Hong
000759	Wuhan Zhongbai Group Co Ltd	No.129, Jianghan Road, Hankou, Wuhan	430021	86-27-82859668	86-27-82210291	Yang Xiaohong
000760	Hubei Axle Stock Co Ltd	No.178, Jingjiang Avenue, Douhudi Town, Gong'an County, Hubei Prov.	434300	86-716-5225925	86-716-5228925	Chen Lin
000761	Bengang Steel Plates Co Ltd	No.16, Renmin Road, Pingshan District, Benxi City, Liaoning Prov.	117000	86-414-7828360	86-414-7828360	Liang Guangde
000762	Tibet Mineral Development Co Ltd	No.14, Zhaji Road, Lahsa, Tibet	850000	86-891-6324952	86-891-6336738	Liu Xiaojiang
000763	Jinzhou Petrochemical Co Ltd	No.2, Chongqing Road, Guta District, Jinzhou, Liaoning	121001	86-416-4159024	86-416-4159024	Wang Huaijiang
000765	Wuhan Huaxin Hi-Tech Co Ltd	No.779-805, Zhongshan Avenue, Wuhan	430021	86-27-85869480	86-27-85855676	Tu Feizhou
000766	Tonghua Golden Horse Pharmaceutical Industey Co Ltd	No.100-1, Jiangnan Road, Tonghua, Jilin	134001	86-435-3907298	86-435-3907298	Deng Jinchang
000767	Shanxi Zhangze Electric Power Co Ltd	No.59, Yangshi Street, Taiyuan, Shanxi	030002	86-351-3115109	86-351-4069879	Wang Yifeng
000768	Xi'An Aircraft International Corporation	Xifei International, No.1, Hong'an Road, Yanliang District, Xi'an	710089	86-29-6846638 / 86-29-6846976 / 86-29-6846021	86-29-6846031	Hao Zhanfu
000769	Dalian Feifei Aojia Modern Agriculture Co Ltd	27th Floor, Post Wanke Building, No.67, Tongxing Street, Zhongshan District, Dalian	116001	86-411-2820379	86-411-2820510	Gao Changqing
000776	Yan Bian Highway Construction Shares Co Ltd	No.1, Henan Street, Yanji City, Jilin Prov.	133001	86-433-2853913	86-433-2853913	Jin Meihua

Stock Code	Company Name	Address	Postcode	Tel	Fax	Legal representative
000777	Sufa Technology Industry Co Ltd	No.679, Renmin Road, Suzhou	215001	86-512-7533655-2577	86-512-7533 655-2577	Shen Cheng
000778	Xinxing Ductile Iron Pipes Co Ltd	2672 Workshop, North of Shangluoyang Village, Wu'an City, Hebei Prov.	056300	86-310-4020929-7306	86-310-4022368	Zeng Yaogan
000779	Lanzhou Sanmao Industrial Co Ltd	No.82, Yumen Street, Xigu District, Lanzhou, Gansu	730060	86-931-7551627	86-931-7555200	Song Xiaomei
000780	Inner Mongolia Prairie Xingfa Co Ltd	Xingfa Building, Pingzhuang Town, Chifeng City, Inner-Mongolia	024076	86-476-3514285	86-476-3510053	Qi Xiangqian
000782	Guangdong Xinhui Meida Nylon Co Ltd	Shangqian Kou, Jianghui Road, Huicheng Town, Xinhui City, Guangdong Prov.	529100	86-750-6107981	86-750-6107975	Hu Zhenhua
000783	Shijiazhuang Refining-Chemical Co Ltd	Shijiazhuang Refining Chemical Co Ltd , Hebei Prov.	050032	86-311-5161160	86-311-5161138	Teng Fengge
000785	Wuhan Zhongnan Commercial Group Co Ltd	No.9, Zhongnan Road, Wuchang, Wuhan	430071	86-27-87362507	86-27-87307723	Yi Guohua
000786	Beijing New Building Material Public Ltd Company	South of Xisanqi Dong Road, Desheng Menwai, Beijing	100096	86-10-82913831-2818	86-10-82912658	Chang Zhangli
000787	Powerise Information Technology Co Ltd	Building M4, Huoju Town, Changsha High-tech Industry Development Zone, Changsha	410013	86-731-8909008	86-731-8909353	Chen Bei
000788	Southwest Synthetic Pharmaceutical Co Ltd	Heishizishui Kou, Jiangbei District, Chongqing	400025	86-23-67091473-8247	86-23-67091507	Xu Sibin
000789	Jiangxi Wannianqing Cement Co Ltd	Office Building of Jiangxi Cement Factory, Wannian County, Jiangxi Prov.	335506	86-793-3839605 86-793-3839868	86-793-3839776	Ma Xin
000790	Chengdu Hoist Inc., Ltd	6th Floor, A Zuo, Huashen Technology Building, New No.1, No.37, Twelve Bridge Road, Chengdu	610075	86-28-7739541	86-28-7778104	Jiang Zhiyong
000791	Northwest Yongxin Chemical Industry Co Ltd	No.1205,Donggang Dong Road, Lanzhou, Gansu	730020	86-931-8663061	86-931-849604	Cao Yifeng
000792	Qinghai Salt Lake Potash Co Ltd	Cha'er han, Ge'ermu City, Qinghai Prov.		0979-449139	0979-417445	Wu Wenhao
000793	Hainan Minsheng Gas Corporation	Minsheng Building, Sidong Road, Haidian, Haikou City, Hainan Prov.	570208	86-898-66254650	86-898-6255636	Wang Fanghuai

No.	Company	Address	Postal Code	Phone	Contact
000795	Taiyuan Twin Tower Aluminum Oxide Co, Ltd	No.168, Bingzhou Bei Road, Taiyuan	030012	86-351-4930649	86-351-4930832	Zhang Xiaodong
000796	Baoji Department Store (Group) Co Ltd	No.114, Jing'er Road, Baoji, Shaanxi	721000	86-917-3233763	86-917-3215282	Dong Qihuai
000797	China Wuyi Co Ltd	22nd Floor, Wuyi Centre, No.33, East Street, Fuzhou, Fujian	350001	86-591-7510668-521	86-591-7603158	Lin Jinzhu
000798	Cnfc Overseas Fishery Co Ltd	6th Floor, Zhongshui Building, No.31, Minfeng Lane, Xidan, Xicheng District, Beijing	100032	86-10-88067461	86-10-88067463	Chen Ming
000799	Hunan Jinguijiu Company Ltd	Xiangquan Town, Zhenwu Ying, Jishou City, Hunan Prov.	416000	86-743-8312079	86-743-8312178	Wang Benxi
000800	Faw Car Co Ltd	Gate 2, Dongfeng Avenue, Lvyuan Area, Changchun	130011	86-431-5976447	86-431-5908726	Wang Wenquan
000801	Sichuan Hushan Electronic Co Ltd	No.53, Mid-block of Changhong Avenue, Mianyang, Sichuan	621000	86-816-2336252	86-816-2336335	Zhang Yue
000802	Beijing Jingxi Tourism Development Co Ltd	4-5th Floor, Baihua Hotel, No.33, Xinqiao Avenue, Mentougou District, Beijing	102300	86-10-69831967	86-10-69831967	Zeng Ming
000803	Sichuan Meiya Silk (Group) Co Ltd	8th Floor, Telegraphy Building, No.29, Renmin Zhong Road, Shunqing District, Nanchong City, Sichuan Prov.	637000	86-817-2198989 86-817-2256855 86-817-2600868	86-817-2244818 86-817-2602653	Luo Xiongfei
000805	Jiangsu Chinese.Com Co Ltd	No.96, Hehai Road, Xin Area, Changzhou, Jiangsu	213022	86-519-5130805	86-519-5130806	Liu Hongmei
000806	Beihai Yinhe Hi-Tech Industrial Co Ltd	8th Floor, World Trade Building, Yinhai Nan Road, Beihai City, Guangxi	536000	86-779-3202636	86-779-3201888	Ou Qiusheng
000807	Yunnan Aluminium Industry Co Ltd	Chenggong County, Kunming, Yunnan	650502	86-871-7455858	86-871-7455605	Zhang Wenwei
000809	Sichuan No.1 Textile Stock Co Ltd	No.8, East Three Block, Erhuan Road, Chengdu	610053	86-28-4398565	86-28-4398565	Yu Wubo
000810	China Resources Jinhua Co Ltd	No.309, Suizhou Zhong Road, Suining City, Sichuan PROv.	629000	86-825-2226774-2225	86-825-2283399	Zhang Zhengbin
000811	Yantai Moon Co Ltd	No.80, Xishan Road, Zhifu District, Yantai, Shandong	264000	86-535-6243451-6503 86-535-6243558	86-535-6642776	Liu Lixin
000812	Shaanxi Jinye Science Technology And Education Co Ltd Group	No.1, Zhuhong Road, Xi'an	710016	86-29-6246725	86-29-6246715	Wang Jinchun

Stock Code	Company Name	Address	Postcode	Tel	Fax	Legal representative
000813	Xinjiang Tianshan Woollen Textiles Co Ltd	No.1, Yinchuan Road, Urumuqi, Xinjiang	830054	86-991-4311866-6849	86-991-4310472	Wang Weimin
000815	Ningxia Meili Paper Industry Co Ltd	Rouyuan District, Zhongwei County, Ningxia	751700	86-953-7679339	86-953-7679216 86-953-7679339	Yan Xueting
000816	Jiangsu Jianghuai Engine Co Ltd	No.213, Huancheng Xi Road, Yancheng, Jiangsu	224001	86-515-8222889	86-515-8244908	Wang Naiqiang
000817	Liaohe Jinma Oilfield Company Ltd	No.13, Yingbin Road, Zhenxing Street, Xinglongtai District, Panjin City, Liaoning Prov.	124010	86-427-7807584	86-427-7823657	Li Zhongtao
000818	Jin Hua Group Chlor-Alkali Co,	Jinhua Chemical(Group) Co Ltd, Huagong Street, Lianshan District, Huludao City, Liaoning Prov.	125001	86-429-2709065	86-429-2901152	Zhao Zhipeng
000819	Yueyang Xingchang Petro-Chemical Co Ltd	Yunxi District, Yueyang City, Hunan Prov.	414012	86-730-8452594 86-730-8843910	86-730-8439202 86-730-8843910	Peng Dongsheng
000820	Jincheng Paper Co Ltd	Jincheng Street, Linghai City, Liaoning Prov.	121203	86-416-8285084	86-416-8282642	Lv Li
000821	Hubei Jingshan Licht Industry Machinery Stock Co Ltd	No.78,Qingji Avenue, Xinshi Town, Jingshan County, Hubei	431800	86-724-7221560 86-724-7222220-669	86-724-7221560	Chen Zhaojun
000822	Shandong Haihua Company Ltd	Oceanic Chemistry High-tech Industry Development Zone, Weifang, Shandong	262737	86-536-5329379	86-536-5329879	Wu Bingshun
000823	Guangdong Goworld Co Ltd	No.21, Xingye Road, Shantou, Guangdong	515041	86-754-8610992	86-754-8628027	Chen Dongping
000825	Shanxi Taigang Stainless Steel Co Ltd	No.2, Jiancaoping Street, Taiyuan, Shanxi	030003	86-359-3017702	86-359-3017729	Zhang Zhuping
000826	Sdic Yuanyi Industry Co Ltd	No.114, Yanjiang Avenue, Yichang City, Hubei Prov.	443000	86-717-6234470	86-717-6233167	Xu Haitian
000827	Dalian Changxing Industry Co Ltd	21st Floor, Post Wanke Building, No.67, Tongxing Street, Zhongshan District, Dalian	116001	86-411-2654998-8555	86-411-2817598	Qiao Shaohui
000828	Guangdong Fortune Science & Technology Co Ltd	No.39, Keji Road, Huangcun Technology & Industry Garden, Dongguan, Guangdong	523077	86-0769-2402236	86-0769-2402525	Zhang Qingwen
000829	Jiangxi Gannan Fruit Co Ltd	Aolinshen Building, No.20, Hongqi Avenue, Ganzhou, Jiangxi	341000	86-797-8117151	86-797-8117151	Guo Huihu

ID	Company	Address	Postal code	Phone	Fax	Contact
000830	Shandong,Luxi Chemical Co Ltd	No.68, Luhuan Road, Liaocheng, Shandong	252000	86-635-8324227-5066	86-635-8324 227-5080	Liang Hejun
000831	Shanxi Guanlu Co Ltd	No.36, Xinjian Road, Xiezhou Town, Yuncheng, Shanxi	044001	86-359-2825232 86-259-2825474	86-359-2800974	Zheng Qijia
000832	Heilongjiang Longdi Co Ltd	Heping Street, Acheng City, Heilongjiang Prov.	150316	86-451-3717068	86-451-3717473	Liu Keqi
000833	Guangxi Guitang (Group) Co Ltd	Office Building of Guangxi Guitang (Group) Co Ltd	537102	86-775-4262888-22278	86-775-4260088	Li Guigao
000835	Shanghai Longyuan Shuangdeng Industrial Co Ltd	34th Floor, Zhaoshang Bureau Building, No.161, Lujiazui Road, Pudong New District, Shanghai	200120	86-10-64046959	86-10-84017838	Yang Li
000836	Genius Co Ltd	No.3,Huatian Road, Huayuan Industry Zone, Neo-tech Industry Garden, Tianjin	300384	86-22-83710888 86-22-83710188	86-22-83710199	Zhang Tong
000837	Qinchuan Machinery Development Co Ltd of Shaanxi	No.22, Jiangtan Road, Baoji City, Shaanxi Prov.	721009	86-917-3670606	86-917-3390960	Wu Yu
000838	Southwest Chemical Machinery Co Ltd	Lianglukou Town, Shifang City, Sichuan Prov.	618407	86-838-8501521 86-838-8213333-3027	86-838-8204843	Yan Jianjun
000839	Citic Guoan Information Industry Co Ltd	Guo'an Building, No.1, Guandongdian North Street, Chaoyang District, Beijing	100020	86-10-65068509 86-10-65008037	86-10-65061482	Liao Xiaotong
000848	He Bei Cheng De Lolo Company Ltd	No.8, West Area of Chengde High-tech Industry Development Zone, Chengde, Hebei	067000	86-314-2066791-3088	86-314-2063525	Li Wensheng
000850	Anhui Huamao Textile Company Ltd	No.80, Fangzhi Nan Road, Anqing City, Anhui Prov.	246018	86-556-5516615	86-556-5516615	Wang Gongzhu
000851	Guizhou China No.7 Grinding Wheel Co Ltd	Qing Town, Guiyang , Guizhou	551414	86-851-2550469	86-851-2550408	Wu Dongsheng
000852	Kingdream Public Ltd Company	Qianjin Road, Guanghua, Qianjiang, Hubei	433124	86-728-6518598	86-728-6518598	Long Bangcheng
000856	Tangshan Ceramic Corp. Ltd	No.29, Gangyao Road, Lubei District, Tangshan, Hebei	063022	86-315-3291354	86-315-3291354	Zhang Shulai
000858	Wuliangye Yibin Co Ltd	No.150, Minjiang Xi Road, Yibin City, Sichuan Prov.	644007	86-831-35539 88-6858-5878	86-831-3555958	Peng Zhifu
000859	Anhui Guofeng Plastic Industry Co Ltd	No.1, Maanshan Road, Hefei, Anhui	230001	86-551-2885333-3177	86-551-2888835	Ye Gang
000860	Beijing Shunxin Agriculture Co Ltd	Zhanqian Street, Shunyi District, Beijing	101300	86-10-69420860 86-10-69428900	86-10-81499846	Tian Jianguo

Stock Code	Company Name	Address	Postcode	Tel	Fax	Legal representative
000861	Maoming Yongye (Group) Co Ltd	No.61, Huanshi Xi Road, Maoming City, Guangdong Prov.	525024	86-668-2327411-8888	86-668-2326412	Wang Hongxin
000862	Wu Zhong Instrument Co Ltd	No.67, Chaoyang Street, Litong District, Wuzhong City, Ningxia	751100	86-953-2069058	86-953-2069057	Feng Pingru
000863	Shenzhen Dawncom Business Technology And Service Co Ltd	No.127, Nujiang Street, Huanggu District, Shenyang	110036	86-24-86794049	86-24-86794029	Zhou Jun
000866	Sinopec Yangzi Petrochemical Company Ltd	B, Building 16, Nanjing High-tech Industry Development Zone, Nanjing	210061	86-25-7787735 86-25-7787739	86-25-7787755	Wu Pengming
000868	Anhui Ankai Automobile Co Ltd	No.1, Gefei Road, Hefei City, Anhui Prov.	230051	86-551-4844712	86-551-4844888	Wang Jun
000869	Yantai Changyu Pioneer Wine Company Ltd	No.174, Shihuiyao Road, Yantai, Shandong	264001	86-535-6691268 86-535-6647864	86-535-6691268 86-535-6691266	Qu Weimin
000876	Sichuan New Hope Agribusiness Co Ltd	No.45, Block 4, Renmin Nan Road, Chengdu, Sichuan	610041	86-28-5249289	86-28-5232842	Zeng Yong
000877	Xinjiang Tianshan Cement Co Ltd	Attached No.1 to No.55, East Road of Cangfang Gou, Urumuqi, Xinjiang	830006	86-991-5615516	86-991-5659425	Zhou Linying
000878	Yunnan Copper Industry Co Ltd	No.111, Renmin Dong Road, Kunming, Yunnan	650051	86-871-3126709 86-871-3133502	86-871-3138100	Guan Hong
000880	Shandong Juli Company Ltd	No.69, Changsong Road, Weifang, Shandong	261021	86-536-8555878-8979	86-5360-8557207	Guo Yong
000881	China Dalian International Cooperation (Group) Holdings Ltd	Foreign Economic and Trade Building, No.219, Huanghe Road, Xigang District, Dalian	116011	86-411-3780066 86-411-3780139	86-411-3780186	Li Feng
000882	China Commerce Company Ltd	Chinese Stock Share, Huanglian Commercial Building, No.4, Area 5, Anzhen Xili, Chaoyang District, Beijing	100029	86-10-88086606	86-10-88086598	Li Cuifang
000883	Hubei Triring Co Ltd	No.356, Wuluo Road, Wuhan, Hubei	430070	86-27-87273368	86-27-87271902	He Yixin
000885	Luoyang Chundu Foodstuff Company Ltd	No.126, Chundu Road, Xigong District, Luoyang, Henan	471001	86-379-2312471	86-379-2312752	Chang Hu
000886	Hainan Expressway Co Ltd	Express Way Building, NO.16, Airport Road, Haikou	570203	86-898-66701555	86-898-66790647	Chen Qiuzhong

000887	Anhui Feicai Vehicle Co Ltd	Xuannan Road, Xuancheng City, Anhui Prov.	242000	86-563-2612500-2998	86-563-2612555	Chen Hui
000888	Emei Shan Tourism Company Ltd	No.168, Mingshan Xi Road, Emei Mount. City, Sichuan Prov.	614200	86-833-5544568	86-833-5526666	Zhou Dongliang
000889	Qinhuang Dao Hualian Business Building Holding Co Ltd	No.152, Hebei Avenue, Haigang District, Qinhuangdao	066000	86-335-3023349	86-335-3045671	Yin Gang
000890	Jiangsu Fasten Co Ltd	No.203,Tongjiang Bei Road, Jiangyin, Jiangsu	214433	86-510-6119890	86-510-6106634	Zhang Yue
000892	Chongqing Changfeng Communication Co Ltd	18th Floor, Building A, City Square, No. 39,Wusi Road, Yuzhong District, Chongqing	400010	86-23-63782700	86-23-63782555	Hu Jin
000893	Guangzhou Refrigeration Co Ltd	No.12, Renhe Avenue, Renhe Town, Baiyun District, Guangzhou, Guangdong	510470	86-20-86453838	86-20-86450724	Shi Geyan
000895	Henan Shuanghui Investment & Development Co Ltd	7th Floor, Shuanghui Building, No.1, Shuanghui Road, Luohe, Henan	462000	86-395-2622616-6158	86-395-2623398	Yi Jiyang
000897	Tianjin Jinbin Development Co Ltd	Jinbin Building,No. 2, First Avenue, Tianjin Development Zone	300457	86-22-66201301	86-22-66202480	Wu Gang
000898	Angang New Steel Company Ltd	No. 396, Nanzhonghua Road, Tiedong District, Anshan, Liaoning	114003	86-412-6326603	86-412-6727772	Fu Jihui
000899	Jiangxi Ganneng Co Ltd	No.125, Huoju Avenue, High-tech Industry Development Zone, Nanchang, Jiangxi	330029	86-793-8109899	86-793-8106120	Li Tianxiao
000900	Xiandai Investment Co Ltd	No.52,Xin'an Li, Furong Zhong Road, Changsha	410005	86-731-2232363	86-731-2232303	Chen Manlin
000901	Harbin Fenghua Aerospace Hi-Tech Co Ltd	No.178, Zhongshan Road, Dongli District, Harbin	150040	86-451-2624810	86-451-2624810	Wang Yuwei
000902	China Garments Co Ltd	27th Floor, Zhongfu Building, No.99, Jianguo Road, Beijing	100020	86-10-65817498	86-10-65812147	Guo Heng
000903	Kunming Yunnei Power Co Ltd	No.715, Chuanjin Road, Kunming, Yunnan	650224	86-871-5625802	86-871-5633176	Cai Jianming
000905	Xiamen Road & Bridge Co. Ltd	8th Floor, Qiaoxing Building, Mid-Jiahe Road, Xiamen	361009	86-592-5326897	86-592-5326893	Miao Luping
000906	Southern Building Materials Co Ltd	No.49, Wuyi Zhong Road, Changsha, Hunan (Headquarter)	410011	86-731-2225271 / 86-731-4452516	86-731-4453546	Tan Changshou
000908	Hunan Tianyi Science And Technology Co Ltd	Tianyue Avenue, Pingjiang Development Zone, Pingjiang, Hunan	414500	86-0731-5795176 / 86-0731-5795175		Ouyang Zhuyu

Stock Code	Company Name	Address	Postcode	Tel	Fax	Legal representative
000909	Soyea Techonlogy Co Ltd	No.1, Jiaogong Road, Xihu District, Hangzhou	310012	86-571-88271038	86-571-88271038	Ding Yi
000910	Jiangsu Dare Advanced Packing Material Co Ltd	Danjing Road, Danyang Econ & Tech Development Zone, Jiangsu	212300	86-511-6883666 86-511-6882222-2143	86-511-6885000	Wang Yi
000911	Nanning Sugar Manufacturing Co Ltd	No.48, Tinghong Road, Nanning, Guangxi	530031	86-771-4914317	86-771-4910755	Wang Guoqing
000912	Sichuan Lutianhua Company Ltd	No.220, Zhong Tongren Road, Chengdu, Sichuan	610031	86-830-4122275	86-830-4123559	Nie Changhai
000913	Zhejing Qianjiang Motorcycle Co Ltd	Wanchang Road, Taiping Town, Wenling City, Zhejiang Prov.	317500	86-576-6139218 86-576-6139250	86-576-6139081	Lin Xianjin
000915	Shandong Shanda Wit Science And Technology Co Ltd	4th Floor, Start-up Centre, Shandong University Technological Garden, No.71Jingshi Road, Jinan, Shandong	250061	86-0531-5198006	86-539-2666189	Liu Hongwei
000916	Huabei Expressway Co Ltd	18th Floor, Jincheng Centre, No.22, Area 4, Qunfang Yuan, Fangzhuang, Fengtai District, Beijing	100078	86-10-67602600	86-10-67602601	Zhou Huiping
000917	Hunan TV & Broadcast Intermediary Co Ltd	East of Liuyang River Bridge, Changsha, Hunan	410003	86-731-4251998	86-731-4252096	Yuan Chuxian
000918	Hunan Yahua Seeds Co Ltd	18–19th Floor, Yahua Building, No.509, Bayi Road, Changsha, Hunan	410011	86-731-2566572 86-731-2565818	86-731-2566602	Xu Yuanzhong
000919 000920	Jinling Pharmaceutical Company Ltd South Huiton Co Ltd	No.238, Zhongyang Road, Nanjing Huoju Building, Xintian Avenue, Guiyang, Guizhou	210009 550018	86-25-3112999-8513 86-851-4470866	86-25-3112486 86-851-4470866	Xu Junyang Gao Xizhong
000921	Guangdong Kelon Electrical Holdings Company Ltd	No.8, Ronggang Road, Ronggui Town, Shunde, Guangdong	528303	86-765-8362570	86-765-8361055	Yu Chuyuan
000922	Acheng Relay Co Ltd	Hedong Street, Acheng City, Heilongjiang Prov.	150302	86-451-5652601	86-451-5645213	Wang Yongli
000923	Xuanhua Construction Machinery Co Ltd	No.21, Dongsheng Road, Xuanhua District, Zhangjiakou, Hebei	075105	86-31-33012255-2248	86-31-33055369	Pang Tingmin
000925	Zhejiang Zheda Haina Science & Technology Co Ltd	6th Floor, Zilan Hotel, No. 7-3, Zheda Road, Hangzhou	310013	86-571-87961070	86-571-87961070	Zhu Guoying
000926	Hubel Fuxing Science And Technique Co Ltd	No.1, Fuxing Street, Chenhu Town, Hanchuan City, Hubei Prov.	431608	86-712-8740018	86-712-8740018	Feng Dongxing
000927	Tianjin Automotive Xiali Co Ltd	South of Mazhuang, Guofang Road, Xiqing District, Tianjin	300073	86-022-23056020	86-022-23056034	Meng Junkui

ID	Company	Address	Post Code	Phone	Fax	Contact
000928	Jilin Carbon Co Ltd	No.9, Heping Street, Changyi District, Jilin City, Jilin Prov.	132002	86-432-2749010	86-432-2749375	Wang Dezhang
000929	Lan Zhou Huanghe Enterprise Co Ltd	22nd Floor, Jinyuan Building, Zhongshan Road, Lanzhou	730030	86-931-8449054	86-931-8449005	Wei Fuxin
000930	Anhui Bbca Biochemical Co Ltd	No. 73, Daqing Road, Bengbu City, Anhui Prov.	233010	86-552-4926486	86-552-4926733	He Hongman
000931	Beijing Centergate Technologies (Holding) Co Ltd	Zhongguancun Technology Development Building, No.32, Zhongguancun South Avenue, Haidian District, Beijing	100081	86-10-62140168	86-10-62140038	Guo Huliang
000932	Hunan Valin Steel Tube & Wire Co Ltd	20th Floor, Hualing Building, No.269, Furong Zhong Road, Changsha, Hunan	410011	86-731-2245196	86-731-2245196	Wang Jun
000933	Henan Sheng Huo Coal Industry And Electricity Power Co Ltd	Guangming Road, Xincheng District, Yongcheng City, Henan Prov.	476600	86-370-5114055	86-370-5114822	Wang Peishun
000935	Sichuan Shuangma Cement Co Ltd	Erlangmiao Town, Jiangyou City, Sichuan Prov.	621716	86-816-3721498	86-816-3721498	Pu Xiaohong
000936	Jiangsu Huaxicun Co Ltd	4th Floor, Jinta Building, Huaxi Village, Jiangyin, Jiangsu	214420	86-510-6217188	86-510-6201744	Bian Wubiao
000937	Hebei Jinniu Energy Resources Co Ltd	No 191, Zhongxing Xi Avenue, Xingtai, Hebei	054021	86-319-2068242	86-319-2068888	Liu Yanchun
000938	Tsinghua Unisplendour Corporation Ltd	Tsinghua University Ziguang Building, Haidian District, Beijing	100084	86-10-62770008	86-10-62770880	Qi Lian
000939	Wuhan Kaidi Electric Power Co Ltd	22nd Floor, Jiangtian Building, No 586, Wuluo Road, Wuchang District, Wuhan	430070	86-27-8765171 / 86-27-8765172-122	86-27-87655218	Cao Weiheng
000948	Yunnan Nantian Electronics Information Co Ltd	No.455, Huangcheng Dong Road, Kunming, Yunnan	650041	86-871-3366327	86-871-3317398	Jiang Dong
000949	Xinxiang Chemical Fiber Co Ltd	No.1, Jinyuan Road, Beizhan District, Xinxiang City, Henan Prov.	453011	86-373-3978813	86-373-3911359	Zhu Weiping
000950	Chongqing Min Feng Grochem Co Ltd (Cma)	No.30, Jingkou Economic Building, Shapingba District, Chongqing	400033	86-23-65180743	86-23-65180655	Cao Ruoyu
000951	Shandong Xiaoya Electrical Appliance Co Ltd	No 44, North Industry Road, Jinan, Shandong	250101	86-531-8980541	86-531-8980541	Zhang Xishun
000952	Hubei Guangji Pharmaceutical Co Ltd	No.1, Jiangdi Road, Wuxue City, Hubei Prov., China	435400	86-713-6216068	86-713-6212108	Wang Hongyong

Stock Code	Company Name	Address	Postcode	Tel	Fax	Legal representative
000953	Guangxi Hechi Chemical Co Ltd	Hechi City, Guangxi	547007	86-778-2266195 86-778-2266867	86-778-2266195	Wei Wenfu
000955	Hainan Xinlong Nonwovens Co Ltd	17ᵗʰ Floor, Dihao Building, Zhujiang Square, No.2, Kunbei Road, Haikou, Hainan	570102	86-898-66717055 86-898-66712769	86-898-66723136	Wei Yi
000956	Sinopec Zhongyuan Petroleum Co Ltd	No.87, Ruida Road, High-tech Industry Development Zone, Zhengzhou, Henan	450001	86-393-4893571	86-393-4893831	Li Honghai
000957	Zhongtong Bus & Holding Co Ltd	No.10, Jianshe Dong Road, Liaocheng, Shandong	252000	86-635-8322765	86-635-832905	Jiang Mingzhu
000958	Shijiazhuang Dongfang Thermoelectric Co Ltd	161, Jian Hua Nan Street, Shijiazhuang, Hebei	050031	86-311-5053913	86-311-5053924	Hu Junfang
000959	Beijing Shougang Co Ltd	Shijingshan Lu, Shijingshan District, Beijing	100041	86-10-88293727	86-10-68873028	Zhang Yan
000960	Yunnan Tin Co Ltd	Hi-Tech Industries Development Zone, Kunming	650118	86-873-2448667	86-873-2448308	Yang Yimin
000961	Dalian Jinniu Co Ltd	4, Gongxing Lu, Ganjingzi District, Dalian, Liaoning	116031	86-411-6679594	86-411-6678899	Zhou Jianping
000962	Ningxia Orient Tantalum Industry Co Ltd	Yejin Lu, Da Wu Kou District, Shizuishan, NIngxia	753000	86-952-2012012-6003	86-952-2037628	Zhang Zongguo

'B' Shares Listed on Shanghai Stock Exchange

Stock Code	Company Name	Address	Postcode	Tel	Fax	Legal representative
900901	SVA Electron Co Ltd	26ᵗʰ Floor, Century Commercial Building, No.97,Changshou Road, Shanghai	200060	86-21-62980202-646 86-21-62980202-647	86-21-62982121	Hu Zhikui
900902	Shanghai Erfangji Co Ltd	No.687, Shichang Zhong Road, Shanghai	200434	86-21-65318888-3981	86-21-65421963	Zhu Jianzhong
900903	Dazhong Transportion (Group) Co Ltd	12ᵗʰ Floor, Dazhong Building, No.1515, Zhongshan XI Road, Shanghai	200235	86-21-64289122	86-21-64288660	Gu Hua
900904	Shanghai Wingsung Data Technology Co Ltd	11ᵗʰ Floor, No.2669, Xietu Road, Shanghai	200030	86-21-64397553 86-21-64399900	86-21-54590737	Lu Zhengzhi
900905	China First Pencil Co Ltd	24ᵗʰ Floor, No.550, Xujiahui Road, Shanghai	200025	86-21-64453300	86-21-64720802	Zhou Fuliang
900906	China Textile Machinery Stock Ltd	No.1687, Changyang Road, Shanghai	200090	86-21-65432970	86-21-65455130	Shi Lifen
900907	Shanghai Rubber Belt Co Ltd	No.630, Haimen Road, Shanghai	200086	86-21-65415210-234 86-21-235021-5123957	86-21-65123671	Yu Binghan
900908	Shanghai Chlor-Alkali Chemical Co Ltd	No.4747, Longwu Road, Shanghai	200241	86-21-64342640	86-21-64341341	Xu Peiwen
900909	Shanghai Tyre & Rubber Co, Ltd	No.560 ,Xujiahui Road, Shanghai	200025	86-21-64735577	86-21-64735921	Zhou Jianhui
900910	Shanghai Highly (Group) Co Ltd	No.2555, Changyang Road, Shanghai	200090	86-21-65660000	86-21-65670941	Zhong Lei
900911	Shanghai Jinqiao Export Processing Zone Development Co, Ltd	No.28, Xinjinqiao Road, Pudong, Shanghai	201206	86-21-58991818	86-21-58991533 86-21-58991812	Chen Enhua
900912	Shanghai Wai Gaoqiao Free Trade Zone Development Co Ltd	No.889,Yanggao Bei Road, Pudong, Shanghai	200131	86-21-58669217	86-21-58680808	Gao Haiming
900913	Shanghai Lian Hua Fibre Corporation	No.4290, Huyi Road, Jiading District, Shanghai	201800	86-21-59528713	86-21-59528433	Li Shounan
900914	Shanghai Jin Jiang Tower Co Ltd	No.161, Changle Road, Shanghai	200020	86-21-64151188-653	86-21-64726815	Wang Junxing
900915	Shanghai Forever Co Ltd	No.209, Liaoyuan Xi Road, Shanghai	200092	86-21-65136974	86-21-65139966	Yuan Zhijian
900916	Phoenix Co Ltd	No.168, Gaoyang Road, Shanghai	200080	86-21-65954641 86-21-65950100-611	86-21-65952565 86-21-65956731	Cao Qi
900917	Shanghai Haixin Group Co Ltd	10ᵗʰ Floor, Jinling Haixin Building, No.666, Fuzhou Road, Shanghai	200001	86-21-63917000	86-21-63917678	Chen Mouliang
900918	Shanghai Yaohua Pilkington Glass Company Ltd	No.100, Jiyang Road, Pudong Xin District, Shanghai	200126	86-21-58839305	86-21-58801554	Jin Minli
900919	Shanghai Dajiang Group Stock Co Ltd	No.26, Guyang Nan Road, Songjiang District, Shanghai	201600	86-21-57817566 86-21-57817571	86-21-57820072	Gu Deming

Code	Company	Address	Postal Code	Tel	Fax	Contact
900920	Shanghai Diesel Engine Company Limited	No.2636, Jungong Road, Shanghai	200432	86-21-65745656-2207	86-21-65749845	Liang Baoquan
900921	Daying Moden Agricultural Co Ltd	No.127, Qilianshan Road, Shanghai	200331	86-21-62509596	86-21-62506181	Jiang Wei
900922	Shanghai Sanmao Textile Co Ltd	No.1150, Xuchang Road, Shanghai	200082	86-21-65121377	86-21-65453247	Zhang Lifang
900923	Shanghai Friendship Group Incorporated Company	10th Floor, No.518,Shangcheng Road, Shanghai	200120	86-21-58799358	86-21-58883303	Wang Longsheng
900924	Shanggong Co Ltd	12th Floor, Oriental Building, No.1500, Century Avenue, Pudong New District, Shanghai	200122	86-21-68407700-617	86-21-63302939	Zhang Yifeng
900925	Shanghai Shangling Electric Appliances Co Ltd	No.2, Jianping Road, Shanghai	200135	86-021-58857888-3436	86-021-5858624	Cao Jun
900926	Shanghai Baosight Software Co Ltd	No.515, Guoshoujing Road, Zhangjiang Hi-tech Garden, Pudong New District, Shanghai	201203	86-21-50801155-1353	86-21-38953436	Cheng Jian
900927	Shanghai Material Trading Centre Co Ltd	No.2550, Zhongshan Bei Road, Shanghai	200063	86-21-62570000-8522	86-21-62168718	Cai Jiade
900928	Shanghai Automation Instrumentation Co Ltd	7F, Yixiang Building, No1559, Yan'an Xi Road, Shanghai	200050	86-62800705	86-62801680	Huang Dingfa
900929	Shanghai China International Travel Service Co Ltd	No.1277, Beijing XI Road, Shanghai	200040	86-21-62898899-239	86-21-62893487	Zhu Eyan
900930	Shanghai Posts & Telecommunications Equipment Co Ltd	No.700, Yishan Road, Shanghai	200233	86-21-64834310	86-21-64333435	Yang Jialin
900932	Shanghai Lujiazui Finance & Trade Zone Development Co Ltd	No.981, Pudong Avenue, Shanghai	200135	86-21-58878888	86-21-58877100	Zhu Wei
900933	Huaxin Cement Co Ltd	No.897, Huangshi Avenue, Huangshi, Hubei	435002	86-714-6224971	86-714-6235204	Wang Ximing
900934	Shanghai New Asia (Group) Co Ltd	4th Floor, No.285, Tianmu Xi Road, Shanghai	200070	86-21-63536304	86-21-63533021	Kang Ming
900935	Shanghai Jintai Company Limited	No.400, Wenshui Road, Shanghai	200072	86-21-56657316	86-21-56657534	Shen Huiming
900936	Inner Mongolia Eerduosi Cashmere Products Co Ltd	No.102, Dalate Nan Road, Dongsheng, Inner-Mongolia	017000	86-477-8346294	86-477-8336699	Li Chengjun
900937	Heilongjiang Electric Power Company Limited	No.209, Dacheng Street, Nangang District, Harbin	150001	86-451-2525998	86-451-2525878	Mei Junchao
900938	Tianjin Marine Shipping Co Ltd	No.207, Machang Road, Hexi District, Tianjin	300204	86-22-23288000	86-22-23286115	Song Tao
900939	Shanghai Huili Building Materials Co Ltd	No.4131, Chuanzhou Road, Zhoupu, Pudong, Shanghai	201318	86-21-68112933	86-21-58113874	Tao Yaling

Stock Code	Company Name	Address	Postcode	Tel	Fax	Legal representative
900940	Shanghai Worldbest Co Ltd	31st Floor, Zhaoshang Bureau Building, No.161, Lujiazui Dong Road, Pudong, Shanghai	200120	86-21-58823020	86-21-58825887	Zhang Lesheng
900941	Eastern Communications Co Ltd	No.398, Wensan Road, Hangzhou, Zhejiang, China	310013	86-571-88865242 86-571-88865228	86-571-88865243	Guo Duanduan
900942	Huangshan Tourism Development Co Ltd	Spring at Huangshan Beauty Spot, Huangshan City, Anhui Prov.	242709	86-559-5561113	86-559-5561110	He Jie
900943	Shanghai Kaikai Industry Co Ltd	24th Floor, No.888, Wanhangdu Road, Shanghai	200042	86-21-62127558	86-21-62125575	Xu Xiaobai
900945	Hainan Airlines Co Ltd	Haihang Development Building, No.29, Haixiu Road, Haikou, Hainan	570206	86-898-66739961	86-898-66739960	Zhang Shanghui
900946	Jinan Qingqi Motorcycle Co Ltd	No.34, Heping Road, Lixia District, Jinan, Shandong	250014	86-531-6414419	86-531-6960676	Han Jinke
900947	Shanghai Zhenhua Port Machinery Co Ltd	No.3470, Pudong Nan Road, Shanghai	200125	86-21-58396666	86-21-58399555	Gao LIjuan
900948	Inner Mongolia Yitai Coal Company Limited	Yimei Group Office Building, E'er duosi Xi Street, Dongsheng City, Inner-Mongolia	017000	86-477-8524944	86-477-8530722	Tian Shangwan
900949	Zhejiang Southeast Electric Power Co Ltd	No.451, Fengqi Road, Hangzhou, Zhejiang , China	310006	86-571-87068779-2658	86-571-87077321	Dai Jiancheng
900950	Jiangsu Xincheng Real Estate Co Ltd	No.145, Wuyibei Road, Hutang Town, Wujin City, Jiangsu Prov.	213161	86-519-6506246	86-519-6507245	Tang Yunlong
900951	Dahua Group Dalian Chemical Industry Co, Limited	No.10, Gongxing Road, Ganjingzi District, Dalian, Liaoning	116032	86-411-6672312-4192	86-411-6671948	Li Jiantao
900952	Jinzhou Port Co Ltd	No.1, Block 1, Jingang Avenue, Jinzhou Econ & Tech Development Zone, Liaoning	121007	86-416-3586372	86-416-3582841	Yu Jianping
900953	Worldbest Kama Machinery Co Ltd	6th Floor, Huayuan World Square, No.1958, Zhongshan Bei Road, Shanghai	200063	86-21-62031188-6612	86-21-62030851	Wang Chiwei
900955	Shanghai Matsuoka Co Ltd	8th Floor, 841, Yan'an Zhong Lu, Shanghai	200040	86-21-62893080	86-21-62893088	Wang Weimin
900956	Huangshi Dongbei Electrical Appliance Co Ltd	5, Wu Huan Lu, Tieshan District, Huangshi, Hubei	435006	86-714-5415858	86-714-5415588	Zhu Jinming
900957	Shanghai Lingyun Curtain Wall Science & Technology Co Ltd	18 Floor, Jiaxing Building, 877, Dong Fang Lu Pudong New District, Shanghai	200122	86-21-50818005	86-21-50819380	Liao YIngzheng

'B' Shares Listed on Shenzhen Stock Exchange

Stock Code	Company Name	Address	Postcode	Tel	Fax	Legal representative
200002	China Vanke Co Ltd	27, Shuibei Er Road, Luohu District, Shenzhen, P.R.C.	518020	86-755-5606666	86-755-5601764	Xiao Li
200003	Gintian Industry (Group) Co Ltd	23–26th Floor, Jintian Building, 1199, Heping Road, Shenzhen	518010	86-755-5573548	86-755-5592045 86-755-5591994	Peng Wei
200011	Shenzhen Properties & Resources Development (Group) Ltd	39/F and 42/F, International Trade Centre, Renmin Road South, Shenzhen	518014	86-755-2253020	86-755-2251997	Guo Yumei
200012	China Southern Glass Holding Co Ltd	Southern Glass Building, #1, the 6th Industrial Road, SheKou, ShenZhen, China	518067	86-755-6695970	86-755-6675733	Wu Guobin
200013	Shenzhen Petrochemical Industry (Group) Co Ltd	SPEC Building, Hongli (W.) Rd, Futian District, Shenzhen, PRC	518028	86-755-3344355	86-755-3324057	Cai Jianping
200015	Shenzhen Zhonghao (Group) Ltd	9/F, 10/F Zhonghao Building, Bagua Si Road, Bagualing Industrial Zone, Futian District, Shenzhen	518029	86-755-2260864	86-755-2262272	Jiang Yonglin
200016	Konka Group Company, Ltd	No. 1 Buxin Road, Shenzhen City, Guangdong Province, China	518053	86-755-6608866	86-755-6600082	Chen Xumu
200017	Shenzhen China Bicycle Company (Holdings) Ltd	3008, Buxin Road, Shenzhen, Guangdong, China	518019	86-755-5516998	86-755-5516620	Li Hai
200018	Shenzhen Victor Onward Textile Industrial Co Ltd	18/F, Wah Chong Centre, 899#, Hong Kong.	518001	86-755-2320942 86-852-24281823	86-755-2339100 86-852-24805666	Ren Yuanwei Cheung Sha Wan Road, Kowloon
200019	Shenzhen Shenbao Industrial Co Ltd	No.1058, Wenjin N. RD., Luohu District, Shenzhen	518020	86-755-5507480	86-755-5507480	Xu Yuqiao
200020	Shenzhen Huafa Electronics Co Ltd	6th Floor, Building 411, Huafa Bei Road, Futian District, Shenzhen	518031	86-755-3352207	86-755-3352207	Hu Jianping
200022	Shenzhen Chiwan Wharf Holdings (CWH) Ltd	11–12/F, Chiwan Petroleum Building, Chiwan, Shenzhen, PRC	518068	86-755-6694620	86-755-6694297	Pei Jiangyuan
200024	China Merchants Shekou Holdings Co Ltd	30th Floor, New Times Square, Shekou Industry Zone, Nanshan District, Shenzhen	518067	86-755-6819610	86-755-6819680	Chen Ken
200025	Shenzhen Tellus Holding Co Ltd	3rd Floor, Teli Building, Shuibei II Road, Luohu District, Shenzhen	518020	86-755-5536888-315	86-755-5536658	Li Shengchang
200026	Shenzhen Fiyta Holdings Ltd	Fiyta Building, 163, Zhenhua Road, Shenzhen	518041	86-755-3217888-8218	86-755-3348369	Hao Huiwen

Code	Company	Address	Postcode	Phone	Phone	Contact
200028	Shenzhen Accord Pharmaceutical Co Ltd	11th Floor, World Trade Centre Building, Renmin Nan Road, Shenzhen, Guangdong	518014	86-755-2251782	86-755-2222353	Chen Changbing
200029	Shenzhen Special Economic Zone Real Estate & Properties (Group) Co Ltd	45–48th Floor, Shenfang Square, 3005, Renmin Nan Road, Shenzhen	518001	86-755-2293000-4718 / 86-755-2293000-4715 / 86-755-2293000-4719	86-755-2294024	Ye Huanbao
200030	Guangdong Shegnrun Group Co Ltd	Jiahua Building, Huaqiang Bei Road, Shenzhen	518031	86-755-3361666-255	86-755-3361777	Pan Shiming
200037	Shenzhen Nanshan Power Station Co Ltd	18, Yueliang wan Road, Nanshan District, Shenzhen, Guangdong	518052	86-755-6072818-208 / 86-755-6650052-208	86-755-6650642	Fu Bo
200039	China International Marine Containers Group Co Ltd	5th Floor, Financial Centre, Shekou Industry Zone, Shenzhen, Guangdong	518067	86-755-6691130	86-755-6826579	Wu Fapei
200041	Shenzhen Benelux Enterprise Co Ltd	Building 11, Nanyou Zhongxing Industry City, Nanshan District, Shenzhen	518062	86-755-6068614 / 86-755-6068025	86-755-6068031	Shen Yanlei
200045	Shenzhen Textile (Holdings) Co Ltd	6th Floor, Shenfang Building, 3, Huaqiang Bei Road, Futian District, Shenzhen	518031	86-755-3776043	86-755-3776139	Chao Jin
200053	Shenzhen Chiwan Petroleum Supply Base Co Ltd	Chiwan Base Building, Shenzhen, Guangdong, China	518068	86-755-6694211	86-755-6694227	Cui Wei
200054	Shenzhen North Jianshe Motorcycle Co Ltd	47, Zheng Street, Xiejia Wan, Chongqing	400050	86-23-68483175	86-23-68482330	Ju Bing
200055	China Fangda Group Co Ltd	Technology Building, Fang Da Town, Xililongjing, Nanshan District, Shenzhen, P.R.C.	518055	86-755-6788571-6622	86-755-6788353	Lu Weiwei
200056	Shen Zhen International Enterprise Co Ltd	23rd Floor, Development Centre Building, Renmin Nan Road, Shenzhen	518001	86-755-2285564	86-755-2285573	Xie Wei
200057	Shenzhen Great Ocean Shipping Co Ltd	Room 1805, A Zuo, Electric Technology Building, Futian District, Shenzhen	518031	86-755-3781732	86-755-3780771	Yan Zhongyu
200058	Shenzhen Seg Co Ltd	16th Baohua Building, Huaqiang Bei Road, Futian District, Shenzhen	518031	86-755-3675060	86-755-3779770	Zheng Dan
200152	Shandong Airlines Co Ltd	Yaoqiang International Airport, Jinan, Shandong	250107	86-531-8737888	86-531-8737889	Zheng Baoan
200160	Chengde Dixian Textile Co Ltd	Dixian Building, Xiaban Town, Chengde, Hebei	067400	86-314-3011218	86-314-3182013	Wang Huilai

Stock Code	Company Name	Address	Postcode	Tel	Fax	Legal representative
200168	Guangdong Rieys Company Ltd	22nd Floor, B Zuo, Shengtingyuan Hotel, Huaqiang Bei Road, Shenzhen	518280	86-755-2075639	86-755-3789806	Zhou Haolin
200413	Shijiazhuang Baoshi Electronic Glass Co Ltd	9, Huanghe Avenue, High-tech Industry Development Zone, Shijiazhuang, Hebei	050035	86-311-6044705	86-311-6041503	Luo Lina
200418	Wuxi Little Swan Co Ltd	67, Huiqian Road, Wuxi, Jiangsu	214035	86-510-3704003-2192	86-510-3704031	Qiao Li
200429	Guangdong Provincial Expressway Development Co Ltd	85, Baiyun Road, Guangzhou, Guangdong	510100	86-20-83731365 86-20-83731388-230	86-20-83731384	Huo Haibin
200468	Nanjing Postel Telecommunications Co Ltd	1, Putian Road, Qinhuai District, Nanjing	210012	86-25-2418518-2278	86-25-2309954	Xiao Zhaokai
200488	Shandong Chenming Paper Holdings Ltd	595, Shengcheng Street, Shouguang, Shandong	262700	86-536-5280011	86-536-5228900	Hao Yun
200505	Hainan Pearl River Holdings Co Ltd	29th Floor, Dihao Building, Zhujiang Square, Binhai Avenue, Haikou, Hainan	570125	86-898-6763723 86-898-6717888	86-898-6776026	Feng Pai
200512	Tsann Kuen (China) Enterprise Co Ltd	88, Xinglong Road, Huli Industry Zone, Xiamen	361006	86-592-6030228	86-592-6035905	Tian Zhuying
200513	Livzon Pharmaceutical Croup Inc	Guihua Bei Road, Zhujiang, Guangdong	519020	86-756-8135888	86-756-8886002	Wang Wuping
200521	Hefei Meiling Co Ltd	48, Wuhu Road, Hefei	230001	86-551-2884961-394	86-551-2885502	Xue Hui
200530	Dalian Refrigeration Co Ltd	888, Xinan Road, Shahekou District, Daliang	116033	86-411-6653081-8100	86-411-6641470	Lv Lianzhen
200539	Guangdong Electric Power Development Co Ltd	10th Floor, Baili Commercial Centre, Guangfa Garden, 198, Huanshi Dong Road, Guangzhou, Guangdong	510075	86-20-87609276	86-20-87609909	Zhang Dewei
200541	Foshan Electrical And Lighting Co Ltd	15, Fenjiang Bei Road, Foshan, Guangdong	528000	86-0757-2813838-282 86-0757-2814805	86-0757-2816276	Lin Yihui
200550	Jiangling Motors Corporation Co Ltd	509, Yingbing Bei Avenue, Nanchang, Jiangxi	330001	86-791-5232888-6178	86-791-5232839	Xiong Zhongping
200553	Hubei Sanonda Co Ltd	93, Beijing Dong Road, Jingzhou, Hubei	434001	86-716-8314802	86-716-8316796	Li Zhongxi
200570	Changchai Company,Ltd	123, Huaide Zhong Road, Changzhou, Jiangsu, China	213002	86-519-6600448 86-519-6603656-3155	86-519-6630954	Zhang Jianhe
200581	Weifu High Technology Co Ltd	107, Renmin Xi Road, Wuxi	214031	86-510-2719579	86-510-2751025	Liu Yonglin
200596	Anhui Gujing Distillery Co Ltd	Gujing Town, Bozhou, Anhui	236820	86-558-5710085	86-558-5710006	Wang Feng

Code	Company	Address	Postcode	Phone 1	Phone 2	Contact
200613	Hainan Dadonghai Tourism Centre (Holdings) Co Ltd	Da Dong Hai, Sanya City	572021	86-898-88219888-8264	86-898-88212298	Liu Juntao
200625	Chongqing Changan Automobile Co Ltd	260, Jianxin Dong Road, Jiangbei District, Chongqing	400023	86-23-67591249 86-23-67591568	86-23-67866055 86-23-67870261	Cui Yunjiang
200706	Wafangdian Bearing Co Ltd	1, Block 1, Beigongji Street, Wafangdian City, Liaoning, China	116300	86-411-5509888-3829	86-411-5500794	Zhang Xinghai
200725	Boe Technology Group Co Ltd	10, Jiuxianqiao Road, Chaoyang District, Beijing	100016	86-10-64370756	86-10-64366264	Chen Yanshun
200726	Luthai Textile Co Ltd	81, Songling Dong Road, Zichuan District, Zibo, Shandong	255100	86-533-5185166	86-533-5182188	Qin Guiling
200761	Bengang Steel Plates Co Ltd	16, Renmin Road, Pingshan District, Benxi, Liaoning	117000	86-414-7828360	86-414-7828360	Liang Guangde
200770	Wuhan Boiler Co Ltd	586, Wuluo Road, Wuhan, Hubei	430070	86-27-87657327	86-27-87883008	Chen Xingzhi
200771	Hangzhou Steam Turbine Co Ltd	357, Shiqiao Road, Hangzhou	310022	86-571-85780198	86-571-85780433	He Jianghang
200869	Yantai Changyu Pioneer Wine Company Ltd	174, Huiyao Road, Yantai, Shandong	264001	86-535-6691268 86-535-6647864	86-535-6691268 86-535-6691266	Qu Weimin
200986	Foshan Huaxin Packaging Co Ltd	20th Floor, Jinghua Building, Jihua Road, Foshan	528000	86-757-3981729	86-757-3981025	Chen Haiyan
200992	Shandong Zhonglu Oceanic Fisheries Company Ltd	57, Lishan Road, Jinan, Shandong	250013	86-531-6944881	86-531-6955357	Li Wenyi

'H' Shares Listed on Hong Kong Stock Exchange

Stock Code	Company	Registered Address	Postcode	Telephone	Fax
0038	First Tractor Co Ltd	154 Jianshe Road, Luoyang City, Henan, China	471003	86-379-4970038	86-379-4978838
0042	Northeast Electrical Transmission & Transformation Machinery Manufacturing Co Ltd	16 Bei Er Zhong Road, Tiexi District, Shenyang, Liaoning Province, China	110025	86-24-25851243	86-24-25618447
0107	Sichuan Expressway Co Ltd	252 Wuhouci Da Jie, Chengdu, Sichuan, China	610041	86-28-5585124	86-28-5582022
0161	CATIC Shenzhen Holdings Ltd Company	Level 25, Hangdu Building, Shennan Road, Central, CATIC Zone, Futian District, Shenzhen, China	518041	86-755-3790218	86-755-3790228
0168	Tsingtao Brewery Co Ltd	56 Dengzhou Road, Qing Dao City, Shandong Province, China	266000	86-532-5713831	86-532-5713240
0177	Jiangsu Expressway Co Ltd	Jiangsu Communication Building, No. 69 Shigu Road, Nanjing , China	210000	86-25-4200999	86-23-68849520
0187	Beiren Printing Machiery Holdings Ltd	No. 44 Guangqu Road South, Chaoyang District, Beijing, China	100022	86-10-67748470	86-10-67714086
0300	Kunming Machine Tool Co Ltd	23 Ciba Road, Kunming City, Yunnan Province, China	650203	86-871-5212409	86-871-5150317
0317	Guangzhou Shipyard International Co Ltd	40 South Fangcun Main Road, Guangzhou, China	510382	86-20-81896411	86-20-81891575
0323	Maanshan Iron & Steel Co Ltd	No. 8 Hong Qi Zhong Road, Maanshan City, Anhui Province, China	243003	86-555-2888158	86-555-2887284
0325	Beijing Yanhua Petrochemical Co Ltd	No.1 Beice, Yingfeng Erli, Fangshan District, Beijing, China	102500	86-10-69345924	86-10-69345448
0338	Shanghai Petrochemical Co Ltd	Jinshanwei, Shanghai, China	200540	86-21-57943143	86-21-57940050
0347	Angang New Steel Co Ltd	396 Nan Zhong Hua Road, Tie Dong District, Anshan city, Liaoning, China	114003	86-412-6334293	86-412-6727772
0350	Jingwei Textile Machinery Co Ltd	No. 2 Ping street, High and New Industrial Development Zone, Xuefu Road, Taiyuan, Shanxi, China	030601	86-354-2421587	86-354-2421574
0358	Jiangxi Copper Co Ltd	15 Yejin Avenue Guixi City, Jiangxi, China	335424	86-701-3777011	86-701-3777013
0368	Jilin Chemical Industrial Co Ltd	No. 31 East Zunyi Road, Longtan District, Jilin City Jilin, China	132021	86-432-3038671	86-432-3037738
0525	Guang Shen Railway Co Ltd	1052 Heping Road, Shenzhen, Guangdong Province, China	518000	86-755-5589684	86-755-5589684
0548	Shenzhen Expressway Co Ltd	19/F Tower, United Plaza, 5022 Binhe Road N; Shenzhen, China	518033	86-755-3246586	86-755-3231633
0553	Nanjing Panda Electronics Co Ltd	1-2/F, Block 5, North Wing Nanjing New & High Technology Development Zone, Nanjing, China	210002	86-25-4801144	86-25-4820729
0576	Zhejiang Expressway Co.,Ltd.	19/F World Trade Center, 15 Shuguang, Hangzhou, Zhejiang, China	310000	86-571-7985588	86-571-7985599

Code	Company	Address	Postal	Tel 1	Tel 2
0588	Beijing North Star Co Ltd	No. 8 Bei Si Huan Zhong Road, Chao Yang District, Beijing, China	100101	86-10-64991277	86-10-64991967
0670	China Eastern Airlines Corporation Ltd	2550 Hongqiao Road, Shanghai,China	200335	86-21-62686268	86-21-62686116
0719	Shandong Xinhua Pharmaceutical Co Ltd	14 Dongyi Road, Zhangdian District, Zibo City, Shandong, China	255005	86-5333-2184223	86-5333-2287508
0874	Guangzhou Pharmaceutical Co Ltd	NO.45 Sha Mian Bei St, Guang Zhou, China	510132	86-20-81885712	86-20-81876408
0902	Huaneng Power Internatioanl, Inc.	No. 40 Xueyuan Nanlu, Haidian District, Beijing, China	100088	86-10-62254466	86-10-62232910
0914	Anhui Conch Cement Co Ltd	Wuhu city, Anhui, China	241000	86-553-3114546	86-553-3114550
0921	Guangdong Kelon Electrical Holdings Co.,Ltd.	8 Ronggang Road, Rongqi, Shunde, Guangdong, China	528303	86-765-6621955	86-765-6629355
0991	Beijing Datang Power Generation Company	No.482 Guanganmennei Street, Xuanwu District, Beijing, China	100053	86-10-83581910	86-10-83581911
0995	Anhui Expressway Co Ltd	219 Anqing Road, Hefei, Anhui, China	230061	86-551-2843563	86-551-2821539
1033	Yizheng Chemical Fibre Co Ltd	Yizheng City 211900, Jiangsu Province, China	211900	86-514-3231888	86-514-3235880
1053	Chongqing Iron & Steel Co Ltd	Chongqing City, China	630081	86-23-68845430	86-23-68849520
1056	China Southern Airlines Co Ltd	Baiyun International Airport, Guangzhou, Guangdong, China	510406	86-20-86124738	86-20-86659040
1065	Tianjin Bohai Chemical Industry (Group) Co Ltd	No. 10 Hubei Road, Heping District, Tianjin, China	300050	86-22-23135112	86-22-23135107
1072	Dongfang Electrical Machinery Co Ltd	13 Huanghe Xi Road, Deyang, Sichuan, China	618000	86-838-2409358	86-838-2402125
1108	Luoyang Glass Co Ltd	No. 9 Tanggong Zhonglu, Xigong District, Luoyang, Henan, China	471009	86-379-3908552	86-379-3938594
1122	QingLing Motors Co Ltd.	No. 1 Xiexing Rd, Zhong Liangshan, Jiu Longpo District, Chongqing, Sichuan, China	400052	86-23-65212133	86-23-68830397
1128	Zhenhai Refining & Chemical Co Ltd	Yufan, Zhenhai District, Ningbo, Zhejiang, China	315207	86-574-6444447	86-574-6456155
1133	Harbin Power Equipment Co Ltd	Block 3, Nangang District high Technology Production Base, Harbin, China	150000	86-451-2135727	86-451-2135700
1138	China Shipping Development Co.,Ltd.	700 Dong Da Ming Road, Shanghai, China	200080	86-21-65966666	86-21-65966160
1171	Yanzhou Coal Mining Co Ltd	40 Fushan road, Zoucheng, Shandong, China	273500	86-537-5383310	86-537-538331
1202	Chengdu Telecommunications Cable Co Ltd	High-Tech Development Zone, Wai Nan Shen Xian Shu, Chengdu, Sichuan, China	610042	86-28-5189711	86-28-5184474

Organization Structure of China Securities Regulatory Commission

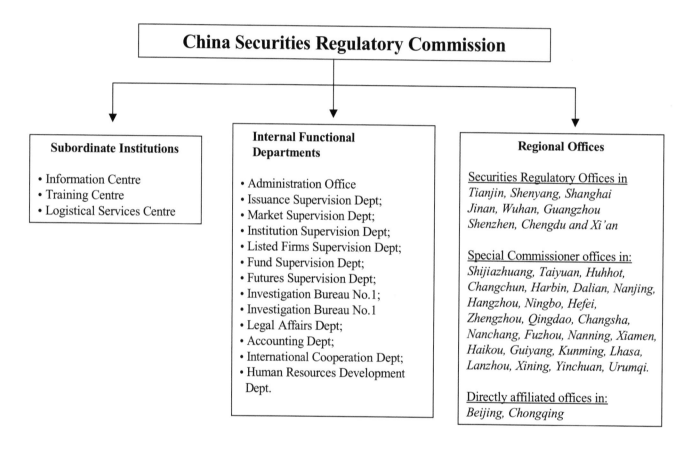

China Securities Regulatory Commission

Subordinate Institutions

- Information Centre
- Training Centre
- Logistical Services Centre

Internal Functional Departments

- Administration Office
- Issuance Supervision Dept;
- Market Supervision Dept;
- Institution Supervision Dept;
- Listed Firms Supervision Dept;
- Fund Supervision Dept;
- Futures Supervision Dept;
- Investigation Bureau No.1;
- Investigation Bureau No.1
- Legal Affairs Dept;
- Accounting Dept;
- International Cooperation Dept;
- Human Resources Development Dept.

Regional Offices

Securities Regulatory Offices in
Tianjin, Shenyang, Shanghai Jinan, Wuhan, Guangzhou Shenzhen, Chengdu and Xi'an

Special Commissioner offices in:
Shijiazhuang, Taiyuan, Huhhot, Changchun, Harbin, Dalian, Nanjing, Hangzhou, Ningbo, Hefei, Zhengzhou, Qingdao, Changsha, Nanchang, Fuzhou, Nanning, Xiamen, Haikou, Guiyang, Kunming, Lhasa, Lanzhou, Xining, Yinchuan, Urumqi.

Directly affiliated offices in:
Beijing, Chongqing

Appendix I

Editorial Contributors: Contact Details

Other

Cable & Wireless plc
Ms Michelle Ye
Director of China
Cable and Wireless Plc
Beijing Representative Office
Unit 1418, South Tower, the Kerry Centre
No 1, Guang Hua Road
Beijing 100020
PR China
Tel: (86) 10 6561 6622
Fax: (86) 10 6561 2388
Email: michelle.ye@cw.com

China-Britain Business Council
Abford House
15 Wilton Road
London SW1V 1LT
Tel: 020 7828 5176
Fax: 020 7630 5780
Email: enquiries@cbbc.org
Website: www.cbbc.org

Denton Wilde Sapte
Hong Kong
Edward R J Neunuebel
43/F Cheung Kong Center
2 Queen's Road, Central
Hong Kong
Tel: (852) 28206 272
Fax: (852) 28106 434
Email: erjn@dentonwildesapte.com.hk

Beijing
Unit 12, Level 5, Tower E1
The Towers
Oriental Plaza
No 1 East Chang An Avenue
Beijing 100738
Tel: (86) 10 8518 6680
Fax: (86) 10 8518 6678

Herbert Smith
Beijing
Jeremy Xiao
14th Floor
Units 1410-1415
China World Tower 1
1 Jianguomenwai
Beijing 100004
Tel: (86) 10 6505 6512
Email: jeremy.xiao@herbertsmith.com

Brussels
Craig Pouncey
15 Rue Guimard
1040 Brussels
Tel: (322) 511 7450
Email: craig.pouncey@herbertsmith.com

London
Jonathan Scott
Exchange House
Primrose Street
London EC2A 2HS
Tel: 020 7466 3917

HSBC Holdings plc
Level 21, 8 Canada Square
London E14 5HQ
Fax: 020 7992 4615
Contacts – China Affairs:
Clare Hammond
Tel: 020 7991 0283
Email: clarehammond@hsbc.com
Michelle Zhang
Tel: 020 7992 1183
Email: michellezhang@hsbc.com

Society of Motor Manufacturers and Traders (SMMT)
Mark Norcliffe
Forbes House
Halkin Street
London SW1X 7DS
Tel: 020 7235 9230
Fax: 020 7344 1675
Email: mnorcliffe@smmt.co.uk

PricewaterhouseCoopers
Beijing
Eric Goujon
11ᵗʰ Floor China World Tower 1
1 Jian Guo Men Wai Avenue
Beijing 100004, PRC
Tel: (86) 10 6505 3333
Fax: (86) 10 8529 9000
Email: eric.goujon@cn.pwcglobal

Kerry Center, 18th Floor
1 Guang Hua Lu, Chao Yang District
Beijing 100020, PRC
Tel: (86) 10 6561 2233
Fax: (86) 10 8529 9000

Chongqing
Room 1905, 19th Floor
Metropolitan Tower, 68 Zhou Rong Road
Chongqing 400010, PRC
Tel: (86) 23 6374 0008
Fax: (86) 23 6374 0990

Dalian
1705 Gold Name Tower
68 Renmin Lu, Zhongshan District
Dalian 116001, PRC
Tel: (86) 411 271 4468/78
Fax: (86) 411 271 4498

Guangzhou
Room 3312, 3308 Office Tower
CITIC Plaza, 233 Tianhe North Road
Guangzhou 510620, PRC
Tel: (86) 20 8363 3168
Fax: (86) 20 8363 4941

HongKong
21st Floor, Edinburgh Tower
The Landmark, 15 Queen's Road
Central, Hong Kong SAR, PRC
Tel: (852) 2289 8888
Fax: (852) 2577 2692

23rd Floor, Prince's Building
Central, Hong Kong SAR, PRC
Tel: (852) 2289 8888
Fax: (852) 2577 2692

Shanghai
12th & 19th Floor, Shanghai ShuiOn Plaza
333 Huai Hai Zhong Road
Shanghai 200020, PRC
Tel: (86) 21 6386 3388
Fax: (86) 21 6386 9000/3300

Shenzhen
Room 3706, Shun Hing Square
Di Wang Commercial Centre
5002 Shennan Road East
Shenzhen 518008, PRC
Tel: (86) 755 8246 1717
Fax: (86) 755 8246 1730

28/F Shenzhen International Financial Bldg.
2022 Jianshe Road
Shenzhen 518001, PRC
Tel: (86) 755 8229 8288
Fax: (86) 755 8228 0044

Suzhou
11/F, International Building
#2 Su Hua Road
Suzhou Industrial Park
Jiangsu Province, Suzhou 215021, PRC
Tel: (86) 512 6288 6860
Fax: (86) 512 6288 6870

Tianjin
37th Floor, Golden Emperor Building
20, Nanjing Road
Hexi District
Tianjin 300041, PRC
Tel: (86) 22 2330 6789
Fax: (86) 22 2339 3662

Xian
Room 301, 3rd Floor
Zhong Da International, No.30 Nanda Street
Xian 710002, PRC
Tel: (86) 29 720 3336
Fax: (86) 29 720 3335

The United States-China Business Council
Washington
Bob Kapp
1818 N Street NW
Suite 200
Washington DC 20036
Tel: (1) 202 429 0340
Fax: (1) 202 775 2478
Email: Bkapp@uschina.org

Beijing
CITIC Building
Suite 10-01
19 Jianguomenwai Dajie
Beijing 100004
Tel: (86) 10 6592 0727
Fax: (86) 10 6512 5854
Email: uscbc@eastneet.com.cn

Shanghai
Jinjiang Hotel
2312 West Building
59 Mar Ming Road
Shanghai 200020
Tel: (86) 21 6415 2579
Fax: (86) 21 6415 2584
Email: uscbc@uninet.com.cn

Appendix I

Editorial Contributors: Contact Details

China

China Securities Regulatory Commission
Jin Yang Plaza
16 Jin Rong Street
Xi Cheng District
Beijing 100032
China
Tel: (86) 10 88061141
Fax: (86) 10 66210206
Website: www.csrc.gov.cn

China Import and Export Bank
Jinyun Tower B
No.43A Xizhimenbei Street
Beijing 100044
China
Tel: (86) 10 62278899
Fax: (86) 10 62212024
Website: www.eximbank.gov.cn

Mr Liu Xiangdong
Vice Ministerial Chair
Ministry of Foreign Trade and Economic
Cooperation
2 Dong Chang An Street
Beijing 100731
China

Mr Hu Jingyan
Director General
Foreign Investment Department
Ministry of Foreign Trade and Economic
Cooperation
2 Dong Chang An Street
Beijing 100731
China
Tel: (86) 10 65197304
Fax: (86) 10 65197322

Ms Li Shantong
Director General
Research Dept. of Development Strategy and
Regional Economy
Development Research Centre of the State Council
No.225 Chaonei Street
Beijing 100010
China
Tel: (86) 10 65276661
Fax: (86) 10 65232937

Mr Ma Shaobo
Capital Account Administration Dept
State Administration of Foreign Exchange
Hua Rong Building
18 Fu Cheng Lu
Haidian District
Beijing 100037
China

Mr Wang Xuekun
Director
Division of Economic Analysis
Dept. of Policy Research
Ministry of Foreign Trade and Economic
Cooperation
2 Dong Chang An Street
Beijing 100731
China
Tel: (86) 10 65198498
Fax: (86) 10 6519 7151

Mr Shi Yonghai
Chairman
China Association of International Trade
2 Dong Chang An Street
Beijing 100731
China
Tel: (86) 10 65197955
Fax: (86) 10 65245899

Mr Li Yong
Deputy Secretary General
China Association of International Trade
2 Dong Chang An Street
Beijing 100731
China
Tel: (86) 10 65197955
Mobile: 13801 093 386
Fax: (86) 10 64295362
Email: lycmtd@public3.bta.net.cn /
yonglii@yahoo.com.cn

Mr Fan Weimin
Patent Attorney
CCPIT Patent & Trademark Law Office
10/F Ocean Plaza
158 Fuxingmennei Street
Beijing 100031
China
Tel: (86) 10 6641 2345
Fax: (86) 10 6641 5678

Mr Liu Baocheng
Professor
Dean
Sino US School of International Management
University of International Business and Econonics
(UIBE)
Room 1401 Chengxin Building
Hu Xin Dong Jie
Chaoyang District
Beijing 100029
China
Tel: (86) 10 6449 4628
Fax: (86) 10 6449 4627
Email: simdean@uibe.edu.cn
Website: www.sim-gbs.org

Mr Chen Duo
Senior Researcher
Deputy Director-General
Hong Kong and Macao Research Institute
Hong Kong and Macao Affairs Office of the State
Council
77 Yue Tan Nan Jie
Xicheng District
Beijing 100045
Tel: (86) 10 68517366
Fax: (86) 10 6851 3574

Mr Du Xishuang
Director
Senior Statistician
National Bureau of Statistics
75 Yue Tan Nan Jie
San Li He
Beijing 100826
China
Tel: (86) 10 68573311 ext 80133
Fax: (86) 10 6857 6322

Wu Naiwen
Vice Chairman
China Customs Research Society
6 Jian Guo Men Nei Street
Beijing 100730
China
Tel: (86) 10 6519 5202
Fax: (86) 10 6519 5797

Editorial Department
China Chemical News and China Chemical Industry
Yearbook
53 Xiaoguanjie
Andingmenwai
Beijing 100029 China
Tel: (86) 10 64444034/5 815
Fax:(86) 10 64431546
Email: q-ssl@mail.cncic.gov.cn
Website: www.chemnews.com.cn
Contact: Sun Shanlin or Chen Yu

Dr Lu Chunshan
Deputy Division Chief
Economic Restructuring Office of the State Council
22 Xi An Men Da Jie
Beijing 100017
China

Ni Hongxing
Director
Department of International Cooperation
Ministry of Agriculture
11 Nong Zhan Guan Nan Li
Beijing 100026
China
Tel: (86) 10 6419 1573
Fax: (86) 10 6419 2453

Chen Congcong
Guanghua Management School
Beijing University
Tel: (86) 10 6276 3162
Mobile: 13911 121 214

Prof T S Chan, Associate Vice President and
Academic Dean
Chair Professor in Marketing
Lingnan University
8 Castle Peak Road
Tuen Mun
Hong Kong
Tel (86) 852 26168302

Dr Wei-ping Wu
Department of Marketing and International Business
Lingnan University
8 Castle Peak Road
Tuen Mun
Hong Kong
Tel: (86) 852 26168236
Email: wpwu@ln.edu.hk

Che Yanhua
Marketing Communications and CRM Manager
Volkswagen China Import
Level 13, South Tower
Beijing Terry Center
No.1 Guanghua Road
Chaoyang District
Beijing 100020
China
Tel: (86) 8529 7888 ext 2203
Mobile: 13901 089 084
Fax: 8529 6790
Email: may.che@volkswagen.com.cn

Dr Gao Chunping
Manager
Strategic Planning Department
Shijiazhuang Pharmaceutical Group Co Ltd
276 Zhong Shan Xi Lu
Shijiazhuang 050051
Hebei Province
China
Tel: (86) 311 7037021
Fax: (86) 311 7023481

Directory of Local Authorities of Foreign Trade and Economic Cooperation

1. Beijing Municipal Foreign Trade & Economic Cooperation Commission
No.190 Chaonei Street, Dong Cheng District,
Beijing China
Post code: 100010
Tel: 010-65236688
http://www.bjfetc.gov.cn/fetc/fabu/english/index.jsp

2. Tianjin Municipal Commission of Foreign Trade & Economic Cooperation
80 Qufu Road, Heping District,
Tianjin, China
Tel: 022-87310501 022-87310502
Fax: 022-87310589
E-mail: webmaster@goldentianjin.net.cn
http://www.goldentianjin.net.cn/EN/edefault.asp

3. Hebei Provinical Commission of Foreign Trade & Economic Cooperation
184, Er Duan, Heping Xi Road,
Shijiazhuang, Hebei Province, China
Postcode: 050071
Tel: 0311-7044842 0311-7029523
Fax: 0311-7041570

4. Shanxi Provinical Commission of Foreign Trade & Economic Cooperation Bureau
15, Xin Jian Road
Taiyuan, Shanxi Province
China
Postcode: 030002
Tel: 0351-4041722
Fax: 0351-4081004
E-mail: sxdbc@ec.com.cn

5. Inner Mongolia Autonomous Region Foreign Trade & Economic Cooperation Bureau
138, Zhong Shan Xi Lu
Huhhot, Inner Mongolia Autonomous Region
China
Postcode: 010020
Tel: 0471-6964301
Fax: 0471-6962138
E-mail: nmgwjmt@public.hh.nm.cn
nmgftec@mail.ec.com.cn

6. Liaoning Provinical Foreign Trade & Economic Cooperation Bureau
45-1, Bei Ling Street, Huanggu District
Shenyang, Liaoning Province
China
Postcode: 110032
Tel: 024-6892544024-6892225
Fax: 024-6893858

7. Jilin Provinical Foreign Trade & Economic Cooperation Bureau
119, Ren Min Street
Changchun, Jilin Province
Postcode: 130021
Tel: 0431-26441910431-5626905
Fax: 0431-5624772

8. Heilongjiang Provincial Foreign Trade & Economic Cooperation Bureau
55, He Ping Lu, Dongli District
Harbin, Heilongjiang
China
Postcode: 150001
Tel: 0451 2626987 0451-2621455   2621001

9. Shanghai Municipal Commission Foreign Trade and Economic Cooperation
2104, #55 Lou Shan Guan Road
Shanghai, China
Postcode: 200335
Tel: 021-62756811, 62752200, 62751950
Fax: 021-62751159

10. Zhejiang Provincial Foreign Trade & Economic Cooperation Bureau
18, Jiao Chang Road
Hangzhou, Zhejiang Province
China
Postcode: 310006
Tel: 0571-87706099
Fax: 0571-87706029

11. Jiangsu Provincial Commission of Foreign Trade & Economic Cooperation
50, Zhong Hua Road
Nanjing, Jiangsu Province
Postcode: 210008
Tel: 025-2254455,2254466
Fax: 025-7712072

12. Anhui Provinical Commission of Foreign Trade & Economic Cooperation
85, Chang Jiang Road
Hefei, Anhui Province
Postcode: 230001
Tel: 0551-3631900 0551-3637766
Fax: 0551-3631872

13. Fujian Provincial Foreign Trade & Economic Cooperation Bureau
Floor 13-17, Shi Fa Building
92, Liu Yi Bei Lu
Fuzhou, Fujian Province
China
Postcode: 350013
Tel: 0591-7841917 0591-7853616
Fax: 0951-7856133

14. Jiangxi Provincial Foreign Trade & Economic Cooperation Bureau
60, Zhanqian Road
Nancang, Jiangxi Province
Postcode: 330002
Tel: 0791-6246328 0791-6227281
Fax: 0791-6246307

15.Shandong Provincial Commission of Foreign Trade & Economic Cooperation
121, Hei Hu Quan Xi Lu
Jinan, Shandong Province
Postcode: 250011
Tel: 0531-6917061 0532-2870493
Fax: 0531-6912793

16. Hubei Provincial Foreign Trade & Economic Cooperation Bureau
8, Jiang Han Bei Lu
Wuhan, Hubei Province
China
Postcode: 430022
Tel: 027-85773850 85774233
Fax: 027-85773668

17. Henan Provincial Foreign Trade & Economic Cooperation Bureau
115, Wen Hua Road
Zhengzhou, Henan Province
China
Postcode: 450003
Tel: 0371-3941359
Fax: 0371-3945422

18. Guangdong Provinical Commission of Foreign Trade & Economic Cooperation
Fl. 8, Foreign Trade Tower
351, Tian He Lu
Guangzhou, Guangdong Province
China
Postcode: 510620
Tel: 020-87592165 020-87577168
Fax: 020-87592219

19.Hunan Provinical Commission of Foreign Trade & Economic Cooperation
80, Wu Yi Dong Lu
Changsha, Hunan Province
Postcode: 410001
Tel: 0731-2295145 0731-2295060
Fax: 0731-2295160

20.Guangxi Zhuang Autonomous Region Foreign Trade & Economic Cooperation Bureau
137, Qi Xing Road
Nanning, Guangxi
China
Postcode: 530002
Tel: 0711-2813165 0771-2800676
Fax: 0771-5851581

21. Hainan Provincial Foreign Trade & Economic Cooperation Bureau
Expert Building, Qiongyuan Hotel
Qiong Yuan Road,
Haikou, Hainan Province
China
Postcode: 570203
Tel: 0898-5337135 0898-5342896
Fax: 0898-5338762

22. Sichuan Provincial Foreign Trade & Economic Cooperation Bureau
4, Chenghua Road
Chengdu, Sichuan Province
China
Postcode: 610081
Tel: 028-83235033
Fax: 028-83226033-6708
E-mail: webmaster@scbg.org.cn

23. Yunnan Provincial Foreign Trade & Economic Cooperation Bureau
576, Beijing Road
Kunming, Yunnan Province
Postcode: 650011
Tel: 0871-3135001 0871-3135371
Fax: 0871-3123541

24.Chongqing Municipal Commission of Foreign Trade & Economic Cooperation
65, Xi Jian Bei Lu
Chongqing, China
Postcode: 630020
Tel: 0811-67523525 0811-67528098
Fax: 0811-67853458

25. Shaanxi Foreign Trade & Economic Cooperation Bureau
Provincial Government Office Complex
Xi'an, Shaanxi Province
Postcode: 710004
Tel: 029-7291591 029-7291583
Fax: 029-7291618

26. Guizhou Provincial Foreign Trade & Economic Cooperation Bureau
21, Beijing Road
Guiyang, Guizhou Province
Postcode: 550004
Tel: 0851-6822341
Fax: 0851-6826509

27. Qinghai Provincial Foreign Trade & Economic Cooperation Bureau
102, Shu Lin Xiang
Xining, Qinghai Province
China
Postcode: 810007
Tel: 0971-8174514 0971-8176744
Fax: 0971-8176805

28. Tibet Autonomous Region Foreign Trade & Economic Cooperation Bureau
184, Beijing Zhong Road
Lhasa, Tibet Autonomous Region
China
Postcode: 850001
Tel: 0891-6339337 0891-6322448
Fax: 0891-6335733

29.Xinjiang Uygur Autonomous Region Foreign Trade & Economic Cooperation Bureau
11, Tuanjie Road
Urumqi, Xinjiang Uygur Autonomous Region
Postcode: 830001
Tel: 0991-2877270 0991-2860255
Fax: 0991-2860255

30. Gansu Provincial Foreign Trade & Economic Cooperation Bureau
386, Ding Xi Road
Lanzhou, Ganxu Province
China
Postcode: 730000
Tel: 0931-8619767
Fax: 0931-8618083   8619394

31. Ningxia Hui Autonomous Region Foreign Trade & Economic Cooperation Bureau
199, Jiefang Xi Road
Yinchuan, Ningxia Autonomous Region
China
Postcode: 750001
Tel: 0951-5044277 0951-5044850
Fax: 0951-5044239

Contact details of the foreign trade and economic cooperation commissions in key coastal cities

Beihai City Foreign Trade & Economic Cooperation Bureau
4, Bei Bu Wan Dong Lu
Beihai, Guangxi
China
Postcode: 536000
Tel: 0779-2059509
Fax: 0779-2052748

Dalian City Foreign Trade & Economic Cooperation Bureau
219, Huang He Lu, Xigang District
Dalian, Liaoning Province
China
Postcode: 116011
Tel: 0411- 3698000 3686165
Fax: 0411-3686246

Fuzhou City City Foreign Trade & Economic Cooperation Commission
93, Wu Shan Lu
Fuzhou, Fujian Province
China
Postcode: 350001
Tel: 0591-555308
Fax: 0591-557232

Guangzhou City Foreign Trade & Economic Cooperation Commission
158, Dong Feng Xi Lu
Guangzhou, Guangdong Province
China
Postcode: 510049
Tel: 020-8886 6455
Fax: 020-81097902

Lianyungang City Foreign Trade & Economic Cooperation Bureau
9, Hai Lian Dong Lu
Lianyungang, Jiangsu Province
China
Postcode: 222006
Tel: 0518-5805793
http://ftecb.lyg.gov.cn/

Nantong City Foreign Trade & Economic Cooperation Bureau
51, Gong Nong Lu
Nantong, Jiangsu Province
China
Tel: 0513 3562336

Ningbo City Commission of Foreign Trade & Economic Cooperation
190, Ling Qiao Lu
Ningbo, Zhejiang Province
China
Postcode: 315000
Tel: 0574-87310963
Fax: 0574-87328288

Qingdao City Foreign Trade & Economic Cooperation Bureau
Block A, Qingdao World Trade Centre
6, Xiang Gang Zhong Lu, Shi Nan District
Qingdao, Shandong Province
China
Postcode: 266071
Tel: 0532- 5918108
Fax: 0532-3836036
E-mail: qdfert@fert.qingdaochina.com
http://www.qingdaochina.com/

Qinhuangdao City Foreign Trade & Economic Cooperation Bureau
78, You Yi Lu, Harbour District
Qinghuangdao, Hebei Province
China
Postcode: 066002
Tel: 0335-3428988
Fax: 0335-3411560

Wenzhou City Foreign Trade & Economic Cooperation Bureau
8, Li Ming Xi Lu
Wenzhou, Zhejiang Province
China
Postcode: 325000
Tel: 0571-85156707
Fax: 0571-85155825

Yantai City Foreign Trade & Economic Cooperation Bureau
71, Jian She Lu, Zhi Fu District
Yantai, Shandong
China
Postcode: 264000
Tel: 0535-6254375 6245518

Zhanjiang City Foreign Trade & Economic Cooperation Bureau
Xi Men, 31, Nan Fang Lu, Chi Kan
Zhanjiang, Guangdong Province
China
Postcode: 524038
Tel: 0759-3339742
Fax: 0759-3336897

Shenzhen City Foreign Trade & Economic Cooperation Bureau
8 Shang Bu Zhong Lu
Shenzhen, Guangdong Province
Postcode: 518006
Tel: 0755-2240972
Fax; 0755-2243803

Shantou City Foreign Trade & Economic Cooperation Bureau

3, Da Hua Lu
Shantou, Guangdong Province
China
Postcode: 515031
Tel: 0754-8274257
Fax: 0754-8271037

Special Commissioner's offices of the Ministry of Foreign Trade and Economic Cooperation in 16 cities

Qingdao
12, Yan Er Dao Lu, Shi Nan District
Qingdao, Shandong Province
Postcode: 266071
Tel: 0532-5734278
Fax: 0532-5734682

Dalian
2, Zhong Shan Guang Chang, Zhong Shan District
Dalian, Liaoning Province
Postcode: 116002
Tel: 0411-2630778
Fax: 0411-2630213

Tianjin
59, Nan Jing Road, Heping District
Tianjin, China
Postcode: 300042
Tel: 022-23317060 23307724
Fax: 022-23308071

Shanghai
1, Yong Fu Lu, Xuhui District
Shanghai, China
Postcode: 200031
Tel: 021-64317212
Fax: 021-64335268

Guangzhou
117, Liu Hua Lu
Guangzhou, Guangdong Province
China
Postcode: 510014
Tel: 020-86677314
Fax: 020-86677314

Shenzhen
Fl. 4, Haian Centre
229, Bin He Lu, Fu Tian District
Shenzhen, Guangdong Province
China
Postcode: 518032
Tel: 0755-83797220
Fax: 0755-83797143

Haikou
Fl.7, Anhai Tower
Huahai Road
Kaikou, Hainan Province
Postcode: 570105
Tel: 0898-66776186
Fax: 0898-66776957

Nanning
17, Yuan Hu Nan Lu
Nanning, Guangxi
China
Postcode: 530022
Tel: 0771-5867858
Fax: 0771-5867740

Nanjing
Fl. 7, World Trade Tower
50, Zhong Hua Lu
Nanjing, Jiangsu Province
China
Postcode: 210001
Tel: 025-2251925
Fax: 025-2253474
E-mail: njtb@moftec.gov.cn

Wuhan
8, Jiang Han Bei Lu
Wuhan, Hubei Province
Postcode: 430021
Tel: 027-85774211
Fax: 027-85774298

Zhenzhou
115, Wen Hua Lu
Zhengzhou, Henan Province
China
Postcode: 450003
Tel: 0371-3576207 0371-3576205 0371-3576206
Fax: 0371-3942780

Fuzhou
Fl.9, Foreign Trade Tower
Wu Si Lu
Fuzhou, Fujian Province
China
Postcode: 350001
Tel: 0591-7536473
Fax: 0591-7500312

Xi'an
Fl. 5, 68, Huan Cheng Nan Lu Zhong Duan
Xi'an, Sha'anxi Province
China
Postcode: 710054
Tel: 029-7861934
Fax: 029-7861932

Chengdu
18, Fu Qing Xi Nan Jie
Xi San Duan, Yi Huan Lu
Chengdu, Sichuan Province
China
Postcode: 610031
Tel: 028-87734181
Fax: 028-87781984

Hangzhou
18, Jiao Chang Lu, Xia Cheng District
Hangzhou, Zhejiang Province
China
Postcode: 310006
Tel: 0571-87706098
Fax: 0571-87706019

Kunming
B9, Wan Xing Garden, Guanshang
Kunming, Yunnan Province
China
Postcode: 650200
Tel: 0871-7181299 0871-7183566 0871-7183508
Fax: 0871-7181396

Appendix III

Commercial Offices of PRC Embassies Worldwide

Afghanistan
Sardar Shah Mahmoud Ghazi Wai, Kabul,
Afghanistan
Tel: +93-20446, +93-25551, +93-22340

Albania
Rruga Skenderbej Nr.57 Tirane Albania
Tel: 00355-4-232077, 253505
Fax: 00355-42-32077
E-mail: cnemec@icc.al.eu.org
ekzet@adanet.net.al

Algeria
34, Bd, Des Martyrs, Alger, Algerie
Tel: 00213-21-693189 00213-21-691865
Fax: 00213-21-692362
E-mail: dz@moftec.gov.cn; becchine@wissal.dz

Angola
Caixa Postal No.704, Rua Fernao Mendes Pinto No.
26–28
Bairro Alvalade, Luanda, Angola
Tel: 002442-322803
Fax: 002442-322803
E-mail: luo.taiheng@netangola.com

Antigua and Barbuda
Mckinnons Way, St. John's, Antigua, W.I. P. O. Box
1355
Tel: 001-809-4626414
Fax: 001-809-4620986

Argentina
La Pampa 3410 Buenos Aires Argentina
Tel: 0054-1-5541258, 5542613
Fax: 0054-1-5538939
E-mail: ofeccocn@ba.net

Armenia
Nork-Marash, 9-th Street, house 39, Yerevan,
Republic of Armenia 375048
Tel: 00374-1-655022, 651311, 653569
Fax: 00374-1-587898
E-mail: zzyswc@ns.r.am

Australia
15 Coronation Drive Yarralumla, Act 2600
Canberra, Australia
Tel: 0061-2-62734785
Fax: 0061-2-62734987
E-mail: commerce@chinaembassy.org.au

Sydney, Australia
68 George Street, Redfern, New South Wales 2016,
Australia
Tel: 0061-2-6987788, 6987838
Fax: 0061-2-6987373
E-mail: eco@all.com.au

Melbourne, Australia
75–77 Irving Road, Toorak, Vic. 3142 Australia
Tel: 0061-3-95095547
Fax: 0061-3-98220320
E-mail: amjsch@netlink.com.au

Austria
A-1030 Wien, Metternichgasse 4, 1030 Vienna, Austria
Tel: (00431) 7143149-19/20/21
Fax: (00431) 7143149-22
E-mail: handelsabtchina@aon.at

AZERBAIJAN
94 Str. T. Aliev, 370069, Azerbaijan, Baku
Tel: 99412-656214; 656215
Fax: 99412-988880
Mob.tel.: 99450-2155718; 2155008
E-mail: zgswc@azeri.com
az@moftec.gov.cn

Bangladesh
Plot, 15, Park Road, Block-I, Baridhara, Dhaka, Bangladesh
Tel: 00880-2-8823968, 8825272, 8823313
Fax: 00880-2-8823082
E-Mail: checodhk@mail.citech-bd.com

The Bahamas
3rd Orchard Terrace Village Road, Nassau, The Bahamas
P. O. Box SS6389
Tel: 1-242-3931960, 1-242-3931029
Fax: 1-242-3930733
E-mail: moftec_bahamas@sohu.com

Bahrain
Villa 928, Road 3118, Manama 331, State of Bahrain
Postal Address: P. O. BOX 5260, Manama, Bahrain
Tel: 973-233339
Fax: 973-272790
E-mail: chinacom@batelco.com.bh

Barbados
Maxwell Coast Road, Christ Church, Barbados, W. I.
P. O. Box 34A,
Tel: 001-246-4283384
Fax: 001-246-4285860
E-mail: ecocom@sunbeach.net

Belarus
No.42, 22a Krasnoarmeiskaya Str.220030 Minsk Belarus
Tel: 00375-17-2891413 2292925 2292928
Fax: 00375-17-2105841
E-mail: swchu@solo.by

Belgium
Boulevard General Jacques 19 1050 Bruxelles, Belgique
Tel: 0032-2-6404210
Fax: 0032-2-6403595
E-mail:comoffchnmsn@pophost.eunet.be

Benin
Route No. 2 De l'Aeroport Zone Des Ambassades Cotonou, Benin 08-0167 (or) 08-0462 Cotonou, Benin
Tel: 00229-301909, 301097
Fax: 00229-301639

Bolivia
Calle H No. 100, Achumani, Sectors San Ramon, La Paz, Bolivia
Tel: 00591-2-794567
Fax: 00591-2-797577

Bosnia and Herzegovina
Brace Begica 17, 71000 Sarajevo
Tel: 00387-215107
Fax: 00387-215108
E-mail: ecobh@bih.net.ba

Botswana
3097 North Ring Road Gaborone Botswana
P. O. Box 1031 Gaborone Botswana
Tel: 00267-353270, 352209
Fax: 00267-300156

Brazil
SHIS QL 8, Conjunto 5, Casa 20, Lago Sul, Brasilia-DF
CEP: 71620-255, Brasilia – DF, Brasil
Tel: 0055-61-2481446/2485205/2480776
Fax: 0055-61-2482139
E-mail: sanab843@bsb.nutecnet.com.br
webmaster@chinaembaco.org.br

Sao Paulo, Brazil
Rua Estados Unidos, 170-Jardim America-CEP
01437 Sao Paulo-SP-Brasil
Tel: 0055-11-2829877, 8522663
Fax: 0055-11-30641813
E-mail: conchi@sti.com.br

Rio de Janeiro, Brazil
Rua Muniz Barretots Botafogo, Kio De Janeird CEP
22251-090 Brasil
Tel: 0055-21-5514878
Fax: 0055-21-5515736, 5514533
E-mail: comeeco@uol.com.br

Brunei
Simpang 462 Lot 38868 KG Sungai Tilong Jalan
Muara
Negara Brunei Darussalam
Tel: 006732 340891
Fax: 006732 335163 338277
E-mail: embcc@brunet.bn

Bulgaria
Sofia 3, 9, 'Pler Degelder' Str, 1113, Sofia, Bulgaria
Tel: 00359-2-724988, 9712032
Fax: 00359-2-9712416
E-mail: chinabiz@cn-bg.com

Burundi
Sur La Parcelle 675 a Vugizo, Bujumbura, Burundi
Tel: 00257-224246, 222558
Fax: 00257-221962
Telex:5137 BCCHINE BDI
E-mail: conec@crinf.com

Cabo Verde
C.P. No. 8, Praia; Achada De Santo Antonio Praia
Republica
De Cabo Verde
Tel: 00238-623029
Fax: 00238-623007
E-mail: cv@moftec.gov.cn

Cambodia
No. 156 BLC Mao Tsetung Pohnom Peuh,
Cambodia
Tel: 00855-23-720923
Fax: 00855-23-720924

Cameroun
B.P. 11608 Yaounde Cameroun Ambassade De
Chine
Tel: 00237-209522, 203191
Fax: 00237-210091

Douala, Cameroun
B.P. 2983, Douala, Cameroun
Tel: 00237-3425437
Fax: 00237-3422268
E-mail: consulchina@iccnet2000.com
douala@moftec.gov.cn

Canada
401 King Edward Avenue, Ontario Canada K1N
9C9 TEL : Fax:
Tel: 1-613-236-8828
Fax: 1-613-236-5078
E-mail: ecoffice@buildlink.com

Vancouver, Canada
3380 Granville Street, Vancouver, B.C. Canada
V6H 3K3
Tel: 001-604-7364021
Fax: 001-604-7364343
Telex: 04-54659
E-mail: ecomms@infoserve.net

Toronto, Canada
240 St. George Street, Toronto, Ontario, Canada,
M5R 2P4
Tel: 001-416-3246455, 3246454
Fax: 001-416-3246468

Calgary, Canada
Suite 100, 1011-6th Avenue SW Calgary Alberta
Canada T2P 0W1
Tel: 001-403-264-3322
Fax: 001-403-264-6656

Central Africa
Avenue des Martyrs Bangui, Republique
Centragricaine
Tel: 00236-614682
Fax: 00236-614358

Chile
Casilla 3417; Av. Pedro De Valdivia 1032,
Providencia, Santiago, Chile
Tel: 0056-2-2239988
Fax: 0056-2-2232465

Comores
B.P. 442 Moroni Comores
Tel: 00269-732937
Fax: 00269-732937
E-mail:jingsc@snpt.km

Congo
466, Av. Colonel Lukusa, Kinshasa/Gombe,
D'Congo
Tel: 00243-12-26210, 83076, 46507
Fax: 001-212-3769255

Cote D'Ivoire
06 B.P. 206 Abidjan 06 Cote D'Ivoire
Tel: 00225-22420102
Fax: 00225- 22426373
E-mail: ci@moftec.gov.cn

Brazzaville, Congo
Avenue Monseigneur Augouard, Brazzaville, Congo
B.P. 2838, Brazzaville, Congo
Tel: 00242-830952
Fax: 00242-837702

Colombia
Cra.16 No.98-30, Bogota D.C, Republica de
Colombia
Tel: 00571-6222879 6223103
Fax: 00571-6223114
E-mail: ecocnco@hotmail.com
co@moftec.gov.cn

Croatia
Bukovacka 8A 10000 Zagreb Croatia
Tel: 00385-1-2421646, 2304546
Fax: 00385-1-2304484, 2421686
E-mail: e.c.office.chn@zg.tel.hr

Cuba
La, Calle 42, No. 313, 5 Avenid Miramar Playa,
Ciudad De La Habana, Cuba
Tel: 0053-7-332585
Fax: 0053-7-331021
E-mail: ecomochn@ip.etecsa.cu

Cyprus
P. O. Box 7088, No. 17 Agapinor Street, Nicosia,
Cyprus
Tel: 00357-2-375252
Fax: 00357-2-376699
E-mail: shangwu@cytanet.com.cy

Czech Republic
Velvyslsnectvi Cinske Li Dove
Republiky Obchodni
Oddeleni Pelleova 22 16000 Praha 6-Bubenec
Tel: 0042-2-24311324, 33028872
Fax: 0042-2- 33028876
E-mail: ec.embcn@cmail.cz

Denmark
Oeregaards Alle 12, DK - 2900 Hellerup,
Copenhagen Denmark
Tel: 0045-39611013
Fax: 0045-39612913
Telex: 0045-19106 CHCOEM DK
E-mail: ecc@post7.tele.dk

Djibouti
Rue De Nairobi, Heron, Djibouti B.P. 4001 Djibouti
Tel: 00253-350575
Fax: 00253-354174

Dominica
Calle Repoblacion Forestal No. 7, Edificio
Don Samudl, Los Millones, Apartado Postal 3513,
Santo
Domingo, Republica Dominicana
Tel: 00566-2620, 7063, 8430, 567-3480
Fax: (1-809)566-2620

Ecuador
Av. Atahualpa No. 349 Y Av. Amazonas Quito-
Ecuador
Casilla 17-110-5143
Tel: 00593-2-2444362, 2433474
Fax: 00593-2-2433474
E-mail: ecocnec@hotmail.com

Egypt
22, Bahgat Aly Street, Zamalek, Cairo, Egypt
Tel: 00202-3404316, 3417423
Fax: 00202-7358728, 7362094
E-mail: ccechina@soficom.com.eg

Equatorial Guinea
Calle De Independencia 26-B-2 Consejero
Economico-Comercial De La Embajada De La
Republica
Popular China En La Republica De Guinea
Ecuatorial; P. O. Box
Malabo, No. 44
Tel: 00240-9-3440
Fax: 00240-9-3459

Eritrea
Eritrea Asmara Zone 4 Adm. 02 Street No. 702
Hause No. 74, P. O. Box 204
Tel: 002911-182273
Fax: 002911-182200

ESTONIA
Juhkentali 21 EE0001 Tallinn Estonia
Tel: 00372-6607867, 6607868
Fax: 00372- 6607818
E-mail: chincoff@online.ee

Ethiopia
High 24, Kebele 13, House, No. 729 Jimma Road,
Addis, Ababa, Ethiopia
P. O. Box 5643
Tel: 002511-712266
Fax: 002511-710059, 713066

Fiji
147 Queen Elizabeth Drive, Private Mail Bag,
Suva, Fiji
Tel: 00679-3304817ext.17
Fax: 00679-3304564

Finland
Vahanityntie 4 00570 Helsinki 57, Finland
Tel: 00358-9-6848416, 6849641
Fax: 00358-9-6849595
E-mail: fin.shangwu@kolumbus.fi
Telex:126055 CHINA SF

France
21, Rue De L'Amiral D'Estaing 75016 Paris, France
Tel: 0033-1-53577000
Fax: 0033-1-47209471
E-mail: shangwu@amb-chine.fr
eccochn@sysium.com

Gabon
B.P. 3914 Libreville Gabon
Tel: 00241-732873, 738839
Fax: 00241-738645, 738887

GEORGIA
52 Barnov Str., 380008 Tbilisi, Georgia
Tel: 0099532-983953
Fax: 0099532-931276
E-mail: gzj@access.sanet.ge

Germany
Selma-Lagerloef-Str. 11, 13189 Berlin
Tel 0049 30 47901910
Fax: 0049-30-4710230
E-mail: mail@trade-embassy-china.de
trade-embassy.china@snafu.de
www.trade-embassy-china.de

Bonn, Germany
Friedrich-Ebert-Str. 59 53177 Bonn Bad Godesberg,
F.R.Germany
Tel: 0049-228-955940
Fax: 0049-228-356781
E-mail: trade-bonn.cn@debitel.net

Hamburg, Germany
Elbchaussee 268 22605. Hamburg, Germany
Tel: 0049-40-82276012, 82276016
Fax: 0049-40-82276021
E-mail: trade.consulate.cn.hh@t-online.de

Ghana
P. O. Box M344 Airport Residential Area Accra,
Ghana
Tel: 00233-21-777462, 772541
Fax: 00233-21-777462, 772541
E-mail: jshchu@ghana.com

Greece
Diadochou Pavlou 7, P, Psychikon, 154
52 Athens, Greece
Tel: 0030-1-6723281
Fax: 0030-1-6741575
Telex:226848 CPRC GR
E-mail: eccoprc@otenet.gr

Guinea
Bureau Du Conseiller Economique
Et Commercial Pres Ambassade De La Republique
Populaire De Chine En Republique
De Guinee B.P. 714 Conakry Republique
De Guinee
Tel: (224)464366
Fax: 001-212-4794818

Guinea-Bissau
Av. Francisco Joao Mendes, Bissau, Guine-Bissau
Tel: 00245-203637
Fax: 00245-203590

Guyana
52, Brickdam, Georgetown, Cooperative Republic
Guyana
P. O. Box.101195
Tel: 00592-226-9965, 592-226-7428
Fax: 00592-226-4308
E-mail:guyecoc@networksgy.com
Website:www.guyana-in.com

Hungary
1068 Budapest Benczur U. 17 Hungary
Tel: 0036-1-3225242
Fax: 0036-1-3229067
E-mail: shangwu@elender.hu

Iceland
Vidimelur 25, Reykjavik, Iceland
P. O. Box 7290 Reykjavik
Tel: 00354-1-5526322
Fax: 00354-1-5623922
E-mail: chinacom@chinacommercial.is

Indonesia
JL. Mega Kuningan, Barat 10, No. 2, Jakarta 12950
Indonesia
Tel: 0062-21-5761047, 5761048, 5761049,
5761050
Fax: 0062-21-5761051
E-mail: cydcww@indosat.net.id/
muxinh@indosat.net.id

India
No. 50, D-Shantipath Chanakyapuri New Delhi-
110021, India
Tel: 0091-11-4672687
Fax: 0091-11-6111099
E-mail: chinacom@del6.vsnl.net.in
chinacom@ndf.vsnl.net.in

Bombay, India
P. O. Box 189, GPO, Mumdai 400001, India
Tel: 0091-22-24915863
Fax: 0091-22-24924945

Iran
No.180, Farmanieh Ave., Tehran Iran
Tel: 0098-21-2561567
Fax: 0098-21-2292283
E-mail: chinacom@neda.net
chinacom@dci.co.ir

Iraq
P. O. Box 15097, Al-Yarmuk, Baghdad, Iraq
Tel: 00964-1-5567897, 5562740
Telex: 2195 CHINCOM IK

Ireland
77, Allesbury Road, Dublin 4, Ireland
Tel: 00353-1-2600580
Fax: 00353-1-2696966
Telex:91834 CODE EI
E-mail: chinacomm@tinet.ie

Israel
94, Derech Namir Road, Tel Aviv, 62337, Israel
Tel: 00972-3-5465922
Fax: 00972-3-5465926
E-mail: il@moftec.gov.cn

Italy
Via Della Camilluccia 613, 00135 Roma, Italy
Tel: 0039-6-36308534, 36303856
Fax: 0039-6-36308552
Telex: 622162 CINAC I
E-mail: gckli@tin.it/qigaoh@tin.it
Uffcomcina.uffcomcina@tin.it

Milan, Italy
Via Paleocapa, 4-2-21 Milano, Italia
Tel: 0039-2-72021905, 72021988
Fax: 0039-2-86452219

Kazakhstan
No.137, Furmanov Street, Almaty, Kazakhstan
Tel: +7-3272-533618
Fax: NA
E-mail: ekcochina@asdc.kz

Korea, Democratic People's Republic of
Kinmaeuli Dong, Mao Lang Bong District,
Pyongyang, Democratic People's Republic of Korea
Tel: 00850-2-3813119, 3813120
Fax: 00850-2-3813425, 3813442

Korea, Republic of
Tel: 00822-22537521
Fax: 00822-22537524
cninkr@thrunet.com

Pusan of the Republic of Korea
1418, U-2 Dong, Haeundae, Busan, Korea
TEL: 82-51-742-4991-2
FAX: 82-51-742-5446

Kuwait
Al-Shamiya, Block 8, Street 85, House No.4, Kuwait
Postal address: P. O. Box 25713
SAFAT, 13118 Safat, Kuwait
Tel: 00965-4822816-4822817-4817843
Fax: 00965-4822867-4822873
E-mail: ecocom@qualitynet.net

KYRGHYZ
Manac Ave.6 Bishkek 720017 Republic of Kyrgyz
Tel: 00996-312 665366 224893 224693 224732
660134
Fax: 00996-312 663148
E-mail: moftec@mail.elcat.kg

Jamaica
8, Seaview Ave, Kingston 10, Jamaica W.I.
Tel: 001-876-9276816
Fax: 001-876-9787780
E-mail: chinaemba@cwjamaica.com

Japan
5-8-16 Mono-Azabu, Minato-Ku, Tokyo, Japan
Tel: 0081-3-3440-2011
Fax: 0081-3-3446-8242
E-mail: cecj@ma.kcom.or.jp

Sapporo, JAPAN
5-1 Nishi 23-Chome Minam 13-J0 Chuo-Ku
Sapporo Japan
Tel: 0081-11-5635563
Fax: 0081-11-5631818

Fukuoka, Japan
Fukuoka-Shi Chiuo-Ku Jigyohama 1-3-3 Japan
Tel: 0081-92-713-7532
Fax: 0081-92-781-8906

Osaka, Japan
Utsubohonmach1 3-Chome Osaka Japan
Tel: 0081-6-4459471 0081-6-4459481
Fax: 0081-6-4459476

Jordan
No. 21, Zahran St. Southern Um Uthaina, Amman,
Jordan
423 Um Essomaq & Khelda, Amman, 11821, Jordan
Postal Add: P. O. Box: 423 Amman 11821 Jordan
Tel: 00962-6-5516194
Fax: 00962-6-5537417
E-mail: jojsc@hotmail.com

Kenya
Ngong Road, Nairobi, Kenya
P. O. Box 48190, 47030, Nairobi
Tel: 00254-2-726180, 726179
Fax: 00254-2-713451, 726179
E-mail: chinakenya@yahoo.com
http://www.chinakenya.com

Laos
Ruelle Vatnak Muong Sisattanak, Vientiane, Laos
Tel: 00856-21-253025 00856-21-253026
Fax: 00856-21-253024
Mobile phone: 00856-020-513992

LATVIA
2 Darba Str. LV-1046. Riga, Latvia
Tel: 00371-7805475
Fax: 00371-7805470
E-mail: econ-ch@apollo.lv

Lebanon
71 Rue Nicolas Ibrahim Sursock, Ramlet El-Baida,
Beirut, Lebanon
Postal add.: P. O. Box 114-5098, Beirut
Tel: 00961-1-822493
Fax: 00961-1-826672
E-mail: becelb@hotmail.com
shixu_1999@hotmail.com

Lesotho
1st Floor, Block 2, 257 Oxford Road, Zuovo,
Johannesburg
Tel: 011-8046311
Fax: 011-788-2428

Lithuania
Blindziu 34, LT-2004 Vilnius, Lithuania
Tel: 00370-2-722375/722259/722223
Fax: 00370-2-722161
E-mail: chinesecomoffice@tdd.lt

Libya
Near the petrol station No. 37, Kalkalish Street,
Tipoli, Libya
P. O. Box 6310 Andalus, Tipoli
Tel: 00218-21-4832237, 4831224, 4831234,
4838052
Fax: 00218-21-4831225, 4831877
Email: eccolibya@sina.com

Luxembourg
Boulevard General Jacques 19 1050 Bruxelles,
Belgique
Tel: 0032-0032-2-6404210
Fax: 0032-2-6403595
E-mail: comoffchnmsn@pophost.eunet.be

Malaysia
No. 39, Jalan Uiu Kelang, 68000 Ampang, Selangor
Darul
Ehsan, Malaysia
Tel: 0060-3-4513226, 4513555
Fax: 0060-3-4513233
E-mail: comembmy@tm.net.my

Kuching, Malaysia
340 Fortune Garden, Lorong 5, Jalan Stampin
Timur, off Kuching By-pass, 93350
Kuching, Sarawak, Malaysia
Tel: 0060-82-461344
Fax: 0060-82-461424
E-mail: zhicun@tm.net.com

Malta
10, Oscar Testa Street, Attard BZN 02, Malta
Tel: 00-356-21433047, 21421891
Fax: 00-356-21421892
E-mail: eccochn@kemmunet.net.mt

MADAGASCAR
Nanisana-Ambatobe, Antananarivo,
Republic of Madagascar
Tel: 261-20-2240856
Fax: 00261-20-2244529

Macedonia
St. Oslo 22-B 91000 Skopje Republic of Macedonia
Tel: 00389 2 369658 369668
Fax: 00389 2 369688
E-mail: eco@mt.net.mk

Mali
B.P.1614, Bamako, Mali
Tel: 00223-223823
Fax: 00223-229019
E-mail: bcecmali@spider.toolnet.org

Maroc
2, Rue Mekki El-Bitaouri Souissi-Rabat-Maroc
Tel: 00212-7-752718, 754940
Fax: 00212-7-756966, 755769

Mauritanie
B.P. 5534, Nouakchott, R.I de Mauritanie
Tel: 0022-2-5251205/5252347
Fax: 0022-2-5258634
E-mail : bcecacm@opt.mr

Mauritius
Royal Road, Belle Rose, Rose Hill, Mauritius
Tel: 00230-4549113, 6755635
Fax: 00230-4540362, 6743523
Telex: 4829 CHINCOM IW
E-mail: ecocnemb@intnet.mu
mu@moftec.gov.cn

Mexico
Calle Platon No. 317, Col Polanco Mexico,
D.F.11560
Mexico, D.F.
Tel: 0052-5-2808592, 2802970
Fax: 0052-5-2804847, 2821646
Telex:1763515 OCCHME
E-mail: ecocnmex@infoabc.com

Micronesia
P. O. Box 1836 Kolonia, Pohnpei
Federated States of Micronesia 96941
Tel: 00691-320-5072
Fax: 00691-320-7074

MOLDOVA
Str. Anton Crihan Nr. 30 2009, Chisinau, Republica
Moldova
Tel: 00373-2-213072, 222257, 225345
Fax: 00373-2-223335
E-mail: chnmd@chnmd.mld.net

Mongolia
No. 5 Frienship Street Ulanbator Mongolia
Tel: 009716-323940
Fax: 009716-311943

Mozambique
Av. Do Zimbabwe N.1088 Maputo, Av. De Kim lL
Sung N.974
Maputo C.P.2545;C.P.1105
Tel: 00258-1-490306, 491879
Fax: 00258-1-490306, 491879
E-mail: coocai@teledata.mz

Myanmar
No. 53, Pyidaungsu Yeiktha Road, Yangon,
Myanmar
Tel: 0095-2-35944
Fax: 0095-1-220386

Namibia
66 Gevers Street, Windhoek, Namibia
P. O. Box 21350
Tel: 00264-61-222702, 220210, 221460
Fax: 00264-61-221325
E-mail: nmbyjsc@iafrica.com.na

Nepal
Baluwater, Kathmandu, Nepal
Tel: 00977-1-434792
E-mail: ecco@info.com.np

The Netherlands
Groot Haesebroekseweg 2A 2243 EA Wassenaar,
The Netherlands
Tel: 0031-(0)70-5115559
Fax: 0031-(0)70-5111206
E-mail: coce@xs4all.nl

New Zealand
104A Korokoro Road, Lower Hutt, P. O. Box 12342,
Thorndon, Wellington, New Zealand
Tel: 00644-5870407
Fax: 00644-5870407
E-mail: chinaeco@paradise.net.nz
http://www.chinaeco.org.nz

Niger
Boite Postale: 10777 Niamey Republique Du Niger
Tel: 00227-752859, 722126
Fax: 00227-752861, 722106
E-mail: ambbcec@intnet.ne

Nigeria
161A, Adeola Odeku Street, Victoria Island, Lagos,
Nigeria
P. O. Box 72697 V/I, Lagos
Tel: 00234-1-2612404, 2612414
Fax: 00234-1-2612414

Norway
Inkognitogaten 11 0258 Oslo 2 Norway
Tel: 0047-22-560270, 438666, 449638
Fax: 0047-22-447230
E-mail: cnembn@online.no
zhouxinjian@moftec.gov.cn

Oman
Shati Al-Qurum, WAY3021, House No. 1784 3315
Ruwis Mascat, Sultanate of Oman
P. O. Box 3471 Ruwi, Post Code 112, Muscat,
Sultanate Of Oman
Tel: 00968-697804
Fax: 00968-697482
E-mail: chinaceo@omantel.net.om

Pakistan
P. O. Box 2601, House No. 11, Street No. 19, F-8/2,
Islamabad, Pakistan
Tel: 0092-51-252426
Fax: 0092-51-256887
E-mail: ecco@comsats.net.pk

Karachi, Pakistan
43-6-B, Block 6, P.E.C.H.S.Karachi
Tel: 0092-21-4530523, 4530526
Fax: 0092-21-4530525

Panama
Edificio Torre Cosmos Campo Alegre, Calle Manuel
Maria Zcazabella Vista, Panama, Apartado 87-4631
Zona
7, Panama Republica De Panama
Tel: 00507-654061, 654062
Fax: 00507-2654051, 2130265

Papua New Guinea
Sir John Guise Drive, Waigani, Papua New Guinea,
P. O. Box 1351, Boroko, PNG
Tel: 00675-3251190
Fax: 675-3258247

Peru
Av. del Parque Norte 315, Corpac, San Isidro, Lima,
Peru
P. O. Box 170140, Lima 17 PERU
Tel: 51-1-2261757, 2261728
Fax: 51-1-4750016
E-mail: ofcembch@amnet.com.pe
ofcechina@ofcechina.org.pe

The Philippines
No. 10, Flame Tree Road, South Forbes Park,
Makati City
1200, Metro Manila, Philippines
Tel: 0063-2-8195991 0063-2-8195992
0063-2-8939067
Fax: 0063-2-8184553

Cebu, The Philippines
4th Fl. Eeurd Pacific Bldg, F. Gonzales Compound,
Camputhaw St. Lahug Cebu City, 6000,
The Philippines
Tel: 006332-2316217 006332-2316218 006332-
2316219
Fax: 006332-2315697
Tel: (During Holidays): 006332-2548727 006332-
2548728
E-mail: wy-zh@hotmail.com

Poland
Str. Bonifraterska 1, 00-203 Warsaw, Poland
Tel: 0048-22-8313861, 8313836
Fax: 0048-22-6354211
E-mail: brhchiem@ipgate.pl
Telex: 813589 CHINA PL

Portugal
Rua Antonio De Saldanha, No 42, 1400, Lisboa,
Portugal
Tel: 00351-21-3041266, 301 1947
Fax: 00351-21-3014950
Email: chinaembacom@mail.telepac.pt
http://www.secom-china.com.pt

Qatar
No. 63, Al-Sham Street, West Bay Area, Doha
Postal Address: P. O. Box 17514, Doha, Qatar
Tel: 00974-4835680
Fax: 00974-4835184
E-mail: qcec@qatar.net.qa

Romania
Soseaua Nordului No.2, Bucharest, Romania
Tel: 0040-1-2321923
Fax: 0040-1-2307786
Telex: 11324 CHIAB R
E-mail: embchina@dial.kappa.ro

Russia
Tel: 007-095-9382111 1431544
Fax: 007-095-9382005
E-mail: shcach@dol.ru

Rwanda
B.P. 519 OU 182, Kigali, Rwanda
Tel: 00250-84965
Fax: 00250-84965
E-mail: becom@rwandal.com

Saudi Arabia
P. O. Box 99882 Riyadh 11625 Saudi Arabia
Tel: 00966-1-4655655 00966-1-4622485
Fax: 00966-1-4629617
00966-1-4629617
E-mail: comm-china@sol.net.sa

Jeddah, Saudi Arabia
Al-Andulous Road, Andulous Dist. (2) P. O. Box
51373 Jeddah
21543 Jeddah, Kingdom of Saudi Arabia
Tel: 00966-2-6605430
Fax: 00966-2-6606546

Seychelles
P. O. Box 680 Victoria Mahe-Seychelles
Tel: 00248-266808
Fax: 00248-266866
E-mail: ecchina@seychelles.net

Sierra Leone
P. O. Box 778 B28, Kong Harman Road, Freetown
Sierra Leone
Tel: 00232-22-240075(Economic Section), 240490
(Commercial Section), 240086
Fax: 00232-22-240086
E-mail: ecco@sierratel.sl

Singapore
150 Tanglin Road, Singapore 247969
Tel: 0065-67351716 64121900
Fax: 0065-67338590
E-mail: ecco@bizcn-sg.org.sg
jscsg@singnet.com.sg

Slovak Republic
Jeseneskeho 7, 811, 01, Bratislava, Slovenska
Republika
Tel: 00421-2-52920154
Fax: 00421-2-52920153
E-mail: ekocn@ekocn.sk

Slovenia
Malci Beliceve 123 1000 Ljubljana, Republic of
Slovenia
Tel: 00386-61-272759 00386-1-2005871/72/73
Fax: 00386-61-233838 00386-1-2005878
E-mail: ecco@china-embassy.si

South Africa
797 Park Street Clydesdale (Hatfiled) Pretoria 0083
R.S.A
Tel: (0027)-12-3440428, (0027)-12-3441404
Fax: (0027)-12-3440439
E-mail: commercial@chinese-embassy.co.za

Spain
Arturo Soria 142, Piso 2-A 28043 Madrid, Espana
Tel: 34-91-4132776/914135892/234 2244
Fax: 34-915194675
E-mail: prchina@es.dominios.net
C/. Arturo Soria, 142, 2A, 28043 Madrid, Spain

Sri Lanka
120/3A Wijerama Mawatha, Colombo 07, Sri Lanka
Tel: 00941-684576-7
Fax: 00941-684578, 684579
E-mail: mhwtt@yahoo.com

Sudan
Manshia District, Khartoum, Sudan
P. O. Box 1425 Khartoum-Sudan
Tel: 00249-11-272274, 224816
Fax: 00249-11-272274

Suriname
4 Erosstraat, Paramaribo Suriname
P. O. Box 8116, Paramaribo, Suriname
Tel: 00597-451251/452352
Fax: 00597-452560
E-mail: ecco@sr.net

Sweden
Ringvagen 56 181 34 Lidingo, Sweden
Tel: 0046-8-7674083, 7679625, 7678740
Fax: 0046-8-7318404
E-mail: moftec.swe@swipnet.se

Switzerland
Widmannstr.7, 3074 Muri, Bern, Switzerland
Tel: 0041-31-9511401
Fax: 0041-31-9510575
E-mail: admin@sinoswiss.net

Syria
P. O. Box 2455, Damascus, Syria
Tel: 00963-11-6133008 /6133086
Fax: 00963-11-6133019
Telex: (0492) 413217 CHINEC SY
E-mail: eccoces@scs-net.org

Tajikistan
No. 143, Rudaki Street, Dushanbe, Republic of
Tajikistan
Tel: 00992-372-244183, 242007
Fax: 00992-372-510024

Tanzania
No. 1390, Msasani Penisula Tanzania Plot No 3621
Msasani, Road Dares
Salaam (Economic)
Tel: 00255-51-68198, 41288
Fax: 00255-51-66177

Thailand
57, Ratchadapisake Road, Bangkok 10310, Thailand
Tel: 0066-2-2457038 0066-2-2472122 0066-2-
2474506
Fax: 0066-2-2472123
E-mail: clian@mozart.inst.cn.th

Songkhla, Thailand
9 Sadao Rood, Songkhla 9000 Thailand
Tel: 0066-74-322034 0066-74-325045
Fax: 0066-74-323772
E-mail: clian@mozart.inst.cn.th

Tonga
P. O. Box 877, Vuna Road, Nuku'alofa,
Kingdom of Tonga
Tel: 00676-24554 22899
Fax: 00676-22899 24595
E-mail: chinaton@kalianet.to

Togo
11, Rue Tevi-Benissan a Tokoin-Lycee B.P. 4714-
Lome-Togo
Tel: 00228-215470, 215243
Fax: 00228-218390, 215470
E-mail: sinoecom@cafe.lg

Trinidad and Tobago
40 Elizabeth Street, St. Clail Port of Spain,
Trinidad, W.I.
Tel: 001-809-6285556
Fax: 001-809-6288020

Tunis
Route De La Marsa KMG El Aouina 2405 Cite
Taieb M'Hiri
Tunis, Tunisie
Tel: 00216-1-845805
Fax: 00216-1-841996
E-mail: bcec.ambachine@email.ati.tn

Turkey
Horasan Sokak No.8, 06700 Gaziosmanpasa -
Ankara/Turkey
Ankara-Turkey
Tel: 0090-312-4377107
Fax: 0090-312-4466762
E-mail: tr@moftec.gov.cn

Istanbul, Turkey
The Economic and Commercial Section of the
Chinese Consulate in Istanbul Mecidiyekoy, Ortaklar
Cad. 14,
Istanbul, Turkey
Tel: 0090-212-2666590
Fax: 0090-212-2992632
Telex:26906 CCGT TR
E-mail: sws@netone.com.tr

Turkmenistan
744000 Turkmenistan Ashgabat Str.
Sota Rustawely, 15
Tel: 00993-12 350269, 352308, 351928
Fax: 00993-12 510888
E-mail: ecchina@online.tm

Uganda
Plot 112-114-116, Luthuli Ave. Bugolobi
P. O. Box 8858 Kampala Uganda
Tel: 00256-41-220572, 220578, 220570
Fax: 00256-41-220379
E-mail: cnecoug@infocom.co.ug

Ukraine
11, Lane Zemliancky, 252014, Kiev, Ukraine 01014
Tel: 380-44-2947710, 2948810
Fax: 380-44-2948040
E-mail: chinacom@ukrpack.net

United Arab Emirates
Al Falah Street, 10 th Lane, 35-1 Sector P. O. Box
25455 Abu, Dhabi-U.A.E.
Tel: 00971-2-6427073
Fax: 00971-2-764402
E-mail: Comchiem@emirates.net.ae

Dubai, UAE
P. O. Box 9374 Dubai-U.A.E.
Tel: 00971-4-448032 00971-4-449445
Fax: 00971-4-448099
Email: moftec@emirates.net.ae

United Kingdom
Cleveland Court, 1–3 Leinster Gardens, London
W2 6DP, The United Kingdom
Tel: 0044-171-2620253, 2623911, 7238923
Fax: 0044-171-7062777
Telex: 896440 CLEFSL G
E-mail: public@checo.demon.co.uk

United States of America
2133 Wisconsin Ave., NW Washington D.C.,
20007, USA
Tel: 001-202-625-3380, 3360
Fax: 001-202-337-5864, 5845
E-mail: chinacom@erols.com

San Francisco, United States
1450 Laguna Street, San Francisco, CA94115, USA
Tel: 001-415-5634858, 5634874
Fax: 001-415-5630494
Telex:497021 CCSF

New York, United States
520 12 Avenue, New York, N.Y.10036, USA
Tel: 001-212-212£3307404, 3307427, 3307428
Fax: 001-212-5020248

Los Angeles, United States
443 Shatto Place, Los Angeles, CA90020, USA
Tel: (213)807-8016, 8017, 8026
Fax: (213)380-1961

Houston, United States
3417 Montrose Boulevard, Houston, Texas 77006,
USA
Tel: 001-713-5244064, 5240780, 5240778
Fax: 001-713-5243547
E-mail: moftec@wt.net

Chicago, United States
104 West Erie Street, Chicago IL. 60610 USA
Tel: 001-312-8030115
Fax: 001-312-8030114
E-mail: ccgc@ais.net

Uruguay
Calle Palma y Ombues No 6016, Montevideo
Tel: 00598-2-6043899
Fax: 00598-2-6042637

Uzbekistan
No. 79, Akademik Yahyo G'Ulomoy Street, Tashkent
700047, Republic of Uzbekistan
Tel: 00-998-71-1206246

Vanuatu
Elluk Hill, Port Vila, Republic of Vanuatu
Postal Address: P. O. Box 210, Port Vila,
Republic of Vanuatu
Tel: 00678 28860
Fax: 00678 22730
E-mail: vu@moftec.gov.cn

Venezuela
Quinta La Orquidea Calle San Francisco Desviacion
San Pedro Urb. Prados Del Este Apartado 80520,
Zona Postal 1080-A
Caracas, Venezuela
Tel: 0058-2-9761678, 9762896

Vietnam
So Nha 46.52 Pho Hoang Dieu, Hanoi, Vietnam
Tel: 00966-2-6606546
E-mail: cscgc@dmp.net.sa

Ho Chi Minh City, Vietnam
So Nha 39 Ngnyen Thi Minh Khai, District 1, Ho
Chi Minh City, Vietnam
Tel: 00848-8292463
Fax: 00848-8231142

Western Samoa
Private Bag, Vailima, Apia, Western Samoa
Tel: 00685-20802
Fax: 00685-21115
E-mail: encco@samoa.net
encco@samoa.ws

Yemem
Al-Zubeiry Street, Sana'a, Yemen
Tel: 00967-1-275339, 275411
Fax: 00967-1-275339, 272298
E-mail: chinaeco-com@y.net.ye

Aden, Yemen
150# Andrus Street, Khormaksar, Aden, Republic of
Yemen
P. O. Box 6160 Khormaksay, Aden, Yemen
Tel: 00967-2- 232630, 230968 71103966,
71103926
00967-2-235599 ext. 121, 131, 132, 127, 123, 231,
125, 128
Fax: 00967-2-231377
E-mail: ecoccga@y.net.ye, liuchang@y.net.ye

Yugoslavia
Vasilija Gacese 5, 11000 Belgrad, Yugoslavia
Tel: 00381-11-651630, 651638
Fax: 00381-11-650726
Telex:12492 CNCCO YU
E-mail: yu@moftec.gov.cn

Zambia
United Nations Avenue, Lusaka, Zambia
P. O. Box 31205 Lusaka, Zambia
Tel: 00260-1-253601, 262363, 264123
Fax: 00260-1-262363, 253001

Zanzibar
P. O. Box 1200 Zanzibar, Tanzania Chinese
Consulate in Zanzibar
Tel: 0255-054-30816
Fax: 0255-054-32681

Zimbabwe
10, Cork Road, Avondale, Harare, Zimbabwe
P. O. Box 40 Harare, Zimbabwe; P .O. Box 1340,
Harare, Zimbabwe
Tel: 00263-4-735194, 730516
Fax: 00263-4-700264, 735252
E-mail: eccoprc@samara.co.zw

**The Permanent Mission of the People's Republic of
China to the United Nations**
West. 66th Street New York, N.Y. 10023
Tel: 001-212-6556100 001-212-6556152
Fax: 001-212-6556112
E-mail: fazhanzu@yahoo.com

**The Permanent Mission of the People's Republic of
China to the United Nations Industrial
Development Organization**
Untere Donaustrasse 41, 1020 Vienna, Austria
Tel: 00431-2163367, 2169380
Fax: 00431-2169389

**The Permanent Mission of the People's Republic of
China to the United Nations and Other
International Organizations in Vienna**
Poetzleinsdorfer Strasse 42 1180 Vienna, Austria
Tel: 0043-0222-471364 0043-0222-478338

**The Permanent Mission of the People's Republic of
China to the United Nations Office in Geneva and
Other International Organizations in Switzerland**
Chemin De Surville 11 1213 Petit-Lancy, Geneva,
Switzerland
Tel: 0041-22-7937013, 7933270
Fax: 0041-22-7937014
E-mail: eto.cn@ties.itu.int

**Bureau du Sonseiller Economique et Commercial
de la Mission de la Republique Populaire de China
a la Communaute Europeenne**
Boulevard General Jacques 19 1050 Bruxelles,
Belgique
Tel: 0032-2-6404210
Fax: 0032-2-6403595
E-mail:comoffchnmsn@pophost.eunet.be
BD General Jacques 19, 1050 Brussels, Belgium

Note: the above list of the commercial offices of the
Chinese embassies and consulate generals is compiled
with information available. Those not included
herein are due to absence of relevant information.

Appendix IV

PRC Accounting Standards and
Financial Regulations vs IAS and US GAAP

PricewaterhouseCoopers

SUBJECT	US GAAP	IAS	People's Republic of China *Accounting Standards and Accounting Systems for Business Enterprises*
Special purpose entities	Consolidate based on risks and rewards. Specific guidance for consolidation of lease arrangements involving SPEs. Specific criteria have to be met for transfers of financial assets.	Consolidate where the substance of the relationship indicates control.	Not specified in the regulations.
Foreign currency translation – individual companies	Translate transactions at rate on date of transaction; monetary assets/liabilities at balance sheet rate; non-monetary items at the historical rate. Difference taken to equity.	Similar to US GAAP.	Translate transactions at rate stipulated by the People's Bank of China (PBOC) rate on date of transaction or 1st day of the month in which the transactions took place. Monetary assets/liabilities denominated in foreign currencies at the balance sheet date are translated into RMB at the exchange rates stipulated by PBOC at the balance sheet date. Translation difference recorded as part of equity.
Foreign entities within consolidated financial statements	Use closing rate for balance sheets, average rate for income statements. Take exchange differences to equity. Include in gain or loss on disposal of a subsidiary.	Similar to US GAAP.	Use closing rate for balance sheets, average rate for income statements. Take exchange differences to equity.
Hyperinflation – foreign entity	Remeasure local currency statements using the reporting currency as the functional currency.	Adjust local statements of foreign entity to current price levels prior to translation.	Not specified in regulations.
Types	All business combinations are acquisitions.	An acquisition is the most common. Uniting of interests/pooling severely restricted.	No effective rules although the Exposure Draft on Business Combination suggests that the purchase method should be used. In practice, most acquisitions are accounted for using the purchase method of accounting.
Purchase method – fair values on acquisition	Fair value the assets and liabilities of acquired entity but specific rules for acquired in-process research and development (generally expensed). Some plant closure and restructuring liabilities relating solely to the acquired entity may be provided in fair value exercise, if specific criteria about restructuring plans are met.	Fair value the assets and liabilities of acquired entity. Similar to US GAAP, but more stringent recognition criteria regards timing of implementation of the plan.	No effective rules but the Exposure Draft suggests that fair value of assets and liabilities acquired should be used. Existing regulations do not address this. The Exposure Draft suggests that foreseeable costs of integration, restructuring and redundancy charges should form part of the acquisition costs.

Purchase method – goodwill	Capitalize but do not amortize. Goodwill should be tested for impairment at least annually at the reporting unit level.	Capitalize and amortize over useful life, normally not longer than 20 years.	If the acquiree retains its status as a legal person, then any excess of the cost of the acquisition over the acquiree's net assets book value (not fair value) would be 'equity investment difference'. This difference should be amortized over the investment period as stipulated in the investment contract or a period not exceeding 10 years. If the acquiree does not continue to be a legal person, then any excess of the cost of the acquisition over the acquiree's net assets fair value would be recognized as 'goodwill'.
Uniting of interests method	Prohibited.	Severely restricted to "true mergers of equals". Requirements focus on lack of identification of an acquirer.	Not specified in regulations.
Revenue recognition	Four key criteria have been established. Detailed guidance for specific transactions.	Based on several criteria, In principle similar to US GAAP, which require the recognition of revenue when risks and rewards have been transferred and the revenue can be measured reliably.	Revenue is recognized when risks and rewards have been transferred, ceases 'control' on the goods sold, and the revenue (and associated costs) can be measured reliably.
Construction contracts	Accounted for using the percentage of completion method. Completed contract method permitted.	Accounted for using the percentage of completion method. Completed contract method prohibited.	Accounted for using the percentage of completion method.
Interest income	Accrual basis	Similar to US GAAP	Similar to US GAAP.
General	Accrual basis.	Similar to US GAAP	Similar to US GAAP.
Interest expense	Interest expense recognized on an accrual basis. Effective yield (known as interest method) method used to amortize non-cash finance charges.	Interest expense recognized on an accrual basis. Effective yield method used to amortize non-cash finance charges.	Similar to US GAAP.
Inventories – valuation	Carry at lower of cost or net realizable value (NRV)	Carry at lower of cost and NRV.	Similar to US GAAP.
Inventories – determining cost	Use FIFO, LIFO, or weighted average method to determine cost. More common use of LIFO.	Use FIFO, LIFO (rarely used), or weighted average method to determine cost.	Use FIFO, LIFO, weighted average, moving average, and specific identification method to determine cost.
Inventories – provision for obsolescence losses	Recognise based on general rule for making provisions.	Similar to US GAAP.	Similar to US GAAP.
Property, plant and equipment – revaluation	Revaluations are not permitted.	Use historical cost or revalued amounts. Frequent valuations of entire classes of assets required.	Carried at historical costs. Revaluations are not permitted.

SUBJECT	US GAAP	IAS	People's Republic of China Accounting Standards and Accounting Systems for Business Enterprises
Property, plant and equipment – depreciation	Depreciate over the useful life of the asset, generally by the straight-line method.	Similar to US GAAP.	Depreciate over the estimated useful life of the assets by straight-line method, double-declining method, production method, sum-of-the-years-digits method etc. Useful life and depreciation method is based on management judgement. Assets above RMB2,000 and expected to be used for two or more periods should be capitalized.
Property, plant and equipment – Asset retirement costs	The present value of future retirement costs should be capitalized as part of the P, P&E.	Asset retirement costs should be accrued for. However, discounting is not required.	Not specified in regulations.
Capitalization of borrowing costs	Compulsory when relates to construction of certain assets.	Permitted for qualifying assets.	Borrowing costs on project-specific borrowings should be capitalized as part of the cost of acquiring or constructing a tangible fixed asset.
Investment property	Treat as for other properties (depreciated cost).	Measure at depreciated cost or fair value and recognize changes in fair value in the income statement.	Not specified in regulations.
Impairment of assets	If impairment indicated, account it as follows: For assets to be held and used, impairment assessed on undiscounted cash flows. If less than carrying amount, measure impairment loss using market value or discounted cash flows. Reversals of losses prohibited. For assets held for disposal, impairment based on lower of carrying amount and fair value.	If impairment indicated, write down assets to higher of net selling price and value in use based on discounted cash flows. If no loss arises, reconsider useful lives of those assets. Reversals of losses permitted in certain circumstances.	Similar to US GAAP but reversals of impairment reserves allowed under certain circumstances.
Acquired intangible assets	Capitalize purchased intangible assets and amortize over useful life, and review for impairment. Intangibles may also be assigned an indefinite useful life, these must not be amortized but reviewed for impairment at least annually. Revaluations are not permitted.	Capitalize if recognition criteria met; intangible assets must be amortized over useful life, normally no longer than 20 years. Revaluations are permitted in rare circumstances.	Capitalize purchased intangible assets and amortize over useful life normally no less than 10 years.

Internally generated intangible assets	Expense both research and development costs as incurred. Some software and website development costs must be capitalized.	Expense research costs as incurred. Capitalize and amortize development costs only if stringent criteria are met.	Expense research and development costs as incurred. Capitalize expenditures such as registration fees and legal fees incurred for legal application of obtaining the asset, and amortize over its estimated useful life.
Leases – classification	Finance lease if substantially all risks and rewards of ownership transferred. Substance rather than form is important.	Similar to US GAAP. Substance rather than form is more important than that of US GAAP.	Similar to US GAAP.
Leases – lessor accounting	Record amounts due under finance leases as a receivable. Allocate gross earnings to give constant rate of return based on (pre-tax) net investment method. Specific rules for leveraged leases.	Similar to US GAAP.	Similar to US GAAP.
Leases – lessee accounting	Record finance leases as asset and obligation for future rentals. Normally depreciate over useful life of asset. Apportion rental payments to give constant interest rate on outstanding obligation. Generally charge operating lease rentals on straight-line basis.	Similar to US GAAP.	Similar to US GAAP except that the aggregate of the future lease payments is presented as a liability undiscounted. The difference between the asset value (calculated as the net present value of future lease payments) and the aggregate of future lease payments is systematically allocated to costs.
Leases – sale and leaseback transactions.	Defer and amortize profits up to certain limits. Immediately recognize losses. Consider specific strict criteria if a real estate transaction.	For a finance lease defer and amortize profit arising on sale, if an operating lease arises then profit recognition depends on sale proceeds compared to fair value of the asset.	For a finance lease, defer and amortize profit arising on sale as an adjustment to depreciation. For an operating lease, defer and amortize profit on sale according to the proportion of the lease payments during the lease.
Financial assets – security investments	Depends on classification of investment – if held to maturity or originated by the entity then carry at amortised cost, otherwise at fair value. Unrealised gains/losses on trading securities recognized in the income statement and on available-for-sale investments recognized in comprehensive income (equity).	Similar to US GAAP, except unrealized gains/losses on available-for-sale securities recognized in either equity, or the income statement.	Security investments are accounted for as short and long-term investments. Only short-term investments are required to be carried at the lower of cost or market, unless impairment other than temporary exist in long-term investments.
Financial instruments – impairment of securities	When a decline in fair value below the amortized cost basis is other than temporary, recognition of impairment loss on a security is required.	Similar to US GAAP, less guidance than US GAAP.	Similar to US GAAP. Should review fair value of long-term investment securities at least annually.

SUBJECT	US GAAP	IAS	People's Republic of China Accounting Standards and Accounting Systems for Business Enterprises
Financial assets – loans	Normally capitalised by principal amounts. Write-down of specific account is required when impaired.	Similar to US GAAP.	Similar to US GAAP.
Financial assets - Allowance for credit losses	Generally established based on experiences and/or analysis of recoverability. Commonly general provisions and provisions for specific accounts are made.	Similar to US GAAP.	Similar to US GAAP.
Derecognition of financial assets	Recognize and derecognize assets based on control. Legal isolation of assets even in bankruptcy necessary for derecognition.	Recognize and derecognize assets based on control.	Not specified in regulations.
Provisions – general	Record provisions relating to present obligations from past events if outflow of resources is probable and can be reliably estimated. Rules for specific situations (employee termination costs, environmental liabilities, loss contingencies).	Record provisions relating to present obligations from past events if outflow of resources is probable and can be reliably estimated.	General concept similar to US GAAP although there are no specific guidance on employee termination and restructuring costs. In practice, best practice would be to have them accrued as the liability arises.
Provision – compensated absences Provisions – restructuring	Required to recognise the obligation. Recognise restructuring provisions if management approval and communication for involuntary employee terminations have been made.	Similar to US GAAP. Similar to US GAAP, however need detailed formal plan announced or implementation effectively begun.	No rules for compensated absences. No specific rules for restructuring.
Employee benefits – pension costs (defined benefit plans) paid	Must use projected unit credit method to determine benefit obligation.	Similar to US GAAP, although several minor differences.	Not addressed in existing regulations. In practice, employee benefit expenses will only be recognized as
Employee benefits – other	Account for post-retirement benefits as pensions. More detailed guidance given for termination benefits. Account for termination indemnity plans as pensions.	Similar to US GAAP. Rules also given for termination benefits arising from redundancies and other post-employment and long-term employee benefits. Termination indemnity similar to US GAAP.	No standards for post-retirement benefits.
Contingencies	Disclose unrecognized possible losses and potential gains.	Similar to US GAAP.	Similar to US GAAP.

Deferred income taxes general approach	Use full provision method, (some exceptions) driven by balance sheet temporary differences. Recognize all deferred tax assets and then provide valuation allowance if recovery is less than 50% likely.	Similar to US GAAP. Recognize deferred tax assets if recovery is probable. A number of specific differences in application.	May choose tax payable method or tax effect accounting – deferral method / liability method. If deferred tax method is used, then application is more similar to IAS.
Deferred income taxes – main exceptions	The exceptions are treated as permanent differences.	Non-deductible goodwill and temporary differences on initial recognition of assets and liabilities which do not impact accounting or taxable profit. Similar to US GAAP.	The exceptions are treated as permanent differences.
Government grants	Recognise as deferred income and amortize. May offset capital grants against asset values.	Similar to US GAAP.	Recognized as income upon receipt.
Financial liabilities – classification	Generally where an instrument is not a share, classify as liability when obligation to transfer economic benefit exists. Redeemable preference shares normally mezzanine category (between debt and equity).	Classify capital instruments depending on substance of obligations of the issuer. Mandatorily redeemable preference shares are classified as liabilities.	Generally where an instrument is not a share, classify as liability when obligation to transfer economic benefit exists. Financial liabilities exist beyond 1 year is not discounted. Not specified regarding redeemable preference shares in regulations.
Convertible debt	Convertible debt is usually recognized as a liability.	Account for convertible debt on split basis, allocating proceeds between equity and debt	Similar to US GAAP.
Derecognition of financial liabilities	Derecognize liabilities when extinguished. The difference between the carrying amount and the amount paid is recognized in the income statement.	Similar to US GAAP.	Similar to US GAAP.
Derivatives and hedging			
Derivatives – not qualifying as a hedging instruments	Fair value and the change in fair values charged to income.	Similar to US GAAP.	No regulations specified in this area.
Derivatives – qualifying as a hedging instruments	Recognized at fair value	Similar to US GAAP.	No regulations specified in this area.
Derivatives – hedging criteria	Numerous requirements including designation, documentation, and periodical testing of effectiveness by each hedging instruments.	Similar to US GAAP.	No regulations specified in this area.

SUBJECT	US GAAP	IAS	People's Republic of China Accounting Standards and Accounting Systems for Business Enterprises
Derivatives and other financial instruments – measurement of financial instruments and hedging activities	Measure derivatives and hedge instrument at fair value; recognise changes in fair value in income statement except for effective cash flow hedges defer in equity until effect of the underlying transaction is recognized in the income statement.	Similar to US GAAP, except gains/losses on hedge instrument used to hedge forecast transaction, included in cost of asset/liability (basis adjustment).	No regulations specified in this area.
Derivatives and other financial instruments – measurement of hedges of foreign entity investments	Gains/losses on hedges of foreign entity investments recognised in equity. Gains/losses held in equity must be transferred to the income statement on disposal of investment. All hedge ineffectiveness recognized in the income statement.	Gains/losses on hedges of foreign entity investments recognised in equity, including hedge ineffectiveness on non-derivatives. For derivatives, recognize hedge ineffectiveness in the income statement. Gains/losses held in equity must be transferred to the income statement on disposal of investment.	No regulations specified in this area.

Index

Index of Advertisers

Other titles in this series from Kogan Page

Doing Business with Azerbaijan
Doing Business with Bahrain
Doing Business with the Czech Republic
Doing Business with Egypt
Doing Business with Georgia
Doing Business with Germany
Doing Business with Hungary
Doing Business with India
Doing Business with Iran
Doing Business with Kazakhstan
Doing Business with Libya

Doing Business with Oman
Doing Business with Poland
Doing Business with Qatar
Doing Business with Russia
Doing Business with Saudi Arabia
Doing Business with Spain
Doing Business with South Africa
Doing Business with Turkey
Doing Business with Ukraine
Doing Business with United Arab Emirates